DEWEY
Decimal Classification ®

DEWEY

Decimal Classification and Relative Index

Devised by

MELVIL DEWEY

Edition 19

Edited under the direction of
BENJAMIN A. CUSTER

Volume 3
Relative Index

FOREST PRESS
A Division of
Lake Placid Education Foundation

ALBANY, N.Y. 12206 U.S.A.
1979

Library of Congress Cataloging in Publication Data

Dewey, Melvil, 1851–1931.
  Dewey decimal classification and relative index.
  First published anonymously in 1876 under title: A classification and
subject index. 2d ed. published under title: Decimal classification and
relativ index.

  CONTENTS: v. 1. Introduction. Tables.—v. 2. Schedules.—v. 3. Relative index.

  1. Classification, Dewey decimal. I. Custer, Benjamin Allen, 1912–   . II. Title.
Z696.D519 1979   0.25.4'3   77–27967
ISBN 0–910608–19–9 (v. 1)

Vol. 3: ISBN 0–910608–21–0
3-vol. set: ISBN 0–910608–23–7

Contents

Volume 1

Contents

Volume 2

Volume 3

Relative Index

Use of the Index

Full instructions on use of the index may be found in the Editor's Introduction, section 11.

Alphabeting is word by word. A hyphenated word is filed as one word.

Abbreviations are filed as if spelled out; their meanings are identified in the table immediately following this page.

Grouping of digits: Digits are printed in groups of three purely for ease in reading and copying. The spaces are not part of the numbers, and the groups are not related to those shown in DDC numbers on Library of Congress cataloging records.

Tables: A number preceded by "*s.s.–*" may be found in Table 1, by "*area–*" in Table 2, by "*lit. sub.–*" in Table 3, by "*lang. sub.–*" in Table 4, by "*r.e.n.–*" in Table 5, by "*lang.–*" in Table 6, by "*pers.–*" in Table 7, by "*law s.s.–*" in the list of specially extended standard subdivisions enumerated under centered heading 342–347. Such numbers are never used alone.

Abbreviations Used in the Index

Abbreviations are alphabeted letter by letter

admin.	administration(s)	Conn.	Connecticut
adv.	advertisement(s), advertising	cpd(s).	compound(s)
agric.	agricultural, agriculture	crit.	criticism
Ala.	Alabama	crys.	crystal(s), crystallography
Alta.	Alberta	dec.	decoration(s), decorative
anal.	analysis, analytic(al)	Del.	Delaware
anc. hist.	ancient history	dept(s).	department(s)
&	and	desc.	description, descriptive
anthr.	anthropological, anthropology	econ.	economic(s)
appl(s).	application(s), applied	econ. geol.	economic geology
arch.	architectural, architecture	ed.	education(al)
Ariz.	Arizona	elect.	electric(al), electricity
Ark.	Arkansas	Eng.	England
ASSR	Autonomous Soviet Socialist Republic	eng.	engineering, engineers
		equip.	equipment
bact.	bacteria, bacteriological, bacteriology	exp.	experiment(s), experimental
		Fla.	Florida
B.C.	British Columbia	Ga.	Georgia
biog.	biographical, biography	gen.	general
biol.	biological, biology	gen. wks.	general works
bldg(s).	building(s)	geog.	geographical, geography
bus.	business(es)	geog. subd.	geographical subdivisions
bus. tech.	business technology	geol.	geological, geology
Calif.	California	Ger.	Germany
Can.	Canada	govt.	government(s), governmental
cent.	century	Gt. Brit.	Great Britain
chem.	chemical, chemistry	hist.	historical, history
chem. tech.	chemical technology	hist. subd.	historical subdivisions
clim.	climate(s), climatological, climatology	home econ.	home economics
		Ia.	Iowa
Co.	County	Ida.	Idaho
coll(s).	collected, collecting, collection(s)	Ill.	Illinois
		illus.	illustration(s)
Colo.	Colorado	Ind.	Indiana
comm.	commerce, commercial	ind.	industrial, industries, industry
commun.	communication(s)	indiv.	individual
comp.	comparative	inorg. chem.	inorganic chemistry
condit.	condition(s)	inst.	institution(s), institutional

instr.	instrument(s), instrumental	N.H.	New Hampshire
int.	interior, internal	N. Ire.	Northern Ireland
int. dec.	interior decoration	N.J.	New Jersey
internat.	international	N.M.	New Mexico
Ire.	Ireland	N.S.	Nova Scotia
isl(s).	island(s)	N.S.W.	New South Wales
jur.	jurisdiction(s)	N.T.	New Testament
Kan.	Kansas	N.Ter.Aust.	Northern Territory Australia
Ky.	Kentucky	N.Y.	New York
La.	Louisiana	N.Z.	New Zealand
lang.–	*language* [Table 6]	O.	Ohio
lang. sub.–	*language subdivision* [Table 4]	Okla.	Oklahoma
lang(s).	language(s)	Ont.	Ontario
law s.s.–	*law standard subdivision*	Ore.	Oregon
ling.	lingual, linguistics	org. chem.	organic chemistry
lit.	literary, literature(s)	O.T.	Old Testament
lit. sub.–	*literature subdivision* [Table 3]	Pa.	Pennsylvania
		paleob.	paleobotany
Man.	Manitoba	paleon.	paleontology
Mass.	Massachusetts	paleoz.	paleozoology
math.	mathematical, mathematics	Par.	Parish
Md.	Maryland	path.	pathological, pathology
Me.	Maine	P.E.I.	Prince Edward Island
meas.	measures	perf.	performance
mech.	mechanical, mechanics	pers.	personnel
mech. eng.	mechanical engineering	*pers.–*	*persons* [Table 7]
med.	medical, medicine	pharm.	pharmacological, pharmacology
med. sci.	medical science	phil.	philosophical, philosophy
medv. hist.	medieval history	phys.	physiological, physiology
met.	meteorological, meteorology	pol.	political, politics
Mex.	Mexico	pol. sci.	political science
mf.	manufacture(s), manufacturing	prac.	practical, practice
Mich.	Michigan	proc.	procedure, process(es), processing
mil.	military		
mil. sci.	military science	prod.	producing, production, products
min.	mineral(s), mineralogical, mineralogy	prof.	profession(s), professional
		psych.	psychological, psychology
Minn.	Minnesota	pub.	public
misc.	miscellaneous, miscellany	qual.	qualitative, quality
Miss.	Mississippi	quan.	quantitative, quantity
Mo.	Missouri	Qld.	Queensland
mod. hist.	modern history	Que.	Quebec
Mont.	Montana	rec.	recreation(al)
mt(s).	mountain(s)	reg.	regulation(s), regulatory
nat.	national, natural	rel.	religion(s), religious
N.B.	New Brunswick	*r.e.n.–*	*racial, ethnic, national groups* [Table 5]
N.C.	North Carolina		
N.D.	North Dakota	res.	reservoir
Neb.	Nebraska	R.I.	Rhode Island
Nev.	Nevada	RSFSR	Russian Soviet Federated Socialist Republic
Nfld.	Newfoundland		

Abbreviations Used in the Index

s.a.	*see also*	Ter.	Territory
Sask.	Saskatchewan	Tex.	Texas
S. Aust.	South Australia	transp.	transport, transportation
S.C.	South Carolina	trmt.	treatment
sci.	science(s), scientific	U.S.	United States
Scot.	Scotland	USSR	Union of Soviet Socialist
S.D.	South Dakota		Republics
sep.	separate, separation(s)	Va.	Virginia
soc.	social, socialization, sociology	vet.	veterinary
spec.	specific	vet. sci.	veterinary science
s.s.–	*standard subdivision* [Table 1]	Vic.	Victoria
SSR	Soviet Socialist Republic	vs.	versus
St.	Saint	Vt.	Vermont
subj.	subject(s)	Wash.	Washington
sys.	system(s), systematic(s)	W. Aust.	Western Australia
Tas.	Tasmania	Wis.	Wisconsin
tech.	technical, technique,	W.Va.	West Virginia
	technological, technology	Wyo.	Wyoming
Tenn.	Tennessee	zool.	zoological, zoology

Relative Index

A

ABM
mil. eng.
soc. & econ. aspects *see*
Secondary industries
tech. & mf.   623.451 94
ACTH
production
physiology
human   612.492
other aspects see
Secretion
ADC
soc. services   362.713
misc. aspects see Young
people soc. services to
ADP *see* Automatic data proc.
ALGOL *see* Program ianguages
AM
broadcasting stations *see*
Broadcasting stations
radio systems *see* Long-wave
systems
AP (ammunition)
mil. eng.
soc. & econ. aspects *see*
Secondary industries
tech. & mf.   623.451 8
AP (journalism)   070.435
APC
mil. eng.
soc. & econ. aspects *see*
Secondary industries
tech. & mf.   623.451 8
Aabenraa Denmark   *area*–489 5
Aaland Isls. Finland   *area*–489 73
Aalborg Denmark   *area*–489 5
Aardvarks *see* Tubulidentata
Aardwolves *see* Proteles
Aargau Switzerland   *area*–494 5
Aarhus Denmark   *area*–489 5
Abacá *see* Manila hemp
Abacuses
arithmetic   513.028
s.a. spec. appls. e.g.
Accounting
other aspects see Calculating
machines

Abandoned children
soc. services   362.73
misc. aspects see Young
people soc. services to
other aspects see Children
s.a.   *pers.*–069 45
Abattoir residues
fertilizers
production
soc. & econ. aspects *see*
Secondary industries
technology   668.624 3
use agric.   631.843
s.a. spec. crops; also
spec. types of culture
e.g. Floriculture
Abattoirs *see* Slaughterhouses
Abbeville Co. S.C.   *area*–757 35
Abbey
buildings *see* Monastic
buildings
establishments *see* Religious
congregations
schools   377.3
misc. aspects see Schools
Abbott
John J.C. admin.
Can. hist.   971.055
s.a. spec. events & subj.
e.g. Courts
Abbreviated longhand
writing systems   653.2
s.a. spec. appls. e.g.
Practical pharmacy
Abbreviations   410
polyglot dictionaries   413.1
spec. langs.
desc. & anal.   *lang. sub.*–1
dictionaries   *lang. sub.*–31
usage   *lang. sub.*–8
spec. subj.   *s.s.*–014 8
Abdias
Bible   224.91
other aspects see Prophetic
books (O.T.)
Abdication
monarchs
pub. admin.   351.003 6
spec. jur.   354

Abortion
  criminal *see* Criminal
    abortion
  induced
    criminology *see* Criminal
      abortion
    ethics
      philosophy   179.76
      religion
        Buddhism   294.356 976
        Christianity   241.697 6
        comp. rel.   291.569 76
        Hinduism   294.548 697 6
        s.a. other spec. rel.
      soc. aspects   363.46
      other aspects see Moral
        issues
    legal aspects   344.041 9
      spec. jur.   344.3–.9
    spontaneous *see* Spontaneous
      abortion
    surgical *see* Surgical
      abortion
Abra Philippines   *area*–599 1
Abrading tools
  soc. & econ. aspects *see*
    Secondary industries
  tech. & mf.   691.92
    s.a. spec. appls. e.g.
      Surface finishing
Abram Greater Manchester Eng.
               area–427 36
Abrasions
  statistics   312.304 713
  surgery   617.13
    anesthesiology   617.967 13
    s.a. Veterinary sciences
Abrasive materials   553.65
  econ. geol.   553.65
  mining
    soc. & econ. aspects *see*
      Primary industries
    technology   622.365
    prospecting   622.186 5
  road eng.
    technology   625.763
    other aspects see Roads
  s.a. other spec. uses e.g.
    Lapidary work
Abreaction *see* Subconscious
    depth psych.
Abridgments
  musical scores & parts *see*
    Scores (music)
  other kinds see spec. subj.
Abrogation pub. debt
  pub. finance   336.368
  misc. aspects see Public
    borrowing
Abrupt deviations genetics 575.29
  animals   591.159

Abrupt deviations genetics (continued)
  man   573.229
  microorganisms   576.139
  plants   581.159
  s.a. spec. organisms
Abruptio placentae *see*
    Placental dystocia
Abruzzi e Molise Italy *area*–457 1
Absaroka Range Wyo. *area*–787 4
Abscesses *see* Pustular
    eruptions
Abscission
  plant phys.   581.31
  s.a. spec. plants
Absences
  employment *see* Leaves
    (absence)
  mil. offense *see* Offenses
    mil. law
  school *see* Truancy
Absentee
  ownership
    land econ.   333.4
    s.a. spec. kinds and prod.
      e.g. Textiles
      manufacturing
  voting
    pol. sci.   324.65
Absenteeism
  employment *see* Leaves
    (absence)
  mil. offense *see* Offenses
    mil. law
  school *see* Truancy
Absinthe *see* Compound liquors
Absolute
  metapysics   111.6
  monarchies
    pol. sci.   321.6
    s.a. spec. jur.
  rights pol. sci.   323.401
  standards elect. measurement
    see Primary standards
    elect. measurement
  temperature *see* Low
    temperatures
Absolution Christian rel.
  doctrines   234.166
  rites   265.64
  withholding *see* Censures rel.
    law
Absolutism
  pol. form *see spec. kinds*
    e.g. Absolute
    monarchies
  religion
    Christianity   234.9
    other rel. see Humankind
    rel. doctrines

Absorbency
  skin
    human phys.   612.791
    other aspects see
      Integumentary organs
Absorber oil
  chem. tech.   665.538 4
  other aspects see Petroleum
Absorption
  atmospheric optical phenomena
    meteorology   551.566
      artificial modification   551.686 6
      weather forecasting   551.646 6
      spec. areas   551.65
  electronic waves *see* Wave
      transmission
  gases
    physical chem. *see* Surface
      phenomena
    physics   533.1
    technology   660.284 23
      nat. gases   665.73
    s.a. other spec. prod.
  heat
    astrophysics   523.013 34
    s.a. spec. celestial
      bodies
    physics   536.34
    spec. states of matter   530.4
  light
    optics
      gen. wks.
        astrophysics   523.015 326
        s.a. spec. celestial
          bodies
        physics   535.326
        spec. states of matter   530.4
      spectroscopy
        astrophysics   523.015 843
        s.a. spec. celestial
          bodies
        physics   535.843
        spec. states of matter   530.4
  liquids
    physical chem. *see* Surface
      phenomena
    physics   532.6
    technology   660.284 23
    s.a. spec. prod. e.g.
      Coal-tar chemicals
  nutrition
    physiology
      med. sci.   612.38
      human phys.   612.38
      vet. phys.   636.089 238
      s.a. spec. animals
    other aspects see Digestion
  radiations met. *see*
      Radiations meteorology
  soils agric. *see* Physics soil
    sci.

Absorption (continued)
  sound
    engineering   620.21
    s.a. spec. appls. e.g.
      Music bldgs. for
    physics   534.208
      spec. states of matter   530.4
    surface chem. *see* Surface
      phenomena physical
      chem.
Abstinence
  ethics *see* Consumption ethics
  rel. self-discipline *see*
    Asceticism
Abstract
  algebra   512.02
    s.a. spec. topics of algebra
      e.g. Fields; *also*
      spec. appls. e.g.
      Engineering
  algebraic geometry   512.33
    s.a. spec. appls. e.g.
      Engineering
  analysis   515.7
    s.a. spec. appls. e.g.
      Engineering
  art *see* Abstractionism
  expressionism *see*
    Abstractionism
  groups
    sociology   302.33
  harmonic analysis   515.785
    s.a. spec. appls. e.g.
      Engineering
  measure theory   515.783
    s.a. spec. appls. e.g.
      Engineering
  motion *see* Kinematics
    mechanics
  spaces *see* Metric geometry
  subjects
    art representation *see*
      Abstractions art
      representation
  thought
    psychology *see* Abstraction
      ideation psych.
Abstraction
  ideation psych.   153.24
    animals   156.324
    children   155.413
    s.a. psych. of other spec.
      groups
  painting   759.06
    spec. places   759.1–.9
Abstractionism
  arts
    gen. wks.   709.040 52
      spec. places   709.1–.9
    painting   759.065 2
      spec. places   759.1–.9

Academic (continued)
  sermons
    Christianity   252.55
    other rel. see Preaching
  year   371.23
  law   344.079 2
    spec. jur.   344.3–.9
    s.a. spec. levels of ed.;
        also Special education
  s.a. Educational; *also*
        School
Academicians
  biog. & work *see spec. subj.*
      e.g. Lexicographers
  s.a.   *pers.*–090 1
Academies (organizations) *see*
        Organizations
Academies (schools) *see*
        Secondary schools
Acadia
  Colony Can.
    history   971.601
    s.a.   *area*–716
  Nat. Park Me.   *area*–741 45
  Par. La.   *area*–763 56
Acanthaceae *see* Personales
Acanthocephala
  culture & hunting   639.753
  zoology   595.13
  other aspects see Worms
Acanthopterygii
  culture   639.375 8
  fishing
    commercial   639.275 8
    sports   799.175 8
  zoology   597.58
  other aspects see Teleostei
Acanthus family *see* Personales
Acari
  zoology   595.42
  other aspects see Arachnida
Acariasis *see* Integument
        diseases
Acarina
  zoology   595.42
  other aspects see Arachnida
Acarnania Greece   *area*–495 1
  ancient   *area*–383
Acceleration
  biophysics
    extraterrestrial
      gen. wks.   574.191 934
      animals   591.191 934
      microorganisms   576.119 193 4
      plants   581.191 934
      s.a. spec. organisms
    med. sci.   612.014 534
      animals   636.089 201 453 4
        s.a. spec. animals
      man   612.014 534

Acceleration
  biophysics (continued)
    terrestrial
      gen. wks.   574.191 34
      animals   591.191 34
      microorganisms   576.119 134
      plants   581.191 34
      s.a. spec. organisms
    med. sci.   612.014 414
      animals   636.089 201 441 4
        s.a. spec. animals
      man   612.014 414
    s.a. spec. functions,
        systems, organs
  education
    individualized instruction
        see Individualized
        instruction
    promotion *see* Promotion
        education
  kinematics   531.112
    misc. aspects see Dynamics
  nuclear physics *see* Particles
        (matter) acceleration
Accelerator effect
  macroeconomics   339.41
Accelerators
  nuclear physics *see* Particles
        (matter) acceleration
  rubber tech. *see* Compounding
        rubber mf.
Accelerometers
  aircraft eng.   629.135 2
    s.a. spec. appls. e.g.
        Military engineering
  s.a. other spec. uses
Accent
  prosody *see* Poetry gen. wks.
        rhetoric
  speech *see* Intonation
        linguistics
Acceptances *see* Commercial
        paper
Access roads
  highway transp.
    commerce   388.13
    law *see* Roads law; *also*
        Streets local transp.
        law
  other aspects see Roads
Accessibility
  buildings *see* Location
        buildings
Accession *see* Acquisitions
Accessories
  automobiles
    law   343.094 4
      spec. jur.   343.3–.9
    soc. & econ. aspects *see*
        Secondary industries

Relative Index

|---|---|
Accessories	
automobiles (continued)	
tech. & mf.	629.27
s.a. spec. appls.	
costume soc. customs	391.44
to crime	
criminal law	345.03
spec. jur.	345.3–.9
other kinds see Equipment	
s.a. other spec. subj. e.g.	
Clothing	
Accessory	
cathedral structures	
architecture	726.69
building	690.669
other aspects see	
Religious-purpose	
bldgs.	
college structures	
architecture	727.38
building	690.738
other aspects see	
Educational buildings	
contracts *see* Contracts	
domestic structures	
architecture	728.9
building	690.89
other aspects see	
Residential buildings	
equipment	
railroad rolling stock	
technology	625.25
other aspects see Rolling	
stock railroads	
other kinds see Equipment	
s.a. other spec. subj.	
monastic structures	
architecture	726.79
building	690.679
other aspects see	
Religious-purpose	
bldgs.	
rel. bldgs.	
architecture	726.4
building	690.64
other aspects see	
Religious-purpose	
bldgs.	
s.a. spec. kinds e.g.	
Accessory cathedral	
structures	
sinuses *see* Nasal sinuses	
Accidents	
catastrophic *see* Disasters	
control	
pub. admin.	350.783
central govts.	351.783
spec. jur.	353–354
local govts.	352.3
insurance	368.384
industrial casualty	368.7

Accidents	
insurance (continued)	
private law	346.086 384
spec. jur.	346.3–.9
soc. insurance	368.42
pub. admin. *see* Social	
insurance pub. admin.	
soc. law	344.022
spec. jur.	344.3–.9
transportation	368.2
other aspects see Insurance	
s.a. other spec. kinds	
law	346.032 2
spec. jur.	346.3–.9
s.a. Safety law	
metaphysics	111.1
prevention *see* Safety	
psych. influence	155.936
soc. path.	363.1
spec. situations	
mining eng.	622.8
s.a. other spec. activities	
statistics	312.4
deaths	312.27
Accipitridae	
hunting	
commercial	639.128 916
sports	799.248 916
paleozoology	568.9
zoology	598.916
other aspects see Aves	
Acclimation	
ecology *see* Climates ecology	
hygiene	613.1
misc. aspects see Hygiene	
Accomack Co. Va.	*area*–755 16
Accommodation	
disorders of eye	
optometry	617.755
geriatrics	618.977 755
pediatrics	618.920 977 55
pub. health	614.599 7
statistics	312.304 775 5
other aspects see	
Diseases	
process	
sociology	303.6
Accommodations *see spec. kinds*	
e.g. Eating-places	
Accompaniment (music)	
music theory	781.66
s.a. spec. mediums	
Accordion music	786.97
recordings	789.912 697
Accordions	
mf. tech.	681.816 97
misc. aspects see Musical	
instruments	
musical art	786.97
Accountability	
criminals	364.3

Accountability (continued)
  government
    pub. admin. *see* Government
      malfunctioning
    rel. doctrines
      Christianity   233.4
      other rel. see Humankind
        rel. doctrines
Accountants
  biog. & work   657.092
  s.a.   *pers.*–657
Accounting
  home econ.   640.42
  management policy   658.151 1
    spec. subj.   *s.s.*–068 1
  mil. admin.   355.622
    s.a. spec. mil. branches
  organization law   346.063
    spec. jur.   346.3–.9
  pub. admin.   350.723 1
    central govts.   351.723 1
      spec. jur.   353–354
    local govts.   352.17
  technology   657
    soc. & econ. aspects *see*
      Secondary industries
Accounting-machines *see*
      Business machines
Accounts
  payable
    accounting trmt.   657.74
      s.a. spec. kinds of
        enterprise e.g.
        Insurance accounting
  receivable
    accountinq trmt.   657.72
      s.a. spec. kinds of
        enterprise e.g.
        Insurance accounting
  capital *see* Working capital
  security *see* Credit
Accreditation of schools
  education
    gen. wks   371.204
      s.a. spec. levels of ed.;
        also Special education
    govt. supervision   379.158
Accrington Lancashire Eng. *area*–427 625
Acculturation
  sociology   303.482
Accumulator
  panels elect. power *see*
      Control devices
      electrodynamic eng.
  substations elect. power
    soc. & econ. aspects *see*
      Secondary industries
    technology   621.312 6
Accumulators
  elect. eng. *see* Applied
      electrochemistry

Accumulators (continued)
  hydraulic-power tech.
    soc. & econ. aspects *see*
      Secondary industries
    tech. & mf.   621.254
      s.a. spec. appls. e.g.
        Steam engineering
  steam eng.
    soc. & econ. aspects *see*
      Secondary industries
    tech. & mf.   621.197
      s.a. spec. appls. e.g.
        Steam locomotives
Accuracy drills & tests
  shorthand   653.15
    s.a. spec. systems e.g.
      Gregg
  typewriting   652.307
    s.a. other spec. activities
Acer *see* Maple trees
Aceraceae *see* Sapindales
Acetaldehyde *see* Aldehydes
Acetales *see* Thermoplastic
      plastics
Acetamide *see* Amides
Acetanilid
  org. chem.   547.542
  pharmacology   615.314 2
    analgesics   615.783
    other aspects see Drugs
  toxicology   615.951 42
  s.a. other spec. appls. e.g.
      Lackers
Acetates
  lackers
    manufacturing
      soc. & econ. aspects *see*
        Secondary industries
      technology   667.75
  plastics *see* Thermoplastic
      plastics
  textiles
    arts   746.044 64
      s.a. spec. processes e.g.
        Weaving
    dyeing   667.346 4
    manufacturing
      soc. & econ. aspects *see*
        Secondary industries
      technology   677.464
        special-process fabrics   677.6
    org. chem.   547.856 4
    other aspects see Textiles
    s.a. spec. prod. e.g.
      Clothing
  other aspects see Esters
Acetobacteriaceae *see*
      Eubacteriales
Acetone *see* Ketones
Acetonitrile *see* Nitriles

Acorns (continued)
  other aspects see Oak
Acoustical
  detection methods
    geophysical prospecting   622.159
    s.a. spec. methods e.g.
      Sonar
  engineering   620.21–.25
    s.a. spec. appls. e.g.
      Buildings construction
  engineers
    biog. & work   620.209 2
    s.a.   *pers.*–620 2
  insulated construction   693.834
  properties
    bldg. materials   691
    crystals   548.84
    s.a. spec. substances
    eng. materials   620.112 94
    s.a. spec. materials; also
      spec. uses e.g. Roads
    lumber mf. tech.   674.132
  systems
    wire telegraphy
      technology   621.382 3
      s.a. spec. appls. e.g.
        Communication
        facilities
      other aspects see
        Telegraphy wire
Acoustics
  arch. design   729.29
    structural elements   729.3
    s.a. spec. kinds of bldgs.
  music   781.22
    s.a. spec. mediums
  other aspects see Sound
Acquired characteristics
  evolution theory   575.016 6
Acquisition
  of organizations
    management of reorganization
      658.16
  of public lands
    law   343.025 2
    spec. jur.   343.3–.9
  of real property
    law   346.043 62
    spec. jur.   346.3–.9
  of territory
    internat. law   341.42
    pol. sci.   325.32
  s.a. spec. commodities &
    services e.g.
      livestock 636.081;
      also Procurement
Acquisitions
  library econ.   025.2
  museum econ.   069.51–.52
  s.a. other institutions
Acre Brazil   *area*–811 2

Acreage allotments
  agric. econ.   338.18
    law   343.076
    spec. jur.   343.3–.9
Acridine dyes *see* Dyes
Acrobatics
  circuses   791.34
  equipment mf.   688.764 7
    soc. & econ. aspects *see*
      Secondary industries
  sports   796.47
  other aspects see Sports
Acrobats
  biog. & work   791.340 92
  s.a.   *pers.*–791 3
Acromegaly *see* Pituitary gland
    diseases
Acronyms
  polyglot dictionaries   413.1
  spec. langs.
    desc. & anal.   *lang. sub.*–1
    dictionaries   *lang. sub.*–31
  spec. subj.   *s.s.*–014 8
  other aspects see Words
Acrostics recreation   793.73
Acrothoracica *see* Cirripedia
Acrylic painting
  arts   751.426
  indiv. artists   759.1–.9
Acrylics
  plastics
    chem. tech.   668.423 2
    org. chem.   547.843 223 2
    other aspects see Plastics
    s.a. spec. prod. e.g.
      automobile windows
      629.26
  textiles
    arts   746.044 742
      s.a. spec. processes e.g.
        Weaving
    dyeing   667.347 42
    manufacturing
      soc. & econ. aspects *see*
        Secondary industries
      technology   677.474 2
        special-process fabrics   677.6
    org. chem.   547.857 42
    other aspects see Textiles
    s.a. spec. prod. e.g.
      Clothing
Acrylonitrile rubbers *see*
    Synthetic rubber
Act of Union
  Canada hist.   971.039
Acting
  dramatic performances
    motion pictures   791.430 28
    radio   791.440 28

Acting
  dramatic performances (continued)
    stage   792.028
      s.a. spec. kinds e.g.
        Tragedies (drama)
    television   791.450 28
Actiniaria *see* Anthozoa
Actinide series metals
  chemistry
    inorganic   546.42–.44
    organic   547.054 2–.054 4
      s.a. spec. groupings e.g.
        Aliphatic compounds
    soc. & econ. aspects *see*
      Secondary industries
    technology   661.042–.044
    organic   661.895
      s.a. spec. prod.
    eng. materials   620.189 292–.189 294
      s.a. spec. uses
    metallography   669.952 92–.952 94
    metallurgy   669.292–.294
    physical & chem.   669.962 92–.962 94
    pharmacology   615.242–.244
      misc. aspects see
        Pharmacology
    products
      mf. tech.   673.292–.294
      other aspects see
        Nonferrous metal
          products
    toxicology   615.925 42–.925 44
      misc. aspects see
        Toxicology
      other aspects see Metal;
        also Metals
Actinidiaceae *see* Theales
Actinium
  chemistry
    inorganic   546.421
    organic   547.054 21
      s.a. spec. groupings e.g.
        Aliphatic compounds
    soc. & econ. aspects *see*
      Secondary industries
    technology   661.042 1
    organic   661.895
      s.a. spec. prod.
    eng. materials   620.189 292 1
      s.a. spec. uses
    metallography   669.952 921
    metallurgy   669.292 1
    physical & chem.   669.962 921
    pharmacology   615.242 1
      misc. aspects see
        Pharmacology
    products
      mf. tech.   673.292 1
      other aspects see
        Nonferrous metals
          products

Actinium (continued)
    toxicology   615.925 421
      misc. aspects see
        Toxicology
      other aspects see Metal;
        also Metals
Actinomycetaceae *see*
      Actinomycetales
Actinomycetales
  botany   589.92
  med. aspects
    disease organisms   616.014 2
    gen. pharm.   615.329 92
      toxicology   615.952 992
    vet. pharm.   626.089 532 992
      toxicology   636.089 595 299 2
  paleobotany   561.9
    other aspects see Plants
Actinomycosis *see* Fungus
      diseases
Actinopoda
  culture   639.731 3
  zoology   593.13
    other aspects see Protozoa
Actinopterygii *see* Teleostei
Actinotherapy *see* Radiotherapy
Action
  freedom of civil right pol.
        sci.   323.44
  games
    indoor   793.4
    outdoor *see* Outdoor sports
  human
    metaphysics   128.4
  toys
    manufacturing
      soc. & econ. aspects *see*
        Secondary industries
    technology   688.728
Activated
  carbons *see* Adsorbent carbons
  sludge process
    sewage trmt.
      technology   628.354
      other aspects see Sewage
        treatment
Activation analysis
  anal. chem.
    gen. wks.   543.088 2
      qualitative   544.982
      quantitative   545.822
    organic   547.308 82
      qualitative   547.349 82
      quantitative   547.358 22
      s.a. spec. elements & cpds.
Activities *see spec. subj. e.g.*
        Public administration
Activity
  method
    education *see* Project
      method education

Activity (continued)
  therapies   615.851 5
    s.a. spec. diseases
Acton London Eng.   *area*–421 84
Actors
  biog. & work
    motion pictures   791.430 280 92
    radio   791.440 280 92
    stage   792.028 092
    television   791.450 280 92
  occupational ethics   174.979 1–.979 2
  persons   *pers.*–792 1
    motion pictures   *pers.*–791 4
    radio   *pers.*–791 4
    stage   *pers.*–792 1
    television   *pers.*–791 4
Actresses *see* Actors
Acts of Apostles
  Bible   226.6
    pseudepigrapha   229.92
  other aspects see New
        Testament
Actual grace
  Christian doctrines   234.1
Actuarial science   368.01
  s.a. spec. kinds of insurance
Actuaries *see* Insurance
        personnel
Acuity
  visual perception
    psychology
      gen. wks.   152.142 2
      animals   156.214 22
      children   155.412
      s.a. psych. of other
        spec. groups
    influences   155.911 422
Acupressure therapeutics   615.822
  misc. aspects see Physical
        therapies
  s.a. spec. diseases
Acupuncture therapeutics   615.892
  s.a. spec. diseases
Acyclic cpds. *see* Aliphatic
        compounds
Acylation
  chem. eng.   660.284 41
  org. chem.   547.21
  s.a. spec. elements, cpds.,
      prod.
Ada Co. Ida.   *area*–796 28
Adages
  folk lit.   398.9
Adair Co.
  Iowa   *area*–777 73
  Kentucky   *area*–769 675
  Missouri   *area*–778 264
  Oklahoma   *area*–766 89
Adamawa *see* Benue-Niger

Adams
  County
    Colorado   *area*–788 81
    Idaho   *area*–796 26
    Illinois   *area*–773 44
    Indiana   *area*–772 73
    Iowa   *area*–777 76
    Mississippi   *area*–762 26
    Nebraska   *area*–782 397
    North Dakota   *area*–784 89
    Ohio   *area*–771 86
    Pennsylvania   *area*–748 42
    Washington   *area*–797 34
    Wisconsin   *area*–775 56
  John admin.
    U.S. hist.   973.44–.45
    s.a. spec. events & subj.
      e.g. Courts
  John Quincy admin.
    U.S. hist.   973.55
    s.a. spec. events & subj.
      e.g. Courts
Adana Turkey   *area*–564
Adaptability
  psychology   155.24
    aged people   155.672
    children   155.413
    situational   155.9
    s.a. psych. of other spec.
      groups
Adaptations
  life sci. *see* Ecology
Adaptive
  control systems
    automation eng.   629.836
    s.a. spec. appls. e.g.
      Underwater guided
      missiles
Added-value taxes
  law   343.055
    spec. jur.   343.3–.9
  pub. admin.   350.724 7
    central govts.   351.724 7
    spec. jur.   353–354
    local govts.   352.135
  pub. finance   336.271 4
Adder's tongue ferns *see*
      Eusporangiated ferns
Addictions
  abnormal psych.   157.6
    animals   156.7
    children   155.454
  ethics *see* Consumption ethics
  law   344.044 6
    spec. jur.   344.3–.9
  med. sci.
    gen. med.   616.86
    geriatrics   618.976 86
    hygiene   613.8
    pediatrics   618.928 6

13

Adhesives
gen. wks.
  eng. materials (continued)
    shipbuilding   623.820 799
    structures   624.189 9
    s.a. other spec. uses
  manufacturing
    chem. tech.   668.3
    soc. & econ. aspects *see*
      Secondary industries
  s.a. other spec. uses
  masonry materials *see* Masonry
    adhesives
Adipose tissues *see* Connective
  tissue
Adirondack Mts. N.Y.   *area*–747 53
Adiyaman Turkey   *area*–565
Adjar ASSR   *area*–479 2
Adjectives *see* Words
Adjudication
  internat. law   341.55
Adjustable bearings *see*
  Bearings
Adjustments
  insurance claims   368.014
  s.a. spec. kinds of
    insurance
  statistical math.   519.86
  s.a. spec. appls. e.g.
    Engineering
  to environment *see* Ecology
  wage & salary admin. *see*
    Compensation personnel
    admin.
  s.a.   *s.s.*–028 8
Adlerian systems
  psychology   150.195 3
  s.a. spec. subj. & branches
    of psych. e.g.
    Psychoneuroses
Adlington Lancashire Eng. *area*–427 615
Administration
  of justice
    crimes against
      criminology   364.134
      law   345.023 4
        spec. jur.   345.3–.9
      soc. theology
        Christianity   261.833 134
        comp. rel.   291.178 331 34
        s.a. other spec. rel.
    law   347
      criminal   345.05
      spec. jur.   345.3–.9
    s.a. Management; *also spec.*
      organizations e.g.
      United Nations
Administrative
  areas civic art   711.551
  assistants
    office management   651.3

Administrative (continued)
  counties local pub. admin. 352.007 3
  courts
    law   342.066 4
      spec. jur.   342.3–.9
      spec. subj.   *law s.s.*–026 9
    law   342.06
      spec. jur.   342.3–.9
  personnel
    libraries   023.4
    s.a. spec. library
      activities e.g.
      Cataloging
    museums   069.63
    s.a. spec. museum
      activities e.g.
      Selection procedures
    office services   651.3
    schools   371.201 1–.201 3
    s.a. spec. levels of ed.;
      also Special education
    s.a. other spec.
      organizations &
      activities
  procedure
    law   342.066
      spec. jur.   342.3–.9
  regulations
    law   348.025
      spec. jur.   348.3–.9
    U.S.
      Federal   348.732 5
      state & local   348.74–.79
    spec. subj.   *law s.s.*–026 36
  revenues pub. finance   336.16
    misc. aspects see Nontax
      revenues
  rooms
    library bldgs.   022
    museum bldgs.   069.24
    s.a. other spec. activities
  secretaries
    office management   651.3
  services
    armed forces   355.341
    s.a. spec. mil. branches
    s.a. other spec. activities
  s.a. Managerial; *also other*
    spec. subj.
Administrators
  gen. wks. *see* Managers
  public *see* Public
    administrators
Admiralty
  courts *see* Specialized courts
  departments *see* Defense
    (military) pub. admin.
    departments
  Islands   *area*–937
  law   343.096
    spec. jur.   343.3–.9

Adsorption-analysis
  anal. chem. (continued)
   s.a. spec. elements & cpds.
Adult
  baptism
   Christian doctrines   234.161 3
   Christian rites   265.13
  development *see* Development
   (biology)
  education   374
   finance
    law   344.076 84
     spec. jur.   344.3–.9
   spec. subj.   *s.s.*–071 5
Adulterations
  control meas.
   offenses *see* Public health
    offenses
   product safety *see* Product
    safety
  s.a. spec. prod. e.g. Foods
Adultery *see* Extramarital sex
  relations
Adults
  criminal offenders   364.37
  education *see* Adult education
  hygiene   613.043 4–.043 8
  journalism for   070.483 4
  meditations for
   Christianity   242.64
   other rel. see Worship
  personal rel.
   Christianity   248.84
   other rel. see Personal
    religion
  prayers for
   Christianity   242.84
   other rel. see Worship
  psychology   155.6
  recreation   790.192
   indoor   793.019 2
   outdoor   796.019 2
  rel. associations
   Christianity   267.1
   other rel. see Religious
    associations
  soc. theology
   Christianity   261.834 24
   comp. rel.   291.178 342 4
   s.a. other spec. rel.
  sociology   305.24
  Sunday school divisions
   Christianity   268.434
   other rel. see Religious
    instruction
  writing easy books for
   rhetoric   808.067
  other spec. subj.   *pers.*–056
  s.a. Men; *also* Women;
   also Middle-aged
   people

Adunata
  paleozoology   563.91
Adur West Sussex Eng.   *area*–422 69
Advaita philosophy   181.482
Advanced
  elementary schools   373.236
   govt. supervision & support   379
  placement higher ed.   378.105
  societies
   sociology   301.74
Advances *see spec. subj. e.g.*
  Glaciers
Advent
  devotional lit.   242.33
  rel. observance   263.91
  Roman Catholic liturgy   264.027 2
  sermons   252.61
  theology
   incarnation   232.1
   second coming   232.6
Advent Christian Church   286.73
  misc. aspects see Adventists
   (denominations)
Adventists (denominations)   286.7
  Christian life guides   248.486 7
  church buildings
   architecture   726.586 7
   building   690.658 67
   other aspects see
    Religious-purpose
    bldgs.
  doctrines   230.67
   creeds   238.67
  general councils   262.567
  govt. & admin.   262.067
   parishes   254.067
  missions   266.67
  moral theology   241.046 7
  music
   arts   783.026 67
    recordings   789.912 302 667
    s.a. spec. instruments;
     also spec. kinds e.g.
     Liturgical music
   religion
    pub. worship   264.067 02
    significance   246.7
  private prayers for   242.806 7
  pub. worship   264.067
  rel. associations
   adults   267.186 7
   men   267.246 7
   women   267.446 7
   young adults   267.626 7
  rel. instruction   268.867
  rel. law   262.986 7
  schools   377.867
  secondary training   207.126 7
  sermons   252.067
  theological seminaries   207.116 7
  s.a. other spec. aspects

Aerodynamics
mechanics (continued)
  physics — 533.62
  meteorology — 551.515 3
Aeroelasticity
  aeronautical aerodynamics — 629.132 362
  s.a. spec. appls. e.g.
    Flying
Aeromechanics
  aeronautical eng. — 629.132 3
  s.a. spec. appls. e.g.
    Flying
  engineering — 620.107
  s.a. spec. appls. e.g.
    Aerospace engineering
  physics — 533.6
Aeronautical engineers
  biog. & work — 629.130 092
  s.a. spec. kinds e.g. wing
    designers
    629.134 320 92
  s.a. — *pers.*–629 1
Aeronautics
  lit. & stage trmt. *see* Things
  soc. & econ. aspects *see*
    Secondary industries
  technology — 629.13
  s.a. spec. appls. e.g.
    Military engineering
  s.a. Aviation
Aeroplanes *see* Airplanes
Aerosols
  colloid chem. — 541.345 15
    applied — 660.294 515
    organic — 547.134 515
    s.a. spec. elements, cpds.,
      prod.
  meteorology
    artificial modification — 551.68
    gen. wks. — 551.511 3
      atmospheric electricity — 551.564
      s.a. other spec. aspects
    weather forecasting — 551.64
    spec. areas — 551.65
Aerospace
  engineering
    soc. & econ. aspects *see*
      Secondary industries
    technology — 629.1
      military — 623.66
    other aspects see
      Transportation
      engineering
  engineers
    biog. & work — 629.109 2
    s.a. spec. kinds e.g.
      Aeronautical engineers
    s.a. — *pers.*–629 1
  medicine — 616.980 21
    s.a. spec. diseases

Aerospace (continued)
  photography technique — 778.35
    mil. eng. — 623.72
Aerostatics
  aeronautical eng. — 629.132 2
    s.a. spec. appls. e.g.
      Flying
  mechanics
    engineering *see* Statics
      eng. mech.
    physics — 533.61
    meteorology — 551.515 2
Aerosteam engines
  stationary
    soc. & econ. aspects *see*
      Secondary industries
    tech. & mf. — 621.166
    s.a. spec. appls. e.g.
      Power plants
Aerotherapeutics — 615.836
  misc. aspects see Physical
    therapies
  s.a. spec. diseases
Aerotropism *see* Tropisms
Aesthetics
  arts — 701.17
    literature — 801.93
    s.a. other spec. art forms
  philosophy — 111.85
Aetolia Greece — *area*–495 1
  ancient — *area*–383
Aextoxicaceae *see* Celastrales
Afan West Glamorgan Wales
  — *area*–429 85
Afars territory — *area*–677 1
Affection
  psychology *see* Emotions
  virtues *see* Virtues
Affective processes
  psychology *see* Emotions
Affenpinscher dogs
  animal husbandry — 636.76
  other aspects see Dogs
Affidavits *see* Witnesses law
Affiliated broadcasting stations
  see Broadcasting
    stations
Affiliation law *see* Paternity
  law
Affine geometry — 516.4
  s.a. spec. appls. e.g.
    Engineering
Affinity
  law — 346.015
    spec. jur. — 346.3–.9
Affixes *see* Words
Afflicted people
  parochial activities for
    Christianity — 259.4
    other rel. see Pastoral
      theology

Afflicted people (continued)
  personal rel.
    Christianity   248.86
    other rel. see Personal
      religion
  sermons
    Christianity   252.56
    other rel. see Preaching
Afforestation
  silviculture   634.956
  s.a. spec. trees
Afghan
  language *see* Pashto language
  people   *r.e.n.*–915 9
  rugs textile arts   746.758 1
  s.a. Afghanistan; *also other*
    spec. subj. e.g. Arts
Afghanistan   *area*–581
Africa   *area*–6
African
  languages
    linguistics   496
    literatures   896
    s.a.   *lang.*–96
  people   *r.e.n.*–96
  regional organizations
    internat. law   341.249
    treaties   341.026 39
  sleeping sickness *see*
    Trypanosomiasis
  violets *see* Personales
  s.a. Africa; *also other*
    spec. subj. e.g. Arts
African Methodist Episcopal
    Church   287.83
  misc. aspects see Methodist
African Methodist Episcopal Zion
    Church   287.83
  misc. aspects see Methodist
Afrikaans
  language
    linguistics   439.36
    literature   839.36
    s.a.   *lang.*–393 6
  s.a. South Africa; *also*
    other spec. subj. e.g.
    Arts
Afro-American
  cookery   641.592 960 73
  people   *r.e.n.*–960 73
Afro-Asian bloc
  regional subj. trmt.   *area*–171 65
  s.a. spec. countries
Afro-Asiatic languages
  linguistics   492
  literatures   892
  s.a.   *lang.*–92
After-dinner
  speaking *see* Public speaking
  speeches *see* Public speeches

Aftereffects of drugs
  pharmacodynamics   615.704 3
  misc. aspects see
    Pharmacology
Afterimages
  visual perception
  psychology
    gen. wks.   152.148
    animals   156.214 8
    children   155.412
    s.a. psych. of other
      spec. groups
    influences   155.911 48
Afternoon
  influence on crime   364.22
  lit. & stage trmt. *see* Times
  prayer *see* Prayer gen. wks.
  weekday schools rel.
    instruction *see*
      Religious instruction
    eccelesiastical
      theology
Afyon-Karahisar Turkey   *area*–562
Agadir Morocco   *area*–646
Agalega isl. Indian Ocean   *area*–694
Agapes Christian rites   265.9
Agar
  food *see* Gelatins
  other aspects see Phaeophyta
Agaricaceae
  agric. pathogen   632.422 3
    s.a. spec. plants; also
      spec. types of culture
      e.g. Forestry
  botany   589.222 3
  med. aspects
    gen. pharm.   615.329 222 3
    toxicology   615.952 922 23
    vet. pharm.   636.089 532 922 23
    toxicology   636.089 595 292 223
  other aspects see Fungi
Agaricales
  agric. pathogens   632.422
    s.a. spec. plants; also
      spec. types of culture
      e.g. Forestry
  botany   589.222
  med. aspects
    gen. pharm.   615.329 222
    toxicology   615.952 922 2
    vet. pharm.   636.089 532 922 2
    toxicology   636.089 595 292 22
  other asoects see Fungi
Agateware *see* Enamels
Agavaceae *see* Agavales
Agavales
  botany   584.43
  floriculture   635.934 43
  med. aspects
    crop prod.   633.884 43

Agavales
  med. aspects (continued)
    gen. pharm.   615.324 43
      toxicology   615.952 443
    vet. pharm.   636.089 532 443
      toxicology   636.089 595 244 3
    paleobotany   561.4
    other aspects see Plants
Agave
  fibers
    agriculture   633.577
      soc. & econ. aspects *see*
        Primary industries
    other aspects see Agavales
  sisalina *see* Agave fibers
Agdestidaceae *see* Chenopodiales
Age
  levels incidence
    population statistics   312.92
  requirements
    employees *see* Personal
      qualifications
    voting *see* Voting
      qualifications
Aged people
  architecture for   720.43
  asylums for *see* Aged people
    institutions for
  employees
    pers. admin.
      gen. management   658.304 2
      spec. subj.   *s.s.*–068 3
    pub. admin.   350.1
      central govts.   351.1
      spec. jur.   353–354
      local govts.   352.005 1
  ethics   170.202 26
  etiquette   395.126
  food preparation for
    home econ.   641.562 7
  housing meas.   363.59
    misc. aspects see Housing
  income taxes
    law   343.052 6
    spec. jur.   343.3–.9
  institutions for
    buildings
      architecture   725.56
      building   690.556
      other aspects see Public
        structures
    soc. services   362.61
    misc. aspects see Aged
      people sociology soc.
      services
  insurance *see* Old-age &
    survivors' insurance
  labor
    economics   331.398

Aged people
  labor (continued)
    pub. admin.   350.838 6
      central govts.   351.838 6
      spec. jur.   353–354
      local govts.   352.943 86
  law   346.013
    spec. jur.   346.3–.9
  libraries for   027.622
    administration   025.197 622
    buildings
      architecture   727.826 22
      functional planning   022.316 22
    catalogs *see* Library
      catalogs
    reference services   025.527 762 2
    selection for   025.218 762 2
    use studies   025.587 622
    user orientation   025.567 622
    s.a. other spec. activities
      e.g. Cataloging
  med. sci.
    geriatrics   618.97
    hygiene   613.043 8
    physiology   612.67
  meditations for
    Christianity   242.65
    other rel. see Worship
  parochial activities for
    Christianity   259.3
    other rel. see Pastoral
      theology
  personal living   646.79
  personal rel.
    Christianity   248.85
    other rel. see Personal
      religion
  prayers for
    Christianity   242.85
    other rel. see Worship
  psychology   155.67
  recreation   790.192 6
    indoor   793.019 26
    outdoor   796.019 26
  sermons for
    Christianity   252.56
    other rel. see Preaching
  soc. theology
    Christianity   261.834 26
    comp. rel.   291.178 342 6
    s.a. other spec. rel.
  sociology   305.26
    soc. insurance   368.43
      accident & health   368.426
      pub. admin. *see* Social
        insurance pub. admin.
    soc. services   362.6
      govt. control   350.846
      central govts.   351.846
      spec. jur.   353–354
      local govts.   352.944 6

Agricultural
chemicals
manufacturing (continued)
soc. & econ. aspects *see*
Secondary industries
use *see* Agricultural
chemistry
chemistry ... 630.24
s.a. spec. appls. e.g. Pest
control
civilization ... 909
classes
biog. & work ... 630.92
s.a. spec. kinds e.g.
Fruit growers
occupational ethics
philosophy ... 174.963
religion
Buddhism ... 294.356 496 3
Christianity ... 241.649 63
comp. rel. ... 291.564 963
Hinduism ... 294.548 649 63
s.a. other spec. rel.
other aspects see Lower
classes
climatology ... 630.251 6
communities
sociology ... 307.72
cooperatives econ. ... 334.683
credit
financial econ. ... 332.71
institutions *see*
Agricultural banks
prod. econ. ... 338.18
other aspects see Credit
economics *see* Agricultural
industries economics
enterprises *see* Agricultural
industries
equipment
manufacturing
soc. & econ. aspects *see*
Secondary industries
technology ... 681.763
shortages
prod. econ. ... 338.14
use ... 631.3
s.a. spec. crops; also
spec. types of culture
e.g. Floriculture
s.a. spec. kinds e.g. Farm
fences
experiment
buildings
architecture ... 727.563
building ... 690.756 3
other aspects see
Educational buildings
stations ... 630.724
s.a. Agricultural research
extension work ... 630.715

Agricultural (continued)
finance
prod. econ. ... 338.13
geology ... 630.25
high schools ... 373.246 3
govt. supervision & support ... 379
implements *see* Agricultural
equipment
industries
accounting ... 657.863
govt. control
activities ... 351.823 3
spec. jur. ... 353–354
departments ... 351.082 33
spec. jur. ... 353–354
labor econ. ... 331.763
active employment ... 331.125 3
aged workers ... 331.398 83
collective bargaining ... 331.890 43
employment conditions ... 331.204 3
ind. relations ... 331.043
labor force ... 331.119 3
market ... 331.129 3
need ... 331.123 3
opportunities ... 331.124 3
pensions ... 331.252 9
strikes ... 331.892 83
unemployment ... 331.137 83
unions ... 331.881 3
wages ... 331.283
women workers ... 331.483
young workers ... 331.383
labor law *see* Labor law
prod. econ. ... 338.1
organization ... 338.763
cooperatives ... 334.683
mergers ... 338.836 3
restrictive practices ... 338.826 3
products *see* Agricultural
products
regulation
law ... 343.076
spec. jur. ... 343.3–.9
instruments *see* Agricultural
equipment
insurance
crops ... 368.122
livestock ... 368.56
other aspects see Insurance
land
agriculture *see* Soils
agriculture
other aspects see Rural
lands
life
civilization ... 909
machinery *see* Agricultural
equipment
meteorology ... 630.251 5
pests *see* Pests agriculture
physics ... 630.23

Aid (continued)
  to education
    law   344.076 3
      spec. jur.   344.3–.9
    s.a. Welfare services
Aids to perfection
  rel. self-discipline *see*
    Asceticism
Aiken Co. S.C.   *area*–757 75
Aikido
  equipment mf.   688.768 154
    soc. & econ. aspects *see*
      Secondary industries
  sports   796.815 4
  other aspects see Sports
Ailanthus family *see* Rutales
Ailerons
  aircraft eng.
    soc. & econ. aspects *see*
      Secondary industries
    tech. & mf.   629.134 33
Aiming
  mil. gunnery   623.557
    s.a. spec. appls. e.g.
      Naval gunnery
Ain France   *area*–444 4
Aïn-Sefra Algeria   *area*–657
Ainu *see* Paleosiberian
Air
  bags
    automobiles   629.276
  bases
    mil. eng.   623.661 3
    mil. sci.   358.417
    spec. wars
      World War 1   940.443
      World War 2   940.544 3
      s.a. other spec. wars;
        also hist. of spec.
        countries
  chem. tech.   665.82
    soc. & econ. aspects *see*
      Secondary industries
  combat *see* Air warfare
  compression *see*
    Air-compression
  compressors pneumatic eng.
    technology   621.51
    s.a. spec. appls. e.g.
      Sandblasts
    other aspects see Pneumatic
      engineering
  conditioning *see*
    Air-conditioning
  controllers   *pers.*–629 1
  currents
    aeronautics
      aerodynamics   629.132 3
      aerostatics   629.132 2
      flying eng.   629.132 4

Air
  currents
    aeronautics (continued)
      s.a. spec. appls. e.g.
        Flying
    meteorology *see* Wind
      systems
    other aspects see
      Aerodynamics
  engines
    soc. & econ. aspects *see*
      Secondary industries
    tech. & mf.   621.42
    s.a. spec. appls. e.g.
      Pumps
  facilities
    mil. transp. tech.   623.66
    s.a. spec. appls. e.g.
      Takeoff procedures
    s.a. spec. subj. e.g.
      Airplanes
  filters internal combustion
    engines
    automobiles *see* Fuel
      systems internal
      combustion engines
      automobiles
    s.a. other spec. appls.
  forces
    law   343.018 4
      spec. jur.   343.3–.9
    mil. sci.   358.4
    s.a. Air-force; *also*
      Armed forces
  freight *see* Freight
    transportation
  fronts met.   551.551 2
    artificial modification 551.685 12
    weather forecasting   551.645 12
    spec. areas   551.65
  guns
    art metalwork   739.73
    customs   399
    mil. eng.   623.441
  holes *see* Air pockets
  hygiene of   613.19
    misc. aspects see Hygiene
  mail
    postal commun.   383.144
    other aspects see Postal
      communication
  masses met.   551.551 2
    artificial modification 551.685 12
    weather forecasting   551.645 12
    spec. areas   551.65
  mechanics
    engineering   620.107
    s.a. spec. appls. e.g.
      Aerospace engineering
    physics   533.6

Air (continued)
  medium for projectiles
    solid dynamics   531.552
  motors *see* Air engines
  navigation *see* Navigation
  pockets
    aeronautical aerodynamics   629.132 327
    s.a. spec. appls. e.g.
      Flying
  pollution
    control
      law
        international   341.762 3
        municipal   344.046 342
        spec. jur.   344.3–.9
      pub. admin.   350.823 24
        central govts.   351.823 24
        spec. jur.   353–354
        local govts.   352.942 324
    plant injuries agric.   632.19
    s.a. spec. plants; also
      spec. types of agric.
      e.g. Forestry
    sanitary eng.
      soc. & econ. aspects *see*
        Secondary industries
      technology   628.53
      s.a. spec. appls. e.g.
        Internal-combustion
        engines
      soc. aspects   363.739 2
  pressures biophysics *see*
    Pressure biophysics
  propulsion
    soc. & econ. aspects *see*
      Secondary industries
    technology   621.42
    s.a. spec. appls. e.g.
      Air-compression-powered
      locomotives
  raids *see* Air-raids
  resistance
    aeronautical aerodynamics   629.132 34
    s.a. spec. appls. e.g.
      Flying
    exterior ballistics
      mil. eng.   623.415
  resources
    economics   333.92
    govt. control
      law   346.046 92
      spec. jur.   346.3–.9
      pub. admin. *see* Natural
        resources govt. control
        pub. admin.
  rights
    economics   333.92
    sale & gift   333.339
  routes *see* Routes transp.
    services

Air (continued)
  screws
    aircraft eng.
      soc. & econ. aspects *see*
        Secondary industries
      tech. & mf.   629.134 36
    seasoning lumber mf.
      soc. & econ. aspects *see*
        Secondary industries
      technology   674.382
    sports   797.5
    misc. aspects see Sports
  supply *see* Air-supply
  temperatures met.   551.525
    artificial modification   551.682 5
    weather forecasting   551.642 5
    spec. areas   551.65
  terminal buildings *see* Air
    transportation
    buildings
  traffic control
    commerce *see* Traffic
      control
    engineering   629.136 6
    military   623.666
    s.a. other spec. appls.
  transportation
    accidents   363.124
    misc. aspects see
      Transportation
      accidents
    buildings
      architecture   725.39
      building   690.539
      law
        international   341.756 77
        municipal   343.097 7
        spec. jur.   343.3–.9
      other aspects see Public
        structures
      s.a. Airport facilities
    commerce   387.7
    engineering *see* Aeronautics
    facilities civic art   711.78
    govt. control   351.877 7
      spec. jur.   353–354
    hazards
      soc. path.   363.124
    insurance   368.24
    misc. aspects see
      Insurance
    law
      international   341.756 7
      municipal   343.097
      spec. jur.   343.3–.9
    personnel
      biog. & work   387.709 2
      s.a.   *pers.*–387 7
    safety
      law
        international   341.756 7

Air
  transportation
    safety
      law (continued)

municipal	343.097
spec. jur.	343.3–.9
pub. meas.	363.124

        govt. control *see*
          Safety pub. admin.
      other asepcts see
        Transportation
  turbines *see* Air propulsion
  utilization *see* Air resources
  warfare

law of war	341.63
mil. sci.	358.4

    technology *see* Military
      engineering
    s.a. spec. wars
    other aspects see Gases
  s.a. Aerial
Airborne

infantry mil. sci.	356.166

Air-breathing engines
  aircraft eng.
    soc. & econ. aspects *see*
      Secondary industries

tech. & mf.	629.134 352–.134 353

Airbrush
  drawing

drawing	741.29
indiv. artists	741.092
spec. appls.	741.5–.7
spec. subj.	743.4–.8
painting	751.494
indiv. artists	759.1–.9

Air-compression engineering
  automobile engines
    soc. & econ. aspects *see*
      Secondary industries

tech. & mf.	629.250 7
parts & systems	629.259 4

    s.a. spec. appls. e.g.
      Motorcycles
  other aspects see Pneumatic
    engineering
Air-compression-powered
  automobiles

commerce	388.34

    engineering

gen. tech. & mf.	629.229 4
maintenance	629.287 94
models	629.221 94
operation	629.284 94

      s.a. other spec. aspects
        e.g. Brakes; *also*
        spec. appls. e.g.
        Driving motor vehicles
    soc. & econ. aspects *see*
      Secondary industries
  other aspects see Land
    vehicles

Air-compression-powered (continued)
  engines *see* Air engines
  locomotives

commerce	385.365
special-duty	385.5

    engineering
      technology

gen. wks.	625.265
accessory equip.	625.25
running gear	625.21
monorail	625.28

    other aspects see Rolling
      stock railroads
Air-conditioning
  effect

library bldgs.	022.8
museum bldgs.	069.29

  engineering
    soc. & econ. aspects *see*
      Secondary industries

technology	697.93

    aircraft
      soc. & econ. aspects
        see Secondary
        industries

tech. & mf.	629.134 42

    automobiles
      soc. & econ. aspects
        see Secondary
        industries

tech. & mf.	629.277
buildings	697.93
mines	622.42

    railroad cars *see*
      Passenger-train cars

ships	623.853 7
design	623.814 537
spec. craft	623.812

  engineers

biog. & work	697.930 92
s.a.	*pers.–697*
hygiene	613.5

    misc. aspects see Hygiene
  management

households	644.5
industry	658.25
spec. subj.	*s.s.–068 2*
pipe fitting	696.2

Aircraft
  accidents

disaster relief soc. welfare	361.58

    statistics *see* Aviation
      accidents
  air transportion law

international	341.756 75
municipal	343.097 5
spec. jur.	343.3–.9
commerce	387.732–.733
govt. control	351.877 732–.877 733
spec. jur.	353–354

Aircraft (continued)
detection civil defense *see*
  Civil defense
engineering
 soc. & econ. aspects *see*
  Secondary industries
 tech. & mf.   629.133
  military eng.   623.741–.746
  s.a. other spec. appls.
engineers
 biog. & work   629.133 092
 s.a.   *pers.–629 1*
failures
 air transp. hazards   363.124 16
flying
 sports   797.52–.55
 other aspects see Sports
gunnery mil. eng.   623.555
hangars *see* Air
  transportation
  buildings
influences psychology   155.965
marketing *see* Marketing
navigators
 biog. & work   629.132 510 92
 s.a.   *pers.–629 1*
noise
 aeronautical aerodynamics   629.132 3
 soc. aspects   363.741
 other aspects see Noise
 s.a. spec. appls. e.g.
  Flying
operation
 commerce   387.740 44
 govt. control   351.877 740 44
  spec. jur.   353–354
 law
  international   341.756 75
  municipal   343.097 5
  spec. jur.   343.3–.9
ordnance
pollution by
 soc. aspects   363.731
 other aspects see Pollution
racing
 sports   797.52
 other aspects see Sports
sanitation *see* Public
  carriers sanitation
Aircraft-carriers
engineering   623.825 5
 design   623.812 55
 models   623.820 155
naval forces
 materiel   359.83
 organization   359.325 5
 seamanship   623.882 55
other aspects see Vessels
 (nautical)

Air-cushion vehicles
land transp.
 commerce   388.35
 govt. control   350.878 3
  central govts.   351.878 3
  spec. jur.   353–354
  local govts.   352.918 3
 other aspects see Land
  vehicles
soc. & econ. aspects *see*
  Secondary industries
technology   629.3
 mil. eng.   623.748
water transp. *see* Vessels
 (nautical)
Aird Highland Scot.   *area*–411 75
Airdrie Strathclyde Scot.   *area*–414 46
Airdromes *see* Airports
Aireborough West Yorkshire Eng.
     area–428 19
Airedales
animal husbandry   636.755
other aspects see Dogs
Airflow
aeronautical aerodynamics   629.132 32
 s.a. spec. appls. e.g.
  Flying
other aspects see
 Aerodynamics
Airfoils aircraft eng.
soc. & econ. aspects *see*
  Secondary industries
tech. & mf.   629.134 32
 s.a. spec. appls. e.g.
  Military engineering
Air-force
cookery home econ.   641.573
departments
 U.S. govt.   353.63
 other jur. see Defense
  (military) pub. admin.
  departments
personnel
 biog. & work   358.400 92
  s.a. hist. of spec.
   countries & spec. wars
 s.a.   *pers.–358*
s.a. Military
Airframes aircraft eng.
soc. & econ. aspects *see*
  Secondary industries
tech. & mf.   629.134 31
 s.a. spec. appls. e.g.
  Military engineering
Air-freight *see* Freight
  transportation
Airline
companies
 commerce   387.706 5
 govt. control   351.877 706 5
  spec. jur.   353–354

Airline
  companies (continued)
    law
      international   341.753
      municipal   346.06
        spec. jur.   346.3–.9
    cookery home econ.   641.575 4
    terminals *see* Airports
Airmen *see* Pilots aerial
Air-mileage indicators
  aircraft eng.   629.135 1
Airplanes
  aeronautical eng.
    gen. tech. & mf.   629.133 34
      components & tech.   629.134
      models   629.133 134
      operation   629.132 521
      soc. & econ. aspects *see*
        Secondary industries
    military   623.746
    s.a. other spec. appls.
  commerce   387.733 4
    misc. aspects see Aircraft
      commerce
  paper
    handicrafts   745.592
  other aspects see Aircraft
Airport
  activities
    freight *see* Freight
      services
    passenger *see* Passenger
      services
  buildings
    comm. aspects *see* Airport
      facilities
    tech. aspects *see* Air
      transportation
      buildings
  facilities
    civic art   711.78
    commerce   387.736 2
    govt. control   350.877 736 2
      central govts.   351.877 736 2
        spec. jur.   353–354
      local govts.   352.917 736 2
    law *see* Airports air
      transp. law
    s.a. Air transportation
      buildings
Airports
  air transp. law
    international   341.756 77
    municipal   343.097 7
      spec. jur.   343.3–.9
  commerce   387.736
  construction
    engineering *see* Airports
      engineering
    mil. sci.   358.22

Airports (continued)
  engineering   629.136
    mil. transp.   623.66
    s.a. other spec. appls.
  govt. control   350.877 736
    central govts.   351.877 736
      spec. jur.   353–354
    local govts.   352.917 736
Air-position indicators
  aircraft eng.   629.135 1
Air-pressure control
  spacecraft eng.
    gen. wks.   629.470 44
      unmanned   629.460 44
    life-support systems   629.477 5
      unmanned   629.467 5
    other aspects see
      Spacecraft
Air-raid
  shelters
    mil. eng.   623.38
  warning systems
    mil. eng.   623.737
    other aspects see Warning
      systems
Air-raids
  civilian protection *see* Civil
    defense
  history
    World War 1   940.442
    World War 2   940.544 2
    s.a. other spec. wars; also
      hist. of spec. places
  mil. sci.   358.42
Air-return equipment
  air-conditioning eng.   697.932 5
Airships
  aeronautical eng.
    gen. tech. & mf.   629.133 24
      components & tech.   629.134
      models   629.133 124
      operation   629.132 522
      soc. & econ. aspects *see*
        Secondary industries
    military   623.743
    s.a. other spec. appls.
  commerce   387.732 4
    misc. aspects see Aircraft
      commerce
  other aspects see Aircraft
Airsickness *see* Motion sickness
Airspace
  internat. law   341.46
Air-speed indicators
  aircraft eng.   629.135 2
    s.a. spec. appls. e.g.
      Military engineering
Airstrips
  engineering
    gen. wks.   629.136 12
    details   629.136 3–.136 8

Airstrips
  engineering (continued)
    military   623.661 2
    s.a. other spec. appls.
  other aspects see Airports
Air-supply
  control
    spacecraft eng.   629.477 5
      unmanned   629.467 5
      other aspects see
        Spacecraft
    s.a. other spec.
      environments
  equipment
    air-conditioning eng.   697.932 5
    s.a. other spec. tech.
Air-taxi
  accidents   363.124 93
    misc. aspects see
      Transportation
      accidents
Air-to-air
  guided missiles mil. eng.
    soc. & econ. aspects *see*
      Secondary industries
    tech. & mf.   623.451 91
  missile-launching forces
    mil. sci.   358.43
Air-to-surface
  guided missiles mil. eng.
    soc. & econ. aspects *see*
      Secondary industries
    tech. & mf.   623.451 92
  missile-launching forces
    mil. sci.   358.42
Air-to-underwater
  guided missiles mil. eng.
    soc. & econ. aspects *see*
      Secondary industries
    tech. & mf.   623.451 93
  missile-launching forces
    mil. sci.   358.42
Air-turbine engines *see* Air
    engines
Airways
  navigation   629.132 51
  routes *see* Routes transp.
    services
Aisén Chile   *area*–836 2
Aisne France   *area*–443 45
Aiti Japan   *area*–521 6
Aitkin Co. Minn.   *area*–776 72
Aizoaceae *see* Caryophyllales
Ajlun Jordan   *area*–569 54
Ajman   *area*–535 7
Ajmer India   *area*–544
Akan states hist.   966.701
  s.a. spec. events & subj.
    e.g. Commerce
Akaniaceae *see* Sapindales

Akbar reign India hist.   954.025 4
  s.a. spec. events & subj.
    e.g. Commerce
Akershus Norway   *area*–482
Akhaia Greece *see* Achaea
Akhenaton reign Egypt hist.   932.014
  s.a. spec. events & subj.
    e.g. Commerce
Akhmimic *see* Coptic
Akimiski Isl. Northwest Ter.
                  area–719 4
Akita
  dog animal husbandry   636.73
    misc. aspects see Dogs
  Japan   *area*–521 1
Akkadian
  period Mesopotamia hist.   935.01
    s.a. spec. events & subj.
      e.g. Arts
  s.a. East Semitic
Aklan Philippines   *area*–599 5
Akmolinsk USSR   *area*–584 5
Akron O.   *area*–771 36
Alabama
  River   *area*–761 2
  state   *area*–761
Alabama (ship)
  battle with Kearsarge
    U.S. hist.   973.754
Alabamine *see* Astatine
Alabaster *see* Gypsum
Alachua Co. Fla.   *area*–759 79
Aladdin ovens
  cookery   641.588
Alagoas Brazil   *area*–813 5
Alajuela Costa Rica   *area*–728 65
Alamance Co. N.C.   *area*–756 58
Alamanni *see* Alemanni
Alameda Co. Calif.   *area*–794 65
Alamosa Co. Colo.   *area*–788 36
Aland Isls. Finland   *area*–489 73
Alangiaceae *see* Araliales
Alarm systems
  engineering
    fire safety engineering   628.922 5
    gen. wks. *see*
      Public-address systems
    mil. eng.   623.73
  other aspects see Warning
    systems
Alaska
  Gulf *see* Alaskan Pacific
    seawaters
  Range   *area*–798 3
  state   *area*–798
Alaskan
  malamutes
    animal husbandry   636.73
    other aspects see Dogs
  Pacific seawaters
    oceanography   551.466 34

Alaskan
  Pacific seawaters (continued)
    regional subj. trmt.   *area*–164 34
    other aspects see Pacific
      Ocean
Alastrim
  gen. med.   616.913
  geriatrics   618.976 913
  pediatrics   618.929 13
  pub. health   614.521
  statistics   312.391 3
    deaths   312.269 13
  other aspects see Diseases
Alaudidae
  hunting
    commercial   639.128 812
    sports   799.248 812
  paleozoology   568.8
  zoology   598.812
  other aspects see Aves
Álava Spain   *area*–466 5
Alba Romania   *area*–498 4
Albacete Spain   *area*–467 71
Albacores *see* Acanthopterygii
Albacutya Lake Vic.   *area*–945 9
Albania (Balkans)   *area*–496 5
Albania (Caucasus) ancient   *area*–395
Albanian
  language
    linguistics   491.991
    literature   891.991
    s.a.   *lang.*–919 91
  people   *r.e.n.*–919 91
  s.a. Albania (Balkans); *also*
    other spec. subj. e.g.
      Arts
Albany
  city
    New York   *area*–747 43
    W. Aust.   *area*–941 2
  County
    New York   *area*–747 42
    Wyoming   *area*–787 95
Albatrosses *see*
    Procellariiformes
Albay Philippines   *area*–599 1
Albemarle
  Co. Va.   *area*–755 482
  Sound
    oceanography   551.461 48
    regional subj. trmt.   *area*–163 48
    other aspects see Atlantic
      Ocean
Alberga S. Aust.   *area*–942 38
Albert
  Co. N.B.   *area*–715 31
  Lake   *area*–676 1
  1 reign Belgium hist.   949.304 1
    s.a. spec. events & subj.
      e.g. Commerce

Albert (continued)
  2 reign Ger. hist.   943.028
    s.a. spec. events & subj.
      e.g. Commerce
Alberta   *area*–712 3
Albigensian churches   284.4
  Christian life guides   248.484 4
  doctrines   230.44
    creeds   238.44
  general councils   262.544
  govt. & admin.   262.044
    parishes   254.044
  missions   266.44
  moral theology   241.044 4
  private prayers for   242.804 4
  pub. worship   264.044
  rel. associations
    adults   267.184 4
    men   267.244 4
    women   267.444 4
    young adults   267.624 4
  rel. instruction   268.844
  rel. law.   262.984 4
  schools   377.844
  secondary training   207.124 4
  sermons   252.044
  theological seminaries   207.114 4
    s.a. other spec. aspects
Albigensians
  biog. & work   284.4
  Christian church hist.
    heresies   273.6
    persecutions   272.3
  s.a.   *pers.*–244
Albinism *see* Pigmentary changes
    skin
Alboran Sea *see* Western
    Mediterranean Sea
Al-Bukhari Hadith   297.124 1
Albumin glues
  chem. tech.   668.32
  other aspects see Adhesives
Albumins
  org. chem.   547.752
  other aspects see Proteins
Albuminuria *see* Urine diseases
Albuquerque N.M.   *area*–789 61
Albury N.S.W.   *area*–944 8
Alcae *see* Charadriiformes
Alcantarines *see* Franciscans
Alcedines *see* Coraciiformes
Alcester Warwickshire Eng.
    area–424 89
Alchemy   540.112
Alcohol cookery   641.585
Alcoholic beverages   641.21
  comm. proc.   663.1
  ethics
    philosophy   178.1
    religion
      Buddhism   294.356 81

Ales	641.23
comm. proc.	663.42
home econ.	
cookery	641.623
preparation	641.873
other aspects see Alcoholic	
beverages	
Alessandri Rodriguez admin. Chile	
hist.	983.064 4
s.a. spec. events & subj.	
e.g. Commerce	
Alessandria Italy	*area*–451 4
Alethopteris paleobotany	561.597
Aleurone grains cytology	574.874
animals	591.874
plants	581.874
s.a. spec. organisms	
Aleut *see* Eskimo Aleut	
Aleutian Isls.	
election district Alaska	*area*–798 4
Alexander	
County	
Illinois	*area*–773 999
North Carolina	*area*–756 795
reign Russia hist.	
1	947.072
2	947.081
3	947.082
s.a. spec. events & subj.	
e.g. Commerce	
Alexandra Vic.	*area*–945 3
Alexandria	
Egypt	*area*–621
Virginia	*area*–755 296
Alexandrian philosophy	186.4
Alexandrina Lake S. Aust.	*area*–942 33
Alexia *see* Aphasias	
Alexis	
reign Russia hist.	947.048
s.a. spec. events & subj.	
e.g. Commerce	
Aleyrodoidea *see* Homoptera	
Alfalfa Co. Okla.	*area*–766 22
Alfalfas	
agriculture	633.31
soc. & econ. aspects *see*	
Primary industries	
other aspects see	
Papilionaceae; *also*	
Field crops	
Alfonso	
12-13 reigns Spain hist.	946.08
s.a. spec. events & subj.	
e.g. Commerce	
Alford Licolnshire Eng.	*area*–425 32
Alfred	
reign Eng. hist.	942.016 4
s.a. spec. events & subj.	
e.g. Commerce	
Alfreton Derbyshire Eng.	*area*–425 16

Algae	
botany	589.3
culture	635.939 3
med. aspects	
gen. pharm.	615.329 3
toxicology	615.952 93
vet. pharm.	636.089 532 93
toxicology	636.089 595 293
paleobotany	561.93
other aspects see Plants	
Algarve Portugal	*area*–469 6
Algebra	512
elementary ed.	372.73
s.a. spec. appls. e.g.	
Engineering	
Algebra of sets *see* Boolean	
algebra	
Algebraic	
geometry	516.35
abstract	512.33
classical	516.35
s.a. spec. appls. e.g.	
Engineering	
number theory	512.74
s.a. spec. appls. e.g.	
Engineering	
numbers *see* Algebraic number	
theory	
operations	512.92
s.a. spec. topics of	
algebra; also spec.	
appls. e.g.	
Engineering	
progressions	512.93
topology	514.2
s.a. spec. appls. e.g.	
Engineering	
varieties *see* Varieties	
algebraic	
Alger Co. Mich.	*area*–774 932
Algeria	*area*–65
Algerians	*r.e.n.*–927 65
Algicides	
production	
soc. & econ. aspects *see*	
Secondary industries	
technology	668.652
use agric.	632.952
s.a. spec. crops; also spec.	
types of culture e.g.	
Floriculture	
Algiers	
city	*area*–653
War	
U.S. hist.	973.53
Algol *see* Program languages	
Algoma District Ont.	*area*–713 132
Algonkian-Mosan	
languages	
linguistics	497.3
literatures	897.3

Algonkian-Mosan
languages (continued)
  s.a.   *lang.*–973
peoples   *r.e.n.*–97
  s.a. other spec. subj. e.g.
       Arts
Algonquin Provincial Park   *area*–713 147
Algorithms *see* Mathematical
     models
Al-Homina Morocco   *area*–642
Alicante Spain   *area*–467 65
Alice Springs N. Ter. Aust.
                area–942 91
Alicyclic compounds
  chem. tech.
    hydrocarbons   661.815
    org. chem.   547.51–.58
  other aspects see Organic
     chemicals
  s.a. spec. cpds. & spec.
     prod.
Alienated
  classes *see* Lower classes
Alienation
  real property
    law   346.043 6
    spec. jur.   346.3–.9
  soc. interaction   302.5
Aliens
  pol. sci.
    naturalization   323.623
    pol. status   323.631
    law
      international   341.484
      municipal   342.083
      spec. jur.   342.3–.9
  other aspects see Ethnic
     groups
Alimentary tract *see* Digestive
     system
Alimony
  law   346.016 6
  spec. jur.   346.3–.9
Aliphatic compounds
  chem. tech.
    hydrocarbons   661.814
    org. chem.   547.4
  other aspects see Organic
     chemicals
  s.a. spec. cpds. & spec.
     prod.
Alismataceae *see* Alismatales
Alismatales
  botany   584.721
  floriculture   635.934 721
  med. aspects
    crop prod.   633.884 721
    gen. pharm.   615.324 721
    toxicology   615.952 472 1
    vet. pharm.   636.089 532 472 1
    toxicology   636.089 595 247 21

Alismatales (continued)
  paleobotany   561.4
  other aspects see Plants
Alizarines *see* Hydroxyketone
    dyes
Al Jadida Morocco   *area*–643
Al-Jazira Desert Iraq   *area*–567 4
Alkali metals
  chemistry
    industrial   661.038
      chlorates   661.35
      hydroxides   661.35
      organic   661.895
    soc. & econ. aspects see
      Secondary industries
    s.a. spec. prod.
    inorganic   546.38
    organic   547.053 8
    s.a. spec. groupings e.g.
      Aliphatic compounds
  construction
    building   693.772 5
  materials
    building   691.872 5
    engineering   620.189 6
    s.a. spec. uses
  metallography   669.957 25
  metallurgy   669.725
    physical & chem. 669.967 25
    soc. & econ. aspects see
      Secondary industries
  mineral aspects see Minor
     metals
  pharmacology   615.238
    misc. aspects see
      Pharmacology
  products
    mf. tech.   673.725
    other aspects see
      Nonferrous metals prod.
  toxicology   615.925 38
    misc. aspects see
      Toxicology
  other aspects see Metal;
    also Metals
Alkalimetry *see* Neutralization
    volumetric anal.
Alkaline
  batteries *see* Secondary
    batteries
  earth metals
    chemistry
      industrial   661.039
        chlorates   661.35
        hydroxides 661.35
        organic   661.895
      soc. & econ. aspects
        see Secondary
        industries
      s.a. spec. prod.
      inorganic   546.39

Alkaline
  earth metals
    chemistry (continued)
      organic   547.053 9
      s.a. spec. groupings
        e.g. Aliphatic
          compounds
    construction
      building   693.772 5
    materials
      building   691.872 5
      engineering   620.189 6
      s.a. spec. uses
    metallography   669.957 25
    metallurgy   669.725
      physical & chem.   669.967 25
      soc. & econ. aspects *see*
        Secondary industries
    mineral aspects *see* Minor
      metals
    pharmacology   615.239
      misc. aspects see
        Pharmacology
    products
      mf. tech.   673.725
      other aspects see
        Nonferrous metals prod.
    toxicology   615.925 39
      misc. aspects see
        Toxicology
      other aspects see Metal;
        also Metals
  environments ecology   574.526 5
    animals   591.526 5
    microorganisms   576.15
    plants   581.526 5
    s.a. spec. organisms
  posions *see* Alkalis
    toxicology
  salts *see* Simple salts metals
  soils
    plants grown in
      floriculture   635.955
      s.a. spec. plants
  storage batteries *see*
    Secondary batteries
Alkalinity
  soil science   631.42
  soil conditioners   631.825
    misc. aspects see Soil
      conditioners
    s.a. spec. crops; also spec.
      types of culture e.g.
      Floriculture
Alkalis
  inorg. chem.   546.38–.39
  toxicology   615.922
    misc. aspects see
      Toxicology
  other aspects see Bases
    (proton acceptors)

Alkaloidal
  crops
    agriculture   633.7
    soc. & econ. aspects *see*
      Primary industries
    foods   641.337
      cookery   641.637
  plants
    botany   581.63
    s.a. spec. plants
    crops *see* Alkaloidal crops
Alkaloids
  biochemistry
    gen. wks.   574.192 42
      animals   591.192 42
      microorganisms   576.119 242
      plants   581.192 42
      s.a. spec. organisms
    med. sci.   612.015 72
      animals   636.089 201 572
      s.a. spec. animals
      man   612.015 72
    org. chem.   547.72
    pharmacognosy   615.321
    misc. aspects see
      Pharmacology
    s.a. spec. uses e.g.
      Antipyretics
Alkanes *see* Paraffins (chem.
    cpds.)
Alkenes *see* Olefins
Alkylation
  chem. eng.   660.284 41
  org. chem.   547.21
  s.a. spec. elements, cpds.,
    prod.
Alkynes *see* Acetylenics
All-age schools
  gen. wks.   373.23
    elementary ed.   372.24
    secondary ed.   373.23
  govt. supervision & support 379
Allah *see* God
Allamakee Co. Ia.   *area*–777 33
All-cargo services
  air freight
    commerce   387.744
    law *see* Freight services
      law
    other aspects see Freight
      transportation
Allegan Co. Mich.   *area*–774 14
Allegany Co.
  Maryland   *area*–752 94
  New York   *area*–747 84
Alleghany Co.
  North Carolina   *area*–756 832
  Virginia   *area*–755 816
Allegheny
  Co. Pa.   *area*–748 85

Allegheny (continued)
  Mountains   *area*–748 7
    Pennsylvania   *area*–748 7
    West Virginia   *area*–754 8
  River   *area*–748 6
Allegory
  art representation   704.946
    paintings   753.6
    s.a. other spec. art forms
  lit. qual. *see* Symbolism lit.
        qual.
  rel. texts
    Bible   220.68
    s.a. spec. parts of Bible
    Hadith   297.124 068
    s.a. spec. Hadith
    Koran   297.122 68
      spec. parts   297.122 9
    Midrash   296.140 68
    s.a. spec. works
    Talmudic lit.   296.120 68
    s.a. spec. works
  stage qual.   792.090 915
    s.a. other spec. dramatic
        mediums e.g.
        Television; *also spec.*
        kinds of drama e.g.
        Tragedies (drama)
Allen
  Bog Leinster Ire.   *area*–418 5
  County
    Indiana   *area*–772 74
    Kansas   *area*–781 94
    Kentucky   *area*–769 732
    Ohio   *area*–771 42
  Par. La.   *area*–763 58
Allendale Co. S.C.   *area*–757 77
Allende Gossens admin. Chile
    hist.   983.064 6
  s.a. spec. events & subj.
        e.g. Commerce
Allene *see* Olefins
Allenstein Poland   *area*–438 3
Allerdale Cumbria Eng.   *area*–427 87
Allergenic plants botany   581.67
  s.a. spec. plants
Allergies
  cookery for   641.563 1
  gen. med.   616.97
  geriatrics   618.976 97
  pediatrics   618.929 7
  pub. health   614.599 3
  statistics   312.397
    deaths   312.269 7
  other aspects see Diseases
Alley cats *see* Cats
Alleys *see* Streets
Alliaceous plants
  agriculture   635.26
    soc. & econ. aspects *see*
        Primary industries

Alliaceous plants (continued)
  foods   641.352 6
    preparation
      commercial   664.805 26
      domestic   641.652 6
  other aspects see
        Amaryllidales; *also*
        Vegetables
Alliances
  internat. politics   327.116
    spec. countries   327.3–.9
Allied forces
  mil. sci.   355.356
  s.a. spec. mil. branches
  s.a. Allies
Allier France   *area*–445 7
Allies
  World War 1 hist.   940.332
    s.a. spec. aspects e.g.
        Diplomatic history
  World War 2 hist.   940.533 2
    s.a. spec. aspects e.g.
        Diplomatic history
  s.a. hist. of other spec.
        wars
Alligator pears *see* Avocados
Alligators *see* Crocodilia
Alliopteris paleobotany   561.597
Allium cepa *see* Onions
Alloa Central Scot.   *area*–413 15
Allocation *see* Consumption
        govt. control
Allodium
  land econ.   333.323 2
  property law *see* Land tenure
        law
Alloeocoela *see* Turbellaria
Allopathy
  therapeutics   615.531
    misc. aspects see
        Therapeutics
  s.a. spec. diseases
Allorhythmia *see* Arrhythmia
Allotheria paleozoology   569.17
Allotments
  loan flotation
    pub. finance   336.344
      misc. aspects see Public
        borrowing
Allotriognathi *see*
        Acanthopterygii
Allowances *see* Compensation
Alloy
  binary systems
    metallurgy   669.94
    s.a. spec. metals
  steels *see* Steel
Alloys
  chemistry
    inorganic   546.37
      spec. kinds   546.38–.68

Alloys
  chemistry (continued)
    other aspects see Metals
      chemistry
    eng. materials   620.16
      foundations   624.153 6
      naval design   623.818 2
      shipbuilding   623.820 7
      structures   624.182
      s.a. other spec. uses
    manufacturing *see* Metals
      products
    metallography   669.95
    metallurgy
      manufacturing
        soc. & econ. aspects *see*
          Secondary industries
      technology   669
    pharmacology   615.237
      misc. aspects see
        ' Pharmacology
    toxicology   615.925 37
      misc. aspects see
        Toxicology
Allspice *see* Spices; *also*
    Myrtales
All-Star games
  baseball sports   796.357 784
All-terrain vehicles *see*
    Off-road vehicles
Alluvial mining
  technology   622.32
    spec. deposits   622.33–.39
Alluvium geology   551.35
All-volunteer army
  mil. sci.   355.223 62
All-year school   371.236
  s.a. spec. levels of ed.;
    also Special education
Almanacs
  general *see* Serials
  nautical   528
Almería Spain   *area*–468 1
Almonds
  agriculture   634.55
    soc. & econ. aspects *see*
      Primary industries
  foods   641.345 5
    preparation
      commercial   664.804 55
      domestic   641.645 5
  other aspects see Rosaceae;
    also Nuts
Almsgiving
  Islamic moral theology   297.54
Almshouses
  bldg. aspects *see* Poor people
    institution buildings
  welfare   362.585
    misc. aspects see Young
      people soc. services to

Al-Nasai Hadith   297.124 5
Alnwick Northumberland Eng.
    area–428 87
Alodia kingdom hist.   962.402
  s.a. spec. events & subj.
    e.g. Commerce
Alodium
  land econ.   333.323 2
  property law *see* Land tenure
    law
Aloes
  cathartics   615.732
  other aspects see Liliales
Alopecia *see* Scalp diseases
Alor Indonesia   *area*–598 6
Alpaca wool textiles
  arts   746.043 2
    s.a. spec. processes e.g.
      Weaving
  dyeing   667.332
  manufacturing
    soc. & econ. aspects *see*
      Secondary industries
    technology   677.32
      special-process fabrics   677.6
  other aspects see Textiles
  s.a. spec. prod. e.g. Men's
    clothing
Alpacas
  animal husbandry   636.296
  other aspects see Tylopoda
Alpena Co. Mich.   *area*–774 81
Alpenhorn music   788.49
  recordings   789.912 849
Alpenhorns
  mf. tech.   681.818 49
    misc. aspects see Musical
      instruments
  musical art   788.49
Alpes-de-Haute-Provence   *area*–449 5
Alpes-Maritimes France   *area*–449 41
Alpha
  cellulose
    manufacturing
      soc. & econ. aspects *see*
        Secondary industries
      technology   676.4
  decay radioactivity
    astrophysics   523.019 752 2
      s.a. spec. celestial
        bodies
    physics   539.752 2
      spec. states of matter   530.4
      s.a. spec. physical
        phenomena e.g. Heat
  particles *see* Nuclei
  radiations *see* Particle
    radiations
Alphabetic subject catalogs
  books   017.5–.8
  other spec. kinds   *s.s.*–021 6

Alternators
 internal combustion engines
  see Ignition systems
  & devices
Althorns *see* Saxhorns
Altimeters
 aircraft eng. 629.135 2
  s.a. spec. appls. e.g.
  Military engineering
Al-Tirmidhi Hadith 297.124 4
Altitude sickness
 gen. med. 616.989 3
 geriatrics 618.976 989 3
 pediatrics 618.929 893
 statistics 312.398 93
  deaths 312.269 893
  other aspects see Diseases
 s.a. spec. diseases
Altitudes
 biophysics *see* Pressure
  biophysics
Alto
 Adige Italy *area*–453 83
 Alentejo Portugal *area*–469 52
 horns *see* Saxhorns
 Paraguay *area*–892 27
 Paraná Paraguay *area*–892 132
Alton Hampshire Eng. *area*–422 74
Altoona Pa. *area*–748 76
Altrincham Greater Manchester
  Eng. *area*–427 31
Altruism
 ethical systems 171.8
  applications 172–179
Altrusa clubs 369.5
Alumina
 refractory materials *see*
  Refractory materials
Aluminography *see* Aluminum
  lithography
Aluminum
 arts
  decorative 739.57
  other aspects see Metals
  arts
 bronze *see* Copper
 chemistry
  inorganic 546.673
  organic 547.056 73
   s.a. spec. groupings e.g.
   Aliphatic compounds
  soc. & econ. aspects *see*
   Secondary industries
  technology 661.067 3
  organic 661.895
   s.a. spec. prod.
 compounds
  chemistry *see* Aluminum
   chemistry

Aluminum
 compounds (continued)
  plant nutrition *see* Trace
   elements plant
   nutrition
 construction
  architecture 721.044 772 2
   s.a. spec. kinds of
   bldgs.
  building 693.772 2
 lithography
  graphic arts
   processes 763.23
   products 769
  materials
   buildings 691.872 2
   engineering 620.186
    foundations 624.153 86
    naval design 623.818 26
    shipbuilding 623.820 7
    structures 624.182 6
    s.a. other spec uses
 metallography 669.957 22
 metallurgy 669.722
  physical & chem. 669.967 22
  soc. & econ. aspects *see*
   Secondary industries
 mineral aspects
  econ. geol. 553.492 6
  mining 622.349 26
  prospecting 622.184 926
  s.a. spec. minerals
 pharmacology 615.267 3
  misc. aspects see
   Pharmacology
 products
  arts *see* Aluminum arts
  mf. tech. 673.722
  other aspects see
   Nonferrous metals
   products
 roofing
  bldg. construction 695
 soaps
  chem. tech. 668.125
  soc. & econ. aspects *see*
   Secondary industries
 toxicology 615.925 673
  misc. aspects see
   Toxicology
 other aspects see Metal;
  also Metals
Alumni *pers.*–379
Alunite mineralogy 549.755
Alva Central Scot. *area*–413 15
Alveolar abscesses *see* Gums
  (anatomy) diseases
Alvsborg Sweden *area*–486
Alyn & Deeside Clwyd Wales
  area–429 36
Alyth Tayside Scot. *area*–412 8

Amaas *see* Alastrim
Amador Co. Calif.   *area*–794 42
Amalgamations
   firms *see* Mergers
   prod. econ.   338.83
Amalgams
   fillings & inlays dentistry   617.675
   other aspects see Mercury
     (elements)
Amambay Paraguay   *area*–892 137
Amapá Brazil   *area*–811 6
Amara Iraq   *area*–567 5
Amaranth family *see*
     Chenopodiales
Amaranthaceae *see* Chenopodiales
Amaryllidaceae *see*
     Amaryllidales
Amaryllidales
   botany   584.25
   floriculture   635.934 25
   med. aspects
     crop prod.   633.884 25
     gen. pharm.   615.324 25
     toxicology   615.952 425
     vet. pharm.   636.089 532 425
     toxicology   636.089 595 242 5
   paleobotany   561.4
   other aspects see Plants
Amaryllis family *see*
     Amaryllidales
Amasya Turkey   *area*–563
Amateur
   circuses   791.39
   motion pictures
     performing arts   791.433
   photography
     cinematography   778.534 9
     projection   778.554 9
   radio stations
     engineering   621.384 166
     s.a. spec. appls. e.g.
      Radiotelephony
     internat. law   341.757 7
     other aspects see Radio
   theater performing arts   792.022 2
   workshops   684.08
   s.a. spec. activities &
     prod.
   s.a. other spec. activities
Amaurosis *see* Blindness
Amaurotic idiocy
   gen. med.   616.858 845
   geriatrics   618.976 858 845
   pediatrics   618.928 588 45
   psychology   157.8
   pub. health   362.3
   statistics   312.385 884 5
Amazon River   *area*–811
   Brazil   *area*–811
   Peru   *area*–854 3

Amazonas
   Brazil   *area*–811 3
   Colombia   *area*–861 7
   Peru   *area*–854 6
   Venezuela   *area*–876 4
Ambari hemp
   agriculture   633.56
   soc. & econ. aspects *see*
     Primary industries
   other aspects see Malvales
Ambassadors *see* Envoys
Amber
   carvings
     dec. arts   736.6
   rel. significance
     Christianity   247.866
     comp. rel.   291.37
     s.a. other spec. rel.
   other aspects see Fossil gums
     & resins
Amber Valley Derbyshire Eng.
      area–425 16
Amble Northumberland Eng.
      area–428 87
Ambleside Cumbria Eng.   *area*–427 83
Amblyopia *see* Blindness
Amblypygi
   zoology   595.453 6
   other aspects see Arachnida
Amblystomoidea *see* Caudata
Ambrosian chants *see* Chants
     sacred music
Ambulance service
   mil. sci.
     gen. wks. *see* Health
      services military
     history
      World War 1   940.475 3
      World War 2   940.547 53
     s.a. other spec. wars;
      also hist. of spec.
      places
   soc. services   362.18
   misc. aspects see Health
     services
Ambulances
   engineering
     gen. tech. & mf.   629.222 34
     maintenance   629.287 234
     models   629.221 234
     operation   629.283 34
     spec. appls.
      mil. eng.   623.747 24
      s.a. other spec. appls.
     s.a. other spec. aspects
      e.g. Brakes
   soc. & econ. aspects *see*
     Secondary industries
   mil. equip.   355.83
   s.a. spec. mil. branches

Ambulances (continued)
  sanitation *see* Health care
    facilities sanitation
Ambush tactics
  mil. sci.   355.422
    s.a. spec. mil. branches
Ameba *see* Amoebina
Amelanchier *see* Juneberries
Amelia Co. Va.   *area*–755 634
Amenhetep reign Egypt hist.   932.014
  s.a. spec. events & subj.
    e.g. Commerce
Amenhotep reign Egypt hist.   932.014
  s.a. spec. events & subj.
    e.g. Commerce
Amenorrhea *see* Menstruation
    disorders
American
  aboriginal *see* American
    native
  Artic seawaters
    oceanography   551.468 7
    regional subj. trmt.   *area*–163 27
    other aspects see Atlantic
      Ocean
  Baptist Convention   286.131
    misc. aspects see Baptist
  buffaloes
    animal husbandry   636.292
    other aspects see Bovoidea
  Evangelical Lutheran Church 284.133 2
    misc. aspects see Lutheran
  Falls Res. Ida.   *area*–796 49
  football
    equipment mf.   688.763 32
      soc. & econ. aspects *see*
        Secondary industries
    sports   796.332
    other aspects see Sports
  Independent Party U.S.
    pol. sci.   324.273 3
    s.a. spec. subj. of concern
      e.g. Social problems
  Indian *see* American native
    languages
    aboriginal *see* American
      native languages
    European *see spec. langs.*
      e.g. English language
  Legion   369.186 1
  literature
    English   810
    other languages   830–890
  Lutheran Church   284.131
    misc. aspects see Lutheran
  native
    architecture   722.91
      misc. aspects see
        Architectural schools
    languages
      linguistics   497

American
  native
    languages (continued)
      literatures   897
      s.a.   *lang.*–97
    people
      North American   *r.e.n.*–97
      South American   *r.e.n.*–98
    troops in
      U.S. Revolution   973.343
      U.S. War of 1812   973.524 2
      World War 1   940.403
      World War 2   940.540 3
      s.a. other spec. wars;
        also hist. of spec.
        countries
      Wars 1790-91
        U.S. hist.   973.42
    songs
      U.S.   784.751
        recordings   789.912 475 1
      other countries   784.769 7
        recordings   789.912 476 97
    other aspects see Primitive
    s.a. North America; *also*
        South America; *also*
        other spec. subj. e.g.
        Arts
  Nazi Party U.S.
    pol. sci.   324.273 38
    s.a. spec. subj. of concern
      e.g. Social problems
  Party U.S.
    pol. sci.   324.273 2
    s.a. spec. subj. of concern
      e.g. Social problems
  pronounciation Eng. lang.   421.54
  quarter horse
    animal husbandry   636.133
    other aspects see Horses
  Reformed Christians
    biog. & work
      gen. wks.   285.709 2
      s.a. spec. kinds
    s.a.   *pers.*–257
  revised version Bible   220.520 4
    s.a. spec. parts of Bible
  Revolution
    history   973.3
  saddle horse
    animal husbandry   636.13
    other aspects see Horses
  Samoa   *area*–961 3
  socialism econ.   335.3
  spelling Eng. lang.   421.55
  standard version Bible   220.520 4
    s.a. spec. parts of Bible
    s.a. other spec. subj. e.g.
      Arts
Americanisms Eng. lang.   427.97
Americans (U.S.)   *r.e.n.*–13

Americas *see* Western
    Hemisphere; *also spec.*
    places e.g. North
    America, Brazil
Americium
  chemistry   546.441
Amerindian *see* American native
Amersham Buckinghamshire Eng.
    area–425 9
Amesbury Wiltshire Eng. *area*–423 19
Amethysts *see* Gems
Amharas   *r.e.n.*–928
Amharic language *see* Ethiopic
    languages
Amherst
  Co. Va.   *area*–755 496
  governorship India hist. 954.031 3
    s.a. spec. events & subj.
      e.g. Commerce
Amides
  org. chem.   547.042
    s.a. spec. groupings e.g.
      Aliphatic compounds
  synthetic drugs pharm. 615.314 2
    misc. aspects see
      Pharmacology
  synthetic poisons 615.951 42
    misc. aspects see
      Toxicology
  other aspects see Nitrogen
    compounds
  s.a. spec. prod.; also other
    spec. appls.
Amiiformes
  culture   639.374 1
  fishing
    commercial   639.274 1
    sports   799.174 1
  paleozoology   567.4
  zoology   597.41
  other aspects see Pisces
Amination
  chem. eng.   660.284 45
  org. chem.   547.25
  s.a. spec. elements, cpds.,
    prod.
Amindivi Isls. India *area*–548 1
Amines
  org. chem.   547.042
    s.a. spec. groupings e.g.
      Aliphatic compounds
  synthetic drugs pharm. 615.314 2
    misc. aspects see
      Pharmacology
  synthetic poisons 615.951 42
    misc. aspects see
      Toxicology
  other aspects see Nitrogen
    compounds
  s.a. spec. prod.; also other
    spec. appls.

Amino acids
  proteins
    org. chem.   547.75
    other aspects see Proteins
  other aspects see Acids
Amirantes isl. *area*–695
Amish   289.73
  misc. aspects see Mennonite
    churches
Amite Co. Miss. *area*–762 24
Amitosis
  cytology   574.876 22
    animals   591.876 22
    plants   581.876 22
    s.a. spec. organisms
Amman Jordan *area*–569 58
Ammanford Dyfed Wales *area*–429 68
Ammeters
  electric current measurement 621.374 4
    s.a. spec. appls. e.g.
      Ignition systems &
      devices
Ammiaceae *see* Umbellales
Ammodytoidea *see*
    Acanthopterygii
Ammonia
  chem. tech.   661.34
    soc. & econ. aspects *see*
      Secondary industries
  other aspects see Nitrogen
  s.a. spec. prod.
Ammonite
  language
    linguistics   492.47
    literature   892.4
    s.a. *lang.*–924
  people   *r.e.n.*–924
  s.a. other spec. subj. e.g.
    Arts
Ammonitoidea paleozoology 564.53
Ammonium
  chlorate *see* High explosives
  chloride fertilizers *see*
    Ammonium fertilizers
  compounds *see* Nitrogen
    compounds; *also spec.*
    cpds.
  fertilizers
    production
      soc. & econ. aspects *see*
        Secondary industries
      technology   668.624 1
    use agric.   631.841
      s.a. spec. crops; also
      spec. types of culture
      e.g. Floriculture
  hydroxide
    chem. tech.   661.34
    soc. & econ. aspects *see*
      Secondary industries
    s.a. spec. prod.

Ammonium (continued)
  nitrates fertilizers *see*
    Nitrate fertilizers
  picrate *see* High explosives
  salts
    chem. tech.   661.5
      soc. & econ. aspects *see*
        Secondary industries
    s.a. spec. prod.
  sulfate fertilizers *see*
    Ammonium fertilizers
Ammunition
  mil. eng.
    soc. & econ. aspects *see*
      Secondary industries
    tech. & mf.   623.45
    s.a. spec. appls. e.g.
      Demolition operations
  mil. sci.   355.825
    s.a. spec. mil. branches
  small arms
    mf. tech.   683.406
    other aspects see Small
      arms
    s.a. spec. kinds e.g.
      Carbines
Ammunition-ships *see* Supply
  ships military
Amnesias
  gen. med.   616.852 32
  geriatrics   618.976 852 32
  pediatrics   618.928 523 2
  psychology   157.3
  statistics   312.385 232
Amnesty
  penology   364.65
Amniotic fluid
  diseases
    obstetrics   618.34
    pub. health   614.599 2
    statistics   312.304 834
      deaths   312.260 483 4
    other aspects see Diseases
  other aspects see Pregnancy
Amoeba *see* Amoebina
Amoebiasis *see* Amoebic
  dysentery
Amoebic dysentery
  gen. med.   616.935 3
  geriatrics   618.976 935 3
  pediatrics   618.929 353
  pub. health   614.516
  statistics   312.393 53
    deaths   312.269 353
  other aspects see Diseases
Amoebina
  culture   639.731 17
  zoology   593.117
  other aspects see Protozoa
Amorites   *r.e.n.*–921

Amos
  Bible   224.8
  other aspects see Prophetic
    books (O.T.)
Amoy dialect
  linguistics   495.17
  literature   895.1
  s.a.   *lang.*–951 7
Ampelidaceae *see* Rhamnales
Ampere-hour
  meters
    electric current
      measurement   621.374 4
    s.a. spec. appls. e.g.
      Ignition systems &
      devices
Amphetamine *see* Stimulants
Amphibia
  agric. pests   632.676
    s.a. spec. types of culture
      e.g. Forestry; *also*
      spec. crops
  conservation tech.   639.977 6
  culture
    technology   639.37
    soc. & econ. aspects *see*
      Primary industries
    other aspects see Agriculture
  drawing tech.   743.676
  food   641.396
    cookery   641.696
  hunting
    commercial
      soc. & econ. aspects *see*
        Primary industries
      technology   639.13
    sports   799.257 6
  paleozoology   567.6
  resources
    economics   333.957
    govt. control
      law   346.046 957
        spec. jur.   346.3–.9
      pub. admin. *see*
        Biological resources
        govt. control pub.
        admin.
  zoology   597.6
  other aspects see Animals
Amphibian planes
  aeronautical eng.
    gen. tech. & mf.   629.133 348
      components & tech.   629.134
      models   629.133 134 8
      operation   629.132 524 8
    military   623.746 042–.746 044
    s.a. spec. kinds e.g.
      Trainers (aircraft)
    soc. & econ. aspects *see*
      Secondary industries
    s.a. other spec. appls.

Amphibian planes (continued)
  commerce   387.733 48
    misc. aspects see Aircraft
      commerce
Amphibians *see* Amphibia
Amphibious
  air-cushion vehicles
    technology   629.325
    mil. eng.   623.748 5
      soc. & econ. aspects *see*
        Secondary industries
    other aspects see
      Air-cushion vehicles
  landing craft *see*
    Landing-craft
  warfare   359.96
Amphiboles mineralogy   549.66
Amphicoela
  zoology   597.83
  other aspects see Anura
Amphidiscophora *see*
  Hyalospongiae
Amphilothales *see* Pyrrophyta
Amphineura *see* Crepipoda
Amphipoda
  fishing sports   799.255 371
  zoology   595.371
  other aspects see
    Eumalacostraca
Amphitheaters
  architecture   725.827
  building   690.582 7
  other aspects see Public
    structures
Amphoteric salts *see* Simple
  salts metals
Amplification
  light
    optics
      astrophysics   523.015 58
        s.a. spec. celestial
          bodies
      physics   535.58
        spec. states of matter   530.4
    s.a. Lasers
  s.a. Amplifiers
Amplifiers
  closed-loop automation eng.   629.831 5
    s.a. spec. appls. e.g.
      Thermostats
  electronic circuits
    tech. & mf.   621.381 535
    microelectronics   621.381 735
    microwave electronics   621.381 325
    radiowave electronics   621.381 535
    x- & gamma-ray
      electronics   621.381 6
    s.a. spec. appls. e.g.
      Television

Amplifiers
  electronic circuits (continued)
    other aspects see Microwave
      electronics; Radiowave
      electronics; X-ray
      electronics
  radio *see* Circuits radio eng.
Amplitude
  modulation systems *see*
    Long-wave systems radio
  modulators electronic circuits
    tech. & mf.   621.381 536 2
    microelectronics   621.381 736 2
    microwave electronics   621.381 326 2
    radiowave electronics   621.381 536 2
    x- & gamma-ray
      electronics   621.381 6
      s.a. spec. appls. e.g.
        Radar
    other aspects see Microwave
      electronics; Radiowave
      electronics; X-ray
      electronics
  sound
    engineering   620.21
      s.a. spec. appls. e.g.
        Reproducers sound
    physics   534.34
    spec. states of matter   530.4
Ampthill Bedfordshire Eng. *area*–425 63
Amputations *see* Extremities
  surgery
Amputees *see* Crippled people
Amsterdam
  city Netherlands   *area*–492 3
  island   *area*–699
Amulets
  Islamic practice   297.33
  numismatics   737.23
  occultism   133.44
  rel. significance
    Christianity   247.872 3
    comp. rel.   291.37
    s.a. other spec. rel.
Amundsen
  Gulf *see* American Arctic
    seawaters
  Sea
    oceanography   551.469 4
    regional subj. trmt.   *area*–167 4
    other aspects see Antarctic
      waters
Amur
  River   *area*–577
  RSFSR   *area*–577
Amusement
  areas civic art   711.558
  features journalism   070.444
  park bldgs.
    architecture   725.76
    building   690.576

Amusement
park bldgs. (continued)
  other aspects see Public
    structures
parks
  landscape design   712.5
  recreation   791.068
Amusements *see* Recreation
Amvets   369.186 2
Amylases *see* Saccharolytic
    enzymes
Ana *see* Quotations
Anabantoidea *see*
    Acanthopterygii
Anabaptist
church bldgs.
  architecture   726.584 3
  building   690.658 43
  other aspects see
    Religious-purpose
    bldgs.
churches   284.3
  Christian life guides   248.484 3
doctrines   230.43
  creeds   238.43
general councils   262.543
govt. & admin.   262.043
  parishes   254.043
missions   266.43
moral theology   241.044 3
private prayers for   242.804 3
pub. worship   264.043
rel. associations
  adults   267.184 3
  men   267.244 3
  women   267.444 3
  young adults   267.624 3
rel. instruction   268.843
rel. law   262.984 3
schools   377.843
secondary training   207.124 3
sermons   252.043
theological seminaries   207.114 3
s.a. other spec. aspects
Anabaptists
biog. & work   284.3
s.a.   *pers.*–243
Anabolism *see* Metabolism
Anacanthini *see* Acanthopterygii
Anacardiaceae *see* Sapindales
Anacardiaceous fruits
agriculture   634.44
  soc. & econ. aspects *see*
    Primary industries
foods   641.344 4
  preparation
    commercial   664.804 44
    domestic   641.644 4
other aspects see Sapindales;
  also Fruits

Anacardium occidentale *see*
  Cashew nuts
Anaconda Mont.   *area*–786 87
Anaerobic
digestion sewage trmt.
  technology   628.354
  other aspects see Sewage
    treatment
respiration
  pathology   574.212 8
    animals   591.212 8
    plants   581.212 8
    s.a. spec. organisms
  physiology   574.128
    animals   591.128
    microorganisms   576.112 8
    plants   581.128
    s.a. spec. organisms
Anaesthetics
pharmacodynamics   615.781
other aspects see Drugs
Anagrams
recreation   793.73
Analgesics
pharmacodynamics   615.783
other aspects see Drugs
Analogue
computers
  electronic data proc.   001.64
    spec. subj.   *s.s.*–028 54
  electronic eng.   621.381 957
instruments
  manufacturing
    soc. & econ. aspects
      see Secondary
      industries
    technology   681.1
  other aspects see Computers
Analogue-to-digital converters
electronic eng.   621.381 959 6
other aspects see Computers
Analogy
logic   169
nat. rel.   219
Analysis
commodities
  foods
    comm. proc.   664.07
    other aspects see Foods
    s.a. spec. foods e.g.
      Meats
  minerals   549.1
    spec. minerals   549.2–.7
  pharmaceuticals   615.190 1
    misc. aspects see
      Pharmacology
    s.a. spec. drugs
engineering   620.004 22
  aircraft eng.   629.134 1
    parts   629.134 3

Anam   *area*–597
Anambra Nigeria   *area*–669 4
Ananas comosus *see* Pineapples
Ananda Mahidol reign Thailand
   hist.   959.304 3
   s.a. spec. events & subj.
      e.g. Commerce
Anaphase *see* Mitosis
Anaphrodisiacs
   pharmacodynamics   615.766
   other aspects see Drugs
Anaphylaxis *see* Allergies
Anapsida *see* Chelonia
Anarchism
   economics   335.83
   pol. ideology   320.57
     soc. theology *see* Political
       ideologies soc.
       theology
Anarchist communities econ.   335.9
Anarchists
   biog. & work   335.830 92
   s.a.   *pers.*–335
Anarchy pol. sci.   321.07
Anaspidacea *see* Syncarida
Anatolia   *area*–561
Anatolian languages
   linguistics   491.998
   literatures   891.998
   s.a.   *lang.*–919 98
Anatomy
   drawing arts
     animals   743.6
     humans   743.49
   embryology
     gen. wks.   574.332
     animals   591.332
     microorganisms   576.133 2
     plants   581.332
     s.a. spec. organisms
   med. sci.   611.013
     animals   636.089 101 3
     s.a. spec. animals
     man   611.013
   gen. wks.   574.4
     animals   591.4
     microorganisms   576.14
     plants   581.4
     s.a. spec. organisms
   med. sci.   611
     animals   636.089 1
     s.a. spec. animals
     man   611
   pathology *see* Pathological
     anatomy
Anaxagorean philosophy   182.8
Ancash Peru   *area*–852 1
Ancestors
   rel. worship
     comp. rel.   291.213
     s.a. spec. rel.

Ancestors (continued)
   s.a.   *pers.*–043
Ancestry genealogy   929.1
Anchor ice physical geol.   551.344
Anchorage Alaska   *area*–798 3
Anchorages port eng.
   technology   627.22
   s.a. spec. appls. e.g.
       Military engineering
   other aspects see Liquids
     engineering
Anchors shipbuilding *see* Gear
     shipbuilding
Ancient
   architecture   722
     misc. aspects see
       Architectural schools
   civilization   930
   elements occultism   135.42
   governmental forms
     pol. sci.   321.14
   history   930
   law   340.53
   philosophy   180
     s.a. spec. branches & subj.
       e.g. Metaphysics
   religions   291.044
   remedies
     therapeutics   615.899
     s.a. spec. diseases
   sculpture   732
   Western architecture   722.6
     misc. aspects see
       Architectural schools
   world
     regional subj. trmt.   *area*–3
     other spec. subj.   *s.s.*–090 1
Ancistrocladaceae *see* Ochnales
Ancona Italy   *area*–456 71
Andalusia Spain   *area*–468
Andalusite mineralogy   549.62
Andaman
   & Nicobar Isls. India   *area*–548 8
   Sea
     oceanography   551.467 65
     regional subj. trmt.   *area*–165 65
     other aspects see Indian
       Ocean
Andamanese *see* Negrito
Andante *see* Musical forms
Andantino *see* Musical forms
Anderson Co.
   Kansas   *area*–781 672
   Kentucky   *area*–769 463
   South Carolina   *area*–757 25
   Tennessee   *area*–768 73
   Texas   *area*–764 229
Andes   *area*–8
Andesite *see* Volcanic rocks

Angles (configurations) (continued)
geodetic surveying 526.33
geometry
gen. wks. *see*
Configurations geometry
trisection 516.204
molecular structure *see*
Stereochemistry
Angles (tribe) *r.e.n.–2*
Anglesey Wales *area–429 21*
Anglesite
mineralogy 549.752
Anglican
cathedral bldgs.
architecture 726.65
building 690.665
other aspects see
Religious-purpose
bldgs.
chants *see* Chants sacred
music
church
buildings
architecture 726.583
building 690.658 3
other aspects see
Religious-purpose
bldgs.
s.a. Anglican cathedral
bldgs.
music
arts 783.026 3
recordings 789.912 302 63
s.a. spec. instruments;
also spec. kinds e.g.
Liturgical music
religion
pub. worship 264.030 2
significance 246.7
churches 283
Christian life guides 248.483
doctrines 230.3
creeds 238.3
general councils 262.53
govt. & admin. 262.03
parishes 254.03
missions 266.3
moral theology 241.043
private prayers for 242.803
pub. worship 264.03
rel. associations
adults 267.183
men 267.243
women 267.443
young adults 267.623
rel. instruction 268.83
rel. law 262.983
schools 377.83
secondary training 207.123
sermons 252.03
theological seminaries 207.113

Anglican
churches (continued)
s.a. other spec. aspects
Anglicans
biog. & work 283.092
s.a. *pers.–23*
Angling
sports 799.12
other aspects see Fishing
Anglo-American
songs 784.755
recordings 789.912 475 5
s.a. other spec. subj.
Anglo-Dutch Wars hist. 949.204
Anglo-Egyptian Sudan
history 962.403
s.a. *area–624*
Anglo-Indians *r.e.n.–914 11*
Anglo-Saxon
languages
linguistics 429
literature 829
s.a. *lang.–29*
peoples *r.e.n.–2*
s.a. other spec. subj. e.g.
Arts
Angola *area–673*
Angolese
people *r.e.n.–967 3*
s.a. other spec. subj. e.g.
Arts
Angoon election district Alaska
area–798 2
Angora
cats
animal husbandry 636.83
other aspects see Cats
Turkey *area–563*
Angoulême House France hist. 944.028
s.a. spec. events & subj.
e.g. Commerce
Angoumois France *area–446 5*
Angra do Heroísmo Portugal
area–469 9
Anguilla *area–729 73*
Angular momentum
nuclei *see* Nuclei
particles *see* Particles
(matter)
rays *see* Rays (beams)
Angus Scot. *area–412 6*
Anhalt Ger. *area–431 9*
Anhidrosis *see* Sweat glands
diseases
Anhimae *see* Anseriformes
Anhwei China *area–512 25*
Anhydrite
mineralogy 549.752
Anhydrous sulfates
mineralogy 549.752

Animal (continued)
  oils
    comm. proc. — 665.2
      soc. & econ. aspects *see*
        Secondary industries
  pathology *see* Pathology
  performances — 791.8
    circuses — 791.32
  pests
    agriculture — 632.6
      s.a. spec. plants; also
        spec. types of culture
        e.g. Forestry
    home econ. — 648.7
    sanitary eng. — 628.963–.969
      other aspects see Pests
  physiology *see* Physiology
  plankton zool. — 592
  power *see* Power
  psychology — 156.2–.7
  racing
    equip. mf. — 688.7
      soc. & econ. aspects *see*
        Secondary industries
    sports — 798
  reserves *see* Wildlife
        reserves
  sacrifices
    rel. worship
      comp. rel. — 291.34
      s.a. spec. rel.
  viruses
    med. sci. — 616.019 4
    virology — 576.648 4
  wastes
    disposal
      law — 344.046 22
        spec. jur. — 344.3–.9
      other aspects see Wastes
        control
    pollution water-supply eng.
      technology — 628.168 46
      other aspects see Water
        supply engineering
    sanitary eng.
      technology — 628.746 6
      other aspects see
        Sanitary engineering
  weapons zoology — 591.57
    s.a. spec. animals
Animal-derived
  drugs
    pharmacology — 615.36
    other aspects see Drugs
  fats *see* Animal fats
  foods *see* Animal foods
  glues
    chem. tech. — 668.32
    other aspects see Adhesives

Animal-derived (continued)
  oils
    comm. proc. — 665.2
      soc. & econ. aspects *see*
        Secondary industries
  poisons
    toxicology — 615.94
      misc. aspects see
        Toxicology
  waxes
    comm. proc. — 665.13
    other aspects see Waxes
Animal-drawn omnibuses *see*
        Omnibuses animal-drawn
Animals
  art representation — 704.943 2
    drawing tech. — 743.6
    painting — 758.3
    s.a. other spec. art forms
  cruelty to *see* Animals
        treatment of
  disease carriers
    pub. health — 614.43
      misc. aspects see Public
        health
  husbandry *see* Animal
        husbandry
  lit. trmt.
    folk lit.
      sociology
        legendary — 398.469
        real — 398.369
      texts & lit. crit. — 398.245
    gen. wks.
      collections
        legendary — 808.803 75
        real — 808.803 6
      hist. & crit.
        legendary — 809.933 75
        real — 809.933 6
    spec. lits.
      collections
        legendary — *lit. sub.*–080 375
        real — *lit. sub.*–080 36
      hist. & crit.
        legendary — *lit. sub.*–093 75
        real — *lit. sub.*–093 6
      s.a. spec. lit. forms
  rel. worship
    comp. rel. — 291.212
    s.a. spec. rel.
  resources
    economics — 333.954
    govt. control
      law — 346.046 954
        spec. jur. — 346.3–.9
      pub. admin. *see*
        Biological resources
        govt. control pub.
        admin.

Animals (continued)
  stage trmt.
    gen. wks.
      legendary   792.090 937 5
      real   792.090 936
    s.a. other spec. dramatic
        mediums e.g.
        Television; *also spec.*
        kinds of drama e.g.
        Tragedies (drama)
  treatment of
    criminology   364.187
    law   345.028 7
      spec. jur.   345.3–.9
    soc. theology
      Christianity   261.833 187
      comp. rel.   291.178 331 87
    s.a. other spec. rel.
  ethics
    philosophy   179.3
    religion
      Buddhism   294.356 93
      Christianity   241.693
      comp. rel.   291.569 3
      Hinduism   294.548 693
    s.a. other spec. rel.
  use in haulage
    mining eng.   622.65
    s.a. other spec. appls.
  zoological sciences   590
Animated cartoons
  drawing   741.58
    indiv. artists   741.092
  drawings   741.59
  moving pictures
    arts   791.433
    photographic tech.   778.534 7
Animism
  philosophy *see* Pantheism
            philosophy
  religion
    comparative   291.21
    s.a. spec. rel.
Anion
  separation & identification
    qual. anal. chem.   544.13
      organic   547.341 3
    s.a. spec. elements &
        cpds.
Anis *see* Cuculiformes
Anise *see* Umbellales
Aniseikonia ophthalmology   617.758
  geriatrics   618.977 758
  pediatrics   618.920 977 58
  pub. health   614.599 7
  statistics   312.304 775 8
  other aspects see Diseases
Anisoptera *see* Odonata
Anisotropy crystals
  optical crystallography   548.9
    s.a. spec. substances

Anjou region France   *area*–441 8
Ankara Turkey   *area*–563
Ankles
  diseases
    regional med. trmt.   617.584
    s.a. spec. systems &
        organs
    surgery   617.584
      anesthesiology   617.967 584
    other aspects see Diseases
  fractures   617.158
  orthopedic surgery   617.398
Anklets
  precious metalwork   739.278
  other aspects see Jewelry
Ankole
  kingdom
    history   967.610 1
    s.a. spec. events & subj.
        e.g. Commerce
    s.a.   *area*–676 1
Ann Cape Mass.   *area*–744 5
Annaba Algeria   *area*–655
Annam   *area*–597
Annamese *see* Vietnamese
Annam-Muong languages
  linguistics   495.92
  literatures   895.92
  s.a.   *lang.*–959 2
Annan Dumfries & Galloway Scot.
                             area–414 83
Annandale & Eskdale Dumfries &
            Galloway Scot.   *area*–414 83
Annapolis
  city Md.   *area*–752 56
  Co. N.S.   *area*–716 33
Annatto family *see* Bixales
Anne
  Arundel Co. Md.   *area*–752 55
  Eng. hist.   942.069
  Gt. Brit. hist.   941.069
  Russia hist.   947.061
  saint
    Christian doctrines   232.933
    private prayers to   242.75
  Scotland history   941.106 9
  s.a. spec. events & subj.
      e.g. Commerce
Annealing
  glassmaking   666.129
    s.a. spec. kinds of glass
  metal prod. *see* Heat
            treatment
Annelida
  culture & hunting   639.754
  zoology   595.14
  other aspects see Worms
Annexation
  local govt.
    pub. admin.   352.006

Annihilation
  nuclear interactions *see*
      Interactions nuclear
      reactions
Annihilationism
  rel. doctrines
      Christianity   236.23
      other rel. see Eschatology
Anniversaries
  armed forces   355.16
      s.a. spec. mil. branches
  Sunday-school services
      Christianity   268.7
      other rel. see Religious
          instruction
      s.a. other spec. subj.
Annobón   *area*–669 96
Annona *see* Annonaceous fruits
Annonaceae *see* Annonales
Annonaceous fruits
  agriculture   634.41
      soc. & econ. aspects *see*
          Primary industries
  foods   641.344 1
      preparation
          commercial   664.804 41
          domestic   641.644 1
      other aspects see Annonales;
          also Fruits
Annonales
  botany   583.115
  floriculture   635.933 115
  forestry   634.973 115
  med. aspects
      crop prod.   633.883 115
      gen. pharm.   615.323 115
          toxicology   615.952 311 5
      vet. pharm.   636.089 532 311 5
          toxicology   636.089 595 231 15
  paleobotany   561.3
      other aspects see Plants
Annotations
  rel. books *see* Commentaries
  s.a. other spec. subj.
Announce systems *see*
      Public-address systems
Announcements
  etiquette   395.4
Announcing
  radio tech.   791.443
  television tech.   791.453
Annual
  leave *see* Leaves (absence)
  publications *see* Serials
  variations
      air temperatures met.   551.525 3
          weather forecasting   551.642 53
          spec. areas   551.65

Annual (continued)
  wages
      labor econ.   331.216 2
      *s.a. spec. classes of
          labor e.g.* Women
Annuals (plants)
  floriculture   635.931 2
      s.a. Herbaceous plants
Annuities
  insurance   368.37
      misc. aspects see Insurance
      other aspects see Pensions
Annulment of marriage
  law   346.016 6
      spec. jur.   346.3–.9
      s.a. Divorce
Annunciation Christian doctrine   232.912
Anodynes
  pharmacodynamics   615.783
      other aspects see Drugs
Anointing sick *see* Extreme
      unction
Anoka Co. Minn.   *area*–776 65
Anomalies *see* Teratology
Anomalodesmacea *see* Pelecypoda
Anomochloeae *see* Pooideae
Anomocoela
  zoology   597.85
      other aspects see Anura
Anomura
  culture   639.544
  fishing
      commercial   639.544
      sports   799.255 384 4
  zoology   595.384 4
      other aspects see Decapoda
          (crustaceans)
Anonales *see* Annonales
Anonymous works
  bibliographies   014
  spec. subj.   016
Anopla *see* Nemertea
Anoplura
  culture   638.575 12
  paleozoology   565.75
  zoology   595.751 2
      other aspects see Insecta
Anostraca *see* Branchiopoda
Anoxemia *see* Altitude sickness
Anschluss Austria hist.   943.605 2
      *s.a. spec. events & subj.
          e.g.* Commerce
Anseres *see* Anseriformes
Anseriformes
  hunting
      commercial   639.128 41
      sports   799.248 41
  paleozoology   568.4
  zoology   598.41
      other aspects see Aves
Anson Co. N.C.   *area*–756 753

Anthropology (continued)
museums
  desc. & colls.   301.074
  museology   069.930 1
  s.a. spec. activities
    e.g. Display
  s.a. spec. kinds e.g.
    Physical anthropology
Anthropometric design
automobiles *see* Design
  automobiles
Anthropometry   573.6
criminal   364.125
Anthropomorphism nat. rel.   211
Anthroposophy
religion   299.935
Antiaircraft
artillery
  mil. sci.   358.13
  other aspects see Artillery
defenses
  naval warfare   359.981
  spec. wars *see* Aerial
    operations military
Antiasthmatics
pharmacodynamics   615.72
other aspects see Drugs
Anti-ballistic missiles
mil. eng.
  soc. & econ. aspects *see*
    Secondary industry
  tech. & mf.   623.451 94
Antibiotics
biochemistry
  gen. wks.   574.192 46
    animals   591.192 46
    microorganisms   576.119 246
    plants   581.192 46
  s.a. spec. organisms
  med. sci.   612.015 76
    animals   636.089 201 576
    s.a. spec. animals
    man   612.015 76
  org. chem.   547.76
  pharmacology   615.329
  other aspects see Drugs
Antibodies immunology
pathology
  gen. wks.   574.293
    animals   591.293
    plants   581.293
  s.a. spec. organisms
  med. sci.   616.079 3
    animals   636.089 607 93
    s.a. spec. animals
    man   616.079 3
  s.a. spec. diseases
physiology
  med. sci.   612.118 223

Antibodies immunology
physiology (continued)
  other aspects see
    Circulatory fluids
    physiology
Antichrist
Christian doctrines   236
Anticlericalism *see* Religious
  groups & state
Anticoagulants
pharmacodynamics   615.718
other aspects see Drugs
Anticonvulsants
pharmacodynamics   615.784
other aspects see Drugs
Anticosti Isl. Que.   *area*–714 17
Anticyclogenesis *see*
  Anticyclones met.
Anticyclones met.   551.551 4
artificial modification   551.685 14
weather forecasting   551.645 14
spec. areas.   551.65
Antidiaphoretics
pharmacodynamics   615.74
other aspects see Drugs
Antidiuretics
pharmacodynamics   615.761
other aspects see Drugs
Antidotes toxicology   615.908
misc. aspects see Toxicology
Antiemetics
pharmacodynamics   615.73
other aspects see Drugs
Antienzymes *see* Enzymes
Antietam Battle
U.S. Civil War hist.   973.733 6
Antifederalist Party
U.S.
  pol. sci.   324.273 26
  s.a. spec. subj. of concern
    e.g. Social problems
Antifreeze solutions
internal combustion engines
  automobiles *see*
    Cooling-systems
    internal combustion
    engines automobiles
Antigens immunology
pathology
  gen. wks.   574.292
    animals   591.292
    plants   581.292
  s.a. spec. organisms
  med. sci.   616.079 2
    animals   636.089 607 92
    s.a. spec. animals
    man   616.079 2
  s.a. spec. diseases
physiology
  med. sci.   612.118 222

Antigens immunology
  physiology (continued)
    other aspects see
      Circulatory fluids
      physiology
Antigonish Co. N.S.   *area*–716 14
Antigua   *area*–729 74
Antiguans   *r.e.n.*–969 729 74
Anti-Lebanon   *area*–569 14
Antilles   *area*–729
Antimacassars
  textile arts   746.95
Antimatter *see* Matter
Antimilitarism
  mil. sci.   355.021 3
Antimissile missiles
  mil. eng.
    soc. & econ. aspects *see*
      Secondary industries
    tech. & mf.   623.451 94
Antimission Baptists   286.4
  misc. aspects see Baptist
Antimonides
  mineralogy   549.32
Antimony
  chemistry
    inorganic   546.716
    organic   547.057 16
    s.a. spec. groupings e.g.
      Aliphatic compunds
    technology   661.071 6
    soc. & econ. aspects *see*
      Secondary industries
    s.a. spec. prod.
  materials
    building   691.875
    engineering   620.189 5
      foundations   624.153 895
      naval design   623.818 295
      shipbuilding   623.820 7
      structures   624.182 95
  metallography   669.957 5
  metallurgy   669.75
    physical & chem.   669.967 5
    soc. & econ. aspects *see*
      Secondary industries
  mineral aspects
    econ. geol.   553.47
    marketing *see* Marketing
    mineralogy   549.25
    mining
      technology   622.347
      prospecting   622.184 7
    s.a. spec. uses; also spec.
      minerals
  phamacology   615.271 6
    misc. aspects see
      Pharmacology
  products
    mf. tech.   673.75

Antimony
  products (continued)
    other aspects see
      Nonferrous metals
      products
    toxicology   615.925 716
      misc. aspects see
        Toxicology
    other aspects see Metal;
      also Metals
Antinauseants
  pharmacodynamics   615.73
  other aspects see Drugs
Antineutrinos
  astrophysics
    gen. wks.   523.019 721 5
    acceleration   523.019 737 5
    s.a. spec. celestial bodies
  physics
    gen. wks.   539.721 5
    acceleration   539.737 5
    spec. states of matter   530.4
    s.a. spec. physical
      phenomena e.g. Heat
Antineutrons
  astrophysics
    gen. wks.   523.019 721 3
    acceleration   523.019 737 3
    s.a. spec. celestial bodies
  physics
    gen. wks.   539.721 3
    acceleration   539.737 3
    spec. states of matter   530.4
    s.a. spec. physical
      phenomena e.g. Heat
Antinomianism heresies
  Christian church hist.   273.6
Antioch Turkey   *area*–564
Antioquia Colombia   *area*–861 26
Antioxidants
  rubber tech. *see* Compounding
    rubber mf.
Antiparticles *see* Particles
    (matter)
Antipersonnel devices
  mil. eng.
    soc. & econ. aspects *see*
      Secondary industries
    tech. & mf.   623.451 4
Antiphonal readings *see*
    Responsive readings
Antipodes Isls.   *area*–931 1
Antiprotons *see* Nucleons
Antipyretics
  pharmacodynamics   615.75
  other aspects see Drugs
Antique
  furniture   749.1
    spec. periods   749.2
  Philippines   *area*–599 5

Antiques
  dec. arts   745.1
    s.a. spec. kinds
Antiquities *see* Ancient; *also*
        Archaeology
Anti-Semitism
  pol. sci.   323.119 24
  psychology   155.9
Antisepsis
  obstetrics   618.89
  vet. med.   636.089 889
    s.a. spec. animals
  surgery   617.910 1
    misc. aspects see Diseases
    s.a. spec. diseases
Antisocial
  compulsions *see*
      Obsessive-compulsive
      neuroses
  persons   *pers.*–069 2
Antispasmodics
  pharmacodynamics 615.784
  other aspects see Drugs
Antistrophe *see* Poetry gen.
    wks. rhetoric
Antisubmarine warfare
  history
    World War 1   940.451 6
    World War 2   940.545 16
    s.a. other spec. wars
Antisynclines
  structural geol.   551.86
    s.a. spec. aspects e.g.
      Prospecting
Antitank artillery
  mil. sci.   358.12
  other aspects see Artillery
Antitoxins
  pharmacology   615.375
  other aspects see Drugs
Anti-Trinitarianism *see*
    Unitarianism
Antitrust law   343.072
  spec. jur.   343.3–.9
Antivenins *see* Antitoxins
Antlerite
  mineralogy   549.755
Antlers *see* Integumentary
    organs
Antofagasta Chile *area*–831 3
Antoniaceae *see* Loganiales
Antonians *see* Antonines
Antonines
  rel. orders   255.18
    church hist.   271.18
    ecclesiology 262.24
Antonyms
  spec. langs.
    nonstandard forms *lang. sub.*–7
    standard forms
      dictionaries *lang. sub.*–31

Antonyms
  spec. langs.
    standard forms (continued)
      usage   *lang. sub.*–8
  spec. subj.   *s.s.*–014
  other aspects see Words
Antrim
  Co. Mich.   *area*–774 85
  district N. Ire. *area*–416 12
  former co. Ire. *area*–416 1
Ants *see* Formicidae
Antwerp Belgium *area*–493 2
Anura
  culture   639.378
  hunting
    commercial   639.13
    sports   799.257 8
  paleozoology 567.8
  zoology   597.8
  other aspects see Amphibia
Anus
  anatomy
    human   611.35
    other aspects see Nutritive
      organs
  diseases
    gen. wks.   616.35
      neoplasms 616.992 35
      tuberculosis 616.995 35
    geriatrics   618.976 35
    pediatrics   618.923 5
    pub. health 614.593 5
    statistics   312.335
      deaths   312.263 5
    surgery   617.555
      anesthesiology 617.967 555
    other aspects see Diseases
  physical anthropometry 573.635
  physiology
    human   612.36
    other aspects see Nutrition
  tissue biology human 611.018 935
Anvil music   789.4
  recordings   789.912 94
Anvils (musical instruments)
  mf. tech.   681.819 4
    misc. aspects see Musical
      instruments
  musical art   789.4
Anxiety
  mental pub. health 614.582 2
  neuroses
    gen. med.   616.852 23
    geriatrics   618.976 852 23
    pediatrics   618.928 522 3
    psychology 157.3
    statistics   312.385 223
  other aspects see Mental
    illness
Anzoátegui Venezuela *area*–875 2
Aomori Japan   *area*–521 1

Aorta
  diseases   616.138
    geriatrics   618.976 138
    pediatrics   618.921 38
    public health   614.591 38
    statistics   312.313 8
    deaths   312.261 38
    other aspects see Diseases
Aosta Italy   *area*–451 1
Apache Co. Ariz.   *area*–791 37
Apachean *see* Na-Dene
Apalachicola River Fla.   *area*–759 92
Apartheid pol. ideology   320.56
  soc. theology *see* Political
      ideologies soc.
      theology
Apartment
  hotels
    architecture   728.314
    building   690.831 4
    housekeeping   647.92
    other aspects see
      Residential buildings
  houses
    architecture   728.314
    building   690.831 4
    housekeeping   647.92
    other aspects see
      Residential buildings
  sales
    commerce   381.19
    misc. aspects see
      Commerce
Apartment-house districts
  civic art   711.58
Apatites
  mineralogy   549.72
  other aspects see Phosphate
      fertilizers
Apennines   *area*–45
Aperients
  pharmacodynamics   615.732
  other aspects see Drugs
Apes *see* Pongidae
Apetalae
  botany   583.9
  floriculture   635.933 9
  med. aspects
    crop prod.   633.883 9
    gen. pharm.   615.323 9
      toxicology   615.952 39
    vet. pharm.   636.089 532 39
      toxicology   636.089 595 239
  paleobotany   561.3
  other aspects see Plants
Aphaniptera *see* Siphonaptera
Aphasias
  gen. med.   616.855 2
  geriatrics   618.976 855 2
  pediatrics   618.928 552
  psychology   157.5

Aphasias (continued)
  pub. health   614.58
  statistics   312.385 52
  other aspects see Mental
      illness
Aphasmidia *see* Nematoda
Aphid flies *see* Cyclorrhapha
Aphidoidea *see* Homoptera
Aphids *see* Homoptera
Aphrodisiacs
  pharmacodynamics   615.766
  other aspects see Drugs
Aphyllophorales *see* Agaricales
Apiaceae *see* Umbellales
Apiarists *see* Beekeepers
Apiary establishment agric.   638.11
Apiculture *see* Apidae culture
Apidae
  agric. pests   632.799
    s.a. spec. types of culture
      e.g. Forestry; *also*
      spec. crops
  conservation tech.   639.975 799
  culture
    soc. & econ. aspects *see*
      Primary industries
    technology   638.1
    other aspects see
      Agriculture
  drawing tech.   743.657 99
  paleozoology   565.79
  zoology   595.799
  other aspects see Animals
Apium
  graveolens *see* Celery
  graveolens rapaceum *see*
    Celeriac
Aplacophora *see* Crepipoda
Apocalypses
  Bible
    N.T.
      pseudepigrapha   229.94
      St. John   228
      O.T. pseudepigrapha 229.913
    liturgy   264.3–.4
      spec. denominations 264.01–.09
Apocrypha
  Bible   229
  liturgy   264.3–.4
    spec. denominations   264.01–.09
Apocryphal
  wisdom literature
    deuterocanonical books 229.3
    other aspects see Apocrypha
Apocynaceae *see* Apocynales
Apocynales
  botany   583.72
  floriculture   635.933 72
  med. aspects
    crop prod.   633.883 72

Apocynales
  med. aspects (continued)
    gen. pharm.   615.323 72
    toxicology   615.952 372
    vet. pharm.   636.089 532 372
    toxicology   636.089 595 237 2
  paleobotany   561.3
  other aspects see Plants
Apocynum cannabinum *see* Indian
    hemp
Apoda (amphibians)
  culture   639.377
  hunting
    commercial   639.13
    sports   799.257 7
  paleozoology   567.7
  zoology   597.7
  other aspects see Amphibia
Apoda (crustaceans) *see*
    Cirripedia
Apoda (echinoderms) *see*
    Holothurioidea
Apodes
  culture   639.375 1
  fishing
    commercial   639.275 1
    sports   799.175 1
  zoology   597.51
  other aspects see Teleostei
Apodi *see* Apodiformes
Apodiformes
  hunting
    commercial   639.128 899
    sports   799.248 899
  paleozoology   568.8
  zoology   598.899
  other aspects see Aves
Apogee
  celestial bodies *see* Orbits
Apollo project astronautics   629.454
Apologetics
  doctrinal theology
    Christianity   239
    comp. rel.   291.2
    Islam   297.29
    other rel. see Doctrinal
        theology
  s.a. other spec. subj.
Aponogetonaceae *see*
    Aponogetonales
Aponogetonales
  botany   584.743
  floriculture   635.934 743
  med. aspects
    crop. prod.   633.884 743
    gen. pharm.   615.324 743
    toxicology   615.952 474 3
    vet. pharm.   636.089 532 474 3
    toxicology   636.089 595 247 43
  paleobotany   561.4
  other aspects see Plants

Apophyllite
  mineralogy   549.67
Apoplexy *see* Cerebrovascular
    diseases
Apostasiaceae *see* Haemodorales
Apostasy *see* Heresy
Apostates
  polemics against
    Christianity   239.7
    Islam   297.297
    other rel. see Doctrinal
        theology
Apostle Isls. Wis.   *area*–775 21
Apostles
  art representation
    arts   704.948 62
    s.a. spec. art forms
  Christian rel.
    paintings   247.562
    sculpture   247.3
  biog. & work   225.92
  Creed
    Christian doctrines   238.11
    private prayers   242.723
  lit. & stage trmt. *see*
      Persons
Apostleship
  spiritual gift
    Christian doctrines   234.13
Apostolic
  apologetics Christian doctrines 239.1
  Christians
    biog. & work   270
    s.a. spec. periods
    coll. writings   281.1–.4
    s.a.   *pers.*–211
  Church   281.1
    history   270.1–.3
  letters rel. law   262.91
  polemics
    Christian doctrines   239.1
  succession Christian church
        govt.   262.11
Apostolicity Christian church 262.72
Appalachian Mts.   *area*–74
  Canada   *area*–714
  North Carolina   *area*–756 8
  U.S.   *area*–74
Appanoose Co. Ia.   *area*–777 89
Apparatus *see* Equipment
Apparel *see* Clothing
Apparent
  movement visual *see* Movements
        perception visual
  time chronology   529.1
Apparitions
  of Mary
    Christian doctrines   232.917
  s.a. Ghosts

Applied (continued)
  liquid mechanics *see* Liquids
      engineering
  mathematics   519
    s.a. appls. to spec. subj.
       e.g. Civil engineering
  mechanics
    gen. wks.   620.1
    s.a. spec. appls. e.g.
       Aerospace engineering
  personnel
    biog. & work   620.100 92
    s.a.   *pers.*–620 1
  nutrition
    animal husbandry   636.085 2
    s.a. spec. feeds; also
      spec. animals
    home econ.   641.1
    hygiene   613.2
      misc. aspects see Hygiene
  optics *see* Light (radiation)
      engineering
  physicists
    biog. & work   621.092
    s.a. spec. kinds
    s.a.   *pers.*–621
  physics
    gen. wks
    soc. & econ. aspects *see*
      Secondary industries
    technology   621
    s.a. spec. appls. e.g.
      Aerospace engineering
    mil. eng.   623.045
    other aspects see
      Engineering
    s.a. other spec. appls.
  psychology   158
    s.a. appls. to spec. subj.
      e.g. Personnel
      management
  sciences *see* Technology
  scientists *see* Technologists
  sociology   360
  solid mechanics   620.105
  s.a. spec. appls. e.g.
      Aerospace engineering
  sonics   620.21–.25
  s.a. spec. appls. e.g.
      Buildings construction
  spectroscopy
    soc. & econ. aspects *see*
      Secondary industries
    technology   621.361
    s.a. spec. appls. e.g.
      Military engineering
  statics *see* Statics eng.
    mech.
  subsonics   620.28
  ultrasonics   620.28
  s.a. other spec. subj.

Appling Co. Ga.   *area*–758 784
Appliqué
  textile arts   746.445
  s.a. spec. prod. e.g.
      Hangings
Appointment powers
  chief executives *see* Powers
      chief executives
  legislative bodies
    law *see* Legislative powers
    law
      pol. sci.   328.345 5
      spec. jur.   328.4–.9
Appointments *see spec. subj.*
Appomattox Co. Va.   *area*–755 625
Apportionment
  legislative bodies
    law *see* Representation law
    pol. sci.   328.334 52
    spec. jur.   328.4–.9
Appraisals
  desc. research *see*
      Descriptive research
  land econ.   333.332
  tax admin. *see* Valuation tax
    admin.
Appreciation
  arts   701.1
  literature   801
  music   780.15
    s.a. spec. mediums
    s.a. other spec. art forms
  s.a. other spec. subj. e.g.
      Money
Apprehension
  police services *see* Arrest
  psychology *see* Perception
Apprentices
  labor econ.   331.55
  labor law *see* Labor law
  spec. subj.   *s.s.*–073
Apprenticeship
  centers
    secondary ed.   373.27
  labor law *see* Labor law
  training
    education   373.27
    labor econ.   331.259 22
    s.a. spec. classes of
      labor e.g. Women
    personnel admin. *see* Job
      training
Approach
  manned space flight
    gen. wks.
      lunar flights   629.454 4
      planetary flights 629.455
    s.a. spec. appls. e.g.
      Space warfare
  piloting
    seamanship   623.892 9

Approaches		**Apterygota**	
Christian church arch.	726.591	agric. pests	632.71
s.a. other spec. subj.		*s.a. spec. types of culture*	
Appropriations		*e.g.* Forestry; *also*	
budgeting		*spec. crops*	
pub. admin.	350.722 36	culture	638.571
central govts.	351.722 36	paleozoology	565.71
spec. jur.	353–354	zoology	595.71
local govts.	352.123 6	*other aspects see* Insecta	
legislative bodies *see*		**Aptitude**	
Financial powers		requirements	
Approved plans		employee *see* Personal	
library acquisitions	025.233	qualifications	
Approximations		tests	
mathematics	511.4	psychology	153.94
algebra	512.924	animals	156.394
arithmetic	513.24	children	155.413
s.a. other spec. branches of		*s.a. psych. of other spec.*	
math.; also spec.		*groups*	
appls. e.g.		**Aptitudes**	
Engineering		determination palmistry	133.62
Appurtenances		ed. grouping *see* Homogeneous	
sewers	628.25	grouping	
s.a. spec. appls. e.g.		psychology	153.9
Water drainage		animals	156.39
s.a. other spec. subj.		children	155.413
Apraxia *see* Aphasias		*s.a. psych. of other spec.*	
Apricots		*groups*	
agriculture	634.21	**Apuania** Italy	*area*–455 4
soc. & econ. aspects *see*		**Apulia** Italy	*area*–457 5
Primary industries		ancient	*area*–377
foods	641.342 1	**Apure** Venezuela	*area*–874 2
preparation		**Apurimac** Peru	*area*–852 94
commercial	664.804 21	**Aqaba** Gulf *see* Red Sea	
domestic	641.642 1	**Aqaid** Islam	297.2
other aspects see Rosaceae;		**Aquaplaning**	
also Fruits		sports	797.173
Aprons		*other aspects see* Sports	
comm. mf.		**Aquariums**	
soc. & econ. aspects *see*		museums *see* Museums	
Secondary industries		use fish culture	639.34
technology	687.19	*s.a. spec. kinds of fish*	
leather	685.22	**Aquatic**	
domestic mf.	646.48	biol. resources	
Apses		economics	333.952
Christian church arch.	726.593	govt. control	
Aptandraceae *see* Olacales		law	346.046 952
Apterous insects		spec. jur.	346.3–.9
culture	638.575 1	pub. admin. *see*	
paleozoology	565.75	Biological resources	
zoology	595.751	govt. control pub.	
other aspects see Insecta		admin.	
Apterygiformes		biology *see* Hydrographic	
hunting		biology	
commercial	639.128 54	ecology life sci.	574.526 3
sports	799.248 54	animals	591.526 3
paleozoology	568.5	microorganisms	576.15
zoology	598.54	plants	581.526 3
other aspects see Aves		*s.a. spec. organisms*	

Aquatic (continued)
  plants
    floriculture   635.967 4
      s.a. spec. plants
    sports   797
      misc. aspects see Sports
    s.a. Water
Aquatinting
  graphic arts
    processes   766.3
    products   769
Aqueducts
  water-supply eng.
    technology   628.15
      other aspects see Water
                supply engineering
Aqueous
  deposits *see* Water
  humor eyes
    human phys.   612.844
      other aspects see Eyes
  solutions *see* Water solutions
Aquifoliaceae *see* Celastrales
Aquila Italy   *area*–457 11
Aquilariaceae *see* Thymelaeales
Aquitaine France   *area*–447
Arab
  architecture   722.3
    misc. aspects see
              Architectural schools
  countries   *area*–174 927
    s.a. spec. countries
  domination Iran hist.   955.02
    s.a. spec. events & subj.
        e.g. Commerce
  language *see* Arabic
  Leaque
    internat. law   341.247 7
    treaties   341.026 377
  people   *r.e.n.*–927
  rule
    Algeria hist.   965.02
      s.a. spec. events & subj.
          e.g. Commerce
    Egypt hist.   962.02
      s.a. spec. events & subj.
          e.g. Commerce
    Ethiopia hist.   962.02
      s.a. spec. events & subj.
          e.g. Commerce
    Libya hist.   961.202
      s.a. spec. events & subj.
          e.g. Commerce
    Morocco hist.   964.02
      s.a. spec. events & subj.
          e.g. Commerce
    North Africa hist.   961.022
      s.a. spec. events & subj.
          e.g. Commerce

Arab
  rule (continued)
    Tunisia hist.   961.102
      s.a. spec. events & subj.
          e.g. Commerce
    Zanzibar hist.   967.810 2
      s.a. spec. events & subj.
          e.g. Commerce
    s.a. Arabian; *also* Arabic
Arabesques
  musical form
    gen. wks. *see* Musical forms
    piano   786.42
      recordings   789.912 642
    s.a. other spec. mediums
Arabia   *area*–53
  ancient   *area*–394
Arabian
  Desert Egypt   *area*–623
  horses
    animal husbandry   636.112
      other aspects see Horses
  Peninsula *see* Arabia
  Sea
    oceanography   551.467 37
    regional subj. trmt.   *area*–165 37
      other aspects see Indian
              Ocean
  s.a. Arab; *also* Arabic
Arabic
  language
    linguistics   492.7
    literatures   892.7
    s.a.   *lang.*–927
  people   *r.e.n.*–927
  texts
    Bible   220.46
      s.a. spec. parts of Bible
    Hadith   297.124 04
      s.a. spec. works
    Koran   297.122 4
      s.a. spec. works
    s.a. spec. Arab countries
        e.g. Syria; *also*
        other spec. subj. e.g.
        Arts; *also* Arab;
        also Arabian
Arabs   *r.e.n.*–927
Araceae *see* Arales
Arachis hypogaea *see* Peanuts
Arachnida
  agric. pests   632.654
    s.a. spec. types of culture
        e.g. Forestry; *also*
        spec. crops
  conservation tech.   639.975 4
  disease carriers
    pub. health   614.433
      misc. aspects see Public
              health
  drawing tech.   743.654

Arachnida (continued)	
paleozoology	565.4
zoology	595.4
other aspects see Arthropoda	
Arad Romania	*area*–498 4
Aradoidea *see* Heteroptera	
Arafura Sea	
oceanography	551.465 75
regional subj. trmt.	*area*–164 75
other aspects see Pacific	
Ocean	
Aragon Spain	*area*–465 5
Aragonite	
mineralogy	549.785
Aragua Venezuela	*area*–873 4
Aral Sea	*area*–587
Arales	
botany	584.64
floriculture	635.934 64
med. aspects	
crop prod.	633.884 64
gen. pharm.	615.324 64
toxicology	615.952 464
vet. pharm.	636.089 532 464
toxicology	636.089 595 246 4
paleobotany	561.4
other aspects see Plants	
Araliaceae *see* Araliales	
Araliales	
botany	583.687
floriculture	635.933 687
forestry	634.973 687
med. aspects	
crop prod.	633.883 687
gen. pharm.	615.323 687
toxicology	615.952 368 7
vet. pharm.	636.089 532 368 7
toxicology	636.089 595 236 87
paleobotany	561.3
other aspects see Plants	
Aramaic	
languages	
linguistics	492.2
literatures	892.2
s.a.	*lang.*–922
people	*r.e.n.*–922
texts	
Midrash	296.140 4
s.a. spec. works	
Talmudic lit.	296.120 4
s.a. spec. works	
s.a. other spec. subj. e.g.	
Arts	
Arameans	*r.e.n.*–922
Aran Isls. Ireland	*area*–417 48
Araneae *see* Araneida	
Araneida	
zoology	595.44
other aspects see Arachnida	
Aransas Co. Tex.	*area*–764 122

Aranyakas	
Vedic literature	294.592 1
Arapahoe Co. Colo.	*area*–788 82
Arapaimas *see* Isospondyli	
Ararat Vic.	*area*–945 7
Arauca Colombia	*area*–861 38
Araucanian	
language	
linguistics	498
literature	898
s.a.	*lang.*–98
people	*r.e.n.*–98
s.a. other spec. subj.	
Araucaria family *see*	
Coniferales	
Araucariaceae *see* Coniferales	
Arauco Chile	*area*–834 2
Arbil Iraq	*area*–567 2
Arbitration	
employee relations	
personnel admin.	
gen. management	658.315 4
spec. subj.	*s.s.*–068 3
pub. admin.	350.174
central govts.	351.174
spec. jur.	353–354
local govts.	352.005 174
internat. law	341.522
labor econ.	331.891 43
labor law *see* Labor law	
municipal law	347.09
spec. jur.	347.3–.9
U.S.	
Federal	347.739
state & local	347.74–.79
spec. subj.	*law s.s.*–026 9
sociology	303.6
Arboriculture *see* Forestry	
Arborvitae *see* Coniferales	
Arbroath Tayside Scot.	*area*–412 6
Arbuckle Mts. Okla.	*area*–766 5
Arc	
brazing *see* Brazing metal	
products	
cutting *see* Cutting metal	
products	
electric *see* Disruptive	
discharge	
furnaces elect. eng.	
soc. & econ. aspects *see*	
Secondary industries	
tech. & mf.	621.396
s.a. spec. appls. e.g.	
Metallurgy	
length integral geometry	516.362
s.a. spec. appls. e.g.	
Engineering	
lighting eng.	
soc. & econ. aspects *see*	
Secondary industries	

Arc
  lighting eng. (continued)
    technology   621.325
      s.a. spec. appls. e.g.
        Military engineering
  melting *see* Melting metal
      products
  welding
    metal products
      mf. tech.   671.521 2
        ferrous metals   672.521 2
        s.a. other spec. metals
      other aspects see Welding
Arcades
  architecture
    construction   721.2
    design & decoration   729.33
  building   690.12
  s.a. spec. kinds of bldgs.
Arcadia Greece   *area*–495 2
  ancient   *area*–388
Arch
  bridges
    structural eng.   624.6
    other aspects see Bridges
        (structures)
    dams *see* Masonry dams
Archaeoceti paleozoology   569.5
Archaeocyatha paleozoology   563.47
Archaeologists
  biog. & work
    gen. wks.   930.109 2
    s.a. geog. of spec. places
  occupational ethics   174.993
  s.a.   *pers.*–93
Archaeology   930.1
  & rel. nat. rel.   215.8
  cultural relations
    internat. law   341.767 7
  law   344.094
    spec. jur.   344.3–.9
  pub. admin. *see* History pub.
      admin.
  spec. places
    ancient   931–939
    Bible   220.93
      s.a. spec. parts of
          Bible
    modern   940–990
  s.a. spec. subj. e.g.
      Commerce
Archaeopteris paleobotany   561.597
Archaeornithes paleozoology   568.22
Archaisms   417.2
  spec. langs.   *lang. sub.*–7
Archangel RSFSR   *area*–472 3
Archangels *see* Angels
Archangiaceae *see*
        Myxobacterales
Archbishops *see* Bishops
        (clergy)

Archean *see* Archeozoic era
Archeogastropoda *see*
        Prosobranchia
Archeology *see* Archaeology
Archeozoic era
  geology   661.712
    s.a. spec. aspects e.g.
        Economic geology
  paleontology *see* Precambrian
      eras
Archer
  Co. Tex.   *area*–764 543
  River Qld.   *area*–943 8
Archers
  biog. & work.   799.320 92
  s.a.   *pers.*–799 3
Archery
  sports   799.32
  other aspects see Sports
Arches (structural element)
  architecture
    construction   721.41
    design & decoration   729.33
  building   690.141
  structural eng.
    gen. wks.   624.177 5
    concretes   624.183 45
      s.a. other spec.
          materials
    naval arch.   623.817 75
    s.a. other spec. appls.
  s.a. spec. kinds of
      structures
Arches (structures)
  architecture   725.96
  building   690.596
Arch-gravity dams *see* Masonry
        dams
Archiannelida
  culture & hunting   639.754 2
  zoology   595.142
  other aspects see Worms
Architarbi paleozoology   565.49
Architects
  biog. & work   720.92
    s.a. spec. kinds of
        structures
  occupational ethics   174.972
  s.a.   *pers.*–72
Architectural
  acoustics sound eng.   690
  construction   721
    s.a. spec. kinds of bldgs.
  decoration   729
    rel. significance
      Christianity   247.4
      other rel. see Arts rel.
          significance
    s.a. spec. kinds of bldgs.
  design   729
    s.a. spec. kinds of bldgs.

Arezzo Italy	*area*–455 9
Arfon Gwynedd Wales	*area*–429 25
Argenteuil Co. Que.	*area*–714 23
Argentina	*area*–82
Argentine	
literature	860
people	*r.e.n.*–688 2
Republic	*area*–82
s.a. other spec. subj. e.g.	
Arts	
Argentinians	*r.e.n.*–688 2
Argentite	
mineralogy	549.32
Argentum *see* Silver	
Arges Romania	*area*–498 2
Argillaceous rocks *see*	
Sedimentary rocks	
Argobba language *see* Ethiopic	
languages	
Argolis Greece	*area*–495 2
ancient	*area*–388
Argon	
chemistry	
inorganic	546.753
technology	661.075 3
soc. & econ. aspects *see*	
Secondary industries	
s.a. spec. prod.	
pharmacology	615.275 3
misc. aspects see	
Pharmacology	
toxicology	615.925 753
misc. aspects see	
Toxicology	
other aspects see Rare gases	
Argonne France	*area*–443 8
Argot *see* Slang	
Argovie Switzerland	*area*–494 5
Argument	
logic	168
Arguments	
law *see* Pretrial procedure	
s.a. other spec. subj.	
Argyll & Bute Scot.	*area*–414 23
Ariana (ancient region)	*area*–396
Arianism	
heresies Christian church hist.	273.4
Arid lands	
ecology life sci.	574.526 5
animals	591.526 5
microorganisms	576.15
plants	581.526 5
s.a. spec. organisms	
other aspects see Deserts	
Ariège France	*area*–448 8
Aristocracy (social class) *see*	
Nobility (social class)	
Aristolochiaceae *see*	
Aristolochiales	
Aristolochiales	
botany	583.922

Aristolochiales (continued)	
floriculture	635.933 922
med. aspects	
crop prod.	633.883 922
gen. pharm.	615.323 922
toxicology	615.952 392 2
vet. pharm.	636.089 532 392 2
toxicology	636.089 595 239 22
paleobotany	561.3
other aspects see Plants	
Aristotelian philosophy	185
Aristotype process	
photography	772.14
Arithmetic	513
elementary ed.	372.72
s.a. spec. appls. e.g.	
Engineering	
Arithmetical progressions *see*	
Progressions	
Arizona	*area*–791
Arkabutla Res. Miss.	*area*–762 85
Arkansas	
Co. Ark.	*area*–767 86
River	*area*–767 3
Arkansas	*area*–767 3
Colorado	*area*–788 53
Kansas	*area*–781 4
Oklahoma	*area*–766 8
state	*area*–767
Arkhangelsk RSFSR	*area*–472 3
Arksey South Yorkshire Eng.	
	area–428 27
Arlington Co. Va.	*area*–755 295
Arm (anatomy) *see* Arms	
(anatomy)	
Armadale Lothian Scot.	*area*–413 3
Armadillos *see* Edentata	
Armageddon	
Christian doctrines	236.9
Armagh Ireland	
city	*area*–416 62
district	*area*–416 61
former co.	*area*–416 6
Armaments *see* Ordnance	
Armature winding *see* Armatures	
(electricity)	
Armatures (electricity)	
generators	
electrodynamic eng.	
soc. & econ. aspects *see*	
Secondary industries	
tech. & mf.	621.316
s.a. spec. appls. e.g.	
Military engineering	
other aspects see	
Electrodynamics	
Armatures (sculpture)	731.3
spec. periods & schools	732–735
Armed	
forces	
& state pol. sci.	322.5

Arms (military) (continued)
  control
    internat. relations
      pol. sci.   327.174
        spec. countries   327.3–.9
      mil. sci.   355.03
    customs   399
    manual
      horse cavalry   357.185
      infantry   356.184
    other aspects see Ordnance
Armstrong Co.
  Pennsylvania   *area*–748 88
  Texas   *area*–764 833
Army
  departments
    U.S. govt.   353.62
    other jur. see Defense
      (military) pub. admin.
      departments
  of the Cumberland Society   369.15
  other aspects see Armed
    services
Arnatto family *see* Bixales
Arnhem Land N. Ter. Aust.
      area–942 95
Arnold
  Benedict treason
    U.S. hist.   973.382
  Nottinghamshire Eng.   *area*–425 28
Aromatic
  compounds
    chem. tech.
      hydrocarbons   661.816
      org. chem.   547.6
    other aspects see Organic
      chemicals
    s.a. spec. cpds. & spec.
      prod.
  herbs *see* Herbs
  teas
    comm. proc.   663.96
    other aspects see
      Nonalcoholic beverages
Aromatization
  chem. eng.   660.284 41
  org. chem.   547.21
  s.a. spec. elements, cpds.,
    prod.
Aroostook
  Co. Me.   *area*–741 1
  River Me.   *area*–741 1
Arpad dynasty
  Hungary hist.   943.902
  s.a. spec. events & subj.
    e.g. Commerce
Arpeggios
  exercises
    keyboard string instr.   786.34

Arraignment
  criminal law   345.072
    spec. jur.   345.3–.9
Arran
  Isls. Ireland   *area*–417 48
  Scotland   *area*–414 61
Arrangement
  flowers
    dec. arts   745.92
  library materials   025.81
  museology   069.53
  statistical method   001.422 4
    spec. subj. *see* Statistical
      method
Arrangement (music)
  music theory   781.64
  s.a. spec. mediums
Arrangments
  musical scores & parts *see*
    Scores (music)
Arrest
  criminal law   345.052 7
    spec. jur.   345.3–.9
  police services   363.232
    misc. aspects see Law
      enforcement
Arrested mental development *see*
  Mental deficiency
Arrhythmia
  gen. med.   616.128
  geriatrics   618.976 128
  pediatrics   618.921 28
  pub. health   614.591 28
  statistics   312.312 8
    deaths   312.261 28
  other aspects see Diseases
Arrondissements
  local govt. admin.   352.007 3
Arrow Rock Res. Ida   *area*–796 29
Arrow-grass family *see*
  Juncaginales
Arrowroot
  agriculture   633.68
  soc. & econ. aspects *see*
    Primary industries
  foods
    comm. proc.   664.23
  other aspects see
    Zingiberales; *also*
    Starches
Arrows *see* Bows (weapons)
Arroyos *see* Depressions
  (geomorphology)
Ars antiqua
  musical style
    gen. wks.   780.902
    spec. places   780.91–.99
  s.a. spec. mediums

Ars nova
  musical style
    gen. wks.   780.902
      spec. places   780.91–.99
    s.a. spec. mediums
Arsenal buildings *see* Military
          buildings
Arsenals
  armed forces   355.73
    s.a. spec. mil. branches
Arsenates
  chemistry *see* Arsenic
          chemistry
  mineralogy   549.72
Arsenic
  chemistry
    inorganic   546.715
    organic   547.057 15
      s.a. spec. groupings e.g.
          Aliphatic compounds
    technology   661.071 5
      soc. & econ. aspects *see*
          Secondary industries
      s.a. spec. prod.
  eng. materials   620.189 5
    s.a. spec. uses
  metallography   669.957 5
  metallurgy   669.75
    physical & chem.   669.967 5
    soc. & econ. aspects *see*
          Secondary industries
  mineral aspects
    econ. geol.   553.47
    mineralogy   549.25
    mining
      technology   622.347
      prospecting   622.184 7
    s.a. spec. uses; also spec.
          minerals
  pharmacology   615.271 5
    misc. aspects see
          Pharmacology
  products
    mf. tech.   673.75
    other aspects see
          Nonferrous metals
          products
  toxicology   615.925 715
    misc. aspects see
          Toxicology
  other aspects see Metal;
          also Metals
Arson
  criminology   364.164
  law   345.026 4
    spec. jur.   345.3–.9
  soc. theology
    Christianity   261.833 164
    comp. rel.   291.178 331 64
    s.a. other spec. rel.

Art
  gallery buildings *see* Art
          museum buildings
  metalwork *see* Metals arts
  metalworkers
    biog. & work   739.092
      s.a. spec. metals
    s.a.   *pers.*–739
  museum bldgs.
    architecture   727.7
    building   690.77
    other aspects see
          Educational buildings
  music   780.43
    s.a. spec. mediums
  needlework   746.4
    s.a. spec. prod.
  papers
    mf. tech.   676.282 5
    other aspects see Papers
          pulp prod.
  rel. attitude toward
    Christianity   261.57
    other rel. see Religious
          attitudes secular
          disciplines
    s.a. Arts rel. significance
  school bldgs.
    architecture   727.47
    building   690.747
    other aspects see
          Educational buildings
  songs   784.3
    recordings   789.912 43
  stonework *see* Stone sculpture
  therapy   615.851 56
    s.a. spec. diseases
  woodwork *see* Wood arts
  s.a. Arts
Art deco
  gen. wks.   709.040 12
    spec. places   709.1–.9
  painting   759.061 2
    spec. places   759.1–.9
  sculpture   735.230 412
    spec. places   730.9
  s.a. other spec. art forms
Art nouveau
  architecture   724.91
    spec. places   720.9
    other aspects see
          Architectural schools
  gen. wks.
    19th cent.   709.034 9
    20th cent.   709.040 14
    spec. places   709.1–.9
  painting
    19th cent.   759.059
    20th cent.   759.061 4
    spec. places   759.1–.9

Art nouveau (continued)
  sculpture   735.230 414
    spec. places   730.9
  s.a. other spec. art forms
Arta Greece   *area*–495 3
Arterial
  circulation
    human phys.   612.133
    other aspects see
        Circulation (biology)
  hypertension *see* Hypertension
  roads *see* Roads
  streets *see* Streets
Arteries
  anatomy
    human   611.13
    other aspects see
        Circulatory organs
  diseases
    gen. wks.   616.13
      neoplasms   616.992 13
      tuberculosis   616.995 13
      geriatrics   618.976 13
      pediatrics   618.921 3
      pub. health   614.591 3
      statistics   312.313
        deaths   312.261 3
    surgery   617.413
      anesthesiology   617.967 413
    other aspects see Diseases
  physical anthropometry   573.613
  physiology
    human   612.133
    other aspects see
        Circulatory organs
  tissue biology human   611.018 913
Arteriosclerosis
  gen. med.   616.136
  geriatrics   618.976 136
  pediatrics   618.921 36
  pub. health   614.591 36
  statistics   312.313 6
    deaths   312.261 36
  other aspects see Diseases
Arteritis *see* Blood vessels
        diseases
Artesian wells
  water-supply sources
    technology   628.114
    other aspects see Water
        supply engineering
Arthabaska Co. Que.   *area*–714 565
Arthritis
  gen. med.   616.722
  geriatrics   618.976 722
  pediatrics   618.927 22
  pub. health   614.597 22
  statistics   312.372 2
    deaths   312.267 22
  other aspects see Diseases

Arthropoda
  conservation tech.   639.975 2
  culture
    technology   639.7
    soc. & econ. aspects *see*
        Primary industries
    other aspects see
        Agriculture
  drawing tech.   743.652
  paleozoology   565.2
  zoology   595.2
  other aspects see Animals
Arthur
  Chester A. admin.
    U.S. hist.   973.84
    s.a. spec. events & subj.
        e.g. Courts
  Co. Neb.   *area*–782 785
  king reign
    Eng. hist.   942.014
    s.a. spec. events & subj.
        e.g. Commerce
  Range Tas.   *area*–946 2
  River Tas.   *area*–946 5
Arthurian romances *see* Persons
        lit. trmt. folk lit.
Artibonite Haiti   *area*–729 44
Artichokes
  agriculture   635.32
    soc. & econ. aspects *see*
        Primary industries
  foods   641.353 2
    preparation
      commercial   664.805 32
      domestic   641.653 2
  other aspects see Asterales;
        also Vegetables
Articles
  Anglican liturgy   264.037
  of Confederation U.S. hist.   973.318
Articles (linguistics) *see*
        Words
Articulata *see* Crinoidea
Articulation
  education   371.218
  s.a. spec. levels of ed.;
        also Special education
Articulations
  anatomy
    human   611.72
    other aspects see Skeletal
        organs
  physical anthropometry   573.672
  physiology
    human   612.75
    other aspects see Motor
        functions
  tissue biology human   611.018 972
Artifacts
  archaeology *see* Archaeology
  library trmt. *see* Realia

Artificial
  environments
    hygiene   613.5
      misc. aspects see Hygiene
  eyes
    ophthalmology *see*
      Prosthetic
      ophthalmology
  flies (fishing sports)
    manufacturing
      soc. & econ. aspects *see*
        Secondary industries
    technology   688.791 2
  flowers
    arrangements   .745.92
    handicrafts   745.594 3
  harbors
    mil. transp. tech.   623.64
  insemination
    animal husbandry   636.082 45
      s.a. spec. animals
    ethics *see* Sexual ethics
    gynecology   618.17
    hygiene   613.94
  intelligence cybernetics   001.535
  islands hydraulic eng.
    technology   627.98
      s.a. spec. appls. e.g.
        Military engineering
      other aspects see Liquids
        engineering
  languages
    linguistics   499.99
    literatures   899.99
    s.a.   lang.–999 9
  leather *see* Imitation leather
  legs mf.
    mf. tech.   685.38
      other aspects see Footwear
  light
    plants grown in floriculture   635.954
      s.a. spec. plants
      s.a. other spec. uses
  limbs surgery *see* Extremities
    surgery
  marble *see* Artificial stones
  masonry materials *see*
    Artificial stones
  minerals
    manufacturing
      soc. & econ. aspects *see*
        Secondary industries
    technology   666.86–.88
  modification of weather   551.68
  mutations *see* Radiations
    genetics
  organs plastic surgery *see*
    Plastic surgery
  ponds *see* Ponds

Artificial (continued)
  radioactivity
    astrophysics   523.019 753
      s.a. spec. celestial
        bodies
    physics   539.753
      spec. states of matter   530.4
      s.a. spec. physical
        phenomena e.g. Heat
  respiration *see* Asphyxiation
    surgical trmt.
  road surfaces eng.
    technology   625.8
      other aspects see Roads
  satellites
    flight
      soc. & econ. aspects *see*
        Secondary industries
      technology   629.434
        s.a. spec. appls. e.g.
          Space warfare
      tracking *see* Tracking
    use in commun. ind. *see*
      Communications
      satellites
    use in weather forecasting   551.635 4
      spec. areas   551.65
      spec. elements   551.64
      other aspects see Unmanned
        spacecraft
    s.a. other spec. uses
  stones
    architecture   721.044 4
      s.a. spec. structural
        elements; also spec.
        types of bldgs.
    bldg. construction   693.4
    bldg. materials   691.3
    eng. materials   620.139
    foundations   624.153 39
    structures   624.183 2
      s.a. other spec. uses
    manufacturing
      soc. & econ. aspects *see*
        Secondary industries
      technology   666.89
  teeth
    dentistry   617.69
  tissue
    plastic surgery *see* Plastic
      surgery
    s.a. Synthetics; *also other*
      spec. subj.
Artificial-light
  photography tech.   778.72
Artigas Uruguay   *area*–895 36
Artillery
  art metalwork   739.742
  ballistics
    mil. eng.   623.51

Artillery (continued)
  defense vs.
    mil. eng.   623.3
  forces mil. sci.   358.1
    naval   359.981
  installations armed forces   355.73
    s.a. spec. mil. branches
  mil. eng.
    soc. & econ. aspects *see*
      Secondary industries
    tech. & mf.   623.41
  mil. sci.   355.821
    s.a. spec. mil. branches
  projectiles mil. eng.
    gen. wks.
      soc. & econ. aspects *see*
        Secondary industries
    tech. & mf.   623.451 3
  nuclear *see* Nuclear weapons
  schools
    armed forces   355.73
    s.a. spec. mil. branches
  units *see* Artillery forces
  warfare *see* Artillery forces
  other aspects see Ordnance
Artiodactyla
  animal husbandry   636.973
  hunting
    commercial   639.117 3
    sports
      big game   799.277 3
      small game   799.259 73
  paleozoology   569.73
  zoology   599.73
  other aspects see Mammalia
Artisans *see* Industrial
    occupations
Artistic
  dancing performing arts   793.32
  lettering dec. arts   745.61
  themes
    lit. trmt.
      folk lit.
        sociology   398.357
        texts & lit. crit.   398.27
      gen. wks.
        collections   808.803 57
        hist. & crit.   809.933 57
      spec. lits.
        collections   *lit. sub.*–080 357
        hist. & crit.   *lit. sub.*–093 57
      s.a. spec. lit. forms
  stage trmt.   792.090 935 7
    s.a. other spec. dramatic
      mediums e.g.
      Television; also spec.
      kinds of drama e.g.
      Tragedies (drama)
s.a. other spec. subj.

Artists
  biog. & work   709.2
    s.a. spec. kinds
  marks   *s.s.*–027 8
  occupational ethics   174.97
  s.a.   *pers.*–7
Artocarpus altilis *see*
    Breadfruit
Artois France   *area*–442 7
Arts   700
  advertising operations   659.132 3
  applied *see* Technology
  cultural relations
    internat. law   341.767 7
  decorative   745
    misc. aspects see Fine arts
  fine *see* Fine arts
  industrial *see* Technology
  influence on crime   364.254
  law   344.097
    spec. jur.   344.3–.9
  lit. & stage trmt. *see*
    Artistic themes lit.
    trmt.; *also* Artistic
    themes stage trmt.
  literary *see* Literature
  obscenity *see* Obscenity in
    art
  relation to music   780.08
  rel. significance
    Buddhism   294.343 7
    Christianity   246
    comp. rel.   291.37
    Hinduism   294.537
    Islam   297.3
    Judaism   296.4
    s.a. other spec. rel.; also
      Religious symbolism art
      representation
  soc. aspects   306.4
  study & teaching   700.7
    elementary ed.   372.5
    special ed.   371.904 4
    s.a. spec. groups of
      students e.g. Blind
      people
  s.a. Art; *also* Disciplines
    (systems)
Artvin Turkey   *area*–566 2
Aruba   *area*–729 86
Arum family *see* Arales
Arun West Sussex Eng.   *area*–422 67
Arunachal Pradesh India *area*–541 63
Arundel West Sussex Eng. *area*–422 67
Arundineae *see* Pooideae
Arundinelleae *see* Pooideae
Arusha Tanzania   *area*–678 26
Arusi Ethiopia   *area*–632
Aryan *see* Indo-Iranian

Ashes
  fertilizers *see* Potassium
    fertilizers
  s.a. Refuse
Asheville N.C.   *area*–756 88
Ashfield Nottinghamshire Eng.
    area–425 25
Ashford Kent Eng.   *area*–422 392
Ashington Northumberland Eng.
    area–428 86
Ashland Co.
  Ohio   *area*–771 29
  Wisconsin   *area*–775 21
Ashley Co. Ark.   *area*–767 83
Ashmore Isl. Australia   *area*–948
Ashoka reign India hist.   934.045
  s.a. spec. events & subj.
    e.g. Commerce
Ashtabula Co. O.   *area*–771 34
Ashton-in-Makerfield Greater
    Manchester Eng. *area*–427 36
Ashton-under-Lyne Greater
    Manchester Eng. *area*–427 35
Asia   *area*–5
Asia Minor   *area*–561
  ancient   *area*–392
Asian
  Arctic seawaters
    oceanography   551.468 5
    regional subj. trmt.   *area*–163 25
    other aspects see Atlantic
      Ocean
  influenza *see* Influenzas
  regional organizations
    internat. law   341.247
    treaties   341.026 37
  s.a. other spec. subj. e.g.
    Arts; *also* Asiatic
Asiatic
  cholera
    gen. med.   616.932
    geriatrics   618.976 932
    pediatrics   618.929 32
    pub. health   614.514
    statistics   312.393 2
    deaths   312.269 32
    other aspects see Diseases
  s.a. Asian
Asimina triloba *see* Annonaceous
    fruits
Askrigg North Yorkshire Eng.
    area–428 48
Asocial persons   *pers.*–069 2
Asotin Co. Wash.   *area*–797 42
Asparagus
  agriculture   635.31
    soc. & econ. aspects *see*
      Primary industries
  foods   641.353 1
    preparation
      commercial   664.805 31

Asparagus
  foods
    preparation (continued)
      domestic   641.653 1
    other aspects see Liliales;
      also Vegetables
Aspects
  planets astrology   133.53
Aspen
  Ridge Ida.   *area*–796 45
  trees *see* Poplar
Asphalts
  bituminous materials *see*
    Bituminous materials
  petroleum products
    chem. tech.   665.538 8
    other aspects see Petroleum
  pitch *see* Pitch (carbonaceous
    material)
  waxes
    comm. prcc.   665.4
    soc. & econ. aspects *see*
      Secondary industries
  s.a. other spec. appls.
Asphyxiating gases
  toxicology   615.91
  misc. aspects see
    Toxicology
Asphyxiation
  prevention *see* Safety
  statistics   312.304 718
    deaths   312.260 471 8
  surgical trmt.   617.18
    anesthesiology   617.967 18
  s.a. Veterinary sciences
Aspidochirota *see*
    Holothurioidea
Aspidogastrea *see* Trematoda
Aspidorhynchoidea
  paleozoology   567.4
Aspirates *see* Notations
  languages
Aspull Greater Manchester Eng.
    area–427 36
Assam India   *area*–541 62
Assamese
  language
    linguistics   491.45
    literature   891.45
    s.a.   *lang.*–914 5
  people   *r.e.n.*–914 5
  s.a. Assam India; *also*
    Burmese; *also other*
    spec. subj. e.g. Arts
Assassination
  criminology   364.152 4
  law   345.025 24
    spec. jur.   345.3–.9
  soc. theology
    Christianity   261.833 152 4
    comp. rel.   291.178 331 524

Assassination
  soc. theology (continued)
    s.a. other spec. rel.
  other aspects see Homicide
Assateague Isl.   *area*–752 21
Assault & battery
  criminology   364.155 5
  law
    crimes   345.025 55
      spec. jur.   345.3–.9
    torts   346.033
      spec. jur.   346.3–.9
  soc. theology
    Christianity   261.833 155 5
    comp. rel.   291.178 331 555
    s.a. other spec. rel.
Assaying
  metallurgy   669.92
    s.a. spec. metals
  pharmaceutical chem.   615.190 18
    misc. aspects see
            Pharmacology
    s.a. spec. drugs
Assemblage
  arts   702.814
Assemblers
  computer programming *see*
            Software programming
Assemblies
  of God *see* Miscellaneous
            Christian denominations
  pol. sci. *see* Legislative
            branch of govt.
  religion *see* Congregations
  sociology   302.3
Assembling products
  factory eng.   670.42
    spec. prod.
      aircraft   629.134 2
      s.a. other spec. prod.
  prod. management   658.533
    spec. subj.   *s.s.*–068 5
Assembly
  chem. plants   660.281
    s.a. spec. prod.
  civil right
    law   342.085 4
      spec. jur.   342.3–.9
    pol. sci.   323.47
  halls *see* Auditorium
            buildings
  League of Nations
    internat. law   341.222 2
  United Nations
    internat. law   341.232 2
  unlawful *see* Public order
            crimes against
Assembly-line processes *see*
            Assembling products
Assemblymen *see* Legislators
Assens Denmark   *area*–489 4

Asses
  animal husbandry   636.18
    soc. & econ. aspects *see*
            Primary industries
  products
    dairy products *see* Dairy
            products
    other prod. see spec. prod.
      e.g. Hides
  other aspects see Equidae
Assessment
  taxes
    law   343.042
      spec. jur.   343.3–.9
    pub. admin.   350.724
      central govts.   351.724
        spec. jur.   353–354
      local govts.   352.13
    pub. finance   336.2
Assignment of contracts
  law   346.022
    spec. jur.   346.3–.9
Assimilation
  physiology
    med. sci.   612.39
      human phys.   612.39
      vet. phys.   636.089 239
    s.a. spec. animals
    other aspects see
            Metabolism
Assiniboine River Man.   *area*–712 73
Assistance *see spec. kinds e.g.*
            Subsidies
Associated Press
  journalism   070.435
Associate-degree
  nurses & nursing   610.730 692
Association   366
  civil right pol. sci.   323.47
  football *see* Soccer
  psychology
    ideation   153.22
      animals   156.322
      children   155.413
      s.a. psych. of other spec.
            groups
    learning   153.152 6
      animals   156.315 26
      children   155.413
      s.a. psych. of other spec.
            groups
Associational ecology *see*
            Synecology
Associationism
  psychology   150.194 4
    s.a. spec. subj. & branches
            of psych.
Associations   366
  religion *see* Ecclesiastical
            theology
  sociology   302.3

Associations (continued)
  songs 784.66
    recordings 789.912 466
  other aspects see
       Organizations
  s.a. spec. kinds e.g. Learned
      societies
Associative algebras 512.24
  s.a. spec. appls. e.g.
      Engineering
Ass's milk
  dairy tech. 637.17
  other aspects see Dairy
      products
Assumption
  of Mary
    Christian doctrines 232.914
  of Moses
    pseudepigrapha 229.913
    other aspects see Apocrypha
  Par. La. *area*–763 43
Assurance *see* Insurance
Assyrian
  Empire Mesopotamia hist. 935.03
    s.a. spec. events & subj.
      e.g. Arts
  rule Palestine hist. 933.03
    s.a. spec. events & subj.
      e.g. Commerce
  s.a. East Semitic
Assyro-Babylonian *see* East
      Semitic
Astasiaceae *see* Euglenophyta
Astatine
  chemistry
    inorganic 546.735
    organic 547.02
    s.a. spec. groupings e.g.
      Aliphatic compounds
  technology 661.073 5
    soc. & econ. aspects *see*
      Secondary industries
    s.a. spec. prod.
  pharmacology 615.273 5
    misc. aspects see
      Pharmacology
  toxicology 615.925 735
    misc. aspects see
      Toxicology
  other aspects see Halogen
Asteraceae *see* Asterales
Asterales
  botany 583.55
  floriculture 635.933 55
  forestry 634.973 55
  med. aspects
    crop prod. 633.883 55
    gen. pharm. 615.323 55
      toxicology 615.952 355
    vet. pharm. 636.089 532 355
      toxicology 636.089 595 235 5

Asterales (continued)
  paleobotany 561.3
  other aspects see Plants
Asteroidea
  culture 639.739 3
  paleozoology 563.93
  zoology 593.93
  other aspects see Animals
Asteroids
  astronomy
    description 523.44
    theory 521.544
  flights to
    manned 629.455 4
    unmanned 629.435 44
  regional subj. trmt. *area*–992 4
  other aspects see Celestial
      bodies
Asterozoa *see* Asteroidea
Asters *see* Asterales
Asthenic reactions
  gen. med. 616.852 8
  geriatrics 618.976 852 8
  pediatrics 618.928 528
  psychology 157.3
  pub. health 614.58
  statistics 312.385 28
  other aspects see Mental
      illness
Asthma
  gen. med. 616.238
  geriatrics 618.976 238
  pediatrics 618.922 38
  pub. health 614.592 38
  statistics 312.323 8
    deaths 312.262 38
  other aspects see Diseases
Asti Italy *area*–451 5
Astigmatism *see* Refraction
      errors
Astrakhan RSFSR *area*–478 5
Astral projection
  spiritualism 133.9
Astrapotheria paleoz. 569.75
Astrobiology
  & religion nat. rel. 215.24
  gen. wks. 574.999
    animals 591.999
    plants 581.999
  s.a. spec. organisms
Astrodomes
  architecture 725.827
  building 690.582 7
  other aspects see Public
      structures
Astrodynamics *see* Celestial
      mechanics
Astrolabes *see* Extrameridional
      instruments
Astrolatry
  comp. rel. 291.212

Atavism
genetics (continued)
microorganisms   576.139
plant   581.15
s.a. spec. organisms
influence on crime   364.24
Atcham Salop Eng.   *area*–424 54
Atchison Co.
Kansas   *area*–781 36
Missouri   *area*–778 113
Atelectasis *see* Lungs diseases
Atentaculata *see* Ctenophorae
Athabascan *see* Na-Dene
Athabaska
Lake Sask.   *area*–712 41
River Alta.   *area*–712 32
Athanasian Creed
Christian doctrines   238.144
Athapascan *see* Na-Dene
Atharvaveda
Indic rel.   294.592 15
Atheca *see* Chelonia
Atheism
comp. rel.   291.14
nat. rel.   211.8
Atheists
biog. & work   211.809 2
polemics against
Christanity   239.7
Islam   297.297
other rel. see Doctrinal
theology
s.a.   *pers.*–291
Athelstan
reign Eng. hist.   942.017 1
s.a. spec. events & subj.
e.g. Arts
Atheneum libraries *see*
Proprietary libraries
Athenian supremacy Greece hist. 938.04
s.a. spec. events & subj.
e.g. Commerce
Athens
city Greece   *area*–495 12
ancient   *area*–385
Co. O.   *area*–771 97
Atherstone Warwickshire Eng.
area–424 81
Atherton Greater Manchester Eng.
area–427 36
Atherton Qld.   *area*–943 6
Athletes
biog. & work   796.092
s.a. spec. kinds
hygiene   613.71
occupational ethics   174.979 6
s.a.   *pers.*–796
Athlete's foot *see* Parasitic
skin diseases

Athletic
club bldgs.
architecture   725.85
building   690.585
other aspects see Public
structures
exercises
equipment mf.   688.764
soc. & econ. aspects *see*
Secondary industries
sports   796.4
other aspects see Sports
fields
civic art   711.558
sports   796.420 68
games *see* Sports
gloves & mitts
mf. tech.   685.43
other aspects see Handwear
services armed forces *see*
Recreational services
armed forces
sports *see* Sports
wounds & injuries
statistics   312.304 710 27
deaths   312.260 471 027
surgery   617.102 7
anesthesiology   617.967 102 7
s.a. spec. wounds e.g.
Abrasions
Athletics *see* Sports
Athos Mount Greece   *area*–495 6
Atitlán Guatemala   *area*–728 16
Atkinson Co. Ga.   *area*–758 822
Atlanta Ga.   *area*–758 231
Atlantic
City N.J.   *area*–749 85
Coastal Plain
Maryland   *area*–752 1
North Carolina   *area*–756 1
South Carolina   *area*–757 6
U.S.   *area*–75
Virginia   *area*–755 1
Co. N.J.   *area*–749 84
Ocean
biology   574.921
botany   581.921
zoology   591.921
s.a. spec. organisms
fishing sports   799.166 1
islands   *area*–97
oceanography   551.461
currents   551.471
submarine geology   551.460 8
regional subj. trmt.   *area*–163
transocean flights   629.130 911
Provinces Canada   *area*–715
region subj. trmt.   *area*–182 1
regional organizations
internat. law   341.243
treaties   341.026 33

Attaché cases
  manufacturing
    soc. & econ. aspects *see*
        Secondary industries
    technology   685.51
Attachment
  law *see* Remedies law
Attack
  games
    recreation *see spec. games*
  operations mil. sci.   355.4
    s.a. spec. mil branches
  plans *see* Attack operations
        mil. sci.
Attala Co. Miss.   *area*–762 644
Attendance
  work
    labor econ.   331.257 2
      s.a. spec. classes of
          labor e.g. Women
      other aspects see Work
          periods
  s.a. other spec. subj.
Attention
  psychology
    learning   153.153 2
      animals   156.315 32
      children   155.413
      s.a. psych. of other spec.
          groups
    perception   153.733
      animals   156.373 3
      children   155.413
      s.a. psych. of other spec.
          groups
Attenuation
  wave propagation *see* Wave
          propagation
Attenuators electronic circuits
        see Amplitude
        modulators
Attica Greece   *area*–495 1
  ancient   *area*–385
Attics
  household management   643.5
Attitude training
  employees
    personnel admin.
      gen. management   658.312 44
        executive management 658.407 124 4
      spec. subj.   *s.s.*–068 3
    pub. admin.   350.15
      central govts.   351.15
        spec. jur.   353–354
      local govts.   352.005 15
Attitudes
  psychology   152.452
    animals   156.245 2
    children   155.412
    s.a. psych. of other spec.
        groups

Attitudes (continued)
  soc. control   303.38
  students   371.81
    s.a. spec. levels of ed.;
        also Special education
Attorneys *see* Lawyers
Attorneys-general
  advisory opinions
    law   348.05
      spec. jur.   348.3–.9
    U.S.
      Federal   348.735
      state & local   348.74–.79
    spec. subj.   *law s.s.*–026 5
  offices *see* Justice pub.
        admin.
  pub. admin. *see* Justice pub.
        admin. departments
Attraction
  magnetism *see* Magnetic
        phenomena
  soc. interaction   302
Attractive
  adaptations *see* Protective
        adaptations
  nuisance
    law   346.036
      spec. jur.   346.3–.9
Attributes
  Christian church   262.72
  of God
    rel. doctrines
      Christianity   231.4
      nat. rel.   212.7
    other rel. see God
  sensory perception *see*
        Sensory perception
Aube France   *area*–443 31
Aubergines *see* Eggplants
Auchterarder Tayside Scot.   *area*–412 8
Auchtermuchty Fife Scot.   *area*–412 92
Auckland
  governorship India hist.   954.031 4
    s.a. spec. events & subj.
        e.g. Commerce
  Islands   *area*–931 1
  province & city N.Z.   *area*–931 22
Auction
  bridge
    equipment mf.   688.754 14
      soc. & econ. aspects *see*
          Secondary industries
    recreation   795.414
  catalogs
    articles   *s.s.*–029 4
    books
      general
        alphabetic subject   017.7
        author   018.3
        classified   017.3
        dictionary   019.3

Auction	
catalogs	
books (continued)	
spec. subj.	016
Auctions *see* Distribution	
channels	
Aude France	*area*–448 7
Audenshaw Greater Manchester	
Eng.	*area*–427 35
Audience participation programs	
radio performances	791.445
television performances	791.455
Audiences	
mass communication	302.23
soc. interaction	302.33
Audio	
inputs electronic data proc.	
see Inputs electronic	
data proc.	
outputs electronic data proc.	
see Outputs	
electronic data proc.	
records	
communication	001.554
Audio-lingual study	
appl. ling.	418
spec. langs.	*lang. sub.*–83
Audiologists *see* Medical	
scientists	
Audiology	
med. sci.	
hearing correction	617.89
geriatrics	618.977 89
pediatrics	618.920 978 9
otology *see* Otology	
music	781.22
s.a. spec. mediums	
physiology *see* Hearing	
function physiology	
psychology *see* Auditory	
perception	
Audiovisual	
aids *see* Audiovisual	
materials	
apparatus	
library bldgs.	022.9
museum bldgs.	069.32
devices *see* Audiovisual	
materials	
materials	
art appreciation use	701.1
bibliographies	011.37
spec. kinds	012–016
catalogs	
general	017–019
spec. kinds	012–016
ed. use	371.335
s.a. spec. levels of ed.;	
also Special education	
library trmt.	025.177
acquisitions	025.287

Audiovisual	
materials	
library trmt. (continued)	
cataloging	025.347
s.a. other spec.	
activities	
rel. communication	
Christian local church	254.3
parochial activities	259.7
other rel. see	
Ecclesiastical theology	
rel. instruction	
Christianity	268.635
other rel. see Religious	
instruction	
reviews	028.137
other aspects see	
Communication devices	
s.a. spec. materials &	
devices e.g. Motion	
pictures	
records	
communication	001.553
technology	621.380 44
s.a. spec. kinds e.g.	
Cinematography	
treatment	*s.s.*–020 8
Audit	
reports	657.452
s.a. spec. kinds of	
enterprise e.g.	
Insurance	
Auditing	
accounting records	657.45
s.a. spec. kinds of	
enterprise e.g.	
Insurance accounting	
mil. admin.	355.622
s.a. spec. mil. branches	
pub. admin.	350.723 2
central govts.	351.723 2
spec. jur.	353–354
local govts.	352.17
Audition *see* Audiology	
Auditorium	
buildings	
architecture	725.83
building	690.583
other aspects see Public	
structures	
rooms *see* Instructional	
spaces education	
Auditory	
aids *see* Auditory materials	
canals	
diseases	617.83
geriatrics	618.977 83
pediatrics	618.920 978 3
statistics	312.304 783
deaths	312.260 478 3
other aspects see Ears	

Auditory (continued)
  devices *see* Auditory
    materials
  materials
    educational use   371.333
     s.a. spec. levels of ed.;
      also Special education
    other aspects see
     Audio-visual materials
  memory
    psychology   153.133
     animals   156.313 3
     children   155.413
     s.a. psych. of other spec.
      groups
  perception
    psychology
     gen. wks.   152.15
     animals   156.215
     children   155.412
     s.a. psych. of other
      spec. groups
    influence   155.911 5
Audits *see spec. subj. e.g.*
    Defense (military) pub.
     admin.
Audrain Co. Mo.   *area*–778 332
Audubon Co. Ia.   *area*–777 486
Auglaize Co. O.   *area*–771 43
Augsburg Confession
  Christian doctrines   238.41
Augsburg League War
  history   949.204
Augusta
  city Me.   *area*–741 6
  Co. Va.   *area*–755 916
Augustana Evangelical Lutheran
    Church   284.133 3
  misc. aspects see Lutheran
Augustinian monastic bldgs.
  architecture   726.774
  building   690.677 4
  other aspects see
     Religious-purpose
      bldgs.
Augustinians
  rel. orders   255.4
    church hist.   271.4
    ecclesiology   262.24
Auks *see* Charadriiformes
Aunis France   *area*–446 4
Aunts   *pers.*–046
Aural
  nervous system
    diseases
     gen. wks.   617.886
     geriatrics   618.977 886
     pediatrics   618.920 978 86
     pub. health   614.599 8
     statistics   312.304 788 6
     deaths   312.260 478 86

Aural
  nervous system
    diseases (continued)
     other aspects see
      Diseases
    other aspects see Ears
Aurangzeb reign India hist.   954.025 8
  s.a. spec. events & subj.
    e.g. Commerce
Aureomycin
  pharmacology   615.329 92
  other aspects see
    Antibiotics
Aurès Algeria   *area*–655
Auricles (ears)
  diseases   617.82
    geriatrics   618.977 82
    pediatrics   618.920 978 2
    statistics   312.304 782
    deaths   312.260 478 2
  other aspects see Ears
Auricles (heart) *see* Heart
Aurora Co. S.D.   *area*–783 375
Auroras
  geomagnetism
    astrophysics   523.018 876 8
    s.a. spec. celestial
     bodies
  physics   538.768
    spec. states of matter   530.4
Aurum *see* Gold
Au Sable River Mich.   *area*–774 7
Ausable River N.Y.   *area*–747 53
Ausdehnungslehre   512.5
  s.a. spec. appls. e.g.
    Engineering
Aust-Agder Norway   *area*–482
Austerity
  rel. self-discipline *see*
    Asceticism
Austin
  city Tex.   *area*–764 31
  Co. Tex   *area*–764 252
  Lake W. Aust.   *area*–941 3
Austral
  Islands   *area*–962 2
  region Chile   *area*–836
Australasia   *area*–9
Australia   *area*–94
Australian
  aboriginal
    languages
     linguistics   499.15
     literatures   899.15
     s.a.   *lang.*–991 5
    people   *r.e.n.*–991 5
    s.a. other spec. subj. e.g.
     Arts
  Alps   *area*–94
  Capital Ter.   *area*–947

Australian (continued)	
football	
equipment mf.	688.763 36
soc. & econ. aspects *see*	
Secondary industries	
sports	796.336
other aspects see Sports	
literature	820
pitcher-plant family *see*	
Saxifragales	
Australians	*r.e.n.*–24
Austria	*area*–436
Austrian	
domination Italy hist.	945.07
s.a. spec. events & subj.	
e.g. Commerce	
literature	830
school econ.	330.157
Succession War	
history	940.253 2
s.a. spec. countries	
winter peas *see* Field peas	
Austrians	*r.e.n.*–36
Austroasiatic	
languages	
linguistics	495.93
literatures	895.93
s.a.	*lang.*–959 3
Austrobaileyaceae *see* Laurales	
Austronesian languages	
linguistics	499.2–.5
literatures	899.2–.5
s.a.	*lang.*–922–995
Autarchy	
pol. sci.	321.6
s.a. spec. jur.	
Autarky prod. econ.	338.9
Autauga Co. Ala.	*area*–761 463
Autecology	
life sci.	574.522
animals	591.522
microorganisms	576.15
plants	581.522
s.a. spec. organisms	
Authenticating	
fine arts	702.88
s.a. techs. in spec. art	
forms	
Authenticity	
Bible	220.1
s.a. spec. parts of Bible	
Koran	297.122 1
spec. suras	297.122 9
Author catalogs books	018
Authoritarian	
ethics *see* Authority ethical	
systems	
states	
pol. sci.	321.9
s.a. spec. jur.	

Authority	
ecclesiastical theology	
Christianity	262.8
other rel. see	
Ecclesiastical theology	
ethical systems	
philosophy	171.1
applications	172–179
religion	
Christianity	241.2
other rel. see Moral	
theology	
files	
library cataloging	
names	025.322
subjects	025.47
soc. control	303.36
sociology	301.155 2
Authorizations	
pub. expenditures	
pub. admin.	350.722 34
central govts.	351.722 34
spec. jur.	353–354
local govts.	352.123 4
Authorized version	
Bible	220.520 3
s.a. spec. parts of Bible	
Authors	
biog. & work	809
s.a. spec. kinds e.g. Poets	
occupational ethics	174.98
relations with publishers	070.52
s.a.	*pers.*–8
Authorship	
Bible	220.66
s.a. spec. parts of Bible	
techniques	808.02
Author-title indexing	
library operations	025.322
Autism	
medicine	616.898 2
geriatrics	618.976 898 2
pediatrics	618.928 982
Auto courts *see* Hotels	
Autobiographies *see* Biographies	
Autoclaves	
chem. eng.	660.283
s.a. spec. prod.	
Autocracies	
pol. sci.	321.5
s.a. spec. jur.	
Autocratic	
chief executives	
pub. admin.	351.003 16
spec. jur.	353–354
Auto-da-fé	
church hist.	272.2
Autogiros *see* Vertical-lift	
aircraft	
Autographs	929.88

Autogyros *see* Vertical-lift
   aircraft
Autoimmune diseases   616.978
  geriatrics   618.976 978
  pediatrics   618.929 78
  pub. health   614.599 3
  statistics   312.397 8
  deaths   312.269 78
  other aspects see Diseases
Autoimmunity *see* Immunology
Auto-instructional methods
  education   371.394 4
  s.a. spec. levels of ed.;
    also Special education
Automata *see* Automatons
Automatic
  control *see* Automation
  data proc.   001.63
    management   658.053
    office services   651.83
    spec. subj.   *s.s.*–028 53
  equipment
    printing composition
      soc. & econ. aspects *see*
      Secondary industries
      technology   686.225 44
    s.a. other spec. appls.
  firearms portable
    art metalwork   739.744 24
    mil. eng.
      soc. & econ. aspects *see*
      Secondary industries
      tech. & mf.   623.442 4
      mil. sci.   355.824 24
    s.a. spec. mil. branches
  movements
    psychology   152.32–.33
    animals   156.232–.233
    children   155.412
    s.a. psych. of other spec.
      groups
  pilots aircraft eng.   629.135 2
  s.a. spec. appls. e.g.
    Military engineering
  pistols *see* Automatic
    firearms
  rifles *see* Automatic firearms
  signals
    tech. & mf.   621.389
    soc. & econ. aspects *see*
      Secondary industries
    s.a. spec. appls. e.g.
      Military engineering
    s.a. Signals
  sprinkling devices
    fire extinction tech.   628.925 2
    s.a. spec. appls. e.g.
      ships 623.865

Automatic (continued)
  switchboard systems
    wire telephony
      technology   621.385 7
      s.a. spec. appls. e.g.
        military use 623.733
      other aspects see
        Telephony wire
  switchboards
    wire telephony *see*
      Telephone switchboards
      wire telephony
    other aspects see Telephony
      wire
  systems
    wire telegraphy
      technology   621.382 4
      s.a. spec. appls. e.g.
        military use 623.732
      other aspects see
        Telegraphy wire
    wire telephony *see*
      Automatic switchboard
      systems
    s.a. other spec.
      technologies
  train control
    technology   625.27
    other aspects see Railroads
  transmission-devices
    automobiles
      soc. & econ. aspects *see*
      Secondary industries
      tech. & mf.   629.244 6
      s.a. spec. appls. e.g.
        Driving motor vehicles
  utterances spiritualism   133.93
  writings spiritualism   133.93
  s.a. other spec. subj.
Automation
  chem. plants   660.281
  s.a. spec. prod.
  engineering
    soc. & econ. aspects *see*
      Secondary industries
    technology   629.8
    s.a. spec. appls. e.g.
      Military engineering
  engineers
    biog. & work   629.809 2
    s.a.   *pers.*–629 8
  factory eng.   670.427
    s.a. spec. prod. of mf.
  machine tools *see* Machine
    tools
  postal commun.   383.24
    other aspects see Postal
      communication

Automation (continued)
  production
    economics
      primary ind. *see*
        Efficiency prod. econ.
        primary ind.
      secondary ind.   338.454
      other aspects see
        Efficiency prod. econ.
    management   658.514
    spec. subj.   *s.s.*–068 5
  sociology *see* Technology
    sociology
  training
    employees personnel admin.
      see Job training
  s.a. other spec. appls.
Automatism
  metaphysics   127
Automatons
  automation eng.
    soc. & econ. aspects *see*
      Secondary industries
    tech. & mf.   629.892
    s.a. spec. appls. e.g.
      Crops production
  chess players rec.   794.17
  cybernetics   001.535
Automats
  food services   642.5
  other aspects see
    Eating-places
Automobile
  cars *see* Freight cars
  courts *see* Hotels
  driving *see* Driving motor
    vehicles
  racers
    biog. & work   796.720 92
    s.a.   *pers.*–796 7
  racing
    sports   796.72
    other aspects see Sports
  other aspects see Motor
    vehicle
Automobiles
  art representation   704.949 629 2
  s.a. spec. art forms
  as refuse
    pub. sanitation
      technology   628.440 42
    other aspects see Refuse
      pub. sanitation
  commerce   388.342–.348
  engineering
    soc. & econ. aspects *see*
      Secondary industries
    tech. & mf.   629.2
    military eng.   623.747
    s.a. other spec. appls.

Automobiles (continued)
  pollution by
    soc. aspects   363.731
    other aspects see Pollution
  safety aspects *see* Vehicular
    transp.
  sports   796.7
    misc. aspects see Sports
  other aspects see Land
    vehicles
Automorphic functions
  calculus   515.9
    s.a. spec. appls. e.g.
      Engineering
  gen. wks. *see* Functions
    (mathematics)
  number theory   512.7
    s.a. spec. appls. e.g.
      Engineering
Automorphisms
  categories
    topological algebras   512.55
    s.a. spec. appls. e.g.
      Engineering
  geometry   516.1
    Euclidean   516.21
    s.a. other spec. geometries
  s.a. other spec. branches of
    math.; also spec.
    appls. e.g.
    Engineering
Automotive *see* Automobile;
  also Automobiles
Autonomic nervous system
  anatomy
    human   611.83
    other aspects see Nervous
      system
  diseases   616.88
    geriatrics   618.976 88
    pediatrics   618.928 8
    pub. health   614.598 8
    statistics   312.388
    deaths   312.268 8
    other aspects see Diseases
  physical anthropometry   573.683
  physiology
    animal phys.   591.188
    s.a. spec. animals,
      functions, systems,
      organs
    human   612.89
  tissue biology human   611.018 983
Autonomous
  authorities
    pub. admin.   350.009 1
      central govts.   351.009 1
      spec. jur.   353–354
      local govts.   352.009 2

Autonomy
  ethical systems *see*
      Conscience ethical
      systems
  pol. sci. *see* Sovereignty of
      states
Autopilots aircraft eng.   629.135 2
  s.a. spec. appls. e.g.
      Military engineering
Autopsies
  med. diagnosis
    gen. med.   616.075 9
    surgery   617.075 9
    s.a. spec. diseases
  other aspects *see* Diseases
Autos *see* Automobiles
Autosuggestion *see* Hypnotism
Autotrophic plants
  food synthesis *see*
      Photosynthesis
Autotypes
  printing *see* Plates mech.
      printing tech.
Autumn
  plants flowering in
    floriculture   635.953
    s.a. spec. plants
  other aspects *see* Seasons
Auvergne France   *area*–445 9
Auxiliary
  foods
    comm. proc.   664.58
    soc. & econ. aspects *see*
      Secondary industries
    cookery   641.81
  generating units
    electrodynamic eng. *see*
      Generation elect. power
    wire telephony *see*
      Power-supply equipment
      wire telephony
    other aspects see
      Electrodynamics
  power systems
    spacecraft eng.   629.474 4
    unmanned   629.464 4
    other aspects see
      Spacecraft
  routes marine transp.
    commerce   387.523
    govt. control   351.877 523
    spec. jur.   353–354
    law *see* Marine
      transportation law
  spacecraft astronautics
    soc. & econ. aspects *see*
      Secondary industries
    technology   629.44
    s.a. spec. appls. e.g.
      Space warfare
  s.a. other spec. subj.

Auxins
  org. chem.   547.734 2
  other aspects see Hormones
Avalanches
  disasters
    history   904.5
    s.a. spec. places
  snow formations
    meteorology   551.578 48
    weather forecasting   551.647 848
    spec. areas   551.65
Avarice *see* Vices
Ave Maria
  private prayers   242.74
Aveiro Portugal   *area*–469 35
Avellino Italy   *area*–457 21
Avena *see* Oats
Aveneae *see* Pooideae
Average
  costs prod. econ.   338.514 2
  statistical math.   519.533
  s.a. spec. appls. e.g.
      Engineering
Averrhoaceae *see* Rutales
Avery Co. N.C.   *area*–756 862
Aves
  agric. pests   632.68
    s.a. spec. types of culture
      e.g. Forestry; *also*
      spec. crops
  animal husbandry
    technology   636.5–.6
    soc. & econ. aspects *see*
      Primary industries
    other aspects see
      Agriculture
  conservation tech.   639.978
  control
    agricultural *see* Aves
      agric. pests
    home econ.   648.7
    sanitary eng.   628.968
  drawing tech.   743.68
  hunting
    commercial
      technology   639.12
      soc. & econ. aspects
      see Primary
      industries
    sports   799.24
  paleozoology   568
  resources
    economics   333.958
    govt. control
      law   346.046 958
      spec. jur.   346.3–.9
    pub. admin. *see*
      Biological resources
      govt. control pub.
      admin.
  zoology   598

Aves (continued)
  other aspects see Animals
  s.a. Birds
Avesta Zoroastrianism   295.82
Avestan language
  linguistics   491.52
  literature   891.52
  s.a.   *lang.*–915 2
Aveyron France   *area*–447 4
Aviary birds
  animal husbandry   636.686
    soc. & econ. aspects *see*
        Primary industries
Aviation
  accidents
    statistics   312.44
      deaths   312.274
  fuels
    chem. tech.   665.538 25
    other aspects see Petroleum
  insurance   368.093
    liability   368.576
    other aspects see Insurance
  medicine   616.980 213
    s.a. spec. diseases
  meteorology   629.132 4
    s.a. spec. appls. e.g.
        Flying
  psychology   155.965
    s.a. Aeronautics
Aviators *see* Pilots aerial
Aviculture *see* Aves animal
        husbandry
Ávila
  Camacho Mexico hist.   972.082 6
    s.a. spec. events & subj.
        e.g. Commerce
  Spain   *area*–463 59
Avitaminoses
  gen. med.   616.392–.396
  geriatrics   618.976 392–.976 396
  pediatrics   618.923 92–.923 96
  pub. health   614.593 92–.593 96
  statistics   312.339 2–.339 6
    deaths   312.263 92–.263 96
  other aspects see Diseases
Avocados
  agriculture   634.653
    soc. & econ. aspects *see*
        Primary industries
  foods   641.346 53
    preparation
      commercial   664.804 653
      domestic   641.646 53
    other aspects see Laurales;
        also Fruits
Avocets *see* Charadriiformes
Avon
  Co. Eng.   *area*–423 9
  Rivers Eng.
    East   *area*–423 19

Avon
  Rivers Eng. (continued)
    Lower   *area*–423 9
    Upper   *area*–424 4
  Avonmouth Avon Eng.   *area*–423 93
Avoyelles Par. La.   *area*–763 71
Awadhi *see* Eastern Hindi
        languages
Awards
  mil. discipline
    law *see* Discipline armed
        forces law
  music   780.79
    s.a. spec. mediums
  research   001.44
  other spec. fields   *s.s.*–079
Awe Loch Strathclyde Scot.
                                  area–414 23
Awnings
  home econ.   645.3
Axbridge Somerset Eng.   *area*–423 81
Axes
  tools *see* Disassembling tools
  weapons *see* Edged weapons
Axholme Isle Humberside Eng.
                                  area–428 35
Axial-flow pumps *see*
        Centrifugal pumps
Axinite
  mineralogy   549.64
Axiology   121.8
Axioms *see* Symbolic logic
Axis Powers
  World War 2 hist.   940.533 4
    s.a. spec. aspects e.g.
        Diplomatic history
        World War 2
Axles
  mech. eng. *see* Bearings
  mechanics   531.8
  motor land vehicles
    front *see* Front axles
    rear *see* Rear axles
  railroad rolling stock
    technology   625.21
    other aspects see Rolling
        stock
Axminster Devon Eng.   *area*–423 57
Axons
  human anatomy & phys.   611.018 8
  other aspects see Tissue
        biology
Axum kingdom hist.   963.01
  s.a. spec. events & subj.
        e.g. Commerce
Ayachucho Peru   *area*–852 92
Aydin Turkey   *area*–562
Aye-ayes *see* Prosimii
Ayers Rock-Mount Olga Nat. Park
        N. Ter. Aust.   *area*–942 91

Aylesbury Vale Buckinghamshire	
Eng.	*area*–425 93
Ayr	
Qld.	*area*–943 6
Scotland	*area*–414 64
Ayrshire	
cattle	
animal husbandry	636.225
other aspects see Cattle	
Scot.	*area*–414 6
Aysén Chile	*area*–836 2
Ayub Khan admin. Pakistan hist.	
	954.904 5
s.a. spec. events & subj.	
e.g. Commerce	
Ayutthaya period Thailand hist.	959.302 3
s.a. spec. events & subj.	
e.g. Commerce	
Azaleas *see* Ericales	
Azerbaijan	*area*–553
Iran	
East	*area*–553
West	*area*–554
USSR	*area*–479 1
Azerbaijani *see* Turkic; *also*	
Azerbaijan	
Azimuth	
geodetic astronomy	526.63
Azlons *see* Protein textiles	
Azo cpds.	
org. chem.	547.043
s.a. spec. groupings e.g.	
Aliphatic compounds	
synthetic drugs pharm.	615.314 3
misc. aspects see	
Pharmacology	
synthetic poisons	615.951 43
misc. aspects see	
Toxicology	
other aspects see Nitrogen	
compounds	
Azo-oxy dyes	
manufacturing	
chem. tech.	667.253
soc. & econ. aspects *see*	
Secondary industries	
org. chem.	547.863
Azores	*area*–469 9
Azo-tetrazo dyes	
manufacturing	
chem. tech.	667.253
soc. & econ. aspects *see*	
Secondary industries	
org. chem.	547.863
Azotobacteriaceae *see*	
Eubacteriales	
Azov Sea *see* Black Sea	
Aztec	
architecture	722.91
misc. aspects see	
Architectural schools	

Aztec (continued)	
other subj. see	
Macro-Penutian	
Azua Dominican Republic	*area*–729 372
Azuay Ecuador	*area*–866 24
Azurite	
mineralogy	549.785

B

BMR	
human phys.	612.39
other aspects see Metabolism	
Bab el Mandeb *see* Aden Gulf	
Babbitt metal *see* Tin	
Babcock test	
dairy tech.	637.127 6
Babergh Suffolk Eng.	*area*–426 48
Babies *see* Infants	
Babirusas *see* Suiformes	
Babism	
art representation	704.948 978 8
s.a. spec. art forms	
calendars	529.327 88
cookery	641.567 788
philosophy	181.078 8
regions	*area*–176 788
religion	297.88
rel. holidays	394.268 297 88
schools	377.978 8
Babist temples & shrines	
architecture	726.178 8
building	690.617 88
other aspects see	
Religious-purpose	
bldgs.	
Babists	
biog. & work	297.880 92
s.a.	*pers.*–297 8
Baboons *see* Cercopithecidae	
Babouvism	
socialist school econ.	335.2
Babur reign India hist.	954.025 2
s.a. spec. events & subj.	
e.g. Commerce	
Baby	
foods	
manufacturing	
soc. & econ. aspects *see*	
Secondary industries	
technology	664.62
sitters' handbooks	
home econ.	649.102 48
Babylonian	
Empire Mesopotamia hist.	935.02
s.a. spec. events & subj.	
e.g. Arts	
rule Palestine hist.	933.03
s.a. spec. events & subj.	
e.g. Commerce	
Talmud	296.125

Babylonian (continued)
  s.a. East Semitic
Baca Co. Colo.   *area*–788 99
Bacau Romania   *area*–498 1
Baccarat
  equipment mf.   688.754 2
    soc. & econ. aspects *see*
        Secondary industries
  recreation   795.42
Bacchus Marsh Vic.   *area*–945 2
Bachelor girls *see* Unmarried
    women
Bachelors *see* Unmarried men
Bacillaceae *see* Eubacteriales
Bacillariophyceae
  botany   589.481
  med. aspects
    gen. pharm.   615.329 481
      toxicology   615.952 948 1
    vet. pharm.   636.089 532 948 1
      toxicology   636.089 595 294 81
  paleobotany   561.93
  other aspects see Plants
Bacillary
  diseases   616.931
    geriatrics   618.976 931
    pediatrics   618.929 31
    pub. health   614.512
    statistics   312.393 1
      deaths   312.269 31
    other aspects see Diseases
  dysentery   616.935 5
    geriatrics   618.976 935 5
    pediatrics   618.929 355
    pub. health   614.516
    statistics   312.393 55
      deaths   312.269 355
    other aspects see Diseases
Bacitracin
  pharmacology   615.329 95
  other aspects see Antibiotics
Back
  play
    American football   796.332 24
    rugby   796.333 26
    soccer   796.334 25
  yards landscape design   712.6
Back (anatomy)
  muscles
    human anatomy   611.731
    other aspects see Muscles
  regional med. trmt.   617.56
    s.a. spec. systems & organs
  surgery   617.56
    anesthesiology   617.967 56
    orthopedic   617.37
    s.a. Veterinary sciences
Backbone *see* Spinal column
Backfield play *see* Back play
Backgammon *see* Dice games

Backhand
  tennis   796.342 23
Backpacking *see* Walking
    (sports)
Backward *see* Mentally deficient
Bacon Co. Ga.   *area*–758 787
Bacon (meat) *see* Pork
Bacs-Kiskun Hungary   *area*–439 8
Bacteria *see* Schizomycetes
Bacteriaceae *see* Eubacteriales
Bacterial
  diseases
    agric. sci.
      animals   636 089 692
        s.a. spec. animals
      plants   632.32
        s.a. spec. plants; also
          spec. types of culture
          e.g. Forestry
    gen. wks.   574.232 2
      animals   591.232 2
      plants   581.232 1
        s.a. spec. organisms
    med. sci.
      blood diseases   616.94
        geriatrics   618.976 94
        pediatrics   618.929 4
        pub. health   614.577
        statistics   312.394
          deaths   312.269 4
        other aspects see
          Diseases
      gen. med.   616.92
        geriatrics   618.976 92
        pediatrics   618.929 2
        pub. health   614.57
        statistics   312.392
          deaths   312.269 2
        other aspects see
          Diseases
    s.a. spec. systems, organs,
      diseases; also Medical
      bacteriology
  relapsing fever *see* Relapsing
    fevers
  viruses
    med. sci.   616.019 4
    virology   576.648 2
Bactericides
  production
    soc. & econ. aspects *see*
      Secondary industries
    technology   668.653
  use agric.   632.953
    s.a. spec. crops; also spec.
      types of culture e.g.
      Floriculture
Bacterins
  pharmacology   615.372
  other aspects see Druqs

Bacteriological
counts milk
  dairy tech.   637.127 7
examination
  med. sci.
    gen. med.   616.075 81
    surgery   617.075 81
    s.a. spec. diseases
    other aspects see
    Diseases
warfare *see* Biological
  warfare
Bacteriologists
biog. & work   589.900 92
  other aspects see Scientists
s.a.   *pers.*–589
Bacteriology   589.9
agricultural   630.289 9
  s.a. Microbiology; *also*
    Medical bacteriology
Bacteriophages *see* Bacterial
  viruses
Bactria   *area*–396
Bacup Lancashire Eng.   *area*–427 63
Bad debts
  tax reductions *see* Business
    losses tax reductions
Badajoz Spain   *area*–462 7
Badenoch & Strathspey Highland
    Scot.   *area*–411 92
Baden-Württemberg Ger.   *area*–434 6
Badgers *see* Mustelidae
Badges
mil. discipline   355.134 2
  s.a. spec. mil. branches
Badlands
  North Dakota   *area*–784 9
  South Dakota   *area*–783 93
Badminton
equipment mf.   688.763 45
  soc. & econ. aspects *see*
    Secondary industries
players
  biog. & work   796.345 092
  s.a.   *pers.*–796 34
sports   796.345
other aspects see Sports
Baffin
Bay *see* American Arctic
  seawaters
Isl. Northwest Ter.   *area*–719 5
region Can.   *area*–719 5
Bag
papers
  mf. tech.   676.287
  other aspects see Papers
    pulp prod.
punching *see* Boxing

Bagasse
fuel
  manufacturing
    soc. & econ. aspects *see*
      Secondary industries
    technology   662.65
plastics mf.   668.411
  s.a. spec. kinds of
    plastics
pulp
  mf. tech.   676.14
  other aspects see Pulp
Bagdad Iraq   *area*–567 4
Baggage
cars *see* Passenger-train cars
insurance   368.2
  misc. aspects see Insurance
services passenger transp.
  law *see* Passenger services
  other aspects see Passenger
    transportation
Baghdad Iraq   *area*–567 4
Bagheli *see* Eastern Hindi
  languages
Bagot Co. Que.   *area*–714 525
Bagpipe music   788.925
recordings   789.912 892
Bagpipes
mf. tech.   681.818 92
  misc. aspects see Musical
    instruments
musical art   788.92
Bags
paper
  mf. tech.   676.33
  soc. & econ. aspects *see*
    Secondary industries
Bagshot Surrey Eng.   *area*–422 13
Baguios *see* Hurricanes
Bahai
faith
  art representation   704.948 978 9
    s.a. spec. art forms
  calendars   529.327 89
  cookery   641.567 789
  philosophy   181.078 9
  regions   *area*–176 789
  religion   297.89
  rel. holidays   394.268 297 89
  schools   377.978 9
music *see* Bahai sacred music
sacred music
  arts   783.029 789
  recordings   789.912 302 978 9
  s.a. spec. instruments;
    also spec. kinds e.g.
    Liturgical music
religion
  pub. worship   297.893 8
  significance   297.893 7

Bahai (continued)
  temples & shrines
    architecture   726.178 9
    building   690.617 89
    other aspects see
        Religious-purpose
        bldgs.
Bahais
  biog. & work   297.890 92
  s.a. spec. kinds e.g.
      Clergy
  s.a.   *pers.*–297 9
Bahama Isls.   *area*–729 6
Bahamians   *r.e.n.*–969 729 6
Bahasa
  Indonesia
    linguistics   499.221
    literature   899.221
    s.a.   *lang.*–992 21
  Malaysia
    linguistics   499.28
    literature   899.28
    s.a.   *lang.*–992 8
Bahawalpur Pakistan   *area*–549 16
Bahia Blanca
  oceanography   551.464 68
  regional subj. trmt.   *area*–163 68
  other aspects see Atlantic
      Ocean
Bahia state Brazil   *area*–814 2
Bahnaric languages *see*
      Mon-Khmer languages
Bahr el Ghazal Sudan   *area*–629 4
Bahrein
  people   *r.e.n.*–927 536 5
  state   *area*–536 5
Bail
  criminal law   345.072
  spec. jur.   345.3–.9
Baildon West Yorkshire Eng.
      area–428 17
Bailey
  bridges
    structural eng.   624.37
    other aspects see Bridges
      (structures)
  Co. Tex.   *area*–764 844
Bailiffs   *pers.*–349
  occupational ethics   174.3
Bailments
  law   346.025
  spec. jur.   346.3–.9
Bain system telegraphy *see*
      Automatic systems wire
      telegraphy
Bairnsdale Vic.   *area*–945 6
Bait casting
  angling
    sports   799.12
  other aspects see Fishing
Baixo Alentejo Portugal   *area*–469 55

Baja
  California Mex.   *area*–722
  Verapaz Guatemala   *area*–728 152
Baker
  County
    Florida   *area*–759 13
    Georgia   *area*–758 967
    Oregon   *area*–795 75
  Island   *area*–969 9
Bakery goods
  comm. proc.   664.752
  home proc.
    auxiliary dishes   641.81
    pastries   641.865
Bakewell Derbyshire Eng.   *area*–425 13
Baking
  clays *see* Firing clays
  cookery tech.   641.71
Baking-aids
  manufacturing
    soc. & econ. aspects *see*
      Secondary industries
    technology   664.68
Baking-powder
  manufacturing
    soc. & econ. aspects *see*
      Secondary industries
    technology   664.68
Baking-soda
  manufacturing
    soc. & econ. aspects *see*
      Secondary industries
    technology   664.68
Bakongo kingdom hist.   967.301
  s.a. spec. events & subj.
      e.g. Commerce
Bala Gwynedd Wales   *area*–429 29
Balaenicipites *see*
      Ciconiiformes
Balalaikas *see* Guitars
Balance
  design *see* Aesthetics
  of payments
    internat. banking   332.152
    internat. comm.   382.17
  of power internat. rel.   327.112
  of trade internat. comm.   382.17
  sheets
    accounting   657.3
    s.a. spec. kinds of
      enterprise e.g.
      Insurance accounting
    financial management *see*
      Reporting financial
      management
    investment analysis   332.632 042
Balancing
  machine eng.
    technology   621.816
    s.a. spec appls. e.g.
      Reciprocating engines

Balancing
machine eng. (continued)
   other aspects see Mechanics
Balanitaceae *see* Malpighiales
Balanoglossida *see*
      Enteropneusta
Balanophoraceae *see* Santalales
Balanopsidaceae *see*
      Balanopsidales
Balanopsidales
  botany   583.961
  floriculture   635.933 961
  forestry   634.973 961
  med. aspects
    crop prod.   633.883 961
    gen. pharm.   615.323 961
      toxicology   615.952 386 1
    vet. pharm.   636.089 532 396 1
      toxicology 636.089 595 239 61
  paleobotany   561.3
  other aspects see Plants
Balcones Escarpment Tex.   *area*–764 87
Balconies
  architectural
    construction   721.84
    design & decoration   729.39
  building   690.184
  finish carpentry   694.6
  s.a. spec. kinds of bldgs.
Balcony
  furnishings home econ.   645.8
  gardening floriculture   635.967 1
  motifs *see* Ornaments arts
Bald
  cypress family *see*
      Coniferales
  Mts. Tenn.   *area*–768 91
Baldachins *see* Canopies
Baldness *see* Scalp diseases
Baldock Hertfordshire Eng. *area*–425 81
Baldwin Co.
  Alabama   *area*–761 21
  Georgia   *area*–758 573
Bale Ethiopia   *area*–632
Bâle Switzerland   *area*–494 3
Baleares Spain   *area*–467 5
Balearic Sea
  oceanography   551.462 2
  regional subj. trmt.   *area*–163 82
  other aspects see Atlantic
      Ocean
Baleen whales *see* Mysticeti
Balers
  agriculture   631.36
  use   631.56
    s.a. spec. crops; also
      spec. types of culture
      e.g. Floriculture
  mf. tech.   681.763 1
  soc. & econ. aspects *see*
    Secondary industries

Bali
  isl. Indonesia   *area*–598 6
  Sea *see* Southern Sunda Isls.
    seas
Balikesir Turkey   *area*–562
Balinese *see* Indonesian
Baling crops
  agriculture   631.56
  s.a. spec. crops
Balkan
  Mts. Bulgaria   *area*–497 7
  Peninsula   *area*–496
  Wars hist.   949.6
  s.a. hist. of spec.
      countries
Balkars   *r.e.n.*–942
Ball
  bearings *see* Bearings
  games
    indoor
      equipment mf.   688.747
      soc. & econ. aspects
        see Secondary
        industries
      recreation   794.7
    outdoor & gen.
      equipment mf.   688.763
      soc. & econ. aspects
        see Secondary
        industries
      sports   796.3
      other aspects see Sports
  lightning
    meteorology   551.563 4
      artificial modification 551.686 34
      weather forecasting   551.646 34
      spec. areas   551.65
Ballachulish Highland Scot. *area*–411 85
Ballades   784.3
  recordings   789.912 43
Ballads
  literature
    gen. wks.
      collections   808.814 4
      hist. & crit.   809.144
      rhetoric   808.144
      juvenile   808.068 144
    spec. lits.   *lit. sub.*–104 4
    indiv. authors   *lit. sub.*–11–19
    other aspects see Poetry
  music
    gen. wks.   781.5
      piano *see* Romantic music
      piano
      voice   784.3
    s.a. other spec. mediums
    recordings   789.912
Ballarat Vic.   *area*–945 7
Ballard Co. Ky.   *area*–769 96

Ballast
railroad eng.
  technology   625.141
  other aspects see Permanent
    way
Ballater Grampian Scot. *area*–412 4
Ballet
  dancers *see* Dancers
  music   782.95
    recordings   789.912 295
    stage performance   792.8
Ballina N.S.W. *area*–944 3
Ballistic missiles
  mil. eng.
    soc. & econ. aspects *see*
      Secondary industries
    tech. & mf.   623.451 9
Ballistics
  criminal investigation *see*
    Physical evidence
  electron *see* Ionization of
    gases electronics
  solid dynamics
    engineering
      gen. wks.   620.105
      s.a. spec. appls. e.g.
        Aerospace engineering
      mil. eng.   623.51
      s.a. other spec. appls.
        e.g. Target shooting
    physics   531.55
Ballistocardiography
  medicine   616.120 754
Balloons
  aircraft *see* Lighter-than-air
    aircraft
  latex *see* Dipped latex
    products
Ballots
  law *see* Election procedures
    law
  pol. sci.   324.65
Ballroom
  dance music
    piano   786.46
      recordings   789.912 646
    s.a. other spec. mediums
  dancing recreation   793.33
  s.a. Dance hall bldgs.
Balls (dances)
  recreation   793.38
Balls (rec. equip.)
  manufacturing
    soc. & econ. aspects *see*
      Secondary industries
    technology
      athletic sports   688.763
      indoor   688.747
  recreation
    athletic
      American football   796.332 028

Balls (rec. equip.)
  recreation
    athletic (continued)
      s.a. other spec. games
      indoor   794.7
Ballycastle N. Ire. *area*–416 15
Ballyclare N. Ire. *area*–416 18
Ballymena N. Ire. *area*–416 13
Ballymoney N. Ire. *area*–416 14
Balneotherapy   615.853
  s.a. spec. diseases
Balqa Jordan *area*–569 55
Balranald N.S.W. *area*–944 8
Balsam
  fig family *see* Guttiferales
  fir *see* Fir
Balsaminaceae *see* Geraniales
Baltic
  languages
    linguistics   491.9
    literature   891.9
    s.a. *lang.*–919
  Sea
    oceanography   551.461 34
    regional subj. trmt. *area*–163 34
    other aspects see Atlantic
      Ocean
Baltimore
  city Md. *area*–752 6
  Co. Md. *area*–752 71
Balto-Slavic languages
  linguistics   491.8
  literatures   891.8
  s.a. *lang.*–918
Baluchi
  language
    linguistics   491.59
    literature   891.59
    s.a. *lang.*–915 9
  people *r.e.n.*–915 9
  s.a. other spec. subj. e.g.
    Arts
Baluchistan *area*–549 15
  Iran *area*–558 3
  Pakistan *area*–549 15
Balustrades
  architectural
    construction   721.8
    design & decoration   729.39
  building   690.18
  finish carpentry   694.6
  other aspects see Ornaments
    arts
  s.a. spec. kinds of bldgs.
Bambara *see* Mandingo
Bamberg Co. S.C. *area*–757 78
Bamboo
  agriculture   633.58
    soc. & econ. aspects *see*
      Primary industries

Bamboo (continued)
　products
　　fibers *see* Unaltered
　　　　vegetable fibers
　　pulp
　　　mf. tech.   676.14
　　　other aspects see Pulp
　　other aspects see Pooideae
Bambusa *see* Bamboo
Bambuseae *see* Pooideae
Banach
　algebras & groups   512.55
　s.a. spec. appls. e.g.
　　　Engineering
　spaces   515.732
　s.a. spec. appls. e.g.
　　　Engineering
Bananas
　agriculture   634.772
　　soc. & econ. aspects *see*
　　　Primary industries
　foods   641.347 72
　　preparation
　　　commercial   664.804 772
　　　domestic   641.647 72
　　other aspects see
　　　Zingiberales; *also*
　　　Fruits
Banat   *area*–498 4
　Romania   *area*–498 4
　Yugoslavia   *area*–497 1
Banbridge N. Ire.   *area*–416 57
Banbury Oxfordshire Eng.   *area*–425 73
Banchory Grampian Scot.   *area*–412 4
Band
　directors
　　biog. & work   785.092
　　s.a.   *pers.*–785
　music   785.12
　　recordings   789.912 512
Banda Sea *see* Southern Sunda
　　Isls. seas
Bandages *see* Surgical gauzes
Bandaging *see* Surgical
　　dressings
Bandera Co. Tex.   *area*–764 885
Bandicoots *see* Marsupialia
Banding birds
　ornithology   598.072 32
Bandits *see* Offenders
Bandonians *see* Accordions
Bands   785.067
　s.a. spec. kinds of music
Bandundu Zaïre   *area*–675 116
Banff
　Alberta   *area*–712 33
　& Buchan Grampian Scot.   *area*–412 25
　Scotland   *area*–412 25

Bangalore torpedoes
　mil. eng.
　　soc. & econ. aspects *see*
　　　Secondary industries
　　tech. & mf.   623.454 5
Bangladesh   *area*–549 2
　arts *see* South Asian arts
　people   *r.e.n.*–914 12
　s.a. other spec. subj. e.g.
　　　Arts
Bangor
　Gwynedd Wales   *area*–429 25
　Maine   *area*–741 3
　Northern Ireland   *area*–416 53
Bang's disease
　vet. med.   636.208 969 57
Banjo music   787.75
　recordings   789.912 77
Banjoists
　biog. & work   787.709 2
　s.a.   *pers.*–787
Banjos
　mf. tech.   681.817 7
　　misc. aspects see Musical
　　　instruments
　musical art   787.7
Bank
　accounts
　　economics   332.175 2
　　　misc. aspects see Banking
　currency *see* Paper money
　deposit insurance   368.854
　　misc. aspects see Insurance
　for International Settlements   332.155
　　misc. aspects see Banks
　　　(finance)
　holding companies econ.   332.16
　　misc. aspects see Banks
　　　(finance)
　mergers econ.   332.16
　　misc. aspects see Banking
　notes *see* Paper money
　reserves macroeconomics   339.53
Bankers
　biog. & work   332.109 2
　ethics *see* Business ethics
　s.a.   *pers.*–332
Banking
　economics   332.1
　　cooperatives   334.2
　law
　　international   341.751
　　municipal   346.082
　　　spec. jur.   346.3–.9
　　pub. admin.   351.825 2
　　　spec. jur.   353–354
　services
　　economics   332.17
Bankruptcy
　economics
　　private   332.75

Baptistries
Christian churches arch.　726.596
detached *see* Accessory rel.
　bldgs.
Baptists
biog. & work　286.092
s.a. spec. denominations
persecutions church hist.　272.8
s.a.　*pers.*–261
Bar mitzvahs
etiquette　395.24
Jewish rites　296.442 4
soc. customs　392.14
Baraga Co. Mich.　*area*–774 973
Barahona Dominican Republic
　area–729 324
Baraita Talmudic lit.　296.126 3
Baranya Hungary　*area*–439 7
Barb horses
animal husbandry　636.11
other aspects see Horses
Barbadians　*r.e.n.*–969 729 81
Barbados　*area*–729 81
Barbary States　*area*–61
Barbecue cookery　641.578 4
Barbecuing
cookery technique　641.76
Barbell exercises *see*
　Calisthenics
Barbels *see* Ostariophysi
Barber Co. Kan.　*area*–781 82
Barbering
personal care
technology　646.74
soc. & econ. aspects *see*
　Secondary industries
soc. customs　391.5
Barberries
agriculture　634.724
soc. & econ. aspects *see*
　Primary industries
foods　641.347 4
preparation
commercial　664.804 74
domestic　641.647 4
other aspects see
　Berberidales; *also*
　Fruits
Barbers
biog. & work　646.724 092
s.a.　*pers.*–646 7
Barbershops
sanitation　363.729 9
law　344.046 4
spec. jur.　344.3–.9
pub. admin.　350.772
central govts.　351.772
spec. jur.　353–354
local govts.　352.6
other aspects see Barbering
Barbets *see* Piciformes

Barbeuiaceae *see* Chenopodiales
Barbeyaceae *see* Urticales
Barbiturates *see* Narcotics
Barbour Co.
Alabama　*area*–761 32
West Virginia　*area*–754 59
Barbuda　*area*–729 74
Barcaldine Qld.　*area*–943 5
Barcelona Spain　*area*–467 2
Barcoo River Qld.　*area*–943 5
Bare wires *see* Uninsulated
　wires
Barents Sea *see* European Arctic
　seawaters
Bargain theory
wages econ.　331.210 1
s.a. spec. classes of labor
　e.g. Women
Barge canals
hydraulic eng.
soc. & econ. aspects *see*
　Secondary industries
technology　627.138
construction details　627.131–.136
s.a. spec. appls. e.g.
　Military engineering
transportation
commerce　386.48
govt. control　351.876 48
spec. jur.　353–354
law *see* Inland-waterway
　transp.
Bargello
textile arts　746.442
s.a. spec. prod. e.g.
　Hangings
Barges *see* Towed vessels
Bari Italy　*area*–457 51
Barinas Venezuela　*area*–874 3
Barite
mineralogy　549.752
other aspects see Pigment
　materials
Baritone
horn music　788.445
recordings　789.912 844
horns
mf. tech.　681.818 44
misc. aspects see Musical
　instruments
musical art　788.44
voice solos *see* Men's solos
Barium
chemistry
inorganic　546.395
organic　547.053 95
s.a. spec. groupings e.g.
　Aliphatic compounds
technology　661.039 5
organic　661.895

Barium
  chemistry
    technology (continued)
      soc.& econ. aspects *see*
        Secondary industries
      s.a. spec. prod.
    mineral aspects *see* Minor
      metals
    pharmacology   615.239 5
      misc. aspects see
        Pharmacology
    toxicology   615.925 395
      misc. aspects see
        Toxicology
    other aspects see Alkaline
      earth metals
Barking London Eng.   *area*–421 75
Barkly Tableland N. Ter. Aust.
                              area–942 95
Barks
  forest prod.   634.985
    soc. & econ. aspects *see*
      Primary industries
    s.a. spec. trees
Barlee Lake W. Aust.   *area*–941 6
Barley
  agriculture
    food crops   633.16
    forage crops   633.256
    soc. & econ. aspects *see*
      Primary industries
  foods   641.331 6
    cookery   641.631 6
  other aspects see Pooideae;
    also Cereal grains
Barlow governorship India hist. 954.031 2
  s.a. spec. events & subj.
    e.g. Commerce
Barmera S. Aust.   *area*–942 33
Barmouth Gwynedd Wales   *area*–429 29
Barnabite monastic bldgs.
  architecture   726.775
  building   690.677 5
  other aspects see
    Religious-purpose
      bldgs.
Barnabites
  rel. orders   255.52
    church hist.   271.52
    ecclesiology   262.24
Barnacles *see* Cirripedia
Barnard Castle Durham Eng.
                              area–428 61
Barnes
  Co. N.D.   *area*–784 32
  London Eng.   *area*–421 95
Barnet London Eng.   *area*–421 87
Barnoldswich Lancashire Eng.
                              area–427 645
Barnouic isl.   *area*–423 49

Barns
  agriculture   631.22
    s.a. spec. crops
  bldg. aspects
    architecture   728.922
    building   690.892 2
    other aspects see
      Residential buildings
Barnsley South Yorkshire Eng.
                              area–428 25
Barnstable Co. Mass.   *area*–744 92
Barnstaple Devon Eng.   *area*–423 52
Barnwell Co. S.C.   *area*–757 76
Barometers *see*
  Measuring-instruments
Barometric
  leveling
    geodetic surveying   526.37
  pressures
    biophysics *see* Pressure
      biophysics
    meteorology *see* Atmospheric
      pressure met.
    physics   533.6
Baroque art
  architecture   724.19
    spec. places   720.9
    other aspects see
      Architectural schools
  design & dec.   745.443
    spec. places   745.449
  gen. wks.   709.032
    spec. places   709.1–.9
  music
    gen. wks.   780.903 2
    spec. places   780.91–.99
    s.a. spec. mediums
  painting   759.046
    spec. places   759.1–.9
  sculpture   735.21
    spec. places   730.9
  s.a. other spec. art forms
Barotse kingdom   968.940 1
  s.a. spec. events & subj.
    e.g. Commerce
Barra Hebrides Scot.   *area*–411 4
Barraba N.S.W.   *area*–944 4
Barracks
  mil. quarters   355.71
    s.a. spec. mil. branches
  other aspects see Military
    buildings
Barracuda *see* Acanthopterygii
Barrage balloons
  mil. eng.   623.744
Barrages
  water diversion *see* Water
    diversion

Barrel organs
  mf. tech.   681.82
    misc. aspects see Musical
        instruments
  musical art   789.71
Barrels
  wooden
    mf. tech.   674.82
    other aspects see Wood
        products
Barren Co. Ky.   *area*–769 72
Barrhead Strathclyde Scot. *area*–414 41
Barrier
  islands
    geomorphology   551.423
    regional subj. trmt.   *area*–142
Barrine Lake Qld.   *area*–943 6
Barristers *see* Lawyers
Barron Co. Wis.   *area*–775 18
Barrow
  Co. Ga.   *area*–758 195
  election district Alaska   *area*–798 7
  Isl. Nat. Park W. Aust.
                  area–941 3
  River Leinster Ire.   *area*–418
  Strait *see* American Arctic
      seawaters
Barrowford Lancashire Eng. *area*–427 645
Barrow-in-Furness Cumbria Eng.
                  area–427 81
Barry
  County
    Michigan   *area*–774 16
    Missouri   *area*–778 76
  South Glamorgan Wales *area*–429 89
Bars (drinking places)
  home arrangement   643.4
  public *see* Drinking-places
Bars (structural element)
  structural eng.
    gen. wks.   624.177 4
    concretes   624.183 44
    s.a. other spec.
      materials
    naval arch.   623.817 74
    s.a. other spec. appls.
Bartenders' manuals & recipes 641.874
Barter instruments econ.   332.55
Bartholomew Co. Ind.   *area*–772 24
Barton Co.
  Kansas   *area*–781 52
  Missouri   *area*–778 71
Barton-upon-Humber Humberside
      Eng.   *area*–428 32
Bartow Co. Ga.   *area*–758 365
Baruch
  deuterocanonical book   229.5
  other aspects see Apocrypha
Barwon River N.S.W.   *area*–944 9

Baryons
  astrophysics
    gen. wks.   523.019 721 64
    acceleration   523.019 737 64
    s.a. spec. celestial bodies
  physics
    gen. wks.   539.721 64
    acceleration   539.737 64
    spec. states of matter   530.4
    s.a. spec. physical
      phenomena e.g. Heat
Barytone *see* Baritone
Basal
  ganglions *see* Ganglions basal
  metabolism
    human phys.   621.39
    other aspects see
      Metabolism
Basalts
  mineralogy   549.114 26
    spec. minerals   549.2–.7
  petrology   552.26
  other aspects see Natural
    stones
Bascule bridges
  structural eng.   624.82
  other aspects see Bridges
    (structures)
Base lines
  geodetic surveying   526.33
Baseball
  equipment mf.   688.763 57
    gloves & mitts
    mf. tech.   685.43
      other aspects see
      Handwear
    soc. & econ. aspects *see*
      Secondary industries
  players
    biog. & work   796.357 092
    s.a.   *pers.*–796 35
    sports   796.357
  other aspects see Sports
Basel Switzerland   *area*–494 3
Basellaceae *see* Chenopodiales
Basements
  household management   643.5
Basenji dogs
  animal husbandry   636.753
  other aspects see Dogs
Base-running
  baseball sports   796.357 27
Bases (military) *see*
    Installations armed
    forces
Bases (proton acceptors)
  chem. tech.   661.3
  soc. & econ. aspects *see*
    Secondary industries
  s.a. spec. prod.

Bases (proton acceptors) (continued)
metals
  chemistry
    inorganic   546.32
    spec. kinds   546.38–.68
    other aspects see Metals
      chemistry
  pharmacology   615.232
    misc. aspects see
      Pharmacology
  toxicology   615.925 32
    misc. aspects see
      Toxicology
  spec. elements *see spec.*
    elements
Bases (structures) *see*
  Foundations (supports)
Bashkir
  ASSR   *area*–478 7
  s.a. Turkic
Basic
  English
    linguistics   428
    rhetoric   808.042
  slag fertilizers *see*
    Phosphorus fertilizers
  sulfates mineralogy   549.755
  training mil. sci.   355.54
    s.a. spec. mil. branches
    s.a. other spec. subj.
Basidiomycetes
  agric. pathogens   632.42
    s.a. spec. plants; also
      spec. types of culture
      e.g. Forestry
  botany   589.22
  med. aspects
    gen. pharm.   615.329 22
    toxicology   615.952 922
    vet. pharm.   636.089 532 922
    toxicology   636.089 595 292 2
  other aspects see Plants
Basidium fungi *see*
  Basidiomycetes
Basil 3 reign Russia hist.   947.042
  s.a. spec. events & subj.
    e.g. Commerce
Basildon Essex Eng.   *area*–426 772
Basilians
  rel. orders   255.17
  church hist.   271.17
  ecclesiology   262.24
Basilicas *see* Christian church
  (general) buildings
Basilicata Italy   *area*–457 7
Basilisks
  lit. & stage trmt.
    folk lit. texts & lit. crit.   398.245 4
    other aspects see Animals
  zoology *see* Lacertilia

Basingstoke Hampshire Eng.
                                   area–422 71
Basket
  rope suspension bridges
    structural eng.   624.52
    other aspects see Bridges
      (structures)
  stars *see* Ophiuroidea
Basketball
  equipment mf.   688.763 23
    soc. & econ. aspects *see*
      Secondary industries
  players
    biog. & work   796.323 092
    s.a.   *pers.*–796 32
  sports   796.323
  other aspects see Sports
Basketry
  elementary ed.   372.55
  handicrafts   746.412
    s.a. spec. prod.
  plants
    agriculture   633.58
      soc. & econ. aspects *see*
        Primary industries
  textiles *see* Unaltered
    vegetable fibers
Basle Switzerland   *area*–494 3
Basommatophora *see* Pulmonata
Basotho   *area*–681 6
Basotho-Qwaqwa Orange Free
  State   *area*–685 91
Basque
  language
    linguistics   499.92
    literature   899.92
    s.a.   *lang.*–999 2
  people   *r.e.n.*–999 2
  Provinces of Spain   *area*–466
    s.a. other spec. subj. e.g.
      Arts
Basra Iraq   *area*–567 5
Bas-relief *see* Relief (art)
Bas-Rhin France   *area*–443 835
Bass (music)
  horns *see* Serpents (horns)
  voice solos *see* Men's solos
  s.a. spec. instruments e.g.
    Clarinets
Bass Strait
  Islands   *area*–946 7
  oceanography   551.467 76
  regional subj. trmt.   *area*–165 76
    other aspects see Indian
      Ocean
Bassarisks *see* Procyonidae
Bassenthwaite Cumbria Eng.
                                   area–427 87
Basses (fishes) *see*
  Acanthopterygii
Basses-Alpes France   *area*–449 5

Basses-Normandie France *area*–442
Basses-Pyrénées France *area*–447 9
Basset
  horn music 788.625
    recordings 789.912 862
  horns
    mf. tech. 681.818 62
      misc. aspects see Musical
        instruments
    musical art 788.62
Basse-taille *see* Enamels
Bassetlaw Nottinghamshire Eng.
  area–425 21
Basso continuo *see* Thorough
  bass
Bassoon music 788.85
  recordings 789.912 88
Bassoons
  mf. tech. 681.818 8
    misc. aspects see Musical
      instruments
  musical art 788.8
Basswood
  trees
    forestry 634.972 7
      soc. & econ. aspects *see*
        Primary industries
    other aspects see Tiliales;
      also Trees
  woods *see* Hardwoods
Bast fibers
  textiles
    arts 746.041
      s.a. spec. processes e.g.
        Weaving
    dyeing 667.31
    manufacturing
      soc. & econ. aspects *see*
        Secondary industries
      technology 677.1
        special-process fabrics 677.6
    other aspects see Textiles
    s.a. spec. prod.
Bastard
  jute *see* Ambari hemp
Bastardy *see* Illegitimacy
Bastocladiales *see*
  Uniflagellate molds
Bastrop Co. Tex. *area*–764 32
Basutoland
  history 968.160 2
  s.a. *area*–681 6
Bas-Zaïre *area*–675 114
Bat
  flies *see* Cyclorrhapha
  games
    equip. mf. 688.763 5
      soc. & econ. aspects *see*
        Secondary industries
    sports 796.35
    other aspects see Sports

Bat (continued)
  tick flies *see* Cyclorrhapha
Batan Isls. Philippines *area*–599 1
Batanes Philippines *area*–599 1
Batangas Philippines *area*–599 1
Batavian Republic Netherlands
  hist. 949.205
    s.a. spec. events & subj.
      e.g. Commerce
Batemans Bay N.S.W. *area*–944 7
Bates Co. Mo. *area*–778 43
Bath
  city Avon Eng. *area*–423 98
  County
    Kentucky *area*–769 555
    Virginia *area*–755 87
  mitzvahs
    etiquette 395.24
    Jewish rites 296.443
    soc. customs 392.14
Bathgate Lothian Scot. *area*–413 3
Bathhouse bldgs.
  domestic *see* Accessory
    domestic structures
  public
    architecture 725.73
    building 690.573
    other aspects see Public
      structures
Bathing
  hygiene 613.41
    misc. aspects see Hygiene
  other aspects see Cleanliness
Bathing-beaches *see* Beaches
Bathing-caps *see* Molded rubber
  prod.
Bathing-suits *see* Sportswear
Bathrobes *see* Lounging garments
Bathrooms
  furnishings 645.6
  household management 643.52
  plumbing 696.182
  residential int. dec. 747.78
    s.a. spec. dec.
Baths
  therapy 615.853
    s.a. spec. diseases
  other aspects see Bathing
Bathurst
  Isl. N. Ter. Aust. *area*–942 95
  Isl. Northwest Ter. Can.
    area–719 5
  N.S.W. *area*–944 5
Bathynellacea *see* Syncarida
Bathyscaphes & bathyspheres
  engineering 623.827
    design 623.812 7
    models 623.820 17
  seamanship 623.882 7
  other aspects see Vessels
    (nautical)

Bazaars
  fund raising
    soc. welfare — 361.7
    s.a. other spec. uses
Bazooka rockets
  mil. eng.
    soc. & econ. aspects *see*
      Secondary industries
    tech. & mf. — 623.455
Bazookamen armed forces — 356.162
Bazookas
  mil. eng. — 623.442 6
Beach activities
  recreation
    equipment mf. — 688.765 3
      soc. & econ. aspects *see*
        Secondary industries
    sports — 796.53
    other aspects see Sports
Beaches
  civic planning — 711.558
  formation & erosion
    physical geol. — 551.36
    geomorphology — 551.457
  landscape arch. — 714
  pub. sanitation *see*
    Recreational facilities
      pub. sanitation
    other aspects see Coastal
      regions
Beacons
  radio
    engineering — 621.384 191
    s.a. spec. appls. e.g.
      Navigation
    use
      navigation
        seamanship — 623.893 2
        other aspects see
          Navigation
      other aspects see Radio
  visible
    hydraulic eng.
      technology — 627.924
      s.a. spec. appls. e.g.
        Military engineering
      other aspects see Liquids
        engineering
      seamanship — 623.894 4
Beaconsfield
  Buckinghamshire Eng. — *area*–425 98
  Tasmania — *area*–946 5
Bead tests blowpipe anal. *see*
  Blowpipe analysis
Beadle Co. S.D. — *area*–783 274
Beads
  embroidery — 746.5
  s.a. spec. prod. e.g.
    Hangings
  handicrafts — 745.582
    spec. objects — 745.59

Beagles
  animal husbandry — 636.753
  other aspects see Dogs
Beaked whales *see* Odontoceti
Beakers
  chem apparatus — 542.2
  s.a. spec. appls. e.g.
    Organic chemistry
  s.a. other spec. uses
Beaminster Dorset Eng. — *area*–423 31
Beams (light)
  optics
    astrophysics — 523.015 5
    *s.a. spec. celestial
      bodies*
    physics — 535.5
      spec. states of matter — 530.4
Beams (structural element)
  structural eng.
    gen. wks. — 624.177 23
    concretes — 624.183 423
    *s.a. other spec.
      materials*
    naval arch. — 623.817 723
    s.a. other spec. appls.
    wooden bldg. construction — 694.2
Beans *see spec. kinds e.g.*
  Kidney beans
Bear
  Lake Co. Ida. — *area*–796 44
  River Divide Wyo. — *area*–787 84
Beards
  personal care — 646.724
  soc. customs — 391.5
Bearing walls *see* Walls
Bearings
  automobile wheels
    soc. & econ. aspects *see*
      Secondary industries
    tech. & mf. — 629.248
  clockwork
    mf. tech. — 681.112
      soc. & econ. aspects *see*
        Secondary industries
  gen. machine eng.
    soc. & econ. aspects *see*
      Secondary industries
    tech. & mf. — 621.822
    s.a. spec. appls. e.g.
      Windlasses
  internal combustion engines
    automobiles
      soc. & econ. aspects *see*
        Secondary industries
      tech. & mf. — 629.252
  railroad rolling stock
    technology — 625.21
    other aspects see Rolling
      stock railroads
  other aspects see Mechanics
  s.a. other spec. uses

Bedwellty Gwent Wales   *area*–429 93
Bedworth Warwickshire Eng.
             area–424 83
Bee
   Co. Tex.   *area*–764 117
   eaters *see* Coraciiformes
   flies *see* Orthorrhapha
   lice *see* Cyclorrhapha
   venoms
     toxicology   615.942
     misc. aspects see
         Toxicology
Beech
   family *see* Fagales
   trees
     forestry   634.972 5
     soc. & econ. aspects see
         Primary industries
     other aspects see Trees
   woods *see* Hardwoods
Beechworth Vic.   *area*–945 5
Beef
   breeds of cattle
     animal husbandry   636.22–.28
     other aspects see Cattle
   food   641.362
     cookery   641.662
   other aspects see Red meats
Beefwood family *see*
         Casuarinales
Beekeepers
   biog. & work   638.109 2
   other aspects see
         Agricultural classes
   s.a.   *pers.*–638
Beekeeping *see* Apidae culture
Beelzebub *see* Devils
Beers   641.23
   comm. proc.   663.42
   home econ.
     cookery   641.623
     preparation   641.873
   other aspects see Alcoholic
         beverages
Bees *see* Apidae
Beeston Nottinghamshire Eng.
             area–425 26
Beeswax
   prod. tech.   638.17
   soc. & econ. aspects see
         Primary industries
Beetles *see* Coleoptera
Beetling textiles *see* Finishing
         textiles
Beets
   agriculture
     soc. & econ. aspects see
         Primary industries
     technology
       field crops   633.41
       garden crops   635.11

Beets
   agriculture
     technology (continued)
       sugar crops   633.63
   foods   641.351 1
     preparation
       commercial   664.805 11
       domestic   641.651 1
   sugars & sirups
     comm. proc.   664.123
     other aspects see Sugars
   other aspects see
         Chenopodiales; *also*
         Vegetables
Bega N.S.W.   *area*–944 7
Begemdir Ethiopia   *area*–634
Beggars *see* Poor people
Beggiatoaceae *see*
         Thiobacteriales
Beginners *see* Novices
Begonia family *see* Cucurbitales
Begoniaceae *see* Cucurbitales
Behavior
   child rearing   649.64
   comp. psych.   156
   consumers *see* Consumer
         behavior
   ecology   574.5
   ed. psych.   370.153
   gen. psych.   150
   modification
     education
       classroom discipline   371.102 4
       instruction   371.393
       psychology   370.15
       spec. ed.   371.904 3
       s.a. spec. groups of
         students
       s.a. spec. levels of ed.
   therapy *see* Behavior
       therapy
   soc. psych.   302
   therapy
     psychiatry   616.891 42
     geriatrics   618.976 891 42
     pediatrics   618.928 914 2
     other aspects see Medical
         sciences
   s.a. Conduct; Animal
       behavior; Plant
       behavior
Behavioral
   genetics   155.7
   sciences   300
Behaviorism
   psychology   150.194 3
   s.a. spec. subj. & branches
       of psych.
Beheira Egypt   *area*–621
Being
   metaphysics   111

Belorussian
language
  linguistics — 491.799
  literature — 891.799
  s.a. — *lang.*–917 99
  people — *r.e.n.*–917 99
  s.a. Belorussia; *also other*
    spec. subj. e.g. Arts
Belper Derbyshire Eng. — *area*–425 16
Belt
  buckles
    precious metalwork — 739.278
    other aspects see Jewelry
Belt-driven elevators *see*
    Elevators (lifts)
Beltrami Co. Minn. — *area*–776 82
Belts
  clothing
    comm. mf.
      soc. & econ. aspects *see*
        Secondary industries
      technology — 687.19
        leather — 685.22
    domestic mf. — 646.48
    s.a. Supporting garments
  conveyers
    machine eng.
      soc. & econ. aspects *see*
        Secondary industries
      tech. & mf. — 621.867 5
      s.a. spec. appls. e.g.
        Internal transportation
    pedestrian traffic *see*
      Pedestrian traffic
    other aspects see Mechanics
  drives *see* Belts power
    transmission
  power transmission
    machine eng.
      soc. & econ. aspects *see*
        Secondary industries
      tech. & mf. — 621.852
      s.a. spec. appls. e.g.
        Military engineering
    other aspects see Mechanics
  pulleys *see* Belts power
    transmission
  safety equip. *see* Safety
    equipment
Beltways *see* Expressways
Belvoir Vale Nottinghamshire Eng.
    area–425 29
Bemba kingdom hist. — 968.940 1
  s.a. spec. events & subj.
    e.g. Commerce
Ben
  Hill Co. Ga. — *area*–758 852
  Lomond Nat. Park Tas. — *area*–946 4
  Lomond Tas. — *area*–946 4
Benalla Vic. — *area*–945 5
Benbecula Hebrides Scot. — *area*–411 4

Bench marks
  geodetic surveying — 526.32
Bench-scale plants
  chem. eng. — 660.280 71
  s.a. spec. products
Bendel Nigeria — *area*–669 3
Bendigo Vic. — *area*–945 4
Bending
  eng. materials *see* Flexure
  metals
    arts
      decorative — 739.14
      s.a. spec. metals; also
        spec. products e.g.
        Jewelry
    fine *see* Direct-metal
      sculpture
    technology *see* Mechanical
      working
  stresses
    crystals — 548.842
    s.a. spec. substances
    gen. wks.
      engineering *see* Dynamics
    physics — 531.382 2
Bending-tools
  soc. & econ. aspects *see*
    Secondary industries
  tech. & mf. — 621.982
  s.a. spec. appls. e.g.
    Military engineering
Bends (curves)
  liquid flow
    mechanics
      engineering *see* Dynamics
      eng. mech.
      physics — 532.55
Bends (disease) *see*
    Decompression sickness
Benedictine monastic bldgs.
  architecture — 726.771
  building — 690.677 1
  other aspects see
    Religious-purpose
    bldgs.
Benedictines
  rel. orders
    church hist. — 271.1
      women's — 271.97
    ecclesiology — 262.24
    gen. wks. — 255.1
      women's — 255.97
Benedictus *see* Common of the
    Mass
Benefices
  rel. law *see* Things rel. law
Beneficial organisms
  econ. biol. — 574.61
    animals — 591.61
    microorganisms — 576.162
    plants — 581.61

Beneficial organisms
  econ. biol. (continued)
    s.a. spec. organisms
Benefit societies
  economic   334.7
    s.a. Insurance
Benefits
  employees *see* Employee
      benefits
  insurance   368.014
    s.a. spec. kinds of
        insurance
  veterans'
    mil. sci.   355.115
  warfare
    mil. sci.   355.023
Benelux countries   *area*–492
Benevento Italy   *area*–457 23
Benevolence
  ethics *see* Love ethics
Benevolent societies *see*
      Benefit societies
Benewah Co. Ida.   *area*–796 93
Benfleet Essex Eng.   *area*–426 792
Bengal
  Bangladesh   *area*–549 2
  Bay
    oceanography   551.467 64
    regional subj. trmt.   *area*–165 64
    other aspects see Indian
        Ocean
  East Pakistan   *area*–549 2
  province Indian Empire *area*–541 4
  state India   *area*–541 4
Bengali
  language
    linguistics   491.44
    literature   891.44
    s.a.   *lang.*–914 4
  people   *r.e.n.*–914 4
  s.a. Bengal; *also*
      Bangladesh; *also other*
      spec. subj. e.g. Arts
Benguela Angola   *area*–673 4
Benguet Philippines   *area*–599 1
Beni Bolivia   *area*–844 2
Beni Suef Egypt   *area*–622
Benign
  neoplasms
    gen. med.   616.993
    geriatrics   618.976 993
    pediatrics   618.929 93
    pub. health   614.599 9
    statistics   312.399 3
      deaths   312.269 93
    other aspects see Diseases
  tumors *see* Benign neoplasms
Beni-Mellal Morocco   *area*–644

Benin
  early kingdom hist.   966.901 5
    s.a. spec. events & subj.
      e.g. Commerce
  former Dahomey   *area*–668 3
  modern country   *area*–668 3
  state of Nigeria   *area*–669 3
Bennett
  Co. S.D.   *area*–783 65
  Richard Bedford admin.
    Canada hist.   971.062 3
    s.a. spec. events & subj.
      e.g. Courts
Bennettitales paleobotany   561.592
Bennington Co. Vt.   *area*–743 8
Benson Co. N.D.   *area*–784 39
Bent
  Co. Colo.   *area*–788 97
  grasses
    agriculture   633.23
    soc. & econ. aspects *see*
      Primary industries
    other aspects see Pooideae;
      also Field crops
Bentinck governorship India hist. 954.031 4
  s.a. spec. events & subj.
    e.g. Commerce
Bentley with Arksey South
    Yorkshire Eng.   *area*–427 27
Benton Co.
  Arkansas   *area*–767 13
  Indiana   *area*–772 972
  Iowa   *area*–777 61
  Minnesota   *area*–776 67
  Mississippi   *area*–762 89
  Missouri   *area*–778 493
  Oregon   *area*–795 34
  Tennessee   *area*–768 33
  Washington   *area*–797 51
Bentonite *see* Clays
Benue Nigeria   *area*–669 5
Benue-Niger languages
  linguistics   496.36
  literatures   896.36
  s.a.   *lang.*–963 6
Benzenes
  fuel
    manufacturing
      chem. tech.   662.669
    soc. & econ. aspects *see*
      Secondary industries
  org. chem.   547.611
  s.a. spec. cpds.
Benzie Co. Mich.   *area*–774 632
Beowulf
  Anglo-Saxon poetry   829.3
Berber
  languages
    linguistics   493.3
    literatures   893.3
    s.a.   *lang.*–933

Berber (continued)
people   *r.e.n.*–933
rule
  Algeria hist.   965.02
   s.a. spec. events & subj.
    e.g. Commerce
  Morocco hist.   964.02
   s.a. spec. events & subj.
    e.g. Commerce
  s.a. other spec. subj. e.g.
    Arts
Berberidaceae *see* Berberidales
Berberidales
  botany   583.117
  floriculture   635.933 117
  forestry   634.973 117
  med. aspects
   crop prod.   633.883 117
   gen. pharm.   615.323 117
    toxicology   615.952 311 7
   vet. pharm.   636.089 532 311 7
    toxicology   636.089 595 231 17
  paleobotany   561.3
  other aspects see Plants
Berberis *see* Barberries
Berbice Guyana   *area*–881 6–881 7
Bereaved people
  parochial activities for
   Christianity   259.6
   other rel. see Pastoral
    theology
  other aspects see Afflicted
    people
Bereavement
  devotions for *see* Consolatory
    devotions
  soc. aspects *see* Families
    dissolution
Bergamo Italy   *area*–452 4
Bergen Co.
  New Jersey   *area*–749 21
  Norway   *area*–483
Bergius process
  synthetic petroleum tech.   662.662 2
Bergsonism
  philosophy   143
   indiv. philosophers   180–190
  s.a. spec. branches of phil.
    e.g. Metaphysics
Berhou isl.   *area*–423 47
Beriberi
  gen. med.   616.392
  geriatrics   618.976 392
  pediatrics   618.923 92
  pub. health   614.593 92
  statistics   312.339 2
   deaths   312.263 92
  other aspects see Diseases
Bering
  Sea
   oceanography   551.465 51

Bering
  Sea (continued)
   regional subj. trmt.   *area*–164 51
   other aspects see Pacific
    Ocean
  Strait *see* Bering Sea
Berith milah
  Jewish rites   296.442 2
Berkeley
  city Calif.   *area*–794 67
  County
   South Carolina   *area*–757 93
   West Virginia   *area*–754 97
  Gloucestershire Eng.   *area*–424 19
Berkelium
  chemistry   546.444
Berkhamsted Hertfordshire Eng.
    area–425 84
Berks Co. Pa.   *area*–748 16
Berkshire
  County
   England   *area*–422 9
   Massachusetts   *area*–744 1
  Hills Mass.   *area*–744 1
Berlin
  city Ger.   *area*–431 55
  Res. O.   *area*–771 37
Bermondsey London Eng.   *area*–421 64
Bermuda   *area*–729 9
Bern Switzerland   *area*–494 5
Bernalillo Co. N.M.   *area*–789 61
Bernardines *see* Cistercians
Bernese
  mountain dog
   animal husbandry   636.73
   other aspects see Dogs
Bernier & Dorre Isls. Nat. Park
  W. Aust.   *area*–941 3
Berri S. Aust.   *area*–942 33
Berrien Co.
  Georgia   *area*–758 862
  Michigan   *area*–774 11
Berries
  agriculture   634.7
   soc. & econ. aspects *see*
    Primary industries
  foods   641.347
   preparation
    commercial   664.804 7
    domestic   641.647
  other aspects see Fruits
Berry
  Isls. Bahamas   *area*–729 6
  region France   *area*–445 5
Berseem
  agriculture   633.327
   soc. & econ. aspects *see*
    Primary industries
  other aspects see
    Papilionaceae; *also*
    Field crops

Berthier Co. Que.   *area*–714 43
Bertholletia excelsa *see* Brazil
    nuts
Berths
  port eng.
    soc. & econ. aspects *see*
      Secondary industries
    technology   627.312
    s.a. spec. appls. e.g.
      Approach piloting
Bertie Co. N.C.   *area*–756 163
Berwickshire Borders Scot.   *area*–413 95
Berwick-upon-Tweed Northumberland
    Eng.   *area*–428 89
Berycoidea *see* Acanthopterygii
Beryl
  mineralogy   549.64
Beryllium
  chemistry
    inorganic   546.391
    organic   547.053 91
    s.a. spec. groupings e.g.
      Aliphatic compounds
    technology   661.039 1
    organic   661.895
    soc. & econ. aspects *see*
      Secondary industries
    s.a. spec. prod.
  compounds *see* Beryllium
    chemistry
  construction
    architecture   721.044 772 4
    s.a. spec. kinds of
      bldgs.
    building   693.772 4
  materials
    building   691.872 4
    engineering   620.189 4
    foundations   624.153 894
    naval design   623.818 294
    shipbuilding   623.820 7
    structures   624.182 94
    s.a. other spec. uses
  metallography   669.957 24
  metallurgy   669.724
    physical & chem.   669.967 24
    soc. & econ. aspects *see*
      Secondary industries
  mineral aspects
    econ. geol.   553.492 3
    mining   622.349 23
    prospecting   622.184 923
    s.a. spec. minerals
  pharmacology   615.239 1
    misc. aspects *see*
      Pharmacology
  products
    mf. tech.   673.724
    other aspects see
      Nonferrous metals
      products

Beryllium (continued)
  toxicology   615.925 391
    misc. aspects see
      Toxicology
    other aspects see Metal;
      also Metals
Bessarabia   *area*–477 5
Bessbrook N. Ire.   *area*–416 58
Bessel functions   515.53
  s.a. spec. appls. e.g.
    Engineering
Bessemer
  converter practice
    metallurgy   669.142 3
  steel
    technology   669.142 3
    other aspects see Ferrous
      metals
Bestiality
  sexual relations *see* Sexual
    deviations
Beta
  decay
    radioactivity
      astrophysics   523.019 752 3
      s.a. spec. celestial
        bodies
      physics   539.752 3
      spec. states of matter   530.4
      s.a. spec. physical
        phenomena e.g. Heat
  functions
    mathematics   515.52
    s.a. spec. appls. e.g.
      Engineering
  particles
    astrophysics
      gen. wks.   523.019 721 12
      acceleration   523.019 737 12
      s.a. spec. celestial
        bodies
    physics
      gen. wks.   539.721 12
      acceleration   539.737 12
      spec. states of matter   530.4
  radiations *see* Particle
    radiations
  vulgaris *see* Beets
  vulgaris cicla *see* Chard
Beta-ray spectroscopy *see* Beta
    particles
Betatrons
  physics   539.734
  s.a. spec. physical
    phenomena e.g. Heat
Betatron-synchrotrons
  physics   539.735
  s.a. spec. physical
    phenomena e.g. Heat
Bethel election district Alaska
    area–798 4

Bethesda Gwynedd Wales   *area*–429 25
Bethnal Green London Eng. *area*–421 5
Beton *see* Concretes
Betrayal
   by Judas
     Christian doctrines   232.961
   of country *see* Treason
Betrothals
   etiquette   395.22
   other aspects see Courtship
Betsimisaraka kingdom hist.   969.101
   s.a. spec. events & subj.
       e.g. Commerce
Betting
   ethics
     philosophy   175.9
     religion
       Buddhism   294.356 59
       Christianity   241.659
       comp. rel.   291.565 9
       Hinduism   294.548 659
       s.a. other spec. rel.
   horse racing   798.401
   systems
     recreation   795.01
Betula *see* Birch trees
Betulaceae *see* Fagales
Betws-y-Coed Gwynedd Wales
           area–429 27
Bevel gears
   machine eng.
     soc. & econ. aspects *see*
       Secondary industries
     tech. & mf.   621.833 2
     s.a. spec. appls. e.g.
       Military engineering
   other aspects see Mechanics
Beverages   641.2
   health & safety
     soc. aspects   363.192 9
     misc. aspects see Foods
       health & safety
   home econ.
     cookery   641.62
     preparation   641.87
   hygiene   613.3
     misc. aspects see Hygiene
   manufacturing
     soc. & econ. aspects *see*
       Secondary industries
     technology   663
   technologists
     biog. & work   663.092
     s.a. spec. kinds of drink
   s.a.   *pers.*–663
Beverley Humberside Eng. *area*–428 36
Bewdley Hereford & Worcester
       Eng.   *area*–424 41
Bexar Co. Tex.   *area*–764 35
Bexhill East Sussex Eng.   *area*–422 52
Bexley London Eng.   *area*–421 77

Bhagavad Gita Hinduism   294.592 4
Bhakti Yoga   294.543
Bhedabheda phil.   181.484 2
Bhojpuri *see* Bihari
Bhopal India   *area*–543
Bhumibol Adulyadej reign
       Thailand hist.   959.304 4
   s.a. spec. events & subj.
       e.g. Commerce
Bhutan   *area*–549 8
Bhutanese people   *r.e.n.*–914 18
Bhutto admin. Pakistan hist.   954.910 5
   s.a. spec. events & subj.
       e.g. Commerce
Biafran War Nigeria hist.   966.905
   s.a. spec. events & subj.
       e.g. Commerce
Biala Podlaska Poland   *area*–438 4
Bialystok Poland   *area*–438 3
Bias bindings *see* Passementerie
Bibb Co.
   Alabama   *area*–761 82
   Georgia   *area*–758 552
Bible
   Christians
     Methodist denomination   287.53
       misc. aspects see
       Methodist
   lit. hist. & crit.   809.935 22
   meditations   242.5
   prayers   242.722
   readings *see* Scripture
     readings
   schools *see* Religious
     instruction
Biblical
   Aramaic language
     linguistics   429.29
     literature   892.29
     texts Bible   220.42
     s.a.   *lang.*–922 9
   characters & events
     art representation
       arts   704.948 4
       s.a. spec. art forms
     Christian rel.
       paintings   247.54
       sculpture   247.3
   Greek language
     linguistics   487.4
     s.a.   *lang.*–87
   precepts moral theology
     Christianity   241.52–.54
     Judaism   296.385
   Sabbath rel. observance
     Christianity   263.1
     Judaism   296.41
   theology
     Christianity   230
     Judaism   296.31–.33

Bibliographers
biog. & work 010.92
s.a. *pers.*–091
Bibliographic
analysis
library sci. 025.3
Classification *see* Bliss's
Bibliographic
Classification
control
library sci. 025.3
description
library sci. 025.324
Bibliographical centers
library cooperation 021.64
Bibliographies 011
Bibliography 010
historical 002
Bibliotherapy 615.851 6
s.a. spec. diseases
Bicameral legislatures
constitutional law *see*
Legislative branch of
govt. law
pol. sci. 328.39
spec. jur. 328.4–.9
Bicester Oxfordshire Eng. *area*–425 73
Bichon Frise
animal husbandry 636.72
other aspects see Dogs
Bicycle
paths
commerce 388.12
local 388.411
other aspects see Roads;
also Streets
transp. facilities
civic art 711.72
troops
armed forces 357.52
Bicycles
commerce 388.347 2
engineering
gen. tech. & mf. 629.227 2
maintenance 629.287 72
models 629.221 72
operation 629.284 72
s.a. other spec. aspects
e.g. Brakes; *also*
spec. appls. e.g.
Ground transportation
soc. & econ. aspects *see*
Secondary industries
riding & racing *see* Cycling
safety aspects *see* Vehicular
transp.
other aspects see Land
vehicles
Bicycling *see* Cycling
Bicyclists *see* Cyclists

Bidding (games)
contract bridge 795.415 2
s.a. other spec. games
Biddulph Staffordshire Eng. *area*–424 61
Bideford Devon Eng. *area*–423 51
Bids
govt. contracts
pub. admin. 350.711 2
central govts. 351.711 2
spec. jur. 353–354
local govts. 352.161 2
Bie Angola *area*–673 4
Bielsko-Biala Poland *area*–438 6
Biennials
floriculture 635.931 4
s.a. spec. plants
Bienville Par. La. *area*–763 93
Biflagellate
molds
agric. pathogens 632.451
s.a. spec. types of
culture e.g. Forestry;
also spec. plants
botany 589.251
med. aspects
gen. pharm. 615.329 251
toxicology 615.952 925 1
vet. pharm. 636.089 532 925 1
toxicology 636.089 595 292 51
paleobotany 561.92
other aspects see Plants
Big
bang theory cosmogony 523.18
Bend
area Tex. *area*–764 93
Nat. Park Tex. *area*–764 932
Black
Mts. Ky. *area*–769 154
River Mass. *area*–762 4
Blue River *area*–781 2
business
management 658.023
financial 658.159
personnel 658.303
prod. econ. 338.644
Cypress Swamp Fla. *area*–759 44
game hunting
industries 639.11
misc. aspects see Hunting
industries
sports 799.26
Horn
County
Montana *area*–786 38
Wyoming *area*–787 33
Mts. Wyo. *area*–787 3
Sandy River *area*–754 4
Kentucky *area*–769 2
West Virginia *area*–754 4
Sioux River *area*–783 3
Iowa *area*–777 1

Big
Sioux River (continued)
South Dakota   *area*–783 3
Stone Co. Minn.   *area*–776 432
s.a. other spec. subj.
Bigamy
criminology   364.183
law   345.028 3
spec. jur.   345.3–.9
soc. theology
Christianity   261.833 183
comp. rel.   291.178 331 83
s.a. other spec. rel.
other aspects see Polygamy
Biggar
Saskatchewan   *area*–712 42
Strathclyde Scot.   *area*–414 69
Biggleswade Bedfordshire Eng.
    area–425 63
Bignoniaceae *see* Bignoniales
Bignoniales
botany   583.54
floriculture   635.933 54
forestry   634.973 54
med. aspects
crop prod.   633.883 54
gen. pharm.   615.323 54
toxicology   615.952 354
vet. pharm.   636.089 532 354
toxicology   636.089 595 235 4
paleobotany   561.3
other aspects see Plants
Bigotry *see* Vices
Bihar India   *area*–541 2
Bihari
language
linguistics   491.45
literature   891.45
s.a.   *lang.*–914 5
people   *r.e.n.*–914 5
s.a. Bihar; *also other spec.*
subj. e.g. Arts
Bihor Romania   *area*–498 4
Bikeways *see* Bicycle paths
Bikini isl.   *area*–968 3
Bilaspur India   *area*–545 2
Bilateral
secondary schools   373.25
trade agreements
internat. comm.   382.93–.99
internat. law   341.754 026 6
treaties
internat. law
texts   341.026 6
other aspects see
Treaties
Bile
acids
biochemistry
gen. wks.
animals   574.192 437
animals   591.192 437

Bile
acids
biochemistry
gen. wks. (continued)
microorganisms   576.119 243 7
plants   581.192 437
s.a. spec. organisms
med. sci.   612.015 737
animals   636.089 201 573 7
man   612.015 737
s.a. spec. functions,
systems, organs
org. chem.   547.737
ducts
diseases
gen. wks.   616.365
neoplasms   616.992 36
tuberculosis   616.995 36
geriatrics   618.976 365
pediatrics   618.923 65
pub. health   614.593 65
statistics   312.336 5
deaths   312.263 65
other aspects see Biliary
tract
Bilecik Turkey   *area*–563
Bilharziasis *see* Fluke-caused
diseases
Biliary tract
anatomy
human   611.36
other aspects see Nutritive
organs
diseases
gen. wks.   616.36
neoplasms   616.992 36
tuberculosis   616.995 36
geriatrics   618.976 36
pediatrics   618.923 6
pub. health   614.593 6
statistics   312.336
deaths   312.263 6
surgery   617.556
anesthesiology   617.967 556
other aspects see Diseases
physical anthropometry   573.636
physiology
human   612.35
other aspects see Nutrition
tissue biology human   611.018 936
Bilinear forms
algebra   512.944
s.a. spec. appls. e.g.
Engineering
geometry   516.35
s.a. spec. appls. e.g.
Engineering
Bilingual
education *see* Ethnic groups
education special ed.
Bilingualism   401

Billboards
  outdoor advertising   659.134 2
Billiard players
  biog. & work   794.720 92
    s.a.   *pers.*–794 7
Billiards
  equipment mf.   688.747 2
    soc. & econ. aspects *see*
      Secondary industries
  recreation   794.72
Billiatt Nat. Park S. Aust.
      area–942 33
Billinge-and-Winstanley
    Merseyside Eng. *area*–427 57
Billingham-on-Tees Cleveland Eng.
      area–428 51
Billings Co. N.D.   *area*–784 94
Bills (proposed laws)
  pol. sci.   328.378
    spec. jur.   328.4–.9
  texts   348.01
    spec. jur.   348.3–.9
      U.S.   348.731
        spec. states & localities   348.74–.79
    spec. subj.   *law s.s.*–026 2
Bills of exchange *see*
    Commercial paper
Biloela Qld.   *area*–943 5
Bimetallic standards money
  economics   332.423
  other aspects see Money
Bimini Isls. Bahamas   *area*–729 6
Binary
  invariants algebra   512.944
    s.a. spec. appls. e.g.
      Engineering
  numeration system   513.52
    s.a. spec. appls. e.g.
      Electronic data
      processing
  salts *see* Simple salts metals
  stars *see* Visual binary stars
Binders (agric. equip.) *see*
    Harvesting-machinery
Binding
  books *see* Bookbinding
  force of treaties *see*
    Treaties
Bingham Co. Ida.   *area*–796 51
Binghamton N.Y.   *area*–747 76
Bingley West Yorkshire Eng.
      area–428 17
Bingol Turkey   *area*–566 7
Binocular
  imbalance *see* Ocular
    neuromuscular mechanism
    diseases
  vision *see* Spatial perception
    visual

Binoculars
  mf. tech.   681.412
    components   681.42–.43
  other aspects see Optical
    instruments
Binocular-vision photography
    see Stereoscopic
    photography
Binomial equations *see*
    Polynomial equations
Bioastronautics biophysics
  gen. wks.   574.191 9
    animals   591.191 9
    microorganisms   576.119 19
    plants   581.191 9
    s.a. spec. organisms
  med. sci.   612.014 5
    animals   636.089 201 45
      s.a. spec. animals
    man   612.014 5
Biobibliographies *see* Persons
    bibliographies
Bío-Bío Chile   *area*–834 3
Biochemical
  analysis
    qual. anal. chem.   544.94
    organic   547.349 4
    s.a. spec. elements &
      cpds.
  genetics
    cytology   574.873 224
    animals   591.873 224
    plants   581.873 224
Biochemistry
  gen. wks.   574.192
    animals   591.192
    microorganisms   576.119 2
    plants   581.192
    s.a. spec. organisms
  industrial   660.63
    s.a. spec. prod.
  med. sci.
    brain
      human phys.   612.822
      other aspects see Nervous
      system
    gen. wks.   612.015
    animals   636.089 201 5
      s.a. spec. animals
    man   612.015
    heart
      human phys.   612.173
      other aspects see
      Circulatory organs
    muscles
      human phys.   612.744
      other aspects see
      Movements
    nerves
      human phys.   612.814

Biochemistry
  med. sci.
    nerves (continued)
      other aspects see Nervous
        system
    red corpuscles
      human phys.   612.111 1
      other aspects see
        Circulatory fluids
    respiration
      human phys.   612.22
      other aspects see
        Respiration
    skin
      human phys.   612.792
      other aspects see
        Integumentary organs
    white corpuscles
      human phys.   612.112 1
      other aspects see
        Circulatory fluids
    s.a. other spec. functions,
      systems, organs
  soil science   631.417
  s.a. spec. crops; also spec.
    types of culture e.g.
    Floriculture
Bioclimatology ecology
  life sci.   574.522 2
  animals   591.522 2
  microorganisms   576.15
  plants   581.522 2
  s.a. spec. organisms
Biodegradation
  resistance to
    eng. materials   620.112 23
    s.a. spec. materials &
      spec. uses
Bioecology *see* Ecology
Bioelectricity biophysics
  gen. wks.   574.191 27
  animals   591.191 27
  microorganisms   576.119 127
  plants   581.191 27
  s.a. spec. organisms
  med. sci.   612.014 27
  animals   636.089 201 427
  s.a. spec. animals
  man   612.014 27
  s.a. spec. functions, systems,
    organs
Bioenergetics biophysics
  gen. wks.   574.191 21
  animals   591.191 21
  microorganisms   576.119 121
  plants   581.191 21
  s.a. spec. organisms
  med. sci.   612.014 21
  animals   636.089 201 421
  s.a. spec. animals
  man   612.014 21

Bioenergetics biophysics (continued)
  s.a. spec. functions, systems,
    organs
Biofeedback *see* Proprioceptive
    perceptions psychology
Biogenesis   577
Biogeochemical prospecting
  mining eng.   622.12
Biogeochemistry ecology
  life sci.   574.522 2
  animals   591.522 2
  microorganisms   576.15
  plants   581.522 2
  s.a. spec. organisms
Biogeography   574.9
  animals   591.9
  microorganisms   576.19
  plants   581.9
  s.a. spec. organisms
Biographers
  biog. & work   920
  occupational ethics   174.992
  s.a.   *pers.*–92
Biographies   920
  spec. fields   *s.s.*–092
Biological
  chemistry *see* Biochemistry
  clocks *see* Biological rhythms
  control agric. pests   632.96
    s.a. spec. plants; also
      spec. types of culture
      e.g. Forestry
  determinants
    indiv. psych.   155.234
  devices mil.
    ammunition
      tech. & mf.   623.451 6
      soc. & econ. aspects
        see Secondary
        industries
    control internat. law   341.735
    nonexplosive
      tech. & mf.   623.459 4
      soc. & econ. aspects
        see Secondary
        industries
  drives *see* Physiological
    drives psych.
  forces mil. sci.   358.38
  instruments
    manufacturing
      soc. & econ. aspects *see*
        Secondary industries
    technology   681.757
    s.a. spec. kinds
  laboratory bldgs.
    architecture   727.557 4
    building   690.755 74
    other aspects see
      Educational buildings

Biophysics
gen. wks.	574.191
animals	591.191
microorganisms	576.119 1
plants	581.191
s.a. spec. organisms	

med. sci.
blood
human phys.	612.118 1

other aspects see
    Circulatory fluids
brain
human phys.	612.822

other aspects see Nervous
    system
gen. wks.	612.014
animals	636.089 201 4

s.a. spec. animals
man	612.014
heart
human phys.	612.171

other aspects see
    Circulatory organs
muscles
human phys.	612.741

other aspects see
    Movements
nerves
human phys.	612.813

other aspects see Nervous
    system
nervous system
human phys.	612.804 3

other aspects see Nervous
    system
respiration
human phys.	612.21

other aspects see
    Respiration
skin
human phys.	612.791

other aspects see
    Integumentary organs
white corpuscles
human phys.	612.112 2

other aspects see
    Circulatory fluids
s.a. other spec. functions,
    systems, organs

Biopsies diagnoses *see*
    Microscopic examination
    diagnosis

Biosynthesis
gen. wks.	574.192 9
animals	591.192 9
microorganisms	576.119 29
plants	581.192 9
s.a. spec. organisms	

med. sci.
	612.015 4
animals	636.089 201 54
s.a. spec. animals

Biosynthesis
med. sci. (continued)
man	612.015 4
s.a. spec. functions, systems,
    organs

Biotechnologists
biog. & work	620.809 2
s.a.	*pers.*–620 8
Biotechnology	620.8
s.a. spec. appls. e.g.
    Aerospace engineering

Biotin *see* Vitamins

Birational transformations
algebraic geometry	516.35
s.a. spec. appls. e.g.
    Engineering
gen. wks. *see* Transformations

Birch trees
forestry	634.972 6
soc. & econ. aspects *see*
    Primary industries
other aspects see Fagales;
    also Trees

Birchip Vic.	*area*–945 9

Bird
dogs
animal husbandry	636.752
other aspects see Dogs
lice *see* Mallophaga
watching ornithology	598.072 34
Birdbanding ornithology	598.072 32

Birdhouses *see* Accessory
    domestic structures

Birds
air transp. hazard	363.124 12
census taking ornithology	598.072 32
disease carriers
pub. health	614.434
misc. aspects see Public
    health
s.a. Aves; *also* Wildlife

Birds of paradise *see*
    Paradisaeidae

Birds of prey *see* Falconiformes

Bird's-eye fabrics *see*
    Dobby-weave fabrics

Bird's-nest fungi *see*
    Lycoperdales

Biremes
engineering	623.821
design	623.812 1
models	623.820 11
seamanship	623.882 1
other aspects see Vessels
    (nautical)

Birkenhead Merseyside Eng.	*area*–427 51

Birmingham
Alabama	*area*–761 781
England	*area*–424 96

Bismuth (continued)
  materials
    building   691.875
    engineering   620.189 5
    s.a. spec. uses
  metallography   669.957 5
  metallurgy   669.75
    physical & chem.   669.967 5
    soc. & econ. aspects *see*
      Secondary industries
  mineralogy   549.25
    s.a. spec. minerals
  mining
    technology   622.347
      prospecting   622.184 7
  pharmacology   615.271 8
    misc. aspects see
      Pharmacology
  products
    mf. tech.   673.75
    other aspects see
      Nonferrous metals
      products
  toxicology   615.925 718
    misc. aspects see
      Toxicology
  other aspects see Metal;
    also Metals
  s.a. other spec. uses; also
    spec. minerals
Bismuthinite
  mineralogy   549.32
Bison
  animal husbandry   636.292
  other aspects see Bovoidea
Bistrita-Nasaud Romania *area*–498 4
Bithynia ancient *area*–392 5
Biting lice *see* Mallophaga
Bitlis Turkey *area*–566 7
Bitterns *see* Ciconiiformes
Bitterroot Range *area*–786 8
  Idaho *area*–796 6
  Montana *area*–786 8
Bittersweet
  Celastraceae *see* Celastrales
  Solanaceae *see* Solanales
Bitumen *see* Pitch (carbonaceous
    material)
Bituminous
  coal   553.24
    econ. geol.   553.24
    mining
      soc. & econ. aspects *see*
        Primary industries
      technology   622.334
        prospecting   622.182 4
    processing   662.622 4
    other aspects see Coals
    s.a. spec. uses

Bituminous (continued)
  concrete pavement eng. *see*
    Bituminous materials
    road eng.
  materials
    bldg. materials   691.96
    eng. materials   620.196
      foundations   624.153 96
      naval design   623.818 96
      shipbuilding   623.820 7
      structures   624.189 6
    s.a. other spec. uses
  road eng.
    technology   625.85
      sidewalks   625.885
    other aspects see Roads
  shale   553.23
    econ. geol.   553.23
    mining
      soc. & econ. aspects *see*
        Primary industries
      technology   622.333
        prospecting   622.182 3
    processing   662.622 3
    other aspects see Coals
    s.a. spec. uses
Bivalve mollusks *see* Pelecypoda
Bivalvia *see* Pelecypoda
Bivouac
  mil. sci.   355.412
  s.a. spec. mil. branches
Bixaceae *see* Bixales
Bixales
  botany   583.138
  floriculture   635.933 138
  forestry   634.973 138
  med. aspects
    crop prod.   633.883 138
    gen. pharm.   615.323 138
      toxicology   615.952 313 8
    vet. pharm.   636.089 532 313 8
      toxicology   636.089 595 231 38
  paleobotany   561.3
  other aspects see Plants
Blaby Leicestershire Eng. *area*–425 4
Black
  Africa *area*–67
  arts   133.4
  Belt Ala. *area*–761 4
  books occultism   133.43
  Country Eng. *area*–424 9
  currants
    agriculture   634.721 7
    other aspects see Currants
  death
    Europe hist.   940.17
      s.a. hist. of spec.
        countries
    medical aspects *see* Bubonic
      plague
  earth area RSFSR *area*–473 5

Bladder (urinary)
anatomy (continued)
   other aspects see Excretory
      organs
diseases
  gen. wks.   616.62
    neoplasms   616.992 62
    tuberculosis   616.995 62
  geriatrics   618.976 62
  pediatrics   618.926 2
  pub. health   614.596 2
  statistics   312.362
    deaths   312.266 2
  surgery   617.462
    anesthesiology   617.967 462
  other aspects see Diseases
physical anthropometry   573.662
physiology
  human   612.467
  other aspects see Excretion
tissue biology human   611.018 962
Bladderwort family *see*
    Personales
Bladen Co. N.C.   *area*–756 32
Bladensburg Battle
  War of 1812 hist.   973.523 8
Blading roads
  technology   625.761
  other aspects see Roads
Blaenau Gwent Gwent Wales
         area–429 95
Blaenavon Gwent Wales *area*–429 97
Blagoyevgrad Bulgaria *area*–497 74
Blaina Gwent Wales   *area*–429 95
Blaine Co.
  Idaho   *area*–796 32
  Montana   *area*–786 15
  Nebraska   *area*–782 772
  Oklahoma   *area*–766 31
Blair Co. Pa.   *area*–748 75
Blairgowrie & Rattray Tayside
    Scot.   *area*–412 8
Blairmore Alta.   *area*–712 34
Blanche Lake S. Aust. *area*–942 37
Blanco Co. Tex.   *area*–764 64
Bland Co. Va.   *area*–755 765
Blandford Forum Dorset Eng.
         area–423 32
Blankets
  household equip.   643.53
  manufacturing
    soc. & econ. aspects *see*
        Secondary industries
  technology   677.626
  other aspects see Textiles;
    also Bedclothing
Blasphemy
  criminology   364.188
  ethics
    philosophy   179.5

Blasphemy
ethics (continued)
  religion
    Buddhism   294.356 95
    Christianity   241.695
    comp. rel.   291.569 5
    Hinduism   294.548 695
    s.a. other spec. rel.
  law   345.028 8
    spec. jur.   345.3–.9
  soc. theology
    Christianity   261.833 188
    comp. rel.   291.178 331 88
    s.a. other spec. rel
Blast
  deformation
    structural theory *see*
      Mechanical deformation
      structural theory
  injuries
    statistics   312.304 719
      deaths   312.260 471 9
    surgery   617.19
      anesthesiology 617.967 19
    s.a. Veterinary sciences
Blast-furnace
  gas
    chem. tech.   665.772
  practice   669.141 3
    misc. aspects see Ferrous
      metals
Blasting
  foundation eng. *see*
      Excavation foundation
      eng.
  underground mining 622.23
    spec. deposits 622.33–.39
  underwater eng.   627.74
    s.a. spec. appls. e.g.
      Military engineering
    s.a. other spec. appls.
Blasting-caps *see* Detonators
Blastoidea paleozoology 563.92
Blast-resistant construction
  buildings   693.854
  mil. eng.   623.38
Blattaria
  culture   638.572 2
  paleozoology   565.72
  zoology   595.722
  other aspects see Insecta
Blaydon Tyne & Wear Eng. *area*–428 73
Blazonry   929.6
Bleaching
  clothing
    home econ.   646.6
  ind. oils & gases 665.028 3
    s.a. spec. prod.
  soc. & econ. aspects *see*
      Secondary industries
  technology   667.14

Bleaching (continued)
  s.a. other spec. prod. & subj.
    e.g. Hairdressing
Bleckley Co. Ga.   *area*–758 525
Bledsoe Co. Tenn.   *area*–768 76
Bleeding
  therapeutics   615.899
  s.a. spec. diseases
Bleeding heart *see* Rhoeadales
Blekinge Sweden   *area*–486
Blended waxes
  comm. proc.   665.19
  other aspects see Waxes
Blenders
  use
    cookery   641.589
    s.a. other spec. uses
  other aspects see Electrical
      appliances
Blending
  ind. oils & gases   665.028 3
  s.a. spec. prod.
  nonalcoholic brewed beverages
    comm. proc.
      coffee   663.935
      tea   663.945
    s.a. other spec.
      beverages
  other aspects see Beverages
  petroleum distillates   665.534
  s.a. spec. prod.
  s.a. other spec. prod. &
    subj.
Blennies *see* Acanthopterygii
Blennioidea *see* Acanthopterygii
Blepharoplasts *see* Cytoplasm
Blessings at meals *see* Prayer
    gen. wks.
Bletchley Buckinghamshire Eng.
      area–425 91
Blighted areas
  civic art   711.5
Blights *see* Pathology
Blimps *see* Lighter-than-air
    aircraft
Blind
  children
    psychology   155.451 1
    rearing home econ.   649.151 1
  employees
    pers. admin.
      gen. management   658.304 5
      spec. subj.   *s.s.*–068 3
      pub. admin.   350.1
      central govts.   351.1
      spec. jur.   353–354
      local govts.   352.005 1
  man's bluff recreation   793.4

Blind (continued)
  people
    education   371.911
    law   344.079 111
      spec. jur.   344.3–.9
    library services *see*
      Disabled people
      libraries for
    museum services   069.17
    printing for *see* Raised
      characters
    soc. services to   362.418
    other aspects see Disabled
      people
    s.a.   *pers.*–081 61
  play
    chess   794.17
Blindman's bluff recreation   793.4
Blindness
  ophthalmology   617.712
    geriatrics   618.977 712
    pediatrics   618.920 977 12
    pub. health   614.599 7
    statistics   312.304 771 2
    other aspects see Diseases
  soc. path.   362.41
  soc. theology *see* Social
    problems soc. theology
  s.a. Blind people
Blinds
  architectural
    construction   721.82
    design & decoration   729.39
  building   690.182
  home econ.   645.3
  wooden bldg. construction   694.6
  s.a. spec. kinds of bldgs.
Blinkers *see* Electrooptical
    devices
Bliss's Bibliographic
    Classification   025.434
  special materials   025.34
  spec. subj.   025.46
Blister beetles *see*
    Mordelloidea
Blitz tactics
  mil. sci.   355.422
  s.a. spec. mil. branches
Blizzards *see* Snowstorms
Block
  books hist. & crit.   092
  diagraming *see* Flowcharting
    programming
  Isl. R.I.   *area*–745 8
  printing
    graphic arts *see* Relief
      (art) printing graphic
      arts
    textiles *see* Printing
      processes textiles

Blockades
  internat. law
    law of war   341.63
    peaceful   341.58
    mil. sci.   355.44
    s.a. spec. mil. branches
    World War 1 hist.   940.452
    World War 2 hist.   940.545 2
    s.a. other spec. wars
Blockbusters (ammunition)
  mil. eng.
    soc. & econ. aspects *see*
        Secondary industries
    tech. & mf.   623.451 7
Blocking
  American football   796.332 26
Blood
  analysis
    criminal investigation *see*
        Physical evidence
    med. sci.
      gen. med.   616.075 61
        surgery   617.075 61
      s.a. spec. diseases
    other aspects see
      Diseases
  banks
    health services   362.17
    misc. aspects see Medical
      services
  chemistry
    human phys.   612.12
    other aspects see
      Circulatory fluids
  diseases   616.15
    cancer   616.994 18
    geriatrics   618.976 15
    pediatrics   618.921 5
    pub. health   614.591 5
    puerperal diseases
      obstetrics   618.77
      pub. health   614.599 2
      statistics   312.304 877
      deaths   312.260 487 7
    statistics   312.315
    deaths   312.261 5
    other aspects see Diseases
  drugs affecting
    pharmacodynamics   615.718
    other aspects see Drugs
  elements
    tissue biology
      human anatomy & phys. 611.018 5
      other aspects see Tissue
        biology
  human phys.   612.11
  plasma
    banks
      health services   362.17
      misc. aspects see
        Medical services

Blood
  plasma (continued)
    human anatomy & phys. 611.018 5
    misc. aspects see Tissue
      biology
  transfusions
    therapeutics   615.65
    misc. aspects see
      Medication methods
    s.a. spec. diseases
  pressure
    human phys.   612.14
    other aspects see
      Circulation (biology)
  River battle Natal hist.   968.404 2
  transfusions
    therapeutics   615.65
    misc. aspects see
      Medication methods
    s.a. spec. diseases
  vessels
    anatomy
      human   611.13
      other aspects see
        Circulatory organs
    diseases
      gen. wks.   616.13
        neoplasms   616.992 13
        tuberculosis   616.995 13
      geriatrics   618.976 13
      pediatrics   618.921 3
      pub. health   614.591 3
      statistics   312.313
        deaths   312.261 3
      surgery   617.413
        anesthesiology   617.967 413
      other aspects see
        Diseases
    physical anthropometry 573.613
    physiology
      human   612.13
      other aspects see
        Circulatory organs
    tissue biology
      human   611.018 913
    other aspects see Circulatory
      fluids
Blood-forming system
  diseases   616.41
    geriatrics   618.976 41
    pediatrics   618.924 1
    pub. health   614.594 1
    statistics   312.341
      deaths   312.264 1
    other aspects see Diseases
  drugs affecting
    pharmacodynamics   615.718
    other aspects see Drugs
Bloodletting therapeutics   615.899
  s.a. spec. diseases
Bloodsworth Isl. Md.   *area*–752 27

Bloodwort family *see*
    Haemodorales
Blotting papers
  mf. tech.   676.284 4
  other aspects see Papers pulp
    prod.
Blount Co.
  Alabama   *area*–761 72
  Tennessee   *area*–768 885
Blouses
  comm. mf.   687.115
    children's   687.13
    women's   687.12
  domestic mf.   646.435
  other aspects see Clothing
Blowers
  air-conditioning eng.   697.932 5
  gen. eng.
    soc. & econ. aspects *see*
      Secondary industries
    tech. & mf.   621.61
  marine engine auxiliaries *see*
    Engine auxiliaries
    shipbuilding
  other aspects see Dynamics
  s.a. other spec. uses
Blowflies *see* Cyclorrhapha
Blowing
  glassmaking   666.122
  s.a. spec. kinds of glass
  s.a. other spec. prod. &
    subj.
Blown glass *see* Glassware
Blowpipe analysis
  anal. chem.
    gen. wks.   543.086
      qualitative   544.3
      quantitative   545.43
    organic   547.308 6
      qualitative   547.343
      quantitative   547.354 3
    s.a. spec. elements & cpds.
    minerals   549.133
      spec. minerals   549.2–.7
Blowpipes (chem. equip.)   542.5
  s.a. spec. appls. e.g.
    Organic chemistry
Blowpipes (weapons)
  hunting & shooting sports   799.202 82
Blue
  Earth Co. Minn.   *area*–776 21
  Mt. Res. Ark.   *area*–767 37
  Mts.
    N.S.W.   *area*–944 5
    Oregon   *area*–795 7
    Washington   *area*–797 46
  Nile
    province Sudan   *area*–626 4
    River   *area*–626 4
  Ridge   *area*–755
    Georgia   *area*–758 273

Blue
  Ridge (continued)
    North Carolina   *area*–756 8
    South Carolina   *area*–757 2
    Virginia   *area*–755
Bluebell family *see* Campanales
Blueberries
  agriculture   634.737
    soc. & econ. aspects *see*
      Primary industries
  foods   641.347 37
    preparation
      commercial   664.804 737
      domestic   641.647 37
  other aspects see Ericales;
    also Fruits
Blue-collar
  classes *see* Lower classes
  workers
    labor econ.   331.79
    unions   331.880 42
    other aspects see
      Industrial occupations
    labor law *see* Labor law
Bluegrass
  Kentucky   *area*–769 3
  music *see* Country music
Bluegrasses
  agriculture   633.21
    soc. & econ. aspects *see*
      Primary industries
  other aspects see Pooideae;
    also Field crops
Blue-green algae *see* Cyanophyta
Blueprinting
  soc. & econ. aspects *see*
    Secondary industries
  technology   686.42
Blueprints
  bldg. construction   692.1
  tech. drawing *see* Copies
    tech. drawing
Blues
  music theory   781.573
    recordings   789.912 157 3
  songs   784.53
    recordings   789.912 453
  s.a. spec. mediums
Bluestones   553.53
  econ. geol.   553.53
  mining
    soc. & econ. aspects *see*
      Primary industries
    technology   622.353
      prospecting   622.185 3
  s.a. spec. uses
Blyth Valley Northumberland Eng.
    area–428 84
Bo tree
  Buddhism   294.343 5
  other aspects see Urticales

Boaco Nicaragua   *area*–728 526
Boadicea queen Eng. hist.   936.204
   s.a. spec. events & subj.
      e.g. Commerce
Board
  games
    equip. mf.   688.74
     soc. & econ. aspects *see*
       Secondary industries
    recreation   794
  of trade
    buildings *see* Exchange
       buildings
Boarding
  nat. leathers
   manufacturing
     soc. & econ. aspects *see*
       Secondary industries
    technology   675.25
  schools
    secondary ed.   373.222
Boardinghouses
  housekeeping   647.94
   s.a. spec. housekeeping
     activities e.g.
      Housecleaning home
      econ.
  sanitation *see* Residential
      buildings sanitation
  other aspects see Dwellings
Boards *see* Governing boards
Boars *see* Suiformes
Boat racing
  sports   797.14
   misc. aspects see Sports
Boatbuilding *see* Vessels
    (nautical) engineering
Boathouses
  architecture   725.87
  building   690.587
  other aspects see Public
     structures
Boating
  accidents
    statistics *see* Recreation
     accidents
  seamanship   623.88
  sports   797.1
   misc. aspects see Sports
Boatmen
  biog. & work   797.109 2
  s.a.   *pers.*–797 1
Boats *see* Vessels (nautical)
Bobbin laces
  textile arts   746.222
  other aspects see Laces
    fabrics
Bobbins
  manufacturing *see* Textile-
    technology instruments
    & machinery

Bobbins (continued)
  textiles
    handicrafts *see* Weaving
     arts
    manufacturing *see* Looms
     textiles mf.
Bocas del Toro Panama   *area*–728 712
Bocking Essex Eng.   *area*–426 715
Bodies
  automobiles
    soc. & econ. aspects *see*
      Secondary industries
    tech. & mf.   629.26
   s.a. other spec. kinds
Bodmin Cornwall Eng.   *area*–423 71
Bodmin Moor Cornwall Eng.
        area–423 71
Body
  care
    children home econ.   649.4
    other aspects see Personal
      grooming
  contours soc. customs   391.62
  heat biochemistry
    med. sci.   612.014 26
    animals   636.089 201 426
     s.a. spec. animals
    man   612.014 26
    zoology   596.019 12
     s.a. spec. vertebrates
  measurements *see*
     Anthropometry
  relation to mind
    metaphysics   128.2
   s.a. Human body
Body-building
  personal care   646.75
Bodywork
  automobiles *see* Bodies
     automobiles
Boehmeria *see* Ramie
Boeotia Greece   *area*–495 1
  ancient   *area*–384
Boer War hist.
  1st   968.204 6
  2d   968.048
   s.a. spec. countries & spec.
     provinces
Bog mosses *see* Sphagnales
Bog of Allen Leinster Ire.   *area*–418 5
Boggabri N.S.W.   *area*–944 4
Bognor Regis West Sussex Eng.
        area–422 67
Bogong Mount Vic.   *area*–945 5
Bogotá Colombia   *area*–861 4
Bogs
  drainage *see* Drainage
  ecology life sci. *see*
     Wetlands ecology life
     sci.

Bogus wrapping papers
    mf. tech.   676.287
    other aspects see Papers pulp
        prod.
Bohemia   *area*–437 1
Bohemia-Moravia Protectorate
        Czechoslovakia hist.   943.703
    s.a. spec. events & subj.
        e.g. Commerce
Bohemian *see* Czech
Bohemium *see* Rhenium
Bohol Philippines   *area*–599 5
Boiler
    furnaces *see* Furnaces steam
        eng.
    insurance   368.7
        misc. aspects see Insurance
    operations steam eng.
        soc. & econ. aspects *see*
            Secondary industries
        technology   621.194
        s.a. spec. appls. e.g.
            Steam automobiles
Boiler-house practices
    steam eng. *see* Boiler
        operations steam eng.
Boilers
    bldg. heating equip.   697.07
    s.a. spec. kinds e.g. Steam
        heating
    marine engine auxiliaries *see*
        Engine auxiliaries
        shipbuilding
    steam eng.
        soc. & econ. aspects *see*
            Secondary industries
        tech. & mf.   621.184
        s.a. spec. appls. e.g.
            Military engineering
Boiling
    cookery technique   641.73
    effect of heat *see*
        Liquid-to-gas
        vaporization effect of
        heat
Boiling-point elevation *see*
        Colligative properties
        solutions
Boiling-points physics   536.443
Boils *see* Furuncles
Boina kingdom hist.   969.101
    s.a. spec. events & subj.
        e.g. Commerce
Bois Blanc Isl. Mich.   *area*–774 923
Boise
    city Ida.   *area*–796 28
    Co. Ida.   *area*–796 74
Bojutsu *see* Fencing (swordplay)
Bokhara rugs
    textile arts   746.758 7
Bokmal *see* Norwegian

Bolas
    hunting & shooting sports   799.202 82
Boldon Tyne & Wear Eng.   *area*–428 75
Bolides *see* Meteoroids
Bolivar Co. Miss.   *area*–762 43
Bolívar
    dept. Colombia   *area*–861 14
    province Ecuador   *area*–866 16
    state Venezuela   *area*–876 3
Bolivia (country)   *area*–84
Bolivia (game) *see* Rummy
Bolivian
    literature   860
    people   *r.e.n.*–688 4
    s.a. other spec. subj. e.g.
        Arts
Bollinger Co. Mo.   *area*–778 94
Bollington Cheshire Eng.   *area*–427 16
Bologna Italy   *area*–454 1
Bolshevik *see* Communist
Bolshevism *see* Communism
Bolsover Derbyshire Eng.   *area*–425 15
Bolton Greater Manchester Eng.
        area–427 37
Bolts
    locksmithing
        mf. tech.   683.31
        other aspects see Hardware
    machine eng.
        soc. & econ. aspects *see*
            Secondary industries
        tech. & mf.   621.882
        s.a. spec. appls. e.g.
            Automobiles
    other aspects see Mechanics
Boltzmann statistics *see*
        Classical statistical
        mechanics
Bolu Turkey   *area*–563
Bolyai geometry   516.9
    s.a. spec. appls. e.g.
        Engineering
Bolzano Italy   *area*–453 83
Bomaderry N.S.W.   *area*–944 7
Bombacaceae *see* Tiliales
Bombala N.S.W.   *area*–944 7
Bombardment (military)
    defense against
        mil. eng.   623.3
    gen. wks. *see* Disasters
Bombardment (nuclear)
    nuclear interactions *see*
        Interactions nuclear
        reactions
Bombay India   *area*–547 92
Bombers
    mil. aircraft eng.   623.746 3
Bombing forces
    air warfare   358.42
Bombings *see* Bombardment
        (military)

Bombproof construction
buildings — 693.854
mil. eng. — 623.38
Bombs
disposal units
mil. sci. — 358.2
mil. eng.
tech. & mf. — 623.451
soc. & econ. aspects *see*
Secondary industries
Bombsights
ordnance
soc. & econ. aspects *see*
Secondary industries
tech. & mf. — 623.46
Bombycillidae
hunting
commercial — 639.128 852
sports — 799.248 852
paleozoology — 568.8
zoology — 598.852
other aspects see Aves
Bon
Homme Co. S.D. — *area*–783 395
Secours *see* Sisters of Bon
Secours
Bonaire isl. — *area*–729 86
Bonaparte Archipelago W. Aust.
area–941 4
Bonaventure Co. Que. — *area*–714 78
Bond
Co. Ill. — *area*–773 873
papers
mf. tech. — 676.282 3
other aspects see Papers
pulp prod.
Bonded fabrics
arts — 746.046 9
s.a. spec. processes e.g.
Weaving
manufacturing
soc. & econ. aspects *see*
Secondary industries
technology — 677.69
other aspects see Textiles
s.a. spec. prod.
Bonding
metal prod.
mf. tech. — 671.58
ferrous metals — 672.58
s.a. other spec. metals
other aspects see Joining
Bonds (binders)
molecular structure
theoretical chem.
distances *see*
Stereochemistry
gen. wks. — 541.224
organic — 547.122 4
s.a. spec. elements &
cpds.

Bonds (securities)
accounting trmt. — 657.75
s.a. spec. kinds of
enterprise e.g.
Insurance accounting
capital *see* Fixed capital
govt. finance *see* Public
securities
investment finance — 332.632 3
govt. control *see*
Securities govt.
control
law — 346.092 2
spec. jur. — 346.3–.9
issues capital management — 658.152 24
spec. subj. — *s.s.*–068 1
Bonds (surety)
bail *see* Bail
employees
insurance — 368.83
misc. aspects see
Insurance
obligations
insurance — 368.84
misc. aspects see
Insurance
Bône Algeria — *area*–655
Bone
carving
dec. arts — 736.6
rel. significance
Christianity — 247.866
comp. rel. — 291.37
s.a. other spec. rel
char *see* Adsorbent carbons
marrow
diseases *see* Blood-forming
system diseases
human phys. — 612.491
tissue biology
human anatomy & phys. — 611.018 4
other aspects see Tissue
biology
other aspects see Secretion
meal fertilizers *see*
Phosphorus fertilizers
tissues
human anatomy & phys. — 611.018 4
other aspects see Tissue
biology
Bones
anatomy
human — 611.71
other aspects see Skeletal
organs
diseases
gen. wks. — 616.71
neoplasms — 616.992 71
tuberculosis — 616.995 71
geriatrics — 618.976 71
pediatrics — 618.927 1

Books (continued)
  lit. & stage trmt. *see*
      Artistic themes
  mailing
      postal commun.   383.124
      other aspects see Postal
          commun.
  manufacturing   686
      soc. & econ. aspects *see*
          Secondary industries
      s.a. spec. activities e.g.
          Printing
  preparation for storage
      library econ.   025.7
  preservation
      library operations   025.84
  publishing   070.5
  repair
      library operations   025.7
  restoration
      library operations   025.7
  soc. & econ. aspects *see*
      Secondary industries
  sociology   302.23
  s.a. Book
Booksellers' catalogs
  general
      alphabetic subject   017.8
      author   018.4
      classified   017.4
      dictionary   019.4
  spec. subj.   016
Bookselling   658.809 070 57
  to libraries   025.233
  other aspects see Marketing
Boolean algebra   511.324
  s.a. spec. math. branches;
      also spec. appls. e.g.
      Electronic data
      processing
Boomerangs
  customs   399
  mil. eng.   623.441
  sports
      gen. wks. *see* Throwing
      hunting   799.202 82
Boone
  County
      Arkansas   *area*–767 18
      Illinois   *area*–773 29
      Indiana   *area*–772 54
      Iowa   *area*–777 544
      Kentucky   *area*–769 363
      Missouri   *area*–778 29
      Nebraska   *area*–782 51
      West Virginia   *area*–754 39
  Res. Tenn.   *area*–768 96
Boosters
  detonators *see* Detonators

Boosters (continued)
  elect. power *see*
      Direct-current
      machinery
Boothferry Humberside Eng.
                                      area–428 35
Boothia Gulf *see* American
      Arctic seawaters
Bootle Merseyside Eng.   *area*–427 59
Bootlegging *see* Revenue
      offenses
Boots
  mf. tech.   685.31
  other aspects see Footwear
Bophuthatswana Transvaal   *area*–682 94
Boquerón Paraguay   *area*–892 24
Boracite
  mineralogy   549.735
Borage family *see* Boraginales
Boraginaceae *see* Boraginales
Boraginales
  botany   583.77
  floriculture   635.933 77
  med. aspects
      crop prod.   633.883 77
      gen. pharm.   615.323 77
      toxicology   615.952 377
      vet. pharm.   636.089 532 377
      toxicology   636.089 595 237 7
  paleobotany   561.3
  other aspects see Plants
Boran dialect *see* Cushitic
      languages
Borates   553.633
  econ. geol.   553.633
  mineralogy   549.735
  mining
      soc. & econ. aspects *see*
          Primary industries
  technology   622.363 3
      prospecting   622.186 33
  s.a. spec. uses
Borax *see* Borates
Borden
  Co. Tex.   *area*–764 853
  Robert L. admin.
      Can. hist.   971.061 2
      s.a. spec. events & subj.
          e.g. Courts
Border
  Country Scot.   *area*–413 7
  defenses
      mil. sci.   355.45
      s.a. spec. mil. branches
  patrols
      police services   363.285
      other aspects see Law
          enforcement

Borders
plants grown for
  floriculture   635.963
   s.a. spec. plants
Scotland   *area*–413 7
Bordertown S. Aust.   *area*–942 34
Boring
operations
  underground mining   622.24
  spec. deposits   622.33–.39
tools
  soc. & econ. aspects *see*
    Secondary industries
  tech. & mf.   621.945
   s.a. spec. appls. e.g.
    Tunnels
Boris Godunov reign Russia hist.   947.044
  s.a. spec. events & subj.
    e.g. Commerce
Bornean *see* Indonesian
Borneo   *area*–598 3
  Indonesia   *area*–598 3
  Malaysia   *area*–595 3
Bornholm Denmark   *area*–489 2
Borno Nigeria   *area*–669 5
Bornu kingdom hist.   966.901 3
  s.a. spec. events & subj.
    e.g. Commerce
Boron
chemistry
  inorganic   546.671
  organic   547.056 71
   s.a. spec. groupings e.g.
    Aliphatic compounds
  technology   661.067 1
  organic   661.895
  soc. & econ. aspects *see*
    Secondary industries
  s.a. spec. prod.
compounds
  chemistry *see* Boron
    chemistry
econ. geol.   553.92
fuels
  manufacturing
    chem. tech.   662.86
  soc. & econ. aspects *see*
    Secondary industries
mining
  soc. & econ. aspects *see*
    Primary industries
  technology   622.392
  prospecting   622.189 2
pharmacology   615.267 1
  misc. aspects see
    Pharmacology
plant nutrition *see* Trace
    elements plant
    nutrition

Boron (continued)
toxicology   915.925 671
  misc. aspects see
    Toxicology
  other aspects see Minor
    metals
  s.a. spec. uses; also spec.
    minerals
Boroughs
local govt.   352.007 2
  other aspects see Local;
    also Urban
Borrowing
authorization
  legislative bodies *see*
    Financial powers
capital sources
  capital management   658.152 24
  spec. subj.   *s.s.*–068 1
pub. finance *see* Public
    borrowing
Borsod-Abauj-Zemplen Hungary
    area–439 9
Borstals penology   365.42
  misc. aspects see Penal
    institutions
Borzois
animal husbandry   636.753
  other aspects see Dogs
Boscastle Cornwall Eng.   *area*–423 71
Bose-Einstein statistics
physics   530.133 2
spec. states of matter   530.4
  s.a. spec. branches of
    physics
Bosnia & Hercegovina Yugoslavia
    area–497 42
Bosons
nuclear physics *see* Particles
    (matter)
Bosphorus *see* Black Sea
Bosporus *see* Black Sea
Bosque Co. Tex.   *area*–764 518
Bosses (structural geol.)   551.88
  s.a. spec. aspects e.g.
    Prospecting
Bossier Par. La.   *area*–763 97
Boston
city Mass.   *area*–744 61
Lincolnshire Eng.   *area*–425 37
Massacre U.S. hist.   973.311 3
Mountains
  Arkansas   *area*–767 1
  Oklahoma   *area*–766 8
Port Bill U.S. hist.   973.311 6
Tea Party U.S. hist.   973.311 5
terriers
  animal husbandry   636.72
  other aspects see Dogs
Bosworth Leicestershire Eng.
    area–425 49

Bot flies *see* Cyclorrhapha
Botanic medicine
  therapeutics   615.537
    misc. aspects see
        Therapeutics
    s.a. spec. diseases
Botanical
  garden bldgs.
    architecture   727.558
    other aspects see
        Educational buildings
  gardens   580.744
  landscape design   712.5
  laboratory bldgs.
    architecture   727.558
    other aspects see
        Educational buildings
  sciences   580
    Biblical trmt.   220.858
    s.a. spec. parts of Bible
    curriculums   375.58
    documentation   025.065 8
    libraries   026.58
      misc. aspects see Special
        libraries
    library acquisitions   025.275 8
    library classification   025.465 8
    subject headings   025.495 8
    other aspects see Sciences
  s.a. Plant; *also* Vegetable
Botanists
  biog. & work   581.092
  s.a. spec. kinds
  other aspects see Scientists
  s.a.   *pers.*–58
Botany   581
  museums
    desc. & colls.   581.074
    museology   069.958 1
    s.a. spec. activities
      e.g. Display
  other aspects see Botanical
    sciences
Botetourt Co. Va.   *area*–755 83
Botha admin. South Africa hist.
      968.052
  s.a. spec. events & subj.
    e.g. Commerce
Bothnia Gulf *see* Baltic Sea
Bothriocidaroida
  paleozoology   563.95
Botosani Romania   *area*–498 1
Botswana
  people   *r.e.n.*–968 1
  republic   *area*–681 1
Bottineau Co. N.D.   *area*–784 61
Bottle
  nipples
    latex *see* Dipped latex
      products
  trees *see* Tiliales

Bottled water *see* Potable water
Bottles
  glass
    dec. arts   748.82
    technology   666.192
  s.a. other spec. materials
Bottling
  alcoholic beverages
    comm. proc.   663.19
    s.a. spec. beverages e.g.
      Wines
    other aspects see Alcoholic
      beverages
  s.a. other spec. subj.
Bottoms
  petroleum
    chem. tech.   665.538 8
    other aspects see Petroleum
  ships *see* Hulls shipbuilding
Botulism
  gen. med.   616.931 5
  geriatrics   618.976 931 5
  pediatrics   618.929 315
  pub. health   614.512 5
  statistics   312.393 15
    deaths   312.269 315
  other aspects see Diseases
Bouches-du-Rhône France   *area*–449 1
Boudicca queen Eng. hist.   936.204
  s.a. spec. events & subj.
    e.g. Commerce
Bougainville Solomon Isls.
      area–935
Boulder
  clays
    physical geol.   551.314
  Co. Colo.   *area*–788 63
Boundaries
  local govts.   352.003
  of states
    internat. law   341.42
  property law *see* Land tenure
    law
Boundary
  Co. Ida.   *area*–796 98
  layers
    aeronautical aerodynamics   629.132 37
    s.a. spec. appls. e.g.
      Flying
    astronautics   629.415 1
    s.a. spec. appls. e.g.
      Space warfare
  lighting systems airports *see*
    Lighting airports
  rivers
    internat. law   341.442
  surveying   526.92
Boundary-value problems   515.35
  calculus of finite differences   515.62
  differential equations   515.35

Boundary-value problems (continued)
  s.a. spec. appls. e.g.
      Engineering
Bourbon Co.
  Kansas   *area*–781 97
  Kentucky   *area*–769 423
Bourbonnais France   *area*–445 7
Bourbons
  France hist.   944.03
  Spain hist.   946.054
  s.a. spec. events & subj.
      e.g. Courts
Bourgeoisie *see* Middle classes
Bourgogne France   *area*–444
Bourke N.S.W.   *area*–944 9
Bourne Lincolnshire Eng. *area*–425 38
Bournemouth Dorset Eng. *area*–423 38
Bournonite
  mineralogy   549.35
Bourse *see* Exchange
Boutonneuse fever *see* Tick
      typhus
Boutonnieres
  flower arrangement   745.923
Bouvet Isl.   *area*–971 3
Bouvier des Flandres
  animal husbandry   636.73
  other aspects see Dogs
Bovey Tracey Devon Eng. *area*–423 55
Bovines *see* Bovoidea
Bovoidea
  agric. pests   632.697 358
  animal husbandry   636.2
  soc. & econ. aspects *see*
      Primary industries
  conservation tech.   639.979 735 8
  drawing tech.   743.697 358
  hunting
    commercial
      technology   639.117 358
      soc. & econ. aspects
        see Primary
        industries
    sports
      big game   799.277 358
      small game   799.259 735 8
  paleozoology   569.73
  products
    dairy products *see* Dairy
      products
    meats
      food   641.362
        cookery   641.662
      production *see* Red meats
    other prod. see spec. prod.
      e.g. Hides
  zoology   599.735 8
  other aspects see Animals
Bowdon Greater Manchester Eng.
              area–427 31

Bowed instruments
  manufacture   681.817 01
    spec. kinds   681.817 1–.817 4
  musical art   787.01
    spec. kinds   787.1–.4
Bowell
  Mackenzie admin.
    Can. hist.   971.055
  s.a. spec. events & subj.
    e.g. Commerce
Bowels *see* Intestines
Bowen Qld.   *area*–943 6
Bowfins *see* Amiiformes
Bowie Co. Tex.   *area*–764 197
Bowl games
  American football sports 796.332 72
Bowland Forest Lancashire Eng.
              area–427 685
Bowlers
  biog. & work   794.609 2
  s.a.   *pers.*–794 6
Bowling (cricket)
  sports   796.358 22
Bowling (game)
  alley bldgs. *see* Indoor game
      bldgs.
  equipment mf.   688.746
  soc. & econ. aspects *see*
      Secondary industries
  recreation   794.6
  s.a. Lawn bowling
Bowman Co. N.D.   *area*–784 92
Bows (weapons)
  art metalwork   739.73
  customs   399
  mil. eng.   623.441
  use in sports   799.202 85
    shooting at targets 799.32
    shooting game   799.215
Box
  Butte Co. Neb.   *area*–782 94
  Elder Co. Utah   *area*–792 42
Boxcars *see* Freight cars
Boxers (dogs)
  animal husbandry   636.73
  other aspects see Dogs
Boxers (pugilists)
  biog. & work   796.830 92
  s.a.   *pers.*–796 8
Boxes
  paper & paperboard
    mf. tech.   676.32
  other kinds & aspects see
      Containers
Box-girder bridges
  structural eng.   624.4
  other aspects see Bridges
      (structures)

Boxing	
equipment mf.	688.768 3
soc. & econ. aspects *see*	
Secondary industries	
ethics *see* Combat sports	
ethics	
law *see* Recreation law	
sports	796.83
other aspects see Sports	
Boy Scouts	369.43
camp sports	796.542 2
Boyacá Colombia	*area*–861 37
Boycott	
internat. law	341.58
Boycotts	
internat. pol.	327.117
spec. countries	327.3–.9
labor econ.	331.893
labor law *see* Labor law	
Boyd Co.	
Kentucky	*area*–769 27
Nebraska	*area*–782 723
Boyer River Ia.	*area*–777 4
Boyle Co. Ky.	*area*–769 523
Boyne River Leinster Ire.	*area*–418 22
Boys	
club bldgs. *see* Indoor game	
bldgs.	
criminal offenders	364.36
hygiene	613.042 32
journalism for	070.483 26
psychology	155.432
publication for	
bibliographies	011.624 1
spec. kinds	012–016
catalogs	
general	017–019
spec. kinds	012–016
reviews	028.162 41
s.a. spec. forms e.g. Books	
rearing home econ.	649.132
recreation	790.194
indoor	793.019 4
outdoor	796.019 4
rel. associations	
Christianity	267.7
other rel. see Religious	
associations	
sex hygiene	613.953
societies	369.42
other aspects see Children	
Boysenberries	
agriculture	634.718
soc. & econ. aspects *see*	
Primary industries	
foods	641.347 18
preparation	
commercial	664.804 718
domestic	641.647 18
other aspects see Rosaceae;	
also Fruits	

Bozcaada Turkey	*area*–562
Brabant Belgium	*area*–493 3
Bracelets	
precious metalwork	739.278
other aspects see Jewelry	
Brachiopoda	
culture	639.7
paleozoology	564.8
zoology	594.8
other aspects see	
Molluscoidea	
Brachycephalidae	
zoology	597.87
other aspects see Anura	
Brachyura	
culture	639.542
fishing	
commercial	639.542
sports	799.255 384 2
food *see* Seafoods	
zoology	595.384 2
other aspects see Decapoda	
(crustaceans)	
Bracing equipment	
aircraft eng.	
soc. & econ. aspects *see*	
Secondary industries	
tech. & mf.	629.134 37
Bracken Co. Ky.	*area*–769 325
Brackish waters regional subj.	
trmt.	*area*–169
Brackley Northamptonshire Eng.	
	area–425 59
Bracknell Berkshire Eng.	*area*–422 98
Bradford	
city West Yorkshire Eng.	*area*–428 17
County	
Florida	*area*–759 15
Pennsylvania	*area*–748 57
Bradford-on-Avon Wiltshire Eng.	
	area–423 15
Bradley Co.	
Arkansas	*area*–767 63
Tennessee	*area*–768 873
Bradyodonti	
paleozoology	567.3
Braemar Grampian Scot.	*area*–412 4
Braga Portugal	*area*–469 12
Bragança Portugal	*area*–469 2
Brahma *see* God	
Brahma Samaj	
Hinduism	294.556 2
misc. aspects see Hinduism	
Brahmanas	
Vedic literature	294.592 1
Brahmanism *see* Hinduism	
Brahmanists *see* Hindus	
Brahmaputra River	*area*–54
Brahui	
language	
linguistics	494.83

Branchiura
  fishing (continued)
    sports   799.255 31
    paleozoology   565.31
    zoology   595.31
    other aspects see Crustacea
Brandenburg Ger.   *area*–431 5
Brandies   641.253
  comm. proc.   663.53
  other aspects see Alcoholic
      beverages
Branding
  animal husbandry   636.081 2
  s.a. spec. animals
Brandon
  & Byshottles Durham Eng.
                area–428 65
  Manitoba   *area*–712 73
Brands
  preferences *see* Consumer
      preferences
  sales promotion   658.827
    spec. subj.   *s.s.*–068 8
Brandywine Creek Pa. *area*–748 14
Brant Co. Ont.   *area*–713 47
Brantford Ont.   *area*–713 48
Brantley Co. Ga.   *area*–758 753
Bras d'Or Lake N.S.   *area*–716 9
Brasilia Brazil   *area*–817 4
Brasov Romania   *area*–498 4
Brass
  arts
    decorative   739.52
    other aspects see Metal
      arts
  bands   785.067 1
    s.a. spec. kinds of music
  ensembles   785.068
    s.a. spec. kinds of music
  instruments
    manufacture   681.818 01
      spec. kinds   681.818 1–.818 4
    musical art   788.01
      spec. kinds   788.1–.4
  other aspects see Copper
Brassica
  napobrassica *see* Rutabagas
  oleraceae *see* Cabbages
    capitata *see* Cauliflower
    gemmifera *see* Brussels
      sprouts
    italica *see* Broccoli
  rapa *see* Turnips
Brassicaceae *see* Cruciales
Brassieres
  comm. mf.   687.25
  other aspects see Underwear
Bravery *see* Courage
Brawling *see* Public order crime
      against
Braxton Co. W.Va.   *area*–754 66

Braziers
  bldg. heating   697.1
  ceramic arts   738.8
  rel. significance
    Christianity   247.888
    comp. rel.   291.37
    s.a. other spec. rel.
Brazil   *area*–81
Brazil nuts
  agriculture   634.575
    soc. & econ. aspects *see*
      Primary industries
  foods   641.345 75
    preparation
      commercial   664.804 575
      domestic   641.645 75
  other aspects see Myrtales,
      also Nuts
Brazilian
  literature   869
  people   *r.e.n.*–698
  s.a. other spec. subj. e.g.
    Arts
Brazing
  metal prod.
    dec. arts   739.14
      s.a. spec. metals; also
        spec. prod. e.g.
        Jewelry
    fine arts *see* Direct-metal
      sculpture
    mf. tech.   671.56
      ferrous metals   672.56
      s.a. other spec. metals
    other aspects see Joining
Brazoria Co. Tex.   *area*–764 137
Brazos
  Co. Tex.   *area*–764 242
  River Tex.   *area*–764 1
Breach
  of contract
    law   346.022
  of peace *see* Public order
    crimes against
Bread-dough handicrafts 745.5
Breadfruit
  agriculture   634.39
    soc. & econ. aspects *see*
      Primary industries
  foods   641.343 9
    preparation
      commercial   664.804 39
      domestic   641.643 9
  other aspects see Urticales;
    also Fruits
Breads
  comm. proc.   664.752 3
  cookery home econ. 641.815
Breakbone fever *see* Dengue
    fever

Break-even analysis
financial management *see*
Income financial
management
Breakfast
foods
comm. proc. 664.756
rooms
household management 643.4
Breakfasts
cookery home econ. 641.52
soc. customs 384.15
Breaking
properties affecting
eng. materials 620.112 6
s.a. spec. materials &
spec. uses
Breaks in work day *see* Rest
periods
Breakwaters *see* Protective
structures port eng.
Breast
gen. wks. *see* Mammary glands
male *see* Male breast
Breastbone *see* Sternum
Breast-feeding
home econ. 649.3
Breathing
diesel engines 621.436 1
land vehicles 629.250 61
marine vehicles 623.872 361
s.a. other spec. appls.
man
hygiene 613.192
vocal music 784.932
s.a. Respiration
Breathitt Co. Ky. *area*–769 19
Brechin Tayside Scot. *area*–412 6
Brechou isl. *area*–423 47
Breckinridge Co. Ky. *area*–769 854
Breckland Norfolk Eng. *area*–426 14
Brecknock Powys Wales *area*–429 56
Breconshire Wales *area*–429 56
Brecqhou isl. *area*–423 47
Bredbury & Romiley Greater
Manchester Eng. *area*–427 34
Breeder reactors
nuclear tech. 621.483 4
s.a. spec. appls. e.g.
Generation elect. power
other aspects see Nuclear
reactions
Breeding
habits *see* Reproductive
adaptations
methods
animal husbandry 636.082
s.a. spec. animals
plants *see* Plant
propagation

Breeding
methods (continued)
trees
silviculture 634.956
s.a. spec. trees
purposes
animal husbandry for 636.088 1
s.a. spec. animals
records
animal husbandry 636.082 2
s.a. spec. animals
Breeds
genetic factor
animal breeding 636.082 1
s.a. spec. animals
Breezes *see* Wind systems
Bremen Ger. *area*–435 2
Bremer Co. Ia. *area*–777 34
Bremsstrahlung *see* X rays
Brent London Eng. *area*–421 85
Brentford & Chiswick London Eng.
area–421 82
Brentwood Essex Eng. *area*–426 76
Brescia Italy *area*–425 6
Breslau Poland *area*–438 5
Brest Belorussia *area*–476 52
Bretagne *area*–441
Brethren
Church of the 286.5
misc. aspects see Baptist
Breton
language
linguistics 491.68
literature 891.68
s.a. *lang.*–916 8
people *r.e.n.*–916 8
s.a. Brittany; *also other*
spec. subj. e.g. Arts
Brevard Co. Fla. *area*–759 27
Breviaries
Roman Catholic liturgy 264.024
Brevicipitidae
zoology 597.89
other aspects see Anura
Brewarrina N.S.W. *area*–944 9
Brewed beverages
alcoholic 641.23
comm. proc. 663.3
cookery 641.62
composite dishes 641.873
other aspects see Alcoholic
beverages
nonalcoholic
comm. proc. 663.9
other aspects see
Nonalcoholic beverages
Brewster Co. Tex. *area*–764 932
Brezhnev regime USSR hist. 947.085 3
s.a. spec. events & subj.
e.g. Commerce
Briansk RSFSR *area*–476 2

Briard
  animal husbandry   636.73
  other aspects see Dogs
Bribery
  of officials *see* Political
      corruption
  of voters *see* Electoral
      offenses
Bric-a-brac *see* Ornaments arts
Brick pavements
  road eng.
    technology   625.82
    sidewalks   625.882
  other aspects see Roads
Bricklayers
  biog. & work   693.210 92
  s.a.   *pers.*–693
Bricks
  arch. construction   721.044 21
    s.a. spec. structural
      elements; also spec.
      types of bldgs.
  bldg. construction   693.21
  bldg. materials   691.4
  ceramic arts   738.6
  eng. materials   620.142
    foundations   624.153 42
    naval design   623.818 36
    shipbuilding   623.820 7
    structures   624.183 6
    s.a. other spec. uses
  rel. significance
    Christianity   247.886
    comp. rel.   291.37
    s.a. other spec. rel.
  technology   666.737
  other aspects see Structural
      clay products
Bridal *see* Weddings
Bridal wreath *see* Rosales
Brides
  purchase soc. customs   392.4
Bridge
  circuits
    elect. measurement *see*
      Resistance elect.
      measurement
    radiowave electronics *see*
      Testing-devices
      radiowave electronics
  dams *see* Movable dams
  engineers
    biog. & work   624.209 2
    other aspects see Civil
      engineers
  of Allan Central Scot.   *area*–413 12
  whist
    equipment mf.   688.754 13
      soc. & econ. aspects *see*
        Secondary industries
    recreation   795.413

Bridge (game)
  equipment mf.   688.754 13–.754 15
    soc. & econ. aspects *see*
      Secondary industries
  recreation   795.413–.415
Bridgend Mid Glamorgan Wales
        area–429 71
Bridges (dentistry)   617.692
Bridges (electrical)
  elect. measurement *see*
      Resistance elect.
      measurement
  radiowave electronics *see*
      Testing-devices
      radiowave electronics
Bridges (structures)
  agric. structures   631.28
  architecture   725.98
  building   690.598
  forest management   634.93
  highway transp.
    commerce   388.132
    law *see* Roads law
  ice *see* Ice crossings
  mil. eng.   623.67
  mil. sci.   358.22
  pub. works
    pub. admin.   350.864 5
      central govts.   351.864 5
      spec. jur.   353–354
      local govts.   352.74
  rail transp. *see* Stationary
      facilities railroads
  structural eng.   624.2
  s.a. other spec. occurrences
    e.g. Roads
Bridgeton N.J.   *area*–749 95
Bridgnorth Salop Eng.   *area*–424 59
Bridgwater Somerset Eng.   *area*–423 81
Bridle paths *see* Roads
Bridlington Humberside Eng.
        area–428 39
Bridport Dorset Eng.   *area*–423 31
Brie cheeses
  dairy tech.   637.353
  other aspects see Cheeses
Briefcases
  manufacturing
    soc. & econ. aspects *see*
      Secondary industries
  technology   685.51
Briefs
  rel. law   262.91
  s.a. Appellate procedure
Brierfield Lancashire Eng.   *area*–427 645
Brigades
  mil. organization   355.31
  s.a. spec. mil. branches
Brigand troops
  mil. sci.   356.15
Brigg Humberside Eng.   *area*–428 32

Brighouse West Yorkshire Eng.
    area–428 12
Brightlingsea Essex Eng.   *area*–426 725
Brightness
  celestial bodies
    Jupiter   523.452
    Mars   523.432
    Mercury   523.412
    moon   523.32
    Neptune   523.481 2
    Pluto   523.482 2
    Saturn   523.462
    Uranus   523.472
    Venus   523.422
    s.a. other spec. bodies
  perception psych.
    gen. wks.   152.143
      animals   156.214 3
      children   155.412
    s.a. psych. of other spec.
      groups
    influences   155.911 43
Brighton East Sussex Eng.   *area*–422 56
Bright's disease *see* Nephritis
Brigs *see* Modern wind-driven
    vessels
Brill's disease *see* Epidemic
    typhus
Brindisi Italy   *area*–457 54
Brines *see* Saline waters
Brining foods   641.46
  commercial   664.028 6
  domestic   641.46
  other aspects see Foods
  s.a. spec. foods e.g. Meats
Brinjal *see* Eggplants
Briquettes
  manufacturing
    soc. & econ. aspects *see*
      Secondary industries
    technology   662.65
Brisbane
  city Qld.   *area*–943 1
  River Qld.   *area*–943 2
  Waters Nat. Park N.S.W.
                 area–944 2
Briscoe Co. Tex.   *area*–764 839
Bristles
  animal husbandry for   636.088 45
  s.a. spec. animals
  products
    manufacturing
      soc. & econ. aspects *see*
        Secondary industries
    technology   679.6
Bristletails
  zoology   595.713
  other aspects see Apterygota
Bristol
  Bay election district Alaska
                 area–798 4

Bristol (continued)
  board *see* Paperboard
  Channel *see* British western
      seawaters
  city
    Avon Eng.   *area*–423 93
    Virginia   *area*–755 726
  County
    Massachusetts   *area*–744 85
    Rhode Island   *area*–745 5
Britain *see* British Isles
British
  Columbia   *area*–711
  Commonwealth   *area*–171 241
    s.a. spec. countries &
      regions
  Empire *see* British
    Commonwealth
  Guiana   *area*–881
  Honduras   *area*–728 2
  Isles   *area*–41
    ancient   *area*–361
  North America Act
    Canada hist.   971.049
  people   *r.e.n.*–2
  period Cyprus hist.   956.450 3
    s.a. spec. events & subj.
      e.g. Commerce
  pronunciation Eng. lang.   421.55
  sculpture   730.941
    ancient   732.6
  spelling Eng. lang.   421.55
  system
    mensuration   530.813
    s.a. spec. branches of
      physics
    metrology   389.15
  Virgin Isls.   *area*–729 725
  western seawaters
    oceanography   551.461 37
    regional subj. trmt.   *area*–163 37
    other aspects see Atlantic
      Ocean
    s.a. spec. kinds e.g.
      English; *also other*
      spec. subj. e.g. Arts
Brittany   *area*–441
Brittle stars *see* Ophiuroidea
Brittleness
  eng. materials
    properties affecting   620.112 6
    s.a. spec. materials &
      spec. uses
Brixham Devon Eng.   *area*–423 595
Broaching-tools
  soc. & econ. aspects *see*
    Secondary industries
  tech. & mf.   621.954
    s.a. spec. appls. e.g.
      Agricultural equipment

Broad
  beans
    agriculture   635.651
      soc. & econ. aspects *see*
        Primary industries
    foods   641.356 51
      preparation
        commercial   664.805 651
        domestic   641.656 51
      other aspects see
        Papilionaceae; *also*
        Vegetables
  River S.C.   *area*–757 41
Broadcast
  advertising   659.14
  drama
    gen. wks.
      collections   808.822
      hist. & crit.   809.22
      'rhetoric   808.22
      juvenile   808.068 22
    presentation   791.44–.45
    spec. lits.   *lit. sub.*–202
    indiv. authors   *lit. sub.*–21–29
    other aspects see Drama
Broadcasting
  activities
    radio *see*
      Radiocommunication
    television *see* Television
      communication
  channels commun. ind.
    commerce
      radio   384.545 2
      television   384.554 52
        subscription   384.554 7
      govt. control   351.874
      spec. jur.   353–354
    law *see* Television
      communication law
  frequencies *see* Broadcasting
    channels
  networks
    commun. ind.
      commerce
        radio   384.545 5
        television   384.554 55
          subscription   384.554 7
        govt. control   351.874
        spec. jur.   353–354
      law *see* Television
        communication law
    financial aspects *see*
      Communications media
  satellites *see* Communications
    satellites
  services
    commerce
      radio   384.544
      television   384.554 4
        community antenna   384.555 64

Broadcasting
  services
    commerce
      television (continued)
        subscription   384.554 7
      govt. control   351.874
      spec. jur.   353–354
    law *see* Radiocommunication
      law
  stations
    commun. ind.
      commerce
        radio   384.545 3
        television   384.554 53
          community antenna   384.555 65
          subscription   384.554 7
        govt. control   351.874
        spec. jur.   353–354
      law *see*
        Radiocommunication law
    engineering
      radio *see* Stations radio
        engineering
      television   621.388 62
      misc. aspects see
        Television
      s.a. spec. appls. e.g.
        Astronautics
    financial aspects *see*
      Communications media
Broadcloth *see spec. composition*
  e.g. Cotton textiles
Broadford Vic.   *area*–945 3
Broad-gauge railroads
  transportation *see* Railroad
    transportation
  other aspects see Railroad
Broadland Norfolk Eng.   *area*–426 17
Broad-leaved trees
  woods *see* Hardwoods
Broadloom carpets & rugs *see*
  Rugs
Broadsides
  direct advertising   659.133
  library trmt.   025.172
    acquisitions   025.282
    cataloging   025.342
    s.a. other spec. activities
Broadstairs Kent Eng.   *area*–422 357
Broadwater Co. Mont.   *area*–786 664
Brocades *see* Jacquard-weave
  fabrics
Brocatelles *see* Jacquard-weave
  fabrics
Broccoli
  agriculture   635.35
    soc. & econ. aspects *see*
      Primary industries
  foods   641.353 5
    preparation
      commercial   664.805 35

Broccoli
  foods
    preparation (continued)
      domestic   641.643 5
    other aspects see Cruciales;
      also Vegetables
Brochures
  museology   069.57
  s.a. other spec. subj.
Broiling
  cookery technique   641.76
Broken
  Hill N.S.W.   *area*–944 9
  homes *see* Families
    dissolution
Brokerage firms
  govt. control *see* Investments
    govt. control
  investment econ.   332.62
  law   346.092 6
    spec. jur.   346.3–.9
Brokopondo Surinam   *area*–883 9
Bromates
  chem. tech.   661.42
  other aspects see Industrial
    chemicals
Bromberg Poland   *area*–438 2
Brome Co. Que.   *area*–714 64
Bromeliaceae *see* Bromeliales
Bromeliales
  botany   584.22
  floriculture   635.934 22
  med. aspects
    crop prod.   633.884 22
    gen. pharm.   615.324 22
      toxicology   615.952 422
    vet. pharm.   636.089 532 422
      toxicology 636.089 595 242 2
  paleobotany   561.4
  other aspects see Plants
Bromides
  chem. tech.   661.42
  other aspects see Industrial
    chemicals
Bromine
  chemistry
    inorganic   546.733
    organic   547.02
    s.a. spec. groupings e.g.
      Aliphatic compounds
  technology   661.073 3
    soc. & econ. aspects *see*
      Secondary industries
    s.a. spec. prod.
  pharmacology   615.273 3
    misc. aspects see
      Pharmacology
  toxicology   615.925 733
    misc. aspects see
      Toxicology
  other aspects see Halogen

Bromites
  chem. tech.   661.42
  other aspects see Industrial
    chemicals
Bromley London Eng.   *area*–421 78
Bromoil process
  photographic printing   773.8
Bromsgrove Hereford & Worcester
    Eng.   *area*–424 42
Bromyard Hereford & Worcester
    Eng.   *area*–424 47
Bronchi
  anatomy
    human   611.23
    other aspects see
      Respiratory organs
  diseases
    gen. wks.   616.23
      neoplasms   616.992 23
      tuberculosis   616.995 23
    geriatrics   618.976 23
    pediatrics   618.922 3
    pub. health   614.592 3
    statistics   312.323
      deaths   312.262 3
    surgery   617.544
      anesthesiology 617.967 544
    other aspects see Diseases
  physical anthropometry   573.623
  physiology
    human   612.2
    other aspects see
      Respiration
  tissue biology human   611.018 923
Bronchial asthma *see* Asthma
Bronchiectasis *see* Bronchi
    diseases
Bronchitis
  gen. med.   616.234
  geriatrics   618.076 234
  pediatrics   618.922 34
  pub. health   614.592 34
  statistics   312.323 4
    deaths   312.262 34
  other aspects see Diseases
Bronchopneumonia *see* Pneumonias
Broncos
  animal husbandry   636.16
  other aspects see Horses
Bronx Co. N.Y.   *area*–747 275
Bronze
  Age
    archaeology   930.15
  arts
    decorative   739.512
    other aspects see Metals
      arts
  sculpture
    dec. arts   739.512
    fine arts
      casting tech.   731.456

Bronze
  sculpture
    fine arts (continued)
      other aspects see Metals
        sculpture
  other aspects see Copper

Brooches
  precious metalwork   739.278
  other aspects see Jewelry

Brooke Co. W. Va.   *area*–754 13
Brookings Co. S.D.   *area*–783 272
Brooklyn N.Y.   *area*–747 23

Brooks Co.
  Georgia   *area*–758 874
  Texas   *area*–764 475

Brooks (streams) *see* Streams

Broomcorn
  millet
    agriculture
      food crops   633.171 7
      forage crops   633.257 17
    other aspects see Millets
  sorghum
    agriculture
      food crops   633.174 7
      forage crops   633.257 47
    other aspects see Sorghums

Broome
  Co. N.Y.   *area*–747 75
  W. Aust.   *area*–941 4

Brooms
  manufacturing
    soc. & econ. aspects *see*
      Secondary industries
    technology   679.6

Brotherhoods
  religion *see* Religious
    congregations
  s.a. other spec. subj.

Brothers
  of the Christian Schools *see*
    Christian Brothers
  rel. orders
    Christianity   255.092
      church hist.   271.092
      ecclesiology   262.24
    other rel. see Religious
      congregations
  siblings *see* Siblings

Brotton Cleveland Eng.   *area*–428 54
Broward Co. Fla.   *area*–759 35

Brown
  algae *see* Phaeophyta
  coal   553.22
    econ. geol.   553.22
    mining
      soc. & econ. aspects *see*
        Primary industries
      technology   622.332
        prospecting   622.182 2
      processing   662.622 2

Brown
  coal (continued)
    other aspects see Coals
    s.a. spec. uses
  County
    Illinois   *area*–773 473
    Indiana   *area*–772 253
    Kansas   *area*–781 34
    Minnesota   *area*–776 31
    Nebraska   *area*–782 736
    Ohio   *area*–771 796
    South Dakota   *area*–783 144
    Texas   *area*–764 548
    Wisconsin   *area*–775 61
  John raid
    U.S. Civil War causes   973.711 6
  wrapper papers
    mf. tech.   676.287
    other aspects see Papers
      pulp prod.

Brownhills West Midlands Eng.
               area–424 92

Brownian motion
  particle dynamics   531.163

Brownies
  lit. & stage trmt. *see*
    Supernatural beings

Brownouts
  mil. eng.   623.77

Broxbourne Hertfordshire Eng.
               area–425 87

Broxtowe Nottinghamshire Eng.
               area–425 26

Bruce Co. Ont.   *area*–713 21

Brucellosis *see* Undulant fever

Brucite
  mineralogy   549.53

Bruises *see* Contusions

Brule Co. S.D.   *area*–783 381

Brunch
  cookery home econ.   641.53
  soc. customs   394.15

Brunei   *area*–595 5

Brunelliaceae *see* Cunoniales
Bruniaceae *see* Hamamelidales
Brunoniaceae *see* Goodeniales

Brunswick Co.
  North Carolina   *area*–756 29
  Virginia   *area*–755 575

Bruny Isl. Tas.   *area*–946 2

Brush
  disposal silviculture   634.955
    s.a. spec. trees
  drawing arts   741.26
    indiv. artists   741.092
    spec. appls.   741.5–.7
    spec. subj.   743.4–.8

Brushes
  manufacturing
    soc. & econ. aspects *see*
      Secondary industries

Brushes
  manufacturing (continued)
    technology 679.6
  use in painting
    buildings 698.102 82
      s.a. spec. surfaces e.g.
        Floors painting bldgs.
    s.a. other spec. uses
Brushes (generators)
  electrodynamic eng.
    soc. & econ. aspects *see*
      Secondary industries
    tech. & mf. 621.316
      s.a. spec. appls. e.g.
        Ignition systems &
        devices
    other aspects see
      Electrodynamics
Brushing
  clothing
    home econ. 646.6
Brussels
  city Belgium area–493 3
  griffon
    animal husbandry 636.76
    other aspects see Dogs
  sprouts
    agriculture 635.36
      soc. & econ. aspects *see*
        Primary industries
    foods 641.353 6
      preparation
        commercial 664.805 36
        domestic 641.653 6
      other aspects see
        Cruciales; *also*
        Vegetables
Bruttium ancient area–377
Bryales *see* Musci
Bryan Co.
  Georgia area–758 732
  Oklahoma area–766 62
Bryansk RSFSR area–476 2
Bryce Canyon Nat. Park Utah
                     area–792 52
Brynmawr Gwent Wales area–429 95
Bryophyta
  botany 588
  floriculture 635.938
  med. aspects
    crop prod. 633.888
    gen. pharm. 615.322
      toxicology 615.952 8
    vet. pharm. 636.089 532 2
      toxicology 636.089 595 28
  paleobotany 561.8
  other aspects see Plants
Bryozoa
  culture 639.7
  paleozoology 564.7
  zoology 594.7

Bryozoa (continued)
  other aspects see
    Molluscoidea
Brythonic *see* Celtic
Bubbles *see* Surface phenomena
Bubonic plague
  gen. med. 616.923 2
  geriatrics 618.976 923 2
  pediatrics 618.929 232
  pub. health 614.573 2
  statistics 312.392 32
    deaths 312.269 232
  other aspects see Diseases
Buccal *see* Mouth
Buccaneers
  travel 910.453
    misc. aspects see Travel
Bucerotes *see* Coraciiformes
Buchan Caves Vic. area–945 6
Buchanan
  County
    Iowa area–777 382
    Missouri area–778 132
    Virginia area–755 752
  James admin.
    U.S. hist. 973.68
      s.a. spec. events & subj.
        e.g. Commerce
Bucharest Romania area–498 2
Buck-bean family *see*
  Gentianales
Buckets
  mining eng. 622.68
  s.a. other spec. uses
Buckfastleigh Devon Eng. area–423 55
Buckhaven & Methill Fife Scot.
                     area–412 95
Buckie Grampian Scot. area–412 23
Buckingham
  city Eng. area–425 93
  Co. Va. area–755 623
Buckinghamshire Eng. area–425 9
Buckles
  precious metalwork 739.278
  other aspects see Jewelry
Buckley Clwyd Wales area–429 36
Bucks Co.
  chickens
    animal husbandry 636.581
    other aspects see Chickens
  Pennsylvania area–748 21
Buckthorn family *see* Rhamnales
Buckwheat
  agriculture
    food crops 633.12
    forage crops 633.252
    soc. & econ. aspects *see*
      Primary industries
  flour & metal
    comm. proc. 664.725

Buckwheat (continued)
foods   641.331 2
  cookery   641.631 2
other aspects see
       Polygonales; *also*
       Cereal grains
Bucuresti Romania   *area*–498 2
Budapest Hungary   *area*–439 1
Buddha
  art representation *see*
       Buddhism art
       representation
  religion   294.363
Buddhism
  art representation   704.948 943
  s.a. spec. art forms
  calendars   529.324 3
  cookery   641.567 43
  philosophy   181.043
  regions subj. trmt.   *area*–176 43
  religion   294.3
  rel. holidays   394.268 294 3
  schools   377.943
Buddhist
  arts *see* South Asian arts
  monastic bldgs.
    architecture   726.784 3
    building   690.678 43
    other aspects see
       Religious-purpose
       bldgs.
  music *see* Buddhist sacred
       music
  philosophy   181.043
  regions subj. trmt.   *area*–176 43
  religion *see* Buddhism
  sacred music
    arts   783.029 43
    recordings   789.912 302 943
    s.a. spec. instruments;
      also spec. kinds e.g.
      Liturgical music
    religion
      pub. worship   294.343 8
      significance   294.343 7
  temples & shrines
    architecture   726.143
    building   690.614 3
    other aspects see
       Religious-purpose
       bldgs.
Buddhists
  biog. & work   294.309 2
  s.a. spec. kinds e.g.
      Clergy; *also spec.*
      branches
  s.a.   *pers.*–294 3
Buddleiaceae *see* Loganiales
Bude-Stratton Cornwall Eng.
        area–423 71

Budgerigars
  animal husbandry   636.686 4
  soc. & econ. aspects *see*
       Primary industries
  other aspects see
       Psittaciformes
Budget
  counseling
    soc. services *see* Poor
      people soc. services
  instructions *see* Budget
    manuals
  manuals
    pub. admin.   350.722 202 02
    central govts.   351.722 202 02
    spec. jur.   353–354
    local govts.   352.122 020 2
  rules *see* Budget manuals
  systems
    pub. admin. *see* Budgeting
      admin.
Budgeting
  financial management   658.154
    spec. subj.   *s.s.*–068 1
  legislative bodies *see*
      Financial powers
  pub. admin.   350.722
    central govts.   351.722
    spec. jur.   353–354
    local govts.   352.12
  s.a. other spec. appls.; also
      Money-saving
Budgets
  deficits
    macroeconomics   339.523
    home econ.   640.42
  in brief *see* Digests of
    budgets
  pub. admin.   350.722 52
    central govts.   351.722 52
    spec. jur.   353–354
    local govts.   352.125 2
  pub. law   343.034
    spec. jur.   343.3–.9
  surpluses
    macroeconomics   339.523
  other aspects see Finance
Budleigh Salterton Devon Eng.
        area–423 57
Buds
  use in plant propagation   631.533
  s.a. spec. crops; also spec.
      types of culture e.g.
      Floriculture
Buena Vista
  city Va.   *area*–755 851
  Co. Ia.   *area*–777 18
Buenos Aires Argentina
  city   *area*–821 1
  province   *area*–821 2

Buffalo
berries
  agriculture   634.74
  soc. & econ. aspects *see*
    Primary industries
  foods   641.347 4
  preparation
    commercial   664.804 74
    domestic   641.647 4
  other aspects see
    Rhamnales; *also*
    Fruits
city N.Y.   *area*–747 97
County
  Nebraska   *area*–782 45
  South Dakota   *area*–783 31
  Wisconsin   *area*–775 48
Mount Vic.   *area*–945 5
Buffaloes
animal husbandry   636.293
bison   636.292
other aspects see Bovoidea
Buffers
railroad eng.
  technology   625.25
  other aspects see Rolling
    stock railroads
Buffet-car cookery home econ.   641.576
Buffets (furniture) *see*
  Cabinets (furniture)
Buffing
metal prod.
  mf. tech.   671.72
    ferrous metals   672.72
    s.a. other spec. metals
  other aspects see Finishing
Buffing-tools *see* Lapping-tools
Bufonidae
zoology   597.87
other aspects see Anura
Buganda
kingdom
  history   967.610 1
  s.a. spec. events & subj.
    e.g. Commerce
s.a.   *area*–676 1
Bugey France   *area*–444 4
Bugging equipment *see*
  Eavesdropping devices
Bugle
corps *see* Band
music   788.15
recordings   789.912 81
Bugles
mf. tech.   681.818 1
  misc. aspects see Musical
    instruments
musical art   788.1
Bugs *see* Heteroptera

Builders
biog. & work   690.092
  s.a. spec. kinds
s.a.   *pers.*–69
Building
& loan associations
  banking econ.   332.32
  other aspects see Banks
    (finance)
construction *see* Buildings
  construction
cooperatives econ.   334.1
laws *see* Secondary industries
  govt. control
materials
  arch. construction   721.044
  technology   691
  s.a. spec. kinds of bldgs. &
    materials
papers
  mf. tech.   676.289
  other aspects see Papers
    pulp prod.
s.a. Construction
Buildings
architecture   720
art representation *see*
  Architecture art
  representation
capital *see* Fixed capital
civic art   711.6
codes
  enforcement *see* Civil laws
    enforcement
construction
  mil. sci.   358.3
  pub. admin.   352.922
    procurement   350.712
    s.a. spec. levels of
    govt.
  soc. & econ. aspects *see*
    Secondary industries
  technology   690
inspection
  local govt. control   352.92
investment finance   332.632 43
  misc. aspects see Real
    property
landscape design   717
local Christian parishes   254.7
management & disposal
  pub. admin.   350.713 3
  central govts.   351.713 3
  spec. jur.   353–354
  local govts.   352.163 3
procurement
  pub. admin.   350.712 3
  central govts.   351.712 3
  spec. jur.   353–354
  local govts.   352.162 3
sale & rental   333.338

Buildings (continued)
  taxes *see* Property taxes
  other aspects see Structures
  s.a. spec. kinds & other spec.
      uses e.g. Library
        buildings
Builth Wells Powys Wales   *area*–429 56
Built-in furniture
  dec. arts   749.4
  mf. tech.   684.16
    outdoor   684.18
  wooden bldg. construction   694.6
  other aspects see Furniture
Buka Isls. Solomons   *area*–935
Bukhara rugs
  textile arts   746.758 7
Bukidno Philippines   *area*–599 7
Bukoba Tanzania   *area*–678 27
Bukovina   *area*–498 4
  Romania   *area*–498 4
  Ukraine   *area*–477 18
Bulacan Philippines   *area*–599 1
Bulbs (lamps) *see* Electric
    lighting
Bulbs (plants)
  crop prod.   631.526
  s.a. spec. crops; also spec.
      types of culture e.g.
        Floriculture
  plants grown from
    floriculture   635.944
    s.a. spec. plants
  use in plant propagation   631.532
  s.a. spec. crops; also spec.
      types of culture e.g.
        Floriculture
  s.a. Edible bulbs
Bulganin regime USSR hist.   947.085 2
  s.a. spec. events & subj.
      e.g. Commerce
Bulgaria   *area*–497 7
Bulgarian
  language
    linguistics   491.81
    literature   891.81
    s.a.   *lang.*–918 11
  Macedonia   *area*–497 74
  people   *r.e.n.*–918 11
  s.a. Bulgaria; *also other*
      spec. subj. e.g. Arts
Bulk
  carrier (ships) *see* Cargo
      ships powered
  mailings
    postal commun.   383.124
    other aspects see Postal
      communication
  modulus
    engineering *see* Dynamics
    physics   531.381
Bulkley Mts. B.C.   *area*–711 2

Bull
  mastiff
    animal husbandry   636.73
    other aspects see Dogs
  Moose Party U.S.
    pol. sci.   324.273 2
    s.a. spec. subj. of concern
      e.g. Social problems
  Run Battles
    U.S. hist.
      1861   973.731
      1862   973.732
  Shoals Lake Ark.   *area*–767 193
Bulldogs
  animal husbandry   636.72
  other aspects see Dogs
Bulldozers *see* Work automobiles
Bulletin boards
  ed. use   371.335 6
    s.a. spec. levels of ed.;
      also Special education
  management use   658.455
Bullets
  mil. eng.
    soc. & econ. aspects *see*
      Secondary industries
    tech. & mf.   623.455
Bullfights
  ethics *see* Animal combat
    sports
  performing arts   791.82
Bullis fever
  gen. med.   616.922 6
  geriatrics   618.976 922 6
  pediatrics   618.929 226
  pub. health   614.526 6
  statistics   312.392 26
    deaths   312.269 226
  other aspects see Diseases
Bullitt Co. Ky.   *area*–769 453
Bulloch Co. Ga   *area*–758 766
Bullock Co. Ala.   *area*–761 483
Bulls *see spec. animals e.g.*
    Cattle
Bumpers
  automobiles   629.276
Bunbury W. Aust.   *area*–941 2
Buncombe Co. N.C.   *area*–756 88
Bundaberg Qld.   *area*–943 2
Bundling *see* Courtship
Bungalows *see* Single-story
    houses
Bungay Suffolk Eng.   *area*–426 41
Bunker
  Hill Battle
    U.S. hist.   973.331 2
  oils
    chem. tech.   665.538 8
    other aspects see Petroleum

Bunsen burners
  chemistry   542.4
    s.a. spec. appls. e.g.
        Organic chemistry
Buntings *see* Fringillidae
Bunts
  wheat disease   633.119 427
Bunya
  Mts. Qld.   *area*–943 2
  Nat. Park Qld.   *area*–943 2
Bunyoro
  kingdom
    history   967.610 1
    s.a. spec. events & subj.
      e.g. Commerce
  s.a.   *area*–676 1
Buoyancy
  statics *see* Statics
Buoys
  hydraulic eng.
    technology   627.924
    s.a. spec. appls. e.g.
      Piloting seamanship
    other aspects see Liquids
      engineering
  navigation   623.894 4
  other aspects see Navigation
    aids
Burdekin River Qld.   *area*–943 6
Burdur Turkey   *area*–562
Bureau Co. Ill.   *area*–773 372
Bureaucracy
  pub. admin.   350.001
    central govts.   351.001
    U.S. govts.
      federal   353.01
      states   353.911
        spec. states   353.97–.99
        other   354
    local govts.   352
  sociology   302.35
Burettes *see*
    Measuring-instruments
Burgas Bulgaria   *area*–497 78
Burgenland Austria   *area*–436 15
Burgess Hill West Sussex Eng.
                area–422 65
Burgesses *see* Legislators
Burghead Grampian Scot. *area*–412 23
Burglar alarms
  engineering *see*
    Public-address systems
  other aspects see Warning
    systems
Burglarproofing
  household management 643.16
Burglary *see* Larceny
Burgos Spain   *area*–463 53
Burgundian *see* East Germanic
Burgundy France   *area*–444
Burhou isl.   *area*–423 47

Burial
  of dead
    customs   393.1
    rites *see* Death rel. rites
    other aspects see Dead
      bodies disposal human
  of Jesus Christ
    Christian doctrines 232.964
  of refuse
    technology   628.445 64
    other aspects see Refuse
      pub. sanitation
  of sewage sludge
    technology   628.364–.366
    other aspects see Sewage
      disposal
Buriat
  ASSR   *area*–575
  other aspects see Mongolic
Buried treasure
  lit. & stage trmt. *see* Things
  travel   910.453
    misc. aspects see Travel
Burke Co.
  Georgia   *area*–758 65
  North Carolina   *area*–756 85
  North Dakota   *area*–784 72
Burlap *see* Hemp textiles
Burleigh Co. N.D.   *area*–784 77
Burleson Co. Tex.   *area*–764 241
Burlesque
  stage presentation   792.7
Burlington
  city Vt.   *area*–743 17
  Co. N.J.   *area*–749 61
Burma   *area*–591
Burmanniaceae *see* Burmanniales
Burmanniales
  botany   584.13
  floriculture   635.934 13
  med. aspects
    crop prod.   633.884 13
    gen. pharm.   615.324 13
      toxicology   615.952 413
    vet. pharm.   636.089 532 413
      toxicology   636.089 595 241 3
  paleobotany   561.4
  other aspects see Plants
Burmese
  arts *see* Southeast Asian arts
  cats
    animal husbandry 636.825
    other aspects see Cats
  language
    linguistics   495.8
    literature   895.8
    s.a.   *lang.*–958
  people   *r.e.n.*–958
  s.a. Burma; *also other spec.*
    subj.
Burnet Co. Tex.   *area*–764 63

Burnet-Llano region Tex.	*area*–764 6
Burnett	
Co. Wis.	*area*–755 14
River Qld.	*area*–943 2
Burnham-on-Crouch Essex Eng.	
	area–426 756
Burnham-on-Sea Somerset Eng.	
	area–423 81
Burnie Tas.	*area*–946 5
Burning	
explosives *see* Propellant	
explosives	
Burnley Lancashire Eng.	*area*–427 642
Burns	
first aid *see* First aid	
statistics	312.304 711
deaths	312.260 471 1
surgery	617.11
anesthesiology	617.967 11
s.a. Veterinary sciences	
Burntisland Fife Scot.	*area*–412 95
Bur-reed family *see*	
Sparganiaceae	
Burros *see* Asses	
Burry Port Dyfed Wales	*area*–429 67
Bursa Turkey	*area*–563
Bursae	
diseases	
gen. wks.	616.76
neoplasms	616.992 75
tuberculosis	616.995 75
geriatrics	618.976 76
pediatrics	618.927 6
pub. health	614.597 6
statistics	312.376
deaths	312.267 6
surgery	617.475
anesthesiology	617.967 475
other aspects see Diseases	
human anatomy	611.75
physical anthropometry	573.675
physiology	
human	612.75
other aspects see Movements	
tissue biology human	611.018 975
Burseraceae *see* Rutales	
Bursitis *see* Bursae diseases	
Burt Co. Neb.	*area*–782 243
Burton	
Latimer Northamptonshire Eng.	
	area–425 52
upon Trent Staffordshire Eng.	
	area–424 65
Burundi	*area*–675 72
Burundis	*r.e.n.*–967 572
Bury	
Greater Manchester Eng.	*area*–427 38
Saint Edmunds Suffolk Eng.	
	area–426 44
Buryat	
ASSR	*area*–575

Buryat (continued)	
other aspects see Mongolic	
Burying-beetles	
zoology	595.764 2
other aspects see Polyphaga	
Bus	
cookery	641.575 2
drivers	
biog. & work	388.322 092
s.a.	*pers.*–388
services *see* Passenger	
transportation	
stations *see* Bus terminals &	
stops	
stops *see* Bus terminals &	
stops	
terminal bldgs.	
transportation aspects *see*	
Bus terminals & stops	
terminals & stops	
activities *see* Passenger	
services	
facilities	
gen. wks.	
commerce	388.33
govt. control	350.878 3
central govts.	351.878 3
spec. jur.	353–354
local govts.	352.918 3
law	
international	341.756 882
municipal	343.094 82
spec. jur.	343.3–.9
local	
commerce	388.473
govt. control	350.878 473
central govts.	351.878 473
spec. jur.	353–354
local govts.	352.918 473
law	343.098 2
spec. jur.	343.3–.9
transportation	
gen. wks.	
commerce	388.322
govt. control	350.878 322
central govts.	351.878 322
spec. jur.	353–354
local govts.	352.918 322
law	
international	341.756 882
municipal	343.094 82
spec. jur.	343.3–.9
local transit	
commerce	388.413 22
govt. control	350.878 413 22
central govts.	351.878 413 22
spec. jur.	353–354
local govts.	352.918 413 22
law	343.098 2
spec. jur.	343.3–.9

Business (continued)

libraries	027.69
administration	025.197 69
buildings	
architecture	727.826 9
functional planning	022.316 9
catalogs *see* Library	
catalogs	
reference services	025.527 769
selection for	025.218 769
use studies	025.587 69
user orientation	025.567 69
s.a. other spec. activities	
e.g. Cataloging	
location	
economics	338.09
management	658.11
losses	
tax reductions	
law	343.052 36
spec. jur.	343.3–.9
pub. finance	336.206
s.a. spec. kinds of	
taxes e.g. Income	
taxes	
machines	
manufacturing	
soc. & econ. aspects *see*	
Secondary industries	
technology	681.14
management	658
spec. subj.	*s.s.*–068
news	
reporting	070.433
use in investment analysis	332.632 042
offenses	
criminology	364.168
law	345.026 8
spec. jur.	345.3–.9
soc. theology	
Christianity	261.833 168
comp. rel.	291.178 331 68
s.a. other spec. rel.	
school bldgs.	
architecture	727.465
building	690.746 5
other aspects see	
Educational buildings	
security management	658.47
success	650.1
taxes	
law	343.068
spec. jur.	343.3–.9
pub. admin. *see* Taxes pub.	
admin.	
pub. finance econ.	336.207
other aspects see Managerial	
sciences	
s.a. Commercial; *also*	
Mercantile; *also*	
Economic	

Busing school students	
education	
ethnic aspects	370.193 42
gen. wks.	371.872
s.a. spec. levels of ed.;	
also Special education	
law	344.079 8
spec. jur.	344.3–.9
Buskerud Norway	*area*–482
Busoga	
kindgom	
history	967.610 1
s.a. spec. events & subj.	
e.g. Commerce	
s.a.	*area*–676 1
Busts	
sculpture	731.74
spec. periods & schools	732–735
Butadiene-styrene rubbers *see*	
Synthetic rubber	
Butane	
chem. tech.	665.773
soc. & econ. aspects *see*	
Secondary industries	
Butcher papers	
mf. tech.	676.287
other aspects see Papers pulp	
prod.	
Bute Scot.	*area*–414 23
Butene	
chem. tech.	665.773
soc. & econ. aspects *see*	
Secondary industries	
Butler Co.	
Alabama	*area*–761 37
Iowa	*area*–777 29
Kansas	*area*–781 88
Kentucky	*area*–769 755
Missouri	*area*–778 93
Nebraska	*area*–782 322
Ohio	*area*–771 75
Pennsylvania	*area*–748 91
Butlers *see* Household employees	
Butomaceae *see* Butomales	
Butomales	
botany	584.73
floriculture	635.934 73
med. aspects	
crop. prod.	633.884 73
gen. pharm.	615.324 73
toxicology	615.952 473
vet. pharm.	636.089 532 473
toxicology	636.089 595 247 3
paleobotany	561.4
other aspects see Plants	
Butte	
city Mont.	*area*–786 68
County	
California	*area*–794 32
Idaho	*area*–796 59
South Dakota	*area*–783 43

C

C* algebras
  & groups   512.55
    s.a. spec. appls. e.g.
        Engineering
CARE
  soc. welfare   361.77
    spec. problems & groups   362.363
    other aspects see Welfare
      services
CAT
  air transp. hazard   363.124 12
CATV *see* Community antenna
    television
CBW
  biological *see* Biological
    warfare
  chemical mil. sci.   358.34
CENTO
  mil. sci.   355.031 095 6
COBOL *see* Program languages
COD mail
  postal commun.   383.184
  other aspects see Postal
    communication
CPM *see* Systems analysis
Caaguazú Paraguay   *area*–892 134
Caazapá Paraguay   *area*–892 127
Cab drivers *see* Taxicab drivers
Cabalah
  Jewish mysticism
    experience   296.71
    movement   296.833
    Judaistic sources   296.16
Cabalistic traditions
  occultism   135.4
Cabañas El Salvador   *area*–728 426
Cabarets
  stage performance   792.7
Cabarrus Co. N.C.   *area*–756 72
Cabbages
  agriculture   635.34
    soc. & econ. aspects *see*
      Primary industries
  foods   641.353 4
    preparation
      commercial   664.805 34
      domestic   641.653 4
  other aspects see Cruciales;
    also Vegetables
Cabell Co. W. Va.   *area*–754 42
Cabin pressurization
  aircraft eng.
    soc. & econ. aspects *see*
      Secondary industries
    tech. & mf.   629.134 42
  s.a. other spec. appls.
Cabinda Angola   *area*–673 1

Cabinet
  members
    biog. & work *see spec.*
      countries & spec.
      subj.
    s.a.   *pers.*–352 1
    Mts. Mont.   *area*–786 8
  organs *see* Reed organs
  systems
    pol. sci.   321.804 3
    s.a. spec. jur.
Cabinets (furniture)
  dec. arts   749.3
  mf. tech.   684.16
    outdoor   684.18
  other aspects see Furniture
Cabinets (govt. agencies)
  pub. admin.   351.004
    U.S. govt.   353.04
    other central govts.   354
Cabinetwork
  arts *see* Wood arts
  furniture *see* Wood furniture
Cabins
  aircraft eng.
    soc. & econ. aspects *see*
      Secondary industries
    tech. & mf.   629.134 45
  buildings
    architecture   728.73
    building   690.873
    other aspects see
      Residential buildings
Cable
  commun. systems *see* Wire
    communications systems
  railways
    technology   625.5
    other aspects see Mountain
      railways
  television *see* Community
    antenna television
Cables
  elect. circuits
    electrodynamic eng.
      soc. & econ. aspects *see*
        Secondary industries
      tech. & mf.   621.319 34
      s.a. spec. appls. e.g.
        Underground lines
    other aspects see
      Electrodynamics
  knotting & splicing   623.888 2
  metal prod. *see* Drawn metal
    prod.
  structural eng.
    gen. wks.   624.177 4
    concretes   624.183 44
    s.a. other spec.
      materials
    naval arch.   623.817 74

Caerleon Gwent Wales   *area*–429 91
Caernarvon Gwynedd Wales*area*–429 25
Caernarvonshire Wales   *area*–429 2
Caerphilly Mid Glamorgan Wales
       area–429 76
Caesalpiniaceae
   botany   583.323
   floriculture   635.933 323
   forestry   634.973 323
   med. aspects
     crop prod.   633.883 323
     gen. pharm.   615.323 323
       toxicology   615.952 332 3
     vet. pharm.   636.089 532 332 3
       toxicology   636.089 595 233 23
   paleobotany   561.3
   other aspects see Plants
Caesarean section
   obstetrical surgery   618.86
   vet. med.   636.089 886
     s.a. spec. animals
Caesium *see* Cesium
Café
   Filho admin. Brazil hist.   981.061
     s.a. spec. events & subj.
       e.g. Commerce
   orchestras   785.066 2
     s.a. spec. kinds of music
Cafés
   food services   642.5
   other aspects see
       Eating-places
Cafeterias
   food services   642.5
   other aspects see
       Eating-places
Caffeine *see* Alkaloids
Cagayan Philippines   *area*–599 1
Cage birds
   animal husbandry   636.686
   soc. & econ. aspects *see*
       Primary industries
Cages (elevators)
   mining eng.   622.68
Cages (shelter)
   animal husbandry   636.083 1
   s.a. spec. animals
Cagliari Sardinia   *area*–459 1
Caicos Isls.   *area*–729 61
Cairngorm Mts. Grampian Scot.
       area–412 4
Cairns Qld.   *area*–943 6
Cairo Egypt   *area*–621 6
Caisson disease *see*
       Decompression sickness
Caissons
   foundation eng.   624.157
   s.a. spec. appls. e.g.
       Bridges (structures)
       structural eng.
   gun mounts *see* Gun mounts

Caistor Lincolnshire Eng.   *area*–425 31
Caithness Scot.   *area*–411 62
Cajamarca Peru   *area*–851 5
Cake mixes
   comm. proc.   664 753
Cakes (animal feeds) *see*
       Formula feeds
Cakes (pastry)
   comm. proc.   664.752 5
   cookery home econ.   641.865 3
Calabria Italy (heel) ancient
       area–377
Calabria Italy (toe)   *area*–457 8
Calamian Isls. Philippines
       area–599 4
Calamitales
   paleobotany   561.72
Calamopityaceae
   paleobotany   561.595
Calanoida *see* Copepoda
Calaveras Co. Calif.   *area*–794 44
Calaverite
   mineralogy   549.32
Calcarea *see* Calcispongiae
Calcasieu
   Lake La.   *area*–763 52
   Par. La.   *area*–763 54
Calciferol *see* Vitamins
Calcimining
   buildings   698.2
   s.a. other spec. appls.
Calcispongiae
   culture   639.734 2
   fishing   639.734 2
   paleozoology   563.4
   zoology   593.42
   other aspects see Porifera
Calcites
   mineralogy   549.782
   other aspects see Cementing
       materials
Calcium
   chemistry
     inorganic   546.393
     organic   547.053 93
     s.a. spec. groupings e.g.
       Aliphatic compounds
   technology   661.039 3
     organic   661.895
     soc. & econ. aspects *see*
       Secondary industries
     s.a. spec. prod.
   cyanamide fertilizers *see*
       Cyanamide fertilizers
   mineral aspects *see* Minor
       metals
   nitrates fertilizers *see*
       Nitrate fertilizers
   pharmacology   615.239 3
     misc. aspects see
       Pharmacology

Calcium (continued)
  salts
    plant nutrition *see*
      Macronutrient elements
      plant nutrition
  soaps
    chem. tech.   668.125
    soc. & econ. aspects *see*
      Secondary industries
  toxicology   615.925 393
    misc. aspects see
      Toxicology
    other aspects see Alkaline
      earth metals
    s.a. other spec. appls.
Calculating machines
  manufacturers   *pers.*–681
  manufacturing
    soc. & econ. aspects *see*
      Secondary industries
    technology   681.14
Calculators *see* Calculating
    machines
Calculi
  biliary *see* Gall bladder
    diseases
  urinary *see* Kidney stones
Calculus   515
  s.a. spec. appls. e.g.
    Engineering
Calcutta India   *area*–541 4
Caldas Colombia   *area*–861 35
Calderdale West Yorkshire Eng.
            area–428 12
Caldwell
  County
    Kentucky   *area*–769 815
    Missouri   *area*–778 185
    North Carolina   *area*–756 845
    Texas   *area*–764 33
  Par. La.   *area*–763 76
Caledonia Canal Scot.   *area*–411 75
Caledonia Co. Vt.   *area*–743 34
Calendars
  chronology   529.3
  illustration   741.682
  religious
    Anglican liturgy   264.031
    Roman Catholic liturgy   264.021
    other aspects see Church
      year
Calendering
  paper *see* Finishing paper
  rubber mf.
    soc. & econ. aspects *see*
      Secondary industries
    technology   678.27
    s.a. spec. kinds of rubber
      e.g. Natural rubber
  textiles *see* Finishing
    textiles

Calendulas *see* Asterales
Calgary Alta.   *area*–712 33
Calhoun Co.
  Alabama   *area*–761 63
  Arkansas   *area*–767 64
  Florida   *area*–759 943
  Georgia   *area*–758 956
  Illinois   *area*–773 853
  Iowa   *area*–777 43
  Michigan   *area*–774 22
  Mississippi   *area*–762 81
  South Carolina   *area*–757 72
  Texas   *area*–764 121
  West Virginia   *area*–754 29
Calibration
  elect. instruments
    soc. & econ. aspects *see*
      Secondary industries
    technology   621.372
    other aspects see
      Electricity
    s.a. other spec. appls.
California
  Gulf *see* Southeast Pacific
    Ocean
  state   *area*–794
Californium
  chemistry   546.448
Caligoida *see* Copepoda
Caliphate
  Islamic doctrines   297.24
  Islamic organization   297.65
Calisthenics
  child care
    home econ.   649.57
  equipment mf.   688.764 1
    soc. & econ. aspects *see*
      Secondary industries
  hygiene   613.71
  sports   796.41
  therapeutics   615.824
    misc. aspects see Physical
      therapies
    s.a. spec. diseases
    other aspects see Sports
Call systems *see* Public-address
    systems
Calla lilies *see* Arales
Callabonna Lake S. Aust.   *area*–942 37
Callahan Co. Tex.   *area*–764 726
Callander Central Scot.   *area*–413 12
Callao Peru   *area*–852 6
Callaway Co. Mo.   *area*–778 335
Calles Mexico hist.   972.082 3
  s.a. spec. events & subj.
    e.g. Commerce
Calligraphy
  dec. arts   745.61
  s.a. Handwriting

Calling
  apparatus wire telegraphy *see*
    Instrumentation wire
     telegraphy
  of apostles
    Jesus Christ doctrines   232.95
Calliopsis *see* Asterales
Callipteris
  paleobotany   561.597
Callithricidae
  animal husbandry   636.982
  hunting
    commercial   639.118 2
    sports   799.259 82
  zoology   599.82
  other aspects see Primates
Callitrichiaceae *see* Lythrales
Callixylon
  paleobotany   561.55
Callosities *see* Hypertrophies
  skin
Calloway Co. Ky.   *area*–769 92
Calne Wiltshire Eng.   *area*–423 12
Caloosahatchee River Fla.   *area*–759 48
Calories
  appl. nutrition
    home econ.   641.104 2
  counters
    home econ.   641.104 2
    other aspects see
     Calorimeters
  other aspects see Nutrition
Calorimeters
  astrophysics   523.013 62
  s.a. spec. celestial bodies
  physics   536.62
    spec. states of matter   530.4
  other aspects see
    Measuring-instruments
Calorimetry
  astrophysics   523.013 6
  s.a. spec. celestial bodies
  physics   536.6
    spec. states of matter   530.4
  s.a. spec. appls. e.g.
    Engineering chemical
Caltanissetta Sicily   *area*–458 21
Calumet Co. Wis.   *area*–775 66
Calumny *see* Defamation
Calurea fertilizers *see* Ureas
  fertilizers
Calvados France   *area*–442 2
Calvert Co. Md.   *area*–752 44
Calves *see spec. animals e.g.*
    Cattle
Calvinistic
  Baptists   286.1
  misc. aspects see Baptist
  church
    buildings
     architecture   726.584 2

Calvinistic
  church
    buildings (continued)
     building   690.658 42
    other aspects see
     Religious-purpose
     bldgs.
    music
     arts   783.026 42
     recordings   789.912 302 642
     s.a. spec. instruments;
      also spec. kinds e.g.
      Liturgical music
    religion
     pub. worship   264.042 02
     significance   246.7
  churches in Europe   284.2
  Christian life guides   248.484 2
  doctrines   230.42
    creeds   238.42
  general councils   262.542
  govt. & admin.   262.042
    parishes   254.042
  missions   266.42
  moral theology   241.044 2
  private prayers for   242.804 2
  pub. worship   264.042
  rel. associations
    adults   267.184 2
    men   267.244 2
    women   267.444 2
    young adults   267.624 2
  rel. instruction   268.842
  rel. law   262.984 2
  schools   377.842
  secondary training   207.124 2
  sermons   252.042
  theological seminaries   207.114 2
  s.a. other spec. aspects
  s.a. Presbyterian
Calvinists
  biog. & work   284.209 2
  s.a.   *pers.*–242
Calycanthaceae
  botany   583.374
  floriculture   635.933 374
  med. aspects
    crop. prod.   633.883 374
    gen. pharm.   615.323 374
    toxicology   615.952 337 4
    vet. pharm.   636.089 532 337 4
    toxicology   636.089 595 233 74
  paleobotany   561.3
  other aspects see Plants
Calyceraceae *see* Valerianales
Calyxes
  plant anatomy   582.046 3
  s.a. spec. plants
Camaguey Cuba   *area*–729 156
Camaldolese *see* Cluniacs
Camarines Philippines   *area*–599 1

Camp (continued)
  meetings
    Christian rel. practices   269.24
  programs
    parochial work
      Christianity   259.8
      other rel. see Pastoral
        theology
Campaigns
  mil. sci.
    analysis   355.48
    s.a. spec. mil. branches
    history *see hist. of spec.*
      countries & wars
  s.a. other spec. kinds e.g.
      Political campaigns
Campanales
  botany   583.57
  floriculture   635.933 57
  forestry   634.973 57
  med. aspects
    crop prod.   633.883 57
    gen. pharm.   615.323 57
      toxicology   615.952 357
    vet. pharm.   636.089 532 357
      toxicology   636.089 595 235 7
  paleobotany   561.3
  other aspects see Plants
Campania Italy   *area*–457 2
  ancient   *area*–377
Campaniles *see* Towers
    (structures)
Campanulaceae *see* Campanales
Campaspe River Vic.   *area*–945 4
Campbell
  County
    Georgia   *area*–758 23
    Kentucky   *area*–769 34
    South Dakota   *area*–783 17
    Tennessee   *area*–768 72
    Virginia   *area*–755 672
    Wyoming   *area*–787 12
  island N.Z.   *area*–931 1
Campbell Town Tas.   *area*–946 3
Campbellites *see* Disciples of
    Christ (Church)
Campbelltown
  New South Wales   *area*–944 6
  Stathclyde Scot.   *area*–414 23
Campeche
  Bay *see* Mexico Gulf
  state Mex.   *area*–726 4
Camperdown Vic.   *area*–945 7
Campers (vehicles)
  automobiles
    commerce   388.346
    dwellings *see* Trailers
      automobile dwellings
    engineering
      gen. tech. & mf.   629.226
        maintenance   629.287 6

Campers (vehicles)
  automobiles
    engineering
      gen. tech. & mf. (continued)
        models   629.221 6
        operation   629.284 6
        s.a. other spec. aspects
          e.g. Brakes; *also*
          spec. appls. e.g.
          Travel
    soc. & econ. aspects *see*
      Secondary industries
    other aspects see Land
      vehicles
  cookery   641.575
Campfires
  sports   796.545
Camphor trees *see* Laurales
Camphors
  chemistry *see* Terpenes
Camping
  equipment
    armed forces   355.81
    s.a. spec. mil. branches
    manufacturing
      soc. & econ. aspects *see*
        Secondary industries
    technology   685.53
  sports   796.54
  other aspects see Sports
Campobasso Italy   *area*–457 19
Camps
  mil. quarters   355.71
    basic training operations   355.544
    logistics   355.412
    s.a. spec. mil. branches
  s.a. other spec. kinds e.g.
      Trailer camps
Campstools *see* Camping
    equipment
Campuses *see* Grounds
Cams
  machine eng.
    soc. & econ. aspects *see*
      Secondary industries
    tech. & mf.   621.838
    s.a. spec. appls. e.g.
      High-compression-
        ignition engines
  other aspects see Mechanics
Canaanite-Phoenician
  languages *see* Canaanitic
    languages
  people   *r.e.n.*–926
  s.a. other spec. subj. e.g.
    Arts
Canaanitic languages
  linguistics   492.6
  literatures   892.6
  s.a.   *lang.*–926
Canada   *area*–71

Canadian
Arctic   *area*–719 9
Co. Okla.   *area*–766 39
football
  equipment mf.   688.763 35
  soc. & econ. aspects *see*
    Secondary industries
  sports   796.335
  other aspects see Sports
literature
  English   810
  French   840
Pacific seawaters
  oceanography   551.466 33
  regional subj. trmt.   *area*–164 33
  other aspects see Pacific
    Ocean
people   *r.e.n.*–11
pronunciation Eng. lang.   421.52
River   *area*–766 1
Shield *see* Laurentian Plateau
spelling Eng. lang.   421.52
s.a. other spec. subj. e.g.
    Arts
Canaigre
culture   633.87
  soc. & econ. aspects *see*
    Primary industries
  other aspects see Polygonales
Canakkale Turkey   *area*–562
Canal
port facilities *see* Port
    facilities
ports *see* Ports
    inland-waterway
transportation
  commerce   386.4
  govt. control   351.876 4
    spec. jur.   353–354
  law *see* Inland-waterway
    transp.
terminals
  activities
    freight *see* Freight
      services transp.
      terminals
    passenger *see* Passenger
      services transp.
      terminals
  facilities
    freight *see* Freight
      terminals facilities
    passenger *see* Passenger
      terminals facilities
  other aspects see
    Inland-waterway transp.
Canalboats *see* Towed vessels
Canalized rivers
hydraulic eng. *see* Canals
    hydraulic eng.

Canalized rivers (continued)
transportation *see* River
    transportation
Canals
hydraulic eng.
  soc. & econ. aspects *see*
    Secondary industries
  technology   627.13
  s.a. spec. appls. e.g.
    Inland-waterway transp.
  other aspects see Liquids
    engineering
internat. law   341.446
irrigation *see* Irrigation
Canandaigua Lake N.Y.   *area*–747 86
Canapés
cookery   641.812
Cañar Ecuador   *area*–866 23
Canaries *see* Finches
Canary
grasses *see* Pooideae
Islands   *area*–649
Canasta *see* Rummy
Canaveral Cape Fla.   *area*–759 27
Canberra Australia   *area*–947 1
Cancellation *see spec. subj.*
    e.g. Labor contracts
Cancellation (philately)   769.567
Cancers *see* Malignant neoplasms
Candelabras *see*
    Lighting-fixtures
Candelilla wax
comm. proc.   665.12
  other aspects see Waxes
Candies
comm. proc.   664.153
  misc. aspects see Sugars
home cookery   641.853
Candleberry wax
comm. proc.   665.12
  other aspects see Waxes
Candler Co. Ga.   *area*–758 773
Candles
handicrafts   745.593 32
lighting tech.   621.323
  s.a. spec. appls.
Candlesticks
ceramic arts   738.8
handicrafts   745.593 3
rel. significance
  Christianity   247.888
  comp. rel.   291.37
  s.a. other spec. rel.
  other apsects see Containers
Cane
fruits
  agriculture   634.71
    soc. & econ. aspects *see*
      Primary industries

Cane
  fruits (continued)
    foods 641.347 1
      preparation
        commercial 664.804 71
        domestic 641.647 1
      other aspects see Rosaceae;
        also Fruits
    sugars & syrups
      comm. proc. 664.122
      other aspects see Sugars
Canea Greece *area*–499 8
Canellaceae *see* Bixales
Canelones Uruguay *area*–895 14
Canendiyú Paraguay *area*–892 133
Canes (fibers) *see* Unaltered
      vegetable fibers
Canes (sticks)
  dress customs 391.44
Canes (sugar)
  agriculture 633.61
    soc. & econ. aspects *see*
      Primary industries
  foods 641.336
    cookery 641.636
  other aspects see
      Panicoideae; *also*
      Sugars
Canidae
  agric. pests 632.697 444 2
    s.a. spec. types of culture
      e.g. Forestry; *also*
      spec. crops
  animal husbandry
    technology 636.974 442
      soc. & econ. aspects *see*
        Primary industries
  conservation tech. 639.979 744 42
  control
    agricultural *see* Canidae
      agric. pests
    home econ. 648.7
    sanitary eng. 628.969 7
  drawing tech. 743.697 444 2
  hunting
    commercial
      technology 639.177 444 2
        soc. & econ. aspects
          see Primary
          industries
    sports 799.259 744 42
  paleozoology 569.74
  zoology 599.744 42
  other aspects see Animals
  s.a. Dogs
Canine police services *see*
      Crime prevention
Canines *see* Dogs
Cankiri Turkey *area*–563
Canna family *see* Zingiberales
Cannabiaceae *see* Urticales

Cannabis sativa
  hemp *see* Hemp
  marijuana *see* Marijuana
  med. sci.
    addictive aspects *see*
      Addictive drugs use
    pharmacodynamics 615.782 7
    misc. aspects see Drugs
Cannaceae *see* Zingiberales
Canned
  foods
    cookery 641.612
    health & safety
      soc. aspects 363.192 9
      misc. aspects see Foods
        health & safety
  water *see* Potable water
Cannel coal 553.23
  econ. geol. 553.23
  mining
    soc. & econ. aspects *see*
      Primary industries
    technology 622.333
    prospecting 622.182 3
  processing 662.622 3
  other aspects see Coals
  s.a. spec. uses
Cannibalism
  soc. customs 394.9
Canning
  foods 641.42
    commercial 664.028 2
    domestic 641.42
  governorship India hist. 954.031 7
    s.a. spec. events & subj.
      e.g. Commerce
  other aspects see Foods
  s.a. spec. foods e.g. Meats
Cannock Chase Staffordshire Eng.
      area–424 67
Cannon Co. Tenn. *area*–768 535
Cannons
  art metalwork 739.742
  mil. eng.
    soc. & econ. aspects *see*
      Secondary industries
    tech. & mf. 623.42
      s.a. spec. appls
  s.a. Guns artillery
Canoe club bldgs.
  architecture 725.87
  building 690.587
  other aspects see Public
      structures
Canoeing
  sports 797.122
    racing 797.14
  other aspects see Sports
Canoes *see* Hand-propelled
      vessels

Capacitors
  electrostatics
    electrodynamic eng.
      soc. & econ. aspects *see*
        Secondary industries
      tech. & mf. — 621.315
      s.a. spec. appls. e.g.
        Electrostatics
    engineering
      physics — 537.242
        spec. states of matter — 530.4
    other aspects see
      Electrodynamics
  radio
    engineering — 621.384 133
    s.a. spec. appls. e.g.
      Radiotelephony
    other aspects see Radio
  television
    engineering — 621.388 33
    s.a. spec. appls. e.g.
      Astronautics
    other aspects see
      Television
Capacity
  determination aircraft eng. — 629.134 57
  s.a. spec. appls. e.g.
    Military engineering
  of persons
    law — 346.013
      spec. jur. — 346.3–.9
  to commit crime
    law — 345.04
      spec. jur. — 345.3–.9
Cape
  Barren Isl. Tas. — *area*–946 7
  Breton
    Co. N.S. — *area*–716 95
    Highlands Nat. Park N.S.
       — *area*–716 91
    Isl. N.S. — *area*–716 9
  Cod
    Bay
      oceanography — 551.461 45
      regional subj. trmt. — *area*–163 45
      other aspects see
        Atlantic Ocean
    Massachusetts — *area*–744 92
  Fear River N.C. — *area*–756 2
  Girardeau Co. Mo. — *area*–778 96
  Le Grand Nat. Park W. Aust.
     — *area*–941 7
  May Co. N.J. — *area*–749 98
  of Good Hope South Africa
     — *area*–687
  Range Nat. Park W. Aust.
     — *area*–941 3
  Town South Africa — *area*–687
  Verde Isls. & Republic — *area*–665 8
  York Peninsula Qld. — *area*–943 8

Capers
  food *see* Condiments
  other aspects see
    Capparidales
Capets France hist. — 944.021
  s.a. spec. events & subj.
    e.g. Commerce
Capillaries
  anatomy
    human — 611.15
    other aspects see
      Circulatory organs
  diseases
    gen. wks. — 616.148
      neoplasms — 616.992 15
      tuberculosis — 616.995 15
    geriatrics — 618.976 148
    pediatrics — 618.921 48
    pub. health — 614.591 48
    statistics — 312.314 8
      deaths — 312.261 48
    surgery — 617.415
      anesthesiology — 617.967 415
    other aspects see
      Cardiovascular system
  physical anthropometry — 573.615
  physiology
    human — 612.135
    other aspects see
      Circulatory organs
  tissue biology human — 611.018 915
Capillarity *see* Surface
    phenomena
Capillary
  analysis *see*
    Adsorption-analysis
  circulation
    human phys. — 612.135
    other aspects see
      Circulation (biology)
Capital
  accounting — 657.76
  s.a. spec. kinds of
    enterprise e.g.
      Insurance accounting
  budgets financial management
    see Budgeting
    financial management
  cities
    planning arts — 711.45
  costs capital management *see*
    Capital sources capital
    management
  District Paraguay — *area*–892 121
  expenditures financial
    management
  estimates
    budgeting
      pub. admin. — 350.722 253 4
        central govts. — 351.722 253 4
        spec. jur. — 353–354

Captive balloons
aeronautical eng.
  gen. tech. & mf. (continued)
    marketing *see* Marketing
    models   629.133 122
    operation   629.132 522
    military   623.744
  soc. & econ. aspects *see*
    Secondary industries
Captives
  law of war   341.67
  war customs   399
Captivity
  status
    armed forces   355.113
    s.a. spec. mil. branches
Capture
  nuclear interactions *see*
    Interactions nuclear
    reactions
Capuchín monastic bldgs.
  architecture   726.773 6
  building   690.677 36
  other aspects see
    Religious-purpose
    bldgs.
Capuchins
  rel. orders   255.36
    church hist.   271.36
    ecclesiology   262.24
Capusiaceae *see* Celastrales
Caquetá Colombia   *area*–861 64
Car cards
  transp. adv.   659.134 4
Carabaos *see* Buffaloes
Carabobo Venezuela   *area*–873 2
Caraboidea *see* Adephaga
Caracas Venezuela   *area*–877
Caracciolini *see* Minor Clerks
  Regular
Caradon Cornwall Eng.   *area*–423 74
Caramels *see* Candies
Carangoidea *see* Acanthopterygii
Caras-Severin Romania   *area*–498 4
Caravans (vehicles) *see* Campers
  (vehicles)
Caravels
  engineering   623.821
    design   623.812 1
    models   623.820 11
  seamanship   623.882 1
  other aspects see Vessels
    (nautical)
Caraway *see* Herbs; *also*
  Umbellales
Carazo Nicaragua   *area*–728 516
Carbines
  art metalwork   739.744 25
  hunting & shooting sports   799.202 832
    game   799.213
    targets   799.31

Carbines (continued)
  mil. enq.
    soc. & econ. aspects *see*
      Secondary industries
    tech. & mf.   623.442 5
Carbohydrases *see* Saccharolytic
  enzymes
Carbohydrate
  cookery   641.563 8
  metabolism disorders
    gen. med.   616.399 8
    geriatrics   618.976 399 81
    pediatrics   618.923 998
    pub. health   614.593 998
    statistics   312.339 98
      deaths   312.263 998
    other aspects see Diseases
Carbohydrates
  appl. nutrition
    home econ.   641.13
    hygiene   613.28
  biochemistry
    gen. wks.   574.192 48
      animals   591.192 48
      microorganisms   576.119 248
      plants   581.192 48
    s.a. spec. organisms
    med. sci.   612.015 78
      animals   636.089 201 578
      s.a. spec. animals
      man   612.015 78
    s.a. spec. functions,
      systems, organs
  biosynthesis
    gen. wks.   574.192 94
      animals   591.192 94
      microorganisms   576.119 294
      plants   581.192 94
    s.a. spec. organisms
    med. sci.   612.015 44
      animals   636.089 201 544
      s.a. spec. animals
      man   612.015 44
    s.a. spec. functions,
      systems, organs
  blood chemistry
    human phys.   612.12
    other aspects see
      Circulatory fluids
  metabolism
    human phys.   612.396
    other aspects see
      Metabolism
  org. chem.   547.78
Carbon
  black *see* Adsorbent carbons
  chemistry
    inorganic   546.681
    organic   547
    technology   661.068 1
      organic   661.8

Carbon
  chemistry
    technology (continued)
      soc. & econ. aspects *see*
        Secondary industries
      s.a. spec. prod.
  County
    Montana   *area*–786 652
    Pennsylvania   *area*–748 26
    Utah   *area*–792 566
    Wyoming   *area*–787 86
  dioxide
    chem. tech.   665.89
    soc. & econ. aspects *see*
        Secondary industries
    fire extinction tech.   628.925 4
      s.a. spec. appls. e.g.
        Forest fires
    removal
      respiration
        human phys.   612.22
      other aspects see
        Respiration
    therapy *see*
        Aerotherapeutics
  mineralogy   549.27
    s.a. spec. minerals
  pharmacology   615.268 1
    misc. aspects see
      Pharmacology
  processes
    photographic printing   773.1
  toxicology   615.925 681
    misc. aspects see
      Toxicology
  other aspects see Nonmetallic
      elements
Carbonaceous ores   553.2
  econ. geol.   553.2
  mining
    soc. & econ. aspects *see*
      Primary industries
    technology   622.33
    prospecting   622.182
  s.a. spec. uses; also spec.
      minerals
Carbonado *see* Abrasive
      materials
Carbonated beverages
  comm. proc.   663.62
  other aspects see
      Nonalcoholic beverages
Carbonates
  mineralogy   549.78
Carboniferous periods
  geology   551.751–.752
    s.a. spec. aspects e.g.
        Economic geology
  paleontology *see*
        Mississippian period

Carboxylic acids
  chemistry   547.037
    applied   661.86
    s.a. spec. acids
Carbro process
  photographic printing   773.1
Carbuncles *see* Furuncles
Carbureted-blue gas
  chem. tech.   665.772
    soc. & econ. aspects *see*
      Secondary industries
Carburetors
  internal-combustion engines
    soc. & econ. aspects *see*
      Secondary industries
    tech. & mf.   621.437
      automobiles   629.253 3
      marine vehicles   623.872 37
      s.a. other spec. appls.
Carchi Ecuador   *area*–866 11
Carcinomas *see* Malignant
      neoplasms
Card
  catalogs
    library sci.
      spec. catalogs   016–019
      theory   025.313
  game bldgs. *see* Indoor game
      bldgs.
  games
    equipment mf.   688.754
      soc. & econ. aspects *see*
        Secondary industries
    ethics *see* Games ethics
    recreation   795.4
  players
    biog. & work   795.409 2
    s.a.   *pers.*–795
  tricks recreation   795.438
  weaving *see* Weaving
Cardboard *see* Paperboard
Cárdenas Mexico hist.   972.082 5
  s.a. spec. events & subj.
      e.g. Commerce
Cardiac
  asthma *see* Heart diseases
  muscle tissue
    human anatomy and phys.   611.018 6
    other aspects see Tissue
        biology
Cardiff South Glamorgan Wales
                        area–429 87
Cardigan Wales   *area*–429 61
Cardigans *see* Sweaters
Cardinal sins
  Christian moral theology   241.3
Cardinals (birds) *see*
        Fringillidae
Cardinals (clergy)
  biog. & work   262.135 092
  Christian church govt.   262.135

Cardinals (clergy) (continued)
  creation of
    Roman Catholic liturgy   264.022
    other aspects see Roman
      Catholics
Carding textiles
  arts   746.11
  manufacturing
    soc. & econ. aspects *see*
      Secondary industries
    technology   677.028 21
    s.a. spec. kinds of
      textiles
Cardiography
  med. sci.   616.120 754
Cardiology
  med. sci.   616.12
    geriatrics   618.976 12
    pediatrics   618.921 2
    vet. med.   636.089 612
    s.a. spec. animals
    other aspects see Medical
      sciences
  s.a. Heart
Cardiopteridaceae *see*
  Celastrales
Cardiovascular system
  anatomy
    human   611.1
    other aspects see
      Circulatory organs
  diseases
    gen. wks.   616.1
      neoplasms   616.992 1
      tuberculosis   616.995 1
    geriatrics   618.976 1
    nursing   610.736 91
    pediatrics   618.921
    perinatal   618.326 1
    pub. health   614.591
    statistics   312.31
      deaths   312.261
    surgery   617.41
      anethesiology   617.967 41
    other aspects see Diseases
  drugs affecting
    pharmacodynamics   615.71
    other aspects see Drugs
  physical anthropometry   573.61
  physiology
    human   612.13–.18
    other aspects see
      Circulatory organs
  tissue biology human   611.018 91
Care *see spec. subj.*
Careers *see* Occupations
Carey Lake W. Aust.   *area*–941 6
Cargados Carajos Shoals   *area*–698

Cargo
  airplanes
    freight services *see*
      Freight transportation
    technology
      gen. wks. *see* Aeronautics
      military   623.746 5
  insurance   368.2
    misc. aspects see Insurance
  ships
    powered
      engineering   623.824 5
      design   623.812 45
      models   623.820 145
      use in petroleum transp.   665.543
      seamanship   623.882 45
      other aspects see Vessels
        (nautical)
    wind-driven *see* Merchant
      ships wind-driven
  transportation *see* Freight
    transportation
Cargo-handling equipment
  port eng.
    soc. & econ. aspects *see*
      Secondary industries
    technology   627.34
    s.a. spec. appls. e.g.
      Military engineering
Caria ancient   *area*–392 4
Cariamae *see* Gruiformes
Caribbean
  islands   *area*–729
  Sea
    oceanography   551.463 5
    regional subj. trmt.   *area*–163 65
    other aspects see Atlantic
      Ocean
Caribbees   *area*–729 7–729 8
Cariboo Mts. B.C.   *area*–711 2
Caribou Co. Ida.   *area*–796 45
Caribous
  animal husbandry   636.294
  other aspects see Cervoidea
Carica papaya *see* Papayas
Caricaceae *see* Cucurbitales
Caricatures *see* Cartoons
Caries *see* Cavities (teeth)
Carillon music   789.55
  recordings   789.912 95
Carillons
  mf. tech.   681.819 5
  misc. aspects see Musical
    instruments
  musical art   789.5
Carinthia Austria   *area*–436 6
Carleton Co.
  New Bruswick   *area*–715 52
  Ontario   *area*–713 83
Carlisle
  city Cumbria Eng.   *area*–427 87

Carlisle (continued)
Co. Ky.   *area*–769 97
Carlow Ireland   *area*–418 82
Carlsbad Caverns Nat. Park N.M.
                        area–789 42
Carlton
   city Nottinghamshire Eng.
                        area–425 28
   Co. Minn.   *area*–776 73
Carmarthen Dyfed Wales   *area*–429 65
Carmelite
   convent bldgs.
     architecture   726.779 71
     building   690.677 971
     other aspects see
          Religous-purpose bldgs.
   monastic bldgs.
     architecture   726.777 3
     building   690.677 73
     other aspects see
          Religious-purpose
          bldgs.
Carmelites
   rel. orders
     church hist.   271.73
       women's   271.971
     ecclesiology   262.24
     gen. wks.   255.73
       women's   255.971
Carnallite
   mineralogy   549.4
Carnarvon
   Range Nat. Park Qld.   *area*–943 5
   W. Aust.   *area*–941 3
Carnations *see* Caryophyllales
Carnauba wax
   comm. proc.   665.12
   other aspects see Waxes
Carnegie Lake W. Aust.   *area*–941 6
Carnforth Lancashire Eng.   *area*–427 69
Carnivals
   performing arts   791.1
   soc. customs   394.25
Carnivora
   agric. pests   632.697 4
     s.a. spec. types of culture
       e.g. Forestry; *also*
       spec. crops
   animal husbandry
     technology   636.974
     soc. & econ. aspects *see*
       Primary industries
   conservation tech.   639.979 74
   drawing tech.   743.697 4
   hunting
     commercial
       soc. & econ. aspects *see*
         Primary industries
       technology   639.117 4
     sports
       big game   799.277 4

Carnivora
   hunting
     sports (continued)
       small game   799.259 74
     paleozoology   569.74
     zoology   599.74
     other aspects see Animals
Carnivores *see* Carnivora
Carnosa *see* Demospongiae
Carnot cycle
   thermodynamics
     astrophysics   523.013 71
       s.a. spec. celestial
         bodies
     physics   536.71
     spec. states of matter   530.4
Carnoustie Tayside Scot.   *area*–412 6
Caro, Joseph
   Judaistic sources   296.182
Carob beans *see* Leguminous
       fruits
Caroline
   County
     Maryland   *area*–752 31
     Virginia   *area*–755 362
   Isl. Line Isls.   *area*–964
   Isls. Micronesia   *area*–966
Carolingian
   dynasty
     France hist.   944.01
     Ger. hist.   943.010 21
     s.a. spec. events & subj.
         e.g. Commerce
   lettering dec. arts   745.619 74
Carols
   sacred music   783.62–.65
   recordings   789.912 362–.912 365
Carotid glands
   anatomy
     human   611.47
     other aspects see Secretory
         organs
   diseases
     gen. wks.   616.48
       neoplasms   616.992 47
       tuberculosis   616.995 47
     geriatrics   618.976 48
     pediatrics   618.924 8
     pub. health   614.594 8
     statistics   312.348
       deaths   312.264 8
     other aspects see Diseases
   physical anthropometry   573.647
   physiology
     human   612.492
     other aspects see Secretion
   tissue biology human   611.018 947
Carpal bones *see* Upper
       extremities bones
Carpathian Mts. Ukraine   *area*–477 18
Carpathos Greece   *area*–499 6

Casein
  glues
    chem. tech.   668.32
    other aspects see Adhesives
  painting *see* Water-color
    painting
  plastics *see* Protein plastics
  textiles *see* Protein textiles
Caserta Italy   *area*–457 25
Cases (containers) *see*
    Containers
Cases (grammar) *see* Grammar
    (linguistics)
Cases (law)
  international
    reports & decisions   341.026 8
    source of law   341.1
  municipal   348.04
    spec. jur.   348.3–.9
    U.S.
      Federal   348.734
      state & local   348.74–.79
  spec. subj.   *law s.s.*–026 4
Casework
  soc. services   361.32
  spec. problems & groups   362–363
  other aspects see Welfare
    services
Casey Co. Ky.   *area*–769 66
Cash
  accounting trmt.   657.72
    s.a. spec. kinds of
      enterprise e.g.
      Insurance accounting
  balance theory
    money econ.   332.401
  capital *see* Working capital
  receipts
    agriculture
      prod. econ.   338.13
  registers
    manufacturing
      soc. & econ. aspects *see*
        Secondary industries
      technology   681.14
    use *see* Data processing
  rental
    land econ.   333.562
Cashew nuts
  agriculture   634.573
    soc. & econ. aspects *see*
      Primary industries
  foods   641.345 73
    preparation
      commercial   664.804 573
      domestic   641.645 73
  other aspects see Sapindales;
    also Nuts
Cashmere
  textiles *see* Goat-hair
    textiles

Cashmere (continued)
  s.a. Kashmir
Casino
  buildings
    architecture   725.76
    building   690.576
    other aspects see Public
      structures
  New South Wales   *area*–944 3
Casks
  wooden
    mf. tech.   674.82
    other aspects see Wood
      products
Caspian Sea
  region   *area*–479
    ancient   *area*–396
    modern   *area*–479
      Iran   *area*–551
      USSR   *area*–479
  waters   *area*–168
Casquets isl.   *area*–423 48
Cass Co.
  Illinois   *area*–773 465
  Indiana   *area*–772 86
  Iowa   *area*–777 72
  Michigan   *area*–774 12
  Minnesota   *area*–776 86
  Missouri   *area*–778 42
  Nebraska   *area*–782 272
  North Dakota   *area*–784 13
  Texas   *area*–764 195
Cassations *see* Romantic music
    orchestra
Cassava
  agriculture   633.682
    soc. & econ. aspects *see*
      Primary industries
  foods
    comm. proc.   664.23
    other aspects see
      Euphorbiales; *also*
      Starches;
Casserole dishes
  cookery   641.821
Cassettes *see* Tape recorders &
    recordings
Cassia Co. Ida.   *area*–796 39
Cassiterite
  mineralogy   549.524
Cassowaries *see* Casuariiformes
Cast
  glass *see* Glassware
  iron
    technology   669.141 3
    other aspects see Iron
  latex products
    manufacturing
      soc. & econ. aspects *see*
        Secondary industries
      technology   678.533

Catalan (continued)
  s.a. Catalonia; *also other*
    spec. subj. e.g. Arts
Catalases *see*
    Oxidizing-reducing
    enzymes
Catalepsy *see* Dissociative
    reactions
Catalog cards
  preparation
    libray operations 025.317
Cataloging
  library econ. 025.3
  museology 069.52
Catalogs
  library sci. *see* Library
    catalogs
  mailing
    postal commun. 383.124
    other aspects see Postal
      communication
  museology *s.s.*–074
  of articles *s.s.*–021 6
  of books 010
  of music scores 016.78
  of recordings 010
  of stars 523.890 8
  s.a. other spec. kinds e.g.
    Trade catalogs
Catalonia *area*–467
Catalonian *see* Catalan
Catalpa family *see* Bignoniales
Catalysis
  physical chem. 541.395
    applied 660.299 5
    organic 547.139 5
  s.a. spec. aspects e.g. Low
    temperatures
  s.a.spec. elements & cpds.
Catalytic cracking
  petroleum 665.533
  s.a. spec. prod. e.g.
    Gasolines
Catamarca Argentina *area*–824 5
Catanduanes Isl. Philippines
    .... *area*–599 1
Catania Sicily *area*–458 13
Catanzaro Italy *area*–457 81
Catapults
  art metalwork 739.73
  customs 399
  mil. eng. 623.441
Cataracts (eyes) *see*
    Crystalline lens
    diseases
Cataracts (water) *see*
    Waterfalls
Catastrophes *see* Disasters
Catatonia *see* Schizophrenia
Catawba
  Co. N.C. *area*–756 785

Catawba (continued)
  River S.C. *area*–757 45
Catbirds *see* Mimidae
Catboats *see* Modern wind-driven
    vessels
Catch basins
  sewers 628.25
  s.a. spec. appls. e.g.
    Water drainage
Catch-as-catch-can wrestling
    see Free-style
    wrestling
Catchers' mitts
  mf. tech. 685.43
  other aspects see Handwear
Catches (songs) *see* Choral
    music
Catching
  baseball 796.357 23
  s.a. other spec. sports
Catchword indexing
  library operations 025.486
Catechetics
  rel. instruction
    Christianity 268.6
    other rel. see Religious
      instruction
Catechisms
  doctrinal theology
    Christianity 238
    other rel. see Doctrinal
      theology
Catechols
  org. chem. 547.633
  s.a. spec. cpds.
Categories
  topological algebras 512.55
  s.a. spec. appls. e.g.
    Engineering
Caterers
  biog. & work 642.409 2
  s.a. *pers.*–642
Catering 642.4
  armed forces 355.341
  s.a. spec. mil. branches
Caterpillars *see* Lepidoptera
Catfishes *see* Ostariophysi
Catharine
  reign Russia hist.
    1 .... 947.061
    s.a. spec. events & subj.
      e.g. Commerce
    2 .... 947.063
    s.a. spec. events & subj.
      e.g. Commerce
Catharism
  heresy
    Christian church hist. 273.6
Catharist
  churches 284.4
    Christian life guides 248.484 4

Cattle (continued)
  products
    dairy products *see* Dairy
      products
    meats *see* Beef
    other see spec. prod. e.g.
      Hides
  other aspects see Bovoidea
Cattle-cars *see* Freight cars
Cauca Colombia   *area*–861 53
Caucasian *see* Caucasic
Caucasic
  language
    linguistics   499.96
    literature   899.96
    s.a.   *lang.*–999 6
  people   *r.e.n.*–999 6
  s.a. other spec. subj. e.g.
    Arts
Caucasoids   *r.e.n.*–034
Caucasus
  Mts. & region   *area*–479
    ancient   *area*–395
  rugs
    textile arts   746.759
Cauchy integral calculus   515.43
  s.a. spec. appls. e.g.
    Engineering
Caucuses
  pol. sci.
    nominating procedure   324.52
    spec. parties   324.24–.29
    party organization *see* Party
      organization gen. wks.
Caudal anesthesia *see* Regional
      anesthesia
Caudata
  culture   639.376 5
  hunting
    commercial   639.13
    sports   799.257 65
  paleozoology   567.6
  zoology   597.65
  other aspects see Amphibia
Cauliflower
  agriculture   635.35
    soc. & econ. aspects *see*
      Primary industries
  foods   641.353 5
    preparation
      commercial   664.805 35
      domestic   641.653 5
  other aspects see Cruciales;
      also Vegetables
Caulobacteriaceae *see*
      Caulobacteriales
Caulobacteriales
  botany   589.94
  med. aspects
    disease organisms   616.014 4

Caulobacteriales
  med. aspects (continued)
    gen. pharm.   615.329 94
      toxicology   615.952 994
    vet. pharm.   636.089 532 994
      toxicology   636.089 595 299 4
  paleobotany   561.9
  other aspects see Plants
Causation
  metaphysics   122
Cause
  metaphysics   122
Caustic
  potash
    chem. tech.   661.332
      soc. & econ. aspects *see*
        Secondary industries
      s.a. spec. prod.
  soda
    chem. tech.   661.322
      soc. & econ. aspects *see*
        Secondary industries
      s.a. spec. prod.
Cautín Chile   *area*–834 6
Cavalcades *see* Processions
Cavalier Co. N.D.   *area*–784 37
Cavalry forces & warfare
  mil. sci.   357
Cavan Ireland   *area*–416 98
Caves
  exploring
    equipment mf.   688.765 25
      soc. & econ. aspects *see*
        Secondary industries
    sports   796.525
    other aspects see Sports
  geomorphology   551.447
  psych. influences   155.964
  other aspects see Openings
      (physiography)
Cavies *see* Hystricomorpha
Cavitation
  fluid mech.
    engineering *see* Dynamics
    physics   532.059 5
      gases   533.295
        air   533.629 5
      liquids   532.595
Cavite Philippines   *area*–599 1
Cavities (teeth)
  dentistry
    gen. wks. & surgery   617.67
      anesthesiology   617.967 67
    pub. health   614.599 6
    statistics   312.304 767
    other aspects see Diseases
Cavity resonators
  microwave electronics *see*
      Resonators microwave
      electronics
Cayenne Guyane   *area*–882 3

Cayley algebra 512.53
  s.a. spec. appls. e.g.
          Engineering
Cayman Isls. *area*–729 21
Cayo Belize *area*–728 25
Cayuga
  Co. N.Y. *area*–747 68
  Lake N.Y. *area*–747 68
Ceará Brazil *area*–813 1
Cebidae
  animal husbandry 636.982
  hunting
    commercial 639.118 2
    sports 799.259 82
  zoology 599.82
  other aspects see Primates
Cebu Philippines *area*–599 5
Cecil Co. Md. *area*–752 38
Cecum
  anatomy
    human 611.345
    other aspects see Nutritive
          organs
  diseases
    surgery 617.554 5
      anesthesiology 617.967 554 5
    other aspects see
          Intestines diseases
  physical anthropometry 573.634 5
  physiology
    human 612.33
    other aspects see Nutrition
  tissue biology human 611.018 934 5
Cedar
  County
    Iowa *area*–777 66
    Missouri *area*–778 743
    Nebraska *area*–782 58
  River Ia. *area*–777 6
  trees
    forestry 634.975 6
      soc. & econ. aspects *see*
          Primary industries
    other aspects see
          Coniferales; *also*
          Trees
  woods *see* Softwoods
Cedrus *see* Cedar trees
Ceiling coverings
  home econ. 645.2
  s.a. spec. kinds e.g.
          Wallpaper
Ceilings
  architectural
    construction 721.7
    design & decoration 729.34
  building 690.17
  int. dec. 747.3
  painting bldgs. 698.147
  wood bldg. construction 694.2
  s.a. spec. kinds of bldgs.

Celastraceae *see* Celastrales
Celastrales
  botany 583.271
  floriculture 635.933 271
  forestry 634.973 271
  med. aspects
    crop prod. 633.883 271
    gen. pharm. 615.323 271
      toxicology 615.952 327 1
    vet. pharm. 636.089 532 327 1
      toxicology 636.089 595 232 71
  paleobotany 561.3
  other aspects see Plants
Celebes
  isl. Indonesia *area*–598 4
  Sea *see* Malay Archipelago
          inner seas
Celebrations
  armed forces 355.16
    s.a. spec. mil. branches
  cookery for 641.568
  hist. events
    law 344.091
      spec. jur. 344.3–.9
    s.a. spec. events
  pub. admin. *see history pub.*
          admin.
  soc. customs 394.2
  s.a. other spec. subj.; also
          Memorials
Celeriac
  agriculture 635.128
    soc. & econ. aspects *see*
          Primary industries
  foods 641.351 28
    preparation
      commercial 664.805 128
      domestic 641.651 28
  other aspects see Umbellales;
          also Vegetables
Celery
  agriculture 635.53
    soc. & econ. aspects *see*
          Primary industries
  foods 641.355 3
    preparation
      commercial 664.805 53
      domestic 641.655 3
  other aspects see Umbellales;
          also Vegetables
Celery-root *see* Celeriac
Celesta music 789.6
  recordings 789.912 96
Celestas
  mf. tech. 681.819 6
    misc. aspects see Musical
          instruments
  musical art 789.6

Celestial
  bodies
    astronomy
      description   523
      theory   521.5
      internat. law   341.47
      lit. & stage trmt.
        folk lit. soc.   398.362
      other aspects see Natural
        phenomena
    magnetism *see* Geomagnetism
    s.a. spec. celestial bodies
      e.g. Stars
  command systems
    aeronautics
      soc. & econ. aspects *see*
        Secondary industries
      technology   629.132 6
  coordinates
    spherical astronomy   522.7
    s.a. spec. celestial
      bodies
  hierarchy *see* Angels
  mechanics
    astronomy   521.1
    s.a. spec. celestial
      bodies
    space flight   629.411 1
    s.a. spec. appls. e.g.
      Space warfare
  navigation   527
  seamanship   623.89
  sphere
    spherical astronomy   522.7
    s.a. spec. celestial
      bodies
Celestines
  rel. orders   255.16
    church hist.   271.16
    ecclesiology   262.24
Celestite
  mineralogy   549.752
Celibacy
  clergymen
    pastoral theology
      Christianity   253.2
      other rel. see Pastoral
        theology
  ethics *see* Sexual ethics
  psychology   155.3
  rel. self-discipline *see*
    Asceticism
  soc. customs   392.6
  other aspects see Sexual
    relations
Cell differentiation   574.876 12
  animals   591.876 12
  plants   581.876 12
  s.a. spec. organisms
Cellists *see* Violoncellists
Cello *see* Violoncello

Cellobiose
  org. chem.   547.781 5
  other aspects see Sugar
Cells
  biology *see* Cytology
  monasticism *see* Accessory
    monastic structures
Cellular therapy
  med. sci.   615.66
  s.a. spec. diseases and
    groups of diseases
Cellulases *see* Saccharolytic
    enzymes
Cellulose
  acetates *see* Acetates
  cpds. supports photosensitive
    surfaces *see* Supports
    photosensitive surfaces
  derivatives
    organic chemicals
      chem. tech.   661.802
      other aspects see Organic
        chemicals
    eng. materials   620.197
    foundations   624.153 97
    naval design   623.818 97
    shipbuilding   623.820 7
    structures   624.189 7
    s.a. other spec. uses
    org. chem.   547.782
    other aspects see
      Carbohydrates
Cellulosics
  gen. wks.
    chem. tech   668.44
    org. chem.   547.843 24
    other aspects see Plastics
    s.a. spec. prod.
  textiles
    arts   746.044 6
    s.a. spec. processes e.g.
      Weaving
    dyeing   667.346
    manufacturing
      soc. & econ. aspects *see*
        Secondary industries
      technology   677.46
        special-process fabrics   677.6
    org. chem.   547.856
    other aspects see Textiles
    s.a. spec. prod.
Celtic
  languages
    linguistics   491.6
    literature   891.6
    s.a.   *lang.–916*
  people   *r.e.n.–916*
  period Eng. hist.   936.202
    s.a. spec. events & subj.
      e.g. Commerce
  regions ancient   *area–364*

Central (continued)
  generating stations
    electrodynamic eng. *see*
      Generation elect. power
  governments
    constitutional law   342.042
      spec. jur.   342.3–.9
    pub. admin.   351
      U.S.   353
      other   354
  heating
    buildings   697.03
    s.a. spec. kinds e.g.
      Steam heating
  nervous system *see* Nervous
    system
  Pacific
    islands   *area*–96
    seawaters   *area*–164 9
  Powers
    World War 1 hist.   940.334
    s.a. spec. aspects e.g.
      Diplomatic history
  Province
    Iran   *area*–552 5
    Kenya   *area*–676 26
  region Scot.   *area*–413 1
  stations
    air-conditioning eng.   697.933
    s.a. spec. types of
      bldgs.
    electric power *see*
      Generation elect. power
    steam eng.
      soc. & econ. aspects *see*
        Secondary industries
      technology   621.19
      s.a. spec. appls. e.g.
        District heating
    wire telephony *see*
      Telephony wire
  tendency
    statistical math.   519.533
    s.a. spec. appls.e.g.
      Engineering
  Treaty Organization
    mil. sci.   355.031 095 6
Centrales *see* Bacillariophyceae
Centralization
  library sci.   021.6
  local school districts   379.153 5
  management tech.
    pub. admin.   350.007 3
    central govts.   351.007 3
      spec. jur.   353–354
    local govts.   352.000 473
  s.a. other spec. subj.
Central-Southern Region China
    area–512
Centre
  Co. Pa.   *area*–748 53

Centre (continued)
  region France   *area*–445
Centrechinoida *see* Echinoidea
Centrifugal
  casting
    arts *see* Casting sculpture
    metal prod.
      manufacturing   671.254
      ferrous metals   672.254
      s.a. other spec. metals
      other aspects see Foundry
        practice
  fans & blowers
    engineering
      soc. & econ. aspects *see*
        Secondary industries
      tech. & mf.   621.63
      s.a. spec. appls.
      e.g. Ventilation
    other aspects see Dynamics
  forces
    physics mech.   531.113
    solids   531.35
    other aspects see
      Dynamics
  pumps
    engineering
      soc. & econ. aspects *see*
        Secondary industries
      tech. & mf.   621.67
      s.a. spec. appls. e.g.
        Water supply
        engineering
    other aspects see Dynamics
Centrifuging
  latex mf. *see* Preliminary
    operations latex mf.
Centripetal forces
  physics mech.   531.113
  solids   531.35
  other aspects see Dynamics
Centrist parties
  pol. sci.   324.24–.29
  s.a. spec. events & subj.
    e.g. Social problems
Centrolepidaceae *see* Juncales
Centrosomes *see* Cytoplasm
Century plants *see* Agave
Cephalaspidomorphi
  paleozoology   567.2
Cephalocarida
  culture   639.5
  fishing
    commercial   639.5
    sports   799.255 31
  paleozoology   565.31
  zoology   595.31
  other aspects see Crustacea
Cephalochordata
  zoology   596.4
  other aspects see Chordata

Cerebellum
physiology
  animal — 591.188
    s.a. spec. animals,
    functions, systems,
    organs
  human — 612.827
  other aspects see Brain
Cerebral
commissures
  human phys. — 612.826
  other aspects see Brain
palsy
  gen. med. — 616.836
  geriatrics — 618.976 836
  pediatrics — 618.928 36
  pub. health — 614.598 36
  statistics — 312.383 6
  deaths — 312.268 36
  other aspects see Diseases
peduncles
  human phys. — 612.826
  other aspects see Brain
Cerebrospinal fluid
  human phys. — 612.804 2
  other aspects see Nervous
    system
Cerebrovascular diseases
  gen. med. — 616.81
  geriatrics — 618.976 81
  pediatrics — 618.928 1
  pub. health — 614.598 1
  statistics — 312.381
  deaths — 312.268 1
  other aspects see Diseases
Cerebrum
physiology
  animal — 591.188
    s.a. spec. animals,
    functions, systems,
    organs
  human — 612.825
  other aspects see Brain
Ceredigion Dyfed Wales — *area*–429 61
Ceremonial robes *see* Symbolic
    garments
Ceremonials
armed forces — 355.17
  s.a. spec. mil. branches
Roman Catholic liturgy — 264.022
Ceremonies
official
  soc. customs — 394.4
rel. worship *see* Public
    worship
soc. customs *see* Social
    customs
Ceresin *see* Pitch (carbonaceous
    material)
Cerigo *see* Kythera

Cerium
chemistry
  inorganic — 546.412
  organic — 547.054 12
    s.a. spec. groupings e.g.
      Aliphatic compounds
  technology — 661.041 2
  organic — 661.895
    soc. & econ. aspects *see*
      Secondary industries
    s.a. spec. prod.
eng. materials — 620.189 291 2
  s.a. spec. uses
metallography — 669.952 912
metallurgy — 669.291 2
  physical & chem. — 669.962 912
pharmacology — 615.241 2
  misc. aspects see
    Pharmacology
products
  mf. tech. — 673.291 2
  other aspects see
    Nonferrous metals
    products
toxicology — 615.925 412
  misc. aspects see
    Toxicology
  other aspects see
    Cerium-group metals
Cerium-group metals
econ. geol. — 553.494 3
mining
  soc. & econ. aspects *see*
    Primary industries
  technology — 622.349 43
  prospecting — 622.184 943
  other aspects see Metal;
    also Metals
  s.a. spec. uses; also spec.
    minerals
Cerro
  Gordo Co. Ia. — *area*–777 25
  Largo Uruguay — *area*–895 23
Certainty
epistemology — 121.63
Certhiidae
hunting
  commercial — 639.128 823
  sports — 799.248 823
paleozoology — 568.8
zoology — 598.823
  other aspects see Aves
Certificates
of indebtedness
  pub. finance — 336.32
  other aspects see Public
    debt
research — 001.44
  s.a. other spec. subj.

Certification *see spec. subj.*
    e.g. Births
      certification
Certified milk
  dairy tech.
    skim   637.147 1
    whole   637.141
    other aspects see Milk
Certitude
  epistemology   121.63
Cerussite
  mineralogy   549.785
Cervical
  infections *see* Uterine
      infections
  pregnancy *see* Extrauterine
      pregnancy
Cervicitis *see* Uterine
    infections
Cervix
  uterus *see* Uterus
Cervoidea
  agric. pests   632.697 357
  s.a. spec. types of culture
    e.g. Forestry; *also*
      spec. crops
  animal husbandry 636.294
  conservation tech. 639.979 735 7
  drawing tech.   743.697 357
  hunting
    commercial
      technology   639.117 357
      soc. & econ. aspects
        see Primary
        industries
    sports
      big game   799.277 357
      small game   799.259 735 7
  products
    meats
      food   641.362 94
        cookery   641.662 94
      production *see* Red meats
    other prod. see spec. prod.
      e.g. Hides
  zoology   599.735 7
  other aspects see Animals
Cesar Colombia   *area*–861 23
Cesium
  chemistry
    inorganic   546.385
    organic   547.053 85
    s.a. spec. groupings e.g.
      Aliphatic compounds
  technology   661.038 5
    organic   661.895
    soc. & econ. aspects *see*
      Secondary industries
    s.a. spec. prod.
  mineral aspects *see* Minor
    metals

Cesium (continued)
  pharmacology   615.238 5
    misc. aspects see
      Pharmacology
  toxicology   615.925 385
    misc. aspects see
      Toxicology
  other aspects see Alkali
    metals
Cessnock N.S.W.   *area*–944 2
Cesspools
  engineering   628.742
Cestoda *see* Cestoidea
Cestodaria *see* Cestoidea
Cestode-caused diseases *see*
    Tapeworm-caused
    diseases
Cestodes *see* Cestoidea
Cestoidea
  culture & hunting 639.752 1
  zoology   595.121
  other aspects see Worms
Cetacea
  animal husbandry
    technology   636.95
    soc. & econ. aspects *see*
      Primary industries
  conservation tech. 639.979 5
  drawing tech.   743.695
  paleozoology   569.5
  whaling
    commercial
      technology   639.28
      soc. & econ. aspects
        see Primary
        industries
    sports   799.275
  zoology   599.5
  other aspects see Animals
Ceuta Morocco   *area*–642
Cévennes Mts. France *area*–448
Ceylon   *area*–549 3
Ceylonese
  people   *r.e.n.*–914 13
  s.a. spec. subj. e.g. Arts
Chachalacas *see* Cracidae
Chaco
  Boreal Paraguay   *area*–892 2
  department Paraguay *area*–892 26
  province Argentina   *area*–823 4
  War hist.   989.207
Chad
  country   *area*–674 3
  languages
    linguistics   493.7
    literatures   893.7
    s.a.   *lang.*–937
  people   *r.e.n.*–967 43
  s.a. other spec. subj. e.g.
    Arts

Chadderton Greater Manchester
    Eng.   *area*–427 393
Chaetodontoidea *see*
    Acanthopterygii
Chaetognatha
  culture & hunting   639.758 6
  zoology   595.186
  other aspects see Worms
Chaetophorales *see* Chlorophyta
Chaffee Co. Colo.   *area*–788 47
Chafing dish cookery   641.58
Chagas' diseases *see*
    Trypanosomiasis
Chagatay language *see* Turkic
    languages
Chagos Isls.   *area*–697
Chailletiaceae
  botany   583.373
  floriculture   635.933 373
  forestry   634.973 373
  med. aspects
    crop prod.   633.883 373
    gen. pharm.   615.323 373
      toxicology   615.952 337 3
    vet. pharm.   636.089 532 337 3
      toxicology   636.089 595 233 73
  paleobotany   561.3
  other aspects see Plants
Chain
  banking
    economics   332.16
    other aspects see Banking
  drives *see* Chain power
    transmission
  gangs *see* Convict labor
  gearing *see* Gears
  hoists
    machine eng.
      soc. & econ. aspects *see*
        Secondary industries
      tech. & mf.   621.863
      s.a. spec. appls. e.g.
        Internal transportation
    other aspects see Mechanics
  indexing *see* Precoordinate
    indexing
  lightning *see* Disruptive
    discharge
  nuclear reactions
    astrophysics   523.019 761
    s.a. spec. celestial
      bodies
    physics   539.761
    spec. states of matter   530.4
    s.a. spec. physical
      phenomena e.g. Heat
  power transmission
    machine eng.
      soc. & econ. aspects *see*
        Secondary industries

Chain
  power transmission
    machine eng. (continued)
      tech. & mf.   621.859
      s.a. spec. appls. e.g.
        Materials-handling
        equip.
    other aspects see Mechanics
  reactions
    physical chem.   541.393
      applied   660.299 3
      organic   547.139 3
    s.a. spec. aspects e.g.
      Low temperatures
    s.a. spec. elements, cpds.,
      prod.
  stores
    advertising 659.196 588 702–.196 588 703
    commerce   381.2
      misc. aspects see
        Commerce
    pub. relations
        659.296 588 702–.296 588 703
    retail marketing   658.870 2–.870 3
Chains (mechanisms) *see* Machine
    engineering
Chain-stitch fabrics
  arts   746.046 6
    s.a. spec. processes e.g.
      Weaving
  manufacturing
    soc. & econ. aspects *see*
      Secondary industries
    technology   677.66
  other aspects see Textiles
  s.a. spec. prod.
Chair
  cars *see* Passenger-train cars
  lifts *see* Telpherage
Chairs
  dec. arts   749.32
  ecclesiastical furniture *see*
    Seats ecclesiastical
    furniture
  mf. tech.   684.13
    outdoor   684.18
  other aspects see Furniture
Chalatenango El Salvador   *area*–728 421
Chalcanthite
  mineralogy   549.755
Chalcidice Greece   *area*–495 6
Chalcocite
  mineralogy   549.32
Chaldean *see* Neo-Babylonian
Chaldeans
  rel. orders   255.18
    church hist.   271.18
    ecclesiology   262.24
Chaldee *see* Biblical Aramaic
Chalices *see* Containers

Chants
  sacred music   783.5
    recordings   789.912 35
Chapbooks
  folk lit.   398.5
Chapel-en-le-Frith Derbyshire
      Eng.   *area*–425 11
Chapels
  detached *see* Accessory rel.
      bldgs.
  side
    Christian church arch.   726.595
Chaperonage
  soc. customs   392.6
Chaplain services
  armed forces
    gen. wks.   355.347
    s.a. spec. mil. branches
    spec. wars
      U.S. Civil War   973.778
      World War 1   940.478
      World War 2   940.547 8
      s.a. other spec. wars
Chaplains *see* Clergy
Chapping
  gen. med.   616.58
  geriatrics   618.976 58
  pediatrics   618.925 8
  pub. health   614.595 8
  statistics   312.358
  other aspects see Diseases
Chapter houses *see* Accessory
      cathedral structures
Characeae *see* Chlorophyta
Character
  determination palmistry   133.62
  disorders
    abnormal psych.   157.7
    gen. med.   616.858
    geriatrics   618.976 858
    pediatrics   618.928 58
    pub. health   614.58
    statistics   312.385 8
    other aspects see Mental
      illness
  education   370.114
    s.a. spec. levels of ed.
  influence on crime   364.24
  of Jesus Christ
    Christian doctrines   232.903
  psychology   155.2
  training
    child rearing   649.7
    penal institutions *see*
      Welfare services gen.
      wks. penal institutions
Character-recognition
  cybernetics   001.534
  devices *see*
      Pattern-recognition
      devices

Characters (persons)
  lit. element
    gen. wks.
      collections   808.802 7
      hist. & crit.   809.927
    spec. lits.
      collections   *lit. sub.*–080 27
      hist. & crit.   *lit. sub.*–092 7
    s.a. spec. lit. forms
  stage element   792.090 927
    s.a. other spec. dramatic
      mediums e.g.
      Television; also spec.
      kinds of drama e.g.
      Tragedies (drama)
Characters (symbols)
  printing   686.21
Charades
  indoor amusements   793.24
Charadrii *see* Charadriiformes
Charadriiformes
  hunting
    commercial   639.128 33
    sports   799.248 33
  paleozoology   568.3
  zoology   598.33
  other aspects see Aves
Charales *see* Chlorophyta
Charbon *see* Anthrax
Charcoal
  cookery   641.58
  manufacturing
    chem. tech.   662.74
    soc. & econ. aspects *see*
      Secondary industries
  reactions blowpipe anal. *see*
      Blowpipe analysis
Charcoal-drawing
  arts   741.22
    indiv. artists   741.092
    spec. appls.   741.5–.7
    spec. subj.   743.4–.8
Chard
  agriculture   635.42
    soc. & econ. aspects *see*
      Primary industries
  foods   641.354 2
    preparation
      commercial   664.805 42
      domestic   641.654 2
  other aspects see
      Chenopodiales; *also*
      Vegetables
Chard Somerset Eng.   *area*–423 89
Chardonnet-process textiles *see*
      Nitrocellulose textiles
Charente France
  department   *area*–446 5
  river   *area*–446 5
Charente-Inférieure France   *area*–446 4
Charente-Maritime France   *area*–446 4

Charms
  Islamic worship 297.33
  occultism 133.44
Charnwood Leicestershire Eng.
                              area–425 47
Charter
  services
    transportation
      freight *see* Freight
        transportation
      passenger *see* Passenger
        transportation
  United Nations
    internat. law 341.232
Charters *see spec. subj. e.g.*
        Municipal incorporation
Charters Towers Qld.   area–943 6
Charts
  aeronautical use 629.132 54
  gen. wks.
    spec. subj. *see* Statistical
        method spec. subj.
    other aspects see Graphic
        materials
  geography 912
  statistical method 001.422 6
    spec. subj. *s.s.*–018 2
Charwomen *see* Household
        employees
Chase Co.
  Kansas area–781 59
  Nebraska area–782 87
Chasing (treatment)
  metals
    arts *see* Decorative
        treatment sculpture
Chasms *see* Depressions
        (geomorphology)
Chassis
  automobiles
    soc. & econ. aspects *see*
        Secondary industries
    tech. & mf. 629.24
    s.a. spec. appls. e.g.
        Military engineering
Chastity
  ethics *see* Sexual ethics
  rel. self-discipline *see*
        Asceticism
Chasubles *see* Ecclesiastical
        vestments
Chateau Clique
  Lower Canada
    Canada hist. 971.038
Châteauguay Co. Que. area–714 33
Chateaux
  architecture 728.82
  building 690.882
  other aspects see Residential
        buildings

Chatham
  County
    Georgia area–758 724
    North Carolina area–756 59
  Islands area–931 1
  Kent Eng. area–422 323
Chattahoochee
  Co. Ga. area–758 476
  River area–758
Chattanooga Tenn. area–768 82
Chattel
  mortgages *see* Secured
        transactions
Chattels *see* Personal property
Chatteris Cambridgeshire Eng.
                              area–426 53
Chattisgarhi *see* Eastern Hindi
        languages
Chattooga Co. Ga. area–758 344
Chaunceys Line Reserve Nat. Park
        S. Aust. area–942 32
Chausey isls. area–423 48
Chausseys isls. area–423 48
Chautauqua Co.
  Kansas area–781 918
  New York area–747 95
Chaves Co. N.M. area–789 43
Cheadle & Gatley Greater
        Manchester Eng. area–427 34
Cheadle Staffordshire Eng. area–424 61
Cheam London Eng. area–421 92
Cheat River W. Va. area–754 8
Cheatham Co. Tenn. area–768 462
Cheating *see* Vices
Cheboygan Co. Mich. area–774 87
Chebyshev polynomials 515.55
  s.a. spec. appls. e.g.
        Engineering
Chechen *see* Caucasic
Chechen-Ingush ASSR area–479 7
Checkers
  equipment mf. 688.742 2
    soc. & econ. aspects *see*
        Secondary industries
  recreation 794.22
Checking accounts
  banking econ. 332.175 2
  other aspects see Banking
Checklists
  employee selection *see*
        Selection procedures
        employees
  of cases
    law 348.048
      spec. jur. 348.3–.9
      U.S.
        Federal 348.734 8
        state & local 348.74–.79
      spec. subj. *law s.s.*–026 48

Chemical
warfare (continued)
  law of war — 341.63
  mil. eng.
    defense — 623.3
    offense *see* Chemical
      devices mil. eng.
  mil. sci. — 358.34
wastes
  disposal
    law — 344.046 22
      spec. jur. — 344.3–.9
    other aspects see Wastes
      control
weapons *see* Chemical devices
    mil.
s.a. Chemistry
Chemicals
fire extinction tech. — 628.925 4
  s.a. spec. appls. e.g.
    Forest fires
photography — 771.5
  gen. tech. — 770.283
  spec. proc. & fields — 772–778
pollution by
  soc. aspects — 363.738 4
  other aspects see
    Pollutants
pub. safety — 363.179
  law — 344.042 4
    spec. jur. — 344.3–.9
  other aspects see Hazardous
    materials
textiles *see* Materials
    textiles mf.
Chemiculture — 631.585
s.a. spec. crops
Chemisorption
surface chem. *see* Surface
    phenomena
Chemistry — 540
& religion
  nat. rel. — 215.4
applied — 660
  misc. aspects see
    Technology
astronomy — 523.02
  s.a. spec. celestial bodies
Biblical treatment — 220.854
  s.a. spec. parts of Bible
cells *see* Cytochemistry
curriculums — 375.54
documentation — 025.065 4
libraries — 026.54
  misc. aspects see Special
    libraries
library acquisitions — 025.275 4
library classification — 025.465 4

Chemistry (continued)
soil science — 631.41
  s.a. spec. crops; also spec.
    types of culture e.g.
    Floriculture
subject headings — 025.495 4
other aspects see Sciences
s.a. Chemical; *also spec.*
    fields e.g.
    Geochemistry
Chemists
biog. & work — 540.92
  s.a. spec. kinds
  other aspects see Scientists
  s.a. — *pers.*–541
Chemnitz Ger. — *area*–432 1
Chemosynthesis
plant nutrition
  pathology — 581.213 343
  physiology — 581.133 43
  s.a. spec. plants
Chemotherapy
therapeutics *see* Drug therapy
Chemung Co. N.Y. — *area*–747 78
Chemurgy — 660.282
s.a. spec. prod.
Chenango
Co. N.Y. — *area*–747 73
River N.Y. — *area*–747 73
Chenille *see* Pile-weave fabrics
Chenopodiaceae *see*
  Chenopodiales
Chenopodiales
botany — 583.913
floriculture — 635.933 913
forestry — 634.973 913
med. aspects
  crop prod. — 633.883 913
  gen. pharm. — 615.323 913
    toxicology — 615.952 391 3
  vet. pharm. — 636.089 532 391 3
    toxicology — 636.089 595 239 13
paleobotany — 561.3
other aspects see Plants
Chepstow Gwent Wales — *area*–429 98
Cheques
economics — 332.76
law *see* Negotiable
    instruments law
Cher France — *area*–445 52
Cheremis
language *see* Middle Volga
    languages
people — *r.e.n.*–945 6
s.a. other spec. subj. e.g.
    Arts
Cherimoya *see* Annonaceous
    fruits
Cherkassy Ukraine — *area*–477 14
Chernigov Ukraine — *area*–477 15
Chernovtsy Ukraine — *area*–477 18

Cherokee
County
   Alabama — *area*–761 65
   Georgia — *area*–758 253
   Iowa — *area*–777 17
   Kansas — *area*–781 99
   North Carolina — *area*–756 99
   Oklahoma — *area*–766 88
   South Carolina — *area*–757 42
   Texas — *area*–764 183
lang. & people *see* Hokan-Siouan
Res. Tenn. — *area*–768 92
Cherokees Lake of Okla. — *area*–766 91
Cherries
agriculture — 634.23
   soc. & econ. aspects *see*
      Primary industries
foods — 641.342 3
   preparation
      commercial — 664.804 23
      domestic — 641.642 3
other aspects see Rosaceae;
      also Fruits
Cherry
   Co. Neb. — *area*–782 732
   woods *see* Hardwoods
Chertsey Surrey Eng. — *area*–422 11
Cherubim *see* Angels
Chervil *see* Herbs; *also*
      Umbellales
Cherwell Oxfordshire Eng. — *area*–425 73
Chesapeake Bay
   region — *area*–755 18
   waters
      oceanography — 551.461 47
      regional subj. trmt. — *area*–163 47
   other aspects see Atlantic
      Ocean
Chesham Buckinghamshire
      Eng. — *area*–425 97
Cheshire
   cheese
      dairy tech. — 637.354
   other aspects see Cheeses
   County
      England — *area*–427 1
      New Hampshire — *area*–742 9
   swine
      animal husbandry — 636.484
   other aspects see Swine
Cheshunt Hertfordshire
      Eng. — *area*–425 87
Chesil Beach Dorset Eng. — *area*–423 31
Chess
   equipment mf. — 688.741
   soc. & econ. aspects *see*
      Secondary industries
   players
      biog. & work — 794.109 2
      s.a. — *pers.*–794 1
   recreation — 794.1

Chessmen — 794.1
   manufacture — 688.741
Chest
   bones
      anatomy
         human — 611.712
         other aspects see
            Skeletal organs
      diseases *see* Bones diseases
      physical anthropometry — 573.671 2
      physiology
         human — 612.75
         other aspects see
            Movements
      tissue biology human — 611.018 971 2
   deformities
      statistics — 312.304 737 4
      surgery — 617.374
         anesthesiology — 617.967 374
      s.a. Veterinary sciences
   muscles
      human anatomy — 611.735
      other aspects see Muscles
   s.a. Thorax
Chester
   Cheshire Eng. — *area*–427 14
   County
      Pennsylvania — *area*–748 13
      South Carolina — *area*–757 47
      Tennessee — *area*–768 265
   River Md. — *area*–752 34
   White swine
      animal husbandry — 636.484
      other aspects see Swine
Chesterfield
   County
      South Carolina — *area*–757 63
      Virginia — *area*–755 594
   Derbyshire Eng. — *area*–425 12
   Isls. New Caledonia — *area*–932
Chester-le-Street Durham
      Eng. — *area*–428 69
Chestnut
   beans *see* Chick-peas
   Ridge Pa. — *area*–748 8
   trees
      forestry — 634.972 4
      soc. & econ. aspects *see*
         Primary industries
      other aspects see Fagales;
         also Trees
   woods *see* Hardwoods
Chestnuts
   agriculture — 634.53
      soc. & econ. aspects *see*
         Primary industries
   foods — 641.345 3
      preparation
         commercial — 664.804 53
         domestic — 641.645 3

Chilblains (continued)
geriatrics	618.976 58
pediatrics	618.925 8
pub. health	614.595 8
statistics	312.358
other aspects see Diseases	

Child
abuse	
criminology *see* Assault & battery	
soc. path.	362.704 4
sociology *see* Abused children	
care	
home econ.	649.1
development	
human phys.	612.65
other aspects see Development (biology)	
guidance clinics	
soc. services	362.74
misc. aspects see Young people soc. services to	
labor *see* Children's labor	
offenders *see* Juvenile delinquents	
support	
law	346.017 2
spec. jur.	346.3–.9
welfare *see* Young people soc. services	
s.a. Children	

Childbirth
human physiology	612.63
preparation	
obstetrics	618.24
other aspects see Parturition	

Childhood in Nazareth
Jesus Christ	
Christian doctrines	232.927

Child-parent relationships *see* Parent-child relationships

Children
art representation	704.942 5
drawing tech.	743.45
painting	757.5
s.a. other spec. art forms	
as cooks	641.512 3
criminal offenders *see* Juvenile delinquents	
cruelty to *see* Children treatment of	
ethics	170.202 22
etiquette	395.122
food prep. by	
home econ.	641.512 3
food prep. for	
home econ.	641.562 2
grooming	646.704 6
hygiene	613.043 2

Children (continued)
journalism for	070.483 2
meditations for	
Christianity	242.62
other rel. see Worship	
parochial activities for	
Christianity	259.22
other rel. see Pastoral theology	
personal rel.	
Christianity	248.82
other rel. see Personal religion	
physical fitness	
hygiene	613.704 2
prayers for	
Christianity	242.82
other rel. see Worship	
psychology	155.4
publications for	
bibliographies	011.625 4
spec. kinds	012–016
catalogs	
general	017–019
spec. kinds	012–016
reviews	028.162 54
s.a. spec. forms e.g. Books	
reading	
library sci.	028.534
rearing of	
customs	392.13
home econ.	649.122–.124
recreation	790.192 2
indoor	793.019 22
outdoor	796.019 22
soc. services to	362.795
misc. aspects see Young people soc. services to	
treatment of	
ethics	
philosophy	179.2
religion	
Buddhism	294.356 92
Christianity	241.692
comp. rel.	291.569 2
Hinduism	294.548 692
s.a. other spec. rel.	
World War 1 hist.	940.316 1
World War 2 hist.	940.531 61
writing for	
rhetoric	808.068
other aspects see Young people; *also* Persons	
other spec. subj.	*pers.*–054
s.a. Child; *also* Boys; *also* Girls	

Children's
books	
illustration	741.642
clothing	
child care	649.4

Chiliasm
rel. doctrines
  Christianity   236.3
  other rel. see Eschatology
Chilled
dishes
  cookery tech.   641.79
Chilliwack B.C.   *area*–711 33
Chiloé Chile   *area*–835 6
Chilognatha *see* Diplopoda
Chilopoda *see* Opisthogoneata
Chiltern Buckinghamshire Eng.
                area–425 97
Chilterns Eng.   *area*–425
Chilton Co. Ala.   *area*–761 81
Chimaerae
  culture   639.373 8
  fishing
    commercial   639.273 8
    sports   799.173 8
  zoology   597.38
  other aspects see
        Chondrichthyes
Chimaltenango Guatemala *area*–728 161
Chimborazo Ecuador   *area*–866 17
Chimeras *see* Chimaerae
Chimes
  mf. tech.   681.819 5
  misc. aspects see Musical
       instruments
  musical art   789.5
  recordings   789.912 95
Chimneys
  bldg. heating   697.8
  steam eng. *see* Furnaces steam
       eng.
  other aspects see Roofs
Chimpanzees *see* Pan (animal)
Ch'in & Chin dynasties China
       hist.   931.04
  s.a. spec. events & subj.
      e.g. Commerce
China
  cabinets *see* Cabinets
    (furniture)
  country   *area*–51
    ancient   *area*–31
  jute
    agriculture   633.56
    soc. & econ. aspects *see*
       Primary industries
    other aspects see Malvales
  Sea *see* East China Sea;
      also South China Sea
Chinaberry tree *see* Sapindales
Chinandega Nicaragua   *area*–728 511
Chinaware *see* Porcelain
Chinchilla cats
  animal husbandry   636.83
  other aspects see Cats
Chinchilla Qld.   *area*–943 3

Chinchillas *see* Hystricomorpha
Chinese
  architecture   722.11
    misc. aspects see
       Architectural schools
  chess
    equip. mf.   688.741 8
    soc. & econ. aspects *see*
       Secondary industries
    recreation   794.18
  communism
    economics   335.434 5
    pol. ideology   320.532 3
    soc. theology *see*
       Political ideologies
       soc. theology
  flower arrangements
    dec. arts   745.922 51
  ink
    painting   751.425 1
      indiv. artists   759.1–.9
  jute *see* China jute
  language
    linguistics   495.1
    literature   895.1
    s.a.   *lang.*–951
  lettering
    dec. arts   745.619 951
  people   *r.e.n.*–951
  rugs
    textile arts   746.751
  sculpture   732.71
  wood oil
    comm. proc.   665.333
    soc. & econ. aspects *see*
       Secondary industries
  s.a. China; *also other spec.*
       subj. e.g. Arts
Ch'ing dynasty China hist.   951.03
  s.a. spec. events & subj.
      e.g. Arts
Chingford London Eng.   *area*–421 72
Chinghai China   *area*–514 7
Chingma *see* China jute
Chinook *see* Macro-Penutian
Chinooks *see* Local wind systems
Chinquapin trees *see* Chestnut
    trees
Chios Greece   *area*–499
  ancient   *area*–391 3
Chip
  boards
    mf. tech.   676.183
    other aspects see Pulp
  carving wood *see* Wood
    sculpture
Chipewyan *see* Na-Dene
Chipmunks *see* Sciuromorpha
Chipped soaps
  manufacturing
    chem. tech.   668.124

Chipped soaps
  manufacturing (continued)
    soc. & econ. aspects *see*
      Secondary industries
Chippenham Wiltshire Eng.
                  area–423 12
Chippewa
  County
    Michigan   *area*–774 91
    Minnesota   *area*–776 39
    Wisconsin   *area*–775 44
  River Wis.   *area*–775 4
Chippewaian *see* Na-Dene
Chipping
  Campden Gloucestershire Eng.
                  area–424 17
  golf   796.352 34
  Norton Oxfordshire Eng. *area*–425 71
  Sodbury Avon Eng.   *area*–423 91
Chiquimula Guatemala   *area*–728 141
Chiriquí Panama   *area*–728 711
Chirognomy palmistry   133.62
Chiromancy palmistry   133.64
Chiropody
  med. sci.   617.585
    vet. med.   636.089 758 5
    s.a. spec. animals
  other aspects see Feet
      diseases
Chiropractic
  therapeutics   615.534
    misc. aspects see
      Therapeutics
  s.a. spec. diseases
Chiroptera
  animal husbandry   636.94
  hunting
    commercial   639.114
    sports   799.259 4
  paleozoology   569.4
  zoology   599.4
  other aspects see Mammalia
Chisago Co. Minn.   *area*–776 61
Chiseling *see* Carving
Chislehurst London Eng. *area*–421 78
Chi-square test
  statistical math.   519.56
    s.a. spec. appls. e.g.
      Engineering
Chita RSFSR   *area*–575
Chitral Pakistan   *area*–549 122
Chittagong Bangladesh *area*–549 23
Chittenden Co. Vt.   *area*–743 17
Chivalry
  lit. & stage trmt. *see* Human
      qualities
  soc. customs   394.7
Chives *see* Alliaceous plants
Chkalov RSFSR   *area*–478 7
Chlaenaceae *see* Theales

Chlamydobacteriaceae *see*
    Chlamydobacteriales
Chlamydobacteriales
  botany   589.93
  med. aspects
    disease organisms   616.014 3
    gen. pharm.   615.329 93
    toxicology   615.952 993
    vet. pharm.   636.089 532 993
    toxicology 636.089 595 299 3
  paleobotany   561.9
  other aspects see Plants
Chloanthaceae *see* Verbenales
Chloranthaceae *see* Piperales
Chlorates
  chem. tech.   661.42
  other aspects see Industrial
    chemicals
Chlorideae *see* Pooideae
Chlorides
  chem. tech.   661.42
  other aspects see Industrial
    chemicals
Chlorination
  water-supply trmt.
    technology   628.166 2
    other aspects see Water
      supply engineering
Chlorine
  chemistry
    inorganic   546.732
    organic   547.02
    s.a. spec. groupings e.g.
      Aliphatic compounds
  technology   661.073 2
    soc. & econ. aspects *see*
      Secondary industries
    s.a. spec. prod.
  pharmacology   615.273 2
    misc. aspects see
      Pharmacology
  toxicology   615.925 732
    misc. aspects see
      Toxicology
  other aspects see Halogen
Chlorite
  mineralogy   549.67
Chlorites
  chem. tech.   661.42
  other aspects see Industrial
    chemicals
Chlorococcales *see* Chlorophyta
Chloromonadida *see* Mastigophora
Chlorophylls
  org. chem.   547.593
  s.a. spec. cpds.
Chlorophyta
  botany   589.47
  med. aspects
    gen. pharm.   615.329 47
    toxicology   615.952 947

Chlorophyta
  med. aspects (continued)
    vet. pharm.   636.089 532 947
      toxicology   636.089 595 294 7
    paleobotany   561.93
    other aspects see Plants
Chloroplasts *see* Plastids
Chloroprene rubbers *see*
    Synthetic rubber
Chocó Colombia   *area*–861 27
Chocolate
  beverage *see* Cocoa beverage
  other aspects see Cacao
Choctaw
  County
    Alabama   *area*–761 395
    Mississippi   *area*–762 694
    Oklahoma   *area*–766 63
  lang. & people *see*
    Hokan-Siouan
Choice
  freedom *see* Freedom of choice
  mathematics   511.65
    s.a. spec. math. branches;
      also spec. appls. e.g.
      Engineering
  of college ed.   378.198
  of entry
    library cataloging   025.322
  of vocation
    economics   331.702
    education   371.425
    s.a. spec. levels of ed.;
      also Special education
    s.a. Vocational guidance
  psychology   153.83
    animals   156.383
    children   155.413
    s.a. psych. of other spec.
      groups
  soc. interaction   302
  s.a. other spec. subj.
Choir
  lofts
    Christian church arch. 726.593
  stalls *see* Canopies
Choirs
  sacred music   783.8
Choiseul Isls. Solomons   *area*–935
Choking *see* Asphyxiation
Cholecalciferol *see* Vitamins
Cholera
  Asiatic *see* Asiatic cholera
  morbus *see* Stomach diseases
Cholesterol
  biochemistry *see* Sterols
    biochemistry
  blood chem.
    human phys.   612.12
    other aspects see
      Circulatory fluids

Cholesterol (continued)
  org. chem.   547.731
Cholic acids
  org. chem.   547.737
Cholicosis *see* Pneumoconiosis
Choluteca Honduras   *area*–728 351
Chondrichthyes
  culture   639.373
  fishing
    commercial   639.273
    sports   799.173
  paleozoology   567.3
  zoology   597.3
  other aspects see Pisces
Chondrodite
  mineralogy   549.62
Chong-kie *see* Chinese chess
Chontales Nicaragua   *area*–728 527
Choptank River Md.   *area*–752 31
Choral
  music
    gen. wks.
      sacred
        liturgical *see*
          Liturgical music
        nonliturgical   783.4
      secular
        with orchestra   784.2
        without orchestra 784.1
    recordings   789.912 41
  speaking
    rhetoric   808.55
    juvenile   808.068 55
    other aspects see
      Speaking
  texts
    gen. wks.
      collections   808.855
      hist. & crit.   809.55
    spec. lits.   *lit. sub.*–505
    indiv. authors *lit. sub.*–51–59
    other aspects see
      Speeches
Chordariales *see* Phaeophyta
Chordata
  agric. pests   632.66
    s.a. spec. types of culture
      e.g. Forestry; *also*
      spec. crops
  conservation tech.   639.976
  drawing tech.   743.66
  fishing & hunting
    commercial
      soc. & econ. aspects *see*
        Primary industries
      technology   639
    other aspects see Fishing
      industries; *also*
      Hunting industries
  sports   799
  paleozoology   566

Christian (continued)
  sacred music
    arts   783.026
      recordings   789.912 302 6
    s.a. spec. instruments;
      also spec. kinds e.g.
        Liturgical music
    religion *see* Sacred music
      religion
  Science *see* Church of Christ
    Scientist
  Scientists
    biog. & work   289.509 2
    s.a.   *pers.–285*
  socialism
    economics   335.7
    pol. ideology   320.531 2
      soc. theology *see*
        Political ideologies
        soc. theology
  virtues
    moral theology   241.4
    personal rel.   248.4
    s.a. Church
Christianity   200
  and other religions *see*
    Interreligious
      relations
  art representation
    arts   704.948 2
    s.a. spec. art forms
    rel. significance   246
  Islamic polemics vs.   297.293
  lit. & stage trmt. *see*
    Religious concepts
Christians
  biog. & work   209.2
  s.a. spec. kinds e.g.
    Clergy; *also spec.*
      denominations
  other aspects see Religious
    believers
  s.a.   *pers.–2*
Christmas
  carols *see* Christmas music
  devotional lit.   242.33
  Island   *area–964*
    Australia   *area–948*
    Line Isls.   *area–964*
  liturgical music *see* Festive
    music Christian liturgy
  music   783.65
    recordings   789.912 365
    s.a. spec. kinds e.g.
      Oratorios sacred
  rel. observance   263.91
  Roman Catholic liturgy   264.027 2
  seals
    prints   769.57
  sermons   252.61
  soc. customs   394.268 282

Christmas (continued)
  other aspects see Holidays
Christology
  Christian doctrines   232
Chromates
  mineralogy   549.752
Chromatic
  radiations *see* Visible light
    spectroscopy
Chromatics *see* Color
Chromatin *see* Nucleus cells
    cytology
Chromatographic analysis
  anal. chem.
    gen. wks.   543.089
      qualitative   544.92
      quantitative   545.89
    organic   547.308 9
      qualitative   547.349 2
      quantitative   547.358 9
    s.a. spec. elements & cpds.
Chromatography *see*
    Chromatographic
      analysis
Chrome
  refractory materials *see*
    Refractory materials
Chromite
  mineralogy   549.526
Chromium
  arts
    decorative   739.58
    other aspects see Metals
      arts
  chemistry
    inorganic   546.532
    organic   547.055 32
    s.a. spec. groupings e.g.
      Aliphatic compounds
  technology   661.053 2
    organic   661.895
    soc. & econ. aspects *see*
      Secondary industries
    s.a. spec. prod.
  construction
    architecture   721.044 773 4
    s.a. spec. kinds of
      bldgs.
    building   693.773 4
  materials
    engineering   620.189 34
    foundations   624.153 893 4
    naval design   623.818 293 4
    structures   624.182 934
    s.a. other spec. uses
  metallography   669.957 34
  metallurgy   669.734
    physical & chem.   619.967 34
    soc. & econ. aspects *see*
      Secondary industries

Church
authority (continued)
other rel. see
Ecclesiastical theology
calendar
chronology | 529.44
camps
sports | 796.542 2
etiquette | 395.53
fathers *see* Apostolic
Christians
finance
Christianity | 254.8
other rel. see
Ecclesiastical theology
flower arrangements
dec. arts | 745.926
furnishings
rel. significance
Christianity | 247
other rel. see Arts rel.
significance
government
Christianity | 262
other rel. see
Ecclesiastical theology
grounds
landscape design | 712.7
history
Christianity | 270
spec. denominations | 280
s.a. other spec. rel.
holidays
soc. customs | 394.268 28
Lancashire Eng. | *area*–427 625
law *see* Religious law
members *see* Laity
membership
Christianity | 254.5
other rel. see
Ecclesiastical theology
nature Christian ecclesiology | 262.7
of Christ | 286.63
misc. aspects see Disciples
of Christ Church
of Christ Scientist | 289.5
buildings
architecture | 726.589 5
building | 690.658 95
other aspects see
Religious-purpose
bldgs.
Christian life guides | 248.489 5
doctrines | 230.95
general councils | 262.595
govt. & admin. | 262.095
parishes | 254.095
missions | 266.95
moral theology | 241.049 5

Church
of Christ Scientist (continued)
music
arts | 783.026 95
recordings | 789.912 302 695
s.a. spec. instruments;
also spec. kinds e.g.
Liturgical music
religion
pub. worship | 264.095 02
significance | 246.7
private prayers for | 242.809 5
pub. worship | 264.095
rel. associations
adults | 267.189 5
men | 267.249 5
women | 267.449 5
young adults | 267.629 5
rel. instruction | 268.895
rel. law | 262.989 5
schools | 377.895
secondary training | 207.129 5
sermons | 252.095
theological seminaries | 207.119 5
s.a. other spec. aspects;
also Christian
Scientists
of England *see* Anglican
churches
of God (Adventists) | 286.73
misc. aspects see
Adventists
(denominations)
of God in Christ | 289.73
misc. aspects see Mennonite
churches
of Jesus Christ of Latter-Day
Saints | 289.33
misc. aspects see
Latter-Day Saints
Church
of the Brethren | 286.5
misc. aspects see Baptist
of the Nazarene *see*
Miscellaneous Christian
denominations
of the New Jerusalem | 289.4
buildings
architecture | 726.589 4
building | 690.658 94
other aspects see
Religious-purpose
bldgs.
Christian life guides | 248.489 4
doctrines | 230.94
creeds | 238.94
general councils | 262.594
govt. & admin. | 262.094
parishes | 254.094
missions | 266.94
moral theology | 241.049 4

Church
of the New Jerusalem (continued)
music
arts   783.026 94
recordings   789.912 302 694
s.a. spec. instruments;
also spec. kinds e.g.
Liturgical music
religion
pub. worship   264.094 02
significance   246.7
private prayers for   242.809 4
pub. worship   264.094
rel. associations
adults   267.189 4
men   267.249 4
women   267.449 4
young adults   267.629 4
rel. instruction   268.894
rel. law   262.989 4
schools   377.894
secondary training   207.129 4
sermons   252.094
theological seminaries   207.119 4
s.a. other spec. aspects;
also New Jerusalemites
organization
Christianity   262
other rel. see
Ecclesiastical theology
polity
Christianity   262
other rel. see
Ecclesiastical theology
precepts
Christian moral theology   241.57
programs
Christianity   254.6
other rel. see
Ecclesiastical theology
renewal ecclesiology   262.001 7
schools
gen. ed. *see* Christian
church (general)
schools
libraries   027.83
administration   025.197 83
buildings
architecture   727.828 3
functional planning   022.318 3
catalogs *see* Library
catalogs
reference services   025.527 783
selection for   025.218 783
use studies   025.587 83
user orientation   025.567 83
s.a. other spec.
activities e.g.
Cataloging

Church
schools (continued)
rel. instruction *see*
Religious instruction
ecclesiastical theology
Slavonic language *see* Old
Bulgarian language
Stretton Salop Eng.   *area*–424 57
suppers
food services   642.4
year
devotional lit.
Christianity   242.3
other rel. see
Meditations
rel. observance
Christianity   263.9
other rel. see Times rel.
observance
Roman Catholic pub. worship
     264.021
sermons
Christianity   252.61–.67
other rel. see Preaching
s.a. Christian
Churches
accounting   657.832
haunted
occultism   133.122
of God *see* Miscellaneous
Christian denominations
welfare services *see*
Religious organizations
welfare services
Churchill
city Man.   *area*–712 71
Co. Nev.   *area*–793 52
River Man.   *area*–712 71
Churchyards *see* Cemeteries
Churrigueresque architecture   724.19
spec. places   720.9
other aspects see
Architectural schools
Chutneys
comm. proc.   664.58
soc. & econ. aspects *see*
Secondary industries
Chuvash
ASSR   *area*–478 3
language *see* Turkic languages
people   *r.e.n.*–945 6
s.a. other spec. subj. e.g.
Arts
Chymotrypsin *see* Enzymes
Chytridiales *see* Uniflagellate
molds
Chytrids *see* Uniflagellate
molds
Cicadas *see* Homoptera
Cicadoidea *see* Homoptera
Cicer arietinum *see* Chick-peas

Cichorium
  endiva *see* Endive
  intybus *see* Chicory
Ciconiae *see* Ciconiiformes
Ciconiiformes
  hunting
    commercial — 639.128 34
    sports — 799.248 34
  paleozoology — 568.3
  zoology — 598.34
  other aspects see Aves
Cidaroida *see* Echinoidea
Cider — 641.2
  comm. proc.
    fermented — 663.2
    sweet — 663.63
  other aspects see Beverages
Ciechanow Poland — *area*–438 4
Ciego de Avila Cuba — *area*–729 153
Cienfuegos Cuba — *area*–729 143
Cigarette
  cases *see* Smokers' supplies
  holders *see* Smokers' supplies
  lighters *see* Smokers'
    supplies
Cigarettes
  mf. tech. — 679.73
  other aspects see Tobacco
Cigars
  mf. tech. — 679.72
  other aspects see Tobacco
Ciliary bodies
  eyes *see* Uveas eyes
Ciliata
  culture — 639.731 72
  zoology — 593.172
  other aspects see Protozoa
Cilicia — *area*–564
  ancient — *area*–393 5
Ciliophora
  culture — 639.731 7
  paleozoology — 563.17
  zoology — 593.17
  other aspects see Protozoa
Cimarron
  Co. Okla. — *area*–766 132
  River — *area*–766 3
Cimicoidea *see* Heteroptera
Cinchona *see* Rubiales
Cincinnati
  city O. — *area*–771 78
  society — 369.13
Cinclidae
  hunting
    commercial — 639.128 832
    sports — 799.248 832
  paleozoology — 568.8
  zoology — 598.832
  other aspects see Aves
Cinder blocks
  technology — 666.894

Cinder blocks (continued)
  other aspects see Artificial
    stones
Cinema *see* Motion pictures
Cinematography — 778.53
Cineraria *see* Asterales
Cinnabar
  mineralogy — 549.32
Cinnamon *see* Spices; *also*
    Laurales
Cinque Ports Eng. — *area*–422 352
Ciphers (cryptography) — 652.8
Circaeasteraceae *see*
    Berberidales
Circassian *see* Caucasic
Circle-geometry — 516.184
  s.a. spec. geometries; also
    spec. appls. e.g.
      Engineering
Circles
  geometry
    gen. wks. *see*
      Configurations geometry
  squaring — 516.204
Circuit breakers *see* Control
    devices electrodynamic
    eng.
Circuitry *see* Circuits
Circuits
  closed-loop automation eng. — 629.831 3
    s.a. spec. appls. e.g.
      Automatons
  computer eng. — 621.381 953 5
    analogue — 621.381 957 35
    combinations & related — 621.381 959
    digital — 621.381 958 35
    other aspects see Computers
    s.a. spec. appls. e.g. Data
      processing
  elect. power transmission
    electrodynamic eng. — 621.319 2
      s.a. spec. appls. e.g.
        Lighting engineering
    other aspects see
      Electrodynamics
  gamma-ray electronics *see*
      Gamma-ray circuits
  microelectronics
    soc. & econ. aspects *see*
      Secondary industries
    tech. & mf. — 621.381 73
      s.a. spec. appls. e.g.
        Tracking
    other aspects see
      Electronics
  microwave electronics
    technology — 621.381 32
      s.a. spec. appls. e.g.
        Radar engineering
    other aspects see Microwave
      electronics

Circuits (continued)
radar eng.   621.384 81
  misc. aspects see Radar
  s.a. spec. appls. e.g.
    Navigation
radio & microwave electronics
  astrophysics   523.018 753 4
    s.a. spec. celestial
     bodies
  physics   537.534
    spec. states of matter   530.4
radio eng.   621.384 12
  misc. aspects see Radio
  s.a. spec. appls. e.g.
    Radiotelephony
radiowave electronics
  technology   621.381 53
    s.a. spec. appls. e.g.
     Radiocontrol
  other aspects see Radiowave
    electronics
receiving sets
  radio
    engineering   621.384 136 1
    s.a. spec. appls. e.g.
     Radiotelephony
    other aspects see Radio
  television
    engineering   621.388 361
    s.a. spec. appls. e.g.
     Astronautics
    other aspects see
     Television
television eng.   621.388 12
  other aspects see
    Television
  s.a. spec. appls. e.g.
    Astronautics
x-ray electronics *see* X-ray
  circuits
s.a. other spec. appls.
Circulars
direct advertising   659.133
postal commun.   383.124
  misc. aspects see Postal
    communication
spec. subj.   *s.s.*–029
Circulation
atmosphere
  meteorology   551.517
library services   025.6
museum services   069.13
steam *see* Transmission steam
theory
  money econ.   332.401
Circulation (biology)
brain
  human phys.   612.824
  other aspects see Nervous
    system

Circulation (biology) (continued)
pathology
  gen. wks.   574.211
  animals   591.211
  plants   581.211
  s.a. spec. organisms
  med. sci.   616.1
  animals   636.089 61
    s.a. spec. animals
  man   616.1
physiology
  gen. wks.   574.11
  animals   591.11
  microorganisms   576.111
  plants   581.11
  s.a. spec. organisms
  med. sci.   612.1
  animals   636.089 21
    s.a. spec. animals
  man   612.1
  s.a. spec. functions,
    systems, organs
Circulatory
fluids
  pathology
    gen. wks.   574.211 3
    animals   591.211 3
    plants   581.211 3
    s.a. spec. organisms
    med. sci.   616.15
    animals   636.089 615
     s.a. spec. animals
    man   616.15
  physiology
    gen. wks.   574.113
    animals   591.113
    microorganisms   576.111 3
    plants   581.113
    s.a. spec. organisms
    med. sci.   612.11–.12
    animals   636.089 211–.089 212
     s.a. spec. animals
    man   612.11–.12
organs
  anatomy
    gen. wks.   574.41
    animals   591.41
    microorganisms   576.14
    plants   581.41
    s.a. spec. organisms
    med. sci.   611.1
    animals   636.089 11
     s.a. spec. animals
    man   611.1
  pathology
    anatomical   574.221
    animals   591.221
    plants   581.221
    s.a. spec. organisms

Circulatory
  organs
    pathology (continued)
      medical *see* Circulation
        (biology) pathology
        med. sci.
        physiological   574.211 6
          animals   591.211 6
          plants   581.211 6
        s.a. spec. organisms
      physiology
        gen. wks.   574.116
          animals   591.116
          microorganisms   576.111 6
          plants   581.116
        s.a. spec. organisms
        med. sci.   612.13–.18
          animals   636.089 213–.089 218
          s.a. spec. animals
        man   612.13–.18
Circumcision
  Jesus Christ
    Christian doctrines   232.924
  Jewish rites   296.442 2
  soc. customs   392.12
  surgery   617.463
Circumnavigational travel   910.41
  misc. aspects see Travel
Circumnutation
  plants
    pathology   581.218 5
    physiology   581.185
    s.a. spec. plants
Circumstantial evidence
  criminal investigation   363.256
  law   347.064
    criminal   345.064
  other aspects see Evidence
Circumterrestrial flights
  astronautics
    manned
      soc. & econ. aspects *see*
        Secondary industries
      technology   629.454
      s.a. spec. appls. e.g.
        Space warfare
Circus
  performers
    biog. & work   791.309 2
    s.a. spec. kinds e.g.
      Acrobats
    s.a.   *pers.*–791 3
  use
    animal husbandry for   636.088 8
    s.a. spec. animals
Circuses
  ethics *see* Public
    entertainment ethics
  performing arts   791.3
Cire perdue casting *see*
    Precision casting

Cirencester Gloucestershire Eng.
        area–424 17
Cirques
  physical geol.   551.315
Cirrhosis
  gen. med.   616.362 4
  geriatrics   618.976 362 4
  pediatrics   618.923 624
  pub. health   614.593 624
  statistics   312.336 24
    deaths   312.263 624
  other aspects see Diseases
Cirripedia
  culture   639.5
  fishing
    commercial   639.5
    sports   799.255 35
  paleozoology   565.35
  zoology   595.35
  other aspects see Crustacea
Ciskei Cape of Good Hope   *area*–687 92
Cis-polydienes *see* Synthetic
    rubber
Cistaceae *see* Bixales
Cistercian
  monastic bldgs.
    architecture   726.771 2
    building   690.677 12
    other aspects see
      Religious-purpose
      bldgs.
Cistercians
  rel. orders
    church hist.   271.12
    women's   271.97
    ecclesiology   262.24
    gen. wks.   255.12
    women's   255.97
Citadels
  mil. eng.   623.1
  other aspects see Military
    buildings
Citations
  mil. discipline   355.134
  s.a. spec. mil. branches
Citators
  to cases
    law   348.047
    spec. jur.   348.3–.9
    U.S.
      Federal   348.734 7
      state & local   348.74–.79
    spec. subj.   *law s.s.*–026 48
  to laws
    law   348.027
    spec. jur.   348.3–.9
    U.S.
      Federal   348.732 7
      state & local   348.74–.79
    spec. subj.   *law s.s.*–026 38
Citharas *see* Harps

Cities
  local govt.   352.007 24
  sociology   307.76
  s.a. City
Citizen-executive relations *see*
        Executive-citizen
        relations
Citizens & state
  ethics *see* Citizenship ethics
  pol. sci.   323
Citizen's band radio
  technology   621.384 54
    s.a. spec. appls. e.g. Fire
      fighting
  other aspects see
      Radiotelephony
Citizenship
  elementary ed.   372.832
  ethics
    philosophy   172.1
    religion
      Buddhism   294.356 21
      Christianity   241.621
      comp. rel.   291.562 1
      Hinduism   294.548 621
      s.a. other spec. rel.
  law
    international   341.482
    municipal   342.083
    spec. jur.   342.3–.9
  loss of
    penology   364.68
    pol. sci.   323.6
Citrons
  agriculture   634.331
    soc. & econ. aspects *see*
      Primary industries
  foods   641.343 31
    preparation
      commercial   664.804 331
      domestic   641.643 31
  other aspects see Rutales;
    also Fruits
Citrullus vulgaris *see*
    Watermelons
Citrus
  aurantifolia *see* Limes
    (fruit)
  aurantium *see* Oranges (fruit)
  Co. Fla.   *area*–759 72
  fruits
    agriculture   634.35
    soc. & econ. aspects *see*
      Primary industries
    foods   641.343 5
    preparation
      commercial   664.804 35
      domestic   641.643 5
    other aspects see Fruits
  limonia *see* Lemons
  medica *see* Citrons

Citrus (continued)
  paradisi *see* Grapefruit
  trees *see* Rutales
City
  buildings
    architecture   725.13
    building   690.513
    other aspects see Public
      structures
  club bldgs. *see* Clubhouse
    buildings
  gas
    chem. tech.   665.772
    soc. & econ. aspects *see*
      Secondary industries
  managers
    local govt. admin.   352.008 4
  planners
    biog. & work   711.092
    s.a.   *pers.*–71
  planning
    civic art   711.4
    law   346.045
      spec. jur.   346.3–.9
    pub. admin.   352.96
  states
    pol. sci.   321.06
    s.a. spec. jur.
  s.a. Urban; *also* Cities;
    also Municipal
Cityscapes
  art representation   704.944
  painting   758.7
  s.a. other spec. art forms
Ciudad Real Spain   *area*–464 5
Civets *see* Viverridae
Civic
  areas civic art   711.551
  art   711
  duties ethics *see* Citizenship
    ethics
Civics   320.4
  elementary ed.   372.832
Civil
  actions
    legal procedure   347.053
    spec. jur.   347.3–.9
    other aspects see Legal
      procedures
  architecture *see* Public
    structures
  commotion insurance   368.125
  defense   363.35
  law
    international   341.72
    municipal   344.053 5
      spec. jur.   344.3–.9
    pub. admin.   350.755
      central govts.   351.755
      spec. jur.   353–354
      local govts.   352.935 5

Civil (continued)	
disobedience	
law	342.085 4
spec. jur.	342.3–.9
disorders	
disaster relief	363.349 7
misc. aspects see	
Disasters	
sociology	303.62
engineering	
gen. wks.	
soc. & econ. aspects *see*	
Secondary industries	
technology	624
mil. eng.	623.047
s.a. other spec. appls.	
engineers	
biog. & work	624.092
s.a. spec. kinds	
s.a.	*pers.–624*
freedóm	
pub. admin. ethics *see*	
Public administration	
ethics	
s.a. Civil rights	
government *see* Government	
law systems	340.56
laws	
enforcement	
legal aspects	344.052 33
spec. jur.	344.3–.9
soc. services	363.233
other aspects see Law	
enforcement	
liberty *see* Civil rights	
medals	
numismatics	737.223
penalties	
penology	364.68
procedure *see* Legal procedure	
resistance	
ethics *see* Citizenship	
ethics	
rights	
law	
international	341.481
municipal	342.085
spec. jur.	342.3–.9
pol. sci.	323.4
pub. admin.	350.811
central govts.	351.811
spec. jur.	353–354
local govts.	352.941 1
rel. to soc. welfare	361.614
violations & denials	
criminology	364.132 2
law	345.023 22
spec. jur.	345.3–.9
pub. admin.	350.996
central govts.	351.996
spec. jur.	353–354

Civil	
rights	
violations & denials	
pub. admin. (continued)	
local govts.	352.002
soc. theology	
Christianity	261.833 132 2
comp. rel.	291.178 331 322
s.a. other spec. rel.	
workers	
biog. & work	323.409 2
s.a.	*pers.–323*
service	
administration	350.6
central govts.	351.6
spec. jur.	353–354
local govts.	352.005 6
examinations	
pub. admin.	350.3
central govts.	351.3
spec. jur.	353–354
local govts.	352.005 3
spec. subj.	*s.s.–076*
law	342.068
spec. jur.	342.3–.9
personnel	
biog. & work	351.000 92
s.a. admin. of spec.	
jur.	
investigation pub. admin.	350.992
central govts.	351.992
spec. jur.	353–354
local govts.	352.002
labor econ.	331.795
labor force	331.119 042
market	331.129 042
other aspects see	
Industrial occupations	
labor law *see* Labor law	
law	342.068
spec. jur.	342.3–.9
s.a.	*pers.–352 7*
s.a. spec. occupations &	
kinds	
uniforms *see* Uniforms	
violence	
sociology	303.62
war	
citizenship ethics *see*	
Citizenship ethics	
internat. law	341.68
warfare mil. sci.	355.021 84
wars	
history	904.7
U.S.	973.7
societies	369.15–.17
s.a. hist. of other spec.	
countries	
sociology	303.64

Civilian
  manpower
    mil. sci.   355.23
  works
    labor econ.   331.79
      labor force   331.119 042
      market   331.129 042
      other aspects see
           Industrial occupations
    labor law *see* Labor law
Civilization
  Bible   220.95
    s.a. spec. parts of Bible
  hist. & crit.
    areal & group trmt.   930–990
    gen. trmt.   909
      ancient   930
    other aspects see History
  lit. trmt. *see* Places lit.
      trmt.
  sociology   306
Civil-military relations
  pol. sci.   322.5
Clackamas Co. Ore.   *area*–795 41
Clackmannan Scot.   *area*–413 15
Clacton Essex Eng.   *area*–426 725
Cladding *see* Coating metal
      products
Cladocera *see* Branchiopoda
Cladocopa *see* Ostracoda
Cladophorales *see* Chlorophyta
Cladoselachii
  paleozoology   567.3
Claiborne
  County
    Mississippi   *area*–762 285
    Tennessee   *area*–768 944
  Par. La.   *area*–763 94
Claiming
  library acquisitions   025.236
Claims
  adjustment
    insurance   368.014
    s.a. spec. kinds of
      insurance
  sales management *see* Customer
    relationships sales
    management
  settlement
    govt. contracts
      pub. admin.   350.711 3
        central govts.   351.711 3
        spec. jur.   353–354
      local govts.   352.161 3
Clairaudience
  parapsychology   133.85
Clairvoyance
  parapsychology   133.84
Clairvoyants
  biog. & work   133.840 92
  s.a.   *pers.*–13

Clallam Co. Wash.   *area*–797 99
Clam shrimps *see* Branchiopoda
Clamps *see* Holding-equipment
Clams
  culture   639.44
  fishing
    commercial   639.44
    sports   799.254 11
  food *see* Mollusca food
  other aspects see Pelecypoda
Clandestine publications *see*
      Underground
      publications
Clans
  ecology life sci. *see*
      Populations ecology
      life sci.
Clare
  County
    Ireland   *area*–419 3
    Michigan   *area*–774 71
  S. Aust.   *area*–942 32
  Suffolk Eng.   *area*–426 44
Clarence River N.S.W. *area*–944 3
Clarendon Co. S.C.   *area*–757 81
Clarinet music   788.625
  recordings   789.912 862
Clarinetists
  biog. & work   788.620 92
  s.a.   *pers.*–788
Clarinets
  mf. tech.   681.818 62
  misc. aspects see Musical
      instruments
  musical art   788.62
Clarion Co. Pa.   *area*–748 69
Clark Co.
  Arkansas   *area*–767 49
  Idaho   *area*–796 57
  Illinois   *area*–773 71
  Indiana   *area*–772 185
  Kansas   *area*–781 77
  Kentucky   *area*–769 54
  Missouri   *area*–778 343
  Nevada   *area*–793 13
  Ohio   *area*–771 49
  South Dakota   *area*–783 22
  Washington   *area*–797 86
  Wisconsin   *area*–775 28
Clarke
  County
    Alabama   *area*–761 245
    Georgia   *area*–758 18
    Iowa   *area*–777 856
    Mississippi   *area*–762 673
    Virginia   *area*–755 98
  Isl. Tas.   *area*–946 7
  Range Qld.   *area*–943 6
Clarkia *see* Lythrales
Clarksburg W.Va.   *area*–754 58

Class
  actions
    legal procedure 347.053
      spec. jur. 347.3–.9
    other aspects see Legal
        procedure
  conflict
    influence on crime 364.256
  periods *see* Class schedules
  schedules 371.242 1
    s.a. spec. levels of ed.;
      also Special education
  struggle
    labor union theory
      economics 331.880 1
    Marxist theory
      economics 335.411
Classes
  museum services 069.15
  school organization 371.25
    s.a. spec. levels of ed.;
      also Special education
  sociology *see* Social classes
  s.a. other spec. subj. e.g.
      Mail services
Classical
  algebraic geometry 516.35
    s.a. spec. appls. e.g.
      Engineering
  architecture 722.6
    misc. aspects see
      Architectural schools
  dances
    music *see* Dance music
  dancing
    performing arts 793.32
    economics 330.153
  languages
    linguistics 480
    literatures 880
    s.a.   *lang.–8*
  mechanics *see* Mechanics
  music 780.43
    s.a. spec. mediums
  physics *see* Physics
  religion 292
    persons in   *pers.–292*
  religious temples & shrines
    architecture 726.12
    other aspects see
        Religious-purpose
        bldgs.
  revival arts
    architecture 724.2
      spec. places 720.9
      other aspects see
        Architectural schools
    design & dec. 745.555 1
      spec. places 745.449
    gen. wks. 709.034 1
      spec. places 709.1–.9

Classical
  revival arts (continued)
    painting 759.051
      spec. places 759.1–.9
    sculpture 735.22
      spec. places 730.9
    s.a. other spec. art forms
  secondary schools 373.242
    govt. supervision & support 379
  statistical mechanics
    physics 530.132
    spec. states of matter 530.4
    s.a. spec. branches of
        physics
  typology
    indiv. psych. 155.262
  s.a. Ancient
Classicism
  lit. qual.
    gen. wks.
      collections 808.801 42
      hist. & crit. 809.914 2
    spec. lits.
      collections   *lit. sub.–080 142*
      hist. & crit.   *lit. sub.–091 42*
    s.a. spec. lit. forms
  stage qual. 792.090 914 2
    s.a. other spec. dramatic
        mediums e.g.
        Television; *also spec.*
        kinds of drama e.g.
        Tragedies (drama)
Classification
  jobs *see* Job classification
  library operations 025.42
  mil. personnel 355.223 6
    s.a. spec. mil. branches
  security
    armed forces 355.343 3
      s.a. spec. mil. branches
  s.a.   *s.s.–012*
  s.a. other spec. subj.
Classified catalogs
  library sci.
    spec. catalogs 017.1–.4
    theory 025.315
Classroom
  control *see* Classroom
      discipline
  discipline 371.102 4
    s.a. spec. levels of ed.;
      also Special education
  management *see* Teaching
Classrooms *see* Instructional
    spaces education
Clastidiaceae *see* Cyanophyta
Clatsop Co. Ore.   *area*–795 46
Clauses *see* Grammar
    (linguistics)
Clavariaceae *see* Agaricales

Clear-channel broadcasting
    stations
  radio
    engineering   621.384 162
    s.a. spec. appls. e.g.
      Radiotelephony
    other aspects see Radio
Clearfield Co. Pa.   *area*–748 61
Clearing
  canal eng. *see* Earthwork
      canal eng.
  land
    agriculture   631.61
    s.a. spec. crops
  road eng. *see* Roadbeds
  s.a. other spec. subj.
Clearwater
  County
    Idaho   *area*–796 88
    Minnesota   *area*–776 83
  Mts. Ida.   *area*–796 82
  River Ida.   *area*–796 85
Cleavage
  crystal   548.843
  s.a. spec. substances
  minerals *see* Mechanical
      properties minerals
  structural geol.   551.84
  s.a. spec. aspects e.g.
      Prospecting
Cleburne Co.
  Alabama   *area*–761 64
  Arkansas   *area*–767 285
Cleethorpes Humberside Eng.
            area–428 33
Cleft palate *see* Palate
    diseases
Clemency
  criminology   364.6
  ethics *see* Virtues
Cleobury Mortimer Salop Eng.
            area–424 57
Cleopatra reign Egypt hist.   932.021
  s.a. spec. events & subj.
    e.g. Commerce
Clepsydras
  mf. tech.   681.111
Clerestories
  Christian church arch.   726.594
Clergy
  biog. & work
    Christianity   253.209 2
    s.a. spec. denominations;
      also spec. kinds e.g.
      Theologians
    comp. rel.   291.610 92
    s.a. other spec. rel.
  ecclesiology *see* Governing
      leaders ecclesiology
  life & duties
    Christianity   253

Clergy
  life & duties (continued)
    other rel. see Governing
      leaders
    meditations
      private devotions
        Christianity   242.692
      other rel. see
        Meditations
    occupational ethics
      philosophy   174.1
      religion
        Buddhism   294.356 41
        Christianity   241.641
        comp. rel.   291.564 1
        Hinduism   294.548 641
        s.a. other spec. rel.
    personal rel.
      Christianity   248.892
      other rel. see Personal
        religion
    prayers for
      private devotions
        Christianity   242.892
      other rel. see Prayers
        private devotions
    rel. law *see* Persons rel. law
    retreats
      rel. practices
        Christianity   269.692
      other rel. see Spiritual
        renewal
    sermons for
      Christianity   252.592
      other rel. see Preaching
    s.a.   *pers.*–2
Clerical
  occupations
    labor econ. *see* Service
      occupations labor econ.
  personnel
    office services   651.37
  services
    management
      pub. admin.   350.714
        central govts.   351.714
        spec. jur.   353–354
        local govts.   352.164
Clerihews *see* Humorous poetry
Clerks
  gen. wks. *see* Office
      personnel
  of court
    law *see* Court officials law
  regular
    rel. orders   255.5
      church hist.   271.5
      ecclesiology   262.24
Regular of the Mother of God
  rel. orders   255.57
    church hist.   271.57

Clerks
Regular of the Mother of God
rel. orders (continued)
ecclesiology   262.24
Clermont
Co. O.   *area*–771 794
Queensland   *area*–423 96
Clethraceae *see* Ericales
Clevedon Avon Eng.   *area*–423 96
Cleveland
bay horse
animal husbandry   636.14
other aspects see Horses
city O.   *area*–771 32
County
Arkansas   *area*–767 69
England   *area*–428 5
North Carolina   *area*–756 775
Oklahoma   *area*–766 37
Grover
U.S. hist.
1 admin.   973.85
2 admin.   973.87
s.a. spec. events & subj.
e.g. Commerce
Hills North Yorkshire Eng.
area–428 49
Click beetles *see* Elateroidea
Clifford algebra   512.57
s.a. spec. appls. e.g.
Engineering
Clifton Forge Va.   *area*–755 811
Climacteric
disorders
female *see* Menopause
disorders
gen. wks. *see* Menopause
disorders
male
gen. med.   616.693
geriatrics   618.976 693
pub. health   614.596 93
statistics   312.369 3
other aspects see
Diseases
human phys.   612.665
other aspects see Development
(biology)
Climate-induced illnesses   616.988
geriatrics   618.976 988
pediatrics   618.929 88
statistics   312.398 8
deaths   312.269 88
other aspects see
Environmental diseases
s.a. spec. diseases
Climates
city planning
arts   711.42
earth sciences   551.62

Climates (continued)
ecology
life sci.   574.542
animals   591.542
man   573.4
microorganisms   576.15
plants   581.542
s.a. spec. organisms
sociology   304.25
soc. theology
Christianity   261.836 25
comp. rel.   291.178 362 5
s.a. other spec. rel.
hygiene   613.11
misc. aspects see Hygiene
influence on crime   364.22
psych. influences   155.915
Climatological diseases *see*
Climate-induced
illnesses
Climatologists
biog. & work   551.609 2
other aspects see Scientists
s.a.   *pers.*–551
Climatology   551.6
misc. aspects see Earth
sciences
Climatotherapy   615.834
misc. aspects see Physical
therapies
s.a. spec. diseases
Climbing mountains *see* Mountain
climbing
Climbing-plants *see* Vines
Clinch
Co. Ga.   *area*–758 812
Mts. Tenn.   *area*–768 932
River Tenn.   *area*–768 73
Clinic buildings *see* Office
buildings
Clinical
diagnosis *see* Diagnoses
medicine   616.07
psychology   157.9
Clinics
civic art   711.555
safety aspects *see* Health
care facilities
sanitation *see* Health care
facilities sanitation
soc. services   362.12
misc. aspects see Hospitals
Clinton Co.
Illinois   *area*–773 875
Indiana   *area*–772 553
Iowa   *area*–777 67
Kentucky   *area*–769 653
Michigan   *area*–774 24
Missouri   *area*–778 155
New York   *area*–747 54
Ohio   *area*–771 765

Clinton Co. (continued)
  Pennsylvania   *area*–748 54
Clip spot embroidery *see*
      Machine embroidery
Clipper ships *see* Merchant
      ships wind-driven
Clippings
  library trmt.   025.172
    acquisitions   025.282
    cataloging   025.342
    s.a. other spec. activities
Cliques
  sociology   302.34
  s.a. spec. organizations
Clitheroe Lancashire Eng.   *area*–427 685
Clitoris *see* Vulva
Clive governorship India hist.   954.029 6
  s.a. spec. events & subj.
      e.g. Commerce
Cloaks
  comm. mf.   687.147
  domestic mf.   646.457
  other aspects see Clothing
Clock towers *see* Towers
      (structures)
Clockcases
  art metalwork   739.3
  dec. arts   749.3
Clockmakers
  biog. & work   681.113 092
  s.a.   *pers.*–681 1
Clocks
  mf. tech.   681.113
    soc. & econ. aspects *see*
      Secondary industries
  time measurement   529.78
Clockworks
  mf. tech.   681.112
    soc. & econ. aspects *see*
      Secondary industries
Clog dancing
  performing arts   793.324
Clogs
  mf. tech.   685.32
  other aspects see Footwear
Cloisonné
  ceramic arts   738.42
  other aspects see Enamels
Cloisters
  cathedral *see* Accessory
      cathedral structures
  monastic *see* Accessory
      monastic structures
Cloncurry Qld.   *area*–943 7
Clonmel Munster Ire.   *area*–419 25
Clontarf Battle
  Ireland hist.   941.501
Close corporations
  law   346.066 8
  other aspects see
      Corporations

Closed shop
  labor econ.   331.889 2
  law *see* Labor law
Closed stacks
  library operations   025.81
Closed-circuit
  stations
    television
      engineering   621.388 63
      s.a. spec. appls. e.g.
        Astronautics
      other aspects see
        Television
  television
    commerce   384.555
    govt. control   351.874 555
    spec. jur.   353–354
    law *see* Television
      communication law
Closed-cycle turbine engines
    see Simple
      gas-turbine engines
Closed-loop systems
  automation eng.
    soc. & econ. aspects *see*
      Secondary industries
  technology   629.83
    s.a. spec. appls. e.g.
      Automatons
Close-up photography
  technique   778.324
Closings
  real estate
    law   346.043 73
      spec. jur.   346.3–.9
Cloth
  covers
    bookbinding   686.343
    gen. wks. *see* Textiles
Clothbound books
  publishing   070.573
  other aspects see Books
Clothes dryers
  mf. tech.   683.88
  other aspects see Household
      appliances
Clothing   646.3
  academic
    higher ed.   378.28
  armed forces
    costume   355.14
    equipment   355.81
    s.a. spec. mil. branches
  care of
    home econ.   646.6
  comm. mf.
    soc. & econ. aspects *see*
      Secondary industries
    technology   687
  domestic mf.   646
  hygiene   613.482

Coach
  horses (continued)
    other aspects see Horses
Coaches
  railroad *see* Passenger-train
    cars
Coaching
  athletic sports   796.077
    s.a. spec. activities
  horses
    sports   798.6
    s.a. other spec. subj.
Coagulants
  pharmacodynamics   615.718
  other aspects see Drugs
Coagulation
  blood
    diseases *see* Hemorrhagic
      diseases
    human phys.   612.115
    other aspects see
      Circulatory fluids
  water-supply trmt.
    technology   628.162 2
    other aspects see Water
      supply engineering
  s.a. other spec. subj.
Coahoma Co. Miss.   *area*–762 44
Coahuila Mex.   *area*–721 4
Coal
  Co. Okla.   *area*–766 67
  gas
    chem. tech.   665.772
    soc. & econ. aspects *see*
      Secondary industries
  heating
    buildings   697.042
    s.a. spec. kinds e.g.
      Steam heating
  oil
    chem. tech.   665.538 3
    other aspects see Petroleum
  tar
    org. chem.   547.82
Coalition
  forces
    mil. sci.   355.356
    s.a. spec. mil. branches
  War hist.   949.204
Coals   553.24
  econ. geol.   553.24
  mining
    law   343.077 52
      spec. jur.   343.3–.9
    technology   622.334
      prospecting   622.182 4
  processing
    soc. & econ. aspects *see*
      Secondary industries
    technology   662.62

Coals (continued)
  resources
    economics   333.822
    govt. control
      law   346.046 822
        spec. jur.   346.3–.9
      pub. admin. *see*
        Subsurface resources
        govt. control pub.
        admin.
  supply
    law   343.092 7
      spec. jur.   343.3–.9
  other aspects see Fuels
  s.a. spec. uses e.g. Steam
    engineering; *also*
    spec. minerals
Coal-tar chemicals
  chem. tech.   661.803
  other aspects see Organic
    chemicals
Coalville Leicestershire Eng.
        area–425 48
Coast
  artillery
    armed forces   358.16
    mil. eng.
      soc. & econ. aspects *see*
        Secondary industries
      tech. & mf.   623.417
  guard
    mil. sci.   359.97
    police services   363.286
    misc. aspects see Law
      enforcement
  vessels
    engineering   623.826 3
      design   623.812 63
      models   623.820 163
    naval forces
      materiel   359.83
      organization   359.326 3
    seamanship   623.882 63
    other aspects see Vessels
      (nautical)
  province Kenya   *area*–676 23
  Ranges   *area*–795
    British Columbia   *area*–711 3
    California   *area*–794 1
    Oregon   *area*–795
    Washington   *area*–797 9
  region Tanzania   *area*–678 23
Coastal
  changes
    physical geol.   551.36
  defenses
    mil. sci.   355.45
    s.a. spec. mil. branches
  operations
    mil. sci.   355.423
    s.a. spec. mil. branches

Coastal (continued)
Plain Atlantic *see* Atlantic
    Coastal Plain
pools *see* Special salt-water
    forms
regions
  geology   551.45
  reclamation *see* Shore
    reclamation eng.
  regional subj. trmt.   *area*–146
  resources
    economics   333.917
    recreational   333.784
    govt. control
      law   346.046 917
      spec. jur.   346.3–.9
      pub. admin. *see* Land
      resources govt. control
      pub. admin.
routes *see* Coastwise routes
Coasting
snow sports
  equip. mf.   688.769 5
  soc. & econ. aspects *see*
    Secondary industries
  sports   796.95
other aspects see Sports
Coasts
geomorphology   551.457
other aspects see Coastal
    regions
Coastwise routes
marine transp.
  commerce   387.524
  govt. control   351.877 524
  spec. jur.   353–354
law *see* Marine
    transportation
Coatbridge Strathclyde Scot.
    area–414 46
Coated
papers
  mf. tech.   676.283
  other aspects see Papers
    pulp prod.
powders *see* Propellant
    explosives
Coating
gen. wks.
  technology   667.9
  s.a. spec. appls. e.g.
    Bodies automobiles
latex mf.
  soc. & econ. aspects *see*
    Secondary industries
  technology   678.527
  s.a. spec. kinds of latexes
    e.g. Natural latexes
metal products
  mf. tech.   671.73
  ferrous metals   672.73

Coating
metal products
  mf. tech. (continued)
    s.a. other spec. metals
    other aspects see Finishing
  paper
    mf. tech.   676.235
    spec. papers   676.28
  s.a. other spec. subj.
Coatings
manufacturing
  soc. & econ. aspects *see*
    Secondary industries
  technology   667.9
painting material
  arts   751.2
  indiv. artists   759.1–.9
Coatis *see* Procyonidae
Coats
children's *see* Children's
    clothing
Isl. Northwest Ter.   *area*–719 4
men's *see* Men's clothing
women's *see* Women's clothing
other aspects see Outer
    garments
Coats-of-arms
genealogy   929.82
Cob *see* Sun-dried blocks
Cobaeaceae *see* Bignoniales
Cobalt
chemistry
  inorganic   546.623
  organic   547.056 23
  s.a. spec. groupings e.g.
    Aliphatic compounds
  technology   661.062 3
  organic   661.895
  soc. & econ. aspects *see*
    Secondary industries
  s.a. spec. prod.
construction
  building   693.773 3
materials
  building   691.873 3
  engineering   620.189 33
  s.a. spec. uses e.g. Colors
metallography   669.957 33
metallurgy   669.733
  physical & chem.   669.967 33
  soc. & econ. aspects *see*
    Secondary industries
mineral aspects
  econ. geol.   553.48
  marketing *see* Marketing
  mining
    technology   622.348
    prospecting   622.184 8
  s.a. spec. minerals

Cobalt (continued)
  pharmacology   615.262 3
    misc. aspects see
        Pharmacology
  products
    mf. tech.   673.733
    other aspects see
        Nonferrous metals
        products
  soaps
    chem. tech.   668.125
    soc. & econ. aspects *see*
        Secondary industries
  toxicology   615.925 623
    misc. aspects see
        Toxicology
  other aspects see Metal;
    also Metals
Cobar N.S.W.   *area*–944 9
Cobb
  Co. Ga.   *area*–758 245
  Isl. Va.   *area*–755 15
Cobbling
  soc. & econ. aspects *see*
    Secondary industries
  technology   685.310 2–.310 4
Cobnuts *see* Filberts
Cobol *see* Program languages
Cobourg Peninsula Fauna Reserve
    N. Ter. Aust.   *area*–942 95
Cocaine *see* Alkaloids
Coccidiosis *see* Protozoan
    diseases
Coccoidea *see* Homoptera
Cochabamba Bolivia   *area*–842 3
Cochin China *see* French
    Indochina
Cochineal
  culture   638.3
    misc. aspects see
        Agriculture
  dyes
    comm. proc.   667.26
    other aspects see Dyes
Cochise Co. Ariz.   *area*–791 53
Cochlea
  ear *see* Internal ear
Cochlospermaceae *see* Bixales
Cochoas *see* Turdidae
Cochran Co. Tex.   *area*–764 845
Cochrane District Ont. *area*–713 142
Cockateels *see* Parrots
Cockatoos *see* Parrots
Cocke Co. Tenn.   *area*–768 895
Cockenzie & Port Seton Lothian
    Scot.   *area*–413 6
Cockermouth Cumbria Eng. *area*–427 87
Cockfighting
  ethics *see* Animal combat
    sports
  performing arts   791.8

Cockney dialect   427.1
Cockroaches *see* Blattaria
Cocks (birds) *see spec. kinds*
    e.g. Pheasants
Cocks (mechanical)
  machine eng.
    soc. & econ. aspects *see*
        Secondary industries
    tech. & mf.   621.84
    s.a. spec. appls. e.g.
        Plumbing
  other aspects see Mechanics
Cocksfoots *see* Orchard grasses
Cocktails *see* Alcoholic
    beverages
Coclé Panama   *area*–728 721
Coco family *see* Tiliales
Cocoa
  beverage
    comm. proc.   663.92
    cookery   641.877
    other aspects see
        Nonalcoholic beverages
  butter
    comm. proc.   665.354
    soc. & econ. aspects *see*
        Secondary industries
  other aspects see Cacao
Coconino Co. Ariz.   *area*–791 33
Coconut
  milk
    comm. proc.   663.64
    other aspects see Beverages
  oil
    comm. proc.   665.355
    soc. & econ. aspects *see*
        Secondary industries
Coconuts
  agriculture
    fiber crops
      soc. & econ. aspects *see*
        Primary industries
      technology   633.58
    food crops
      soc. & econ. aspects *see*
        Primary industries
      technology   634.61
  foods   641.346 1
    preparation
      commercial   664.804 61
      domestic   641.646 1
    processing *see* Coconuts
      processing
  processing
    foods
      soc. & econ. aspects *see*
        Secondary industries
      technology   664.8
    textiles
      soc. & econ. aspects *see*
        Secondary industries

Coconuts
  processing
    textiles (continued)
      technology   677.18
    other aspects see Palmales;
      also Fruits
Cocopara Fauna Reserve N.S.W.
                                          area–944 8
Cocos
  islands   *area*–699
  nucifera *see* Coconuts
Cod
  Cape *see* Cape Cod
  liver oil
    pharmacology   615.34
    other aspects see Drugs
Code telegraphy
  commun. ind.
    commerce   384.14
    wire   384.14
      submarine cable   384.44
    wireless   384.524
  govt. control   351.874
  spec. jur.   353–354
  law *see* Telegraphy law
Codes
  cryptography *see* Cryptography
  of conduct *see* Conduct
  of law *see* Legal codes
  telegraphy
    eng. aspects *see* Telegraphy
    wire
  s.a. other spec. subj.
Codex iuris canonici
  rel. law   262.93
Codices
  Bible   220.4
    s.a. spec. parts of Bible
Codification
  internat. law   341.026 7
  municipal law   348.004
  spec. jur.   348.3–.9
    U.S.   348.730 4
      spec. states & localities   348.74–.79
Coding
  programming   001.642 4
    spec. subj.   *s.s.*–028 542 4
  theory mathematics   519.4
Codington Co.S.D.   *area*–783 23
Cods *see* Acanthopterygii
Coeducation   376
Coefficient of restitution
  engineering *see* Dynamics
  physics   531.382 3
Coefficients of expansion
  effect of heat
    astrophysics   523.013 41
    s.a. spec. celestial
      bodies
  physics   536.41
    spec. states of matter   530.4

Coelenterata
  culture   639.735
  paleozoology   563.5
  zoology   593.5
  other aspects see Animals
Coelum *see* Peritoneum
Coenopteridales
  paleobotany   561.73
Coenzyme A *see* Enzymes
Coercion
  internat. law   341.58
  soc. accommodation   303.6
  soc. control   303.36
Coeur d'Alene Mts. Ida.   *area*–796 91
Coffea *see* Coffee
Coffee
  agriculture   633.73
    soc. & econ. aspects *see*
      Primary industries
  comm. proc.   663.93
  County
    Alabama   *area*–761 34
    Georgia   *area*–758 823
    Tennessee   *area*–768 64
  foods   641.337 3
    cookery of   641.877
    cookery with   641.637 3
  grounds
    fortunetelling   133.324 4
  hygiene *see* Beverages
  substitutes
    comm. proc.   663.97
  other aspects see
      Nonalcoholic beverages;
      also Rubiales; *also*
      Alkaloids
Cofferdam methods
  underwater foundation eng.   624.157
    s.a. spec. appls. e.g.
      Military engineering
Coffey Co. Kan.   *area*–781 645
Coffins
  use *see* Burial of dead
  other aspects see Cabinets
      (furniture)
Coffs Harbour N.S.W.   *area*–944 3
Cog railways
  engineering   625.33
  other aspects see Mountain
      railways
Coggshall Essex Eng.   *area*–426 715
Cognac *see* Brandies
Cognition
  metaphysics   121
  psychology
    educational   370.152
    general   153.4
      animals   156.34
      children   155.413
    s.a. psych. of other spec.
      groups

Cogs *see* Spur gears
Coherent optics *see* Physical
      optics
Cohesion
  crystals   548.843
    s.a. spec. substances
  minerals *see* Mechanical
      properties minerals
  surface chem. *see* Surface
      phenomena
Cohomology groups   514.23
  s.a. spec. appls. e.g.
      Engineering
Cohorts
  mil. organization   355.31
    s.a. spec. mil. branches
Coimbra
  da Luz admin. Brazil hist.   981.062
    s.a. spec. events & subj.
      e.g. Commerce
  Portugal   *area*–469 35
Coinage
  law   343.032
    spec. jur.   343.3–.9
  monetary policy *see* Monetary
      policy
  profits
    pub. revenues
      economics   336.16
      other aspects see Nontax
        revenues
Coins
  investment econ.   332.63
  numismatics   737.4
  rel. significance
    Christianity   247.874
    comp. rel.   291.37
    s.a. other spec. rel.
Coir textiles
  arts   746.041 8
    s.a. spec. processes e.g.
      Weaving
  dyeing   667.318
  manufacturing
    soc. & econ. aspects *see*
      Secondary industries
    technology   677.18
      special-process fabrics   677.6
  other aspects see Textiles
  s.a. spec. prod.
Cojedes Venezuela   *area*–874 6
Coke
  Co. Tex.   *area*–764 723
  gas
    chem. tech.   665.772
    soc. & econ. aspects *see*
      Secondary industries
  heating
    buildings   697.042
    s.a. spec. kinds e.g.
      Steam heating

Coke (continued)
  manufacturing
    chem. tech.   662.72
    soc. & econ. aspects *see*
      Secondary industries
Coke-oven gas
  chem. tech.   665.772
  soc. & econ. aspects *see*
      Secondary industries
Cola
  agriculture   633.76
  soc. & econ. aspects *see*
      Primary industries
  foods   641.337 6
    cookery   641.637 6
  other aspects see Tiliales;
      also Alkaloids
Colac Vic.   *area*–945 7
Colaciaceae *see* Euglenophyta
Colas
  comm. proc.   663.62
  other aspects see
      Nonalcoholic beverages
Colbert Co. Ala.   *area*–761 915
Colchagua Chile   *area*–833 3
Colchester
  County N.S.   *area*–716 12
  Essex Eng.   *area*–426 723
Colchis ancient   *area*–395
Cold
  climates
    hygiene   613.111
      misc. aspects see Hygiene
  dishes
    cookery tech.   641.79
  frames
    agric.   631.34
    use   631.583
      s.a. spec. crops; also
        spec. types of culture
        e.g. Floriculture
    mf. tech.   681.763 1
    soc. & econ. aspects *see*
      Secondary industries
  fronts
    meteorology *see* Air fronts
      met.
  Harbor Battle
    U.S. Civil War hist.   973.736
    s.a. Cryo-
Cold-blooded vertebrates
  agric. pests   632.67
    s.a. spec. types of culture
      e.g. Forestry; *also*
      spec. crops
  conservation tech.   639.977
  control
    agricultural *see*
      Cold-blooded
      vertebrates agric.
      pests

Collection (continued)
  systems
    water-supply eng.
      technology   628.142
      other aspects see Water
        supply engineering
    s.a. other spec. subj.
Collections
  desc. research *see*
    Descriptive research
  museology   069.5
  spec. objects   *s.s.*–074
  texts *see* Anthologies
  s.a. spec. kinds e.g. Museum
    collections
Collective
  bargaining
    labor econ.   331.89
    labor law *see* Labor law
    personnel admin.
      gen. management   658.315 4
      spec. subj.   *s.s.*–068 3
    pub. admin.   350.174
      central govts.   351.174
      spec. jur.   353–354
      local govts.   352.005 174
    pub. admin. *see* Industrial
      relations pub. admin.
  security *see* Alliances
  s.a. Corporate
Collectivism
  economics   335
  pol. ideology   320.53
  soc. theology *see* Political
    ideologies soc.
    theology
Collects
  Anglican liturgy   264.036
  s.a. other spec.
    denominations
College & university *see*
  University & college
College of Cardinals *see*
  Cardinals (clergy)
Colleges & universities *see*
  Universities & colleges
Collembola
  zoology   595.715
  other aspects see Apterygota
Colleton Co. S.C.   *area*–757 95
Collie W. Aust.   *area*–941 2
Collier Co. Fla.   *area*–759 44
Colliers *see* Cargo ships
Collies
  animal husbandry   636.73
  other aspects see Dogs
Colligative properties
  solutions
    physical chem.
      electrolytic   541.374 5
      applied   660.297 45

Colligative properties
  solutions
    physical chem.
      electrolytic (continued)
        organic   547.137 45
        gen. wks.   541.341 5
        applied   660.294 15
        organic   547.134 15
      s.a. spec. elements,
        cpds., prod.
Collin Co. Tex.   *area*–764 556
Collingsworth Co. Tex.   *area*–764 831
Collision
  nuclear interactions *see*
    Interactions nuclear
    reactions
  prevention sea safety   623.888 4
Collodions
  prac. pharm.   615.42
  misc. aspects see
    Pharmacology
Colloid chemistry *see* Colloids
Colloidal
  fuels
    manufacturing
      chem. tech.   662.82
      soc. & econ. aspects *see*
        Secondary industries
  mixtures
    metals *see* Alloys
    other see spec. elements
Colloids
  physical chem.   541.345 1
  applied   660.294 51
  organic   547.134 51
  s.a. spec. elements, cpds.,
    prod.
Colloquialisms   417.2
  spec. langs.   *lang. sub.*–7
Collotype printing
  soc. & econ. aspects *see*
    Secondary industries
  technology   686.232 5
Collusion *see* Administration of
  justice crimes against
Colne
  Lancashire Eng.   *area*–427 645
  Valley West Yorkshire Eng.
        area–428 13
Cologne Ger.   *area*–435 5
Colognes *see* Perfumes
Colombia   *area*–861
Colombian
  literature   860
  people   *r.e.n.*–688 61
  s.a. other spec. subj. e.g.
    Arts
Colón
  Ecuador   *area*–866 5
  Honduras   *area*–728 313
  Panama   *area*–728 732

Color-materials
  ceramic
    arts
      decorative   738.12
      fine   731.2
      spec. periods & schools   732–735
    industries
      economics   338.476 664 2
      soc. & econ. aspects *see*
        Secondary industries
      technology   666.42
Color-photography   778.6
  motion pictures
    cinematography   778.534 2
    projection   778.554 2
  photomicrography   778.31
Color-programs
  television performances   791.453
Colors
  armed forces   355.15
    s.a. spec. mil. branches
  minerals *see* Optical
    properties minerals
  plants grown for floriculture   635.968
    s.a. spec. plants
  rel. significance
    Christianity   246.6
    other rel. see Arts rel.
      significance
  table settings
    home econ.   642.8
  technology   667
    soc. & econ. aspects *see*
      Secondary industries
  s.a. Colors; *also other*
    spec. subj.
Color-television
  soc. & econ. aspects *see*
    Secondary industries
  technology   621.388 04
  s.a. spec. aspects e.g.
    Circuits; *also spec.*
    appls. e.g. Space
    communication
Colossendeomorpha *see*
  Pycnogonida
Colossians
  Bible   227.7
  other aspects see New
    Testament
Colquitt Co. Ga.   *area*–758 975
Colts *see* Equidae
Columbae *see* Columbiformes
Columbia
  city S.C.   *area*–757 71
  County
    Arkansas   *area*–767 59
    Florida   *area*–759 83
    Georgia   *area*–758 635
    New York   *area*–747 39
    Oregon   *area*–795 47

Columbia
  County (continued)
    Pennsylvania   *area*–748 38
    Washington   *area*–797 46
    Wisconsin   *area*–775 81
  River   *area*–797
    British Columbia   *area*–711 45
    Oregon   *area*–795 4
    Washington   *area*–797
Columbiana Co. O.   *area*–771 63
Columbiformes
  hunting
    commercial   639.128 65
    sports   799.248 65
  paleozoology   568.6
  zoology   598.65
  other aspects see Aves
Columbines *see* Ranales
Columbite
  mineralogy   549.528
Columbium *see* Niobium
Columbus
  Christopher discoveries hist.   970.015
    North America   970.015
    South America   980.01
    s.a. hist. & geog. of spec.
      places
  city O.   *area*–771 57
  Co. N.C.   *area*–756 31
Columelliaceae *see* Personales
Column chromatography *see*
    Liquid chromatography
Columnar
  epithelia
    human anatomy & phys.   611.018 7
    other aspects see Tissue
      biology
  structures
    architectural
      construction   721.3
      design & decoration   729.32
      building   690.13
      s.a. spec. kinds of bldgs.
Columns
  arch. & bldg. *see* Columnar
    structures
  journalism   070.442
    spec. subj.   070.449
  structural eng.
    gen. wks.   624.177 2
    concrete   624.183 42
    s.a. other spec.
      materials
    naval arch.   623.817 72
    s.a. other spec. appls.
Colusa Co. Calif.   *area*–794 33
Colwyn Clwyd Wales   *area*–429 31
Colydioidea
  culture   638.576 9
  paleozoology   565.76
  zoology   595.769

Combustion (continued)
  diesel engines   621.436 1
    land vehicles   629.250 61
    marine vehicles   623.872 361
    s.a. other spec. appls.
  heat eng.   621.402 3
    s.a. spec. appls. e.g.
      Spark-ignition engines
  thermochemistry
    physical chem.   541.361–.362
      applied   660.296 1–.296 2
      organic   547.136 1–.136 2
    s.a. spec. elements,
      cpds., prod.
Comedies (drama)
  gen. wks.
    collections   808.825 23
    hist. & crit.   809.252 3
    rhetoric   808.252 3
    juvenile   808.068 252 3
  spec. lits.   *lit. sub.–205 23*
    indiv. authors   *lit. sub.–21–29*
  stage presentation   792.23
  other aspects see Drama
Comedy
  lit. qual.
    gen. wks.
      collections   808.801 7
      hist. & crit.   809.917
    spec. lits.
      collections   *lit. sub.–080 17*
      hist. & crit.   *lit. sub.–091 7*
    s.a. spec. lit forms
  stage performance   792.2
  stage qual.   792.090 917
    s.a. other spec. dramatic
      mediums e.g.
      Television; *also spec.*
      kinds of drama e.g.
      Tragedies (drama)
Comets
  astronomy
    description   523.6
    theory   521.76
  regional subj. trmt.   *area*–993
  other aspects see Celestial
      bodies
Comfort
  engineering   620.8
    s.a. spec. appls. e.g.
      Aerospace engineering
  equipment
    aircraft eng.
      soc. & econ. aspects *see*
        Secondary industries
      tech. & mf.   629.134 42
    automobiles
      soc. & econ. aspects *see*
        Secondary industries
      tech. & mf.   629.277

Comfort (continued)
  stations
    pub. health   363.729 4
      govt. control   352.6
      law   344.046 4
        spec. jur.   344.3–.9
    pub. sanitation eng.
      soc. & econ. aspects *see*
        Secondary industries
      technology   628.45
    other aspects see Public
      structures
Comic opera *see* Opera
Comics
  ethics *see* Reading ethics
  influence on crime   364.254
  other aspects see Cartoons
Cominform
  pol. sci.   324.1
Coming-of-age customs   392.15
Comintern
  pol. sci.   324.1
Commagene
  ancient   *area*–393 6
Command systems
  aeronautics
    soc. & econ. aspects *see*
      Secondary industries
    technology   629.132 6
Commandeering
  mil. resources   355.28
    s.a. spec. mil. branches
Commander Isls.   *area*–577
Commando tactics
  mil. sci.   355.422
    s.a. spec. mil. branches
Commandos
  armed forces   356.167
Commelinaceae *see* Commelinales
Commelinales
  botany   584.38
  floriculture   635.934 38
  med. aspects
    crop prod.   633.884 38
    gen. pharm.   615.324 38
      toxicology   615.952 438
    vet. pharm.   636.089 532 438
      toxicology   636.089 595 243 8
  paleobotany   561.4
  other aspects see Plants
Commemorations *see* Celebrations
Commemorative
  medals
    numismatics   737.222
  stamps
    philately   769.563
  s.a. other spec. subj.
Commencement sermons
  Christianity   252.55
  other rel. see Preaching

Commercial
buildings (continued)
  other aspects see Public
    structures
catalogs   *s.s.*–029 4
credit
  economics   332.742
  other aspects see Credit
education *see* Business high
  schools
fishing *see* Fishing
  industries
gardening
  horticulture   635
    misc. aspects see
      Agriculture
high schools *see* Business
  high schools
lands *see* Urban lands
languages   401.3
  s.a. spec. langs. e.g.
    Swahili
law   346.07
  spec. jur.   346.3–.9
leases
  law   346.043 462
    spec. jur.   346.3–.9
paper
  credit   332.77
  exchange medium   332.55
  misc. aspects see Money
  law *see* Negotiable
    instruments
policy   380.13
  domestic comm.   381.3
  internat. comm.   382.3
publishers   070.592
revenues
  pub. finance   336.11–.15
  misc. aspects see Nontax
    revenues
s.a. Business
Commercials
broadcast advertising   659.14
radio performances   791.443
television performances   791.453
Commewijne Surinam   *area*–883 7
Commission government
local admin.   352.008 5
Commissioned officers
armed forces   355.332
  s.a. spec. mil. branches
Commissioners
pub. admin.   350.009
  central govts.   351.009
    spec. jur.   353–354
  local govts.   352.008 5
s.a.   *pers.*–352 3
Commissioning
mil. personnel   355.223 6
  s.a. spec. mil. branches

Commissions
libraries   021.82
pub. admin. *see* Independent
  government agencies
s.a. other spec. subj.
Commitment
religion *see* Religious
  experience
Committees
legislative bodies
  law *see* Organization of
    legislative bodies law
  pol. sci.   328.365
    spec. jur.   328.4–.9
  s.a. spec. organizations
sociology   302.34
s.a. other spec. subj.
Commodities
evaluation
  materials management *see*
    Procurement materials
    management
exchange
  govt. control   351.826
    spec. jur.   353–354
  investment econ.   332.644
  law
    international   341.754
    municipal   343.08
      spec. jur.   343.3–.9
  investment finance   332.632 8
  govt. control   351.826
    spec. jur.   353–354
  law   343.08
    spec. jur.   343.3–.9
  prod. econ. *see* Products
    economics
  s.a. other spec. subj. e.g.
    Consumption
Commodity
brokers
  financial econ.   332.62
  govt. control   351.826
    spec. jur.   353–354
  law   343.08
    spec. jur.   343.3–.9
exchange bldgs. *see* Exchange
  buildings
futures *see* Commodities
  investment finance
markets *see* Commodities
  exchange
standards
  money
    economics   332.422–.425
    other aspects see Money
  taxes *see* Excise taxes
Common
carriers
  truck transp.
    commerce   388.324 3

Communication	
facilities (continued)	
gen. wks. *see*	
Communications	
mil. resources	355.27
s.a. spec. mil. branches	
misuse	
criminology	364.147
law	345.024 7
spec. jur.	345.3–.9
soc. theology	
Christianity	261.833 147
comp. rel.	291.178 331 47
s.a. other spec. rel.	
railroads	
gen. wks.	
commerce	385.316
govt. control	350.875 316
central govts.	351.875 316
spec. jur.	353–354
local govts.	352.915 316
law *see* Railroad	
transportation law	
local	
commerce	388.42
govt. control	350.878 42
central govts.	351.878 42
spec. jur.	353–354
local govts.	352.918 42
special-duty	
commerce	385.5
govt. control	350.875 5
central	351.875 5
spec. jur.	353–354
local govts.	352.915 5
s.a. other spec. appls. &	
occurrences	
forces	
mil. sci.	358.24
air warfare	358.46
naval sci.	359.983
lines in bldgs.	
arch. design	729.25
structural elements	729.3
s.a. spec. kinds of	
bldgs.	
management use	658.45
media *see* Communications	
media	
office services	651.7
pub. admin.	350.714 2
central govts.	351.714 2
spec. jur.	353–354
local govts.	352.164 2
personnel	
biog. & work	380.309 2
s.a. spec. kinds of	
services	
s.a.	*pers.–384*
s.a. Communication	
engineers	

Communication (continued)	
psychic *see* Psychic	
psychology	153.6
animals	156.36
children	155.413
s.a. psych. of other spec.	
groups	
services	
police	363.24
misc. aspects see Police	
services	
other aspects see	
Communication systems	
sociology	302.2
spec. subj.	*s.s.*–014 1
systems	
electronic eng. *see* Systems	
electronic eng.	
library bldgs.	022
museum bldgs.	069.29
radio	
engineering	621.384 15
s.a. spec. appls. e.g.	
Radiotelephony	
other aspects see Radio	
spacecraft eng.	629.474 3
unmanned	629.464 3
other aspects see	
Spacecraft	
television	
engineering	621.388 5
s.a. spec. appls. e.g.	
Astronautics	
other aspects see	
Television	
other aspects see	
Communication services	
s.a. other spec. appls. &	
occurrences	
tactics	
mil. sci.	355.415
s.a. spec. mil. branches	
Communications	380.3
law	
international	341.757
municipal	343.099
spec. jur.	343.3–.9
media	
accounting	657.84
influence on crime	364.254
religious work	
Christianity	254.3
other rel. see	
Ecclesiastical theology	
s.a. Mass media	
pub. admin.	350.873–.874
central govts.	351.873–.874
spec. jur.	353–354
local govts.	352.913–.914

Community (continued)
  suppers
    food services | 642.4
Community-school relations | 370.193 1
Commutation of sentence
  penology | 364.65
Commutative
  algebras | 512.24
    s.a. spec. appls. e.g.
      Engineering
  groups
    algebra | 512.2
    s.a. spec. appls. e.g.
      Engineering
Commutators
  generators
    electrodynamic eng.
      soc. & econ. aspects *see*
        Secondary industries
      tech. & mf. | 621.316
        s.a. spec. appls. e.g.
          Electric locomotives
      other aspects see
        Electrodynamics
Commuter services *see* Urban
      transportation
Como Italy | *area*–452 3
Comoro Isls. | *area*–694
Compaction
  road eng. *see* Roadbeds
Companies
  firms *see* Corporations
  mil. organization | 355.31
    s.a. spec. mil. branches
Company
  towns *see* Cities
  unions
    labor econ. | 331.883 4
    labor law *see* Labor law
Comparative
  advantage
    econ. law
      internat. comm. | 382.104 2
      prod. econ. | 338.604 6
  cytology
    life sci. | 574.878
  education | 370.195
  government
    pol. sci. | 320.3
  law | 340.2
  librarianship | 020.9
  linguistics | 410
  literature | 809
  psychology | 156
    social | 302
  religion | 291
  s.a. other spec. subj.

Compass
  variations
    spherical astronomy | 522.7
    s.a. spec. celestial
      bodies
Compasses
  gen. wks. *see* Navigation
    technology
  radio *see* Radio compasses
  ships *see* Nautical
      instruments
Compassion
  ethics *see* Virtues
  psychology *see* Emotions
Compends | *s.s.*–020 2
Compensation
  armed forces
    administration | 355.64
    law *see* Armed services law
    s.a. spec. mil. branches
  income distribution
    macroeconomics | 339.21
  labor
    economics | 331.21
    spec. occupations | 331.28
    s.a. spec. classes of
      workers
  law
    international | 341.763 6
    municipal | 344.012 1
    spec. jur. | 344.3–.9
  pub. admin. | 350.835
    central govts. | 351.835
    spec. jur. | 353–354
    local govts. | 352.943
  legislators
    law *see* Membership
      legislative bodies
    pol. sci. | 328.333
    spec. jur. | 328.4–.9
  neuroses *see* Traumatic
      neuroses
  personnel admin.
    gen. management | 658.32
    executive management | 658.407 2
    spec. subj. | *s.s.*–068 3
    law of pub. admin. | 342.068 6
    pub. admin. | 350.123 2
      central govts. | 351.123 2
      spec. jur. | 353–354
      local govts. | 352.005 123 2
  pub. executives
    law *see* Executive branches
      law
  scales
    labor
      economics | 331.22
      s.a. spec. classes of
        workers e.g. Women
      law *see* Labor law

Complex-valued functions (continued)
   s.a. spec. appls. e.g.
      Engineering
Complications *see spec. kinds*
      e.g. Surgical
        complications
Complin *see* Office hours
Components

air-conditioning eng.	697.932
computer eng.	621.381 953
analogue	621.381 957 3
combinations & related	621.381 959
digital	621.381 958 3

   other aspects see Computers
   s.a. spec. uses e.g. Data
      processing
microelectronics
   soc. & econ. aspects *see*
      Secondary industries

tech. & mf.	621.381 71

   s.a. spec. appls. e.g.
      Tracking
   other aspects see
      Electronics
microwave electronics

technology	621.381 33

   s.a. spec. appls. e.g.
      Radar engineering
   other aspects see Microwave
      electronics
radio

engineering	621.384 13

   s.a. spec. appls. e.g.,
      Radiotelephony
   other aspects see Radio
receiving sets
   radio

engineering	621.384 136 1

   s.a. spec. appls. e.g.
      Radiotelephony
   other aspects see Radio
television

engineering	621.388 361

   s.a. spec. appls. e.g.
      Astronautics
   other aspects see
      Television
solutions

phys. chem.	541.348
applied	660.294 8
organic	547.134 8

   s.a. spec. elements,
      cpds., prod.

spacecraft eng.	629.472
unmanned	629.462

   other aspects see
      Spacecraft
television

engineering	621.388 3

   s.a. spec. appls. e.g.
      Astronautics

Components
   television (continued)
      other aspects see
        Television
   s.a. other spec. apparatus,
      equip., materials
Composers *see* Musicians
Composing machines

mf. tech.	681.61

   soc. & econ. aspects *see*
      Secondary industries
Compositae *see* Asterales
Composite
   checks
      payroll admin. *see* Payroll
        administration
   commodity standards
      money

economics	332.425

      other aspects see Money
   current
      transmission

electrodynamic eng.	621.319 15

      s.a. spec. appls. e.g.
        Lighting airports
      soc. & econ. aspects *see*
        Secondary industries
      other aspects see
        Electrodynamics
   foods

cookery	641.8

      manufacturing
      soc. & econ. aspects *see*
        Secondary industries

technology	664.65

   materials

engineering	620.118

      s.a. spec. uses
   furniture

mf. tech.	684.106

      other aspects see
        Furniture
      s.a. spec. prod.
   media
      arts

gen. wks.	709.040 7
spec. places	709.1–.9
painting	759.067
spec. places	759.1–.9
sculpture	735.230 47
spec. places	730.9

      s.a. other spec. art
        forms
   woods

mf. tech.	674.834–.836

      other aspects see Wood
        products
   s.a. other spec. subj.
Composites

arts	702.81

Compression (continued)
  sickness
    gen. med. — 616.989 4
    geriatrics — 618.976 989 4
    pediatrics — 618.929 894
    statistics — 312.398 94
     deaths — 312.269 894
    other aspects see Diseases
    s.a. spec. diseases
  stresses
    crystals — 548.842
    s.a. spec. substances
    gen. wks.
     engineering *see* Dynamics
     physics — 531.382 2
Compromise
  of 1850 — 973.64
   U.S. Civil War cause — 973.711 3
  sociology — 303.6
Compton Co. Que. — *area*–714 68
Compulsion of testimony
  law *see* Witnesses law
Compulsions
  sociopathic *see* Sociopathic
    personality
Compulsive
  defrauding & lying
    gen. med. — 616.858 45
    psychology — 157.7
    pub. health — 614.58
    statistics — 312.385 845
    other aspects see Mental
     illness
Compulsory
  education
    law — 344.079
     spec. jur. — 344.3–.9
    labor — 331.117 3
    s.a. spec. classes of labor
     e.g. Women
    s.a. other spec. subj.
Computation machines *see*
    Computers; *also*
    Calculating machines
Computations
  astronomy — 522
   s.a. spec. clestial bodies
  mathematics — 511
   s.a. spec. math. branches;
    also spec. appls. e.g.
    Engineering
   s.a. other spec. subj.,
    operations, proc.
Computer
  combinations
    electronic eng.
     soc. & econ. aspects *see*
     Secondary industries
     tech. & mf. — 621.381 959 2
    s.a. spec. appls. e.g.
    Data processing

Computer
  combinations (continued)
    other aspects see Computers
  communications
    telephony
     commerce — 384.648
     govt. control — 351.874 648
      spec. jur. — 353–354
     law *see* Telephony law
  control
    automation eng.
     soc. & econ. aspects *see*
     Secondary industries
     technology — 629.895
    s.a. spec. appls. e.g.
    Factory operations
  games
    recreation — 794
    mathematics — 519.4
  programmers
    professional library
     positions — 023.2
  programming — 001.642
    spec. subj. — *s.s.*–028 542
  security
    management — 658.478
Computer-based
  instruction *see*
    Teaching-machines
Computerization
  office records — 651.59
  other aspects see Data
    processing
Computerized matching
  employee selection *see*
    Selection procedures
    employees
Computer-operated equipment
  printing composition
    soc. & econ. aspects *see*
    Secondary industries
    technology — 686.225 44
Computers
  business use
    law — 346.07
     spec. jur. — 346.3–.9
  chemistry use — 542.8
  s.a. spec. appls. e.g.
    Organic chemistry
  electronic data proc. *see*
    Electronic data
    processing
  electronic eng.
    soc. & econ. aspects *see*
    Secondary industries
    tech. & mf. — 621.381 95
    s.a. spec. uses e.g. Data
    processing
Comtism
  philosophy *see* Positivism
    philosophy

Concretes
  eng. materials (continued)
    naval design   623.818 34
    shipbuilding   623.820 7
      hulls   623.845 4
    structures   624.183 4
    s.a. other spec. uses
  manufacturing
    soc. & econ. aspects *see*
      Secondary industries
    technology   666.893
  other aspects see Masonry
Concubinage
  soc. customs   392.6
  sociology *see* Extramarital
    sex relations
Condemnation
  Jesus Christ
    Christian doctrines   232.962
  real property
    law   343.025 2
      spec. jur.   343.3–.9
Condensation
  chem. eng.   660.284 48
  control
    bldg. construction   693.893
  effect of heat
    astrophysics   523.013 443
    s.a. spec. celestial
      bodies
    physics   536.443
      spec. states of matter   530.4
    meteorology   551.574 1
      artificial modification   551.687 41
      weather forecasting   551.647 41
      spec. areas   551.65
    physical chem.   541.393
      applied   660.299 3
      organic   547.28
    s.a. spec. aspects e.g. Low
      temperatures
  products
    atmospheric optical phenomena
      meteorology   551.567
        artificial modification   551.686 7
        weather forecasting   551.646 7
        spec. areas   551.65
    s.a. spec. elements, cpds.,
      prod.
Condensed milk
  dairy tech.
    skim   637.147 23–.147 24
    whole   637.142 3–.142 4
    other aspects see Milk
Condensers
  electrostatics *see* Capacitors
      electrostatics
  marine engine auxiliaries *see*
      Engine auxiliaries
      shipbuilding

Condensers (continued)
  steam eng.
    soc. & econ. aspects *see*
      Secondary industries
    tech. & mf.   621.197
    s.a. spec. appls. e.g.
      Steam locomotives
Condiments
  agriculture   633.84
  soc. & econ. aspects *see*
    Primary industries
  foods   641.338 4
    preparation
      commercial   664.54
      soc. & econ. aspects
        see Secondary
        industries
    domestic   641.638 4
Conditional
  equations   515.254
    algebra   512.94
    calculus   515.254
      complex variables   515.925 4
      real variables   515.825 4
    s.a. other spec. functions
      & equations; also spec.
      appls. e.g.
      Engineering
  immortality
    rel. doctrines
      Christianity   236.23
      other rel. see
        Eschatology
  probabilities   519.2
    s.a. spec. appls. e.g.
      Engineering
  sales *see* Secured
    transactions
Conditioned reflexes
  psychology   152.322 4
    animals   156.232 24
    children   155.412
  s.a. psych. of other spec.
    groups
Conditions *see spec. subj. e.g.*
    Economic conditions
Condobolin N.S.W.   *area*–944 9
Condominiums
  law *see* Horizontal property
    law
Condors *see* Cathartidae
Conduct
  armed forces   355.133
    law   343.014
      spec. jur.   343.3–.9
    s.a. spec. mil. branches
  ethics   170.44
  etiquette *see* Etiquette
  legislators
    law *see* Membership
      legislative

Conduct (continued)
  moral theology
    Christianity   241.5
    other rel. see Moral
        theology
  personal rel.
    Christianity   248.4
    comp. rel.   291.44
    Judaism   296.74
    s.a. other spec. rel.
  pub. executives
    law *see* Executive branches
        law
  s.a. Behavior
Conducting
  musical performance
    music theory   781.635
    s.a. spec. mediums
Conduction
  electrodynamics
    astrophysics   523.018 762
    *s.a. spec. celestial
        bodies*
    physics   537.62
    spec. states of matter   530.4
  heat
    astrophysics   523.013 23
    *s.a. spec. celestial
        bodies*
    engineering *see*
        Transmission heat
        engineering
    physics   536.23
    spec. states of matter   530.4
  heating
    elect. eng.
      soc. & econ. aspects *see*
        Secondary industries
      technology   621.396
      s.a. spec. appls. e.g.
        Metallurgy
Conductivity
  atmospheric electricity
    meteorology   551.561
  electricity
    material property *see*
        Conduction
        electrodynamics
    electrolytic *see* Electrolytic
        solutions
  heat
    material property
      astrophysics   523.013 201 2
      *s.a. spec. celestial
          bodies*
      physics   536.201 2
      spec. states of matter   530.4
  other elect. aspects see
      Electromagnetic
      properties

Conductometric methods
  anal. chem.
    gen. wks.   543.087 11
      qualitative   544.971 1
      quantitative   545.311
    organic   547.308 711
      qualitative   547.349 711
      quantitative   547.353 11
    s.a. spec. elements & cpds.
Conductors (music) *see*
        Musicians
Conduits
  drainage *see* Drainage
  irrigation *see* Irrigation
  water-supply eng.
    technology   628.15
    other aspects see Water
        supply engineering
  *s.a. other spec. occurrences
      e.g.* Underground lines
      elect. circuits
Condylarthra
  paleozoology   569.75
Conecuh Co. Ala.   *area*–761 263
Conejos Co. Colo.   *area*–788 33
Cones (botany)
  dec. arts   745.925
Cones (geometry) *see*
        Configurations geometry
Confectionery *see* Candies
Confederate
  States of America
    U.S. hist.   973.713
  sympathizers
    U.S. Civil War hist.   973.718
  Veterans society   369.17
Confederated
  Benedictines
    rel. orders   255.11
      church hist.   271.11
      ecclesiology   262.24
Confederation
  of the Rhine
    Ger. hist.   943.06
    U.S. hist.   973.318
Confederations
  pol. sci.   321.02
  s.a. spec. jur.
Conference
  calls
    telephone commun. *see*
        Telephone calls
  committees
    legislative bodies
      pol. sci.   328.365 7
      spec. jur.   328.4–.9
Conference of People Called
        Methodists   287.53
  misc. aspects see Methodist
Conferences
  gen. wks. *see* Organizations

235

Conferences (continued)	
management use	658.456 2
Confessionals *see* Sacramental	
furniture	
Confessions	
Christian doctrines	234.166
Christian rites	265.62
criminal law	345.06
spec. jur.	345.3–.9
of faith	
doctrinal theology	
Christianity	238
other rel. see Doctrinal	
theology	
pub. worship	
Christianity	264.5
spec. denominations	264.01–.09
other rel. see Public	
worship	
Configurations	
geometry	516.15
Euclidean	516.215
s.a. other spec. geometries;	
also spec. appls. e.g.	
Engineering	
Configurative chemistry *see*	
Stereochemistry	
Confinement	
childbirth *see* Parturition	
penology *see* Penal	
institutions	
Confirmation	
etiquette	395.24
rel. doctrines	
Christianity	234.162
comp. rel.	291.22
s.a. other spec. rel.	
rel. rites	
Christianity	265.2
comp. rel.	291.38
Judaism	
bar mitzvah	296.442 4
bath mitzvah	296.443
s.a. other spec. rel.	
sermons	
Christianity	252.1
s.a. other spec. rel.	
soc. customs	392.14
Conflict of interest	
govt. officials	
law	342.068 4
spec. jur.	342.3–.9
pub. admin.	350.995
central govts.	351.995
spec. jur.	353–354
local govts.	352.002
Conflict of laws	
internat. law	340.9
municipal law	342.042
spec. jur.	342.3–.9

Conflicts	
depth psych.	154.24
animals	156.4
international	
law	341.5
pol. sci.	327.16
spec. countries	327.3–.9
s.a. War; *also* Wars	
of duties ethical systems *see*	
Conscience ethical	
systems	
sociology	303.6
s.a. other spec. kinds e.g.	
Industrial conflicts	
Conformal	
mapping	
calculus	515.9
s.a. spec. appls. e.g.	
Engineering	
projections	
maps	526.82
transformations	
algebraic geometry	516.35
s.a. spec. appls. e.g.	
Engineering	
gen. wks. *see*	
Transformations	
Conformity	
psychology	153.854
animals	156.385 4
children	155.413
s.a. psych. of other spec.	
groups	
soc. interaction	302.5
Confraternities	
Christian pious societies	248.06
Confraternity version	
Bible	220.520 5
s.a. spec. parts of Bible	
Confucianism	
art representation	704.948 995 12
s.a. spec. art forms	
calendars	529.329 512
cookery	641.567 951 2
philosophy	181.095 12
regions	*area*–176 951 2
religion	299.512
rel. holidays	394.268 299 512
sacred music	
arts	783.029 951 2
recordings	789.912 302 995 12
s.a. spec. instruments;	
also spec. kinds e.g.	
Liturgical music	
religion	
pub. worship	299.512 38
significance	299.512 37
schools	377.995 12
Confucianists	
biog. & work	299.512 092
s.a.	*pers.*–299 512

Coniferous trees (continued)
  woods *see* Softwoods
  other aspects see
      Coniferales; *also*
      Trees
Conifers *see* Coniferales
Conisbrough South Yorkshire Eng.
      area–428 27
Coniston Water Cumbria Eng.
      area–427 83
Conjugales *see* Chlorophyta
Conjugated proteins
  org. chem.   547.754
  other aspects see Proteins
Conjugation (linguistics) *see*
      Grammar (linguistics)
Conjugation (sexual)
  pathology   574.216 62
    animals   591.216 62
    plants   581.216 62
    s.a. spec. organisms
  physiology   574.166 2
    animals   591.166 2
    microorganisms   576.116 62
    plants   581.166 2
    s.a. spec. organisms
Conjugations (molecules) *see*
      Linkages molecular
      structure
Conjunctions (linguistics) *see*
      Words
Conjunctiva
  diseases   617.77
    geriatrics   618.977 77
    pediatrics   618.920 977 7
    statistics   312.304 777
  human phys.   612.841
  other aspects see Eyes
Conjunctivitis   617.773
  geriatrics   618.977 773
  pediatrics   618.920 977 73
  pub. health   614.599 7
  statistics   312.304 777 3
  other aspects see Diseases
Conjurers *see* Magicians
      (conjurers)
Conjuring
  recreation   793.8
Connacht Ireland   *area*–417 1
Connah's Quay Clwyd Wales
       area–429 36
Connaraceae *see* Sapindales
Connaught Ireland   *area*–417 1
Connecticut
  Lakes N.H.   *area*–742 1
  River   *area*–74
    Connecticut   *area*–746
    Massachusetts   *area*–744 2
    upper   *area*–742
  state   *area*–746

Connecting rods
  internal-combustion engines
    soc. & econ. aspects *see*
      Secondary industries
    tech. & mf.   621.827
      marine vehicles   623.872 37
      s.a. other spec. appls.
  machine eng.
    soc. & econ. aspects *see*
      Secondary industries
    tech. & mf.   621.827
    s.a. spec. appls. e.g.
      Steam engines
  other aspects see Mechanics
Connections (mathematics)
  algebraic geometry   516.35
  topology   514.3
  s.a. spec. appls. e.g.
    Engineering
Connective tissue
  histology
    gen. wks.   611.018 2
      misc. aspects see Tissue
      biology
    motor system   611.018 974
  motor system
    anatomy
      med. sci.   611.74
      animals   636.089 174
      s.a. spec. animals
      man   611.74
      zoology   591.47
      s.a. spec. animals
    diseases
      gen. wks.   616.77
        neoplasms   616.992 74
        tuberculosis   616.995 74
      geriatrics   618.976 77
      pediatrics   618.927 7
      pub. health   614.597 7
      statistics   312.377
      deaths   312.267 7
      other aspects see
      Diseases
    pathology
      med. sci. *see* Connective
      tissue motor system
      diseases
    zoology
      gen. wks.
        anatomical   591.218 52
        physiological   591.227
      s.a. spec. animals
    physical anthropometry   573.674
    physiology
      med. sci.   612.75
      animals   636.089 275
      s.a. spec. animals
      man   612.75
      zoology   591.185 2
      s.a. spec. animals

Consolidated
  financial statements 657.3
    s.a. spec. kinds of
        enterprise e.g.
          Insurance accounting
  statutes *see* Legal codes
Consolidation
  soil mechanics
    foundation eng. 624.151 362
    s.a. spec. appls. e.g.
        Roads engineering
Consolidations
  land econ. 333.33
  local school districts 379.153 5
  management 658.16
  real estate
    law 346.043 6
    spec. jur. 346.3–.9
  s.a. other spec subj.
Consonants *see* Notations
        languages
Consortia *see spec. kinds e.g.*
        Library consortia
Conspiracy *see* Criminal
        offenses
Constables
  law *see* Court officials law
  s.a. Police
Constance Lake *area*–434 6
Constanta Romania *area*–498 3
Constantine Algeria *area*–655
Constantinople *see* Istanbul
Constantinopolitan Creed
  Christian doctrines 238.14
Constants
  atomic structure
    theoretical chem. 541.242
      organic 547.124 2
    s.a. spec. elements &
        cpds.
  celestial bodies
    earth 525.1
    Jupiter 523.451
    Mars 523.431
    Mercury 523.411
    moon 523.31
    Neptune 523.481 1
    Pluto 523.482 1
    Saturn 523.461
    stars 523.81
      spec. systems 523.84–.85
    sun 523.71
    Uranus 523.471
    Venus 523.421
    s.a. other spec. bodies
  physics 530.8
    s.a. spec. branches of
        physics
Constellations
  atlases 523.890 3

Constipation
  gen. med. 616.342 8
  geriatrics 618.976 342 8
  pediatrics 618.923 428
  pub. health 614.593 428
  other aspects see Diseases
Constituencies
  representation pol. sci. 324.63
Constitution
  celestial bodies *see* Physical
        constitution
  s.a. other spec. subj.
Constitutional
Act 1791
  Canada hist. 971.028
  amendments
    law 342.03
      spec. jur. 342.3–.9
  Church *see* Roman Catholic
        schisms
  conventions
    law
      history 342.029 2
        spec. jur. 342.2–.9
      proceedings 342.024 2
  guarantees *see* Civil rights
  history 342.029
    spec. jur. 342.3–.9
  law 342
  monarchies
    pol. sci. 321.87
  period
    U.S. hist. 973.4
    s.a. hist of other spec.
        countries
  position
    chief executives
      pub. admin. 350.003
        central govts. 351.003
        U.S. govts.
          federal 353.03
          states 353.913
          other 354
        local govts. 352.008
    s.a. other spec. officials
  reform *see* Constitutional
        amendments
  revision *see* Constitutional
        amendments
Constitutionalism *see*
        Democratic states
Constitutions
  history *see spec. countries*
  labor unions
    labor econ. 331.871
    s.a. spec. classes of
        workers e.g. Women
  labor law *see* Labor law
  law 342.02
    spec. jur. 342.3–.9

Consumer
  affairs
    pub. admin.
      departments *see* Executive
        departments
    attitudes *see* Consumer
      preferences
  behavior
    marketing management   658.834 2
    spec. subj.   *s.s.*–068 8
  cooperatives
    advertising   659.196 588 707
    economics   334.5
    pub. relations   659.296 588 707
    retail marketing   658.870 7
  credit
    economics   332.743
    marketing management   658.883
    spec. subj.   *s.s.*–068 8
    other aspects see Credit
    s.a. Secured transactions
  education
    curriculums   375.008 5
    s.a. spec. levels of ed.;
      also Special education
    home econ.   640.73
      foods   641.31
      furnishings   645.042
      s.a. other spec. subj.
  finance institutions
    economics   332.35
    other aspects see Credit
      institutions
  income
    macroeconomics   339.22
  information
    commerce   381.33
  movements   381.32
  preferences
    marketing management   658.834 3
    spec. subj.   *s.s.*–068 8
  protection
    commerce   381.34
    govt. control
      activities   350.820 42
        central govts.   351.820 42
        spec. jur.   353–354
      local govts.   352.942
      departments *see* Executive
        departments
    law   343.071
      spec. jur.   343.3–.9
  psychology *see* Consumer
    behavior
  reactions *see* Consumer
    preferences
  research
    marketing management   658.834
    spec. subj.   *s.s.*–068 8
Consumerism
  commerce   381.3

Consumption
  ethics
    philosophy   178
    religion
      Buddhism   294.356 8
      Christianity   241.68
      comp. rel.   291.568
      Hinduism   294.548 68
      s.a. other spec. rel.
  govt. control
    activities   350.82
      central govts.   351.82
        spec. jur.   353–354
      local govts.   352.942
    departments *see* Executive
      departments
    law   343.07
      spec. jur.   343.3–.9
    natural resources   333.717
    s.a. spec. kinds of
      resources e.g.
      Shorelands
  macroeconomics   339.47
    relation to savings   339.43
  natural resources   333.713
    s.a. spec. kinds of
      resources e.g.
      Shorelands
  purposes
    animal husbandry for   636.088 3
    s.a. spec. animals
  soc. aspects   306.3
Contact
  allergies
    gen. med.   616.973
    geriatrics   618.976 973
    pediatrics   618.929 73
    pub. health   614.599 3
    statistics   312.397 3
      deaths   312.269 73
    other aspects see Diseases
  lenses
    mf. tech.   681.42
    optometry   617.752 3
  printing
    photography *see* Positives
Contactors
  generators
    electrodynamic eng.
      soc. & econ. aspects *see*
        Secondary industries
      tech. & mf.   621.316
      s.a. spec. appls. e.g.
        Electric locomotives
    other aspects see
      Electrodynamics
Contacts
  elect. power *see* Control
    devices electrodynamic
    eng.

Continental (continued)
  shelves
    jurisdiction
      internat. law 341.448
    other aspects see
        Continents
  wind systems
    meteorology 551.518 4
      artificial modification 551.681 84
      weather forecasting 551.641 84
      spec. areas 551.65
  wrestling
    equipment mf. 688.768 122
      soc. & econ. aspects *see*
          Secondary industries
    sports 796.812 2
    other aspects see Sports
Continents
  geomorphology 551.41
  lit. & stage trmt. *see* Places
  other spec. subj. *area*–141
  s.a. spec. continents
Continuation schools
  adult ed. 374.8
Continued fractions 515.243
  number theory 512.73
    s.a. spec. appls. e.g.
        Engineering
  series *see* Series calculus
Continuity
  functions
    calculus 515.222
      complex variables 515.922 2
      real variables 515.822 2
      s.a. other spec. functions
          & equations; also spec.
          appls. e.g.
          Engineering
    s.a. other spec. subj.
Continuous
  bridges
    structural eng. 624.33
    other aspects see Bridges
        (structures)
  casting
    arts *see* Casting sculpture
    metal prod.
      mf. tech. 671.256
        ferrous metals 672.256
        s.a. other spec. metals
      other aspects see Foundry
          practice
  creation theory
    cosmogony 523.18
  functions
    gen. wks. *see* Functions
        (mathematics)
    spaces 515.73
      s.a. spec. appls. e.g.
          Engineering

Continuous (continued)
  processes
    prod. management 658.533
      spec. subj. *s.s.*–068 5
  systems
    radar
      engineering 621.384 85
      s.a. spec. appls. e.g.
          Military engineering
      other aspects see Radar
Continuous-combustion
  turbine engines *see* Simple
      gas-turbine engines
Continuum
  mechanics *see* Mechanics
Contortions
  sports 796.47
    equipment mf. 688.764 7
      soc. & econ. aspects *see*
          Secondary industries
    other aspects see Sports
  structural geol. 551.87
    s.a. spec. aspects e.g.
        Engineering
Contour
  surveying 526.981
Contouring
  soil conservation 631.455
    s.a. spec. crops
Contra Costa Co. Calif. *area*–794 63
Contraband *see* Revenue offenses
Contrabasses *see* Double basses
Contraception
  ethics *see* Sexual ethics
  technique 613.94
Contract
  bridge
    equipment mf. 688.754 15
      soc. & econ. aspects *see*
          Secondary industries
    recreation 795.415
  carriers
    truck transp.
      commerce 388.324 3
      govt. control 351.878 324 3
        spec. jur. 353–354
      law *see* Truck
          transportation
  freedom of
    civil right
      pol. sci. 323.442
    negotiation
      labor econ. 331.891 2
    system
      convict labor *see* Convict
          labor
    workers
      labor econ. 331.542
      labor law *see* Labor Law
Contracting
  bldg. construction 692.8

Control
mechanisms
  biology (continued)
    physiology
      gen. wks. | 574.188
        animals | 591.188
        microorganisms | 576.118 8
        plants | 581.188
        s.a. spec. organisms
      med. sci. | 612.022
        human phys. | 612.022
        vet. phys. | 636.089 202 2
        s.a. spec. animals
      s.a. spec. functions,
          systems, organs
  of flight
    aeronautical aerodynamics | 629.132 36
    s.a. spec. appls. e.g.
        Flying
  of markets
    price determination
      economics | 338.523
      spec. ind. | 338.1–.4
  of nuclear reactors
    technology | 621.483 5
    other aspects see Nuclear
        reactions
  processes biology *see* Control
          mechanisms biology
  rods
    technology | 621.483 5
    other aspects see Nuclear
        reactions
  surfaces
    aircraft eng.
      soc. & econ. aspects *see*
          Secondary industries
      tech. & mf. | 629.134 33
  systems
    electronic eng. *see* Systems
        electronic eng.
    s.a. other spec. appls.
  theory
    automation eng.
      gen. wks.
        closed loop systems | 629.831 2
        open loop systems | 629.82
      s.a. spec. appls. e.g.
          Automatons
  towers
    air transp.
      bldg. aspects *see* Air
          transportation
          buildings
      facilities *see* Airport
          facilities
      lighting systems *see*
          Lighting airports
      traffic control *see*
          Traffic control
  s.a. other spec. subj.

Controlled money
  economics | 332.427
  other aspects see Money
Controlled subject vocabularies
  library sci. | 025.49
Controlled-environment
  agriculture
    crop prod. | 631.583
    floriculture | 635.982
    s.a. spec. crops; also
        other spec. types of
        culture
Controllers *see* Finance; *also*
            Financial
Controls
  export trade | 382.64
    misc. aspects see Export
        trade
Controversial knowledge | 001.9
  s.a. spec. subj.
Contusions
  statistics | 312.304 713
  surgery | 617.13
    anesthesiology | 617.967 13
    s.a. Veterinary sciences
Conundrums *see* Riddles
Conurbations *see* Metropolitan
          areas
Convalescent
  homes *see* Extended care
          facilities
  serums
    pharmacology | 615.375
    other aspects see Drugs
Convalescents
  recreation | 790.196
    indoor | 793.019 6
    outdoor | 796.019 6
Convection
  heat
    astrophysics | 523.013 25
    s.a. spec. celestial
        bodies
    engineering *see*
        Transmission heat
        engineering
    physics | 536.25
    spec. states of matter | 530.4
Convective heating
  local bldg. heating | 697.2
Convenience
  engineering for | 620.8
    s.a. spec. appls. e.g.
        Aerospace engineering
  equipment
    automobiles
      soc. & econ. aspects *see*
          Secondary industries
      tech. & mf. | 629.277

Convenience (continued)
  stores
    commerce 381.1
    misc. aspects see
      Commerce
Convent
  buildings *see* Monastic
    buildings
  schools
    education 376.5
Conventional
  housing
    architecture 728.3
    building 690.83
    other aspects see
      Residential buildings
  warfare
    mil. sci. 355.021 7
      strategy 355.430 7
      s.a. spec. mil.
        branches
    s.a. other spec. subj.
Conventions
  gen. wks. *see* Organizations
  labor unions
    labor econ. 331.874
  s.a. other spec. subj.
Conventions (treaties)
  internat. law 341.026
Convents *see* Religious
    congregations
Conventual monastic bldgs.
  architecture 726.773 7
  building 690.677 37
  other aspects see
    Religious-purpose
    bldgs.
Conventuals
  rel. orders 255.37
    church hist. 271.37
    ecclesiology 262.24
Conversation
  ethics
    philosophy 177.2
  religion
    Buddhism 294.356 72
    Christianity 241.672
    comp. rel. 291.567 2
    Hinduism 294.548 672
    s.a. other spec. rel.
  etiquette 395.59
  rhetoric 808.56
    juvenile 808.068 56
  other aspects see Speaking
Conversationalists
  biog. & work 809.5
  s.a. spec. lits.
  s.a. *pers.*–85

Conversations
  literature
    gen. wks.
      collections 808.856
      hist. & crit. 809.56
    spec. lits. *lit. sub.*–506
    indiv. authors *lit. sub.*–51–59
    other aspects see Speeches
Converse Co. Wyo. *area*–787 16
Conversion
  rel. experience
    Christianity 248.24
    other rel. see Religious
      experience
  tables
    mensuration 530.81
    s.a. spec. branches of
      physics
    s.a. other spec. subj.
Converter substations
  elect. power *see* Modification
    elect. power
Converters
  direct-current *see*
    Direct-current
    machinery
  electrodynamic eng.
    soc. & econ. aspects *see*
      Secondary industries
    tech. & mf. 621.313
    s.a. spec. appls. e.g.
      Electric locomotives
  electronic circuits
    tech. & mf. 621.381 532 2
    microelectronics 621.381 732 2
    microwave electronics 621.381 322 2
    radiowave electronics 621.381 532 2
    x- & gamma-ray electronics 621.381 6
    s.a. spec. appls. e.g.
      Receiving sets
    other aspects see Microwave
      electronics; Radiowave
      electronics; X-ray
      electronics
Convertible tops
  automobiles
    soc. & econ. aspects *see*
      Secondary industries
    tech. & mf. 629.26
Convertiplanes *see*
    Vertical-lift aircraft
Converts
  rel. experience
    Christianity 248.24
    other rel. see Religious
      experience
Convex
  programming math. 519.76
    s.a. spec. appls. e.g.
      Engineering

Convex (continued)
  sets
    geometry   516.08
      s.a. spec. geometries;
        also spec. appls. e.g.
          Engineering
  surfaces
    gen. wks. *see* Surfaces
    mathematics
    integral geometry   516.362
      s.a. spec. appls. e.g.
        Engineering
Conveyancing
  law   346.043 8
  spec. jur.   346.3–.9
Conveying-equipment
  machine eng.
    soc. & econ. aspects *see*
      Secondary industries
    tech. & mf.   621.867
      s.a. spec. appls. e.g.
        Military engineering
    other aspects see Mechanics
    s.a. Carriers
Conveyor belts
  rubber prod.
    soc. & econ. aspects *see*
      Secondary industries
    technology   678.36
    s.a. spec. kinds of rubber
      e.g. Natural rubber
Conveyors
  mining eng.   622.66
Convict labor
  labor econ.   331.51
  penology   365.65
  law   344.035 65
    spec. jur.   344.3–.5
Convicts
  penology *see* Prison economy
  s.a.   *pers.*–069 2
Convocation sermons
  Christianity   252.55
  other rel. see Preaching
Convolutions
  cerebrum
    human phys.   612.825
    other aspects see Brain
  mathematics *see*
    Transformations
Convolvulaceae *see* Solanales
Convulsions
  symptomatology
    neurological diseases   616.845
    vet. sci.   636.089 684 5
    s.a. spec. animals
Conway
  Co. Ark.   *area*–767 31
  Gwynedd Wales   *area*–429 27
  Range Nat. Park Qld.   *area*–943 6

Cook
  County
    Georgia   *area*–758 876
    Illinois   *area*–773 1
    Minnesota   *area*–776 75
  Inlet *see* Alaskan Pacific
    seawaters
  Islands   *area*–962 3
  Strait *see* Tasman Sea
Cooke Co. Tex.   *area*–764 533
Cookery   641.5
  domestic customs   392.37
Cookies
  comm. proc.   664.752 5
  home proc.   641.865 4
Cooking-greens
  agriculture   635.4
    soc. & econ. aspects *see*
      Primary industries
  foods   641.354
    preparation
      commercial   664.805 4
      domestic   641.654
  other aspects see Vegetables
Cooking-oils
  comm. proc.   664.36
  other aspects see Fats
Cooking-utensils
  mf. tech.   683.82
  other aspects see Household
    appliances
Cookout cookery   641.578
Cooks
  biog. & work   641.509 2
  other aspects see Household
    employees
  s.a.   *pers.*–641
Cookstown N. Ire.   *area*–416 43
Coolants
  nuclear reactors   621.483 36
  refrigeration eng.
    technology   621.564
    s.a. spec. appls. e.g.
      Military engineering
  other aspects see Low
    temperatures
    engineering
Coolgardie W. Aust.   *area*–941 6
Coolidge
  Calvin admin.
    U.S. hist.   973.915
    s.a. spec. events & subj.
      e.g. Commerce
Coolies *see* Unskilled workers
Cooling
  engines
    diesels   621.436 1
    land vehicles   629.250 61
    marine vehicles   623.872 361
    s.a. other spec. appls.
    s.a. other spec. kinds

Coosa
Co. Ala.	*area*–761 59
River Ala.	*area*–761 6
Cootamundra N.S.W.	*area*–944 8

Coots *see* Gruiformes
Copán Honduras	*area*–728 384
Copeland Cumbria Eng.	*area*–427 84
Copenhagen Denmark	*area*–489 1

Copepoda
culture	639.5
fishing	
commercial	639.5
sports	799.255 34
paleozoology	565.34
zoology	595.34

other aspects *see* Crustacea
Copiah Co. Miss.	*area*–762 52

Copies
art	702.872
paintings	751.5
indiv. artists	759.1–.9
s.a. techs. in other spec. art forms	
tech. drawing	604.25
spec. subj.	*s.s.*–022 1

Copolymerization
chem. eng.	660.284 48
physical chem.	541.393
applied	660.299 3
organic	547.28
s.a. spec. aspects e.g. Low temperatures	

s.a. spec. elements, cpds., prod.

Copper

Age
archaeology	930.15

arts
decorative	739.511

other aspects *see* Metals arts

chemistry
inorganic	546.652
organic	547.056 52

s.a. spec. groupings e.g. Aliphatic compounds
technology	661.065 2
organic	661.895

soc. & econ. aspects *see* Secondary industries

s.a. spec. prod.

compounds
chemistry *see* Copper chemistry
plant nutrition *see* Trace elements plant nutrition

construction
architecture	721.044 73

s.a. spec. kinds of bldgs.

Copper
construction (continued)
building	693.73

materials
building	691.83
engineering	620.182
foundations	624.153 82
naval design	623.818 22
shipbuilding	623.820 7
structures	624.182 2

s.a. other spec. uses
metallography	669.953
metallurgy	669.3
physical & chem.	669.963

soc. & econ. aspects *see* Secondary industries

mineral aspects
econ. geol.	553.43
mineralogy	549.23

mining
technology	622.343
prospecting	622.184 3

s.a. spec. minerals
pharmacology	615.265 2

misc. aspects see Pharmacology

products
arts *see* Copper arts
mf. tech.	673.3

other aspects see Nonferrous metals products

roofing
bldg. construction	695

soaps
chem. tech.	668.125

soc. & econ. aspects *see* Secondary industries

sulfate trmt.
water-supply
technology	628.166 2

other aspects see Water supply engineering
toxicology	615.925 652

misc. aspects see Toxicology

other aspects see Metal; *also* Metals

s.a. spec. uses

Copper-aluminum alloys *see* Copper

Copper-beryllium alloys *see* Copper

Copper-coated
utensils
use in cookery	641.589

s.a. other spec. subj.

Coppersmithing *see* Copper products

Copra
comm. proc.	665.355

Copra (continued)
  other aspects see Oils
Coptic
  Church   281.7
   buildings
    architecture   726.581 7
    building   690.658 17
    other aspects see
      Religious-purpose
      bldgs.
   Christian life guides   248.481 7
   doctrines   230.17
    creeds   238.19
   general councils   262.517
   govt. & admin.   262.017
    parishes   254.017
   missions   266.17
   moral theology   241.041 7
   music
    arts   783.026 17
     recordings   789.912 302 617
     s.a. spec. instruments;
      also spec. kinds e.g.
      Liturgical music
   religion
    pub. worship   264.017 02
    significance   246.7
   private prayers for   242.801 7
   pub. worship   264.017
   rel. associations
    adults   267.181 7
    men   267.241 7
    women   267.441 7
    young adults   267.621 7
   rel. instruction   268.817
   rel. law   262.981 7
   schools   377.817
   secondary training   207.121 7
   sermons   252.017
   theological seminaries   207.111 7
   s.a. other spec. aspects
  language
   linguistics   493.2
   literature   893.2
   s.a.   *lang.*–932
  people   *r.e.n.*–932
  period Egypt hist.   932.023
   s.a. spec. events & subj.
    e.g. Commerce
  texts
   Bible   220.49
   s.a. spec. parts of Bible
  s.a. other spec. subj. e.g.
    Arts
Copts   *r.e.n.*–932
Copulation
  gen. wks. *see* Conjugation
    (sexual)
  humankind *see* Sex
Copying *see* Copies

Copying-machines *see*
    Photoduplication
Copyreading
  journalism   070.415
Copyright
  deposits
   libraries   021.84
    acquisitions   025.26
     govt. aspects   021.8
  law
   international   341.758 2
   municipal   346.048 2
    spec. jur.   346.3–.9
  pub. admin. *see* Secondary
    industries govt.
    control pub. admin.
Copywriting
  advertising operations   659.132 2
Coquet River Northumberland
    Eng.   *area*–428 87
Coquimbo Chile   *area*–832 3
Coracii *see* Coraciiformes
Coraciiformes
  hunting
   commercial   639.128 892
   sports   799.248 892
  paleozoology   568.8
  zoology   598.892
  other aspects see Aves
Coracles *see* Hand-propelled
    vessels
Coral
  fungi *see* Agaricales
  reefs *see* Reefs
  Sea
   oceanography   551.465 76
   regional subj. trmt.   *area*–164 76
   other aspects see Pacific
    Ocean
Corals *see* Anthozoa
Corangamite Lake Vic.   *area*–945 7
Corby Northamptonshire Eng.
    area–425 51
Corchorus *see* Jute
Cord & pulley
  mechanics   531.8
Cordage
  metal prod. *see* Drawn metal
    prod.
  shipbuilding *see* Gear
    shipbuilding
  textiles
   arts   746.047 1
   s.a. spec. proc.
   manufacturing
    soc. & econ. aspects *see*
     Secondary industries
    technology   677.71
   other aspects see Textiles
   s.a. spec. prod.

Cordaitales
  paleobotany   561.55
Cordaiteae
  paleobotany   561.55
Cordials *see* Compound liquors
Cordierite
  mineralogy   549.64
Cordite *see* Propellant
     explosives
Córdoba
  Argentina   *area*–825 4
  Colombia   *area*–861 12
  Spain   *area*–468 4
Cordova McCarthy
  election district Alaska   *area*–798 3
Cords *see* Passementerie
Corduroy
  fabric *see* Pile-weave fabrics
  roads *see* Wood pavements
Core of earth
  geophysics   551.112
Coreoidea *see* Heteroptera
Coreopsis *see* Asterales
Corfu Greece   *area*–495 5
Corgis
  animal husbandry   636.73
  other aspects see Dogs
Coriander
  crops *see* Herbs
Coriariaceae *see* Coriariales
Coriariales
  botany   583.29
  floriculture   635.933 29
  med. aspects
    crop. prod.   633.883 29
    gen. pharm.   615.323 29
      toxicology   615.952 329
    vet. pharm.   636.089 532 329
      toxicology   636.089 595 232 9
  paleobotany   561.3
  other aspects see Plants
Corinth Gulf *see* Ionian Sea
Corinthia Greece   *area*–495 2
  ancient   *area*–387
Corinthians
  Bible   227.2–.3
  other aspects see New
       Testament
Cork Ireland   *area*–419 5
Cork (material)
  manufacturing
    soc. & econ. aspects *see*
       Secondary industries
    technology   674.9
  s.a. spec. prod.
Corkboard *see* Insulating
     materials
Corkwood family *see*
     Leitneriales
Cormorants *see* Pelecaniformes

Corn
  agriculture
    field crops
      food   633.15
      forage   633.255
    garden crops   635.67
    soc. & econ. aspects *see*
       Primary industries
  flour & meal
    comm. proc.   664.725
    foods   641.356 7
    preparation
      commercial   664.805 67
      domestic   641.656 7
  oil
    comm. proc.   664.369
    other aspects see Oils
  sugars & syrups
    comm. proc.   664.133
    other aspects see Sugars
  textiles *see* Protein textiles
  other aspects see
       Panicoideae; *also*
       Vegetables
  s.a. spec. kinds e.g. Sweet
     corn
Cornaceae *see* Araliales
Corn-derived
  plastics *see* Protein plastics
  s.a. other spec. subj.
Corneas
  diseases   617.719
    geriatrics   618.977 719
    pediatrics   618.920 977 19
    statistics   312.304 771 9
  human phys.   612.841
  other aspects see Eyes
Cornet music   788.15
  recordings   789.912 81
Cornetists
  biog. & work   788.109 2
  s.a.   *pers.*–788
Cornets
  mf. tech.   618.818 1
    misc. aspects see Musical
       instruments
  musical art   788.1
Cornices
  roofs *see* Roofs
  snow formations *see* Snow
     formations
Cornish
  chickens
    animal husbandry   636.587 2
    other aspects see Chickens
  language
    linguistics   491.67
    literature   891.67
    s.a.   *lang.*–916 7
  people   *r.e.n.*–916 7

Cornish (continued)
s.a. Cornwall; *also other*
    spec. subj. e.g. Arts

Cornmeal
  comm. proc.   664.725

Corns (hypertrophies) *see*
    Hypertrophies skin

Cornstalk pulp
  mf. tech.   676.14
  other aspects see Pulp

Cornstarch
  food
    comm. proc.
      soc. & econ. aspects *see*
        Secondary industries
    technology   664.22

Cornwall Eng.   *area*–423 7

Cornwallis
  governorship India hist.   954.031 1–.031 2
    s.a. spec. events & subj.
      e.g. Commerce
  Isl. Northwest Ter.   *area*–719 5

Corollas *see* Reproductive
    organs

Coronagraphs
  astronomy   522.5
    s.a. spec. celestial bodies
  other aspects see Optical
    instruments

Coronary
  atherosclerosis
    gen. med.   616.123 2
    geriatrics   618.976 123 2
    pediatrics   614.591 23
    pub. health   614.591 232
    statistics   312.312 32
      deaths   312.261 232
    other aspects see Diseases
  care units
    med. sci.   616.120 25
  diseases   616.123
    geriatrics   618.976 123
    pediatrics   618.921 23
    pub. health   614.591 23
    statistics   312.312 3
      deaths   312.261 23
    other aspects see Diseases

Coronas (electronics) *see*
    Disruptive discharge

Coronas (sun)
  astronomy   523.75

Coronatae *see* Scyphozoa

Coronation Gulf *see* American
    Arctic seawaters

Coronations
  art represntation   704.949 9
    painting   756
    s.a. other spec. art forms
  history *see hist. of spec.*
    countries
  soc. customs   394.4

Coroners
  law *see* Court officials law
  occupational ethics   174.3
  s.a.   *pers.*–349

Coronie Surinam   *area*–883 2

Corowa N.S.W.   *area*–944 8

Corozal Belize   *area*–728 21

Corpora quadrigemina
  human phys.   612.826 4
  other aspects see Brain

Corporal punishment
  education   371.542
    s.a. spec. levels of ed.;
      also Special education
  penology   364.67
  other aspects see Punishment

Corporate
  bonds
    investment finance   332.632 34
    misc. aspects see Bonds
      (securities)
  income tax reductions
    law *see* Tax reductions law
    pub. finance   336.243 16
  income taxes
    law   343.067
    spec. jur.   343.3–.9
    pub. admin. *see* Income
      taxes pub. admin.
    pub. finance   336.243
  management
    law   346.066 4
    spec. jur.   346.3–.9
  organization
    law   346.066 2
    spec. jur.   346.3–.9
  ownership
    land econ.   333.324
  profits
    income distribution
      macroeconomics   339.21
  securities
    financial econ.   332.632 044
    other aspects see
      Securities
  states
    pol. sci.   321.94
    s.a. spec. jur.

Corporation taxes
  law   343.067
  spec. jur.   343.3–.9
  other aspects see Taxes
  s.a. Corporate income taxes

Corporations
  accounting   657.95
  law   346.066
    misc. aspects see
      Organizations law
  management   658.045
    initiation   658.114 5
  prod. econ.   338.74

Corporations (continued)
pub. relations 659.285
s.a. Municipal incorporation;
also spec. fields of
enterprise e.g.
Telecommunication
Corps
mil. organization 355.31
s.a. spec. mil. branches
Corpulence *see* Obesity
Corpus iuris canonici
rel. law 262.923
Corpus striatum
human phys. 612.825
other aspects see Brain
Corpuscles *see* Blood
Corpuscular
radiation
meteorology 551.527 6
weather forecasting 551.642 76
spec. areas 551.65
theory
electricity
astrophysics 523.018 714
s.a. spec. celestial
bodies
physics 537.14
spec. states of matter 530.4
light
astrophysics 523.015 12
s.a. spec. celestial
bodies
physics 535.12
spec. states of matter 530.4
Correctional institutions *see*
Penal institutions
Corrections
astronomy 522.9
s.a. spec. celestial bodies
s.a. other spec. subj.
Correlation
analysis
statistical math. 519.537
s.a. spec. appls. e.g.
Engineering
Correspondence
courses
adult ed. 374.4
spec. subj. *s.s.*–071 54
schools *see* Correspondence
courses
Correspondence (communication)
see Letters
(correspondence)
Correspondence (mathematics)
see Transformations
Correspondences
nat. rel. 219
Corrèze France *area*–446 7
Corrientes Argentina *area*–822 2

Corrodentia
culture 638.573 2
paleozoology 565.73
zoology 595.732
other aspects see Insecta
Corrosion
resistance to
eng. materials 620.112 23
s.a. spec. materials &
spec. uses
Corrosion-resistant construction
see Resistant
construction
Corrosive materials
pub. safety 363.179
misc. aspects see Hazardous
materials
Corrugated paperboard boxes
mf. tech. 676.32
other aspects see Containers
Corruption *see spec. subj.*
Corryong Vic. *area*–945 5
Corsages
flower arrangement 745.923
Corse *see* Corsica
Corse de Sud France *area*–449 452
Corsets *see* Supporting garments
Corsiaceae *see* Burmanniales
Corsica *area*–449 45
ancient *area*–379
Corsicans *r.e.n.*–58
Corson Co. S.D. *area*–783 52
Cortés Honduras *area*–728 311
Cortex
cerebrum
human phys. 612.825
other aspects see Brain
Cortin
org. chem. 547.734 5
pharm. & phys. *see* Adrenal
hormones
other aspects see Hormones
Cortisone
pharm. & phys. *see* Adrenal
hormones
Cortland Co. N.Y. *area*–747 72
Coruh Turkey *area*–566 2
Corum Turkey *area*–563
Coruña Spain *area*–461 1
Corundum
eng. materials 620.198
foundations 624.153 98
naval design 623.818 98
shipbuilding 623.820 7
structures 624.189 8
s.a. other spec. uses
mineralogy 549.523
other aspects see Abrasive
materials

Costa (continued)
  Rica   *area*–728 6
  Rican
    literature   860
    people   *r.e.n.*–687 286
    s.a. spec. subj. e.g. Arts
Costilla Co. Colo.   *area*–788 35
Cost-output ratio
  prod. econ. *see* Efficiency
      prod. econ.
Costs
  govt. procurement
    pub. admin.   350.712 044
      central govts.   351.712 044
        spec. jur.   353–354
      local govts.   352.162 044
  law   347.077
    spec. jur.   347.3–.9
    other aspects see Legal
      procedure
  macroeconomics   339.42
  prod. econ.   338.51
    misc. aspects see Finance
      prod. econ.
  recovery
    govt. contracting
      pub. admin.   350.711 3
        central govts. 351.711 3
         spec. jur.   353–354
        local govts.   352.161 3
  warfare
    mil.sci.   355.023
  other aspects see Finance
  s.a. other spec. subj.
Costume jewelry
  manufacturers
    biog. & work   688.209 2
    s.a.   *pers.*–688
  manufacturing
    soc. & econ. aspects *see*
      Secondary industries
    technology   688.2
  other aspects see Jewelry
Costumes *see* Clothing
Costuming
  dramatic performances
    motion pictures   791.430 26
    stage   792.026
    s.a. spec. kinds e.g.
      Tragedies (drama)
    television   791.450 26
Cost-volume-profit analysis
  financial management *see*
    Income financial
    management
Cotabato Philippines   *area*–599 7
Côte-d'Or France   *area*–444 2
Côtes-du-Nord France   *area*–441 2
Cotillions
  recreation   793.35
Cotopaxi Ecuador   *area*–866 14

Cotswold Gloucestershire Eng.
              area–424 17
Cotswolds Gloucestershire Eng.
              area–424 17
Cottage
  cheeses
    dairy tech.   637.356
    other aspects see Cheeses
  industries *see* Domestic
      industries
Cottages
  architecture   728.37
  building   690.837
  other aspects see Residential
      buildings
Cottbus Ger.   *area*–431 5
Cotter pins *see* Cotters
Cotters
  machine eng.
    soc. & econ. aspects *see*
      Secondary industries
    tech. & mf.   621.883
    s.a. spec. appls. e.g.
      Agricultural equipment
  other aspects see Mechanics
Cottle Co. Tex.   *area*–764 751
Cotton
  Co. Okla.   *area*–766 49
  derivatives
    polysaccharides
      org. chem.   547.782
      other aspects see
        Carbohydrates
  family *see* Malvales
  plants
    agriculture   633.51
    soc. & econ. aspects *see*
      Primary industries
  textiles
    arts   746.042 1
      s.a. spec. proc. e.g.
        Weaving
    dyeing   667.321
    manufacturing
      soc. & econ. aspects *see*
        Secondary industries
      technology   677.21
      special-process fabrics 677.6
    other aspects see Textiles
    s.a. spec. prod.
Cottonseed oil
  comm. proc.   664.363
  other aspects see Oils
Cottonseeds
  flour & meal
    comm. proc.   644.726
    other aspects see Seeds
Cottonwood
  Co. Minn.   *area*–776 28
  trees *see* Salicales

Cotylosauria
paleozoology   567.92
Couches *see* Upholstered
   furniture
Couching
   textile arts *see* Embroidery
Cougars
   animal husbandry   636.89
   other aspects see Cats
Cough remedies
   pharmacodynamics   615.72
   other aspects see Drugs
Coulometers
   electric current measurement   621.374 4
   s.a. spec. appls. e.g.
     Ignition systems &
     devices
Coulometric
   methods
     anal. chem.
       gen. wks.   543.087 4
         qualitative   544.974
         quantitative   545.34
       organic   547.308 74
         qualitative   547.349 74
         quantitative   547.353 4
     s.a. spec. elements &
       cpds.
Coulsdon & Purley London Eng.
       area–421 91
Council
   League of Nations
     internat. law   341.222 3
Council of Europe
   members
     regional subj. trmt.   *area*–177
Council-manager form
   local govt. admin.   352.008 4
Councilors of state
   biog. & work *see spec.*
       countries & spec.
       subj.
   s.a.   *pers.*–352 1
Councils
   of state
     pub. admin.   351.004
       U.S. govts.   353.914
       other spec. jur.   354
     s.a. other spec. kinds
Counsel
   gift of the Holy Spirit
     Christian doctrines   234.12
   right to
     procedural right
       criminal law   345.056
       spec. jur.   345.3–.9
Counseling
   armed forces   355.347
   s.a. spec. mil. branches
   crime prevention   364.48

Counseling (continued)
   education   371.4
     law   344.079 4
       spec. jur.   344.3–.9
     special ed.   371.9
     s.a. spec. levels of ed.
   pastoral theology
     Christianity   253.5
     other rel. see Pastoral
       theology
   personnel admin.
     gen. management   658.385
       executive management   658.407 85
       spec. subj.   *s.s.*–068 3
     pub. admin.   350.16
       central govts.   351.16
       spec. jur.   353–354
       local govts.   352.005 16
     soc. services   361.06
     soc. work   361.323
     spec. problems & groups   363–364
     other aspects see Welfare
       services
Counselors
   religion *see* Clergy
Counter displays
   advertising operations   659.157
Countercultures
   sociology   306.1
Counterfeit
   coins
     numismatics   737.4
   paper money
     arts   769.55
   philatelic issues
     prints   769.562
Counterfeiting
   economics   332.9
   internat. law   341.77
   other aspects see Revenue
     offenses
Counterglow *see* Zodiacal light
Counterintelligence services
   armed forces   355.343 3
   s.a. spec. mil. branches
Countermeasures
   mech. vibrations
     engineering   620.37
     s.a. spec. appls. e.g.
       Reciprocating engines
   noise
     acoustical eng.   620.23
     s.a. spec. appls. e.g.
       Soundproofing bldg.
       construction
   s.a. other spec. subj.
Countermining
   mil. eng.   623.3
Countermonopoly
   labor union theory   331.880 1

Counterpoint
  music theory — 781.42
    spec. forms — 781.5
  s.a. spec. mediums
Counter-Reformation
  Christian church hist. — 270.6
    spec. denominations — 280
Counters
  numismatics — 737.3
  rel. significance
    Christianity — 247.873
    comp. rel. — 291.37
    s.a. other spec. rel.
Counties
  local govt. admin. — 352.007 3
  s.a. spec. counties
Counting
  circuits electronic *see* Pulse
    circuits
  machines
    manufacturing
      soc. & econ. aspects *see*
        Secondary industries
      technology — 681.14
  s.a. other spec. subj.
Countries
  lit. & stage trmt. *see* Places
  s.a. spec. countries
Country
  club bldgs. *see* Clubhouse
    buildings
  clubs
    landscape design — 712.7
  music — 780.42
    songs — 784.52
      recordings — 789.912 452
    s.a. other spec. mediums
  Party Australia
    pol. sci. — 324.294 04
    s.a. spec. subj. of concern
      e.g. Social problems
  s.a. Rural; *also*
    Agricultural
County
  boroughs
    local govt. — 352.007 24
  buildings
    architecture — 725.13
    building — 690.513
    other aspects see Public
      structures
  Court
    England
      law — 347.420 21
  libraries
    buildings
      architecture — 727.824 22
    catalogs *see* Library
      catalogs
  planning
    civic art — 711.3

County
  planning (continued)
    economics — 338.9
    soc. sci. *see* Planning soc.
    welfare
  s.a. Local governments
Coup d'état
  pol. sci. — 321.09
Coupar Angus Tayside Scot. *area*–412 8
Coupling
  nuclear interactions *see*
    Interactions nuclear
    reactions
Couplings
  machine eng.
    soc. & econ. aspects *see*
      Secondary industries
    tech. & mf. — 621.825
    s.a. spec. appls. e.g.
      Rolling stock railroads
  railroad eng.
    technology — 625.25
    other aspects see Rolling
      stock railroads
  other aspects see Mechanics
Courage
  ethics
    philosophy — 179.6
    religion
      Buddhism — 294.356 96
      Christianity — 241.696
      comp. rel. — 291.569 6
      Hinduism — 294.548 696
      s.a. other spec. rel.
Courland — *area*–474 3
Course
  celestial navigation — 527.5
Courses *see* Curriculums
Court
  buildings
    architecture — 725.15
    building — 690.515
    other aspects see Public
      structures
  calendars *see* Judicial
    administration
  decisions
    law
      international
        source of law — 341.1
        texts — 341.026 8
      municipal — 348.044
        spec. jur. — 348.3–.9
      U.S.
        Federal — 348.734 4
        state & local — 348.74–.79
      spec. subj. — *law s.s.*–026 43
  management *see* Judicial
    administration
  of Appeal
    England law — 347.420 32

Coverdale Bible	220.520 1
s.a. spec. parts of Bible	
Covered girder bridges	
structural eng.	624.37
other aspects see Bridges	
(structures)	
Coverlets	
woven felt fabrics	
manufacturing	
soc. & econ. aspects *see*	
Secondary industries	
technology	677.626
other aspects see Textiles	
Covers	
bookbinding	686.34
Covers (philately)	769.565
Covetousness *see* Vices	
Covington	
city Va.	*area*–755 812
County	
Alabama	*area*–761 27
Mississippi	*area*–762 545
Cowardice	
ethics	
philosophy	179.6
religion	
Buddhism	294.356 96
Christianity	241.696
comp. rel.	291.569 6
Hinduism	294.548 696
s.a. other spec. rel.	
Cowbridge South Glamorgan	
Wales	*area*–429 89
Cowdenbeath Fife Scot.	*area*–412 98
Cowes Isle of Wight Eng.	*area*–422 82
Coweta Co. Ga.	*area*–758 423
Cowfish *see* Odontoceti	
Cowley Co. Kan.	*area*–781 89
Cowlitz	
Co. Wash.	*area*–797 88
River Wash.	*area*–797 82
Cowpeas *see* Black-eyed peas	
Cowpox	
gen. med.	616.913
geriatrics	618.976 913
pediatrics	618.929 13
pub. health	614.521
statistics	312.391 3
deaths	312.269 13
other aspects see Diseases	
Cowra N.S.W.	*area*–944 5
Cow's milk *see* Milk	
Cows *see spec. animals e.g.*	
Cattle	
Coyotes *see* Canidae	
Coypus *see* Hystricomorpha	
Crabgrass	
agric. pests *see* Weeds	
other aspects see Panicoideae	
Crabs	
food	641.395

Crabs (continued)	
other aspects	
gen. wks. *see* Brachyura	
hermits & king *see* Anomura	
Cracidae	
hunting	
commercial	639.128 614
sports	799.248 614
paleozoology	568.6
zoology	598.614
other aspects see Aves	
Crack resistance	
materials	
properties	620.112 6
s.a. spec. materials & spec.	
uses	
Crackers	
comm. proc.	664.752
home proc.	641.81
Cracking processes	
petroleum	665.533
s.a. spec. prod. e.g.	
Gasolines	
Cradle	
Mt. Tas.	*area*–946 3
Mountain-Lake Saint Clair Nat.	
Park Tas.	*area*–946 3
roll	
Sunday schools	
Christianity	268.432
other rel. see Religious	
instruction	
Craft	
air *see* Aircraft	
nautical *see* Vessels	
(nautical)	
space *see* Spacecraft	
unions	
labor econ.	331.883 2
labor law *see* Labor law	
Crafts	
gen. wks.	
arts	745
industry	680
spec. ed.	371.904 4
s.a. spec. groups of	
students	
s.a. spec. crafts	
Craftsmen *see* Industrial	
occupations	
Craftsmen's marks	*s.s.*–027 8
Craig Co.	
Oklahoma	*area*–766 98
Virginia	*area*–755 795
Craigavon N. Ire	*area*–416 64
Craighead Co. Ark.	*area*–767 98
Crail Fife Scot.	*area*–412 92
Cranberries	
agriculture	634.76
soc. & econ. aspects *see*	
Primary industries	

Crematories
  architecture   725.597
  building   690.559 7
  other aspects see Public
      structures
Cremona Italy   *area*–452 7
Crenshaw Co. Ala.   *area*–761 36
Creodonta
  paleozoology   569.74
Crepes
  cookery   641.8
Creping
  paper *see* Finishing paper
  textiles *see* Finishing
      textiles
  s.a. other spec. subj.
Crepipoda
  culture   639.481 9
  paleozoology   564.19
  zoology   594.19
  other aspects see Mollusca
Crescent Lake Tas.   *area*–946 3
Cresses
  agriculture   635.56
  soc. & econ. aspects *see*
      Primary industries
  foods   641.355 6
    preparation
      commercial   664.805 56
      domestic   641.655 6
  other aspects see Cruciales;
      also Vegetables
Crests
  genealogy   929.82
Creswick Vic.   *area*–945 3
Cretaceous period
  geology   551.77
  s.a. spec. aspects e.g.
      Economic geology
  paleontology   560.176 6
    spec. fossils   561–569
Crete
  island   *area*–499 8
    ancient   *area*–391 8
  Sea
    oceanography   551.462 8
    regional subj. trmt.   *area*–163 88
    other aspects see Atlantic
      Ocean
Cretinism
  gen. med.   616.858 848
  pediatrics   618.928 588 48
  psychology   157.8
  pub. health   362.3
  statistics   312.385 884 8
Creuse France   *area*–446 8
Crewe & Nantwich Cheshire Eng.
      area–427 12

Crewelwork
  textile arts   746.446
  s.a. spec. prod. e.g.
      Hangings
Crewkerne Somerset Eng.   *area*–423 89
Crews
  naval organization   359.31
Crib deaths   618.920 078
Cribbage
  equip. mf.   688.754 1
  soc. & econ. aspects *see*
      Secondary industries
  recreation   795.41
Criblé engraving
  graphic arts
    processes   765.6
    products   769
Cribwork
  underwater foundation eng.   624.157
  s.a. spec. appls. e.g.
      Military engineering
Criccieth Gwynedd Wales   *area*–429 23
Cricket
  game
    equipment mf.   688.763 58
    soc. & econ. aspects *see*
      Secondary industries
    sports   796.358
    other aspects see Sports
  players
    biog. & work   796.358 092
    s.a.   *pers.*–796 35
Crickets *see* Orthoptera
Crieff Tayside Scot.   *area*–412 8
Crime
  & press
    law   345.056
      spec. jur.   345.3–.9
  correction *see* Penology
  gen. wks. *see* Criminology
  lit. & stage trmt. *see* Social
      themes
  prevention   363.232
    criminology   364.4
    management   658.473
    penology   364.601
    police work
      pub. admin.   350.75
      central govts.   351.75
      spec. jur.   353–354
      local govts.   352.935
    soc. welfare
      pub. admin.   350.849 2
      central govts.   351.849 2
      spec. jur.   353–354
      local govts.   352.944 92
  rel. aspects *see* Sin
  soc. theology
    Christianity   261.833
    comp. rel.   291.178 33
    s.a. other spec. rel.

Crime (continued)
  victims *see* Victims of crime
Crimea   *area*–477 17
Crimean War hist.   947.073
Crimes
  gen. wks. *see* Criminal
    offenses
  violent *see* Violent crimes
Criminal
  abortion
    criminology   364.185
    law   345.028 5
      spec. jur.   345.3–.9
    soc. theology
      Christianity   261.833 185
      comp. rel.   291.178 331 85
      s.a. other spec. rel.
  anthropology   364.2
  anthropometry   364.125
  classes *see* Offenders
  courts
    law   345.01
      spec. jur.   345.3–.9
  intent
    law   345.04
      spec. jur.   345.3–.9
  investigation
    law enforcement   363.25
      misc. aspects see Law
        enforcement
    mil. sci.   355.133 23
      s.a. spec. mil. branches
  jurisdiction
    internat. law   341.488
  law
    international   341.77
    municipal   345
  libel *see* Defamation
  offenses
    criminology   364.1
    insurance against   368.48
      misc. aspects see
        Insurance
    law
      criminal   345.02
        spec. jur.   345.3–.9
      military   343.014
        spec. jur.   343.3–.9
      religious
        Christianity
          Roman Catholic
            Codex iuris
              canonici   262.935
            early codes   262.92
            other denominations   362.98
          other rel. see
            Religious law
      soc. theology
        Christianity   261.833 1
        comp. rel.   291.178 331
        s.a. other spec. rel.

Criminal
  offenses (continued)
    s.a. Offenses military law
  practice
    law   345.05
      spec. jur.   345.3–.9
  procedure
    law   345.05
      spec. jur.   345.3–.9
  psychology *see* Offenders
  responsibility
    law   345.04
      spec. jur.   345.3–.9
  usury *see* Financial offenses
Criminalistics   363.25
Criminally insane people
  penology   365.46
  other aspects see Penal
    institutions
  s.a. Mentally ill people
Criminals *see* Offenders
Criminologists
  biog. & work   364.92
  s.a.   *pers.*–364
Criminology   364
  curriculums   375.364
Crimson clovers
  agriculture   633.327
  soc. & econ. aspects *see*
    Primary industries
  other aspects see
    Papilionaceae; *also*
    Field crops
Crinoidea
  culture   639.739 1
  paleozoology   563.91
  zoology   593.91
  other aspects see Animals
Crippled
  children
    psychology   155.451 6
    rearing home econ.   649.151 6
  people
    soc. services   362.438
    other aspects see Disabled
      people
    s.a.   *pers.*–081 66
  students
    education   371.916
    law   344.079 116
      spec. jur.   344.3–.9
Crisana Romania   *area*–498 4
Crisp Co. Ga.   *area*–758 893
Criteria
  epistemology   121.65
Critical
  appraisal *see* Criticism
  care *see* Intensive care
  ethics
    philosophy   170.42

264

Critical (continued)
  path method *see* Systems
    analysis
  phenomena *see* Phase changes
    effect of heat
  philosophy   142
    indiv. phil.   180–190
    s.a. spec. branches of phil.
      e.g. Metaphysics
  realism
    philosophy   149.2
    indiv. phil.   180–190
    s.a. spec. branches of
      phil. e.g. Metaphysics
  size
    nuclear eng.
      technology   621.483 1
      s.a. spec. appls. e.g.
        Military engineering
      other aspects see Nuclear
        reactions
Criticism
  arts
    gen. wks.
      theory   701.18
      works of art   709
      spec. subj.   704.94
    literature *see* Literary
      criticism
    s.a. other spec. art forms
  sacred books *see* Exegesis
  s.a. other spec. subj.
Crittenden Co.
  Arkansas   *area*–767 94
  Kentucky   *area*–769 893
Croatia   *area*–497 2
Croatian
  people   *r.e.n.*–918 23
  other aspects see
    Serbo-Croatian
  s.a. Croatia
Croats   *r.e.n.*–918 23
Crocheted
  fabrics
    arts   746.046 62
    s.a. spec. processes e.g.
      Weaving
    manufacturing
      soc. & econ. aspects *see*
        Secondary industries
      technology   677.662
    other aspects see Textiles
    s.a. spec. prod.
  rugs
    textile arts   746.73
Crocheting
  textile arts   746.434
  s.a. spec. prod.
Crockery *see* Earthenware
Crockett Co.
  Tennessee   *area*–768 225

Crockett Co. (continued)
  Texas   *area*–764 875
Crocodiles *see* Crocodilia
Crocodilia
  culture   639.398
  hunting
    commercial   639.148
    sports   799.279 798
  paleozoology   567.98
  zoology   597.98
  other aspects see Reptilia
Crocoite
  mineralogy   549.752
Crocuses *see* Iridales
Crohn's disease *see* Ileitis
Cro-Magnon man   573.3
Cromarty Scot.   *area*–411 72
Cromdale Highland Scot.   *area*–411 92
Cromer Norfolk Eng.   *area*–426 12
Crompton Greater Manchester Eng.
      area–427 393
Cromwells
  Eng. hist.   942.064–.065
  Gt. Brit. hist.   941.064–.065
  Scotland hist.   941.106 4–.106 5
  s.a. spec. events & subj.
    e.g. Commerce
Crook & Willington Durham Eng.
      area–428 64
Crook Co.
  Oregon   *area*–795 83
  Wyoming   *area*–787 13
Crooked Isl. Bahamas   *area*–729 6
Crookes tubes *see* Photoelectric
    devices
Crookwell N.S.W.   *area*–944 5
Crops   631
  loans
    economics   332.71
    other aspects see Credit
  pathology   632
  production
    agriculture   631.5
  rotation
    effect
      agric. econ.   338.162
      soil conservation   631.452
    s.a. spec. crops
Croquet
  equipment mf.   688.763 54
    soc. & econ. aspects *see*
      Secondary industries
  recreation   796.354
  other aspects see Sports
Crosby
  Co. Tex.   *area*–764 848
  Merseyside Eng.   *area*–427 59
Crosier Fathers
  rel. orders   255.19
    church hist.   271.19
    ecclesiology   262.24

Crosiers of the Red Star
 rel. orders   255.19
  church hist.   271.19
  ecclesiology   262.24
Cross
 Co. Ark.   *area*–767 93
 examination *see* Examination
  of witnesses
 River Nigeria   *area*–669 4
 sections
  nuclear reactions *see*
   Nuclear reactions
 Timbers Belt Tex.   *area*–764 54
Crossbreeding
 animals
  husbandry   636.082 43
  s.a. spec. animals
Cross-cultural psychology   155.8
Crosses
 rel. significance   246.558
Crossings
 railroad eng.
  technology   625.163
  other aspects see Permanent
   way
Crossopterygii
 culture   639.374 6
 fishing
  commercial   639.274 6
  sports   799.174 6
 paleozoology   567.4
 zoology   597.46
 other aspects see Pisces
Crossosomataceae *see*
   Dilleniales
Cross-stitch *see* Embroidery
Crossword puzzles
 recreation   793.732
Croup
 gen. med.   616.201
 pediatrics   618.922 01
 pub. health   614.592 01
 statistics   312.320 1
 deaths   312.262 01
 other aspects see Diseases
Crow Wing Co. Minn.   *area*–776 71
Crowbars *see* Disassembling
   tools
Crowberry family *see*
   Celastrales
Crowds
 control   363.32
 law   344.053 2
  spec. jur.   344.3–.9
 pub. admin.   350.75
  central govts.   351.75
   spec. jur.   353–354
  local govts.   352.935
 sociology   302.33
Crowfoot family *see* Ranales
Crowley Co. Colo.   *area*–788 94

Crown Court
 England law   345.420 14
Crowns
 dentistry   617.692
 jewelry *see* Jewelry
Crows *see* Corvidae
Croydon London Eng.   *area*–421 91
Crozet Isls.   *area*–699
Cruciales
 botany   583.123
 floriculture   635.933 123
 med. aspects
  crop prod.   633.883 123
  gen. pharm.   615.323 123
   toxicology   615.952 312 3
  vet. pharm.   636.089 532 312 3
   toxicology   636.089 595 231 23
 paleobotany   561.3
 other aspects see Plants
Crucible steel
 technology   669.142 9
 other aspects see Ferrous
   metals
Crucibles
 chem. apparatus   542.2
 s.a. spec. appls. e.g.
   Organic chemistry
Cruciferae *see* Cruciales
Crucifixes
 rel. significance   246.558
Crucifixion
 Christian doctrines   232.963
Crude
 drugs
  pharmacognosy   615.321
  misc. aspects see
    Pharmacology
 gelatin
  manufacturing
   chem. tech.   668.34
   soc. & econ. aspects *see*
     Secondary industries
 rubbers *see* Raw rubber
 turpentines *see* Turpentines
Cruelty
 ethics
  philosophy   179.1–.4
  religion
   Buddhism   294.356 91–.356 94
   Christianity   241.691–.694
   comp. rel.   291.569 1–.569 4
   Hinduism   294.548 691–.548 694
   s.a. other spec. rel.
 to animals *see* Animals
   treatment of
 to children *see* Children
   treatment of
Cruisers
 engineering   623.825 3
 design   623.812 53
 models   623.820 153

Cruisers (continued)
  naval forces
    materiel — 359.83
    organization — 359.325 3
    seamanship — 623.882 53
    other aspects see Vessels
      (nautical)
Crusades
  history
    Christian church — 270.4-.5
    Europe — 940.18
    general — 909.07
    s.a. spec. countries
  journalism — 070.412
Crushed stone
  pavement eng. *see* Stone
    pavements road eng.
Crushers (agric. tools)
  agriculture — 631.314
    use *see spec. uses e.g.*
      Tillage
      s.a. spec. crops; also
        spec. types of culture
        e.g. Floriculture
  mf. tech. — 681.763 1
    soc. & econ. aspects *see*
      Secondary industries
Crushing
  chem. eng. — 660.284 22
    s.a. spec. prod.
  ore
    mining eng. — 622.73
    spec. ores — 622.33-.39
Crushing-tools
  soc. & econ. aspects *see*
    Secondary industries
  tech. & mf. — 621.914
    s.a. spec. appls. e.g.
      Scrap metals
Crust
  earth
    geophysics — 551.13
Crustacea
  agric. pests — 632.653
    s.a. spec. types of culture
      e.g. Forestry; *also*
      spec. crops
  conservation tech. — 639.975 3
  culture
    technology — 639.5
      soc. & econ. aspects *see*
        Primary industries
    other aspects see
      Agriculture
  drawing tech. — 743.653
  fishing
    commercial
      technology — 639.5
        soc. & econ. aspects
          see Primary
          industries

Crustacea
  fishing
    commercial (continued)
      other aspects see Fishing
        industries
    law *see* Fishing law
    sports — 799.255 3
  food — 641.395
    cookery — 641.695
  paleozoology — 565.3
  zoology — 595.3
    other aspects see Animals
Crutches
  mf. tech. — 685.38
    other aspects see Footwear
Cryobiology *see* Cryogenic
  temperatures biophysics
Cryogenic
  engineers
    biog. & work — 621.590 92
    s.a. — *pers.*–621
  fluids
    pub. safety — 363.179
      misc. aspects see
        Hazardous materials
  temperatures
    biophysics
      extraterrestrial
        gen. wks — 574.191 967
        animals — 591.191 967
        microorganisms — 576.119 196 7
        plants — 581.191 967
        s.a. spec. organisms
      med. sci. — 621.014 567
        animals — 636.089 201 456 7
          s.a. spec. animals
        humankind — 612.014 567
      terrestrial
        gen. wks. — 574.191 67
        animals — 591.191 67
        microorganisms — 576.119 167
        plants — 581.191 67
        s.a. spec. organisms
      med. sci. — 612.014 467
        animals — 636.089 201 446 7
          s.a. spec. animals
        humankind — 612.014 467
      s.a. spec. functions,
        systems, organs
      other aspects see Low
        temperatures
Cryogenics
  technology — 621.59
    s.a. spec. appls. e.g. Deep
      freezing foods
    other aspects see Low
      temperatures
Cryolite
  mineralogy — 549.4

Cryolite (continued)
  synthetic
    manufacturing
      soc. & econ. aspects *see*
        Secondary industries
      technology   666.86
Cryometry
  astrophysics   523.013 54
    s.a. spec. celestial bodies
  physics   536.54
    spec. states of matter   530.4
Cryosurgery   617.05
  misc. aspects see Diseases
  s.a. spec. diseases
Cryotherapy   615.832 9
  misc. aspects see Physical
    therapies
  s.a. spec. diseases
Cryptanalysis
  services
    armed forces   355.343 2
    s.a. spec. mil. branches
  technique   652.8
Crypteroniaceae *see* Lythrales
Cryptobranchoidea *see* Caudata
Cryptocerata *see* Heteroptera
Cryptococcales *see*
    Deuteromycetes
Cryptodira *see* Chelonia
Cryptogamia
  botany   586
  floriculture   635.936
  med. aspects
    crop prod.   633.886
    gen. pharm.   615.326
      toxicology   615.952 6
    vet. pharm.   636.089 532 6
      toxicology   636.089 595 26
  paleobotany   561.6
  other aspects see Plants
Cryptogams *see* Cryptogamia
Cryptograms
  rel. significance *see*
    Symbolism rel.
    significance
Cryptography
  mil. sci.   358.24
  technique   652.8
  verbal commun.   001.543 6
Cryptomonadida *see* Mastigophora
Cryptonemiales *see* Rhodophyta
Crypts *see* Mortuary tombs &
    chapels
Crystal
  conduction counters
    radioactivity detection
      astrophysics   523.019 776
      s.a. spec. celestial
      bodies
      physics   539.776
        spec. states of matter   530.4

Crystal
  conduction counters
    radioactivity detection
      physics (continued)
        s.a. spec. physical
          phenomena e.g. Heat;
          also spec. appls.
          e.g. Civil defense
    devices
      electronics *see*
        Semiconductors
      radiowave electronics
  gazing
    parapsychology   133.322
  growth   548.5
    misc. aspects see
      Crystallography
  lasers *see* Solid-state lasers
  lattices
    crystallography   548.81
    s.a. spec. substances
  rotation
    optical crystallography   548.9
    s.a. spec. substances
  sets
    radio
      engineering   621.384 136 6
      s.a. spec. appls. e.g.
        Radiotelephony
      other aspects see Radio
  structure
    crystallography   548.81
    s.a. spec. substances
Crystal (glassware) *see*
    Glassware
Crystalline
  lens
    diseases
      gen. wks.   617.742
      geriatrics   618.977 742
      pediatrics   618.920 977 42
      statistics   312.304 774 2
    human phys.   612.844
    other aspects see Eyes
  limestones *see* Metamorphic
    rocks
  precipitation *see* Snowfall
Crystallization   548.5
  chem. eng.   660.284 298
  sugar prod.
    comm. prod.   664.115
    cane   664.122 5
    s.a. other kinds
    other aspects see Sugars
  s.a. other spec. prod. &
    substances
Crystallograms
  crystallography   548.83
  s.a. spec. substances
Crystallographers
  biog. & work   548.092

Crystallographers (continued)
 s.a.   *pers.*–548
Crystallographic
 mineralogy   549.18
 spec. minerals   549.2–.7
 properties eng. materials   620.112 99
 s.a. spec. materials & spec.
 uses
Crystallography   548
 curriculums   375.548
 documentation   025.065 48
 library acquisitions   025.275 48
 library classification   025.465 48
 mineralogy   549.18
 subject headings   025.495 48
 other aspects see Sciences
 s.a. spec. appls. e.g.
 Petrology
Csongrad Hungary   *area*–439 8
Ctenolphonaceae *see*
 Malpighiales
Ctenophorae
 culture   639.738
 paleozoology   563.8
 zoology   593.8
 other aspects see Animals
Ctenostoma *see* Gymnolaemata
Cuando Cubango Angola   *area*–673 5
Cuanza Angola   *area*–673 2
Cub Scouts   369.43
Cuba   *area*–729 1
Cuban
 communism
 economics   335.434 7
 pol. ideology   320.532 3
 soc. theology *see*
 Political ideologies
 soc. theology
 itch *see* Alastrim
 literature   860
 people   *r.e.n.*–687 291
 s.a. other spec. subj. e.g.
 Arts
Cubature
 calculus   515.43
 s.a. spec. appls. e.g.
 Engineering
Cube roots
 number theory algebra   512.72
 s.a. spec. appls. e.g.
 Engineering
Cubes
 geometry
 duplication   516.204
 gen. wks. *see*
 Configurations
Cubic equations *see* Polynomial
 equations

Cubism
 arts
 gen. wks.   709.040 32
 spec. places   709.1–.9
 painting   759.063 2
 spec. places   759.1–.9
 sculpture   735.230 432
 spec. places   730.9
Cubomedusae *see* Scyphozoa
Cuckfield West Sussex Eng.
      area–422 65
Cuckoo
 shrikes
 zoology   598.8
 other aspects see
 Passeriformes
Cuckoos *see* Cuculiformes
Cucujoidea
 zoology   595.764 3
 other aspects see Polyphaga
Cuculi *see* Cuculiformes
Cuculiformes
 hunting
 commercial   639.128 74
 sports   799.248 74
 paleozoology   568.7
 zoology   598.74
 other aspects see Aves
Cucumbers
 agriculture   635.63
 soc. & econ. aspects *see*
 Primary industries
 foods   641.356 3
 preparation
 commercial   664.805 63
 domestic   641.656 3
 other aspects see
 Cucurbitales; *also*
 Vegetables
Cucumis
 melo *see* Muskmelons
 sativus *see* Cucumbers
Cucurbita
 maxima *see* Squashes
 pepo *see* Pumpkins
Cucurbitaceae *see* Cucurbitales
Cucurbitales
 botany   583.46
 floriculture   635.933 46
 forestry   634.973 46
 med. aspects
 crop prod.   633.883 46
 gen. pharm.   615.323 46
 toxicology   615.952 346
 vet. pharm.   636.089 532 346
 toxicology   636.089 595 234 6
 paleobotany   561.3
 other aspects see Plants
Cudworth South Yorkshire Eng.
      area–428 25
Cuenca Spain   *area*–464 7

Cuffs
  comm. mf.
    soc. & econ. aspects *see*
        Secondary industries
    technology   687.19
    domestic mf.   646.48
Cuirasses *see* Defensive arms
Cuitlatec *see*
        Miskito-Matagalpan
Culberson Co. Tex.   *area*–764 94
Culebra Puerto Rico   *area*–729 59
Cullen Grampian Scot.   *area*–412 23
Cullman Co. Ala.   *area*–761 73
Culpeper Co. Va.   *area*–755 392
Culross Fife Scot.   *area*–412 98
Cultivated
  areas
    ecology *see* Land ecology
            life sci.
  silk textiles
    arts   746.043 91
    s.a. spec. proc. e.g.
        Weaving
    dyeing   667.339 1
    manufacturing
      soc. & econ. aspects *see*
          Secondary industries
      technology   677.391
        special-process fabrics   677.6
    other aspects see Textiles
    s.a. spec. prod.
Cultivation
  crops
    agriculture   631.5
  roadsides
    technology   625.77
    other aspects see Roads
Cultivators
  agriculture   631.316
  use   631.5
    s.a. spec. crops; also
        spec. types of culture
        e.g. Floriculture
  mf. tech.   681.763 1
    soc. & econ. aspects *see*
        Secondary industries
Cultural
  affairs
    govt. control
      activities   350.85
        central govts.   351.85
          spec. jur.   353–354
        local govts.   352.945
      govt. depts. *see*
          Executive departments
      soc. law   344.09
        spec. jur.   344.3–.9
    anthropologists
      biog. & work   306.092
      s.a.   *pers.*–309
    anthropology   306

Cultural (continued)
  areas
    civic art   711.57
  exchanges
    law
      international   341.767
      municipal   344.08
        spec. jur.   344.3–.9
    pub. admin. *see* Cultural
        affairs govt. control
    sociology   303.482
  factors
    educational sociology   370.193 4
    mental pub. health   362.204 2
  institutions
    sociology   306.4
  organizations *see*
        Organizations
  processes
    sociology   306
  relations
    internat. law   341.767
  role
    libraries   021.26
Culturally deprived
  children
    psychology   155.456 7
    rearing
      home econ.   649.156 7
  students
    education   371.967
    law   344.079 167
      spec. jur.   344.3–.9
Culture
  pub. reg. & control *see*
        Cultural affairs govt.
        control
  other aspects see
        Civilization
Cultured milk
  dairy tech.
    skim   637.147 6
    whole   637.146
    other aspects see Milk
Culverts
  drainage
    road eng.
      technology   625.734 2
      other aspects see Roads
    other aspects see Drainage
Cumacea
  fishing sports   799.255 381
  paleozoology   565.38
  zoology   595.381
  other aspects see
        Eumalacostraca
Cumberland
  city Md.   *area*–752 95
  County
    England   *area*–427 8
    Illinois   *area*–773 73

Cumberland
 County (continued)
  Kentucky   *area*–769 683
  Maine   *area*–741 91
  New Jersey   *area*–749 94
  North Carolina   *area*–756 373
  Nova Scotia   *area*–716 11
  Pennsylvania   *area*–748 43
  Tennessee   *area*–768 75
  Virginia   *area*–755 615
 Gap Tenn.   *area*–768 944
 Isl. Ga.   *area*–758 746
 Lake Ky.   *area*–769 63
 Mountains
  Kentucky   *area*–769 1
  Tennessee   *area*–768 944
 Plateau Tenn.   *area*–768 7
 Presbyterian Church 285.135
  misc. aspects see
    Presbyterian
 River Tenn.   *area*–768 5
Cumbernauld & Kilsyth Strathclyde
  Scot.   *area*–414 38
Cumbrae Isls. Scot.   *area*–414 61
Cumbria Eng.   *area*–427 8
Cumbrian Mts. Eng.   *area*–427 8
Cuming Co. Neb.   *area*–782 232
Cumnock & Doon Valley Strathclyde
  Scot.   *area*–414 67
Cundinamarca Colombia *area*–861 4
Cuneiform inscriptions 417.7
 s.a. spec. langs.
Cuneo Italy   *area*–451 3
Cunnamulla Qld.   *area*–943 4
Cunninghame Strathclyde Scot.
        area–414 61
Cunoniaceae *see* Cunoniales
Cunoniales
 botany   583.397
 floriculture   635.933 397
 forestry   634.973 397
 med. aspects
  crop prod.   633.883 397
  gen. pharm.   615.323 397
   toxicology   615.952 339 7
  vet. pharm. 636.089 532 339 7
   toxicology 636.089 595 233 97
 paleobotany   561.3
 other aspects see Plants
Cup
 fungi *see* Ascomycetes
 games
  soccer
   spec. games   796.334 74
   type   796.334 64
Cupar Fife Scot.   *area*–412 92
Cupboards *see* Cabinets
   (furniture)
Cupoidea *see* Adephaga
Cupolated roofs *see* Roofs

Cuprammonium textiles
 arts   746.044 62
  s.a. spec. processes e.g.
    Weaving
 dyeing   667.346 2
 manufacturing
  soc. & econ. aspects *see*
    Secondary industries
  technology   677.462
   special-process fabrics 677.6
 org. chem.   547.856 2
 other aspects see Textiles
 s.a. spec. prod.
Cupressaceae *see* Coniferales
Cupressus *see* Cypress trees
Cuprite
 mineralogy   549.522
Cuprum *see* Copper
Cups *see* Containers
Curaçao isl.   *area*–729 86
Curassows *see* Cracidae
Curates *see* Clergy
Curbs
 road eng.
  technology   625.888
  other aspects see Roads
Curculionoidea
 agric. pests   632.768
  s.a. spec. types of culture
    e.g. Forestry; *also*
     spec. crops
 culture   638.576 8
 paleozoology   565.76
 zoology   595.768
 other aspects see Insecta
Curettage *see* Dilation &
   curettage
Curfew
 crime prevention meas. 364.4
Curia Romana
 papal admin.   262.136
Curicó Chile   *area*–833 4
Curing
 nonalcoholic brewed beverages
  comm. proc.
   coffee   663.934
   tea   663.944
   s.a. other spec.
    beverages
  other aspects see Beverages
 s.a. other spec. subj.
Curiosities   001.93
 s.a. spec. subj.
Curium
 chemistry   546.442
Curlews *see* Charadriiformes
Curling (sport) *see* Ice games
Curly grass family *see*
   Filicales

Currants
 agriculture   634.721
  soc. & econ. aspects *see*
   Primary industries
 foods   641.347 21
  preparation
   commercial   664.804 721
   domestic   641.647 21
  other aspects see Cunoniales;
   also Fruits
Currency
 arts   769.55
 law   343.032
  spec. jur.   343.3–.9
 movements
  internat. comm.   382.174
 papers
  mf. tech.   676.282 6
  other aspects see Papers
   pulp prod.
 regulation
  legislative bodies *see*
   Financial powers
 other aspects see Paper money
Current
 assets
  accounting trmt.   657.72
  s.a. spec. kinds of
   enterprise e.g.
    Insurance accounting
 awareness programs
  library operations   025.525
 liabilities
  accounting trmt.   657.74
  s.a. spec. kinds of
   enterprise e.g.
    Insurance accounting
 operations
  capital sources
   capital management   658.152 26
   spec. subj.   *s.s.*–068 1
 transactions
  balance of payments
   internat. comm.   382.17
Currents *see spec. kinds e.g.*
   Air currents, Electric
   currents, Ocean
   currents
Curriculums   375
 elementary ed.   372.19
 exceptional students   371.9
 govt. supervision   379.155
 higher ed.   378.199
 law   344.077
  spec. jur.   344.3–.9
 rel. instruction
  Christianity   268.6
  other rel. see Religious
   instruction
 secondary ed.   373.19
Curries *see* Condiments

Currituck Co. N.C.   *area*–756 132
Curry Co.
 New Mexico   *area*–789 27
 Oregon   *area*–795 21
Curses
 folklore   398.41
Curtain dams *see* Movable dams
Curtains
 comm. mf.   684.3
 domestic mf.   646.21
 textile arts   746.94
 window furnishings   645.3
 other aspects see Furnishings
Curumbenya Fauna Reserve N.S.W.
     area–944 5
Curvature
 differential geometry   516.363
  s.a. spec. appls. e.g.
   Engineering
 integral geometry   516.362
  s.a. spec. appls. e.g.
   Enqineering
 s.a. Curves
Curve fittinq
 mathematics   511.42
  s.a. spec. math. branches;
   also spec. appls. e.g.
    Engineering
Curved constructions
 architecture
  construction   721.4
  design & decoration   729.33–.34
 building   690.14
 s.a. spec. kinds of bldgs.
Curves
 abstract algebraic geometry   512.33
  s.a. spec. appls. e.g.
   Engineering
 differential & integral
   qeometry   516.36
  s.a. spec. appls. e.g.
   Engineering
 projective & affine planes
  algebraic geometry   516.352
   s.a. spec. appls. e.g.
    Engineering
 other aspects see
   Configurations
Curvilinear systems *see*
   Coordinate systems
Curzon governorship India hist.   954.035 5
 s.a. spec. events & subj.
  e.g. Commerce
Cuscatlán El Salvador   *area*–728 424
Cuscutaceae *see* Polemoniales
Cush
 ancient region   *area*–397 8
 sovereignty Egypt hist.   932.015
  s.a. spec. events & subj.
   e.g. Commerce

Cutting
  metal prod. (continued)
    manufacturing
      soc. & econ. aspects *see*
        Secondarv industries
      technology   671.53
        ferrous metals   672.53
        s.a. other spec. metals
    plants grown for
      floriculture   635.966
        s.a. spec. plants
    trees
      silviculture   634.952
        s.a. spec. trees
    s.a. other spec. subj.
Cuttings
  plants grown from
    floriculture   635.948
      s.a. spec. plants
  use in plant propagation   631.535
    s.a. spec. crops; also spec.
      types of culture e.g.
      Floriculture
Cutting-tools
  soc. & econ. aspects *see*
    Secondary industries
  tech. & mf.   621.93
    s.a. spec. appls. e.g.
      Clothing comm. mf.
Cuttlefish *see* Decapoda
  (mollusks)
Cutwork
  textile arts *see* Embroidery
Cuyahoga Co. O.   *area*–771 31
Cuyo Isls. Philippines   *area*–599 4
Cuzco Peru   *area*–853 7
Cwmamman Dyfed Wales   *area*–429 68
Cwmbran Gwent Wales   *area*–429 97
Cyanamide
  fertilizers
    production
      soc. & econ. aspects *see*
        Secondary industries
      technology   668.624 1
    use agric.   631.841
      s.a. spec. crops; also
        spec. types of culture
        e.g. Floriculture
Cyanastraceae *see* Liliales
Cyanite
  mineralogy   549.62
Cyanophyceae *see* Cyanophyta
Cyanophyta
  botany   589.46
  med. aspects
    gen. pharm.   615.329 46
    toxicology   615.952 946
    vet. pharm.   636.089 532 946
    toxicology   636.089 595 294 6
  paleobotany   561.93
  other aspects see Plants

Cyathea family *see* Filicales
Cyatheaceae *see* Filicales
Cybernetics   001.53
  & religion
    nat. rel.   215
Cycadaceae *see* Cycadales
Cycadales
  botany   585.9
  floriculture   635.935 9
  forestry   634.975 99
  med. aspects
    crop prod.   633.885 9
    gen. pharm.   615.325 9
    toxicology   615.952 59
    vet. pharm.   636.089 532 59
    toxicology   636.089 595 259
  paleobotany   561.591
  other aspects see Plants
Cycadeoidaceae
  paleobotany   561.592
Cycadeoidales
  paleobotany   561.592
Cycadophyta
  paleobotany   561.59
Cycads *see* Cycadales
Cyclades Greece   *area*–499
  ancient   *area*–391 5
Cyclamen *see* Primulales
Cyclanes *see* Paraffins (chem.
  cpds.)
Cyclanthaceae *see* Cyclanthales
Cyclanthales
  botany   584.62
  floriculture   635.934 62
  med. aspects
    crop prod.   633.884 62
    gen. pharm.   615.324 62
    toxicology   615.952 462
    vet. pharm.   636.089 532 462
    toxicology   636.089 595 246 2
  paleobotany   561.4
  other aspects see Plants
Cyclenes *see* Olefins
Cycles *see* Evolution
Cycles (mathematics)   512.33
  s.a. spec. appls. e.g.
    Engineering
Cycles (vehicles)
  commerce   388.347
  engineering
    gen. tech. & mf.   629.227
    maintenance   629.287 7
    models   629.221 7
    operation   629.284 7
    s.a. other spec. aspects
      e.g. Brakes; *also*
      spec. appls. e.g.
      Military engineering
  soc. & econ. aspects *see*
    Secondary industries

Cycles (vehicles) (continued)
  other aspects see Land
      vehicles
Cyclic
  compounds
    org. chem.   547.5
    s.a. spec. cpds.
  groups
    algebra   512.2
    s.a. spec. appls. e.g.
      Engineering
Cyclical unemployment
  labor econ.   331.137 047
  s.a. spec. classes of labor
    e.g. Women
Cycling
  sports   796.6
  other aspects see Sports
Cycling paths *see* Bicycle paths
Cyclists
  biog. & work   796.609 2
  s.a.   *pers.*–796 6
Cyclo rubbers
  manufacturing
    soc. & econ. aspects *see*
      Secondary industries
  technology   678.68
Cycloalkanes *see* Paraffins
    (chem. cpds.)
Cyclogenesis *see* Cyclones
    (low-pressure systems)
Cycloidal steam engines
  stationary
    soc. & econ. aspects *see*
      Secondary industries
    tech. & mf.   621.166
    s.a. spec. appls. e.g.
      Power plants
Cyclones (hurricanes) *see*
    Hurricanes
Cyclones (low-pressure systems)
  meteorology   551.551 3
    artificial modification 551.685 13
    weather forecasting   551.645 13
    spec. areas   551.65
Cyclones (tornadoes) *see*
    Tornadoes
Cyclonite *see* High explosives
Cycloolefins *see* Olefins
Cycloparaffins *see* Paraffins
    (chem. cpds.)
Cyclopedias *see* Encyclopedias
Cyclopoida *see* Copepoda
Cyclops *see* Copepoda
Cyclopteris
  paleobotany   561.597
Cycloramas
  dec. arts   745.8
  painting arts   751.74
    indiv. artists   759.1–.9

Cycloramas
  painting arts (continued)
    s.a. spec. subj., tech.,
      equip.
Cyclorrhapha
  culture   638.577 4
  paleozoology   565.77
  zoology   595.774
  other aspects see Insecta
Cyclosilicates
  mineralogy   549.64
Cyclostomata (Agnatha) *see*
    Agnatha
Cyclostomata (Molluscoidea) *see*
    Gymnolaemata
Cyclostomi *see* Agnatha
Cyclothymia *see*
    Manic-depressive
    psychoses
Cyclotrons
  physics   539.733
  s.a. spec. physical
    phenomena e.g. Heat
Cydonia oblonga *see* Quinces
Cygnet Tas.   *area*–946 2
Cylinder
  bridges
    structural eng.   624.4
    other aspects see Bridges
      (structures)
  records & recorders *see*
    Recordings
Cylinders
  geometry *see* Configurations
    geometry
  internal combustion engines
    soc. & econ. aspects *see*
      Secondary industries
    tech. & mf.   621.437
      automobiles   629.252
      marine vehicles   623.872 37
    s.a. other spec. appls.
  structural eng. element
    gen. wks.   624.177 2
    concretes   624.183 42
    s.a. other spec.
      materials
    naval arch.   623.817 72
    s.a. other spec. appls.
Cylindrical functions   515.53
  s.a. spec. appls. e.g.
    Engineering
Cymbal music   789.25
  recordings   789.912 92
Cymbals
  mf. tech.   681.819 2
    other aspects see Musical
      instruments
  musical art   789.2
Cymric *see* Welsh
Cynara scolymus *see* Artichokes

Cynewulf
    Anglo-Saxon poetry   829.4
Cynic philosophy   183.4
Cynocrambaceae *see*
        Chenopodiales
Cynomorium *see* Santalales
Cynon Valley Mid Glamorgan
      Wales   *area*–429 73
Cyperaceae *see* Cyperales
Cyperales
  botany   584.84
  floriculture   635.934 84
  forage crops   633.2
    soc. & econ. aspects *see*
      Primary industries
    other aspects see Plants;
      also Field crops
  med. aspects
    crop prod.   633.884 84
    gen. pharm.   615.324 84
      toxicology   615.952 484
    vet. pharm.   636.089 532 484
      toxicology   636.089 595 248 4
  paleobotany   561.4
  other aspects see Plants
Cypress
  trees
    forestry   634.975 5
    soc. & econ. aspects *see*
      Primary industries
    other aspects see
      Coniferales; *also*
      Trees
  woods *see* Softwoods
Cyprinodontes *see* Mesichthyes
Cyprinoidea *see* Ostariophysi
Cypriot
  architecture   722.32
  misc. aspects see
    Architectural schools
  people   *r.e.n.*–895
  s.a. Cyprus; *also other*
    spec. subj. e.g. Arts
Cyprus   *area*–564 5
  ancient   *area*–393 7
Cyprus fever *see* Undulant fever
Cyrenaic
  philosophy   183.5
  s.a. other spec. subj. e.g.
    Arts
Cyrenaica   *area*–612
  ancient   *area*–397 5
Cyrillaceae *see* Celastrales
Cyrillic
  alphabet
    linguistics   411
    s.a. spec. langs.
    printing   686.219 18
  lettering
    dec. arts   745.619 918

Cystic fibrosis *see* Pancreas
    diseases
Cystitis
  gen. med.   616.623
  geriatrics   618.976 623
  pediatrics   618.926 23
  pub. health   614.596 23
  statistics   312.362 3
    deaths   312.266 23
  other aspects see Diseases
Cystoidea
  paleozoology   563.97
Cysts *see* Neoplasms
Cythera *see* Kythera
Cytinaceae *see* Aristolochiales
Cytochemistry   574.876 042
  animals   591.876 042
  plants   581.876 042
  s.a. spec. organisms
Cytogenetics
  cytology   574.873 223
    animals   591.873 223
    plants   581.873 223
    s.a. spec. organisms
Cytological examination
  med. sci.
    gen. med.   616.075 82
    surgery   617.075 82
    s.a. spec. diseases
    other aspects see Diseases
Cytology
  life sci.
    gen. wks.   574.87
    animals   591.87
    plants   581.87
    s.a. spec. organisms
  med. sci.   611.018 1
    animals   636.089 101 81
    s.a. spec. animals
    man   611.018 1
Cytopathology *see* Pathology
    cells cytology
Cytoplasm
  cytology   574.873 4
    animals   591.873 4
    plants   581.873 4
    s.a. spec. organisms
Czech
  language
    linguistics   491.86
    literature   891.86
    s.a.   *lang.*–918 6
  people   *r.e.n.*–918 6
  s.a. Czechoslovakia; *also*
    other spec. subj. e.g.
    Arts
Czechoslovakia   *area*–437
Czechoslovaks   *r.e.n.*–918 6
Czestochowa Poland   *area*–438 5

D

Dakota Co. (continued)
Nebraska   *area*–782 224
Dalbeattie Dumfries & Galloway
       Scot.   *area*–414 92
Dalby Qld.   *area*–943 3
Dale
   Co. Ala.   *area*–761 33
   Hollow Res. Tenn.   *area*–768 49
Dalhousie governorship India
       hist.   954.031 5
   s.a. spec. events & subj.
       e.g. Commerce
Dalkeith Lothian Scot.   *area*–413 5
Dallam Co. Tex.   *area*–764 812
Dallas
   city Tex.   *area*–764 281 2
   County
     Alabama   *area*–761 45
     Arkansas   *area*–767 67
     Iowa   *area*–777 57
     Missouri   *area*–778 813
     Texas   *area*–764 281 1
Dalmatia Yugoslavia   *area*–497 2
Dalmatian
   dogs
     animal husbandry   636.72
     other aspects see Dogs
   language
     linguistics   457.994 972
     literature   850
     s.a.   *lang.*–57
   people   *r.e.n.*–57
   s.a. Dalmatia; *also other*
       spec. subj. e.g. Arts
Dalton-in-Furness Cumbria Eng.
       area–427 81
Daly
   River Fauna Reserve N. Ter.
       Aust.   *area*–942 95
   Waters N. Ter. Aust.   *area*–942 95
Damage *see spec. subj. e.g.*
       Disasters
Daman India   *area*–547 99
Damascening metals
   arts *see* Decorative treatment
       sculpture
Damascus Syria   *area*–569 14
Damasks *see* Jacquard-weave
       fabrics
Damietta Egypt   *area*–621
Dampers
   steam eng. *see* Furnaces steam
       eng.
Dampier Archipelago W. Aust.
       area–941 3
Damping
   aeronautical aerodynamics   629.132 364
   s.a. spec. appls. e.g.
       Flying
   sound *see* Absorption sound

Dampness control
   bldg. construction   693.893
Dams
   hydraulic eng.
     soc. & econ. aspects *see*
       Secondary industries
     technology   627.8
      s.a. spec. appls. e.g.
       Military engineering
     other aspects see Liquids
       engineering
   pub. admin.   351.867
     spec. jur.   353–354
   s.a. Farm dams
Damselflies *see* Odonata
Damson plums
   agriculture   634.227
   other aspects see Plums
Dance
   etiquette   395.59
   flies *see* Orthorrhapha
   hall bldgs.
     architecture   725.86
     building   690.586
     other aspects see Public
       structures
   music
     gen. wks.
      music theory   781.55
      recordings   789.912 155
      orchestra   785.41
      recordings   789.912 541
      piano   786.45
      recordings   789.912 645
      s.a. other spec. mediums
     orchestras   785.066 6
     s.a. spec. kinds of music
     songs   784.3
      recordings   789.912 43
     therapy   615.851 55
      s.a. spec. diseases
Dancers
   biog. & work   793.309 2
     ballet   792.809 2
   persons   *pers.*–793 3
     ballet   *pers.*–792 8
Dances
   musical form *see* Dance music
   soc. customs   394.3
Dancing
   arts   793.3
     ballet   792.82
   ethics
     philosophy   175.3
     religion
      Buddhism   294.356 53
      Christianity   241.653
      comp. rel.   291.565 3
      Hinduism   294.548 653
      s.a. other spec. rel.

Dancing (continued)
  games
    outdoor recreation   796.13
  rel. significance
    Christianity   246.7
    other rel. see Arts rel.
      significance
Dandelions
  agriculture   635.51
    soc. & econ. aspects *see*
      Primary industries
  foods   641.355 1
    preparation
      commercial   664.805 51
      domestic   641.655 1
    other aspects see Asterales;
      also Vegetables
Dandruff *see* Scalp diseases
Dane Co. Wis.   *area*–775 83
Danes *see* Danish
Daniel
  Bible   224.5
  other aspects see Prophetic
    books (O.T.)
Daniell integrals   515.43
  s.a. spec. appls. e.g.
    Engineering
Daniels Co. Mont.   *area*–786 213
Danish
  language
    linguistics   439.81
    literature   839.81
    s.a.   *lang.*–398 1
  people   *r.e.n.*–398 1
  s.a. Denmark country; *also*
    other spec. subj. e.g.
      Arts
Dano-Norwegian *see* Norwegian
Danube River   *area*–496
  Germany   *area*–434 8
Danville Va.   *area*–755 666
Danzig Poland   *area*–438 2
Daphniphyllaceae *see*
  Hamamelidales
Daqahliya Egypt   *area*–621
Dar es Salaam Tanzania   *area*–678 23
Dard
  languages
    linguistics   491.499
    literatures   891.499
    s.a.   *lang.*–914 99
  people   *r.e.n.*–914 99
  s.a. other spec. subj. e.g.
    Arts
Dardanelles *see* Black Sea
Dare Co. N.C.   *area*–756 175
Darfield South Yorkshire Eng.
    area–428 25
Darfur Sudan   *area*–627
Darien Gulf *see* Caribbean Sea
Darién Panama   *area*–728 74

Dark ages *see* Medieval
Darke Co. O.   *area*–771 47
Darkness
  lit. & stage trmt. *see* Times
  plants grown in floriculture   635.954
    s.a. spec. plants
Darkrooms
  photography   771.1
    gen. tech.   770.283
    spec. proc. & fields   772–778
Darling
  Downs Qld.   *area*–943 3
  Range W. Aust.   *area*–941 2
  River N.S.W.   *area*–944 9
Darlington
  Co. S.C.   *area*–757 66
  Durham Eng.   *area*–428 63
Darned laces
  textile arts   746.22
Darning
  home econ.   646.204
Dart River Devon Eng.   *area*–423 592
Darters (birds) *see*
  Pelecaniformes
Dartford Kent Eng.   *area*–422 312
Dartmoor Devon Eng.   *area*–423 53
Dartmouth Devon Eng.   *area*–423 592
Darton South Yorkshire Eng.
    area–428 25
Darts
  equip. mf.   688.743
    soc. & econ. aspects *see*
      Secondary industries
  recreation   794.3
Darwen Lancashire Eng.   *area*–427 623
Darwin N. Ter. Aust.   *area*–942 95
Darwinian theories
  evolution   575.016 2
Dascylloidea
  zoology   595.764 6
  other aspects see Polyphaga
Dassies *see* Hyracoidea
Data
  base
    electronic data proc. *see*
      Storage of electronic
      data processing
  cells
    electronic data proc. *see*
      Inputs electronic data
      proc.
  processing   001.6
  research use *see* Research
  spec. subj.
    research   *s.s.*–072
    technique   *s.s.*–028 5
    s.a. spec. appls. e.g.
      Documentation
Dates (chronology)   902.02
  s.a. hist. of spec. countries,
    places, subj.

Dates (fruit)
  agriculture   634.62
  soc. & econ. aspects *see*
    Primary industries
  foods   641.346 2
    preparation
      commercial   664.804 62
      domestic   641.646 2
  other aspects see Palmales;
    also Fruits
Dating (archeological tech.)   930.102 85
  s.a. spec. places & subj.
Dating (courtship) *see*
  Courtship
Datiscaceae *see* Cucurbitales
Daucus carota *see* Carrots
Daufuskie Isl. S.C.   *area*–757 99
Daughters
  gen. wks.   *pers.*–044 1
  of Rebekah
    organization   366.38
    persons
      biog. & work   366.380 92
      s.a.   *pers.*–366 3
  of the American Revolution 369.135
  of the Confederacy   369.17
Dauphin Co. Pa.   *area*–748 18
Dauphiné France   *area*–449 6
Dauplin Lake Man.   *area*–712 72
Davao Philippines   *area*–599 7
Davenport
  Iowa   *area*–777 69
  Range N. Ter. Aust. *area*–942 91
Davenports
  dec. arts   749.3
  other aspects see Upholstered
    furniture
Daventry Northamptonshire Eng.
                  area–425 56
Davey Port Tas.   *area*–946 2
David reign Palestine hist. 933.02
  s.a. spec. events & subj.
    e.g. Commerce
Davidson Co.
  North Carolina   *area*–756 68
  Tennessee   *area*–768 55
Davie Co. N.C.   *area*–756 69
Daviess Co.
  Indiana   *area*–772 385
  Kentucky   *area*–769 864
  Missouri   *area*–778 183
Davis
  County
    Iowa   *area*–777 97
    Utah   *area*–792 27
  Mts. Tex.   *area*–764 934
  Strait
    oceanography   551.461 42
    regional subj. trmt. *area*–163 42
    other aspects see Atlantic
      Ocean

Davison Co. S.D.   *area*–783 374
Dawes Co. Neb.   *area*–782 93
Dawley Salop Eng.   *area*–424 56
Dawlish Devon Eng.   *area*–423 55
Dawn
  earth astronomy   525.7
  lit. & stage trmt. *see* Times
Dawson
  city Yukon   *area*–719 1
  County
    Georgia   *area*–758 263
    Montana   *area*–786 24
    Nebraska   *area*–782 46
    Texas   *area*–764 854
Day
  camps
    sports   796.542 3
  care
    child welfare   362.712
      misc. aspects see Young
        people soc. services to
  Co. S.D.   *area*–783 142
  nurseries *see* Day care
  of the Lord
    Christian eschatology 236.9
  schools
    secondary ed.   373.222
Daydreams *see* Secondary
  consciousness
Daylesford Vic.   *area*–945 3
Daylight-saving time   529.75
Daymarks
  hydraulic eng.
    technology   627.924
    s.a. spec. appls. e.g.
      Piloting seamanship
    other aspects see Liquids
      engineering
  navigation
    seamanship   623.894 4
Days
  lit. & stage trmt. *see* Times
  of work *see* Work periods
  time interval   529.2
Dayton O.   *area*–771 73
Deacons *see* Clergy
Dead
  bodies
    disposal
      animal *see* Animal
        carcases disposal
      customs   393
      human
        soc. aspects   363.75
        govt. control   350.772
          central govts. 351.772
          spec. jur.   353–354
          local govts. 352.6
        law   344.045
          spec. jur.   344.3–.9
        technology   614.6

Deaths (continued)
  effect on family *see* Families
        dissolution
  law *see* Persons law
  lit. & stage trmt. *see* Life
        cycle
  psych. influences   155.937
  soc. theology
    Christianity   261.836 64
    comp. rel.   291.178 366 4
    s.a. other spec. rel.
  sociology   304.64
  statistics   312.2
  s.a. Maternal deaths
De Baca Co. N.M.   *area*–789 44
Debarkation
  maneuvers
    mil. sci.   355.422
    s.a. spec. mil. branches
Debaters
  biog. & work   809.5
  s.a. spec. lits.
  s.a.   *pers.*–85
Debates
  literature
    gen. wks.
      collections   808.853
      hist. & crit.   809.53
    spec. lits.   *lit. sub.*–503
    indiv. authors   *lit. sub.*–51–59
    other aspects see Speeches
  s.a. other spec. subj. e.g.
        Constitutional
        conventions law
        proceedings
Debating
  rhetoric   808.53
  other aspects see Speaking
  s.a. Discussion
Debt
  ceiling *see* Debt limits
  collection
    law   346.077
    spec. jur.   346.3–.9
  limits
    pub. finance   336.346
    misc. aspects see Public
        borrowing
  management
    bus. tech.   658.152 6
    spec. subj.   *s.s.*–068 1
    macroeconomics   339.523
    personal finance   332.024 02
    pub. finance   336.36
    misc. aspects see Public
        borrowing
Debtor-creditor relationships
  law   346.077
  spec. jur.   346.3–.9

Debtors'
  prisons
    penology   365.4
    misc. aspects see Penal
        institutions
  relief
    law   346.077
    spec. jur.   346.3–.9
Deburring *see* Finishing metal
    products
Debuts
  etiquette   395.24
  soc. customs   392.15
Decalcomania
  dec. arts   745.74
Decalog *see* Ten Commandments
Decapoda (crustaceans)
  culture   639.54
  fishing
    commercial   639.54
    sports   799.255 384
  paleozoology   565.38
  zoology   595.384
  other aspects see Crustacea
Decapoda (mollusks)
  culture   639.485 8
  paleozoology   564.58
  zoology   594.58
  other aspects see Mollusca
Decatur Co.
  Georgia   *area*–758 993
  Indiana   *area*–772 16
  Iowa   *area*–777 875
  Kansas   *area*–781 143
  Tennessee   *area*–768 32
Decay
  bldg. materials
    wood   691.12
    s.a. other spec. materials
  eng. materials *see*
        Deterioration
  schemes radioactivity *see*
        Radioactivity
  soc. change   303.45
Deccan hemp *see* Ambari hemp
Deccan India   *area*–548
Deceleration
  biophysics
    extraterrestrial
      gen. wks.   574.191 934
      animals   591.191 934
      microorganisms   576.119 193 4
      plants   581.191 934
      s.a. spec. organisms
    med. sci.   612.014 534
      animals   636.089 201 453 4
      s.a. spec. animals
    man   612.014 534
    terrestrial
      gen. wks.   574.191 34
      animals   591.191 34

Decompression sickness (continued)
  other aspects see Diseases
Decorated glass *see* Glassware
Decorating glass   748.6
Decoration
  arts   745.4
    music
      music theory   781.67
      s.a. spec. mediums
    plastic arts *see* Decorative
      treatment
    s.a. other spec. art forms
  automobiles
    soc. & econ. aspects *see*
      Secondary industries
    tech. & mf.   629.26
Decorations
  genealogy   929.81
  medals
    numismatics   737.223
    mil. discipline   355.134 2
    s.a. spec. mil. branches
  Sunday schools
    Christianity   268.5
    other rel. see Religious
      instruction
Decorative
  arts   745
    misc. aspects see Fine arts
  coatings *see* Coatings
  coloring   745.7
  cords *see* Passementerie
  lettering   745.61
  sculpture   731.72
    spec. periods & schools   732–735
  treatment
    ceramic
      arts *see* Decorative
        treatment sculpture
      technology   666.45
    sculpture
      dec. arts
        ceramics   738.15
          specialized tech.   738.4–.8
        metals   739.15
        s.a. spec. metals;
        * also spec. prod.*
        * e.g.* Jewelry
      fine arts   731.4
        spec. periods & schools   732–735
  values
    arts   701.8
    s.a. spec. art forms
  s.a. Ornamental; *also other*
    spec. subj.
Decorators *see* Interior
    decorators
Decoupage
  handicrafts   745.546
Decoys
  handicrafts   745.593

Decoys (continued)
  s.a. spec. uses e.g.
    Anseriformes hunting
Decrees *see* Law
Decubitus
  ulcers *see* Ulcerations skin
Dedication Feast *see* Hanukkah
Dedications
  rel. rites
    Christianity   265.92
    other rel. see Public
      worship
Deductions
  wage & salary admin. *see*
    Compensation personnel
    admin.
Deductive reasoning
  logic   162
  psychology   153.433
    animals   156.343 3
    children   155.413
    s.a. psych. of other spec.
      groups
Dee River Grampian Scot.   *area*–412 4
Deeds
  property law   346.043 8
    spec. jur.   346.3–.9
Deep freezing foods   641.453
  commercial   664.028 53
  domestic   641.453
  other aspects see Foods
  s.a. spec. foods e.g. Meats
Deep-sea surveys
  oceanography   551.460 7
    s.a. spec. bodies of water
Deer
  flies *see* Orthorrhapha
  Isl. Me.   *area*–741 45
  Lodge Co. Mont.   *area*–786 87
Deers
  animal husbandry   636.294
  other aspects see Cervoidea
Deeside Clwyd Wales   *area*–429 36
Defamation
  criminology   364.156
  ethics
    philosophy   177.3
  religion
    Buddhism   294.356 73
    Christianity   241.673
    comp. rel.   291.567 3
    Hinduism   294.548 673
    s.a. other spec. rel.
  law
    crimes   345.025 6
      spec. jur.   345.3–.9
    torts   346.034
      spec. jur.   346.3–.9
  soc. theology
    Christianity   261.833 156
    comp. rel.   291.178 331 56

Defamation
  soc. theology (continued)
    s.a. other spec. rel.
Default
  pub. finance
    economics   336.368
    other aspects see Public
      borrowing
Defecation
  human phys.   612.36
  other aspects see Digestion
Defectives *see* Mentally
    deficient
Defenceless Mennonites   289.73
  misc. aspects see Mennonite
    churches
Defendants
  legal actions
    law
      criminal   345.050 44
        spec. jur.   345.3–.9
      gen. wks.   347.052
        spec. jur.   347.3–.9
      other aspects see Legal
        procedure
Defense (legal)
  criminal law   345.050 44
    spec. jur.   345.3–.9
Defense (military)
  citizenship ethics *see*
        Citizenship ethics
  contracts
    law *see* Public contracts
      law
    mil. admin.   355.621 1
    s.a. spec. mil. branches
  law   343.01
    spec. jur.   343.3–.9
  operations
    mil. eng.   623.3
    mil. sci.   355.4
    s.a. spec. mil. branches
  plans *see* Defense (military)
      operations
  pub. admin.
    departments   351.06
      U.S. govt.   353.6
      other spec. jur.   354
Defenseless Mennonites   289.73
  misc. aspects see Mennonite
    churches
Defensive
  arms
    art metalwork   739.75
    customs   399
    mil. eng.   623.441
  play
    games *see spec. games*

Deferrals
  budgeting
    pub. admin. *see*
        Supplementary budgeting
        pub. admin.
Defiance Co. O.   *area*–771 14
Deficiency
  budgeting
    pub. admin.   350.722 4
      central govts.   351.722 4
      spec. jur.   353–354
      local govts.   352.124
    budgets
      pub. admin.   350.722 54
      central govts.   351.722 54
      spec. jur.   353–354
      local govts.   352.124
  diseases   616.392–.396
    geriatrics   618.976 392–.976 396
    pediatrics   618.923 92–.923 96
    pub. health   614.593 92–.593 96
    statistics   312.339 2–.339 6
    deaths   312.263 92–.263 96
    other aspects see Diseases
Definite integrals   515.43
  s.a. spec. appls. e.g.
      Engineering
Deflagratory explosives *see*
      Propellant explosives
Deflaking
  cereal grains
    comm. proc.   664.720 3
    s.a. spec. grains & prod.
    other aspects see Cereal
      grains
Deflation
  economics   332.41
Deflections
  structural theory
    gen. wks.   624.171 4
    spec. elements   624.177 2–.177 9
    naval arch.   623.817 14
    s.a. other spec. appls.
Defluoridation
  water-supply trmt.
    technology   628.166 7
    other aspects see Water
      supply engineering
Deformation
  crystals   548.842
    s.a. spec. substances
  earth's crust
    geophysics   551.14
  eng. materials *see* Mechanical
      deformation
  minerals *see* Mechanical
      properties minerals
  rocks
    geology   551.8
    s.a. spec. appls. e.g.
      Prospecting

Deformation (continued)
solid dynamics
engineering *see* Dynamics
physics — 531.382
Deformities
anatomy *see* Teratology
psych. influences — 155.916
statistics — 312.304 737
surgery — 617.37
anesthesiology — 617.967 37
s.a. Veterinary sciences
Degeneration
biology *see* Pathology
Degenerative diseases
heart *see* Heart diseases
Degradation (geology) *see*
Erosion
Degrees
academic *see* Academic degrees
Dehumidification
air-conditioning *see*
Air-conditioning
chem. eng. — 660.284 29
s.a. spec. prod.
Dehumidifiers
air-conditioning eng. — 697.932 3
Dehydrated foods
cookery — 641.614
Dehydrating
foods — 641.44
commercial — 664.028 4
domestic — 641.44
other aspects see Foods
s.a. spec. foods e.g. Meats
Dehydration
phys. & psych. *see* Thirst
Dehydrogenases *see*
Oxidizing-reducing
enzymes
Dehydrogenation
chem. eng. — 660.284 43
physical chem. — 541.393
applied — 660.299 3
organic — 547.23
s.a. spec. aspects e.g. Low
temperatures
s.a. spec. elements, cpds.,
prod.
Deir ez Zor Syria — area–569 12
Deism
nat. rel. — 211.5
Deists
biog. & work — 211.509 2
polemics against
Christianity — 239.5
other rel. see Doctrinal
theology
s.a. — pers.–291
Deities *see* Gods
De Kalb Co.
Alabama — area–761 66

De Kalb Co. (continued)
Georgia — area–758 225
Illinois — area–773 28
Indiana — area–772 77
Missouri — area–778 153
Tennessee — area–768 532
Dekkan India — area–548
Delagoa Bay
oceanography — 551.467 24
regional subj. trmt. — area–165 24
other aspects see Indian
Ocean
Delany system telegraphy *see*
Automatic systems wire
telegraphy
Delaware
Bay
oceanography — 551.461 46
regional subj. trmt. — area–163 46
other aspects see Atlantic
Ocean
County
Indiana — area–772 65
Iowa — area–777 385
New York — area–747 36
Ohio — area–771 535
Oklahoma — area–766 91
Pennsylvania — area–748 14
Indian *see* Algonkian-Mosan
River — area–749
state — area–751
Water Gap Pa. — area–748 25
Delegates
nominating conventions *see*
Nomination procedures
Deleterious organisms
agriculture *see* Pests
econ. biol. — 574.65
animals — 591.65
microorganisms — 576.165
plants — 581.65
s.a. spec. organisms
Delhi India — area–545 6
Delicts *see* Torts law
Delinquency *see* Crime
Delinquent
children
education — 371.93
law — 344.079 13
spec. jur. — 344.3–.9
psychology — 155.453
rearing — 649.153
s.a. Juvenile delinquents
people — pers.–069 2
Delirium tremens *see* Alcoholism
Delmarva Peninsula — area–752 1
Del Norte Co. Calif. — area–794 11
Deloraine Tas. — area–946 3
Delos Greece — area–499
Delphiniums *see* Ranales

Delta
  Amacuro Venezuela   *area*–876 2
  County
    Colorado   *area*–788 18
    Michigan   *area*–774 94
    Texas   *area*–764 273
Deltas
  geomorphology   551.456
  other aspects see Shorelands
Delusional states *see* Paranoia
Delusions   001.96
  s.a. spec. subj. e.g. mirages
    551.565
Delyn Clwyd Wales   *area*–429 33
Demand
  deposits
    banking econ.   332.175 2
    other aspects see Banking
  econ. theory   338.521 2
  meters *see* Energy elect.
    measurement
  prod. econ.
    commun. services
      telecommunications   384.041
        radiobroadcasting   384.543
        telegraphy   384.13
          submarine cable   384.43
          wire   384.13
          wireless   384.523
        telephony   384.63
          wire   384.63
          wireless   384.533
        television   384.554 3
          cable television   384.555 63
          subscription   384.554 7
    highways
      commerce   388.11
    transportation
      commerce
        air   387.71
        inland waterway   386.1
        maritime   387.51
        motor   388.32
        railway   385.1
        special-duty   385.5
        urban transp.   388.404 2
  s.a. Supply-&-demand
Dematerialization
  spiritualism   133.92
Dementia praecox *see*
    Schizophrenia
Demerara Guyana   *area*–881 4–881 5
Demineralization
  sewage trmt.
    technology   628.358
    other aspects see Sewage
      treatment
  water-supply trmt.
    technology   628.166 6
    other aspects see Water
      supply engineering

Demobilization
  mil. resources   355.29
    s.a. spec. mil. branches
Democracies
  pol. sci. *see* Democratic
    states
Democracy
  soc. theology *see* Political
    ideologies soc.
    theology
Democratic
  Labour Party Australia
    pol. sci.   324.294 06
    s.a. spec. subj. of concern
      e.g. Social problems
  Party
    U.S.
      pol. sci.   324.273 6
      s.a. spec. subj. of
        concern e.g. Social
        problems
  Republican Party *see*
    Democratic Party U.S.
  socialism
    economics   335.5
    pol. ideology   320.531 5
    soc. theology *see*
      Political ideologies
      soc. theology
  states
    pol. sci.   321.8
    pure   321.4
    s.a. spec. jur.
Democritean philosophy   182.7
Demodulation
  electronic circuits *see*
    Demodulators electronic
    circuits
Demodulators
  electronic circuits
    tech. & mf.   621.381 536
      microelectronics   621.381 736
      microwave electronics   621.381 326
      radiowave electronics   621.381 536
      x- & gamma-ray electronics 621.381 6
    s.a. spec. appls. e.g.
      Receiving sets
    other aspects see Microwave
      electronics; Radiowave
      electronics; X-ray
      electronics
Demography *see* Populations
DeMolay
  members
    biog. & work   366.170 92
    s.a.   *pers.*–366 1
    order   366.17

Demolition
blocks
  mil. eng.
    soc. & econ. aspects *see*
      Secondary industries
    tech. & mf.   623.454 5
operations
  mil. eng.   623.27
  s.a. spec. appls.
  mil. sci.   358.23
Demoniac possession
  occultism   133.426
Demonology
  occultism   133.42
Demons *see* Devils
Demonstrations
  advertising operations   659.15
  s.a. other spec. appls.
Demospongiae
  culture   639.734 6
  fishing   639.734 6
  paleozoology   563.4
  zoology   593.46
  other aspects see Porifera
Demotic
  Egyptian *see* Egyptian
      languages
  Greek *see* Greek languages
      modern
Demotions
  armed forces   355.112
  s.a. spec. mil. branches
  employees
    personnel admin.
      disciplinary meas. *see*
        Penalties employee
        discipline
      gen. management   658.312 7
        executive management   658.407 127
        spec. subj.   *s.s.*–068 3
      pub. admin.   350.14
        central govts.   351.14
          spec. jur.   353–354
        local govts.   352.005 14
Demulcents
  pharmacodynamics   615.735
  other aspects see Drugs
Demythologizing
  rel. books
    interpretation *see*
      Mythological
      interpretation
Denbigh Clwyd Wales   *area*–429 37
Denbighshire Wales   *area*–429 3
Denby Dale West Yorkshire Eng.
      area–428 13
Dendrochirota *see*
      Holothurioidea
Dendrologists
  biog. & work   582.160 092
  other aspects see Scientists

Dendrologists (continued)
  s.a.   *pers.*–58
Dendrology *see* Trees botany
Dene *see* Na-Dene
Dengue fever
  gen. med.   616.921
  geriatrics   618.976 921
  pediatrics   618.929 21
  pub. health   614.571
  statistics   312.392 1
    deaths   312.269 21
  other aspects see Diseases
Denholme West Yorkshire Eng.
      area–428 17
Denial
  church authority
    Christianity
      262.8
    other rel. see
      Ecclesiastical theology
  epistemology   121.5
Deniliquin N.S.W.   *area*–944 8
Denizli Turkey   *area*–562
Denjoy integrals   515.43
  s.a. spec. appls. e.g.
    Engineering
Denmark
  country   *area*–489
  Strait *see* European Arctic
    seawaters
Denny & Dunipace Central Scot.
      area–413 18
Denominations
  Christianity   280
  s.a. spec. subj. e.g.
    Doctrinal theology
  other rel. see Sects
Density
  crystals   548.845
  s.a. spec. substances
  physics mech.   531.14
  solids   531.54
  other states of matter see
    Mass (substance)
    physics mech.
  sea water
    oceanography   551.460 1
    s.a. spec. bodies of
      water
  other aspects see Mechanical
    properties
  s.a. other spec. subj.
Density-pumps
engineering
  soc. & econ. aspects *see*
    Secondary industries
  tech. & mf.   621.699
  s.a. spec. appls. e.g.
    Water supply
    engineering
  other aspects see Dynamics
Dent Co. Mo.   *area*–778 86

Dental
assistants
  prof. duties &
     characteristics   617.602 33
  other aspects see Dentists
diseases *see* Teeth diseases
insurance   368.382 3
  misc. aspects see Insurance
pulp
  diseases   617.634 2
    geriatrics   618.977 634 2
    statistics   312.304 763 42
    other aspects see Teeth
school bldgs.
  architecture   727.461 76
  building   690.746 176
  other aspects see
    Educational buildings
services *see* Health services
technicians
  law   344.041 3
    spec. jur.   344.3–.9
  prof. duties &
    characteristics   617.602 33
  other aspects see Dentists
s.a. Teeth
Dentinal materials
products
  manufacturing
    soc. & econ. aspects *see*
      Secondary industries
  technology   679.4
Dentine *see* Tooth tissues
Dentistry
law   344.041 3
  spec. jur.   344.3–.9
med. sci.   617.6
  geriatrics   618.977 6
  pediatrics   617.645
  vet. med.   636.089 76
    s.a. spec. animals
  other aspects see Medical
    sciences
s.a. Dental
Dentists
biog. & work   617.600 92
prof. duties & characteristics   617.602 32
law   344.041 3
  spec. jur.   344.3–.9
other aspects see Medical
  scientists
s.a.   *pers.*–617 6
Dentition disorders
dentistry   617.643
  pub. health   614.599 6
  statistics   312.304 764 3
  other aspects see Diseases
Denton
  Co. Tex.   *area*–764 555
  Greater Manchester Eng.   *area*–427 35
D'Entrecasteaux Isls.   *area*–953

Dentures
  dentistry   617.692
Denumerative geometry   516.213
Denver city & Co. Colo.   *area*–788 83
Deodorants
  air pollution *see* Air
    pollution
  pharmacodynamics   615.778
  other aspects see Drugs
Deodorization
  sewers   628.23
  s.a. other spec. subj.
Deoxyribonucleic acid
  cytology   574.873 282
    animals   591.873 282
    plants   581.873 282
    s.a. spec. organisms
Department stores
  advertising   659.196 588 71
  pub. relations   659.296 588 71
  retail marketing   658.871
Departmental organization
  management *see* Organization
    of management
Departments
  pub. admin. *see* Executive
    departments
  s.a. other spec. subj.
Dependence
  psychology
    personality trait   155.232
Dependencies *see* Dependent
  states
Dependent
  children
    soc. services   362.713
      misc. aspects see Young
        people social services
        to
  states
    law
      constitutional   342.041 3
        spec. jur.   342.3–.9
      international   341.27
    pol. sci.   321.08
      s.a. spec. jur.
  trials
    probabilities   519.2
      s.a. spec. appls. e.g.
        Engineering
Dependents
  soc. services
    aged people *see* Aged people
      sociology
    children *see* Dependent
      children
    young people *see* Young
      people soc. services to
Deportation
  penology   364.68

Deposit insurance	368.854
misc. aspects see Insurance	
Deposition	
electrometallurgy *see*	
Electrometallurgy	
physical geol.	551.303
water action	551.353
wind action	551.373
s.a. other spec. agents	
Depositions	
law *see* Witnesses law	
Deposits	
libraries	
acquisitions	025.26
govt. aspects	021.8
moisture	
meteorology	551.574
artificial modification	551.687 4
weather forecasting	551.647 4
spec. areas	551.65
ocean floor	
submarine geol.	551.460 83–.460 84
s.a. spec. bodies of water	
pub. revenues	336.15
misc. aspects see Nontax revenues	
Depreciation	
allowances	
tax reductions	
law	343.052 34
spec. jur.	343.3–.9
pub. finance	336.206
s.a. spec. kinds of taxes e.g. Income taxes	
assets	
accounting trmt.	657.73
s.a. spec. kinds of enterprises e.g. Insurance accounting	
s.a. other spec. subj. e.g. Money	
Depredation	
criminology	364.164
law	345.026 4
spec. jur.	345.3–.9
soc. theology	
Christian rel.	261.833 164
comp. rel.	291.178 331 64
s.a. other spec. rel.	
Depressants	
heart	
pharmacodynamics	615.716
other aspects see Drugs	
nerves	
addictive aspects *see* Addictive drugs use	
pharmacodynamics	615.782
other aspects see Drugs	

Depressions (economics)	
econ. cycles	
prod. econ.	338.542
personal finance	332.024 02
Depressions (geomorphology)	
geology	551.44
ocean floor	551.460 84
s.a. spec. bodies of water	
regional subj. trmt	*area*–144
Depressions (mental states)	
gen. med.	616.852 7
geriatries	618.976 852 7
pediatrics	618.928 527
psychology	157.3
statistics	312.385 27
Depressive	
neuroses *see* Depressions (mental states)	
psychoses & reactions *see* Manic-depressive psychoses	
Deptford London Eng.	*area*–421 63
Depth	
effects	
biophysics *see* Pressure biophysics	
psychology	154
animals	156.4
Deputy chief executives	
biog. & work *see hist. of spec. countries*	
law	342.062
spec. jur.	342.3–.9
pub. admin.	350.003 18
central govts.	351.003 18
U.S.	
federal	353.031 8
states	353.913 18
spec. states	353.97–.99
other	354
local govts.	352.008
s.a.	*pers.*–351 2
Dera	
Ismail Khan Pakistan	*area*–549 124
Syria	*area*–569 14
Derby	
Eng.	*area*–425 17
W. Aust.	*area*–941 4
Derbyshire Eng.	*area*–425 1
Der-Ezza Syria	*area*–569 12
Der ez Zor Syria	*area*–569 12
Derivation (linguistics) *see* Etymology	
Derived	
organic chemicals	
chem. tech.	661.802–.804
other aspects see Organic chemicals	
proteins	
org. chem.	547.756
other aspects see Proteins	

Derived (continued)
  sensory perception
    psychology
      gen. wks.   152.182 8
        animals   156.218 28
        children   155.412
      s.a. psych. of other
        spec. groups
      influences   155.911 828
  spaces
    topology   514.320 3
    s.a. spec. appls. e.g.
      Engineering
Dermaptera
  culture   638.572 1
  paleozoology   565.72
  zoology   595.721
  other aspects see Insecta
Dermatitis *see* Papular
  eruptions
Dermatology   616.5
  geriatrics   618.976 5
  pediatrics   618.925
  vet. med.   636.089 65
  s.a. spec. animals
  other aspects see Medical
    sciences
  s.a. Integument
Dermoptera
  animal husbandry   636.934
  hunting
    commercial   639.113 4
    sports   799.259 34
  paleozoology   569.34
  zoology   599.34
  other aspects see Mammalia
Derrick cars
  railroad *see* Work cars
Derricks
  machine eng.
    soc. & econ. aspects *see*
      Secondary industries
    tech. & mf.   621.872
    s.a. spec. appls. e.g.
      Buildings construction
  other aspects see Mechanics
Derringers *see* Pistols
Derry Ireland *see* Londonderry
  Ireland
Dervishes
  Islam   297.42
Derwent
  River
    Derbyshire Eng.   *area*–425 1
    Tasmania   *area*–946 2
    Yorkshire Eng.   *area*–428 4
    Water Cumbria Eng.   *area*–427 87
  Derwentside Durham Eng.   *area*–428 68
Desai Morarji admin. India
  hist.   954.052

Desai Morarji admin. India (continued)
  s.a. spec. events & subj.
    e.g. Civil rights
Desalinization
  water-supply eng.
    technology   628.167
    other aspects see Water
      supply engineering
Des Allemands Lake La.   *area*–763 32
Desborough Northamptonshire
  Eng.   *area*–425 52
Descendants   *pers.*–044
Descent into hell
  Jesus Christ
    Christian doctrines   232.967
Deschutes
  Co. Ore.   *area*–795 87
  River Ore.   *area*–795 6
Description
  lit. element
    gen. wks.
      collections   808.802 2
      hist. & crit.   809.922
    spec. lits.
      collections   *lit. sub.*–080 22
      hist. & crit.   *lit. sub.*–092 2
    s.a. spec. lit. forms
  stage element   792.090 922
    s.a. other spec. dramatic
      mediums e.g.
      Television; *also spec.*
      kinds of drama e.g.
      Tragedies (drama)
  s.a. spec. subj.
Descriptive
  astronomy   523
  bibliography   010.42
  cataloging
    library operations   025.32
    special materials   025.34
  geometry
    abstract   516.6
    s.a. spec. appls. e.g.
      Engineering
  government   320.4
    pub. admin.   350
  music
    piano   786.43
    recordings   789.912 643
    s.a. other spec. musical
      mediums
  poetry
    gen. wks
      collections   808.816
      hist. & crit.   809.16
      rhetoric   808.16
      juvenile   808.068 16
    spec. lits.   *lit. sub.*–106
      indiv. authors   *lit. sub.*–11–19
  other aspects see Poetry

Descriptive (continued)
probabilities   519.24
  s.a. spec. appls. e.g.
    Engineering
research   001.433
  spec. subj.   *s.s.–072 3*
statistics
  mathematics   519.53
  s.a. spec. appls. e.g.
    Engineering
  s.a. other spec. subj.
Descriptors
  library subj. vocabularies 025.49
Desegregation *see* Social
    classes
Desensitizing
  negatives *see* Negatives
Desert
  region
    Chile   *area–831*
  s.a. other spec. areas
  warfare
    mil. sci.   355.423
  s.a. spec. mil. branches
Desertion
  family dissolution *see*
    Families dissolution
Deserts
  ecology life sci.   574.526 52
    animals   591.526 52
    microorganisms   576.15
    plants   581.526 52
  s.a. spec. organisms
  reclamation eng. *see*
    Irrigation land
    reclamation eng.
  regional subj. trmt.   *area–154*
  s.a. spec. deserts
Desha Co. Ark.   *area–767 85*
Desiccated *see* Dried
Design
  aircraft eng.   629.134 1
    parts   629.134 3
  anthropometry   620.82
  s.a. spec. appls. e.g.
    Aerospace engineering
  arts   745.4
  automobiles
    soc. & econ. aspects *see*
      Secondary industries
    technology   629.231
    spec. parts   629.24–.27
  bridges   624.25
  s.a. spec. appls. e.g.
    Military engineering
  canals
    technology   627.131
    other aspects see Liquids
      engineering
  elementary ed.   372.52

Design (continued)
  engineering   620.004 25
  s.a. spec. branches of eng.
  machine eng.
    technology   621.815
  s.a. spec. appls. e.g.
    Materials-handling
      equip.
  other aspects see Mechanics
  metaphysics *see* Teleology
  operations research *see*
    Operations research
  patterns
    clothing
      comm. mf.
        soc. & econ. aspects
        see Secondary
         industries
        technology   687.042
      domestic mf.   646.407 2
  protection
    law   346.048 4
      spec. jur.   346.3–.9
  railroad eng.
    technology   625.11
    other aspects see Railroads
  road eng.
    technology   625.725
    other aspects see Roads
  spacecraft eng.   629.471
    unmanned   629.461
    other aspects see
      Spacecraft
  structural eng.   624.177 1
    naval arch.   623.817 71
    s.a. other spec. appls.
  s.a. other spec. apparatus,
    equip., materials
Designs
  textiles
    manufacturing
      soc. & econ. aspects *see*
        Secondary industries
      technology   677.022
    s.a. spec. kinds of
      textiles
  s.a.   *s.s.–022 2*
  s.a. Patterns
Désirade Guadeloupe   *area–729 76*
Desks
  mf. tech.   684.14
  other aspects see Furniture
Desmans *see* Insectivora
Desmarestiales *see* Phaeophyta
Des Moines
  city Ia.   *area–777 58*
  Co. Ia.   *area–777 96*
  River Ia.   *area–777*
Desmomonadales *see* Pyrrophyta
Desmospongiae *see* Demospongiae

Desmostyliformes
  paleozoology   569.5
De Soto
  County
    Florida   *area*–759 59
    Mississippi   *area*–762 87
  Par. La.   *area*–763 63
Des Plaines River Ill.   *area*–773 2
Desserts
  cookery   641.86
Destiny
  metaphysics   123
  religion
    Christianity   234.9
    other rel. see Humankind
      rel. doctrines
Destitute persons *see* Poor
      people
Destroyer escorts
  engineering   623.825 4
    design   623.812 54
    models   623.820 154
  naval forces
    materiel   359.83
    organization   359.325 4
  seamanship   623.882 54
  other aspects see Vessels
        (nautical)
Destroyers
  engineering   623.825 4
    design   623.812 54
    models   623.820 154
  naval forces
    materiel   359.83
    organization   359.325 4
  seamanship   623.882 54
  other aspects see Vessels
        (nautical)
Destruction
  of universe
    astronomic theories 523.19
  s.a. other spec. subj.
Destructive forces
  resistance to
    eng. materials   620.11
Destructors
  mil. eng.
    soc. & econ. aspects *see*
      Secondary industries
    tech. & mf.   623.454 5
Desulfuration
  coal
    fuel tech.   662.623
Detail
  drawings
    bldg. construction   692.2
  finishing
    bldg. construction   698

Detection
  criminal investigation 363.25
  misc. aspects see Law
      enforcement
  electronic circuits *see*
      Detectors electronic
      circuits
Detective
  fiction *see* Mystery fiction
  plays *see* Melodrama
Detectors
  electronic circuits
    tech. & mf.   621.381 536
      microelectronics 621.381 736
      microwave electronics 621.381 326
      radiowave electronics 621.381 536
      x- & gamma-ray electronics 621.381 6
    s.a. spec. appls. e.g.
      Receiving sets
    other aspects see Microwave
      electronics; Radiowave
      electronics; X-ray
      electronics
Detention homes
  penology   365.34
  other aspects see Penal
      institutions
Detergents
  manufacturing
    chem. tech.   668.14
    soc. & econ. aspects *see*
      Secondary industries
  pollution
    water-supply eng.
      technology   628.168 23
      other aspects see Water
        supply engineering
Deterioration
  eng. materials   620.112 2
    s.a. spec. materials & spec.
      uses
  soc. change   303.45
  s.a. other spec. subj.
Determinants
  algebra   512.943 2
    s.a. spec. appls. e.g.
      Engineering
  indiv. psych.   155.23
  s.a. other spec. subj.
Determination
  of functions
    calculus   515.232
      complex variables 515.923 2
      real variables   515.823 2
    s.a. other spec. functions
      & equations; also spec.
      appls. e.g.
      Engineering
  s.a. other spec. subj.

Determinative
  mineralogy   549.1
    spec. minerals   549.2–.7
  procedures
    illumination eng.
      soc. & econ. aspects *see*
        Secondary industries
      technology   621.321 1
        exterior   621.322 9
        interior   621.322 5–.322 8
      s.a. spec. kinds e.g.
        Incandescent lighting
    s.a. other spec. subj.
Determinism
  metaphysics   123
  religion
    Christianity   234.9
    other rel. see Humankind
    rel. doctrines
Deterrents
  internat. investment   332.673 2
  s.a. other spec. subj.
Detonators
  manufacturing
    soc. & econ. aspects *see*
      Secondary industries
    technology   662.4
    mil. eng.   623.454 2
    s.a. spec. appls. e.g.
      Demolition
Detroit
  city Mich.   *area*–774 34
  River Mich.   *area*–774 33
Deuel Co.
  Nebraska   *area*–782 913
  South Dakota   *area*–783 25
Deuterium
  gen. wks.
    inorg. chem.   546.212
  oxide *see* Water
Deuterocanonical books *see*
  Apocrypha
Deuteromycetes
  agric. pathogens   632.44
  s.a. spec. types of culture
    e.g. Forestry; *also*
    spec. plants
  botany   589.24
  med. aspects
    gen. pharm.   615.329 24
      toxicology   615.952 924
    vet. pharm.   636.089 532 924
      toxicology   636.089 595 292 4
  other aspects see Plants
Deuteronomy
  Bible   222.15
  other aspects see Historical
    books (O.T.)
Deuterons *see* Nuclei
Deux-Montagnes Co. Que.   *area*–714 25
Deux-Sèvres France   *area*–446 2

Devaluation
  currency
    economics   332.414
      foreign exchange   332.452
    other aspects see Money
Developable surfaces
  gen. wks. *see* Surfaces
  mathematics
    integral geometry   516.362
  s.a. spec. appls. e.g.
    Engineering
Developed regions
  regional subj. trmt.   *area*–172 2
  s.a. spec. areas
Developing
  negatives *see* Negatives
  positives *see* Positives
Developing-apparatus
  photography   771.4
    gen. tech.   770.283
    spec. proc. & fields   772–778
Developing-regions
  regional subj. trmt.   *area*–172 4
  s.a. spec. areas
Developing-solutions
  photography   771.54
    gen. tech.   770.283
    spec. proc. & fields   772–778
Development (biology)
  cytology   574.876 1
    animals   591.876 1
    plants   581.876 1
  s.a. spec. organisms
  gen. wks   574.3
    animals   591.3
    microorganisms   576.13
    plants   581.3
  s.a. spec. organisms
  med. sci.   612.65–.67
    animals   636.089 265–.089 267
    s.a. spec. animals
    man   612.65–.67
Development (history) *see*
  History
Development (improvement)
  expenditures
    estimates
      budgeting
        pub. admin.   350.722 253 6
          central govts.   351.722 253 6
            spec. jur.   353–354
          local govts.   352.122 536
  land econ.   333.38
  management
    pub. admin.   350.007 8
      central govts.   351.007 8
        spec. jur.   353–354
      local govts.   352.000 478

Diadems *see* Jewelry
Diagnoses
  med. sci.
    gen. med.   616.075
    surgery   617.075
    s.a. spec. diseases
  other aspects see Diseases
Diagnostic
  graphology
    indiv. psych.   155.282
  radiology services
    soc. welfare   362.17
    misc. aspects see Medical
      services
  s.a. other spec. subj.
Diagrams
  spec. subj.   *s.s.*–022 3
  other aspects see Graphic
    materials
Dialectical materialism
  Marxist econ.   335.411 2
  philosophy   146.32
    indiv. phil.   180–190
  s.a. spec. branches of phil.
    e.g. Metaphysics
Dialectology   417.2
  spec. langs.   *lang. sub.*–7
Dialects
  linguistics *see* Dialectology
  literatures *see spec. lits.*
Dialing
  equipment
    wire telephony *see* Terminal
      equipment wire
      telephony
  systems
    telephone commun.
      commerce   384.65
      wire   384.65
      wireless   384.535
Dialog
  lit. element
    gen. wks.
      collections   808.802 6
      hist. & crit.   809.926
    spec. lits.
      collections   *lit. sub.*–080 26
      hist. & crit.   *lit. sub.*–092 6
    s.a. spec. lit. forms
  stage element   792.090 926
    s.a. other spec. dramatic
      mediums e.g.
      Television; *also spec.*
      kinds of drama e.g.
      Tragedies (drama)
Dialogs *see* Drama
Dials
  time measurement   529.78
  s.a. other spec. uses
Dialypetalanthaceae *see*
  Rubiales

Dialysis *see* Diffusion analysis
Dialyzers
  chem. apparatus   542.6
  s.a. spec. appls. e.g.
    Organic chemistry
Diamagnetic substances *see*
  Diamagnetism
Diamagnetism
  astrophysics   523.018 842
  s.a. spec. celestial bodies
  physics   538.42
    spec. states of matter   530.4
Diamantina River Qld.   *area*–943 5
Diammonium phosphates
  impregnation
    wood bldg. materials   691.15
Diamonds
  gen. wks.   553.82
    econ. geol.   553.82
  glyptics   736.23
  mineralogy   549.27
  mining
    soc. & econ. aspects *see*
      Primary industries
    technology   622.382
      prospecting   622.188 2
  rel. significance
    Christianity   247.862 3
    comp. rel.   291.37
    s.a. other spec. rel.
  industrial *see* Abrasive
    materials
  synthetic
    manufacturing
      soc. & econ. aspects *see*
        Secondary industries
      technology   666.88
  s.a. spec. uses
Dianetics   158.9
Diapensiaceae *see* Ericales
Diaphragm
  anatomy
    human   611.26
    other aspects see
      Respiratory organs
  diseases
    neoplasms   616.992 26
    surgery   617.547
      anesthesiology   617.967 547
    tuberculosis   616.995 26
    other aspects see Diseases
  physical anthropometry   573.626
  physiology
    human   612.2
    other aspects see
      Respiration
  tissue biology human   611.018 926
Diapsida
  paleozoology   567.94
Diaries
  biography *see* Biographies

Diaries (continued)
  literature *see* Journals
    (writings) literature
Diarrhea
  gen. med.   616.342 7
  geriatrics   618.976 342 7
  pediatrics   618.923 427
  pub. health   614.593 427
  statistics   312.334 27
    deaths   312.263 427
  other aspects see Diseases
  s.a. Epidemic diarrhea
Diaspore
  clay *see* Clays
  mineralogy   549.525
Diastase *see* Enzymes
Diastrophism   551
Diatessaron
  Gospels   226.1
Diathermy
  therapeutics   615.832 3
    misc. aspects see Physical
      therapies
    s.a. spec. diseases
Diatomaceous earth
  econ. & mining aspects *see*
    Earthy materials
  materials aspects *see*
    Insulating materials
  mineral aspects *see*
    Sedimentary rocks
Diatoms *see* Bacillariophyceae
Diatrymiformes
  paleozoology   568.3
Diaz Ordaz Mexico hist.   972.083 1
  s.a. spec. events & subj.
    e.g. Commerce
Diazines
  org. chem.   547.593
  s.a. spec. cpds.
Diazonitrophenol *see* High
    explosives
Diazotization
  chem. eng.   660.284 45
  org. chem.   547.25
  s.a. spec. elements, cpds.,
    prod.
Diazotype processes
  photographic printing   773.7
Dibranchia *see* Cephalopoda
Dice games
  equipment mf.   688.751
    soc. & econ. aspects *see*
      Secondary industries
  etbics *see* Games ethics
  recreation   795.1
Dichapetalaceae *see* Rosales
Dickens Co. Tex.   *area*–764 741
Dickenson Co. Va.   *area*–755 745
Dickey Co. N.D.   *area*–784 54

Dickinson Co.
  Iowa   *area*–777 123
  Kansas   *area*–781 56
  Michigan   *area*–774 955
Dickson Co. Tenn.   *area*–768 44
Dicksonia family *see* Filicales
Dicksoniaceae *see* Filicales
Diclidantheraceae *see*
    Styracales
Dicotyledones *see* Dicotyledons
Dicotyledons
  botany   583
  floriculture   635.933
  forestry   634.972
  med. aspects
    crop prod.   633.883
    gen. pharm.   615.323
      toxicology   615.952 3
    vet. pharm.   636.089 532 3
      toxicology   636.089 595 23
  paleobotany   561.3
  other aspects see Plants
Dictating equipment
  use office services   651.74
Dictation
  music teaching   780.77
    s.a. spec. mediums
  office services
    giving dictation   651.74
    taking dictation   653.14
Dictators
  biog. & work *see hist. of*
    spec. countries
  s.a.   *pers.*–351 4
Dictatorships
  pol. sci.   321.9
  s.a. spec. jur.
Dictionaries
  linguistics
    polyglot   413
    spec. langs.
      nonstandard forms
          lang. sub.–7
      standard forms   *lang. sub.*–3
  spec. subj.   *s.s.*–03
Dictionary catalogs   019
Dictyosiphonales *see* Phaeophyta
Dictyotales *see* Phaeophyta
Didactic poetry
  gen. wks.
    collections   808.815
    hist. & crit.   809.15
    rhetoric   808.15
    juvenile   808.068 15
  spec. lits.   *lit. sub.*–105
  indiv. authors   *lit. sub.*–11–19
  other aspects see Poetry
Didiereaceae *see* Sapindales
Didymium *see* Praseodymium
Die casting *see* Permanent mold
    casting

Diefenbaker
John George admin.
  Can. hist. — 971.064 2
    s.a. spec. events & subj.
      e.g. Commerce
Dielectric furnaces
  elect. eng.
    soc. & econ. aspects *see*
      Secondary industries
    tech. & mf. — 621.396
      s.a. spec. appls. e.g.
        Heat engineering
Dielectricity
  spec. substances *see*
    Electromagnetic
      properties
Dielectrics
  astrophysics — 523.018 724
    s.a. spec. celestial bodies
  physics — 537.24
    spec. states of matter — 530.4
Diencephalon
  human phys. — 612.826 2
  other aspects see Brain
Dies *see* Molding-equipment
Diesel
  engines *see* High-compression-
    ignition engines
  fuels
    chem. tech. — 665.538 4
    other aspects see Petroleum
Diesel-electric locomotives
  commerce — 385.366 2
    special-duty — 385.5
  engineering
    soc. & econ. aspects *see*
      Secondary industries
    technology
      gen. wks. — 625.266 2
        accessory equipment — 625.25
        running gear — 625.21
        monorail — 625.28
  other aspects see Rolling
    stock railroads
Diesel-hydraulic locomotives
  commerce — 385.366 4
    special-duty — 385.5
  engineering
    soc. & econ. aspects *see*
      Secondary industries
    technology
      gen. wks. — 625.266 4
        accessory equipment — 625.25
        running gear — 625.21
        monorail — 625.28
  other aspects see Rolling
    stock railroads
Diesel-powered
  submarines
    engineering — 623.825 72
      design — 623.812 572

Diesel-powered
  submarines
    engineering (continued)
      models — 623.820 157 2
    naval forces — 359.325 72
      materiel — 359.83
      organization — 359.325 72
    seamanship — 623.882 572
    other aspects see Vessels
      (nautical)
    s.a. other spec. subj.
Diet cookery
  home econ. — 641.563
Dietary laws
  Judaism — 296.73
  other rel. see Personal
    religion
Dietetic salts
  manufacturing
    soc. & econ. aspects *see*
      Secondary industries
    technology — 664.4
Dietetics *see* Applied nutrition
Dietotherapy — 615.854
  s.a. spec. diseases
Diets (food) *see* Applied
  nutrition
Diets (legislatures) *see*
  Legislative branch of
    govt.
Difference
  algebras — 512.56
    s.a. spec. appls. e.g.
      Engineering
  equations — 515.625
    s.a. spec. appls. e.g.
      Engineering
Difference-differential equations — 515.38
  s.a. spec. appls. e.g.
    Engineering
Differences
  indiv. psych. — 155.22
  s.a. other spec. subj.
Differentiable manifolds
  geometry *see* Differential
    geometry
  topology — 514.72
    s.a. spec. appls. e.g.
      Engineering
Differential
  algebras — 512.56
    s.a. spec. appls. e.g.
      Engineering
  analyzers *see* Analogue
    computers
  calculus — 515.33
    s.a. spec. appls. e.g.
      Engineering
  diagnosis *see* Diagnoses med.
    sci.

Digestive system
  anatomy
    human   611.3
    other aspects see Nutritive
        organs
  diseases
    gen. wks.   616.3
      neoplasms   616.992 3
      tuberculosis   616.995 3
    geriatrics   618.976 3
    pediatrics   618.923
    pub. health   614.593
    statistics   312.33
      deaths   312.263
    surgery   617.43
      anesthesiology   617.967 43
    other aspects see Diseases
  drugs affecting
    pharmacodynamics   615.73
    other aspects see Drugs
  physical anthropometry   573.63
  physiology
    human   612.3
    other aspects see Nutrition
  tissue biology human   611.018 93
Digests
  of budgets
    pub. admin.   350.722 53
      central govts.   351.722 53
        spec. jur.   353–354
      local govts.   352.125 3
  of cases
    law   348.046
      spec. jur.   348.3–.9
      U.S.
          Federal   348.734 6
          state & local   348.74–.79
      spec. subj.   *law s.s.*–026 48
  of laws
    law   348.026
      spec. jur.   348.3–.9
      U.S.
          Federal   348.732 6
          state & local   348.74–.79
      spec. subj.   *s.s.*–026 38
  s.a.   *s.s.*–020 2
Digital
  computers
    electronic data proc.   001.64
    spec. subj.   *s.s.*–028 54
    electronic eng.   621.381 958
    other aspects see Computers
  instruments
    manufacturing
      soc. & econ. aspects *see*
        Secondary industries
      technology   681.1
  representations
    arithmetic   513.5
    s.a. spec. appls. e.g.
      Computers

Digitalis
  pharmacodynamics   615.711
  other aspects see Drugs;
    also Personales
Digital-to-analogue converters
  electronic eng.   621.381 959 6
  other aspects see Computers
Dihydroxy aromatics
  org. chem.   547.633
  s.a. spec. cpds.
Dikes
  drainage *see* Drainage
  flood control eng. *see* Water
    retention
  structural geol.   551.88
  s.a. spec. aspects e.g.
    Prospecting
Dilation
  & curettage
    surgery   618.145 8
    vet. sci.   636.089 814 58
    s.a. spec. animals
  heart
    human phys.   612.171
    other aspects see
      Circulatory organs
Diligence *see* Virtues
Dill
  culture *see* Herbs
  other aspects see Umbellales
Dillenia family *see* Dilleniales
Dilleniaceae *see* Dilleniales
Dilleniales
  botany   583.112
  floriculture   635.933 112
  forestry   634.973 112
  med. aspects
    crop prod.   633.883 112
    gen. pharm.   615.323 112
      toxicology   615.952 311 2
    vet. pharm.   636.089 532 311 2
      toxicology 636.089 595 231 12
  paleobotany   561.3
  other aspects see Plants
Dillon Co. S.C.   *area*–757 85
Diluents
  chem. tech.   661.807
  oil-soluble paints
    technology   667.624
    other aspects see Paints
  painting bldgs.   698.102 82
  s.a. spec. surfaces e.g.
    Floors
  other aspects see Organic
    chemicals
Dilute solutions
  physical chem. *see* Solutions
    physical chem.
Dilution
  thermochemistry   541.362
    applied   660.296 2

Diodes (continued)
  other aspects see
    Semiconductors
Diophantine
  analysis   512.74
    s.a. spec. appls. e.g.
      Engineering
  equations   512.74
    s.a. spec. appls. e.g.
      Engineering
  inequalities   512.73
    s.a. spec. appls. e.g.
      Engineering
Dioptrics *see* Refraction light
  optics
Diorama paintings
  arts   751.74
    indiv. artists   759.1–.9
    s.a. spec. subj., tech.,
      equip.
Dioramas
  dec. arts   745.8
  library trmt. *see* Models
    library trmt.
Diorites *see* Plutonic rocks
Dioscorea *see* Yams
Dioscoreaceae *see* Dioscoreales
Dioscoreales
  botany   584.27
  floriculture   635.934 27
  med. aspects
    crop prod.   633.884 27
    gen. pharm.   615.324 27
      toxicology   615.952 427
    vet. pharm.   636.089 532 427
      toxicology   636.089 595 242 7
  paleobotany   561.4
  other aspects see Plants
Diospyros *see* Persimmons
Dipentodontaceae *see* Olacales
Diphenyl hydrocarbons
  org. chem.   547.613
    s.a. spec. cpds.
Diphenylmethane dyes
  manufacturing
    chem. tech.   667.254
    soc. & econ. aspects *see*
      Secondary industries
  org. chem.   547.864
Diphtheria
  gen. med.   616.931 3
  geriatrics   618.976 931 3
  pediatrics   618.929 313
  pub. health   614.512 3
  statistics   312.393 13
    deaths   312.269 313
  other aspects see Diseases
Diphthongs *see* Notations
  languages
Diplasiocoela
  zoology   597.89

Diplasiocoela (continued)
  other aspects see Anura
Diplomacy
  internat. law   341.33
  internat. relations
    pol. sci.   327.2
Diplomas
  education   371.291 2
    s.a. spec. levels of ed.;
      also Special education
  prints
    arts   769.5
Diplomatic
  agencies & procedures
    law
      constitutional   342.041 2
        spec. jur.   342.3–.9
      international   341.33
  causes of warfare
    mil. sci.   355.027 2
      s.a. hist. of spec. wars &
        spec. places
  customs   399
  history   327
    Spanish-American War   973.892
    U.S. Civil War   973.72
    U.S. Mexican War   973.622
    U.S. Revolutionary War   973.32
    U.S. War of 1812   973.522
    Vietnamese War   959.704 32
    World War 1   940.32
    World War 2   940.532
    s.a. other spec. wars
  relations
    rupture
      internat. law   341.58
Diplomatics *see* Paleography
Diplopia *see* Ocular
  neuromuscular mechanism
    diseases
Diplopoda
  paleozoology   565.61
  zoology   595.61
  other aspects see Arthropoda
Dipnoi
  culture   639.374 8
  fishing
    commercial   639.274 8
    sports   799.174 8
  paleozoology   567.4
  zoology   597.48
  other aspects see Pisces
Dipole moments
  electrostatics
    astrophysics   523.018 724 3
      s.a. spec. celestial
        bodies
    physics   537.243
      spec. states of matter   530.4

Dipped
  latex products
    manufacturing
      soc. & econ. aspects *see*
        Secondary industries
      technology   678.533
    s.a. spec. kinds of latexes
      e.g. Natural latexes
  rubber products
    manufacturing
      soc. & econ. aspects *see*
        Secondary industries
      technology   678.36
    s.a. spec. kinds of rubber
      e.g. Natural rubber
Dippers (birds) *see* Cinclidae
Dipping
  animals
    husbandry   636.083 3
    s.a. spec. animals
  gen. wks.
    technology   667.9
    s.a. spec. appls. e.g.
      Bodies automobiles
  latex mf.
    soc. & econ. aspects *see*
      Secondary industries
    technology   678.527
    s.a. spec. kinds of latexes
      e.g. Natural latexes
  s.a. other spec. prod.
Dips
  structural geol.   551.85
  s.a. spec. aspects e.g.
    Prospecting
Dipsacaceae *see* Valerianales
Dipsocoroidea *see* Heteroptera
Dipsomania *see* Alcoholism
Diptera
  culture   638.577
  paleozoology   565.77
  zoology   595.77
  other aspects see Insecta
Dipterocarpaceae *see* Ochnales
Diptychs *see* Easel paintings
Dir Pakistan   *area*–549 122
Dirachmaceae *see* Tiliales
Direct
  advertising   659.133
  currents
    astrophysics   523.018 761
    s.a. spec. celestial
      bodies
    engineering *see*
      Electrodynamics
    physics   537.61
      spec. states of matter   530.4

Direct (continued)
  energy conversion
    elect. power
      electromagnetic eng.   621.312 4
        s.a. spec. appls. e.g.
          Solar energy-powered
          autos
      soc. & econ. aspects *see*
        Secondary industries
      other aspects see
        Electrodynamics
  examination *see* Examination
    of witnesses
  lighting
    illumination eng.
      soc. & econ. aspects *see*
        Secondary industries
      technology   621.321 2
        exterior   621.322 9
        interior   621.322 5–.322 8
      s.a. spec. kinds e.g.
        Incandescent lighting
      s.a. spec. appls. e.g.
        Lighting airports
  nuclear-powered
    generation
      electrodynamic eng.
        soc. & econ. aspects
          see Secondary
          industries
        technology   621.312 56
        s.a. spec. appls.
          e.g. Electric
          railroads
        other aspects see
          Electrodynamics
  processes
    color photography   778.63
    motion pictures   778.534 2
    photomicrography   778.31
  selling *see* Personal selling
  taxes
    pub. finance   336.294
  s.a. other spec. subj.
Direct-current
  machinery
    electrodynamic eng.
      soc. & econ. aspects *see*
        Secondary industries
      tech. & mf.   621.313 2
        s.a. spec. appls. e.g.
          Electric locomotives
      other aspects see
        Electrodynamics
  transmission
    electrodynamic eng.   621.319 12
      s.a. spec. appls. e.g.
        Surface rail systems
      soc. & econ. aspects *see*
        Secondary industries

Direct-current
transmission (continued)
   other aspects see
    Electrodynamics
Direct-distant-dialing systems
  see Automatic
   switchboard systems
Direct-driven hoists
  mining eng.   622.67
Directed lighting
  illumination eng. *see* Flood
   lighting illumination
   eng.
Direct-fluid-pressure
   displacement pumps
  engineering
   soc. & econ. aspects *see*
    Secondary industries
   tech. & mf.   621.699
    s.a. spec. appls. e.g.
     Water supply
     engineering
  other aspects see Dynamics
Direction
  dramatic performances
   motion pictures   791.430 233
   radio   791.440 233
   stage   792.023 3
    s.a. spec. kinds e.g.
     Tragedies (drama)
   television   791.450 233
  geography *see* Navigation
  management tech.
   pub. admin.   350.007 4
    central govts.   351.007 4
    spec. jur.   353–354
    local govts.   352.000 474
  musical ensembles
   music theory   781.635
    s.a. spec. mediums
Directional
  antennas *see* Antennas
  derivatives
   calculus   515.33
    s.a. spec. appls. e.g.
     Engineering
   geometry   516.36
    s.a. spec. appls. e.g.
     Engineering
  gyros
   aircraft eng.   629.135 2
    s.a. spec. appls. e.g.
     Military engineering
Directionality
  sound
   engineering   620.21
    s.a. spec. appls. e.g.
     Music bldgs. for
   physics   534.203
    spec. states of matter   530.4

Direction-finding
  devices
   aircraft eng.   629.135 1
   navigation
    seamanship   623.893 2–.893 3
    other aspects see
     Navigation
  procedures
   celestial navigation   527.5
   radio
    engineering   621.384 191
     s.a. spec. appls. e.g.
      Navigation
    other aspects see Radio
Directives
  sociology   302.24
Direct-mail advertising   659.133
Direct-metal sculpture   731.41
  spec. periods & schools 732–735
Directories   *s.s.*–025
Directors
  dramatic performances
   biog. & work
    motion pictures   791.430 233 092
    radio   791.440 233 092
    stage   792.023 309 2
    television   791.450 233 092
    ocupational ethics 174.979 1–.979 2
   persons
    motion pictures   *pers.*–791 4
    radio   *pers.*–791 4
    stage   *pers.*–792 1
    television   *pers.*–791 4
  management   658.422
   s.a. other spec. activities;
    also Officers
Directory
  advertising   659.132
  France hist.   944.045
   s.a. spec. events & subj.
    e.g. Commerce
Direct-positive processes
  photography   772.1
Dirigible balloons *see* Airships
Dirk Hartogs Isl. W. Aust.
             area–941 3
Dirks *see* Edged weapons
Dirouilles isl.   *area*–423 49
Dirt *see* Soil; Soils
Disability
  compensation for
   veterans
    law   343.011 6
     spec. jur.   343.3–.9
   income insurance   368.386
   misc. aspects see Insurance
  mental health factor
   pub. health   362.2
   soc. path.   362.4
   soc. theology *see* Social
    problems soc. theology

Disasters	
soc. action	
law (continued)	
municipal	344.053 4
spec. jur.	344.3–.9
pub. admin.	350.754
central govts.	351.754
spec. jur.	353–354
local govts.	352.935 4
sociology	
social change	303.485
Disc records & recordings *see*	
Recordings	
Discarding	
library econ.	025.216
museology	069.51
Discarnate spirits	
spiritualism	133.9
Discharge	
armed forces	355.114
law	343.012
spec. jur.	343.3–.9
s.a. spec. mil. branches	
electronics *see* Electronics	
employees *see* Dismissal	
Discharged offenders	
rehabilitation & welfare	364.8
Discifloral plants	
botany	583.2
floriculture	635.933 2
forestry	634.973 2
med. aspects	
crop prod.	633.883 2
gen. pharm.	615.323 2
toxicology	615.952 32
vet. pharm.	636.089 532 32
toxicology	636.089 595 232
paleobotany	561.3
other aspects see Plants	
Disciples of Christ Church	286.6
adherents	
biog. & work	286.609 2
s.a. spec. denominations	
s.a.	*pers.–266*
buildings	
architecture	726.586 6
building	690.658 66
other aspects see	
Religious-purpose	
bldgs.	
Christian life guides	248.486 6
doctrines	230.66
creeds	238.66
general councils	262.566
govt. & admin.	262.066
parishes	254.066
missions	266.66
moral theology	241.046 6
music	
arts	783.026 66
recordings	789.912 302 666

Disciples of Christ Church	
music	
arts (continued)	
s.a. spec. instruments;	
also spec. kinds e.g.	
Liturgical music	
religion	
pub. worship	264.066 02
significance	246.7
private prayers for	242.806 6
pub. worship	264.066
rel. associations	
adults	267.186 6
men	267.246 6
women	267.446 6
young adults	267.626 6
rel. instruction	268.866
rel. law	262.986 6
schools	377.866
secondary training	207.126 6
sermons	252.066
theological seminaries	207.116 6
s.a. other spec. aspects	
Discipline	
armed forces	
gen. wks.	355.13
s.a. spec. mil. branches	
law	343.014
spec. jur.	343.3–.9
child rearing	649.64
classrooms *see* Classroom	
discipline	
employees	
personnel admin.	
gen. management	658.314
executives	658.407 14
spec. subj.	*s.s.*–068 3
law of pub. admin.	342.068 4
spec. jur.	342.3–.9
pub. admin.	350.147
central govts.	351.147
spec. jur.	353–354
local govts.	352.005 147
judges	
law *see* Judges law	
labor unions	
labor econ.	331.873
s.a. spec. classes of	
workers e.g. Women	
labor law *see* Labor law	
legislative bodies	
law *see* Membership	
legislative bodies law	
pol. sci.	328.366
spec. jur.	328.4–.9
prisons	365.643
law	344.035 643
spec. jur.	344.3–.9
pub. executives	
law *see* Executive branches	
law	

Discriminatory practices (continued)
  labor law *see* Labor law
  soc. aspects *see* Social
      structure
  s.a. other spec. subj.
Discs *see* Recordings
Discus throwing *see* Throwing
Discussion
  groups
    adult ed.   374.22
  literature
    private *see* Conversations
    public *see* Public
        discussions
  method
    education   371.37
    s.a. spec. levels of ed.;
        also Special education
  rhetoric
    private *see* Conversations
    public *see* Public
        discussions
Disease-causing microbes
  mil. sci. & eng.
    ammunition *see* Biological
        devices mil. eng.
    gen. wks. *see* Biological
        warfare
Diseases
  bees
    apiculture   638.15
  biology *see* Pathology
  carriers
    pub. health   614.43
    law   344.043
      spec. jur.   344.3–.9
    misc. aspects see Public
        health
  control
    law   344.043
      spec. jur.   344.3–.9
    pub. admin.   350.776
      central govts.   351.776
      spec. jur.   353–354
      local govts.   352.4
    pub. health   614.44
    misc. aspects see Public
        health
    wildlife conservation tech.   639.96
    s.a. spec. kinds of
        animals
  distribution
    pub. health   614.42
    misc. aspects see Public
        health
  floriculture   635.923
    s.a. spec. plants
  grape culture   634.823

Diseases (continued)
  incidence
    pub. health   614.42
    misc. aspects see Public
        health
    med. sci.   616
    vet. med.   636.089 6
    s.a. spec. animals
  plants *see* Plant diseases
        agriculture
  prevention   614.44
    misc. aspects see Public
        health
  reports
    pub. health   614
    misc. aspects see Public
        health
  resistance to
    eng. materials *see*
        Deterioration eng.
        materials
  statistics   312.3
    deaths   312.26
  trees
    forestry   634.963
    s.a. spec. trees
  s.a. Illness
Diseconomies of scale
  prod. econ.   338.514 4
Disembodied spirits
  occultism   133.14
    communication   133.9
Dishes
  home econ.
    cleaning   648.56
    use   642.7
  other aspects see Containers
Dishwashers
  mf. tech.   683.88
  plumbing   696.184
  other aspects see Household
      appliances
Dishwashing home econ.   648.56
Disincarnation
  rel. doctrines *see*
      Eschatology
Disinfection
  control meas.
    pub. health   614.48
    misc. aspects see Public
        health
  sewage trmt.
    technology   628.32
    other aspects see Sewage
        treatment
  water-supply trmt.
    technology   628.166 2
    other aspects see Water
        supply engineering

Disruptive discharge
electronics (continued)
  atmospheric electricity
    meteorology 551.563 2
      artificial modification 551.686 32
      weather forecasting 551.646 32
      spec. areas 551.65
    physics 537.52
    spec. states of matter 530.4
Diss Norfolk Eng. *area*–426 19
Dissent
  political
    law 342.085 4
    spec. jur. 342.3–.9
  religious *see* Religious
    freedom
  soc. action *see* Protest soc.
    action
Dissertations
  bibliographies 011.7
    spec. kinds 012–016
  catalogs
    general 017–019
    spec. kinds 012–016
  preparation
    rhetoric 808.02
Dissociative reactions
  gen. med. 616.852 3
  geriatrics 618.976 852 3
  pediatrics 618.928 523
  psychology 157.3
  pub. health 614.58
  statistics 312.385 23
  other aspects see Mental
    illness
Dissolution *see spec. subj.*
  e.g. Families
    dissolution
Dissolving
  gases
    chem. apparatus 542.7
    s.a. spec. appls. e.g.
      Organic chemistry
Dissonance
  sound
    engineering 620.23
    s.a. spec. appls. e.g.
      Pest control
    physics 534.352
    spec. states of matter 530.4
Distance
  celestial bodies *see*
    Constants celestial
    bodies
  geography *see* Navigation
Distant prospection
  parapsychology 133.323 9

Distillation
  alcoholic beverages
    comm. proc. 663.16
    s.a. spec. beverages e.g.
      Brandies
    illicit *see* Revenue
      offenses
    other aspects see Alcoholic
      beverages
  saline water conversion
    technology 628.167 2
    other aspects see Water
      supply engineering
Distilled liquors 641.25
  comm. proc. 663.5
  cookery 641.625
    composite dishes 641.874
  other aspects see Alcoholic
    beverages
Distilling apparatus
  chemistry 542.4
    s.a. spec. appls. e.g.
      Organic chemistry
Distomatosis *see* Fluke-caused
    diseases
Distortion
  of celestial bodies *see*
    Refraction atmospheric
    optical phenomena
Distortions
  photographic tech. *see*
    Special effects
    photography
Distribution
  channels
    marketing management 658.84
    spec. subj. *s.s.*–068 8
  controls
    air-conditioning eng. 697.932 5
  cooperatives
    economics 334.5
  management *see* Marketing
    management
  of coal
    fuel tech. 662.624
  of elect. power *see*
    Transmission elect.
    power
  of ind. gases 665.74
    s.a. spec. gases
  of labor force 331.111
    s.a. spec. classes of
      workers e.g. Women
  of petroleum 665.54
    s.a. spec. products
  of sea water
    oceanography 551.460 1
    s.a. spec. bodies of
      water
  soc. aspects 306.3

Distribution (continued)
spaces functional analysis
 see Distribution
 theory functional
 analysis
systems
 water-supply eng.
  technology   628.144
 other aspects see Water
  supply engineering
theory
 functional analysis   515.782
 s.a. spec. appls. e.g.
  Engineering
 primes   512.73
 s.a. spec. appls. e.g.
  Engineering
transformers *see* Transformers
s.a. other spec. subj. e.g.
 Fogs
Distributions
algebra   512.925
arithmetic   513.25
s.a. spec. appls. e.g.
 Business arithmetic
Distributive education *see*
 Business high schools
Distributor brands
sales promotion *see* Brands
 sales promotion
Distributors
internal-combusion engines
 see Ignition systems
 & devices
District
Court
 Scotland
  law   345.411 012
courts
 U.S. law
  Federal   347.732 2
heating
 buildings   697.54
nursing
 med. sci.   610.734 3
of Columbia   *area*–753
Districts
legislative bodies *see*
 Election districts
local govt.
 pub. admin.   352.007 3
Disturbances
atmosphere
 meteorology   551.552–.559
 artificial modification
       551.685 2–.685 9
 weather forecasting   551.645 2–.645 9
 spec. areas   551.65
s.a. other spec. kinds e.g.
 Riots

Ditchers
railroad *see* Work cars
Ditches
drainage *see* Drainage
irrigation *see* Irrigation
Ditching operations
soil reclamation   631.62
s.a. spec. crops; also spec.
 types of culture e.g.
  Floriculture
Diu India   *area*–547 99
Diuretics
pharmacodynamics   615.761
other aspects see Drugs
Diurnal variations
air temperatures
 meteorology   551.525 3
  weather forecasting   551.642 53
  spec. areas   551.65
geomagnetism
 astrophysics   523.018 874 2
 s.a. spec. celestial
  bodies
 physics   538.742
 spec. states of matter   530.4
Divers
hydraulic eng. *see* Hydraulic
  engineers
sports
 biog. & work   797.2
 s.a.   *pers.*–797 2
Diversification
prod. management   658.503
spec. subj.   *s.s.*–068 5
Divertimenti *see* Romantic music
  orchestra
Divestment
management   658.16
Divide Co. N.D.   *area*–784 71
Divided catalogs
library sci.   025.315
Dividend policy
financial management *see*
  Profits management
  financial management
Dividends
accounting trmt.   657.76
s.a. spec. kinds of
 enterprise e.g.
  Insurance accounting
stock valuation
 investment finance   332.632 21
Dividers
roadside barriers
 technology   625.795
 other aspects see Roads
Divination
parapsychology   133.3
rel. worship
 comp. rel.   291.32
 Islam   297.32

Divination
rel. worship (continued)
  s.a. other spec. rel.
Divinatory
arts *see* Divination
graphology   137
signs
  parapsychology   133.334
Divine
law
  Christianity   241.2
  other rel. see Moral
    theology
purpose of God
rel. doctrines
  Christianity   231.7
  other rel. see God
right of kings
  pol. sci.   321.6
  s.a. spec. jur.
services *see* Public worship
Diving
aeronautical aerodynamics   629.132 31
  s.a. spec. appls. e.g.
    Flying
underwater   627.72
engineering   627.72
sports   797.2
  misc. aspects see Sports
  s.a. spec. appls. e.g.
    Military engineering
Diving
aeronautical aerodynamics   629.132 31
  s.a. spec. appls. e.g.
    Flying
underwater   627.72
engineering   627.72
sports   797.2
  misc. aspects see Sports
  s.a. spec. appls. e.g.
    Military engineering
Divining rods
parapsychology   133.323
Divinities *see* Gods
Divinity
of Jesus Christ
  Christian doctrines   232.8
Division   512.92
algebra   512.92
arithmetic   513.2
  s.a. spec. appls. e.g.
    Business arithmetic
of cells biology *see*
    Reproduction of cells
of powers pub. admin. *see*
    Separation of powers
Divisionism *see*
    Neo-Impressionism
Divisions
mil. organization   355.31
  s.a. spec. mil. branches

Divorce
ethics *see* Family ethics
Jewish rites   296.444
law   346.016 6
  spec. jur.   346.3–.9
soc. theology
  Christian rel.   261.835 89
  comp. rel.   291.178 358 9
  s.a. other spec. rel.
sociology   306.89
statistics   312.5
Divorced people
psychology   155.643
  s.a.   *pers.*–065 3
Diwaniya Iraq   *area*–567 5
Dixie Co. Fla.   *area*–759 812
Dixiecrat Party U.S.
pol. sci.   324.273 3
  s.a. spec. subj. of concern
    e.g. Social problems
Dixon
Co. Neb.   *area*–782 223
Entrance *see* Canadian Pacific
    seawaters
Diyala Iraq   *area*–567 4
Diyarbakir Turkey   *area*–566 7
Dizziness
symptomatology
  neurological diseases   616.841
  vet. sci.   636.089 684 1
  s.a. spec. animals
Djakarta Indonesia   *area*–598 2
Djibouti   *area*–677 1
Dnepr River   *area*–477 1
Dnepropetrovsk Ukraine   *area*–477 16
Dnestr River   *area*–477 18
Dnieper River   *area*–477 1
Dniepropetrovsk Ukraine   *area*–477 16
Dniester River   *area*–477 18
Dobby-weave fabrics
arts   746.046 15
  s.a. spec. proc. e.g.
    Weaving
manufacturing
  soc. & econ. aspects *see*
    Secondary industries
  technology   677.615
  other aspects see Textiles
  s.a. spec. prod.
Doberman pinschers
animal husbandry   636.73
  other aspects see Dogs
Dobrich Bulgaria   *area*–497 77
Dobrogea Romania   *area*–498 3
Dobruja   *area*–498 3
Bulgaria   *area*–497 77
Romania   *area*–498 3
Dobson flies *see* Neuroptera
Dock buildings *see* Marine
    transportation
    buildings

Docks (loading platforms) *see*
        Bus terminals & stops;
        also Truck terminals
Docks (port facility)
    construction
        mil. sci.   358.22
    port eng.
        soc. & econ. aspects *see*
            Secondary industries
        technology   627.31
        military   623.64
    other aspects see Port
        facilities
Doctoral dissertations *see*
        Dissertations
Doctors
    of medicine *see* Physicians
Doctrinal
    controversies
        Christian church hist.   273
    theology
        Buddhism   294.342
        Christianity   230
        comp. rel.   291.2
        Hinduism   294.52
        Islam   297.2
        Judaism   296.31–.33
        nat. rel.   210
        s.a. other spec. rel.
Documentalists *see* Information
        scientists
Documentary
    evidence
        criminal investigation   363.256 5
    law
        criminal law   345.064
        gen. wks.   347.064
        other aspects see Evidence
    films
        journalism   070.1
        s.a. spec. activities
            e.g. Reporting
        performing arts   791.435 3
Documentation   025
Documents
    library trmt.   025.173 4
        acquisitions   025.283 4
        cataloging   025.343 4
        s.a. other spec. activities
Doddridge Co. W. Va.   *area*–754 56
Dodecanese   *area*–499 6
    ancient   *area*–391 6
Dodge Co.
    Georgia   *area*–758 532
    Minnesota   *area*–776 153
    Nebraska   *area*–782 235
    Wisconsin   *area*–775 82
Dodoma Tanzania   *area*–678 26
Dodos *see* Columbiformes
Dodworth South Yorkshire Eng.
                            area–428 25

Dog cabbage family *see*
        Chenopodiales
Dogbane family *see* Apocynales
Dogmas *see* Doctrinal theology
Dogmatic theology *see* Doctrinal
        theology
Dogmatism
    philosophy   148
        indiv. phil.   180–190
        s.a. spec. branches of phil.
            e.g. Metaphysics
Dogs
    animal husbandry   636.7
        soc. & econ. aspects *see*
            Primary industries
    experimental animals
        med. sci.   619.7
    other aspects see Canidae
Dogwood family *see* Araliales
Doilies *see* Table linens
Doldrums *see* Planetary wind
        systems
Dolerites *see* Plutonic rocks
Dolgano-Nenets Nat. Region *area*–575
Dolgellau Gwynedd Wales   *area*–429 29
Dolj Romania   *area*–498 4
Doll
    clothing
        handicrafts   745.592 21
    furniture
        handicrafts   745.592 3
        mf. tech.   688.723
        other aspects see Toys
Dollar Central Scot.   *area*–413 15
Dollhouses
    handicrafts   745.592 3
    mf. tech.   688.723
    other aspects see Toys
Dolls
    child care   649.552
    handicrafts   745.592 21
    mf. tech.   688.722 1
    other aspects see Toys
Dolomite
    mineralogy   549.782
    soil conditioners   631.821
        misc. aspects see Soil
            conditioners
    other aspects see Sedimentary
        rocks
Dolores Co. Colo.   *area*–788 26
Dolphins (animals) *see*
        Odontoceti
Dolphins (mooring structures)
        see Mooring
        structures
Dombes France   *area*–444 4
Domes
    buildings
        architectural
            construction   721.46

Domes
 buildings
  architectural (continued)
   design & decoration   729.34
   building construction   690.146
   s.a. spec. kinds of bldgs.
  structural eng.
   gen. wks.   624.177 5
   concretes   624.183 45
   s.a. other spec.
    materials
   naval arch.   623.817 75
   s.a. other spec. appls.
Domestic
 accidents
  statistics   312.42
  deaths   312.272
 activities
  pollution by
   soc. aspects   363.731
   other aspects see
    Pollution
 animals
  insurance *see* Livestock
  production *see* Animal
   husbandry
 architecture   728
 arts *see* Home economics
 cats
  animal husbandry   636.82–.83
  other aspects see Cats
 commerce   381
  govt. control
   activities   350.826
    central govts.   351.826
    spec. jur.   353–354
    local govts.   352.942 5
   govt. depts. *see*
    Executive departments
   law   343.088
    spec. jur.   343.3–.9
  customs   392.3
 economy *see* Home economics
 employees *see* Household
  employees
 food services   642.1
 hazards
  soc. path.   363.13
  s.a. spec. kinds e.g. Fire
   hazards
 industries
  management *see* Small
   businesses management
  prod. econ.   338.634
  technology *see spec. ind.*
 investments
  economics   332.672
  misc. aspects see
   Investments
 medicine   616.024
  misc. aspects see Diseases

Domestic (continued)
 relations
  law   346.015
   spec. jur.   346.3–.9
  sociology   306.8
 requirements
  water-supply eng.
   technology   628.17
   other aspects see Water
    supply engineering
 safety
  law   344.047
   spec. jur.   344.3–.9
  pub. meas.   363.13
   govt. control *see* Safety
    pub. admin.
  s.a. spec. aspects e.g.
   Fire safety
 sciences *see* Home economics
 servants *see* Household
  employees
 trade *see* Domestic commerce
 traders
  biog. & work   381.092
  s.a.   *pers.*–381
 trunk routes
  air transp. *see* Routes
   transp. services
 waste pollution
  water-supply eng.
   technology   628.168 2
   other aspects see Water
    supply engineering
 wastes *see* Wastes control
 s.a. Home; *also other spec.*
  subj.
Domestic (municipal) law   342–347
 relation to internat. law   341.04
Domestica plums
 agriculture   634.227
 other aspects see Plums
Domicile
 law *see* Persons law
Dominations (angels) *see* Angels
Dominica West Indies   *area*–729 841
Dominican
 convent bldgs.
  architecture   726.779 72
  building   690.677 972
  other aspects see
   Religious-purpose
   bldgs.
 monastic bldgs.
  architecture   776.772
  building   690.677 2
  other aspects see
   Religious-purpose
   bldgs.
 Republic   *area*–729 3
  literature   860
  people   *r.e.n.*–687 293

Dosimetry (continued)	
biophysics	
extraterrestrial	
gen. wks.	574.191 95
animals	591.191 95
microorganisms	576.119 195
plants	581.191 95
s.a. spec. organisms	
med. sci.	612.014 55
animals	636.089 201 455
s.a. spec. animals	
man	612.014 55
terrestrial	
gen. wks.	574.191 5
animals	591.191 5
microorganisms	576.191 15
plants	381.191 5
s.a. spec. organisms	
med. sci.	612.014 48
animals	636.089 201 448
s.a. spec. animals	
man	612.014 48
s.a. spec. functions,	
systems, organs	
physics	539.77
spec. states of matter	530.4
s.a. spec. physical	
phenomena e.g. Heat	
Dositheus Confession	
Christian doctrines	238.19
Dotted Swiss *see* Machine	
embroidery	
Douay version	
Bible	220.520 2
s.a. spec. parts of Bible	
Double	
basses	
instruments	
mf. tech.	681.817 41
misc. aspects see	
Musical instruments	
musical art	787.41
music	787.415
recordings	789.912 741
images	
photography *see* Special	
effects photography	
reed instruments	
manufacture	681.818 056
spec. kinds	681.818 7–.818 8
musical art	788.056
spec. kinds	788.7–.8
salts metals	
chemistry	
inorganic	546.343
spec. kinds	546.38–.68
other aspects see Metals	
chemistry	
pharmacology	615.234 3
misc. aspects see	
Pharmacology	

Double	
salts metals (continued)	
toxicology	615.925 343
misc. aspects see	
Toxicology	
stars *see* Visual binary stars	
sulfides	
mineralogy	549.35
taxation	
internat. law	341.484
pub. finance	336.294
Doubles	
tennis sports	796.342 28
Doubs France	*area*–444 6
Doubt	
epistemology	121.5
Dougherty Co. Ga.	*area*–758 953
Douglas	
County	
Colorado	*area*–788 86
Georgia	*area*–758 243
Illinois	*area*–773 68
Kansas	*area*–781 65
Minnesota	*area*–776 45
Missouri	*area*–778 832
Nebraska	*area*–782 254
Nevada	*area*–793 59
Oregon	*area*–795 29
South Dakota	*area*–783 383
Washington	*area*–797 31
Wisconsin	*area*–775 11
Res. Tenn.	*area*–768 924
Doune Central Scot.	*area*–413 12
Douro Litoral Portugal	*area*–469 15
Dove River Derbyshire Eng.	*area*–425 13
Dover	
city	
Delaware	*area*–751 5
Kent Eng.	*area*–422 352
Strait *see* English Channel	
Doves *see* Columbiformes	
Down Ire.	
district	*area*–416 56
former co.	*area*–416 5
Downham Market Norfolk Eng.	
	area–426 13
Downpatrick N. Ire.	*area*–416 56
Downs district Qld.	*area*–943 3
Down's syndrome *see* Mongolism	
Downy mildews *see*	
Peronosporales	
Dowry	
customs	392.5
Dowsing	
parapsychology	133.323
Doxologies	
private prayers	
Christianity	242.721
other rel. see Prayers	
private devotions	

Draft
  horses
    animal husbandry   636.15
    other aspects see Horses
  use
    animal husbandry for   636.088 2
    s.a. spec. animals
Draft (conscription)
  armed forces
    law   343.012 2
    spec. jur.   343.3–.9
    other aspects see Induction
        military
Drafted labor
  economics   331.117 32
  s.a. spec. classes of labor
    e.g. Women
Drafting (drawing)
  procedures
    tech. drawing   604.24
    spec. subj.   *s.s.*–022 1
  rooms
    tech. drawing   604.22
    spec. subj.   *s.s.*–022 1
Drafting (requisitioning) *see*
    Draft (conscription)
Drafts *see* Commercial paper
Draftsmen
  biog. & work   741.092
  occupational ethics   174.974 3
  s.a.   *pers.*–743
Drag
  aeronautical aerodynamics 629.132 34
  s.a. spec. appls. e.g.
    Flying
Dragging
  roads
    technology   625.761
    other aspects see Roads
Dragonfishes *see* Isospondyli
Dragonflies *see* Odonata
Dragons
  lit. & stage trmt.
    folk lit. texts & lit. crit. 398.245 4
    other aspects see Animals
Drainage
  agric. soil reclamation   631.62
    s.a. spec. crops; also spec.
      types of culture e.g.
      Floriculture
  airport runways
    aeronautical eng.   629.136 35
    military   623.663 5
    s.a. other spec. appls.
  land reclamation eng.
    soc. & econ. aspects *see*
      Secondary industries
    technology   627.54
    s.a. spec. appls. e.g.
      Landscape architecture

Drainage
  land reclamation eng. (continued)
    other aspects see Liquids
      engineering
  mining
    engineering   622.5
  pollution
    water-supply eng.
      technology   628.168 32
      other aspects see Water
        supply engineering
  road eng.
    technology   625.734
    other aspects see Roads
  soil mechanics
    foundation eng.   624.151 36
    s.a. spec. appls. e.g.
      Roads engineering
Drainage-winds *see* Local wind
    systems
Drainpipes *see* Roofs
Drake Passage
  oceanography   551.469 3
  regional subj. trmt.   *area*–167 3
  other aspects see Antarctic
    waters
Drama
  elementary ed.   372.66
  gen. wks.
    collections   808.82
    crit. theory   801.952
      textual   801.959
    hist. & crit.   809.2
    rhetoric   808.2
    juvenile   808.068 2
  rel. significance
    Christianity   246.7
    other rel. see Arts rel.
      significance
  spec. lits.   *lit. sub.*–2
  stage presentation *see*
    Theater
Drama (nome) Greece   *area*–495 6
Dramatic
  films
    performing arts   791.435 2
  method
    education *see*
      Teaching-methods
    rel. instruction
      Christianity   268.67
      other rel. see Religious
        instruction
  music   782
    recordings   789.912 2
    voice training   784.95
  poetry
    gen. wks.
      collections   808.812
      hist. & crit.   809.12

Dramatic
  poetry
    gen. wks. (continued)
      rhetoric   808.12
      juvenile   808.068 12
    spec. lits.   *lit. sub.*–102
    indiv. authors   *lit. sub.*–11–19
    other aspects see Poetry
  programs
    radio performances   791.445
    television performances   791.455
Dramatists
  biog. & work   809.2
  s.a. spec. lits.
  other aspects see Authors
  s.a.   *pers.*–82
Draped figures
  art representation   704.942 2
  drawing tech.   743.5
  painting   757.23
  s.a. other spec. art forms
Draperies
  comm. mf.   684.3
  domestic mf.   646.21
  int. dec.   747.5
  s.a. spec. kinds of bldgs.;
    also spec. dec.
  textile arts   746.94
  window furnishings home econ. 645.3
  other aspects see Furnishings
Draughts (game) *see* Checkers
Dravida
  languages
    linguistics   494.81
    literatures   894.81
    s.a.   *lang.*–948 1
  people   *r.e.n.*–948
Dravidian
  languages
    linguistics   494.8
    literatures   894.8
    s.a.   *lang.*–948
  people   *r.e.n.*–948
  s.a. other spec. subj. e.g.
    Arts
Drawbacks
  internat. comm.   382.7
Drawing (delineating)
  arts   741
    study & teaching   740.071
    elementary ed.   372.52
  maps   526.86
  technical   604.2
Drawing (pulling)
  glassmaking   666.124
  s.a. spec. kinds of glass

Drawing (pulling) (continued)
  metals
    arts
      decorative   739.14
      s.a. spec. metals; also
        spec. prod. e.g.
        Jewelry
    fine *see* Direct-metal
      sculpture
    mf. tech.   671.34
      ferrous metals   672.34
      s.a. other spec. metals
    other aspects see
      Mechanical working
Drawing-papers
  mf. tech.   676.282 5
  other aspects see Papers pulp
    prod.
Drawing-rooms *see* Living rooms
Drawings
  arts   741
  bldg. construction   692.1
  other aspects see Pictures
Drawn
  metal prod.
    mf. tech.   671.84
    ferrous metals   672.84
    s.a. other spec. metals
    other aspects see Primary
      metal prod.
  work
    textile arts *see* Embroidery
Dreadnoughts *see* Battleships
Dream books   135.3
Dreams
  human phys.   612.821
  popular psych.   135.3
  psychology   154.63
    animals   156.4
  other aspects see Nervous
    functions
Dred Scott decision
  U.S. Civil War cause   973.711 5
Dredgers (ships)
  engineering   623.828
    design   623.812 8
    models   623.820 18
  seamanship   623.882 8
  other aspects see Vessels
    (nautical)
Dredging operations
  underwater eng.   627.73
  foundations   624.157
  s.a. spec. appls. e.g.
    Bridges (structures)
Drenthe Netherlands   *area*–492 1
Dresden Ger.   *area*–432 1
Dress *see* Clothing
Dressers (furniture) *see*
  Cabinets (furniture)

Driver information
  highway services (continued)
    law   343.094 6
      local   343.098 2
      spec. jur.   343.3–.9
    local
      commerce   388.413 124
      govt. control   350.878 413 124
        central govts.   351.878 413 124
        spec. jur.   353–354
        local govts.   352.918 413 124
Drivers' licenses
  law   343.094 6
    spec. jur.   343.3–.9
Drives (power transmission) *see*
          Power transmission
Drives (psychology)
  physiological *see*
          Physiological drives
          psychology
  other kinds see Motivation
Drive-shafts
  automobiles
    soc. & econ. aspects *see*
          Secondary industries
    tech. & mf.   629.245
    s.a. spec. appls. e.g.
          Military engineering
Driveways
  road eng.
    technology   625.889
  other aspects see Roads
Driving
  horses
    sports   798.6
    other aspects see Sports
  motor vehicles
    soc. & econ. aspects *see*
          Secondary industries
    sports   796.7
    misc. aspects see Sports
    technology   629.283
    s.a. spec. appls. e.g.
          Military engineering
Driving-belts
  rubber
    manufacturing
      soc. & econ. aspects *see*
          Secondary industries
      technology   678.36
    s.a. spec. kinds of rubber
        e.g. Natural rubber
Drogheda Leinster Ire.   *area*–418 256
Droitwich Hereford & Worcester
      Eng.   *area*–424 49
Drôme France   *area*–449 8
Dromedaries
  animal husbandry   636.295
  other aspects see Ruminantia
Dromore N. Ire.   *area*–416 57

Drones (aircraft)
  mil. eng.   623.746 9
Dronfield Derbyshire Eng.   *area*–425 14
Dropouts
  education *see* School dropouts
Droseraceae *see* Sarraceniales
Drought relief
  agric. econ.   338.18
Droughts
  adaptations ecology *see*
          Weather ecology
  agric. econ.   338.14
  disasters
    soc. action   363.349 2
  diseases caused by
    agriculture *see* Droughts
          plant injuries
    gen. wks. *see* Environmental
          diseases
  meteorology   551.577 3
    artificial modification   551.687 73
    weather forecasting   551.647 73
    spec. areas   551.65
  plant injuries
    agriculture   632.12
    s.a. spec. plants; also
        spec. types of culture
        e.g. Forestry
  other aspects see Disasters
Drowning *see* Asphyxiation
Droxford Hampshire Eng.   *area*–422 735
Droylsden Greater Manchester Eng.
          area–427 35
Drug
  abuse
    programs
      pers. admin.
        gen. management   658.382 2
        spec. subj.   *s.s.*–068 3
      pub. admin.   350.16
        central govts.   351.16
        spec. jur.   353–354
        local govts.   352.005 16
    s.a. Addictive drugs use
  allergies
    gen. med.   616.975
    geriatrics   618.976 975
    pediatrics   618.929 75
    pub. health   614.599 3
    statistics   312.397 5
      deaths   312.269 75
    other aspects see Diseases
  shock therapy *see* Shock
      (convulsions) therapy
  therapy   615.58
    dentistry   617.606 1
    ophthalmology   617.706 1
    otology   617.806 1
    psychiatry   616.891 8
      geriatrics   618.976 891 8
      pediatrics   618.928 918

Drying (continued)
  positives *see* Positives
  s.a. other spec. subj.
Drying-processes
  chem. eng.   660.284 26
    s.a. spec. prod.
Dryopoidea
  zoology   595.764 5
  other aspects see Polyphaga
Drypoint
  graphic arts
    processes   767.3
    products   769
Dry-weather photography   778.75
Dual
  geometries   516.35
    s.a. spec. appls. e.g.
        Engineering
  nationality
    pol. sci.   323.634
  personalities *see* Multiple
      personalities
  s.a. other spec. subj.
Dualism
  nat. rel.   211.33
  philosophy   147.4
    Hindu   181.484
    indiv. phil.   180–190
    s.a. spec. branches of phil.
      e.g. Metaphysics
Duality
  functional analysis   515.782
  s.a. spec. appls. e.g
      Engineering
Duarte Dominican Republic *area*–729 367
Dubai   *area*–535 7
Dubbo N.S.W.   *area*–944 5
Dublin Ireland   *area*–418 3
Dubois Co. Ind.   *area*–772 37
Dubuque Co. Ia.   *area*–777 39
Ducane Range Tas.   *area*–946 3
Duchesne Co. Utah   *area*–792 22
Ducie Isl.   *area*–961 8
Duck
  River Tenn.   *area*–768 434
  roofing
    bldg. construction   695
Duckbills *see* Monotremata
Ducks
  animal husbandry   636.597
    soc. & econ. aspects *see*
      Primary industries
  products
    eggs
      food   641.375 97
      cookery   641.675 97
      prod. tech.   637.597
      soc. & econ. aspects *see*
        Primary industries

Ducks
  products (continued)
    meats
      food   641.365 97
        cookery   641.665 97
    production *see* Poultry
      products meats
    other prod. see spec. prod.
      e.g. Feathers
    other aspects see
      Anseriformes
Duckweed family *see* Arales
Ductility
  materials   620.112 5
    s.a. spec. materials & spec.
      uses
Ductless glands *see* Endocrine
      system
Dude ranching & farming
  equipment mf.   688.765 6
    soc. & econ. aspects *see*
      Secondary industries
  sports   796.56
  other aspects see Sports
Dudley West Midlands Eng. *area*–424 93
Dueling
  ethics
    philosophy   179.7
    religion
      Buddhism   294.356 97
      Christianity   241.697
      comp. rel.   291.569 7
      Hinduism   294.548 697
      s.a. other spec. rel.
  soc. customs   394.8
Dues
  checkoff
    labor econ.   331.889 6
Duets
  by instrument *see spec.*
    instruments
  chamber music
    recordings   789.912 572
    scores & parts   785.72
    treatises   785.702
  songs
    recordings   789.912
    scores & parts   784.82
    sacred   783.675 2
    secular   784.306 2
Dufferin
  Co. Ont.   *area*–713 41
  governorship India hist.   954.035 4
    s.a. spec. events & subj.
      e.g. Commerce
Dufftown Grampian Scot.   *area*–412 23
Dugongs *see* Sirenia
Dukeries Nottinghamshire Eng.
         area–425 21
Dukes Co. Mass.   *area*–744 94

Dukinfield Greater Manchester
    Eng.   *area*–427 35
Dulaim Iraq   *area*–567 4
Dulcimer music   787.945
  recordings   789.912 794
Dulcimers
  mf. tech.   681.817 94
  misc. aspects see Musical
    instruments
  musical art   787.94
Duluth Minn.   *area*–776 771
Dulverton Somerset Eng. *area*–423 85
Dumbarton Strathclyde Scot.
                area–414 25
Dumbbells *see* Calisthenics
Dumbwaiters *see* Elevators
    (lifts)
Dumfries Scot.   *area*–414 86
Dummy construction
  mil. sci. & eng. *see*
    Camouflage
Dumortierite
  mineralogy   549.62
Dump trucks *see* Trucks
Dumps
  refuse disposal
    technology   628.445 62
  other aspects see Refuse
    pub. sanitation
Dun Laoghaire Leinster Ire.
                area–418 38
Dunbar Lothian Scot.   *area*–413 6
Dunbartonshire Scot.   *area*–414 25
Dunblane Central Scot. *area*–413 12
Duncan Strathclyde Scot. *area*–414 23
Dundas Co. Ont.   *area*–713 75
Dundee Tayside Scot.   *area*–412 7
Dundy Co. Neb.   *area*–782 86
Dune buggies *see* Private
    automobiles
Dunedin N.Z.   *area*–931 57
Dunes
  ecology life sci.   574.526 5
    animals   591.526 5
    microorganisms   576.15
    plants   581.526 5
    s.a. spec. organisms
  formation
    physical geol.   551.375
  stabilization *see* Shore
    reclamation eng.
Dunfermline Fife Scot. *area*–412 98
Dung
  beetles
    zoology   595.764 9
  other aspects see Polyphaga
  flies *see* Cyclorrhapha
Dungannon N. Ire.   *area*–416 45
Dungeness Kent Eng.   *area*–422 395
Dungog N.S.W.   *area*–944 2
Dunipace Central Scot. *area*–413 18

Dunkards *see* Dunkers
Dunkers   286.5
  misc. aspects see Baptist
Dunklin Co. Mo.   *area*–778 993
Dunn Co.
  North Dakota   *area*–784 82
  Wisconsin   *area*–775 43
Duns Borders Scot.   *area*–413 95
Dunstable Bedfordshire
    Eng.   *area*–425 65
Dunster Somerset Eng. *area*–423 85
Duodecimal numeration system 513.56
  s.a. spec. appls. e.g.
    Engineering
Duodenal ulcers
  gen. med.   616.343 3
  geriatrics   618.976 343 3
  pediatrics   618.923 433
  pub. health   614.593 433
  statistics   312.334 33
    deaths   312.263 433
  other aspects see Diseases
Duodenitis *see* Enteritis
Duodenum *see* Small intestines
Du Page Co. Ill.   *area*–773 24
Duplex
  houses
    architecture   728.312
    building   690.831 2
    other aspects see
      Residential buildings
  telegraphy *see* Acoustical
    systems wire telegraphy
Duplex-process
  steel tech.   669.142 3
  misc. aspects see Ferrous
    metals
Duplicating-machines
  manufacturing
    soc. & econ. aspects *see*
      Secondary industries
    technology   681.6
Duplicating-techniques
  photoduplication *see*
    Photoduplication
  printing *see* Printing
    processes
Duplication
  of cubes
    geometry   516.204
  processes
    library econ.   025.129
    office use   652.4
Duplin Co. N.C.   *area*–756 382
Dura *see* Brain
Durability
  engineering   620.004 54
  other aspects see Materials

Durable
  press fabrics
    manufacturing
      soc. & econ. aspects *see*
        Secondary industries
      technology   677.68
    other aspects see Textiles
    s.a. spec. prod.
Durango Mex.   *area*–721 5
Duration
  snow cover
    meteorology   551.578 461
      weather forecasting   551.647 846 1
      spec. areas   551.65
    s.a. other spec. subj.
Durazno Uruguay   *area*–895 24
Durban South Africa   *area*–684
Duress
  legal defense
    criminal law   345.04
    spec. jur.   345.3–.9
Durham
  County
    England   *area*–428 6
    North Carolina   *area*–756 563
    Ontario   *area*–713 56
  district Eng.   *area*–428 65
  mission
    Canada hist.   971.039
  Regional Municipality Ont.
         area–713 56
Duroc-Jersey swine
  animal husbandry   636.483
  other aspects see Swine
Durra
  agriculture
    food crops   633.174 7
    forage crops   633.257 47
    other aspects see Sorghums
Dursley Gloucestershire Eng.
         area–424 19
Düsseldorf Ger.   *area*–435 5
Dust
  atmosphere *see* Particulates
  atmospheric electricity *see*
      Aerosols meteorology
  storms
    disasters
      soc. action   363.349 2
      misc. aspects see
        Disasters
    meteorology   551.559
      artificial modification   551.685 9
      weather forecasting   551.645 9
      spec. areas   551.65
Dust-caused respiratory diseases
      see Pneumoconiosis
Dusting
  housecleaning   648.5

Dusting (continued)
  pest control
    agriculture   632.94
    s.a. spec. plants; also
      spec. types of culture
      e.g. Forestry
Dusting-on processes
  photographic printing   773.2
Dutch
  Antilles   *area*–729 86
  cheeses
    dairy tech.   637.356
    other aspects see Cheeses
  East India Company
    Indonesia hist.   959.802 1
    s.a. spec. events & subj.
      e.g. Commerce
  East Indies
    history   959.802 2
    s.a.   *area*–598
  Guiana   *area*–883
  language
    linguistics   439.31
    literature   839.31
    s.a.   *lang.*–393 1
  people   *r.e.n.*–393 1
  Republic Netherlands hist.   949.204
    s.a. spec. events & subj.
      e.g. Commerce
  West Indies   *area*–729 86
  s.a. Netherlands; *also other*
      spec. subj. e.g. Arts
Dutchess Co. N.Y.   *area*–747 33
Duties (obligations)
  ethics   170
  moral theology *see* Conduct
  of citizens
    pol. sci.   323.65
  of judges
    law   347.012
    spec. jur.   347.3–.9
  of legislators
    law   342.052
    spec. jur.   342.3–.9
  of pub. executives
    law   342.06
    spec. jur.   342.3–.9
    pub. admin.   350.003 2
      central govts.   351.003 2
      spec. jur.   353–354
      local govts.   352.008
  other spec. activities   *s.s.*–023
Duties (taxes) *see* Customs
    (tariffs)
Dutra admin. Brazil hist.   981.061
  s.a. spec. events & subj.
      e.g. Commerce
Duval Co.
  Florida   *area*–759 12
  Texas   *area*–764 463
Dvaita phil.   181.484 1

Dysenteries
  gen. med.   616.935
  geriatrics   618.976 935
  pediatrics   618.929 35
  pub. health   614.516
  statistics   312.393 5
    deaths   312.269 35
  other aspects see Diseases
Dyslexia
  education *see* Linguistically
    handicapped students
  gen. med.   616.855 3
  geriatrics   618.976 855 3
  pediatrics   618.928 553
  psychology   157.5
  pub. health   614.58
  statistics   312.385 53
  other aspects see Mental
    illness
Dysmenorrhea *see* Menstruation
    disorders
Dyspepsia
  gen. med.   616.332
  geriatrics   618.976 332
  pediatrics   618.923 32
  pub. health   614.593 32
  statistics   312.333 2
    deaths   312.263 32
  other aspects see Diseases
Dysprosium
  chemistry
    inorganic   546.417
    organic   547.054 17
    s.a. spec. groupings e.g.
      Aliphatic compounds
  technology   661.041 7
    organic   661.895
    soc. & econ. aspects *see*
      Secondary industries
    s.a. spec. prod.
  eng. materials   620.189 291 7
    s.a. spec. uses
  metallography   669.952 917
  metallurgy   669.291 7
    physical & chem.   669.962 917
  pharmacology   615.241 7
    misc. aspects see
      Pharmacology
  products
    mf. tech.   673.291 7
    other aspects see
      Nonferrous metals
      products
  toxicology   615.925 417
    misc. aspects see
      Toxicology
  other aspects see
    Yttrium-group metals
Dystocia *see* Parturition
    disorders

Dystrophy *see* Muscular
    dystrophy

E

EDP *see* Electronic data
    processing
EEC *see* European Economic
    Community
EFTA *see* European Free Trade
    Association
EPR *see* Paramagnetic resonance
E region
  ionosphere
    geomagnetism   538.767 3
ESP parapsychology   133.8
Eagle Co. Colo.   *area*–788 44
Eagles *see* Accipitridae
Ealing London Eng.   *area*–421 84
Ear training method
  music teaching   780.77
    s.a. spec. mediums
Earby Lancashire Eng.   *area*–427 645
Eardrums *see* Tympanic membranes
Eared seals *see* Otariidae
Earless seals *see* Phocidae
Earlsferry Fife Scot.   *area*–412 92
Early
  Christian
    art
      architecture   723.1
        spec. places   720.9
        other aspects see
          Architectural schools
      design & dec.   745.442
        spec. places   745.449
      gen. wks.   709.02
        spec. places   709.1–.9
      painting   759.02
        spec. places   759.1–.9
      rel. significance   246.2
      sculpture   734.22
        spec. places   730.9
      *s.a. other spec. art
        forms*
    philosophy   189
    s.a. other spec. subj.
  church *see* Apostolic Church
  Co. Ga.   *area*–758 962
  suspension bridges
    structural eng.   624.52
    other aspects see Bridges
      (structures)
  s.a. other spec. subj.
Earmuffs *see* Muffs
Earnings *see* Compensation
Earphones
  comm. eng.
    soc. & econ. aspects *see*
      Secondary industries

Earphones
  comm. eng. (continued)
    tech. & mf. — 621.380 282
    s.a. spec. appls. e.g.
      Receiving sets radio
Earrings
  precious metalwork — 739.278
  other aspects see Jewelry
Ears
  anatomy
    human — 611.85
    other aspects see Sense
      organs
  configurations
    identification of criminals
      see Identification
        criminals
  diseases
    gen. wks. — 617.8
      neoplasms — 616.992 85
      tuberculosis — 616.995 85
    geriatrics — 618.977 8
    pediatrics — 618.920 978
    pub. health — 614.599 8
    statistics — 312.304 78
      deaths — 312.260 478
    surgery — 617.805 9
      anesthesiology — 617.967 8
    other aspects see Diseases
  physical anthropometry — 573.685
  physiology
    human — 612.85
    other aspects see Sensory
      functions
  tissue biology human — 611.018 985
Earth
  age
    geology — 551.7
    nat. rel — 215.5
  astronomy — 525
  currents
    geomagnetism — 538.748
  geography *see* Geography
  haulage
    canal eng. *see* Earthwork
      canal eng.
    road eng. *see* Roadbeds
  magnetism *see* Geomagnetism
  pigments *see* Pigment
    materials
  sciences — 550
    Biblical trmt. — 220.855
    s.a. spec. parts of Bible
    curriculums — 375.55
    documentation — 025.065 5
    libraries — 026.55
      misc. aspects see Special
        libraries
    library acquisitions — 025.275 5
    library classification — 025.465 5
    museums — 069.955

Earth
  sciences (continued)
    subject headings — 025.495 5
    other aspects see Sciences
  structure — 551.1
  temperatures
    meteorology — 551.523
      weather forecasting — 551.642 3
      spec. areas — 551.65
  s.a. Terrestrial
Earthenware
  ceramic arts — 738.3
    processes — 738.1
  manufacturing
    soc. & econ. aspects *see*
      Secondary industries
    technology — 666.6
  rel. significance
    Christianity — 247.883
    comp. rel. — 291.37
    s.a. other spec. rel.
Earth-fill dams
  hydraulic eng.
    soc. & econ. aspects *see*
      Secondary industries
    technology — 627.83
    s.a. spec. appls. eg.
      Military engineering
    other aspects see Liquids
      engineering
Earthquake-resistant construction
  buildings — 693.852
Earthquakes
  deformation
    structural theory — 624.176 2
    spec. elements — 624.177 2–.177 9
    s.a. spec. appls. e.g.
      Roads engineering
  disasters
    soc. action — 363.349 5
    geophysics — 551.22
    other aspects see Disasters
Earthwork
  canal eng.
    technology — 627.132
    s.a. spec. appls. e.g.
      Military engineering
    other aspects see Liquids
      engineering
  dam eng.
    technology — 627.81
    spec. dams — 627.82–.85
    s.a. spec. appls. e.g.
      Military engineering
    other aspects see Liquids
      engineering
  foundation eng. *see*
    Excavation foundation
      eng.
  highway eng.
    technology — 625.73

Earthwork
  highway eng. (continued)
    other aspects see Roads
  mining   622.2
  railroad eng.
    technology   625.12
    other aspects see Permanent
      way
Earthworms *see* Oligochaeta
Earthy
  materials   553.6
    econ. geol.   553.6
    mining
      soc. & econ. aspects *see*
        Primary industries
      technology   622.36
      prospecting   622.186
    s.a. spec. uses e.g.
      Buildings construction
  minerals
    synthetic
      manufacturing
        soc. & econ. aspects
          see Secondary
          industries
        technology   666.86
Earwigs *see* Dermaptera
Easel paintings
  arts   751.72
    indiv. artists   759.1–.9
  s.a. spec. subj., tech.,
    equip.
Easements
  law
    international   341.4
    municipal   346.043 5
      spec. jur.   346.3–.9
Easington Durham Eng.   *area*–428 67
Easingwold North Yorkshire Eng.
           area–428 49
East   *area*–5
  Africa   *area*–676
  Anglia   *area*–426
  Asia   *area*–5
  Asians   *r.e.n.*–95
  Avon River Eng.   *area*–423 19
  Azerbaijan Iran   *area*–553
  Baton Rouge Par. La. *area*–763 18
  Bengal   *area*–549 2
  Berbice Guyana   *area*–881 7
  Berlin Ger.   *area*–431 552
  Cambridgeshire Eng. *area*–426 56
  Cameroon   *area*–671 13
  Carroll Par. La.   *area*–763 82
  China Sea
    oceanography   551.465 57
    regional subj. trmt. *area*–164 57
    other aspects see Pacific
      Ocean
  Coast N.Z.   *area*–931 22
  Demerara Guyana   *area*–881 5

East (continued)
  Dereham Norfolk Eng.   *area*–426 14
  Devon Eng.   *area*–423 57
  European Economic Organization
    international
      commerce   382.914 7
      economics   337.147
      law   341.242
        econ. functions 341.750 61
  Feliciana Par. La.   *area*–763 16
  Flanders Belgium   *area*–493 1
  Friesian cattle
    animal husbandry   636.234
    other aspects see Cattle
  Galicia Ukraine   *area*–477 18
  Germanic
    languages
      linguistics   439.9
      literatures   839.9
      s.a.   *lang.*–399
    s.a. other spec. subj. e.g.
      Arts
  Germany   *area*–431–432
  Grinstead West Sussex Eng.
           area–422 65
  Ham London Eng.   *area*–421 76
  Hampshire Eng.   *area*–422 74
  Hertfordshire Eng.   *area*–425 83
  India Company
    India hist.   954.031
    s.a. spec. events & subj.
      e.g. Commerce
    s.a. Dutch East India
      Company
  Indian *see* Indic
  Indies   *area*–598
  Iranian language *see* Avestan
  Kilbride Strathclyde Scot.
           area–414 54
  Lansing Mich.   *area*–774 27
  Lindsey Lincolnshire Eng. *area*–425 32
  Linton Lothian Scot. *area*–413 6
  Lothian Scot.   *area*–413 6
  Malaysia   *area*–595 3
  Northamptonshire Eng. *area*–425 54
  Pakistan   *area*–549 2
  Prussia   *area*–438 3
  Retford Nottinghamshire Eng.
           area–425 21
  Riding Yorkshire   *area*–428 3
  Scandinavian
    languages
      linguistics   439.7–.8
      literatures   839.7–.8
      s.a.   *lang.*–397–398
    people   *r.e.n.*–397–398
    s.a. other spec. subj. e.g.
      Arts
  Semitic
    languages
      linguistics   492.1

Eastern (continued)
Star
  members
    biog. & work   366.180 92
    s.a.   *pers.*–366 1
  order   366.18
world   *area*–5
s.a. East; *also other spec.*
    subj.
Easthampstead Berkshire Eng.
            area–422 98
Eastland Co. Tex.   *area*–764 547
Eastleigh Hampshire Eng. *area*–422 772
Eastwood
  Nottinghamshire Eng. *area*–425 26
  Strathclyde Scot.   *area*–414 51
Eating
  customs   394.12
Eating-places
  bldgs. aspects *see* Restaurant
    buildings
  cookery   641.572
  financial aspects *see*
    Restaurants
  food services   642.5
  household management 647.95
  sanitation   363.729 6
  law   344.046 4
    spec. jur.   344.3–.9
    pub. admin.   350.772
    central govts.   351.772
      spec. jur.   353–354
    local govts.   352.6
Eaton Co. Mich.   *area*–774 23
Eau Claire
  city Wis.   *area*–775 46
  Co. Wis.   *area*–775 45
Eavesdropping devices
  microelectronics
    soc. & econ. aspects *see*
      Secondary industries
    tech. & mf.   621.381 792
    s.a. spec. appls. e.g.
      Interception of
      communication
  other aspects see Electronics
Ebbw Vale Gwent Wales *area*–429 95
Ebenaceae *see* Ebenales
Ebenaceous fruits
  agriculture   634.45
  soc. & econ. aspects *see*
    Primary industries
  foods   641.344 5
    preparation
      commercial   664.804 45
      domestic   641.644 5
  other aspects see Ebenales;
    also Fruits
Ebenales
  botany   583.685
  floriculture   635.933 685

Ebenales (continued)
  forestry   634.973 685
  med. aspects
    crop prod.   633.883 685
    gen. pharm.   615.323 685
    toxicology   615.952 368 5
    vet. pharm.   636.089 532 368 5
    toxicology   636.089 595 236 85
  paleobotany   561.3
  other aspects see Plants
Ebony family *see* Ebenales
Ebro River Spain   *area*–465
Ebullioscopy *see* Colligative
    properties
Ecaudata *see* Anura
Eccentrics
  machine eng.
    soc. & econ. aspects *see*
      Secondary industries
    tech. & mf.   621.827
    s.a. spec. appls. e.g.
      Cams
  other aspects see Mechanics
Eccles Greater Manchester Eng.
            area–427 32
Eccleshall Staffordshire Eng.
            area–424 64
Ecclesiastes
  Bible   223.8
  other aspects see Poetic
    books (O.T.)
Ecclesiastical
  law *see* Religious law
  theology
    Buddhism   294.365
    Christianity   260
    comp. rel.   291.65
    Islam   297.65
    Judaism   296.67
    s.a. other spec. rel.
  vestments
    rel. significance
      Christianity   247.792
      s.a. other spec. rel.
    other aspects see Symbolic
      garments
  s.a. Religious
Ecclesiasticus
  deuterocanonical book 229.4
  other aspects see Apocrypha
Ecclesiology (architecture) *see*
    Religious-purpose
    bldgs.
Ecclesiology (organization)
  Christianity   262
  other rel. see Ecclesiastical
    theology
Eccrinales *see* Nonflagellate
    molds
Echeneoidea *see* Acanthopterygii

Economic (continued)
  cooperation
    internat. comm.   337.1
    internat. law   341.75
  determinism
    Marxian econ.   335.413
  development
    govt. control *see*
      Production govt.
      control
    internat. banking   332.153
      misc. aspects see Banking
    law
      international   341.759
      municipal   343.074
        spec. jur.   343.3–.9
    prod. econ.   338.9
      internat. organizations   338.883
  effects *see spec. subj.*
  ethics *see* Occupational
      ethics
  factors
    influence on crime   364.2
  fluctuations
    prod. econ.   338.54
  geography   330.91–.99
  geology   553
    misc. aspects see Earth
      sciences
  growth
    macroeconomics   339.5
    prod. econ.   338.9
  history   330.9
    spec. wars *see* Social
      history
  institutions
    sociology   306.3
  integration
    internat. econ.   337.1
  microbiology *see* Economic
      biology
  order
    soc. theology
      Christianity   261.85
      comp. rel.   291.178 5
      s.a. other spec. rel.
  penalties
    penology   364.68
  planning   338.9
    internat. econ.   337
    law   343.075
      spec. jur.   343.3–.9
  rent land econ.   333.012
  resources
    development
      internat. banking   332.153
        misc. aspects see
        Banking
      mil. sci.   355.2
        s.a. spec. mil. branches

Economic (continued)
  rights
    pol. sci.   323.46
  services
    to employees
      personnel admin.
        gen. management   658.383
        executive
          management   658.407 83
        spec. subj.   *s.s.*–068 3
      pub. admin.   350.162
        central govts.   351.162
          spec. jur.   353–354
        local govts.   352.005 162
  situation   330.9
  stabilization
    law   343.034
      spec. jur.   343.3–.9
    macroeconomics   339.5
  welfare powers
    legislative bodies
      law *see* Legislative
        powers law
      pol. sci.   328.341 3
        spec. jur.   328.4–.9
  zoology *see* Economic biology
  s.a. other spec. subj.
Economics   330
  Biblical trmt.   220.833
    s.a. spec. parts of Bible
  curriculums   375.33
  documentation   025.063 3
  forestry   634.92
    s.a. spec. trees
  internat. pol.   327.111
    spec. countries   327.3–.9
  journalism   070.449 33
  libraries   026.33
    misc. aspects see Special
      libraries
  lit. & stage trmt. *see* Social
      themes
  soc. aspects   306.3
  other aspects see Social
      sciences
Economies of scale
  prod. econ.   338.514 4
Economists
  biog. & work   330.092
    s.a. spec. kinds
  s.a.   *pers.*–339
Ecrehous isl.   *area*–423 49
Ecstasy *see* Secondary emotions
Ectocarpales *see* Phaeophyta
Ectoparasitic diseases   616.968
  geriatrics   618.976 968
  pediatrics   618.929 68
  pub. health   614.558
  statistics   312.396 8
    deaths   312.269 68
  other aspects see Diseases

Ectopic pregnancy *see*
     Extrauterine pregnancy
Ectoplasm
  spiritualism   133.92
Ectoprocta *see* Bryozoa
Ector Co. Tex.   *area*–764 862
Ecuador   *area*–866
Ecuadorean
  literature   860
  people   *r.e.n.*–688 66
  s.a. other spec. subj. e.g.
     Arts
Ecumenical
  councils
    Christian church hist.
      Middle Ages   270.2
      modern period 270.82
    Christian ecclesiology 262.5
  movement
    Christian church hist. 270.82
Ecumenicalism
  ecclesiology   262.001 1
Eczema
  gen. med.   616.521
  geriatrics   618.976 521
  pediatrics   618.925 21
  pub. health   614.595 21
  statistics   312.352 1
  other aspects see Diseases
Edam cheeses
  dairy tech.   637.354
  other aspects see Cheeses
Eddy
  County
    New Mexico *area*–789 42
    North Dakota *area*–784 512
  currents
    electrodynamic eng. *see*
      Machinery electrical
  Mary Baker
    Christian Science writings 289.52
Edemas
  symptoms *see* Symptoms of
    disease
Eden
  Cumbria Eng. *area*–427 86
  N.S.W. *area*–944 7
  River Cumbria *area*–427 86
Edentata
  animal husbandry 636.931
  hunting
    commercial 639.113 1
    sports 799.259 31
  paleozoology 569.31
  zoology 599.31
  other aspects see Mammalia
Edeyrnion Clwyd Wales *area*–429 37
Edgar
  Co. Ill. *area*–773 69

Edgar (continued)
  reign Eng. hist. 942.017 3
  s.a. spec. events & subj.
    e.g. Commerce
Edgecombe Co. N.C. *area*–756 46
Edged weapons
  art metalwork 739.72
  customs 399
  mil. eng. 623.441
Edgefield Co. S.C. *area*–757 37
Edgers *see spec. uses e.g.*
  Sawmill operations
Edgings
  plants grown for
    floriculture 635.963
    s.a. spec. plants
Edible
  bulbs
    agriculture 635.2
    soc. & econ. aspects *see*
      Primary industries
    foods 641.352
    preparation
      commercial 664.805 2
      domestic 641.652
    other aspects see
      Vegetables
  flowers
    agriculture 635.3–.5
    soc. & econ. aspects *see*
      Primary industries
    foods 641.353–.355
    preparation
      commercial 664.805 3–.805 5
      domestic 641.653–.655
    other aspects see
      Vegetables
  fruits
    agriculture 635.6
    soc. & econ. aspects *see*
      Primary industries
    foods 641.356
    preparation
      commercial 664.805 6
      domestic 641.656
    other aspects see
      Vegetables
  leaves
    agriculture 635.3–.5
    soc. & econ. aspects *see*
      Primary industries
    foods 641.353–.355
    preparation
      commercial 664.805 3–.805 5
      domestic 641.653–.655
    other aspects see
      Vegetables
  oysters
    culture 639.411
    other aspects see Oysters

Edible (continued)	
plants	
botany	581.632
s.a. spec. plants	
roots *see* Root crops	
seeds	
agriculture	635.6
soc. & econ. aspects *see*	
Primary industries	
foods	641.356
preparation	
commercial	664.805 6
domestic	641.656
other aspects see	
Vegetables	
stems	
agriculture	635.3–.5
soc. & econ. aspects *see*	
Primary industries	
foods	641.353–.355
preparation	
commercial	664.805 3–.805 5
domestic	641.653–.655
other aspects see	
Vegetables	
tubers *see* Tuber crops	
Edinburgh Scot.	*area*–413 4
Edirne Turkey	*area*–563
Edisto Isl. S.C.	*area*–757 99
Editing	
films cinematography	778.535
journalism	070.41
manuscripts	808.02
Edition bookbinding	
soc. & econ. aspects *see*	
Secondary industries	
technology	686.303 4
s.a. spec. operations &	
materials	
Editorial	
policy	
journalism	070.412
techniques *see* Editing	
Editorials	
journalism	070.442
spec. subj.	070.449
Edmonson Co. Ky.	*area*–769 752
Edmonton	
Alberta	*area*–712 33
London Eng.	*area*–421 89
Edmund	
reign Eng. hist.	
1	942.017 2
2	942.017 4
s.a. spec. events & subj.	
e.g. Commerce	
Edmunds Co. S.D.	*area*–783 15
Edo period Japan	
history	952.025
s.a. spec. events & subj.	
e.g. Courts	

Edom	*area*–394 6
Edred	
reign Eng. hist.	942.017 2
s.a. spec. events & subj.	
e.g. Commerce	
Educable retarded persons	
child psych.	155.452 82
child rearing home econ.	649.152 82
education	371.928 2
law	344.079 128 2
spec. jur.	344.3–.9
Education	370
Biblical trmt.	220.837
s.a. spec. parts of Bible	
child care at home	649.68
curriculums	375.37
depts. pub. admin.	350.085 1
central govts.	351.085 1
spec. jur.	353–354
local govts.	352.945 1
documentation	025.063 7
ethical systems	171.7
applications	172–179
govt. control	379
activities	350.851
central govts.	351.851
spec. jur.	353–354
local govts.	352.945 1
govt. depts. *see* Education	
depts.	
journalism	070.449 37
law	344.07
spec. jur.	344.3–.9
libraries	026.37
misc. aspects see Special	
libraries	
library acquisitions	025.273 7
library classification	025.463 7
of employees	
personnel admin.	
gen. management	658.312 4
executives	658.407 124
spec. subj.	*s.s.*–068 3
pub. admin.	350.15
central govts.	351.15
spec. jur.	353–354
local govts.	352.005 15
of veterans	
mil. sci.	355.155 2
penal institutions	365.66
law	344.035 66
spec. jur.	344.3–.9
pub. admin. ethics *see* Public	
administration ethics	
religion *see* Religious	
instruction	
rel. role in *see* Society soc.	
theology	
spec. subj.	
elementary	372.3–.8
other levels	*s.s.*–071

Education (continued)

subject headings	025.493 7
topics journalism	070.444
other aspects see Disciplines (systems)	
s.a. Training	

Educational

administration	371.2
s.a. spec. levels of ed.; *also* Special education	
areas	
civic art	711.57
assistance	370.196 5
buildings	
air-conditioning	697.937
architecture	727
building	690.7
care	647.99
interior decoration	747.87
lighting	
exterior	621.322 9
interior	621.322 7
exchanges	
gen. wks.	
students	370.196 2
teachers	370.196 3
higher ed.	
students	378.35
law	
international	341.767
municipal	344.08
spec. jur.	344.3–.9
factors	
mental pub. health	362.204 2
s.a. other spec. subj.	
films	
performing arts	791.435 3
guidance *see* Intellectual guidance	
institutions	
libraries for	027.7–.8
administration	025.197 7–.197 8
buildings	
architecture	727.827–.828
building	690.782 7–.782 8
functional planning	022.317–.318
other aspects see Educational buildings	
catalogs *see* Library catalogs	
reference services	025.527 77–.527 78
selection for	025.218 77–.218 78
use studies	025.587 7–.587 8
user orientation	025.567 7–.567 8
s.a. other spec. activities e.g. Cataloging	
level	
population statistics	312.9
programs	
radio performances	791.445

Educational

programs (continued)	
television performances	791.455
psychology	370.15
quotient *see* Academic prognosis	
relations	
internat. law	341.767
requirements	
employees *see* Occupational requirements	
voting *see* Voting qualifications	
s.a. other spec. groups	
role	
libraries	021.24
s.a. other spec. enterprises	
services	
museology	069.1
s.a. other spec. enterprises	
sociology	370.193
therapy	615.851 6
s.a. spec. diseases	
toys	
mf. tech.	688.725
other aspects see Toys	
s.a. School; *also* Academic; *also other spec. subj.*	

Education-school bldgs.

architecture	727.437
building	690.743 7
other aspects see Educational buildings	

Educators

biog. & work	370.92
s.a. spec. levels of ed.	
occupational ethics	174.937
s.a.	*pers.–37*

Edward

Lake Congo	*area–675 17*
reign	
Eng. hist.	
1	942.035
2	942.036
3	942.037
4	942.044
5	942.045
6	942.053
7	942.082
8	942.084
Confessor	942.019
Elder	942.016 5
Martyr	942.017 3
Gt. Brit. hist.	
1	941.035
2	941.036
3	941.037
4	941.044

Edward
  reign
    Gt. Brit. hist. (continued)
      5   941.045
      6   941.053
      7   941.082
      8   941.084
      Confessor   941.019
      Elder   941.016 5
      Martyr   941.017 3
    Scotland hist.
      7   941.108 2
      8   941.108 4
    s.a. spec. events & subj.
      e.g. Commerce
  River N.S.W.   *area*–944 8
Edwards
  County
    Illinois   *area*–773 791
    Kansas   *area*–781 782
    Texas   *area*–764 882
    Plateau Tex.   *area*–764 87
Edwy
  reign Eng. hist.   942.017 2
  s.a. spec. events & subj.
    e.g. Commerce
Eels *see* Apodes
Eelworms *see* Nematoda
Effect
  metaphysics   122
  s.a. other spec. subj.
Efficiency
  employees
    personnel admin.
      gen. management   658.314
      executives   658.407 14
      spec. subj.   *s.s.*–068 3
    pub. admin.   350.147
      central govts.   351.147
        spec. jur.   353–354
      local govts.   352.005 147
  engineering for   620.8
  s.a. spec. appls. e.g.
    Aerospace engineering
  prod. econ.   338.06
    highways
      commerce   388.11
    primary ind.
      agriculture   338.16
      mineral ind.   338.26
      other   338.3
    secondary ind.   338.45
      communication   380.3
        gen. telecommun.   384.041
        postal   383.24
        telegraphy   384.13
          submarine cable   384.43
          wire   384.13
          wireless   384.523
        telephony   384.63
          wire   384.63

Efficiency
  prod. econ.
    secondary ind.
      communication
        telephony (continued)
          wireless   384.533
      transportation   380.59
        air   387.71
        inland waterway   386.1
        maritime   387.51
        motor   388.32
        railway   385.1
          special-duty   385.5
        urban transp.   388.404 2
    prod. management   658.515
    spec. subj.   *s.s.*–068 5
    s.a. other spec. subj.
Effingham Co.
  Georgia   *area*–758 722
  Illinois   *area*–773 796
Effluvium *see* Air pollution
Egadi Isls. Sicily   *area*–458 24
Egbert
  reign Eng. hist.   942.016 1
  s.a. spec. events & subj.
    e.g. Commerce
Egg cells
  gametogenesis *see*
    Gametogenesis
  histogenesis *see* Histogensis
Egg Highland Scot.   *area*–411 85
Eggplants
  agriculture   635.646
    soc. & econ. aspects *see*
      Primary industries
  foods   641.356 46
    preparation
      commercial   664.805 646
      domestic   641.656 46
    other aspects see Solanales;
      also Vegetables
Eggs
  animal husbandry for   636.088 42
    s.a. spec. animals
  biology *see* Embryology
  decorating   745.594 4
  feeds
    animal husbandry   636.087 6
    s.a. spec. animals
  other aspects see Poultry
    products
Egham Surrey Eng.   *area*–422 11
Ego
  depth psych.   154.22
    animals   156.4
Egoism
  ethical systems   171.9
    applications   172–179
Egrets *see* Ciconiiformes
Egypt   *area*–62
  ancient   *area*–32

Elasticity	
crystals	548.842
s.a. spec. substances	
earth's crust	
geophysics	551.14
eng. materials	620.112 32
spec. properties	620.112 5–.112 6
spec. stresses	620.112 4
s.a. spec. materials & spec.	
uses	
flow fluid mech.	
engineering *see* Dynamics	
physics	532.053 5
gases	533.28
air	533.628
liquids	532.58
muscles	
human phys.	612.741
other aspects see Movements	
solid dynamics	
engineering *see* Dynamics	
physics	531.382 3
Elastomer technology	
instr. & machinery	
manufacturing	
soc. & econ. aspects *see*	
Secondary industries	
technology	681.766 8
s.a. spec. kinds	
Elastomers	
eng. materials	620.194
foundations	624.153 94
naval design	623.818 94
structures	624.189 4
s.a. other spec. uses	
manufacturing	
soc. & econ. aspects *see*	
Secondary industries	
technology	678
org. chem.	547.842
Elastoplastics	
manufacturing	
soc. & econ. aspects *see*	
Secondary industries	
technology	678.73
org. chem.	547.842 73
Elateroidea	
agric. pests	632.765
s.a. spec. types of culture	
e.g. Forestry; *also*	
spec. crops	
culture	638.576 5
paleozoology	565.76
zoology	595.765
other aspects see Insecta	
Elatinaceae *see* Caryophyllales	
Elazig Turkey	*area*–566 7
Elba Italy	*area*–455 6
Elbert Co.	
Colorado	*area*–788 87
Georgia	*area*–758 163

Elblag Poland	*area*–438 2
Elbows	
diseases	
regional med. trmt.	617.574
s.a. spec. systems &	
organs	
surgery	617.574
anesthesiology	617.967 574
other aspects see Diseases	
fractures	617.157
orthopedic surgery	617.397
Elcho Isl. N. Ter. Aust.	*area*–942 95
Elderberries	
agriculture	634.74
soc. & econ. aspects *see*	
Primary industries	
foods	641.347 4
preparation	
commercial	664.804 74
domestic	641.647 4
other aspects see Rubiales;	
also Fruits	
Elderly people *see* Aged people	
Elders (religion) *see* Clergy	
Eldon Range Tas.	*area*–946 6
El Dorado Co. Calif.	*area*–794 41
Eleatic philosophy	182.3
Elected officials	
lists	
pub. admin.	350.22
central govts.	351.22
spec. jur.	353–354
local govts.	352.005 2
Election	
districts	
legislative representation	
law *see* Representation	
law	
pol. sci.	328.334 5
spec. jur.	328.4–.9
law	342.07
spec. jur.	342.3–.9
officials	324.65
procedures	
law	342.075
spec. jur.	342.3–.9
pol. sci.	324.6
rel. doctrines *see*	
Eschatology rel.	
doctrines	
returns	324.9
soteriology	
Christianity	234
Judaism	296.3ll
other rel. see Eschatology	
rel. doctrines	
Elections	
labor unions	
labor econ.	331.874
pol. sci.	324.6
history	324.9

Electric
  lighting
    shipbuilding (continued)
      technology   623.852
        design   623.814 52
        spec. craft   623.812
    other aspects see Lighting
  locomotives
    commerce   385.363
      special-duty   385.5
    engineering
      technology
        gen. wks.   625.263
          accessory equip. 625.25
          running gear   625.21
          monorail   625.28
      other aspects see Rolling
        stock railroads
  megaphone systems *see*
    Public-address systems
  motors
    soc. & econ. aspects *see*
      Secondary industries
    tech. & mf.   621.462
    s.a. spec. appls. e.g.
      Elevators (lifts)
  portable heaters
    bldg. heating   697.24
  potentials
    electrostatics
      astrophysics   523.018 721
      s.a. spec. celestial
        bodies
      physics   537.21
        spec. states of matter 530.4
    measurement
      technology   621.374 3
      s.a. spec. appls. e.g.
        Ignition systems &
        devices
      other aspects see
        Electricity
  power
    civic planning   711.8
    distribution *see*
      Transmission elect.
      power
    failure *see* Transmission
      elect. power
    generation *see* Generation
      elect. power
    govt. control   350.872 2
      central govts.   351.872 2
      spec. jur.   353–354
      local govts.   352.912 2
    law   343.092 9
      spec. jur.   343.3–.9
    lines maintenance
      forest management 634.93
      s.a. spec. trees

Electric
  power (continued)
    measurement
      technology   621.374 6
      s.a. spec. appls. e.g.
      Electric lighting
      other aspects see
      Electricity
    mining eng.   622.48
    soc. services   363.62
    supply *see* Utilities
    transmission *see*
      Transmission elect.
      power
    utilization
      economics   333.793 2
      govt. control
        law   346.046 793 2
        spec. jur.   346.3–.9
      pub. admin. *see* Natural
      resources govt. control
      pub. admin.
    other aspects see Power
  propulsion
    gen. wks.
      soc. & econ. aspects *see*
      Secondary industries
      technology   621.46
    spacecraft eng.   629.475 5
      unmanned   629.465 5
      other aspects see
      Spacecraft
    s.a. other spec. appls.
      e.g. Electric
      locomotives
  radiant panel heating
    buildings   697.72
    s.a. other spec. uses
  railroads
    electrification   621.33
    gen. wks. *see* Railroads
    local
      technology   625.6
      other aspects see
      Railroads
  shavers
    manufacturing
      soc. & econ. aspects *see*
      Secondary industries
      technology   688.5
  shock therapy
    psychiatry   616.891 22
    geriatrics   618.976 891 22
    pediatrics   618.928 912 2
    other aspects see Medical
      sciences
  signs
    advertising operations 659.136
  slow cookery   641.588 4

Electric (continued)
  submarines *see*
      Electric-powered
      submarines
  supply meters *see* Energy
      elect. measurement
  welding metal prod.
    mf. tech.   671.521
      ferrous metals   672.521
      s.a. other spec. metals
    other aspects see Welding
  s.a. Electrical; *also other*
      spec. subj.
Electrical
  analysis *see* Electrical
      methods
  apparatus
    chemistry   542.8
      s.a. spec. appls. e.g.
        Organic chemistry
    s.a. other spec. subj.
  appliances
    mf. tech.   683.83
      other aspects see Household
        appliances
    s.a. spec. kinds
  communication
    technology   621.380 412
      s.a. spec. appls. e.g.
        Military engineering
      other aspects see
        Communication
    s.a. spec. kinds e.g.
        Public-address systems
  diagnosis med. sci.
    gen. med.   616.075 4
      surgery   617.075 4
      s.a. spec. diseases
    other aspects see Diseases
  engineering
    gen. wks.
      soc. & econ. aspects *see*
        Secondary industries
      technology   621.3
      military   623.76
    s.a. other spec. appls.
  engineers
    biog. & work   621.309 2
      s.a. spec. kinds e.g.
        lighting engineers
        621.322 092
    s.a.   pers.–621 3
  equipment
    pub. safety   363.189
      misc. aspects see
        Hazardous machinery
    technology *see spec. uses*
  household appliances *see*
      Electrical appliances

Electrical (continued)
  injuries
    statistics   312.304 712 2
      deaths   312.260 471 22
    surgery   617.122
      anesthesiology   617.967 122
    s.a. Veterinary sciences
  installations
    local govt. control   352.923
  measurements *see* Measurement
      elect. eng.
  methods
    anal. chem.
      gen. wks.   543.087 1
      qualitative   544.971
      quantitative   545.31
      organic   547.308 71
      qualitative   547.349 71
      quantitative   547.353 1
      s.a. spec. elements &
        cpds.
    geophysical prospecting   622.154
    s.a. other spec. activities
  properties
    spec. substances *see*
        Electromagentic
        properties
  resistance thermometry
    astrophysics   523.013 53
      s.a. spec. celestial
        bodies
    physics   536.53
      spec. states of matter   530.4
  separation
    ores
      mining eng.   622.77
      spec. ores   622.33–.39
    s.a. other spec. subj.
  storms *see* Thermal convective
      storms
  systems
    aircraft eng.   629.135 4
    internal combustion engines
        see Ignition systems
        & devices
    shipbuilding
      soc. & econ. aspects *see*
        Secondary industries
      technology   623.850 3
      design   623.814 503
      spec. craft   623.812
      s.a. spec. systems
    s.a. other spec. appls
  toys
    manufacturing
      soc. & econ. aspects *see*
        Secondary industries
      technology   688.728
  s.a. Electric; *also other*
      spec. subj.

Electricity
  astrophysics   523.018 7
    s.a. spec. celestial bodies
  biophysics
    extraterrestrial
      gen. wks.   574.191 97
        animals   591.191 97
        microorganisms   576.119 197
        plants   591.191 97
      s.a. spec. organisms
      med. sci.   612.014 57
        animals   636.089 201 457
        s.a. spec. animals
        man   612.014 57
    terrestrial
      gen. wks   574.191 7
        animals   591.191 7
        microorganisms   576.119 17
        plants   581.191 7
      s.a. spec. organisms
      med. sci.   612.014 42
        animals   636.089 201 442
        s.a. spec. animals
        man   612.014 42
  s.a. spec. functions,
    systems, organs
  engineering *see* Electrical
    engineering
  meteorology *see* Atmospheric
    electricity meteorology
  physics   537
    spec. states of matter   530.4
  s.a. Electric power
Electric-power
  plants
    automobiles
      soc. & econ. aspects *see*
        Secondary industries
      tech. & mf.   629.250 2
        parts & systems   629.259 3
      s.a. other spec. appls.
    systems
      spacecraft eng.   629.474 45
      unmanned   629.464 43
      other aspects see
        Spacecraft
      s.a. other spec. appls.
Electric-powered
  automobiles
    commerce   388.34
    engineering
      gen. tech. & mf.   629.229 3
        maintenance   629.287 93
        models   629.221 93
        operation   629.284 93
      s.a. other spec. aspects
      e.g. Brakes; *also*
      spec. appls. e.g.
        Driving motor vehicles
    soc. & econ. aspects *see*
      Secondary industries

Electric-powered
  automobiles (continued)
    other aspects see Land
      vehicles
  submarines
    engineering   633.825 72
    design   623.812 572
    models   623.820 157 2
    naval forces
      materiel   359.83
      organization   359.325 72
    seamanship   623.882 572
    other aspects see Vessels
      (nautical)
Electrification
  soc. & econ. aspects *see*
    Secondary industries
  technology   621.394
  s.a. spec. appls. e.g.
    Railroads
    electrification
Electroacoustical communication
    see Electrical
      communication
Electroanalysis *see* Electrical
    methods
Electrocapillarity
  astrophysics   523.018 724 5
    s.a. spec. celestial bodies
  physics   537.245
    spec. states of matter   530.4
Electrocardiography
  med. sci.   616.120 754 7
Electrochemistry
  applied *see* Applied
    electrochemistry
  physical chem.   541.372–.377
    applied   660.297 2–.297 7
    organic   547.137 2–.137 7
    s.a. spec. elements, cpds.,
      prod.
Electroconvulsive therapy *see*
    Electric shock therapy
Electrocution
  gen. wks. *see* Deaths
  punishment *see* Capital
    punishment
Electrodeposited
  latex prod.
    manufacturing
      soc. & econ. aspects *see*
        Secondary industries
      technology   678.538
    s.a. spec. kinds of latexes
      e.g. Natural latexes
  rubber prod.
    manufacturing
      soc. & econ. aspects *see*
        Secondary industries
      technology   678.36

Relative Index

Electrodeposited
rubber prod. (continued)
s.a. spec. kinds of rubber
e.g. Natural rubber
Electrodeposition
anal. chem. *see* Coulometric
methods
latex mf.
soc. & econ. aspects *see*
Secondary industries
technology ... 678.527
s.a. spec. kinds of latexes
e.g. Natural latexes
s.a. other spec. appls.
Electrodes
elect. lighting *see* Electric
lighting
electrolytic solutions
physical chem. ... 541.372 4
applied ... 660.297 24
organic ... 547.137 24
s.a. spec. elements,
cpds., prod.
Electrodiagnosis med. sci. *see*
Electrical diagnosis
med. sci.
Electrodialysis
saline water conversion
technology ... 628.167 42
other aspects see Water
supply engineering
Electrodynamics
astrophysics ... 523.018 76
s.a. spec. celestial bodies
engineering
soc. & econ. aspects *see*
Secondary industries
technology ... 621.31
s.a. spec. appls. e.g.
Electric engines
physics ... 537.6
spec. states of matter ... 530.4
Electrodynamometers *see*
Electric power
measurement
Electroencephalography
med. sci. ... 616.804 754 7
Electroforming
metal prod.
manufacturing
soc. & econ. aspects *see*
Secondary industries
technology ... 671.4
ferrous metals ... 672.4
s.a. other spec. metals
s.a. other spec. appls.
Electrolysis
physical chem. *see*
Electrolytic solutions
saline water conversion
technology ... 628.167 3

Electrolysis
saline water conversion (continued)
other aspects see Water
supply engineering
Electrolyte
conductivity *see* Electrolytic
solutions
Electrolytic
casting
metal sculpture
fine arts tech. ... 731.457
other aspects see Casting
sculpture
converters *see* Rectifiers
dissociation *see* Ionization
electrolytic solutions
solutions
physical chem. ... 541.372
applied ... 660.297 2
organic ... 547.137 2
s.a. spec. elements,
cpds., prod.
Electromagnetic
analysis *see* Electromagnetic
methods
engineering
soc. & econ. aspects *see*
Secondary industries
technology ... 621.34
s.a. spec. appls. e.g.
Electric motors
engineers
biog. & work ... 621.340 92
s.a. ... pers.–621 3
furnaces
elect. eng.
soc. & econ. aspects *see*
Secondary industries
tech. & mf. ... 621.396
s.a. spec. appls. e.g.
Heat treatment
methods
anal. chem.
gen. wks. ... 543.087
qualitative ... 544.97
quantitative ... 545.3
organic ... 547.308 7
qualitative ... 547.349 7
quantitative ... 547.353
s.a. spec. elements &
cpds.
phenomena
celestial bodies
Jupiter ... 523.452
Mars ... 523.432
Mercury ... 523.412
moon ... 523.32
Neptune ... 523.481 2
Pluto ... 523.482 2
Saturn ... 523.462

343

Electromagnetic
 phenomena
  celestial bodies (continued)
   stars | 523.82
    spec. systems | 523.84–.85
   sun | 523.72
   Uranus | 523.472
   Venus | 523.422
   s.a. other spec. bodies
   s.a. other spec. subj.
  properties
   crystals | 548.85
    s.a. spec. substances
   eng. materials | 620.112 97
    s.a. spec. materials &
     spec. uses
   minerals | 549.127
   spec. minerals | 549.2–.7
  radiations *see* Radiations
  theory
   gen. wks.
    physics | 530.141
     spec. states of matter | 530.4
     s.a. spec. branches of
      physics
   light
    astrophysics | 523.015 14
     s.a. spec. celestial
      bodies
    physics | 535.14
     spec. states of matter | 530.4
  s.a. Magnetic
Electromagnets
 generators
  electrodynamic eng.
   soc. & econ. aspects *see*
    Secondary industries
   tech. & mf. | 621.316
    s.a. spec. appls. e.g.
     Electric motors
   other aspects see
    Electrodynamics
  other aspects see Temporary
   magnets
Electrometallurgy
 soc. & econ. aspects *see*
  Secondary industries
 technology | 669.028 4
 s.a. spec. metals
Electrometers *see* Electric
  potentials measurement
Electron
 ballistics *see* Ionization of
  gases electronics
 magnetic resonance *see*
  Paramagnetic resonance
 metallography | 669.950 282
  s.a. spec. metals
 microscopes
  physics | 535.332 5
   spec. states of matter | 530.4

Electron
 microscopes (continued)
  use
   biology | 578.45
   chem. anal. *see*
    Microscopic analysis
   gen. sci. | 502.825
   s.a. other spec. uses
 optics
  astrophysics | 523.018 756
   s.a. spec. celestial
    bodies
  physics | 537.56
   spec. states of matter | 530.4
 paramagnetic resonance *see*
  Paramagnetic resonance
 spin resonance *see*
  Paramagnetic resonance
 theory of metals *see* Solids
Electronic
 aids
  geonavigation
   seamanship | 623.893
   other aspects see
    Navigation
  s.a. other spec.subj.
 apparatus
  chemistry | 542.8
   s.a. spec. appls. e.g.
    Organic chemistry
  s.a. other spec. subj.
 audiocommunication | 001.554 4
  misc. aspects see
   Electronic
    communication
 chess players
  engineering | 621.381 9
  recreation | 794.17
 command systems
  aeronautics
   soc. & econ. aspects *see*
    Secondary industries
   technology | 629.132 6
  communication
   technology | 621.380 413
    s.a. spec. appls. e.g.
     Military engineering
   other aspects see
    Communication
   s.a. spec. kinds e.g. Radio
 control
  automation eng. | 629.804 3
   s.a. spec. appls. e.g.
    Machine tools; *also*
    spec. systems e.g.
     Closed-loop systems
   s.a. other spec. appls.
  converters *see* Rectifiers
  data processing | 001.64
   s.a. | *s.s.*–028 54

Electrostatic photoduplication
soc. & econ. aspects *see*
Secondary industries
technology — 686.44
Electrostatics
astrophysics — 523.018 72
s.a. spec. celestial bodies
engineering
soc. & econ. aspects *see*
Secondary industries
technology — 621.312 6
physics — 537.2
spec. states of matter — 530.4
Electrostriction
astrophysics — 523.018 724 6
s.a. spec. celestial bodies
physics — 537.246
spec. states of matter — 530.4
Electrotherapy — 615.845
misc. aspects see Physical
therapies
s.a. spec. diseases
Electrotypes
printing *see* Plates mech.
printing tech.
Electuaries
vet. pharm. — 636.089 54
Elegiac poetry *see* Lyric poetry
Elementary
education — 372
law — 344.074
spec. jur. — 344.3–.9
number theory — 512.72
s.a. spec. appls. e.g.
Engineering
school
buildings
architecture — 727.1
building — 690.71
other aspects see
Educational buildings
libraries — 027.822 2
administration — 025.197 822 2
buildings
architecture — 727.828 222
functional planning — 022.318 222
catalogs *see* Library
catalogs
geog. trmt. — 027.823–.829
reference studies — 025.527 782 22
selection for — 025.218 782 22
use studies — 025.587 822 2
user orientation — 025.567 822 2
s.a. other spec.
activities e.g.
Cataloging
teachers
prof. ed. — 370.712 2
schools & courses — 370.732 62

Elementary (continued)
schools — 372.1
finance
law — 344.976 82
spec. jur. — 344.3–.9
s.a. other spec. subj.
Elements (chemistry)
chemistry — 546
mineralogy — 549.2
Elements (meteorology) — 551.5
Elephant
Butte Res. N.M. — *area*–789 62
fish *see* Chimaerae
seas *see* Phocidae
Elephantiasis *see* Filarial
diseases
Elephants *see* Proboscidea
Eleuthera Isl. Bahamas — *area*–729 6
Eleutherozoa *see* Echinodermata
Elevated railways
commerce — 388.44
govt.control — 350.878 44
central govts. — 351.878 44
spec. jur. — 353–354
local govts. — 352.918 44
law *see* Local railways law
technology — 625.44
other aspects see Railroads
Elevated-railway stations *see*
Railroad terminals
Elevations (architecture) *see*
Vertical plane
Elevations (physiography)
geomorphology — 551.43
ocean floor — 551.460 84
s.a. spec. bodies of water
regional subj. trmt. — *area*–143
other aspects see
Physiographic regions
Elevator liability insurance — 368.56
misc. aspects see Insurance
Elevators (aircraft)
engineering
soc. & econ. aspects *see*
Secondary industries
tech. & mf. — 629.134 33
Elevators (grain)
agriculture — 631.23
s.a. spec. crops
Elevators (lifts)
building element
architectural
construction — 721.833
design & decoration — 729.39
building — 690.183 3
s.a. spec. kinds of bldgs.
machine eng.
soc. & econ. aspects *see*
Secondary industries
tech. & mf. — 621.877
mining eng. — 622.68

Elevators (lifts)
  tech. & mf. (continued)
    s.a. other spec. appls.
  other aspects see Mechanics
Elevenses
  cookery for
    home econ.   641.53
  soc. customs   394.15
Eleventh century
  history   909.1
  applications to spec. subj.
                  s.s.–090 21
  s.a. spec. countries
Elgin
  Co. Ont.   *area*–713 34
  earl 8th governorship India
    hist.   954.035 1
    s.a. spec. events & subj.
      e.g. Commerce
  earl 9th governorship India
    hist.   954.035 5
    s.a. spec. events & subj.
      e.g. Commerce
  Grampian Scot.   *area*–412 23
Elian philosophy   183.7
Elie & Earlsferry Fife Scot.
                area–412 92
Elis Greece   *area*–495 2
  ancient   *area*–388
Elite classes *see* Upper classes
Elitist systems
  pol. sci.   321.5
  s.a. spec. jurisdictions
Elixirs
  prac. pharm.   615.42
  misc. aspects see
      Pharmacology
Elizabeth
  city N.J.   *area*–749 37
  empress of Russia
    history   947.062
    s.a. spec. events & subj.
      e.g. Commerce
  Isls. Mass.   *area*–744 94
  queen
    1
      Eng. hist.   942.055
      Gt. Brit. hist.   941.055
      persecutions of Catholics
        Cristian church hist.   272.7
    2
      Eng. hist   942.085
      Gt. Brit. hist.   941.085
      Scot. hist.   941.108 5
    s.a. spec. events & subj.
      e.g. Commerce
Elizabeth City Co. Va.   *area*–755 412
Elizabethan
  architecture   724.1
  spec. places   720.9

Elizabethan
  architecture (continued)
    other aspects see
      Architectural schools
  s.a. other spec. subj.
Elk
  County
    Kansas   *area*–781 915
    Pennsylvania   *area*–748 65
    Mts. Colo.   *area*–788 41
  River
    Maryland   *area*–752 38
    West Virginia   *area*–754 6
Elkhart Co. Ind.   *area*–772 81
Elkhorn River Neb.   *area*–782 5
Elko Co. Nev.   *area*–793 16
Elks (animals)
  animal husbandry   636.294
  other aspects see Cervoidea
Elks (order)   366.5
  members
    biog. & work   366.509 2
    s.a.   *pers.*–366 5
Elland West Yorkshire Eng.
                area–428 12
Ellenborough governorship India
    hist.   954.031 5
  s.a. spec. events & subj.
      e.g. Commerce
Ellesmere
  Isl. Northwest Ter.   *area*–719 5
  Port and Neston Cheshire Eng.
                area–427 17
  Salop Eng.   *area*–424 53
Ellice Isls.   *area*–968 1
Elliott
  Co. Ky.   *area*–769 255
  Key Fla.   *area*–759 38
Ellipses *see* Configurations
      geometry
Ellipsoids *see* Configurations
      geometry
Elliptic
  equations   515.353
    s.a. spec. appls. e.g.
      Engineering
  functions   515.983
    s.a. spec. appls. e.g.
      Engineering
Ellis Co.
  Kansas   *area*–781 19
  Oklahoma   *area*–766 155
  Texas   *area*–764 281 5
Ellon Grampian Scot.   *area*–412 32
Ellsworth
  Co. Kan.   *area*–781 535
  Land Antarctica   *area*–989
Elm
  family *see* Urticales

Elm (continued)
trees
  forestry   634.972 8
  soc. & econ. aspects *see*
    Primary industries
  other aspects see Trees
  woods *see* Hardwoods
Elmbridge Surrey Eng.   *area*–422 145
Elmira N.Y.   *area*–747 79
Elmore Co.
  Alabama   *area*–761 52
  Idaho   *area*–796 29
Elocution *see* Speaking
El Oro Ecuador   *area*–866 31
El Paraíso Honduras   *area*–728 34
El Paso Co.
  Colorado   *area*–788 56
  Texas   *area*–764 96
El Progreso Guatemala   *area*–728 153
El Salvador   *area*–728 4
El Seibo Dominican Republic
     area–729 384
Elstree Hertfordshire Eng.   *area*–425 895
Elves
  lit. & stage trmt. *see*
    Supernatural beings
Ely
  city Eng.   *area*–426 56
  Isle Eng.   *area*–426 53
Emaciation
  deficiency disease
    gen. med.   616.396
    geriatrics   618.976 396
    pediatrics   618.923 96
    pub. health   614.593 96
    statistics   312.339 6
    deaths   312.263 96
  other aspects see Diseases
Emancipation
  pol. sci.   326
  Proclamation
    U.S. Civil War result   973.714
Emanuel Co. Ga.   *area*–758 684
Embalming
  death customs   393.3
  preparation tech.
    biol. specimens   579.2
  other aspects see Dead bodies
    disposal
Embankments
  canal eng. *see* Earthwork
    canal eng.
  road eng. *see* Roadbeds
  structural eng.   624.162
  other aspects see Shorelands
  s.a. other spec. appls.
Embargoes
  internat. comm.   383.53
  other aspects see Import
    trade
  internat. law   341.58

Embassies
  pub. admin.
    activities   351.892
    spec. jur.   353–354
    departments *see* Foreign
      affairs pub. admin.
      departments
Embassy buildings *see* Official
    residence buildings
Embellishment (music)
  music theory   781.67
  s.a. spec. mediums
Ember Days
  devotional lit.   242.37
  rel. observance   263.97
  Roman Catholic liturgy   264.027 2
  sermons   252.67
Embezzlement *see* Larceny
Embiodea *see* Embioptera
Embioptera
  culture   638.573 7
  paleozoology   565.73
  zoology   595.737
  other aspects see Insecta
Emblems
  rel. significance
    Christianity   246.55
    other rel. see Arts rel.
      significance
Embolisms
  arteries
    gen. med.   616.135
    geriatrics   618.976 135
    pediatrics   618.921 35
    pub. health   614.591 35
    statistics   312.313 5
    deaths   312.261 35
    other aspects see Diseases
  veins
    gen. med.   616.145
    geriatrics   618.976 145
    pediatrics   618.921 45
    pub. health   614.591 45
    statistics   312.314 5
    deaths   312.261 45
    other aspects see Diseases
Embossing
  nat. leathers
    manufacturing
      soc. & econ. aspects *see*
        Secondary industries
      technology   675.25
  s.a. other spec. techs.
Embrithopoda
  paleozoology   569.6
Embroidered rugs
  textile arts   756.74
Embroidery
  machine *see* Machine
    embroidery

Embroidery (continued)
  textile arts   746.44
    s.a. spec. products
Embryo
  development
    human phys.   612.646
    other aspects see
      Development (biology)
Embryological genetics *see*
    Physiological genetics
Embryology
  life sci.
    gen. wks.   574.33
      animals   591.33
      microorganisms   576.133
      plants   591.33
      s.a. spec. organisms
    med. sci.   612.64
      animals   636.089 264
      s.a. spec. animals
      man   612.64
Embryotomy
  obstetrical surgery   618.83
  vet. med.   636.089 883
    s.a. spec. animals
Emerald Qld.   *area*–943 5
Emeralds   553.86
  econ. geol.   553.86
  mining
    soc. & econ. aspects *see*
      Primary industries
    technology   622.386
    prospecting   622.188 6
  s.a. spec. uses
Emergency
  first aid *see* First aid
  generating units *see*
    Auxiliary generating
    units
  health services
    mental illness   362.28
    misc. aspects see Mental
      health services
    physical illness   362.28
    misc. aspects see Medical
      services
  labor
    economics   331.117 32
    s.a. spec. classes of labor
      e.g. Women
  legislation
    law   343.012–.019
    spec. jur.   343.3–.9
  mass cookery   641.577
  planning *see* Disasters soc.
    action
  services
    telephony *see* Telephone
      calls

Emergency (continued)
  surgery
    med. sci.   617.026
    misc. aspects see
      Diseases
    s.a. spec. diseases
Emerging states
  pol. sci.   320.17
Emery
  abrasives *see* Abrasive
    materials
  Co. Utah   *area*–792 57
  wheels
    soc. & econ. aspects *see*
      Secondary industries
    tech. & mf.   621.923
    s.a. spec. appls. e.g.
      Grinding
Emetics
  pharmacodynamics   615.731
  other aspects see Drugs
Emicon music *see* Electronic
  music
Emicons
  musical art   789.99
  other aspects see Musical
    instruments
Emigration
  law   342.082
    spec. jur.   342.3–.9
  pol. sci.   325.2
  other aspects see Migration
Emilia-Romagna Italy   *area*–454
Eminent domain
  land econ.   333.13
  law   343.025 2
    spec. jur.   343.3–.9
Emission
  control devices
    internal combustion engines
      automobiles
        soc. & econ. aspects
          see Secondary
          industries
        tech. & mf.   629.252 8
  light
    optics
      astrophysics   523.015 3
      s.a. spec. celestial
        bodies
    physics   535.3
      spec. states of matter   530.4
    theory *see* Corpuscular
      theory light
  radiations meteorology *see*
    Radiations meteorology
Emmenagogues
  pharmacodynamics   615.766
  other aspects see Drugs
Emmet Co.
  Iowa   *area*–777 125

Emmet Co. (continued)
  Michigan   *area*–774 88
Emmons Co. N.D.   *area*–784 78
Emotional
  disturbances *see* Mental
      illness
  illness *see* Mental illness
Emotionally-disturbed
  children
    psychology   155.454
    rearing home econ.   649.154
    soc. services   362.74
      misc. aspects see Young
          people soc. services to
    persons   *pers.*–082 4
    soc. services *see* Mentally
        ill people
  students
    education   371.94
    law   344.079 14
      spec. jur.   344.3–.9
Emotions
  ed. psych.   370.153
  psychology   152.4
    animals   156.24
    children   155.412
    s.a. psych. of other spec.
        groups
  religion   200.19
    s.a. spec. rel.
Empathy
  ethics *see* Virtues
  psychology *see* Emotions
Empedoclean philosophy   182.5
Empennages *see* Airframes
Emperors *see* Monarchs
Empetraceae *see* Celastrales
Emphysema
  gen. med.   616.248
  geriatrics   618.976 248
  pediatrics   618.922 48
  pub. health   614.592 48
  statistics   312.324 8
    deaths   312.262 48
    other aspects see Diseases
Empires
  pol. sci.   321.02
    s.a. spec. jurisdictions
  regional subj. trmt.   *area*–171 2
Empirical
  remedies
    therapeutics   615.88
      s.a. spec. diseases
  tests *see* Experimental
      research
Empiricism
  philosophy   146.44
  indiv. phil.   180–190
    s.a. spec. branches of phil.
        e.g. Metaphysics

Employee
  benefits
    labor econ.   331.255
      s.a. spec. classes of
          labor e.g. Women
    labor law *see* Labor law
    personnel admin.
      gen. management   658.325
        executives   658.407 25
        spec. subj.   *s.s.*–068 3
      law of pub. admin.   342.068 6
        spec. jur.   342.3–.9
      pub. admin.   350.123 4
        central govts.   351.123 4
          spec. jur.   353–354
        local govts.   352.005 123 4
  control of industry *see*
      Worker control of
      industry
  development
    pers. admin.
      gen. management   658.312 4
        spec. subj.   *s.s.*–068 3
      pub. admin.   350.15
        central govts.   351.15
          spec. jur.   353–354
        local govts.   352.005 15
  discipline *see* Discipline
      employees
  organizations
    personnel admin.
      gen. management   658.315 3
        spec. subj.   *s.s.*–068 3
      pub. admin.   350.173
        central govts.   351.173
          spec. jur.   353–354
        local govts.   352.005 173
    s.a. Labor unions
  participation
      gen. management   658.315 2
        spec. subj.   *s.s.*–068 3
      pub. admin.   350.172
        central govts.   351.172
          spec. jur.   353–354
        local govts.   352.005 172
  rights
    civil service personnel
      law   342.068 4
        spec. jur.   352.3–.9
  selection
    personnel admin.
      gen. management   658.311 2
        executives   658.407 112
        spec. subj.   *s.s.*–068 3
      pub. admin.   350.132
        central govts.   351.132
          spec. jur.   353–354
        local govts.   352.005 132

Enamels (continued)
glass
  arts   748.6
manufacturing
  soc. & econ. aspects *see*
    Secondary industries
  technology   666.2
rel. significance
  Christianity   247.884
  comp. rel.   291.37
  s.a. other spec. rel.
teeth *see* Tooth tissue
Enargite
  mineralogy   549.35
Encampment tactics
  mil. sci.   355.412
  s.a. spec. mil. branches
Encaustic painting
  arts   751.46
  indiv. artists   759.1–.9
Encephalitis
  gen. med.   616.832
  geriatrics   618.976 832
  pediatrics   618.928 32
  pub. health   614.598 32
  statistics   312.383 2
  deaths   312.268 32
  other aspects see Diseases
Enchanters
  rel. leaders
    comp. rel.   291.62
    s.a. spec. rel.
Enclosed-arc lighting *see*
  Luminous-tube lighting
Enclosure
  land econ.   333.2
Encyclicals
  rel. law   262.91
Encyclopedias   030
  spec. subj.   *s.s.*–03
Encyclopedists
  biog. & work   030.92
  Christian polemics vs.   239.6
  s.a.   *pers.*–093
End
  games
    chess   794.124
  of world *see* Eschatology
  papers
    handicrafts *see* Paper
      handicrafts
Enderbury Isl.   *area*–968 1
Enderby Land Antarctica   *area*–989
Endive
  agriculture   635.55
  soc. & econ. aspects *see*
    Primary industries
  foods   641.355 5
  preparation
    commercial   664.805 55
    domestic   641.655 5

Endive (continued)
  other aspects see Asterales;
    also Vegetables
Endocarditis *see* Endocardium
Endocardium
  diseases
    gen. med.   616.11
    geriatrics   618.976 11
    pediatrics   618.921 1
    pub. health   614.591 1
    statistics   312.311
    deaths   312.261 1
    other aspects see Diseases
  other aspects see Heart
Endocrine
  drugs
    pharmacology   615.36
    other aspects see Drugs
  secretion
    pathology
      gen. wks.   591.214 2
      s.a. spec. animals
      med. sci.   616.43–.48
      animals   636.089 643–.089 648
      s.a. spec. animals
      man   616.43–.48
    physiology
      gen. wks.   591.142
      s.a. spec. animals
      med. sci.   612.4
      human phys.   612.4
      vet. phys.   636.089 24
      s.a. spec. animals
  system
    anatomy
      human   611.4
      other aspects see
        Secretory organs
    diseases
      gen. wks.   616.4
      neoplasms   616.992 4
      tuberculosis   616.995 4
      geriatrics   618.976 4
      pediatrics   618.924
      pub. health   614.594
      statistics   312.34
      deaths   312.264
      surgery *see* Glandular
        organs diseases
    physical anthropometry   573.64
    physiology
      human   612.4
      other aspects see
        Secretion
    tissue biology human   611.018 94
Endocrinology
  med. sci.   616.4
    geriatrics   618.976 4
    pediatrics   618.924
  vet. med.   636.089 64
    s.a. spec. animals

Engineering (continued)

curriculums — 375.62

design — 620.004 25

   s.a. spec. appls. e.g.

     Aeronautics

drawing — 604.2

forces

  mil. sci.

    land forces — 358.2

    naval — 359.982

geology — 624.151

  railroads

    technology — 625.122

    other aspects see

      Permanent way

  roads

    technology — 625.732

    other aspects see Roads

  s.a. other spec. appls.

graphics — 604.2

industries

  ind. relations — 331.042

    s.a. spec. aspects e.g. '

      Compensation

  management — 658.92

  organizations — 338.762

    cooperative — 334.682

    mergers — 338.836 2

    restrictive practices — 338.826 2

  prod. econ. — 338.476 2

    efficiency — 338.456 2

    finance — 338.436 2

installations

  armed forces — 355.74

  s.a. spec. mil. branches

libraries — 026.62

  misc. aspects see Special

    libraries

library acquisitions — 025.276 2

library classification — 025.466 2

lit. & stage trmt. *see*

    Scientific themes

mechanics — 620.1

museums

  desc. & colls. — 620.007 4

  museology — 069.962

  s.a. spec. activities

    e.g. Display

optics — 621.36

school bldgs.

  architecture — 727.46

  building — 690.746

  other aspects see

    Educational buildings

subject headings — 025.496 2

systems

  shipbuilding

    soc. & econ. aspects *see*

      Secondary industries

Engineering

systems

  shipbuilding (continued)

    technology — 623.85

    design — 623.814 5

      spec. craft — 623.812

    spacecraft eng. — 629.474

    unmanned — 629.464

    other aspects see

      Spacecraft

  s.a. other spec. appls.

  other aspects see Technology

  s.a. spec. branches & appls.

Engineers

biog. & work — 620.009 2

  s.a. spec. kinds

occupational ethics — 174.962

s.a. — *pers.–62*

Engines *see* Power plants

England — *area–42*

ancient — *area–362*

English

Channel

  oceanography — 551.461 36

  regional subj. trmt. — *area–163 36*

  transchannel flights — 629.130 911 36

  other aspects see Atlantic

    Ocean

horn music — 788.75

  recordings — 789.912 87

horns

  mf. tech. — 681.818 7

    misc. aspects see Musical

      instruments

  musical art — 788.7

language

  linguistics — 420

  literature — 820

  s.a. — *lang.–21*

Longhorn cattle

  animal husbandry — 636.226

  other aspects see Cattle

people — *r.e.n.–21*

revised version Bible — 220.520 4

  s.a. spec. parts of Bible

sheepdog

  animal husbandry — 636.73

  other aspects see Dogs

socialism econ. — 335.1

sparrow *see* Ploceidae

texts

  Bible — 220.52

    s.a. spec. parts of Bible

  s.a. other spec. works

Toy Spaniel

  animal husbandry — 636.76

  other aspects see Dogs

s.a. England; *also other*

    spec. subj. e.g. Arts

Engraved
  plates
    printing *see* Plates mech.
        printing tech.
  seals
    numismatics   737.6
    rel. significance
      Christianity   247.876
      comp. rel.   291.37
      s.a. other spec. rel.
Engraving
  gems *see* Lapidary work
  glass
    arts   748.6
    technology   666.1
      soc. & econ. aspects *see*
          Secondary industries
  graphic arts   760
  s.a. other spec. mediums
Engravings *see* Prints
Enigmas
  gen. wks.   001.94
    s.a. spec. subj.
  recreation   793.73
Eniwetok   *area*–968 3
Enlisted personnel
  armed forces   355.338
Enlistment
  mil. personnel   355.223 62
  s.a. spec. mil. branches
Enna Sicily   *area*–458 12
Enoch
  pseudepigrapha   229.913
  other aspects see Apocrypha
Enopla *see* Nemertea
Enoree River S.C.   *area*–757 31
Ensembles *see spec. kinds e.g.*
        Instrumental ensembles
Entablatures *see* Walls
Entails
  land econ.   333.323 4
Enteric
  diseases   616.93
    geriatrics   618.976 93
    pediatrics   618.929 3
    pub. health   614.51
    statistics   312.393
      deaths   312.269 3
    other aspects see Diseases
  fever *see* Typhoid fever
Enteritis
  gen. med.   616.344
    geriatrics   618.976 344
    pediatrics   618.923 44
    pub. health   614.593 44
    statistics   312.334 4
      deaths   312.263 44
    other aspects see Diseases
Enterobacteriaceae *see*
        Eubacteriales

Enterobiasis
  gen. med.   616.965 4
    geriatrics   618.976 965 4
    pediatrics   618.929 654
    pub. health   614.555 4
    statistics   312.396 54
      deaths   312.269 654
    other aspects see Diseases
Enteropneusta
  culture   639.739 93
  paleozoology   563.993
  zoology   593.993
  other aspects see Animals
Entertainers
  biog. & work   791.092
    s.a. spec. kinds
  occupational ethics   174.979 1
  s.a.   *pers.*–791
Entertaining
  food service   642.4
Entertainment
  advertising   659.13
  equipment
    automobiles
      soc. & econ. aspects *see*
          Secondary industries
      tech & mf.   629.277
    etiquette   395.3
  media
    accounting   657.84
  s.a. Recreation
Entertainments
  indoor amusements   793.2
Enthusiasm
  learning
    psychology   153.153 3
    animals   156.315 33
    children   155.413
    s.a. psych. of other spec.
        groups
Entiat Range Wash.   *area*–797 59
Entire functions   515.98
  s.a. spec. appls. e.g.
        Engineering
Entombment *see* Burial
Entomologists
  biog. & work   595.700 92
  other aspects see Scientists
  s.a.   *pers.*–595
Entomology   595.7
  s.a. Medical entomology
Entomorphthorales *see*
        Nonflagellate molds
Entoprocta
  culture & hunting   639.758 8
  zoology   595.188
  other aspects see Worms
Entotrophi
  zoology   595.714
  other aspects see Apterygota
Entrance N.S.W.   *area*–944 2

Entrance requirements
  schools   371.217
    s.a. spec. levels of ed.;
      also Special education
Entrances
  Christian church arch.   726.591
  s.a. other spec. bldgs.; also
      Porches
Entre
  Douro e Minho Portugal   *area*–469 1
  Ríos Argentina   *area*–822 1
Entrees
  cookery home econ.   641.82
Entrepreneurial classes *see*
    Middle classes
Entrepreneurs
  biog. & work   338.040 92
  s.a. spec. enterprises
  management   658.42
  s.a.   *pers.*–338
Entrepreneurship
  economics   338.04
  income distribution   339.21
Entropy
  thermodynamics
    astrophysics   523.013 73
    s.a. spec. celestial
      bodies
    physics   536.73
    spec. states of matter   530.4
  other aspects see
    Thermodynamics
Entry
  bibliographic
    library cataloging   025.322
Enumeration
  mathematics   511.62
  s.a. spec. math. branches;
      also spec. appls. e.g.
      Engineering
Enuresis
  symptomatology
    neurological diseases   616.849
Environment
  control
    agriculture *see*
      Controlled-environment
      agriculture
  lit. & stage trmt. *see* Social
      themes
  physical anthr.   573.4
    racial characteristics   572.3
  resources *see* Natural
      resources
  use in psychiatry *see* Milieu
      therapy psychiatry
  s.a. Natural environments;
      also Ecology
Environmental
  design
    arts   711

Environmental
  design (continued)
    crime prevention   364.49
  diseases
    gen. pathology   574.24
      animals   591.24
      plants   581.24
    s.a. spec. organisms
    med. sci.   616.98
      geriatrics   618.976 98
      pediatrics   618.929 8
      statistics   312.398
      deaths   312.269 8
    other aspects see
      Diseases
    s.a. spec. diseases,
      systems, organs
  engineering   620.8
    s.a. spec. appls. e.g.
      Aerospace engineering
  factors
    genetics   575.22
      animals   591.152
      man   573.222
      microorganisms   576.139
      plants   581.152
    s.a. spec. organisms
    mental pub. health   362.204 2
  health
    engineering   620.85
    s.a. spec. branches of
      eng. & spec. appls.
      e.g. Aerospace
      engineering
  injuries
    plants
      agriculture   632.1
      s.a. spec. plants; also
        spec. types of culture
        e.g. Forestry
  medicine
    gen. wks.   616.98
    geriatrics   618.976 98
    pediatrics   618.929 8
    statistics   312.398
    deaths   312.269 8
    other aspects see Diseases
  pollution *see* Pollution
  protection
    law
      international   341.762
      municipal   344.046
      spec. jur.   344.3–.9
  psychology   155.9
  sanitation *see* Sanitation
  studies
    curriculums   375.008 3
    s.a. spec. levels of ed.;
      also Special education

Environments (art style)
gen. wks.	709.040 74
spec. places	709.1–.9
painting	759.067 4
spec. places	759.1–.9
sculpture	735.230 474
spec. places	730.9

  s.a. other spec. art forms

Envoys
biog. & work	327.092
s.a.	*pers.*–352 2

Envy *see* Vices

Enzymes
  biochemistry
gen. wks.	574.192 5
animals	591.192 5
microorganisms	576.119 25
plants	581.192 5

    s.a. spec. organisms
med. sci.	612.015 1
animals	636.089 201 51

    s.a. spec. animals
man	612.015 1

  s.a. spec. functions,
    systems, organs
  blood chem.
human phys.	612.12

    other aspects see
      Circulatory fluids
org. chem.	547.758
pharmacology	615.35

    misc. aspects see Drugs
  other aspects see Proteins

Eoanura
paleozoology	567.8

Eocanthocephala *see*
  Acanthocephala

Eocene epoch
geology	551.784

  s.a. spec. aspects e.g.
    Economic geology
  paleontology *see* Cenozoic era

Eolipile steam engines
  stationary
    soc. & econ. aspects *see*
      Secondary industries
tech & mf.	621.166

    s.a. spec. appls. e.g.
      Power plants

Eolithic Age
archaeology	930.1

Eosuchia
paleozoology	567.94

Epacridaceae *see* Ericales
Ephedra family *see* Gnetales
Ephedraceae *see* Gnetales
Ephedrine *see* Stimulants
Ephemeral
  verse *see* Light verse
  s.a. other spec. subj.

Ephemerides
astrology	133.55
nautical almanacs	528

Ephemeroptera
culture	638.573 4
paleozoology	565.73
zoology	595.734

  other aspects see Insecta

Ephesians
Bible	227.5

  other aspects see New
    Testament

Epic
  poetry
    gen. wks.
collections	808.813
hist. & crit.	809.13
rhetoric	808.13
juvenile	808.068 13

spec. lits.	*lit. sub.*–103	
indiv. authors	*lit. sub.*–11–19	

    other aspects see Poetry
  s.a. Mythology

Epicaridea *see* Isopoda

Epicurean philosophy 187

Epidemic
  diarrhea
pub. health	614.517

    other aspects see Diarrhea
  parotitis *see* Mumps
  roseola *see* Measles
  typhus
gen. med.	616.922 2
geriatrics	618.976 922 2
pediatrics	618.929 222
pub. health	614.526 2
statistics	312.392 22
deaths	312.269 222

    other aspects see Diseases

Epidemics (diseases)
  disaster relief
soc. welfare	361.54

  sociology
effect on populations	304.62
social change	303.485

  other aspects see Diseases

Epidemics (mathematics)	519.85

  s.a. spec. appls. e.g.
    Engineering

Epidemiology
pub. health	614.4

    misc. aspects see Public
      health

Epidermis *see* Skin

Epidote
mineralogy	549.63

Epigastric regions abdomen *see*
  Abdomen

Epiglottis *see* Larynx

Epigrams
gen. colls.	808.882

Epigrams (continued)
  spec. lits.   *lit. sub.*–802
    spec. periods   *lit. sub.*–81–89
Epigraphy *see* Paleography
Epilepsy
  gen. med.   616.853
  geriatrics   618.976 853
  pediatrics   618.928 53
  pub. health   614.598 53
  statistics   312.385 3
    deaths   312.268 53
  other aspects see Diseases
Epinastic movements *see* Nastic
        movements
Epipolasida *see* Demospongiae
Epirus Greece   *area*–495 3
  ancient   *area*–382
Episcopal
  palaces
    architecture   726.9
    building   690.69
    rel. purpose   291.35
    s.a. spec. rel.
    other aspects see
        Religious-purpose
        bldgs.
  systems
    Christian church leaders   262.17
    Christian ecclesiology   262.3
  thrones *see* Seats
        ecclesiastical
        furniture
Episcopalians *see* Anglicans
Epistemology   121
  misc. aspects see Philosophy
Epistle of Jeremy
  Apocrypha   229.5
  other aspects see Apocrypha
Epistles
  Anglican liturgy   264.036
  Bible   227
    pseudepigrapha   229.93
  other aspects see New
        Testament
Epitaphs
  genealogy   929.5
Epithelial tissue
  human anatomy & phys.   611.018 7
  other aspects see Tissue
        biology
Epitomes   *s.s.*–020 2
Epoxies
  plastics
    chem. tech.   668.422 6
    org. chem.   547.843 222 6
    other aspects see Plastics
    s.a. spec. products
Epoxy resins
  manufacturing
    chem. tech.   668.374

Epoxy resins
  manufacturing (continued)
    soc. & econ. aspects *see*
        Secondary industries
Epping
  Essex Eng.   *area*–426 74
  Forest Essex Eng.   *area*–426 74
Epsom & Ewell Surrey Eng.
              area–422 15
Epsom salts
  pharmacodynamics   615.732
  other aspects see Drugs
Epsomite
  mineralogy   549.755
Equal
  econ. opportunity
    govt. promotion
      pub. admin.   350.820 44
        central govts.   351.820 44
        spec. jur.   353–354
        local govts.   352.942
  employment opportunity
    govt. promotion *see*
      Employment services
    pub. admin.
    govt. service   350.104
      central govts.   351.104
      spec. jur.   353–354
      local govts.   352.005 104
  opportunity programs *see spec.*
    kinds of programs e.g.
    employment programs
    331.133
  protection of laws
    pol. sci.   323.42
Equal-area projections maps   526.85
Equalization
  taxes *see* Assessment taxes
Equateur Zaïre   *area*–675 13
Equation
  of exchange theory
    money econ.   332.401
  of time chronology   529.1
Equations   511.33
  theory   515.25
    algebra   512.94
    calculus   515.25
  s.a. spec. math. branches;
    also spec. appls. e.g.
    Engineering
Equator province Congo   *area*–675 13
Equatoria Sudan   *area*–629 5
Equatorial
  Guinea   *area*–671 8
  Islands   *area*–964
  telescopes *see*
      Extrameridional
      instruments
  s.a. Tropical

Eragrosteae *see* Pooideae
Erath Co. Tex.   *area*–764 551
Erbil Iraq   *area*–567 2
Erbium
  chemistry
    inorganic   546.418
    organic   547.054 18
    s.a. spec. groupings e.g.
      Aliphatic compounds
  technology   661.041 8
    organic   661.895
    soc. & econ. aspects *see*
      Secondary industries
    s.a. spec. prod.
  eng. materials   620.189 291 8
    s.a. spec. uses
  metallography   669.952 918
  metallurgy   669.291 8
    physical & chem.   669.962 918
  pharmacology   615.241 8
    misc. aspects see
      Pharmacology
  products
    mf. & tech.   673.291 8
    other aspects see
      Nonferrous metal
      products
  toxicology   615.925 418
    misc. aspects see
      Toxicology
  other aspects see
    Yttrium-group metals
Eremitical rel. orders
  Christianity
    church hist.   271.02
      women's   271.902
    ecclesiology   262.24
    gen. wks.   255.02
      women's   255.902
  other rel. see Religious
    congregations
Eremosynaceae *see* Saxifragales
Eretrian philosophy   183.7
Erewash Derbyshire Eng.   *area*–425 18
Erfurt Ger.   *area*–432 2
Ergodic theory   515.42
  s.a. spec. appls. e.g. Atomic
    physics
Ergonomics   620.82
  s.a. spec. appls. e.g.
    Aerospace engineering
Ergosterol *see* Sterols
Ergot *see* Ascomycetes
Ericaceae *see* Ericales
Ericales
  botany   583.62
  floriculture   635.933 62
  forestry   634.973 62
  med. aspects
    crop prod.   633.883 62

Ericales
  med. aspects (continued)
    gen. pharm.   615.323 62
      toxicology   615.952 362
    vet. pharm.   636.089 532 362
      toxicology   636.089 595 236 2
  paleobotany   561.3
  other aspects see Plants
Erie
  County
    New York   *area*–747 96
    Ohio   *area*–771 22
    Pennsylvania   *area*–748 99
  Lake
    Battle War of 1812 hist.   973.525 4
    regional subj. trmt.   *area*–771 2
    Ontario   *area*–713 3
Eriobotrya japonica *see* Loquats
Eriocaulaceae *see* Eriocaulales
Eriocaulales
  botany   584.81
  floriculture   635.934 81
  med. aspects
    crop prod.   633.884 81
    gen. pharm.   615.324 81
      toxicology   615.952 481
    vet. pharm.   636.089 532 481
      toxicology   636.089 595 248 1
  paleobotany   561.4
  other aspects see Plants
Erith London Eng.   *area*–421 77
Eritrea Ethiopia   *area*–635
Erogeneity
  sex psych.   155.31
Erosion
  physical geol.   551.302
    water action   551.352
    wind action   551.372
    s.a. other spec. agents
  soil
    technology   627.52
    agriculture   631.45
    land reclamation   627.52
Erosions
  uterus & cervix
    gynecology
      gen. wks.   618.143
      anesthesiology   617.968 1
      geriatrics   618.978 143
      pediatrics   618.920 981 43
      pub. health   614.599 2
      statistics   312.304 814 3
    other aspects see
      Diseases
Erotica
  arts   704.942 8
  literature
    gen. wks.
      collections   808.803 538
      hist. & crit.   809.933 538

Erotica
  arts
    literature (continued)
      spec. lits.
        collections   *lit. sub.*–080 353 8
        hist. & crit.   *lit. sub.*–093 538
      s.a. spec. lit. forms
      painting   757.8
      stage   792.090 935 38
        s.a. other spec. dramatic
            mediums e.g.
            Television; also spec.
            kinds of drama e.g.
            Tragedies (drama)
    s.a. other spec. art forms
    other aspects see Pornography
Errantia *see* Polychaeta
Errhines
  pharmacodynamics   615.72
  other aspects see Drugs
Error
  detectors & correctors
    closed-loop automation eng. 629.831 5
    s.a. spec. appls. e.g.
      Thermostats
  theory
    mathematics   511.43
    s.a. spec. math. branches;
      also spec. appls. e.g.
      Engineering
Errors   001.96
  logic   165
  psychology   153.74
    animals   156.374
    children   155.413
    s.a. psych. of other spec.
      groups
  s.a. spec. subj.
Erse *see* Scottish Gaelic
Erudition   001.2
Eruptive
  diseases
    gen. med.   616.91
    geriatrics   618.976 91
    pediatrics   618.929 1
    pub. health   614.52
    statistics   312.391
      deaths   312.269 1
    other aspects see Diseases
  fevers *see* Tick typhus
  variable stars
    astronomy
      description   523.844 6
      theory   521.584 46
    other aspects see Celestial
      bodies
Erysipelas
  gen. med.   616.942
  geriatrics   618.976 942
  pediatrics   618.929 42
  pub. health   614.577

Erysipelas (continued)
  statistics   312.394 2
    deaths   312.269 42
  other aspects see Diseases
Erythrite
  mineralogy   549.72
Erythrocytes *see* Red corpuscles
Erythropalaceae *see* Celastrales
Erythroxylaceae *see*
    Malpighiales
Erzincan Turkey   *area*–566 7
Erzurum Turkey   *area*–566 2
Esaki diodes *see* Diodes
    semiconductors
Escalators
  building element *see* Stairs
  machine eng.
    soc. & econ. aspects *see*
      Secondary industries
    tech. & mf.   621.867 6
    s.a. spec. appls. e.g.
      Internal transportation
  other aspects see Mechanics
Escalloniaceae *see* Cunoniales
Escambia Co.
  Alabama   *area*–761 265
  Florida   *area*–759 99
Escape
  equipment
    aircraft eng.
      soc. & econ. aspects *see*
        Secondary industries
      tech. & mf.   629.134 386
  velocity
    celestial mech. *see*
      Celestial mechanics
    physics   531.555 2
Escapements
  clockwork
    tech. & mf.   681.112
    soc. & econ. aspects *see*
      Secondary industries
Escapes
  penology *see* Security
    penology
Eschatology
  rel. doctrines
    Christianity   236
    comp. rel.   291.23
    Islam   297.23
    Judaism   296.33
    nat. rel.   218
    s.a. other spec. rel.
Escuintla Guatemala   *area*–728 163
Esdras
  Apocrypha   229.1
  other aspects see Apocrypha
  s.a. Ezra; also Nehemiah
Esfahan Iran   *area*–559 5
Esher Surrey Eng.   *area*–422 145

Eskdale Dumfries & Galloway Scot.
     area–414 83
Eskimo
 dogs
  animal husbandry 636.73
  other aspects see Dogs
 other subj. see Eskimo-Aleut
Eskimo-Aleut
 languages
  linguistics   497.1
  literatures   897.1
  s.a.   *lang.*–971
 people   *r.e.n.*–97
 s.a. other spec. subj. e.g.
   Arts
Eskimos   *r.e.n.*–97
Eskisehir Turkey   *area*–563
Esmeralda Co. Nev. *area*–793 35
Esmeraldas Ecuador *area*–866 35
Esophagus
 anatomy
  human   611.32
  other aspects see Nutritive
   organs
 diseases
  gen. wks.   616.32
   neoplasms 616.992 32
   tuberculosis 616.995 32
  geriatrics   618.976 32
  pediatrics   618.923 2
  pub. health   614.593 2
  statistics   312.332
   deaths   312.263 2
  surgery   617.548
   anesthesiology 617.967 548
  other aspects see Diseases
 physical anthropometry 573.632
 physiology
  human   612.315
  other aspects see Nutrition
 tissue biology human 611.018 932
Esoteric
 societies   366.1–.5
 traditions
  occultism   135.4
Espaillat Dominican Republic
     area–729 362
Esparto
 plants
  agriculture   633.58
  soc. & econ. aspects *see*
   Primary industries
Esperance
 Nat. Park W. Aust. *area*–941 7
 W. Aust.   *area*–941 7
Esperanto language
 linguistics   499.992
 literature   899.992
 s.a.   *lang.*–999 92

Espionage
 industrial *see* Industrial
  espionage
 international
  ethics *see* International
   relations ethics
  internat. relations 327.12
   spec. countries 327.3–.9
  spec. wars *see*
   Unconventional warfare
  war laws   341.63
  other aspects see Political
   offenses
 labor econ.
  management meas. 331.894
Espírito Santo Brazil *area*–815 2
Essayists
 biog. & work 809.4
 s.a. spec. lits.
 other aspects see Authors
 s.a.   *pers.*–84
Essays
 belles-lettres
  gen. wks.
   collections 808.84
   crit. theory 801.954
    textual 801.959
   hist. & crit. 809.4
   rhetoric 808.4
    juvenile 808.068 4
   spec. lits. *lit. sub.*–4
  gen. colls. *see* Anthologies
Essence
 metaphysics   111.1
Essences
 drugs   615.42
  misc. aspects see
   Pharmacology
 flavorings
  comm. proc. 664.52
  soc. & econ. aspects *see*
   Secondary industries
 perfumes *see* Perfumes
Essenes
 Judaism   296.81
 misc. aspects see Judaism
Essential
 hypertension *see* Hypertension
 oils
  chem. tech. 661.806
  org. chem. 547.71
  other aspects see Organic
   chemicals
Essequibo Guyana *area*–881 2
Essequibo Islands Guyana *area*–881 3
Essex Co.
 England   *area*–426 7
 Massachusetts *area*–744 5
 New Jersey *area*–749 31
 New York *area*–747 53
 Ontario   *area*–713 31

Essex Co. (continued)
  Vermont   *area*–743 25
  Virginia   *area*–755 34
Essonne France   *area*–443 65
Es Suweida Syria   *area*–569 14
Established church *see*
              Religious groups &
              state
Establishments
  armed forces *see*
              Installations armed
              forces
  s.a. Organizations
Estates (financial)
  accounting trmt.   657.47
  s.a. spec. kinds of
              enterprise e.g.
              Insurance accounting
  administration
    law   346.056
    spec. jur.   346.3–.9
  planning
    financial econ.   332.024 01
    law   343.053
    spec. jur.   343.3–.9
  taxation
    law   343.053 2
    spec. jur.   343.3–.9
    pub. admin.   350.724 76
      central govts.   351.724 76
        spec. jur.   353–354
      local govts.   352.135
    pub. finance   336.276
Estates (grounds)
  landscape design   712.6
Estelí Nicaragua   *area*–728 524
Esterases *see* Lipolytic enzymes
Esterification
  chem. eng.   660.284 44
  org. chem.   547.24
  s.a. spec. elements, cpds.,
              prod.
Esters
  chem. tech.   661.83
  org. chem.   547.038
  s.a. spec. groupings e.g.
              Aliphatic compounds
  synthetic drugs pharm.   615.313 8
    misc. aspects see
              Pharmacology
  synthetic poisons   615.951 38
    misc. aspects see
              Toxicology
  other aspects see Organic
              chemicals
  s.a. spec. prod.; also other
              spec. appls.
Esther
  Bible   222.9
    Apocrypha   229.27

Esther (continued)
  other aspects see Historical
              books (O.T.)
Esthetics *see* Aesthetics
Esthonia   *area*–474 1
Esthonian *see* Estonian
Estill Co. Ky.   *area*–769 59
Estimates
  budgeting
    pub. admin.   350.722 25
      central govts.   351.722 25
        spec. jur.   353–354
      local govts.   352.122 5
Estimation
  theory   511.4
    probabilities   519.287
    statistical math.   519.544
    s.a. spec. appls. e.g.
              Engineering
  s.a. other spec. branches of
              math.; also spec.
              appls. e.g. insurance
              underwriting 369.012
Estivation *see* Seasonal changes
              ecology
Eston Cleveland Eng.   *area*–428 54
Estonia   *area*–474 1
Estonian
  language
    linguistics   494.545
    literature   894.545
    s.a.   *lang.*–945 45
  people   *r.e.n.*–945 45
  SSR   *area*–474 1
  s.a. Estonia; *also other*
              spec. subj. e.g. Arts
Estremadura
  Portugal   *area*–469 4
  Spain   *area*–462 6
Estrogens *see* Sex hormones
Estrone *see* Sex hormones
Estuaries
  ecology life sci.   574.526 365
    animals   591.526 365
    microorganisms   576.15
    plants   581.526 365
    s.a. spec. organisms
  hydraulic eng.
    technology   627.124
    s.a. spec. appls. e.g.
              Military engineering
  other aspects see Liquids
              engineering
  other aspects see Special
              salt-water forms
Etch tests
  minerals   549.133
  spec. minerals   549.2–.7
Etching
  glass
    arts   748.6

Etching	
glass (continued)	
technology	666.1
soc. & econ. aspects *see*	
Secondary industries	
graphic arts	
processes	767.2
products	769
Etchings *see* Prints	
Eternal	
life *see* Immortality	
reward & punishment	
rel. doctrines	
Christianity	236.2
other rel. see	
Eschatology	
Eternity	
metaphysics *see* Time	
rel. doctrines	
Christianity	236.21
other rel. see Eschatology	
Ethelbald	
reign Eng. hist.	942.016 3
s.a. spec. events & subj.	
e.g. Commerce	
Ethelbert	
reign Eng. hist.	942.016 3
s.a. spec. events & subj.	
e.g. Commerce	
Ethelred	
reign Eng. hist.	
1	942.016 3
2	942.017 4
s.a. spec. events & subj.	
e.g. Commerce	
Ethelwulf	
reign Eng. hist.	942.016 2
s.a. spec. events & subj.	
e.g. Commerce	
Ethers	
chem. tech.	661.84
org. chem.	547.035
s.a. spec. groupings e.g.	
Aliphatic compounds	
synthetic drugs pharm.	615.313 5
misc. aspects see	
Pharmacology	
synthetic poisions	615.951 35
misc. aspects see	
Toxicology	
other aspects see Organic	
chemicals	
Ethical	
education	370.114
s.a. spec. levels of ed.	
school	
economics	330.155
Ethics	
& law	340.112

Ethics (continued)	
philosophy	170
misc. aspects see	
Philosophy	
religion	
Buddhism	294.35
Christianity	241
comp. rel.	291.5
Hinduism	294.548
s.a. other spec. rel.	
s.a. Values	
Ethiopia (Abyssinia)	*area*-63
Ethiopia (Sudan) ancient	*area*-397 8
Ethiopian	
Church *see* Abyssinian Church	
War hist.	963.043
s.a. spec. events & subj.	
e.g. Commerce	
Ethiopians	*r.e.n.*-928
Ethiopic	
languages	
linguistics	492.8
literatures	892.8
s.a.	*lang.*-928
people	*r.e.n.*-928
texts	
Bible	220.46
s.a. spec. parts of Bible	
s.a. Ethiopia; *also other*	
spec. subj. e.g. Arts	
Ethnic	
cookery	641.592
differences *see* Racial	
differences	
groups	
& state	323.11
area trmt.	323.13–.19
appls. to spec. subj.	*s.s.*-089
child rearing home econ.	649.157
civilization *see* Ethnic	
groups history	
criminal offenders	364.34
discrimination *see spec.*	
aspects e.g. Ethnic	
groups sociology	
education	
sociology	370.193 42
special ed.	371.97
law	344.079 17
spec. jur.	344.3–.9
students	371.82
s.a. spec. levels of	
ed.; also Special	
education	
s.a. spec. subj. e.g.	
School dropouts	
govt. services to	350.814
central govts.	351.814
spec. jur.	353–354
local govts.	352.941 4

Eugenics
medical ethics (continued)
  religion
    Buddhism · 294.356 425
    Christianity · 241.642 5
    comp. rel. · 291.564 25
    Hinduism · 294.548 642 5
    s.a. other spec. rel.
  techniques · 613.94
Euglenaceae *see* Euglenophyta
Euglenida (zoology) *see*
    Mastigophora
Euglenoids (botany) *see*
    Euglenophyta
Euglenophyta
  botany · 589.44
  med. aspects
    gen. pharm. · 615.329 44
    toxicology · 615.952 944
    vet. pharm. · 636.089 532 944
    toxicology · 636.089 595 294 4
  paleobotany · 561.93
  other aspects see Plants
Eulerian integrals
  mathematics · 515.52
  s.a. spec. appls. e.g.
    Engineering
Eumalacostraca
  culture · 639.5
  fishing
    commercial · 639.5
    sports · 799.255 37
  paleozoology · 565.37
  zoology · 595.37
  other aspects see Crustacea
Eumycetozoa *see* Mycetozoa
Eumycophyta
  agric. pathogens · 632.4
  s.a. spec. plants; also
    spec. types of culture
    e.g. Forestry
  botany · 589.22-.25
  med. aspects
    gen. pharm. · 615.329 22-.329 25
    toxicology · 615.952 922-.952 925
    vet. pharm. 636.089 532 922-.089 532 925
    toxicology
      636.089 595 292 2-.089 595 292 5
  other aspects see Plants
Eungella Nat. Park Qld. · *area*-943 6
Euphausiacea
  culture · 639.54
  fishing
    commercial · 639.54
    sports · 799.255 385
  paleozoology · 595.385
  other aspects see Crustacea
Euphonium music · 788.445
  recordings · 789.912 844

Euphoniums
  mf. tech. · 681.818 44
  misc. aspects see Musical
    instruments
  musical art · 788.44
Euphorbiaceae *see* Euphorbiales
Euphorbiales
  botany · 583.95
  floriculture · 635.933 95
  forestry · 634.973 95
  med. aspects
    crop prod. · 633.883 95
    gen. pharm. · 615.323 95
    toxicology · 615.952 395
    vet. pharm. · 636.089 532 395
    toxicology · 636.089 595 239 5
  paleobotany · 561.3
  other aspects see Plants
Euphrates River *see* Mesopotamia
    Iraq
Eupomatiaceae *see* Annonales
Eurasia · *area*-5
Eurasians · *r.e.n.*-042
Eure France · *area*-442 4
Eure-et-Loir France · *area*-445 1
Eureka Co. Nev. · *area*-793 32
Euro Vic. · *area*-945 5
Europe · *area*-4
  ancient · *area*-36
European
  Arctic seawaters
    oceanography · 551.468 4
    regional subj. trmt. · *area*-163 24
    other aspects see Atlantic
      Ocean
  Common Market *see* European
    Economic Community
  Economic Community
    international
      commerce · 382.914 2
      economics · 337.142
      law · 341.242 2
        econ. functions · 341.750 614
        treaties · 341.026 322
  Free Trade Association
    international
      commerce · 382.914 3
      economics · 337.143
      law · 341.242
        econ. functions · 341.750 61
        treaties · 341.026 32
  Investment Bank
    economics · 332.153 4
    other aspects see Banks
      (finance)
  regional organizations
    internat. law · 341.242
    treaties · 341.026 32
  s.a. other spec. subj. e.g.
    Arts

Evangelistic
  music
    gen. wks.
      scores & parts
        congregational   783.95
        1-9 parts   783.675
        treatises   783.7
      recordings   789.912 3
    rel. orders *see* Preaching
      orders
  sermons
    Christianity   252.3
  writings
    private devotions
      Christianity   243
      other rel. see Religious
        experience
Evans Co. Ga   *area*–758 763
Evaporated milk
  dairy tech.
    skim   637.147 22
    whole   637.142 2
  other aspects see Milk
Evaporation
  chem eng.   660.284 26
    s.a. spec. prod.
  control water-supply eng.
    technology   628.132
    other aspects see Water
      supply engineering
  food preservation tech. *see*
      Drying foods
  meteorology   551.572
    artificial modification 551.687 2
    weather forecasting   551.647 2
      spec. areas   551.65
  milk
    dairy tech.   637.133 5
    s.a. spec. varieties e.g.
      Whole milk
  physical transformation *see*
    Vaporization
Evapotranspiration
  meteorology   551.572
    artificial modification 551.687 2
    weather forecasting   551.647 2
      spec. areas   551.65
Evasion
  taxes
    ethics *see* Citizenship
      ethics
    other aspects see Revenue
      offenses
Evening
  colleges
    higher ed.   378.154 4
  prayer *see* Prayer gen. wks.
  prayers
    Anglican liturgy   264.034
  time of day
    influence on crime   364.22

Evening
  time of day (continued)
    lit. & stage trmt. *see*
      Times
  s.a. Night
Evenki Nat. Region RSFSR *area*–575
Events *see* History
Events (art style)
  gen. wks.   709.040 74
    spec. places   709.1–.9
  painting   759.067 4
    spec. places   759.1
  sculpture   735.230 474
    spec. places   730.9
  s.a. other spec. art forms
Everglades Fla.   *area*–759 39
Everlasting
  flowers (Asterales) *see*
    Asterales
  plants floriculture   635.973
    s.a. spec. plants
Everyday
  life
    art representation   704.949
    painting   754
    s.a. other spec. art
      forms
    lit. & stage trmt. *see*
      Social themes
  living
    personal rel. *see* Conduct
  s.a. Daily
Evesham
  Hereford & Worcester Eng.
                area–424 49
  Vale Hereford & Worcester Eng.
                area–424 49
Eviction (law) *see* Ejectment &
    recovery
Evidence
  analysis
    criminal investigation 363.256
    law   345.052
      spec. jur.   345.3–.9
    pub. admin. *see* Law
      enforcement pub. admin.
  epistemology   121.65
  law
    criminal law   345.06
      spec. jur.   345.3–.9
    gen. wks.   347.06
      spec. jur.   347.3–.9
    other aspects see Legal
      procedure
  procurement
    criminal investigation 363.252
    law   345.052
      spec. jur.   345.3–.9
    pub. admin. *see* Law
      enforcement pub. admin.

Evil
  eye
    occultism 133.425
  spirits
    occultism 133.423
    other aspects see Devils
Evil (concept)
  freedom of choice
    rel. doctrines
      Christianity 233.7
      nat. rel. 216
      other rel. see Humankind
        rel. doctrines
  justification *see* Theodicy
  metaphysics 111.84
Evolutes
  integral geometry 516.362
  s.a. spec. appls. e.g.
    Engineering
Evolution
  ethical systems 171.7
    applications 172–179
  life sci. 575
    animals 591.38
    man 573.2
    microorganisms 576.138
    plants 581.38
  mathematics *see* Root
    extraction
  metaphysics 116
  vs. creation
    rel. doctrines
      Christianity 231.765
      nat. rel. 213
      other rel. see Creation
        rel. doctrines
  s.a. other spec. subj.
Evolutional psychology 155.7
Evolutionary
  cycles
    life sci. 575.7
    animals 591.38
    plants 581.38
    s.a. spec. organisms
Evolutionism
  philosophy 146.7
  indiv. phil. 180–190
  s.a. spec. branches of phil.
    e.g. Metaphysics
Évora Portugal *area*–469 52
Evros Greece *area*–495 7
Ewe
  language *see* Kwa languages
  people *r.e.n.*–963
  s.a. other spec. subj. e.g.
    Arts
Ewell Surrey Eng. *area*–422 15
Ewes *see* Sheep
Ewings Morass Fauna Reserve Vic.
    area–945 6

Examination
  of conscience *see* Contrition
  of witnesses *see* Courtroom
    procedure law
Examinations
  civil service *see* Civil
    service examinations
  education *see* Tests education
  mil. personnel 355.223 6
    s.a. spec. mil. branches
  spec. subj. *s.s.*–076
Examples
  psychology 155.9
  s.a. spec. subj.
Exanthemata *see* Tick typhus
Excavation
  archaeological tech. 930.102 83
  foundation eng.
    soc. & econ. aspects *see*
      Secondary industries
  technology 624.152
    s.a. spec. appls. e.g.
      Tunnels structural eng.
  road eng. *see* Roadbeds
  other aspects see Earthwork
Excelsior
  mf. tech. 674.84
  other aspects see Wood
    products
Exceptional
  children
    education 371.9
    psychology 155.45
    rearing home econ. 649.15
  students
    education 371.9
Excerpts
  musical scores & parts *see*
    Scores (music)
  s.a. Anthologies
Exchange
  buildings
    architecture 725.25
    building 690.525
    other aspects see Public
      structures
  rates
    foreign exchange 332.456
    other aspects see Money
  work library econ. 025.26
    govt. aspects 021.8
  s.a. spec. kinds & subj. of
    exchange e.g. Foreign
    exchange, Securities;
    also Marketing
Exchanges
  commodities *see* Commodities
    exchange
  libraries
    acquisitions 025.26
    govt. aspects 021.8

Exchanges (continued)
  securities *see* Securities
    exchange
Exchequers *see* Finance
    departments
Excise taxes
  law   343.055 3
    spec. jur.   343.3–.9
  pub. admin.   350.724 71
    central govts.   351.724 71
      spec. jur.   353–354
    local govts.   352.135
  pub. finance   336.271
Excisions
  extremities *see* Extremities
    surgery
Excluded
  classes *see* Lower classes
Excommunication *see* Penalties
    rel. law
Excretion
  cells cytology   574.876 4
    animals   591.876 4
    plants   581.876 4
    s.a. spec. organisms
  pathology
    gen. wks.   574.214
    animals   591.214 9
    plants   581.214
    s.a. spec. organisms
  med. sci.
    digestive
      gen. med.   616.342
      geriatrics   618.976 342
      pediatrics   618.923 42
      pub. health   614.593 42
      statistics   312.334 2
      deaths   312.263 42
      other aspects see
        Diseases
    urinary *see* Urogenital
      system diseases
  physiology
    gen. wks.   574.14
    animals   591.149
    microorganisms   576.114
    plants   581.14
    s.a. spec. organisms
    med. sci.   612.46
      human phys   612.46
      vet. phys.   636.089 246
      s.a. spec. animals
Excretory organs
  anatomy
    gen. wks.   574.44
    animals   591.44
    microorganisms   576.14
    plants   581.44
    s.a.spec. organisms

Excretory organs
  anatomy (continued)
    med. sci.   611.6
    animals   636.089 16
      s.a. spec. animals
    man   611.6
  pathology
    gen. wks.   574.224
    animals   591.224
    plants   581.224
    s.a. spec. organisms
    med. sci. *see* Excretion
Exe River Devon Eng.   *area*–423 5
Execution
  of judgment
    law *see* Judgments law
  of wills
    law   346.056
    spec. jur.   346.3–.9
Execution (music)
  music theory   781.63
  s.a. spec. mediums
Executive
  branches of govt.
    law   342.06
    spec. jur.   342.3–.9
    pol. sci.   350
  budgets
    pub. admin.   350.722 2
    central govts.   351.722 2
      spec. jur.   353–354
    local govts.   352.122
  classes *see* Middle classes
  control by legislature
    law *see* Legislative powers
      law
    pol. sci.   328.345 6
    spec. jur.   328.4–.9
  dept. bldgs.
    architecture   725.12
    building   690.512
    other aspects see Public
      structures
  departments
    law   342.064
    spec. jur.   342.3–.9
    pub. admin.   350.004
    central govts.   351.004
      U.S. govts.
        federal   353.04
        states   353.914
        other   354
    local govts.   352.008
  publications
    bibliographies   011.534
      spec. kinds   012–016
    catalogs
      general   017–019
      spec. kinds   012–016
    s.a. spec. forms e.g.
      Books

Exercise (continued)
  hygiene   613.71
    misc. aspects see Hygiene
  therapeutics *see* Therapeutic
      exercises
Exercises   *s.s.*–076
Exeter Devon Eng.   *area*–423 56
Exhaust
  diesel engines   621.436 1
    land vehicles   629.250 61
    marine vehicles   623.872 361
    s.a. other spec. appls.
  pollution *see* Air pollution
  s.a. other spec. aspects &
      occurrences
Exhaust-driven turbine engines
      see Simple
      gas-turbine engines
Exhaust-fans *see* Centrifugal
      fans & blowers
Exhibit cases
  library bldgs.   022.9
  museum bldgs.   069.31
Exhibition
  buildings
    architecture   725.91
    building   690.591
    other aspects see Public
        structures
  purposes
    animal husbandry for   636.088 8
    s.a. spec. animals
Exhibitions *see* Exhibits
Exhibits
  advertising operations   659.152
  museology   069.5
  spec. subj.   *s.s.*–074
  s.a. spec. kinds e.g. Museum
      collections
Exhortation
  spiritual gift
    Christian doctrines   234.13
Exhortations
  pub. worship
    Christianity   264.6
      spec. denominations   264.01–.09
    other rel. see Public
        worship
Existence
  metaphysics   111.1
  of God
    nat. rel.   212.1
    other rel. see God rel.
        doctrines
Existential
  schools
    psychology   150.192
    s.a. spec. subj. &
        branches of psych.

Existential (continued)
  theology
    Protestantism *see*
        Protestantism
Existentialism
  lit. & stage trmt. *see*
      Philosophy
  philosophy   142.78
    ethical systems   171.2
      applications   172–179
    indiv. phil.   180–190
    s.a. other spec. branches of
        phil.
Exmoor Somerset Eng.   *area*–423 85
Exmouth Devon Eng.   *area*–423 57
Exobiology *see* Astrobiology
Exocrine
  glands *see* Glandular organs
  secretion
    pathology   591.214 3
    s.a. spec. animals
    physiology
      gen. wks.   591.143
      s.a. spec. animals
      med. sci.   612.4
        human phys.   612.4
        vet. phys.   636.089 24
      s.a. spec. animals
Exocycloida *see* Echinoidea
Exodontics *see* Extraction
      dental surgery
Exodus
  Bible   222.12
  other aspects see Historical
      books (O.T.)
Ex-offenders
  labor econ.   331.51
  labor law *see* Labor law
Exogenous process
  physical geol.   551.3
Exorcism
  of demons
    occultism   133.427
  rel. rites
    Christianity   265.94
    other rel. see Public
        worship
Exorcists
  rel. leaders
    comp. rel.   291.62
    s.a. spec. rel.
Exoskeletons *see* Skeletal
      organs
Exothermic reactions
  thermochemistry   541.362
    applied   660.296 2
    organic   547.136 2
    s.a. spec. elements, cpds.,
        prod.

Expanding
  universe theories
    astronomy   523.18
  vaults
    architectural
      construction   721.45
      design & decoration   729.34
    building   690.145
    s.a. spec. kinds of bldgs.
Expansion
  effect of heat
    astrophysics   523.013 41
      s.a. spec. celestial
        bodies
    physics   536.41
    spec. states of matter   530.4
  of enterprises
    management   658.406
  of functions
    calculus   515.234
      complex variables   515.923 4
      real variables   515.823 4
      s.a. other spec. functions
        & equations; also spec.
        appls. e.g.
        Engineering
Expansions
  mathematics   511.4
  s.a. spec. appls. e.g.
    Engineering
Expatriation
  pol. sci.   323.64
Expectancies
  law *see* Future interests
    property law
Expectant parents' handbooks
  child care   649.102 42
  medicine   618
Expectation   519.287
  probabilities   519.287
  statistical math.   519.54
    s.a. spec. appls. e.g.
      Engineering
  s.a. spec. appls. e.g.
    Engineering
Expectorants
  pharmacodynamics   615.72
  other aspects see Drugs
Expediting
  receiving operations
    materials management *see*
      Receiving operations
      materials management
  shipping operations
    materials management   658.788 6
    spec. subj.   *s.s.*–068 7
Expeditionary forces
  mil. sci.   355.352
    s.a. spec. mil. branches

Expenditure
  public
    macroeconomics   339.522
Expenditures
  public   336.39
    budgeting
      control
        pub. admin.   350.722 32
        central govts.   351.722 32
        spec. jur.   353–354
        local govts.   352.123 2
      estimates
        pub. admin.   350.722 253
        central govts.   351.722 253
        spec. jur.   353–354
        local govts.   352.122 53
    law   343.034
      spec. jur.   343.3–.9
    macroeconomics   339.522
    pub.admin.   350.72
      central govts.   351.72
      spec. jur.   353–354
      local govts.   352.1
    other aspects see Finance
Expenses
  financial management   658.155
    spec. subj.   *s.s.*–068 1
  legislators *see* Membership
    legislative bodies
  pub. executives law *see*
    Executive branches law
Experience
  human
    metaphysics   128.4
Experimental
  biology   574.072 4
  botany   581.072 4
    s.a. spec. plants
  design *see* Operations
    research
  lit. works
    gen. colls.   808.887
    spec. lits.   *lit. sub.*–807
      spec. periods   *lit. sub.*–81–89
  medicine   619
    ethics
      philosophy   174.28
      religion
        Buddhism   294.356 428
        Christianity   241.642 8
        comp. rel.   291.564 28
        Hinduism   294.548 642 8
        s.a. other spec. rel.
  purposes
    animal husbandry for   636.088 5
      s.a. spec. animals
  research   001.434
    spec. subj.   *s.s.*–072 4
  schools   371.04
    s.a. spec. levels of ed.

Experimental (continued)
zoology   591.072 4
   s.a. spec. animals
   s.a. other spec. subj.
Experimentation
   medical ethics
    on animals
     philosophy   179.4
     religion
      Buddhism   294.356 94
      Christianity   241.694
      comp. rel.   291.569 4
      Hinduism   294.548 694
      s.a. other spec. rel.
    on humans *see* Experimental
     medicine
Expert
   testimony
    crime detection   364.127 8
    law
     criminal   345.067
     spec. jur.   345.3–.9
     gen. wks.   347.067
     spec. jur.   347.3–.9
    other aspects see
     Evidence
   witnesses *see* Expert
    testimony
Expertizing
   fine arts   702.88
   s.a. techs. in spec. art
    forms
Experts
   management *see* Consultants
    management use
Exploding wire phenomena
   electronics *see* Electronics
Explorations
   geography   910.9
    ancient world   913.04
     spec. places   913.1–.9
    modern world
     spec. places
      by continent   914–919
      general   910.09
   history *see spec. countries*
   mining eng. *see* Prospecting
   oceanography   551.460 7
   s.a. spec. bodies of water
   recreation   796.52
    equipment mf.   688.765 2
     soc. & econ. aspects *see*
      Secondary industries
    other aspects see Sports
Explorers
   biog. & work   910.92
   s.a. geog. of spec. places
   s.a.   *pers.–91*
Explorers (organization)   369.43

Explosions
   disasters
    soc. action   363.349 7
    misc. aspects see
     Disasters soc. action
   gen. hist.
    collections   904.7
    s.a. hist. of spec. places
Explosive forming *see*
   Mechanical working
Explosives
   control   363.33
   law   344.053 3
    spec. jur.   344.3–.9
   pub. admin.   350.75
    central govts.   351.75
     spec. jur.   353.354
    local govts.   352.935
   s.a. Arms (military)
    control
   manufacturing
    soc. & econ. aspects *see*
     Secondary industries
    technology   662.2
    mil. eng.   623.452
    s.a. spec. appls. e.g.
     Demolition operations
   pub. safety   363.179
   technologists
    biog. & work   662.209 2
    s.a.   *pers.–662*
   s.a. Hazardous materials
Exponents   512.922
   algebra   512.922
   arithmetic   513.22
   s.a. spec. appls. e.g.
    Business arithmetic
Export
   licensing   382.64
   subsidies   382.63
   taxes
    pub. finance   336.263
    other aspects see Customs
     (tariffs)
   trade   382.6
    govt. control
     activities   351.827 6
     spec. jur.   353–354
    departments *see* Executive
     departments
    law   343.087 8
     spec. jur.   343.3–.9
    marketing management   658.848
    spec. subj.   *s.s.–068 8*
Exporters *see* Foreign traders
Export-Import Bank
   economics   332.154
   other aspects see Banks
    (finance)
Exposing
   positives *see* Positives

Expositions
  buildings *see* Exhibition
        buildings
  industrial   607.34
  s.a. Exhibits; *also* Fairs
Expository
  programs
    radio performances   791.445
    television performances   791.455
  writing   808.066
    juvenile   808.068 8
Exposure
  of corpses
    death customs   393.4
  of person
    ethics *see* Personal
        appearance ethics
Exposure-meters
  photography   771.37
    gen. tech.   770.282
    spec. proc. & fields   772–778
Express services (freight)
  commerce
    air   387.744
    bus   388.322 2
    inland-waterway   386.244
      canal   386.404 24
      ferry   386.6
      lake   386.544
      river   386.354
    maritime   387.544
    rail
      gen. & standard   385.23
      special-duty   385.5
    truck   388.324
  govt. control
    gen. wks.   351.875–.878
    spec. jur.   353–354
  law *see* Freight services law
Expression
  dramatic *see* Acting
  linguistics *see* Linguistics
  music theory   781.63
  of emotions
    psychology   152.42
    animals   156.242
    children   155.412
    s.a. psych. of other spec.
      groups
  speaking
    preaching
      Christianity   251.03
      other rel. see Preaching
    other aspects see Speaking
  s.a. spec. mediums
Expressionism
  arts
    architecture   724.91
      spec. places   720.9
    other aspects see
      Architectural schools

Expressionism (continued)
  gen. wks.   709.040 42
    spec. places   709.1–.9
  painting   759.064 2
    spec. places   759.1–.9
  sculpture   735.230 442
    spec. places   730.9
  s.a. other spec. art forms
Expressive movements
  psychology   152.384
    animals   156.238 4
    children   155.412
    s.a. psych. of other spec.
      groups
Expressways
  commerce   388.12
  local   388.411
  law *see* Roads law; *also*
      Streets law
  other aspects see Roads
Expropriation
  economics   338.924
  land   333.13
  real property
    law   343.025 2
    spec. jur.   343.3–.9
Expulsions
  school ed.   371.543
  s.a. spec. levels of ed.;
    also Special education
Extemporization
  music theory   781.65
  s.a. spec. mediums
Extended
  care facilities
    gen. wks.
      soc. services   362.16
      misc. aspects see
        Hospitals
    other aspects see Health
      care facilities
    psychiatric
      soc. services   362.23
      misc. aspects see
        Mental health services
    other aspects see Health
      care facilities
  family
    soc. theology
      Christianity   261.835 85
      comp. rel.   291.178 358 5
      s.a. other spec. rel.
    sociology   306.85
Extended-coverage insurance   368.129
  misc. aspects see Insurance
Extenders
  chem. tech.   661.807
    misc. aspects see Organic
      chemicals
  oil-soluble paints
    technology   667.623

Extenders
  oil-soluble paints (continued)
    other aspects see Paints
Extension
  cords
    exterior wiring *see*
      Exterior wiring elect.
      circuits
    interior wiring *see*
      Interior wiring elect.
      circuits
  departments
    universities   378.155 4
  theory
    algebra   512.4
    s.a. spec. appls. e.g.
      Engineering
  units library sci.   021.62
Exterior
  algebras   512.57
    s.a. spec. appls. e.g.
      Engineering
  ballistics
    mil. eng.   623.514
  lighting eng.
    soc. & econ. aspects *see*
      Secondary industries
    technology   621.322 9
    s.a. spec. appls. e.g.
      Spectaculars
  painting buildings   698.12
  wiring elect. circuits
    electrodynamic eng.   621.319 25
    s.a. spec. appls. e.g.
      Flood lighting
    other aspects see
      Electrodynamics
  s.a. Outdoor
External
  affairs *see* Foreign affairs
  auditing *see* Auditing
  degrees
    higher ed.   378.03
  ear
    diseases
      gen. wks.   617.81
        neoplasms   616.992 85
        tuberculosis   616.995 85
      geriatrics   618.977 81
      pediatrics   618.920 978 1
      pub. health   614.599 8
      statistics   312.304 781
        deaths   312.260 478 1
      surgery   617.810 59
        anesthesiology   617.967 81
      other aspects see
        Diseases
    physiology
      human   612.851
      other aspects see Sensory
        functions

External
  ear (continued)
    other aspects see Ears
  medication
    therapeutics   615.67
    misc. aspects see
      Medication methods
    s.a. spec. diseases
  structure
    crystallography   548.12
    s.a. other spec. subj.
  s.a. other spec. subj.
Exterritoriality
  internat. law   341.488
Extinct
  animals
    paleozoology   560
    zoology   591.042
    s.a. spec. animals
  birds
    paleozoology   568
    zoology   598.042
  mammals
    paleozoology   569
    zoology   599.004 2
Extinction of species
  biology *see* Evolutionary
    cycles
Extortion
  criminology   364.165
  law   345.026 5
    spec. jur.   345.3–.9
  soc. theology
    Christianity   261.833 165
    comp. rel.   291.178 331 65
    s.a. other spec. rel.
Extraction
  dental sUrgery
    med. sci.   617.66
    vet. med.   636.089 766
    s.a. spec. animals
  foods
    gen. wks.
      comm. proc.   664.022
      other aspects see Foods
    sugars & syrups
      comm. proc.   664.113
      cane   664.122 3
      s.a. other kinds
      other aspects see Sugars
    s.a. other spec. foods
  ind. oils & gases   665.028 2
    s.a. spec. prod.
  obstetrical surgery   618.82
    vet. med.   636.089 882
    s.a. spec. animals
  s.a. other spec. subj.
Extractive
  industries *see* Primary
    industries

Extruded
latex prod.
manufacturing (continued)
technology — 678.538
s.a. spec. kinds of latexes
e.g. Natural latexes
metal prod.
mf. tech. — 671.84
ferrous metals — 672.84
s.a. other spec. metals
other aspects see Primary
metal prod.
rubber prod.
manufacturing
soc. & econ. aspects *see*
Secondary industries
technology — 678.35
s.a. spec. kinds of rubber
e.g. Natural rubber
Extrusion
metal prod.
arts
decorative — 739.14
s.a. spec. metals; also
spec. prod. e.g.
Jewelry
fine *see* Direct-metal
sculpture
mf. tech. — 671.34
ferrous metals — 672.34
s.a. other spec. metals
other aspects see
Mechanical working
plastics mf. — 668.413
s.a. spec. kinds of
plastics
rubber mf.
soc. & econ. aspects *see*
Secondary industries
technology — 678.27
s.a. spec. kinds of rubber
e.g. Natural rubber
Eye
banks
health services — 362.17
misc. aspects see Medical
services
muscles *see* Movements of eyes
training
music teaching method — 780.77
s.a. spec. mediums
Eye (locality) Suffolk Eng. — *area*–426 45
Eyeballs
diseases
gen. wks. — 617.74
neoplasms — 616.992 84
tuberculosis — 616.995 84
geriatrics — 618.977 74
pediatrics — 618.920 977 4
pub. health — 614.599 7
statistics — 312.304 774

Eyeballs
diseases (continued)
surgery — 617.740 59
anesthesiology — 617.967 74
other aspects see Diseases
tissue biology human — 611.018 984
other aspects see Eyes
Eyebar-chain suspension bridges
structural eng. — 624.55
other aspects see Bridges
(structures)
Eye-ear-nose-throat diseases
see
Otorhinolaryngology
Eyeglasses
dress customs — 391.44
mf. tech. — 681.411
components — 681.42–.43
optometry — 617.752 2
other aspects see Optical
instruments
Eyelids
diseases
gen. wks. — 617.771
geriatrics — 618.977 771
pediatrics — 618.920 977 71
statistics — 312.304 777 1
physiology
human — 612.847
other aspects see Sensory
functions
other aspects see Eyes
Eyemouth Borders Scot. — *area*–413 95
Eyes
anatomy
human — 611.84
other aspects see Sense
organs
diseases
gen. wks. — 617.7
neoplasms — 616.992 84
tuberculosis — 616.995 84
geriatrics — 618.977 7
pediatrics — 618.920 977
pub. health — 614.599 7
statistics — 312.304 77
deaths — 312.260 477
other aspects see Diseases
s.a. Otorhinolaryngology
personal care — 646.726
physical anthropometry — 573.684
physiology
human — 612.84
other aspects see Sensory
functions
surgery *see* Optical surgery
tissue biology human — 611.018 984
Eyewitnesses *see* Witnesses
Eyre
Creek Qld. — *area*–943 5
Lake S. Aust. — *area*–942 38

Factors of production

economics	338.01
income distribution	339.21
prod. efficiency *see*	
Efficiency prod. econ.	
spec. kinds	331–333

Factory

buildings *see* Industrial	
buildings	
inspection	
automobiles	
soc. & econ. aspects *see*	
Secondary industries	
technology	629.234
spec. parts	629.24–.27
s.a. other spec. prod.	
operations	
engineering	670.42
s.a. spec. prod. of mf.	
ships	
engineering	623.824 8
design	623.812 48
models	623.820 148
seamanship	623.882 48
other aspects see Vessels	
(nautical)	
system	
prod. econ.	338.65
s.a. Industrial	

Factory-outlet stores

commerce	381.1
misc. aspects see Commerce	

Faculae

sun	523.74

Faculties (schools) *see*
  Teachers

Faculty

councils	
universities & colleges	378.101 1
school	
psych. system	150.192
s.a. spec. subj. &	
branches of psych.	
senates	
universities & colleges	378.101 1

Fads

soc. movements	303.484

Faeroes	*area*–491 5

Faeroese

language	
linguistics	439.699
literature	839.699
s.a.	*lang.*–396 99
people	*r.e.n.*–396 9
s.a. Faeroes; *also other*	
spec. subj. e.g. Arts	

Fagaceae *see* Fagales

Fagales

botany	583.976
floriculture	635.933 976

Fagales (continued)

forestry	634.973 976
lumber trees	634.972
med. aspects	
crop prod.	633.883 976
gen. pharm.	615.323 976
toxicology	615.952 397 6
vet. pharm.	636.089 532 397 6
toxicology	636.089 595 239 76
paleobotany	561.3
other aspects see Plants	

Fagopyrum *see* Buckwheat

Fagus *see* Beech trees

Failings (human) *see* Vices

Failsworth Greater Manchester	
Eng.	*area*–427 393

Failure

business *see* Bankruptcy	
education	371.28
s.a. spec. levels of ed.;	
also Special education	
elect. power *see* Transmission	
elect. power	

Fair play

ethics *see* Recreation ethics	

Fairbanks election district

Alaska	*area*–798 6

Fairfax

city Va.	*area*–755 292
Co. Va.	*area*–755 291

Fairfield Co.

Connecticut	*area*–746 9
Ohio	*area*–771 58
South Carolina	*area*–757 49

Fairgrounds

landscape design	712.5

Fairies

lit. & stage trmt. *see*	
Supernatural beings	

Fairs

distribution channels	
commerce	381.18
misc. aspects see	
Commerce	
marketing management *see*	
Distribution channels	
soc. customs	394.6
s.a. Expositions	

Fairways

port. eng.	
technology	627.23
s.a. spec. appls. e.g.	
Harbor piloting	
other aspects see Liquids	
engineering	

Fairy

chess	
equip. mf.	688.741 8
soc. & econ. aspects *see*	
Secondary industries	
recreation	794.18

Families (continued)
  religion *see* Personal
    religion
  soc. theology
    Christianity ... 261.835 8
    comp. rel. ... 291.178 358
    s.a. other spec. rel.
  soc. welfare ... 362.82
    govt. control ... 350.848 2
    central govts. ... 351.848 2
    spec. jur. ... 353–354
    local govts. ... 352.944 82
    law *see* Welfare services
      law
  sociology ... 306.8
  worship
    Christianity ... 249
    comp. rel. ... 291.43
    Judaism ... 296.4
    s.a. other spec. rel.
Families (mathematics) ... 512.33
  s.a. spec. appls. e.g.
    Engineering
Family
  cars
    driving
      recreation ... 796.78
      technology ... 629.283 2
  Compact
    Can. hist. ... 971.038
  corporations
    law ... 346.066 8
      misc. aspects see
        Organizations law
  counseling
    soc. services ... 362.828 6
      misc. aspects see
        Families soc. welfare
  ethics
    philosophy ... 173
    religion
      Buddhism ... 294.356 3
      Christianity ... 241.63
      comp. rel. ... 291.563
      Hinduism ... 294.548 63
      s.a. other spec. rel.
  law *see* Domestic relations
    law
  libraries *see* Private
    libraries
  life
    home econ. ... 646.78
    soc. customs ... 392.3
  names ... 929.42
  planning
    pub. admin. ... 350.815
      central govts. ... 351.815
      spec. jur. ... 353–354
      local govts. ... 352.941 5
    technique ... 613.94

Family
  planning (continued)
    other aspects see
      Population controls
    psychotherapy
      psychiatry ... 616.891 56
      geriatrics ... 618.976 891 56
      pediatrics ... 618.928 915 6
      other aspects see Medical
        sciences
  relationships
    appl. psych. ... 158.24
    children ... 155.418
      s.a. psych. of other spec.
        groups
      s.a. spec. activities
        e.g. Home nursing
    ethics *see* Family ethics
    soc. theology
      Christianity ... 261.835 87
      comp. rel. ... 291.178 358 7
      s.a. other spec. rel.
    sociology ... 306.87
  rooms
    household management ... 643.55
    int. dec. ... 747.791
      s.a. spec. dec.
  size *see* Births
  state
    pol. sci. ... 321.12
      s.a. spec. jur.
  welfare law *see* Welfare
    services law
  s.a. Marriage; Domestic;
    Household
Famine *see* Hunger
Famous problems
  geometry ... 516.204
Fan vaults *see* Rib & fan vaults
Fancy-weave fabrics
  arts ... 746.046 1
    s.a. spec. processes e.g.
      Weaving
  manufacturing
    soc. & econ. aspects *see*
      Secondary industries
    technology ... 677.61
    other aspects see Textiles
    s.a. spec. prod.
Fancywork *see spec. kinds e.g.*
    Embroidery
Fan-jet engines
  aircraft eng.
    soc. & econ. aspects *see*
      Secondary industries
    tech. & mf. ... 629.134 353 7
Fannin Co.
  Georgia ... *area*–758 293
  Texas ... *area*–764 265
Fanning Isl. ... *area*–964

Farmhouses
  buildings (continued)
    other aspects see
      Residential buildings
Farming   631
  other aspects see Agriculture
Farms
  in animal husbandry   636.01
    s.a. spec. animals
  other aspects see
    Agricultural industries
Farmyard manures
  fertilizer
    production
      soc. & econ. aspects *see*
        Secondary industries
      technology   668.636 1
    use agric.   631.861
    s.a. spec. crops; also
        spec. types of culture
        e.g. Floriculture
Farnborough Hampshire Eng.
          area–422 725
Farne Isl. Northumberland Eng.
          area–429 89
Farnham Surrey Eng.   *area*–422 19
Farnworth Greater Manchester
    Eng.   *area*–411 62
Faro (game)
  equipment mf.   688.754 2
    soc. & econ. aspects *see*
      Secondary industries
  recreation   795.42
Faro Portugal   *area*–469 6
Farquhar Isls.   *area*–694
Farr Highland Scot.   *area*–411 62
Fars Iran   *area*–557 2
Farsi language *see* Persian
    language
Farsightedness *see* Refraction
    errors
Faruk reign Egypt hist.   962.052
  s.a. spec. events & subj.
    e.g. Commerce
Fasciae
  diseases
    gen. wks.   616.75
      neoplasms   616.992 74
      tuberculosis   616.995 74
    geriatrics   618.976 75
    pediatrics   618.927 5
    pub. health   614.597 5
    statistics   312.375
    other aspects see Diseases
  other aspects see Connective
    tissue
Fascism
  economics   335.6
  pol ideology   320.533

Fascism (continued)
  soc. theology *see* Political
    ideologies soc.
    theology
  s.a. spec. countries
Fascist
  parties
    pol. sci.   324.24–.29
    s.a. spec. subj. of concern
      e.g. Social problems
  regime
    Italy hist.   945.091
    s.a. spec. events & subj.
      e.g. Commerce
  states
    pol. sci.   321.94
    s.a. spec. jur.
Fashion
  design
    textile arts   746.92
    drawing   741.672
    modeling
      advertising operations   659.152
    soc. movements   303.484
    s.a. Clothing
Fast (denial) *see* Fasting
Fast (rapid)
  nuclear reactors
    technology   621.483 4
    s.a. spec. appls. e.g.
      Generation elect. power
    other aspects see Nuclear
      reactions
  s.a. other spec. subj.
Fasteners
  machine eng.
    soc. & econ. aspects *see*
      Secondary industries
    tech. & mf.   621.88
    s.a. spec. appls. e.g.
      Agricultural equipment
  other aspects see Mechanics
  s.a. Fastenings
Fastening-equipment
  soc. & econ. aspects *see*
      Secondary industries
  tech. & mf.   621.97
    s.a. spec. appls. e.g.
      Automobiles
Fastenings
  bookbinding   686.35
  buildings
    architecture   721.8
    construction   690.18
    design & dec.   729.39
    s.a. spec. kinds of bldgs.
  s.a. other spec. techs.; also
      Fasteners
Fasting
  days
    chronology   529.44

Fauvism
  arts (continued)
    painting   759.064 3
      spec. places   759.1–.9
    sculpture   735.230 443
      spec. places   730.9
    s.a. other spec. art forms
Faversham Kent Eng.   *area*–422 33
Fawley Hampshire Eng.   *area*–422 75
Fayette Co.
  Alabama   *area*–761 87
  Georgia   *area*–758 426
  Illinois   *area*–773 797
  Indiana   *area*–772 623
  Iowa   *area*–777 35
  Kentucky   *area*–769 47
  Ohio   *area*–771 813
  Pennsylvania   *area*–748 84
  Tennessee   *area*–768 21
  Texas   *area*–764 251
  West Virginia   *area*–754 71
Fear
  mental pub. health   614.582 2
  of the Lord
    gift of Holy Spirit
      Christian doctrines   234.12
  psychology *see* Primitive
            emotions
  other aspects see Mental
            illness
Feast days
  chronology   529.44
  sermons
    Christianity   252.6
    other rel. see Preaching
  soc. customs   394.2
  other aspects see Church year
Feasts
  rel. rites
    Christianity   265.9
    Judaism   296.43
    other rel. see Public
            worship
Feather products
  manufacturing
    soc. & econ. aspects *see*
            Secondary industries
    technology   679.47
Featherbedding
  labor econ.   331.889 6
Feathers
  birds raised for
    animal husbandry   636.61
    chickens   636.508 845
    *s.a. other spec. kinds of
            poultry*
  other aspects see
            Integumentary organs
  s.a. spec. uses e.g. Clothing
Featherstone West Yorkshire Eng.
                           area–428 15

Feathertop Mount Vic.   *area*–945 5
Features
  character anal.
    physiognomy   138
Febrifuges
  pharmacodynamics   615.75
  other aspects see Drugs
Feces
  human phys.   612.36
  other aspects see Digestion
Federal
  court reports
    U.S. law   348.734 1
  courts
    U.S. law   347.732
  governments *see* Central
            governments
  Register
    U.S. govt.   353.000 5
  Republic of Germany   *area*–43
  states
    pol. sci.   321.02
    s.a. spec. jur.
    s.a. National
Federalism
  constitutional law   342.042
    spec. jur.   342.3–.9
Federalist Party U.S.
  pol. sci.   324.273 22
  *s.a. spec. subj. of concern
            e.g.* Social problems
Federal-local relations *see*
            National-local
            relations
Federal-state relations *see*
            National-state
            relations
Federation of Arab Republics
                           area–62
Fee simple
  ownership
    land econ.   333.323 2
  property law *see* Land
            tenure law
Feebleminded *see* Mentally
            deficient
Feeblemindedness *see* Mental
            deficiency
Feedback
  characteristics
    closed-loop automation eng.   629.831 4
    s.a. spec. appls. e.g.
            Thermostats
  circuits
    tech. & mf.   621.381 535
      microelectronics   621.381 735
      microwave electronics   621.381 325
      radiowave electronics   621.381 535
      x- & gamma-ray electronics   621.381 6
    s.a. spec. appls. e.g.
            Television

Felling	
trees	
forestry	634.982
s.a. spec. trees	
Tyne & Wear Eng.	*area*–428 73
Fellowships	
education	378.33
s.a. Special education	
other aspects see	
Scholarships	
Feloidea	
animal husbandry	636.974 42
hunting	
commercial	639.117 442
sports	
big game	799.277 442
small game	799.259 744 2
zoology	599.744 2
other aspects see Carnivora	
Felonies *see* Criminal offenses	
Felsites *see* Volcanic rocks	
Felt roofing	
bldg. construction	695
Feltham London Eng.	*area*–421 82
Felting	
textiles	
manufacturing	
soc. & econ. aspects *see*	
Secondary industries	
technology	677.028 24
s.a. spec. kinds of	
textiles & spec. prod.	
Felts *see* Nonwoven fabrics;	
also Woven felts	
Feluccas *see* Modern wind-driven	
vessels	
Female	
breast *see* Mammary glands	
genital organs	
anatomy	
human	611.65
other aspects see	
Reproductive organs	
diseases	
gen. wks.	618.1
neoplasms	616.992 65
tuberculosis	616.995 65
geratrics	618.978 1
pediatrics	618.920 981
pub. health	614.599 2
statistics	312.304 81
deaths	312.260 481
surgery	618.1
anesthesiology	617.968 1
other aspects see	
Diseases	
physical anthropometry	573.665
physiology	
human	612.62
other aspects see	
Reproduction	
Female	
genital organs (continued)	
tissue biology human	611.018 965
reproductive system *see*	
Female genital organs	
sexual disorders	
gynecology	618.17
geriatrics	618.978 17
pediatrics	618.920 981 7
pub. health	614.599 2
statistics	312.304 817
other aspects see	
Diseases	
voices	
songs *see* Women's vocal	
music	
Females	
hygiene	613.042 4
misc. aspects see Hygiene	
s.a.	*pers.*–042
s.a. spec. female groups e.g.	
Women	
Femininity	
sex psych.	155.333
Femur *see* Lower extremities	
bones	
Fencers	
biog. & work	796.860 92
s.a.	*pers.*–796 8
Fences	
landscape design	717
roadside barriers	
technology	625.795
other aspects see Roads	
s.a. Farm fences	
Fencing (stolen goods) *see*	
Larceny	
Fencing (swordplay)	
equipment mf.	688.768 6
soc. & econ. aspects *see*	
Secondary industries	
sports	796.86
other aspects see Sports	
Fenders	
automobiles	
soc. & econ. aspects *see*	
Secondary industries	
tech. & mf.	629.26
Fenian	
activities	
Canada hist.	971.048
Fenland Cambridgeshire Eng.	
	area–426 53
Fennel *see* Umbellales	
Fens Eng.	*area*–426
Fentress Co. Tenn.	*area*–768 69
Ferdinand	
reign	
Germany	
1	943.032
2	943.042

Ferrous
  metals (continued)
    materials
      building 691.7
      engineering 620.17
        foundations 624.153 7
        naval design 623.818 21
        shipbuilding 623.820 7
        structures 624.182 1
        s.a. other spec. uses
      metallography 669.951
      metallurgy 669.1
        physical & chem. 669.961
        soc. & econ. aspects *see*
            Secondary industries
      mineral aspects *see* Iron
    products
      arts *see* Ferrous metals
          arts
      manufacturing
        soc. & econ. aspects
            see Secondary
            industries
        technology 672
        s.a. spec. prod.
      roofing
        bldg. construction 695
        other aspects see Metal;
            also Metals
    sulfate
      soil conditioners 631.825
        misc. aspects see Soil
            conditioners
Ferrum *see* Iron
Ferry
  Co. Wash. *area*–797 25
  houses *see* Marine
          transportation
          buildings
  terminals
    activities and facilities
        see Ferry
            transportation
  transportation
    commerce 386.6
    govt. control 350.876 6
      central govts. 351.876 6
      spec. jur. 353–354
      local govts. 352.916 6
    law *see* Water
            transportation law
Ferryboats
  engineering 623.823 4
    design 623.812 34
    models 623.820 134
    seamanship 623.882 34
    other aspects see Vessels
            (nautical)
Fertility
  human *see* Births

Fertility (continued)
  soil science 631.422
    s.a. spec. crops; also spec.
        types of culture e.g.
        Floriculture
Fertilizers
  conversion refuse
    soc. & econ. aspects *see*
        Secondary industries
    technology 631.877
  production
    soc. & econ. aspects *see*
        Secondary industries
    technology 668.62
    use agric. 631.81
      effect on prod. econ. 338.162
      s.a. spec. crops; also spec.
          types of culture e.g.
          Floriculture
  wastes *see* Soil improvement
          wastes
Fertilizer-spreaders
  agriculture 631.33
    use 631.816
      s.a. spec. crops; also
          spec. types of culture
          e.g. Floriculture
  mf. tech. 681.763 1
    soc. & econ. aspects *see*
        Secondary industries
Ferungulata
  animal husbandry 636.97
  hunting
    commercial 639.117
    sports
      big game 799.277
      small game 799.259 7
  paleozoology 569.7
  zoology 599.7
  other aspects see Mammalia
Fescue grasses *see* Pooideae
Festivals
  Anglican liturgy 264.031
  arts 700.79
    s.a. spec. art forms
  dress for
    customs 391.8
  music 780.79
    s.a. spec. mediums
  performing arts 791.6
  rel. rites
    Christianity 265.9
    Judaism 296.43
    other rel. see Public
        worship
  soc. customs 394.2
  Sunday-school services
    Christianity 268.7
    other rel. see Religious
        instruction

Fibrations	512.33
s.a. spec. appls. e.g.	
Engineering	
Fibrin	
blood	
human phys.	612.115
other aspects see	
Circulatory fluids	
Fibrinoplastin	
blood	
human phys.	612.115
other aspects see	
Circulatory fluids	
Fibrous	
cartilage	
human anatomy & phys.	611.018 3
other aspects see Tissue	
biology	
tunics eyes	
physiology	
human	612.841
other aspects see Sensory	
functions	
other aspects see Eyes	
Fibrovascular bundles	
plant	
anatomy	581.41
pathology	581.221
s.a. spec. plants	
Fibula *see* Lower extremities	
bones	
Ficoidaceae *see* Caryophyllales	
Fiction	
folklore	398.2
gen. wks.	
collections	808.83
crit. theory	801.953
textual	801.959
hist. & crit.	809.3
rhetoric	808.3
juvenile	808.068 3
spec. lits.	*lit. sub.*–3
Fiction writers	
biog. & work	809.3
s.a. spec. lits.	
s.a.	*pers.*–83
Fictions	
logic	165
Fictitious *see* Legendary	
Ficus	
carica *see* Figs	
elastica	
agriculture	633.895 2
soc. & econ. aspects *see*	
Primary industries	
Fidelity bonds	
insurance	368.83
misc. aspects see Insurance	

Fiduciary	
accounting	657.47
s.a. spec. kinds of	
enterprise e.g.	
Insurance accounting	
trusts	
law	
gen. wks.	346.059
spec. jur.	346.3–.9
taxes	
law	343.064
spec. jur.	343.3–.9
other aspects see Taxes	
Field	
artillery	
armed forces	358.12
mil. eng.	
soc. & econ. aspects *see*	
Secondary industries	
tech. & mf.	623.412
athletics	
equipment mf.	688.764 2
soc. & econ. aspects *see*	
Secondary industries	
sports	796.42
other aspects see Sports	
cores	
generators *see*	
Electromagnets	
generators	
crops	
agriculture	633
soc. & econ. aspects *see*	
Primary industries	
feeds	
animal husbandry	636.086
s.a. spec. animals	
effect	
transistors	
gen. wks.	
tech. & mf.	621.381 528 4
s.a. spec. appls.	
e.g. Radiocontrol	
other aspects see	
Transistors	
extensions	
number theory	512.74
s.a. spec. appls. e.g.	
Engineering	
generators *see* Auxiliary	
generating units	
glasses	
mf. tech.	681.412
components	681.42–.43
other aspects see Optical	
instruments	
hockey	
equipment mf.	688.763 55
soc. & econ. aspects *see*	
Secondary industries	

Field
  hockey (continued)
    players
      biog. & work   796.355 092
      s.a.   *pers.*–796 35
    sports   796.355
    other aspects see Sports
  kitchens
    mil. training operations   355.544
  peas
    agriculture   633.369
    soc. & econ. aspects *see*
      Primary industries
    other aspects see
      Papilionaceae; *also*
      Field crops
  theories
    physics   530.14
      spec. states of matter   530.4
      s.a. spec. branches of
        physics
  theory   512.32
    numbers   512.74
    s.a. spec. appls. e.g.
      Engineering
  psychology   150.198 4
    s.a. spec. subj. &
      branches of psych.
  training
    mil. sci.   355.544
    s.a. spec. mil. branches
  trips
    ed. method *see* Laboratory
      method
    museum services   069.15
  units
    elect. power generation *see*
      Auxiliary generating
      units
  work
    statistical method   001.422 2
    spec. subj. *see*
      Statistical method
      spec. subj.
Fielding
  baseball   796.357 24–.357 25
  cricket   796.358 23
Fields
  algebra   512.3
  s.a. spec. appls. e.g.
    Engineering
Fife
  music   788.515
    recordings   789.912 851
  Scotland   *area*–412 9
Fifes
  mf. tech.   681.818 51
  misc. aspects see Musical
    instruments
  musical art   788.51

Fifteenth century
  history   909.4
    appls. to spec. subj.   *s.s.*–090 24
  s.a. spec. countries
Fifth Republic
  France history   944.083
  s.a. spec. events & subj.
    e.g. Arts
Fighter-bombers
  mil. aircraft eng.   623.746 3
Fighters (aircraft)
  mil. aircraft eng.   623.746 4
Fighting
  animal husbandry for   636.088 8
  s.a. spec. animals
  sports *see* Combat sports
Fighting-forces
  air warfare   358.43
Figs
  agriculture   634.37
  soc. & econ. aspects *see*
    Primary industries
  foods   641.343 7
    preparation
      commercial   664.804 37
      domestic   641.643 7
  other aspects see Urticales;
    also Fruits
Figured madras fabrics *see*
    Dobby-weave fabrics
Figures
  art representation *see* Human
    figures
  of speech rhetoric   808
Figurines
  ceramic arts   738.82
  earthenware
    technology   666.68
    other aspects see
      Earthenware
  porcelain
    technology   666.58
    other aspects see Porcelain
  rel. significance
    Christianity   247.888 2
    comp. rel.   291.37
    s.a. other spec. rel.
  other aspects see Ornaments
    arts
Fiji
  islands   *area*–961 1
  Sea
    oceanography   551.465 77
    regional subj. trmt.   *area*–164 77
    other aspects see Pacific
      Ocean
Fijians   *r.e.n.*–995
Filaments *see* Electric lighting
Filarial diseases   616.965 2
  geriatrics   618.976 965 2
  pediatrics   618.929 652

Filarial diseases (continued)
   pub. health 614.555 2
   statistics 312.396 52
      deaths 312.269 652
   other aspects see Diseases
Filariasis *see* Filarial
      diseases
Filberts
   agriculture 634.54
   soc. & econ. aspects *see*
      Primary industries
   foods 641.345 4
    preparation
      commercial 664.804 54
      domestic 641.645 4
   other aspects see Fagales;
      also Nuts
File cabinets
   use records management 651.54
   other aspects see Cabinets
      (furniture)
Filers
   office services 651.374 3
   other aspects see Office
      personnel
Files (furniture) *see* File
      cabinets
Files (tools) *see* Filing-tools
Filey North Yorkshire Eng. *area*–428 47
Filial ethics *see* Family ethics
Filicales
   botany 587.31
   floriculture 635.937 31
   med. aspects
    crop prod. 633.887 31
    gen. pharm. 615.327 31
     toxicology 615.952 731
    vet. pharm. 636.089 532 731
     toxicology 636.089 595 273 1
   paleobotany 561.73
   other aspects see Plants
Filicineae
   botany 587.3
   floriculture 635.937 3
   med. aspects
    crop prod. 633.887 3
    gen. pharm. 615.327 3
     toxicology 615.952 73
    vet. pharm. 636.089 532 73
     toxicology 636.089 595 273
   paleobotany 561.73
   other aspects see Plants
Filing
   library econ. 025.317
   records management 651.53
Filing-cabinets *see* File
      cabinets
Filing-tools
   soc. & econ. aspects *see*
      Secondary industries

Filing-tools (continued)
   tech. & mf. 621.924
   s.a. spec. appls. e.g.
      Surface finishing
Filipino *see* Tagalog
Fillers
   plastics mf. 668.411
   s.a. spec. kinds of
      plastics
Filling station bldgs. *see*
      Motor vehicle transp.
      bldgs.
Fillings
   dentistry 617.675
Fillmore
   County
    Minnesota *area*–776 16
    Nebraska *area*–782 342
   Millard admin.
    U.S. hist. 973.64
    s.a. spec. events & subj.
      e.g. Commerce
Fills
   road eng. *see* Roadbeds
Film
   music 782.85
    recordings 789.912 285
   musicals *see* Musical shows
   records & recorders *see*
      Recordings
Filmed programs
   television performances 791.453
Films
   exposure
    photographic tech. 770.282
     spec. fields 778
   photosensitive surfaces
    photography 771.532 4
     gen. tech. 770.283
     spec. proc. & fields 772–778
   pictorial materials
    library trmt. 025.177 3
     acquisitions 025.287 3
     cataloging 025.347 3
     s.a. other spec.
      activities
    museology 069.57
     circulation 069.134
    other aspects see
      Audiovisual
    s.a. spec. kinds e.g.
      Motion pictures
   plastic
    chem. tech. 668.495
    other aspects see Plastics
   surface chem. *see* Surface
      phenomena
   thin
    physics *see* Solids
    technology *see*
      Microelectronics

Finance
  prod. econ. (continued)
    transportation
      commerce | 380.59
        air | 387.71
        inland waterway | 386.1
        maritime | 387.51
        motor | 388.32
        railway | 385.1
          special-duty | 385.5
        urban | 388.404 2
      govt. control | 350.875–.878
        central govts. | 351.875–.878
          spec. jur. | 353–354
        local govts. | 352.915–.918
      law *see* Transportation
          law
    public *see* Public finance
  s.a. other spec. subj. e.g.
      Schools finance
Financial
  accounting | 657.48
    s.a. spec. kinds of
        enterprise e.g.
        Insurance accounting
  administration
    armed forces | 355.622
      s.a. spec. mil branches
    management | 658.15
      spec. subj. | *s.s.*–068 1
    pub. admin. *see* Public
        finance pub. admin.
  aid
    crime prevention | 364.44
    soc. services | 361.05
      spec. problems & groups | 362–363
      other aspects see Welfare
          services
  assistance *see* Financial aid
  clerks
    office services | 651.37
  economics | 332
  institution bldgs.
    architecture | 725.24
    building | 690.524
    other aspects see Public
        structures
  institutions
    accounting | 657.833
    economics | 332.1–.3
    govt. control
      activities | 351.825
        spec. jur. | 353–354
  news *see* Business news
  offenses
    criminology | 364.168
    law | 345.026 8
      spec. jur. | 345.3–.9
    soc. theology
      Christianity | 261.833 168
      comp. rel. | 291.178 331 68

Financial
  offenses
    soc. theology (continued)
      s.a. other spec. rel.
  pages *see* Business news
  powers
    legislative bodies
      law *see* Legislative
          powers law
      pol. sci. | 328.341 2
        spec. jur. | 328.4–.9
  reporting
    accounting | 657.3
      s.a. spec. kinds of
          enterprise e.g.
          Insurance accounting
  security
    personal finance | 332.024 01
  statements
    accounting *see* Financial
        reporting accounting
    pub. admin. *see* Accounting
        pub. admin.
  strength measurement
    accounting | 657.48
      s.a. spec. kinds of
          enterprise e.g.
          Insurance accounting
  success | 650.12
  support by govts.
    libraries | 021.83
  transactions
    govt. control
      activities | 351.825
        spec. jur. | 353–354
      govt. depts. *see*
          Executive departments
    s.a. Business
Financiers
  biog. & work | 332.092
  ethics *see* Business ethics
  s.a. | *pers.*–332
Finbacks *see* Mysticeti
Finches
  animal husbandry | 636.686 2
    soc. & econ. aspects *see*
        Primary industries
  other aspects see
      Fringillidae
Finchley London Eng. | *area*–421 87
Findochty Grampian Scot. | *area*–412 23
Fine
  arts | 700
    Biblical trmt. | 220.87
      s.a. spec. parts of Bible
  curriculums | 375.7
  documentation | 025.067
  govt. control
    activities | 350.854
      central govts. | 351.854
        spec. jur. | 353–354

Finnish
Evangelical Lutheran Church   284.133 4
  misc. aspects see Lutheran
language
  linguistics   494.541
  literature   894.541
  s.a.   *lang.*–945 41
people   *r.e.n.*–945 41
s.a. Finland; *also other*
        spec. subj. e.g. Arts
Finnmark Norway   *area*–484 5
Finno-Ugric
  languages
    linguistics   494.5
    literatures   894.5
    s.a.   *lang.*–945
  people   *r.e.n.*–945
  s.a. other spec. subj. e.g.
          Arts
Finns   *r.e.n.*–945 41
Fins
  aircraft eng.
    soc. & econ. aspects *see*
            Secondary industries
    tech. & mf.   629.134 33
  s.a. other spec. occurrences
Finsbury London Eng.   *area*–421 43
Finsler geometry   516.375
  s.a. spec. appls.
Fiqh   340.59
Fir
  trees
    forestry   634.975 4
    soc. & econ. aspects *see*
            Primary industries
    other aspects see
            Coniferales; *also*
            Trees
  woods *see* Softwoods
Fire
  alarms
    communication *see* Warning
            systems
    engineering   628.922 5
    s.a. spec. appls. e.g.
            Forest fires
  control (artillery)
    mil. gunnery   623.558
  control (combustion) *see* Fire
          safety
  doors *see* Fire safety
          engineering
  escapes
    engineering *see* Fire safety
            engineering
  exits
    safety meas. *see* Fire
            safety
  extinction *see* Fire fighting
  fighters
    biog. & work   363.370 92

Fire
  fighters (continued)
    other aspects see Welfare
            personnel
    s.a.   *pers.*–363 3
  fighting
    equipment
      airport eng.   629.136 8
      military   623.668
      s.a. other spec. appls.
    shipbiilding *see* Safety
            equipment shipbuilding
    soc. services   363.378
      misc. aspects see Fire
            safety
    other aspects see Fire
            fighting technology
    s.a. other spec.
            installations
    soc. & econ. aspects *see*
            Secondary industries
    technology   628.925
    seamanship   623.888 6
      s.a. other spec. appls.
            e.g. Forest fires
  hazards
    soc. path.   363.37
  hoses
    fire extinction tech.   628.925 2
      s.a. spec. appls. e.g.
            Forest fires
  insurance   368.11
    misc. aspects see Insurance
  lit. & stage trmt.
    folk lit. soc.   398.364
    other aspects see Natural
            phenomena
  prevention *see* Fire safety
  rel. worship
    comp. rel.   291.212
    s.a. spec. rel.
  resistance trmt.
    wood bldg. materials   691.15
  retardants
    soc. & econ. aspects *see*
            Secondary industries
    technology   628.922 3
      s.a. spec. appls. e.g.
            Flame-resistant fabrics
  safety
    engineering
      soc. & econ. aspects *see*
            Secondary industries
      technology   628.922
        s.a. spec. appls. e.g.
            Forest fires
    law   344.053 7
      spec. jur.   344.3–.9

First
aid
  med. sci.
    gen. med.   616.025 2
    surgery   617.026 2
    s.a. spec. diseases
    other aspects see
      Diseases
  stations
    armed forces   355.72
    s.a. spec. mil.
      branches
  editions
    hist. & crit.   094.4
Empire
  France hist.   944.05
  s.a. spec. events & subj.
    e.g. Arts
Instance
  Court of
    Scotland
      law   345.411 016 2
  names   929.44
Republic
  France hist.   944.042
  s.a. spec. events & subj.
    e.g. Arts
First-aid equip. *see* Safety
    equipment
First-class mail
  postal commun.   383.122
  other aspects see Postal
    communication
Fiscal
  policy
    law   343.034
      spec. jur.   343.3–.9
    macroeconomics   339.52
    pub. finance   336.3
  tariffs
    internat. comm.   382.72
    other aspects see Customs
      (Tariffs)
Fischer-Tropsch processes
  coal
    synthetic petroleum tech.   662.662 3
Fish
  culturists
    biog. & work   639.309 2
    s.a.   *pers.*–639 3
  feeds from
    animal husbandry   636.087 6
    s.a. spec. animals
  foods from   641.392
    cookery   641.692
    other aspects see Seafoods
  hatcheries   639.311
  s.a. spec. kinds of fish
  lice *see* Branchiura

Fish (continued)
  oil
    industrial
      comm. proc.   665.2
      soc. & econ. aspects
        see Secondary
          industries
    s.a. Pisces
Fisher Co. Tex.   *area*–764 732
Fisheries *see* Fishing
Fishermen
  biog. & work
    industries   639.209 2
    sports   799.109 2
  persons
    industries   *pers.*–639 2
    sports   *pers.*–799 1
Fishers Isl. N.Y.   *area*–747 25
Fishes *see* Pisces
Fishguard Dyfed Wales   *area*–429 62
Fishing
  equipment (sports)
    manufacturing
      soc. & econ. aspects *see*
        Secondary industries
      technology   688.791
  industries   639.2–.3
    bus. organizations   338.763 92–.763 93
    cooperatives   334.683 92–.683 93
    mergers   338.836 392–.836 393
    restrictive practices
                                  338.826 392–.826 393
    govt. control
      activities   351.823 62
        spec. jur.   353–354
      govt. depts.   351.082 362
        spec. jur.   353–354
    ind. relations   331.043 92–.043 93
    s.a. spec. aspects e.g.
      Compensation
    prod. econ.   338.372
  law
    international   341.762 2
    municipal   343.076 2
      spec. jur.   343.3–.9
  sports   799.1
    misc. aspects see Sports
Fish-liver oils
  pharmacology   615.34
  other aspects see Drugs
Fission
  biol. reproduction *see*
    Vegetative generation
  nuclear
    astrophysics   523.019 762
    s.a. spec. celestial
      bodies
    physics   539.762
      spec. states of matter   530.4
      s.a. spec. physical
        phenomena e.g. Heat

Flags 929.92
 mil. sci. 355.15
  s.a. spec. mil. branches
 nonverbal commun. *see* Flag
  signals
Flagstones 553.53
 econ. geol. 553.53
 marketing *see* Marketing
 mining
  prod. econ. 338.275 3
  technology 622.353
   prospecting 622.185 3
 road eng.
  technology 625.81
   sidewalks 625.881
  other aspects see Roads
 other aspects see Natural
  stones
 s.a. other spec. uses
Flakes
 animal feeds *see* Formula
  feeds
Flaking
 drying & dehydrating foods
  comm. proc. 664.028 43
 other aspects see Foods
 s.a. spec. foods e.g. Meats
Flame
 tests
  blowpipe anal. *see* Blowpipe
   analysis
 thermochemistry *see*
   Combustion
   thermochemistry
 throwers *see* Chemical devices
  mil. eng.
 violets *see* Personales
Flameproof fabrics
 manufacturing
  soc. & econ. aspects *see*
   Secondary industries
  technology 677.689
 other aspects see Textiles
 s.a. spec. prod.
Flame-resistant fabrics
 manufacturing
  soc. & econ. aspects *see*
   Secondary industries
  technology 677.689
 other aspects see Textiles
 s.a. spec. prod.
Flamingos *see* Ciconiiformes
Flammable materials
 pub. safety 363.179
  misc. aspects see Hazardous
   materials
Flanders
 Belgium area–493 1
 France area–442 8
Flangers
 railroad *see* Work cars

Flannel fabrics
 arts 746.046 24
  s.a. spec. processes e.g.
   Weaving
 manufacturing
  soc. & econ. aspects *see*
   Secondary industries
  technology 677.624
 other aspects see Textiles
 s.a. spec. prod.
Flaps
 aircraft eng.
  soc. & econ. aspects *see*
   Secondary industries
  tech. & mf. 629.134 33
 s.a. other spec. occurrences
Flare stars *see* Eruptive
  variable stars
Flares
 shipbuilding
  soc. & econ. aspects *see*
   Secondary industries
  technology 623.86
   design 623.814 6
   spec. craft 623.812
 sun
  astronomy 523.75
 s.a. Pyrotechnical devices
Flash welding *see*
   Resistance-welding
Flash-bulb photography 778.72
Flashcards
 library trmt. 025.179 6
  acquisitions 025.289 6
  cataloging 025.349 6
Flashings *see* Roofs
Flashless powders *see*
   Propellant explosives
Flasks
 chem. apparatus 542.2
  s.a. spec. appls. e.g.
   Organic chemistry
Flat
 racing
  horses
   equip. mf. 688.78
    soc. & econ. aspects
    see Secondary
     industries
   sports 798.43
   other aspects see Sports
  other animals
   equip. mf. 688.78
    soc. & econ. aspects
    see Secondary
     industries
   sports 798.8
   other aspects see Sports
Flatboats *see* Towed vessels
Flatcars *see* Freight cars

Flathead
Co. Mont.   *area*–786 82
Lake Mont.   *area*–786 832
Flatirons
elect. appliances *see*
Electrical appliances
use home econ.   648.1
Flats
architecture   728.314
building   690.831 4
housekeeping   647.92
other aspects see Residential
buildings
Flattery
ethics
philosophy   177.3
religion
Buddhism   294.356 73
Christianity   241.673
comp. rel.   291.567 3
Hinduism   294.548 673
s.a. other spec. rel.
Flatware *see* Tableware
Flatworms *see* Platyhelminthes
Flautists *see* Flutists
Flavoring aids
food tech.
processing   664.5
soc. & econ. aspects *see*
Secondary industries
s.a. spec. kinds
Flavoring-producing plants
agriculture   633.82
soc. & econ. aspects *see*
Primary industries
foods   641.338
preparation
commercial   664.5
domestic   641.638
Flax
agriculture   633.52
soc. & econ. aspects *see*
Primary industries
textiles
arts   746.041 1
s.a. spec. processes e.g.
Weaving
dyeing   667.311
manufacturing
soc. & econ. aspects *see*
Secondary industries
technology   677.11
special-process fabrics 677.6
other aspects see Textiles
s.a. spec. prod.
other aspects see
Malpighiales
Flaxseed oil
comm. proc.   665.352
soc. & econ. aspects *see*
Secondary industries

Flea-borne typhus *see* Murine
typhus
Fleas
disease carriers
pub. health   614.432 4
misc. aspects see Public
health
other aspects see
Siphonaptera
Fleet Hampshire Eng.   *area*–422 723
Fleets
naval organization   359.31
Fleetwood Lancashire Eng.   *area*–427 682
Fleming Co. Ky.   *area*–769 56
Flemings   *r.e.n.*–393 2
Flemish
language
linguistics   439.32
literatures   839.32
s.a.   *lang.*–393 2
people   *r.e.n.*–393 2
s.a. Flanders; *also other*
spec. subj. e.g. Arts
Flesh flies *see* Cyclorrhapha
Fleshing
nat. leathers
manufacturing
soc. & econ. aspects *see*
Secondary industries
technology   675.22
Fleshy-finned fishes *see* Dipnoi
Flettner rotors *see* Wind
engines
Flexible
algebras   512.24
s.a. spec. appls. e.g.
Engineering
connections
power transmission *see*
Power transmission
polymers
org. chem.   547.843
working periods
labor econ.   331.257 2
s.a. spec. classes of
workers e.g. Women
other aspects see Work
periods
Flexitime *see* Flexible working
periods
Flexure
resistance to
eng. materials   620.112 44
spec. properties   620.112 5–.112 6
s.a. spec. materials &
spec. uses
Flickers *see* Piciformes

Flies
  disease carriers
    pub. health   614.432 2
    misc. aspects see Public
      health
    other aspects see Diptera
Flight
  aerial *see* Aeronautics
  crews *see* Aircraft operation
  guides
    aeronautics   629.132 54
  instrumentation
    aircraft eng.   629.135 2
    s.a. spec. appls. e.g.
      Military engineering
  into Egypt
    Christian doctrines   232.926
  lit. & stage trmt. *see*
    Scientific themes
  operations
    aeronautics
      soc. & econ. aspects *see*
        Secondary industries
      technology   629.132 52
  systems
    spacecraft eng.   629.474 2
      unmanned   629.464 2
      other aspects see
        Spacecraft
  simulators
    aeronautics   629.132 520 78
    manned space flight   629.450 078
  tests
    aircraft eng.   629.134 53
    s.a. spec. appls. e.g.
      Military engineering
  vehicles *see* Aerospace
    engineering
Flights
  air force organization   358.413 1
Flin Flon Man.   *area*–712 72
Flinders
  Chase Nat. Park S. Aust.
         area–942 35
  Isl. Tas.   *area*–946 7
  Ranges S. Aust.   *area*–942 37
  River Qld.   *area*–943 7
Flint
  city Mich.   *area*–774 37
  Island   *area*–964
  material *see* Abrasive
    materials
  River
    Georgia   *area*–758 9
    Michigan   *area*–774 37
Flintshire Wales   *area*–429 33
Floater insurance   368.2
  misc. aspects see Insurance

Floating
  airports
    engineering
      gen. wks.   629.136 1
      details   629.136 3–.136 8
      military   623.661
      s.a. other spec. appls.
        e.g. Air
        transportation
      other aspects see Airports
  bridges
    structural eng.   624.87
    other aspects see Bridges
      (structures)
  debts
    pub. finance   336.32
  docks
    soc. & econ. aspects *see*
      Secondary industries
    technology   623.83
  foundations
    engineering   624.156
    s.a. spec. appls. e.g.
      Military engineering
Floatplanes *see* Seaplanes
Floats (displays)
  performing arts   791.6
Floats (fishing sports)
  manufacturing
    soc. & econ. aspects *see*
      Secondary industries
    technology   688.791
Flocculation
  water-supply trmt.
    technology   628.162 2
    other aspects see Water
      supply engineering
Flock books
  animal husbandry   636.082 2
  s.a. spec. animals
Flood lighting
  illumination eng.
    soc. & econ. aspects *see*
      Secondary industries
    technology   621.321 4
      exterior   621.322 9
      interior   621.322 5–.322 8
    s.a. spec. kinds e.g.
      Incandescent lighting
    s.a. spec. appls. e.g.
      Photography
Flooding
  irrigation *see* Irrigation
  mil. eng.   623.31
Floods
  control
    engineering
      soc. & econ. aspects *see*
        Secondary industries

Floods
  control
    engineering (continued)
      technology   627.4
        s.a. spec. appls. e.g.
          Military engineering
        other aspects see Liquids
          engineering
    facilities
      civic art   711.8
      forest use   634.99
    pub. admin.
      pub. works   350.86
      resources   350.823 29
        central govts.   351.823 29
        spec. jur.   353–354
        local govts.   352.942 329
      s.a. spec. levels of
        govt.
  disasters
    soc. action   363.349 3
    misc. aspects see
      Disasters
  geology   551.489
  plant injuries from
    agriculture   632.17
    s.a. spec. plants; also
      spec. types of culture
      e.g. Forestry
  warning systems *see* Warning
    systems
  wreckage studies *see* Floods
    control
  other aspects see Disasters
Floodwaters *see* Ground waters
Floor
  coverings
    bldg. details   698.9
    home econ.   645.1
  systems
    bridge eng.   624.283
      analysis & design   624.253
    s.a. spec. appls. e.g.
      Suspension bridges
Floors
  architectural
    construction   721.6
    design & decoration   729.37
  building   690.16
  cleaning
    home econ.   648.5
    int. dec.   747.4
    s.a. spec. dec.
  painting bldgs.   698.146
  wood bldg. construction   694.2
  s.a. spec. kinds of bldgs.
Flora *see* Plants
Floral
  arts   745.92
  oils
    chem. tech.   668.42

Floral
  oils (continued)
    soc. customs   391.63
  waters
    chem. tech.   668.42
    soc. customs   391.63
Florence
  city Italy   *area*–455 1
  County
    South Carolina   *area*–757 84
    Wisconsin   *area*–775 32
Flores
  dept. Uruguay   *area*–895 26
  isl. Indonesia   *area*–598 6
  Sea *see* Southern Sunda Isls.
    seas
Floriculture   635.9
  misc. aspects see Agriculture
Florida
  dept. Uruguay   *area*–895 25
  Keys   *area*–759 41
  state   *area*–759
  Straits
    oceanography   551.464 63
    regional subj. trmt.   *area*–163 63
    other aspects see Atlantic
      Ocean
Florina Greece   *area*–495 6
Flotation
  ores
    mining eng.   622.752
    spec. ores   622.33–.39
Flotillas
  naval organization   359.31
Flours
  comm. proc.   664.720 7
    wheat   664.722 72
    s.a. other spec. grains &
      prod.
    other aspects see Cereal
      grains
Flow
  charting *see* Flowcharting
  charts
    systems analysis *see*
      Systems analysis
  phenomena
    aeronautical aerodynamics
      see Airflow
    compressed-air tech.   621.53
      s.a. spec. appls. e.g.
        Sandblasting
    eng. mech. *see* Dynamics
    hydraulic eng. *see*
      Hydraulics engineering
    physics mech.   531.11
      fluids   532.051
      gases   533.21–.28
        air   533.621–.628
      liquids   532.51
      particles   531.163

Flow
  phenomena
    physics mech. (continued)
      solids   531.3
  welding
    metal products
      mf. tech.   671.529
        ferrous metals   672.529
        s.a. other spec. metals
      other aspects see Welding
Flowcharting
  programming   001.642 3
  spec. subj.   *s.s.*–028 542 3
Flowcharts
  systems analysis *see* Systems
      analysis
Flower beds
  plants grown for
    floriculture   635.962
    s.a. spec. plants
Flowering
  fern family *see* Filicales
  moss family *see* Ericales
  plants
    botany   582.13
    spec. plants *see*
        Angiospermae
Flowers
  arrangement
    dec. arts   745.92
  art representation
    painting   758.42
    other aspects see Plants
  cookery with   641.6
  dress customs   391.44
  floriculture   635.9
    misc. aspects see
        Agriculture
  lit. & stage trmt.
    folk lit. soc.   398.368 213
    other aspects see Plants
        lit. & stage trmt.
  plant anatomy   582.046 3
    s.a. spec. plants
  use in table setting
    home econ.   642.8
  s.a. Edible flowers
Flowmeters *see*
      Measuring-instruments
Flow-of-funds
  accounts
    macroeconomics   339.26
  measurement
    accounting   657.48
    s.a. spec. kinds of
        enterprise e.g.
        Insurance accounting
Floyd Co.
  Georgia   *area*–758 35
  Indiana   *area*–772 19
  Iowa   *area*–777 26

Floyd Co. (continued)
  Kentucky   *area*–769 22
  Texas   *area*–764 841
  Virginia   *area*–755 712
Fluctuations
  mathematics   519.85
    s.a. spec. appls. e.g.
        Engineering
    s.a. other spec. subj. e.g.
        prices 338.528
Flues
  bldg. heating   697.8
  steam eng. *see* Furnaces steam
      eng.
Fluidics
  automation eng. *see* Hydraulic
      control automation eng.
Fluidization
  chem. eng.   660.284 292
    s.a. spec. prod.
Fluidized nuclear reactors
  technology   621.483 4
    s.a. spec. appls. e.g.
        Generation elect. power
    other aspects see Nuclear
        reaction
Fluid-power tech.
  engineering   620.106
    s.a. spec. appls. e.g.
        Aerospace engineering
Fluids
  biochemistry
    gen. wks.   574.192 12
      animals   591.192 12
      microorganisms   576.119 212
      plants   581.192 12
      s.a. spec. organisms
    med. sci.   612.015 22
      animals   636.089 201 522
      s.a. spec. animals
      man   612.015 22
      s.a. spec. functions,
          systems, organs
  heat transmission *see*
      Convection heat
  mechanics   532
  engineering   620.106
    s.a. spec. appls. e.g.
        Aerospace engineering
  physics   532
  s.a. Gases; *also* Liquids
Fluid-state
  lasers
    light amplification
      soc. & econ. aspects *see*
          Secondary industries
      tech. & mf.   621.366 2
        s.a. spec. appls. e.g.
            Tracking

Flying (continued)
  lemurs *see* Dermoptera
  saucers   001.942
  techniques
    aeronautics
      soc. & econ. aspects *see*
        Secondary industries
      technology   629.132 5
      s.a. spec. appls. e.g.
        Military engineering
    sports   797.52-.55
    misc. aspects see Sports
Flying-boats *see* Seaplanes
Flyovers *see* Bridges
    (structures)
Foam
  glass
    technology   666.157
    other aspects see Glass
  latex prod.
    manufacturing
      soc. & econ. aspects *see*
        Secondary industries
      technology   678.532
    s.a. spec. kinds of latexes
      e.g. Natural latexes
Foamed plastics
  chem. tech.   668.493
  other aspects see Plastics
Foams
  colloid chem. *see* Hydrosols
    colloid chem.
  in solids *see* Solid
    disperoids colloid
    chem.
Foard Co. Tex.   *area*-764 748
Focusing
  cameras
    photographic tech.   770.282
    spec. fields   778
Focusing-apparatus
  photography   771.37
  gen. tech.   770.282
  spec. proc. & fields   772-778
Fodder grasses *see* Pooideae
Foehns *see* Local wind systems
Foggia Italy   *area*-457 57
Fogs
  colloid chem. *see* Aerosols
    colloid chem.
  meteorology   551.575
    artificial modification   551.687 5
    weather forecasting   551.647 5
    spec. areas   551.65
  other aspects see Weather
Foils
  use in cookery   641.589
Foix France   *area*-448 8
Folding boxes
  mf. tech.   676.32
  other aspects see Containers

Folds
  structural geol.   551.87
  s.a. spec. aspects e.g.
    Prospecting
Foliage plants
  floriculture   635.975
  s.a. spec. plants
Folk
  arts   745
  beliefs
    folklore   398.41
  literature   398.2
  medicine   615.882
  s.a. spec. diseases
  music   781.7
    recordings   789.912 17
    s.a. spec. mediums
  rock music *see* Rock (music)
  songs
    music   784.4
    recordings   789.912 44
  s.a. other spec. subj.
Folkestone Kent Eng.   *area*-422 395
Folklore   398
Folklorists
  biog. & work   398.092
  s.a.   *pers.*-39
Folkways
  sociology   390
Folly Isl. S.C.   *area*-757 99
Fond du Lac Co. Wis.   *area*-775 68
Fondants *see* Candies
Fondues
  cookery   641.8
Fonts
  baptismal *see* Sacramental
    furniture
Foochow
  dialect
    linguistics   495.17
    literature   895.1
    s.a.   *lang.*-951 7
Food
  additives *see* Additives foods
  allergies
    gen. med.   616.975
    geriatrics   618.976 975
    pediatrics   618.929 75
    pub. health   614.599 3
    statistics   312.397 5
      deaths   312.269 75
    other aspects see Diseases
  board *see* Paperboard
  cartons
    paper
      manufacturing
        soc. & econ. aspects
        see Secondary
        industries
      technology   676.34

Forage crops	
agriculture	633.2
soc. & econ. aspects *see*	
Primary industries	
other aspects see Field crops	
Foraminifera	
culture	639.731 2
paleozoology	563.12
zoology	593.12
other aspects see Protozoa	
Forbes N.S.W.	*area*–944 5
Force	
metaphysics	118
sociology *see* Coercion	
Forceps *see* Medical instruments	
Forces	
dynamics	531.113
misc. aspects see Dynamics	
statics *see* Statics	
Forcing	
plants	
crop prod.	631.544
s.a. spec. crops; also	
spec. types of culture	
e.g. Floriculture	
s.a. other spec. subj.	
Forcipulata *see* Asteroidea	
Ford	
County	
Illinois	*area*–773 62
Kansas	*area*–781 76
Gerald Rudolph admin.	
U.S. hist.	973.925
s.a. spec. events & subj.	
e.g. Commerce	
Fordingbridge Hampshire Eng.	
	area–422 75
Forearms *see* Upper extremities	
Forebrain	
human phys.	612.825
other aspects see Brain	
Forecasting	003
business	338.544
future *see* Divination	
investments	332.678
management use	658.403 55
production	658.503 6
spec. subj.	*s.s.*–068 5
natural resources	
consumption	333.713
requirements	333.712
s.a. spec. kinds of	
resources e.g.	
Shorelands	
sales	658.818
spec. subj.	*s.s.*–068 8
weather	551.63
s.a. other spec. subj.	
Forehand	
tennis	796.342 22
s.a. other spec. games	

Foreign	
affairs	
pub. admin.	
activities	351.89
spec. jur.	353–354
departments	351.01
spec. jur.	353–354
other aspects see	
International relations	
aid	
economics	338.91
law	343.074 8
spec. jur.	343.3–.9
other aspects see Economic	
assistance	
bodies	
removal	
surgery	617.146
anesthesiology	617.967 146
s.a. Veterinary	
sciences	
commerce *see* International	
commerce	
econ. relations	
internat. econ.	337.3–.9
enterprises *see* International	
organizations	
exchange	
economics	332.45
other aspects see Money	
law *see* Monetary exchange	
law	
groups *see* Minority groups	
income	
taxation	
law	343.052 48
spec. jur.	343.3–.9
other aspects see Income	
taxes	
investments econ.	332.673
legions	
mil. organization	355.35
licensing	
management	658.18
missions	
Christianity	266.023
other rel. see Missions	
(religion)	
news reporting	070.449
policy	
pol. sci.	327.11
spec. countries	327.3–.9
relations *see* International	
relations	
students education	371.82
s.a. spec. levels of ed.;	
also Special education	
trade *see* International	
commerce	
traders	
biog. & work	382.092

Forging
  metals
    arts
      decorative   739.14
        s.a. spec. metals; also
          spec. prod. e.g.
          Jewelry
      fine *see* Direct-metal
        sculpture
    blacksmithing   682
    mf. tech.   671.332
      ferrous metals   672.332
      s.a. other spec. metals
    other aspects see
      Mechanical working
    s.a. spec. prod.
Forgiveness
  Christian sacrament *see*
    Absolution Christian
    rel.
  rel. doctrines
    Christianity   234.5
    other rel. see Humankind
      rel. doctrines
For-hire
  carriers *see* Common carriers
Fork lifts
  machine eng.
    soc. & econ. aspects *see*
      Secondary industries
    tech. & mf.   621.863
      s.a. spec. appls. e.g.
        Internal transportation
    other aspects see Mechanics
Forks (tableware) *see* Tableware
Forktails *see* Turdidae
Forlì Italy   *area*–454 8
Form
  books
    law
      criminal   345.05
        spec. jur.   345.3–.9
      gen. wks.   347.055
        spec. jur.   347.3–.9
      other spec. subj.   law s.s.–026 9
      other aspects see Legal
        procedure
  criticism
    rel. books
      Bible   220.663
        s.a. spec. parts of
          Bible
      Hadith   297.124 066 3
        s.a. spec. Hadith
      Koran   297.122 663
        spec. parts   297.122 9
      Midrash   296.140 663
        s.a. spec. types
      Talmudic lit.   296.120 663
        s.a. spec. works

Form (continued)
  letters
    office use   651.752
Form (concept)
  arts   701.8
    s.a. spec. art forms
  metaphysics   117
Formal *see spec. subj.*
Format publishing   686
Formation
  deposits
    econ. geol.   553.1
      spec. deposits   553.2–.8
    thermochemistry
      physical chem.   541.362
        applied   660.296 2
        organic   547.136 2
        s.a. spec. elements,
          cpds., prod.
    s.a. other spec. subj. e.g.
      Fogs
Formations
  atmosphere *see* Atmospheric
    formations met.
  sports
    American football   796.332 22
    soccer   796.334 22
    s.a. other spec. games
Formby Merseyside Eng.   *area*–427 59
Formentera Spain   *area*–467 5
Formicidae
  culture   638.579 6
  paleozoology   565.79
  zoology   595.796
  other aspects see Insecta
Formosa
  island   *area*–512 49
  province Argentina   *area*–823 5
  Strait *see* East China Sea
Formosans   *r.e.n.*–992 5
Forms
  design
    pub. admin.   350.714 4
      central govts.   351.714 4
        spec. jur.   353–354
      local govts.   352.164 4
  employee selection *see*
    Selection procedures
    employees
  law
    criminal   345.05
      spec. jur.   345.3–.9
    gen. wks.   347.055
      spec. jur.   347.3–.9
    other spec. subj.   law s.s.–026 9
    other aspects see Legal
      procedure
  sculpture   731.5
    spec. periods & schools   732–735

Foundation
engineering
  soc. & econ. aspects *see*
    Secondary industries
  technology   624.152–.158
  other aspects see Earthwork
  s.a. spec. appls. e.g.
    Bridges (structures)
garments
  comm. mf.   687.25
  other aspects see Underwear
Foundations (organizations)
law   346.064
welfare   361.763
  spec. problems & groups   362–363
  other aspects see Welfare
    services
other aspects see
  Organizations
Foundations (supports)
bridges   624.284
  analysis & design   624.254
  s.a. spec. appls. e.g.
    Suspension bridges
bldg. aspects
  arch. construction   721.1
  building   690.11
  s.a. spec. kinds of bldgs.
roads *see* Roadbeds
s.a. other spec. appls.
Founders
of religions
  comp. rel.   291.63
  s.a. spec. rel.
Foundlings *see* Abandoned
  children
Foundry practice
metal prod.
  manufacturing
    soc. & econ. aspects *see*
      Secondary industries
    technology   671.2
      ferrous metals   672.2
    s.a. other spec. metals
Fountain Co. Ind.   *area*–772 47
Fountains
landscape design   714
sculpture   731.72
  spec. periods & schools   732–735
Fouquieriaceae *see* Tamaricales
Four Corners region
southwest U.S.   *area*–788 27
Fourier
analysis   515.243 3
  complex variables   515.924 33
  real variables   515.824 33
  s.a. other spec. functions &
    equations; also spec.
    appls. e.g.
      Engineering

Fourier (continued)
transform
  operational calculus   515.723
  s.a. spec. appls. e.g.
    Engineering
Fourierism
socialist school
  economics   335.23
Four-o'clock family *see*
  Thymelaeales
Four-quarter school year   371.236
  s.a. spec. levels of ed.;
    also Special education
Fourteenth century
history   909.3
  appls. to spec. subj.   *s.s.*–090 23
  s.a. spec. countries
Fourth
dimension
  physics *see* Relativity
    theories physics
Republic
  France
    history   944.082
    s.a. spec. events & subj.
      e.g. Arts
Fourth-class mail
postal commun.   383.125
  other aspects see Postal
    communication
Four-year colleges
higher ed.   378.154 2
Fowey Cornwall Eng.   *area*–423 72
Fowl *see spec. kinds e.g.*
  Chickens
Fox River Wis.   *area*–775 6
Foxe Basin *see* American Arctic
  seawaters
Foxes *see* Canidae
Foxgloves *see* Personales
Fractional
distillation
  chem. eng.   660.284 25
  petroleum   665.532
  s.a. other spec. prod.
exponents *see* Exponents
Fractionation
process
  air
    chem tech.   665.82
    soc. & econ. aspects
      see Secondary
      industries
  ind. oils & gases   665.028 3
  s.a. spec. prod.
  s.a. other spec substances
Fractions
arithmetic   513.26
  s.a. spec. appls e.g.
    Practical pharmacy

Franco regime	
Spain hist.	946.082
s.a. spec. events & subj.	
e.g. Courts	
Francoaceae *see* Saxifragales	
Franco-German War	
history	943.082
Franconia Ger.	*area–*433
Franconian	
emperors	
Ger. hist.	943.023
s.a. spec events & subj.	
e.g. Commerce	
language	
linguistics	437.3
literature	830
s.a.	*lang.–*32
s.a. Franconia; *also other*	
spec. subj. e.g. Arts	
Frankeniaceae *see* Tamaricales	
Frankfort Ky.	*area–*769 432
Frankfurt	
am Main Ger.	*area–*434 1
an der Oder Ger.	*area–*431 5
Franking privileges	
postal commun.	383.120 2
other aspects see Postal	
communication	
Frankish rule Italy hist.	945.02
s.a. spec. events & subj.	
e.g. Commerce	
Frankland Range Tas.	*area–*946 2
Franklin	
city Va.	*area–*755 553
County	
Alabama	*area–*761 913
Arkansas	*area–*767 34
Florida	*area–*759 91
Georgia	*area–*758 135
Idaho	*area–*796 42
Illinois	*area–*773 94
Indiana	*area–*772 15
Iowa	*area–*777 28
Kansas	*area–*781 66
Kentucky	*area–*769 432
Maine	*area–*741 72
Massachusetts	*area–*744 22
Mississippi	*area–*762 27
Missouri	*area–*778 63
Nebraska	*area–*782 377
New York	*area–*747 55
North Carolina	*area–*756 54
Ohio	*area–*771 56
Pennsylvania	*area–*748 44
Tennessee	*area–*768 63
Texas	*area–*764 213
Vermont	*area–*743 13
Virginia	*area–*755 68
Washington	*area–*797 33
D. Roosevelt Lake Wash.	*area–*797 23
District Can.	*area–*719 5

Franklin (continued)	
Par. La.	*area–*763 77
state	
Tenn. hist.	976.803
Franklinite	
mineralogy	549.526
Franz Josef Land RSFSR	*area–*985
Fraser	
Isl. Qld.	*area–*943 2
River B.C.	*area–*711 2
Fraserburgh Grampian Scot.	
	*area–*412 25
Fraternal	
club bldgs. *see* Clubhouse	
buildings	
insurance	368.363
misc. aspects see Insurance	
Fraternities	
education	371.855
s.a. spec. levels of ed.;	
also Special education	
Fraternity songs *see* University	
& college songs	
Fraud	
personality disorder *see*	
Compulsive defrauding	
& lying	
Frauds	
criminology	364.163
law	345.026 3
spec. jur.	345.3–.9
occultism	133
soc. theology	
Christianity	261.833 163
comp. rel.	291.178 331 63
s.a. other spec. rel.	
Fraudulent	
advertising & promotion	
postal commun.	383.120 5
other aspects see Postal	
offenses	
s.a. other spec. subj.	
Frazil ice	
physical geol.	551.344
Freaks	
circuses	791.35
biog. & work	791.350 92
s.a.	*pers.–*791 3
Frechet algebras	
& groups	512.55
s.a. spec. appls. e.g.	
Engineering	
Frederick	
city Md.	*area–*752 88
County	
Maryland	*area–*752 87
Virginia	*area–*755 992
reign Ger. hist.	
German emperor	943.084
Holy Roman emperor	
1 Barbarossa	943.024

French (continued)
language
  linguistics   440
  literature   840
  s.a.   *lang.*–41
pastry
  cookery   641.865 9
people   *r.e.n.*–41
Polynesia   *area*–962
Revolution
  history   944.04
Riviera   *area*–449
socialism
  economics   335.2
Somaliland   *area*–677 1
Sudan
  history   966.230 3
  s.a.   *area*–662 3
Territory of the Afars and the
    Issas   *area*–677 1
troops
  in American Revolution   973.347
  s.a. hist. of other spec.
    wars
West Indies   *area*–729 76
s.a. France; *also other*
    spec. subj. e.g. Arts
Frenchman Flat Nev.   *area*–793 34
Frenchmans Cap Nat. Park Tas.
    area–946 6
Frequencies
signals
  commun. eng.
    technology   621.380 432
    s.a. spec. appls. e.g.
      Space communication
    other aspects see
      Communication
  s.a. other spec. subj. e.g.
    Atmospheric pressure
    met.
Frequency
allocation
  radio *see* Measurement radio
  television *see* Measurement
    television
bridges *see* Frequency
    measurement
converters
  asynchronous *see*
    Asynchronous machinery
  synchronous *see* Synchronous
    converters
distributions
  statistical math.   519.532
  s.a. spec. appls. e.g.
    Engineering
measurement
  electricity   621.374 7
    standards   621.372
  radio *see* Measurement radio

Frequency
measurement (continued)
  television *see* Measurement
    television
  other aspects see
    Electricity
  s.a. other spec. appls.
modulators
  electronic circuits
    tech. & mf.   621.381 536 3
    microelectronics   621.381 736 3
    microwave electronics   621.381 326 3
    radiowave electronics   621.381 536 3
    x- & gamma-ray
      electronics   621.381 6
    s.a. spec. appls. e.g.
      Radar engineering
    other aspects see
      Microwave electronics;
      Radiowave electronics;
      X-ray electronics
sound *see* Pitch (sound)
s.a. other spec. subj.
Frequency-modulation systems
radio
  engineering   621.384 152
  s.a. spec. appls. e.g.
    Radiotelephony
  other aspects see Radio
Fresco painting
arts   751.44
  indiv. artists   759.1–.9
Fresh
eggs
  chicken culture   637.541
  misc. aspects see
    Chickens products
  other fowl   637.59
waters
  hydrology   551.48
  regional subj. trmt.   *area*–169
  s.a. Potable water
  s.a. other spec. subj.
Fresh-water
aquariums
  fish culture   639.344
  s.a. spec. kinds of fish
biology   574.929
  animals   591.929
  plants   581.929
  s.a. spec. organisms
ecology
  life sci.   574.526 32
  animals   591.526 32
  microorganisms   576.15
  plants   581.526 32
  s.a. spec. organisms
fish culture   639.31
  s.a. spec. kinds of fish

Frigid Zones (continued)
diseases   616.988 1
   geriatrics   618.976 988 1
   pediatrics   618.929 881
   statistics   312.398 81
    deaths   312.269 881
   other aspects see
     Environmental diseases
   s.a. spec. diseases
earth astronomy   525.5
regional subj. trmt.   *area*–11
s.a. Cold-weather
Frigidity
   gen. med.   616.858 32
   geriatrics   618.976 858 32
   psychology   157.7
   pub. health   614.58
   statistics   312.385 832
   other aspects see Diseases;
     also Mental illness
Frimley & Camberley Surrey Eng.
     area–422 13
Fringe benefits
   pub. admin.   350.835
    central govts.   351.835
    spec. jur.   353–354
    local govts.   352.943 5
   other aspects see Employee
     benefits
Fringe-finned ganoids *see*
     Polypteriformes
Fringes *see* Passementerie
Fringillidae
   hunting
    commercial   639.128 883
    sports   799.248 883
   paleozoology   568.8
   zoology   598.883
   other aspects see Aves
Frinton Essex Eng.   *area*–426 725
Frio Co. Tex.   *area*–764 442
Frisian
   language
    linguistics   439.2
    literature   839.2
    s.a.   *lang.*–392
   people   *r.e.n.*–392
   s.a. Old Low Germanic; *also*
     other spec. subj. e.g.
      Arts
Friulian *see* Rhaeto-Romanic
Friuli-Venezia Giulia
    Italy   *area*–453 9
Frog meats
   preservation   641.495
    commercial   664.95
    domestic   641.495
Frogbit family *see* Butomales
Frogmen
   armed forces   359.984
Frogmouths *see* Caprimulgiformes

Frogs (animals)
   zoology   597.87–.89
   other aspects see Anura
Frogs (track)
   railroad eng.
    technology   625.163
    other aspects see Permanent
     way
Frome
   Lake S. Aust.   *area*–942 37
   Somerset Eng.   *area*–423 83
Fromm system
   psychology   150.195 7
   s.a. spec. subj. & branches
     of psych.
Fronds
   plant
    anatomy   581.497
    pathology   581.229 7
    physiology   581.104 27
    s.a. spec. plants
Front
   axles
    automobiles
     soc. & econ. aspects *see*
      Secondary industries
     tech. & mf.   629.247
     s.a. spec. appls. e.g.
      mil. vehicles   623.747
   yards
    landscape design   712.6
Frontenac Co.
   Ontario   *area*–713 71
   Quebec   *area*–714 69
Frontier
   Co. Neb.   *area*–782 835
   defenses
    mil. sci.   355.45
    s.a. spec. mil. branches
   troops
    armed forces   355.351
    s.a. spec. mil. branches
Fronts
   meteorology *see* Air fronts
     met.
   mil. hist. *see hist. of spec.*
     wars
Frosinone Italy   *area*–456 22
Frost
   air temperature variations
    meteorology   551.525 3
     artificial modification   551.682 53
     weather forecasting   551.642 63
     spec. areas   551.65
   geol. agent   551.38
   s.a. Low temperatures
Frostbite
   gen. med.   616.58
   geriatrics   618.976 58
   pediatrics   618.925 8
   pub. health   614.595 8

Fuel (continued)
 systems
  internal combustion engines
   automobiles
    soc. & econ. aspects
    see Secondary
     industries
    tech. & mf.   629.253
     s.a. spec. appls.
      e.g.
      Military
      engineering
  s.a. other spec kinds
Fueling
 transp. equipment
  commerce
   airplanes   387.736 4
   buses & trucks   388.33
    local   388.473
   ferries   386.6
   ships & boats   387.168
    inland-waterway transp.   386.868
   trains   385.26
    special-duty   385.5
 s.a. other spec. equip.
Fuels
 aircraft eng.   629.134 351
  spec. engines   629.134 352–.134 355
 bldg. heating   697.04
 cookery   641.58
 heat eng.   621.402 3
  s.a. spec. appls. e.g.
   Heating library bldgs.
 internal-combustion engines
  automobiles   629.253 8
   s.a. spec. appls. e.g.
    Military engineering
  s.a. other spec. kinds
 manufacturing
  soc. & econ. aspects *see*
    Secondary industries
  technology   662.6
 marine engines   623.874
 metallurgical furnaces   669.81
  s.a. spec. metals
 nuclear reactors
  technology   621.483 35
   s.a. spec. appls. e.g.
    Generation elect. power
  other aspects see Nuclear
    reactions
 spacecraft *see* Propulsion
    systems spacecraft
 steam generation   621.182
  s.a. spec. appls e.g. Steam
    automobiles
 utilization
  land econ.   333.82
 s.a. spec. kinds e.g. Coals
Fugitive slaves
 U.S. Civil War cause   973.711 5

Fugues (mind)
 gen. med.   616.852 32
 geriatrics   618.976 852 32
 pediatrics   618.928 523 2
 psychology   157.3
 statistics   312.385 232
Fugues (music)
 spec. instruments
  organ   786.82
   recordings   789.912 682
  piano   786.42
   recordings   789.912 642
 s.a. other spec instruments
 theory   781.42
Fujairah   *area*–535 7
Fujiyama Japan   *area*–521 66
Fukien China   *area*–512 45
Fukui Japan   *area*–521 5
Fukuoka Japan   *area*–522
Fukushima Japan   *area*–521 1
Fulani
 empire   966.901 8
  s.a. spec. events & subj.
   e.g. Commerce
 language *see* West-Atlantic
    (Niger-Congo) languages
 people   *r.e.n.*–963
 s.a. other spec. subj. e.g.
    Arts
Fulas   *r.e.n.*–963
Fulgoroidea *see* Homoptera
Fulham London Eng.   *area*–421 33
Full employment policies
 macroeconomics   339.5
Fuller's earth *see* Clays
Full-scale
 plants
  chem. eng.   660.280 73
   s.a. spec. prod.
  s.a. other spec. subj.
Full-term infants
 pediatrics   618.920 12
  s.a. spec. diseases
Fully-boned fishes *see*
    Teleostei
Fulmars *see* Procellariiformes
Fulton Co.
 Arkansas   *area*–767 22
 Georgia   *area*–758 23
 Illinois   *area*–773 48
 Indiana   *area*–772 87
 Kentucky   *area*–769 99
 New York   *area*–747 47
 Ohio   *area*–771 115
 Pennsylvania   *area*–748 72
Fulwood Lancashire Eng.   *area*–427 665
Fumariaceae *see* Rhoeadales
Fumaroles
 geology   551.23
 physical geog.   910.02
  s.a. spec. places

Fungi
botany   589.2
med. aspects
    disease organisms   616.015
      vet sci.   636.089 601 5
    gen. pharm.   615.329 2
      toxicology   615.952 92
    vet. pharm.   636.089 532 92
      toxicology   636.089 595 292
paleobotany   561.92
other aspects see Plants
Fungi imperfecti *see*
    Deuteromycetes
Fungicides
production
    soc. & econ. aspects *see*
      Secondary industries
    technology   668.652
use
    agriculture   632.952
    s.a. spec. crops; also
      spec. types of culture
      e.g. Floriculture
wood decay prevention
    bldg. materials   691.12
Fungus diseases
med. sci.   616.969
    geriatrics   618.976 969
    pediatrics   618.929 69
    pub. health   614.559
    statistics   312.396 9
      deaths   312.269 69
    other aspects see Diseases
pathology
    gen. wks.   574.232 6
      animals   591.232 6
      plants   581.232 6
    s.a. spec. organisms
    med. sci. *see* Fungus
      diseases med. sci.
    s.a. spec. systems, organs,
      diseases
plant husbandry   632.4
    s.a. spec. plants; also
      spec. types of culture
      e.g. Forestry
Funicular railways
engineering
    technology   625.32
    other aspects see Mountain
      railways
Funnels
chem. apparatus   542.2
    s.a. spec. appls. e.g.
      Organic chemistry
Funnies
journalism   070.444

Fur
goods
    manufacturing
      soc. & econ. aspects *see*
        Secondary industries
      technology   685
seals *see* Otariidae
s.a. Integument; *also* Furs
Furans
org. chem.   547.592
s.a. spec. cpds.
Fur-bearing animals
hunting ind.   639.11
    misc. aspects see Hunting
      industries
Furloughs
armed forces   355.113
    s.a. spec. mil. branches
penology *see* Discipline
    prisons
Furnace methods
pyrometallurgy *see*
    Pyrometallurgy
Furnaces
heat eng.
    soc. & econ. aspects *see*
      Secondary industries
    tech. & mf.   621.402 5
    s.a. spec. appls. e.g.
      Heating library bldgs.
heating equipment
    buildings   697.07
    s.a. spec. kinds e.g.
      Steam heating
steam eng.
    soc. & econ. aspects *see*
      Secondary industries
    tech. & mf.   621.183
    s.a. spec. appls. e.g.
      Steam locomotives
other aspects see Heat
Furnas Co. Neb.   *area*–782 384
Furneaux Group Tas.   *area*–946 7
Furnishings
domestic customs   392.36
home econ.   645
    cleaning   648.5
library bldgs.   022.9
manufacturing
    soc. & econ. aspects *see*
      Secondary industries
    technology   684
museum bldgs.   069.3
rel. significance
    Christianity   247
    other rel. see Arts rel.
      significance
school bldgs.   371.63
    s.a. spec. levels of ed.;
      also Special education

Futurism
  arts
    gen. wks.   709.040 33
      spec. places   709.1–.9
    painting   759.063 3
      spec. places   759.1–.9
    sculpture   735.230 433
      spec. places   730.9
    s.a. other spec. art forms
Fylde Lancashire Eng.   *area*–427 662
Fyn Denmark   *area*–489 4

G

GAR   369.15
GATT *see* General Agreement on
      Tariffs and Trade
GAW *see* Guaranteed-wage plans
GNP
  macroeconomics   339.31
GOP
  pol. sci.   324.273 4
  s.a. spec. subj. of concern
      e.g. Social problems
GR-A *see* Synthetic rubber
GR-I *see* Synthetic rubber
GR-M *see* Synthetic rubber
GR-S *see* Synthetic rubber
Gabbros *see* Plutonic rocks
Gables *see* Roofs
Gabon   *area*–672 1
Gabonese   *r.e.n.*–967 21
Gabrovo Bulgaria   *area*–497 76
Gadaba *see* Munda
Gadolinium
  chemistry
    inorganic   546.416
    organic   547.054 16
    s.a. spec. groupings e.g.
      Aliphatic compounds
    technology   661.041 6
    organic   661.895
    soc. & econ. aspects *see*
      Secondary industries
    s.a. spec. prod.
  eng. materials   620.189 291 6
  s.a. spec. uses
  metallography   669.952 916
  metallurgy   669.291 6
    physical & chem. 669.962 916
  pharmacology   615.241 6
  misc. aspects see
    Pharmacology
  products
    mf. tech.   673.291 6
    other aspects see
      Nonferrous metals
      products
  toxicology   615.925 416
  misc. aspects see
    Toxicology

Gadolinium (continued)
  other aspects see
    Yttrium-group metals
Gadsden Co. Fla.   *area*–759 925
Gaelic
  Irish *see* Irish Gaelic
  Scottish *see* Scottish Gaelic
Gaetulia   *area*–397 7
Gage Co. Neb.   *area*–782 286
Gages
  radiowave electronics *see*
    Testing-devices
    radiowave electronics
  s.a. Measuring-instruments
Gahnite
  mineralogy   549.526
Gaines Co. Tex.   *area*–764 855
Gaining diets
  hygiene   613.24
  misc. aspects see Hygiene
Gainsborough Lincolnshire Eng.
        area–425 31
Gairdner Lake S. Aust. *area*–942 38
Galactose
  org. chem.   547.781 3
  other aspects see Sugar
Galápagos Isls.   *area*–866 5
Galashiels Borders Scot. *area*–413 85
Galati Romania   *area*–498 1
Galatia   *area*–393 2
Galatians
  Bible   227.4
  other aspects see New
    Testament
Galax Va.   *area*–755 715
Galaxies
  astronomy
    description   523.112
    theory   521.582
  other aspects see Celestial
    bodies
Galbulae *see* Piciformes
Galcha *see* Pamir
Galena
  mineralogy   549.32
Galeoidea *see* Selachii
Galicia (eastern Europe) *area*–438 6
  Poland   *area*–438 6
  Ukraine   *area*–477 18
Galicia (Spain)   *area*–461
Galician language
  linguistics   469.794
  literature   869
  s.a.   *lang.*–69
Gall bladder
  diseases
    gen. wks.   616.365
      neoplasms   616.992 36
      tuberculosis 616.995 36
    geriatrics   618.976 365
    pediatrics   618.923 65

Gall bladder
  diseases (continued)
    pub. health   614.593 65
    statistics   312.336 5
    deaths   312.263 65
    other aspects see Biliary
      tract
Galla language *see* Cushitic
  languages
Gallatin Co.
  Illinois   *area*–773 97
  Kentucky   *area*–769 365
  Montana   *area*–786 662
Gallegan *see* Galician
Galleons
  engineering   623.821
    design   623.812 1
    models   623.820 11
  seamanship   623.882 1
  other aspects see Vessels
    (nautical)
Galleries (exhibit halls) *see*
  Museums
Galleys (ships)
  engineering   623.821
    design   623.812 1
    models   623.820 11
  seamanship   623.882 1
  other aspects see Vessels
    (nautical)
Gallflies *see* Hymenoptera
Galli
  hunting
    commercial   639.128 61
    sports   799.248 61
  paleozoology   568.6
  zoology   598.61
  other aspects see Aves
Gallia
  Cisalpina   *area*–372
  Co. O.   *area*–771 89
Gallican schismatic churches
    see Roman Catholic
    schisms
Galliformes *see* Galli
Gallinules *see* Gruiformes
Gallionellaceae *see*
    Caulobacteriales
Gallium
  chemistry
    inorganic   546.675
    organic   547.056 75
    s.a. spec. groupings e.g.
      Aliphatic compounds
  technology   661.067 5
    organic   661.895
    soc. & econ. aspects *see*
      Secondary industries
    s.a. spec. prod.

Gallium (continued)
  pharmacology   615.267 5
    misc. aspects see
      Pharmacology
  toxicology   615.925 675
    misc. aspects see
      Toxicology
  other aspects see Minor
    metals
Galloping horses *see* Horse
  racing
Gallo-Roman period France hist.
     936.402
  s.a. spec. events & subj.
    e.g. Commerce
Galloway
  cattle
    animal husbandry   636.223
    other aspects see Cattle
  former district Scot.   *area*–414 9
  region Scot.   *area*–414 7
Galls
  plant injuries
    agriculture   632.2
    s.a. spec. types of
      culture e.g. Forestry
    botany   581.2
    s.a. spec. plants
Gallstones *see* Gall bladder
  diseases
Galois theory
  algebra   512.32
  s.a. spec. appls
Galoshes *see* Footwear
Galton laws *see* Genetic laws
Galvanic methods
  geophysical prospecting   622.154
Galvanizing metals
  dipping *see* Hot-metal dipping
  electroplating *see*
    Electroplating
Galvanometers
  electric current measurement   621.374 4
  s.a. spec. appls. e.g.
    Ignition systems &
    devices
Galveston Co. Tex.   *area*–764 139
Galway Ireland   *area*–417 4
Gama grasses *see* Pooideae
Gambia   *area*–665 1
Gambian trypanosomiasis *see*
    Trypanosomiasis
Gambians   *r.e.n.*–966 51
Gambier Isls.   *area*–962 2
Gamblers
  biog. & work   795.092
  s.a.   *pers.*–795
Gambling
  ethics
    philosophy   175.9

Gambling
  ethics (continued)
    religion
      Buddhism   294.356 59
      Christianity   241.659
      comp. rel.   291.565 9
      Hinduism   294.548 659
      s.a. other spec. rel.
    mathematics   519.2
    soc. aspects   363.42
    crime   364.172
    customs   394.3
    systems
      recreation   795
    other aspects see Moral
      issues
Gambling-bldgs. *see* Casino
      bldgs.
Gambling-business
    ethics   174.6
Game
  birds
    culture   636.63
  foods   641.391
    cookery   641.691
    other aspects see Meats
  refuges *see* Wildlife reserves
  rooms *see* Recreational areas
  theory
    mathematics   519.3
    s.a. spec. appls. e.g.
      Decision making
Games
  camp sports   796.545
  child care
    home econ.   649.553
  education   371.397
    s.a. spec. levels of ed.;
      also Special education
  ethics
    philosophy   175.4–.5
    religion
      Buddhism   294.356 54–.356 55
      Christianity   241.654–.655
      comp. rel.   291.565 4–.565 5
      Hinduism   294.548 654–.548 655
      s.a. other spec. rel.
  folk lit.   398.8
  indoor
    recreation   793
  library trmt.   025.179 6
    acquisitions   025.289 6
    cataloging   025.349 6
  management use   658.403 53
  of chance
    equipment
      manufacturing
        soc. & econ. aspects
          see Secondary
            industries
        technology   688.75

Games
  of chance (continued)
    recreation   795
      ethics *see* Games ethics
  of skill
    indoor
      equipment
        manufacturing
          soc. & econ. aspects
            see Secondary
              industries
          technology   688.74
      recreation   794
        ethics *see* Games ethics
    outdoor *see* Outdoor sports
    soc. customs   394.3
    other aspects see Recreation
Gametes *see* Gametogenesis
Gametogenesis
  life sci.   574.32
    animals   591.32
    microorganisms   576.132
    plants   581.32
    s.a. spec. organisms
Gamma
  decay
    radioactivity
      astrophysics   523.019 752 4
      s.a. spec. celestial
        bodies
      physics   539.752 4
        spec. states of matter   530.4
        s.a. spec. physical
          phenomena e.g.
            Heat
  functions
    mathematics   515.52
    s.a. spec. appls. e.g.
      Engineering
  globulins
    pharmacology   615.39
    other aspects see Drugs
  particles *see* Gamma rays
  radiations *see* Particle
    radiations
  rays
    astrophysics   523.019 722 2
    s.a. spec. celestial
      bodies
    physics   539.722 2
      spec. states of matter   530.4
      s.a. spec. physical
        phenomena e.g. Heat
Gamma-ray
  analysis
    anal. chem.
      gen. wks.   543.085 86
        qualitative   544.66
        quantitative   545.836
      organic   547.308 586
        qualitative   547.346 6

Gamma-ray
  analysis
    anal. chem.
      organic (continued)
        quantitative   547.358 36
        s.a. spec. elements &
          cpds
    astronomy   522.686
      s.a. spec. celestial bodies
  circuits
    astrophysics   523.018 753 53
      s.a. spec. celestial
        bodies
    physics   537.535 3
      spec. states of matter   530.4
    technology   621.381 6
      s.a. spec. appls. e.g.
        Radiography
  electronics
    astrophysics   523.018 753 5
      s.a. spec. celestial
        bodies
    physics   537.535
      spec. states of matter   530.4
    soc. & econ. aspects *see*
      Secondary industries
    technology   621.381 6
      s.a. spec. appls. e.g.
        Radiography
  photography *see* Radiography
  spectroscopes
    mf. tech.   681.414 8
      components   681.42–.43
    other aspects see Optical
      instruments
  spectroscopy
    astrophysics   523.018 753 52
      s.a. spec. celestial
        bodies
    engineering
      soc. & econ. aspects *see*
        Secondary industries
      technology   621.361 6
        s.a. spec. appls. e.g.
          Materials
          engineering
    physics   537.535 2
      spec. states of matter   530.4
    other aspects see
      Spectroscopy
  tubes
    astrophysics   523.018 753 55
      s.a. spec. celestial
        bodies
    physics   537.535 5
      spec. states of matter   530.4
    technology   621.381 6
      s.a. spec. appls. e.g.
        Radiography
Gammaridea *see* Amphipoda
Gamu-Gofa Ethiopia   *area*–633

Ganapataism
  Hinduism   294.551 5
    misc. aspects see Hinduism
Gandhi Indira admin. India hist.
                                        954.045
    s.a. spec. events & subj.
      e.g. Commerce
Gandhism
  pol. ideology   320.55
    soc. theology *see* Political
      ideologies soc.
      theology
Gang criminality
  soc. path.   364.106 6
Ganges River India   *area*–541
Ganglions
  autonomic system *see*
    Autonomic nervous
    system
  basal
    diseases   616.83
      geriatrics   618.976 83
      pediatrics   618.928 3
      pub. health   614.598 3
      statistics   312.383
      deaths   312.268 3
    other aspects see
      Diseases
  cranial nerves *see* Cranial
    nerves
  spinal nerves *see* Spinal
    nerves
  other aspects see Nerves
Gangrene
  symptoms *see* Symptoms of
    disease
Gangs
  sociology   302.34
    s.a. spec. organizations
Gangsterism
  soc. path.   364.106 6
Gannets *see* Pelecaniformes
Ganoidei
  culture   639.374 1–.374 4
  fishing
    commercial   639.274 1–.274 4
    sports   799.174 1–.174 4
  paleozoology   567.4
  zoology   597.41–.44
  other aspects see Pisces
Ganoids *see* Ganoidei
Gaols
  penology   365.34
  other aspects see Penal
    institutions
Garage bldgs.
  private *see* Accessory
    domestic structures
  public *see* Motor vehicle
    transp. bldgs.

Dewey Decimal Classification

Garage sales
commerce 381.19
  misc. aspects see Commerce
Garages
  automobiles
    soc. & econ. aspects *see*
      Secondary industries
    technology 629.286
    s.a. spec. appls. e.g.
      repairing
      automobiles629.287
Garavances *see* Chick-peas
Garbage
  disposal *see* Solid wastes
    disposal
  fertilizers
    production
      soc. & econ. aspects *see*
        Secondary industries
      technology 668.637 7
    use agric. 631.877
    s.a. spec. crops; also
      spec. types of culture
      e.g. Floriculture
  gen. wks. *see* Refuse
Garbage-disposal units
  mf. tech. 683.88
  plumbing 696.184
  other aspects see Household
    appliances
Garbanzos *see* Chick-peas
Garcia admin. Philippines hist. 959.904 4
  s.a. spec. events & subj.
    e.g. Commerce
Garcinia mangostana *see*
    Mangosteens
Gard France area–448 3
Garda Lake Italy area–452 6
Garden
  Co. Neb. area–782 915
  crops
    feeds
      animal husbandry 636.087 5
      s.a. spec. animals
      horticulture 635
      misc. aspects see
        Agriculture
  eggs *see* Eggplants
  furnishings
    home econ. 645.8
  furniture *see* Outdoor
    furniture
  lighting
    engineering 621.322 9
  peas
    agriculture 635.656
    soc. & econ. aspects *see*
      Primary industries
    foods 641.356 56
      cookery 641.656 56

Garden
  peas (continued)
    other aspects see
      Papilionaceae; *also*
      Vegetables
  sculpture 731.72
    spec. periods & schools 732–735
Gardeners
  biog. & work 635.092
  s.a. spec. kinds e.g. flower
    gardeners 635.9092
  soc. & ethical aspects *see*
    Agricultural classes
  other aspects see Household
    employees
  s.a. pers.–635
Gardenias *see* Rubiales
Gardening
  horticulture *see* Garden crops
  landscape design 712
Gardens
  lit. & stage trmt. *see*
    Natural phenomena
  s.a. Gardening
Gardiners Isl. N.Y. area–747 25
Garfield
  County
    Colorado area–788 16
    Montana area–786 27
    Nebraska area–782 764
    Oklahoma area–766 28
    Utah area–792 52
    Washington area–797 44
  James A. admin.
    U.S. hist. 973.84
    s.a. spec. events & subj.
      e.g. Commerce
Garfishes *see* Mesichthyes
Garforth West Yorkshire Eng.
    area–428 19
Gargoyles
  art *see* Relief (art) arch.
    decoration
Garland Co. Ark. area–767 41
Garlic *see* Alliaceous plants
Garmentmakers
  biog. & work. 687.092
  s.a. spec. kinds of
    garments
  s.a. pers.–687
Garments *see* Clothing
Garnets
  abrasives *see* Abrasive
    materials
  mineralogy 549.62
  synthetic
    manufacturing
      soc. & econ. aspects *see*
        Secondary industries
      technology 666.88

432

Gas (continued)
portable heaters
bldg. heating — 697.24
supply
govt. control — 350.872 3
central govts. — 351.872 3
spec. jur. — 353–354
local govts. — 352.912 3
law — 343.092 6
spec. jur. — 343.3–.9
soc. services — 363.63
other aspects see Utilities
technology
instruments & machinery
manufacturing
soc. & econ. aspects
see Secondary
industries
technology — 681.766 5
s.a. spec. kinds
tubes
radio-wave electronics
soc. & econ. aspects *see*
Secondary industries
tech. & mf. — 621.381 513
s.a. spec. appls. e.g.
Receiving sets
other aspects see
Disruptive discharge
warfare *see* Chemical warfare
welding
metal products
mf. tech. — 671.522
ferrous metals — 672.522
s.a. other spec. metals
other aspects see Welding
other aspects see Fuels
s.a. Gases
Gascogne France — *area*–447 7
Gasconade Co. Mo. — *area*–778 61
Gascony France — *area*–447 7
Gas-detection methods
geophysical prospecting — 622.159
Gaseous poisons
toxicology — 615.91
misc. aspects see
Toxicology
Gaseous-state
lasers
light amplification
soc. & econ. aspects *see*
Secondary industries
tech. & mf. — 621.366 3
s.a. spec. appls. e.g.
Tracking
other aspects see
Amplification light
optics
masers *see* Fluid-state masers
physics & chem. *see* Gases

Gases
atmosphere
meteorology — 551.511 2
artificial modification — 551.681 12
weather forecasting — 551.641 12
spec. areas — 551.65
chem. state of matter — 541.042 3
applied — 600.043
eng. mech. — 620.107
s.a. spec. appls. e.g.
Aerospace engineering
heat
expansion & contraction
astrophysics — 523.013 412
s.a. spec. celestial
bodies
physics — 536.412
physics
mechanics — 533
state of matter — 530.43
sound transmission
engineering — 620.25
s.a. spec. appls. e.g.
Spacecraft engineering
physics — 534.24
specific heats
astrophysics — 523.013 65
s.a. spec. celestial
bodies
physics — 536.65
other aspects see Fluids
Gases (fuels)
chem. tech. — 665.7
extraction
law — 343.077 2
spec. jur. — 343.3–.9
natural *see* Natural gases
pub. safety — 363.179
misc. aspects see Hazardous
materials
radiesthesia
parapsychology — 133.323 7
s.a. Natural gases
Gases (military)
ammunition *see* Chemical
devices mil. eng.
Gases (noxious)
pollution by
soc. aspects — 363.738 7
other aspects see
Pollutants
sanitary eng. — 628.532
Gaskets
rubber *see* Extruded rubber
products
Gas-liquid chromatography *see*
Gas chromatography
Gas-lubricated bearings *see*
Bearings

434

Gasoline
 engines
  piston *see* Spark-ignition
    engines
  reciprocating *see*
    Spark-ignition engines
  turbine *see* Gas-turbine
    engines
 lamps
  lighting tech.   621.323
  s.a. spec. appls. e.g.
    Lighting airports
Gasolines
 chem. tech.   665.538 25–.538 27
 pub. safety   363.179
  misc. aspects see Hazardous
    materials
 other aspects see Petroleum
Gasometric methods *see* Gas
    analysis
Gaspé
 Co. Que.   *area*–714 79
 Peninsula   *area*–714 77
Gaspée
 ship
  burning U.S. hist.   973.311 2
Gas-projecting devices *see*
    Chemical devices mil.
    eng.
Gas-solid chromatography *see*
    Gas chromatography
Gas-to-liquid
 heat transformation *see*
    Condensation effect of
    heat
Gaston Co. N.C.   *area*–756 773
Gas-to-solid
 heat transformation
  physics   536.445
  spec. states of matter   530.4
Gastric
 indigestion *see* Dyspepsia
 secretions
  human phys.   621.32
  other aspects see Digestion
 ulcers
  gen. med.   616.334
  geriatrics   618.976 334
  pediatrics   618.923 34
  pub. health   614.593 34
  statistics   312.333 4
  deaths   312.263 34
  other aspects see Diseases
Gastritis
 gen. med.   616.333
 geriatrics   618.976 333
 pediatrics   618.923 33
 pub. health   614.593 33
 statistics   312.333 3
 deaths   312.263 33
 other aspects see Diseases

Gastroenteritis *see* Stomach
    diseases
Gastroenterology
 med. sci.   616.33
 geriatrics   618.976 33
 pediatrics   618.923 3
 vet. med.   636.089 633
  s.a. spec. animals
  other aspects see Medical
    sciences
 s.a. Stomach
Gastrointestinal *see* Stomach
Gastrojejunal ulcers
 gen. med.   616.343 4
 geriatrics   618.976 343 4
 pediatrics   618.923 434
 pub. health   614.593 434
 statistics   312.334 34
 deaths   312.263 434
 other aspects see Diseases
Gastronomy   641.013
Gastropoda
 culture   639.483
 paleozoology   564.3
 zoology   594.3
 other aspects see Mollusca
Gastroptosis *see* Stomach
    diseases
Gastrotricha
 culture & hunting   639.758 3
 zoology   595.183
 other aspects see Worms
Gas-turbine
 engines
  soc. & econ. aspects *see*
    Secondary industries
  tech. & mf.
   aircraft   629.134 353
   gen. wks.   621.433
    parts & accessories   621.437
   land vehicles   629.250 3
    parts & systems   629.252–.258
   marine vehicles   623.872 33
   s.a. other spec. appls.
  locomotives
   railroad rolling stock
    commerce   385.362
    special-duty   385.5
   engineering
    technology
     gen. wks.   625.262
      accessory equip.   625.25
      running gear   625.21
      monorail   625.28
   other aspects see Rolling
    stock railroads
Gatehouse of Fleet Dumfries &
    Galloway Scot.   *area*–414 92
Gatehouses *see* Accessory
    domestic structures

Gates
  canal eng.
    technology   627.135 2
    s.a. spec. appls. e.g.
      Canal transportation
    other aspects see Liquids
      engineering
  Co. N.C.   *area*–756 153
  landscape design   717
  reservoir eng.
    technology   627.882
    s.a. spec. appls. e.g.
      Military engineering
    other aspects see Liquids
      engineering
Gateshead Tyne & Wear Eng.
                                  area–428 73
Gateways
  architecture   725.96
  building   · 690.596
Gatineau Co. Que.   *area*–714 221
Gatley Greater Manchester Eng.
                                  area–427 34
Gatton Qld.   *area*–943 2
Gauges
  radiowave electronics *see*
      Testing-devices
      radiowave electronics
  s.a. Measuring-instruments
Gaul
  hist.   936.4
  s.a.   *area*–364
Gauley River W. Va.   *area*–754 6
Gaulish language *see* Celtic
      languages
Gaultheria *see* Wintergreen
Gauntlets *see* Handwear
Gauss geometry   516.9
  s.a. spec. appls. e.g.
      Engineering
Gaussian processes
  probabilities   519.2
  s.a. spec. appls. e.g.
      Engineering
Gautama Buddha
  art representation   704.948 943
    s.a. spec. art forms
  religion   294.363
Gauzes
  surgical *see* Surgical gauzes
Gaviiformes
  hunting
    commercial   639.128 442
    sports   799.248 442
  paleozoology   568.4
  zoology   598.442
  other aspects see Aves
Gavleborg Sweden   *area*–487
Gawler S. Aust.   *area*–942 32
Gaylussacia *see* Huckleberries

Gaza
  Mozambique   *area*–679 2
  Strip   *area*–531
Gazankulu Transvaal   *area*–682 92
Gazelles
  animal husbandry   636.293
  other aspects see Bovoidea
Gazetteers   910.3
  s.a.   *s.s.*–03
Gazettes
  pub. documents *see* Official
      gazettes
Gaziantep Turkey   *area*–564
Gdansk Poland   *area*–438 2
Gear
  shipbuilding
    soc. & econ. aspects *see*
        Secondary industries
    technology   623.862
      design   623.814 62
      spec. craft   623.812
Gear-cutting tools
  soc. & econ. aspects *see*
      Secondary industries
  tech. & mf.   621.944
  s.a. spec. appls. e.g.
      Motorboats engineering
Gear-driven hoists
  mining eng.   622.67
Geared wheel
  mechanics   531.8
Gearing *see* Gears
Gears
  clockwork
    mf. tech.   681.112
    soc. & econ. aspects *see*
        Secondary industries
  machine eng.
    soc. & econ. aspects *see*
        Secondary industries
    tech. & mf.   621.833
    s.a. spec. appls. e.g.
      High-compression-
        ignition engines
  other aspects see Mechanics
Geary Co. Kan.   *area*–781 29
Geauga Co. O.   *area*–771 336
Geckos *see* Lacertilia
Gedling Nottinghamshire Eng.
                                  area–425 28
Geelong Vic.   *area*–945 2
Geese
  animal husbandry   636.598
    soc. & econ. aspects *see*
        Primary industries
  products
    eggs
      food   641.375 98
        cookery   641.675 98
      prod. tech.   637.598

Geese
  products
    eggs (continued)
      soc. & econ. aspects *see*
        Primary industries
    meats
      food   641.365 97
        cookery   641.665 97
      production *see* Poultry
        products meats
      other prod. see spec. prod.
        e.g. Feathers
    other aspects see
      Anseriformes
Geez language *see* Ethiopic
  languages
Gegenschein *see* Zodiacal light
Geiger counters *see*
      Geiger-Müller counters
Geiger-Müller counters
  radioactivity detection
    astrophysics   523.019 774
    s.a. spec. celestial
      bodies
    physics   539.774
      spec. states of matter   530.4
    s.a. spec. physical
      phenomena e.g. Heat;
      also spec. appls.
      e.g. Civil defense
Geissolomataceae *see*
      Thymelaeales
Gelatin process
  printing
    soc. & econ. aspects *see*
      Secondary industries
    technology   686.232 5
Gelatins
  cookery   641.864
  food
    comm. proc.   664.26
    soc. & econ. aspects *see*
      Secondary industries
  s.a. Crude gelatin
Gelderland Netherlands   *area*–492 1
Gelidiales *see* Rhodophyta
Gelligaer Mid Glamorgan Wales
                            area–429 76
Gels
  colloid chem. *see* Solid
      disperoids colloid
      chem.
Gem Co. Ida.   *area*–796 27
Gemini project   629.454
Gemmation *see* Vegetative
  generation
Gems   553.8
  econ. geol.   553.8
  eng. materials   620.198
    foundations   624.153 98
    structures   624.189 8

Gems
  eng. materials (continued)
    s.a. other spec. uses
  mining
    soc. & econ. aspects *see*
      Primary industries
    technology   622.38
      prospecting   622.188
  synthetic
    manufacturing
      soc. & econ. aspects *see*
        Secondary industries
      technology   666.88
  s.a. spec. uses
Gender *see* Grammar
      (linguistics)
Genealogists
  biog. & work   929.109 2
  occupational ethics   174.999
  s.a.   *pers.*–99
Genealogy   929.1
General
  Agreement on Tariffs and Trade
    international
      commerce   382.92
      law   341.754
  anesthesia   617.962
    vet. sci.   636.089 796 2
    s.a. spec. animals
  Assembly
    United Nations
      internat. law   341.232 2
  bibliographies   011
  Conference Mennonites   289.73
    misc. aspects see Mennonite
      churches
  libraries   027
    catalogs *see* Library
      catalogs
    s.a. spec. activities e.g.
      Cataloging
  library bldgs.
    architecture   727.82
    building   690.782
    functional planning   022.3
    other aspects see
      Educational buildings
  officers
    armed forces   355.331
      s.a. spec. mil. branches
  paresis
    gen. med.   616.892
    geriatrics   618.976 892
    pediatrics   618.928 92
    pub. health   614.598 92
    statistics   312.389 2
      deaths   312.268 92
  partnerships *see* Partnerships
  secondary schools   373.26
  stores
    advertising   659.196 588 74

General	
stores (continued)	
pub. relations	659.296 588 74
retail marketing	658.874
strikes	
labor econ.	331.892 5
world hist.	909
s.a. other spec. subj.	
Generating-machinery	
electrodynamic eng.	
soc. & econ. aspects *see*	
Secondary industries	
tech. & mf.	621.313
s.a. spec. appls. e.g.	
Surface rail systems	
other aspects see	
Electrodynamics	
Generating-stations	
elect. power	
electrodynamic eng. *see*	
Generation elect. power	
Generation	
elect. power	
soc. & econ. aspects *see*	
Secondary industries	
technology	621.312 1
s.a. spec. appls. e.g.	
Public lighting eng.	
other aspects see	
Electrodynamics	
mech. vibrations	
engineering	620.31
s.a. spec. appls. e.g.	
Mechanotherapy	
sound	
engineering	620.21
s.a. spec. appls. e.g.	
Sonar	
physics	534.1
spec. states of matter	530.4
steam	
soc. & econ. aspects *see*	
Secondary industries	
technology	621.182–.184
s.a. spec. appls. e.g.	
Generation elect. power	
s.a. other spec. subj.	
Generation gap *see* Family	
relationships	
Generators	
internal-combustion engines	
see Ignition systems	
& devices	
static electricity *see* Static	
generators electricity	
s.a. other spec. occurrences	
Genes	
life sci.	575.12
animals	591.15
man	573.212
microorganisms	576.139
Genes	
life sci. (continued)	
plants	581.15
s.a. spec. organisms	
Genesee	
County	
Michigan	*area*–774 37
New York	*area*–747 92
River N.Y.	*area*–747 88
Genesis	
Bible	222.11
other aspects see Historical	
books (O.T.)	
Genetic	
control	
populations	363.98
deviations	
life sci.	575.28
animals	591.158
man	573.228
microorganisms	576.139
plants	581.158
s.a. spec. organisms	
diseases *see* Inherited	
diseases	
engineering *see* Eugenics	
factors	
animal breeding	636.082 1
s.a. spec. animals	
laws	
biology	575.11
man	573.211
makeup	
causes of crime	364.24
life sci.	575.12
animals	591.15
man	573.212
plants	581.15
s.a. spec. organisms	
psychology	155
animals	156.5
screening	
crime prevention meas.	364.41
medicine *see* Inherited	
diseases	
Geneticists	
biog. & work	575.109 2
s.a. spec. kinds e.g. plant	
geneticists 581.15092	
other aspects see Scientists	
s.a.	*pers.*–574
Genetics	
life sci.	575.1
animals	591.15
humankind	573.21
racial characteristics	572.3
microorganisms	576.139
plants	581.15
s.a. spec. organisms; also	
spec. types e.g.	
Nucleic acids cytology	

Genetics (continued)
  soc. theology
    Christianity   261.836 5
    comp. rel.   291.178 365
    s.a. other spec. rel.
  sociology   304.5
Genets *see* Viverridae
Geneva
  canton Switzerland   *area*–494 5
  Co. Ala.   *area*–761 292
Genghis Khan reign Asia hist.
        see Mongol
Geniculate bodies
  human phys.   612.826 2
  other aspects see Brain
Genital organs
  diseases *see* Male (human)
        genital organs diseases
  female *see* Female genital
        organs
  male *see* Male (human) genital
        organs
Genitourinary *see* Urogenital
Genius
  psychology *see* Superior
        intelligence
Geniuses *see* Gifted
Gennadius 2 Confession
  Christian doctrines   238.19
Genoa Italy   *area*–451 82
Genocide
  criminology   364.151
  ethics
    philosophy   179.7
    religion
      Buddhism   294.356 97
      Christianity   241.697
      comp. rel.   291.569 7
      Hinduism   294.548 697
      s.a. other spec. rel.
  law
    international   341.77
    municipal   345.025 1
    spec. jur.   345.3–.9
  soc. theology   364.151
    Christianity   261.833 151
    comp. rel.   291.178 331 51
    s.a. other spec. rel.
Genotypes *see* Genetic makeup
Genova Italy   *area*–451 82
Genre paintings
  arts   754
  indiv. artists   759.1–.9
  s.a. spec. tech. & equip.
Gentian family *see* Gentianales
Gentianaceae *see* Gentianales
Gentianales
  botany   583.75
  floriculture   635.933 75
  med. aspects
    crop prod.   633.883 75

Gentianales
  med. aspects (continued)
    gen. pharm.   615.323 75
    toxicology   615.952 375
    vet. pharm.   636.089 532 375
    toxicology   636.089 595 237 5
  paleobotany   561.3
  other aspects see Plants
Gentleness *see* Virtues
Gentry
  Co. Mo.   *area*–778 145
  genealogy   929.7
  other aspects see Upper
    classes
Geobotanical prospecting
  mining eng.   622.12
Geochemical prospecting
  mining eng.   622.13
Geochemistry   551.9
Geodesics
  integral geometry   516.362
  s.a. spec. appls. e.g.
    Engineering
Geodesists
  biog. & work   526.092
  other aspects see Scientists
  s.a.   *pers.*–526
Geodesy   526.1–.7
Geodetic
  astronomy   526.6
  refraction   526.38
  surveying   526.3
Geognosy   551
Geographers
  biog. & work   910.92
  s.a. geog. of spec. places
  occupational ethics   174.991
  s.a.   *pers.*–91
Geographical
  coordinates   526.61–.63
  treatment
    civilization   930–990
    gen. hist.   930–990
    spec. subj.
      gen. areas   *s.s.*–091
      spec. places   *s.s.*–093–099
  s.a. Places; *also other*
      spec. subj.
Geography
  appls. to spec. subj.   *s.s.*–091–099
  Bible   220.91
  s.a. spec. parts of Bible
  documentation   025.069 1
  gen. wks.
    ancient   913
    general
      spec. places   914–919
      world   910
  journalism   070.449 91

Geography (continued)
libraries   026.91
   misc. aspects see Special
    libraries
library acquisitions   025.279 1
library classification   025.469 1
museums
  desc. & colls.   910.74
  museology   069.991
   s.a. spec. activities
    e.g. Display
study & teaching   910.7
  curriculums   375.91
  elementary ed.   372.891
subject headings   025.499 1
other aspects see Disciplines
  (systems)
s.a. spec. kinds e.g. Medical
  geography
Geologic
  age measurements   551.701
   s.a. spec. eras, periods,
    epochs
  time   551.701
   s.a. spec. eras, periods,
    epochs
Geological
  instruments
   manufacturing
    soc. & econ. aspects *see*
     Secondary industries
    technology   681.755
   s.a. spec. kinds
  prospecting
   mining eng.   622.12
  research
   cooperation
    internat. law   341.767 55
Geologists
  biog. & work   550.92
   s.a. spec. kinds e.g.
    economic geologists
    553.092
  other aspects see Scientists
  s.a.   *pers.–*553
Geology   550
  & religion
   nat. rel.   251.5
  human ecology factor
   soc. theology
    Christianity   261.836 23
    comp. rel.   291.178 362 3
    s.a. other spec. rel.
   sociology   304.23
  libraries   026.55
   misc. aspects see Special
    libraries
  museums
   desc. & colls.   550.74

Geology
  museums (continued)
   museology   069.955
    s.a. spec. activities
     e.g. Display
   other aspects see Earth
    sciences
  s.a. spec. fields e.g.
   Engineering geology
Geomagnetic command systems
  aeronautics
   soc. & econ. aspects *see*
    Secondary industries
   technology   629.132 6
Geomagnetism
  astrophysics   523.018 87
   s.a. spec. celestial bodies
  physics   538.7
   spec. states of matter   530.4
Geomancy   133.333
Geometric
  abstractionism *see*
   Abstractionism
  algebras   512.53
   s.a. spec. appls. e.g.
    Engineering
  design (arts)
   gen. wks.   709.040 3
    spec. places   709.1–.9
   painting   759.063
    spec. places   759.1–.9
   sculpture   735.230 43
    spec. places   730.9
   s.a. other spec. art forms
  probability   519.2
   s.a. spec. appls. e.g.
    Engineering
  progressions *see* Progressions
  topology   514
Geometrical
  crystallography   548.1
   s.a. spec. substances
  optics
   astrophysics   523.015 32
    s.a. spec. celestial
     bodies
   physics   535.32
   spec. states of matter   530.4
Geometries
  over algebras   516.186
   Euclidean   516.218 6
   s.a. other spec. geometries;
    also spec. appls. e.g.
    Engineering
  over groups   516.186
   Euclidean   516.218 6
   s.a. other spec. geometries;
    also spec. appls. e.g.
    Engineering
  over rings   516.186
   Euclidean   516.218 6

Geometries
over rings (continued)
*s.a. other spec. geometries;
also spec. appls. e.g.
Engineering*
Geometry 516
elementary ed. 372.73
of motion *see* Transformations
geometry
of numbers 512.5
*s.a. spec. appls. e.g.
Engineering*
of rational numbers
algebra 512.72
*s.a. spec. appls. e.g.
Engineering*
s.a. spec. appls.
Geomorphologists
biog. & work 551.409 2
other aspects see Scientists
s.a. *pers.*–551
Geomorphology 551.4
Geonavigation
seamanship 623.892
other aspects see Navigation
Geophysical prospecting
mining eng. 622.15
Geophysics 551
Geopolitics
pol. sci. 320.12
internat. relations 327.101 1
George
Co. Miss. *area*–762 165
Lake
New South Wales *area*–944 7
New York *area*–747 51
reign
Eng. hist.
1 942.071
2 942.072
3 942.073
4 942.074
5 942.083
6 942.084
Gt. Brit. hist.
1 941.071
2 941.072
3 941.073
4 941.074
5 941.083
6 941.084
Scotland hist.
1 941.107 1
2 941.107 2
3 941.107 3
4 941.107 4
5 941.108 3
6 941.108 4
*s.a. spec. events & subj.
e.g.* Arts
Town Tas. *area*–946 4

Georgetown
Co. S.C. *area*–757 89
Guyana *area*–881 5
Georgia
Soviet Republic *area*–479 5
state *area*–758
Strait *see* Canadian Pacific
seawaters
Georgian
architecture 724.1
spec. places 720.9
other aspects see
Architectural schools
Bay Ont. *area*–713 15
Georgian (Caucasic)
lang. & people *see* Caucasic
SSR *area*–479 5
Georgina River Qld. *area*–943 5
Geotectonic geology 551.8
s.a. spec. appls. e.g.
Prospecting
Geothermal
energy
resources
economics 333.88
govt. control *see* Natural
resources govt. control
engineering
soc. & econ. aspects *see*
Secondary industries
technology 621.44
s.a. spec. appls. e.g.
Heating buildings
methods
geophysical prospecting 622.159
Gephyrea
culture & hunting 639.757
zoology 595.17
other aspects see Worms
Gera Ger. *area*–432 2
Geraldton W. Aust. *area*–941 2
Geraniaceae *see* Geraniales
Geraniales
botany 583.216
floriculture 635.933 216
med. aspects
crop prod. 633.883 216
gen. pharm. 615.323 216
toxicology 615.952 321 6
vet. pharm. 636.089 532 321 6
toxicology 636.089 595 232 16
paleobotany 561.3
other aspects see Plants
Geranium family *see* Geraniales
Gerbils *see* Myomorpha
Geriatric
diseases 618.97
misc. aspects see Diseases
nursing
med. sci. 610.736 5
surgery 617.97

Geriatric (continued)
therapeutics
  med. sci.   615.547
   misc. aspects see
    Therapeutics
  s.a. spec. diseases
Geriatricians
  biog. & work   618.970 092
  prof. duties & characteristics   618.970 232
  other aspects see Medical
    scientists
  s.a.   *pers.*–618
Geriatrics   618.97
Germ
  cells *see* Gametogenesis
  warfare *see* Biological
    warfare
German
  Baptist Brethren   286.5
   misc. aspects see Baptist
  Democratic Republic   *area*–431–432
  emperors Italy hist.   945.03
   s.a. spec. events & subj.
    e.g. Commerce
  Federal Republic   *area*–43
  language
    linguistics   430
    literature   830
    s.a.   *lang.*–31
  measles
    gen. med.   616.916
    geriatrics   618.976 916
    pediatrics   618.929 16
    pub. health   614.524
    statistics   312.391 6
     deaths   312.269 16
   other aspects see Diseases
  people   *r.e.n.*–31
  police dogs *see* German
    shepherd dogs
  Pomerania   *area*–431 7
  shepherd dogs
    animal husbandry   636.73
   other aspects see Dogs
  silver *see* Nickel
  s.a. Germany; *also* Austria;
   also other spec. subj.
    e.g. Arts
Germanic
  languages
    linguistics   430
    literatures   830
    s.a.   *lang.*–3
  people   *r.e.n.*–3
  regions
    ancient   *area*–363
  religion   293
   persons in   *pers.*–293
  sculpture   730.943
   ancient   732.6

Germanic (continued)
  s.a. other spec. subj. e.g.
    Arts
Germanium
  chemistry
    inorganic   546.684
    organic   547.056 84
   s.a. spec. groupings e.g.
    Aliphatic compounds
  technology   661.068 4
   organic   661.895
   soc. & econ. aspects *see*
    Secondary industries
   s.a. spec. prod.
  pharmacology   615.268 4
   misc. aspects see
    Pharmacology
  toxicology   615.925 684
   misc. aspects see
    Toxicology
  other aspects see Minor
    metals
Germans (dances)
  recreation   793.35
Germany   *area*–43
Germs *see* Microbiology
Gerona Spain   *area*–467 1
Gerontology
  physical   612.67
  social
   soc. theology *see* Social
    problems soc. theology
   s.a. Aged people sociology
Gerroidea *see* Heteroptera
Gerrymandering
  legislative bodies
    pol. sci.   328.334 55
    spec. jur.   328.4–.9
Gers France   *area*–447 71
Gerunds *see* Grammar
    (linguistics)
Gesneriaceae *see* Personales
Gestalt
  psychology   150.198 2
  therapy
    psychiatry   616.891 42
     geriatrics   618.976 891 43
     pediatrics   618.928 914 3
    other aspects see Medical
     sciences
  s.a. spec. subj. & branches of
    psych.
Gestures
  drama *see* Acting
  oratory
   preaching
    Christianity   251.03
   other rel. see Preaching
   other aspects see Speaking
Gettysburg Battle
  U.S. Civil War hist.   973.734 9

Gillespie Co. Tex.	*area*–764 65
Gilliam Co. Ore.	*area*–795 65
Gillingham Kent Eng.	*area*–422 325
Gilmer Co.	
Georgia	*area*–758 295
West Virginia	*area*–754 27
Gilpin Co. Colo.	*area*–788 62
Gilyak *see* Paleosiberian	
Gimps *see* Passementerie	
Gin *see* Compound liquors	
Ginger *see* Spices; *also*	
Zingiberales	
Ginger ales	
comm. proc.	663.62
other aspects see	
Nonalcoholic beverages	
Gingivitis *see* Gums (anatomy)	
diseases	
Ginkgo trees *see* Ginkgoales	
Ginkgoaceae *see* Ginkgoales	
Ginkgoales	
botany	585.7
floriculture	635.935 7
forestry	634.975 97
med. aspects	
crop prod.	633.885 7
gen. pharm.	615.325 7
toxicology	615.952 57
vet. pharm.	636.089 532 57
toxicology	636.089 595 257
paleobotany	561.57
other aspects see Plants	
Ginning	
cotton	
soc. & econ. aspects *see*	
Secondary industries	
technology	677.212 1
Gins *see* Compound liquors	
Ginseng *see* Umbellales	
Gippsland district Vic.	*area*–945 6
Gipsy *see* Romany	
Giraffes	
animal husbandry	636.294
other aspects see Giraffoidea	
Giraffoidea	
hunting	
commercial	639.117 357
sports	799.277 357
zoology	599.735 7
other aspects see Ruminantia	
Girder bridges	
structural eng.	624.37
other aspects see Bridges	
(structures)	
Girders	
structural eng.	
gen. wks.	624.177 23
concretes	624.183 423
s.a. other spec.	
materials	
naval arch.	623.817 723

Girders	
structural eng. (continued)	
s.a. other spec. appls.	
Girdles	
comm. mf.	687.25
other aspects see Underwear	
Giresun Turkey	*area*–565
Girl	
Guides *see* Girl Scouts	
Scouts	369.463
camp sports	796.542 2
Girls	
criminal offenders	364.36
misc. aspects see Juvenile	
delinquents	
hygiene	613.042 42–.042 43
journalism for	070.483 27
psychology	155.433
publications for	
bibliographies	011.624 2
spec. kinds	012–016
catalogs	
general	017–019
spec. kinds	012–016
reviews	028.162 42
s.a. spec. forms e.g. Books	
rearing home econ.	649.133
recreation	790.194
indoor	793.019 4
outdoor	796.019 4
rel. associations	
Christianity	267.8
other rel. see Religious	
associations	
sex hygiene	613.955
societies	369.46
other aspects see Children	
Gironde France	*area*–447 1
Girvan Strathclyde Scot.	*area*–414 64
Given names	929.44
Giza Egypt	*area*–622
Glacial	
action physical geol.	551.313
drift physical geol.	551.314
ecology life sci. *see* Arctic	
ecology life sci.	
epoch *see* Pleistocene epoch	
Glacier	
Co. Mont.	*area*–786 52
Nat. Park Mont.	*area*–786 52
Glaciers	
physical geog.	910.02
s.a. spec. places	
physical geol.	551.312
Glaciology	551.31
Glades Co. Fla.	*area*–759 51
Gladioluses *see* Iridales	
Gladstone Qld.	*area*–943 5
Gladwin Co. Mich.	*area*–774 72
Glamorgan Wales	*area*–429 7

Glanders
gen. med.	616.954
geriatrics	618.976 954
pediatrics	618.929 54
pub. health	614.564
statistics	312.395 4
deaths	312.269 54

other aspects see Diseases

Glands

gen. wks. *see* Glandular
      organs

skin
  biochemistry

human phys.	612.792 1

other aspects see
    Integumentary organs

Glandular

organs

anatomy

human	611.4

other aspects see
    Secretory organs

diseases	616.4
geriatrics	618.976 4
pediatrics	618.924
pub. health	614.594
statistics	312.34
deaths	312.264
surgery	617.44
anesthesiology	617.967 44

other aspects see
    Diseases

drugs affecting

pharmacodynamics	615.74

other aspects see Drugs

physical anthropometry	573.64

physiology

human	612.4

other aspects see
    Secretion

tissue biology human	611.018 94

secretions

skin biochemistry

human phys.	612.792 1

other aspects see
    Integumentary organs

Glanford Humberside Eng.	*area–*428 32
Glarus Switzerland	*area–*494 7
Glascock Co. Ga.	*area–*758 666
Glasgow Scot.	*area–*414 43

Glass

architectural

construction	721.044 96

s.a. spec. kinds of
    bldgs.

decoration *see* Ornamental
    glass

breakage insurance	368.6

misc. aspects see Insurance

bldg. construction	693.96
bldg. materials	691.6

Glass (continued)

dec. arts	748

s.a. spec. uses e.g.
    Windows

eng. materials	620.144
foundations	624.153 44
naval design	623.818 38
shipbuilding	623.820 7
hulls	623.845 8
structures	624.183 8

s.a. other spec. uses

handicrafters

biog. & work

glassware	748.291–.299
stained glass	748.591–.599
s.a.	*pers.–*748

manufacturing

soc. & econ. aspects *see*
    Secondary industries

technology	666.1

optical components

mf. tech.	681.42

other aspects see Optical
    instruments

ornamental *see* Ornamental
    glass

sands *see* Sands

sponges *see* Hyalospongiae

supports for photosensitive
    surfaces *see* Supports
    photosensitive surfaces

textiles *see* Fiber glass

Glasscock Co. Tex.	*area–*764 872

Glass-crabs *see* Stomatopoda

Glasses

musical *see* Musical glasses

optical *see* Eyeglasses

Glasshouse Mts. Qld.	*area–*943 2

Glassware

dec. arts	748.2
table setting home econ.	642.7
technology	666.19

other aspects see Glass

Glastonbury Somerset Eng.	*area–*423 83

Glauberite

mineralogy	549.752

Glaucoma

gen. wks. & surgery	617.741
anesthesiology	617.967 741
geriatrics	618.977 741
pediatrics	618.920 977 41
pub. health	614.599 7
statistics	312.304 774 1

other aspects see Diseases

Glauconite *see* Sedimentary
    rocks

Glavda language *see* Chad
    languages

Glaze

meteorology	551.574 4
artificial modification	551.687 44

Glaze
meteorology (continued)
  weather forecasting   551.647 44
  spec. areas   551.65
Glazes
 ceramic
  arts
   decorative   738.12
   fine   731.2
    spec. periods & schools 732–735
  industries
   soc. & econ. aspects *see*
    Secondary industries
   technology   666.42
Glaziers
 biog. & work   698.509 2
 s.a.   *pers.–*698
Glazing
 clays
  ceramic
   arts *see* Glazing clays
    sculpture
   technology   666.444
  sculpture
   dec. arts   738.144
    specialized tech.   738.4–.8
   fine arts   731.4
    spec. periods & schools 732–735
 nat. leathers
  manufacturing
   soc. & econ. aspects *see*
    Secondary industries
   technology   675.25
 windows
  building   698.5
  prod. econ.   338.476 985
 s.a. other spec. subj.
Glees (songs) *see* Choral music
Gleichenia family *see* Filicales
Gleicheniaceae *see* Filicales
Glen Innes N.S.W.   *area*–944 4
Glenelg River Vic.   *area*–945 7
Glengarry Co. Ont.   *area*–713 77
Glenluce Dumfries & Galloway
     Scot.   *area*–414 95
Glenn Co. Calif.   *area*–794 31
Gliders (aircraft)
 aeronautical eng.
  gen. tech. & mf.   629.133 33
   components & tech. 629.134
   models   629.133 133
   operation   629.132 523
  soc. & econ. aspects *see*
    Secondary industries
  s.a. spec. appls. e.g.
    Gliding sports
 commerce   387.733 3
 other aspects see Aircraft
    commerce

Gliding
 aeronautical aerodynamics 629.132 31
 s.a. spec. appls. e.g.
   Flying
 sports   797.55
  misc. aspects see Sports
Glires
 animal husbandry   636.932
 hunting
  commercial   639.113 2
  sports   799.259 32
 paleozoology   569.32
 zoology   599.32
 other aspects see Mammalia
Global
 analysis topology   514.74
 s.a. spec. appls. e.g.
  Engineering
 differential geometry   516.362
 s.a. spec. appls. e.g.
  Engineering
Globe daisy family *see* Lamiales
Globes *see* Maps
Globular clusters
 stars
  astronomy
   description   523.855
   theory   521.585 5
  other aspects see Celestial
    bodies
Globulariaceae *see* Lamiales
Globulins
 org. chem.   547.752
 other aspects see Proteins
Glockenspiel music   789.6
 recordings   789.912 96
Glockenspiels
 mf. tech.   681.819 6
 misc. aspects see Musical
  instruments
 musical art   789.6
Glomerulonephritis *see*
  Nephritis
Gloria *see* Common of the Mass
Glorioso isl.   *area*–694
Glossaries *see* Dictionaries
Glossolalia *see* Speaking in
  tongues
Glossop Derbyshire Eng. *area*–425 11
Glossopharyngeal neuralgias *see*
  Neuralgias
Glossopteris
 paleobotany   561.597
Glottis
 diseases
  gen. wks.   616.22
   neoplasms   616.992 22
   tuberculosis   616.995 22
  geriatrics   618.976 22
  pediatrics   618.922 2
  pub. health   614.592 2

Glottis	
diseases (continued)	
statistics	312.322
deaths	312.262 2
other aspects see Larynx	
Gloucester	
County	
New Brunswick	*area*–715 12
New Jersey	*area*–749 81
Virginia	*area*–755 32
district Eng.	*area*–424 14
N.S.W.	*area*–944 2
Gloucestershire Eng.	*area*–424 1
Glove compartments automobiles	
soc. & econ. aspects *see*	
Secondary industries	
tech. & mf.	629.277
Glovemakers	
biog. & work	685.409 2
s.a.	*pers.*–685 4
Gloves	
latex *see* Dipped latex	
products	
soc. customs	391.412
other aspects see Handwear	
Glowworms	
zoology	595.764 4
other aspects see Polyphaga	
Gloxinia *see* Personales	
Glucinium *see* Beryllium	
Glucose	
org. chem.	547.781 3
other aspects see Sugar	
Glues *see* Adhesives	
Gluing	
bookbinding	686.35
s.a. other spec. appls.	
Gluttony	
ethics	
philosophy	178.9
religion	
Buddhism	294.356 89
Christianity	241.689
cardinal sin	241.3
comp. rel.	291.568 9
Hinduism	294.548 689
s.a. other spec. rel.	
Glycerin	
manufacturing	
soc. & econ. aspects *see*	
Secondary industries	
technology	668.2
Glycerites	
prac. pharm.	615.42
misc. aspects see	
Pharmacology	
Glycine max *see* Soybeans	
Glycogen	
org. chem.	547.782
other aspects see	
Carbohydrates	

Glyncorrwg West Glamorgan Wales	
	area–429 85
Glyndwr Clwyd Wales	*area*–429 37
Glynn Co. Ga.	*area*–758 742
Glyptics	
dec. arts	736.2
rel. significance	247.862
Glyptographers	
biog. & work	736.209 2
s.a.	*pers.*–736
Gnatcatchers *see* Sylviidae	
Gnathobdellida *see* Hirudinea	
Gnats *see* Orthorrhapha	
Gneisses *see* Metamorphic rocks	
Gnetaceae *see* Gnetales	
Gnetales	
botany	585.1
floriculture	635.935 1
forestry	634.975 91
med. aspects	
crop prod.	633.885 1
gen. pharm.	615.325 1
toxicology	615.952 51
vet. pharm.	636.089 532 51
toxicology	636.089 595 251
paleobotany	561.51
other aspects see Plants	
Gnetum family *see* Gnetales	
Gnomes	
lit. & stage trmt. *see*	
Supernatural beings	
Gnosticism	
religion	299.932
Gnus *see* Bovoidea	
Go(game)	
equip. mf.	688.742
soc. & econ. aspects *see*	
Secondary industries	
recreation	794.2
Goa Daman & Diu India	*area*–547 99
Goal posts	
American football	
manufacture	688.763 32
recreation	796.332 028
s.a. other spec. games	
Goalkeeping	
ice hockey	796.962 27
soccer	796.334 26
s.a. other spec. games	
Goat-hair textiles	
arts	746.043 3
s.a. spec. processes e.g.	
Weaving	
dyeing	667.333
manufacturing	
soc. & econ. aspects *see*	
Secondary industries	
technology	677.33
special-process fabrics	677.6
other aspects see Textiles	
s.a. spec. prod.	

Goats
  animal husbandry   636.39
    soc. & econ. aspects *see*
      Primary industries
  products
    dairy *see* Dairy products
    meats
      food   641.363 9
        cookery   641.663 9
      production *see* Red meats
    other prod. see spec. prod.
      e.g. Hides
  other aspects see Bovoidea
Goat's milk
  dairy tech.   637.17
Goatsuckers *see*
  Caprimulgiformes
Gobi Desert   *area*–517 3
Gobies *see* Acanthopterygii
Gobioidea *see* Acanthopterygii
Goblets *see* Containers
Goblins
  lit. & stage trmt. *see*
    Supernatural beings
God
  art representation
    Christianity *see* Trinity
      art representation
    other rel. see Religion art
      representation
  lit. & stage trmt. *see*
    Religious concepts
  private prayers to
    Christianity   242.72
    other rel. see Prayers
      private devotions
  relation to
    church
      Christianity   262.7
      other rel. see
        Ecclesiastical theology
    history
      Christianity   231.76
      other rel. see God rel.
        doctrines
    human experience
      Christianity   231.7
      other rel. see God rel.
        doctrines
  rel. doctrines
    Christianity   231
    comp. rel.   291.211
    Islam   297.211
    Judaism   296.311
    nat. rel.
      concepts   211
      nature   212
    s.a. other spec. rel.
Godalming Surrey Eng.   *area*–422 19

Goddesses
  art representation *see*
    Religion art
    representation
  rel. worship
    comp. rel.   291.211
    s.a. spec. rel.
Godhead *see* God
Godmanchester Cambridgeshire Eng.
      area–426 54
Gods
  art representation *see*
    Religion art
    representation
  rel. worship
    comp. rel.   291.211
    s.a. spec. rel.
Goethite
  mineralogy   549.525
Gog Magog Hills Cambridgeshire
    Eng.   *area*–426 57
Gogebic Co. Mich.   *area*–774 983
Goiás Brazil   *area*–817 3
Goiter
  gen. med.   616.442
  geriatrics   618.976 442
  pediatrics   618.924 42
  pub. health   614.594 42
  statistics   312.344 2
    deaths   312.264 42
  surgery   617.539 5
  anesthesiology   617.967 539 5
  other aspects see Diseases
Gojjam Ethiopia   *area*–633
Golborne Greater Manchester Eng.
      area–427 36
Gold
  chemistry
    inorganic   546.656
    organic   547.056 56
    s.a. spec. groupings e.g.
      Aliphatic compounds
  technology   661.065 6
    organic   661.895
    soc. & econ. aspects *see*
      Secondary industries
    s.a. spec. prod.
  Coast
    history   966.703
    s.a.   *area*–667
  coins
    money econ.   332.404 2
    misc. aspects see Money
    numismatics   737.43
  compounds
    chemistry *see* Gold
      chemistry
    s.a. spec. appls. e.g. Drug
      therapy
  construction
    building   693.722

Gold (continued)
  letters
    books   096.2
    s.a. other spec. uses
  materials
    building   691.822
    engineering   620.189 22
    s.a spec. uses
  metallography   669.952 2
  metallurgy   669.22
    physical & chem.   669.962 2
    soc. & econ. aspects *see*
      Secondary industries
  mineral aspects
    econ. geol.   553.41
    mineralogy   549.23
    s.a. spec. minerals
    mining
      technology   622.342 2
      prospecting   622.184 1
    s.a. spec. uses; also spec.
      minerals
  movements
    internat. comm.   382.174
  pharmacology   615.265 6
    misc. aspects see
      Pharmacology
  plate
    arts *see* Goldsmithing
    s.a. spec. uses
  products *see* Goldsmithing
  standard
    foreign exchange
      economics   332.452
    money
      economics   332.422 2
      misc. aspects see Money
  toxicology   615.925 656
    misc. aspects see
      Toxicology
  other aspects see Metal;
    also Metals
Golden
  algae *see* Chrysophyta
  Rule
    moral theology
      Christianity   241.54
      other rel. see Moral
        theology
  Valley Co.
    Montana   *area*–786 311
    North Dakota   *area*–784 95
Goldi language *see* Tungusic
Goldsboro N.C.   *area*–756 396
Goldsmithing
  arts
    decorative   739.22
    other aspects see Precious
      metals arts
  mf. tech.   673.22

Goldsmithing (continued)
  other aspects see Nonferrous
    metals products
Golf
  equipment mf.   688.763 52
    soc. & econ. aspects *see*
      Secondary industries
  players
    biog. & work   796.352 092
    s.a.   *pers.*–796 35
  sports   796.352
  other aspects see Sports
Golgi bodies *see* Cytoplasm
Goliad Co. Tex.   *area*–764 123
Gomel Belorussia   *area*–476 56
Go-moku
  equip. mf.   688.742
    soc. & econ. aspects *see*
      Secondary industries
  recreation   794.2
Gomortegaceae *see* Laurales
Gonadotropins *see* Sex hormones
Gonads
  transplants *see* Organs
    (anatomy) transplants
  s.a. Ovaries; *also*
    Testicles
Gonâve Ile de la   *area*–729 4
Gondi
  language
    linguistics   494.823
    literature   894.823
    s.a.   *lang.*–948 23
  people   *r.e.n.*–948
  s.a. other spec. subj. e.g.
    Arts
Gondolas
  cars *see* Freight cars
  ships *see* Hand-propelled
    vessels
Gong music   789.4
  recordings   789.912 94
Gongola Nigeria   *area*–669 5
Gongs
  mf. tech.   681.819 4
    misc. aspects see Musical
      instruments
  musical art   789.4
Goniometric measurement &
    calculations   548.7
  s.a. spec. substances
Gonorhynchoidea *see* Isospondyli
Gonorrhea
  gen. med.   616.951 5
  geriatrics   618.976 951 5
  pediatrics   618.929 515
  pub. health   614.547 8
  statistics   312.395 15
    deaths   312.269 515
  other aspects see Diseases
Gonystylaceae *see* Tiliales

Dewey Decimal Classification

Gonzales Co. Tex.	area–764 257
Goochland Co. Va.	area–755 455
Good	
Friday see Holy Week	
Hope Cape	area–687
luck spells & charms	
occultism	133.443
News Bible	220.52
s.a. spec. parts of Bible	
spirits see Angels	
Goodeniaceae see Goodeniales	
Goodeniales	
botany	583.58
floriculture	635.933 58
med. aspects	
crop prod.	633.883 58
gen. pharm.	615.323 58
toxicology	615.952 358
vet. pharm.	636.089 532 358
toxicology	636.089 595 235 8
paleobotany	561.3
other aspects see Plants	
Goodhue Co. Minn.	area–776 14
Gooding Co. Ida.	area–796 36
Goodness	
freedom of choice	
rel. doctrines	
Christianity	233.7
nat. rel.	216
other rel. see Humankind	
rel. doctrines	
metaphysics	111.84
of God	
rel. doctrines	
Christianity	231.8
nat. rel.	214
other rel. see God	
Goods	
aircraft piloting see	
Commercial aircraft	
piloting	
airplanes see Commercial	
airplanes	
terminals see Freight	
terminals	
transportation see Freight	
transportation	
Goodspeed Bible translation	220.520 9
s.a. spec. parts of Bible	
Goodwill	
property law see Intangible	
property law	
Goole Humberside Eng.	area–428 35
Goondiwindi Qld.	area–943 3
Goose see Geese	
Goose Creek Mts. Ida.	area–796 39
Gooseberries	
agriculture	634.725
soc. & econ. aspects see	
Primary industries	

Gooseberries (continued)	
foods	641.347 25
preparation	
commercial	664.804 725
domestic	641.647 25
other aspects see Cunoniales;	
also Fruits	
Goosefoot family see	
Chenopodiales	
Gordiacea see Nematomorpha	
Gordon	
Co. Ga.	area–758 362
Grampian Scot.	area–412 32
River Tas.	area–946 6
Gore Range Colo.	area–788 45
Gorgana Italy	area–455 6
Gorges see Depressions	
(geomorphology)	
Gorgonzola cheeses	
dairy tech.	637.353
other aspects see Cheeses	
Gorillas	
animal husbandry	636.988 46
hunting	
commercial	639.118 846
sports	799.278 846
zoology	599.884 6
other aspects see Primates	
Gorizia Italy	area–453 92
Gorj Romania	area–498 4
Gorki RSFSR	area–478 1
Gorno Altai Autonomous Region	
RSFSR	area–573
Gorno-Badakhshan Autonomous	
Region Tadzhikistan	
	area–586
Gorzow Wielkopolski Poland	
	area–438 1
Gosford N.S.W.	area–944 2
Gosforth Tyne & Wear Eng.	area–428 76
Goshen Co. Wyo.	area–787 18
Gospel music see Evangelistic	
music	
Gospels	
Anglican liturgy	264.036
Bible	226
pseudepigrapha	229.8
other aspects see New	
Testament	
Gosper Co. Neb.	area–782 387
Gosport Hampshire Eng.	area–422 78
Gossip	
ethics	
philosophy	177.2
religion	
Buddhism	294.356 72
Christianity	241.672
comp. rel.	291.567 2
Hinduism	294.548 672
s.a. other spec. rel.	
Gossypium see Cotton	

Gotaland Sweden	*area*–486
Goteborg och Bohus Sweden*area*–486	
Gothic	
alphabets	686.217 4
art	
architecture	723.5
spec. places	720.9
other aspects see	
Architectural schools	
design & dec.	745.442
spec. places	745.449
gen. wks.	709.022
spec. places	709.1–.9
music	
gen. wks.	780.902
spec. places	780.91–.99
s.a. spec. mediums	
painting	759.022
spec. places	759.1–.9
rel. significance	246.1
sculpture	734.25
spec. places	730.9
s.a. other spec. art forms	
fiction *see* Mystery fiction	
kingdom Italy hist.	945.01
s.a. spec. events & subj.	
e.g. Commerce	
lettering dec. arts	745.619 75
texts	
Bible	220.49
s.a. spec. parts of Bible	
s.a. other spec. works	
tracery art *see* Relief arch.	
(art) decoration	
other aspects see East	
Germanic	
Gothic revival architecture	724.3
spec. places	720.9
other aspects see	
Architectural schools	
Gotland Sweden	*area*–486
Gouache painting *see* Watercolor	
painting	
Goulart admin. Brazil hist.	981.062
s.a. spec. events & subj.	
e.g. Commerce	
Goulburn	
N.S.W.	*area*–944 7
River Vic.	*area*–945 4
Goupiaceae *see* Celastrales	
Gourd family *see* Cucurbitales	
Gourmet cookery	641.514
Gourock Strathclyde Scot.	*area*–414 28
Gout	
gen. med.	616.399 9
geriatrics	618.976 399 9
pub. health	614.593 999
statistics	312.339 99
deaths	312.263 999
other aspects see Diseases	
Gove Co. Kan.	*area*–781 152

Governing	
boards	
libraries	021.82
management	658.422
pub. schools	379.153 1
universities & colleges	378.101 1
s.a. other spec.	
enterprises	
leaders	
ecclesiology	
Christianity	262.1
comp. rel.	291.61
Islam	297.61
Judaism	296.61
s.a. other spec. rel.	
Government	
accounting	657.835
law	343.034
spec. jur.	343.3–.9
areas	
civic art	711.551
auditing	
law *see* Government	
accounting law	
bonds	
investment finance	332.632 32
misc. aspects see Bonds	
(securities)	
buildings	
architecture	725.1
building	690.51
other aspects see Public	
structures	
cities	
planning arts	711.45
corporations	
law	346.067
misc. aspects see	
Organizations law	
pub. admin.	350.009 2
central govts.	351.009 2
spec. jur.	353–354
local govts.	352.009
documents *see* Documents	
employees	
lists	350.2
central govts.	351.2
spec. jur.	353–354
local govts.	352.005 2
pub. admin.	
hist. & desc.	350.4
central govts.	351.4
spec. jur.	353–354
local govts.	352.005 4
s.a. Civil service	
personnel	
expenditures *see* Expenditures	
public	
grants	
prod. econ.	338.922

Government (continued)	
liability	
law	
international	341.26
municipal	342.088
spec. jur.	342.3–.9
pub. admin.	350.91
central govts.	351.91
spec. jur.	353–354
local govts.	352.002
libraries	
catalogs *see* Library	
catalogs	
gen. wks.	027.5
administration	025.197 5
buildings	
architecture	727.825
functional planning	022.315
reference services	025.527 75
selection for	025.218 75
use studies	025.587 65
user orientation	025.567 5
spec. groups	027.65
administration	025.197 65
buildings	
architecture	727.826 5
functional planning	022.316 5
reference services	025.527 765
selection for	025.218 765
use studies	025.587 65
user orientation	025.567 65
s.a. other spec. activities	
e.g. Cataloging	
library bldgs.	
architecture	727.825
building	690.782 5
other aspects see	
Educational buildings	
loans	
law	343.074 2
spec. jur.	343.3–.9
malfunctioning	350.9
central govts.	351.9
spec. jur.	353–354
local govts.	352.002
mortgage insurance	
law	343.074 2
spec. jur.	343.3–.9
notes	
investment finance	332.632 32
misc. aspects see Bonds	
(securities)	
officials *see* Government	
employees	
organizations	350
procurement *see* Procurement	
pub. admin.	

Government (continued)	
property	
maintenance	
pub. admin.	350.713 044
central govts.	351.713 044
spec. jur.	353–354
local govts.	352.163 044
management & disposal	
pub. admin.	350.713 045
central govts.	351.713 045
spec. jur.	353–354
local govts.	352.163 045
utilization	
pub. admin.	350.713 043
central govts.	351.713 043
spec. jur.	353–354
local govts.	352.163 043
publications	
bibliographies	011.53
spec. kinds	012–016
catalogs	
general	017–019
spec. kinds	012–016
library trmt. *see* Documents	
s.a. spec. forms e.g. Books	
publishers	070.595
regulation *see spec. subj.*	
e.g. Exchange rates	
foreign exchange	
savings banks	
economics	332.21
other aspects see Banks	
(finance)	
securities	
financial econ.	332.632 044
other aspects see	
Securities	
spending	
macroeconomics	339.522
surveillance *see* Surveillance	
s.a. Public; *also spec.*	
enterprises e.g. church	
government 262	
Governmental *see* Government	
Governments	
ethics *see* Public	
administration ethics	
investments by	
financial econ.	332.671 52
domestic	332.672 52
international	332.673 12
other aspects see	
Investments	
law	342
pol. sci.	320.2
spiritual gift	
Christian doctrines	234.13
s.a. Political institutions	
Government-sponsored insurance	
see Social insurance	

Governors (control devices)
  internal-combustion engines
    soc. & econ. aspects *see*
        Secondary industries
    tech. & mf.   621.437
      marine vehicles   623.872 37
    s.a. other spec. appls.
  s.a. other spec. kinds
Governors (executives)
  biog. & work *see hist. of*
        spec. places
  pub. admin.   351.003 13
    spec. jur.
      U.S.   353.913 1
        spec. states   353.97–.99
        other   354
  s.a.   *pers.*–351 8
Governors-general
  pub. admin.   351.003 12
    spec. jur.   354
Gower Peninsula West Glamorgan
        Wales   *area*–429 82
Grace
  at meals *see* Prayer gen. wks.
  rel. doctrines
    Christianity   234
    other rel. see Humankind
        rel. doctrines
Graces (music)
  music theory   781.67
  s.a. spec. mediums
Gracias a Dios Honduras   *area*–728 32
Grade
  schools *see* Elementary
  separations
    highway transp.
      commerce   388.13
      local   388.411
    law *see* Roads law; *also*
        Streets law
    other aspects see Roads
    railroad transp. *see*
        Stationary facilities
        railroads
Grades (levels)
  military   355.33
  s.a. spec. mil. branches
  religions *see* Governing
        leaders ecclesiology
  s.a. other spec. kinds
Grades (ratings)
  education   371.272 1
  s.a. spec. levels of ed.;
        also Special education
Gradients *see spec. subj. e.g.*
        Fogs
Grading (leveling)
  canal eng. *see* Earthwork
        canal eng.
  road eng. *see* Roadbeds
  s.a. other spec. appls.

Grading (rating)
  cereal grains
    comm. proc.   664.720 4
    s.a. spec. grains & prod.
    other aspects see Cereal
        grains
  clothing construction
    comm. mf.
      scc. & econ. aspects *see*
        Secondary industries
      technology   687.042
    s.a. spec. garments
  crops agric.   631.567
    s.a. spec. crops
  logs forestry   634.982
    s.a. spec. trees
  lumber mf.
    soc. & econ. aspects *see*
        Secondary industries
    technology   647.5
  students *see* Grades (ratings)
  s.a. other spec. subj.
Gradual *see* Proper of the Mass
Graduate depts. & schools
        universities   378.155 3
Graduated instruments *see*
        Measuring-instruments
Graduate-school songs *see*
        University & college
        songs
Graduation
  customs   394.2
  education   371.291 2
  s.a. spec. levels of ed.;
        also Special education
Grady Co.
  Georgia   *area*–758 986
  Oklahoma   *area*–766 54
Graft *see* Political corruption
Grafting
  plants crop prod.   631.541
    s.a. spec. crops; also spec.
        types of culture e.g.
        Floriculture
  surgery *see* Plastic surgery
Grafting-equipment
  agriculture   631.34
  use   631.541
    s.a. spec. crops; also
        spec. types of culture
        e.g. Floriculture
  mf. tech.   681.763 1
    soc. & econ. aspects *see*
        Secondary industries
Grafton
  Co. N.H.   *area*–742 3
  town N.S.W.   *area*–944 3
Graham
  County
    Arizona   *area*–791 54
    Kansas   *area*–781 163

Graham
County (continued)
  North Carolina   *area*–756 97
  Land Antarctica   *area*–989
  shorthand systems   653.424 4
Grail
  lit. & stage trmt. *see* Things
Grain
  carriers *see* Cargo ships
  elevator bldgs.
    commercial *see* Storage
      elevator buildings
    domestic *see* Agricultural
      structures
  elevators
    agriculture   631.23
    s.a. spec. crops
  sorghums *see* Sorghums
  whiskies *see* Whiskies
Grainger Co. Tenn.   *area*–768 932
Graining woodwork
  buildings   698.32
Grains
  animal feeds
    comm. proc.   664.762
  other aspects see Cereal
    grains
Grallatores
  hunting
    commercial   639.128 3
    sports   799.248 3
  paleozoology   568.3
  zoology   598.3
Grama grasses *see* Pooideae
Graminales
  botany   584.9
  floriculture   635.934 9
  med. aspects
    crop prod.   633.884 9
    gen. pharm.   615.324 9
    toxicology   615.952 49
    vet. pharm.   636.089 532 49
    toxicology   636.089 595 249
  paleobotany   561.49
  other aspects see Plants
Gramineae *see* Graminales
Grammar (linguistics)   415
  spec. langs.
    nonstandard forms *lang. sub.*–7
    standard form
      desc. & anal.   *lang. sub.*–5
      usage   *lang. sub.*–8
  study & teaching   415.071
    elementary ed.   372.61
  s.a. spec. langs.
Grammar schools *see* Academic
    secondary schools
Grammarians
  biog. & work   415.092
  s.a. spec. langs.
  s.a.   *pers.*–4

Grampian
  Mts. Scot.   *area*–412 1
  region Scot.   *area*–412 1
Grampians Vic.   *area*–945 8
Gran Chaco   *area*–823
Granada
  Nicaragua   *area*–728 515
  Spain   *area*–468 2
Granaries
  agriculture   631.23
  s.a. spec. crops
  bldg. aspects *see*
    Agricultural structures
Grand
  Alliance War
    history   949.204
  Army of the Republic   369.15
  Bahama Isl.   *area*–729 6
  Canyon Nat. Park & Monument
    Ariz.   *area*–791 32
  Coulee Wash.   *area*–797 31
  County
    Colorado   *area*–788 65
    Utah   *area*–792 58
  Forks Co. N.D.   *area*–784 16
  Isl. N.Y.   *area*–747 96
  Isle Co. Vt.   *area*–743 12
  juries
    proceedings
      criminal law   345.072
      spec. jur.   345.3–.9
  Kabylia Algeria   *area*–653
  Lake La. (Cameron Par.)
        area–763 52
  Lake La. (Iberia Par.)   *area*–763 49
  Manan Isl. N.B.   *area*–715 33
  opera *see* Opera
  Prairie Tex.   *area*–764 51
  Rapids Mich.   *area*–774 56
  River S.D.   *area*–783 5
  Teton Nat. Park Wyo.   *area*–787 55
  Traverse
    Bay Mich.   *area*–774 64
    Co. Mich.   *area*–774 64
Grandchildren   *pers.*–044 2
Grande Prairie Alta.   *area*–712 31
Grandparents   *pers.*–043 2
Grandstands
  architecture   725.827
  building   690.582 7
  other aspects see Public
    structures
Grange Cumbria Eng.   *area*–427 83
Grangemouth Central Scot. *area*–413 18
Granite
  Belt Nat. Park Qld.   *area*–943 3
  Co. Mont.   *area*–786 88
Granites   553.52
  econ. geol.   553.52
  materials *see* Natural stones

Granites (continued)
  mineralogy & petrology, *see*
      Plutonic rocks
  mining
    soc. & econ. aspects *see*
      Primary industries
    technology   622.352
    prospecting   622.185 2
  s.a. spec. uses
Granma Cuba   *area*–729 163
Grant
  County
    Arkansas   *area*–767 71
    Indiana   *area*–772 69
    Kansas   *area*–781 723
    Kentucky   *area*–769 395
    Minnesota   *area*–776 44
    Nebraska   *area*–782 783
    New Mexico   *area*–789 692
    North Dakota   *area*–784 87
    Oklahoma   *area*–766 23
    Oregon   *area*–795 78
    South Dakota   *area*–783 24
    Washington   *area*–797 32
    West Virginia   *area*–754 92
    Wisconsin   *area*–775 77
  Par. La.   *area*–763 67
  Ulysses S. admin.
    U.S. hist.   973.82
    s.a. spec. events & subj.
      e.g. Courts
Grantham Lincolnshire Eng.
                area–425 38
Grantown-on-Spey Highland Scot.
                area–411 92
Grants
  prod. econ.   338.922
  pub. finance   336.185
  misc. aspects see
      Intergovernmental
      revenues
  s.a. spec. kinds e.g. Land
      grants econ.
Granules
  animal feeds *see* Formula
    feeds
Granville Co. N.C.   *area*–756 535
Grape
  ferns *see* Eusporangiated
    ferns
  wines   641.222
    comm. proc.   663.22
  other aspects see Wines
Grapefruit
  agriculture   634.32
    soc. & econ. aspects *see*
      Primary industries
  foods   641.343 2
    preparation
      commercial   664.804 32
      domestic   641.643 2

Grapefruit (continued)
  other aspects see Rutales;
    also Fruits
Grapes
  agriculture   634.8
    soc. & econ. aspects *see*
      Primary industries
  foods   641.348
    preparation
      commercial   664.804 8
      domestic   641.648
  other aspects see Rhamnales;
    also Fruits
Graphic
  arts   760
    personnel   *pers.*–76
    s.a. spec. kinds e.g.
      Painters (arts)
  development of words *see*
    Etymology
  expressions
    psychology   152.384 5
    animals   156.238 45
    children   155.412
    s.a. psych. of other spec.
      groups
  materials
    ed. use   371.335
    s.a. spec. levels of ed.;
      also Special education
  manufacture
    soc. & econ. aspects *see*
      Secondary industries
    technology   686
    spec. subj.   *s.s.*–022
    s.a. spec. kinds e.g.
      Pictures
  representations
    sound
      engineering   620.21–.25
      physics   534.46
      spec. states of matter 530.4
    tech. drawing *see*
      Production illustration
      tech. drawing
  statics
    structural theory
      gen. wks.   624.171 2
      spec. elements 624.177 2–.177 9
      naval arch.   623.817 12
      s.a. other spec. appls.
    other aspects see Statics
Graphic-arts papers
  mf. tech.   676.282
  other aspects see Papers pulp
    prod.
Graphics
  electronic data proc. *see*
    Outputs electronic data
    proc.

Graphite	553.26
econ. geol.	553.26
eng. materials	620.198
naval design	623.818 98
s.a. other spec. uses	
manufacturing	
chem. tech.	662.92
soc. & econ. aspects *see*	
Secondary industries	
mineralogy	549.27
mining	
technology	622.336
prospecting	622.182 6
synthetic	
manufacturing	
soc. & econ. aspects *see*	
Secondary industries	
technology	666.86
s.a. spec. uses	
Graphitic anthracite coal	553.25
econ. geol.	553.25
mining	
soc. & econ. aspects *see*	
Primary industries	
technology	622.335
prospecting	622.182 5
processing	662.622 5
other aspects see Coals	
s.a. spec. uses	
Graphology	652.1
criminal investigation *see*	
Documentary evidence	
popular psych.	137
Graphs	
mathematics	511.5
s.a. spec. math. branches;	
also spec. appls. e.g.	
Engineering	
spec. subj.	*s.s.*–021 2
statistical method	001.422 6
spec. subj. *see* Statistical	
method spec. subj.	
Graptolitoidea	
paleozoology	563.71
Grass wax	
comm. proc.	665.12
other aspects see Waxes	
Grasses	
dec. arrangements	749.925
horticulture *see* Ground cover	
other aspects see Graminales	
s.a. spec. kinds e.g. Pasture	
grasses	
Grasshoppers *see* Orthoptera	
Grasslands	
ecology life sci.	574.526 43
animals	591.526 43
microorganisms	576.15
plants	581.526 43
s.a. spec. organisms	

Grasslands (continued)	
govt. control	
law	346.046 74
regional subj. trmt.	*area*–153
other aspects see Pasture	
lands	
Grassman algebra	512.57
s.a. spec. appls. e.g.	
Engineering	
Gratiot Co. Mich.	*area*–774 49
Gratitude *see* Virtues	
Gratuities *see* Tipping	
Graubunden Switzerland	*area*–494 7
Graupel *see* Solid amorphous	
precipitation	
Gravel pavement	
engineering *see* Stone	
pavements road eng.	
Gravels	553.626
econ. geol.	553.626
mining	
soc. & econ. aspects *see*	
Primary industries	
technology	622.362 6
prospecting	622.186 26
s.a. spec. uses	
Graves	
Co. Ky.	*area*–769 93
registration service	
mil. admin.	355.69
s.a. spec. mil. branches	
Graves' disease *see*	
Hyperthyroidism	
Gravesend Kent. Eng.	*area*–422 315
Gravesham Kent Eng.	*area*–422 315
Gravestone inscriptions	
genealogy	929.5
Gravestones *see* Monuments	
Graveyards *see* Cemetries	
Gravies *see* Auxiliary foods	
Gravimetric	
analysis	
quan. anal. chem.	545.1
organic	547.351
s.a. spec. elements &	
cpds.	
measuring-apparatus	
chemistry	542.3
s.a. spec. appls. e.g.	
Organic chemistry	
Gravitation	
celestial bodies *see*	
Constants celestial	
bodies	
celestial mech. *see* Celestial	
mechanics	
physics *see* Mass (substance)	
physics mech.	

Great (continued)	
Torrington Devon Eng.	*area*–423 51
Trek	
Cape of Good Hope hist.	968.704 2
s.a. spec. events & subj.	
e.g. Commerce	
Natal hist.	968.404 2
s.a. spec. events & subj.	
e.g. Commerce	
Orange Free State hist.	968.504 2
s.a. spec. events & subj.	
e.g. Commerce	
South Africa hist.	968.042
s.a. spec. events & subj.	
e.g. Commerce	
War (1914-1918)	
history	940.3
s.a. spec. countries & spec.	
subj.	
Western Mts. Tas.	*area*–946 3
Yarmouth Norfolk Eng.	*area*–426 18
Greater	
Antilles	*area*–729 1–729 5
Manchester Metropolitan Co.	
Eng.	*area*–427 3
Grebes *see* Colymbiformes	
Greco-Roman wrestling *see*	
Continental wrestling	
Greco-Turkish War	949.506
Greece	*area*–495
ancient	*area*–38
Greediness	
ethics	
philosophy	178.9
religion	
Buddhism	294.356 89
Christianity	241.689
comp. rel.	291.568 9
Hinduism	294.548 689
s.a. other spec. rel.	
Greek	
alphabets	
printing	686.218
architecture	722.8
misc. aspects see	
Architectural schools	
islands	*area*–499
ancient	*area*–391
languages	
classical	
linguistics	480
literature	880
s.a.	*lang.*–81
modern	
linguistics	489.3
literature	889
s.a.	*lang.*–89
postclassical	
linguistics	487
s.a.	*lang.*–87
lettering dec. arts	745.619 8

Greek (continued)	
Orthodox Church	281.93
misc. aspects see Eastern	
Orthodox	
peoples	
ancient	*r.e.n.*–81
modern	*r.e.n.*–893
philosophy	
ancient	182–185
modern	199.495
religion	292.08
persons in	*pers.*–292
spec. aspects	292.1–.9
sculpture	733.3
texts	
Bible	220.48
s.a. spec. parts of Bible	
s.a. Greece; *also*	
Hellenistic; *also*	
other spec. subj.	
Greek revival architecture	724.23
spec. places	720.9
other aspects see	
Architectural schools	
Greek-letter societies	
education	371.85
s.a. spec. levels of ed.;	
also Special education	
Greeley Co.	
Kansas	*area*–781 413
Nebraska	*area*–782 49
Green	
algae *see* Chlorophyta	
Bay Wis.	*area*–775 3
city	*area*–775 61
County	
Kentucky	*area*–769 695
Wisconsin	*area*–775 86
fodder feeds	
animal husbandry	636.085 51
s.a. spec. feeds; also	
spec. animals	
Lake Wis.	*area*–775 59
manure fertilizers	
production	
soc. & econ. aspects *see*	
Secondary industries	
technology	668.637 4
use agric.	631.874
s.a. spec. crops; also	
spec. types of culture	
e.g. Floriculture	
Mts. Vt.	*area*–743
peppers	
agriculture	635.643
soc. & econ. aspects *see*	
Primary industries	
foods	641.356 43
preparation	
commercial	664.805 643
domestic	641.656 43

Grills (continued)
  electric cookery   641.586
    s.a. spec. situations,
      materials, tech.
Grimes Co. Tex.   *area*–764 243
Grimoire
  occultism   133.43
Grimsby Humberside Eng.   *area*–428 34
Grinding
  cereal grains
    comm. proc.   664.720 3
    s.a. spec. grains & prod.
    other aspects see Cereal
      grains
  chem. eng.   660.284 22
    s.a. spec. prod.
  coal fuel tech.   662.623
  metal prod. *see* Machining
    metal prod.
  ore mining eng.   622.73
  spec. ores.   622.33–.39
Grinding-tools
  soc. & econ. aspects *see*
    Secondary industries
  tech. & mf.   621.92
    s.a. spec. appls. e.g.
      Flours comm. proc.
Grindstones
  soc. & econ. aspects *see*
    Secondary industries
  tech. & mf.   621.923
    s.a. spec. appls. e.g.
      Agricultural equipment
Grisons Switzerland   *area*–494 7
Grodno Belorussia   *area*–476 52
Groined arches & vaults
  architectural
    construction   721.44
    design & decoration   729.33–.34
  building   690.144
  s.a. spec. kinds of bldgs.
Groningen Netherlands   *area*–492 1
Grooming
  animals   636.083 3
    s.a. spec. animals
  personal *see* Personal
    grooming
Groote Eylandt N. Ter. Aust.
      area–942 95
Grooving-machines *see*
    Milling-tools
Gros Ventre Range Wyo.   *area*–787 55
Grosbeaks *see* Fringillidae
Gross
  nat. prod.
    macroeconomics   339.31
  structure
    earth   551.1
    s.a. other spec. subj.
Grosseto Italy   *area*–455 7
Grossulariaceae *see* Cunoniales

Grotesque style
  sculpture   732–735
    s.a. other spec. arts
Grottoes
  geomorphology   551.447
  rel. worship *see* Sacred
    places rel. worship
  other aspects see Openings
    (physiography)
Ground
  cherries *see* Solanales
  cover
    landscape design   716
    plants grown for
      floriculture   635.964
      s.a. spec. plants
  forces mil. sci.   355
  operations mil. sci.   355
  substances connective tissues
    see Connective tissue
  surveying
    photogrammetry   526.982 5
    other aspects see Surveying
  tests
    aircraft eng.   629.134 52
    s.a. spec. appls. e.g.
      Military engineering
  transportation
    commerce   388
    engineering
      soc. & econ. aspects *see*
        Secondary industries
      tech. & mf.   629.049
      military   623.61
      s.a. other spec. appls.
    facilities civic art   711.72–.75
    govt. control   350.878
      central govts.   351.878
      spec. jur.   353–354
      local govts.   352.918
    law *see* Transportation law
    personnel
      biog. & work   388.092
      s.a. spec. kinds e.g.
        Railroad personnel
      s.a.   *pers.*–388
    other aspects see
      Transportation
    s.a. Railroad
      transportation
  warfare mil. sci.   355
  waters   553.79
    econ. geol.   553.79
    extraction
      technology   622.379
      prospecting   622.187 9
    hydraulic eng.
      technology   627.17
      s.a. spec. appls. e.g.
        Sources water-supply
        eng.

Ground
　waters
　　hydraulic eng. (continued)
　　　other aspects see Liquids
　　　　engineering
　　　hydrology　　　　　　　　551.49
　　　regional subj. trmt.　　*area*–169 8
　　　resources
　　　　economics　　　　　　333.910 4
　　　　govt. control
　　　　　law　　　　　346.046 910 4
　　　　　spec. jur.　　　　346.3–.9
　　　　pub. admin. *see* Water
　　　　　resources govt. control
　　　　　pub. admin.
　　　　s.a. spec. aspects e.g.
　　　　　Water supply soc.
　　　　　services
　　　utilization
　　　　land econ.　　　　　　333.910 4
　　　water-supply sources
　　　　technology　　　　　　628.114
　　　　other aspects see Water
　　　　　supply engineering
　　s.a. Land
Ground-control personnel
　aeronautics　　　　　　　*pers.*–629 1
　astronautics　　　　　　　*pers.*–629 4
Ground-effect machines *see*
　　Air-cushion vehicles
Grounding prevention
　sea safety　　　　　　　　623.888 4
Grounding-devices
　electrodynamic eng. *see*
　　　Control devices
　　　electrodynamic eng.
　radio
　　engineering　　　　　　621.384 133
　　s.a. spec. appls. e.g.
　　　Radiotelephony
　　other aspects see Radio
　television
　　engineering　　　　　　621.388 33
　　s.a. spec. appls. e.g.
　　　Astronautics
　　other aspects see
　　　Television
Groundnuts *see* Peanuts
Grounds
　functional use
　　libraries　　　　　　　　022.1
　　local Christian churches　254.7
　　museums　　　　　　　　069.21
　　prisons　　　　　　　　365.5
　　　misc. aspects see Penal
　　　　institutions
　　schools　　　　　　　　371.61
　　　s.a. spec. levels of ed.;
　　　　also Special education
　　s.a. other spec. kinds
　landscape design　　　　712

Grounds (continued)
　management
　　pub. admin. *see* Land
　　　management & disposal
　　　pub. admin.
Groundsels *see* Asterales
Ground-support systems
　astronautics *see* Terrestrial
　　　facilities spacecraft
　　　eng.
Groundwood process
　wood pulp mf.　　　　　676.122
Group
　banking
　　economics　　　　　　332.16
　　other aspects see Banking
　behavior
　　sociology　　　　　　　302.3
　　other aspects see Behavior
　decision making
　　management use　　　　658.403 6
　　other aspects see Decision
　　　making
　education
　　adult ed.　　　　　　　374.2
　guidance
　　education　　　　　　　371.404 4
　　s.a. spec. levels of ed.;
　　　also Special education
　insurance　　　　　　　　368.3
　　misc. aspects see Insurance
　practice med. sci.　　　　610.65
　sex *see* Extramarital sex
　　　relations
　teaching　　　　　　　　371.395
　　s.a. spec. levels of ed.;
　　　also Special education
　theory mathematics　　　512.22
　　s.a. spec. appls. e.g.
　　　Engineering
　therapy
　　psychiatry　　　　　616.891 52
　　　geriatrics　　　618.976 891 52
　　　pediatrics　　　618.928 915 2
　　other aspects see Medical
　　　sciences
　work
　　soc. welfare　　　　　361.4
　　spec. problems & groups　362–363
　　other aspects see Welfare
　　　services
　s.a. other spec. subj.
Groupoids
　algebra　　　　　　　　512.2
　s.a. spec. appls. e.g.
　　Engineering
Groups
　air force organization　358.413 1
　algebra　　　　　　　　512.2
　s.a. spec. appls. e.g.
　　Engineering

Groups (continued)
  blood
    human physiology   612.118 25
    other aspects see
        Circulatory fluids
        physiology
  organisms
    ecology life sci.   574.524 6
      animals   591.524 6
      microorganisms   576.15
      plants   581.524 6
      s.a. spec. organisms
  personal
    art representation   704.942 6
      painting   757.6
      s.a. other spec. art
          forms
    soc. interaction   302.3
    s.a. spec. kinds e.g. Ethnic
        groups
Group-to-group relations
  soc. interaction   302.4
Group-to-person relations
  soc. interaction   302.5
Grouse *see* Tetraonidae
Grouting *see* Earthwork
Growlers
  physical geol.   551.342
Growth
  life sci.
    gen. wks.   574.31
      animals   591.31
      microorganisms   576.131
      plants   581.31
      s.a. spec. organisms
    med. sci.   612.6
      animals   636.089 26
      s.a. spec. animals
      man   612.6
  movements of plants
    pathology   581.218 3
    physiology   581.183
    s.a. spec. plants
  of cells cytology *see*
          Development (biology)
          cytology
  of crystals   548.5
  s.a. spec. substances
  soc. change   303.44
  s.a. other spec. kinds e.g.
          Economic growth
Grubbiaceae *see* Santalales
Grubbing
  canal eng. *see* Earthwork
          canal eng.
  road eng. *see* Roadbeds
Grues *see* Gruiformes
Gruiformes
  hunting
    commercial   639.128 31
    sports   799.248 31

Gruiformes (continued)
    paleozoology   568.3
    zoology   598.31
    other aspects see Aves
Grünberg Poland   *area*–438 1
Grundy Co.
    Illinois   *area*–773 265
    Iowa   *area*–777 537
    Missouri   *area*–778 215
    Tennessee   *area*–768 78
Gruyère cheeses
    dairy tech.   637.354
    other aspects see Cheeses
Guadalajara Spain   *area*–464 9
Guadalcanal Solomons   *area*–935
Guadalquivir River Spain   *area*–468
Guadalupe
  County
    New Mexico   *area*–789 25
    Texas   *area*–764 34
  River Tex.   *area*–764 1
Guadeloupe isl.   *area*–729 76
Guainía Colombia   *area*–861 67
Guairá Paraguay   *area*–892 128
Guajira Colombia   *area*–861 17
Guam   *area*–967
Guanabanas *see* Annonaceous
          fruits
Guanabara Brazil   *area*–815 3
Guanacaste Costa Rica   *area*–728 66
Guanaco wool textiles
  arts   746.043 2
    s.a. spec. proc. e.g.
        Weaving
  dyeing   667.332
  manufacturing
    soc. & econ. aspects *see*
        Secondary industries
    technology   677.32
    special-process fabrics   677.6
  other aspects see Textiles
  s.a. spec. prod.
Guanacos *see* Tylopoda
Guanajuato Mex.   *area*–724
Guano fertilizers
  production
    soc. & econ. aspects *see*
        Secondary industries
    technology   668.636 6
  use agric.   631.866
    s.a. spec. crops; also spec.
        types of culture e.g.
        Floriculture
Guans *see* Cracidae
Guantanamo Cuba   *area*–729 167
Guarani *see* South American
        native

Guaranteed
  minimum income
    soc. welfare   362.582
    misc. aspects see Poor
        people soc. services
Guaranteed-wage plans
  labor econ.   331.23
    s.a. spec. classes of labor
        e.g. Women
  labor law *see* Labor law
Guaranty
  law *see* Secured transactions
Guard cells
  plant anatomy *see* Respiratory
    organs
Guarda Portugal   *area*-469 31
Guardian & ward
  law   346.018
  spec. jur.   346.3-.9
Guarding
  animal husbandry for   636.088 6
    s.a. spec. animals
Guards *see* Safety equipment
Guárico Venezuela   *area*-874 7
Guatemala
  City Guatemala   *area*-728 11
  country   *area*-728 1
  department Guatemala *area*-728 11
Guatemalan
  literature   860
  people   *r.e.n.*-687 281
    s.a. spec. subj. e.g. Arts
Guavas
  agriculture   634.421
    soc. & econ. aspects *see*
      Primary industries
  foods   641.344 21
    preparation
      commercial   664.804 421
      domestic   641.644 21
    other aspects see Myrtales;
      also Fruits
Guayama Puerto Rico   *area*-729 58
Guayaquil Gulf *see* Southeast
    Pacific Ocean
Guayas Ecuador   *area*-866 32
Guayule
  plants
    culture   633.895 9
    other aspects see Asterales
  other aspects see Rubber
Guelph Ont.   *area*-713 43
Guernsey
  cattle
    animal husbandry   636.224
    other aspects see Cattle
  Co. O   *area*-771 92
  island   *area*-423 42
Guerrero Mex.   *area*-727 3
Guerrilla
  forces mil. sci.   356.15

Guerrilla (continued)
  warfare mil. sci.   355.021 84
  tactics   355.425
    s.a. spec. mil. branches
Guests
  seating table service   642.6
Guianas   *area*-88
Guidance
  soc. services *see* Counseling
    soc. services
  space flight
    manned   629.453
    unmanned   629.433
    s.a. spec. appls. e.g.
      Space warfare; *also*
      spec. flights e.g.
      Lunar flights manned
  systems spacecraft *see* Flight
    operations systems
    spacecraft
  other aspects see Counseling
Guidebooks   910.202
  spec. places   913-919
Guided
  aircraft
    aeronautics
      soc. & econ. aspects *see*
        Secondary industries
    technology   629.132 6
    mil. eng.   623.746 9
  missiles
    mil. eng.
      soc. & econ. aspects *see*
        Secondary industries
      tech. & mf.   623.451 9
Guided-missile
  delivery
    postal commun.   383.144
    other aspects see Postal
      communication
  forces mil. sci.   358.17
  warfare defenses
    mil. eng.   623.3
Guided-way systems
  local transp. *see* Local
    railways
Guiding-equipment
  soc. & econ. aspects *see*
    Secondary industries
  tech. & mf.   621.992
    s.a. spec. appls. e.g.
      Military engineering
Guienne France   *area*-447
Guild
  socialism econ.   335.15
  system prod. econ.   338.632
Guildford Surrey Eng. *area*-422 162
Guilford Co. N.C.   *area*-756 62
Guilt
  criminal law   345.04
  spec. jur.   345.3-.9

Guilt (continued)
  rel. doctrines
    Christianity   233.4
    other rel. see Humankind
      rel. doctrines
Guinea
  Equatorial   *area*–671 8
  fowl
    animal husbandry   636.593
    sci. aspects *see* Numididae
    other aspects see Poultry
  Gulf
    islands   *area*–669 9
    oceanography   551.464 73
    regional subj. trmt. *area*–163 73
    other aspects see Atlantic
      Ocean
  Lower   *area*–671
  pigs
    experimental animals
      med. sci.   619.93
    other aspects see
      Hystricomorpha
  republic   *area*–665 2
  Spanish   *area*–671 8
  Upper   *area*–665
Guinea-Bissau   *area*–665 7
Guineans   *r.e.n.*–966 52
Guipúzcoa Spain   *area*–466 1
Guisborough Cleveland Eng.*area*–428 54
Guitar music   787.615
  recordings   789.912 761
Guitarfishes *see* Batoidea
Guitarists
  biog. & work   787.610 92
  s.a.   *pers.*–787
Guitars
  mf. tech.   681.817 61
  misc. aspects see Musical
    instruments
  musical art   787.61
Gujarat India   *area*–547 5
Gujarati
  language
    linguistics   491.47
    literature   891.47
    s.a.   *lang.*–914 71
  people   *r.e.n.*–914 7
  s.a. Gujarat; *also other*
    spec. subj. e.g. Arts
Gujars   *r.e.n.*–914 7
Gulches *see* Depressions
  (geomorphology)
Gulf
  Coast states U.S.   *area*–76
  Co. Fla.   *area*–759 947
  Stream
    oceanography   551.471
Gulfs *see* Seas
Gullies *see* Depressions
  (geomorphology)

Gulls *see* Lari
Gum trees *see* Hamamelidales
Gum-bichromate processes
  photographic printing   773.5
Gumbo *see* Okra
Gumma Japan   *area*–521 3
Gums
  eng. materials   620.192 4
    s.a. spec. uses
  forest prod. *see* Saps
  fossil *see* Fossil gums &
    resins
  manufacturing
    chem. tech.   668.37
    soc. & econ. aspects *see*
      Secondary industries
  org. chem.   547.843 4
Gums (anatomy)
  diseases
    gen. wks.   617.632
    geriatrics   618.977 632
    pub. health   614.599 6
    statistics   312.304 763 2
  other aspects see Teeth
Gumusane Turkey   *area*–565
Gun
  carriages *see* Gun mounts
  dogs
    animal husbandry   636.752
    other aspects see Dogs
  mounts
    art metalwork   739.743
    mil. eng.
      soc. & econ. aspects *see*
        Secondary industries
      tech. & mf.   623.43
  salutes
    mil. discipline   355.134 9
Gunboats *see* Destroyer escorts
Guncotton *see* Propellant
    explosives
Gundagai N.S.W.   *area*–944 8
Gundis *see* Hystricomorpha
Gunmetal *see* Copper
Gunnedah N.S.W.   *area*–944 4
Gunnery
  mil. eng.   623.55
Gunnison Co. Colo   *area*–788 41
Gunpowder *see* Propellant
    explosives
Guns
  artillery
    art metalwork   739.742
    mil. eng.
      soc. & econ. aspects *see*
        Secondary industries
      tech. & mf.   623.42
      s.a. spec. appls. e.g.
        Gunnery

Guns (continued)

control	363.33
law	344.053 3
spec. jur.	344.3–.9
pub. admin.	350.75
central govts.	351.75
spec. jur.	353–354
local govts.	352.935

s.a. Arms (military) control

hunting & shooting sports	799.202 83
game	799.213
targets	799.31

other aspects see Ordnance
s.a. Small arms

Gunshot wounds

statistics	312.304 714 5
deaths	312.260 471 45
surgery	617.145
anesthesiology	617.967 145

s.a. Veterinary sciences

Gunsmithing
soc. & econ. aspects *see*
Secondary industries

technology	683.4

Gunsmiths

biog. & work	683.400 92
s.a.	*pers.*–683

Guntersville Res. Ala. *area*–761 94

Guptas

India hist.	934.06

s.a. spec. events & subj.
e.g. Arts

Gur languages

linguistics	496.35
literatures	896.35
s.a.	*lang.*–963 5

Gurage language *see* Ethiopic
languages

Gurus *see* Clergy

Gustation

animal phys.	591.182 6

s.a. spec. animals

human phys.	612.87

other aspects see Sensory
functions

Gustatory
organs
anatomy

human	611.87

other aspects see Sense
organs

physical anthropometry	573.687

physiology *see* Gustation

tissue biology human	611.018 987

perception psych.

gen. wks.	152.167
animals	156.216 7
children	155.412

s.a. psych. of other spec.
groups

Gustatory
perception psych. (continued)

influences	155.911 67

Gutenberg
discontinuity

geophysics	551.115

Guthrie

Co. Ia.	*area*–777 49
system psych.	150.194 34

s.a. spec. subj. & branches
of psych.

Gutta-percha
trees

culture	633.895 9

other aspects see Ebenales
other aspects see Rubber

Gutters
drainage *see* Drainage
s.a. Roofs

Guttiferae *see* Guttiferales

Guttiferales

botany	583.163
floriculture	635.933 163
forestry	634.973 163

med. aspects

crop prod.	633.883 163
gen. pharm.	615.323 163
toxicology	615.952 316 3
vet. pharm.	636.089 532 316 3
toxicology	636.089 595 231 63
paleobotany	561.3

other aspects see Plants

Guyana	*area*–881
Guyandot River W. Va.	*area*–754 4
Guyane	*area*–882
Guyanese people	*r.e.n.*–969 881
Guysborough Co. N.S.	*area*–716 21

Gwent South Glamorgan Wales

	area–429 9
Gwinnett Co. Ga.	*area*–758 223
Gwydir River N.S.W.	*area*–944 4
Gwynedd Wales	*area*–429 2

Gymnasium bldgs.

architecture	725.85
building	690.585

other aspects see Public
structures

Gymnasiums (physical ed.)

education	371.624

s.a. spec. levels of ed.;
also Special education

sports	796.406 8

Gymnasiums (schools) *see*
Academic secondary
schools

Gymnastics *see* Calisthenics

Gymnodiniales *see* Pyrrophyta

Gymnolaemata

culture	639.7
zoology	594.71

other aspects see Bryozoa

Gymnophiona *see* Apoda
    (amphibians)
Gymnospermae
  botany · 585
  floriculture · 635.935
  forestry · 634.975
  med. aspects
    crop prod. · 633.885
    gen. pharm. · 615.325
      toxicology · 615.952 5
    vet. pharm. · 636.089 532 5
      toxicology · 636.089 595 25
  paleobotany · 561.5
  other aspects see Plants
Gymnosperms *see* Gymnospermae
Gympie Qld. · *area*–943 2
Gynecological nursing · 610.736 78
Gynecologists
  biog. & work · 618.092
  prof. duties & characteristics · 618.102 32
  other aspects see Medical
    scientists
  s.a. · *pers.*–618 1
Gynecology · 618.1
  anesthesiology · 617.968 1
  geriatrics · 618.978 1
  pediatrics · 618.920 981
  vet. med. · 636.089 81
    s.a. spec. animals
  other aspects see Medical
    sciences
Györ-Sopron Hungary · *area*–439 7
Gypsum · 553.635
  econ. geol. · 553.635
  mineralogy · 549.755
  mining
    soc. & econ. aspects *see*
      Primary industries
    technology · 622.363 5
      prospecting · 622.186 35
  plasters
    technology · 666.92
    other aspects see Masonry
      adhesives
  soil conditioners · 631.821
    misc. aspects see Soil
      conditioners
  other aspects see Sedimentary
    rocks
  s.a. other spec. uses
Gypsy *see* Romany
Gyrinoidea *see* Adephaga
Gyrocompasses
  aircraft eng. · 629.135 1
  ships *see* Nautical
    instruments
Gyrodynamics
  solid dynamics
    engineering *see* Dynamics
    physics · 531.34

Gyrohorizons
  aircraft eng. · 629.135 2
    s.a. spec. appls. e.g.
      Military engineering
Gyropilots
  aircraft eng. · 629.135 2
    s.a. spec. appls. e.g.
      Military engineering
Gyroscopes
  dynamics
    engineering *see* Dynamics
    physics · 531.34
  manufacturing
    soc. & econ. aspects *see*
      Secondary industries
    technology · 681.753
Gyrostemonaceae *see*
    Chenopodiales

H

Hafnium (continued)
  toxicology   615.925 514
    misc. aspects see
      Toxicology
    other aspects see Minor
      metals
Hagerstown Md.   *area*–752 92
Hagfishes *see* Agnatha
Haggadah
  Judaism   296.19
  Passover   296.437
Haggai
  Bible   224.97
  other aspects see Prophetic
    books (O.T.)
Hagiographa
  Bible   221.042
Hague Netherlands   *area*–492 3
Haifa Israel   *area*–569 46
Hail
  plant injuries from
    agriculture   632.14
    s.a. spec. plants; also
      spec. types of culture
      e.g. Forestry
  other aspects see Solid
    amorphous precipitation
Hail Mary
  private prayers   242.74
Haile Selassie Ethiopia hist.   963.055
  s.a. spec. events & subj.
    e.g. Commerce
Hailsham East Sussex Eng.
               area–422 51
Hailstones *see* Solid amorphous
    precipitation
Hailstorms
  disasters
    soc. action   363.349 2
    misc. aspects see
      Disasters
  meteorology *see* Thermal
    convective storms
Hainan China   *area*–512 7
Hainaut Belgium   *area*–493 4
Haines election district Alaska
              area–798 2
Hair
  analysis
    criminal investigation *see*
      Physical evidence
  anatomy
    human   611.78
    other aspects see
      Integumentary organs
  animal husbandry for   636.088 45
    s.a. spec. animals
  care   646.724
  diseases   616.546
    geriatrics   618.976 546
    pediatrics   618.925 46

Hair
  diseases (continued)
    pub. health   614.595 46
    statistics   312.354 6
    other aspects see Diseases
  drugs affecting
    pharmacodynamics   615.779
    other aspects see Drugs
  pathology
    gen. wks.   591.218 58
      s.a. spec. animals
    med. sci. *see* Hair diseases
  physical anthropometry   573.678
  physiology
    gen. wks.   591.185 8
      s.a. spec. animals
    med. sci.   612.799
    human   612.799
    veterinary   636.089 279 9
      s.a. spec. animals
  styles
    personal care   646.724 5
    soc. customs   391.5
  textiles *see* Animal fibers
    textiles
  tissue biology human   611.018 978
Hairdressers
  biog. & work   646.724 209 2
  s.a.   *pers.*–646 7
Hairdressing
  soc. customs   391.5
  technology   646.724 2
Hair-follicles *see* Hair
Hairiness *see* Hair diseases
Hairstyling *see* Hair styles
Hairy flies *see* Orthorrhapha
Haiti   *area*–729 4
Haitian
  literature   840
  people   *r.e.n.*–969 729 4
  s.a. other spec. subj. e.g.
    Arts
Hajdu-Bihar Hungary   *area*–439 9
Hajj
  Islamic moral theology   297.55
Hakari Turkey   *area*–566 2
Hakka dialect
  linguistics   495.17
  literature   895.1
  s.a.   *lang.*–951 7
Hakkari Turkey   *area*–566 2
Hala family *see* Pandanales
Halakah
  Judaism   296.18
Haldimand Co. Ont.   *area*–713 37
Haldimand-Norfolk Regional
    Municipality Ont. *area*–713 36
Hale
  County
    Alabama   *area*–761 43
    Texas   *area*–764 842

Halogens (continued)
  s.a. spec. uses; also spec.
    minerals
Haloragidaceae *see* Lythrales
Halos (meteorology) *see*
    Condensation products
    atmospheric optical
    phenomena
Halstead Essex Eng.   *area*–426 715
Haltemprice Humberside Eng.
                             area–428 36
Halton
  Regional Municipality Ont.
                             area–713 533
  town Cheshire Eng.   *area*–427 18
Haltwhistle Northumberland Eng.
                             area–428 81
Ham (meat) *see* Pork
Ham stations *see* Amateur radio
    stations
Hama Syria   *area*–569 13
Hamadan Iran   *area*–555 2
Hamamelidaceae *see*
    Hamamelidales
Hamamelidales
  botany   583.394
  floriculture   635.933 394
  forestry   634.973 394
  med. aspects
    crop prod.   633.883 394
    gen. pharm.   615.323 394
      toxicology   615.952 339 4
    vet. pharm.   636.089 532 339 4
      toxicology   636.089 595 233 94
  paleobotany   561.3
  other aspects see Plants
Hamblen Co. Tenn.   *area*–768 923
Hambleton North Yorkshire Eng.
                             area–428 29
Hambridge Nat. Park S. Aust.
                             area–942 38
Hamburg Ger.   *area*–435 15
Hamburger *see* Beef
Häme Finland   *area*–489 73
Hamilton
  city
    New Zealand   *area*–931 22
    Ontario   *area*–713 52
  County
    Florida   *area*–759 84
    Illinois   *area*–773 95
    Indiana   *area*–772 56
    Iowa   *area*–777 52
    Kansas   *area*–781 415
    Nebraska   *area*–782 354
    New York   *area*–747 52
    Ohio   *area*–771 77
    Tennessee   *area*–768 82
    Texas   *area*–764 549
  Lake Ark.   *area*–767 41
  Strathclyde Scot.   *area*–414 57

Hamilton (continued)
  Victoria   *area*–945 7
Hamilton-Wentworth Regional
    Municipality Ont. *area*–713 52
Hamitic
  languages
    linguistics   493.1–.5
    literatures   893.1–.5
    s.a.   *lang.*–93
  people   *r.e.n.*–93
  s.a. other spec. subj. e.g.
    Arts
Hamito-Semitic languages *see*
    Afro-Asiatic languages
Hamlets
  local govt.   352.007 22
  other aspects see Rural areas
Hamlin Co. S.D.   *area*–783 26
Hammering
  metals *see* Beating metals
  s.a. other spec. subj.
Hammers *see* Fastening-equipment
Hammersley Range W. Aust.
                             area–941 3
Hammersmith London Eng. *area*–421 33
Hammock rope suspension bridges
  structural eng.   624.52
  other aspects see Bridges
    (structures)
Hammurabi reign Mesopotamia
    hist.   935.02
  s.a. spec. events & subj.
    e.g. Commerce
Hampden Co. Mass.   *area*–744 26
Hampshire
  County
    England   *area*–422 7
    Massachusetts   *area*–744 23
    West Virginia   *area*–754 95
  swine
    animal husbandry   636.484
    other aspects see Swine
Hampstead London Eng.   *area*–421 42
Hampton
  city Va.   *area*–755 412
  Co. S.C.   *area*–757 97
Hamsters
  experimental animals
    med. sci.   619.93
  other aspects see Myomorpha
Hanafites
  Islamic sects   297.811
    doctrines   297.204 11
    worship   297.301 1
    s.a. other spec. aspects
Hanbalites
  Islamic sects   297.814
    doctrines   297.204 14
    worship   297.301 4
    s.a. other spec. aspects

Hancock Co.
  Georgia   *area*–758 623
  Illinois   *area*–773 43
  Indiana   *area*–772 58
  Iowa   *area*–777 24
  Kentucky   *area*–769 862
  Maine   *area*–741 45
  Mississippi   *area*–762 14
  Ohio   *area*–771 19
  Tennessee   *area*–768 946
  West Virginia   *area*–754 12
Hand
  bookbinding
    soc. & econ. aspects *see*
      Secondary industries
    technology   686.302
    s.a. spec. operations &
      materials e.g.
      Leather, Hand-sewing
  composition
  printing
    soc. & econ. aspects *see*
      Secondary industries
    technology   686.225 3
  construction
    musical instruments 781.91
    s.a. spec. instruments
    s.a. other spec. subj.
  Co. S.D.   *area*–783 282
  exercises
    keyboard string instruments 786.31
  grenades *see* Grenades
  hammers
    soc. & econ. aspects *see*
      Secondary industries
    tech. & mf.   621.973
    s.a. spec. appls. e.g.
      Carpentry
  haulage
    mining eng.   622.65
    s.a. other spec. subj.
  language *see* Sign language
  organs *see* Barrel organs
  production
    paper mf. tech.   676.22
      spec. papers   676.28
    s.a. other spec. subj.
  pumps
    engineering
    soc. & econ. aspects *see*
      Secondary industries
    tech. & mf.   621.64
    s.a. spec. appls. e.g.
      Water supply
      engineering
    other aspects see Dynamics
  sewing home econ.   646.204 2
  tools
    mechanical
      soc. & econ. aspects *see*
      Secondary industries

Hand
  tools
    mechanical (continued)
      tech. & mf.   621.908
      s.a. spec. appls. e.g.
        Restoration of wooden
        furniture; *also spec.*
        kinds e.g.
        Filing-tools
    use in home woodworking 684.082
  soil-working tools
    agriculture   631.315
      use *see spec. uses e.g.*
      Tillage
      s.a. spec. crops; also
      spec. types of culture
      e.g. Floriculture
    mf. tech.   681.763 1
      soc. & econ. aspects
      see Secondary
      industries
    s.a. other spec. subj.
Handbags
  manufacturing
    soc. & econ. aspects *see*
      Secondary industries
    technology   685.51
Handball
  equipment mf.   688.763 1
  sports   796.31
  other aspects see Sports
Handbill papers
  mf. tech.   676.286
  other aspects see Papers pulp
    prod.
Handbooks   *s.s.*–020 2
Handcars *see* Work cars
Handcrafts *see* Handicrafts
Handedness
  psychology   152.335
    animals   156.233 5
    children   155.412
    s.a. psych. of other spec.
      groups
Hand-forged
  tools
    soc. & econ. aspects *see*
      Secondary industries
    technology   682.4
    s.a. other spec. subj.
Handicapped
  employees *see* Disabled
    employees
  people
    mental *see* Mentally
      deficient people
    physical *see* Disabled
      people
  workers
    labor econ.   331.59
    labor law *see* Labor law

Handicapped
workers (continued)
  pub. admin.   350.836
    central govts.   351.836
      spec. jur.   353–354
    local govts.   352.943 6
Handicaps *see* Disability
Handicrafters
  biog. & work   745.509 2
    s.a. spec. handicrafts
  occupational ethics   174.974 5
  s.a.   *pers.*–745
Handicrafts
  arts   745.5
  elementary ed.   372.55
  industries
    prod. econ.   338.642 5
  technology   684.08
Handkerchiefs
  comm. mf.
    soc. & econ. aspects *see*
      Secondary industries
    technology   687.19
  domestic mf.   646.48
  soc. customs   391.4
Handles
  automobiles
    soc. & econ. aspects *see*
      Secondary industries
    tech. & mf.   629.275
  s.a. other spec. kinds
Handling qualities determination
  aircraft eng.   629.134 57
  s.a. spec. appls. e.g.
    Military engineering
Hand-operated
  telegraphic systems *see*
    Acoustical systems wire
      telegraphy
  s.a. other spec. subj.
Hand-powered
  elevators *see* Elevators
    (lifts)
  s.a. other spec. subj.
Hand-propelled
  vessels
    engineering   623.829
    design   623.812 9
    models   623.820 19
    seamanship   623.882 9
    other aspects see Vessels
      (nautical)
  s.a. other spec. vehicles
Hands
  diseases
    regional med. trmt.   617.575
    s.a. spec. systems &
      organs e.g.
      Cardiovascular system
    surgery   617.575
      anesthesiology   617.967 575

Hands
  diseases (continued)
    other aspects see Diseases
    divinatory reading   133.64
    fractures   617.157
    orthopedic surgery   617.397
    personal care   646.727
    other aspects see Upper
      extremities
Hand-sewing
  bookbinding   686.35
Handwear
  comm. mf.
    soc. & econ. aspects *see*
      Secondary industries
    technology   685.4
  domestic mf.   646.48
  soc. customs   391.41
  other aspects see Clothing
Handwork
  textile arts   746.4
  s.a. spec. prod.
Handwriting   652.1
  analysis
    criminal investigation *see*
      Documentary evidence
    employee selection *see*
      Selection procedures
      employees
    graphology   137
  elementary ed.   372.634
Handwritten shorthand   653.4
Handymen *see* Household
  employees
Hangars *see* Air transportation
  buildings; *also*
  Airport facilities
Hanging
  gen. wks. *see* Asphyxiation
  punishment *see* Capital
    punishment
Hangings
  comm. mf.   684.3
  domestic mf.   646.21
  home econ.   645.2
  int. dec.   747.3
    s.a. spec. kinds of bldgs.;
      also spec. dec.
  textile arts   746.3
  other aspects see Furnishings
Hankel function   515.53
  s.a. spec. appls. e.g.
    Engineering
Hanover
  Co. Va.   *area*–755 462
  House
    Eng. hist.   942.07
    Gt. Brit. hist.   941.07
    Scot. hist.   941.107
    s.a. spec. events & subj.
      e.g. Courts

Hardware
gen. wks.
  manufacturing (continued)
    technology 683
  s.a. other spec. subj. e.g.
    Computers
Hardwoods
  mf. tech. 674.142
    properties 674.13
    structure 674.12
  s.a. Deciduous trees
Hardy Co. W. Va. *area*–754 93
Harelips
  medicine 617.522
Hares *see* Lagomorpha
Harford Co. Md. *area*–752 74
Harghita Romania *area*–498 4
Hariana India *area*–545 58
Haringey London Eng. *area*–421 88
Harlan Co.
  Kentucky *area*–769 154
  Nebraska *area*–782 382
Harlington London Eng. *area*–421 83
Harlow Essex Eng. *area*–426 73
Harmful *see* Deleterious
Harmon Co. Okla. *area*–766 445
Harmonic
  analysis
    calculus 515.243 3
      complex variables 515.924 33
      real variables 515.824 33
    s.a. other spec. functions
      & equations; also spec.
      appls. e.g.
      Engineering
    music *see* Harmony music
      theory
    functions 515.53
    s.a. spec. appls. e.g.
      Engineering
  motions *see* Vibrations
Harmonicas (mouth organs) *see*
  Mouth organs
Harmonicas (musical glasses)
  see Musical glasses
Harmonies
  Gospels 226.1
  interpretation
    Bible 220.65
    s.a. spec. parts of Bible
    Hadith 297.124 065
    s.a. spec. Hadith
    Koran 297.122 65
      spec. parts 297.122 9
    Midrash 296.140 65
    s.a. spec. works
    Talmudic lit. 296.120 65
    s.a. spec. works
Harmoniums *see* Reed organs

Harmony
  arts 701.8
  s.a. spec. art forms
  music theory 781.3
    spec. forms 781.5
  s.a. spec. mediums
  s.a. other spec. subj.
Harness
  horses
    animal husbandry 636.14
    other aspects see Horses
  makers
    biog. & work 685.109 2
    s.a. *pers.*–685 1
  racing
    horses
      equip. mf. 688.78
      soc. & econ. aspects
        see Secondary
        industries
      sports 798.46
    other aspects see Sports
Harnesses *see* Saddlery
Harnett Co. N.C. *area*–756 362
Harney Co. Ore. *area*–795 95
Harold
  Eng. hist.
    1 942.018 2
    2 942.019
  s.a. spec. events & subj.
    e.g. Commerce
Harp music 787.55
  recordings 789.912 75
Harpacticoida *see* Copepoda
Harpenden Hertfordshire Eng.
    area–425 85
Harper Co.
  Kansas *area*–781 845
  Oklahoma *area*–766 153
Harper's Ferry Battle
  U.S. Civil War hist. 973.733 6
Harpists
  biog. & work. 787.509 2
  s.a. *pers.*–787
Harps
  mf. tech. 681.817 5
  misc. aspects see Musical
    instruments
  musical art 787.5
Harpsichord music
  recordings 789.912 64
  scores & parts 786.405
    spec. forms 786.41–.49
    treatises 786.404 21
Harpsichordists
  biog. & work 786.109 2
  s.a. *pers.*–786
Harpsichords
  mf. tech. 681.816 221
  misc. aspects see Musical
    instruments

Hastings (continued)
  marquis governorship India
    hist.   954.031 3
    s.a. spec. events & subj.
        e.g. Commerce
  Warren governorship India hist.
                  954.029 8
    s.a. spec. events & subj.
        e.g. Commerce
Hatay Turkey   *area*–564
Hatcheries
  fish   639.311
    s.a. spec. kinds of fish
    s.a. other spec. kinds
Hatha yoga   613.704 6
Hatred *see* Vices
Hats *see* Headgear
Hattah Lakes Nat. Park Vic.
              area–945 9
Hatteras Cape N.C.   *area*–756 175
Hatters
  biog. & work   646.502 092
  s.a.   *pers.*–646 5
Haulage
  mining eng.   622.6
  s.a. other spec. subj.
Haunted places
  lit. & stage trmt. *see* Places
    s.a. Ghosts
  occultism   133.12
Hausa
  language
    linguistics   493.72
    literature   893.72
    s.a.   *lang.*–937 2
  people   *r.e.n.*–937
  states hist.   966.901 6
    s.a. spec. events & subj.
        e.g. Commerce
    s.a. other spec. subj. e.g.
        Arts
Haute-Corse France   *area*–449 456
Haute-Garonne France *area*–448 6
Haute-Loire France   *area*–448 13
Haute-Marne France   *area*–443 32
Haute-Normandie France *area*–442 4
Hautes-Alpes France   *area*–449 7
Haute-Saône France   *area*–444 53
Haute-Savoie France   *area*–444 9
Hautes-Pyrénées France *area*–447 8
Haute-Vienne France   *area*–446 6
Haute-Zaïre Zaïre   *area*–675 15
Haut-Rhin France   *area*–443 833
Hauts-de-Seine France   *area*–443 64
Havana
  city Cuba   *area*–729 123
  province Cuba   *area*–729 124
Havant Hampshire Eng. *area*–422 795
Haverfordwest Dyfed Wales *area*–429 62
Haverhill Suffolk Eng.   *area*–426 44
Havering London Eng.   *area*–421 74

Hawaii
  Co. Hawaii   *area*–969 1
  Island   *area*–969 1
  state   *area*–969
Hawaiian *see* Polynesian
Hawick Borders Scot.   *area*–413 92
Hawke's Bay N.Z.   *area*–931 25
Hawkesbury River N.S.W. *area*–944 2
Hawkins Co. Tenn.   *area*–768 95
Hawks
  animal husbandry   636.686 9
    soc. & econ. aspects *see*
        Primary industries
  other aspects see
        Accipitridae
Hawsers *see* Ropes; *also*
        Cables
Hawthorns *see* Rosaceae
Hay
  feed *see* Feeds
  Nat. Park W. Aust.   *area*–941 2
  production *see* Forage crops
  town
    New South Wales   *area*–944 8
    Powys Wales   *area*–429 56
Hay fever
  gen. med.   616.202
  geriatrics   618.976 202
  pediatrics   618.922 02
  pub. health   614.599 3
  statistics   312.320 2
    deaths   312.262 02
  other aspects see Diseases
Haydock Merseyside Eng. *area*–427 57
Hayes
  & Harlington London
    Eng.   *area*–421 83
  Co. Neb.   *area*–782 832
  Rutherford B. admin.
    U.S. hist.   973.83
    s.a. spec. events & subj.
        e.g. Courts
Hayle Cornwall Eng.   *area*–423 75
Hayling Isl. Hampshire Eng.
              area–422 795
Hays Co. Tex.   *area*–764 888
Hayti   *area*–729 4
Haywood Co.
  North Carolina   *area*–756 94
  Tennessee   *area*–768 223
Hazardous
  machinery
    pub. safety   363.18
    govt. control   350.783
      central govts.   351.783
      spec. jur.   353–354
      local govts.   352.3
  law
    international   341.765
    municipal   344.047 2
      spec. jur.   344.3–.9

Relative Index

Hazardous (continued)
  materials
    pub. safety   363.17
      govt. control   350.783
        central govts.   351.783
          spec. jur.   353–354
        local govts.   352.3
      law
        international   341.765
        municipal   344.047 2
          spec. jur.   344.3–.9
      technology   604.7
    s.a. other spec. subj.
Hazards
  mining eng.   622.8
  s.a. other spec. subj.
Hazel Grove & Bramhall Greater
        Manchester Eng. *area*–427 34
Hazelnuts *see* Filberts
Hazes *see* Mists
Head
  deformities
    statistics   312.304 737 1
    surgery   617.371
      anesthesiology   617.967 371
      s.a. Veterinary sciences
  human
    anatomy   611.91
    physiology   612.91
    s.a. spec. functions,
        systems, organs e.g.
        Cardiovascular system
  muscles
    human anatomy   611.732
    other aspects see Muscles
  physical anthropometry   573.691
  regional med. trmt.   617.51
    s.a. spec. systems & organs
  surgery   617.51
    anesthesiology   617.967 51
    orthopedic   617.371
    s.a. Veterinary sciences
    other aspects see Regional
        anatomy
Head cabbage
  agriculture   635.347
  other aspects see Cabbages
Headaches
  symptoms
    pathology   616.072
  s.a. Migraine
Headgear
  comm. mf.
    soc. & econ. aspects *see*
        Secondary industries
    technology   687.4
  domestic mf.   646.5
  soc. customs   391.43
  other aspects see Clothing

Headings
  bibliographic
    library cataloging   025.322
  Headlines journalism   070.415
Headmasters
  ed. admin.   371.201 2
  other aspects see School
        administrators
Heads
  of church *see* Clergy
  of govt.
    biog. & work *see hist. of*
        spec. countries
    s.a.   *pers.*–351
  of state
    biog. & work *see hist. of*
        spec. countries
    s.a.   *pers.*–351
Healesville Vic.   *area*–945 2
Healing
  spiritual gift
    Christian doctrines   234.13
Health
  buildings
    architecture   725.5
    building   690.55
    other aspects see Public
        structures
  care facilities
    hazards
      soc. path.   363.15
    safety
      law   344.047
        spec. jur.   344.3–.9
      pub. meas.   363.15
      govt. control *see*
          Safety pub. admin.
    sanitation   363.729 7
      law   344.046 4
        spec. jur.   344.3–.9
      pub. admin.   350.772
        central govts.   351.772
          spec. jur.   353–354
        local govts.   352.6
  centers
    safety aspects *see* Health
        care facilities
    sanitation *see* Health care
        facilities sanitation
    soc. services   362.12
      misc. aspects see
          Hospitals
  columns journalism   070.444
  departments
    pub. admin.   350.077
      central govts.   351.077
        spec. jur.   353–354
      local govts.   352.4
  education *see* Hygiene study &
        teaching

Heat (continued)
  losses
    elect. circuits *see*
        Physical phenomena
        elect. circuits
    of earth's crust geophysics   551.14
    of earth's interior geophysics   551.12
    physics   536
      spec. states of matter   530.4
    pipes
      heat eng.
        soc. & econ. aspects *see*
            Secondary industries
        tech. & mf.   621.402 5
        s.a. spec. appls. e.g.
            Heating buildings
        other aspects see Heat
            engineering
  pollution
    water-supply eng.
      technology   628.168 31
      other aspects see Water
          supply engineering
  properties *see* Thermal
      properties
  prostration *see* Heat sickness
  pumps
    heat eng.
      soc. & econ. aspects *see*
          Secondary industries
      tech. & mf.   621.402 5
      s.a. spec. appls. e.g.
          Heating buildings
      other aspects see Heat
          engineering
    refrigeration eng.
      soc. & econ. aspects *see*
          Secondary industries
      tech. & mf.   621.563
      s.a. spec. appls. e.g.
          Air-conditioning
      other aspects see Low
          temperatures
  radiation ammunition
    mil. eng.
      soc. & econ. aspects *see*
          Secondary industries
      tech. & mf.   623.459 5
  rash *see* Sweat glands
      diseases
  sickness
    gen. med.   616.989
    geriatrics   618.976 989
    pediatrics   618.929 89
    statistics   312.398 9
    other aspects see Diseases
  storage
    solar-energy eng.
      soc. & econ. aspects *see*
          Secondary industries

Heat
  storage
    solar-energy eng. (continued)
      technology   621.471
      s.a. spec. appls. e.g.
          Solar energy-powered
          autos
  stroke *see* Heat sickness
  technology *see* Heat
      engineering
  transfer   536.2
    chem. eng.   660.284 27
    s.a. spec. prod.
    gen. eng.   621.402 2
    metallurgical furnaces   669.85
    s.a. spec. metals
    physics   536.2
  treatment
    metal prod.
      mf. tech.   671.36
        ferrous metals   672.36
      s.a. other spec. metals
      other aspects see
          Mechanical working
    s.a. other spec. materials
    other aspects see Radiations;
        also High
        temperatures
  s.a. Temperatures; *also*
      Thermal
Heaters *see* Heating-equipment
Heath family *see* Ericales
Heath Surrey Eng.   *area*–422 13
Heathcote Vic.   *area*–945 3
Heathens *see* Pagans
Heaths
  ecology life sci. *see* Land
      ecology life sci.
Heating
  buildings   697
  homes
    domestic customs   392.36
    library bldgs.   022.8
    museum bldgs.   069.29
    plant management   658.25
      spec. subj.   *s.s.*–068 2
  work environment *see* Physical
      conditions
  s.a. Temperature; *also other*
      spec. subj.
Heating-apparatus
  chemistry   542.4
    s.a. spec. appls. e.g.
        Organic chemistry
Heating-engineers
  biog. & work   697.009 2
  s.a.   *pers.*–697
Heating-equipment
  air-conditioning eng.   697.932 2
  aircraft & autos *see* Comfort
      equipment

Heating-equipment (continued)
household management 644.1
shipbuilding
soc. & econ. aspects *see*
Secondary industries
technology 623.853 7
design 623.814 537
spec. craft 623.812
Heating-fixtures
furniture arts 749.62
Heating-oils
chem. tech. 665.538 4
other aspects see Petroleum
Heating-pipes
buildings 696.2
Heat-resistant
construction *see* Resistant
construction
glass
technology 666.155
other aspects see Glass
Heaven
rel. doctrines
Christianity 236.24
other rel. see Eschatology
Heavenly bodies *see* Celestial
bodies
Heavier-than-air aircraft
aeronautical eng.
gen. tech. & mf. 629.133 3
components & techniques 629.134
models 629.133 13
operation 629.132 52
soc. & econ. aspects *see*
Secondary industries
military 623.746
components 623.746 049
s.a. other spec. appls.
commerce 387.733
misc. aspects see Aircraft
commerce
operation tech. 629.132 523–.132 528
Heavy
chemicals *see* Industrial
chemicals
equipment
capital *see* Fixed capital
household appliances
mf. tech. 683.88
other aspects see
Household appliances
s.a. spec. kinds
spar *see* Pigment materials
water *see* Water chemistry
s.a. other spec. subj.
Hebburn Tyne & Wear Eng.*area*–428 75
Hebden Royd West Yorkshire Eng.
area–428 12
Hebrew
architecture *see*
Architectural schools

Hebrew (continued)
language
linguistics 492.4
literature 892.4
s.a. *lang.*–924
people *r.e.n.*–924
sculpture 732.3
texts
Bible 220.44
s.a. spec. parts of Bible
Midrash 296.140 4
s.a. spec. works
Talmudic lit. 296.120 4
s.a. spec. works
s.a. Jewish; *also* Israel;
also other spec.
subj.
Hebrews epistle
Bible 227.87
other aspects see New
Testament
Hebrides
isls. Scot. *area*–411 4
inner *area*–411 8
outer *area*–411 4
Sea *see* British western
seawaters
Hebron Jordan *area*–569 51
Hecate Strait *see* Canadian
Pacific seawaters
Heckelphone music 788.85
recordings 789.912 88
Heckelphones
mf. tech. 681.818 8
misc. aspects see Musical
instruments
musical art 788.8
Heckmondwike West Yorkshire
Eng. *area*–428 13
Hedge laurel family *see*
Pittosporales
Hedgehogs *see* Insectivora
Hedges
floriculture 635.976
s.a. spec. plants
s.a. Farm hedges
Hedmark Norway *area*–482
Hedon Humberside Eng. *area*–428 38
Hedonism
ethical systems 171.4
applications 172–179
Heels
rubber *see* Molded rubber
prod.
Heilungkiang China *area*–518 4
Heisenberg representation *see*
Matrix mechanics
physics
Hejaz *area*–538
Helena Mont. *area*–786 615

Helmsley North Yorkshire Eng.
          area–428 46
Helotrephoidea *see* Heteroptera
Helps
  spiritual gift
    Christian doctrines   234.13
Helsinki Finland   *area*–489 71
Helston Cornwall Eng.   *area*–423 76
Helvellyn Cumbria Eng.   *area*–427 86
Hematheia Greece   *area*–495 6
Hematite
  mineralogy   549.523
Hematology
  med. sci.   616.15
    geriatrics   618.976 15
    pediatrics   618.921 5
    vet. med.   636.089 615
    s.a. spec. animals
    other aspects see Medical
        sciences
  s.a. Blood
Hemel Hempstead Hertfordshire
      Eng.   *area*–425 84
Hemic
  disorders *see* Blood diseases
  system *see* Circulatory organs
Hemimorphite
  mineralogy   549.63
Hemiptera
  culture   638.575
  paleozoology   565.75
  zoology   595.75
  other aspects see Insecta
Hemispheres
  cerebrum
    human phys.   612.825
    other aspects see Brain
  regional subj. trmt. *area*–181
Hemlock
  trees
    forestry   634.975 3
    soc. & econ. aspects *see*
        Primary industries
    other aspects see
        Coniferales; *also*
        Trees
  woods *see* Softwoods
Hemlock (poison) *see* Sapindales
Hemoconia
  blood
    human phys.   612.117
    other aspects see
        Circulatory fluids
Hemoglobins
  biochemistry
    diseases *see* Red corpuscles
        diseases
    human phys.   612.111 1
    other aspects see
        Circulatory fluids
  org. chem.   547.754

Hemoglobins (continued)
  other aspects see Proteins
Hemophilia
  gen. med.   616.157 2
  geriatrics   618.976 157 2
  pediatrics   618.921 572
  pub. health   614.591 572
  statistics   312.315 72
    deaths   312.261 572
  other aspects see Diseases
Hemorrhages *see* Hemorrhagic
    diseases
Hemorrhagic diseases   616.157
  geriatrics   618.976 157
  pediatrics   618.921 57
  pub. health   614.591 57
  statistics   312.315 7
    deaths   312.261 57
  other aspects see Diseases
Hemorrhoids *see* Anus diseases
Hemp
  agriculture   633.53
    soc. & econ. aspects *see*
        Primary industries
  pulp
    mf. tech.   676.14
    other aspects see Pulp
  textiles
    arts   746.041 2
      s.a. spec. proc. e.g.
        Weaving
    dyeing   667.312
    manufacturing
      soc. & econ. aspects *see*
        Secondary industries
      technology   677.12
      special-process fabrics 677.6
    other aspects see Textiles
    s.a. spec. prod.
  other aspects see Urticales
  s.a. spec. "hemp" e.g. Manila
    hemp
Hemphill Co. Tex.   *area*–764 817
Hempstead Co. Ark.   *area*–767 54
Hemsworth West Yorkshire Eng.
          area–428 15
Henderson
  County
    Illinois   *area*–773 413
    Kentucky   *area*–769 87
    North Carolina *area*–756 92
    Tennessee   *area*–768 263
    Texas   *area*–764 227
  Island   *area*–961 8
Hendon London Eng.   *area*–421 87
Hendricks Co. Ind.   *area*–772 53
Hendry Co. Fla.   *area*–759 46
Henequen *see* Agave
Henley-in-Arden Warwickshire Eng.
          area–424 89

Henley-on-Thames Oxfordshire Eng.
	*area–*425 79
Hennepin Co. Minn.	*area–*776 57
Henrico Co. Va.	*area–*755 453

Henry
County
Alabama	*area–*761 31
Georgia	*area–*758 435
Illinois	*area–*773 38
Indiana	*area–*772 64
Iowa	*area–*777 95
Kentucky	*area–*769 385
Missouri	*area–*778 462
Ohio	*area–*771 15
Tennessee	*area–*768 34
Virginia	*area–*755 692

Fort capture
U.S. Civil War hist.	973.732

reign
Eng. hist.
1	942.023
2	942.031
3	942.034
4	942.041
5	942.042
6	942.043
7	942.051
8	942.052

France hist.
1	944.021
2	944.028
3	944.029
4	944.031

Gt. Brit. hist.
1	941.023
2	941.031
3	941.034
4	941.041
5	941.042
6	941.043
7	941.051
8	941.052

s.a. spec. events & subj.
e.g. Commerce
Hens *see spec. birds e.g.*
Chickens

Hepaticae
botany	588.33
floriculture	635.938 33

med. aspects
crop prod.	633.888 33
gen. pharm.	615.322 33
toxicology	615.952 833
vet. pharm.	636.089 532 233
toxicology	636.089 595 283 3
paleobotany	561.8

other aspects see Plants
Hepatitic jaundice
gen. med.	616.362 5
geriatrics	618.976 362 5
pediatrics	618.923 625

Hepatitic jaundice (continued)
pub. health	614.593 625
statistics	312.336 25
deaths	312.263 625

other aspects see Diseases
Hepatitis
gen. med.	616.362 3
geriatrics	618.976 362 3
pediatrics	618.923 623
pub. health	614.593 623
statistics	312.336 23
deaths	312.263 623

other aspects see Diseases
Heptarchy Eng. hist.	942.015

s.a. spec. events & subj.
e.g. Commerce
Heraclitean philosophy	182.4
Herakleion Greece	*area–*499 8

Heraldic design
dec. arts	745.66
insignia	929.82
Heraldry	929.6
Hérault France	*area–*448 4

Herb teas
comm. proc.	663.96

other aspects see
Nonalcoholic beverages
Herbaceous
fruits
agriculture	634.77

soc. & econ. aspects *see*
Primary industries
foods	641.347 7

preparation
commercial	664.804 77
domestic	641.647 7

other aspects see Fruits
plants
botany	582.12

misc. aspects see
Spermatophyta
s.a. spec. plants
landscape design	716

shrubs
botany	582.14

misc. aspects see
Spermatophyta
s.a. spec. plants
vines
botany	582.14

misc. aspects see
Spermatophyta
s.a. spec. plants
Herbals
pharmacognosy	615.321

misc. aspects see
Pharmacology
Herbariums
botanical sci.	580.742

Herbicides
  production
    soc. & econ. aspects *see*
      Secondary industries
    technology   668.654
  use agric.   632.954
    s.a. spec. crops; also spec.
      types of culture e.g.
      Floriculture
Herbs
  field crops *see*
    Flavoring-producing
    plants
  garden crops
    agriculture   635.7
    soc. & econ. aspects *see*
      Primary industries
    foods   641.357
      preparation
        commercial   664.805 7
        domestic   641.657
    other aspects see
      Vegetables
Hercegovina Yugoslavia   *area*–497 42
Herdbooks
  animal husbandry   636.082 2
  s.a. spec. animals
Herding
  animal husbandry for   636.088 6
  s.a. spec. animals
Heredia Costa Rica   *area*–728 64
Hereditary
  characteristics
    influence on crime   364.24
    life sci. *see* Genetic
      makeup
  determinants
    indiv. psych.   155.234
    societies   369.2
    members   *pers.*–369 2
Heredity
  life sci.   575.1
    animals   591.15
    man   573.21
    microorganisms   576.139
    plants   581.15
    s.a. spec. organisms
  psychology   155.7
Hereford
  & Worcester Eng.   *area*–424 46
  cattle
    animal husbandry   636.222
    other aspects see Cattle
Heresies
  Christian church hist.   273
  s.a. other spec. rel.
Heresy
  church authority
    Christianity   262.8
    other rel. see
      Ecclesiastical theology

Heresy (continued)
  criminology   364.188
  law   345.028 8
    spec. jur.   345.3–.9
  rel. attitudes toward *see*
    Interreligious
    relations
  soc. theology
    Christianity   261.833 188
    comp. rel.   291.178 331 88
    s.a other spec. rel.
Herkimer Co. N.Y.   *area*–747 61
Herm isl.   *area*–423 46
Hermaphroditism
  pathology   574.216 67
    animals   591.216 67
    human
      gen. med.   616.694
      geriatrics   618.976 694
      pediatrics   618.926 94
      pub. health   614.596 94
      statistics   312.396 4
    other aspects see
      Diseases
    plants   581.216 67
    s.a. spec. organisms
  physiology   574.166 7
    animals   591.166 7
    plants   581.166 7
    s.a. spec. organisms
Hermeneutics
  Bible   220.601
    s.a. spec. parts of Bible
  epistemology   121.68
  Hadith   297.124 060 1
    s.a. spec. Hadith
  Koran   297.122 601
    spec. parts   297.122 9
  Midrash   296.140 601
    s.a. spec. works
  Talmudic lit.   296.120 601
    s.a. spec. works
Hermit crabs *see* Anomura
Hermite polynomials   515.55
  s.a. spec. appls. e.g.
    Engineering
Hermitian spaces   515.73
  s.a. spec. appls. e.g.
    Engineering
Hermits of St. Augustine *see*
    Augustinians
Hernandiaceae *see* Laurales
Hernando Co. Fla.   *area*–759 71
Herne Bay Kent Eng.   *area*–422 34
Hernias
  abdominal
    statistics   312.304 755 9
    deaths   312.260 475 59
    surgery
      gen. wks.   617.559
      anesthesiology   617.967 559

Hernias
abdominal
surgery (continued)
s.a. Veterinary sciences
Heroin *see* Narcotics
Heroism *see* Courage
Herons *see* Ciconiiformes
Herpes zoster *see* Shingles
(disease)
Herpetologists
biog. & work ... 597.609 2
other aspects see Scientists
s.a. ... *pers.*–598
Herpetology ... 597.6
Herrera Panama ... *area*–728 724
Herrings *see* Isospondyli
Hertford
city Eng. ... *area*–425 83
Co. North Carolina ... *area*–756 155
Hertfordshire Eng. ... *area*–425 8
Hertsmere Hertfordshire Eng.
... *area*–425 895
Hertzian waves *see* Radio waves
Hertzog admin. South Africa hist.
... 968.052
s.a. spec. events & subj.
e.g. Commerce
Herzegovina Yugoslavia ... *area*–497 42
Hesperioidea
culture ... 638.578 4
paleozoology ... 565.78
zoology ... 595.784
other aspects see Insecta
Hesperornithiformes
paleozoology ... 568.23
other aspects see Aves
Hesse Ger. ... *area*–434 1
Heston & Isleworth London Eng.
... *area*–421 82
Hetero
nitrogen cpds.
org. chem. ... 547.593
s.a. spec. cpds.
oxygen cpds.
org. chem. ... 547.592
s.a. spec. cpds.
sulfur cpds.
org. chem. ... 547.594
s.a. spec. cpds.
Heterobasidiomycetes *see*
Uredinales
Heterocera
culture ... 638.578 1
silkworms ... 638.2
paleozoology ... 565.78
zoology ... 595.781
other aspects see Insecta
Heterocoela *see* Calcispongiae
Heterocyclic cpds.
chem. tech.
hydrocarbons ... 661.815

Heterocyclic cpds.
chem. tech. (continued)
other aspects see Organic
chemicals
s.a. other cpds.
org. chem. ... 547.59
s.a. spec. cpds.
Heterodontoidea *see* Selachii
Heterogeneous
grouping of students ... 371.252
s.a. spec. levels of ed.;
also Special education
nuclear reactors
technology ... 621.483 4
s.a. spec. appls. e.g.
Generation elect. power
other aspects see Nuclear
reactions
reactions
physical chem. ... 541.393
applied ... 660.299 3
organic ... 547.139 3
s.a. spec. aspects e.g.
Low temperatures
s.a. spec. elements, cpds.,
prod.
s.a. other spec. subj.
Heteromi
paleozoology ... 567.5
Heteropolar bonds
atomic structure
theoretical chem. ... 541.244
organic ... 547.124 4
s.a. spec. elements &
cpds.
Heteroptera
culture ... 638.575 4
paleozoology ... 565.75
zoology ... 595.754
other aspects see Insecta
Heteropyxidaceae *see* Rhamnales
Heterosomata *see*
Acanthopterygii
Heterotrophic plants
food synthesis *see*
Chemosynthesis
Hettinger Co. N.D. ... *area*–784 86
Hetton Tyne & Wear Eng. ... *area*–428 71
Heves Hungary ... *area*–439 8
Hevros Greece ... *area*–495 7
Hex (game)
equip. mf. ... 688.742
soc. & econ. aspects *see*
Secondary industries
recreation ... 794.2
Hexacorallia *see* Anthozoa
Hexactinellida *see*
Hyalospongiae
Hexagen *see* High explosives

Hexagonal
chess
equip. mf.   688.741 8
soc. & econ. aspects *see*
Secondary industries
recreation   794.18
systems crystallography   548.14
s.a. spec. substances
Hexamethylenetriperoxidediamine
see High explosives
Hexasterophora *see*
Hyalospongiae
Hexateuch
Bible   222.1
other aspects see Historical
books (O.T.)
Hexham Northumberland Eng.
area–428 81
Hexokinases *see* Enzymes
Hextose
org. chem.   547.781 3
other aspects see Sugar
Heysham Lancashire Eng.   *area*–427 69
Heywood Greater Manchester Eng.
area–427 393
Hibernation *see* Seasonal
changes ecology
Hibiscus
canabinus *see* Ambari hemp
esculentus *see* Okra
flower & trees *see* Malvales
Hickman Co.
Kentucky   *area*–769 98
Tennessee   *area*–768 434
Hickory
Co. Mo.   *area*–778 496
nuts
agriculture   634.52
soc. & econ. aspects *see*
Primary industries
foods   641.345 2
preparation
commercial   664.804 52
domestic   641.645 2
other aspects see
Juglandales; *also*
Nuts
Hicksite Friends   289.63
misc. aspects see Society of
Friends
Hicoria *see* Hickory nuts
Hidalgo
County
New Mexico   *area*–789 693
Texas   *area*–764 492
state Mex.   *area*–724 6
Hide & seek recreation   796.14
Hides
animal husbandry for   636.088 44
s.a. spec. animals

Hides (continued)
processing
mf. tech.   675.2
other aspects see Leathers
Hierarchy
armed forces   355.33
s.a. spec. mil. branches
ecclesiology *see* Governing
leaders ecclesiology
management *see* Organization
of management
s.a. other spec. subj.
Hieroglyphics *see* Notations
languages
Hierotherapy   615.852
s.a. spec. diseases
Hi-fi
tech. & mf.   621.389 332
s.a. spec. appls. e.g.
music 789.91
other aspects see Reproducers
sound
High
blood pressure *see*
Hypertension
command
armed forces   355.331
s.a. spec. mil. branches
Court of Justice
England
law   347.420 25
Court of Justiciary
Scotland
law   345.411 016
explosives
mil. eng.   623.452 7
technology   662.27
other aspects see
Explosives
German *see* German language
Peak Derbyshire Eng.   *area*–425 11
polymers
org. chem.   547.84
schools *see* Secondary schools
seas
internat. law   341.45
temperatures   536.57
astrophysics   523.013 57
s.a. spec. celestial
bodies
biophysics *see* Heat
biophysics
chemistry *see* High
temperatures reactions
effects
on crops *see* High
temperatures plant
injuries
on life *see* Heat
biophysics

High
  temperatures
    effects (continued)
      on materials   620.112 96
        strength   620.112 17
        s.a. spec. materials &
          uses
      measurement *see* Pyrometry
      physics   536.57
        spec. states of matter   530.4
      plant injuries
        agriculture   632.12
        s.a. spec. plants; also
          spec. types of culture
          e.g. Forestry
      reactions
        physical chem.   541.368 7
          applied   660.296 87
          organic   547.136 87
        s.a. spec. elements,
          cpds., prod.
      resistance to *see* High
        temperatures effects
      other aspects see
        Temperatures
    vacuums
      gas mech.   533.54
      other aspects see Vacuums
  Wycombe Buckinghamshire Eng.
                                        area–425 95
  s.a. other spec. subj.
High-alumina cement
  technology   666.95
  other aspects see Masonry
    adhesives
Higham Ferrars Northamptonshire
    Eng.   *area*–425 54
Highballs *see* Alcoholic
    beverages
Highboys *see* Cabinets
    (furniture)
High-calorie cookery   641.563 4
High-carbohydrate
  cookery   641.563 8
  diets
    hygiene   613.28
    misc. aspects see Hygiene
High-compression-ignition
  engines
    soc. & econ. aspects *see*
      Secondary industries
    tech. & mf.
      gen. wks.   621.436
        parts & accessories   621.437
      land vehicles   629.250 6
        parts & systems   629.252–.258
      marine vehicles   623.872 36
      s.a. other spec. appls.
    other aspects see
      Internal-combustion
      engines

High-energy
  boron fuels
    manufacturing
      chem. tech.   662.86
      soc. & econ. aspects *see*
        Secondary industries
  nuclear reactions
    astrophysics   523.019 76
      s.a. spec. celestial
        bodies
    physics   539.76
      spec. states of matter   530.4
      s.a. spec. physical
        phenomena e.g. Heat
  rate forming *see* Mechanical
      working
Higher
  criticism *see* Literary
      criticism
  education   378
  finance
    law   344.076 84
      spec. jur.   344.3–.9
    law   344.074
      spec. jur.   344.3–.9
High-explosive ammunition
  mil. eng.
    soc. & econ. aspects *see*
      Secondary industries
    tech. & mf.   623.451 7
High-fat
  cookery   641.563 8
  diets
    hygiene   613.28
    misc. aspects see Hygiene
High-fidelity systems *see* Hi-fi
High-frequency
  photopsychography
    technique   778.3
Highland
  County
    Ohio   *area*–771 845
    Virginia   *area*–755 89
  region Scot.   *area*–411 5
  Rim
    Kentucky   *area*–769 6
    Tennessee   *area*–768 4
Highlands Co. Fla.   *area*–759 55
Highly volatile petroleum prod.
  chem. tech.   665.538 2
  other aspects see Petroleum
High-octane-rating gasolines
  chem. tech.   665.538 25
  other aspects see Petroleum
High-protein
  cookery   641.563 8
  diets
    hygiene   613.28
    misc. aspects see Hygiene

High-rise buildings
  fire hazards | 363.379
  misc. aspects see Fire
    safety
High-school
  songs | 784.623
  recordings | 789.912 462 3
High-speed photography | 778.37
  motion pictures | 778.56
High-styrene resins *see*
  Elastoplastics
High-talent employees
  personnel admin.
    gen. management | 658.304 5
    spec. subj. | *s.s.*–068 3
    pub. admin. | 350.1
      central govts. | 351.1
      spec. jur. | 353–354
      local govts. | 352.005 1
High-tension current systems
  see
    Alternating-current
    transmission
High-vacuum tubes *see* Vacuum
  tubes
High-velocity armor-piercing
    ammunition
  mil. eng.
    soc. & econ. aspects *see*
      Secondary industries
    tech. & mf. | 623.451 8
High-voltage
  accelerators
    physics | 539.732
    *s.a. spec. physics
      phenomena e.g.* Heat
  photography
    technique | 778.3
Highway
  costs
    commerce | 388.112
    govt. control | 351.864 2
    spec. jur. | 353–354
  patrol *see* Traffic control
    police services
  post offices
    postal commun. | 383.143
    other aspects see Postal
      communication
  services
    highway transp.
      commerce | 388.312
      govt. control | 351.878 31
      spec. jur. | 353–354
    law | 343.094 2
      spec. jur. | 343.3–.9
    technology | 625.76–.79
  transportation *see* Vehicular
    transp.
  use *see* Roads use
Highways *see* Roads

Hijacking *see* Larceny
Hikers
  biog. & work | 796.510 92
  s.a. | *pers.*–796 5
Hiking *see* Walking (sports)
Hilbert
  spaces | 515.733
  s.a. spec. appls. e.g.
    Engineering
  transform
    operational calculus | 515.723
    s.a. spec. appls. e.g.
      Engineering
Hill
  climbing
    equipment mf. | 688.765 22
    soc. & econ. aspects *see*
      Secondary industries
    sports | 796.522
    other aspects see Sports
  County
    Montana | *area*–786 14
    Texas | *area*–764 283
Hilla Iraq | *area*–567 5
Hillingdon London Eng. | *area*–421 83
Hills
  geomorphology | 551.36
  other aspects see Elevations
    (physiography)
Hillsboro Co. N.H. | *area*–742 8
Hillsborough Co. Fla. | *area*–759 65
Hillsdale Co. Mich. | *area*–774 29
Hilton Head Isl. S.C. | *area*–757 99
Himachal Pradesh India | *area*–545 2
Himalayan
  cats
    animal husbandry | 636.83
    other aspects see Cats
  dialects
    linguistics | 495.4
    literature | 895.49
    s.a. | *lang.*–954 9
Himalayas | *area*–54
Himantandraceae *see* Magnoliales
Hinayana Buddhism | 294.391
  misc. aspects see Buddhism
Hinchinbrook Isl. Nat. Park Qld.
| *area*–943 6
Hinchinbrook Isl. Qld. | *area*–943 6
Hinckley & Bosworth
  Leicestershire Eng.
| *area*–425 49
Hincks Nat. Park S. Aust. | *area*–942 38
Hindi
  language
    linguistics | 491.43
    literature | 891.43
    s.a. | *lang.*–914 31
  people | *r.e.n.*–914 3
  s.a. India; *also other spec.
    subj. e.g.* Arts

Hindley Greater Manchester Eng.
area–427 36
Hindmarsh Lake Vic. area–945 8
Hinds Co. Miss. area–762 51
Hindu
  arts *see* South Asian arts
  Kush area–581
  music *see* Hindu sacred music
  regions subj. trmt. area–176 45
  religion *see* Hinduism
  sacred music
   arts 783.029 45
   recordings 789.912 302 945
   s.a. spec. instruments;
    also spec. kinds e.g.
     Liturgical music
  religion
   pub. worship 294.538
   significance 294.537
  temples & shrines
   architecture 726.145
   building 690.614 5
   rel. significance 294.535
   other aspects see
    Religious-purpose
    bldgs.
  s.a. India; also other spec.
   subj.
Hinduism
  art representation 704.948 945
  s.a. spec. art forms
  calendars 529.324 5
  cookery 641.567 45
  Islamic polemics vs. 297.294
  philosophy 181.41–.48
  regions area–176 45
  religion 294.5
  rel. holidays 394.268 294 5
  schools 377.945
Hindus
  biog. & work 294.509 2
  s.a. spec. kinds e.g.
   Clergy; *also spec.*
   sects
  s.a. pers.–294 5
Hinged arch bridges
  structural eng. 624.6
  other aspects see Bridges
   (structures)
Hingeless arch bridges
  structural eng. 626.6
  other aspects see Bridges
   (structures)
Hinges *see* Hardware
Hinnies *see* Mules (animals)
Hinsdale Co. Colo. area–788 39
Hipbone *see* Lower extremities
  bones
Hippies *see* Lower classes
Hippocastanaceae *see* Sapindales
Hippocrateaceae *see* Celastrales

Hippocrates' theory
  indiv. psych. 155.262
Hippocratic oath
  medical ethics
   philosophy 174.22
   religion
    Buddhism 294.356 422
    Christianity 241.642 2
    comp. rel. 291.564 22
    Hinduism 294.548 642 2
    s.a. other spec. rel.
Hippomorpha
  paleozoology 569.72
  other aspects see Equidae
Hippopotamuses *see* Suiformes
Hips
  deformities
   statistics 312.304 737 6
   surgery 617.376
    anesthesiology 617.967 376
    s.a. Veterinary sciences
  diseases
   regional med. trmt. 617.581
    s.a. spec. systems &
    organs
   surgery 617.581
    anesthesiology 617.967 581
    other aspects see
    Diseases
  muscles
   human anatomy 611.738
   other aspects see Muscles
  other aspects see Pelvic
   region
Hire-purchase *see* Secured
  transactions
Hiring-halls
  labor econ. 331.889 4
Hirohito reign Japan hist. 952.033
  s.a. spec. events & subj.
   e.g. Commerce
Hiroshima Japan area–521 9
Hirudinea
  culture & hunting 639.754 5
  zoology 595.145
  other aspects see Worms
Hirundinidae
  hunting
   commercial 639.128 813
   sports 799.248 813
  paleozoology 568.8
  zoology 598.813
  other aspects see Aves
Hispaniola area–729 3
Histeroidea
  zoology 595.764 6
  other aspects see Polyphaga
Histochemical examination
  med. sci.
   gen. med. 616.075 83
   surgery 617.075 83

Historical (continued)
remedies
  therapeutics   615.88
    s.a. spec. diseases
research   001.432
  spec. subj.   *s.s.*–072 2
school econ.   330.154 2
themes
  lit. trmt.
    folk lit.
      sociology   398.358
      texts & lit. crit.   398.22
    gen. wks.
      collections   808.803 58
      hist. & crit.   809.933 58
    spec. lits.
      collections   *lit. sub.*–080 358
      hist. & crit.   *lit. sub.*–093 58
    s.a. spec. lit. forms
  stage trmt.   792.090 935 8
    s.a. other spec. dramatic
        mediums e.g.
        Television; *also spec.*
        kinds of drama e.g.
        Tradegies (drama)
theory
  folklore   398.17
treatment
  spec. subj.   *s.s.*–09
  s.a. other spec. subj.
Historicity
of Jesus Christ doctrines   232.908
Historiographers *see* Historians
Historiography   907.2
  Christian church hist.   270.09
  s.a. hist. of spec. places;
        also of other spec.
        subj.
History   900
  appls. to spec. subj.   *s.s.*–09
  Biblical events   220.95
    s.a. spec. parts of Bible
  documentation   025.069
  gen. wks.
    ancient   930
    general
      spec. places   940–990
      world   909
    medieval   909.07
      spec. centuries   909.1–.4
      s.a. spec. places
    modern   909.08
      spec. centuries   909.4–.8
      s.a. spec. places
  God in
    rel. doctrines
      Christianity   231.76
      other rel. see Doctrinal
          theology
  journalism   070.449 9

History (continued)
  libraries   026.9
    misc. aspects see Special
        libraries
  library acquisitions   025.279
  library classification   025.469
  museums
    desc. & colls.   907.4
    museology   069.99
    s.a. spec. activities
        e.g. Display
  pub. admin.
    activities   350.859
    central govts.   351.859
      spec. jur.   353–354
    local govts.   352.945 9
    govt. depts. *see* Executive
        departments
  study & teaching   907
    curriculums   375.9
    elementary ed.   372.89
  subject headings   025.499
  other aspects see Disciplines
      (systems)
Hit-&-run tactics
  mil. sci.   355.422
    s.a. spec. mil. branches
Hitchcock Co. Neb.   *area*–782 845
Hitchin Hertfordshire Eng.   *area*–425 81
Hitler
  Adolf Ger. hist.   943.086
    s.a. spec. events & subj.
        e.g. Arts
Hittite
  language *see* Anatolian
      languages
  people   *r.e.n.*–919 9
Hives (apiculture)
  management   638.14
Hives (diseases) *see* Papular
      eruptions
Hjorring Denmark   *area*–489 5
Ho *see* Munda
Hoarding
  macroeconomics   339.43
Hoarfrost
  meteorology   551.574 4
    artificial modification   551.687 44
    weather forecasting   551.647 44
    spec. areas   551.65
Hoatzins *see* Opisthocomi
Hoaxes   001.95
  books hist. & crit.   098.3
    s.a. spec. subj.
Hobart Tas.   *area*–946 1
Hobbies
  recreation   790.13
  spec. subj.   *s.s.*–023
  other aspects see Recreation

Hollow
  concrete blocks (continued)
    other aspects see
      Artificial stones
  tiles
    bldg. construction   693.4
    other aspects see Tiles
  ware
    metal *see* Containers
    rubber *see* Molded rubber
      prod.
Holly family *see* Celastrales
Hollyhocks *see* Malvales
Holmes Co.
  Florida   *area*–759 965
  Mississippi   *area*–762 625
  Ohio   *area*–771 64
Holmfirth West Yorkshire Eng.
                  area–428 13
Holmhead Strathclyde Scot.
                  area–414 67
Holmium
  chemistry
    inorganic   546.417
    organic   547.054 17
    s.a. spec. groupings e.g.
      Aliphatic compounds
  technology   661.041 7
    organic   661.895
    soc. & econ. aspects *see*
      Secondary industries
    s.a. spec. prod.
  eng. materials   620.189 291 7
    s.a. spec. uses
  metallography   669.952 917
  metallurgy   669.291 7
    physical & chem. 669.962 917
  pharmacology   615.241 7
    misc. aspects see
      Pharmacology
  products
    mf. tech.   673.291 7
    other aspects see
      Nonferrous metals
      products
  toxicology   615.925 417
    misc. aspects see
      Toxicology
  other aspects see
    Yttrium-group metals
Holocephali *see* Chimaerae
Holography
  eng. appls.
    soc. & econ. aspects *see*
      Secondary industries
    technology   621.367 5
    s.a. spec. appls. e.g.
      Cartography
  photography   774
  science *see* Interference
    light physics

Holostei *see* Amiiformes
Holothurioidea
  culture   639.739 6
  paleozoology   563.96
  zoology   593.96
  other aspects see Animals
Holotricha *see* Ciliata
Holstein Ger.   *area*–435 12
Holstein-Friesian cattle
  animal husbandry   636.234
  other aspects see Cattle
Holston River Tenn. *area*–768 9
Holsworthy Devon Eng. *area*–423 51
Holt Co.
  Missouri   *area*–778 115
  Nebraska   *area*–782 745
Holy
  Bible *see* Bible
  bldgs. rel. worship *see*
      Sacred places rel.
      worship
  Communion
    Christian doctrines 234.163
    Christian rites   264.36
      spec. denominations 264.01–.09
  days
    observance
      Christianity   263.9
      Judaism   296.43
      other rel. see Times rel.
        observance
    soc. customs   394.268 2
    other aspects see Church
      year
    s.a. Holidays
  Family
    art representation
      arts   704.948 56
      s.a. spec. art forms
    Christian rel.
      paintings   247.556
      sculpture   247.3
    Christian doctrines 232.92
  Ghost *see* Holy Spirit
  Grail
    lit. & stage trmt. *see*
      Things
  Hours
    pub. worship   264.7
      spec. denominations 264.01–.09
  Isl. Northumberland Eng.
                  area–428 89
  Orders
    Christian doctrines 234.164
    Christian rites   265.4
  places
    rel. worship *see* Sacred
      places rel. worship
  Roman Empire
    Church hist.   270
    gen. hist.   943

Home (continued)

remedies

  therapeutics — 615.88

   s.a. spec. diseases

repairs

  home econ. — 643.7

rule

  local govts. — 352.003

selection — 643.12

singing music — 784.96

songs — 784.61

  recordings — 789.912 461

studies *see* Study areas

workshops — 684.08

  s.a. spec. activities &
   prod.

s.a. Domestic; *also* Household

Home-based enterprises *see* Proprietorships

Homelands South Africa *see* Bantustans

Homeless children *see* Abandoned children

Homeless people *see* Poor people

Homemakers

  biog. & work — 640.92

  s.a. — *pers.*–649

Homemaking *see* Home economics

Homeomorphisms

  topology — 514

  s.a. spec. appls. e.g. Engineering

Homeopathy

  therapeutics — 615.532

  misc. aspects see Therapeutics

  s.a. spec. diseases

Homeostasis *see* Control mechanisms biology

Homeroom periods — 371.242 2

  s.a. spec. levels. of ed.;
  also Special education

Homes *see* Dwellings

Homicidal compulsions

  gen. med. — 616.858 44

  geriatrics — 618.976 858 44

  pediatrics — 618.928 584 4

  psychology — 157.7

  pub. health — 614.58

  statistics — 312.385 844

  other aspects see Mental illness

Homicide

  criminology — 364.152

  ethics

   philosophy — 179.7

   religion

    Buddhism — 294.356 97

    Christianity — 241.697

    comp. rel. — 291.569 7

Homicide

  ethics

   religion (continued)

    Hinduism — 294.548 697

    s.a. other spec. rel.

  law — 345.025 2

   spec. jur. — 345.3–.9

  soc. theology

   Christianity — 261.833 152

   comp. rel. — 291.178 331 52

   s.a. other spec. rel.

  statistics *see* Violent crimes

Homiletics *see* Preaching

Homilies *see* Sermons

Homing

  manned space flight

   gen. wks. — 629.453

   s.a. spec. appls. e.g. Space warfare

   s.a. spec. flights e.g. Lunar flights manned

  migration *see* Migration

  systems spacecraft *see* Flight operations systems spacecraft

  unmanned space flight — 629.433

   s.a. spec. appls. e.g. Space warfare

Hominidae *see* Humankind

Hominoidea *see* Pongidae

Homobasidiomycetes *see* Lycoperdales

Homocoela *see* Calcispongiae

Homogeneous

  equations calculus — 515.253

   complex variables — 515.925 3

   real variables — 515.825 3

   s.a. other spec. functions &
   equations; also spec.
   appls. e.g. Engineering

  grouping

   education — 371.254

   s.a. spec. levels of ed.;
   also Special education

  nuclear reactors

   technology — 621.483 4

   s.a. spec. appls. e.g. Generation elect. power

   other aspects see Nuclear reactions

  reactions

   physical chem. — 541.393

    applied — 660.299 3

    organic — 547.139 3

   s.a. spec. aspects e.g. Low temperatures

   s.a. spec. elements, cpds., prod.

  spaces

   gen. wks. *see* Spaces

Homogeneous
spaces (continued)
  topology   514
    s.a. spec. appls. e.g.
      Engineering
systems *see* Coordinate
  systems
Homogenization
  dairy tech.   637.133 4
Homogenized milk
  dairy tech.   637.141
  other aspects see Milk
Homological algebra
  topological algebras   512.55
  s.a. spec. appls. e.g.
    Engineering
Homology groups   514.23
  s.a. spec. appls. e.g.
    Engineering
Homonyms (linguistics)   410
  spec. langs.
    nonstandard forms *lang. sub.*–7
    standard forms
      dictionaries   *lang. sub.*–31
      usage   *lang. sub.*–8
  other aspects see Words
Homopolar bonds
  atomic structure
    theoretical chem.   541.244
    organic   547.124 4
    s.a. spec. elements &
      cpds.
Homoptera
  agric. pests   632.752
  s.a. spec. types of culture
    e.g. Forestry; *also*
      spec. crops
  culture   638.575 2
  paleozoology   565.75
  zoology   595.752
  other aspects see Insecta
Homosexuality
  ethics *see* Sexual ethics
  gen. med.   616.858 34
  geriatrics   618.976 858 34
  pediatrics   618.928 583 4
  psychology   157.7
  soc. issues   363.49
  soc. theology
    Christian rel.   261.835 76
    comp. rel.   291.178 357 6
    s.a. other spec. rel.
  sociology   306.76
  statistics   312.385 834
  other aspects see Moral
    issues; *also* Sexual
    deviations
Homotopy theory   514.24
  s.a. spec. appls. e.g.
    Engineering
Homs Syria   *area*–569 12

Honan China   *area*–511 8
Hondo Japan   *area*–521
Honduran
  literature   860
  people   *r.e.n.*–687 283
  s.a. other spec. subj. e.g.
    Arts
Honduras
  country   *area*–728 3
  Gulf *see* Caribbean Sea
Honesty *see* Virtues
Honey
  guides *see* Piciformes
  plant family *see* Sapindales
Honeybees *see* Apidae
Honeycomb constructions
  structural eng.
    gen. wks.   624.177 9
    spec. materials   624.18
    naval arch.   623.817 79
    s.a. other spec. appls.
Honeydew melons
  agriculture   635.611 7
  other aspects see Muskmelons
Honeyflower family *see*
  Proteales
Honeymoon customs *see* Weddings
  customs
Honeys   641.38
  food   641.38
    cookery   641.68
  prod. tech.   638.16
  soc. & econ. aspects *see*
    Primary industries
Honeysuckle family *see* Rubiales
Hong Kong
  colony   *area*–512 5
  influenza *see* Influenzas
Honiton Devon Eng.   *area*–423 57
Honolulu
  city Hawaii   *area*–969 31
  Co. Hawaii   *area*–969 3
Honor
  rolls
    military
      Spanish-American War   973.896
      U.S. Civil War   973.76
      U.S. Mexican War   973.626
      U.S. Revolution   973.36
      U.S. War of 1812   973.526
      World War 1   940.467
      World War 2   940.546 7
      s.a. other spec. wars;
        also hist. of spec.
        places
    Sunday schools
      Christianity   268.5
      other rel. see Religious
        instruction

Honor (continued)
   systems ed. — 371.59
   s.a. spec. levels of ed.;
       also Special education
Honorary
   degrees — 378.25
   insignia
      mil. discipline — 355.134 2
      s.a. spec. mil. branches
   titles
      spec. fields — *s.s.*–079
Honors
   ed. work method — 371.394 2
   s.a. spec. levels of ed.;
       also Special education
   research — 001.44
Honshu Japan — *area*–521
Hood
   Co. Tex. — *area*–764 522
   Mount Ore. — *area*–795 61
   River Ore. — *area*–795 61
Hoods *see* Headgear
Hoofs *see* Integumentary organs
Hookahs *see* Smokers' supplies
Hooked rugs
   textile arts — 746.74
Hooker Co. Neb. — *area*–782 777
Hooke's law
   solid dynamics
      engineering *see* Dynamics
      physics — 531.382
Hooks
   & eyes clothing *see* Notions
      clothing
   fishing (sports)
      manufacturing
         soc. & econ. aspects *see*
            Secondary industries
         technology — 688.791 2
Hookworm infestations
   gen. med. — 616.965 4
   geriatrics — 618.976 965 4
   pediatrics — 618.929 654
   pub. health — 614.555 4
   statistics — 312.396 54
      deaths — 312.269 654
   other aspects see Diseases
Hooper Isl. Md. — *area*–752 27
Hoopoes *see* Coraciiformes
Hoosic River Mass. — *area*–744 1
Hoover Herbert C. admin.
   U.S. hist. — 973.916
   s.a. spec. events & subj.
      e.g. Panics economics
Hooves *see* Integumentary organs
Hopatcong Lake N.J. — *area*–749 74
Hope *see* Virtues
Hopeh China — *area*–511 5
Hopetoun Vic. — *area*–945 9
Hopewell Va. — *area*–755 586

Hopf algebras & groups — 512.55
   s.a. spec. appls. e.g.
      Engineering
Hopi *see* Macro-Penutian
Hopkins Co.
   Kentucky — *area*–769 823
   Texas — *area*–764 274
Hoplestigmataceae *see* Bixales
Hoplocarida *see* Stomatopoda
Hoppers (cars) *see* Freight cars
Hops
   agriculture — 633.82
      soc. & econ. aspects *see*
         Primary industries
   foods — 641.338 2
      preparation
         commercial — 664.52
         domestic — 641.638 2
   other aspects see Urticales
Horary astrology — 133.56
Horbury West Yorkshire Eng.
            — *area*–428 15
Hordaland Norway — *area*–483
Hordeeae *see* Pooideae
Hordeum *see* Barley
Horehound *see* Lamiales
Horizontal
   bars
      equipment mf. — 688.764 4
         soc. & econ. aspects *see*
            Secondary industries
      sports — 796.44
      other aspects see Sports
   combinations
      prod. econ. — 338.804 2
      other aspects see
         Combinations
         (organizations)
   plane
      arch. design — 729.2
      structural elements — 729.3
      s.a. spec. kinds of
        bldgs.
   property
      law — 346.043 3
         spec. jur. — 346.3–.9
      s.a. other spec. subj.
Hormic psychologies — 150.193 33
   s.a. spec. subj. & branches of
      psych.
Hormones
   biochemistry
      gen. wks. — 574.192 7
      animals — 591.192 7
      microorganisms — 576.119 27
      plants — 581.192 7
      s.a. spec. organisms
   med. sci. — 612.405
      animals — 636.089 240 5
      s.a. spec. animals
      man — 612.405

Hormones (continued)
  human phys.   612.405
    sex   612.61–.62
  org. chem.   547.734
  pharmacology   615.36
    misc. aspects see
        Pharmacology
  other aspects see Secretion
Hormuz Strait *see* Persian Gulf
Horn
  carving
    dec. arts   736.6
  music   788.4
    recordings   789.912 84
  players
    biog. & work   788.409 2
    s.a. spec. kinds of horns
      e.g. Saxhorns
  s.a.   *pers.*–788
Hornbills *see* Coraciiformes
Horncastle Lincolnshire Eng.
              area–425 32
Hornchurch London Eng.   *area*–421 74
Hornets *see* Vespidae
Horney system
  psychology   150.195 7
  s.a. spec. subj. & branches
    of psych.
Horns (anatomy) *see*
    Integumentary organs
Horns (music)
  mf. tech.   681.818 4
  misc. aspects see Musical
    instruments
  musical art   788.4
Hornsby N.S.W.   *area*–944 1
Hornsea Humberside Eng. *area*–428 38
Hornsey London Eng.   *area*–421 88
Hornworts (bryophytes) *see*
    Anthocerotales
Hornworts (spermatophytes) *see*
    Ranales
Horology   529.7
Horoscopes astrology   133.54
Horror
  lit. qual.
    gen. wks.
      collections   808.801 6
      hist. & crit.   809.916
    spec. lits.
      collections   *lit. sub.*–080 16
      hist. & crit.   *lit. sub.*–091 6
    s.a. spec. lit. forms
  stage qual.   792.090 916
  s.a. other spec. dramatic
    mediums e.g.
    Television; *also spec.*
    kinds of drama e.g.
    Tragedies (drama)
Horry Co. S.C.   *area*–757 87

Hors d'oeuvres
  cookery   641.812
Horse
  cavalry armed forces   357.1
  racers
    biog. & work   798.400 92
    other aspects see
      Equestrian sportsmen
  racing
    equip. mf.   688.78
    soc. & econ. aspects *see*
      Secondary industries
    law *see* Recreation law
    sports   798.4
    other aspects see Sports
Horseback riding *see* Riding
    horses
Horse-drawn
  streetcars *see* Surface rail
    systems
  s.a. other spec. vehicles
Horseflies *see* Orthorrhapha
Horsehair worms *see*
    Nematomorpha
Horsemanship
  mil. sci.   357.2
  sports   798.2
  misc. aspects see Sports
Horseradish *see* Condiments;
    also Cruciales
Horses
  animal husbandry   636.1
  soc. & econ. aspects *see*
    Primary industries
  products
    meats
      food   641.361
      cookery   641.661
      other aspects see Red
      meats
    other prod. see spec. prod.
      e.g. Hides
  other aspects see Equidae
Horseshoe crabs *see* Xiphosura
Horseshoeing
  soc. & econ. aspects *see*
    Secondary industries
  technology   682.1
Horseshoes (game) *see* Pitching
    games
Horsetail family *see*
    Sphenopsida
Horsforth West Yorkshire Eng.
              area–428 19
Horsham Vic.   *area*–945 8
Horsham West Sussex Eng. *area*–422 64
Horta Portugal   *area*–469 9
Horticulturalists
  biog. & work   635.092
  s.a. spec. kinds e.g. flower
    gardeners 635.909 2

Horticulturalists (continued)
  other aspects see
    Agricultural classes
  s.a.   *pers.*–635
Horticulture   635
  misc. aspects see Agriculture
Horwich Greater Manchester Eng.
          area–427 37
Hose (clothing) *see* Hosiery
Hose (tubing) *see* Hoses
Hosea
  Bible   224.6
  other aspects see Prophetic
    books (O.T.)
Hoses
  fire
    fire extinction tech.   628.925 2
    s.a. spec. appls. e.g.
      Forest fires
  rubber
    manufacturing
      soc. & econ. aspects *see*
        Secondary industries
      technology   678.36
    s.a. spec. kinds of rubber
      e.g. Natural rubber
Hosiery
  comm. mf.
    soc. & econ. aspects *see*
      Secondary industries
    technology   687.3
  domestic mf.   646.42
  handicrafts *see* Found objects
  soc. customs   391.41
  other aspects see Clothing
Hospital
  buildings
    architecture   725.51
    building   690.551
    other aspects see Public
      structures
  cookery   641.579
  grounds
    landscape design   712.7
  insurance   368.382 7
  misc. aspects see Insurance
  libraries   027.662
    administration   025.197 662
    catalogs *see* Library
      catalogs
    functional planning   022.316 62
    reference services   025.527 766 2
    selection for   025.218 766 2
    use studies   025.587 662
    user orientation   025.567 662
    s.a. other spec. activities
      e.g. Cataloging
  ships
    engineering   623.826 4
     design   623.812 64
     models   623.820 164

Hospital
  ships (continued)
    naval forces
     materiel   359.83
     organization   359.326 4
     seamanship   623.882 64
    other aspects see Vessels
      (nautical)
  other aspects see Health
Hospitality
  ethics
    philosophy   177.1
    religion
     Buddhism   294.356 71
     Christianity   241.671
     comp. rel.   291.567 1
     Hinduism   294.548 671
     s.a. other spec. rel.
  etiquette   395.3
Hospitaller Knights *see* Knights
  of Malta
Hospitallers of St. John of God
  rel. orders   255.49
  church hist.   271.49
  ecclesiology   262.24
Hospitals
  accounting   657.832 2
  animal husbandry   636.083 2
  s.a. spec. animals
  food services   642.5
  law *see* Welfare services law
  liability
    law   346.031
    spec. jur.   346.3–.9
  military
    gen. wks.   355.72
    s.a. spec. mil. branches
    Spanish-American War 973.897 5
    U.S. Civil War   973.776
    U.S. Mexican War   973.627 5
    U.S. Revolution   973.376
    U.S. War of 1812   973.527 5
    World War 1   940.476
    World War 2   940.547 6
  safety aspects *see* Health
    care facilities
  sanitation *see* Health care
    facilities sanitation
  soc. services   362.11
    govt. control   350.841
     central govts.   351.841
      spec. jur.   353–354
     local govts.   352.944 1
    law *see* Welfare services
      law
  s.a. Clinics
Hostels *see* Hotels
Hot
  beverages *see* Beverages
  climates *see* Hot-weather

House
  connections
    sewers   628.25
    s.a. spec. appls. e.g.
      Water drainage
  garments
    comm. mf.   687.11
    dcmestic mf.   646.43
    other aspects see Clothing
  of Lords
    court of last resort
      England
        law   347.420 39
      Scotland
        law   347.411 039
  organs
    journalism   070.486
    management use   658.455
    spec. subj.   *s.s.*–029
  trailers *see* Trailers
    automobile dwellings
Houseboats
  architecture   728.78
  building   690.878
  other aspects see Residential
    buildings
Housecleaning home econ.   648.5
Housecoats *see* Lounging
    garments
Houseflies *see* Cyclorrhapha
Household
  appliances   643.6
    manufacturers
      biog. & work   683.809 2
      s.a.   *pers.*–683
    manufacturing
      soc. & econ. aspects *see*
        Secondary industries
    technology   683.8
    safety
      soc. aspects   363.19
      misc. aspects see
        Product safety
    s.a. spec. kinds
  budgets
    econ. measure
      macroeconomics   339.41
    home econ.   640.42
  employees   640.46
    public   647.2–.6
  equipment   643
    s.a. Household appliances
  expenses home econ.   640.42
  finances home econ.   640.42
  garbage *see* Garbage
  income
    macroeconomics   339.22
  int. dec.   747.98
  security   643.16
  s.a. Home

Housekeepers *see* Household
    employees
Housekeeping   640
  private   648
  public   647
Housemaids *see* Household
    employees
Houseparents
  child welfare   362.732
    misc. aspects see Young
      people soc. services
Houseplants
  floriculture   635.965
  s.a. spec. plants
Houses
  gen. wks. *see* Dwellings
  haunted occultism   133.122
Houses (astrology)   133.53
Housing
  cooperatives
    economics   334.1
  factors in mental pub. health   362.204 2
  home econ.   643.1
  law   344.063 635
    spec. jur.   344.3–.9
  mil. admin.   355.67
    s.a. spec. mil. branches
  of animals
    husbandry   636.083 1
    s.a. spec. animals
  of employees
    personnel admin. *see*
      Economic services to
      employees
  of students *see* Student
    housing
  psych. influences   155.945
  pub. admin.
    activities   350.865
      central govts.   351.865
      spec. jur.   353–354
      local govts.   352.75
    departments *see* Executive
      departments pub. admin.
  renewal civic art   711.59
  services
    appl. soc.   363.5
    for employees *see* Economic
      services to employees
  soc. path.   363.5
Housings
  optical instruments
    mf. tech.   681.43
    other aspects see Optical
      instruments
Houston
  city Tex.   *area*–764 141 1
  County
    Alabama   *area*–761 295
    Georgia   *area*–758 515
    Minnesota   *area*–776 11

Houston
County (continued)
  Tennessee   *area*–768 36
  Texas   *area*–764 235
Hove East Sussex Eng.   *area*–422 54
Hovercraft *see* Air-cushion
  vehicles
Howard Co.
  Arkansas   *area*–767 483
  Indiana   *area*–772 85
  Iowa   *area*–777 312
  Maryland   *area*–752 81
  Missouri   *area*–778 285
  Nebraska   *area*–782 43
  Texas   *area*–764 858
Howden Humberside Eng. *area*–428 35
Howell Co. Mo.   *area*–778 85
Howitzers
  art metalwork   739.742
  mil. eng.
    soc. & econ. aspects *see*
      Secondary industries
    tech. & mf.   623.42
Howland Isl.   *area*–969 9
Hoylake Merseyside Eng. *area*–427 51
Hoyland Nether South Yorkshire
       Eng.   *area*–428 25
Huaceae *see* Malpighiales
Huambo Angola   *area*–673 4
Huancavelica Peru   *area*–852 8
Huánuco Peru   *area*–852 2
Hubbard Co. Minn.   *area*–776 85
Hubs
  automobile wheels
    soc. & econ. aspects *see*
      Secondary industries
    tech. & mf.   629.248
  s.a. other spec. uses
Huckaback fabrics *see*
    Dobby-weave fabrics
Huckleberries
  agriculture   634.732
    soc. & econ. aspects *see*
      Primary industries
  foods   641.347 32
    preparation
      commercial   664.804 732
      domestic   641.647 32
  other aspects see Ericales;
    also Fruits
Hucknall Nottinghamshire Eng.
                area–425 25
Huddersfield West Yorkshire Eng.
                area–428 13
Hudson
  Bay *see* American Arctic
    seawaters
  Co. N.J.   *area*–749 26
  River N.Y.   *area*–747 3
  Strait *see* American Arctic
    seawaters

Hudspeth Co. Tex.   *area*–764 95
Huehuetenango Guatemala *area*–728 171
Huelva Spain   *area*–468 7
Huerfano Co. Colo.   *area*–788 51
Huerta Mexico hist.   972.082 1
  s.a. spec. events & subj.
    e.g. Commerce
Huesca Spain   *area*–465 55
Hugh Capet reign
  France hist.   944.021
  s.a. spec. events & subj.
    e.g. Commerce
Hughenden Qld.   *area*–943 7
Hughes Co.
  Oklahoma   *area*–766 72
  South Dakota   *area*–783 29
Huguenot
  church bldgs.
    architecture   726.584 5
    building   690.658 45
    other aspects see
      Religious-purpose
      bldgs.
  churches   284.5
    Christian life guides 248.484 5
    doctrines   230.45
      creeds   238.45
    general councils   262.545
    govt. & admin.   262.045
      parishes   254.045
    missions   266.45
    moral theology   241.044 5
    private prayers for 242.804 5
    pub. worship   264.045
    rel. associations
      adults   267.184 5
      men   267.244 5
      women   267.444 5
      young adults   267.624 5
    rel. instruction   268.845
    rel. law   262.984 5
    schools   377.845
    secondary training 207.124 5
    sermons   252.045
    theological seminaries 207.114 5
    s.a. other spec. aspects
Huguenots
  biog. & work   284.509 2
  persecutions
    Christian church hist. 272.4
    s.a.   *pers.*–245
Huíla Angola   *area*–673 5
Huila Colombia   *area*–861 54
Hukui Japan   *area*–521 5
Hukuoka Japan   *area*–522
Hukusima Japan   *area*–521 1
Hull
  Co. Que.   *area*–714 221
  system psych.   150.194 34
    s.a. spec. subj. & branches
      of psych.

Hulls
  shipbuilding
    soc. & econ. aspects *see*
      Secondary industries
    technology   623.84
      design   623.814 4
        spec. craft   623.812
    s.a. other spec. uses
Humacao Puerto Rico   *area*–729 59
Human
  attributes *see* Human
    qualities
  body
    lit. & stage trmt.
      folk lit. soc.   398.353
      other aspects see Human
        life
    med. experiments on
      law   344.041 9
        spec. jur.   344.3–.9
  combat *see* Combat sports
  ecology *see* Ecology
  engineering   620.82
    s.a. spec. appls. e.g.
      Aerospace engineering
  evolution
    physical anthr.   573.2
  figures
    art representation   704.942
    drawing tech.   743.4
    painting   757
    s.a. other spec. art
      forms
  laws
    Christianity   241.2
    other rel. see Moral
      theology
  life
    lit. trmt.
      folk lit.
        sociology   398.35
        texts & lit. crit.
          everyday life   398.27
          persons   398.22
      gen. wks.
        collections   808.803 5
        hist. & crit.   809.933 5
      spec. lits.
        collections   *lit. sub.*–080 35
        hist. & crit.   *lit. sub.*–093 5
      s.a. spec. lit. forms
  origin
    metaphysics   128.5
    religion
      Christianity   233.11
      nat. rel.   213
      other rel. see
        Humankind rel.
        doctrines
    other aspects see Life
      origin

Human
  life (continued)
    stage trmt.   792.090 935
    s.a. other spec. dramatic
      mediums e.g.
      Television; *also spec.*
      kinds of drama e.g.
      Tragedies (drama)
  nature
    metaphysics   128.4
    rel. doctrines
      Christianity   233.5
      other rel. see Humankind
        rel. doctrines
  pigmentation
    physical anthr.   573.5
  power *see* Power; *also*
    Manpower
  psychology   150
  qualities
    lit. trmt.
      folk lit. soc.   398.353
      gen. wks.
        collections   808.803 53
        hist. & crit.   809.933 53
      spec. lits.
        collections   *lit. sub.*–080 353
        hist. & crit.   *lit. sub.*–093 53
      other aspects see Human
        life
    stage trmt.   792.090 935 3
    s.a. other spec. dramatic
      mediums e.g.
      Television; *also spec.*
      kinds of drama e.g.
      Tragedy
  races
    physical anthr.   572
    other aspects see Ethnic
      groups
  relations
    psychology *see*
      Interpersonal relations
    pub. admin.   350.81
      central govts.   351.81
        spec. jur.   353–354
      local govts.   352.941
    sociology   302
    training for employees
      personnel admin.
        gen. management   658.312 44
        executives   658.407 124 4
          spec. subj.   *s.s.*–068 3
      pub. admin.   350.15
        central govts.   351.15
          spec. jur.   353–354
        local govts.   352.005 15
  reproduction *see* Sex
  resources *see* Manpower
  rights *see* Civil rights

Humorous poetry
  gen. wks.
    collections   808.817
    hist. & crit.   809.17
    rhetoric   808.17
    juvenile   808.068 17
  spec. lits.   *lit. sub.*–107
    indiv. authors   *lit. sub.*–11–19
  other aspects see Poetry
Humpback whales *see* Mysticeti
Humpbacked flies *see*
    Orthorrhapha
Humphreys Co.
  Mississippi   *area*–762 48
  Tennessee   *area*–768 37
Humulus *see* Hops
Humus
  soil science *see* Biochemistry
    soil science
Hunan China   *area*–512 15
Hundred
  Days France hist.   944.05
  Years' War hist.   944.025
Hunedoara Romania   *area*–498 4
Hungarian
  language
    linguistics   494.511
    literature   894.511
    s.a.   *lang.*–945 11
  people   *r.e.n.*–945 11
  s.a. Hungary; *also other*
    spec. subj. e.g. Arts
Hungary   *area*–439
Hunger
  mechanisms
    human phys.   612.391
    other aspects see
      Metabolism
  perception *see* Visceral
    perceptions
  relief   363.8
    law   344.03
      spec. jur.   344.3–.9
    pub. admin.   350.84
      central govts.   351.84
        spec. jur.   353–354
      local govts.   352.944
    soc. path.   363.8
Hunstanton Norfolk Eng.   *area*–426 13
Hunt Co. Tex.   *area*–764 272
Hunter
  Isl. Tas.   *area*–946 7
  River N.S.W.   *area*–944 2
  system
    psychology   150.194 32
    s.a. spec. subj. &
      branches of psych.
Hunterdon Co. N.J.   *area*–749 71
Hunters
  bicg. & work
    industries   639.109 2

Hunters
  bicg. & work (continued)
    sports   799.292
  persons
    industries   *pers.*–639 1
    sports   *pers.*–799 2
Hunting
  animal husbandry for work   636.088 6
    s.a. spec. animals
  art representation *see*
    Animals art
      representation
  industries   639.1
    bus. organizations   338.763 91
      cooperatives   334.683 91
      mergers   338.836 391
      restrictive practices   338.826 391
    govt. control
      activities   350.823 6
      central govts.   351.823 6
        spec. jur.   353–354
      local govts.   352.942 36
    departments *see* Executive
      departments
    ind. relations   331.043 91
    s.a. spec. aspects e.g.
      Compensation
    prod. econ.   338.372
  Isl. S.C.   *area*–757 99
  products
    commerce   380.143 2–.143 9
    other aspects see Primary
      industries products
    s.a. Hunting industries
  sports   799.2
    ethics *see* Recreation
      ethics
    other aspects see Sports
Hunting-accidents *see*
    Recreation accidents
Hunting-dogs
  husbandry   636.75
  other aspects see Dogs
  sports   799.234
Huntingdon
  County
    Pennsylvania   *area*–748 73
    Quebec   *area*–714 31
  district Cambridgeshire Eng.
      area–426 54
Hunting-horns
  mf. tech.   681.818 41
    misc. aspects see Musical
      instruments
  musical art   788.41
  recordings   789.912 841
Hunting-lodges *see* Seasonal
    houses
Huntington Co. Ind.   *area*–772 71
Huntly Grampian Scot.   *area*–412 32
Huntsmen *see* Hunters

Huon
 Isls. New Caledonia — *area*–932
 River Tas. — *area*–946 2
Huonville Tas. — *area*–946 2
Hupeh China — *area*–512 12
Hurdlers
 biog. & work — 796.426
 s.a. — *pers.*–796 4
Hurdling
 equipment mf. — 688.764 26
 horses — 688.78
 soc. & econ. aspects *see*
  Secondary industries
 sports — 796.426
 horses — 798.45
 other aspects see Sports
Hurdy-gurdies
 mf. tech. — 681.817 9
 misc. aspects see Musical
  instruments
 musical art — 787.9
Hurdy-gurdy music — 787.9
 recordings — 789 912 79
Huron
 County
  Michigan — *area*–774 44
  Ohio — *area*–771 25
  Ontario — *area*–713 22
 Lake — *area*–774
  Michigan — *area*–774
  Ontario — *area*–713 2
 lang. & people *see*
  Hokan-Siouan
Huronian period *see* Proterozoic
  era
Hurricanes
 disasters
  soc. action — 363.349 2
  misc. aspects see
   Disasters
 meteorology — 551.552
  artificial modification — 551.685 2
  weather forecasting — 551.645 2
  spec. areas — 551.65
Husband-wife relationships
 law — 346.016 3
 spec. jur. — 346.3–.9
 other aspects see Family
  relationships
Huskers
 agriculture — 631.36
 use — 631.56
 s.a. spec. crops; also
  spec. types of culture
 mf. tech. — 681.763 1
 soc. & econ. aspects *see*
  Secondary industries
Husking crops
 agriculture — 631.56
 s.a. spec. crops

Hussein Onn admin. Malaysia
 hist. — 959.505 3
 s.a. spec. events & subj.
  e.g. Commerce
Hussite
 church bldgs.
  architecture — 726.584 3
  building — 690.658 43
  other aspects see
   Religious-purpose
   bldgs.
 churches — 284.3
  Christian life guides — 248.484 3
  doctrines — 230.43
   creeds — 238.43
  general councils — 262.543
  govt. & admin. — 262.043
   parishes — 254.043
  missions — 266.43
  moral theology — 241.044 3
  private prayers for — 242.804 3
  pub. worship — 264.043
  rel. associations
   adults — 267.184 3
   men — 267.244 3
   women — 267.444 3
   young adults — 267.624 3
  rel. instruction — 268.843
  rel. law — 262.984 3
  schools — 377.843
  secondary training — 207.124 3
  sermons — 252.043
  theological seminaries — 207.114 3
  s.a. other spec. aspects
 Wars Czechoslovakia hist. — 943.702 2
Hussites
 biog. & work — 284.3
 s.a. — *pers.*–243
Hutches
 animal husbandry — 636.083 1
 s.a. spec. animals
Hutchinson Co.
 South Dakota — *area*–783 384
 Texas — *area*–764 821
Hutias *see* Hystricomorpha
Hutterian Brethren — 289.73
 misc. aspects see Mennonite
  churches
Huyton-with-Roby Merseyside Eng.
  — *area*–427 54
Hwang Ho China — *area*–511
Hyacinths *see* Liliales
Hyaenidae
 animal husbandry — 636.974 427
 hunting
  commercial — 639.117 442 7
  sports — 799.259 744 27
 zoology — 599.744 27
 other aspects see Carnivora
Hyaline cartilage
 human anatomy & phys. — 611.018 3

Hyaline cartilage (continued)
  other aspects see Tissue
      biology
Hyalospongiae
  culture   639.734 4
  fishing   639.734 4
  paleozoology   563.4
  zoology   593.44
  other aspects see Porifera
Hybrid
  computers *see* Computer
      combinations
  s.a. other spec. subj.
Hybrids
  crop. prod.   631.523
    s.a. spec. crops; also spec.
        types of culture e.g.
        Floriculture
  genetics life sci. *see*
      Genetic deviations
Hydatid diseases *see*
      Tapeworm-caused
      diseases
Hyde
  County
    North Carolina   *area*–756 184
    South Dakota   *area*–783 283
  municipality
    Greater Manchester
        Eng.   *area*–427 35
Hyderabad
  India   *area*–548 4
  Pakistan   *area*–549 182
Hydnaceae *see* Agaricales
Hydnoraceae *see* Aristolochiales
Hydrangeaceae *see* Cunoniales
Hydrangeas *see* Cunoniales
Hydrants
  fire extinction tech.   628.925 2
  s.a. spec. appls. e.g.
      Forest fires
Hydrargyrum *see* Mercury
      (element)
Hydras *see* Hydrozoa
Hydration movements
  plants
    pathology   581.218 2
    physiology   581.182
  s.a. spec. plants
Hydraulic
  control
    automation eng.   629.804 2
    s.a. spec. appls. e.g.
        Machine tools; *also*
        spec. systems e.g.
        Closed-loop systems
    s.a. other spec. appls.
  elevators *see* Elevators
        (lifts)
  engineering *see* Hydraulics
      engineering

Hydraulic (continued)
  engineers
    biog. & work   627.092
    s.a.   *pers.*–627
  machinery *see* Hydraulic-power
      technology
  mining *see* Alluvial mining
  rams *see* Rams (hydraulics)
  tackles *see* Tackles
  s.a. other spec. subj.
Hydraulic-power
  engineers
    biog. & work   621.209 2
    s.a.   *pers.*–621
  systems
    spacecraft *see* Auxiliary
        power systems
        spacecraft eng.
    s.a. other spec. appls.
  technology
    prod. tech.   621.2
      s.a. spec. appls. e.g.
          Transmission-devices
    soc. & econ. aspects *see*
        Secondary industries
Hydraulics
  engineering
    power *see* Hydraulic-power
        technology
    soc. & econ. aspects *see*
        Secondary industries
    technology   627
      s.a. spec. appls. e.g.
          Irrigation
  physics   532.1
Hydric *see* Aquatic
Hydrides
  chem. tech.   661.08
  soc. & econ. aspects *see*
      Secondary industries
  s.a. spec. prod.
  s.a. spec. kinds
Hydrocarbons
  chem. tech.   661.81
  org. chem.
    derivatives   547.02–.04
      alicyclic   547.52–.54
      aliphatic   547.42–.44
      aromatic   547.62–.64
    gen. wks.   547.01
      alicyclic   547.51
      aliphatic   547.41
      aromatic   547.61
  other aspects see Organic
      chemicals
Hydrocaryaceae *see* Lythrales
Hydrocephalism
  gen. med.   616.858 843
  geriatrics   618.976 858 843
  pediatrics   618.928 588 43
  psychology   157.8

Hydrometeorology (continued)
  weather forecasting   551.647
    spec. areas   551.65
Hydrophiloidea
  zoology   595.764 1
  other aspects see Polyphaga
Hydrophobia *see* Rabies
Hydrophones
  underwater commun. devices
    soc. & econ. aspects *see*
      Secondary industries
    tech. & mf.   621.389 52
    s.a. spec. appls. e.g.
      Military engineering
Hydrophyllaceae *see*
  Polemoniales
Hydroplanes (aircraft) *see*
  Seaplanes
Hydroplanes (boats) *see* Inboard
  motorboats
Hydroponics   631.585
  s.a. spec. crops
Hydroquinones
  org. chem.   547.633
  s.a. spec. cpds.
Hydrosols
  colloid chem.
    physical chem.   541.345 14
      applied   660.294 514
      organic   547.134 514
    s.a. spec. elements,
      cpds., prod.
Hydrospace
  internat. law   341.45
Hydrosphere physical geol.   551.46–.49
Hydrostachyaceae *see*
  Podostemales
Hydrostatics
  mechanics
    engineering *see* Statics
    eng. mech.
    physics   532.2
Hydrosulfites
  org. chem.   547.063
  s.a. spec. groupings e.g.
    Aliphatic compounds
  synthetic drugs   615.316 3
    misc. aspects see
      Pharmacology
  synthetic poisons   615.951 63
    misc. aspects see
      Toxicology
  other aspects see Sulfur
    compounds
Hydrotherapy   615.853
  s.a. spec. diseases
Hydrous sulfates
  mineralogy   549.755
Hydroxides
  mineralogy   549.53

Hydroxy compounds
  chem. tech.   661.82–.86
  org. chem.   547.03
  s.a. spec. groupings e.g.
    Aliphatic compounds
  synthetic drugs   615.313
    misc. aspects see
      Pharmacology
  synthetic poisons   615.951 3
    misc. aspects see
      Toxicology
  other aspects see Organic
    chemicals
Hydroxyketone dyes
  manufacturing
    chem. tech.   667.256
    soc. & econ. aspects *see*
      Secondary industries
  org. chem.   547.866
Hydrozoa
  culture   639.737 1
  paleozoology   563.71
  zoology   593.71
  other aspects see Animals
Hyenas *see* Hyaenidae
Hyeniales
  paleobotany   561.72
Hygiene
  med. sci.   613
  soc. customs   391.64
  study & teaching   613.07
    elementary ed.   372.37
  vet. sci.   636.089 3
    s.a. spec. animals
  s.a. spec. diseases
Hygienists
  biog. & work   613.092
  other aspects see Medical
    scientists
  s.a.   *pers.*–613
Hygrometry *see* Humidity
Hylidae
  zoology   597.87
  other aspects see Anura
Hylobatinae
  animal husbandry   636.988 2
  hunting
    commercial   639.118 82
    sports   799.278 82
  zoology   599.882
  other aspects see Primates
Hymen
  anatomy
    human   611.67
    other aspects see
      Reproductive organs
  diseases   618.1
    neoplasms   616.992 67
    other aspects see Female
      genital organs diseases
  physical anthropometry   573.667

Hymen (continued)
  physiology
    human   612.62
    other aspects see
      Reproduction
    tissue biology human   611.018 967
Hymenocarina
  paleozoology   565.36
Hymenogastrales *see*
      Lycoperdales
Hymenophyllaceae *see* Filicales
Hymenoptera
  agric. pests   632.79
    s.a. spec. types of culture
      e.g. Forestry; *also*
        spec. crops
  culture   638.579
  paleozoology   565.79
  zoology   595.79
  other aspects see Insecta
Hymnals
  music   783.952
Hymns
  music   783.9
    recordings   789.912 39
  private devotions
    Christianity   245
    comp. rel.   291.43
    Judaism   296.72
  s.a. other spec. rel.
  other aspects see Sacred
      music
Hyndburn Lancashire Eng. *area*–427 625
Hyogo Japan   *area*–521 9
Hyperactivity
  med. sci. *see* Minimal brain
      dysfunction
Hyperadrenalism *see* Adrenal
      glands diseases
Hyperbolas *see* Configurations
      geometry
Hyperbolic
  equations   515.353
    s.a. spec. appls. e.g.
      Engineering
  functions   515.9
    s.a. spec. appls. e.g.
      Engineering
  geometry   516.9
    s.a. spec. appls. e.g.
      Engineering
Hyperboloids *see* Configurations
      geometry
Hyperborean *see* Paleosiberian
Hyperesthesia *see* Cutaneous
      sensory disorders
Hypergeometric polynomials   515.55
  s.a. spec. appls. e.g.
      Engineering
Hypericaceae *see* Guttiferales
Hyperiidea *see* Amphipoda

Hyperkinesia *see* Minimal brain
      dysfunction
Hypermastigida *see* Mastigophora
Hypermetropia *see* Refraction
      errors
Hyperons *see* Baryons
Hyperopia *see* Refraction errors
Hyperparathyroidism *see*
      Parathyroid glands
      diseases
Hyperpinealism *see* Pineal gland
      diseases
Hypersensitivity
  gen. med.   616.97
  geriatrics   618.976 97
  pediatrics   618.929 7
  pub. health   614.599 3
  statistics   312.397
    deaths   312.269 7
  other aspects see Diseases
Hypersonic velocity
  aeronautical aerodynamics   629.132 306
    s.a. spec. phenomena e.g.
      Lift; *also spec.*
      appls. e.g. Flying
  gas flow mech.
    engineering *see* Dynamics
    physics   533.276
      air flow   533.627 6
Hyperspace
  geometry *see* Vector geometry
Hypertension
  gen. med.   616.132
  geriatrics   618.976 132
  pediatrics   618.921 32
  pub. health   614.591 32
  statistics   312.313 2
    deaths   312.261 32
  other aspects see Diseases
Hyperthyroidism
  gen. med.   616.443
  geriatrics   618.976 443
  pediatrics   618.924 43
  pub. health   614.594 43
  statistics   312.344 3
    deaths   312.264 43
  other aspects see Diseases
Hypertrichosis *see* Hair
      diseases
Hypertrophies
  skin
    gen. med.   616.544
    geriatrics   618.976 544
    pediatrics   618.925 44
    pub. health   614.595 44
    statistics   312.354 4
    other aspects see Diseases
  symptoms *see* Symptoms of
      disease
  uterus *see* Malformations
      uterus

Hypertropic arthritis *see*
    Arthritis
Hyperventilation
  gen. med. 616.208
  geriatrics 618.976 208
  pediatrics 618.922 08
  pub. health 614.592 08
  statistics 312.320 8
    deaths 312.262 08
  other aspects see Diseases
Hypesthesia *see* Cutaneous
    sensory disorders
Hyphochytriales *see*
    Uniflagellate molds
Hyphomicrobiales
  botany 589.9
  med. aspects
    disease organisms 616.014
    gen. pharm. 615.329 9
      toxicology 615.952 99
    vet. pharm. 636.089 532 99
      toxicology 636.089 595 299
  paleobotany 561.9
  other aspects see Plants
Hypnotherapy 615.851 2
s.a. spec. diseases
Hypnotics
  addictive aspects *see*
    Addictive drugs
  pharmacodynamics 615.782
  other aspects see Drugs
Hypnotism
  psychology 154.7
  animals 156.4
Hypoadrenalism *see* Adrenal
    glands diseases
Hypochondria
  gen. med. 616.852 5
  geriatrics 618.976 852 5
  pediatrics 618.928 525
  psychology 157.3
  statistics 312.385 25
Hypodermic medication *see*
    Parenteral medication
Hypoglycemia
  gen. med. 616.466
  geriatrics 618.976 466
  pediatrics 618.924 66
  pub. health 614.594 66
  statistics 312.346 6
    deaths 312.264 66
  other aspects see Diseases
Hypoparathyroidism *see*
    Parathyroid glands
    diseases
Hypostatic union
  Christian doctrine 232.8
Hypothalamus
  human phys. 612.826 2
  other aspects see Brain

Hypothermia
  therapeutics *see* Cryotherapy
Hypotheses
  logic 167
    symbolic *see* Symbolic logic
  testing
    statistical math. 519.56
    s.a. spec. appls. e.g.
      Engineering
Hypothyroidism
  gen. med. 616.444
  geriatrics 618.976 444
  pediatrics 618.924 44
  pub. health 614.594 44
  statistics 312.344 4
    deaths 312.264 44
  other aspects see Diseases
Hypoxidaceae *see* Haemodorales
Hyracoidea
  animal husbandry 636.962
  hunting
    commercial 639.116 2
    sports 799.259 62
  paleozoology 569.6
  zoology 599.62
  other aspects see Mammalia
Hyrcania *area*–396
Hysterectomies
  surgery 618.145 3
  vet. sci. 636.089 814 53
    s.a. spec. animals
Hysteresis
  magnetism *see* Magnetic
    phenomena
Hysteria
  gen. med. 616.852 4
  geriatrics 618.976 852 4
  pediatrics 618.928 524
  psychology 157.3
  pub. health 614.58
  statistics 312.385 24
  other aspects see Mental
    illness
Hystricomorpha
  animal husbandry 636.932 34
  hunting
    commercial 639.113 234
    sports 799.259 323 4
  zoology 599.323 4
  other aspects see Rodentia
Hythe Kent Eng. *area*–422 395

I

ICBM
  mil. eng.
    soc. & econ. aspects *see*
      Secondary industries
    tech. & mf. 623.451 954
IQ *see* Intelligence (intellect)
    tests

IRBM
  mil. eng.
    soc. & econ. aspects *see*
      Secondary industries
    tech. & mf.   623.451 953
Ialomita Romania   *area*–498 2
Iasi Romania   *area*–498 1
Ibaraki Japan   *area*–521 3
Iberia
  ancient country   *area*–395
  Par La.   *area*–763 49
Iberian
  Peninsula   *area*–46
    ancient   *area*–366
  sculpture
    ancient   732.6
    later   730.946
Iberville
  Co. Que.   *area*–714 61
  Par. La.   *area*–763 44
Ibises *see* Ciconiiformes
Ibiza Spain   *area*–467 5
Ibn Majah Hadith   297.124 6
Ibo
  language
    linguistics   496.332
    literature   896.332
    s.a.   *lang.*–963 32
  people   *r.e.n.*–963
  s.a. other spec. subj. e.g.
    Arts
Ica Peru   *area*–852 7
Icacinaceae *see* Celastrales
Icarianism
  socialist school econ.   335.2
Ice   551.31
  age *see* Pleistocene epoch
  arch. construction   721.044 91
    s.a. spec. kinds of bldgs.
  ballet *see* Ice skating
  bldg. construction   693.91
  carving dec. arts   736.94
  control road eng.
    technology   625.763
    other aspects see Roads
  cream
    cookery home econ.   641.862
    other aspects see Frozen
      desserts
  crossings
    railroad eng.
      technology   625.147
      other aspects see
        Permanent way
    road eng.
      technology   625.792
      other aspects see Roads
  crystals
    atmospheric electricity *see*
      Aerosols meteorology

Ice (continued)
  fishing
    sports   799.12
    other aspects see Fishing
  formation
    aeronautics   629.132 4
      s.a. spec. appls. e.g.
        Flying
      s.a. other spec. subj.
  games
    equipment mf.   688.769 6
      soc. & econ. aspects *see*
        Secondary industries
    sports   796.96
    other aspects see Sports
  geology   551.31
    econ. geol.   553.7
  hockey
    equipment mf.   688.769 62
      soc. & econ. aspects *see*
        Secondary industries
    players
      biog. & work   796.962 902
      s.a.   *pers.*–796 9
    sports   796.962
    other aspects see Sports
  manufacturing
    soc. & econ. aspects *see*
      Secondary industries
    technology   621.58
      s.a. spec. appls. e.g.
        skating rinks 796.91
  milk
    cookery home econ.   641.862
    other aspects see Frozen
      desserts
  mineralogy   549.522
  removal
    soc. services *see* Highway
      services; *also* Street
      services
    street cleaning   628.466
  roads
    technology   625.792
    other aspects see Roads
  skaters
    biog. & work   796.910 92
    s.a.   *pers.*–796 9
  skates
    mf. tech.   685.361
    other aspects see Footwear
  skating
    sports   796.91
    other aspects see Sports
  sports
    equipment mf.   688.769
      soc. & econ. aspects *see*
        Secondary industries
    recreation   796.9
    other aspects see Sports

Ice (continued)
  storms
    meteorology — 551.559
      artificial modification — 551.685 9
      weather forecasting — 551.645 9
      spec. areas — 551.65
    other aspects see Weather
Icebergs
  physical geol. — 551.342
Iceboating
  sports — 796.97
  other aspects see Sports
Iceboats *see* Pleasure craft
      (nautical) sailing
Iceboxes *see* Refrigerators
Icebreakers
  engineering — 623.828
    design — 623.812 8
    models — 623.820 18
  seamanship — 623.882 8
  other aspects see Vessels
      (nautical)
Icel Turkey — *area*–564
Iceland — *area*–491 2
Icelandic
  language
    linguistics — 439.69
    literature — 839.69
    s.a. — *lang.*–396 91
  people — *r.e.n.*–396 1
  s.a. Iceland; *also* Old
      Norse; *also other*
      spec. subj. e.g. Arts
Ices (desserts) *see* Frozen
      desserts
Ichthyologists
  biog. & work — 597.009 2
  other aspects see Scientists
  s.a. — *pers.*–597
Ichthyology — 597
Ichthyornithiformes
  paleozoology — 568.23
  other aspects see Aves
Ichthyosauria
  paleozoology — 567.93
Ichthyosis *see* Hypertrophies
      skin
Iconography
  arts — 704.9
  s.a. spec. art forms
Icons
  arts
    gen. wks.
      Christianity — 704.948 2
      other religions — 704.948 9
    s.a. spec. art forms
  rel. significance
    Christianity — 246.53
    other rel see Arts rel.
      significance

Icteridae
  hunting
    commercial — 639.128 881
    sports — 799.248 881
  paleozoology — 568.8
  zoology — 598.881
  other aspects see Aves
Id
  depth psych. — 154.22
    animals — 156.4
Ida Co. Ia. — *area*–777 422
Idaho
  Co. Ida. — *area*–796 82
  state — *area*–796
Ideal states
  pol. sci. — 321.07
  s.a. spec. jur.
Idealism
  education — 370.12
  lit. qual.
    gen. wks.
      collections — 808.801 3
      hist. & crit. — 809.913
    spec. lits.
      collections — *lit. sub.*–080 13
      hist. & crit. — *lit. sub.*–091 3
    s.a. spec. lit. forms
  philosophy — 141
    indiv. phil. — 180–190
    s.a. spec. branches of phil.
      e.g. Metaphysics
  stage qual. — 792.090 913
    s.a. spec. mediums e.g.
      Television; *also spec.*
      kinds of drama e.g.
      Tragedies (drama)
Idealistic style
  sculpture — 732–735
  s.a. other spec. subj.
Idealized dances music *see*
      Dance music
Ideals (mathematics)
  algebra — 512.4
    s.a. spec. appls. e.g.
      Engineering
Ideation
  epistemology — 121
  psychology — 153.2
    animals — 156.32
    children — 155.413
    s.a. psych. of other spec.
      groups
Identification
  arts — 702.87
    s.a. techs. in spec. art
      forms
  criminals
    criminal investigation — 363.258
    law — 345.052
      spec. jur. — 345.3–.9

Identification
  criminals
    criminal investigation (continued)
      pub. admin. *see* Law
        enforcement pub. admin.
    minerals   549.1
    spec. minerals   549.2–.7
    s.a. Verification; *also*
        other spec. subj.
Identification-marks   *s.s.*–027
Identity
  psychology   155.2
Ideographs *see* Notations
    languages
Ideologies *see spec. kinds e.g.*
    Anarchism
Ideology (philosophy)   145
  indiv. phil.   180–190
  s.a. spec. branches of phil.
      e.g. Metaphysics
Idiocy *see* Mental deficiency
Idioms *see* Grammar
    (linguistics)
Idiots *see* Severely retarded
    persons
Idlib Syria   *area*–569 13
Idocrase
  mineralogy   549.63
Idolatry
  comp. rel.   291.218
  s.a. spec. rel.
Idols
  rel. worship
    comp. rel.   291.218
    s.a. spec. rel.
Ife kingdom hist.   966.901 5
  s.a. spec. events & subj.
      e.g. Commerce
Ifni   *area*–646
Ifugao Philippines   *area*–599 1
Igbo *see* Ibo
Igloos
  bldg. construction   693.91
Igneous rocks
  mineralogy   549.114 1
  spec. minerals   549.2–.7
  petrology   552.1
  other aspects see Natural
      stones
Ignition
  systems & devices
    internal combustion engines
      soc. & econ. aspects *see*
          Secondary industries
      tech. & mf.   621.437
        automobiles   629.254
        marine vehicles   623.872 37
      s.a. other spec. appls.
  thermochemistry *see*
      Combustion
      thermochemistry

Ignitrons *see* Vacuum tubes
Iguanas *see* Lacertilia
Ikhnaton reign Egypt hist.   932.014
  s.a. spec. events & subj.
      e.g. Commerce
Île-de-France   *area*–443 4
Ileitis
  gen. med.   616.344 5
  geriatrics   618.976 344 5
  pediatrics   618.923 445
  pub. health   614.593 445
  statistics   312.334 45
    deaths   312.263 445
  other aspects see Diseases
Ileum *see* Small intestines
Ilex paraguayensis *see* Maté
Ilford London Eng.   *area*–421 73
Ilfov Romania   *area*–498 2
Ilfracombe Devon Eng.   *area*–423 52
Ilin Philippines   *area*–599 3
Ilium *see* Pelvis
Ilkeston Derbyshire Eng.   *area*–425 18
Ilkley West Yorkshire Eng.
        area–428 17
Ill
  health *see* Illness
  people *see* Sick people
Illawarra Lake N.S.W.   *area*–944 6
Illecebraceae *see* Polygonales
Ille-et-Vilaine France   *area*–441 5
Illegal
  confinement
    torts
      law   346.033
      spec. jur.   346.3–.9
  voting *see* Electoral offenses
  s.a. other spec. subj.
Illegitimacy
  law   346.017
    spec. jur.   346.3–.9
  soc. path.   362.704 4
  other aspects see Sexual
      relations
  s.a. Illegitimate children;
      also Unmarried
      mothers
Illegitimate children
  soc. services   362.71–.73
    misc. aspects see Young
        people soc. services
  s.a.   *pers.*–069 45
  s.a. Illegitimacy
Illiciaceae *see* Magnoliales
Illinois
  River   *area*–773 5
  state   *area*–773
Illness
  devotions for *see* Consolatory
      devotions
  effect on populations   304.64

Illness (continued)
  mental health factor
    pub. health   362.2
    psych. influences   155.916
  rel. rites
    Christianity   265.82
    other rel. see Public
        worship
  soc. path.   362.1–.4
    soc. theology *see* Social
        problems soc. theology
  s.a. Sick people; *also*
        Pathology; *also*
        Diseases
Illumination
  dec. arts   745.67
  engineering
    soc. & econ. aspects *see*
        Secondary industries
    technology   621.321
    s.a. spec. appls. e.g.
        Billboards
  mining eng.   622.47
  s.a. Lighting
Illuminations
  performing arts   791.6
Illusions
  qen. wks. *see* Errors
  s.a. spec. kinds e.g. Optical
        illusions
Illustration
  arts   741.6
Illustrations
  books hist. & crit.   096.1
  communication   001.553
  other aspects see Graphic
        materials
Illyria   *area*–398
Illyrian languages
  linguistics   491.993
  literatures   891.993
  s.a.   *lang.*–919 93
Ilmenite
  mineralogy   549.523
Ilminster Somerset Eng.   *area*–423 89
Ilocos Philippines   *area*–599 1
Iloilo Philippines   *area*–599 5
Ilubabor Ethiopia   *area*–633
Imageless thought
  psychology   153.423
    animals   156.342 3
    children   155.413
    s.a. psych. of other spec.
        groups
Imagery
  psychology   153.3
    animals   156.33
    children   155.413
    s.a. psych. of other spec.
        groups

Images
  arts   704.9
    s.a. spec. art forms
  rel. significance
    Christianity   246.53
    other rel. see Arts rel.
        significance
  rel. worship
    comp. rel.   291.218
    s.a. spec. rel.
Imaginary *see* Legendary
Imagination
  arts & lit. *see* Creation
  human attribute
    metaphysics   128.3
    psychology   153.3
      animals   156.33
      children   155.413
      s.a. psych. of other spec.
          groups
Imamat Islamic doctrines   297.24
Imams Islamic leaders   297.61
Imathia Greece   *area*–495 6
Imbabura Ecuador   *area*–866 12
Imbeciles *see* Trainable
        retarded persons
Imbecility *see* Mental
        deficiency
Imbibition processes
  photographic printing   773.3
Imbros   *area*–562
  ancient   *area*–391 1
Imidazoles
  org. chem.   547.593
  s.a. spec. cpds.
Imitation
  learning proc.
    psychology   153.152 3
      animals   156.315 23
      children   155.413
      s.a. psych. of other spec.
          groups
Imitation leathers
  manufacturing
    soc. & econ. aspects *see*
        Secondary industries
    technology   675.4
    s.a. spec. prod.
Imitation-leather covers
  bookbinding   686.343
Immaculate Conception
  Christian doctrines   232.911
Immature personality
  gen. med.   616.858 2
  geriatrics   618.976 858 2
  pediatrics   618.928 582
  psychology   157.7
  pub. health   614.58
  statistics   312.385 82
  other aspects see Diseases;
        also Mental illness

Impeachment
chief executives | 350.003 6
central govts. | 351.003 6
spec. jur. | 353–354
local govts. | 352.008
govt. officials | 350.993
central govts. | 351.993
spec. jur. | 353–354
local govts. | 352.002
legislative powers *see*
Judicial powers
Impedance
measurement
radio *see* Measurement radio
television *see* Measurement
television
s.a. other spec. subj.
Imperfect
fungi *see* Deuteromycetes
s.a. other spec. subj.
Imperia Italy | *area*–451 87
Imperial
Co. Calif. | *area*–794 99
system
mensuration | 530.813
s.a. spec. branches of
physics
metrology | 389.15
Valley Calif. | *area*–794 99
Imperialism
commerce *see* International
commerce
pol. sci. | 325.32
Impersonation *see* Acting
Impetigo
gen. med. | 616.524
geriatrics | 618.976 524
pediatrics | 618.925 24
pub. health | 614.595 24
statistics | 312.352 4
other aspects see Diseases
Implements *see* Machines; Tools;
also spec. kinds
Import
embargoes *see* Embargoes
tax schedules
pub. finance | 336.265
spec. ccmmodities | 336.266
other aspects see Customs
(tariffs)
taxes
pub. finance | 336.264
spec. commodities | 336.266
other aspects see Customs
(tariffs)
trade | 382.5
govt. control
activities | 351.827 5
spec. jur. | 353–354
departments *see* Executive
departments

Import
trade (continued)
law | 343.087 7
spec. jur. | 343.3–.9
Importers *see* Foreign traders
Imposition
printing | 686.225 6
Impostures *see* Frauds
Impotence
functional
gen. med. | 616.692
geriatrics | 618.976 692
pub. health | 614.596 92
statistics | 312.369 2
neurotic
gen. med. | 616.858 32
geriatrics | 618.976 858 32
psychology | 157.7
pub. health | 614.58
statistics | 312.385 832
other aspects see Diseases;
also Mental illness
Impressing-equipment
soc. & econ. aspects *see*
Secondary industries
tech. & mf. | 621.984
s.a. spec. appls. e.g.
Printing processes
Impression
printing
soc. & econ. aspects *see*
Secondary industries
technology | 686.23
Impressionism
arts
gen. wks. | 709.034 4
spec. places | 709.1–.9
music
gen. wks. | 780.904
spec. places | 780.91–.99
s.a. spec. mediums
painting | 759.054
spec. places | 759.1–.9
s.a. other spec. art forms
Imprisonment
penology *see* Penal
institutions
Improper integrals | 515.43
s.a. spec. appls. e.g.
Engineering
Improvement
eng. materials | 620.11
nat. resources | 333.715
s.a. spec. kinds of
resources e.g.
Shorelands
research prod. management | 658.576
spec. subj. | *s.s.*–068 5
Improvisation (dramatic) *see*
Acting

Incineration
refuse
  technology — 628.445 7
  other aspects see Refuse
  pub. sanitation
sewage disposal
  technology — 628.37
  other aspects see Sewage
  disposal
Incised wounds
  statistics — 312.304 714 3
  deaths — 312.260 471 43
  surgical trmt. — 617.143
  anesthesiology — 617.967 143
  s.a. Veterinary sciences
Incitement *see* Criminal
  offenses
Inclined
  plane mechanics — 531.8
  railways *see* Mountain
  railways
Inclines
canal eng.
  technology — 627.135 3
  s.a. spec. appls. e.g.
  Canal transportation
  other aspects see Liquids
  engineering
Income
  financial management — 658.155 4
  spec. subj. — *s.s.*–068 1
increase
  personal finance — 332.024 01
macroeconomics
  distribution — 339.2
  measurements — 339.3
measurement
  accounting — 657.48
  s.a. spec. kinds of
  enterprise e.g.
  Insurance accounting
policies
  macroeconomics — 339.5
redistribution
  macroeconomics — 339.52
tax reductions
  law *see* Tax reductions law
  pub. finance — 336.241 6
  s.a. spec. kinds e.g.
  Personal income taxes
taxes
  law — 343.052
  spec. jur. — 343.3–.9
  pub. admin. — 350.724 4
  central govts. — 351.724 4
  spec. jur. — 353–354
  local govts. — 352.13
  pub. finance — 336.24
theory money econ. — 332.401
other aspects see Finance

Income-&-expense statements
financial management *see*
  Reporting financial
  management
Income-consumption relations
  macroeconomics — 339.41
Incompatibilities
  logic — 160
  pharmacology *see* Posology
Incompressible airflow
  aeronautical aerodynamics — 629.132 322
  s.a. spec. appls. e.g.
  Flying
Inconvertible money
  economics — 332.427
  other aspects see Money
Incorporated banks
  economics — 332.122
  other aspects see Banks
  (finance)
Incorporation
bus. organizations
  law — 346.066 22
  spec. jur. — 346.3–.9
  local govt. — 352.003
  s.a. Corporations
Incrustation
  arch. decoration — 729.6
  rel. significance
    Christianity — 247.46
    comp. rel. — 291.35
    s.a. other spec. rel.
  s.a. spec. kinds of bldgs.
Incubi
  occultism — 133.423
  other aspects see Devils
Incunabula
  bibliographies — 011.42
  spec. kinds — 012–016
catalogs
  general — 017–019
  spec. kinds — 012–016
  hist. & crit. — 093
Indecent exposure *see* Sex
  offenses
Indemnification
  law of war — 341.66
Independence
  Co. Ark. — *area*–767 26
  U.S. hist. — 973.313
wars
  history — 904.7
  U.S. — 973.3
  s.a. other spec.
  countries
Independencia Dominican Republic
  area–729 325
Independent
government agencies — 350.009
  central govts. — 351.009
  spec. jur. — 353–354

Independent
government agencies (continued)
   local govts.   352.009
  Methodists   287.533
   misc. aspects see Methodist
study plans
   ed. method   371.394 3
    s.a. spec. levels of ed.;
       also Special education
   higher ed.   378.03
trials
   probabilities   519.2
    s.a. spec. appls. e.g.
       Forecasting
Indeterminate
equations   515.253
  algebra   512.74
   s.a. spec. appls. e.g.
      Engineering
  calculus   515.253
   complex variables   515.925 3
   real variables   515.825 3
   s.a. other spec. functions
     & equations; also spec.
     appls. e.g.
     Engineering
  sentence penology   364.62
Indeterminism
  metaphysics   123
Index librorum prohibitorum   098.11
Indexes   *s.s.–*016
of cases
  law   348.048
   spec. jur.   348.3–.9
   U.S.
     Federal   348.734 8
     state & local   348.74–.79
   spec. subj.   *law s.s.–*026 48
of laws
  law   348.028
   spec. jur.   348.3–.9
   U.S.
     Federal   348.732 8
     state & local   348.74–.79
   spec. subj.   *law s.s.–*026 38
s.a. Indices
Indexing
  library operations   025.3
  museology   069.52
  subject   025.48
India   *area–*54
  ancient   *area–*34
Indian
  corn
   agriculture *see* Corn
   grasses *see* Panicoideae
  Desert   *area–*544
  fighting *see* Guerilla
  Head Sask.   *area–*712 44

Indian (continued)
  hemp
   agriculture   633.56
    soc. & econ. aspects *see*
     Primary industries
    other aspects see
     Apocynales
  mallow
   fiber crop *see* China jute
   herbs *see* Herbs
  Ocean
   basin regional subj. trmt.
             *area–*182 4
   biology   574.927
    botany   581.927
    zoology   591.927
    s.a. spec. organisms
   fishing sports   799.166 7
   oceanography   551.467
    currents   551.477
    submarine geology   551.460 8
   regional subj. trmt.   *area–*165
   transocean flights   629.130 917
  pitcher-plant family *see*
    Aristolochiales
  River Fla.   *area–*759 28
  Territory   *area–*766 5
Indian (American) *see* American
  native
Indian (Asian) *see* Indic
Indiana
  Co. Pa.   *area–*748 89
  state   *area–*772
Indianapolis Ind.   *area–*772 52
Indian-pipe family *see* Ericales
Indic
  architecture   722.44
   misc. aspects see
    Architectural schools
  English literature   820
  languages
   linguistics   491.2–.4
   literatures   891.2–.4
   s.a.   *lang.–*912–914
  people   *r.e.n.–*914
  religions   294
   art representation   704.948 94
    s.a. spec. art forms
   persons in
    biog. & work   294.092
    s.a. spec. rel.
    s.a.   *pers.–*294
  religious temples & shrines
   architecture   726.14
   building   690.614
  rugs textile arts   746.754
  sculpture   732.44
  s.a. spec. countries e.g.
    India

Indicators
  radiowave electronics *see*
      Testing-devices
      radiowave electronics
  s.a. other spec. apparatus,
      equip., materials e.g.
      Jet engines
Indices
  number theory
      algebra   512.72
      s.a. spec. appls. e.g.
          Engineering
  s.a. Indexes
Indictment
  criminal law   345.072
      spec. jur.   345.3–.9
Indifference
  rel. attitudes
      Christianity   261.21
      other rel. see
          Interreligious
          relations
Indigenes
  legal status   342.087 2
      spec. jur.   342.3–.9
  s.a.   *r.e.n.–*01
Indigent people *see* Poor people
Indigestion *see* Dyspepsia
Indigo dyes
  comm. proc.   667.26
  other aspects see Dyes
Indigoid dyes
  manufacturing
      chem. tech.   667.257
      soc. & econ. aspects *see*
          Secondary industries
  org. chem.   547.867
Indirect
  evidence *see* Circumstantial
          evidence
  lighting
      illumination eng.
          soc. & econ. aspects *see*
              Secondary industries
          technology   621.321 3
              exterior   621.322 9
              interior   621.322 5–.322 8
          s.a. spec. kinds e.g.
              Incandescent lighting
      s.a. spec. appls. e.g.
              Lighting library bldgs.
  processes
      color photography   778.65–.66
      motion pictures   778.534 2
      photomicrography   778.31
  taxes
      pub. finance   336.294
  s.a. other spec. subj.
Indium
  chemistry
      inorganic   546.677

Indium
  chemistry (continued)
      organic   547.056 77
      s.a. spec. groupings e.g.
          Aliphatic compounds
  technology   661.067 7
      organic   661.895
      soc. & econ. aspects *see*
          Secondary industries
      s.a. spec. prod.
  pharmacology   615.267 7
      misc. aspects see
          Pharmacology
  toxicology   615.925 677
      misc. aspects see
          Toxicology
  other aspects see Minor
          metals
Individual
  observances
      personal rel. *see* Religious
          observances private
  proprietorships *see*
          Proprietorships
  psychology   155.2
  rights *see* Civil rights
  s.a. other spec. subj.
Individual-copy bookbinding *see*
          Library bookbinding
Individualism
  economics   330.153
  philosophy   141.4
      indiv. phil.   180–190
      s.a. spec. branches of phil.
          e.g. Metaphysics
  pol. ideology   320.512
      pol. theology *see* Political
          ideologies soc.
          theology
  soc. interaction   302.5
Individuality psych.   155.2
Individualized instruction
  elementary reading   372.414 7
  gen. wks.   371.394
      s.a. spec. levels of ed.;
          also Special education
Individuals
  taxes
      law   343.062
      spec. jur.   343.3–.9
Indo-Aryan
  period India hist.   934.02
      s.a. spec. events & subj.
          e.g. Commerce; *also*
          Indic
Indo-Aryans   *r.e.n.–*914
Indochina   *area–*597
Indochinese War
  1946-54   959.704 1
  1961-75   959.704 3

Inductive
mathematics 511.2
  s.a. spec. branches; also
    spec. appls. e.g.
    Probabilities
methods
  geophysical prospecting 662.154
  s.a. other spec. operations
reasoning
  psychology 153.432
    animals 156.343 2
    children 155.413
  s.a. psych. of other spec.
    groups
Inductors
radio
  engineering 621.384 133
  s.a. spec. appls. e.g.
    Radiotelephony
  other aspects see Radio
television
  engineering 621.388 33
  s.a. spec. appls. e.g.
    Astronautics
  other aspects see
    Television
Indulgences
Christian rites 265.66
Indus River *area*–549 1
Industrial
accidents
  insurance 368.41
  misc. aspects see
    Insurance
  pub. health *see* Industrial
    safety
  statistics 312.43
    deaths 312.273
advertising 659.131 5
air-conditioning bldgs. 697.931 6
  s.a. spec. types of bldgs.
archaeology 609
  s.a. spec. subj. e.g.
    Metallurgy
areas
  civic art 711.552 4
  sociology 307.3
art & design 745.2
arts 600
  high schools 373.246 7
  govt. supervision & support 379
banks
  economics 332.37
  other aspects see Credit
    institutions; *also*
    Banks (finance)
biochemistry 660.63
  s.a. spec. prod.
biology 660.6
  s.a. spec. prod
botany 581.64

Industrial (continued)
buildings
  architecture 725.4
  building 690.54
  sanitation *see* Industrial
    sanitation
  other aspects see Public
    structures
casualty insurance 368.7
  misc. aspects see Insurance
chemicals
  manufacturing
    chem. tech. 661
    soc. & econ. aspects *see*
      Secondary industries
  s.a. spec. prod.
chemistry 660
chemists
  biog. & work 661.009 2
  s.a. *pers.*–661
cities
  planning
    arts 711.45
  other aspects see Cities
conditions econ. 338.09
conflicts
  labor econ. 331.8
  s.a. spec. classes of
    workers e.g. Women
  labor law *see* Labor law
  sociology 306.3
credit
  economics 332.742
  other aspects see Credit
democracy
  labor theory 331.011 2
  unions 331.880 1
design 745.2
diamonds *see* Abrasive
  materials
diseases 616.980 3
  geriatrics 618.976 980 3
  pediatrics 618.929 803
  statistics 312.398 93
    deaths 312.269 803
  other aspects see Diseases
  s.a. spec. diseases
disputes *see* Industrial
  conflicts
drawing 604.24
  spec. subj. *s.s.*–022 1
economics 338
education *see* Vocational
  education
engineering 658.5
espionage 658.472
  ethics *see* Business ethics
law 343.072
  spec. jur. 343.3–.9

524

Industrial (continued)
  sabotage
    criminology   364.164
    law   345.026 4
      spec. jur.   345.3–.9
    soc. theology
      Christianity   261.833 164
      comp. rel.   291.178 331 64
      s.a. other spec. rel.
  safety
    law   344.046 5
      spec. jur.   344.3–.9
    pub. meas.   363.11
      govt. control *see* Safety
        pub. admin.
  sanitation
    engineering
      soc. & econ. aspects *see*
         Secondary industries
      technology   628.5
      s.a. spec. appls. e.g.
        Internal-combustion
        engines
    law   344.046 4
      spec. jur.   344.3–.9
    pub. admin.   350.772
      central govts.   351.772
        spec. jur.   353–354
      local govts.   352.6
    soc. aspects   363.729 5
  schools
    penology   365.42
    misc. aspects see Penal
      institutions
    secondary ed.   373.246 7
  spectroscopy *see* Applied
    spectroscopy
  stoichiometry   660.7
  s.a. spec. prod.
  surveys econ.   338.09
  toxicology   615.902
    misc. aspects see
      Toxicology
  unions
    labor econ.   331.883 3
    labor law *see* Labor law
  waste
    pollution water-supply eng.
      technology   628.168 3
      other aspects see Water
        supply engineering
    sanitary eng.
      soc. & econ. aspects *see*
        Secondary industries
      technology   628.54
      s.a. spec. appls. e.g.
        Wastes technology
  wastes
    disposal *see* Wastes control
  workers *see* Industrial
    occupations

Industrial (continued)
  s.a. other spec. subj.
Industrial-military complex
  mil. sci.   355.021 3
Industry
  & state pol. sci.   322.3
  application programs *see*
    Software programming
  art representation   704.949 6
    painting   758.6
    s.a. other spec. art forms
  as revenue source
    pub. finance   336.19
  govt. control & reg.
    law   343.07
      spec. jur.   343.3–.9
    pub. admin.
      activities   350.823–.824
      central govts.   351.823–.824
        spec. jur.   353–354
      local govts.   352.942 3–.942 4
    departments *see* Executive
      departments
  location
    prod. econ. *see* Location
      industries prod. econ.
  taxes on *see* Business taxes
  s.a. Public industry
Inequalities
  algebra   512.97
    s.a. spec. topics of
      algebra; also spec.
      appls. e.g.
      Engineering
  calculus   515.26
    complex variables   515.926
    real variables   515.826
    s.a. other spec. functions &
      equations; also spec.
      appls. e.g.
      Engineering
  geometry   516.17
    Euclidean   516.217
    s.a. other spec. geometries;
      also spec. appls. e.g.
      Engineering
Inequality
  time chronology   529.1
  s.a. other spec. subj.
Inert gases *see* Rare gases
Inertia
  moments
    aeronautical aerodynamics   629.132 364
    s.a. spec. appls. e.g.
      Flying
  statics *see* Statics
Infallibility
  Christian church   262.72
  God
    rel. doctrines
      Christianity   231.6

Dewey Decimal Classification

Influence (continued)
social
  control 303.34
  interaction 302
s.a. *s.s.*–013
Influenzas
  gen. med. 616.203
  geriatrics 618.976 203
  pediatrics 618.922 03
  pub. health 614.518
  statistics 312.320 3
  deaths 312.262 03
  other aspects see Diseases
Informal *see spec. subj.*
Information
analysis
  pub. admin. 350.007 22
    central govts. 351.007 22
      spec. jur. 353–354
    local govts. 352.000 472 2
control *see* Censorship
exchanges
  internat. law 341.767 2
freedom of
  civil right
    pol. sci. 323.445
management
  executive management 658.403 8
  office services 651
  prod. management 658.503 6
  spec. subj. *s.s.*–068 5
organizations *see* Libraries
problem solving
  pub. admin. 350.007 22
    central govts. 351.007 22
      spec. jur. 353–354
    local govts. 352.000 472 2
right to *see* Freedom of
    information
science 020
scientists
  biog. & work 020.92
  occupational ethics 174.909 2
  s.a. *pers.*–092
security
  management 658.472
services
  library econ. 025.52
  pub. admin.
    activities 350.819
      central govts. 351.819
        spec. jur. 353–354
      local govts. 352.941 9
    govt. depts. *see*
      Executive departments
sociology 302.24
sources
  library sci. 028.7
  management 658.403 8
specialists
  biog. & work 020.92

Information
specialists (continued)
  s.a. *pers.*–092
storage & retrieval systems 025.04
  law 343.099 9
    spec. jur. 343.3–.9
protection from misuse
  civil right
    pol. sci. 323.448 3
theory cybernetics 001.539
use
  pers. admin. *see* Personnel
    policy & planning
Informational
programs
  management use 658.455
role
  libraries 021.28
Informers
criminal investigation *see*
  Evidence procurement
Infrared
analysis
  anal. chem.
    gen. wks. 543.085 83
      qualitative 544.63
      quantitative 545.833
    organic 547.308 583
      qualitative 547.346 3
      quantitative 547.358 33
  s.a. spec. elements &
    cpds.
photography
  eng. appls.
    soc. & econ. aspects *see*
      Secondary industries
    technology 621.367 2
    s.a. spec. appls. e.g.
      Cartography
  technique 778.34
radiations
  astrophysics 523.015 012
    spectroscopy 523.015 842
  biophysics
    extraterrestrial
      gen. wks. 574.191 952
      animals 591.191 952
      microorganisms 576.119 195 2
      plants 581.191 952
      s.a. spec. organisms
      med. sci. 612.014 552
      animals 636.089 201 455 2
        s.a. spec. animals
      man 612.014 552
    terrestrial
      gen. wks. 574.191 52
      animals 591.191 52
      microorganisms 576.119 152
      plants 581.191 52
      s.a. spec. organisms

Infrared
  radiations
    biophysics
      terrestrial (continued)
        med. sci.   612.014 482
          animals   636.089 201 448 2
            s.a. spec. animals
          man   612.014 482
        s.a. spec. functions,
          systems, organs
    chemistry   541.353 2
    engineering *see* Infrared
      technology
    physics   535.012
      spectroscopy   535.842
    therapeutic use   615.832 2
      misc. aspects see
        Physical therapies
      s.a. spec. diseases
    other aspects see Spectral
      regions radiations
  spectroscopes
    mf. tech.   681.414 2
      components   681.42–.43
    other aspects see Optical
      instruments
  spectroscopy
    astrophysics   523.015 842
      s.a. spec. celestial
        bodies
    engineering
      soc. & econ. aspects *see*
        Secondary industries
      technology   621.361 2
        s.a. spec. appls. e.g.
          Materials engineering
    physics   535.842
      spec. states of matter   530.4
    other aspects see
      Spectroscopy
    technology   621.362
    mil. eng.   623.042
    s.a. other spec. appls.
Infusions
  prac. pharm.   615.42
    misc. aspects see
      Pharmacology
Infusoria *see* Ciliata
Ingestion
  pathology
    gen. wks.   574.213 2
      animals   591.213 2
      plants   581.213 2
      s.a. spec. organisms
    med. sci.   616.3
      animals   636.089 63
      s.a. spec. animals
    man   616.3
  physiology
    gen. wks.   574.132
      animals   591.132

Ingestion
  physiology
    gen. wks. (continued)
      microorganisms   576.113 2
      plants   581.132
      s.a. spec. organisms
    med. sci.   612.31
      human phys.   612.31
      vet. phys.   636.089 231
      s.a. spec. animals
    other aspects see Digestion
Ingham
  Co. Mich.   *area*–774 26
  Queensland   *area*–943 6
Inglenooks
  furniture arts   749.62
Inglewood
  Cumbria Eng.   *area*–427 86
  Queensland   *area*–943 3
  Victoria   *area*–945 4
Ingolfiellidea *see* Amphipoda
Ingot iron
  technology   669.142 3
  other aspects see Ferrous
    metals
Ingush *see* Caucasic
Inhalation
  anesthesia *see* General
    anesthesia
  physiology
    human phys.   612.21
    other aspects see
      Respiration
Inhalatory
  medication therapeutics   615.64
    misc. aspects see
      Medication methods
    s.a. spec. diseases
  therapy   615.836
    misc. aspects see Physical
      therapies
    s.a. spec. diseases
Inhambane Mozambique   *area*–679 3
Inheritance
  evolution theory   575.016 6
  law   346.05
    spec. jur.   346.3–.9
  taxes
    law   343.053 2
      spec. jur.   343.3–.9
    pub. admin.   350.724 76
      central govts.   351.724 76
      spec. jur.   353–354
      local govts.   352.135
    pub. finance   336.276
Inherited
  diseases
    med. sci.   616.042
    other aspects see Diseases

Inherited (continued)
  sin
    rel. doctrines
      Christianity   233.14
      other rel. see Humankind
        rel. doctrines
In-house training *see* Job
    training
Inini Guyane   *area*–882 4
Iniomi *see* Mesichthyes
Inishmore Ireland   *area*–417 48
Initials *see* Lettering
Initial-value problems *see*
    Boundary-value problems
Initiation
  popular psych.   135.4
  soc. customs   392.14
Initiative
  pol. sci.   328.2
  psychology
    personality trait   155.232
    volition *see* Volition
Injection
  diesel engines   621.436 1
    land vehicles   629.250 61
    marine vehicles   623.872 361
    s.a. other spec. appls.
  internal-combustion engines
    automobiles *see* Fuel
      systems internal
      combustion engines
      automobiles
  s.a. other spec. uses
Injections
  immunization *see* Immunization
  therapeutics *see* Parenteral
    medication
Injectors (pumps) *see* Jet pumps
Injunctions
  labor econ.
    labor meas.   331.893
    management meas.   331.894
  labor law *see* Labor law
  other aspects see Remedies
    law
Injuries
  first aid *see* First aid
  law *see* Personal injury law
  of eyes
    statistics   312.304 771 3
    deaths   312.260 477 13
  surgery   617.1
    anesthesiology   617.967 1
    s.a. Veterinary sciences
  surgery
    gen. wks.   617.1
    anesthesiology   617.967 1
    s.a. Veterinary sciences
  s.a. Diseases; *also other*
    spec. parts of body

Injurious organisms *see*
    Deleterious organisms
Ink
  drawing   741.26
    indiv. artists   741.092
    spec. appls.   741.5–.7
    spec. subj.   743.4–.8
  painting   751.425
    indiv. artists   759.1–.9
Inks
  manufacturing
    soc. & econ. aspects *see*
      Secondary industries
    technology   667.4
Inland
  marine insurance   368.23
    misc. aspects see Insurance
  seas
    internat. law   341.444
    other aspects see Special
      salt-water forms
  waters
    hydrology
      fresh   551.48
      salt   551.460 9
    s.a. spec. bodies of water
  waterways
    hydraulic eng.
      soc. & econ. aspects *see*
        Secondary industries
      technology   627.1
      s.a. spec. appls. e.g.
        Military engineering
    other aspects see Liquids
      engineering
Inland-waterway transp.
  commerce   386
  govt. control   351.876
    spec. jur.   353–354
  law
    international   341.756 64
    municipal   343.096 4
      spec. jur.   343.3–.9
  personnel
    biog. & work.   386.092
    s.a. spec. kinds of
      transp.
  s.a.   *pers.*–386
  other aspects see
    Transportation
Inlay trim
  furniture arts   749.5
  wood handicrafts   745.51
Inlays
  dentistry   617.675
  wood bldg. construction   694.6
Inlets
  sewers   628.25
  s.a. spec. appls. e.g.
    Water drainage
  s.a. other spec. occurrences

Inscriptions (continued)

on stone dec. arts	736.5
paleography *see* Paleography	
prints	769.5

Insect

culturists	*pers.*–638
waxes	
comm. proc.	665.13
other aspects see waxes	

Insecta

agric. pests	623.7
s.a. spec. types of culture	
e.g. Forestry; *also*	
spec. crops	
conservation tech.	639.975 7
control	
agricultural *see* Insecta	
agric. pests	
home econ.	648.7
sanitary eng.	628.965 7
culture	
soc. & econ. aspects *see*	
Primary industries	
technology	638
other aspects see	
Agriculture	
disease carriers	
pub. health	614.432
misc. aspects see Public	
health	
drawing tech.	743.657
food	641.396
cookery	641.696
meats preservation	641.495
commercial	664.95
domestic	641.495
paleozoology	565.7
zoology	595.7
other aspects see Animals	

Insecticide-producing plants

agriculture	633.898
soc. & econ. aspects *see*	
Primary industries	

Insecticides

production	
soc. & econ. aspects *see*	
Secondary industries	
technoloqy	668.651
use	
agriculture	632.951
effect on prod. econ.	338.162
s.a. spec. crops; also	
spec. types of culture	
e.g. Floriculture	
s.a. other spec. uses	

Insectivora

agric. pests	632.693 3
s.a. spec. types of culture	
e.g. Forestry; *also*	
spec. crops	

Insectivora (continued)

animal husbandry	
soc. & econ. aspects *see*	
Primary industries	
technology	636.933
conservation tech.	639.979 33
drawing tech.	743.693 3
hunting	
commercial	
soc. & econ. aspects *see*	
Primary industries	
technology	639.113 3
sports	799.259 33
paleozoology	569.33
zoology	599.33
other aspects see Animals	

Insects *see* Insecta

Insecurity

mental pub. health	614.582 2
other aspects see Mental	
illness	

Insemination

artificial *see* Artificial	
insemination	
biological *see* Reproduction	

In-service training

labor econ.	331.259 2
s.a. spec. classes of labor	
e.g. Women	
libraries	023.8
museums	069.63
s.a. spec. activities e.g.	
Selection	
personnel admin. *see* Job	
training	

Insignia

armed forces	
gen. wks.	
honorary	355.134 2
identifying	355.14
s.a. spec. mil. branches	
genealogy	929
rel. significance	
Christianity	246.56
other rel. see Arts rel.	
significance	

Insolation *see* Solar radiation

Insoluble soaps

manufacturing	
chem. tech.	668.125
soc. & econ. aspects *see*	
Secondary industries	

Insolvency *see* Bankruptcy

Insomnia

symptomatology	
neurological diseases	616.849
vet. sci.	636.089 684 9
s.a. spec. animals	

Inspection

automobile eng.	629.282 5

Insulators
  elect. circuits
    electrodynamic eng. (continued)
      tech. & mf. ... 621.319 37
      s.a. spec. appls. e.g.
        Overhead lines
      other aspects see
        Electrodynamics
Insulin
  org. chem. ... 547.734 5
  pharmacology ... 615.365
  physiology
    human phys. ... 612.34
    other aspects see Digestion
  shock therapy *see* Shock
    (convulsions)
  other aspects see Drugs;
    also Hormones
Insurance ... 368
  accounting ... 657.73
    s.a. Insurance companies
      accounting
  companies
    accounting ... 657.836
    investment in
      financial econ. ... 332.671 2
      domestic ... 332.672 2
      other aspects see
        Investments
    loan functions econ. ... 332.38
      misc. aspects see Credit
        institutions
  pub. admin.
    activities ... 351.825 5
    spec. jur. ... 353–354
    govt. depts. *see*
      Executive departments
  financial management ... 658.153
    spec. subj. ... *s.s.*–068 1
  law ... 346.086
    spec. jur. ... 346.3–.9
  personnel
    biog. & work ... 368.009 2
    s.a. ... *pers.*–368
  proceeds
    taxation
      law ... 343.052 4
      spec. jur. ... 343.3–.9
      other aspects see Income
        taxes
  programs labor econ. *see*
    Fringe benefits
  wage & salary admin. ... 658.325 4
    misc. aspects see Employee
      benefits
  s.a. spec. kinds e.g. Life
    insurance
Insured mail
  postal commun. ... 383.182
  other aspects see Postal
    communication

Insurgent warfare
  mil. sci. ... 355.021 84
Insurrections *see* Revolutions;
    also Revolutionary
Intaglio printing
  graphic arts
    processes ... 765–767
    products ... 769
Intaglios
  glyptics ... 736.223
    spec. materials ... 736.23–.28
  rel. significance
    Christianity ... 247.862 23
      spec. materials ... 247.862 3–.862 8
    comp. rel. ... 291.37
    s.a. other spec. rel.
Intake pipes plumbing ... 696.12
Intakes
  water-supply eng.
    technology ... 628.142
    other aspects see Water
      supply engineering
  s.a. other spec. appls.
Intangible
  property
    law ... 346.048
      spec. jur. ... 346.3–.9
    taxes *see* Personal property
      taxes
    risks insurance ... 368.063
Integer programming
  mathematics ... 519.77
    s.a. spec. appls. e.g.
      Engineering
Integers
  number theory
    algebra ... 512.72
    s.a. spec. appls. e.g.
      Engineering
Integral
  calculus ... 515.43
    s.a. spec. appls. e.g.
      Engineering
  domains
    algebra ... 512.4
    s.a. spec. appls. e.g.
      Engineering
  equations ... 514.45
    s.a. spec. appls. e.g.
      Engineering
  geometry ... 516.362
    s.a. spec. appls. e.g.
      Engineering
  inequalities ... 515.46
    s.a. spec. appls. e.g.
      Engineering
  operators ... 515.723
    s.a. spec. appls. e.g.
      Engineering
  transforms *see*
    Transformations

Integrated
  circuits
    microelectronics *see*
      Circuits
      microelectronics
    day school schedule — 371.242
      s.a. spec. levels of ed.;
        also Special education
  optics
    engineering
      soc. & econ. aspects *see*
        Secondary industries
      technology — 621.369 3
        s.a. spec. appls. e.g.
          Cartography
Integration
  calculus — 515.43
    s.a. spec. appls. e.g.
      Engineering
  ed. soc. — 370.193 42
  theory
    calculus — 515.42
      s.a. spec. appls. e.g.
        Eulerian integrals
Integro-differential equations — 515.38
  s.a. spec. appls. e.g.
    Engineering
Integument
  anatomy
    human — 611.77
    other aspects see
      Integumentary organs
  diseases
    gen. wks. — 616.5
      neoplasms — 616.992 77
      tuberculosis — 619.995 77
    geriatrics — 618.976 5
    pediatrics — 618.925
    pub. health — 614.595
    statistics — 312.35
      deaths — 312.265
    surgery — 617.47
      anesthesiology — 617.967 47
    other aspects see Diseases
  pathology
    med. sci. *see* Integument
      diseases
    other aspects see
      Integumentary organs
  physical anthropometry — 573.677
  physiology
    gen. wks. — 591.185 8
      s.a. spec. animals
    med. sci. — 612.79
      animals — 636.089 279
        s.a. spec. animals
      man — 612.79
  tissue biology human — 611.018 977

Integumentary
  organs
    anatomy
      gen. wks. — 574.47
      animals — 591.47
      microorganisms — 576.14
      plants — 581.47
        s.a. spec. organisms
      med. sci. — 611.77
      animals — 636.089 177
        s.a. spec. animals
      man — 611.77
    pathology
      gen. wks. — 574.227
      animals — 591.227
      plants — 581.227
        s.a. spec. organisms
      med. sci. *see* Movements
    s.a. Integument
  system
    drugs affecting
      pharmacodynamics — 615.77
      other aspects see Drugs
Intellectual
  cooperation — 001.14
  development
    soc. theology *see* Religious
      attitudes secular
      disciplines
  disorders *see* Mental
    deficiency
  freedom
    civil right
      pol. sci. — 323.44
  guidance — 371.422
    s.a. spec. levels of ed.;
      also Special education
  life — 001.1
  processes
    psychology — 153
    animals — 156.3
    children — 155.413
      s.a. psych. of other spec.
        groups
Intellectualism
  philosophy *see* Rationalism
    philosophy
Intellectuals
  customs — 390.5
  dress — 391.05
  homes — 392.360 5
  other aspects see Middle
    classes
Intelligence (information)
  services
    armed forces — 355.343 2
      s.a. spec. mil. branches
    spec. wars *see* Unconventional
      warfare
    topography mil. eng. — 623.71

Intercontinental ballistic
   missiles
  mil. eng.
    soc. & econ. aspects *see*
     Secondary industries
    tech. & mf.   623.451 954
Intercultural
  education   370.196
Interdenominational
  cooperation
   Christianity   262.001
   comp. rel.   291.65
   s.a. other spec. rel.
  societies
   Christianity
    adults   267.13
    men   267.23
    women   267.43
    young adults   267.61
   other rel. see Religious
    associations
Interdependence
  prod. econ.   338.9
Interest (income)
  economic   332.82
   distribution   339.21
  rates control
   central banking   332.113
   misc. aspects see
    Banking
  govt. control   351.825
   spec. jur.   353–354
  law   346.073
   spec. jur.   346.3–.9
  taxes
   law   343.052 46
    spec. jur.   343.3–.9
   pub. admin. *see* Income
    taxes pub. admin.
   pub. finance   336.242 6
   corporations   336.243
Interest (psychology)
  learning   153.153 3
   animals   156.315 33
   children   155.413
   s.a. psych. of other spec.
    groups
  teaching approach   371.102 8
   s.a. spec. levels of ed.;
    also Special education
Interests (pressure groups) *see*
  Pressure groups
Interfacial tensions *see*
  Surface phenomena
Interference
  light
   astrophysics   523.015 4
   s.a. spec. celestial
    bodies
   physics   535.4
    spec. states of matter 530.4

Interference (continued)
  microwave electronics
   technology   621.381 31
   s.a. spec. appls. e.g.
    Radar engineering
   other aspects see Microwave
    electronics
  radio waves *see* Waves
   propagation radio
  sound *see* Synthesis sound
  television waves *see* Wave
   propagation television
Interference-eliminators
  electronic circuits
   tech. & mf.   621.381 532
    microelectronics   621.381 732
    microwave electronics 621.381 322
    radiowave electronics 621.381 532
    x- & gamma-ray
     electronics   621.381 6
   s.a. spec. appls. e.g.
    Radiocontrol
   other aspects see Microwave
    electronics; Radiowave
    electronics; X-ray
    electronics
  radio
   engineering   621.384 133
   s.a. spec. appls. e.g.
    Radiotelephony
   other aspects see Radio
  television
   engineering   621.388 33
   s.a. spec. appls. e.g.
    Astronautics
   other aspects see
    Television
Interference-signals
  commun. eng.
   technology   621.380 436
   s.a. spec. appls. e.g.
    Space communication
   other aspects see
    Communication
Interferometers
  optics *see* Interference light
Interferometric analysis
  anal. chem.
   gen. wks.   543.085 3
    qualitative   544.953
    quantitative   545.813
   organic   547.308 53
    qualitative   547.349 53
    quantitative   547.358 13
   s.a. spec. elements & cpds.
Interferons
  virology *see* Viruses
   microbiology
Intergovernmental
  administration   351.09
   U.S. govts.   353.929

Intermediate
state
rel. doctrines (continued)
other rel. see
Eschatology
s.a. other spec. subj.
Interment *see* Burial
Intermetallic compounds
metallurgy 669.94
s.a. spec. metals
Intermittent-combustion turbine
engines *see* Simple
gas-turbine engines
Intermolecular
forces
theoretical chem. 541.226
organic 547.122 6
s.a. spec. elements &
cpds.
physics *see* Molecular physics
Intermunicipal authorities
local govt. 352.009 5
Internal
administration
pub. admin. 350.71
central govts. 351.71
spec. jur. 353–354
local govts. 352.16
auditing 657.458
s.a. spec. kinds of
enterprise e.g.
Insurance accounting
commerce *see* Domestic
commerce
communication
office services 651.79
constitution
celestial bodies *see*
Physical constitution
s.a. other spec. subj.
criticism *see* Literary
criticism
ear
diseases
gen. wks. 617.882
neoplasms 616.992 85
tuberculosis 616.995 85
geriatrics 618.977 882
pediatrics 618.920 978 82
pub. health 614.599 8
statistics 312.304 788 2
deaths 312.260 478 82
surgery 617.880 59
anesthesiology 617.967 882
other aspects see
Diseases
physiology
human 613.858
other aspects see Sensory
functions
other aspects see Ears

Internal (continued)
medicine 616
misc. aspects see Diseases
s.a. spec. diseases
migration
soc. theology
Christianity 261.836 82
comp. rel. 291.178 368 2
s.a. other spec. rel.
sociology 304.82
transportation
materials management 658.781
spec. subj. *s.s.*–068 7
s.a. other spec. subj.
Internal-combustion
engines
automobiles
soc. & econ. aspects *see*
Secondary industries
tech. & mf. 629.250 3–.250 6
parts & systems 629.252–.258
gen. wks.
soc. & econ. aspects *see*
Secondary industries
tech. & mf. 621.43
shipbuilding
soc. & econ. aspects *see*
Secondary industries
tech. & mf. 623.872 3
design 623.814 723
spec. craft 623.812
s.a. other spec. uses; also
spec. kinds e.g.
High-compression-
ignition engines
propulsion
soc. & econ. aspects *see*
Secondary industries
technology 621.43
s.a. spec. appls. e.g.
Gas-turbine locomotives
Internal-combustion-engine
powered generation
electrodynamic eng.
soc. & econ. aspects *see*
Secondary industries
technology 621.312 133
s.a. spec. appls. e.g.
Diesel-electric
locomotives
other aspects see
Electrodynamics
International
affairs *see* International
relations
armed forces
internat. law
role in mutual security 341.72
role in settlement of
conflicts 341.58

International
organizations (continued)
  private
    soc. services — 361.77
    spec. problems & groups 362–263
    other aspects see
      Welfare services
  prod. econ. — 338.88
  pub. relations — 659.289
  publications
    bibliographies — 011.52
    spec. kinds — 012–106
    catalogs
      general — 017–019
      spec. kinds — 012–016
    s.a. spec. forms e.g.
      Books
  role in peaceful settlement
    of conflicts
    internat. law — 341.523
    spec. subj. — *s.s.*–060 1
    other aspects see
      Organizations
  personality
    internat. law — 341.2
  persons
    internat. law — 341.2
  planning
    civic art — 711.2
    soc. services — 361.26
  politics
    history — 900
    pol. sci. *see* Foreign
      policy pol. sci.
  postal conventions
    internat. law — 341.757 3
    postal commun. — 383.41
  Red Cross *see* Red Cross
  relations
    ethics
      philosophy — 172.4
      religion
        Buddhism — 294.356 24
        Christianity — 241.624
        comp. rel. — 291.562 4
        Hinduism — 294.548 624
      s.a. other spec. rel.
    law
      constitutional — 342.041 2
      spec. jur. — 342.3–.9
      international — 341.3
    pol. sci. — 327
    soc. theology
      Buddhism — 294.337 87
      Christianity — 261.87
      comp. rel. — 291.178 7
      Hinduism — 294.517 87
      Islam — 297.197 87
      Judaism — 296.387 87
      s.a. other spec. rel.

International (continued)
  routes
    transp. services *see* Routes
      transp. services
  security forces *see*
    International armed
    forces
  settlements
    internat. banking — 332.155
    misc. aspects see Bankinq
    soc. services — 361.26
    spec. problems & groups — 362–363
    other aspects see Welfare
      services
  studies
    curriculums — 375.008 2
    s.a. spec. levels of ed.;
      also Special education
  style
    architecture — 724.91
    spec. places — 720.9
    other aspects see
      Architectural schools
  subsidiaries *see*
    International
    organizations
  trade *see* International
    commerce
  unions labor econ. — 331.880 91
  warfare mil. sci. — 335.021 82
  s.a. other spec. subj.; also
    Foreign
Internationalized rivers
  internat. law — 341.442
Internment
  camps
    World War 1 hist. — 940.472
    World War 2 hist. — 940.472 2
    s.a. hist. of other spec.
      wars
  status
    armed forces — 355.113
    s.a. spec. mil. branches
Internship *see* Training
Interoccupational mobility — 331.127 2
  law *see* Labor law
  s.a. spec. classes of workers
    e.g. Women
Interoceanic canals
  transportation
    commerce — 386.42
    govt. control — 351.876 42
    spec. jur. — 353–354
    law *see* Inland-waterway
      transp.
Interparliamentary unions
  pol. sci. — 328.306 01
Interpersonal relations
  appl. psych. — 158.2
  children — 155.418

Interpersonal relations
  appl. psych. (continued)
    s.a. psych. of other spec.
      groups; also spec.
      activities
  employees
    personnel admin.
      gen. management   658.314 5
      executive   658.407 145
      spec. subj.   *s.s.*–068 3
      pub. admin.   350.147
      central govts.   351.147
      spec. jur.   353–354
      local govts.   352.005 147
Interphone systems
  wire telephony *see* Telephony
    wire
Interplanetary flights *see*
      Planetary manned
      flights; *also*
      Planetary unmanned
      probes
Interpolation
  mathematics   511.42
    s.a. spec. math. branches;
      also spec. appls. e.g.
      Engineering
Interpretation
  archaeological tech.   930.102 85
  epistemology   121.68
  journalism   070.442
    spec. subj.   070.449
  linguistics *see* Translation
      (linguistics)
  music theory   781.63
    s.a. spec. mediums
  of tongues
    Christian doctrines   234.13
  sacred books *see* Exegesis
  treaties *see* Treaties
  s.a. other spec. subj.
Interpreters
  religion *see* Clergy; *also*
      Theologians
Interpretive dancing
  performing arts   793.32
Interprovincial *see* Interstate
Interregional
  commerce   381.5
    misc. aspects see Commerce
  other aspects see Internal
Interreligious
  relations
    Buddhims   294.337 2
    Christianity   261.2
    comp. rel.   291.172
    Hinduism   294.517 2
    Islam   297.197 2
    Judaism   296.387 2
    s.a. other spec. rel.

Interrogation
  criminal investigation
    law   345.052
      spec. jur.   345.3–.9
    other aspects see Witnesses
Intersections (mathematics)
  algebraic geometry   516.35
    s.a. spec. appls. e.g.
      Engineering
Intersections (roads & streets)
  commerce   388.13
    local   388.411
  law *see* Roads law; *also*
      Streets law
  other aspects see Roads
Interstate
  agreements *see* Interstate
      relations
  commerce   381.5
    misc. aspects see Commerce
  cooperation *see* Interstate
      relations
  disputes *see* Interstate
      relations
  migration *see* Internal
      migration
  planning
    civic art   711.3
    economics   338.9
    soc. sci. *see* Planning soc.
      welfare
  relations
    constitutional law   342.042
      spec. jur.   342.3–.9
    pub. admin.   351.091
      U.S. govts.   353.929 1
      other spec. jur.   354
  rendition
    criminal law   345.052
      spec. jur.   345.3–.9
Interstellar matter
  astronomy
    extragalactic *see* Galaxies
    galaxies *see* Galaxies
    Milky Way
      description   523.113 5
      theory   521.582
    other aspects see Celestial
      bodies
Interstitial nerve tissue
  human anatomy & phys.   611.018 8
  other aspects see Tissue
      bioloqy
Intertestamental works
  Bible *see* Apocrypha
Interurban
  railways
    technology   625.6
      misc. aspects see
      Railroads

Interurban
  railways (continued)
    other aspects see
      Special-purpose
      railroads
Intervals (music)   781.22
  s.a. spec. mediums
Intervention
  internat. law   341.58
Interventionism econ.   330.126
Interviewing
  appl. psych.   158.3
  children   155.418
  s.a. psych. of other spec.
    groups
  employee selection
    gen. management   658.311 24
    executives   658.407 112 4
    spec. subj.   *s.s.*–068 3
    pub. admin.   350.132 5
    central govts.   351.132 5
    spec. jur.   353–354
    local govts.   352.005 132 5
  marketing management   658.830 28
    spec. subj.   *s.s.*–068 8
  social work   361.322
    spec. problems & groups   362–363
    other aspects see Welfare
      services
  s.a. other spec. activities
Interviews *see* Anthologies
Intestate succession *see*
    Succession
Intestinal
  obstructions
    gen. med.   616.342
    geriatrics   618.976 342
    pediatrics   618.923 42
    pub. health   614.593 42
    statistics   312.334 2
    deaths   312.263 42
    other aspects see Diseases
  secretions
    human phys.   612.33
    other aspects see Digestion
Intestines
  anatomy
    human   611.34
    other aspects see Nutritive
      organs
  diseases
    gen. wks.   616.34
    neoplasms   616.992 34
    tuberculosis   616.995 34
    geriatrics   618.976 34
    pediatrics   618.923 4
    pub. health   614.593 4
    statistics   312.334
    deaths   312.263 4
    surgery   617.554
    anesthesiology   617.967 554

Intestines
  diseases (continued)
    other aspects see Diseases
  physical anthropometry   573.634
  physiology
    human   612.23
    other aspects see Nutrition
  tissue biology human   611.018 934
Intibucá Honduras   *area*–728 381
Intonation
  linguistics   414
  spec. langs.
    nonstandard forms
      lang. sub.–7
    standard forms   *lang. sub.*–16
  music   781.22
  s.a. spec. mediums
Intoxications
  abnormal psych.   157.6
  s.a. spec. kinds e.g.
    Metallic intoxication
Intra-arterial injections *see*
    Parenteral medication
Intra-atomic physics *see* Atomic
    physics
Intracoastal routes *see*
    Coastwise routes
Intradermal injections *see*
    Parenteral medication
Intramolecular physics *see*
    Molecular physics
Intramuscular injections *see*
    Parenteral medication
Intranuclear physics *see*
    Nuclear physics
Intraocular lenses
  optometry   617.752 4
Intravenous
  anesthesia *see* General
    anesthesia
  injections *see* Parenteral
    medication
Intrinsic
  differential geometry   516.363
    s.a. spec. appls. e.g.
      Engineering
  variable stars
    astronomy
      description   523.844 2
      theory   521.584 42
    other aspects see Celestial
      bodies
Introit *see* Proper of the Mass
Intrusions (geology)
  structural geol.   551.88
  s.a. spec. aspects e.g.
    Prospecting
Intuition
  epistemology   121.3
  ethical systems   171.2
    applications   172–179

Investigative powers
  legislative bodies (continued)
    pol. sci. — 328.345 2
    spec. jur. — 328.4–.9
Investiture
  clergy *see* Ordination
Investment
  banking
    financial econ. — 332.66
    govt. control *see*
        Securities govt.
        control
    law — 346.066 2
    spec. jur. — 346.3–.9
  capital *see* Fixed capital
  company securities
    financial econ. — 332.632 7
    govt. control *see*
        Securities govt.
        control
    law — 346.092 2
    spec. jur. — 346.3–.9
  counselors
    financial econ. *see*
        Brokerage firms
  financial econ. — 332.6
  guarantees — 368.853
    misc. aspects see Insurance
  guides econ. — 332.678
  macroeconomics — 339.43
  manuals — 332.678
  operations
    capital formation — 332.041 5
  prod. econ. *see* Finance prod.
        econ.
  trusts
    financial econ. *see*
        Investment company
        securities
Investment (foundry practice)
  casting *see* Precision casting
Investments
  bank services
    economics — 332.175 4
    misc. aspects see Banking
  financial
    economics — 332.6
    management *see* Capital
        management financial
        management
    govt. control — 351.825 8
    spec. jur. — 353–354
  income taxation *see* Interest
        (income) taxes
  law
    international — 341.752
    municipal — 346.092
    spec. jur. — 346.3–.9
  pub. revenues
    economics — 336.15

Investments
  pub. revenues (continued)
    other aspects see Nontax
        revenues
Invisibility
  Christian church — 262.72
Invisible world *see* Spiritual
        beings
Invitations
  etiquette — 395.4
Involuntary
  movements
    psychology — 152.32
    animals — 156.232
    children — 155.412
    *s.a. psych. of other spec.
        groups*
  muscle tissues
    human anatomy & phys. — 611.018 6
    other aspects see Tissue
        biology
Involutes
  integral geometry — 516.362
    *s.a. spec. appls. e.g.
        Engineering*
Involution (mathematics) *see*
        Exponents
Involution (physiology) *see*
        Development (biology)
Involutional psychoses *see*
        Manic-depressive
        psychoses
Inyo Co. Calif. — *area*–794 87
Ioannina Greece — *area*–495 3
Iodates
  chem. tech. — 661.42
    other aspects see Industrial
        chemicals
Iodides
  chem. tech. — 661.42
    other aspects see Industrial
        chemicals
Iodine
  chemistry
    inorganic — 546.734
    organic — 547.02
    *s.a. spec. groupings e.g.
        Aliphatic compounds*
  technology — 661.073 4
    soc. & econ. aspects *see*
        Secondary industries
    s.a. spec. prod.
  pharmacology — 615.273 4
    misc. aspects see
        Pharmacology
  toxicology — 615.925 734
    misc. aspects see
        Toxicology
    other aspects see Halogen
Iodites
  chem. tech. — 661.42

Iowa
County
Iowa — *area*–777 653
Wisconsin — *area*–775 78
River Ia. — *area*–777 6
state — *area*–777
Ipomoea batatas *see* Sweet
    potatoes
Ipswich
Queensland — *area*–943 2
Suffolk Eng. — *area*–426 49
Iraklion Greece — *area*–499 8
Iran — *area*–55
ancient — *area*–35
Iranian
languages
linguistics — 491.5
literatures — 891.5
s.a. — *lang.*–915
people — *r.e.n.*–915
other aspects see Persian
s.a. Iran; *also other spec.*
    subj. e.g. Arts
Iraq — *area*–567
Iraqis — *r.e.n.*–927 567
Irasers
physics — 535.012
technology *see* Infrared
    technology
Irbid Jordan — *area*–569 54
Iredell Co. N.C. — *area*–756 793
Ireland — *area*–415
ancient — *area*–361 5
island — *area*–415
Republic — *area*–417
Irian Jaya — *area*–951
Iridaceae *see* Iridales
Iridales
botany — 584.24
floriculture — 635.934 24
med. aspects
crop prod. — 633.884 24
gen. pharm. — 615.324 24
toxicology — 615.952 424
vet. pharm. — 636.089 532 424
toxicology — 636.089 595 242 4
paleobotany — 561.4
other aspects see Plants
Iridescence
minerals *see* Optical
    properties minerals
s.a. other spec. subj.
Iridium
bldg. materials — 691.87
chemistry
inorganic — 546.643
organic — 547.056 43
    s.a. spec. groupings e.g.
      Aliphatic compounds
technology — 661.064 3
organic — 661.895

Iridium
chemistry
technology (continued)
soc. & econ. aspects *see*
    Secondary industries
s.a. spec. prod.
construction
building — 693.77
metallography — 669.957
metallurgy — 669.7
physical & chem. — 669.967
soc. & econ. aspects *see*
    Secondary industries
mineralogy — 549.23
s.a. spec. minerals
pharmacology — 615.264 3
misc. aspects see
    Pharmacology
products
mf. tech. — 673.7
other aspects see
    Nonferrous metals
    products
toxicology — 615.925 643
misc. aspects see
    Toxicology
other aspects see
    Platinum-group metals
Iringa Tanzania — *area*–678 25
Irion Co. Tex. — *area*–764 874
Iris family *see* Iridales
Irises
eyes *see* Uveas eyes
Irish
English literature — 820
Free state
history — 941.708 22
s.a. — *area*–417
Gaelic
languages
linguistics — 491.62
literature — 891.62
s.a. — *lang.*–916 2
people — *r.e.n.*–916 2
s.a. Ireland; *also other*
    spec. subj. e.g. Arts
people — *r.e.n.*–916 2
Sea *see* British western
    seawaters
Irkutsk RSFSR — *area*–575
Irlam Greater Manchester Eng.
    — *area*–427 32
Iron
Age archaeology — 930.16
alloys
technology — 669.141
other aspects see Ferrous
    metals
chemistry
inorganic — 546.621

Iron
  chemistry (continued)
    organic   547.056 21
      s.a. spec. groupings e.g.
        Aliphatic compounds
    technology   661.062 1
      organic   661.895
      soc. & econ. aspects *see*
        Secondary industries
      s.a. spec. prod.
  County
    Michigan   *area*–774 975
    Missouri   *area*–778 883
    Utah   *area*–792 47
    Wisconsin   *area*–775 22
  econ. geol.   553.3
  law
    wages econ. theory   331.210 1
      s.a. spec. classes of
        labor e.g. Women
  metabolism
    human phys.   612.392 4
    other aspects see
      Metabolism
  mineralogy   549.23
    s.a. spec. minerals
  mining
    technology   622.341
    prospecting   622.183
  Mts. Tenn.   *area*–768 984
  pharmacology   615.262 1
    misc. aspects see
      Pharmacology
  salts
    plant nutrition *see*
      Macronutrient elements
      plant nutrition
  soaps
    chem. tech.   668.125
      soc. & econ. aspects *see*
        Secondary industries
  toxicology   615.925 621
    misc. aspects see
      Toxicology
  other aspects see Ferrous
    metals
  s.a. spec. uses
Ironbridge Salop Eng.   *area*–424 56
Ironing
  home econ.   648.1
Ironmasters *see* Ferrous metals
    manufacturers
Ironweed *see* Asterales
Ironwork (blacksmithing)
  soc. & econ. aspects *see*
    Secondary industries
  technology   682.4
  s.a. Ferrous metals arts
Iroquois
  Co. Ill.   *area*–773 64

Iroquois (continued)
  lang. & people *see*
    Hokan-Siouan
Irradiation *see* Radiations
Irregular
  enclosures
    liquid flow mech.
      engineering *see* Dynamics
      physics   532.55
  routes
    marine transp. *see* Tramp
      routes maritime transp.
  sound
    engineering   620.23
      s.a. spec. appls. e.g.
        Pest control
    physics   543.35
      spec. states of matter 530.4
  street patterns
    civic art   711.41
    s.a. other spec. subj.
Irrelevance
  information theory   001.539
Irreligion
  rel. attitudes to
    Christianity   261.21
    other rel. see
      Interreligious
      relations
Irreversible reactions
  physical chem.   541.393
  applied   660.299 3
  organic   547.139 2
  s.a. spec. aspects e.g. Low
    temperatures
  s.a. spec. elements, cpds.,
    prod.
Irrigation
  agriculture   631.7
    s.a. spec. crops; also spec.
      types of culture e.g.
      Floriculture
  govt. control *see* Land
    resources govt. control
  land econ.   333.913
  land reclamation eng.
    soc. & econ. aspects *see*
      Secondary industries
    technology   627.52
      s.a. spec. appls. e.g.
        Rice (cereal)
        agriculture
    other aspects see Liquids
      engineering
  sewage effluent
    technology   628.362 3
    other aspects see Sewage
      disposal
  source of pollution
    water-supply eng.
      technology   628.168 41

Irrigation
  source of pollution
    water-supply eng. (continued)
      other aspects see Water
        supply engineering
Irrigation-farming
  crop prod.   631.587
    s.a. spec. crops; also spec.
      types of culture e.g.
      Floriculture
Irritability
  gen. wks.   591.182 7
    s.a. spec. animals
  med. sci.
    human
      nervous functions   612.816
      sensory functions   612.88
    veterinary
      nervous functions   636.089 281 6
      sensory functions   636.089 288
      s.a. spec. animals
  muscles
    human phys.   612.741
    other aspects see Movements
  skin
    human phys.   612.791
    other aspects see
      Integumentary organs
  other aspects see Nervous
    function
Irvine Strathclyde Scot.   *area*–414 61
Irvingiaceae *see* Malpighiales
Irwin Co. Ga.   *area*–758 855
Irymple Vic.   *area*–945 9
Isabela Philippines   *area*–599 1
Isabella
  Co. Mich.   *area*–774 51
  reign Spain hist.
    1   946.03
    2   946.07
    s.a. spec. events & subj.
      e.g. Commerce
Isagogics
  Bible   220.61
    s.a. spec. parts of Bible
  Hadith   297.124 061
    s.a. spec. Hadith
  Koran   297.122 61
    spec. parts   297.122 9
  Midrash   296.140 61
    s.a. spec. works
  Talmudic lit.   296.120 61
    s.a. spec. works
Isaiah
  Bible   224.1
  other aspects see Prophetic
    books (O.T.)
Isaias *see* Isaiah
Isanti Co. Minn.   *area*–776 64
Ischia Italy   *area*–457 3
Isère France   *area*–449 9

Isfahan Iran   *area*–559 5
Ishikawa Japan   *area*–521 5
Isikawa Japan   *area*–521 5
Isla Gorge Nat. Park Qld.   *area*–943 5
Islam *see* Islamic religion
Islamabad Pakistan   *area*–549 142
Islamic
  architecture *see* Saracenic
    architecture
  calendars   529.327
  conquests India hist.   954.022
    s.a. spec. events & subj.
      e.g. Commerce
  cookery   641.567 7
  law   340.59
  music *see* Islamic sacred
    music
  philosophy   181.07
  regions   *area*–176 71
  religion   297
    art representation   704.948 97
    s.a. spec. art forms
    persons in *see* Muslims
    rel. holidays   394.268 297
  sacred music
    arts   783.029 7
    recordings   789.912 302 97
    s.a. spec. instruments;
      also spec. kinds e.g.
      Liturgical music
    religion   297.38
  schools   377.97
  temples & shrines
    architecture   726.2
    building   690.62
    rel. significance   297.35
    other aspects see
      Religious-purpose
      bldgs.
Island Co. Wash.   *area*–797 75
Islands
  authorities Scot.   *area*–411 2
  ecology life sci.   574.526 7
    animals   591.526 7
    microorganisms   576.15
    plants   581.526 7
    s.a. spec. organisms
  geomorphology   551.42
  regional subj. trmt.   *area*–142
Islands of Langerhans
  anatomy
    human   611.37
    other aspects see Nutritive
      organs
  diseases
    gen. wks.   616.46
      neoplasms   616.992 37
      tuberculosis   616.995 37
    geriatrics   618.976 46
    pediatrics   618.924 6
    pub. health   614.594 6

Islands of Langerhans
  diseases (continued)
    statistics   312.346
      deaths   312.264 6
    surgery   617.557
      anesthesiology   617.967 557
    other aspects see Diseases
  physical anthropometry   573.637
  physiology
    human   612.34
    other aspects see Nutrition
  tissue biology human   611.018 937
Islas de la Bahía Honduras   *area*–728 315
Islay Strathclyde Scot.   *area*–414 23
Isle
  au Haut Me.   *area*–741 53
  of Man   *area*–427 9
  of Wiqht
    Co. Va.   *area*–755 54
    isl. Eng.   *area*–422 8
  Royale Mich.   *area*–774 997
Isleworth London Eng.   *area*–421 82
Islington London Eng.   *area*–421 43
Islwyn Gwent Wales   *area*–429 93
Ismailia Egypt   *area*–621 5
Ismailites *see* Seveners
Isobutylene rubbers *see*
      Synthetic rubber
Isoetales
  botany   587.1
  floriculture   635.937 1
  med. aspects
    crop prod.   633.887 1
    gen. pharm.   615.327 1
      toxicology   615.952 71
    vet. pharm.   636.089 532 71
      toxicology   636.089 595 271
  paleobotany   561.71
  other aspects see Plants
Isolation
  control meas.
    pub. health   614.45
    misc. aspects see Public
      health
  soc. interaction   302.5
Isomers
  molecular structure
    theoretical chem.   541.225 2
    organic   547.122 52
    s.a. spec. elements &
      cpds.
Isometric
  projections *see* Projections
    tech. drawing
  systems crystallography   548.14
    s.a. spec. substances
Isometry *see* Transformations
Isomorphism
  crystallography   548.3
    s.a. spec. substances

Isonitriles
  org. chem.   547.044
    s.a. spec. groupings e.g.
      Aliphatic compounds
  synthetic drugs pharm.   615.314 4
    misc. aspects see
      Pharmacology
  synthetic poisons   615.951 44
    misc. aspects see
      Toxicology
  other aspects see Nitrogen
    compounds
Isopoda
  fishing sports   799.255 372
  zoology   595.372
  other aspects see
    Eumalacostraca
Isoptera
  culture   638.573 6
  paleozoology   565.73
  zoology   595.736
  other aspects see Insecta
Isospondyli
  culture   639.375 5
  fishing
    commercial   639.275 5
    sports   799.175 5
  zoology   597.55
  other aspects see Teleostei
Isostasy   551.12
Isotope structure *see* Nuclear
    structure
Isotopes
  radiochemistry   541.388
    applied   660.298 8
    organic   547.138 8
    s.a. spec. elements, cpds.,
      prod.
Isotropy
  crystals
    optical crystallography   548.9
    s.a. spec. substances
Isparta Turkey   *area*–564
Israel   *area*–569 4
  ancient   *area*–33
Israel-Arab Wars
  history
    1948-49   956.042
    1956   956.044
    1967   956.046
    1973   956.048
    s.a. hist. of spec.
      participants
Israeli
  arts *see* Palestinian arts
Israelis   *r.e.n.*–924
Israelite
  arts *see* Palestinian arts
Issaquena Co. Miss.   *area*–762 412
Issas territory   *area*–677 1

Istanbul Turkey	*area*–563
ancient	*area*–395
Istria Yugoslavia	*area*–497 2
ancient	*area*–373
Itala texts Bible	220.47
s.a. spec. parts of Bible	
Italian	
greyhounds	
animal husbandry	636.76
other aspects see Dogs	
language	
linguistics	450
literature	850
s.a.	*lang.*–51
people	*r.e.n.*–51
Riviera	*area*–451 8
rule Libya hist.	961.203
s.a. spec. events & subj.	
e.g. Commerce	
s.a. Italy; *also other spec.*	
subj. e.g. Arts	
Italic	
alphabets printing	686.217 3
languages	
linguistics	470
literatures	870
s.a.	*lang.*–7
lettering dec. arts	745.619 77
people	*r.e.n.*–4–7
s.a. other spec. subj. e.g.	
Arts	
Italo-Ethiopian War 1935-36	
history	963.056
s.a. hist. of spec.	
countries	
Italy	*area*–45
ancient	*area*–37
Itapúa Paraguay	*area*–892 126
Itasca Co. Minn.	*area*–776 78
Itawamba Co. Miss.	*area*–762 982
Itch perception *see* Derived	
sensory perception	
Iteration	
mathematics	511.42
s.a. spec. math. branches;	
also spec. appls. e.g.	
Engineering	
Ithaca Greece	*area*–495 5
ancient	*area*–383
Ithna Asharites *see* Twelvers	
Ivan	
3 reign Russia hist.	947.041
s.a. spec. events & subj.	
e.g. Commerce	
4 reign Russia hist.	947.043
s.a. spec. events & subj.	
e.g. Commerce	
6 reign Russia hist.	947.061
s.a. spec. events & subj.	
e.g. Commerce	
Ivano-Frankov Ukraine	*area*–477 18

Ivanovo RSFSR	*area*–473 1
Iviza Spain	*area*–457 5
Ivory	
carving	
dec. arts	736.62
rel. significance	
Christianity	247.866 2
comp. rel.	291.37
s.a. other spec. rel.	
Coast	
country	*area*–666 8
people	*r.e.n.*–966 68
products	
manufacturing	
soc. & econ. aspects *see*	
Secondary industries	
technology	679.43
Ivy *see* Umbellales	
Ivy (poison) *see* Sapindales	
Iwate Japan	*area*–521 1
Ixonanthaceae *see* Malpighiales	
Izabal Guatemala	*area*–728 13
Izard Co. Ark.	*area*–767 27
Izmir Turkey	*area*–562

J

Jabots *see* Neckwear	
Jacamars *see* Piciformes	
Jacanas *see* Charadriiformes	
Jack Co. Tex.	*area*–764 544
Jackals *see* Canidae	
Jackets	
house garments	
comm. mf.	687.113
children's	687.13
women's	687.12
domestic mf.	646.433
outdoor garments	
comm. mf.	687.147
domestic mf.	646.457
other aspects see Clothing	
Jacks	
gen. wks. *see* Elevators	
(lifts)	
motor vehicles *see*	
Accessories automobiles	
Jackson	
Andrew admin.	
U.S. hist.	937.56
s.a. spec. events & subj.	
e.g. Constitutional	
law	
city Miss.	*area*–762 51
County	
Alabama	*area*–761 95
Arkansas	*area*–767 97
Colorado	*area*–788 66
Florida	*area*–759 93
Georgia	*area*–758 145
Illinois	*area*–773 994

James
  City Co. Va.   *area*–755 425 1
  epistle
    Bible   227.91
    other aspects see New
       Testament
  Isl. S.C.   *area*–757 99
  reign
    Eng. hist.
      1   942.061
      2   942.067
    Gt. Brit. hist.
      1   941.061
      2   941.067
    Scot. hist.
      1-5   941.104
    s.a. spec. events & subj.
      e.g. Commerce
  River
    Dakota   *area*–783 3
      North Dakota   *area*–784 5
      South Dakota   *area*–783 3
    Virginia   *area*–755 4
  theory indiv. psych.   155.264
Jameson raid Transvaal hist.   968.204 75
Jamesonite
  mineralogy   549.35
Jammu & Kashmir India   *area*–546
Jams *see* Preserves
Jamtland Sweden   *area*–488
Jan Mayen Isl.   *area*–983
Janitors *see* Household
    employees
Jansenism
  doctrinal controversies
    Christian church hist.   273.7
Jansenist Church   284.84
  buildings
    architecture   726.584 84
    building   690.658 484
    other aspects see
      Religious-purpose
      bldgs.
  Christian life guides   248.484 84
  doctrines   230.484
    creeds   238.484
  general councils   262.548 4
  govt. & admin.   262.048 4
    parishes   254.048 4
  missions   266.484
  moral theology   241.044 84
  private prayers for   242.804 84
  pub. worship   264.048 4
  rel. associations
    adults   267.184 84
    men   267.244 84
    women   267.444 84
    young adults   267.624 84
  rel. instruction   268.848 4
  rel. law   262.984 84
  schools   377.848 4

Jansenist Church (continued)
  secondary training   207.124 84
  sermons   252.048 4
  theological seminaries   207.114 84
  s.a. other spec. aspects
Japan
  country   *area*–52
  Current
    oceanography   551.475 5
  Sea
    oceanography   551.465 54
    regional subj. trmt.   *area*–164 54
    other aspects see Pacific
      Ocean
Japanese
  architecture   722.12
    misc. aspects see
      Architectural schools
  chess
    equip. mf.   688.741 8
      soc. & econ. aspects *see*
        Secondary industries
    recreation   794.18
  flower arrangements   745.922 52
  ink painting   751.425 2
    indiv. artists   759.1–.9
  language
    linguistics   495.6
    literature   895.6
    s.a.   *lang.*–956
  medlars *see* Loquats
  people   *r.e.n.*–956
  river fever *see* Scrub typhus
  sculpture   732.72
  spaniel
    animal husbandry   636.76
    other aspects see Dogs
  wrestling *see* Sumo
  s.a. Japan; *also other spec.*
    subj.
Japanning
  dec. arts   745.72
Japans
  manufacturing
    soc. & econ. aspects *see*
      Secondary industries
  technology   667.8
Jargon *see* Slang
Jarrow Tyne & Wear Eng.   *area*–428 75
Jars *see* Containers
Jarvis Isl.   *area*–964
Jasmine *see* Loganiales
Jasper Co.
  Georgia   *area*–758 583
  Illinois   *area*–773 74
  Indiana   *area*–772 977
  Iowa   *area*–777 594
  Mississippi   *area*–762 575
  Missouri   *area*–778 72
  South Carolina   *area*–757 98
  Texas   *area*–764 159

Jassoidea *see* Homoptera

Java

  chickens

    animal husbandry   636.581

    other aspects see Chickens

  isl. Indonesia   *area*–598 2

  jute *see* Ambari hemp

  man   573.3

  Sea *see* Southern Sunda Isls.

    seas

  War hist.   959.802 2

Javanese

  arts *see* Southeast Asian arts

  language

    linguistics   449.222

    literature   899.222

    s.a.   *lang.*–992 22

  people   *r.e.n.*–992 2

  s.a. Java; *also other spec.*

    subj.

Javelin hurling *see* Throwing

Jaws

  diseases

    surgery   617.522

      anesthesiology   617.967 522

    other aspects see Diseases

  fractures   617.156

  orthopedic surgery   617.371

Jay Co. Ind.   *area*–772 67

Jays *see* Corvidae

Jazz

  bands   785.067 2

  s.a. spec. kinds of music

  music

    for orchestra   785.42

      recordings   789.912 542

    for piano   786.46

      recordings   789.912 646

    gen. wks.

      recordings   789.912 157

      theory   781.57

    s.a. other spec. mediums

  orchestras   785.066 7

  s.a. spec. kinds of music

Jealousy *see* Vices

Jeanne d'Arc France hist.   944.026

  s.a. spec. events & subj.

    e.g. Commerce

Jebel Druze Syria   *area*–569 14

Jedburgh Borders Scot.   *area*–413 92

Jeep cavalry

  armed forces   357.54

Jeeps

  mil. eng.   623.747 22

Jeff Davis Co.

  Georgia   *area*–758 827

  Texas   *area*–764 934

Jefferson

  City Mo.   *area*–778 55

  County

    Alabama   *area*–761 78

Jefferson

  County (continued)

    Arkansas   *area*–767 79

    Colorado   *area*–788 84

    Florida   *area*–759 87

    Georgia   *area*–758 663

    Idaho   *area*–796 58

    Illinois   *area*–773 793

    Indiana   *area*–772 13

    Iowa   *area*–777 94

    Kansas   *area*–781 37

    Kentucky   *area*–769 44

    Mississippi   *area*–762 283

    Missouri   *area*–778 67

    Montana   *area*–786 67

    Nebraska   *area*–782 332

    New York   *area*–747 57

    Ohio   *area*–771 69

    Oklahoma   *area*–766 52

    Oregon   *area*–795 85

    Pennsylvania   *area*–748 62

    Tennessee   *area*–768 924

    Texas   *area*–764 145

    Washington   *area*–797 98

    West Virginia   *area*–754 99

    Wisconsin   *area*–775 85

  Par. La.   *area*–763 38

  Thomas admin.

    U.S. hist.   973.46–.48

    s.a. spec. events & subj.

      e.g. Commerce

Jefferson Davis

  Co. Miss.   *area*–762 543

  Par. La.   *area*–763 55

Jeffersonian Republican Party

    U.S.

  pol. sci.   324.273 26

  s.a. spec. subj. of concern

    e.g. Social problems

Jehovah's Witnesses   289.92

  misc. aspects see

    Miscellaneous Christian

    denominations

Jejunitis *see* Enteritis

Jejunum *see* Small intestines

Jekyll Isl. Ga.   *area*–758 742

Jelenia Gora Poland   *area*–438 5

Jellies *see* Preserves

Jellyfish

  culture   639.737

  paleozoology   563.7

  zoology   593.7

  other aspects see Animals

Jellying agents

  processing

    soc. & econ. aspects *see*

      Secondary industries

    technology   664.25–.26

Jenghis Khan

  reign Asia hist. *see* Mongol

Jenkins Co. Ga.   *area*–758 693

Jenkins' Ear War hist.   946.055
Jennies *see* Spinning-machines
Jennings Co. Ind.   *area*–772 17
Jenolan Caves N.S.W.   *area*–944 5
Jerauld Co. S.D.   *area*–783 32
Jerboas *see* Myomorpha
Jeremiah
   Bible   224.2
   other aspects see Prophetic
      books (O.T.)
Jeremiah 2 Answers
   Christian doctrines   238.19
Jeremias *see* Jeremiah
Jeremy
   Apocrypha   229.5
   other aspects see Apocrypha
Jerome Co. Ida.   *area*–796 35
Jersey
   Blue chickens
     animal husbandry   635.581
     other aspects see Chickens
   cattle
     animal husbandry   636.224
     other aspects see Cattle
   City N.J.   *area*–749 27
   Co. Ill.   *area*–773 855
   island   *area*–423 41
Jerusalem
   artichokes
     agriculture
       field crops   633.494
       garden crops   635.24
     soc. & econ. aspects *see*
       Primary industries
     foods   641.352 4
      preparation
       commercial   664.805 24
       domestic   641.652 4
     sugars & syrups
      comm. proc.   664.139
     other aspects see Sugars
     other aspects see
      Asterales; *also*
      Vegetables
   Bible   220.520 7
   city
     ancient   *area*–33
     gen. wks.   *area*–569 44
      Israel   *area*–569 44
      Jordan   *area*–569 52
     sacred place
      Christianity   263.042 569 44
      Islam   297.35
      Judaism   296.4
   corn
     agriculture
      food crops   633.174 7
      forage crops   633.257 47
     other aspects see Sorghums
Jessamine Co. Ky.   *area*–769 483
Jests *see* Humor

Jesuit missions
   Can. hist.   971.016 2
   other aspects see Missions
     (religion)
Jesuits
   monastic bldgs.
     architecture   726.775 3
     building   690.677 53
     other aspects see
      Religious-purpose
      bldgs.
   rel. orders   255.53
   church hist.   271.53
   ecclesiology   262.24
Jesus Christ
   art representation
     arts   704.948 53
     s.a. spec. art forms
     Christian rel.
      painting   247.553
      sculpture   247.3
   Christian doctrines   232
Jesus Isl. Que.   *area*–714 271
Jet
   compressors *see* Air
      compressors
   engines
     soc. & econ. aspects *see*
      Secondary industries
     tech. & mf.
      aircraft   629.134 353
      gen. wks.   621.435 2
       parts & accessories   621.437
      land vehicles   629.250 52
       parts & systems   629.252–.258
      marine vehicles   623.872 352
      s.a. other spec. appls.
   fuels
     chem. tech.   665.538 25
     other aspects see Petroleum
   planes
     aeronautical eng.
      gen. tech. & mf.   629.133 349
       components & tech.   629.134
      models   629.133 134 9
      operation   629.132 524 9
      military   623.746 044
      s.a. spec. kinds e.g.
       Trainers (aircraft)
     s.a. other spec. appls.
     commerce   387.733 49
     other aspects see
      Aircraft commerce
     s.a. Amphibian planes;
      also Seaplanes
   propulsion *see* Jet engines
   pumps
     engineering
      soc. & econ. aspects *see*
      Secondary industries

Jet
  pumps
    engineering (continued)
      tech. & mf.   621.691
        s.a. spec. appls. e.g.
          Water supply
          engineering
        other aspects see Dynamics
    stream *see* Planetary wind
      systems
Jet (coal)   553.22
  econ. geol.   553.22
  mining
    soc. & econ. aspects *see*
      Primary industries
    technology   622.332
    prospecting   622.182 2
    processing   662.622 2
  other aspects see Coals
  s.a. spec. uses
Jethou isl.   *area*–423 47
Jetties *see* Protective
  structures port eng.
Jettons *see* Counters
Jewell Co. Kan.   *area*–781 22
Jewelry
  arts
    decorative
      ceramics   738.4–.5
      precious metals   739.27
    handicrafts   745.594 2
    other aspects see Ornaments
    arts
  dress customs   391.7
Jewelweed family *see* Geraniales
Jewish
  apocalypses
    pseudepigrapha   229.913
    other aspects see Apocrypha
  architecture   722.33
    misc. aspects see
      Architectural schools
  Autonomous Region RSFSR
                                area–577
  chants *see* Chants sacred
    music
  religion *see* Judaism
  sculpture   723.3
  s.a. Hebrew
Jews   *r.e.n.*–924
  polemics against
    Christianity
      apostolic times   239.2
      later times   239.9
    Islam   297.292
    other rel. see Doctrinal
      theology
  religion *see* Judaism

Jew's harp
  mf. tech.   681.818 9
    misc. aspects see Musical
      instruments
  musical art   788.9
    recordings   789.912 89
Jigging ore *see* Gravity
  concentration ores
Jigs *see* Guiding-equipment
Jihad Islamic activity   297.72
Jim Hogg Co. Tex.   *area*–764 482
Jim Wells Co. Tex.   *area*–764 465
Jinnah admin. Pakistan hist.   954.904 2
  s.a. spec. events & subj.
    e.g. Commerce
Jinotega Nicaragua   *area*–728 522
Jipijapa
  agriculture   633.58
    soc. & econ. aspects *see*
      Primary industries
    other aspects see
      Cyclanthales; *also*
      Unaltered vegetable
      fibers
Jiujitsus *see* Jujitsus
Jnana yoga   294.54
Jo Daviess Co. Ill.   *area*–773 343
Joachim Saint
  Christian doctrines   232.933
  private prayers to   242.75
Job
  analysis *see* Job
    classification
  classification
    personnel admin.
      gen. management   658.306
      spec. subj.   *s.s.*–068 3
    law of pub. admin.   342.068 6
      ◦spec. jur.   342.3–.9
    pub. admin.   350.103
      central govts.   351.103
      spec. jur.   353–354
      local govts.   352.005 103
  descriptions
    gen. wks. *see* Job
      classification
    library sci.   023.7
      s.a. spec. activities
        e.g. Cataloging
    museology   069.63
      s.a. spec. activities
      s.a. other spec. appls.
  enrichment
    employee motivation
      pers. admin.
        gen. management   658.314 23
        spec. subj.   *s.s.*–068 3
      pub. admin. *see*
        Motivation employees
        personnel admin. pub.
        admin.

Job (continued)
  qualifications
    labor econ.   331.114 2
    s.a. spec. classes of
        labor e.g. Women
  satisfaction
    employee motivation
      pers. admin.
        gen. management   658.314 22
        spec. subj.   *s.s.*–068 3
      pub. admin. *see*
        Motivation employees
        personnel admin. pub.
        admin.
  tenure labor econ. *see* Worker
        security
  training
    personnel admin.
      gen. management   658.312 43
      executives   658.407 124 3
      spec. subj.   *s.s.*–068 3
    pub. admin.   350.15
      central govts.   351.15
      spec. jur.   353–354
      local govts.   352.005 15
    other aspects see Training
        personnel admin.
  vacancies
    labor econ.   331.124
      law *see* Labor law
    s.a. spec. classes of
        workers e.g. Women
Job (scriptures)
  Bible   223.1
  other aspects see Poetic
        books (O.T.)
Jobbers
  advertising   659.196 588 6
  pub. relations   659.296 588 6
  wholesale marketing *see*
        Wholesale marketing
Job's Daughters   366.18
Jockeys
  biog. & work   798.400 92
Joel
  Bible   224.7
  other aspects see Prophetic
        books (O.T.)
Johannesburg South Africa   *area*–682 21
John
  reign
    Eng. hist.   942.033
    France hist.
    1   944.024
    2   944.025
    Gt. Brit. hist.   941.033
  s.a. spec. events & subj.
        e.g. Courts; *also*
        other spec. countries

John (scriptures)
  Epistles
    Bible   227.94–.96
    other aspects see New
        Testament
  Gospel
    Bible   226.5
      miracles   226.7
      parables   226.8
    other aspects see New
        Testament
  Revelation
    Bible   228
    other aspects see New
        Testament
John Brown's raid
  U.S. Civil War causes   973.711 6
John Dorys *see* Acanthopterygii
John the Baptist
  Christian doctrines   232.94
Johns Isl. S.C.   *area*–757 99
Johnson
  Andrew admin.
    U.S. hist.   973.81
    s.a. spec. events & subj.
        e.g. Impeachment
  County
    Arkansas   *area*–767 33
    Georgia   *area*–758 676
    Illinois   *area*–773 996
    Indiana   *area*–772 515
    Iowa   *area*–777 655
    Kansas   *area*–781 675
    Kentucky   *area*–769 245
    Missouri   *area*–778 455
    Nebraska   *area*–782 276
    Tennessee   *area*–768 99
    Texas   *area*–764 524
    Wyoming   *area*–787 35
  Lyndon B. admin.
    U.S. hist.   973.923
    s.a. spec. events & subj.
        e.g. Health insurance
Johnston
  County
    North Carolina   *area*–756 41
    Oklahoma   *area*–766 68
  Island   *area*–969 9
Johnstone Strathclyde Scot.   *area*–414 41
Johore Malaysia   *area*–595 1
Joinery
  bldg. construction   694.6
  shipbuilding
    soc. & econ. aspects *see*
        Secondary industries
    technology   623.844
Joining
  church
    rel. rites
      Christianity   265.9

Joining
  church
    rel. rites (continued)
      other rel. see Public
        worship
  metals
    arts
      decorative   739.14
      s.a. spec. metals; also
        spec. prod. e.g.
        Jewelry
      fine *see* Direct-metal
        sculpture
    manufacturing
      soc. & econ. aspects *see*
        Secondary industries
      technology   671.5
        ferrous metals   672.5
      s.a. other spec. metals
    s.a. other spec. subj.
Joining-equipment *see*
      Fastening-equipment
Joint
  committees
    legislative bodies
      pol. sci.   328.365 7
      spec. jur.   382.4–.9
  property
    law   346.042
    spec. jur.   346.3–.9
  tenancy
    property law *see* Land
      tenure law
  ventures *see* Unincorporated
    bus. enterprises
Joints (anatomical)
  anatomy
    human   611.72
    other aspects see Skeletal
      organs
  diseases
    gen. wks.   616.72
      neoplasms   616.992 72
      tuberculosis   616.995 72
    geriatrics   618.976 72
    pediatrics   618.927 2
    pub. health   614.597 2
    statistics   312.372
      deaths   312.267 2
    surgery   617.472
      anesthesiology   617.697 472
    other aspects see Diseases
  pathology
    gen. wks.   591.218 52
    s.a. spec. animals
    med. sci. *see* Joints
      (anatomical) diseases
  physical anthropometry   573.672
  physiology
    human   612.75

Joints (anatomical)
  physiology (continued)
    other aspects see Motor
      functions
    tissue biology human   611.018 972
Joints (geological)   551.84
  s.a. spec. aspects e.g.
    Prospecting
Joints (mechanical) *see spec.*
    kinds e.g. Universal
    joints
Joint-stock companies *see*
    Unincorporated bus.
    enterprises
Joists
  wood bldg. construction   694.2
Jokes
  gen. colls.   808.887
  spec. lits.   *lit. sub.–807*
    spec. periods   *lit. sub.–81–89*
  s.a. Humor
Joliette Co. Que.   *area–714 42*
Jolo Philippines   *area–599 9*
Jonah
  Bible   224.92
  other aspects see Prophetic
    books (O.T.)
Jonas *see* Jonah
Jones
  County
    Georgia   *area–758 567*
    Iowa   *area–777 63*
    Mississippi   *area–762 55*
    North Carolina   *area–756 21*
    South Dakota   *area–783 577*
    Texas   *area–764 733*
  Sound *see* American Arctic
    seawaters
Jonkoping Sweden   *area–486*
Jonquils *see* Amaryllidales
Jordan
  algebra   512.53
  s.a. spec. appls. e.g.
    Engineering
  country   *area–569 5*
  River   *area–569 4*
Jordanians   *r.e.n.–927 569 5*
Jornada del Muerto N.M.   *area–789 62*
Joseph
  emperor Ger. hist.
    1   943.051
    2   943.057
    s.a. spec. events & subj.
      e.g. Commerce
  saint
    art represntation *see*
      Saints art
      representation
    Christian doctrines   232.932
    private prayers to   242.75

Joseph Bonaparte reign
  Spain hist.   946.06
    s.a. spec. events & subj.
      e.g. Courts
Josephine Co. Ore.   *area*–795 25
Joshua
  Bible   222.2
  other aspects see Historical
    books (O.T.)
Joshua Tree Nat. Monument Calif.
        area–794 97
Josue *see* Joshua
Joule's law
  thermodynamics
    astrophysics   523.013 71
    s.a. spec. celestial
      bodies
    physics   536.71
    spec. states of matter   530.4
Journalism   070
  curriculums   375.07
  documentation   025.060 7
  libraries   026.07
    misc. aspects see Special
      libraries
  library acquisitions   025.270 7
  library classification   025.460 7
  school bldgs.
    architecture   727.407
    building   690.740 7
    other aspects see
      Educational buildings
  subj. headings   025.490 7
  other aspects see Disciplines
    (systems)
Journalists
  biog. & work   070.92
  occupational ethics   174.909 7
  s.a.   *pers.*–097
Journals (mechanisms)
  machine eng.
    soc. & econ. aspects *see*
      Secondary industries
    tech. & mf.   621.821
    s.a. spec. appls. e.g.
      Windlasses
  other aspects see Mechanics
Journals (publications) *see*
  Serials
Journals (writings)
  literature
    gen. colls.   808.883
    spec. lits.   *lit. sub.*–803
      spec. periods   *lit. sub.*–81–89
    s.a.   *s.s.*–092
  s.a. other spec. subj. e.g.
    Constitutional
      conventions proceedings
Journeys *see* Travel
Joy *see* Secondary emotions
Juab Co. Utah   *area*–792 44

Juan Carlos 1 reign Spain hist.   946.083
  s.a. spec. events & subj.
    e.g. Commerce
Juan de Fuca Strait *see* United
    States Pacific
    seawaters
Jubaland   *area*–677 3
Jubilees
  soc. customs   394.4
  other aspects see
    Celebrations
Judaism
  art representation   704.948 96
    s.a. spec. art forms
  calendars   529.326
  cookery   641.567 6
  philosophy   181.06
  regions   *area*–176 6
  religion   296
  rel. holidays   394.268 296
  schools   377.96
  s.a. Jews
Judaistic
  music *see* Judaistic sacred
    music
  religion *see* Judaism
  sacred music
    arts   783.029 6
      recordings   789.912 302 96
    s.a. spec. instruments;
      also spec. kinds e.g.
      Liturgical music
    religion   296.4
  temples & shrines
    architecture   726.3
    building   690.63
    other aspects see
      Religious-purpose
      bldgs.
Judaists
  biog. & work   296.092
    s.a. spec. kinds e.g.
      Clergy; *also spec.*
      sects & movements
  s.a.   *pers.*–296
  s.a. Jews
Judas's betrayal
  Christian doctrines   232.961
Jude
  Bible   227.97
  other aspects see New
    Testament
Judea   *area*–33
Judean arts *see* Palestinian
  arts
Judeo-German *see* Yiddish
Judeo-Spanish language
  linguistics   467.949 6
  literature   860
  s.a.   *lang.*–67

Jujitsus (continued)
  other aspects see Sports
Jujuy Argentina   *area*–824 1
Julian calendar chronology   529.42
Juliana reign Netherlands hist.   949.207 2
  s.a. spec. events & subj.
      e.g. Commerce
Julianaceae *see* Juglandales
July Monarchy
  France hist.   944.063
  s.a. spec. events & subj.
      e.g. Arts
Jumpers (athletes)
  biog. & work   796.43
  s.a.   *pers.*–796 4
Jumping
  horses
    equip. mf.   688.78
    soc. & econ. aspects *see*
      Secondary industries
    sports   798.25
    other aspects see Sports
  human
    equipment mf.   688.764 32
    soc. & econ. aspects *see*
      Secondary industries
    sports   796.432
    other aspects see Sports
Juncaceae *see* Juncales
Juncaginaceae *see* Juncaginales
Juncaginales
  botany   584.744
  floriculture   635.934 744
  med. aspects
    crop prod.   633.884 744
    gen. pharm.   615.324 744
      toxicology   615.952 474 4
    vet. pharm.   636.089 532 474 4
      toxicology   636.089 595 247 44
  paleobotany   561.4
  other aspects see Plants
Juncales
  botany   584.45
  floriculture   635.934 45
  med. aspects
    crop. prod.   633.884 45
    gen. pharm.   615.324 45
      toxicology   615.952 445
    vet. pharm.   636.089 532 445
      toxicology   636.089 595 244 5
  paleobotany   561.4
  other aspects see Plants
Junction
  diodes *see* Diodes
    semiconductors
  transistors
    gen. wks.
      soc. & econ. aspects *see*
        Secondary industries

Junction
  transistors
    gen. wks. (continued)
      tech. & mf.   621.381 528 2
      s.a. spec. appls. e.g.
        Radiocontrol
    other aspects see
      Transistors
Junctions (elect. lines)
  exterior wiring *see* Exterior
    wiring
  interior wiring *see* Interior
    wiring
Juncture
  linguistics *see* Intonation
    linguistics
June beetles
  zoology   595.764 9
  other aspects see Polyphaga
Juneau
  Co. Wis.   *area*–775 55
  election district Alaska   *area*–798 2
Juneberries
  agriculture   634.74
  soc. & econ. aspects *see*
    Primary industries
  foods   641.347 4
    preparation
      commercial   664.804 74
      domestic   641.647 4
  other aspects see Rosaceae;
    also Fruits
Junee N.S.W.   *area*–944 8
Jungermanniaceae *see* Hepaticae
Jungian
  systems
    psychology   150.195 4
    s.a. spec. subj. &
      branches of psych.
  theory
    indiv. psych.   155.264
Jungle
  diseases *see* Tropical
    diseases
  warfare
    mil. sci.   355.423
    s.a. spec. mil. branches
Jungles *see* Forests
Juniata
  Co. Pa.   *area*–748 47
  River Pa.   *area*–748 45
Junín Peru   *area*–852 4
Junior
  colleges   378.154 3
  departments
    Sunday schools
      Christianity   268.432
      other rel. see Religious
        instruction
  high schools   373.236
    govt. supervision & support   379

Justification	
Christian doctrines	234.7
s.a. other spec. subj.	
Jute	
agriculture	633.54
soc. & econ. aspects *see*	
Primary industries	
pulp	
mf. tech.	676.14
other aspects see Pulp	
textiles	
arts	746.041 3
s.a. spec. proc. e.g.	
Weaving	
dyeing	667.313
manufacturing	
soc. & econ. aspects *see*	
Secondary industries	
technology	677.13
special-process fabrics	677.6
other aspects see Textiles	
s.a. spec. prod.; also spec.	
"jutes" e.g. China	
jute	
other aspects see Tiliales	
Jutiapa Guatemala	*area*–728 143
Jutland Denmark	*area*–489 5
Juvenile	
courts	
criminal law	345.08
spec. jur.	345.3–.9
delinquents	
criminology	364.36
parochial activities for	
Christianity	259.5
other rel. see Pastoral	
theology	
penal institutions	365.42
misc. aspects see Penal	
institutions	
welfare services	364.44
s.a. Delinquent children	
offenders	
criminal law	345.03
spec. jur.	345.3–.9
procedure	
criminal law	345.081
spec. jur.	345.3–.9
s.a. Young; *also* Children's	

K

KWIC indexing	
library operations	025.486
KWOC indexing	
library operations	025.486
Kabardin *see* Caucasic	
Kabardino-Balkar ASSR	*area*–479 7
Kabuki theater	792.095 2
Kabyle language *see* Berber	
languages	

Kadarites	
Islamic sects	297.835
doctrines	297.204 35
worship	297.303 5
s.a. other spec. aspects	
Kadina S. Aust.	*area*–942 35
Kaduna Nigeria	*area*–669 5
Kaffa Ethiopia	*area*–633
Kaffir *see* Kafir	
Kafir	
corn	
agriculture	
food crops	633.174 7
forage crops	633.257 47
other aspects see Sorghums	
grasses *see* Panicoideae	
Kafiri *see* Dard	
Kafirs	*r.e.n.*–914 99
Kafr el Sheikh Egypt	*area*–621
Kagawa Japan	*area*–523
Kagoshima Japan	*area*–522
Kagosima Japan	*area*–522
Kahoolawe Hawaii	*area*–969 22
Kala-azar *see* Leishmaniasis	
Kalahari Desert	*area*–681 1
Kalam	
district Pakistan	*area*–549 122
Islamic doctrine	297.2
Kalamazoo	
city Mich.	*area*–774 18
Co. Mich.	*area*–774 17
River Mich.	*area*–774 1
Kalat Pakistan	*area*–549 153
Kalawao Co. Hawaii	*area*–969 24
Kalbarri Nat. Park W. Aust.	
	area–941 2
Kale	
agriculture	635.347
other aspects see Cabbages	
Kalgoorlie W. Aust.	*area*–941 6
Kalimantan Indonesia	*area*–598 3
Kalinga-Apayao Philippines	*area*–599 1
Kalinin RSFSR	*area*–476 2
Kaliningrad RSFSR	*area*–474 7
Kalisz Poland	*area*–438 4
Kalium *see* Potassium	
Kalkaska Co. Mich.	*area*–774 65
Kallitype processes photography	772.16
Kalmar	
county Sweden	*area*–486
Union hist.	948.03
Denmark	948.902
Norway	948.102
Sweden	948.501
Kalmuck *see* Mongolic	
Kalmyk ASSR	*area*–478 5
Kaluga RSFSR	*area*–476 2
Kamakura period Japan hist.	952.021
s.a. spec. events & subj.	
e.g. Commerce	

Karimata Strait *see* South China
    Sea
Karl-Marx-Stadt Ger.   *area*–432 1
Karma yoga   294.544
Karnak Egypt   *area*–623
Karnataka   *area*–548 7
Karnes Co. Tex.   *area*–764 444
Karpathos Greece   *area*–499 6
  ancient   *area*–391 7
Kars Turkey   *area*–566 2
Karst
  geomorphology   551.447
  other aspects see Openings
    (physiography)
Karting
  sports   796.76
  other aspects see Sports
Karts *see* Racing cars
Kartvelian *see* Caucasic
Kasai Congo   *area*–675 12
Kashmir
  India   *area*–546
  Pakistan   *area*–549 13
Kashmiri *see* Dard
Kashubian
  language
    linguistics   491.857
    literature   891.85
    s.a.   *lang.*–918 51
  people   *r.e.n.*–918 5
  s.a. other spec. subj. e.g.
    Arts
Kashubs   *r.e.n.*–918 5
Kaskaskia River Ill.   *area*–773 8
Kassala Sudan   *area*–629 2
Kastamonu Turkey   *area*–563
Kastoria Greece   *area*–495 6
Katahdin Mt. Me.   *area*–741 25
Katanga
  Congo   *area*–675 18
  early kingdom hist.   967.510 1
  s.a. spec. events & subj.
    e.g. Commerce
  province Zaïre   *area*–675 18
Katanning W. Aust.   *area*–941 2
Katatonia *see* Schizophrenia
Katharevusa *see* Greek language
    modern
Katherine
  Gorge Nat. Park N. Ter. Aust.
     area–942 95
  N. Ter. Aust.   *area*–942 95
Katoomba N.S.W.   *area*–944 5
Katowice Poland   *area*–438 5
Katsu *see* First aid
Kattegat *see* Baltic Sea
Katydids *see* Orthoptera
Kauai
  Co. Hawaii   *area*–969 4
  Isl. Hawaii   *area*–969 41
Kaufman Co. Tex.   *area*–764 277

Kavalla Greece   *area*–495 6
Kaw River Kan.   *area*–781
Kawaguchi geometry   516.377
  s.a. spec. appls. e.g.
    Engineering
Kay Co. Okla.   *area*–766 24
Kayaks *see* Hand-propelled
    vessels
Kayseri Turkey   *area*–564
Kazak *see* Turkic
Kazakh SSR   *area*–584 5
Kazakhstan   *area*–584 5
Keady N. Ire.   *area*–416 61
Kearney Co. Neb.   *area*–782 394
Kearny Co. Kan.   *area*–781 425
Kearsarge (ship)
  battle with Alabama
    U.S.hist.   973.754
Kearsley Greater Manchester Eng.
     area–427 37
Kechua *see* South American
    native
Kedah Malaysia   *area*–595 1
Keene Valley N.Y.   *area*–747 53
Keene's cement
  technology   666.92
  other aspects see Masonry
    adhesives
Keeshonden
  animal husbandry   636.72
  other aspects see Dogs
Keewatin
  period *see* Archeozoic era
  region Can.   *area*–719 4
Kefa Ethiopia   *area*–633
Kefallenia Greece   *area*–495 5
Kegs
  mf. tech.   674.82
  other aspects see Wood
    products
Keighley West Yorkshire Eng.
     area–428 17
Keith
  Co. Neb.   *area*–782 89
  Grampian Scot.   *area*–412 23
Kelantan Malaysia   *area*–595 1
Kelowna B.C.   *area*–711 42
Kelps *see* Phaeophyta
Kelso Borders Scot.   *area*–413 92
Keltic *see* Celtic
Kemerovo RSFSR   *area*–573
Kemper Co. Miss.   *area*–762 683
Kempo
  equip. mf.   688.768 159
  soc. & econ. aspects *see*
    Secondary industries
  sports   796.815 9
  other aspects see Sports
Kempsey N.S.W.   *area*–944 3
Kempston Bedfordshire Eng.
     area–425 61

Ketones (continued)

  synthetic drugs pharm.   615.313 6

    misc. aspects see

      Pharmacology

  synthetic poisons   615.951 36

    misc. aspects see

      Toxicology

  other aspects see Organic

    chemicals

  s.a. spec. prod.; also other

    spec. appls.

Kettering Northamptonshire Eng.

          area–425 52

Kettle River Range Wash.   *area*–797 25

Kettledrums *see* Membranophones

Kettles (geol. formations)   551.315

Keuka Lake N.Y.   *area*–747 82

Kewaunee Co. Wis.   *area*–775 62

Keweenaw

  Co. Mich.   *area*–774 995

  Peninsula Mich.   *area*–774 99

Keweenawan period *see*

  Proterozoic era

Key bugle music   788.455

  recordings   789.912 845

Key bugles

  mf. tech.   681.818 45

    misc. aspects see Musical

      instruments

  musical art   788.45

Key word indexing

  library operations   025.486

Keya Paha Co. Neb.   *area*–782 725

Keyboard

  harmony

    organs   786.7

    string instruments   786.3

  instruments

    gen. wks.

      mf. tech.   681.816

      misc. aspects see

        Musical instruments

    music   786

      recordings   789.912 6

    string

      mf. tech.   681.816 2

      misc. aspects see

        Musical instruments

      musical art   786.2

      music   786.4

        recordings   789.912 64

        training & perf.   786.3

    wind *see* Organs (music)

Keynesianism econ. school   330.156

Keynsham Avon Eng.   *area*–423 97

Keys

  locksmithing

    mf. tech.   683.32

    other aspects see Hardware

Keys (continued)

  wire telegraphy *see*

    Instrumentation wire

    telegraphy

Khabarovsk Territory   *area*–577

Khairpur Pakistan   *area*–549 17

Khakass Autonomous Region *area*–575

Khalaj language *see* Turkic

  languages

Khalji dynasty

  India hist.   954.023 4

  s.a. spec. events & subj.

    e.g. Arts

Khalkha *see* Mongolic

Khalkidiki Greece   *area*–495 6

Khamti

  language

    linguistics   495.919

    literature   895.919

    s.a.   *lang.*–959 19

  people   *r.e.n.*–959 1

  s.a. other spec. subj. e.g.

    Arts

Khanty-Mansi Nat. Region RSFSR

          area–573

Kharkov Ukraine   *area*–477 15

Khartoum Sudan   *area*–626 2

Khasi *see* Mon-Khmer

Khaskovo Bulgaria   *area*–497 75

Kherson Ukraine   *area*–477 17

Khios Greece   *area*–499

Khmelnitski Ukraine   *area*–477 14

Khmer

  Republic   *area*–596

  s.a. Mon-Khmer

Khoi-Khoin *see* Hottentot

Khond

  language

    linguistics   494.824

    literature   894.824

    s.a.   *lang.*–948 24

  people   *r.e.n.*–948

  s.a. other spec. subj. e.g.

    Arts

Khorasan Iran   *area*–559 2

Khotanese language *see* Middle

  Iranian languages

Khouribga Morocco   *area*–643

Khowar language *see* Dard

  languages

Khrushchev regime USSR hist.   947.085 2

  s.a. spec. events & subj.

    e.g. Commerce

Khulna Bangladesh   *area*–549 25

Khurasan Iran   *area*–559 2

Khuzistan Iran   *area*–556

Kiama N.S.W.   *area*–944 7

Kiangsi China   *area*–512 22

Kiangsu China   *area*–511 3

Kiawah Isl. S.C.   *area*–757 99

Kibbutzes
  sociology   307.7
Kicking
  American football   796.332 27
  s.a. other spec. games
Kidder Co. N.D.   *area*–784 57
Kidderminster Hereford &
     Worcester Eng.   *area*–424 41
Kidnaping *see* Abduction
Kidney
  beans
    agriculture   635.652
    soc. & econ. aspects *see*
      Primary industries
    foods   641.356 52
      preparation
        commercial   664.805 652
        domestic   641.656 52
    other aspects see
      Papilionaceae; *also*
      Vegetables
  stones
    gen. med.   616.622
    geriatrics   618.976 622
    pediatrics   618.926 22
    pub. health   614.596 22
    statistics   312.362 2
    deaths   312.266 22
    other aspects see Diseases
Kidneys
  anatomy
    human   611.61
    other aspects see Excretory
      organs
  diseases
    gen. wks.   616.61
      neoplasms   616.992 61
      tuberculosis   616.995 61
    geriatrics   618.976 61
    pediatrics   618.926 1
    pub. health   614.596 1
    statistics   312.361
    deaths   312.266 1
    surgery   617.461
      anesthesiology   617.967 461
    other aspects see Diseases
  physical anthropometry 573.661
  physiology
    human   612.463
    other aspects see Excretion
  tissue biology human   611.018 961
  transplants *see* Organs
    (anatomy) transplants
Kidsgrove Staffordshire Eng.
              area–424 62
Kidwelly Dyfed Wales   *area*–429 67
Kielce Poland   *area*–438 4
Kieselguhr
  econ. & mining aspects *see*
    Earthy materials

Kieselguhr (continued)
  materials aspects *see*
    Insulating materials
  mineral aspects *see*
    Sedimentary rocks
Kiev Ukraine   *area*–477 14
Kievan period Russia hist.   947.02
  s.a. spec. events & subj.
    e.g. Commerce
Kigoma Tanzania   *area*–678 28
Kilcreggan Strathclyde Scot.
              area–414 25
Kildare Ireland   *area*–418 5
Kilimanjaro
  mountain   *area*–678 26
  region Tanzania   *area*–678 26
Kilkeel N. Ire.   *area*–416 58
Kilkenny Ireland   *area*–418 9
Kilkis Greece   *area*–495 6
Killarney Munster Ire.   *area*–419 65
Killer whales *see* Odontoceti
Killifishes *see* Mesichthyes
Kilmarnock & Loudoun Strathclyde
      Scot.   *area*–414 63
Kilmore Vic.   *area*–945 3
Kilns
  ceramic
    arts
      decorative   738.13
      fine   731.3
    technology   666.43
Kiln-seasoning
  lumber mf.
    soc. & econ. aspects *see*
      Secondary industries
    technology   674.384
Kilrenny Fife Scot.   *area*–412 92
Kilsyth Strathclyde Scot. *area*–414 38
Kilwinning Strathclyde Scot.
              area–414 61
Kimball Co. Neb.   *area*–782 973
Kimberley district W. Aust.
              area–941 4
Kimble Co. Tex.   *area*–764 878
Kincardine
  & Deeside Grampian Scot.
              area–412 4
  Highland Scot.   *area*–411 65
Kincardineshire Scot.   *area*–412 4
Kindergarten teachers
  prof. ed.   370.712 2
  schools & courses   370.732 62
Kindergartens   372.218
Kindness
  ethics *see* Love ethics
Kinematics
  atmosphere met.   551.515 1
  machine eng.   621.811
  s.a. spec. appls. e.g.
    Hoisting-equipment

Kinematics (continued)
mechanics   531.112
   misc. aspects see Dynamics
Kinesiology   613.7
   gen. wks. *see* Movements
       biology
   hygiene   613.7
Kinesthetic perception *see*
       Proprioceptive
       perceptions
Kinetic
   art
    gen. wks.   709.040 73
     spec. places   709.1–.9
    painting   759.067 3
     spec. places   759.1–.9
    sculpture   735.230 473
     spec. places   730.9
    s.a. other spec. art forms
   energy
    physics   531.643
     s.a. spec. branches of
       physics
   theories
    physics   530.136
     spec. states of matter   530.4
     s.a. spec. branches of
       physics
Kinetics
   chemistry *see* Chemical
       kinetics
   mechanics   531.113
   misc. aspects see Dynamics
King
   County
    Texas   *area*–764 742
    Washington   *area*–797 77
   crabs *see* Anomura
   Isl. Tas.   *area*–946 7
   Leopold Ranges W. Aust.   *area*–941 4
   vultures *see* Cathartidae
   William Lyon Mackenzie
    admin. Can. hist.
     1-2   971.062 2
     3   971.063 2
     s.a. spec. events & subj.
     e.g. Arts
King & Queen Co. Va.   *area*–755 352
King George Co. Va.   *area*–755 25
King George's War
   U.S. hist.   973.26
   s.a. Austrian Succession War
King James version
   Bible   220.520 3
   s.a. spec. parts of Bible
King Philip's War
   U.S. hist.   973.24
King William
   Co. Va.   *area*–755 355
   Lake Tas.   *area*–946 3

King William's War
   U.S. hist.   973.25
   s.a. other spec. countries
Kingaroy Qld.   *area*–943 2
Kingdom of God
   rel. doctrines
    Christianity   231.72
   other rel. see God
Kingfisher Co. Okla.   *area*–766 32
Kingfishers *see* Coraciiformes
Kingfishes *see* Acanthopterygii
Kinghorn Fife Scot.   *area*–412 95
Kinglake Nat. Park Vic.   *area*–945 2
Kinglets *see* Sylviidae
Kingman Co. Kan.   *area*–781 843
King's
   Co. Ire.   *area*–418 6
   Lynn Eng.   *area*–426 13
Kings
   Canyon Nat. Park Calif.   *area*–794 82
   County
    California   *area*–794 85
    New Brunswick   *area*–715 41
    New York   *area*–747 23
    Nova Scotia   *area*–716 34
    Prince Edward Isl.   *area*–717 7
Kings (chessmen)   794.147
Kings (monarchs) *see* Monarchs
Kings (scriptures)
   Bible   222.5
   s.a. Samuel
   other aspects see Historical
       books (O.T.)
Kingsbridge Devon Eng.   *area*–423 592
Kingsbury Co. S.D.   *area*–783 273
Kingship
   Jesus Christ
    Christian doctrine   232.8
Kingston
   Ont.   *area*–713 72
   S. Aust.   *area*–942 34
   Tas.   *area*–946 2
   upon Hull Humberside Eng.
       area–428 37
   upon Thames London Eng.   *area*–421 94
Kingswood Avon Eng.   *area*–423 94
Kington Hereford & Worcester
       Eng.   *area*–424 44
Kingussie Highland Scot.   *area*–411 92
Kinkajous *see* Procyonidae
Kinlochleven Highland Scot.   *area*–411 85
Kinney Co. Tex.   *area*–764 433
Kinorhyncha *see* Echinodera
Kinross Scot.   *area*–412 8
Kinshasa Congo   *area*–675 112
Kinship
   ethics *see* Family ethics
   genealogy   929
   soc. theology
    Christianity   261.835 83
    comp. rel.   291.178 358 3

Knees (continued)
fractures 617.158
orthopedic surgery 617.398
Knickknacks *see* Ornaments arts
Knife combat
mil. training 355.548
s.a. spec. mil. branches
Knighthood orders
genealogy 929.71
Knightly customs 394.7
Knighton Powys Wales *area*–429 54
Knights
Hospitallers *see* Knights of
Malta
of Malta
rel. orders 255.79
church hist. 271.79
ecclesiology 262.24
of Pythias
association 366.2
members
biog. & work 366.209 2
s.a. *pers.*–366 2
of St. John *see* Knights of
Malta
Knights (chessmen) 799.144
Knitted
fabrics
arts 746.046 61
s.a. spec. proc. e.g.
Weaving
manufacturing
soc. & econ. aspects *see*
Secondary industries
technology 677.661
other aspects see
Textiles
s.a. spec. products
laces
textile arts 746.226
other aspects see Laces
fabrics
rugs
textile arts 746.73
Knitting
textile
arts 746.432
manufacturing
soc. & econ. aspects *see*
Secondary industries
technology 677.028 245
s.a. spec. kinds of textiles
& spec. prod.
Knives
tableware *see* Tableware
tools
soc. & econ. aspects *see*
Secondary industries
tech. & mf. 621.932
s.a. spec. appls. e.g.
Clothing comm. mf.

Knives (continued)
weapons *see* Edged weapons
Knob celery *see* Celeriac
Knobs Ky. *area*–769 5
Knockers
arts *see* Ornaments arts
Knots
combinatorial topoloqy 514.224
s.a. Knotting
Knott Co. Ky. *area*–769 165
Knotted fabrics
arts 746.046 6
s.a. spec. proc. e.g.
Weaving
manufacturing
soc. & econ. aspects *see*
Secondary industries
technology 677.66
other aspects see Textiles
s.a. spec. prod.
Knotting 623.888 2
seamanship 623.888 2
textile arts 746.422
Knottingley West Yorkshire Eng.
area–428 15
Knowledge 001
gift of the Holy Spirit
Christian doctrines 234.12
metaphysics 121
misc. aspects see
Philosophy
of God
Christianity 231.042
nat. rel. 212.6
other rel. see God
psychology *see* Cognition
rel. attitudes *see* Religious
attitudes secular
disciplines
sociology 306.4
s.a. spec. branches of
knowledge
Know-Nothing Party U.S.
pol. sci. 324.273 2
s.a. spec. subj. of concern
e.g. Social problems
Knowsley Merseyside Eng. *area*–427 54
Knox
Bible translation 220.520 9
s.a. spec. parts of Bible
County
Illinois *area*–773 49
Indiana *area*–772 39
Kentucky *area*–769 125
Maine *area*–741 53
Missouri *area*–778 315
Nebraska *area*–782 59
Ohio *area*–771 52
Tennessee *area*–768 85
Texas *area*–764 743
Knoxville Tenn. *area*–768 85

Krypton
  chemistry
    technology (continued)
      s.a. spec. prod.
    other aspects see Rare gases
Ksar-es-Souk Morocco   *area*–645
Kuala Lumpur Malaysia   *area*–595 1
Kuba kingdom hist.   967 510 1
  s.a. spec. events & subj.
    e.g. Commerce
Kubitschek admin. Brazil hist.   981.062
  s.a. spec. events & subj.
    e.g. Commerce
Kublai Khan
  reign Asia hist. *see* Mongol
Kuchean languages
  linguistics   491.996
  literatures   891.996
  s.a.   *lang.*–919 96
Kudus
  animal husbandry   636.293
  other aspects see Bovoidea
Kuibyshev RSFSR   *area*–478 3
Ku-Klux Klan   322.320 973
Kumamoto Japan   *area*–522
Kumquats
  agriculture   634.34
    soc. & econ. aspects *see*
      Primary industries
  foods   641.343 4
    preparation
      commercial   664.804 34
      domestic   641.643 4
  other aspects see Rutales;
    also Fruits
Kundalini
  yoga   294.543
Kung fu
  equipment mf.   688.768 159
  sports   796.815 9
  other aspects see Sports
Kunlun Mts. China   *area*–516
Kuopio Finland   *area*–489 75
Kurdish
  language
    linguistics   491.59
    literature   891.59
    s.a.   *lang.*–915 9
  people   *r.e.n.*–915 9
  s.a. other spec. subj. e.g.
    Arts
Kurdistan   *area*–566 7
  Iran   *area*–555 4
  Iraq   *area*–567 2
  Turkey   *area*–566 7
Kurds   *r.e.n.*–915 9
Kurdzhale Bulgaria   *area*–497 75
Kurgan RSFSR   *area*–573
Kurile Isls.   *area*–577
Ku-ring-gai Chase Nat. Park
  N.S.W.   *area*–944 1

Kurland   *area*–474 3
Kursk RSFSR   *area*–473 5
Kurukh *see* Dravida
Kush   *area*–397 8
Kushitic *see* Cushitic
Kuskokwim election district
    Alaska   *area*–798 4
Kut Iraq   *area*–576 5
Kutahya Turkey   *area*–562
Kutch India   *area*–547 5
Kuvasz
  animal husbandry   636.73
  other aspects see Dogs
Kuwait   *area*–536 7
Kuwaitis   *r.e.n.*–927 536 7
Kwa languages
  linguistics   496.33
  literatures   896.33
  s.a.   *lang.*–963 3
Kwajalein   *area*–968 3
Kwangsi-Chuang Autonomous
    Region China   *area*–512 8
Kwangtung China   *area*–512 7
Kwara Nigeria   *area*–669 5
Kwa-Zulu Natal   *area*–684 91
Kweichow China   *area*–513 4
Kyabram Vic.   *area*–945 4
Kyanite
  mineralogy   549.62
Kyle & Carrick Strathclyde Scot.
    area–414 64
Kyloe cattle
  animal husbandry   636.223
  other aspects see Cattle
Kymi Finland   *area*–489 71
Kyneton Vic.   *area*–945 3
Kyogle N.S.W.   *area*–944 3
Kyoto Japan   *area*–521 91
Kyrie *see* Common of the Mass
Kythera Greece   *area*–495 2
  ancient   *area*–386
Kyushu Japan   *area*–522
Kyustendil Bulgaria   *area*–497 73
Kyusyu Japan   *area*–522

L

L^p spaces   515.73
  s.a. spec. appls. e.g.
    Engineering
LSD *see* Hallucinogenic drugs
La Altagracia Dominican Republic
    area–729 385
Labeling
  law   343.082
    spec. commodities   343.085
    spec. jur.   343.3–.9
  library materials   025.7
  prod. management *see*
    Packaging prod.
    management

Laboratory (continued)
method
 education   371.38
  s.a. spec. levels of ed.;
   also Special education
 rel. instruction
  Christianity   268.68
  other rel. see Religious
   instruction
 rooms school bldgs.
  education   371.623 4
  s.a. spec. levels of ed.;
   also Special education
 s.a. other spec. subj. e.g.
  Diagnoses
Laborers
 biog. & work *see spec. kinds*
  e.g. Carpenters
 s.a.   *pers.*–331 7
Laboring classes
 customs   390.1
  dress   391.01
  homes   392.360 1
 soc. welfare   362.85
  govt. control   350.848 5
   central govts.   351.848 5
   spec. jur.   353–354
   local govts.   352.944 85
  law *see* Welfare services
   law
 other aspects see Lower
  classes
 s.a.   *pers.*–062 3
 s.a. Laborers
Labor-management bargaining *see*
 Collective bargaining
Labor-oriented persons
 biog. & work   331.092
 s.a.   *pers.*–331
Labour Party
 Australia
  pol. sci.   324.294 07
 United Kingdom
  pol. sci.   324.241 07
 s.a. spec. subj. of concern
  e.g. Social problems
Labrador
 Current
  oceanography   551.471 4
 land   *area*–718 2
 Sea
  oceanography   551.461 43
  regional subj. trmt.   *area*–163 43
  other aspects see Atlantic
   Ocean
Laburnum trees *see* Leguminales
Labyrinth
 ear *see* Internal ear
Labyrinthodontia
 paleozoology   567.6
Lac Qui Parle Co. Minn.   *area*–776 38

Laccadive
 Isls. India   *area*–548 1
 Sea *see* Arabian Sea
Laccoliths
 structural geol.   551.88
 s.a. spec. aspects e.g.
  Prospecting
Lacerated wounds
 statistics   312.304 714 3
  deaths   312.260 471 43
 surgical trmt.   617.143
  anesthesiology   617.967 143
 s.a. Veterinary sciences
Lacertilia
 culture   639.395
 hunting
  commercial   639.145
  sports   799.257 95
 paleozoology   567.95
 zoology   597.95
 other aspects see Reptilia
Laces
 fabrics
  arts   746.22
  manufacturing
   soc. & econ. aspects *see*
    Secondary industries
   technology   677.653
  other aspects see Textiles
 s.a. spec. prod.
Lacewings *see* Neuroptera
Lachlan River N.S.W.   *area*–944 9
Lacings *see* Passementerie
Lacistemataceae *see* Piperales
Lackawanna Co. Pa.   *area*–748 36
Lackering
 dec. arts   745.72
 furniture arts   749.5
 woodwork bldgs.   698.34
Lackers
 manufacturing
  soc. & econ. aspects *see*
   Secondary industries
  technology   667.75
Laclede Co. Mo.   *area*–778 815
Lacombe Alta.   *area*–712 33
Laconia Greece *see* Sparta
La Cordillera Paraguay   *area*–892 135
La Coruña Spain   *area*–461 1
Lacquering *see* Lackering
Lacquers *see* Lackers
Lacrimal
 ducts *see* Lacrimal mechanisms
  eyes
 glands *see* Lacrimal
  mechanisms eyes
 mechanisms eyes
  diseases   617.764
   geriatrics   618.977 764
   pediatricts   618.920 977 64
   statistics   312.304 776 4

Lacrimal
 mechanisms eyes (continued)
  physiology
   human   612.847
   other aspects see Sensory
    functions
  other aspects see Eyes
La Croix Lake Minn.   *area*–776 77
La Crosse
 city Wis.   *area*–775 72
 Co. Wis.   *area*–775 71
Lacrosse (game)
 equipment mf.   688.763 47
  soc. & econ. aspects *see*
   Secondary industries
 players
  biog. & work   796.347 092
  s.a.   *pers.*–796 34
 sports   796.347
 other aspects see Sports
Lac-St. Jean Co. Que.   *area*–714 14
Lactation
 diseases
  obstetrics   618.71
  pub. health   614.599 2
  statistics   312.304 871
  other aspects see Diseases
 human phys.   612.664
 other aspects see Secretion
Lactobacteriaceae *see*
  Eubacteriales
Lactoridaceae *see* Magnoliales
Lactose
 org. chem.   547.781 5
 other aspects see Sugar
Lactuca sativa *see* Lettuce
Ladies Isl. S.C.   *area*–757 99
Ladin *see* Rhaeto-Romanic
Ladino *see* Judeo-Spanish
Ladoga Lake RSFSR   *area*–472
Ladrone Isls.   *area*–967
Ladybank Fife Scot.   *area*–412 92
Ladybird beetles *see*
  Colydioidea
La Estrelleta Dominican Republic
    area–729 343
Lafayette
 County
  Arkansas   *area*–767 57
  Florida   *area*–759 816
  Mississippi   *area*–762 83
  Missouri   *area*–778 453
  Wisconsin   *area*–775 79
 Par. La.   *area*–763 47
Lafourche Par. La.   *area*–763 39
Lag b'Omer
 customs   394.268 296
 Judaism   296.439

Lagomorpha
 agric. pests   632.693 22
  s.a. spec. types of culture
   e.g. Forestry; *also*
   spec. crops
 animal husbandry
  technology   636.932 2
  soc. & econ. aspects *see*
   Primary industries
 conservation tech.   639.979 322
 drawing tech.   743.693 22
 hunting
  commercial
   technology   639.113 22
   soc. & econ. aspects
    see Primary
    industries
  sports   799.259 322
 paleozoology   569.322
 zoology   599.322
 other aspects see Animals
Lagomorphs *see* Lagomorpha
Lagoons
 ecology life sci. *see* Aquatic
  ecology life sci.
 fresh-water *see* Fresh-water
  lagoons
 salt-water
  ecology life sci. *see*
   Salt-water ecology life
   sci.
  other aspects see Special
   salt-water forms
 sewage
  technology   628.351
  other aspects see Sewage
   treatment
Lagos Nigeria   *area*–669 1
Lagrange
 Co. Ind.   *area*–772 79
 polynomials   515.55
  s.a. spec. appls. e.g.
   Engineering
Laguerre polynomials   515.55
 s.a. spec. appls. e.g.
  Engineering
Laguna Philippines   *area*–599 1
Lahnda language
 linguistics   491.419
 literature   891.419
 s.a.   *lang.*–914 19
Lahore Pakistan   *area*–549 143
Laissez-faire econ. theory   330.153
Laity
 church govt.
  Christianity   262.15
  comp. rel.   291.64
  Islam   297.61
  Judaism   296.61
  s.a. other spec. rel.

Laity (continued)
  pastoral duties
    Christianity   253.5–.7
    other rel. see Pastoral
        theology
  rel. law *see* Persons rel. law
Lake
  County
    California   *area*–794 17
    Colorado   *area*–788 46
    Florida   *area*–759 22
    Illinois   *area*–773 21
    Indiana   *area*–772 99
    Michigan   *area*–774 68
    Minnesota   *area*–776 76
    Montana   *area*–786 832
    Ohio   *area*–771 334
    Oregon   *area*–795 93
    South Dakota   *area*–783 35
    Tennessee   *area*–768 12
  District Eng.   *area*–427 8
  ice
    physical geol.   551.345
  liners
    engineering   623.824 36
      design   623.812 436
      models   623.820 143 6
    seamanship   623.882 436
    other aspects see Vessels
        (nautical)
  Mead Nat. Recreation Area Nev.
                   area–793 12
  of the Cherokees Okla. *area*–766 91
  of the Ozarks Mo.   *area*–778 493
  of the Woods
    Co. Minn.   *area*–776 81
    lake   *area*–776 79
      Minnesota   *area*–776 79
      Ontario   *area*–713 11
  Pedder Nat. Park Tas. *area*–946 2
  port facilities *see* Port
      facilities
  ports *see* Ports
    inland-waterway
  Reeve Fauna Reserve Vic. *area*–945 6
  Saint John Co. Que.   *area*–714 14
  states U.S.   *area*–77
  transportation
    commerce   386.5
    govt. control   351.876 5
      spec. jur.   353–354
    terminals
      activities
        freight *see* Freight
        services transp.
          terminals
        passenger *see* Passenger
        services transp.
          terminals

Lake
  transportation
    terminals (continued)
      facilities
        freight *see* Freight
        terminals facilties
        passenger *see* Passenger
        terminals facilities
      other aspects see
        Inland-waterway transp.
    other aspects see Fresh-water
    s.a. spec. lakes e.g. Erie
      Lake
Lakes
  ecology life sci.   574.526 322
    animals   591.526 322
    microorganisms   576.15
    plants   581.526 322
    s.a. spec. organisms
  Entrance Vic.   *area*–945 6
  flood-control eng. *see* Water
    storage flood control
    eng.
  hydraulic eng.
    soc. & econ. aspects *see*
      Secondary industries
    technology   627.14
    s.a. spec. appls. e.g.
      Inland-waterway transp.
    other aspects see Liquids
      engineering
  hydrology   551.482
  internat. law   341.444
  regional subj. trmt.   *area*–169 2
  resources
    economics   333.916 3
      recreational   333.784 4
    govt. control
      law   346.046 916 3
        spec. jur.   346.3–.9
      pub. admin. *see* Water
        resources govt. control
        pub. admin.
    s.a. other spec. aspects
      e.g. Water resources
      govt. control pub.
      admin.
  temperatures
    meteorology   551.524 8
      weather forecasting 551.642 48
        spec. areas   551.65
  utilization
    fish culture   639.312
    s.a. spec. kinds of fish
  water-supply sources
    technology   628.112
    other aspects see Water
      supply engineering
Lakonia Greece   *area*–495 2
Lakshadweep India   *area*–548 1

Lancaster
House of (continued)
  s.a. spec. events & subj.
    e.g. Commerce
Sound *see* American Arctic
    seawaters
Lancelets
  zoology   596.4
  other aspects see Chordata
Lances *see* Edged weapons
Land
  appraisal econ.   333.332
  art
    gen. wks.   709.040 76
      spec. places   709.1–.9
    painting   759.067 6
      spec. places   759.1–.9
    sculpture   735.230 476
      spec. places   730.9
    s.a. other spec. art forms
  banks
    economics   332.31
    other aspects see Banks
        (finance)
  birds
    hunting
      commercial   639.122
        misc. aspects see
            Hunting industries
      sports   799.242
    zoology   598.292 2
    other aspects see Aves
    s.a. spec. kinds
  capital *see* Fixed capital
  carnivores *see* Fissipeda
  descriptions
    law   346.043 8
      spec. jur.   346.3–.9
  disposal
    pub. admin. *see* Land
        management & disposal
  drainage
    engineering *see* Drainage
    geology   551.35
  ecology life sci.   574.526 4
    animals   591.526 4
    microorganisms   576.15
    plants   581.526 4
    s.a. spec. organisms
  economics   333
  forces
    mil. sci.   355
      spec. kinds   356–357
  forms
    geomorphology   551.41–.45
    subj. trmt.   *area*–14
  grants econ.   333.16
  gunnery
    mil. eng.   623.551
  income distribution
    macroeconomics   339.21

Land (continued)
  investment finance   332.632 42
    misc. aspects see Real
        property
  law *see* Real property law
  management & disposal
    pub. admin.   350.713 2
      central govts.   351.713 2
        spec. jur.   353–354
      local govts.   352.163 2
  mine laying
    mil. eng.   623.262
    s.a. spec. appls.
  nationalization econ.   331.14
  operations
    history
      Spanish-American War   973.893
      U.S. Civil War   973.33
      U.S. Mexican War   973.623
      U.S. Revolution   973.33
      U.S. War of 1812   973.523
      Vietnamese War   959.704 342
      World War 1   940.41
      World War 2   940.541
      s.a. other spec. wars
    mil. sci.   355
  policy *see* Public lands
  procurement
    pub. admin.   350.712 2
      central govts.   351.712 2
        spec. jur.   353–354
      local govts.   352.162 2
  reclamation
    agriculture *see* Reclamation
        soil sci.
    engineering
      soc. & econ. aspects *see*
          Secondary industries
      technology   627.5
      s.a. spec. appls. e.g.
          Landscape architecture
      other aspects see Liquids
          engineering
  reform
    economics   333.31
    law   346.044
      spec. jur.   346.3–.9
  regions subj. trmt.   *area*–14
  reservations
    armed forces   355.79
    s.a. spec. mil. branches
  resources
    economics   333.73
    govt. control
      law   346.046 73
        spec. jur.   346.3–.9
      pub. admin.   350.823 26
        central govts.   351.823 26
          spec. jur.   353–354
        local govts.   352.942 326

Landing-gear
  aircraft eng.
    soc. & econ. aspects *see*
      Secondary industries
    tech. & mf. — 629.134 381
Landing-lights
  aircraft eng. — 629.135 1
Landing-maneuvers
  mil. sci. — 355.422
  s.a. spec. mil. branches
Landing-systems
  spacecraft *see* Flight
    operations systems
    spacecraft
Landkreise
  local govt. admin. — 352.007 3
Landlocked seas
  internat. law — 341.444
  other aspects see Special
    salt-water forms
Landlords' liability insurance — 368.56
  misc. aspects see Insurance
Landlord-tenant relations
  land econ. — 333.54
  law — 346.043 4
  spec. jur. — 346.3–.9
Landowners
  biog. & work. — 333.009 2
  s.a. — pers.–333
Land's End Cornwall Eng. — area–423 75
Landscape
  architects
    biog. & work — 712.092
    occupational ethics — 174.971
    s.a. — pers.–71
  architecture — 712
  art — 712
  design — 712
Landscapes
  art representation — 704.943 6
  painting — 758.1
  s.a. other spec. art forms
Landslides
  geology — 551.353
Landsmal *see* New Norse
Lane Co.
  Kansas — area–781 45
  Oregon — area–795 31
Langbaurgh Cleveland Eng. — area–428 54
Langeland Denmark — area–489 4
Langerhans islands *see* Islands
  of Langerhans
Langholm Dumfries & Galloway
  Scot. — area–414 83
Langlade Co. Wis. — area–775 354
Langport Somerset Eng. — area–423 89
Langtree Greater Manchester Eng.
   — area–427 36
Language — 400
  bibliographies — 011.2
  spec. kinds — 012–016

Language (continued)
  catalogs
    general — 017–019
    spec. kinds — 012–016
  communication — 001.54
  disorders
    abnormal psych. — 157.4
      children — 155.451 4
    gen. med. — 616.855
    geriatrics — 618.976 855
    pediatrics — 618.928 55
    pub. health — 614.58
    statistics — 312.385 5
    other aspects see Mental
      illness
  groups
    soc. theology
      Christianity — 261.834 7
      comp. rel. — 291.178 347
      s.a. other spec. rel.
    sociology — 305.7
    regions subj. trmt. — area–175
  sociology
    culture — 306
    soc. interaction — 302.22
  translators
    soc. & econ. aspects *see*
      Secondary industries
    tech. & mf. — 621.389 4
    s.a. spec. appls. e.g.
      Translation (linguistics)
Languages — 400
  applications to spec. subj. — s.s.–014
  Biblical trmt. — 220.84
  s.a. spec. parts of Bible
  documentation — 025.064
  incidence statistics — 312.9
  libraries — 026.4
  misc. aspects see Special
    libraries
  library acquisitions — 025.274
  library classification — 025.464
  study & teaching — 407
    curriculums — 375.4
    elementary ed. — 372.6
    spec. ed. — 371.904 4
    s.a. spec. groups of
      students
  subject headings — 025.494
  symbolic logic *see* Symbolic
    logic
  other aspects see Disciplines
    (systems)
Langue d'oc (dialect) — 447.8
Languedoc France — area–448
Languedoc-Roussillon
  France — area–448
Lanier Co. Ga. — area–758 817
Laniidae
  hunting
    commercial — 639.128 862

Laplace transform
 operational calculus   515.723
  s.a. spec. appls. e.g.
   Engineering
Lapland   *area*–489 77
La Plata
 Co. Colo.   *area*–788 29
 estuary *see* Plata estuary
 Mt. Colo.   *area*–788 29
La Porte Co. Ind.   *area*–772 91
Lapp
 language
  linguistics   494.55
  literature   894.55
  s.a.   *lang.*–945 5
 people   *r.e.n.*–945 5
 s.a. Lapland; *also other*
   spec. subj. e.g. Arts
Lappet embroidery *see* Machine
  embroidery
Lappi Finland   *area*–489 77
Lapping-tools
 soc. & econ. aspects *see*
  Secondary industries
 tech. & mf.   621.922
  s.a. spec. appls. e.g.
   Lapidary work
Laprairie Co. Que.   *area*–714 34
Lapsation
 insurance   368.016
  s.a. spec. kinds of
   insurance
Laptev Sea *see* Asian Artic
  seawaters
Lara Venezuela   *area*–872 5
Laramie
 Co. Wyo.   *area*–787 19
 Range Wyo.   *area*–787 9
Larceny
 criminology   364.162
 insurance   368.82
  misc. aspects see Insurance
 law   345.026 2
  spec. jur.   345.3–.9
 prevention museology   069.54
 soc. theology
  Christianity   261.833 162
  comp. rel.   291.178 331 62
  s.a. other spec. rel.
 other aspects see Criminal
  offenses
Larch
 trees
  forestry   634.975 7
  soc. & econ. aspects *see*
   Primary industries
  other aspects see
   Coniferales; *also*
   Trees
 woods *see* Softwoods

Lard
 comm. proc.   664.34
 other aspects see Fats
Larder beetles
 zoology   595.764 6
 other aspects see Polyphaga
Lardizabalaceae *see*
  Berberidales
Large
 industry
  prod. econ.   338.644
 intestines
  anatomy
   human   611.347
   other aspects see
    Nutritive organs
  diseases
   surgery   617.554 7
    anesthesiology   617.967 554 7
   other aspects see
    Intestines diseases
  physical anthropometry   576.634 7
  physiology
   human   612.36
   other aspects see
    Nutrition
  tissue biology human   611.018 934 7
  s.a. other spec. subj.
Large-type publications *see*
  Disabled people
  publications for
Largs Strathclyde Scot.   *area*–414 61
Lari
 hunting
  commercial   629.128 338
  sports   799.248 338
 paleozoology   568.3
 zoology   598.338
 other aspects see Aves
Larimer Co. Colo.   *area*–788 68
La Rioja Argentina   *area*–824 6
Larissa Greece   *area*–495 4
Larix *see* Larch trees
Larks *see* Alaudidae
Larkspur *see* Ranales
Larne N. Ire.   *area*–416 16
La Romana Dominican Republic
      area–729 383
Larue Co. Ky.   *area*–769 713
Larvacea *see* Tunicata
Laryngeal muscles *see* Larynx
Laryngitis *see* Larynx diseases
Laryngology
 med. sci.   616.22
  geriatrics   618.976 22
  pediatrics   618.922 2
  vet. med.   636.089 622
  s.a. spec. animals
  other aspects see Medical
   sciences
 s.a. Larynx

Larynx
  anatomy
    human ... 611.22
    other aspects see
        Respiratory organs
  diseases
    gen. wks. ... 616.22
      neoplasms ... 616.992 22
      tuberculosis ... 616.995 22
    geriatrics ... 618.976 22
    pediatrics ... 618.922 2
    pub. health ... 614.592 2
    statistics ... 312.322
      deaths ... 312.262 2
    surgery ... 617.533
      anesthesiology ... 617.967 533
    other aspects see Diseases
  physical anthropometry ... 573.622
  physiology
    human ... 612.2
    other aspects see
        Respiration
  speech phys. ... 612.78
  tissue biology human ... 611.018 922
La Salle
  County
    Illinois ... *area*–773 27
    Texas ... *area*–764 453
  Par. La. ... *area*–763 75
Las Animas Co. Colo. ... *area*–788 96
Laser
  commun. devices
    soc. & econ. aspects *see*
        Secondary industries
    tech. & mf. ... 621.389 6
    s.a. spec. appls. e.g.
        Tracking
  weapons
    small arms
      mil. eng.
        soc. & econ. aspects
          see Secondary
          industries
        tech. & mf. ... 623.446
Lasers
  engineering
    soc. & econ. aspects *see*
        Secondary industries
    tech. & mf. ... 621.366
    s.a. spec. appls. e.g.
        Tracking
  other aspects see
      Amplification light
      optics
Lasethi Greece ... *area*–499 8
Lashley system psych. ... 150.194 32
  s.a. spec. subj. & branches of
      psych.
Las Palmas Spain ... *area*–649
La Spezia Italy ... *area*–451 83

Lassen
  Co. Calif. ... *area*–794 26
  Volcanic Nat. Park Calif.
    ... *area*–794 24
L'Assomption Co. Que. ... *area*–714 416
Lassos
  hunting & shooting sports ... 799.202 82
Lasswade Lothian Scot. ... *area*–413 5
Last
  Judgment
    Christianity ... 236.9
    other rel. see Eschatology
  resort
    courts of *see* Supreme court
  Supper
    Christian doctrines ... 232.957
  things *see* Eschatology
  words
    Jesus' life
      on cross ... 232.963 5
      to disciples ... 232.958
Las Tunas Cuba ... *area*–729 162
Las Vegas Nev. ... *area*–793 13
Las Villas Cuba ... *area*–729 14
Latah Co. Ida. ... *area*–796 86
Latakia Syria ... *area*–569 13
Latches
  mf. tech. ... 683.31
  other aspects see Hardware
Latent
  heats
    physical chem. ... 541.362
      applied ... 660.296 2
      organic ... 547.136 2
    s.a. spec. elements,
        cpds., prod.
    physics ... 536.42
  radiations
    divinatory use parapsych. ... 133.323
Laterality
  psychology ... 152.335
  animals
  children ... 155.412
  s.a. psych. of other spec.
      groups
Latex paints
  technology ... 667.63
  other aspects see Paints
Latexes
  manufacturing
    soc. & econ. aspects *see*
        Secondary industries
    technology ... 678.5
    org. chem. ... 547.842 5
Lathers
  colloid chem. *see* Hydrosols
      colloid chem.
Lathes
  soc. & econ. aspects *see*
      Secondary industries

Lathes (continued)	
tech. & mf.	621.942
s.a. spec. appls. e.g.	
Woodworking	
Lathwork	
architectural construction	721.044 6
s.a. spec. structural	
elements; also spec.	
types of bldgs.	
bldg. construction	693.6
Latimer Co. Okla.	*area*–766 76
Latin	
alphabets	
printing	686.217
America	*area*–8
American	
literature	860
people	*r.e.n.*–68
s.a. other spec. subj. e.g.	
Arts	
Americans	*r.e.n.*–68
language	
linguistics	470
literature	870
s.a.	*lang.*–71
lettering dec. arts	745.619 7
schools	373.242
govt. supervision & support	379
texts	
Bible	220.47
s.a. spec. parts of Bible	
s.a. other spec. works	
s.a. other spec. subj.	
Latina Italy	*area*–456 23
Latinian languages	
linguistics	479.4
literatures	879.4
s.a.	*lang.*–794
s.a. Latin lanquage	
Latitude	
celestial navigation	527.1
geodetic astronomy	526.61
Latium Italy	*area*–456 2
ancient	*area*–376
Latrines *see* Comfort stations	
La Trobe River Vic.	*area*–945 6
Latrobe Tas.	*area*–946 5
Latter-Day Saints Church	289.3
buildings	
architecture	726.589 3
building	690.658 93
other aspects see	
Religious-purpose	
bldgs.	
Christian life guides	248.489 3
doctrines	230.93
creeds	238.93
general councils	262.593
govt. & admin.	262.093
parishes	254.093

Latter-Day Saints Church (continued)	
members	
biog. & work	289.309 2
s.a. spec. branches	
s.a.	*pers.*–283
missions	266.93
moral theology	241.049 3
music	
arts	783.026 93
recordings	789.912 302 693
s.a. spec. instruments;	
also spec. kinds e.g.	
Liturgical music	
religion	
pub. worship	264.093 02
significance	246.7
private prayers for	242.809 3
pub. worship	264.093
rel. associations	
adults	267.189 3
men	267.249 3
women	267.449 3
young adults	267.629 3
rel. instruction	268.893
rel. law	262.989 3
schools	377.893
secondary training	207.129 3
sermons	252.093
theological seminaries	207.119 3
s.a. other spec. aspects	
Lattice-girder bridges	
structural eng.	624.37
other aspects see Bridges	
(structures)	
Lattice-plant family *see*	
Aponogetonales	
Lattices	
crystals	
crystallography	548.81
s.a. spec. substances	
mathematics	511.33
number theory	512.7
symbolic logic	511.33
s.a. spec. math. branches	
s.a. spec. appls. e.g.	
Engineering	
Latvia	*area*–474 3
Latvian	
language	
linguistics	491.93
literature	891.93
s.a.	*lang.*–919 3
people	*r.e.n.*–919 3
SSR	*area*–474 3
s.a. other spec. subj. e.g.	
Arts	
Laudanum *see* Opium	
Lauder Borders Scot.	*area*–413 85
Lauderdale	
Border Scot.	*area*–413 85

Lauderdale (continued)
  County
    Alabama   *area*–761 99
    Mississippi   *area*–762 676
    Tennessee   *area*–768 16
Lauds *see* Office hours
Launceston
  Cornwall Eng.   *area*–423 71
  Tasmania   *area*–946 5
Launches *see* Motorboats
Launching *see* Takeoff
Launching-pads
  guided missiles
    mil. eng.
      soc. & econ. aspects *see*
          Secondary industries
      tech. & mf.   623.451 9
  spacecraft *see* Terrestrial
          facilities spacecraft
Launch-vehicles
  guided missiles
    mil. eng.
      soc. & econ. aspects *see*
          Secondary industries
      tech. & mf.   623.451 9
Launderers
  biog. & work   648.109 2
  s.a.   *pers.*–648
Laundering
  home econ.   648.1
  soc. & econ. aspects *see*
          Secondary industries
  technology   667.13
Laundries
  plumbing   696.183
  sanitation   363.729 9
  law   344.046 4
    spec. jur.   344.3–.9
  pub. admin.   350.772
    central govts.   351.772
    spec. jur.   353–354
    local govts.   352.6
La Unión El Salvador   *area*–728 434
La Union Philippines   *area*–599 1
Lauraceae *see* Laurales
Laurales
  botany   583.931
  floriculture   635.933 931
  forestry   634.973 931
  med. aspects
    crop prod.   633.883 931
    gen. pharm.   615.323 931
      toxicology   615.952 393 1
    vet. pharm.   636.089 532 393 1
      toxicology   636.089 595 239 31
  paleobotany   561.3
  other aspects see Plants
Laurel
  Co. Ky.   *area*–769 143
  family *see* Laurales
  Hill Pa.   *area*–748 8

Laurel (continued)
  wax
    comm. proc.   665.12
    other aspects see Waxes
Laurencekirk Grampian Scot.
                                          area–412 4
Laurens Co.
  Georgia   *area*–758 535
  South Carolina   *area*–757 31
Laurentian Plateau   *area*–714
  Manitoba   *area*–712 72
  Ontario   *area*–713 1
  Quebec   *area*–714
Laurentides Provincial Park Que.
                                          area–714 4
Laurier
  Wilfred admin.
    Can. hist.   971.056
    s.a. spec. events & subj.
        e.g. Commerce
Lava Beds Nat. Monument Calif.
                                          area–794 21
Lavaca Co. Tex.   *area*–764 255
Laval Co. Que.   *area*–714 271
Lavalieres
  precious metalwork   739.278
  other aspects see Jewelry
Lavalleja Uruguay   *area*–895 21
Lavas
  mineralogy   549.114 22
    spec. minerals   549.2–.7
  petrology   552.22
  other aspects see Natural
          stones
Lavatories
  household management   643.52
  plumbing   696.182
  s.a. Comfort stations
La Vega Dominican Republic
                                          area–729 369
Lavenham Suffolk Eng.   *area*–426 48
Law   340
  Biblical trmt.   220.834
    s.a. spec. parts of Bible
  curriculums   375.34
  documentation   025.063 4
  enforcement
    legal aspects
      internat. criminal law   341.77
      municipal law
        criminal law   345.052
          spec. jur.   345.3–.9
        gen. wks.   344.052 3
          spec. jur.   344.3–.9
      pub. admin.   350.74
        central govts.   351.74
        spec. jur.   353–354
        local govts.   352.2
      soc. services   363.23
  journalism   070.449 33

Law (continued)
  libraries   026.34
    misc. aspects see Special
      libraries
  library acquisitions   025.273 4
  library classification   025.464 3
  lit. & stage trmt. *see* Social
    themes
  of God
    rel. doctrines
      Christianity   241.2
      other rel. see God
  of mass action physical chem.
    see Equilibriums
  of religion *see* Religious law
  reform   340.3
  subject headings   025.493 4
  other aspects see Disciplines
    (systems)
  s.a. Religious law; *also*
    Legal
Lawn
  bowling
    equipment mf.   688.763 1
      soc. & econ. aspects *see*
        Secondary industries
    sports   796.31
    other aspects see Sports
  tennis *see* Tennis
Lawns
  plants grown for
    floriculture   635.964 7
    s.a. spec. plants
Lawrence
  County
    Alabama   *area*–761 92
    Arkansas   *area*–767 25
    Illinois   *area*–773 76
    Indiana   *area*–772 26
    Kentucky   *area*–769 26
    Mississippi   *area*–762 536
    Missouri   *area*–778 75
    Ohio   *area*–771 88
    Pennsylvania   *area*–748 93
    South Dakota   *area*–783 91
    Tennessee   *area*–768 42
  governorship India hist.   954.035 1
  s.a. spec. events & subj.
    e.g. Commerce
Lawrencium
  chemistry   546.449
Laws
  enactment
    pol. sci. *see* Legislative
      procedure
  moral theology
    Christianity   241.2
    other rel. see Moral
      theology

Laws (continued)
  texts   348.02
    spec. jur.   348.3–.9
    U.S.
      Federal   348.732
      state & local   348.74–.79
    spec. subj.   *law s.s.*–026 3
    s.a. Religious law; *also*
      spec. subj. e.g.
      Physics
Law-school bldgs.
  architecture   727.434
  building   690.743 4
  other aspects see Educational
    buildings
Lawsonite
  mineralogy   549.63
Lawyers
  biog. & work   340.092
    s.a. spec. kinds e.g.
      criminal lawyers
      345.009 2
  investments by
    financial econ.   332.671 55
    domestic   332.672 55
    international   332.673 14
  occupational ethics   174.3
  s.a.   *pers.*–344
Laxatives
  pharmacodynamics   615.732
  other aspects see Drugs
Lay
  brothers rel. orders
    Christianity   255.093
    church hist.   271.093
    ecclesiology   262.24
    other rel. see Religious
      congregations
  sisters rel. orders
    Christianity   255.909 3
    church hist.   271.909 3
    ecclesiology   262.24
    other rel. see Religious
      congregations
Layering
  plant propagation   631.534
    s.a. spec. crops; also spec.
      types of culture e.g.
      Floriculture
  plants grown from
    floriculture   635.946
    s.a. spec. plants
Layers
  econ. geol. *see* Stratified
    layers
Layettes *see* Children's
  clothing
Laying on of hands
  rel. rites
    Christianity   265.9

Leaders
ecclesiology *see* Governing
    leaders ecclesiology
s.a. Officers
Leadership
appl. psych. 158.4
  children 155.418
s.a. psych. of other spec.
    groups
s.a. spec. activities
chief executives
  pub. admin. 350.003 23
    central govts. 351.003 23
      spec. jur. 353–354
    local govts. 352.008
management tech. *see*
    Direction management
    tech.
soc. control 698.5
Leading windows 698.5
Leaf
beetles
  zoology 595.764 8
  other aspects see Polyphaga
hoppers *see* Homoptera
miner flies *see* Cyclorrhapha
League
of Augsburg War
  history 949.204
of Nations
  finance 336.091 62
  internat. law 341.22
    treaty series 341.026 1
rugby *see* Rugby football
Leake Co. Miss. *area*–762 653
Leamington Spa Warwickshire Eng.
            area–424 87
Leanness *see* Underweight people
Leapfrog recreation 796.14
Learned societies
buildings
  architecture 727.9
  building 690.79
  other aspects see
    Educational buildings
libraries *see* Nonprofit
    organizations libraries
library bldgs.
  architecture 727.826 8
  building 690.782 68
  other aspects see
    Educational buildings
publishers *see* Institutional
    publishers
Learner-centered ed.
higher 378.03
Learners *see* Students
Learning 001.2
ed. psych. 370.152 3
psychology 153.15
  animals 156.315

Learning
psychology (continued)
  children 155.413
  s.a. psych. of other spec.
    groups
  sociology 303.32
Lease system
convict labor *see* Convict
    labor
Leases
accounting trmt. 657.75
s.a. spec. kinds of
    enterprise e.g.
      Insurance accounting
capital *see* Fixed capital
real property
  economics 333.5
  law 346.043 46
    spec. jur. 346.3–.9
Leasing
personal property
  law 346.047
    spec. jur. 346.3–.9
Least
squares math. 519.4
  appl. to statistics 519.53
Leather
covers bookbinding 686.342
fungi *see* Agaricales
goods
  home sewing 646.1
  manufacturers
    biog. & work 685.092
    s.a. spec. kinds
    s.a. *pers.*–685
  manufacturing
    soc. & econ. aspects *see*
      Secondary industries
    technology 685
Leatherhead Surrey Eng. *area*–422 165
Leathers
arts 745.531
manufacturers
  biog. & work
    artificial leather 675.409 2
    natural leather 675.209 2
    s.a. *pers.*–675
manufacturing
  soc. & econ. aspects *see*
    Secondary industries
  technology 675
  s.a. spec. prod.
Leave periods
labor law *see* Labor law
Leavening agents
manufacturing
  soc. & econ. aspects *see*
    Secondary industries
  technology 664.68
Leavenworth Co. Kan. *area*–781 38

Legal
  aid (continued)
    soc. services   362.58
      misc. aspects see Poor
        people soc. services
  codes
    law   348.023
      spec. jur.   348.3–.9
      U.S.
        federal   348.732 3
        state & local.   348.74–.79
      spec. subj.   *law s.s.*–026 32
    Roman Catholic rel. law   262.92–.93
  counsel
    management use   658.12
  counseling
    soc. welfare   361.38
  decisions
    rel. law *see* Religious law
  notices proc. *see* Legal
        procedure
  officers
    occupational ethics   174.3
    s.a.   *pers.*–349
  personnel
    occupational ethics   174.3
  procedure
    internat. law   341.55
    municipal law
      criminal   345.05
        spec. jur.   345.3–.9
      gen. wks.   347.05
        specialized courts   347.04
        spec. jur.   347.3–.9
        U.S.
          federal   347.735–.738
          local   347.734
            spec. localities   347.74–.79
          state   347.733
            spec. states   347.74–.79
      mil. courts   343.014 3
        spec. jur.   343.3–.9
      spec. subj.   *s.s.*–026 9
  rel. law
    Christianity
      Roman Catholic
        codex iuris canonici   262.934
        early codes   262.92
        other denominations   262.98
      other rel. see Religious
        law
  reasoning   340.11
  systems   340.5
  tender
    money
      economics   332.420 42
      other aspects see Money
    typewriting   652.326
  s.a. Law; *also other spec*
        subj.

Legation buildings *see* Official
        residence buildings
Legations
  pub. admin.
    activities   351.892
      spec. jur.   353–354
    departments *see* Foreign
        affairs pub. admin.
        departments
Legendary
  animals
    lit. & stage trmt.
      folk lit. texts & crit.   398.245 4
      other aspects see Animals
  beings
    lit. & stage trmt. *see*
        Supernatural beings
  minerals
    lit. & stage trmt. *see*
        Minerals
  places
    folk lit. texts & crit.   398.234
    other aspects see Places
  plants
    lit. & stage trmt. *see*
        Plants lit. & stage
        trmt.
  things
    lit. & stage trmt. *see*
        Things
Legendre
  functions   515.53
    s.a. spec. appls. e.g.
        Engineering
  polynomials   515.55
    s.a. spec. appls. e.g.
        Engineering
  transform
    operational calculus   515.723
      s.a. spec. appls. e.g.
        Engineering
Legends
  art representation   704.947
    paintings   753.7
      s.a. other spec. art forms
  folklore   398.2
  religion *see* Religious
        mythology
Leghorn chickens
  animal husbandry   636.55
  other aspects see Chickens
Legions
  mil. organization   355.31
    s.a. spec. mil. branches
Legislation
  pol. sci.   328
Legislative
  bodies
    publications
      bibliographies   011.532
        spec. kinds   012–106

Leguminales (continued)

med. aspects

    crop prod.   633.883 32

    gen. pharm.   615.323 32

      toxicology   615.952 332

    vet. pharm.   636.089 532 332

      toxicology   636.089 595 233 2

    paleobotany   561.3

    other aspects see Plants

Leguminous fruits

agriculture   634.46

    soc. & econ. aspects *see*

              Primary industries

foods   641.344 6

preparation

    commercial   664.804 46

    domestic   641.644 6

other aspects see

         Caesalpiniaceae; *also*

         Fruits

Lehigh Co. Pa.   *area*–748 27

Leicestershire Eng.   *area*–425 4

Leichhardt

Range Qld.   *area*–943 6

River Qld.   *area*–943 7

Leigh

Creek S. Aust.   *area*–942 37

Greater Manchester Eng. *area*–427 36

Leighton-Linslade Bedfordshire

         Eng.   *area*–425 65

Leinster Ireland   *area*–418

Leipzig Ger.   *area*–432 1

Leiria Portugal   *area*–469 42

Leishmaniasis

gen. med.   616.936 4

geriatrics   618.976 936 4

pediatrics   618.929 364

pub. health   614.534

statistics   312.393 64

    deaths   312.269 364

other aspects see Diseases

Leiston-cum-Sizewell Suffolk Eng.

                 area–426 46

Leisure

ed. goal   370.116

    s.a. spec. levels of ed.

influence on crime   364.25

mental health factor   362.204 2

rec. arts   790.013 5

Leitneriaceae *see* Leitneriales

Leitneriales

botany   583.972

floriculture   635.933 972

med. aspects

    crop prod.   633.883 972

    gen. pharm.   615.323 972

      toxicology   615.952 397 2

    vet. pharm.   636.089 532 397 2

      toxicology   636.089 595 239 72

    paleobotany   561.3

other aspects see Plants

Leitrim Ireland   *area*–417 6

Leix Ireland   *area*–418 7

Lemhi Co. Ida   *area*–796 78

Lemmings *see* Myomorpha

Lemnaceae *see* Arales

Lemnos Greece   *area*–499

ancient   *area*–391 1

Lemons

agriculture   634.334

    soc. & econ. aspects *see*

              Primary industries

foods   641.343 34

preparation

    commercial   664.804 34

    domestic   641.643 4

other aspects see Rutales;

        also Fruits

Lempira Honduras   *area*–728 382

Lemuriformes *see* Prosimii

Lemurs *see* Prosimii

flying *see* Dermoptera

Lenawee Co. Mich.   *area*–774 31

Lending *see* Loans

Lenin

Russia hist.   947.084 1

    s.a. spec. events & subj.

        e.g. Commerce

Leningrad RSFSR   *area*–474 5

Lennoaceae *see* Ericales

Lennox & Addington Co. Ont.

                area–713 59

Lennox Hills Central Scot.   *area*–413 12

Lenoir Co. N.C.   *area*–756 385

Leno-weave fabrics

arts   746.046 52

    s.a. spec. proc. e.g.

         Weaving

manufacturing

    soc. & econ. aspects *see*

              Secondary industries

    technology   677.652

other aspects see Textiles

s.a. spec. prod.

Lens culinaris *see* Lentils

Lenses

cameras

    photography   771.352

      gen. tech.   770.282

      spec. proc. & fields   772–778

mf. tech.   681.423

optics *see* Refraction light

         optics

other aspects see Optical

         instruments

Lent

devotional lit.   242.34

rel. observance   263.92

Roman Catholic liturgy   264.027 2

Lenten

cookery home econ.   641.566

Lethal gases
  toxicology — 615.91
    misc. aspects see
      Toxicology
Lethbridge Alta. — *area*–712 34
Letter writers
  biog. & work. — 809.6
    s.a. spec. lits.
  s.a. — *pers.*–86
Lettering
  arch. design — 729.19
    structural elements — 729.3
    s.a. spec. kinds of bldgs.
  bookbinding — 686.36
  decorative — 745.61
  prints — 769.5
  stone — 736.5
  tech. drawing — 604.243
    spec. subj. — *s.s.*–022 1
Letterpress
  mech. printing tech.
    soc. & econ. aspects *see*
      Secondary industries
  technology — 686.231 2
Letters (alphabets)
  inscribing *see* Lettering
  linguistics *see* Notations
    languages
Letters (correspondence)
  biography *see* Biographies
  direct advertising — 659.133
  etiquette — 395.4
  literature
    gen. wks.
      collections — 808.86
      crit. theory — 801.956
        textual — 801.959
      hist. & crit. — 809.6
      rhetoric — 808.6
        juvenile — 808.068 6
    spec. lits. — *lit. sub.*–6
  office services — 651.75
  postal commun. — 383.122
  other aspects see Postal
    communication
Letters of credit *see*
  Commercial paper
Letters rogatory
  internat. law — 341.78
Lettish *see* Latvian
Letts — *r.e.n.*–919 3
Lettuce
  agriculture — 635.52
    soc. & econ. aspects *see*
      Primary industries
  foods — 641.355 2
    preparation
      commercial — 664.805 52
      domestic — 641.655 2
  other aspects see Asterales;
    also Vegetables

Leucite
  mineralogy — 549.68
Leucocytes *see* White corpuscles
Leucocytosis *see* Blood diseases
Leucopenia *see* Blood diseases
Leucoplasts *see* Plastids
Leucotrichia *see* Hair diseases
Leuco- *s.a.* Leuko-
Leukas Greece — *area*–495 5
Leukemias
  gen. med. — 616.994 19
  geriatrics — 618.976 994 19
  pediatrics — 618.929 941 9
  pub. health — 614.599 9
  statistics — 312.399 419
    deaths — 312.269 941 9
  other aspects see Diseases
Leukorrhea
  gynecology — 618.173
    geriatrics — 618.978 173
    pediatrics — 618.920 981 73
  pub. health — 614.599 2
  statistics — 312.304 817 3
  other aspects see Diseases
Leuko- *s.a.* Leuco-
Levant — *area*–56
Levees
  flood control eng. *see* Water
    retention
Leveling
  geodetic surveying — 526.36
Leven Fife Scot. — *area*–412 95
Levers
  mechanics — 531.8
Levis Co. Que. — *area*–714 59
Levisa River Ky. — *area*–769 2
Levitation spiritualism — 133.92
Leviticus
  Bible — 222.13
  other aspects see Historical
    books (O.T.)
Levkas Greece — *area*–495 5
Levulose
  org. chem. — 547.781 3
  other aspects see Sugar
Levy Co. Fla. — *area*–759 77
Lewdness *see* Obscenity
Lewes East Sussex Eng. — *area*–422 57
Lewis
  & Clark Co. Mont. — *area*–786 615
  County
    Idaho — *area*–796 84
    Kentucky — *area*–769 295
    Missouri — *area*–778 345
    New York — *area*–747 59
    Tennessee — *area*–768 432
    Washington — *area*–797 82
    West Virginia — *area*–754 61
  Range Mont. — *area*–786 82
  with Harris Hebrides Scot. — *area*–411 4

Lewisham London Eng.   *area*–421 63
Lexicographers
  biog. & work   413.092
    s.a. spec. langs.
  s.a.   *pers.*–4
Lexicography   413.028
  spec. langs.   *lang. sub.*–302 8
  spec. subj.   *s.s.*–03
Lexicons *see* Dictionaries
Lexington
  Battle U.S. hist.   973.331 1
  city
    Kentucky   *area*–769 47
    Virginia   *area*–755 853
  Co. S.C.   *area*–757 73
Leyburn North Yorkshire Eng.
                    area–428 48
Leyland Lancashire Eng.   *area*–427 67
Leyte Philippines   *area*–599 5
Leyton London Eng.   *area*–421 72
Lhasa apso
  animal husbandry   636.72
  other aspects see Dogs
Liability
  in govt. *see* Government
        liability
  insurance   368.5
    misc. aspects see Insurance
  law   346.02
  of school officials & districts
    law   344.075
    spec. jur.   344.3–.9
Liaoning China   *area*–518 2
Libel *see* Defamation
Liberal
  Catholic Church *see* Roman
        Catholic schisms
  education   370.112
    curriculums   357.008 8
    s.a. spec. levels of ed.;
      also Special education
    s.a. spec. levels of ed.
  parties
    pol. sci.   324.24–.29
    s.a. spec. subj. of concern
      e.g. Social problems
  Party
    Australia
      pol. sci.   324.294 05
    Canada
      pol. sci.   324.271 06
    New York
      pol. sci.   324.274 707
    South Africa
      pol. sci.   324.268 07
    United Kindgom
      pol. sci.   324.241 06
    s.a. spec. subj. of concern
      e.g. Social problems

Liberal (continued)
  theology
    Protestantism *see*
      Protestantism
Liberalism
  philosophy   148
    indiv. phil.   180–190
    s.a. spec. branches of phil.
      e.g. Metaphysics
  pol. ideology   320.51
    soc. theology *see* Political
      ideologies soc.
      theology
Liberality
  ethics *see* Love ethics
Liberia   *area*–666 2
Liberian
  people   *r.e.n.*–966 62
  s.a. spec. subj. e.g. Arts
Libertarian movement
  pol. ideology   320.512
    soc. theology *see* Political
      ideologies soc.
      theology
Liberty
  civil right pol. sci.   323.44
  County
    Florida   *area*–759 923
    Georgia   *area*–758 733
    Montana   *area*–786 13
    Texas   *area*–764 155
  s.a. Freedom
Libido
  sex psych.   155.31
Librarians
  biog. & work   020.92
  occupational ethics   174.909 2
  professional positions   023.2
  s.a.   *pers.*–092
Libraries   027
  accounting   657.832
  community relationships   021.2
  educational institutions   021.3
  govt. control
    activities   350.852
    central govts.   351.852
    spec. jur.   353–354
    local govts.   352.945 2
  govt. depts. *see* Executive
      departments
  govt. relationships   021.8
  law   344.092
    spec. jur.   344.3–.9
  publications for
    bibliographies   011.67
      spec. kinds   012–016
    catalogs
      general   017–019
      spec. kinds   012–016
    reviews   028.167
    s.a. spec. forms e.g. Books

Life
  sciences
    museums (continued)
      museology   069.957
        s.a. spec. activities
          e.g. Display
      subject headings   025.495 7
    other aspects see Sciences
    s.a. spec. kinds e.g.
      Christian life
Lifeboats *see spec. kinds e.g.*
      Hand-propelled vessels
Lifesaving equipment
  shipbuilding *see* Safety
      equipment shipbuilding
Life-support systems
  spacecraft eng.
    manned   629.477
    unmanned   629.467
  other aspects see
      Spacecraft
Liffey River Leinster Ire.   *area*–418 3
Lift
  aeronautical aerodynamics   629.132 33
    s.a. spec. appls. e.g.
      Flying
Lift-bridges
  structural eng.   624.84
  other aspects see Bridges
      (structures)
Lifting
  weights *see* Calisthenics
Lifting-equipment *see*
      Hoisting-equipment
Lifts
  canal eng.
    technology   627.135 3
    s.a. spec. appls. e.g.
      Canal transportation
  other aspects see Liquids
      engineering
Lifts (elevators) *see* Elevators
      (lifts)
Lift-systems
  air-cushion vehicles   629.313
Ligaments
  anatomy
    human   611.72
    other aspects see
      Connective tissue
  diseases
    gen. wks.   616.77
      neoplasms   616.992 72
      tuberculosis   616.995 72
    geriatrics   618.976 77
    pediatrics   618.927 7
    pub. health   614.597 7
    statistics   312.377
      deaths   312.267 7
    other aspects see Diseases
  physical anthropometry   573.672

Ligaments (continued)
  physiology
    human   612.75
    other aspects see Motor
      functions
  tissue biology human   611.018 972
Ligands
  coordination chem. *see*
      Coordination chemistry
Light
  combat vessels
    engineering   623.825 8
      design   623.812 58
      models   623.820 158
    naval forces
      materiel   359.83
      organization   359.325 8
    seamanship   623.882 58
    other aspects see Vessels
      (nautical)
  harness horses
    animal husbandry   636.17
    racing   798.46
    other aspects see Horses
  metals
    arch. construction   721.044 772
      s.a. spec. kinds of
        bldgs.
    bldg. construction   693.772
    bldg. materials   691.872
    metallography   669.957 2
    metallurgy   669.72
      physical & chem.   669.967 2
    soc. & econ. aspects *see*
        Secondary industries
    mineral aspects
      econ. geol.   553.492
      mining
        technology   622.349 2
        prospecting   622.184 92
      s.a. spec. minerals
    products
      mf. tech.   673.72
      other aspects see
        Nonferrous metals
        products
    s.a. spec. uses; also spec.
        metals
  motor trucks *see* Light trucks
  opera *see* Opera
  railways *see* Special-purpose
      railroads
  trucks
    commerce   388.343
    engineering
      gen. tech. & mf.   629.223
        maintenance   629.287 3
        models   629.221 3
        operations   629.284 3

Lighting-fixtures (continued)
ecclesiastical furniture
  built-in arch. decoration   729.98
  rel. significance
    Christianity   247.18
    comp. rel.   291.37
    s.a. other spec. rel.
  furniture arts   749.63
  rel. significance
    Christianity   247.888
    comp. rel.   291.37
    s.a. other spec. rel.
Lightning
  meteorology   551.563
    artificial modification   551.686 3
    weather forecasting   551.646 3
    spec. areas   551.65
  plant injuries
    agriculture   632.15
      s.a. spec. plants; also
        spec. types of culture
        e.g. Forestry
  other aspects see Disasters
Lightning-arresters *see* Control
      devices electrodynamic
      eng.
Lights
  navigation lists   623.894 5
  nonverbal commun. *see*
      Nonverbal language
  rel. significance
    Christianity   246.6
    other rel. see Arts rel.
      significance
  table decorations
    home econ.   642.8
Lightships
  hydraulic eng.   627.923
    s.a. spec. appls. e.g.
      Piloting seamanship
  navigation   623.894 3
  other aspects see Navigation
      aids
Lignin
  recovery from pulp
    technology   676.5
Lignin-derived plastics *see*
      Natural resin-derived
      plastics
Lignite *see* Brown coal
Lignum vitae family *see*
      Malpighiales
Liguria Italy   *area*–451 8
  ancient   *area*–371
Ligurian
  languages *see* Thraco-Phrygian
      languages
  Sea
    oceanography   551.462 2
    regional subj. trmt.   *area*–163 82

Ligurian
  Sea (continued)
    other aspects see Atlantic
      Ocean
Lihou isl.   *area*–423 49
Lihoumel isl.   *area*–423 49
Lij Yasu Ethiopia hist.   963.053
  s.a. spec. events & subj.
      e.g. Commerce
Lilacs *see* Loganiales
Lilaeaceae *see* Juncaginales
Liliaceae
  botany   584.324
  floriculture   635.934 324
  med. aspects
    crop prod.   633.884 324
    gen. pharm.   615.324 324
      toxicology   615.952 432 4
    vet. pharm.   636.089 532 432 4
      toxicology   636.089 595 243 24
  paleobotany   561.4
  other aspects see Plants
Liliales
  botany   584.32
  floriculture   635.934 32
  med. aspects
    crop prod.   633.884 32
    gen. pharm.   615.324 32
      toxicology   615.952 432
    vet. pharm.   636.089 532 432
      toxicology   636.089 595 243 2
  paleobotany   561.4
  other aspects see Plants
Lily family *see* Liliaceae
Lima
  beans
    agriculture   635.653
    soc. & econ. aspects *see*
      Primary industries
    foods   641.356 53
      preparation
        commercial   664.805 653
        domestic   641.656 53
    other aspects see
      Papilionaceae; *also*
      Vegetables
  city Peru   *area*–852 5
Limavady N. Ire.   *area*–416 25
Limbo Christian doctrines
  of fathers   236.6
  of infants   236.7
Limburg
  Belgium   *area*–493 2
  Netherlands   *area*–492 4
Limburger cheeses
  dairy tech.   637.353
  other aspects see Cheeses
Limbus *see* Limbo
Lime mortars *see* Limes
    (cements)
Limerick Ireland   *area*–419 4

Lincoln (continued)
  Heath Eng.   *area*–425 3
  March Eng.   *area*–425 32
  Nat. Park S. Aust.   *area*–942 38
  Par. La.   *area*–763 91
  Sea *see* American Arctic
      seawaters
  Wolds Eng.   *area*–425 32
Lincolnshire Eng.   *area*–425 3
Linden
  family *see* Tiliales
  trees
    forestry   634.972 7
    soc. & econ. aspects *see*
      Primary industries
    other aspects see Tiliales;
      also Trees
Lindsey parts Lincolnshire Eng.
                    area–425 31
Lindsley shorthand system   653.425
Line
  breeding
    animal husbandry   636.082 41
    s.a. spec. animals
  cuts printing
    soc. & econ. aspects *see*
      Secondary industries
    technology   686.232 7
  engraving
    graphic arts
      processes   765.2
      products   769
  geometry   516.183
    Euclidean   516.218 3
    s.a. other spec. geometries;
      also spec. appls. e.g.
      Engineering
  integrals   515.43
    s.a. spec. appls. e.g.
      Engineering
  Islands   *area*–964
  organization
    management *see* Organization
      of management
    mil. sci.   355.330 41
    s.a. spec. mil. branches
  play
    American football   796.332 23
    s.a. other spec. games
Line-&-staff organization
  management *see* Organization
    of management
Linear
  accelerators
    physics   539.733
    s.a. spec. physical
      phenomena e.g. Heat
  algebras   512.5
  s.a. spec. appls. e.g.
    Engineering

Linear (continued)
  closed-loop systems
    automation eng.   629.832
    s.a. spec. appls. e.g.
      Gunnery
  differential equations   515.354
    s.a. spec. appls. e.g.
      Engineering
  equations *see* Polynomial
    equations
  motions
    kinematics   531.112
    misc. aspects see
      Dynamics
  operators   515.724 6
    s.a. spec. appls. e.g.
      Engineering
  programming
    mathematics   519.72
    s.a. spec. appls. e.g.
      Engineering
  topological spaces   515.73
    s.a. spec. appls. e.g.
      Engineering
Line-haul routes
  truck transp. *see* Routes
    transp. services
Linen
  cabinets *see* Cabinets
    (furniture)
  textiles
    gen. wks. *see* Flax textiles
    kitchen
      household equip.   643.3
      s.a. other spec. kinds e.g.
        Table linens
Linens *see spec. kinds e.g.*
    Table linens
Line-of-position method
  celestial navigation   527.3
Line-outs
  rugby   796.333 23
Liners (ships) *see* Merchant
    ships powered
Lines
  elect. power transmission
    electrodynamic eng.   621.319 2
    s.a. spec. appls. e.g.
      Railroads
      electrification
    other aspects see
      Electrodynamics
  geometry *see* Configurations
    geometry
  palmistry   133.64
  wire telephony
    soc. & econ. aspects *see*
      Secondary industries
    tech. & mf.   621.387 84
    s.a. spec. appls. e.g.
      Military engineering

Lines
  wire telephony (continued)
    other aspects see Telephony
      wire
Lineups
  identification of criminals
    see Identification
      criminals
Lingerie *see* Women's underwear
Linguatula
  culture   639.739 92
  paleozoology   563.992
  zoology   593.992
  other aspects see Animals
Linguistic analysis
  philosophy   149.943
    indiv. phil.   180–190
    s.a. spec. branches of phil.
      e.g. Metaphysics
Linguistic philosophies   149.94
  indiv. phil.   180–190
  s.a. spec. branches of phil.
    e.g. Metaphysics
Linguistically handicapped
  children
    psychology   155.451 4
    rearing home econ.   649.151 4
  people
    s.a.   *pers.*–081 64
  students
    education   371.914
    law   344.079 114
      spec. jur.   344.3–.9
Linguistics   410
  spec. langs.   420–490
  other aspects see Languages
Linguists
  biog. & work   409.2
  s.a.   *pers.*–4
Linhares admin. Brazil hist.   981.061
  s.a. spec. events & subj.
    e.g. Commerce
Linin network *see* Nucleus cells
  cytology
Linkages
  molecular structure
    theoretical chem.   541.224
      organic   547.122 4
    s.a. spec. elements &
      cpds.
Links
  combinatorial topology   514.224
  couplings *see* Couplings
  power transmission *see* Power
    transmission
Linlithgow
  governorship India hist.   954.035 9
    s.a. spec. events & subj.
      e.g. Commerce
  Lothian Scot.   *area*–413 3

Linn Co.
  Iowa   *area*–777 62
  Kansas   *area*–781 69
  Missouri   *area*–778 24
  Oregon   *area*–795 35
Linoleum *see* Floor coverings
Linoleum-block printing
  graphic arts
    processes   761.3
    products   769
Linopteris
  paleobotany   561.597
Linotype composition
  printing
    soc. & econ. aspects *see*
      Secondary industries
    technology
      automatic   686.225 44
      manual   686.225 42
Linotypes
  manufacturing
    soc. & econ. aspects *see*
      Secondary industries
    technology   681.61
Linsangs *see* Viverridae
Linseed oil
  comm. proc.   665.352
  soc. & econ. aspects *see*
    Secondary industries
Linslade Bedfordshire Eng. *area*–425 65
Linters
  plastics mf.   668.411
  s.a. spec. kinds of
    plastics
Linum *see* Flax
Lion Gulf
  oceanography   551.462 2
  regional subj. trmt.   *area*–163 82
  other aspects see Atlantic
    Ocean
Lions
  animal husbandry   636.89
  other aspects see Cats
Lions' clubs   369.5
  songs *see* Service club songs
Liopelmidae
  zoology   597.83
  other aspects see Anura
Lip reading
  study & teaching   371.912 7
Lipari Isls. Sicily   *area*–458 11
Lipases *see* Lipolytic enzymes
Lipetsk RSFSR   *area*–473 5
Lipid
  metabolism disorders
    gen. med.   616.399 7
    geriatrics   618.976 399 7
    pediatrics   618.923 997
    pub. health   614.593 997
    statistics   312.339 97
      deaths   312.263 997

Lipid
  metabolism disorders (continued)
    other aspects see Diseases
  synthesis
    plant nutrition
      pathology   581.213 346
      physiology   581.133 46
      s.a. spec. plants
Lipids
  biochemistry
    gen. wks.   574.192 47
    animals   591.192 47
    microorganisms   576.119 247
    plants   581.192 47
    s.a. spec. organisms
    med. sci.   612.015 77
    animals   636.089 201 577
    s.a. spec. animals
    man   612.015 77
    s.a. spec. functions,
      systems, organs
  biosynthesis
    gen. wks.   574.192 93
    animals   591.192 93
    microorganisms   576.119 293
    plants   581.192 93
    s.a. spec. organisms
    med. sci.   612.015 43
    animals   636.089 201 543
    s.a. spec. animals
    man   612.015 43
    s.a. spec. functions,
      systems, organs
  blood chemistry
    human phys.   612.12
    other aspects see
      Circulatory fluids
  metabolism
    human phys.   612.397
    other aspects see
      Metabolism
  org. chem.   547.77
Lipoids *see* Lipids
Lipolytic enzymes
  biochemistry
    gen. wks.   574.192 53
    animals   591.192 53
    microorganisms   576.119 253
    plants   581.192 53
    s.a. spec. organisms
    med. sci.   612.015 13
    animals   636.089 201 513
    s.a. spec. animals
    man   612.015 13
    s.a. spec. functions,
      systems, organs
Lipoproteins
  org. chem.   547.754
  other aspects see Proteins

Lippmann process *see* Direct
    processes color
    photography
Lips
  anatomy
    human   611.317
    other aspects see Nutritive
      organs
  diseases
    surgery   617.522
      anesthesiology   617.967 522
    other aspects see Mouth
      diseases
  personal care   646.726
  physical anthropometry   573.631 7
  physiology
    human   612.31
    other aspects see Nutrition
    speech phys.   612.78
  tissue biology human   611.018 931 7
Lipscomb Co. Tex.   *area*–764 816
Liquefaction
  air
    chem. tech.   665.82
    soc. & econ. aspects *see*
      Secondary industries
  coal
    synthetic petroleum tech.   662.662 2
  effect of heat *see*
      Condensation effect of
      heat
  other tech. aspects see Low
      temperatures
      engineering
Liquefied-hydrocarbon gas
  chem. tech.   665.773
  soc. & econ. aspects *see*
      Secondary industries
Liquefying
  gases
    chem. apparatus   542.7
    s.a. spec. appls. e.g.
      Organic chemistry
Liqueurs *see* Compound liquors
Liquid
  chromatography
    anal. chem.
      gen. wks.   543.089 4
        qualitative   544.924
        quantitative   545.894
      organic   547.308 94
        qualitative   547.349 24
        quantitative   547.358 94
      s.a. spec. elements &
        cpds.
  crystals
    optical crystallography   548.9
    s.a. spec. substances
  precipitation
    meteorology *see* Rain

Llanfyllin Powys Wales	*area*–429 51
Llangollen Clwyd Wales	*area*–429 37
Llanidloes Powys Wales	*area*–429 51
Llanllwchaiarn Powys Wales	
	area–429 51
Llano	
Co. Tex.	*area*–764 62
Estacado	*area*–764 8
New Mexico	*area*–789 3
Texas	*area*–764 8
Llanquihue Chile	*area*–835 4
Llanrwst Gwynedd Wales	*area*–429 27
Llanwrtyd Wells Powys Wales	
	area–429 56
Lliw Valley West Glamorgan Wales	
	area–429 83
Llwchwr West Glamorgan Wales	
	area–429 83
Loaches *see* Ostariophysi	
Loading	
cameras	
photographic tech.	770.282
spec. fields	778
freight	
equipment *see*	
Materials-handling	
equip.	
service *see* Freight	
services	
ore mining eng.	622.69
prod. management	658.54
spec. subj.	*s.s.*–068 5
s.a. other spec. subj.	
Loading-operations	
materials management	658.788 5
spec. subj.	*s.s.*–068 7
sea safety	623.888 1
Loading-programs *see* Software	
programming	
Loads	
aircraft eng.	629.134 57
s.a. spec. appls. e.g.	
Military engineering	
bridge eng.	624.252
s.a. spec. appls. e.g.	
Suspension bridges	
structural theory	
deformation *see* Mechanical	
deformation structural	
theory	
gen. wks.	624.172
spec. elements	624.177 2–.177 9
naval arch.	623.817 2
s.a. other spec. appls.	
Loamy soils	
plants grown in	
floriculture	635.955
s.a. spec. plants	
Loan	
brokers	
economics	332.34

Loan	
brokers (continued)	
other aspects see Credit	
institutions	
collections	
museology	069.56
companies *see* Credit	
institutions	
work library services	025.6
Loanhead Lothian Scot.	*area*–413 5
Loans	
authorization	
legislative bodies *see*	
Financial powers	
economics	332.7
banking services	332.175 3
central banks	332.113
govt. control	351.825
spec. jur.	353–354
flotation	
pub. finance	336.344
misc. aspects see Public	
borrowing	
law	
international	341.751
municipal	346.073
spec. jur.	346.3–.9
pub. revenues	336.15
misc. aspects see Nontax	
revenues	
to students	
higher ed.	378.362
s.a. Credit	
Loasaceae *see* Loasales	
Loasales	
botany	583.453
floriculture	635.933 453
med. aspects	
crop prod.	633.883 453
gen. pharm.	615.323 453
toxicology	615.952 345 3
vet. pharm.	636.089 532 345 3
toxicology	636.089 595 234 53
paleobotany	561.3
other aspects see Plants	
Lobachevski geometry	516.9
s.a. spec. appls. e.g.	
Engineering	
Lobar pneumonia *see* Pneumonias	
Lobbying	
legislative bodies	
pol. sci.	328.38
spec. jur.	328.4–.9
Lobe-finned fishes *see*	
Crossopterygii	
Lobelia family *see* Campanales	
Lobeliaceae *see* Campanales	
Lobsters	
food	641.395
other aspects see Macrura	

Local
anesthesia	617.966
vet. sci.	636.089 796 6
s.a. spec. animals	
bibliographies	015
spec. subj.	016
borrowing & debt	
law	343.037
spec. jur.	343.3–.9
pub. admin.	352.14
pub. finance	336.343 1
broadcasting stations	
radio	
engineering	621.384 164
s.a. spec. appls. e.g.	
Radiotelephony	
other aspects see Radio	
calls	
telephone commun. *see*	
Telephone calls	
channels	
broadcasting *see*	
Broadcasting channels	
Christian church	250
clergy	
church govt.	
Christianity	262.14
other rel. see Governing	
leaders ecclesiology	
pastoral theology	
Christianity	253
other rel. see Pastoral	
theology	
other aspects see Clergy	
control of ed.	
law	344.073
spec. jur.	344.3–.9
courts	
U.S. law	347.734
other aspects see Courts	
debt *see* Local borrowing &	
debt	
differential geometry	516.363
s.a. spec. appls. e.g.	
Engineering	
finance	
economics	336.014
other aspects see Public	
finance	
government	
charters	
law	342.02
spec. jur.	342.3–.9
corporations	
law	342.09
spec. jur.	342.3–.9
law	342.09
spec. jur.	342.3–.9
libraries *see* Government	
libraries	

Local
government (continued)	
personnel	
biog. & work	352.000 92
s.a. spec. kinds; also	
spec. subj. of admin.	
s.a.	*pers.*–354
governments	
pol. sci.	320.8
pub. admin.	352
heating	
buildings	697.02
by source of heat	697.1–.2
s.a. spec. kinds e.g.	
Steam heating	
income *see* Income	
news reporting	070.433
ordinances	
texts	348.022
spec. jur.	348.3–.9
penal institutions	
penology	365.32
other aspects see Penal	
institutions	
planning	
civic art	711.4
law	346.045
spec. jur.	346.3–.9
soc. welfare *see* Planning	
soc. welfare	
sociology	307
railways	
commerce	388.42
govt. control	350.878 42
central govts.	351.878 42
spec. jur.	353–354
local govts.	352.918 42
law	343.098 3
spec. jur.	343.3–.9
technology	625.6
rel. organizations	
Christianity	250
comp. rel.	291.65
Islam	297.65
Judaism	296.65
s.a. other spec. rel.	
routes transp. *see* Routes	
transp. services	
taxation	
law	343.043
spec. jur.	343.3–.9
pub. admin.	352.13
pub. finance	336.201 4
transmission systems	
wire telephony	
soc. & econ. aspects *see*	
Secondary industries	
tech. & mf.	621.387 83
s.a. spec. appls. e.g.	
Communication	
engineering ships	

Local
  transmission systems
    wire telephony (continued)
      other aspects see
        Telephony wire
  transportation *see* Urban
      transportation
  unions
    labor econ.   331.872
      spec. occupations   331.881
  wind systems
    meteorology   551.518 5
      artificial modification   551.681 85
      weather forecasting   551.641 85
      spec. areas   551.65
    s.a. other spec. subj.
Local-federal relations *see*
      National-local
        relations
Localities
  lit. & stage trmt. *see* Places
  s.a. spec. localities
Localization
  auditory perception
    psychology
      gen. wks.   152.158
        animals   156.215 8
        children   155.412
      s.a. psych. of other
        spec. groups
    influences   155.911 58
Local-national relations *see*
      National-local
        relations
Local-provincial relations *see*
      Provincial-local
        relations
Local-state relations *see*
      State-local relations
Location
  buildings
    libraries   022.1
    museums   069.21
  businesses *see* Business
      location
  celestial bodies *see*
        Constants celestial
          bodies
  industries
    prod. econ.
      econ. advantage   338.604 2
      geographical   338.09
Loch Ness Scot.   *area*–411 75
  monster   001.944
Lochaber Highland Scot.   *area*–411 85
Lochalsh Highland Scot.   *area*–411 82
Lochgelly Fife Scot.   *area*–412 98
Lochgilphead Strathclyde Scot.
                                area–414 23
Lochmaben Dumfries & Galloway
      Scot.   *area*–414 83

Loci *see* Configurations
      geometry
Lockerbie Dumfries & Galloway
      Scot.   *area*–414 83
Lockjaw *see* Tetanus
Lockouts
  labor econ.   331.894
  labor law *see* Labor law
Locks (canals)
  engineering
    technology   627.135 2
    s.a. spec. appls. e.g.
        Canal transportation
    other aspects see Liquids
      engineering
Locks (fasteners)
  mf. tech.   683.32
  other aspects see Hardware
Locksmithing
  soc. & econ. aspects *see*
        Secondary industries
  technology   683.3
Locksmiths
  biog. & work   683.309 2
  s.a.   *pers.*–683
Lockup
  printing   686.225 6
Locomotion
  biology
    physiology
      gen. wks.   574.18
        animals   591.185 2
        microorganisms   576.118
      s.a. spec. organisms
    med. sci.   612.76
      human phys.   612.76
      vet. phys.   636.089 276
      s.a. spec. animals
    other aspects see Movements
  psychology   152.382
    animals   156.238 2
    children   155.412
    s.a. psych. of other spec.
      groups
    other aspects see Motor
      functions
Locomotive
  cranes railroad *see* Work cars
  shovels railroad *see* Work
      cars
Locomotives
  mining eng.   622.66
  railroad rolling stock
    commerce   385.36
      special-duty   385.5
    engineering
      technology   625.26
        accessory equipment   625.25
        monorail   625.28
        running gear   625.21

Loire
  department France *area*–445 81
  River France *area*–445
Loire-Atlantique France *area*–441 4
Loire-Inférieure France *area*–441 4
Loiret France *area*–445 2
Loir-et-Cher France *area*–445 3
Loja Ecuador *area*–866 25
Lolland Denmark *area*–489 3
Lolo *see* Nosu
Lombard kingdom Italy hist. 945.01
  s.a. spec. events & subj.
      e.g. Commerce
Lombardy Italy *area*–452
Lomblen Indonesia *area*–598 6
Lombok Indonesia *area*–598 6
Lomond Loch Strathclyde Scot.
      area–414 25
Lomza Poland *area*–438 3
London
  England *area*–421
  Ontario *area*–713 26
Londonderry Ireland
  city *area*–416 23
  district *area*–416 21
  former co. *area*–416 2
Long
  Co. Ga. *area*–758 762
  Eaton Derbyshire Eng. *area*–425 18
  Island
    Bahamas *area*–729 6
    New York *area*–747 21
  Island Sound
    oceanography 551.461 46
    regional subj. trmt. *area*–163 46
    other aspects see Atlantic
        Ocean
  Mynd Salop Eng. *area*–424 57
  s.a. other spec. subj.
Longbenton Tyne & Wear Eng.
      area–428 79
Longdendale Greater Manchester
      Eng. *area*–427 35
Long-distance
  calls
    telephone commun. *see*
        Telephone calls
  transmission systems
    wire telephony
      soc. & econ. aspects *see*
          Secondary industries
      tech. & mf. 621.387 82
        s.a. spec. appls. e.g.
            Reporting journalism
        other aspects see
            Telephony wire
Longevity
  life sci.
    gen. wks. 574.374
      animals 591.374
      microorganisms 576.137 4

Longevity
  life sci.
    gen. wks. (continued)
      plants 581.374
      s.a. spec. organisms
    med. sci. 612.68
      animals 636.089 268
        s.a. spec. animals
      man 612.68
  soc. theology *see* Social
        problems soc. theology
  s.a. Aged people sociology
Longevity-pay
  wage & salary admin. *see*
      Compensation scales
      pers. admin.
Longford
  Ireland *area*–418 12
  Tasmania *area*–946 3
Long-haired domestic cats
  animal husbandry 636.83
  other aspects see Cats
Long-haul routes
  truck transp. *see* Routes
      transp. services
Longitude
  celestial navigation 527.2
  geodetic astronomy 526.62
Long-legged flies *see*
      Orthorrhapha
Long-period variable stars
  astronomy
    description 523.844 26
    theory 521.584 426
  other aspects see Celestial
      bodies
Long-range
  surface-to-surface guided
      missiles
    mil. eng.
      soc. & econ. aspects *see*
          Secondary industries
      tech. & mf. 623.451 954
  weather forecasting 551.636 5
    spec. areas 551.65
    spec. elements 551.64
    s.a. methods e.g. Radar
Longreach Qld. *area*–943 5
Longridge Lancashire Eng. *area*–427 685
Long-term
  capital *see* Fixed capital
  loans
    capital *see* Fixed capital
Long-wave
  electronics
    astrophysics 523.018 753 42
      *s.a. spec. celestial
          bodies*
    physics 537.534 2
      spec. states of matter 530.4

Long-wave
  electronics (continued)
    other aspects see Radiowave
        electronics
  systems radio
    engineering   621.384 153
    s.a. spec. appls. e.g.
        Radiotelephony
    other aspects see Radio
Lonoke Co. Ark.   *area*–767 78
Looe Cornwall Eng.   *area*–423 74
Looking
  nonverbal commun. *see*
        Nonverbal language
  psychology *see* Attention
        psychology perception
Lookout
  Mountain
    Battle U.S. Civil War   973.735 9
    geog. concept   *area*–768 82
      Alabama   *area*–761 6
      Georgia   *area*–758 342
      Tennessee   *area*–768 82
    Point N.S.W.   *area*–944 3
  towers
    maintenance
      forest management   634.93
      s.a. spec. trees
Looms
  textile mf.
    soc. & econ. aspects *see*
        Secondary industries
    technology   677.028 54
    s.a. spec. kinds of
        textiles
Loons *see* Gaviiformes
Loopholes
  taxation *see* Tax reductions
Loose-leaf services
  law   *law s.s.*–026 48
  s.a. other spec. subj.
Loosestrife family *see*
        Lythrales
López Mateos Mexico hist.   972.082 9
  s.a. spec. events & subj.
    e.g. Commerce
López Portillo Mexico hist.   972.083 3
  s.a. spec. events & subj.
    e.g. Commerce
Lopseed family *see* Verbenales
Loquats
  agriculture   634.16
  soc. & econ. aspects *see*
        Primary industries
  foods   641.341 6
    preparation
      commercial   661.804 16
      domestic   641.641 6
  other aspects see Rosaceae;
      also Fruits
Lorain Co. O.   *area*–771 23

Loran
  radio
    engineering   621.384 191
    navigation
      seamanship   623.893 2
      other aspects see
          Navigation
      s.a. other spec. appls.
    other aspects see Radio
Loranthaceae *see* Santalales
Lord Howe Isl.   *area*–948 1
Lord Lyon
  Court of the
    Scotland
      law   347.411 04
Lord's
  Prayer
    Gospels   226.96
    pseudepigrapha   229.8
    other aspects see New
        Testament
  private devotions   242.722
  Supper *see* Holy Communion
Loreto Peru   *area*–854 3
Lories *see* Parrots
Lorises *see* Prosimii
Lorisiformes *see* Prosimii
Lorraine France   *area*–443 8
Lorries *see* Trucks
Los Alamos Co. N.M.   *area*–789 58
Los Altos Guatemala   *area*–728 18
Los Angeles
  city Calif.   *area*–794 94
  Co. Calif.   *area*–794 93
Los Ríos Ecuador   *area*–866 33
Los Santos Panama   *area*–728 723
Loss
  of citizenship
    pol. sci.   323.64
  of memory *see* Forgetting
  of territory *see* Territory
        of states
  s.a. other spec. subj.
Losses
  recovery
    govt. contracting
      pub. admin.   350.711 3
        central govts.   351.711 3
        spec. jur.   353–354
        local govts.   352.161 3
Lossiemouth Grampian Scot.
                            area–412 23
Lost River Range Ida.   *area*–796 72
Lost-Found Nation of Islam in the
        West *see* Black
        Muslims
Lost-wax casting *see* Precision
        casting
Lot France   *area*–447 3
Lotbinière Co. Que.   *area*–714 58
Lot-et-Garonne France   *area*–447 6

Lothair 2 reign
  Ger. hist. — 943.023
  s.a. spec. events & subj.
    e.g. Arts
Lothian Scot. — *area*–413 2
Lotions
  cosmetics *see* Cosmetics
  other aspects see Emulsions
Lots Feast *see* Purim
Lotteries
  advertising operations — 659.17
  ethics — 174.6
  pub. revenues — 336.17
    misc. aspects see Nontax
      revenues
Lotto
  equip. mf. — 688.753
    soc. & econ. aspects *see*
      Secondary industries
  recreation — 795.3
Lotus *see* Trefoils
Loudness
  sound
    engineering — 620.21
    s.a. spec. appls. e.g.
      Music bldgs. for
    physics — 534.33
      spec. states of matter — 530.4
Loudon Co. Tenn. — *area*–768 863
Loudoun
  Co. Va. — *area*–755 28
  Strathclyde Scot. — *area*–414 63
Loudspeakers
  commun. eng.
    soc. & econ. aspects *see*
      Secondary industries
    tech. & mf. — 621.380 282
    s.a. spec. appls. e.g.
      Receiving sets radio
Loughborough Leicestershire Eng.
      area–425 47
Louis
  reign France hist.
    6 — 944.022
    7 — 944.022
    8 — 944.023
    9 — 944.023
    10 — 944.024
    11 — 944.027
    12 — 944.027
    13 — 944.032
    14 — 944.033
    15 — 944.034
    16 — 944.035
    18
      1814-1815 — 944.05
      1815-1824 — 944.061
    s.a. spec. events & subj.
      e.g. Arts
Louis Philippe
  France hist. — 944.063

Louis Philippe (continued)
  s.a. spec. events & subj.
    e.g. Arts
Louisa Co.
  Iowa — *area*–777 926
  Virginia — *area*–755 465
Louisiade Archipelago — *area*–953
Louisiana — *area*–763
Louisville Ky. — *area*–769 44
Lounge cars *see* Passenger-train
      cars
Lounges *see* Upholstered
      furniture
Lounging garments
  comm. mf. — 687.16
  domestic mf. — 646.47
  other aspects see Clothing
Loup
  Co. Neb. — *area*–782 767
  River Neb. — *area*–782 4
Lourenço Marques
  Bay
    oceanography — 551.467 24
    regional subj. trmt. — *area*–165 24
    other aspects see Indian
      Ocean
  city Mozambique — *area*–679 1
Louse flies *see* Cyclorrhapha
Louse-borne typhus *see* Epidemic
      typhus
Louth
  Ireland — *area*–418 25
  Lincolnshire Eng. — *area*–425 32
Love
  charms occultism — 133.442
  Co. Okla. — *area*–766 59
  courtship *see* Courtship
  ethics
    philosophy — 177.7
    religion
      Buddhism — 294.356 77
      Christianity — 241.4
      comp. rel. — 291.567 7
      Hinduism — 294.548 677
  feasts
    Christian rites — 265.9
  fiction
    gen. wks.
      collections — 808.838 5
      hist. & crit. — 809.385
      rhetoric — 808.385
    spec. lits. — *lit. sub.*–308 5
      indiv. authors — *lit. sub.*–31–39
    other aspects see Fiction
  God's
    rel. doctrines
      Christianity — 231.6
      nat. rel. — 212.7
      other rel. see God
    lit. & stage trmt. *see* Life
      cycle

Lower
 extremities
  bones
   anatomy (continued)
    other aspects see
     Skeletal organs
   diseases
    surgery   617.471
     anesthesiology   617.967 471
    other aspects see Bone
     diseases
   fractures   617.158
   physical anthropometry   573.671 8
   physiology
    human   612.75
    other aspects see
     Movements
   tissue biology human   611.018 971 8
  diseases
   regional med. trmt.   617.58
    s.a. spec. systems &
     organs
   surgery   617.58
    anesthesiology   617.967 58
   other aspects see
    Diseases
  human
   anatomy   611.98
   physiology   612.98
    s.a. spec. functions,
     systems, organs e.g.
      Cardiovascular system
  muscles
   human anatomy   611.738
    other aspects see Muscles
   orthopedic surgery   617.398
   physical anthropometry   573.698
Franconia Ger.   *area*–433 3
Guinea   *area*–671
 houses
  legislative bodies
   constitutional law *see*
    Legislative branch of
     govt. law
   pol. sci.   328.32
    spec. jur.   328.4–.9
 middle classes   *pers.*–062 3
Peninsula Mich.   *area*–774
Precambrian era *see* Archezoic
 era
Rio Grande Tex.   *area*–764 4
Saxony Ger.   *area*–435 9
Silurian epoch *see* Ordovician
 period
Lowestoft Suffolk Eng. *area*–426 41
Low-fat
 cookery home econ.   641.563 8
 diets
  hygiene   613.28
   misc. aspects see Hygiene

Low-frequency radiations *see*
 Radio waves
Lowiaceae *see* Zingiberales
Low-income classes   *pers.*–062 4
Lowndes Co.
 Alabama   *area*–761 465
 Georgia   *area*–758 864
 Mississippi   *area*–762 973
Low-protein
 cookery home econ.   641.563 8
 diets
  hygiene
   misc. aspects see Hygiene
Low-salt
 cookery home econ.   641.563 2
 diets
  hygiene   613.28
   misc. aspects see Hygiene
Loxton S. Aust.   *area*–942 33
Loyalists
 U.S. Revolution   973.314
  s.a. other spec. occurrences
Loyalty
 Islands   *area*–933
 oaths
  pub. personnel admin.   350.132 42
   central govts.   351.132 42
    spec. jur.   353–354
   local govts.   352.005 132 42
  political   323.65
Lozère France   *area*–448 15
Luanda Angola   *area*–673 2
Luba kingdom hist.   967.510 1
 s.a. spec. events & subj.
  e.g. Commerce
Lubang Isls. Philippines *area*–599 3
Lubbock Co. Tex.   *area*–764 847
Lublin Poland   *area*–438 4
Lubricants
 internal combustion engines
  automobiles   629.255
   s.a. spec. appls.
 machine eng. *see* Friction
  machine eng.
 plastics mf.   668.411
  s.a. spec. kinds of
   plastics
 s.a. other spec. uses
Lubricating
 nat. leathers
  manufacturing
   soc. & econ. aspects *see*
    Secondary industries
  technology   675.24
Lubricating-greases
 chem. tech.   665.538 5
 other aspects see Petroleum
 s.a. spec. uses
Lubricating-oils
 chem. tech.   665.538 5
 other aspects see Petroleum

Lundy Isls. Devon Eng.	*area*–423 51
Lunenburg Co.	
Nova Scotia	*area*–716 23
Virginia	*area*–755 643
Lung fishes *see* Dipnoi	
Lungs	
anatomy	
human	611.24
other aspects see	
Respiratory organs	
diseases	
gen. wks.	616.24
neoplasms	616.992 24
tuberculosis	619.995 24
geriatrics	618.976 24
pediatrics	618.922 4
pub. health	614.592 4
statistics	312.324
deaths	312.262 4
surgery	617.542
anesthesiology	617.967 542
other aspects see Diseases	
physical anthropometry	573.624
physiology	
human	612.2
other aspects see	
Respiration	
tissue biology human	611.018 924
Luorawetlin *see* Paleosiberian	
Lupines	
agriculture	633.367
soc. & econ. aspects *see*	
Primary industries	
other aspects see	
Papilionaceae; *also*	
Field crops	
Lupinus *see* Lupines	
Lures (fishing sports)	
manufacturing	
soc. & econ. aspects *see*	
Secondary industries	
technology	688.791 2
Lurgan N. Ire.	*area*–416 64
Lusatian *see* Wendish	
Lust *see* Vices	
Luster	
minerals *see* Optical	
properties minerals	
Lute music	787.675
recordings	789.912 767
Lutecium *see* Lutetium	
Lutes	
mf. tech.	681.817 67
misc. aspects see Musical	
instruments	
musical art	787.67
Lutetium	
chemistry	
inorganic	546.419

Lutetium	
chemistry (continued)	
organic	547.054 19
s.a. spec. groupings e.g.	
Aliphatic compounds	
technology	661.041 9
organic	661.895
soc. & econ. aspects *see*	
Secondary industries	
s.a. spec. prod.	
eng. materials	620.189 291 9
s.a. spec. uses	
metallography	669.952 919
metallurgy	669.291 9
physical & chem.	669.962 919
pharmacology	615.241 9
misc. aspects see	
Pharmacology	
products	
mf. tech.	673.291 9
other aspects see	
Nonferrous metals	
products	
toxicology	615.925 419
misc. aspects see	
Toxicology	
other aspects see	
Yttrium-group metals	
Lutheran	
church	
buildings	
architecture	726.584 1
building	690.658 41
other aspects see	
Religious-purpose	
bldgs.	
music	
arts	783.026 41
recordings	789.912 302 641
s.a. spec. instruments;	
also spec. kinds e.g.	
Liturgical music	
religion	
pub. worship	264.041 02
significance	246.7
churches	284.1
Christian life guides	248.484 1
doctrines	230.41
creeds	238.41
general councils	262.541
govt. & admin.	262.041
parishes	254.041
missions	266.41
moral theology	241.044 1
private prayers for	242.804 1
pub. worship	264.041
rel. associations	
adults	267.184 1
men	267.244 1
women	267.444 1
young adults	267.624 1

Lymphatic
  glands (continued)
    physiology
      human   612.42
      other aspects see
        Secretion
    tissue biology human   611.018 946
  system
    anatomy
      human   611.42
      other aspects see
        Secretory organs
    diseases
      gen. wks.   616.42
        neoplasms   616.992 42
        tuberculosis   616.995 42
      geriatrics   618.976 42
      pediatrics   618.924 2
      pub. health   614.594 2
      statistics   312.342
        deaths   312.264 2
      surgery   617.44
        anesthesiology   617.967 44
      other aspects see
        Diseases
    drugs affecting
      pharmacodynamics   615.74
      other aspects see Drugs
    physical anthropometry   573.642
    physiology
      human   612.42
      other aspects see
        Secretion
    tissue biology human   611.018 942
Lymphatics *see* Lymphatic system
Lymphatitis *see* Lymphatic
    system diseases
Lymph-elements
  tissue biology
    human anatomy & phys.   611.018 5
    other aspects see Tissue
      biology
Lymphocytes
  tissue biology
    human anatomy & phys.   611.018 5
    other aspects see Tissue
      biology
Lymphocytic choriomeningitis
    see Viral diseases
Lymphogranuloma venereum
  gen. med.   616.951 8
  geriatrics   618.976 951 8
  pediatrics   618.929 518
  pub. health   614.547
  statistics   312.395 18
    deaths   312.269 518
  other aspects see Diseases
Lymphomatosis *see* Lymphatic
    system diseases

Lymph-plasma
  tissue biology
    human anatomy & phys.   611.018 5
    other aspects see Tissue
      biology
Lynchburg Va.   *area*–755 671
Lynches River S.C.   *area*–757 6
Lynching *see* Administration of
    justice crimes against
Lyndhurst Hampshire Eng. *area*–422 75
Lynn Co. Tex.   *area*–764 851
Lynton Devon Eng.   *area*–423 52
Lynxes
  animal husbandry   636.89
  other aspects see Cats
Lyon
  city France   *area*–445 823
  County
    Iowa   *area*–777 114
    Kansas   *area*–781 62
    Kentucky   *area*–769 813
    Minnesota   *area*–776 363
    Nevada   *area*–793 58
Lyonnais France   *area*–445 8
Lyres *see* Harps
Lyric poetry
  gen. wks.
    collections   808.814
    hist. & crit.   809.14
    rhetoric   808.14
    juvenile   808.068 14
  spec. lits.   *lit. sub.*–104
  indiv. authors   *lit. sub.*–11–19
  other aspects see Poetry
Lytham Saint Annes Lancashire
    Eng.   *area*–427 662
Lythraceae *see* Lythrales
Lythrales
  botany   583.44
  floriculture   635.933 44
  med. aspects
    crop prod.   633.883 44
    gen. pharm.   615.323 44
      toxicology   615.952 344
    vet. pharm.   636.089 532 344
      toxicology 636.089 595 234 4
  paleobotany   561.3
  other aspects see Plants
Lytton governorship India hist. 954.035 3
  s.a. spec. events & subj.
    e.g. Commerce

M

Machine (continued)
  engineering
    soc. & econ. aspects *see*
      Secondary industries
    technology   621.8
      s.a. spec. appls. e.g.
        Factory operations
    other aspects see Mechanics
    friction *see* Friction machine
      eng.
  gunners armed forces   356.162
  guns *see* Automatic firearms
    portable
  laces *see* Laces fabrics
  parts
    mech. eng.   621.82
      s.a. spec. uses e.g.
        Machine tools
  production
    paper
      mf. tech.   676.23
      spec. papers   676.28
    s.a. other spec. appls.
  rifles *see* Automatic firearms
    portable
  sewing home econ.   646.204 4
  sheds
    agriculture   631.25
      s.a. spec. crops; also
        spec. types of culture
        e.g. Floriculture
  shorthand   653.3
  tools
    soc. & econ. aspects *see*
      Secondary industries
    tech. & mf.   621.902
      s.a. spec. appls. e.g.
        Agricultural equipment
        manufacturing
        technology; *also spec.*
        kinds
  translation *see* Translation
    (linguistics)
  s.a. other spec. subj.
Machinery
  balancing
    mech. eng.   621.816
      s.a. spec. machines e.g.
        Machine tools
  electrical
    electrodynamic eng.
      soc. & econ. aspects *see*
        Secondary industries
      tech. & mf.   621.310 42
        s.a. spec. appls. e.g.
          Generation elect. power
      other aspects see
        Electrodynamics
  engineering *see* Machine
    engineering

Machinery (continued)
  insurance   368.7
    misc. aspects see Insurance
  s.a. spec. kinds e.g.
      Agricultural equipment;
      also spec. uses
Machines
  in production *see* Efficiency
    prod. econ.
  in sculpture   731.3
    spec. periods & schools   732–735
  manufacture *see spec. kinds*
  simple mechanics   531.8
  sociology *see* Technology
    sociology
  theory physics   531.8
  other aspects see Equipment
Machine-shop practice
  agriculture   631.304
  gen. wks.
    technology   670.423
      s.a. spec. prod. of mf.
Machining metal prod.
  arts
    decorative   739.14
      s.a. spec. metals; also
        spec. prod. e.g.
        Jewelry
    fine *see* Direct-metal
      sculpture
  mf. tech.   671.35
    ferrous metals   672.35
    s.a. other spec. metals
  other aspects see Mechanical
    working
Machmeters
  aircraft eng.   629.135 2
    s.a. spec. appls. e.g.
      Military engineering
Machynlleth Powys Wales   *area*–429 51
McIntosh Co.
  Georgia   *area*–758 737
  North Dakota   *area*–784 55
  Oklahoma   *area*–766 74
Mackay Qld.   *area*–943 6
McKean Co. Pa.   *area*–748 63
Mackenzie
  Alexander admin.
    Can. hist.   971.052
      s.a. spec. events & subj.
        e.g. Commerce
  District Can.   *area*–719 3
  River Can.   *area*–719 3
McKenzie Co. N.D.   *area*–784 81
Mackerels *see* Acanthopterygii
Mackinac
  Co. Mich.   *area*–774 923
  Isl. Mich.   *area*–774 923
  Straits Mich.   *area*–774 8
McKinley
  Co. N.M.   *area*–789 83

McKinley (continued)
Mt. Alaska — *area*–798 3
William admin.
  U.S. hist. — 973.88
  s.a. spec. events & subj.
    e.g. Courts
McLean Co.
  Illinois — *area*–773 59
  Kentucky — *area*–769 826
  North Dakota — *area*–784 75
Macleay River N.S.W. — *area*–944 3
McLennan Co. Tex. — *area*–764 284
Macleod Alta. — *area*–712 34
McLeod Co. Minn. — *area*–776 52
McMinn Co. Tenn. — *area*–768 865
McMullen Co. Tex. — *area*–764 452
McNairy Co. Tenn. — *area*–768 29
Macomb Co. Mich. — *area*–774 39
Macon Co.
  Alabama — *area*–761 49
  Georgia — *area*–758 513
  Illinois — *area*–773 582
  Missouri — *area*–778 27
  North Carolina — *area*–756 982
  Tennessee — *area*–768 484
Macoupin Co. Ill. — *area*–773 83
McPherson Co.
  Kansas — *area*–781 55
  Nebraska — *area*–782 793
  South Dakota — *area*–783 16
McPherson Range Qld. — *area*–943 2
Macpherson governorship India
  hist. — 954.031 1
  s.a. spec. events & subj.
    e.g. Commerce
Macquarie River N.S.W. — *area*–944 9
Macramé
  textile arts — 746.422 2
  s.a. spec. prod.
Macro methods
  anal. chem. *see* Qualitative
    chemistry
Macroeconomics — 339
Macro-Khoisan languages
  linguistics — 496.1
  literatures — 896.1
  s.a. — *lang.*–961
Macromolecular cpds.
  org. chem. — 547.7
Macronutrient elements
  plant nutrition
    pathology — 581.213 354
    physiology — 581.133 54
  s.a. spec. plants
Macro-Otomanguean
  languages
    linguistics — 497.6
    literatures — 897.6
    s.a. — *lang.*–976
  people — *r.e.n.*–97

Macro-Otomanguean (continued)
  s.a. other spec. subj. e.g.
    Arts
Macro-Penutian
  languages
    linguistics — 497.4
    literatures — 897.4
    s.a. — *lang.*–974
  people — *r.e.n.*–97
  s.a. other spec. subj. e.g.
    Arts
Macroscopic petrology — 552.1–.5
Macrosudanic *see* Chari-Nile
Macrura
  cookery *see* Seafoods
  culture — 639.541
  fishing
    commercial — 639.541
    sports — 799.255 384 1
  zoology — 595.384 1
  other aspects see Decapoda
    (crustaceans)
Madagascar — *area*–691
Madawaska Co. N.B. — *area*–715 54
Madder family *see* Rubiales
Madeira Portugal — *area*–469 8
Madeleine Isls. Que. — *area*–714 797
Madera Co. Calif. — *area*–794 81
Madhvacharya philosophy — 181.484 1
Madhya
  Bharat India — *area*–543
  Pradesh India — *area*–543
Madison
  city Wis. — *area*–775 84
  County
    Alabama — *area*–761 97
    Arkansas — *area*–767 15
    Florida — *area*–759 85
    Georgia — *area*–758 152
    Idaho — *area*–796 55
    Illinois — *area*–773 86
    Indiana — *area*–772 57
    Iowa — *area*–777 81
    Kentucky — *area*–769 53
    Mississippi — *area*–762 623
    Missouri — *area*–778 91
    Montana — *area*–786 663
    Nebraska — *area*–782 54
    New York — *area*–747 64
    North Carolina — *area*–756 875
    Ohio — *area*–771 55
    Tennessee — *area*–768 27
    Texas — *area*–764 237
    Virginia — *area*–755 38
  James admin.
    U.S. hist. — 973.51
    s.a. spec. events & subj.
      e.g. Arts
  Par. La. — *area*–763 81

Madonna & Child
art representation
 arts   704.948 55
  s.a. spec. art forms
Christian rel.
 paintings   247.555
 sculpture   247.3
Madras India   *area*–548 2
Madre de Dios Peru   *area*–854 2
Madrid Spain   *area*–464 1
Madrigals   784.12
 recordings   789.912 412
Madriz Nicaragua   *area*–728 523
Madura Indonesia   *area*–598 2
Madurese *see* Indonesian
Maesteg Mid Glamorgan Wales
     area–429 71
Maffra Vic.   *area*–945 6
Mafia
 Isl. Tanzania   *area*–678 23
 soc. path.   364.106
Magadan   *area*–577
Magahi *see* Bihari
Magallanes Chile   *area*–836 4
Magazine
 illustration   741.652
Magazines (periodicals) *see*
  Serials
Magdalen Isls. Que.   *area*–714 797
Magdalena Colombia   *area*–861 16
Magdeburg Ger.   *area*–431 8
Magellan Strait
 oceanography   551.469 4
 regional subj. trmt.   *area*–167 4
 other aspects see Antarctic
   waters
Maggiore Lake Italy   *area*–451 6
Maggots *see* Diptera
Magherafelt N. Ire.   *area*–416 29
Maghreb   *area*–61
Magi
 art representation *see*
   Biblical characters &
   events
 Christian doctrines   232.923
Magic
 folk lit.
  sociology   398.43
  texts & lit. crit.   398.2
 occultism   133.4
 recreation   793.8
Magicians (conjurers)
 biog. & work   793.809 2
 s.a.   *pers.*–793 8
Magicians (rel. leaders)
 comp. rel.   291.62
 s.a. spec. rel.
Magicians' manuals
 occultism   133.43

Magistrates *see spec. kinds*
   e.g. Justices of the
   peace
Magistrates Court
 England
  law   345.420 12
Magma
 solidified *see* Igneous rocks
 volcanoes   551.21
Magnesia
 cement
  technology   666.95
  other aspects see Masonry
   adhesives
 nome Greece   *area*–495 4
Magnesite
 mineralogy   549.782
Magnesium
 chemistry
  inorganic   546.392
  organic   547.053 92
  s.a. spec. groupings e.g.
   Aliphatic compounds
  technology   661.039 2
  organic   661.895
  soc. & econ. aspects *see*
   Secondary industries
  s.a. spec. prod.
 construction
  architecture   721.044 772 3
  s.a. spec. kinds of
   bldgs.
  building   693.772 3
 materials
  building   691.872 3
  engineering   620.187
   foundations   624.153 87
   naval design   623.818 27
   structures   624.182 7
  s.a. other spec. uses
 metallography   669.957 23
 metallurgy   669.723
  physical & chem.   669.967 23
  soc. & econ. aspects *see*
   Secondary industries
 mineral aspects
  econ. geol.   553.492 9
  mining   622.349 29
  prospecting   622.184 929
  s.a. spec. minerals
 pharmacology   615.239 2
  misc. aspects see
   Pharmacology
 products
  mf. tech.   673.723
  other aspects see
   Nonferrous metals
   products
 salts plant nutrition *see*
   Macronutrient elements
   plant nutrition

Magnetohydrodynamic
  generation
    electrodynamic eng. (continued)
      technology   621.312 45
      s.a. spec. appls. e.g.
        Electric railroads
      other aspects see
        Electrodynamics
    power systems
      spacecraft eng.   629.474 45
        unmanned   629.464 45
      other aspects see
        Spacecraft
    propulsion systems
      spacecraft eng.   629.475 5
        unmanned   629.465 5
      other aspects see
        Spacecraft
Magnetohydrodynamics
  astrophysics   523.018 86
    s.a. spec. celestial bodies
  physics   538.6
    spec. states of matter   530.4
Magnetosphere
  geomagnetism
    astrophysics   523.018 876 6
    s.a. spec. celestial
      bodies
    physics   538.766
      spec. states of matter   530.4
Magnetostriction *see* Magnetic
    phenomena
Magnetrons
  microwave electronics
    soc. & econ. aspects *see*
      Secondary industries
    tech. & mf.   621.381 334
      spec. circuits   621.381 32
      s.a. spec. appls. e.g.
        Radar engineering
    other aspects see Microwave
      electronics
Magnets
  astrophysics   523.018 82
    s.a. spec. celestial bodies
  physics   538.2
    spec. states of matter   530.4
Magnitudes
  stars   523.822
    spec. systems   523.84–.85
Magnolia family *see* Magnoliales
Magnoliaceae *see* Magnoliales
Magnoliales
  botany   583.114
  floriculture   635.933 114
  forestry   634.973 114
  med. aspects
    crop prod.   633.883 114
    gen. pharm.   615.323 114
      toxicology   615.952 311 4

Magnoliales
  med. aspects (continued)
    vet. pharm.   636.089 532 311 4
      toxicology   636.089 595 231 14
  paleobotany   561.3
  other aspects see Plants
Magoffin Co. Ky.   *area*–769 215
Magpie larks
  zoology   598.8
  other aspects see
    Passeriformes
Magpies *see* Corvidae
Magsaysay admin. Philippines
    hist.   959.904 3
  s.a. spec. events and subj.
    e.g. Commerce
Maguey *see* Agave
Magyar *see* Hungarian
Mahabharata
  Hinduism   294.592 3
Maharashtra India   *area*–547 92
Mahaska Co. Ia.   *area*–777 84
Mahayana Buddhism   294.392
  misc. aspects see Buddhism
Mah-jongg
  equipment mf.   688.753
    soc. & econ. aspects *see*
      Secondary industries
  recreation   795.3
Mahl dialect
  linguistics   491.487
  other aspects see Sinhalese
Mahnomen Co. Minn.   *area*–776 94
Mahogany
  family *see* Meliales
  woods *see* Hardwoods
Mahomet the Prophet
  Islam   297.63
Mahometan *see* Islamic
Mahometans *see* Muslims
Mahoning
  Co. O.   *area*–771 39
  River O.   *area*–771 39
Mahratta people   *r.e.n.*–948
Mahri
  language *see* South Arabic
    languages
  people   *r.e.n.*–929
  s.a. other spec. subj. e.g.
    Arts
Maidenhair trees *see* Ginkgoales
Maidenhead Berkshire Eng. *area*–422 96
Maids *see* Household employees
Maidstone Kent Eng.   *area*–422 375
Mail
  cars *see* Passenger-train cars
  handling
    office services   651.759
  openers
    office use   651.759

Maladjustments (continued)
  sociology *see* Social
    pathology
Málaga Spain   *area*–468 5
Malagasy
  language
    linguistics   499.3
    literature   899.3
    s.a.   *lang.*–993
  people   *r.e.n.*–993
  Republic   *area*–691
  s.a. other spec. subj. e.g.
    Arts
Malaita Isls. Solomons   *area*–935
Malan admin. South Africa hist.
           968.056

  s.a. spec. events & subj.
    e.g. Commerce
Malaria
  gen. med.   616.936 2
  geriatrics   618.976 936 2
  pediatrics   618.929 362
  pub. health   614.532
  statistics   312.393 62
    deaths   312.269 362
  other aspects see Diseases
Malatya Turkey   *area*–565
Malawi
  country   *area*–689 7
  people   *r.e.n.*–968 97
  s.a. spec. subj. e.g. Arts
Malay
  Archipelago
    inner seas
      oceanography   551.465 73
      regional subj. trmt.   *area*–164 73
      other aspects see Pacific
        Ocean
    islands   *area*–598
  arts *see* Southeast Asian arts
  languages
    linguistics   499.2
    literature   899.2
    s.a.   *lang.*–992
    people   *r.e.n.*–992
    s.a. other spec. subj. e.g.
      Agriculture
Malaya   *area*–595 1
Malayalam
  language
    linguistics   494.812
    literature   894.812
    s.a.   *lang.*–948 12
    people   *r.e.n.*–948
    s.a. other spec. subj. e.g.
      Arts
Malay-Javanese
  languages
    linguistics   499.22
    literatures   899.22
    s.a.   *lang.*–992 2

Malay-Javanese (continued)
  people   *r.e.n.*–992
  s.a. Malaysia; *also*
    Indonesia; *also other*
    spec. subj. e.g. Arts
Malayo-Polynesian
  languages *see* Oceanic
    languages
  peoples   *r.e.n.*–992–995
  s.a. other spec. subj. e.g.
    Arts
Malays   *r.e.n.*–992
Malaysia   *area*–595
Malden
  & Coombe London Eng.   *area*–421 94
  Island   *area*–964
Maldive Isls.   *area*–549 5
Maldon
  Essex Eng.   *area*–426 756
  Victoria   *area*–945 3
Maldonado Uruguay   *area*–895 15
Male (human)
  breast
    diseases
      gen. wks.   616.49
        neoplasms   616.992 49
        tuberculosis   616.995 49
      geriatrics   618.976 49
      pediatrics   618.924 9
      pub. health   614.594 9
      statistics   312.349
        deaths   312.264 9
      surgery   617.549
        anesthesiology   617.967 549
      other aspects see
        Diseases
  genital organs
    anatomy
      human   611.63
      other aspects see
        Reproductive organs
    diseases
      gen. wks.   616.65
        neoplasms   616.992 63
        tuberculosis   616.995 63
      geriatrics   618.976 65
      pediatrics   618.926 5
      pub. health   614.596 5
      statistics   312.365
        deaths   312.266 5
      surgery   617.463
        anesthesiology   617.967 463
      other aspects see
        Diseases
  physical anthropometry   573.663
  physiology
    human   612.61
    other aspects see
      Reproduction
  tissue biology human   611.018 963

Malpighiales
  med. aspects (continued)
    gen. pharm.   615.323 214
      toxicology   615.952 321 4
    vet. pharm.   636.089 532 321 4
      toxicology   636.089 595 232 14
    paleobotany   561.3
    other aspects see Plants
Malpractice
  law of   346.033
    spec. jur.   346.3–.9
Malta
  fever *see* Undulant fever
  island   *area*–458 5
    ancient   *area*–378
  Knights *see* Knights of Malta
Maltases *see* Saccharolytic
      enzymes
Maltby South Yorkshire Eng.
       area–428 23
Malted beverages
  alcoholic   641.23
    comm. proc.   663.3
  nonalcoholic
    comm. proc.   663.64
    cookery   641.875
  other aspects see Beverages
Maltese
  dogs
    animal husbandry   636.76
    other aspects see Dogs
  language
    linguistics   492.77
    literature   892.7
    s.a.   *lang.*–927
  people   *r.e.n.*–927 7
  s.a. Malta; *also other spec.*
       subj. e.g. Arts
Malto *see* Dravida
Malton North Yorkshire Eng.
       area–428 46
Maltose
  org. chem.   547.781 5
  other aspects see Sugar
Maluku Indonesia   *area*–598 5
Malus *see* Apples
Malvaceae *see* Malvales
Malvales
  botany   583.17
  floriculture   635.933 17
  forestry   634.973 17
  med. aspects
    crop prod.   633.883 17
    gen. pharm.   615.323 17
      toxicology   615.952 317
    vet. pharm.   636.089 532 317
      toxicology   636.089 595 231 7
    paleobotany   561.3
    other aspects see Plants
Malvern Hereford & Worcester
      Eng.   *area*–424 47

Malvern Hills Hereford &
      Worcester Eng.   *area*–424 47
Mammalia
  agric. pests   632.69
  s.a. spec. types of culture
    e.g. Forestry; *also*
      spec crops
  animal husbandry
    technology   636
    soc. & econ. aspects *see*
      Primary industries
    other aspects see
      Agriculture
  conservation tech.   639.979
  control
    agricultural *see* Mammalia
      agric. pests
    home econ.   648.7
    sanitary eng.   628.969
  drawing tech.   743.69
  hunting
    commercial
      technology   639.11
      soc. & econ. aspects
        see Primary
        industries
  paleozoology   569
  resources
    economics   333.959
    govt. control
      law   346.046 959
        spec. jur.   346.3–.9
      pub. admin. *see*
        Biological resources
        govt. control pub.
        admin.
  sports
    big game   799.27
    small game   799.259
  zoology   599
  other aspects see Animals
Mammalogists
  biog. & work   599.009 2
  other aspects see Scientists
  s.a.   *pers.*–599
Mammals *see* Mammalia
Mammary glands
  anatomy
    human   611.49
    other aspects see Secretory
      organs
  diseases
    gen. wks.   618.19
      neoplasms   616.992 49
      tuberculosis   616.995 49
    geriatrics   618.978 19
    pediatrics   618.920 981 9
    pub. health   614.599 2
    statistics   312.304 819
      deaths   312.260 481 9

Mandingo (continued)
  s.a. other spec. subj. e.g.
    Arts
Mandolin music   787.655
  recordings   789.912 765
Mandolins
  mf. tech.   681.817 65
    misc. aspects see Musical
      instruments
  musical art   787.65
Maneuvers
  mil. sci.   355.52
  s.a. spec. mil. branches
Manganese
  chemistry
    inorganic   546.541
    organic   547.055 41
    s.a. spec. groupings e.g.
      Aliphatic compounds
  technology   661.054 1
    organic   661.895
    soc. & econ. aspects *see*
      Secondary industries
    s.a. spec. prod.
  compounds
    chemistry *see* Manganese
      chemistry
    plant nutrition *see* Trace
      elements plant
      nutrition
  construction
    architecture   721.044 773 2
    s.a. spec. kinds of
      bldgs.
    building   693.773 2
  materials
    building   691.873 2
    engineering   620.189 32
      foundations   624.153 893 2
      naval design   623.818 293 2
      structures   624.182 932
    s.a. other spec. uses
  metallography   669.957 32
  metallurgy   669.732
    physical & chem.   669.967 32
    soc. & econ. aspects *see*
      Secondary industries
  mineral aspects
    econ. geol.   553.462 9
    mining
      technology   622.346 29
      prospecting   622.184 629
  pharmacology   615.254 1
    misc. aspects see
      Pharmacology
  products
    mf. tech.   673.732
    other aspects see
      Nonferrous metals
      products

Manganese (continued)
  toxicology   615.925 541
    misc. aspects see
      Toxicology
  other aspects see Metal;
    also Metals
  s.a. spec. uses
Manganite
  mineralogy   549.53
Mange *see* Parasitic skin
  diseases
Mangifera indica *see*
  Anacardiaceous fruits
Mangoes *see* Anacardiaceous
  fruits
Mangosteens
  agriculture   634.655
    soc. & econ. aspects *see*
      Primary industries
  foods   641.346 55
    preparation
      commercial   664.804 655
      domestic   641.646 55
  other aspects see
    Guttiferales; *also*
    Fruits
Mangotsfield Avon Eng.   *area*–423 94
Mangrove family *see* Myrtales
Manguean *see* Macro-Otomanguean
Manhattan N.Y.   *area*–747 1
Manholes
  sewers   628.25
  s.a. spec. appls. e.g.
    Water drainage
Manic psychoses *see*
    Manic-depressive
    psychoses
Manica & Sofala Mozambique
    area–679 4
Manic-depressive psychoses
  gen. med.   616.895
  geriatrics   618.976 895
  pediatrics   618.928 95
  psychology   157.2
  pub. health   614.58
  statistics   312.389 5
  other aspects see Mental
    illness
Manicheism
  religion   299.932
Manicure tools
  manufacturing
    soc. & econ. aspects *see*
      Secondary industries
    technology   688.5
Manicuring
  personal care   646.727
Manifold topology   514.3
  s.a. spec. appls. e.g.
    Engineering

Manifolds
  geometry   516.07
    s.a. spec. geometries; also
        spec. appls. e.g.
        Engineering
  internal-combusion engines
  automobiles
    soc. & econ. aspects *see*
        Secondary industries
    tech. & mf.   629.252
    s.a. other spec. uses
Manihiki Isls.   *area*–962 4
Manihot *see* Cassava
Manila
  city Philippines   *area*–599 1
  hemp
    agriculture   633.571
        soc. & econ. aspects *see*
        Primary industries
    other aspects see
        Zingiberales
  papers
    mf. tech.   676.287
    other aspects see Papers
        pulp. prod.
Maniples *see* Ecclesiastical
        vestments
Manipur India   *area*–541 7
Manisa Turkey   *area*–562
Manistee
  Co. Mich.   *area*–774 62
  River Mich.   *area*–774 6
Manitoba
  Lake Can.   *area*–712 72
  province Can.   *area*–712 7
Manitoulin District Ont.   *area*–713 135
Manitowoc Co. Wis.   *area*–775 67
Manjimup W. Aust.   *area*–941 2
Man-machine ratios
  management
    production   658.514
    spec. subj.   *s.s.*–068 5
Man-made fibers
  eng. materials   620.197
  foundations   624.153 97
  naval design   623.818 97
  shipbuilding   623.820 7
  structures   624.189 7
    s.a. other spec. uses
  textiles
    arts   746.044
        s.a. spec. proc. e.g.
        Weaving
    dyeing   667.34
    manufacturing
        soc. & econ. aspects *see*
        Secondary industries
    technology   677.4
        special-process fabrics   677.6
    org. chem.   547.85
  other aspects see Textiles

Man-made fibers (continued)
  s.a. spec. prod.
Mannar Gulf *see* Arabian Sea
Manned
  space flight
    soc. & econ. aspects *see*
        Secondary industries
    technology   629.45
        s.a. spec. appls. e.g.
        Space warfare
  spacecraft *see* Astronautical
        engineering
Manners (customs) *see* Social
        customs
Manners (etiquette)
  child rearing home econ.   649.6
  other aspects see Etiquette
Manningtree Essex Eng.   *area*–426 725
Mannose
  org. chem.   547.781 3
Mannum S. Aust.   *area*–942 32
Manor house bldgs.
  architecture   728.83
  building   690.883
  other aspects see Residential
        buildings
Man-o'-war birds *see*
        Pelecaniformes
Manpower
  labor econ.   331.11
  mil. resources
    armed forces   355.22
    civilians   355.23
  procurement
    mil. law   343.012
    spec. jur.   343.3–.9
Mansel Isl. Northwest Ter.
            area–719 4
Mansfield
  Nottinghamshire Eng.   *area*–425 23
  Victoria   *area*–945 5
Mansions
  architecture   728.83
  building   690.883
  other aspects see Residential
        buildinqs
Manslaughter
  criminology   364.152 5
  law   345.025 25
    spec. jur.   345.3–.9
  soc. theology
    Christianity   261.833 152 5
    comp. rel.   291.178 331 525
        s.a. other spec. rel.
  other aspects see Homicide
Mantels
  furniture arts   749.62
Mantis shrimps *see* Stomatopoda
Mantises *see* Mantodea
Mantle
  of earth geophysics   551.116

Mantodea
  culture   638.572 5
  paleozoology   565.72
  zoology   595.725
  other aspects see Insecta
Mantova Italy   *area*–452 8
Manual
  alphabet *see* Sign language
  arts
    elementary ed. 372.5
  of arms   355.52
    s.a. spec. mil. branches
  switchboard systems
    wire telephony *see*
      Telephony wire
  switchboards
    wire telephony *see*
      Telephone switchboards
      wire telephony
  training *see* Vocational
    education
  transfer
    switchboards *see* Telephone
      switchboards wire
      telephony
    systems *see* Telephony wire
  trunk switchboards
    wire telephony *see*
      Telephone switchboards
      wire telephony
  trunking systems
    wire telephony *see*
      Telephony wire
  s.a. other spec. subj.
Manuals   *s.s.*–020 2
Manufactured
  gases
    chem. tech. 665.7
    soc. & econ. aspects *see*
      Secondary industries
  s.a. other spec. subj.
Manufacturers
  biog. & work 670.92
  s.a. spec. kinds
  s.a.   *pers.*–67
Manufacturers' outlets
  retail marketing 658.870 5
    advertising 659.196 588 705
    pub. relations 659.296 588 705
  wholesale marketing 658.86
    advertising 659.196 588 6
    pub. relations 659.296 588 6
Manufactures
  soc. & econ. aspects *see*
    Secondary industries
  technology 670
  s.a. spec. prod.

Manufacturing
  cost statements
    financial management *see*
      Reporting financial
      management
  firms 338.76
    accounting 657.867
    cooperatives 334.687
    ind. relations 331.047
      s.a. spec. aspects e.g.
      Labor unions
    mergers 338.836
    pub. relations 659.29
      s.a. spec. aspects e.g.
      Advertising
    restrictive practices 338.826
  industries
    govt. control
      activities 351.824 2
      spec. jur. 353–354
      govt. depts. 351.082 42
      spec. jur. 353–354
    labor econ. 331.767
      active employment 331.125 7
      aged workers 331.398 87
      collective bargaining 331.890 47
      employment conditions 331.204 7
      ind. relations 331.047
      labor force 331.119 7
      market 331.129 7
      need 331.123 7
      opportunities 331.124 7
      pensions 331.252 9
      strikes 331.892 87
      unemployment 331.137 87
      unions 331.881 7
      wages 331.287
      women workers 331.487
      young workers 331.387
      s.a. spec. classes of
       workers e.g. Women
    labor law *see* Labor law
    prod. econ. 338.4
    source of waste
      pollution water-supply eng.
      technology 628.168 37
      other aspects see Water
      supply engineering
      sanitary eng.
      technology 628.547
      other aspects see
      Sanitary engineering
  personnel ethics *see* Business
    ethics
  processes eng. 670.42
  taxes on *see* Business taxes
  s.a. spec. prod.; also
    Industrial
Manures
  animal *see* Animal manures

Marbles
  mining (continued)
    technology — 622.351 2
    prospecting — 622.185 12
    s.a. spec. uses
Marbles (game)
  equip. mf. — 688.762
    soc. & econ. aspects *see*
      Secondary industries
  recreation — 796.2
  other aspects see Sports
Marbling
  bookbinding — 686.36
  woodwork bldgs. — 698.32
Marcgraviaceae *see* Theales
March
  Cambridgeshire Eng. — *area*–426 53
  flies *see* Orthorrhapha
Marchantiaceae *see* Hepaticae
Marche France — *area*–446 8
Marches
  band music *see* Military band
    music
  musical form
    piano music — 786.44
      recordings — 789.912 644
    other aspects see Musical
      forms
  region Italy — *area*–456 7
Marching bands — 785.067 1
  s.a. spec. kinds of music
Marcos admin. Philippines hist. — 959.904 6
  s.a. spec. events & subj.
    e.g. Commerce
Marcy Mt. N.Y. — *area*–747 53
Mardi gras
  recreation — 791.6
  soc. customs — 394.25
Mardin Turkey — *area*–566 7
Mareeba Qld. — *area*–943 6
Maremma Italy — *area*–455 7
Marengo Co. Ala. — *area*–761 392
Mares *see* Horses
Mare's milk
  dairy tech. — 637.17
Margarins
  comm. proc. — 664.32
  other aspects see Fats
Margate Kent Eng. — *area*–422 357
Margays
  animal husbandry — 636.89
  other aspects see Cats
Margiana ancient — *area*–396
Margin buying *see* Speculation
Marginal
  costs prod. econ. — 338.514 2
  productivity theory
    land econ. — 333.012
    wages econ. — 331.210 1
    s.a. spec. classes of
      labor e.g. Women

Marginal (continued)
  utility school econ. — 330.157
Mari
  ASSR — *area*–478 1
  other aspects see Cheremis
Maria Isls. Tas. — *area*–946 4
María Trinidad Sanchez Dominican
    Republic — *area*–729 364
Marianas Isls. — *area*–967
Maribo Denmark — *area*–489 3
Maricopa Co. Ariz. — *area*–791 73
Marie Byrd Land — *area*–989
Marie Galante isl. — *area*–729 76
Maries Co. Mo. — *area*–778 592
Marigolds *see* Asterales
Marijuana
  agriculture — 633.79
    soc. & econ. aspects *see*
      Primary industries
  narcotic aspects *see*
    Narcotics
  other aspects see Urticales;
    also Alkaloids
Marimba music — 789.6
  recordings — 789.912 96
Marimbas
  mf. tech. — 681.819 6
    misc. aspects see Musical
      instruments
  musical art — 789.6
Marin Co. Calif. — *area*–794 62
Marinas
  port eng.
    soc. & econ. aspects *see*
      Secondary industries
    technology — 627.38
    s.a. spec. appls. e.g.
      Nautical facilities
Marinduque Philippines — *area*–599 1
Marine
  aquariums
    fish culture — 639.342
    s.a. spec. kinds of fish
  architecture
    soc. & econ. aspects *see*
      Secondary industries
    tech. & mf. — 623.81
  biology *see* Hydrographic
    biology
  carnivores *see* Pinnipedia
  engineering *see* Power plants
    shipbuilding
  fishes
    culture — 639.32
      spec. kinds — 639.372–.375
    fishing *see* Salt-water
      fishing
    paleozoology — 567
    zoology — 597.092 1–.092 8
    other aspects see Pisces
  forces mil. sci. — 359.96

Marine (continued)
  geology   551.460 8
    s.a. spec. bodies of water
  insurance   368.2
    misc. aspects see Insurance
  scenes
    art representation   704.943 7
      painting   758.2
      s.a. other spec. art
        forms
  transportation
    accidents   363.123
      misc. aspects see
        Transportation
        accidents
  buildings
    architecture   725.34
    building   690.534
      other aspects see Public
        structures
  commerce   387.1-.5
  facilities
    civic art   711.76
    govt. control   351.877 1-.877 5
    spec. jur.   353-354
  law
    international   341.756 62
    municipal   343.096 2
    spec. jur.   343.3-.9
  personnel
    biog. & work   387.092
    s.a.   *pers.*-387 5
  other aspects see
    Transportation
  waters
    geol. agent   551.36
  s.a. Nautical
Mariner project astronautics   629.435 4
Marinette
  city Wis.   *area*-775 34
  Co. Wis.   *area*-775 33
Mariology
  Christian doctrines   232.91
Marion
  County
    Alabama   *area*-761 89
    Arkansas   *area*-767 193
    Florida   *area*-759 75
    Georgia   *area*-758 482
    Illinois   *area*-773 794
    Indiana   *area*-772 52
    Iowa   *area*-777 83
    Kansas   *area*-781 57
    Kentucky   *area*-769 51
    Mississippi   *area*-762 21
    Missouri   *area*-778 353
    Ohio   *area*-771 514
    Oregon   *area*-795 37
    South Carolina   *area*-757 86
    Tennessee   *area*-768 79
    Texas   *area*-764 193

Marion
  County (continued)
    West Virginia   *area*-754 54
    Lake S.C.   *area*-757 81
Marionettes
  handicrafts   745.592 24
  mf. tech.   688.722 4
    misc. aspects see Toys
  performing arts   791.53
Mariopteris
  paleobotany   561.597
Mariotype process
  photographic printing   773.1
Mariposa Co. Calif.   *area*-794 46
Maris   *r.e.n.*-945 6
Marisan language *see* Sabellian
      languages
Marital
  property
    law   346.04
      spec. jur.   346.3-.9
    rights
      law   346.016 3
      spec. jur.   346.3-.9
  s.a. Marriage
Maritime
  law
    international   341.756 6
    municipal   343.096
    spec. jur.   343.3-.9
  Provinces Can.   *area*-715
  Territory RSFSR   *area*-577
  s.a. Marine
Mark
  Bible   226.3
    miracles   226.7
    parables   226.8
  other aspects see New
      Testament
Marker
  drawing   741.26
    indiv. artists   741.092
    spec. appl.   741.5-.7
    spec. subj.   743.4-.8
Market
  analysis & research
    marketing management   658.83
    spec. subj.   *s.s.*-068 8
  areas
    civic art   711.552 2
  Drayton Salop Eng.   *area*-424 53
  gardening *see* Garden crops
  Harborough Leicestershire Eng.
                                              area-425 44
  Rasen Lincolnshire Eng.   *area*-425 31
Marketing
  commerce   380.1
    s.a. spec. kinds e.g.
      Domestic commerce
  firms   380.1
    cooperatives   334.681 380 1

Marketing
 firms (continued)
  ind. relations   331.041 380 1
   s.a. spec. aspects e.g.
    Labor unions
 law   343.084
  spec. commodities   343.085
  spec. jur.   343.3–.9
 management   658.8
  spec. subj.   *s.s.*–068 8
 pub. relations   659.293 801
  s.a. spec. aspects e.g.
   Advertising
 securities
  law   346.092
  spec. jur.   346.3–.9
Markets
 distribution channels
  marketing management *see*
   Distribution channels
 prod. econ.
  commun. services
   motion pictures   384.83
   telecommunications   384.041
    radiobroadcasting   384.543
    telegraphy   384.13
     submarine cable   384.43
     wire   384.13
     wireless   384.523
    telephony   384.63
     wire   384.63
     wireless   384.533
    television   384.554 3
     cable television   384.555 63
     subscription   384.554 7
  transportation
   commerce
    air   387.71
    inland waterway   386.1
    maritime   387.51
    motor   388.32
    railway   385.1
     special-duty   385.5
    urban transp.   388.404 2
Markinch Fife Scot.   *area*–412 95
Marking methods
 silviculture   634.954
  s.a. spec. trees
 s.a. other spec. subj.
Markings
 road traffic controls
  road eng.
   technology   625.794
   other aspects see Roads
  transportation eng.
   technology   629.042
   other aspects see
    Transportation
    engineering
 s.a. other spec. subj.

Markov
 processes   519.233
  s.a. spec. appls. e.g.
   Engineering
 risk   519.287
  s.a. spec. appls. e.g.
   Engineering
Marks
 Christian church   262.72
 s.a.   *s.s.*–027
Marks (ratings) *see* Grades
 (ratings)
Marlberry family *see* Myrsinales
Marlboro Co. S.C.   *area*–757 64
Marlborough
 New Zealand   *area*–931 52
 Wiltshire Eng.   *area*–423 17
Marlins *see* Acanthopterygii
Marlow Buckinghamshire Eng.
    area–425 95
Marls
 cements *see* Cementing
  materials
 soil conditioners   631.821
  misc. aspects see Soil
   conditioners
Marmalades *see* Preserves
Marmara Sea *see* Black Sea
Marmarica   *area*–397 6
Marmora Sea *see* Black Sea
Marmosets *see* Callithricidae
Marmots *see* Sciuromorpha
Marne
 dept. France   *area*–443 2
 river France   *area*–443
Maronites
 rel. orders   255.18
  church hist.   271.18
 ecclesiology   262.24
Marowijne Surinam   *area*–883 8
Marple Greater Manchester Eng.
    area–427 34
Marquesas Isls.   *area*–963 1
Marquetry
 furniture arts   749.5
 wood handicrafts   745.51
Marquette Co.
 Michigan   *area*–774 96
 Wisconsin   *area*–775 58
Marquisettes *see* Leno-weave
 fabrics
Marrakesh Morocco   *area*–646
Marriage
 counseling
  soc. services   362.828 6
  misc. aspects see
   Families soc. welfare
 customs   392.5
 influence on nationality
  internat. law   341.482
  pol. sci.   323.636

Martinique (continued)
people   *r.e.n.*–969 729 82
Martins *see* Hirundinidae
Martinsville Va.   *area*–755 693
Martyniaceae *see* Bignoniales
Martyrs
 Christian church hist. 272
Marwari dialect
 linguistics   491.479 7
 other aspects see Rajasthani
   language
Marxian
 organizations pol. sci. 324
 parties
  pol. sci.   324.24–.29
  s.a. spec. subj. of concern
   e.g. Social problems
 socialism
  economics   335.4
  pol. ideology   320.531 5
  soc. theology *see*
   Political ideologies
   soc. theology
Marxism *see* Marxian socialism
Marxism-Leninism
 economics   335.43
 pol. ideology   320.532 2
 soc. theology *see* Political
  ideologies soc.
  theology
Marxist *see* Marxian
Mary
 Kathleen Qld.   *area*–943 7
 mother of Jesus
  art representation *see*
   Madonna & Child
  Christian doctrines 232.91
  private prayers to 242.74
 queen
  1
   Eng. hist.   942.054
   Gt. Brit. hist. 941.054
   persecutions
    Christian church hist. 272.6
  2
   Eng. hist.   942.068
   Gt. Brit. hist. 941.068
   Scot. hist.   941.106 8
  s.a. spec. events & subj.
   e.g. Literature;
   also Courts
 Virgin *see* Mary mother of
  Jesus
Maryborough
 Queensland   *area*–943 2
 Victoria   *area*–945 3
Maryland   *area*–752
Maryport Cumbria Eng. *area*–427 87
Masaya Nicaragua *area*–728 514
Masbate Philippines *area*–599 5
Mascarene Isls.   *area*–698

Mascots
 occultism   133.44
Masculinity
 sex psych.   155.332
Masers
 microwave electronics
  soc. & econ. aspects *see*
   Secondary industries
  tech. & mf.   621.381 336
  spec. circuits 621.381 32
  s.a. spec. appls. e.g.
   Radar engineering
 other aspects see Microwave
  electronics
Masham North Yorkshire Eng.
     area–428 42
Mashonaland   *area*–689 1
Maskinongé Co. Que. *area*–714 44
Masks (drama)
 gen. wks.
  collections   808.825
  hist. & crit.   809.25
  rhetoric   808.25
  juvenile   808.068 25
 other aspects see Drama
Masks (music)   782.9
 recordings   789.912 29
Masks (sculpture) 731.75
 spec. periods & schools 732–735
Masochism
 gen. med.   616.858 35
 geriatrics   618.976 858 35
 pediatrics   618.928 583 5
 psychology   157.7
 statistics   312.385 835
 other aspects see Sexual
  deviations
Mason Co.
 Illinois   *area*–773 553
 Kentucky   *area*–769 323
 Michigan   *area*–774 61
 Texas   *area*–764 66
 Washington   *area*–797 97
 West Virginia *area*–754 33
Masonic songs *see* Associations
  songs
Masonry
 adhesives
  bldg. materials 691.5
  eng. materials 620.15
  foundations   624.153 5
  s.a. other spec. uses
  manufacturing
   soc. & econ. aspects *see*
    Secondary industries
  technology   666.9
 arch bridges
  structural eng. 624.63
  other aspects see Bridges
  (structures)

Masonry (continued)
dams
hydraulic eng.
soc. & econ. aspects *see*
Secondary industries
technology   627.82
s.a. spec. appls. e.g.
Military engineering
other aspects see Liquids
engineering
materials
arch. construction   721.044 1
s.a. spec. kinds of
bldgs.
bldg. construction   693.1
engineering   620.13
foundations   624.153 3
naval design   623.818 3
shipbuilding   623.820 7
structures   624.183
s.a. other spec. uses
organization   366.1
Masons
biog. & work   693.109 2
s.a.   *pers.*–693
s.a. Freemasons
Masques *see* Masks
Mass
communication
sociology   302.23
other aspects see
Communication
cookery   641.57
examinations ed.   371.262
s.a. spec. levels of ed.;
also Special education
media
pol. sci.   324.73
sociology   302.23
s.a. spec. kinds e.g. Books
Mass (religion)
Christian liturgical music 783.21
recordings   789.912 321
Christian liturgy *see* Holy
Communion Christian
rites
Mass (substance)
action law
physical chem. *see*
Equilibriums
celestial bodies *see*
Constants celestial
bodies
measurements
metrology *see* Measures
physics   530.8
nuclei *see* Nuclei
particles *see* Particles
(matter)
physics mech.   531.14
fluids   532.04

Mass (substance)
physics mech. (continued)
gases   533.15
air   533.6
liquids   532.4
solids   531.5
rays *see* Rays (beams)
spectrographic methods
anal. chem.
gen. wks.   543.087 3
qualitative   544.973
quantitative   545.33
organic   547.308 73
qualitative   547.349 73
quantitative   547.353 3
s.a. spec. elements &
cpds.
transfer
chem. eng.   660.284 23
s.a. spec. prod.
wasting
physical geol.   551.3
Massa e Carrara Italy   *area*–455 4
Massac Co. Ill.   *area*–773 997
Massachusetts
Bay
oceanography   551.461 45
regional subj. trmt.   *area*–163 45
other aspects see Atlantic
Ocean
state   *area*–744
Massacre of innocents
Christian doctrines   232.925
Massage
personal care   646.75
therapeutics   615.822
misc. aspects see Physical
therapies
s.a. spec. diseases
Mass-energy
conservation
physics   531.62
s.a. spec. branches of
physics
equivalence *see* Relativity
theories physics
Massif Central France   *area*–445 9
Master-servant relationships
law   346.024
spec. jur.   346.3–.9
Mastication
human phys.   612.311
rubber mf.
soc. & econ. aspects *see*
Secondary industries
technology   678.22
s.a. spec. kinds of rubber
e.g. Natural rubber
other aspects see Digestion
Mastiffs
animal husbandry   636.73

Mastiffs (continued)
  other aspects see Dogs
Mastigophora
  culture | 639.731 8
  paleozoology | 563.18
  zoology | 593.18
  other aspects see Protozoa
Mastitis *see* Mammary glands
      diseases
Mastoid processes
  diseases
    gen. wks. | 617.87
    geriatrics | 618.977 87
    pediatrics | 618.920 978 7
    statistics | 312.304 787
      deaths | 312.260 478 7
  physiology
    human | 612.854
    other aspects see Sensory
        functions
  other aspects see Ears
Masts
  shipbuilding *see* Gear
      shipbuilding
Masturbation *see* Sexual
      deviations
Mat herbs
  botany | 582.14
  misc. aspects see
      Spermatophyta
  s.a. spec. plants
Matabeleland | *area*–689 1
Matagalpa Nicaragua | *area*–728 525
Matagalpan *see*
      Miskito-Matagalpan
Matagorda Co. Tex. | *area*–764 132
Matane Co. Que. | *area*–714 775
Matanuska Valley Alaska | *area*–798 3
Matanuska-Susitna election
      district Alaska | *area*–798 3
Matanzas Cuba | *area*–729 13
Matapédia Co. Que. | *area*–714 775
Match-cover
  advertising | 659.13
  illustration
    drawings | 741.69
    prints | 769.5
Matches
  manufacturing
    soc. & econ. aspects *see*
        Secondary industries
    technology | 662.5
  s.a. spec. appls. e.g.
      Fireworks safety
Matching numbers
  contests | 790.134
Maté
  agriculture | 633.77
  soc. & econ. aspects *see*
      Primary industries

Mate! (continued)
  foods | 641.337 7
  cookery | 641.637 7
  tea
    comm. proc. | 663.96
    other aspects see
        Nonalcoholic beverages
  other aspects see
      Celastrales; *also*
      Alkaloids
Mate selection
  soc. theology
    Christianity | 261.835 82
    comp. rel. | 291.178 358 2
    s.a. other spec. rel.
  sociology | 306.82
  other aspects see Courtship
Matera Italy | *area*–457 72
Materia medica *see* Drugs
Material remains *see*
      Archaeology
Materialism
  doctrinal controversies
    Christian church hist. | 273.9
  philosophy | 146.3
    indiv. phil. | 180–190
    s.a. spec. branches of phil.
        e.g. Metaphysics
Materialists
  polemics against
    Christianity | 239.8
    Islam | 297.298
  other rel. see Doctrinal
      theology
Materials
  automobiles
    soc. & econ. aspects *see*
        Secondary industries
    technology | 629.232
      spec. parts | 629.24–.27
  buildings | 691
  costs
    financial management | 658.155 3
      spec. subj. | *s.s.*–068 1
  engineering | 620.11
  engineers
    biog. & work | 620.110 92
    s.a. | *pers.*–620 1
  estimation
    structural eng. *see*
        Structural quantity
        surveying
  foundation eng.
    soc. & econ. aspects *see*
        Secondary industries
    tech. & mf. | 624.153
    s.a. spec. appls. e.g.
        Bridges (structures)
        structural eng.
  lit. & stage trmt.
    man-made *see* Things

Materials
  lit. & stage trmt. (continued)
    natural *see* Natural
      phenomena
    management   658.7
      spec. subj.   *s.s.*–068 7
    science   620.11
  shortages
    agriculture
      prod. econ.   338.14
    spacecraft eng.   629.472
      unmanned   629.462
    other aspects see
      Spacecraft
  standards & specifications
    prod. management *see*
      Quality controls prod.
      management
  textiles mf.
    soc. & econ. aspects *see*
      Secondary industries
    technology   677.028 3
    s.a. spec. kinds of
      textiles
    other spec. kinds & uses *s.s.*–028
Materials-handling equip.
  machine eng.
    soc. & econ. aspects *see*
      Secondary industries
    tech. & mf.   621.86
    shipbuilding   623.867
    s.a. other spec. appls.
  other aspects see Mechanics
Materiel
  armed forces   355.8
  s.a. spec. mil. branches
Maternal
  deaths
    obstetrics   618.79
    pub. health   614.599 2
    vet. obstetrics   636.089 879
    s.a. spec. animals
  dystocia
    obstetrics   618.51
    anesthesia   617.968 2
    pub. health   614.599 2
    statistics   312.304 851
    deaths   312.260 485 1
  other aspects see Diseases
Maternity
  hospitals
    safety aspects *see* Health
      care facilities
    soc. services   362.198 2
    misc. aspects see
      Hospitals
  insurance
    soc. insurance   368.424
      pub. admin. *see* Social
        insurance pub. admin.

Maternity
  insurance
    soc. insurance (continued)
      other aspects see
        Insurance
    soc. law   344.022 4
      spec. jur.   344.3–.9
Mathematical
  crystallography   548.7
  s.a. spec. substances
  games
    recreation   793.74
  geography   526
  logic *see* Symbolic logic
  models
    mathematics   511.8
    s.a. spec. math. branches
    operations research *see*
      Models
      (representations)
      operations research
    s.a. other spec. appls.
  physics   530.15
    spec. states of matter   530.4
    s.a. spec. branches of
      physics
  principles
    computer eng. *see*
      Fundamentals computer
      eng.
    s.a.   *s.s.*–015 1
  programming
    management use   658.403 3
    s.a. other spec. appls.
  school econ.   330.154 3
  techniques
    management use   658.403 3
    s.a. other spec. appls.
  s.a. other spec. subj.
Mathematicians
  biog. & work   510.92
  s.a. spec. kinds
  other aspects see Scientists
  s.a.   *pers.*–51
Mathematics   510
  & religion
    nat. rel.   215.1
  appls. to spec. subj.   *s.s.*–015 1
  Biblical trmt.   220.851
    s.a. spec. parts of Bible
  documentation   025.065 1
  libraries   026.51
    misc. aspects see Special
      libraries
  library acquisitions   025.275 1
  library classification   025.465 1
  study & teaching   510.7
    curriculums   375.51
    elementary ed.   372.7

Mathematics
  study & teaching (continued)
    special ed.   371.904 4
      s.a. spec. groups of
        students
    subject headings   025.495 1
    other aspects see Sciences
Mathews Co. Va.   *area*–755 31
Mathieu functions   515.54
  s.a. spec. appls. e.g.
    Engineering
Matins *see* Office hours
Matlock Derbyshire Eng. *area*–425 13
Mato Grosso Brazil   *area*–817 2
Matriarchal
  family
    soc. theology
      Christianity   261.835 85
      comp. rel.   291.178 358 85
      s.a. other spec. rel.
    sociology   306.85
  state
    pol. sci.   321.12
    s.a. spec. jur.
Matrices *see* Matrixes
Matriculation
  schools   371.21
  s.a. spec. levels of ed.;
    also Special education
Matrilineal kinship *see* Kinship
Matrimony
  rel. doctrines
    Christianity   234.165
    s.a. other spec. rel.
  rel. rites
    Christianity   265.5
    Judaism   296.444
    s.a. other spec. rel.
Matrix mechanics
  physics   530.122
  spec. states of matter   530.4
  s.a. spec. branches of
    physics
Matrixes
  algebra   512.943 4
  s.a. spec. appls. e.g.
    Engineering
  molds *see* Molding-equipment
Matruh Egypt   *area*–621
Mats *see* Table linens
Matsu China   *area*–512 49
Matter
  chemistry *see* Chemistry
  metaphysics   117
  physics *see* Physics
  states *see* States of matter
  structure
    astrophysics   523.019 1
    s.a. spec. celestial
      bodies

Matter
  structure (continued)
    physics   539.1
    spec. states of matter   530.4
    s.a. spec. physical
      phenomena e.g. Heat
Matthew
  Bible   226.2
    miracles   226.7
    parables   226.8
    other aspects see New
      Testament
Matthias
  reign Ger. hist.   943.035
  s.a. spec. events & subj.
    e.g. Courts
Matting
  unaltered vegetable fibers
    arts   746.41
    s.a. spec. prod.
    technology *see* Unaltered
      vegetable fibers
Mattresses *see* Beds (furniture)
Maturation *see* Development
    (biology)
Mature people *see* Middle-aged
    people
Maturity
  human phys.   612.663
  other aspects see Development
    (biology)
Maui
  Co. Hawaii   *area*–969 2
  Isl. Hawaii   *area*–969 21
Maule Chile   *area*–833 6
Maumee River O.   *area*–771 1
Maundy Thursday *see* Holy Week
Maurepas Lake La.   *area*–763 32
Mauretania
  ancient country   *area*–397 1
Mauritania   *area*–661
Mauritanian
  people   *r.e.n.*–966 1
  s.a. other spec. subj. e.g.
    Arts
Mauritius   *area*–698 2
Maury
  Co. Tenn.   *area*–768 59
  Mts. Ore.   *area*–795 83
Mauryas
  India hist.   934.04
  s.a. spec. events & subj.
    e.g. Arts
Mausoleums *see* Mortuary tombs &
    chapels
Maverick Co. Tex.   *area*–764 435
Maxima
  mathematics   511.66
    calculus   515.33
    s.a. spec. appls. e.g.
      Engineering

Maxima
  mathematics (continued)
    s.a. other spec. branches;
      also spec. appls. e.g.
      Engineering
Maximal principle methods
  calculus   515.64
    s.a. spec. appls. e.g.
      Engineering
Maximilian
  reign
    Ger. hist.
      1   943.029
      2   943.033
    Mex. hist.   972.07
    s.a. spec. events & subj.
      e.g. Courts
Maxims
  folk lit.   398.9
Maximum-security prisons
  penology   365.33
  other aspects see Penal
    institutions
Maxwell's
  equations *see* Electromagnetic
    theory
  formulas
    thermodynamics
      astrophysics   523.013 71
      s.a. spec. celestial
        bodies
      physics   536.71
      spec. states of matter   530.4
May Day
  soc. customs   394.268 3
Maya
  architecture   722.91
    misc. aspects see
      Architectural schools
    other aspects see
      Macro-Penutian
Mayaca family *see* Commelinales
Mayacaceae *see* Commelinales
Mayaguana Bahamas   *area*–729 6
Mayagüez Puerto Rico   *area*–729 56
Maybole Strathclyde Scot.   *area*–414 64
Maydeae *see* Panicoideae
Mayenne France   *area*–441 6
Mayes Co. Okla.   *area*–766 93
Mayflies *see* Ephemeroptera
Mayflower Descendants   369.12
Mayo
  governorship India hist.   954.035 2
    s.a. spec. events & subj.
      e.g. Commerce
  Ireland   *area*–417 3
Mayonnaise
  comm. proc.   664.37
  other aspects see Fats

Mayor-council form
  local govt.
    pub. admin.   352.008 2–.008 3
Mayors
  local govt.
    pub. admin.   352.008 2–.008 3
Maypops *see* Passion fruit
Mazanderan Iran   *area*–552 3
Mazaruni-Potaro Guyana   *area*–881 9
Mazdaism *see* Zoroastrianism
Mazurkas
  piano music   786.44
    recordings   789.912 644
  other aspects see Dance music
Mbeya Tanzania   *area*–678 28
Mead Lake   *area*–793 12
Meade Co.
  Kansas   *area*–781 75
  Kentucky   *area*–769 852
  South Dakota   *area*–783 44
Meadow-beauty family *see*
    Myrtales
Meadows *see* Grasslands
Meagher Co. Mont.   *area*–786 612
Meals   642.1–.5
  cookery   641.52–.54
  soc. customs   394.15
Meals (milling products)
  comm. proc.   664.720 7
    wheat   664.722 73
    s.a. other spec. grains &
      prod.
  other aspects see Cereal
    grains
Mealybugs *see* Homoptera
Mean
  time chronology   529.1
  value theorems
    calculus   515.33
    s.a. spec. appls. e.g.
      Engineering
  s.a. other spec. subj.
Meander Res. O.   *area*–771 38
Meaning
  epistemology   121.68
Meanings
  linguistics *see* Words
Means
  statistical math.   519.533
    s.a. spec. appls. e.g.
      Engineering
Measles
  gen. med.   616.915
  geriatrics   618.976 915
  pediatrics   618.929 915
  pub. health   614.523
  statistics   312.391 5
    deaths   312.269 15
  other aspects see Diseases
  s.a. German measles

Measurable functions
  gen. wks. *see* Functions
    (mathematics)
  spaces   515.73
    s.a. spec. appls. e.g.
      Engineering
Measure theory
  calculus   515.42
    s.a. spec. appls. e.g.
      Engineering
Measurement
  aircraft eng.   629.134 57
    s.a. spec. appls. e.g.
      Military engineering
  education *see* Tests education
  elect. eng.
    soc. & econ. aspects *see*
      Secondary industries
    technology   621.37
    other aspects see
      Electricity
  engineering   620.004 4
    s.a. spec. branches of eng.
  gases
    chem. apparatus   542.7
    s.a. spec. appls. e.g.
      Organic chemistry
  microwave electronics
    technology   621.381 37
    s.a. spec. appls. e.g.
      Radar engineering
    other aspects see Microwave
      electronics
  radio
    engineering   621.384 17
    s.a. spec. appls. e.g.
      Radiotelephony
    other aspects see Radio
  sound
    engineering   620.21–.25
    s.a. spec. appls. e.g.
      Musical sound
    physics   534.42
    spec. states of matter   530.4
  television
    engineering   621.388 7
    s.a. spec. appls. e.g.
      Astronautics
    other aspects see
      Television
  time   529.7
  water consumption
    technology   628.17
    other aspects see Water
      supply engineering
  other spec. subj.   *s.s.*–028 7
  s.a. other spec. appls.; also
      Mensuration
Measurement-standards eng.
  elect. eng.   621.372

Measurement-standards eng. (continued)
  electronic eng.   621.381 548
    s.a. spec. branches e.g.
      Radar
    s.a. other spec. appls.
Measurement-theory
  physics   530.16
    spec. states of matter   530.16
    s.a. spec. branches of
        physics
Measures
  commerce   388.1
  govt. control   351.821
    spec. jur.   353–354
  law
    international   341.754
    municipal   343.075
    spec. jur.   343.3–.9
Measuring-apparatus *see*
      Measuring-instruments;
      also Measuring-tools
Measuring-devices *see*
      Measuring-instruments;
      also Measuring-tools
Measuring-instruments
  chemistry   542.3
    s.a. spec. appls. e.g.
      Organic chemistry
  gen. wks.
    manufacturing
      soc. & econ. aspects *see*
        Secondary industries
    technology   681.2
  physics   530.7
    s.a. spec. branches of
        physics
  radiowave electronics *see*
      Testing-devices
      radiowave electronics
  s.a. other spec. apparatus,
      equipment, materials,
      uses, kinds
Measuring-tools
  soc. & econ. aspects *see*
      Secondary industries
  tech. & mf.   621.994
    s.a. spec. appls. e.g.
      Carpentry
  s.a. spec. apparatus,
      equipment, materials,
      uses, kinds
Meat
  loaves
    cookery   641.824
  pies
    cookery   641.824
Meath Ireland   *area*–418 22
Meatless high-protein foods
  manufacturing
    soc. & econ. aspects *see*
      Secondary industries

Mechanical (continued)
  pencils
    manufacturing
      soc. & econ. aspects *see*
        Secondary industries
      technology   681.6
  power *see* Power
  processes
    birth control   613.943 5
    printing
      soc. & econ. aspects *see*
        Secondary industries
      technology   686.231
      wood pulp mf.   676.122
  properties
    crystals   548.84
    s.a. spec. substances
    eng. materials   620.112 92
    s.a. spec. materials &
      spec. uses
    minerals   549.121
      spec. minerals   549.2–.7
    solutions
      electolytic   541.374 3
        applied   660.297 43
        organic   547.137 43
      gen. wks.   541.341 3
        applied   660.294 13
        organic   547.134 13
    s.a. spec. elements,
      cpds., prod.
  separation
    ores
      mining eng.   622.75
      spec. ores   622.33–.39
  stokers steam eng. *see*
    Furnaces steam eng.
  systems eng.
    gen. wks. *see* Machine
      engineering
    shipbuilding
      technology   623.850 1
      design   623.814 501
        spec. craft   623.812
    s.a. spec. systems
    s.a. other spec. appls.
  tackles *see* Tackles
  telephones *see*
    Recording-telephones
  toys
    manufacturing
      soc. & econ. aspects *see*
        Secondary industries
      technology   688.728
    recreation   790.133
  treatment
    water-supply eng.
      technology   628.164
      other aspects see Water
        supply engineering

Mechanical (continued)
  vibrations
    engineering   620.3
    s.a. spec. appls. e.g.
      Reciprocating engines
  wave theory of light
    astrophysics   523.015 13
    s.a. spec. celestial
      bodies
    physics   525.13
  working
    metal prod.
      manufacturing
        soc. & econ. aspects
          see Secondary
          industries
        technology   671.32–.34
          ferrous metals   672.32–.34
          s.a. other spec.
            metals
    s.a. other spec. subj.
Mechanics   531
  air
    engineering   620.107
    physics   533.6
  applied   620.1
    states of matter *see spec.*
      states
    s.a. spec. appls. e.g.
      Steam engineering
  astronautics *see* Celestial
    mechanics
  astronomy *see* Celestial
    mechanics
  atmosphere   551.515
  engineering   620.1
    s.a. spec. appls. e.g.
      Aerospace engineering
  fluids   532
    applied   620.106
  gases   533
    applied   620.107
  liquids *see* Hydromechanics
  machinery   621.811
    s.a. spec. machines e.g.
      Pumps
  materials *see* Mechanical
    forces effects eng.
    materials
  particles
    physics   531.16
  physics   531
  soils   624.151 36
    misc. aspects see
      Engineering geology
  solids   531.2–.5
    applied   620.105
  structures   624.171
    spec. structures   624.177
  substances *see* Mechanical
    properties

Mechanism
philosophy   146.6
  indiv. phil.   180–190
  s.a. spec. branches of phil.
    e.g. Metaphysics
Mechanisms
engineering *see* Machine
  engineering
Mechanization
effect
  prod. econ.
    agriculture   338.161
    other aspects see
      Efficiency prod. econ.
  factory eng.   670.427
  s.a. spec. products of mf.
  postal commun.   383.24
  other aspects see Postal
    communication
  s.a. other spec. appls.
Mechanized
cavalry
  armed forces   357.5
  armored   358.18
data processing *see* Data
  processing
indexing *see* Indexing
translation *see* Translation
  (linguistics)
Mechanotherapy   615.822
misc. aspects see Physical
  therapies
s.a. spec. diseases
Mechitarists
rel. orders   255.17
  church hist.   271.17
  ecclesiology   262.24
Mecklenburg
County
  North Carolina   *area*–756 76
  Virginia   *area*–755 645
state Ger.   *area*–431 7
Mecoptera
culture   638.574 4
paleozoology   565.74
zoology   595.744
other aspects see Insecta
Mecosta Co. Mich.   *area*–774 52
Medal of Honor Legion   369.11
Medals
mil. discipline   355.134 2
  s.a. spec. mil. branches
numismatics   737.22
rel. significance
  Christianity   247.872 2
  comp. rel.   291.37
  s.a. other spec. rel
research incentives   001.44
Media
communications *see*
  Communications media

Media (continued)
kits
  library trmt.   025.179 6
  acquisitions   025.289 6
  cataloging   025.349 6
mass *see* Mass media
Median Empire
history   935.04
s.a.   *area*–35
s.a. spec. events & subj.
  e.g. Arts
Mediastinum
anatomy
  human   611.27
  other aspects see
    Respiratory organs
diseases
  gen. wks.   616.27
    neoplasms   616.992 27
    tuberculosis   616.995 27
  geriatrics   618.976 27
  pediatrics   618.922 7
  pub. health   614.592 7
  statistics   312.327
    deaths   312.262 7
  surgery   617.545
    anesthesiology   617.967 545
  other aspects see Diseases
physical anthropometry   573.627
physiology
  human   612.2
  other aspects see
    Respiration
tissue biology human   611.018 927
Mediation
employee relations
  labor econ.   331.891 42
  labor law *see* Labor law
  personnel admin.
    gen. management   658.315 4
    spec. subj.   *s.s.*–068 3
  pub. admin.   350.174
    central govts.   351.174
    spec. jur.   353–354
    local govts.   352.005 174
  internat. law   341.52
Mediatized states *see* Dependent
  states
Medicago sativa *see* Alfalfas
Medical
accounting   657.834
advertising
  ethics   174.26
  techniques   659.196 1
aid *see* Medical services
assistants
  prof. duties &
    characteristics   610.695 3
  services   610.737
  other aspects see Medical
    scientists

Medical (continued)

bacteriology	616.014
s.a. spec. diseases	
care *see* Medical services	
centers *see* Clinics	
chemistry *see* Pharmaceutical	
chemistry	
climatology	616.988
geriatrics	618.976 988
pediatrics	618.929 88
vet. med.	636.089 698 8
s.a. spec. animals	
other aspects see Medical	
sciences	
clinic bldgs. *see* Office	
buildings	
clinics *see* Clinics	
economics	338.476 1
education	
finance	
law	344.076 9
spec. jur.	344.3–.9
emergencies	
med. sci.	616.025
misc. aspects see	
Diseases	
s.a. spec. diseases	
entomology	616.968
geriatrics	618.976 968
pediatrics	618.929 68
vet. med.	636.089 696 8
s.a. spec. animals	
other aspects see Medical	
sciences	
ethics *see* Medical scientists	
occupational ethics	
examinations	
gen. wks.	616.075
s.a. spec. diseases	
mil. sci.	355.223 6
s.a. spec. mil. branches	
folklore *see* Medical sciences	
folklore	
geography	
pub. health	614.42
misc. aspects see Public	
health	
gymnastics *see* Calisthenics	
therapeutics	
helminthology *see*	
Helminthology med. sci.	
history taking	
gen. med.	616.075 1
surgery	617.075 1
s.a. spec. diseases	
other aspects see Diseases	
installations	
armed forces	355.72
s.a. spec. mil. branches	

Medical (continued)

instruments	
manufacturing	
soc. & econ. aspects *see*	
Secondary industries	
technology	681.761
s.a. spec. kinds & uses e.g.	
sphygmomanometers in	
diagnosis of	
hypertension	
616.132 075 4	
insurance	368.382 2
misc. aspects see Insurance	
jurisprudence	614.1
law *see* Public health law	
libraries	026.61
misc. aspects see Special	
libraries	
machinery	
mf. tech.	681.761
s.a. spec. kinds	
malpractice	
law	346.033 2
spec. jur.	346.3–.9
meteorology	616.988
geriatrics	618.976 988
pediatrics	618.929 88
vet. med.	636.089 698 8
s.a. spec. animals	
other aspects see Medical	
sciences	
microbiology	616.01
s.a. spec. diseases	
missionaries *see* Missionaries	
medical	
missions	362.1–.4
museum bldgs.	
architecture	727.661
building	690.766 1
other aspects see	
Educational buildings	
museums	
desc. & colls.	610.74
museology	069.961
s.a. spec. activities	
e.g. Display	
mycology	616.969
geriatrics	618.976 969
pediatrics	618.929 69
vet. med.	636.089 696 9
s.a. spec. animals	
other aspects see Medical	
sciences	
occupations *see* Professional	
occupations	
office bldgs. *see* Office	
buildings	
parasitology	616.96
geriatrics	618.976 96
pediatrics	618.929 6

Medication methods	615.6
vet. sci.	636.089 56
s.a. spec. animals	
Médici admin. Brazil hist.	981.063
s.a. spec. events & subj.	
e.g. Commerce	
Medicinal	
plants	
botany	581.634
s.a. spec. plants	
teas	
comm. proc.	663.96
other aspects see	
Nonalcoholic beverages	
Medicinals *see* Drugs	
Medicine	
Bow Range Wyo.	*area*–787 86
Hat Alta.	*area*–712 34
shows performing arts	791.1
Medicine (discipline) *see*	
Medical sciences	
Medicine-producing plants	
agriculture	633.88
soc. & econ. aspects *see*	
Primary industries	
Medieval	
architecture	723
spec. places	
Oriental	722.1–.5
other	720.9
other aspects see	
Architectural schools	
history	
appls. to spec. subj.	*s.s.*–090 2
Europe	940.1
world	909.07
spec. centuries	909.1–.4
s.a. spec. countries	
law	340.55
philosophy	
Oriental	181
Western	189
s.a. spec. branches & subj.	
e.g. Metaphysics	
remedies	
therapeutics	615.899
s.a. spec. diseases	
sculpture	734
spec. places	730.9
s.a. other spec. subj.	
Medina	
County	
Ohio	*area*–771 35
Texas	*area*–764 42
Islamic worship	297.35
Isle of Wight Eng.	*area*–422 82
Meditation	
personal improvement	
appl. psych.	158.12
children	155.418

Meditation	
personal improvement	
appl. psych. (continued)	
s.a. psych. of other spec.	
groups	
other aspects see Thought	
private worship	
Christianity	248.34
comp. rel.	291.43
other rel. see Worship	
Meditations	
piano music *see* Romantic	
music piano	
private devotions	
Christianity	242
comp. rel.	291.43
Judaism	296.72
s.a. other spec. rel.	
Mediterranean	
fever *see* Undulant fever	
region subj. trmt.	*area*–182 2
Sea	
oceanography	551.462
regional subj. trmt.	*area*–163 8
other aspects see Atlantic	
Ocean	
Medium	
statistical math.	519.533
s.a. spec. appls. e.g.	
Engineering	
Mediums	
painting material	
arts	751.2
indiv. artists	759.1–.9
Medium-security prisons	
penology	365.33
other aspects see Penal	
institutions	
Mediumship	
spiritualism	133.91
Medlars	
agriculture	634.15
soc. & econ. aspects *see*	
Primary industries	
foods	641.341 5
preparation	
commercial	664.804 15
domestic	641.641 5
other aspects see Rosaceae;	
also Fruits	
Medulla	
human anatomy & phys.	611.018 4
other aspects see Tissue	
biology	
Medulla oblongata	
physiology	
animal	591.188
s.a. spec. animals,	
functions, systems,	
organs	
human	612.828

Melodrama (continued)
spec. lits.	*lit. sub.*–205 27
indiv. authors	*lit. sub.*–21–29
stage presentation	792.27

other aspects see Drama

Melody
music theory	781.41
spec. forms	781.5

s.a. spec. mediums

Melons
agriculture	635.61

soc. & econ. aspects *see*
Primary industries
foods	641.356 1
preparation	
commercial	664.805 61
domestic	641.656 1

other aspects see
Cucurbitales; *also*
Fruits
Melos Greece	*area*–499
Melrose Borders Scot.	*area*–413 85
Meltham West Yorkshire Eng.	
	area–428 13

Melting
chem. eng.	660.284 296

s.a. spec. prod.
effect of heat *see* Fusion
effect of heat
metal prod.
mf. tech.	671.24
ferrous metals	672.24

s.a. other spec. metals
other aspects see Foundry
practice
s.a. other spec. appls.
Melton Leicestershire Eng.	*area*–425 46

Melville
city Sask.	*area*–712 44
Island	
N. Ter. Aust.	*area*–942 95
Northwest Ter.	*area*–719 5

Membership
committees
legislative bodies
pol. sci.	328.365 2
spec. jur.	328.4–.9
legislative bodies	
law	342.055
spec. jur.	342.3–.9
pol. sci.	328.33
spec. jur.	328.4–.9
local Christian parishes	254.5
s.a.	*s.s.*–06

s.a. other spec.
organizations
Membracoidea *see* Homoptera
Membranes
cytology
cytology	574.875
animals	591.875
plants	581.875

Membranes
cytology (continued)
s.a. spec. organisms
sound generation *see*
Generation sound
use
saline water conversion
technology	628.167 4

other aspects see Water
supply engineering
s.a. Mucous membranes; *also*
Serous membranes
Membranophone music	789.15
recordings	789.912 91

Membranophones
mf. tech.	681.819 1

misc. aspects see Musical
instruments
musical art	789.1

Memoirs *see* Biographies
Memorandums
office use	651.755

Memorial
buildings
architecture	725.94
building	690.594

other aspects see Public
structures
sermons
Christianity	252.9

other rel. see Preaching
Memorials
Spanish-American War	973.896
U.S. Civil War	973.76
U.S. Mexican War	973.626
U.S. Revolutionary War	973.36
U.S. War of 1812	973.526
World War 1	940.46
World War 2	940.546

s.a. other spec. events
Memorizing
musical performance
music theory	781.634

s.a. spec. mediums
Memory
aids *see* Mnemonic systems
equipment
computer eng.	621.381 953 3
analogue	621.381 957 33
combinations & related	621.381 959
digital	621.381 958 33

other aspects see
Computers
s.a. spec. uses e.g. Data
processing
human attribute
metaphysics	128.3

processes
ed. psych.	370.152 2
psychology	153.12
animals	156.312

Memory
  processes
    psychology (continued)
      children   155.413
      s.a. psych. of other spec.
        groups
Memphis Tenn.   *area*–768 19
Memphremagog Lake Que. *area*–714 64
Men
  art representation   704.942 3
    drawing tech.   743.43
    painting   757.3
    s.a. other spec. art forms
  biography
    gen. colls.   920.71
    spec. fields   *s.s.*–092
  criminal offenders   364.373
  ethics   170.202 42
  etiquette   395.142
  grooming   646.704 4
  hygiene   613.042 34
  journalism for   070.483 46
  meditations for
    Christianity   242.642
    other rel. see Worship
  personal rel.
    Christianity   248.842
    other rel. see Personal
      religion
  physical fitness
    hygiene   613.704 4
  prayers for
    Christianity   242.842
    other rel. see Worship
  psychology   155.632
  recreation   790.194
    indoor   793.019 4
    outdoor   796.019 4
  sex hygiene   613.952
  soc. theology
    Christianity   261.834 3
    comp. rel.   291.178 343
    s.a. other spec. rel.
  sociology   305.3
  other spec. subj.   *pers.*–056 4
  other aspects see Adults
  s.a. spec. groups e.g.
    Unmarried men
Menabe kingdom hist.   969.101
  s.a. spec. events & subj.
    e.g. Commerce
Menard Co.
  Illinois   *area*–773 555
  Texas   *area*–764 877
Mende *see* Mandingo
Mendelevium
  chemistry   546.449
Mendelian laws *see* Genetic laws
Mendicant rel. orders
  Christianity   255.06
    church hist.   271.06

Mendicant rel. orders
  Christianity (continued)
    ecclesiology   262.24
    other rel. see Religious
      congregations
Mending
  books   025.7
  home sewing   646.2
    clothing   646.6
  s.a. other spec. subj.
Mendip
  Hills Somerset Eng.   *area*–423 83
  Somerset Eng.   *area*–423 83
Mendocino Co. Calif.   *area*–794 15
Mendoza Argentina   *area*–826 4
Menelik 2 Ethiopia hist.   963.052
  s.a. spec. events & subj.
    e.g. Commerce
Menifee Co. Ky.   *area*–769 583
Menindee Lakes N.S.W.   *area*–944 9
Meningeal diseases *see* Meninges
  diseases
Meninges
  diseases
    gen. wks.   616.82
      neoplasms   616.992 81
      tuberculosis   616.995 81
    geriatrics   618.976 82
    pediatrics   618.928 2
    pub. health   614.598 2
    statistics   312.382
      deaths   312.268 2
    other aspects see Diseases
  human anatomy & phys.   611.018 8
  other aspects see Tissue
    biology
Meningitis *see* Meninges
  diseases
Menispermaceae *see* Berberidales
Mennonite
  church bldgs.
    architecture   726.589 7
    building   690.658 97
    other aspects see
      Religious-purpose
      bldgs.
  church music
    arts   783.026 97
    recordings   789.912 302 697
    s.a. spec. instruments;
      also spec. kinds e.g.
      Liturgical music
  religion
    pub. worship   264.097 02
    significance   246.7
  churches   289.7
    Christian life guides   248.489 7
    doctrines   230.97
      creeds   238.97
    general councils   262.597

Mennonite
churches (continued)
govt. & admin. 262.097
parishes 254.097
missions 266.97
moral theology 241.049 7
private prayers for 242.809 7
pub. worship 264.097
rel. associations
adults 267.189 7
men 267.249 7
women 267.449 7
young adults 267.629 7
rel. instruction 268.897
rel. law 262.989 7
schools 377.897
secondary training 207.129 7
sermons 252.097
theological seminaries 207.119
s.a. other spec. aspects
Mennonites
biog. & work 289.709 2
s.a. spec. branches
s.a. pers.–287
Menominee
Co. Mich. area–774 953
Co. Wis. area–775 356
River Mich. area–774 95
Menopause
disorders
gynecology 618.175
pub. health 614.599 2
statistics 312.304 817 5
other aspects see
Diseases
s.a. Climacteric
Menorca Spain area–467 5
Menorrhagia *see* Menstruation
disorders
Men's
clothing 646.32
comm. mf.
soc. & econ. aspects *see*
Secondary industries
technology 687
leather & fur 685.2
domestic mf. 646.402
soc. customs 391.1
other aspects see Clothing
s.a. spec. garments & kinds
e.g. Underwear; Men's
outdoor clothing
garments *see* Men's clothing
hats *see* Men's headgear
headgear
comm. mf.
soc. & econ. aspects *see*
Secondary industries
technology 687.41
leather & fur 685.2
domestic mf. 646.502

Men's
headgear (continued)
other aspects see Headgear;
also Men's clothing
house garments
comm. mf. 687.110 42
other aspects see House
garments
outdoor clothing
comm. mf.
soc. & econ. aspects *see*
Secondary industries
technology 687.141
leather & fur 685.2
s.a. spec. garments e.g.
Overcoats
other aspects see Men's
clothing
penal institutions
penology 365.44
other aspects see Penal
institutions
rel. associations
Christianity 267.2
other rel. see Religious
associations
solos
recordings 789.912
scores & parts 784.813
sacred songs 783.675 13
secular songs 784.306 13
songs *see* Men's vocal music
underwear
comm. mf.
soc. & econ. aspects *see*
Secondary industries
technology 687.21
other aspects see Men's
clothing; *also*
Underwear
vocal music
recordings 789.912
scores & parts 784.8
sacred songs 783.675
secular songs 784.306
Menstruation
disorders
gynecology 618.172
pub. health 614.599 2
statistics 312.304 817 2
other aspects see
Diseases
human phys. 612.662
misc. aspects see
Reproduction
Mensuration 530.8
forest econ. 634.928 5
s.a. spec. trees
physics 530.8
s.a. spec. branches of
physics

658

Menticide
  psychology (continued)
    s.a. psych. of other spec.
      groups
Menufiya Egypt   *area*–621
Menus
  meal planning   642.1–.5
Menyanthaceae *see* Gentianales
Menzies
  Robert Gordon admin.
    Australia hist.   994.05
    s.a. spec. events & subj.
      e.g. Arts
Merbein Vic.   *area*–945 9
Mercantile
  credit
    economics   332.742
    marketing management   658.882
    spec. subj.   *s.s.*–068 8
    other aspects see Credit
  s.a.Business
Mercantilism econ. school   330.151 3
Mercaptans *see* Hydrosulfites
Merced Co. Calif.   *area*–794 58
Mercedarians
  rel. orders   255.45
    church hist.   271.45
    ecclesiology   262.24
Mercenary troops
  armed forces   355.35
    s.a. spec. mil. branches
  use
    American Revolution   973.342
    s.a. other spec. wars
Mercer Co.
  Illinois   *area*–773 395
  Kentucky   *area*–769 485
  Missouri   *area*–778 213
  New Jersey   *area*–749 65
  North Dakota   *area*–784 83
  Ohio   *area*–771 415
  Pennsylvania   *area*–748 95
  West Virginia   *area*–754 74
Mercerizing
  textiles *see* Finishing
      textiles
Merchandisers
  biog. & work   658.800 92
  s.a.   *pers.*–658
Merchant
  marine
    schools
      finance
        law   344.076 9
        spec. jur.   344.3–.9
    s.a. Marine transportation
  ships
    powered
      engineering   623.824
      design   623.812 4
      models   623.820 14

Merchant
  ships
    powered (continued)
      seamanship   623.882 4
      other aspects see Vessels
        (nautical)
    wind-driven
      engineering   623.822 4
      design   623.812 24
      models   623.820 214
      seamanship   623.882 24
      other aspects see Vessels
        (nautical)
Mercury
  project astronautics   629.454
Mercury (element)
  chemistry
    inorganic   546.663
    organic   547.056 63
    s.a. spec. groupings e.g.
      Aliphatic compounds
  technology   661.066 3
    organic   661.895
    soc. & econ. aspects *see*
      Secondary industries
    s.a. spec. prod.
  fulminate *see* High explosives
  materials
    building   691.871
    engineering   620.189 1
    s.a. other spec. uses
  metallography   669.957 1
  metallurgy   669.71
    physical & chem.   669.967 1
    soc. & econ. aspects *see*
      Secondary industries
  mineral aspects
    econ. geol.   553.454
    mineralogy   549.23
    mining
      technology   622.345 4
      prospecting   622.184 54
    s.a.spec. minerals
  pharmacology   615.266 3
    misc. aspects see
      Pharmacology
  products
    mf. tech.   673.71
    other aspects see
      Nonferrous metals
        products
  toxicology   615.925 663
    misc. aspects see
      Toxicology
    other aspects see Metal;
      also Metals
    s.a. spec. uses
Mercury (planet)
  astronomy
    description   523.41
    theory   521.541

Mercury (planet)
  astronomy (continued)
    transits   523.91
  flights to
    manned   629.455 1
    unmanned   629.435 41
  regional subj. trmt.   *area*–992 1
  other aspects see Celestial
         bodies
Mercury-vapor lighting eng.
  soc. & econ. aspects *see*
        Secondary industries
  technology   621.327 4
  s.a. spec. appls. e.g.
        Public lighting eng.
Mercy
  killing *see* Euthanasia
  quality *see* Virtues
  sisters *see* Sisters of Mercy
Mergansers *see* Anseriformes
Mergers
  banks
    economics   332.16
    other aspects see Banks
        (finance)
  corporations
    law   346.066 26
    spec. jur.   346.3–.9
  management   658.16
  prod. econ.   338.83
  states
    internat. law   341.26
  transp. ind.
    commerce   380.58
    air   387.71
    inland-waterway   386.1
    maritime   387.51
    motor   388.32
    rail   385.1
      special-duty   385.5
      standard   385.1
    urban   388.404 2
    govt. control 351.878–.878
    spec. jur.   353–354
    law *see* Transportation law
Mérida Venezuela   *area*–871 3
Meriden West Midlands Eng.
             area–424 97
Meridian
  city Miss.   *area*–762 677
  lines
    spherical astronomy 522.7
    s.a. spec. celestial
        bodies
Meridional instruments
  astronomy   522.3
  s.a. spec. celestial bodies
  other aspects see Optical
       instruments

Merina kingdom hist.   969.101
  s.a. spec. events & subj.
      e.g. Commerce
Merino sheep
  animal husbandry   636.36
  other aspects see Sheep
Merioneth Wales   *area*–429 29
Merit
  awards
    wage & salary admin. 658.322 6
    misc. aspects see
       Incentive payments
  Christian doctrines   234
  system *see* Civil service
Meriwether Co. Ga.   *area*–758 455
Mermaids *see* Supernatural
      beings
Mermen *see* Supernatural beings
Meromorphic functions 515.982
  s.a. spec. appls. e.g.
      Engineering
Meropes *see* Coraciiformes
Merostomata *see* Xiphosura
Merovingian dynasty
  France hist.   944.01
  Ger. hist.   943.01
  s.a. spec. events & subj.
      e.g. Courts
Merrick Co. Neb.   *area*–782 423
Merriden W. Aust.   *area*–941 2
Merrimac (ship)
  Battle with Monitor
    U.S. Civil War hist. 973.752
Merrimack
  Co. N.H.   *area*–742 72
  River N.H.   *area*–742 72
Merritt Isl. Fla.   *area*–759 27
Mersey River
  England   *area*–427 5
  Tasmania   *area*–946 5
Merseyside Metropolitan Co. Eng.
            area–427 5
Merthyr Tydfil Mid Glamorgan
       Wales   *area*–429 75
Merton London Eng. *area*–421 93
Merycism *see* Stomach diseases
Mesa
  Co. Colo.   *area*–788 17
  Verde Nat. Park Colo. *area*–788 27
Mesabi Range Minn. *area*–776 77
Mesaxonia *see* Perissodactyla
Mescal   641.259
  comm. proc.   663.59
  other aspects see Alcoholic
      beverages
Mesencephalon
  human phys.   612.826 4
  other aspects see Brain
Mesentery *see* Peritoneum
Mesichthyes
  culture   639.375 3

Mesichthyes (continued)
  fishing
    commercial   639.275 3
    sports   799.175 3
  zoology   597.53
  other aspects see Teleostei
Mesitornithides *see* Gruiformes
Mesmerism
  psychology   .154.72
  animals   156.4
Meso-America *see* Middle America
Mesoenatides *see* Gruiformes
Mesogastropoda *see*
           Prosobranchia
Mesolithic Age
  archaeology   930.13
Mesons
  astrophysics
    gen. wks.   523.019 721 62
    acceleration   523.019 737 62
    s.a. spec. celestial bodies
  physics
    gen. wks.   539.721 62
    acceleration   539.737 62
    spec. states of matter   530.4
    s.a. spec. physical
          phenomena e.g. Heat
Mesopotamia Iraq   *area*–567 4
  ancient   *area*–35
Mesopotamian
  architecture   722.51
    misc. aspects see
          Architectural schools
  sculpture   732.5
  s.a. other spec. subj.
Mesosauria
  paleozoology   567.93
Mesozoic era
  geology   551.76
  s.a. spec. aspects e.g.
          Economic geology
  paleontology   560.176
  spec. fossils   561–569
Mespilus germanica *see* Medlars
Mesquite *see* Mimosaceae
Messapian language *see* Illyrian
          languages
Messenger services
  office services   651.79
Messengers
  office services   651.374 3
Messenia Greece *see* Sparta
Messent Nat. Park S. Aust.
          area–942 34
Messiahs
  Christianity   232.1
  comp. rel.   291.63
  s.a. other spec. rel.
Messiahship
  Jesus Christ   232.1

Messianic prophecies
  Christian doctrines   232.12
Messianism
  Judaistic doctrines   296.33
Messina
  province Sicily   *area*–458 11
  Strait *see* Ionian Sea
Meta Colombia   *area*–861 56
Metabolic
  diseases *see* Metabolism
          diseases
  organs
    life sci.
      anatomy
        gen. wks.   574.43
        animals   591.43
        microorganisms   576.14
        plants   581.43
        s.a. spec. organisms
      med. sci.   611.3–.4
        animals   636.089 13–.089 14
        s.a. spec. animals
        man   611.3–.4
      pathology
        gen. wks.   574.223
        animals   591.223
        plants   581.223
        s.a. spec. organisms
      med. sci. *see*
        Metabolism
Metabolism
  bone diseases
    gen. med.   616.716
    geriatrics   618.976 716
    pediatrics   618.927 16
    pub. health   614.597 16
    statistics   312.371 6
    deaths   312.267 16
    other aspects see Diseases
  cells cytology   574.876 1
    animals   591.876 1
    plants   581.876 1
    s.a. spec. organisms
  diseases   616.39
    geriatrics   618.976 39
    pediatrics   618.923 9
    pub. health   614.593 9
    statistics   312.339
    deaths   312.263 9
    other aspects see Diseases
    s.a. Metabolism bone
         diseases
  drugs affecting
    pharmacodynamics   615.739
    other aspects see Drugs
  pathology
    gen. wks.   574.213 3
    animals   591.213 3
    plants   581.213 3
    s.a. spec. organisms

Metallurgists
  biog. & work   669.009 2
    s.a. spec. metals
    s.a.   *pers.*–669
Metallurgy
  manufacturing
    soc. & econ. aspects *see*
      Secondary industries
    technology   669
Metal-manufacturing instruments
      & machinery
  manufacturing
    soc. & econ. aspects *see*
      Secondary industries
    technology   681.766 9
  s.a. spec. kinds
Metals   669
  arts
    engraving *see* Metal
      engraving
    handicrafts   754.56
      spec. objects   745.59
    sculpture *see* Metals
      sculpture
  casting
    sculpture *see* Metals
      sculpture
  chemistry
    inorganic   546.3
      spec. kinds   546.38–.68
    organic   547.05
    s.a. spec. groupings e.g.
      Aliphatic compounds
    technology   661.03
      organic   661.895
      soc. & econ. aspects *see*
        Secondary industries
      s.a. spec. prod.
  construction
    architecture   721.044 7
    s.a. spec. kinds of
      bldgs.
    building   693.7
  manufacturers
    biog. & work   671.092
      spec. metals
        iron & steel   672.092
        other   673
      s.a.   *pers.*–672–673
  materials
    building   691.7–.8
    engineering   620.16
      foundations   624.153 6
      naval design   623.818 2
      shipbuilding   623.820 7
      structures   624.182
      s.a. other spec. uses
    mil. resources   355.242
    s.a. spec. mil. branches
  mineral aspects
    econ. geol.   553.4

Metals
  mineral aspects (continued)
    mineralogy   549.23–.25
    mining
      technology   622.34
      prospecting   622.184
    resources *see* Mineral
      resources
    s.a. spec. minerals
  pharmacology   615.23
    misc. aspects see
      Pharmacology
  products
    arts *see* Metals arts
    manufacturing
      soc. & econ. aspects *see*
        Secondary industries
      technology   671
    s.a. Metalwork; *also spec.*
      prod.
  radiesthesia parapsych.   133.323 3
  sculpture
    dec. arts   739
    fine arts
      processes
        casting tech.
          bronze   731.456
          others   731.457
          material   731.2
        spec. periods & schools   732–735
    rel. significance
      Christianity
        decorative arts   247.89
        fine arts   247.3
      comp. rel.   291.37
      s.a. other spec. rel.
  structure
    metallurgy   669.95
  supports photosensitive
      surfaces *see* Supports
      photosensitive surfaces
  toxicology   615.925 3
    misc. aspects see
      Toxicology
    s.a. spec. prod. & uses
Metalwork
  arts *see* Metals arts
  shipbuilding
    soc. & econ. aspects *see*
      Secondary industries
    technology   623.843
  s.a. other spec. appls.
Metalworking
  home workshops   684.09
Metamathematics   510.1
Metamorphic rocks
  mineralogy   549.114 4
    spec. minerals   549.2–.7
  petrology   552.4
  other aspects see Natural
    stones

Metamorphoses	
biology	574.334
animals	591.334
microorganisms	576.133 4
plants	581.334
s.a. spec. organisms	
Metaphase *see* Mitosis	
Metaphosphates	
fertilizers *see* Phosphorus	
fertilizers	
Metaphysics	110
misc. aspects see Philosophy	
Metatarsal bones *see* Lower	
extremities bones	
Metatheria *see* Marsupialia	
Metcalfe	
Co. Ky.	*area*–769 693
governorship India hist.	954.031 4
s.a. spec. events & subj.	
e.g. Commerce	
Metempsychosis *see*	
Reincarnation	
Meteoric showers	
astronomy	
description	523.53
theory	521.75
other aspects see Celestial	
bodies	
Meteorites	
astronomy *see* Meteoroids	
mineralogy	549.112
spec. minerals	549.2–.7
Meteoritic hypothesis	
cosmogony	523.12
Meteoroids	
astronomy	
description	523.51
theory	521.75
other aspects see Celestial	
bodies	
effect on space flight	629.416
s.a. spec. appls. e.g.	
Space warfare	
regional subj. trmt.	*area*–993
Meteorological research	
cooperation	
internat. law	341.767 55
Meteorologists	
biog. & work	551.509 2
other aspects see Scientists	
s.a.	*pers.*–551
Meteorology	551.5
aeronautics	629.132 4
s.a. spec. appls. e.g.	
Flying	
libraries	026.551 5
misc. aspects see Special	
libraries	
museums	
desc. & colls.	551.507 4

Meteorology	
museums (continued)	
museology	069.955 15
s.a. spec. activities	
e.g. Display	
other aspects see Earth	
sciences	
Meteors *see* Meteoroids	
Meter	
music	
theory	781.62
s.a. spec. mediums	
prosody *see* Poetry gen. wks.	
rhetoric	
Meters	
elect. power *see* Control	
devices electrodynamic	
eng.	
radiowave electronics *see*	
Testing-devices	
radiowave electronics	
s.a. Measuring-instruments	
Metham West Yorkshire Eng.	
	area–428 13
Methil Fife Scot.	*area*–412 95
Methodist	
church bldgs.	
architecture	726.587
building	690.658 7
other aspects see	
Religious-purpose	
bldgs.	
church music	
arts	783.026 7
recordings	789.912 302 67
s.a. spec. instruments;	
also spec. kinds e.g.	
Liturgical music	
religion	
pub. worship	264.070 2
significance	246.7
churches	287
Christian life guides	248.487
doctrines	230.7
creeds	238.7
general councils	262.57
govt. & admin.	262.07
parishes	254.07
missions	266.7
moral theology	241.047
private prayers for	242.807
pub. worship	264.07
rel. associations	
adults	267.187
men	267.247
women	267.447
young adults	267.627
rel. instruction	268.87
rel. law	262.987
schools	377.87
secondary training	207.127

Methodist
  churches (continued)
    sermons   252.07
    theological seminaries   207.117
    s.a. other spec. aspects
Methodists
  biog. & work   287.092
  s.a. spec. denominations
  s.a.   *pers.–27*
Methodology   *s.s.–018*
Methods   *s.s.–028*
Metric
  differential geometries   516.37
  s.a. spec. appls. e.g.
    Engineering
  geometry   516.1
    Euclidean   516.21
  s.a. other spec. geometries;
    also spec. appls. e.g.
    Engineering
  system
    metrology   389.15
    physics   530.812
    s.a. spec. branches of
      physics
  topology   514.3
Metrication
  activity   389.16
  govt. control *see* Standards
    govt. control
Metritis
  puerperal diseases
    obstetrics   618.73
    pub. health   614.599 2
    statistics   312.304 873
      deaths   312.260 487 3
  other aspects see Diseases
Metrology
  commerce   389
  law
    international   341.754
    municipal   343.075
    spec. jur.   343.3–.9
  s.a. spec. appls. e.g.
    Surveying
Metronomes
  mf. tech.   681.118
  soc. & econ. aspects *see*
    Secondary industries
Metrophanes Confession
  Christian doctrines   238.19
Metropolitan areas
  local govt.   352.009 4
  planning
    civic art   711.43
  sociology   307.76
Metroxylon *see* Sago palm
Meurthe-et-Moselle France *area*–443 823
Meuse
  dept. France   *area*–443 81
  River Belgium   *area*–493 4

Mevagissey Cornwall Eng. *area*–423 72
Mexborough South Yorkshire Eng.
    area–428 27
Mexican
  Hairless dogs
    animal husbandry   636.76
    other aspects see Dogs
  literature   860
  people   *r.e.n.*–687 2
  War
    U.S. hist.   973.62
    s.a. Mexico country; *also*
      other spec. subj. e.g
      Arts
Mexico
  city   *area*–725 3
  country   *area*–72
  Gulf
    oceanography   551.463 4
    regional subj. trmt. *area*–163 64
    other aspects see Atlantic
      Ocean
  state   *area*–725 2
Mezzo-soprano solos *see* Women's
    solos
Mezzotinting
  graphic arts
    processes   766.2
    products   769
Miami
  Beach Fla.   *area*–759 381
  city Fla.   *area*–759 381
  County
    Indiana   *area*–772 84
    Kansas   *area*–781 68
    Ohio   *area*–771 48
  River O.   *area*–771 7
Miao
  language
    linguistics   495
    literature   895
    s.a.   *lang.*–95
  people   *r.e.n.*–95
  s.a. other spec. subj. e.g.
    Arts
Micah
  Bible   224.93
  other aspects see Prophetic
    books (O.T.)
Micas
  mineralogy   549.67
  refractory materials   553.674
    econ. geol.   553.674
    mining   622.367 4
      prospecting   622.186 74
  other aspects see
    Refractory materials
  synthetic
    manufacturing
      soc. & econ. aspects *see*
      Secondary industries

Micas
  synthetic
    manufacturing (continued)
      technology   666.86
Mice
  experimental animals
    med. sci.   619.93
  other aspects see Myomorpha
Michael reign Russia hist.   947.047
  s.a. spec. events & subj.
    e.g. Commerce
Micheas *see* Micah
Michigan
  Lake   *area*–774
  state   *area*–774
Michoacán Mex.   *area*–723 7
Micro methods
  anal. chem.
    gen. wks.
      qualitative   544.8
      quantitative   545.84
    organic
      qualitative   547.348
      quantitative   547.358 4
    s.a. spec. elements & cpds.
Microanalysis
  anal. chem.   543.081
  organic   547.308 1
  s.a. spec. elements & cpds.
Microbe-delivery devices *see*
    Biological devices mil.
    eng.
Microbes
  air pollutants
    sanitary eng.   628.536
  ammunition *see* Biological
    devices mil. eng.
  other aspects see
    Microbiology
Microbiologists
  biog. & work   576.092
  other aspects see Scientists
  s.a.   *pers.*–574
Microbiology   576
  industrial   660
  s.a. spec. prod.
  med. sci.   616.01
  s.a. spec. diseases
  soil sci.   631.46
  s.a. spec. crops
Microcards *see*
    Microreproductions
Microcephalism
  gen. med.   616.858 844
  geriatrics   618.976 858 844
  pediatrics   618.928 588 44
  psychology   157.8
  pub. health   362.3
  statistics   312.385 884 4

Microchemical
  analysis
    anal. chem.
      gen. wks.   543.081 3
        qualitative   544.83
        quantitative   545.843
      organic   547.308 13
        qualitative   547.348 3
        quantitative   547.358 43
      s.a. spec. elements &
        cpds.
    reactions
      minerals   549.133
      spec. minerals   549.2–.7
Microchiroptera *see* Chiroptera
Microcircuits *see* Circuits
    microelectronics
Microclimatology   551.66
Micrococcaceae *see*
    Eubacteriales
Microeconomics   338.5
Microelectronics
  soc. & econ. aspects *see*
    Secondary industries
  technology   621.381 7
  s.a. spec. appls. e.g.
    Interception of
      communication
  other aspects see Electronics
Microfiches *see*
    Microreproductions
Microfilms *see*
    Microreproductions
Microform catalogs
  library sci.
    spec. catalogs   016–019
    theory   025.313
Microforms *see*
    Microreproductions
Micrometers
  astronomy   522.5
  s.a. spec. celestial bodies
  s.a. other spec. uses
Microminiaturization
  electronics *see*
    Microelectronics
Micromorphology
  soil physics   631.43
  s.a. spec. crops; also spec.
    types of culture e.g.
    Floriculture
Micronesia   *area*–965
Micronesian
  language
    linguistics   499.5
    literature   899.5
    s.a.   *lang.*–995
  people   *r.e.n.*–995
  s.a. Micronesia; *also other*
    spec. subj. e.g. Arts

Microwave (continued)
circuit theory
electricity
astrophysics   523.018 712 3
   s.a. spec. celestial
    bodies
physics   537.123
spec. states of matter   530.4
communication *see* Electronic
   communication
cookery   641.588 2
electronics
astrophysics   523.018 753 44
   s.a. spec. celestial
    bodies
engineering
soc. & econ. aspects *see*
   Secondary industries
technology   621.381 3
   s.a. spec. appls. e.g.
    Radar engineering
physics   537.534 4
spec. states of matter   530.4
spectroscopes
mf. tech.   681.414 8
components   681.42–.43
other aspects see Optical
   instruments
spectroscopy
astrophysics   523.018 753 44
   s.a. spec. celestial
    bodies
engineering
soc. & econ. aspects *see*
   Secondary industries
technology   621.361 5
   s.a. spec. appls. e.g.
    Materials engineering
physics *see* Microwave
   electronics physics
other aspects see
   Spectroscopy
Microwaves
biophysics
extraterrestrial
gen. wks.   574.191 951
animals   591.191 951
microorganisms   576.119 195 1
plants   581.191 951
   s.a. spec. organisms
med. sci.   612.014 551
animals   636.089 201 455 1
   s.a. spec. animals
man   612.014 551
terrestrial
gen. wks.   574.191 51
animals   591.191 51
microorganisms   576.119 151
plants   581.191 51
   s.a. spec. organisms

Microwaves
biophysics
terrestrial (continued)
med. sci.   612.014 481
animals   636.089 201 448 1
   s.a. spec. animals
man   612.014 481
   s.a. spec. functions,
    systems, organs
other aspects see Radiations
Microwhipscorpions
zoology   595.452
other aspects see Arachnida
Mid Bedfordshire Eng.   *area*–425 63
Mid Glamorgan Wales   *area*–429 7
Mid Suffolk Eng.   *area*–426 45
Mid Sussex Eng.   *area*–422 65
Mid Wales   *area*–429 5
Midair collisions
transp. accidents   363.124 92
   misc. aspects see
    Transportation
    accidents
Midbrain
human phys.   612.826 4
other aspects see Brain
Midday *see* Noon
Middle
Ages history *see* Medieval
   history
America   *area*–72
American
native
languages
linguistics   497
literatures   897
s.a.   *lang.*–97
people   *r.e.n.*–97
other aspects see
   American native
s.a. other spec. subj.
   e.g. Arts
s.a. Middle America; *also*
   spec. subj. e.g. Arts
Atlantic states U.S.   *area*–74
classes
customs   390.1
dress   391.01
homes   392.360 1
soc. theology
Christianity   261.834 55
comp. rel.   291.178 345 5
   s.a. other spec. rel.
sociology   305.55
other aspects see Social
   classes
s.a.   *pers.*–062 2
Congo
history   967.240 3
s.a.   *area*–672 4

Middle (continued)
  ears
    diseases
      gen. wks. — 617.84
        neoplasms — 616.992 85
        tuberculosis — 616.995 85
      geriatrics — 618.977 84
      pediatrics — 618.920 978 4
      pub. health — 614.599 8
      statistics — 312.304 784
        deaths — 312.250 478 4
      surgery — 617.840 59
        anesthesiology — 617.967 84
      other aspects see
        Diseases
    physiology
      human — 612.854
      other aspects see Sensory
        functions
    other aspects see Ears
  East — *area*–56
    ancient — *area*–394
    regional organizations
      internat. law — 341.247 7
      treaties — 341.026 377
    wars *see* Israel-Arab Wars
  Eastern
    architecture — 722.5
      misc. aspects see
        Architectural schools
      s.a. other spec. subj.
  Egypt — *area*–622
  English language
    linguistics — 427.02
    other aspects see English
      language
  Franconia Ger. — *area*–433 2
  French language
    linguistics — 447.02
    other aspects see French
      language
  games chess — 794.123
  High German language
    linguistics — 437.02
    other aspects see German
      language
  Indic languages
    linguistics — 491.3
    literatures — 891.3
    s.a. — *lang.*–913
  Iranian languages
    linguistics — 491.53
    literatures — 891.53
    s.a. — *lang.*–915 3
  Italian language
    linguistics — 457.02
    other aspects see Italian
      language
  kingdom Egypt hist. — 932.013
    s.a. spec. events & subj.
      e.g. Commerce

Middle (continued)
  Latitude Zones *see* Temperate
    Zones
  management — 658.43
  Persian language *see* Middle
    Iranian languaqes
  Portuguese language
    linguistics — 469.702
    other aspects see
      Portuguese language
  Russian language
    linguistics — 491.770 2
    other aspects see Russian
      language
  Spanish language
    linguistics — 467.02
    other aspects see Spanish
      language
  Volga
    languages
      linguistics — 494.56
      literatures — 894.56
      s.a. — *lang.*–945 6
    s.a. other spec. subj. e.g.
      Arts
  West U.S. — *area*–77
Middle-aged people
  hygiene — 613.043 4
    s.a. spec. sexes
  labor econ. — 331.394
  other aspects see Adults
  s.a. — *pers.*–056 4
Middlesbrough Cleveland Eng. — *area*–428 53
Middlesex Co.
  Connecticut — *area*–746 6
  England — *area*–421 8
  Massachusetts — *area*–744 4
  New Jersey — *area*–749 41
  Ontario — *area*–713 25
  Virginia — *area*–755 33
Middleton Greater Manchester
  Eng. — *area*–427 392
Middlewich Cheshire Eng. — *area*–427 13
Midges *see* Orthorrhapha
Midget car racing
  sports — 796.76
  other aspects see Sports
Midgets
  physical anthr. — 573.8
Midhurst West Sussex Eng. — *area*–422 62
Midi-Pyrénées France — *area*–448 6
Midland Co.
  Michigan — *area*–774 48
  Texas — *area*–764 861
Midlands Eng. — *area*–424
Midlothian Scot. — *area*–414 45
Midrash
  Judaistic sources — 296.14
Midway isl. — *area*–969 9
Mid-Western state Nigeria — *area*–669 3

Midwifery	
law	344.041 5
spec. jur.	344.3–.9
medicine	618.202 33
Mie Japan	*area*–521 8
Mifflin Co. Pa.	*area*–748 46
Mignonette family *see* Resedales	
Migraine	
gen. med.	616.857
geriatrics	618.976 857
pediatrics	618.928 57
pub. health	614.598 57
statistics	312.385 7
Migrant	
children	
psychology	155.456 75
rearing home econ.	649.156 75
students	
education	371.967 5
law	344.079 167 5
spec. jur.	344.3–.9
workers	
labor econ.	331.544
labor law *see* Labor law	
other aspects see Laboring	
classes	
Migration	
ecology	
life sci.	574.52
animals	591.525
microorganisms	576.15
plants	581.52
s.a. spec. organisms	
pol. sci.	325
soc. theology	
Christianity	261.836 8
comp. rel.	291.178 368
s.a. other spec. rel.	
sociology	304.8
Migratory *see* Migrant	
Mihailograd Bulgaria	*area*–497 72
Mikhailovgrad Bulgaria	*area*–497 72
Mikkeli Finland	*area*–489 75
Mikonos Greece	*area*–499
Milam Co. Tex.	*area*–764 288
Milano Italy	*area*–452 1
Mildenhall Suffolk Eng.	*area*–426 43
Mildews	
organisms	
downy *see* Peronosporales	
powdery *see* Ascomycetes	
plant diseases	632.4
s.a. spec. plants; also	
spec. types of culture	
e.g Forestry	
resistance to	
eng. materials	620.112 23
s.a. spec. materials &	
spec. uses	
Mildura Vic.	*area*–945 9
Miles Qld.	*area*–943 3

Milford Haven Dyfed Wales *area*–429 62	
Milieu therapy	
psychiatry	616.891 44
geriatrics	618.976 891 44
pediatrics	618.928 914 4
other aspects see Medical	
sciences	
Militarism	
mil. sci.	355.021 3
soc. theology	
Christianity	261.873
comp. rel.	291.178 73
s.a. other spec. rel.	
Military	
academies *see* Military	
schools	
accounting	657.835
art *see* Military science	
assistance	
internat. law	341.728
mil. sci.	355.032
band music	785.13
recordings	789.912 513
bands	785.067 1
s.a. spec. kinds of music	
buildings	
architecture	725.18
building	690.518
other aspects see Public	
structures	
conduct *see* Discipline armed	
forces	
cookery	641.573
court procedure *see* Courts	
law municipal armed	
services	
courts *see* Courts law	
municipal armed	
services	
customs *see* Social customs	
armed forces	
discipline *see* Discipline	
armed forces	
engineering	
soc. & econ. aspects *see*	
Secondary industries	
technology	623
s.a. spec. appls. e.g.	
Tactics	
engineers	
biog. & work	623.092
s.a.	*pers.*–623 1
ethics *see* Military personnel	
occupational ethics	
government *see* Military	
occupation	
history	
World War 1	940.4
World War 2	940.54
s.a. other spec. wars	
hygiene	613.67

Military (continued)
  installations *see*
    Installations armed
      forces
  institutions
    sociology   306.2
    law   343.01
      spec. jur.   343.3–.9
  life
    gen. wks.   355.1
    s.a. spec. mil. branches
    history
      U.S. Civil War   973.783–.784
      U.S. Revolutionary War   973.38
      U.S. War of 1812   973.528
      Vietnamese War   959.704 38
      World War 1   940.483–.484
      World War 2   940.548 3–.548 4
    s.a. other spec. wars
  medals
    numismatics   737.223
  medicine   616.980 23
    s.a. spec. diseases
  missions
    internat. law   341.728
    mil. sci.   355.032
  models
    handicrafts   745.592 82
  occupation
    law of war   341.66
    mil. sci.   355.49
    result of war   355.028
  operations
    Spanish-American War   973.893
    U.S. Civil War   973.73
    U.S. Mexican War   973.623
    U.S. Revolutionary War   973.33
    U.S. War of 1812   973.523
    Vietnamese War   959.704 34
    World War 1   940.41
    World War 2   940.541
    s.a. other spec. wars
  Order of Foreign Wars of U.S.
     369.11
  organizations & state
    pol. sci.   322.5
  parole law *see* Parole law
  penology
    law   343.014 6
      spec. jur.   343.3–.9
  personnel
    biog. & work   355.009 2
    s.a. spec. kinds; also
      hist. of spec.
      countries & spec. wars
    occupational ethics
      philosophy   174.935 5
      religion
        Buddhism   294.356 493 55
        Christianity   241.649 355
        comp. rel.   291.564 935 5

Military
  personnel
    occupational ethics
      religion (continued)
        Hinduism   294.548 649 355
      s.a. other spec. rel.
    s.a.   *pers.*–355
    police
      mil. sci.   355.34
      use   355.133 23
      s.a. spec. mil. branches
    prisons
      penology   365.48
      other aspects see Penal
        institutions
    probation law *see* Probation
      law
    rel. orders
      Christianity   255.05
        church hist.   271.05
        ecclesiology   262.24
      other rel. see Religious
        congregations
    resources   355.2
    s.a. spec. mil. branches
  schools
    finance
      law   344.076 9
        spec. jur.   344.3–.9
    govt. supervision & support   379
    higher ed.   355.007 11
    s.a. spec. mil. branches
    secondary ed.   355.007 12
    organization
      general   373.222
      vocational   373.243
  science   355
    Biblical trmt.   220.835 5
    s.a. spec. parts of Bible
    curriculums   375.355
    documentation   025.063 55
    journalism   070.449 355
    libraries   026.355
    misc. aspects see Special
      libraries
    library acquisitions   025.273 55
    library classification   025.463 55
    museums   069.935 5
    s.a. spec. activities
      e.g. Display
    subject headings   025.493 55
    other aspects see
      Disciplines (systems)
  services *see* Armed services
  societies   369.2
    members   *pers.*–369 2
  surgery   617.99
  uniforms *see* Uniforms
  units
    Spanish-American War   973.894
    U.S. Civil War   973.74

Military
  units (continued)
    U.S. Mexican War   973.624
    U.S. Revolutionary War   973.34
    U.S. War of 1812   973.524
    World War 1   940.412–.413
    World War 2   940.541 2–.541 3
    s.a. other spec. wars
  s.a. Armed; *also* War
Military-industrial complex
  mil. sci.   355.021 3
Milk
  animal husbandry for   636.088 42
    s.a. spec. animals
  bars *see* Eating places
  food   641.371
    cookery   641.671
  physiology *see* Lactation
  prod. tech.   637.1
    soc. & econ. aspects *see*
        Secondary industries
  programs
    student nutrition *see*
        School lunch programs
  River Mont.   *area–*786 1
  substitutes
    comm. proc.   663.64
    other aspects see
        Nonalcoholic beverages
  s.a. Beverages
Milking
  dairy tech.   637.124
Milkweed family *see* Apocynales
Milky Way
  astronomy
    description   523.113
    theory   521.582
  other aspects see Celestial
      bodies
Mill bldgs. *see* Industrial
      buildings
Millard Co. Utah   *area–*792 45
Mille Lacs
  Co. Minn.   *area–*776 68
  Lake Minn.   *area–*776 68
Milled soaps
  manufacturing
    chem. tech.   668.124
    soc. & econ. aspects *see*
        Secondary industries
Millennium
  rel. doctrines
    Christianity   236.3
    other rel. see Eschatology
Milleporina *see* Hydrozoa
Miller Co.
  Arkansas   *area–*767 56
  Georgia   *area–*758 964
  Missouri   *area–*778 56

Millet
  flour & meal
    comm. proc.   664.725
    other aspects see Cereal
        grains
  grasses *see* Panicoideae
Millets
  agriculture
    food crops   633.171
    forage crops   633.257 1
    soc. & econ. aspects *see*
        Primary industries
  foods   641.331 71
    cookery   641.631 71
  other aspects see
      Panicoideae; *also*
      Cereal grains
Milliammeters
  electric current measurement   621.374 4
    s.a. spec. appls. e.g.
        Ignition systems &
        devices
Milliners
  biog. & work   646.504 092
  s.a.   *pers.–*646 5
Millinery
  commercial mf.   687.42
  domestic mf.   646.504
  other aspects see Headgear
Milling
  crude rubbers *see* Mastication
      rubber mf.
  grains
    comm. proc.   664.72
    s.a. spec. grains & prod.
    other aspects see Cereal
        grains
Milling-plants
  ores
    mining eng.   622.79
    spec. ores   622.33–.39
Millings
  cereal grains
    comm. proc.   664.720 8
      wheat   664.722 8
    s.a. other spec. grains &
        prod.
    other aspects see Cereal
        grains
Milling-tools
  soc. & econ. aspects *see*
      Secondary industries
  tech. & mf.   621.91
    s.a. spec. appls. e.g.
        Small arms
        manufacturing
Millipedes *see* Diplopoda
Millmerran Qld.   *area–*943 3
Millport Strathclyde Scot. *area–*414 61

Mills
buildings *see* Industrial
buildings
County
Iowa — area–777 74
Texas — area–764 512
Milngavie Strathclyde Scot. — area–414 34
Milnrow Greater Manchester Eng.
area–427 392
Milton
Co. Ga. — area–758 23
town Kent Eng. — area–422 33
Milton Keynes Buckinghamshire
Eng. — area–425 91
Milwaukee
city Wis. — area–775 95
Co. Wis. — area–775 94
Mimamsa phil. — 181.42
Mimicry *see* Protective
adaptations
Mimidae
hunting
commercial — 639.128 841
sports — 799.248 841
paleozoology — 568.8
zoology — 598.841
other aspects see Aves
Mimosa family *see* Mimosaceae
Mimosaceae
botany — 583.321
floriculture — 635.933 321
forestry — 634.973 321
med. aspects
crop prod. — 633.883 321
gen. pharm. — 615.323 321
toxicology — 615.952 332 1
vet. pharm. — 636.089 532 332 1
toxicology — 636.089 595 233 21
paleobotany — 561.3
other aspects see Plants
Minarets *see* Islamic temples &
shrines
Minas Gerais Brazil — area–815 1
Mind
lit. & stage trmt.
folk lit. soc. — 398.353
other aspects see Human
life
metaphysics — 128.2
s.a. Psychology
Mindanao Philippines — area–599 7
Mindoro Philippines — area–599 3
Mind-reading — 133.82
Mine
accidents
gen. hist.
collections — 904.7
*s.a. hist. of spec.
places*
mining eng. — 622.8

Mine (continued)
clearance
mil. eng. — 623.26
drainage *see* Drainage mining
health — 622.8
railroads — 622.66
surveys — 622.14
Minehead Somerset Eng. — area–423 85
Minelayers
engineering — 623.826 2
design — 623.812 62
models — 623.820 162
naval forces
materiel — 359.83
organization — 359.326 2
seamanship — 623.882 62
other aspects see Vessels
(nautical)
Minelaying mil. eng. — 623.26
Miner Co. S.D. — area–783 34
Mineral
additives
feeds
animal husbandry — 636.087 7
s.a. spec. animals
County
Colorado — area–788 38
Montana — area–786 84
Nevada — area–793 51
West Virginia — area–754 94
drugs
pharmacology — 615.2
other aspects see Drugs
fertilizers — 553.64
econ. geol. — 553.64
mining
technology — 622.364
prospecting — 622.186 4
*other aspects see
Fertilizers*
foodstuffs — 641.309
industries
govt. control
activities — 351.823 8
spec. jur. — 353–354
departments — 351.082 38
spec. jur. — 353–354
labor econ. — 331.762 2
active employment — 331.125 22
aged workers — 331.398 822
collective bargaining — 331.890 422
employment conditions — 331.204 22
ind. relations — 331.042 2
labor force — 331.119 22
market force — 331.129 22
need — 331.123 22
opportunities — 331.124 22
pensions — 331.252 9
strikes — 331.892 822
unemployment — 331.137 822
unions — 331.881 22

Minerals
 lit. trmt.
  spec. lits.
   collections (continued)
    real   *lit. sub.*–080 36
   hist. & crit.
    legendary   *lit. sub.*–093 71
    real   *lit. sub.*–093 6
   s.a. spec. lit. forms
 metabolism
  human phys.   612.392
  plant nutrition
   pathology   581.213 35
   physiology   581.133 5
   s.a. spec. plants
   other aspects see
    Metabolism
 mil. resources   355.242–.243
  s.a. spec. mil. branches
 stage trmt.
  gen. wks.
   legendary   792.090 937 1
   real   792.090 936
  s.a. spec. mediums e.g.
   Television; *also spec.*
   kinds of drama e.g.
   Tragedies (drama)
Mineral-surfaced asphalt roofing
 bldg. construction   695
Miners
 biog. & work   622.092
 s.a.   *pers.*–622
Mines (ammunition)
 defense against mil. eng.   623.3
 mil. eng.
  clearance   623.26
  laying   623.26
  soc. & econ. aspects *see*
   Secondary industries
  tech. & mf.   623.451 15
  s.a. spec. purposes e.g.
   Antipersonnel devices
Mines (excavations)
 environment technology   622.4
 psych. influences   155.964
 sanitation *see* Industrial
  sanitation
 s.a. Mining
Minesweepers
 engineering   623.826 2
  design   623.812 62
  models   623.820 162
 naval forces   359.326 2
 seamanship   623.882 62
 other aspects see Vessels
  (nautical)
Ming dynasty
 China hist.   951.026
 s.a. spec. events & subj.
  e.g. Arts
Mingo Co. W. Va.   *area*–754 48

Mingrelian *see* Caucasic
Minho Portugal   *area*–469 12
Miniature
 books
  hist. & crit.   099
 cameras
  photography   771.3
  gen. tech.   770.282 2
  spec. proc. & fields   772–778
 computers *see* Minicomputers
 golf
  equipment mf.   688.763 522
  soc. & econ. aspects *see*
   Secondary industries
  sports   796.352 2
  other aspects see Sports
 paintings   751.77
  indiv. artists   759.1–.9
  portraits   757.7
  s.a. other spec. subj.; also
   spec. tech. & equip.
 pinscher
  animal husbandry   636.76
  other aspects see Dogs
 poodle
  animal husbandry   636.72
  other aspects see Dogs   636.72
 Schnauzer
  animal husbandry   636.755
  other aspects see Dogs
 scores music   780.84
 theaters
  performing arts   791.5
  s.a. other spec. subj.
Miniaturization
 electronics *see*
  Microelectronics
 s.a. Models (representations)
Minibikes *see* Motorcycles
Minicomputers
 electronic data proc.   001.640 4
 spec. subj.   *s.s.*–028 540 4
 other aspects see Computers
Minicoy & Amindivi Isls. India
     area–548 1
Minidoka Co. Ida.   *area*–796 33
Minima
 mathematics   511.66
  calculus   515.33
  s.a. other spec. branches;
   also spec. appls. e.g
   Engineering
Minimal
 brain dysfunction
  gen. med.   616.858 9
  geriatrics   618.976 868 9
  pediatrics   618.929 589
  statistics   312.385 89
  other aspects see Diseases
 curves
  gen. wks. *see* Curves

Minimal
  curves (continued)
    integral geometry — 516.362
    s.a. spec. appls. e.g.
      Engineering
  surfaces
    gen. wks. *see* Surfaces
    mathematics
      integral geometry — 516.362
    s.a. spec. appls. e.g.
      Engineering
Minims
  rel. orders — 255.49
    church hist. — 271.49
    ecclesiology — 262.24
Minimum-security prisons
  penology — 365.33
  other aspects see Penal
    institutions
Mining
  communities *see* Cities
  engineering — 622
    source of waste
      sanitary eng.
        technology — 628.542
        other aspects see
          Sanitary engineering
    other aspects see
      Engineering
  engineers
    biog. & work — 622.092
    s.a. — *pers.*–622
  enterprises
    accounting — 657.862
    govt. control
      activities — 351.823 82
        spec. jur. — 353–354
      departments — 351.082 382
        spec. jur. — 353–354
  industries *see* Mineral
    industries
Ministerial
  authority
    Christianity — 262.8
    other rel. see
      Ecclesiastical theology
  counseling
    soc. welfare — 361.38
Ministers
  envoys *see* Envoys
  of justice
    advisory opinions *see*
      Attorneys-general
        advisory opinions
  of religion *see* Clergy
Ministries
  pub. admin. — 351.004
    spec. jur. — 354
Minkowski geometry — 516.93
  metric differential — 516.374

Minkowski geometry (continued)
  s.a. spec. appls. e g.
    Engineering
Minks *see* Mustelidae
Minneapolis Minn. — *area*–776 579
Minnedosa Man. — *area*–712 73
Minnehaha Co. S.D. — *area*–783 371
Minnesota
  River — *area*–776 3
  state — *area*–776
Minoan
  architecture — 722.61
    misc. aspects see
      Architectural schools
  Linear A linguistics — 492.6
  Linear B linguistics — 481.7
Minor
  arts — 745
    misc. aspects see Fine arts
  Clerks Regular — 255.56
    church hist. — 271.56
    ecclesiology — 262.24
  metals
    construction
      architecture — 721.044 779
      s.a. spec. kinds of
        bldgs.
      building — 693.779
    materials
      building — 691.879
      engineering — 620.189 9
      foundations — 624.153 899
      naval design — 623.818 299
      shipbuilding — 623.820 7
      structures — 624.182 99
      s.a. other spec. uses
    metallography — 669.957 9
    metallurgy — 669.79
      physical & chem. — 669.967 9
    soc. & econ. aspects *see*
      Secondary industries
  mineral aspects
    econ. geol. — 553.499
    mining
      technology — 622.349 9
      prospecting — 622.184 99
    s.a. spec. minerals
  products
    mf. tech. — 673.79
    other aspects see
      Nonferrous metals
      products
    s.a. spec. uses
  other aspects see Metal;
    also Metals
  planets *see* Asteroids
  prophets
    Bible — 224.9
    other aspects see Prophetic
      books (O.T.)

Minor (continued)
  surgery
    gen. med.   617.024
    misc. aspects see
      Diseases
    s.a. spec. diseases
    obstetrics   618.85
    vet. med.   636.089 885
    s.a. spec. animals
  wooden products
    mf. tech.   674.88
    other aspects see Wood
      products
Minorca Spain   *area*–467 5
Minority
  businesses *see* Small
    businesses
  enterprises
    prod. econ.   338.642 2
  groups
    employees
      pers. admin.
        gen. management 658.304 1
        spec. subj.   *s.s.*–068 3
      pub. admin.   350.1
        central govts.   351.1
          spec. jur.   353–354
        local govts.   352.005 1
    journalism for   070.484
    libraries for   027.63
      administration   025.197 63
      buildings
        architecture   727.826 3
        functional planning 022.316 3
      catalogs *see* Library
        catalogs
      reference services 025.527 763
      selection for   025.218 763
      use studies   025.587 63
      user orientation 025.567 63
      s.a. other spec.
        activities e.g.
        Cataloging
    opinions
      soc. control   303.387
      s.a. spec. subj. e.g.
        Political science
    parochial activities for
      Christianity   259
      other rel. see Pastoral
        theology
    soc. welfare
      gen. wks.   362.84
        govt. control   350.848 4
          central govts. 351.848 4
          spec. jur.   353–354
        law *see* Welfare
          services law
        local govts.   352.944 84
    young people   362.799

Minority
  groups (continued)
    misc. aspects see Young
      people soc. services to
    other aspects see Social
      structure
    s.a.   *pers.*–069 3
    s.a. other spec. subj.
    rights pol. sci.   323.423
Minors
  law   346.013 5
    spec. jur.   346.3–.9
  s.a. Young people
Minquiers isl.   *area*–423 48
Minsk Belorussia   *area*–476 52
Minstrel
  shows
    performing arts   791.12
  songs *see* Negro songs U.S.
Mint *see* Herbs; *also* Lamiales
Minting practices *see* Monetary
    policy
Minto earl
  1st governorship India hist. 954.031 3
    s.a. spec. events & subj.
      e.g. Commerce
  4th governorship India hist. 954.035 6
    s.a. spec. events & subj.
      e.g. Commerce
Minufiya Egypt   *area*–621
Minutes
  office records   651.77
  s.a. other spec. subj. e.g.
    Constitutional
    conventions law
    proceedings
Minya Egypt   *area*–622
Miocene epoch
  geology   551.787
  s.a. spec. aspects e.g.
    Economic geology
  paleontology *see* Cenozoic era
Miquelon   *area*–718 8
Miracle plays *see* Religious
    plays
Miracles
  Gospels   226.7
    pseudepigrapha 229.8
    other aspects see New
      Testament
  of God
    rel. doctrines
      Christianity   231.73
      other rel. see God
  of Jesus
    Christian doctrines 232.955
  of Mary
    Christian doctrines 232.917
  spiritual gift
    Christian doctrines 234.13

Mirages *see* Refraction
    atmospheric optical
    phenomena
Miranda Venezuela   *area*–873 5
Mirfield West Yorkshire Eng.
    area–428 13
Mirrors
  automobiles eng.   629.276
  dec. arts   748.8
  mf. tech.   681.428
  optics *see* Reflection light
    optics
Misamis Philippines   *area*–599 7
Misappropriation of funds
  criminology   364.132 3
Miscarriage
  mammalogy   599.021 662
  med. sci.
    obstetrics   618.392
    pub. health   614.599 2
    statistics   312.304 839 2
      deaths   312.260 483 92
  other aspects see Diseases
Miscellaneous
  Christian denominations   289.9
    Christian life guides   248.489 9
    church bldgs.
      architecture   726.589 9
      building   690.658 99
      other aspects see
        Religious-purpose
        bldgs.
    church music
      arts   783.026 99
      recordings   789.912 302 699
      s.a. spec. instruments;
      also spec. kinds e.g.
        Liturgical music
    religion
      pub. worship   264.099 02
      significance   246.7
    doctrines   230.99
    creeds   238.99
    govt. & admin.   262.099
    parishes   254.099
    members   *pers.*–289
    missions   266.99
    moral theology   241.049 9
    private prayers for   242.809 9
    pub. worship   264.099
    rel. associations
      adults   267.189 9
      men   267.249 9
      women   267.449 9
      young adults   267.629 9
    rel. instruction   268.899
    rel. law   262.989 9
    schools   377.899
    secondary training   207.129 9
    sermons   252.099
    theological seminaries   207.119 9

Miscellaneous
  Christian denominations (continued)
    s.a. other spec. aspects
    facts books
      American   031.02
      English   032.02
Misdemeanors *see* Criminal
  offenses
Misfeasance *see* Government
  liability
Mishnah
  Talmudic lit.   296.123
Mishnaic period Palestine hist.   956.940 2
  s.a. spec. events & subj.
    e.g. Commerce
Misiones
  Argentina   *area*–822 3
  Paraguay   *area*–892 125
Miskito-Matagalpan
  languages
    linguistics   497.8
    literatures   897.8
    s.a.   *lang.*–978
  people   *r.e.n.*–97
  s.a. other spec. subj. e.g.
    Arts
Missals
  Roman Catholic liturgy   264.023
Missaukee Co. Mich.   *area*–774 66
Misses' clothing *see* Women's
  clothing
Missile-hurling weapons
  art metalwork   739.73
  other aspects see Offensive
    arms
Missiles
  mil. eng.
    soc. & econ. aspects *see*
      Secondary industries
    tech. & mf.   623.451
  s.a. Guided missiles
Missing persons
  police searches   363.233 6
  misc. aspects see Police
    services
Mission
  buildings
    architecture   726.9
    building   690.69
    rel. purpose   291.35
    s.a. spec. rel.
    other aspects see
      Religious-purpose
      bldgs.
  City B.C.   *area*–711 33
  Range Mont.   *area*–786 8
  schools
    education   377.6

Missionaries
  biog. & work
    Christianity   266.009 2
      s.a. spec. kinds of
        missions e.g. Home
        missions; *also spec.*
        denominations
    comp. rel.   291.7
    s.a. other spec. rel.
  medical
    biog. & work   610.92
    prof. duties &
      characteristics   610.695
  occupational ethics
    philosophy   174.1
    religion
      Buddhism   294.356 41
      Christianity   241.641
      comp. rel.   291.564 1
      Hinduism   294.548 641
      s.a. other spec. rel.
  s.a.   *pers.*–2
Missionary
  Ridge Battle
    U.S. Civil War hist.   973.735 9
  societies *see* Missions
    (religion)
  stories
    Christianity   266
Missions (religion)
  Buddhism   294.37
  Christianity   266
  comp. rel.   291.7
  Islam   297.7
  s.a. other spec. rel.
Missisquoi
  Co. Que.   *area*–714 62
  River Vt.   *area*–743 13
Mississippi
  County
    Arkansas   *area*–767 95
    Missouri   *area*–778 983
  Delta La.   *area*–763 3
  River   *area*–77
    Arkansas   *area*–767 8
    lower   *area*–76
    Tennessee   *area*–768 1
    upper   *area*–77
    state   *area*–762
Mississippian period
  geology   551.751
    s.a. spec. aspects e.g.
      Economic geology
  paleontology   560.172 7
    spec. fossils   561–569
Missoula Co. Mont.   *area*–786 85
Missouri
  Compromise hist.   973.54
    U.S. Civil War cause   973.711 3
  River   *area*–78
    Missouri   *area*–778

Missouri
  River (continued)
    Montana   *area*–786 1
    Nebraska   *area*–782 2
    North Dakota   *area*–784 7
    South Dakota   *area*–783 3
    state   *area*–778
Mistassini Ter. Que.   *area*–714 11
Mistletoe family *see* Santalales
Mistrials
  law *see* Trials law
Mists
  colloid chem. *see* Aerosols
    colloid chem.
  meteorology   551.575
    artificial modification   551.687 5
    weather forecasting   551.647 5
    spec. areas   551.65
Mitanni Kingdom
  Mesopotamia hist.   935.02
    s.a. spec. events & subj.
      e.g. Arts
Mitcham London Eng.   *area*–421 93
Mitchell
  County
    Georgia   *area*–758 973
    Iowa   *area*–777 234
    Kansas   *area*–781 23
    North Carolina   *area*–756 865
    Texas   *area*–764 729
  Mt. N.C.   *area*–756 873
  River
    Queensland   *area*–943 7
    Victoria   *area*–945 6
  town Qld.   *area*–943 4
Miters
  rel. significance
    Christianity   246.56
  other aspects see Symbolic
    garments
Mites
  zoology   595.42
  other aspects see Arachnida
Mithraism
  religion   299.15
Mitochondria
  cytology   574.873 42
    animals   591.873 42
    plants   581.873 42
    s.a. spec. organisms
Mitosis
  cytology   574.876 23
    animals   591.876 23
    plants   581.876 23
    s.a. spec. organisms
Mitral valves
  diseases *see* Valvular
    diseases
Mitta Mitta River Vic.   *area*–945 5
Mittelland Switzerland   *area*–494 5
Mittens *see* Handwear

Models (representations) (continued)
 civil aircraft
  soc. & econ. aspects *see*
   Secondary industries
  tech. & mf.   629.133 1
  s.a. spec. appls. e.g.
   studies in stability
   629.132 36
 civilian automobiles
  soc. & econ. aspects *see*
   Secondary industries
  tech. & mf.   629.221
  s.a. spec. appls. e.g.
   Action toys
 handicrafts   745.592 8
 library trmt.   025.179 6
  acquisitions   025.289 6
  cataloging   025.349 6
 manufacturers
  biog. & work   688.109 2
  s.a.   *pers.*–688
 manufacturing
  soc. & econ. aspects *see*
   Secondary industries
  technology   688.1
 mathematics *see* Mathematical
  models
 nautical vessels
  soc. & econ. aspects *see*
   Secondary industries
  tech. & mf.   623.820 1
 operations research   001.424
  spec. subj.   *s.s.*–072 4
 railroads
  soc. & econ. aspects *see*
   Secondary industries
  technology   625.19
 trains
  soc. & econ. aspects *see*
   Secondary industries
  technology   625.19
 s.a.   *s.s.*–022 8
Modena Italy   *area*–454 2
Moderate-income classes   *pers.*–062 3
Moderators
 nuclear reactors
  technology   621.483 37
  s.a. spec. appls. e.g.
   Generation elect. power
  other aspects see Nuclear
   reactions
Modern
 algebra   512
 architecture   724
  spec. places
   Oriental   722.1–.5
   other   720.9
  other aspects see
   Architectural schools

Modern (continued)
 art
  design & dec.   745.444
   spec. places   745.449
  gen. wks.   709.04
   spec. places   709.1–.9
  rel. significance
   Christianity   246.4
   other rel. see Arts rel.
    significance
  s.a. spec. art forms
 constitutionalism *see*
  Democratic states
 geometry   516.04
  s.a. spec. topics of
   geometry; also spec.
   appls. e.g.
   Engineering
 history   909.08
  appls. to spec. subj.   *s.s.*–090 3
  spec. centuries   909.4–.8
  s.a. spec. countries
 painting   759.06
  spec. places   759.1–.9
 philosophy
  Oriental   181
  Western   190
  s.a. spec. branches & subj.
   e.g. Metaphysics
 physics   539
  spec. states of matter   530.4
 sculpture   735
  spec. places   730.9
 suspension bridges
  structural eng.   624.55
  other aspects see Bridges
   (structures)
 wind-driven vessels
  engineering   623.822
   design   623.812 2
   models   623.820 12
  seamanship   623.882 2
  other aspects see Vessels
   (nautical)
 world
  regional subj. trmt.   *area*–4–9
  s.a. other spec. subj.
Modernism
 doctrinal controversies
  Christian church hist.   273.9
Modernization
 management   658.406
 production   658.514
  spec. subj.   *s.s.*–068 5
 pub. admin.   350.007 3
  central govts.   351.007 3
   spec. jur.   353–354
  local govts.   352.000 473
Modesty *see* Virtues

Molecular (continued)
  structure
    astrophysics   523.019 12
      s.a. spec. celestial
        bodies
    cells *see* Structure cells
      cytology
    chemistry   541.22
      organic   547.122
      s.a. spec. elements &
        cpds.
    physics   539.12
      spec. states of matter 530.4
      s.a. spec. physical
        phenomena e.g. Heat
    weights chem.   541.222
      organic   547.122 2
    other aspects see Molecular
      structure chemistry
Molecules
  chemistry *see* Molecular
    structure chemistry
  physics   539.6
Moles (animals) *see* Insectivora
Moles (nevi) *see* Pigmentary
  changes skin
Moleskin *see* Water-repellant
  fabrics
Molinism
  doctrinal controversies
    Christian church hist. 273.7
Molinists
  persecutions
    Christian church hist. 272.5
Molise Italy   *area*–457 19
Molluginaceae *see*
  Caryophyllales
Mollusca
  agric. pests   632.64
  s.a. spec. types of culture
    e.g. Forestry; *also*
    spec. crops
  conservation tech.   639.974
  control
    agricultural *see* Mollusca
      agric. pests
    sanitary eng.   628.964
  culture
    technology   639.4
      soc. & econ. aspects *see*
        Primary industries
    other aspects see
      Agriculture
  drawing tech.   743.64
  fishing
    commercial
      technology   639.4
      soc. & econ. aspects
        see Primary
        industries

Mollusca
  fishing
    commercial (continued)
      other aspects see Fishing
        industries
    law *see* Fishing law
    sports   799.254
  food   641.394
    cookery   641.694
    other aspects see Seafoods
  paleozoology   564
  zoology   594
  other aspects see Animals
Molluscoidea
  agric. pests   632.646
  s.a. spec. types of culture;
    also spec. crops
  conservation tech.   639.974 6
  control
    agricultural *see*
      Molluscoidea agric.
      pests
    sanitary eng.   628.964
  culture
    technology   639.7
      soc. & econ. aspects *see*
        Primary industries
    other aspects see
      Agriculture
  drawing tech.   743.646
  paleozoology   564.6
  zoology   594.6
  other aspects see Animals
Mollusks *see* Mollusca
Molokai isl.   *area*–969 24
Molpadonia *see* Holothurioidea
Molucca Sea *see* Malay
  Archipelago inner seas
Moluccas   *area*–598 5
Molybdates
  mineralogy   549.74
Molybdenite
  mineralogy   549.32
Molybdenum
  chemistry
    inorganic   546.534
    organic   547.055 34
    s.a. spec. groupings e.g.
      Aliphatic compounds
  technology   661.053 4
    organic   661.895
    soc. & econ. aspects *see*
      Secondary industries
    s.a. spec. prod.
  compounds
    chemistry *see* Molybdenum
      chemistry
    plant nutrition *see* Trace
      elements plant
      nutrition

Molybdenum (continued)
construction
  architecture — 721.044 773 4
    s.a. spec. kinds of bldgs.
  building — 693.773 4
materials
  building — 691.873 4
  engineering — 620.189 34
    foundations — 624.153 893 4
    naval design — 623.818 293 4
    shipbuilding — 623.820 7
    structures — 624.182 934
    s.a. other spec. uses
metallography — 669.957 34
metallurgy — 669.734
  physical & chem. — 669.967 34
  soc. & econ. aspects *see* Secondary industries
mineral aspects
  econ. geol. — 553.464 6
  mining
    technology — 622.346 46
    prospecting — 622.184 646
  s.a. spec. minerals
pharmacology — 615.253 4
  misc. aspects see Pharmacology
products
  mf. tech. — 673.734
  other aspects see Nonferrous metals products
toxicology — 615.925 534
  misc. aspects see Toxicology
other aspects see Metal;
  also Metals
s.a. spec uses
Moment
distribution
  structural theory
    gen. wks. — 624.171 5
    spec. elements — 624.177 2–.177 9
    naval arch. — 623.817 15
    s.a. other spec. appls.
magnetism *see* Magnetic phenomena
Moments
of inertia
  aeronautical aerodynamics — 629.132 364
  s.a. spec. appls. e.g. Flying
structural theory
  gen. wks. — 624.171 5
  spec. elements — 624.177 2–.177 9
  naval arch. — 623.817 15
  s.a. other spec. appls.
Momentum transfer
chem. eng. — 660.284 292
  s.a. spec. prod.

Momoyama period Japan hist. — 951.024
  s.a. spec. events & subj.
    e.g. Commerce
Mompa dialect *see* Himalayan dialects
Mon *see* Mon-Khmer
Monaco — *area*–449 49
Monadnock Mt. N.H. — *area*–742 9
Monads
  ontology — 111
  misc. aspects see Philosophy
Monagas Venezuela — *area*–875 6
Monaghan Ireland — *area*–416 97
Monarchies *see spec. kinds e.g.* Absolute monarchies
Monarchist parties
  pol. sci. — 324.24–.29
  s.a. spec. subj. of concern
    e.g. Social problems
Monarchs
  pub. admin. — 351.003 12
    spec. jur. — 354
  rel. worship
    comp. rel. — 291.213
    s.a. spec. rel.
  soc. aspects *see* Royalty
  s.a. — *pers.*–351 1
Monasteries (organizations) *see* Religious congregations
Monastery bldgs. *see* Monastic buildings
Monastic
buildings
  architecture — 726.7
  building — 690.67
  rel. purpose — 291.35
    s.a. spec. rel.
  other aspects see Religious-purpose bldgs.
life
  Christianity — 248.894
  other rel. see Personal religion
orders *see* Religious congregations
schools ed. — 377.3
Monasticism *see* Religious congregations
Monazite
  mineralogy — 549.72
Monetary
exchange
  law
    international — 341.751
    municipal — 343.032
      spec. jur. — 343.3–.9
  policy
    economics — 332.46
      central banking — 332.112

Monoblepharidales *see*
    Uniflagellate molds
Monochromatic photography   778.62
  motion pictures   778.534 2
  photomicrography   778.31
Monochrome television *see*
    Black-&-white
    television
Monoclinic systems
  crystallography   548.14
  s.a. spec. substances
Monocotyledones *see*
    Monocotyledons
Monocotyledons
  botany   584
  floriculture   635.934
  forestry.   634.974
  med. aspects
    crop prod.   633.884
    gen. pharm.   615.324
      toxicology   615.952 4
    vet. pharm.   636.089 532 4
      toxicology   636.089 595 24
  paleobotany   561.4
  other aspects see Plants
Monocycles
  engineering
    gen. tech. & mf.   629.227 1
    maintenance   629.287 71
    models   629.221 71
    operation   629.284 71
    s.a. other spec. aspects
      e.g. Brakes; *also*
      spec. appls. e.g.
      Circuses performing
      arts
  soc. & econ. aspects *see*
    Secondary industries
Monogamy
  soc. theology
    Christianity   261.835 84
    comp. rel.   291.178 358 4
    s.a. other spec. rel.
  sociology   306.84
Monogenea *see* Trematoda
Monohydric hydroxy aromatics
    see Phenols
Monologs
  drama
    gen. wks.
      collections   808.824 5
      hist. & crit.   809.245
      rhetoric   808.245
      juvenile   808.068 245
    spec. lits.   *lit. sub.*–204 5
      indiv. authors   *lit. sub.*–21–29
    other aspects see Drama
  recitations *see* Recitations
    literature
Monomagnesium impregnation
  wood bldg. materials   691.15

Monometallic standards
  money
    economics   332.422
    other aspects see Money
Monomotapas kingdom hist.   968.910 1
  s.a. spec. events & subj.
    e.g. Commerce
Monona Co. Ia.   *area*–777 44
Monongahela River   *area*–748 8
  Pennsylvania   *area*–748 8
  West Virginia   *area*–754 5
Monongalia Co. W. Va.   *area*–754 52
Mononucleosis infectious *see*
    Viral diseases
Monophysite
  church bldgs.
    architecture   726.581 6
    building   690.658 16
    other aspects see
      Religious-purpose
      bldgs.
  church music
    arts   783.026 16
      recordings   789.912 302 616
    s.a. spec. instruments;
      also spec. kinds e.g.
      Liturgical music
  religion
    pub. worship   264.016 02
      significance   246.7
    churches   281.6
    Christian life guides   248.481 6
    doctrines   230.16
      creeds   238.19
    general councils   262.516
    govt. & admin.   262.016
      parishes   254.016
    missions   266.16
    moral theology   241.041 6
    private prayers for   242.801 6
    pub. worship   264.016
    rel. associations
      adults   267.181 6
      men   267.241 6
      women   267.441 6
      young adults   267.621 6
    rel. instruction   268.816
    rel. law   262.981 6
    schools   377.816
    secondary training   207.121 6
    sermons   252.016
    theological seminaries   207.111 6
    s.a. other spec. aspects
Monopoly
  law
    international   341.753
    municipal   343.072
      spec. jur.   343.3–.9
  price determination *see*
    Control of markets

Monopoly (continued)
prod. econ.	338.82
international	338.884

Monorail rolling stock
technology	625.28
other aspects see Rolling	
stock railroads	

Monorailroads
engineering
soc. & econ. aspects *see*	
Secondary industries	
technology	625.103
s.a. spec. subj. e.g.	
Permanent way	
other aspects see Railroads	

transportation
gen. wks.
commerce	385.5
govt. control	350.875 5
central govts.	351.875 5
spec. jur.	353–354
local govts.	352.915 5
law *see* Railroad	
transportation law	

local transit
commerce	388.44
govt. control	350.878 44
central govts.	351.878 44
spec. jur.	353–354
local govts.	352.918 44

Monosaccharides
org. chem.	547.781 3
other aspects see Sugar	

Monosodium glutamate
manufacturing
soc. & econ. aspects *see*	
Secondary industries	
technology	664.4

Monotheism
comp. rel.	291.14
nat. rel.	211.34
other aspects see God	

Monotony studies
prod. management	658.544
spec. subj.	*s.s.*–068 5

Monotremata
animal husbandry	636.91

hunting
commercial	639.111
sports	799.259 1
paleozoology	569.12
zoology	599.1
other aspects see Mammalia	

Monotropaceae *see* Ericales

Monotype composition
printing
soc. & econ. aspects *see*	
Secondary industries	
technology	
automatic	686.225 44
manual	686.225 42

Monotypes
manufacturing
soc. & econ. aspects *see*	
Secondary industries	
technology	681.61

Monroe
County
Alabama	*area*–761 25
Arkansas	*area*–767 87
Florida	*area*–759 41
Georgia	*area*–758 563
Illinois	*area*–773 91
Indiana	*area*–772 255
Iowa	*area*–777 865
Kentucky	*area*–769 685
Michigan	*area*–774 32
Mississippi	*area*–762 975
Missouri	*area*–778 325
New York	*area*–747 88
Ohio	*area*–771 96
Pennsylvania	*area*–748 25
Tennessee	*area*–768 883
West Virginia	*area*–754 78
Wisconsin	*area*–775 54

James admin.
U.S. hist.	973.54
s.a. spec. events & subj.	
e.g. Commerce	

Monsoons *see* Continental wind
systems

Monsters
controversial knowledge	001.944
natural *see* Teratology	
supernatural *see* Supernatural	
beings	

Montage	702.813

Montagne Tremblante Provincial
Park Que.	*area*–714 4
Montague Co. Tex.	*area*–764 541
Montana	*area*–786

Montcalm Co.
Michigan	*area*–774 53
Quebec	*area*–714 415

Monte Carlo
city	*area*–449 49
probabilities	519.282
Monte Cristo Italy	*area*–455 6

Montecristi Dominican Republic
	area–729 352
Montenegro Yugoslavia	*area*–497 45

Monterey
Bay *see* United States Pacific	
seawaters	
Co. Calif.	*area*–794 76
Montessori system ed.	371.392
s.a. spec. levels of ed.;	
also Special Education	
Montevideo Uruguay	*area*–895 13
Montezuma Co. Colo.	*area*–788 27

Montgomery
city Ala.	*area*–761 47

Montgomery (continued)
  County
    Alabama   *area*–761 47
    Arkansas   *area*–767 43
    Georgia   *area*–758 832
    Illinois   *area*–773 82
    Indiana   *area*–772 48
    Iowa   *area*–777 75
    Kansas   *area*–781 93
    Kentucky   *area*–769 553
    Maryland   *area*–752 84
    Mississippi   *area*–762 642
    Missouri   *area*–778 382
    New York   *area*–747 46
    North Carolina   *area*–756 74
    Ohio   *area*–771 72
    Pennsylvania   *area*–748 12
    Tennessee   *area*–768 45
    Texas   *area*–764 153
    Virginia   *area*–755 785
  district Powys Wales   *area*–429 51
Montgomeryshire Wales   *area*–429 51
Monthly wages
  labor econ.   331.216 2
  s.a. spec. classes of labor
      e.g. Women
Months
  lit. & stage trmt. *see* Times
  time interval   529.2
Montmagny Co. Que.   *area*–714 735
Montmorency Co.
  Michigan   *area*–774 83
  Quebec   *area*–714 48
Monto Qld.   *area*–943 5
Montour Co. Pa.   *area*–748 39
Montpelier Vt.   *area*–743 4
Montreal Que.
  city   *area*–714 281
  County   *area*–714 28
  Island   *area*–714 28
Montrose
  Co. Colo.   *area*–788 19
  town Tayside Scot.   *area*–412 6
Montserrat   *area*–729 75
Monumental
  brasses
    dec. arts   739.522
    rubbings *see* Rubbings
        brasses
  reliefs
    sculpture   731.549
    spec. periods and schools 732–735
Monuments
  law   344.094
    spec. jur.   344.3–.9
  memorials
    World War 1   940.465
    World War 2   940.546 5
  other wars see Memorials
  pub. admin. *see* History pub.
    admin.

Monuments (continued)
  sculpture   731.76
  spec. periods & schools 732–735
Moods
  feelings
    psychology   152.454
      animals   156.245 4
      children   155.412
    s.a. psych. of other spec.
      groups
Moody Co. S.D.   *area*–783 36
Moon
  astronomy
    description   523.3
    theory   521.62
  regional subj. trmt.   *area*–991
  other aspects see Celestial
    bodies
  s.a. Lunar
Moon-cars *see* Extraterrestrial
    surface vehicles
    engineering
Moonie River Qld.   *area*–943 4
Moonta S. Aust.   *area*–942 35
Moore Co.
  North Carolina   *area*–756 352
  Tennessee   *area*–768 627
  Texas   *area*–764 822
Mooring
  grounds
    port eng.
      technology   627.22
      s.a. spec. appls. e.g.
        Harbor piloting
    seamanship
    other aspects see Liquids
      engineering
  structures
    port eng.
      soc. & econ. aspects *see*
        Secondary industries
      technology   627.32
      s.a. spec. appls. e.g.
        Approach piloting
Moorish
  architecture *see* Saracenic
    architecture
  dynasties Spain hist.   946.02
  s.a. spec. events & subj.
    e.g. Commerce
  other aspects see Berber
Moors
  ecology life sci. *see* Land
    ecology life sci.
Moose
  animal husbandry   636.294
  other aspects see Cervoidea
Moose Jaw Sask.   *area*–712 44
Moosehead Lake Me.   *area*–741 2
Mopeds *see* Bicycles

Mops
  manufacturing
    soc. & econ. aspects *see*
      Secondary industries
    technology   679.6
Moquegua Peru   *area*–853 4
Mora Co. N.M.   *area*–789 54
Moraceae *see* Urticales
Moraceous fruits
  agriculture   634.36
  soc. & econ. aspects *see*
      Primary industries
  foods   641.343 6
    preparation
      commercial   664.804 36
      domestic   641.643 6
  other aspects see Fruits
Moraines
  physical geol.   551.314
Moral
  determinants
    indiv. psych.   155.234
  education   370.114
  s.a. spec. levels of ed.
  issues
    govt. reg.   350.76
      central govts.   351.76
        spec. jur.   353–354
      local govts.   352.936
    law
      criminal   345.027
        spec. jur.   345.3–.9
      gen. wks.   344.054
        spec. jur.   344.3–.9
    soc. aspects   363.4
      crime   364.17
        soc. theology *see* Crime
        soc. theology
  philosophy *see* Ethics
  Rearmament
    Christian association   267.16
  renewal *see* Religious
      experience
  sense
    ethical systems   171.2
      applications   172–179
  theology
    Buddhism   294.35
    Christianity   241
    comp. rel.   291.5
    Hinduism   294.548
    Islam   297.5
    Judaism   296.385
    s.a. other spec. rel.
  training
    child rearing   649.7
Morale
  armed forces   355.123
  s.a. spec. mil. branches

Morale (continued)
  employees
    personnel admin.
      gen. management   658.314
      executives   658.407 14
      spec. subj.   *s.s.*–068 3
    pub. admin.   350.147
      central govts.   351.147
        spec. jur.   353–354
      local govts.   352.005 147
Morality
  & law   340.112
  plays *see* Religious plays
  s.a. Ethics
Moravia Czechoslovakia   *area*–437 2
Moravian
  church bldgs.
    architecture   726.584 6
    building   690.658 46
    other aspects see
        Religious-purpose
        bldgs.
  church music
    arts   783.026 46
    recordings   789.912 302 646
    s.a. spec. instruments;
        also spec. kinds e.g.
        Liturgical music
  religion
    pub. worship   264.046 02
    significance   246.7
  churches   284.6
    Christian life guides   248.484 6
    doctrines   230.46
      creeds   238.46
    general councils   262.546
    govt. & admin.   262.046
      parishes   254.046
    missions   266.46
    moral theology   241.044 6
    private prayers for   242.804 6
    pub. worship   264.046
    rel. associations
      adults   267.184 6
      men   267.244 6
      women   267.444 6
      young adults   267.624 6
    rel. instruction   268.846
    rel. law   262.984 6
    schools   377.846
    secondary training   207.124 6
    sermons   252.046
    theological seminaries   207.114 6
    s.a. other spec. aspects
  dialects
    linguistics   491.87
    literature   891.87
    s.a.   *lang.*–918 7
  people   *r.e.n.*–918 7

Moravian (continued)
  s.a. Czechoslovakia; *also*
     other spec. subj. e.g.
      Arts

Moravians (rel. group)	
biog. & work	284.609 2
s.a.	*pers.*–246
Moray Scot.	*area*–412 23
Morays *see* Apodes	
Morazán El Salvador	*area*–728 433
Morbidity *see* Diseases	
Morbihan France	*area*–441 3
Morbilli *see* Measles	
Mordelloidea	
culture	638.576 7
paleozoology	565.76
zoology	595.767
other aspects see Insecta	
Morden	
London Eng.	*area*–421 93
Manitoba	*area*–712 73
Mordovian ASSR	*area*–478 3
Mordovinian ASSR	*area*–478 3
Mordva ASSR	*area*–478 3

Mordvin
  language *see* Middle Volga
     languages

people	*r.e.n.*–945 6

  s.a. other spec. subj. e.g.
     Arts

More og Romsdal Norway	*area*–483
Moreau River S.D.	*area*–783 5
Morecambe Lancashire Eng.	*area*–427 69
Moree N.S.W.	*area*–944 4
Morehouse Par. La.	*area*–763 84
Morelos Mex.	*area*–724 9

Mores
  customs *see* Social customs
  ethics *see* Ethics

sociology	306

Moreton-in-Marsh Gloucestershire

Eng.	*area*–424 17

Morgan
  County

Alabama	*area*–761 93
Colorado	*area*–788 74
Georgia	*area*–758 595
Illinois	*area*–773 463
Indiana	*area*–772 513
Kentucky	*area*–769 253
Missouri	*area*–778 53
Ohio	*area*–771 94
Tennessee	*area*–768 74
Utah	*area*–792 26
West Virginia	*area*–754 96

  horses *see* Light harness
    horses

Morgantown W.Va.	*area*–754 53

Morgues

architecture	725.597
building	690.559 7

Morgues (continued)
  other aspects see Public
    structures
Moringaceae *see* Capparidales
Morley West Yorkshire Eng.

	area–428 19

Mormon tea family *see* Gnetales

Mormons	289.33

  misc. aspects see Latter-Day
    Saints Church
Morning

influence on crime	364.22

  lit. & stage trmt. *see* Times
  plants blooming in

floriculture	635.953

    s.a. spec. plants
  prayer *see* Prayer gen. wks.
  prayers

Anglican liturgy	246.033

Morning-glory family *see*
    Solanales

Mornington Vic.	*area*–945 2

Moroccan

people	*r.e.n.*–927 64

  s.a. other spec. subj. e.g.
    Arts

Morocco	*area*–64
Morogoro Tanzania	*area*–678 25
Morona-Santiago Ecuador	*area*–866 43

Moronism *see* Mental deficiency
Morons *see* Educable retarded
    persons
Morphemes *see* Words
Morphine *see* Narcotics
Morphisms

topological algebras	512.55

    s.a. spec. appls. e.g.
     Engineering
Morphogenesis
  embryology *see* Anatomy
    embryology
Morphology (anatomy) *see*
    Anatomy
Morphology (linguistics) *see*
    Grammar (linguistics)

Morrill Co. Neb.	*area*–782 95

Morris Co.

Kansas	*area*–781 58
New Jersey	*area*–749 74
Texas	*area*–764 217
Morrison Co. Minn.	*area*–776 69

Morrow Co.

Ohio	*area*–771 516
Oregon	*area*–795 67

Morse
  code *see* Telegraphy wire
  system telegraphy *see*
    Automatic systems wire
    telegraphy
Mortal sin

Christian doctrines	241.31

Mortality *see* Deaths
Mortars (artillery)
  art metalwork   739.742
  mil. eng.
    soc. & econ. aspects *see*
        Secondary industries
    tech. & mf.   623.42
Mortars (bonding agent) *see*
    Masonry
Mortgage
  insurance   368.852
    misc. aspects see Insurance
  loans
    economics   332.72
    govt. control *see* Credit
      govt. control
Mortgages
  accounting trmt.   657.75
    s.a. spec. kinds of
      enterprise e.g.
      Insurance accounting
  investment econ.   332.632 44
  real property law   346.043 64
  spec. jur.   346.3-.9
  s.a. Secured transactions
Mortlake Vic.   *area*–945 7
Morton
  County
    Kansas   *area*–781 715
    North Dakota   *area*–784 85
  Nat. Park N.S.W. *area*–944 6
Mortuary tombs & chapels
  architecture   726.8
  building   690.68
  rel. purpose   291.35
    s.a. spec. rel.
  other aspects see
      Religious-purpose
      bldgs.
  s.a. Monuments
Morus *see* Mulberries
Moruya N.S.W.   *area*–944 7
Morwell Vic.   *area*–945 6
Mosaic
  disease *see* Viral diseases
    plant culture
  glass
    arts   748.5
  law
    Bible   222.1
    other aspects see
      Historical books (O.T.)
Mosaics   738.5
  in architecture   738.52
  as decoration   729.7
  rel. significance
    Christianity   247.47
    comp. rel.   291.35
    s.a. other spec. rel.
  s.a. spec. kinds of
    bldgs.

Mosan *see* Algonkian-Mosan
Moscow RSFSR   *area*–473 1
Moselle
  dept. France   *area*–443 825
  River   *area*–434 3
Moses
  assumption
    pseudepigrapha   229.913
    other aspects see Apocrypha
Moshi Tanzania   *area*–678 26
Mosks *see* Islamic temples &
    shrines
Moskva RSFSR   *area*–473 1
Moslem *see* Islamic
Moslems *see* Muslims
Mosques *see* Islamic temples &
    shrines
Mosquito
  boats *see* Destroyer escorts
  Range Colo.   *area*–788 59
Mosquitoes
  disease carriers
    pub. health   614.432 3
    misc. aspects see Public
      health
  other aspects see
      Orthorrhapha
Moss
  animals *see* Bryozoa
  Vale N.S.W.   *area*–944 6
Mössbauer spectroscopy
  astrophysics   523.018 753 52
    s.a. spec. celestial bodies
  physics   537.535 2
    spec. states of matter 530.4
Mosses
  black *see* Musci
  bog *see* Sphagnales
  club *see* Lycopsida
  common *see* Musci
  peat *see* Sphagnales
  true *see* Musci
Mossi kingdom hist.   966.250 1
  s.a. spec. events & subj.
    e.g. Commerce
Mossley Greater Manchester Eng.
          area–427 35
Mostaganem Algeria *area*–651
Most-favored-nation trmt. *see*
    Trade agreements
Mosul Iraq   *area*–567 4
Motacillidae
  hunting
    commercial   639.128 854
    sports   799.248 854
  paleozoology   568.8
  zoology   598.854
  other aspects see Aves
Motels *see* Hotels
Motets *see* Choral music
Moth flies *see* Orthorrhapha

Mothers	
meditations for	
Christianity	242.643 1
other rel. see Worship	
personal rel.	
Christianity	248.843 1
other rel. see Personal	
religion	
prayers for	
Christianity	242.843 1
other rel. see Worship	
psychology	155.646 3
working	
labor econ.	331.44
labor law *see* Labor law	
other aspects see Parents	
Motherwell Strathclyde Scot.	
	area–414 49
Moths *see* Heterocera	
Motion	
pictures	
advertising use	659.152
animal husbandry for	636.088 8
s.a. spec. animals	
communication	001.553 2
service	384.8
ed. use	371.335 23
s.a. spec. levels of ed.;	
also Special education	
ethics *see* Public	
entertainment ethics	
influence on crime	364.254
performing arts	791.43
sociology	302.23
other aspects see Films	
pictorial materials	
s.a. Motion-picture	
sickness	
gen. med.	616.989 2
geriatrics	618.976 989 2
pediatrics	618.929 892
statistics	312.398 92
other aspects see Diseases	
s.a. spec. diseases	
studies	
prod. management	658.542 3
spec. subj.	*s.s.*–068 5
psychology *see* Movements	
psychology	
Motion (concept)	
metaphysics *see* Evolution	
Motion-picture	
actors & actresses *see* Actors	
directors	*pers.*–791 4
drama	
gen. wks.	
collections	808.823
hist. & crit.	809.23
rhetoric	808.23
juvenile	808.068 23
presentation	791.43

Motion-picture	
drama (continued)	
spec. lits.	*lit. sub.*–203
indiv. authors	*lit. sub.*–21–29
other aspects see Drama	
performers *see* Actors	
photography	778.53
photomicrography	778.56
producers	
accounting	657.84
projection	778.55
theaters	
accounting	657.84
s.a. Motion pictures	
Motions	
biology *see* Movements biology	
celestial mech. *see* Celestial	
mechanics	
earth astronomy	525.3
mechanics *see* Dynamics	
of celestial bodies	
comets	523.63
spec. comets	523.64
Jupiter	523.453
Mars	523.433
Mercury	523.413
moon	523.33
Neptune	523.481 3
Pluto	523.482 3
Saturn	523.463
stars	523.83
spec. systems	523.84–.85
sun	523.73
Uranus	523.473
Venus	523.423
of nuclei *see* Nuclei	
of particles *see* Particles	
(matter)	
of rays *see* Rays (beams)	
Motions (proposals)	
legal proc.	
criminal	345.05
spec. jur.	345.3–.9
gen. wks.	347.052
spec. courts	347.02–.04
spec. jur.	347.3–.9
spec. subj.	*law s.s.*–026 9
other aspects see Legal	
procedure	
Motivation	
armed forces	355.123
s.a. spec. mil. branches	
ed. psych.	370.154
employees	
personnel admin.	
gen. management	658.314
executive	658.407 14
spec. subj.	*s.s.*–068 3
pub. admin.	350.147
central govts.	351.147
spec. jur.	353–354

Motor
vehicle (continued)
  transportation
    buildings
      architecture   725.38
      building   690.538
      other aspects see
        Public structures
    facilities
      civic art   711.73
  vehicles
    failures
      transp. hazard   363.125 1
    govt. procurement *see*
      Equipment procurement
      pub. admin.
    management
      pub. admin. *see* Equipment
        management
    pollution by
      soc. aspects   363.731
      other aspects see
        Pollution; *also spec.*
        kinds e.g. Motorboats
    safety aspects *see*
      Vehicular transp.
    s.a. spec. kinds e.g.
      Motorcycles
  yachts *see* Inboard motorboats
Motorboating
  sports   797.125
  racing   797.14
  other aspects see Sports
Motorboats
  engineering   623.823 1
  design   623.812 31
  models   623.820 131
  seamanship   623.882 31
  other aspects see Vessels
    (nautical)
Motorcars *see* Automobiles
Motorcycle
  racers
    biog. & work   796.750 92
    s.a.   *pers.*–796 7
  racing
    sports   796.75
    other aspects see Sports
  troops armed forces   357.53
Motorcycles
  commerce   388.347 5
  engineering
    gen. tech. & mf.   629.227 5
    maintenance   629.287 75
    models   629.221 75
    operation   629.284 75
    s.a. other spec. aspects
      e.g. Brakes; *also*
      spec. appls. e.g.
      Military engineering

Motorcycles
  engineering (continued)
    soc. & econ. aspects *see*
      Secondary industries
    safety aspects *see* Vehicular
      transp.
    other aspects see Land
      vehicles
Motoring *see* Driving motor
  vehicles
Motorized infantry
  armed forces   356.11
Motors *see* Power plants
Motorscooters *see* Motorcycles
Motorways *see* Expressways
Moulding-equipment *see*
  Molding-equipment
Moulds *see* Molds
Moultrie Co. Ill.   *area*–773 675
Mount
  Barney Qld.   *area*–943 2
  Beauth Vic.   *area*–945 5
  Buffalo Nat. Park Vic.   *area*–945 5
  Desert Isl. Me.   *area*–741 45
  Elliott Nat. Park Qld.   *area*–943 6
  Field Nat. Park Tas.   *area*–946 2
  Gambier S. Aust.   *area*–942 34
  Isa Qld.   *area*–943 7
  Lofty Ranges S. Aust.   *area*–942 32
  McKinley Nat. Park Alaska
      area–798 3
  Morgan Qld.   *area*–943 5
  Rainier Nat. Park Wash.   *area*–797 78
  Rescue Nat. Park S. Aust.
      area–942 33
  Royal Que.   *area*–714 281
  Spec Nat. Park Qld.   *area*–943 6
Mountain
  Ash Mid Glamorgan Wales
      area–429 73
  breezes *see* Local wind
    systems
  climbing
    accidents *see* Recreation
      accidents
    equipment mf.   688.765 22
      soc. & econ. aspects *see*
        Secondary industries
    sports   796.522
    other aspects see Sports
  lands *see* Mountainous lands
  province Philippines   *area*–599 1
  railways
    commerce   385.6
    engineering
      technology   625.3
      other aspects see
        Railroads
    govt. control   351.875 6
      spec. jur.   353–354

Movements
  biology
    pathology (continued)
      med. sci. — 616.7
        animals — 636.089 67
          s.a. spec. animals
        man — 616.7
    physiology
      gen. wks. — 574.18
        animals — 591.18
        microorganisms — 576.118
        plants — 581.18
          s.a. spec. organisms
      med. sci. — 612.7
        human phys. — 612.7
        vet. phys. — 636.089 27
          s.a. spec. animals
        s.a. spec. functions,
          systems, organs
    of cells cytology — 574.876 4
      animals — 591.876 4
      plants — 581.876 4
        s.a. spec. organisms
    of eyes
      human phys. — 612.846
        other aspects see Sensory
          functions
  perception
    intellectual
      psychology — 153.754
        animals — 156.375 4
        children — 155.413
          s.a. psych. of other
            spec. groups
    visual
      psychology
        gen. wks. — 152.142 5
          animals — 156.214 25
          children — 155.412
            s.a. psych. of other
              spec. groups
        influences — 155.911 425
    psychology — 152.3
      animals — 156.23
      children — 155.412
Movers of personnel *see*
    Materials-handling
    equip.
Moving
  clusters stars
    astronomy
      description — 523.852
      theory — 521.585 2
        other aspects see Celestial
          bodies
  expenses
    employees *see* Economic
      services to employees
  households
    home econ. — 648.9
  pictures *see* Motion pictures

Moving (continued)
  sidewalks *see* Belts conveyors
  stairs *see* Escalators
  street belts *see* Belts
    conveyors
  targets
    gun sports — 799.313
  vans *see* Trucks
Mowbray Leicestershire Eng.
    area–425 46
Mower Co. Minn. — *area*–776 17
Mowers *see* Harvesting-machinery
Mowing crops
  agriculture — 631.55
    s.a. spec. crops
Moxico Angola — *area*–673 4
Moyle N. Ire. — *area*–416 15
Mozambique
  Channel
    oceanography — 551.467 25
    regional subj. trmt. — *area*–165 25
      other aspects see Indian
        Ocean
  country — *area*–679
  people — *r.e.n.*–967 9
    s.a. other spec. subj. e.g.
      Arts
Mthethwa kingdom hist. — 968
    s.a. spec. events & subj.
      e.g. Commerce
Mtwara Tanzania — *area*–678 24
Much Wenlock Salop Eng. — *area*–424 59
Mucilages
  chem. tech. — 668.33
    other aspects see Adhesives
Mucocutaneous leishmaniasis *see*
    Leishmaniasis
Mucorales *see* Nonflagellate
    molds
Mucous membranes
  human anatomy & phys. — 611.018 7
  medication through
    therapeutics — 615.66
      misc. aspects see
        Medication methods
    s.a. spec. diseases
  other aspects see Tissue
    biology
Mud
  fuels
    manufacturing
      chem. tech. — 662.82
      soc. & econ. aspects *see*
        Secondary industries
  puppies *see* Caudata
Mudejar architecture *see*
    Saracenic architecture
Mudflows
  geology — 551.353
Mudgee N.S.W. — *area*–944 5

Mudguards
  automobiles
    soc. & econ. aspects *see*
      Secondary industries
    tech. & mf.   629.26
    s.a. other spec. uses
Muezzins
  Islamic leaders   297.61
Muffin mixes
  comm. proc.   664.753
Mufflers
  internal combustion engines
    automobiles
      soc. & econ. aspects *see*
        Secondary industries
      tech. & mf.   629.252
      s.a. spec. appls. e.g.
        Noise control
Muffs
  comm. mf.
    soc. & econ. aspects *see*
      Secondary industries
    technology   687.19
    fur   685.24
    soc. customs   391.41
Mugiloidea *see* Acanthopterygii
Mugla Turkey   *area*–562
Muhammad
  the Prophet Islam   297.63
  Zahir Shah Afghanistan hist.   958.104 3
  s.a. spec. events & subj.
    e.g. Commerce
Muhammadan *see* Islamic
Muhammadans *see* Muslims
Muhlenberg Co. Ky.   *area*–769 832
Mukurra kingdom hist.   962.402
  s.a. spec. events & subj.
    e.g. Commerce
Mulberries
  agriculture   634.38
    soc. & econ. aspects *see*
      Primary industries
  foods   641.343 8
    preparation
      commercial   664.804 38
      domestic   641.643 8
  other aspects see Urticales;
    also Fruits
Mulch
  tillage
    soil conservation   631.451
    s.a. spec. crops
Mulefoot swine
  animal husbandry   636.484
  other aspects see Swine
Mules (animals)
  animal husbandry   636.18
    soc. & econ. aspects *see*
      Primary industries
  products *see spec. prod. e.g.*
    Hides

Mules (animals) (continued)
  other aspects see Equidae
Mules (footwear) *see* Footwear
Mules (machines) *see*
    Spinning-machines
Mull Strathclyde Scot.   *area*–414 23
Mullica River N.J.   *area*–749 61
Multan Pakistan   *area*–549 145
Multidimensional algebras   512.5
  s.a. spec. appls. e.g.
    Engineering
Multielement vacuum tubes
  radiowave electronics
    soc. & econ. aspects *see*
      Secondary industries
    tech. & mf.   621.381 512 3–.381 512 8
      s.a. spec. appls. e.g.
        Radio eng. & mf.
  other aspects see Vacuum
    tubes
Multiform
  functions *see* Multiformity of
    functions calculus
  processes glassmaking   666.126
    s.a. spec. kinds of glass
Multiformity of functions
  calculus   515.223
    complex variables   515.922 3
    real variables   515.822 3
  s.a. other spec. functions &
    equations; also spec.
    appls. e.g.
    Engineering
Multilateral
  secondary schools   373.25
  trade agreements
    internat. comm.   382.91
    internat. law   341.754 026 5
  treaties
    internat. law
      texts   341.026 5
    other aspects see
      Treaties
Multilinear
  algebras   512.5
    s.a. spec. appls. e.g.
      Engineering
  forms
    algebra   512.944
      s.a. spec. appls. e.g.
        Engineering
    geometry   516.35
      s.a. spec. appls. e.g.
        Engineering
Multilingual
  shorthand systems   653.41
Multinational
  bus. organizations
    prod. econ.   338.88

Multiphase flow	
mechanics	
engineering *see* Dynamics	
physics	532.56
Multiple	
access	
electronic data proc. *see*	
Networks electronic	
data proc.	
art	
gen. wks.	709.040 78
spec. places	709.1–.9
painting	759.067 8
spec. places	759.1–.9
sculpture	735.230 478
spec. places	730.9
s.a. other spec. art forms	
banking	
economics	332.16
other aspects see Banking	
childbirth	
obstetrics	618.25
anesthesia	617.968 2
pub. health	614.599 2
vet. obstetrics	636.089 825
s.a. spec. animals	
column tariffs	
internat. comm.	382.753
misc. aspects see Customs	
(tariffs)	
deficiency states	
gen. med.	616.399
geriatrics	618.976 399
pediatrics	618.923 99
pub. health	614.593 99
statistics	312.339 9
deaths	312.263 99
other aspects see Diseases	
dwelling bldgs.	
architecture	728.31
building	690.831
other aspects see	
Residential buildings	
s.a. spec. activities e.g.	
Housecleaning home	
econ.	
images	
photography *see* Special	
effects photography	
oxides	
mineralogy	549.52
personalities	
gen. med.	616.852 36
geriatrics	618.976 852 36
pediatrics	618.928 523 6
psychology	157.3
statistics	312.385 236
pregnancy	
obstetrics	618.25
anesthesia	617.968 2
pub. health	614.599 2

Multiple	
pregnancy (continued)	
vet. obstetrics	636.089 825
s.a. spec. animals	
sclerosis	
gen. med.	616.834
geriatrics	618.976 834
pediatrics	618.928 34
pub. health	614.598 34
statistics	312.383 4
deaths	312.268 34
other aspects see Diseases	
stars	
astronomy	
description	523.841
theory	521.584 1
other aspects see Celestial	
bodies	
s.a. other spec. subj.	
Multiple-loop systems	
automation eng.	629.833
s.a. spec. appls. e.g.	
Gunnery	
Multiplex telegraphy *see*	
Acoustical systems wire	
telegraphy	
Multiplication	512.92
algebra	512.92
arithmetic	513.2
s.a. spec. appls. e.g.	
Business arithmetic	
Multiplier effect	
macroeconomics	339.43
Multistage programming	
mathematics	519.703
s.a. spec. appls. e.g.	
Engineering	
Multi-story	
buildings	
arch. construction	721.042
s.a. spec. kinds of	
bldgs.	
houses	
architecture	728.372
building	690.837 2
other aspects see	
Residential buildings	
Multituberculata	
paleozoology	569.17
Multivariate analysis	
statistical math.	519.535
s.a. spec. appls. e.g.	
Engineering	
Multnomah Co. Ore.	*area*–795 49
Mu-mesons *see* Muons	
Mummification *see* Embalming	
Mumps	
gen. med.	616.313
geriatrics	618.976 313
pediatrics	618.923 13
pub. health	614.544

Musa
  paradisiaca *see* Plantains
  sapientum *see* Bananas
  textilis *see* Manila hemp
Musaceae *see* Zingiberales
Musales *see* Zingiberales
Muscat & Oman   *area*–535
Muscatine Co. Ia.   *area*–777 68
Musci
  botany   588.2
  floriculture   635.938 2
  med. aspects
    crop prod.   633.888 2
    gen. pharm.   615.322 2
      toxicology   615.952 82
    paleobotany   561.8
    vet. pharm.   636.089 532 22
      toxicology   636.089 595 282
  other aspects see Plants
Muscles
  anatomy
    human   611.73
    other aspects see Muscular
      organs
  diseases
    gen. wks.   616.74
      neoplasms   616.992 73
      tuberculosis   616.995 73
    geriatrics   618.976 74
    pediatrics   618.927 4
    pub. health   614.597 4
    statistics   312.374
      deaths   312.267 4
    surgery   617.473
      anesthesiology   617.967 473
    other aspects see Diseases
  drawing arts
    animals   743.6
    human   743.47
  pathology
    gen. wks.   591.218 52
    s.a. spec. animals
    med. sci. *see* Muscles
      diseases
  physical anthropometry   573.673
  physiology
    medical   612.74
    zoological   591.185 2
    other aspects see Movements
  tissue biology human   611.018 973
Muscogee Co. Ga.   *area*–758 473
Muscular
  dystrophy
    gen. med.   616.748
    geriatrics   618.976 748
    pediatrics   618.927 48
    pub. health   614.597 48
    statistics   312.374 8
      deaths   312.267 48
    other aspects see Diseases

Muscular (continued)
  organs
    anatomy
      med. sci.   611.73
      animals   636.089 173
        s.a. spec. animals
      man   611.73
      zoology   591.47
        s.a. spec. animals
    pathology
      med. sci. *see* Movements
      zoology   591.227
        s.a. spec. animals
    rheumatism
      gen. med.   616.742
      geriatrics   618.976 742
      pediatrics   618.927 42
      pub. health   614.597 42
      statistics   312.374 2
      deaths   312.267 42
      other aspects see Diseases
  tissue
    human anatomy & phys.   611.018 6
    other aspects see Tissue
      biology
Musculoskeletal system
  anatomy
    human   611.7
    other aspects see Motor
      organs
  diseases
    gen. wks.   616.7
      neoplasms   616.992 7
      tuberculosis   616.995 7
    geriatrics   618.976 7
    pediatrics   618.927
    pub. health   614.597
    statistics   312.37
      deaths   312.267
    surgery   617.47
      anesthesiology   617.967 47
    other aspects see Diseases
  drugs affecting
    pharmacodynamics   615.77
    other aspects see Drugs
  physical anthropometry   573.67
  physiology
    human   612.7
    other aspects see Movements
  tissue biology human   611.018 97
  other aspects see Motor
    system
Museologists
  biog. & work   069.092
  occupational ethics   174.909 6
  s.a.   *pers.*–096
Museology   069
  libraries   026.069
    misc. aspects see Special
      libraries
Musettes *see* Bagpipes

Music hall
  stage performance — 792.7
Musical
  aptitude tests
    psychology — 153.947 8
      children — 155.413
      s.a. psych. of other spec.
        groups
  chairs recreation — 793.4
  comedies *see* Musical shows
  drama *see* Dramatic music
  forms
    music theory — 781.5
    recordings — 789.912 15
    s.a. spec. mediums
  glasses
    mf. tech. — 681.819 6
      misc. aspects see Musical
        instruments
  musical art — 789.6
    recordings — 789.912 96
  instruments — 781.91
    manufacturers
      biog. & work — 681.809 2
      s.a. — *pers.*–681 8
  manufacturing
    soc. & econ. aspects *see*
      Secondary industries
    technology — 681.8
  performances
    ethics *see* Public
      entertainment ethics
  programs
    library & museum services
      see Recreational
        services
  psychology *see* Auditory
    perception
  saws *see* Saws (musical
    instruments)
  scores *see* Scores (music)
  shows — 782.81
    recordings — 789.912 281
  sound
    music theory — 781.22
    s.a. spec. mediums
  structure
    music theory — 781.3–.4
      spec. forms — 781.5
    s.a. spec. mediums
Musicians
  biog. & work — 780.92
    s.a. spec. kinds
  occupational ethics — 174.978
  s.a. — *pers.*–78
Musicologists
  biog. & work — 780.010 92
  s.a. — *pers.*–781
Musique concrète *see* Concrete
  music

Muskegon
  Co. Mich. — *area*–774 57
  River Mich. — *area*–774 5
Muskellunges *see* Mesichthyes
Muskets
  art metalwork — 739.744 25
  mil. eng.
    soc. & econ. aspects *see*
      Secondary industries
    tech. & mf. — 623.442 5
Muskingum
  Co. O. — *area*–771 91
  River O. — *area*–771 91
Muskmelons
  agriculture — 635.611
    soc. & econ. aspects *see*
      Primary industries
  foods — 641.356 11
    preparation
      commercial — 664.805 611
      domestic — 641.656 11
  other aspects see
    Cucurbitales; *also*
    Fruits
Muskogee Co. Okla. — *area*–766 82
Muskoka District Municipality
  Ont. — *area*–713 16
Musk-oxen
  animal husbandry — 636.293
  other aspects see Bovoidea
Muskrats *see* Myomorpha
Muslim
  Hadith — 297.124 3
  s.a. Islamic
Muslims
  biog. & work — 297.092
    s.a. spec. kinds e.g.
      Clergy; *also spec.*
        sects
  s.a. — *pers.*–297 1
  s.a. Black Muslims
Muslin *see* Cotton textiles
Musoma Tanzania — *area*–678 27
Musophagi *see* Cuculiformes
Musselburgh Lothian Scot. — *area*–413 6
Mussels
  culture — 639.42
  fishing
    commercial — 639.42
    sports — 799.254 11
  food *see* Mollusca food
  other aspects see Pelecypoda
Musselshall Co. Mont. — *area*–786 312
Mussolini
  Benito Italy hist. — 945.091
    s.a. spec. events & subj.
      e.g. Commerce
Mustaches
  personal care — 646.724
  soc. customs — 371.5

Myodocopa *see* Ostracoda	
Myology *see* Muscles	
Myomorpha	
animal husbandry	636.932 33
hunting	
commercial	639.113 233
sports	799.259 323 3
zoology	599.323 3
other aspects see Rodentia	
Myopia *see* Refraction errors	
Myoporaceae *see* Lamiales	
Myositis	
gen. med.	616.743
geriatrics	618.976 743
pediatrics	618.927 43
pub. health	614.597 43
statistics	312.374 3
deaths	312.267 43
other aspects see Diseases	
Myriapoda *see* Progoneata	
Myricaceae *see* Myricales	
Myricales	
botany	583.974
floriculture	635.933 974
forestry	634.973 974
med. aspects	
crop prod.	633.883 974
gen. pharm.	615.323 974
toxicology	615.952 397 4
vet. pharm.	636.089 532 397 4
toxicology	636.089 595 239 74
paleobotany	561.3
other aspects see Plants	
Myristicaceae *see* Laurales	
Myrobalan family *see* Myrtales	
Myrothamnaceae *see*	
Hamamelidales	
Myrsinaceae *see* Myrsinales	
Myrsinales	
botany	583.677
floriculture	635.933 677
forestry	634.973 677
med. aspects	
crop prod.	633.883 67
gen. pharm.	615.323 677
toxicology	615.952 367 7
vet. pharm.	636.089 532 367 7
toxicology	636.089 595 236 77
paleobotany	561.3
other aspects see Plants	
Myrtaceae *see* Myrtales	
Myrtaceous fruits	
agriculture	634.42
soc. & econ. aspects *see*	
Primary industries	
foods	641.344 2
preparation	
commercial	664.804 42
domestic	641.644 2
other aspects see Fruits	

Myrtales	
botany	583.42
floriculture	635.933 42
forestry	634.973 42
med. aspects	
crop prod.	633.883 42
gen. pharm.	615.323 42
toxicology	615.952 342
vet. pharm.	636.089 532 342
toxicology	636.089 595 234 2
paleobotany	561.3
other aspects see Plants	
Myrtle	
family *see* Myrtales	
wax	
comm. proc.	665.12
other aspects see Waxes	
Myrtleford Vic.	*area*–945 5
Mysia	*area*–392 1
Mysidacea	
fishing sports	799.255 383
paleozoology	565.38
zoology	595.383
other aspects see	
Eumalacostraca	
Mysore India	*area*–548 7
Mystacocarida	
culture	639.5
fishing	
commercial	639.5
sports	799.255 31
paleozoology	565.31
zoology	595.31
other aspects see Crustacea	
Mysteries	001.94
popular psych.	135.4
s.a. spec. subj.	
Mystery	
fiction	
gen. wks.	
collections	808.838 72
hist. & crit.	809.387 2
rhetoric	808.387 2
juvenile	808.068 387 2
spec. lits.	*lit. sub.*–308 72
spec. authors	*lit. sub.*–31–39
other aspects see Fiction	
plays	
religious *see* Religious	
plays	
suspense *see* Melodrama	
Mystic	
philosophy	
medieval western	189.5
traditions occultism	135
Mystical	
body of Christ	
Christian church	262.77
Judaism	296.833
misc. aspects see Judaism	

N

Nails (anatomy)
  anatomy
    human   611.78
    other aspects see
        Integumentary organs
  animal path.   591.218 58
    med. sci. *see* Nails
      (anatomy) diseases
  animal phys.   591.185 8
    med. sci.   612.799
      veterinary   636.089 279 9
    s.a. spec. animals
  diseases   616.547
    geriatrics   618.976 547
    pediatrics   618.925 47
    pub. health   614.595 47
    statistics   312.354 7
    other aspects see Diseases
  drugs affecting
    pharmacodynamics   615.779
    other aspects see Drugs
  human physiology   612.799
  personal care   646.727
  physical anthropometry   573.678
  tissue biology human   611.018 978
Nails (fasteners)
  arts *see* Ornaments arts
  machine eng.
    soc. & econ. aspects *see*
      Secondary industries
    tech. & mf.   621.884
    s.a. spec. appls. e.g.
      Carpentry
  other aspects see Mechanics
Nailsworth Gloucestershire Eng.
      area–424 19
Nairn Scot.   *area*–411 95
Nairobi Kenya   *area*–676 25
Najadaceae *see* Najadales
Najadales
  botany   584.722
  floriculture   635.934 722
  med. aspects
    crop prod.   633.884 722
    gen. pharm.   615.324 722
      toxicology   615.952 472 2
    vet. pharm.   636.089 532 472 2
      toxicology   636.089 595 247 22
  paleobotany   561.4
  other aspects see Plants
Najas family *see* Najadales
Naked-seed plants *see*
      Gymnospermae
Nakhichevan ASSR   *area*–479 1
Namboku period Japan hist.   952.022
  s.a. spec. events & subj.
    e.g. Commerce
Nambour Qld.   *area*–943 2
Name
  authority files
    library cataloging   025.322

Name (continued)
  cards
    arts   769.5
  giving
    soc. customs   392.12
  reference structure
    library cataloging   025.322
Names
  commercial
    property law *see* Intangible
      property law
  fictitious *see* Pseudonymous
    works
  geographical   910.3
    s.a. spec. places
  houses   929.97
  personal   929.4
    law *see* Persons law
  pets   929.97
  ships   929.97
Namibia   *area*–688
Namoi River N.S.W.   *area*–944 4
Namur Belgium   *area*–493 4
Nance Co. Neb.   *area*–782 425
Nandewar Range N.S.W.   *area*–944 4
Nandinaceae *see* Berberidales
Nanking China   *area*–511 3
Nansemond Co. Va.   *area*–755 53
Nantucket
  Co. & Isl. Mass.   *area*–744 97
  Sound
    oceanography   551.461 46
    regional subj. trmt.   *area*–163 46
    other aspects see Atlantic
      Ocean
Nantwich Cheshire Eng.   *area*–427 12
Nantyglo Blaina Gwent Wales
      area–429 95
Napa Co. Calif.   *area*–794 19
Naphthalenes
  org. chem.   547.615
  s.a. spec. cpds.
Naphthas
  chem. tech.   665.538 24
  other aspects see Petroleum
Napierville Co. Que.   *area*–714 35
Napkins *see* Table linens
Naples Italy   *area*–457 3
Napo Ecuador   *area*–866 41
Napoleon
  reign France hist.
    1   944.05
    3   944.07
  s.a. spec. events & subj.
    e.g. Arts
Napoleonic
  wars
    Europe hist.   940.27
    s.a. spec. countries
Napoli Italy   *area*–457 3
Napped fabrics *see* Woven felts

Nasopharynx	
diseases	
gen. wks.	616.212
neoplasms	616.992 21
tuberculosis	616.995 21
geriatrics	618.976 212
pediatrics	618.922 12
pub. health	614.592 12
statistics	312.321 2
deaths	312.262 12
other aspects see Nose	
diseases	
Nassau	
city Bahamas	*area*–729 6
County	
Florida	*area*–759 11
New York	*area*–747 245
Nasser admin. Egypt hist.	962.053
s.a. spec. events & subj.	
e.g. Commerce	
Nastic movements	
plants	
pathology	581.218 33
physiology	581.183 3
s.a. spec. plants	
Nasturtium family *see*	
Geraniales	
Natal South Africa	*area*–684
Natalia republic Natal hist.	968.4
s.a. spec. events & subj.	
e.g. Commerce	
Natantia	
culture	639.543
fishing	
commercial	639.543
sports	799.255 384 3
food *see* Seafoods	
zoology	595.384 3
other aspects see Decapoda	
(crustaceans)	
Natatoriums *see* Swimming pools	
Natchitoches Par. La.	*area*–763 65
Nathalia Vic.	*area*–945 4
National	
advertising	659.131 2
airs *see* National songs &	
hymns	
banks	
economics	332.122 3
other aspects see Banks	
(finance)	
Baptist Convention U.S.A.	286.133
misc. aspects see Baptist	
bibliographies	015
spec. subj.	016
borrowing & debt	
law	343.037
spec. jur.	343.3–.9
pub. admin.	351.726
spec. jur.	353–354
pub. finance	336.343 3

National (continued)	
control of ed.	
law	344.073
spec. jur.	344.3–.9
dances music *see* Dance music	
debt *see* National borrowing &	
debt	
finance	
economics	336.012
other aspects see Public	
finance	
flags *see* Flags	
governments *see* Central	
governments	
groups *see* Ethnic groups	
guards	
armed forces	355.351
s.a. spec. mil. branches	
hymns *see* National songs &	
hymns	
income	
macroeconomics	
distribution	339.2
measurement	339.32
wage theory	331.210 1
Liberation Front	
Vietnamese War hist.	959.704 332 2
libraries *see* Government	
libraries	
memorial cemeteries	
landscape design	718.8
Party South Africa	
pol. sci.	324.268 03
s.a. spec. subj. of concern	
e.g. Social problems	
penal institutions	
penology	365.32
other aspects see Penal	
institutions	
planning	
civic art	711.2
economics	338.9
soc. sci. *see* Planning soc.	
welfare	
product	
macroeconomics	339.3
psychology	155.89
reporter system	
U.S. law	348.734 2
reports of cases	
law	348.041
spec. jur.	348.3–.9
U.S.	
Federal	348.734 1
state & local	348.74–.79
spec. subj.	*law s.s.*–026 42
Republican Party U.S.	
pol. sci.	324.273 23
s.a. spec. subj. of concern	
e.g. Social problems	

Natural
  gases
    resources (continued)
      govt. control
        law 346.046 823 3
          spec. jur. 346.3–.9
        pub. admin. *see*
          Subsurface resources
          govt. control pub.
          admin.
      s.a. spec. uses e.g.
        Heating homes
  history 500
    & religion
      nat. rel. 215.74
    libraries 026.5
      misc. aspects see Special
        libraries
    museum bldgs. *see* Sciences
      museum bldgs.
    museums *see* Sciences
      museums
    s.a. spec. branches e.g.
      Mineralogy
  landscapes design 719
  latexes
    manufacturing
      soc. & econ. aspects *see*
        Secondary industries
    s.a. spec. prod.
  law
    moral theology
      Christianity 241.2
      other rel. see Moral
        theology
    philosophy 171.2
  leathers
    mf. tech. 675.2
    other aspects see Leathers
  perfumes
    chem. tech. 668.542
    other aspects see Perfumes
  phenomena
    lit. trmt.
      folk lit.
        sociology 398.36
        texts & lit. crit.
          living phenomena 398.24
          nonliving phenomena 398.26
      gen. wks.
        collections 808.803 6
        hist. & crit. 809.933 6
      spec. lits.
        collections .... *lit. sub.*–080 36
        hist. & crit. ...... *lit. sub.*–093 6
      s.a. spec. lit. forms
    stage trmt. 792.090 936
      s.a. spec. mediums e.g.
        Television; *also spec.*
        kinds of drama e.g.
        Tragedies (drama)

Natural (continued)
  products
    org. chem. 547.7
  radioactivity
    astrophysics 523.019 752
      s.a. spec. celestial
        bodies
    physics 539.752
      spec. states of matter 530.4
      s.a. spec. physical
        phenomena e.g. Heat
  religion 210
  resin-derived plastics
    chem. tech. 668.45
    org. chem. 547.843 25
    other aspects see Plastics
    s.a. spec. prod.
  resources
    conservation *see*
      Conservation
    economics 333.7
    govt. control
      law 346.046 7
        spec. jur. 346.3–.9
      pub. admin. 350.823 2
        central govts. 351.823 2
          spec. jur. 353–354
        local govts. 352.942 32
  rights
    pol. sci. 323.401
  rubber
    manufacturing
      soc. & econ. aspects *see*
        Secondary industries
      technology 678.62
    org. chem. 547.842 6
    s.a. spec. prod.
  scenes
    art representation 704.943
      painting 758
      s.a. other spec. art
        forms
  sciences 500
    s.a. spec. sci.
  selection
    evolution theory 575.016 2
  stones
    construction
      architecture 721.044 1
        s.a. spec. structural
          elements; also spec.
          types of bldgs.
      building 693.1
    materials
      building 691.2
      engineering 620.132
        foundations 624.153 32
        naval design 623.818 32
        structures 624.183 2
      s.a. other spec. uses
  theology 210

Natural (continued)
  s.a. other spec. subj.
Naturalism
  arts
    gen. wks.   709.034 3
      spec. places   709.1–.9
    painting   759.053
      spec. places   759.1–.9
    sculpture   732–735
    s.a. other spec. art forms
    lit. & stage qual. *see*
      Realism
  philosophy   146
    ethical systems   171.2
    applications   172–179
    indiv. phil.   180–190
    s.a. other spec. branches of
      phil.
  s.a. other spec. arts
Naturalization
  pol. sci.   323.623
  pub. admin.   350.817
    central govts.   351.817
    spec. jur.   353–354
    local govts.   352.941 7
Nature
  art representation *see*
    Natural scenes
  lit. & stage trmt. *see*
    Natural phenomena
  metaphysics   113
  misc. aspects see
    Philosophy
  rel. worship
    comp. rel.   291.212
    s.a. spec. rel.
  study
    elementary ed.   372.357
Natures of Jesus Christ
  Christian doctrines   232.8
Naturopathy
  therapeutics   615.535
  misc. aspects see
    Therapeutics
  s.a. spec. diseases
Nauru   *area*–968 5
Nautical
  almanacs   528
  engineering
    soc. & econ. aspects *see*
      Secondary industries
    technology   623.8
  engineers
    biog. & work   623.809 2
    s.a.   *pers.*–623 8
  facilities
    mil. transp. tech.   623.64
  hygiene   613.68

Nautical (continued)
  instruments
    shipbuilding
      soc. & econ. aspects *see*
        Secondary industries
    technology   623.863
      design   623.814 63
        spec. craft   623.812
  s.a. Marine
Nautiloidea
  culture   639.485 2
  paleozoology   564.52
  zoology   594.52
  other aspects see Mollusca
Nautilus *see* Nautiloidea
Navaho *see* Navajo
Navajo
  Co. Ariz.   *area*–791 35
  rugs
    textile arts   746.72
  other aspects see Na-Dene
Naval
  architecture
    soc. & econ. aspects *see*
      Secondary industries
    technology   623.81
  artillery
    mil. eng.
      soc. & econ. aspects *see*
        Secondary industries
      tech. & mf.   623.418
  bases
    history
      World War 1   940.453
      World War 2   940.545 3
      s.a. other spec. wars
  cookery   641.573
  design
    soc. & econ. aspects *see*
      Secondary industries
    technology   623.81
  forces
    mil. sci.   359
  gunnery
    mil. eng.   623.553
  hygiene   613.68
  medicine   616.980 24
  s.a. spec. diseases
  operations
    Spanish-American War   973.895
    U.S. Civil War   973.75
    U.S. Mexican War   973.625
    U.S. Revolutionary War   973.35
    U.S. War of 1812   973.525
    Vietnamese War   959.704 345
    World War 1   940.45
    World War 2   940.545
    s.a. other spec. wars

Naval (continued)
  personnel
    biog. & work   359.009 2
      s.a. hist. of spec.
        countries & spec. wars
    s.a.   *pers.*–359
    schools   373.243
      govt. supervision & support   379
    ships *see* Warships
  warfare
    law of war   341.63
    mil. sci.   359
    technology *see* Military
      engineering
    s.a. Military; *also* Armed
      forces
Navarra Spain   *area*–465 2
Navarro Co. Tex.   *area*–764 282
Naves
  Christian church arch.   726.592
Navies
  law   343.019
    spec. jur.   343.3–.9
Navigable waters
  land econ.   333.915
Navigation
  Acts
    U.S. hist.   973.311 2
  aids
    commerce
      inland waterways   386.855
        govt. control   350.876 855
          central govts.   351.876 855
            spec. jur.   353–354
          local govts.   352.916 855
      law *see* Ports
      inland-waterway transp.
        law
      maritime transp.   387.155
        govt. control   350.877 155
          central govts.   351.877 155
            spec. jur.   353–354
          local govts.   352.917 155
      law *see* Seaports law
      transp.
  hydraulic eng.
    technology   627.92
      s.a. spec. appls. e.g.
        Piloting seamanship
      other aspects see Liquids
        engineering
  aquatic sports   797.1
  instrumentation
    aircraft eng.   629.135 1
      s.a. spec. appls. e.g.
        Military engineering
      s.a. other spec. appls.
  law
    air transp.
      international   341.756 76

Navigation
  law
    air transp. (continued)
      municipal   343.097 6
      spec. jur.   343.3–.9
    maritime transp.
      international   341.756 76
      municipal   343.096 6
      spec. jur.   343.3–.9
  lights *see* Navigation
    instrumentation
  systems
    spacecraft *see* Flight
      operations systems
      spacecraft
    s.a. other spec. appls.
  technology   629.045
    aeronautics   629.132 51
    manned space flight   629.453
      s.a. spec. appls. e.g.
        Space warfare
      s.a. spec. flights e.g.
        Lunar flights
    seamanship   623.89
    other aspects see
      Transportation
      engineering
Navigators
  biog. & work   629.045 092
  s.a.   *pers.*–629
Navy
  beans *see* Kidney beans
  departments
    U.S. Govt.   353.7
    other jur. see Defense
      (military) pub. admin.
      departments
Nayarit Mex.   *area*–723 4
Nazarene Church *see*
      Miscellaneous Christian
      denominations
Nazareth
  Jesus's childhood
    Christian doctrines   232.927
Nazi parties
  pol. sci.   324.24–.29
  s.a. spec. subj. of concern
    e.g. Social problems
Nazism *see* Fascism
n-dimensional geometries *see*
      Vector geometry
Ndongo kingdom hist.   967.301
  s.a. spec. events & subj.
    e.g. Commerce
Ndwandwe kingdom hist.   968
  s.a. spec. events & subj.
    e.g. Commerce
Neagh Lough Northern Ireland
                                               area–416
Neales S. Aust.   *area*–942 38
Neamt Romania   *area*–498 1

Neglected children *see* Abused children

Negligence
  law   346.032
    spec. jur.   346.3–.9
Negotiable instruments
  law   346.096
    spec. jur.   346.3–.9
Negotiation
  internat. law
    gen. wks.   341.52
    of treaties *see* Treaties
  s.a. other spec. appls.
Negri Sembilan Malaysia   *area*–595 1
Negrito *see* Mon-Khmer
Negro
  Africa   *area*–67
  literature
    gen. wks.
      collections   808.898 96
      hist. & crit.   809.889 6
    spec. lits.
      collections   *lit. sub.*–080 896
      hist. & crit.   *lit. sub.*–098 96
    s.a. spec. lit. forms
  Methodist churches   287.8
    misc. aspects see Methodist
  people   *r.e.n.*–96
  songs
    U.S.
      gen. wks.   784.756
        recordings   789.912 475 6
      spirituals   783.67
        recordings   789.912 367
    other countries   784.769 6
      recordings   789.912 476 96
Negroes
  in U.S. Civil War
    history   973.741 5
  in World War 1
    history   940.403
  in World War 2
    history   940.540 3
  other aspects see Ethnic groups
  s.a.   *r.e.n.*–96
  s.a. African; *also* Negroids
Negroids   *r.e.n.*–036
Negros Philippines   *area*–599 5
Nehemiah
  Bible   222.8
  other aspects see Historical books (O.T.)
Nehemias *see* Nehemiah
Nehru admin. India hist.   954.042
  s.a. spec. events & subj.
    e.g. Commerce
Neighborhood centers
  adult ed.   374.28

Neighborhood centers (continued)
  recreation centers   790.068
  s.a. spec. kinds of recreation
Neighborhoods
  sociology   307.3
Neighbors
  psych. influences   155.925
  relationships with
    appl. psych.   158.25
    children   155.418
  s.a. psych. of other spec. groups; also spec. activities
Neisseriaceae *see* Eubacteriales
Nejd   *area*–538
Nelson
  and Hay Nat. Park W. Aust.   *area*–941 2
  city B.C.   *area*–711 44
  County
    Kentucky   *area*–769 495
    North Dakota   *area*–784 35
    Virginia   *area*–755 493
  provincial district N.Z.   *area*–931 53
  River Man.   *area*–712 71
  town Lancashire Eng.   *area*–427 645
Nemaha Co.
  Kansas   *area*–781 332
  Nebraska   *area*–782 278
Nemalionales *see* Rhodophyta
Nematocera *see* Orthorrhapha
Nematoda
  culture & hunting   639.758 2
  zoology   595.182
  other aspects see Worms
Nematode-caused diseases *see* Roundworm-caused diseases
Nematoidea *see* Nematoda
Nematomorpha
  culture & hunting   639.758 4
  zoology   595.184
  other aspects see Worms
Nemertea
  culture & hunting   639.752 4
  zoology   595.124
  other aspects see Worms
Nene River Northamptonshire Eng.   *area*–425 5
Nenets
  National Region RSFSR   *area*–472 3
  other aspects see Samoyedic
Neo-Babylonian
  Empire Mesopotamia hist.   935.04
  s.a. spec. events & subj.
    e.g. Arts
  other aspects see East Semitic

Neoplastic diseases *see*
    Neoplasms
Neoplasticism *see*
    Abstractionism
Neoplatonism
  philosophic system
    ancient — 186.4
    modern — 141.2
      indiv. phil. — 180–190
    s.a. spec. branches of
      phil. e.g. Metaphysics
Neoplatonists
  Christian polemics vs.
    apostolic times — 239.4
    later times — 239.9
  other rel. see Doctrinal
    theology
Neopsychoanalytic systems
  psychology — 150.195 7
  s.a. spec. subj. & branches
    of psych.
Neorealism
  philosophy — 149.2
    indiv. phil. — 180–190
  s.a. spec. branches of phil.
    e.g. Metaphysics
Neornithes
  paleozoology — 568
  other aspects see Aves
Neosho Co. Kan. — *area*–781 95
Nepal — *area*–549 6
Nepali
  language
    linguistics — 491.49
    literature — 891.49
    s.a. — *lang.*–914 9
  people — *r.e.n.*–914 95
  s.a. Nepal; *also other spec.*
    subj. e.g. Arts
Nepean River N.S.W. — *area*–944 6
Nepenthaceae *see*
    Aristolochiales
Nephelometric methods *see*
    Photometric analysis
Nephews — *pers.*–046
Nephritis
  gen. med. — 616.612
  geriatrics — 618.976 612
  pediatrics — 618.926 12
  pub. health — 614.596 12
  statistics — 312.361 2
  deaths — 312.266 12
  other aspects see Diseases
Nephrology
  med. sci. — 616.61
    geriatrics — 618.976 61
    pediatrics — 618.926 1
    vet. med. — 636.089 661
    s.a. spec. animals
  other aspects see Medical
    sciences

Nephrology (continued)
  s.a. Kidneys
Neptune (planet)
  astronomy
    gen. wks.
      description — 523.481
      theory — 521.548 1
    satellites
      description — 523.988 1
      theory — 521.681
  flights to
    manned — 629.455 81
    unmanned — 629.435 481
  regional subj. trmt. — *area*–992 8
  other aspects see Celestial
    bodies
Neptunium
  chemistry — 546.432
Nerve
  depressants
    addictive aspects *see*
      Addictive drugs
    pharmacodynamics — 615.782
    other aspects see Drugs
  fibers *see* Nerves
  tissue
    human anatomy & phys. — 611.018 8
    other aspects see Tissue
      biology
Nerves
  diseases
    surgery — 617.483
      anesthesiology — 617.967 483
    other aspects see Diseases
  human anatomy — 611.83
  physical anthropometry — 573.683
  physiology
    human — 612.81
    other aspects see Nervous
      functions
  tissue biology human — 611.018 983
  other aspects see Nervous
    system
  s.a. spec. kinds e.g. Cranial
    nerves
Nervous
  functions
    animal phys. — 591.188
    s.a. spec. animals,
      functions, systems,
      organs
  system
    anatomy
      human — 611.8
      zoology — 591.48
      s.a. spec. animals
    diseases
      gen. wks. — 616.8
        neoplasms — 616.992 8
        tuberculosis — 616.995 8
      geriatrics — 618.976 8

Nervous
  system
    diseases (continued)
      pediatrics   618.928
      perinatal   618.326 8
      pub. health   614.598
      statistics   312.38
        deaths   312.268
      surgery   617.48
        anesthesiology   617.967 48
      other aspects see
        Diseases
    drugs affecting
      pharmacodynamics   615.78
      other aspects see Drugs
    pathology
      med. sci. *see* Nervous
        system diseases
      zoology
        anatomical   591.228
        physiological   591.218 8
        s.a. spec. animals
    physical anthropometry   573.68
    physiology
      human   612.8
      other aspects see Nervous
        functions
    tissue biology human   611.018 98
Neshoba Co. Miss.   *area*–762 685
Nesosilicates
  mineralogy   549.62
Ness
  Co. Kan.   *area*–781 46
  Loch Scot.   *area*–411 75
    s.a. Loch Ness monster
Neston Cheshire Eng.   *area*–427 17
Nestorian
  church bldgs.
    architecture   726.581 8
    building   690.658 18
    other aspects see
        Religious-purpose
        bldgs.
  churches   281.8
    Christian life guides   248.481 8
    doctrines   230.18
      creeds   238.19
    general councils   262.518
    govt. & admin.   262.018
      parishes   254.018
    missions   266.18
    moral theology   241.041 8
    private prayers for   242.801 8
    pub. worship   264.018
    rel. associations
      adults   267.181 8
      men   267.241 8
      women   267.441 8
      young adults   267.621 8
    rel. instruction   268.818
    rel. law   262.981 8

Nestorian
  churches (continued)
    schools   377.818
    secondary training   207.121 8
    sermons   252.018
    theological seminaries   207.111 8
    s.a. other spec. aspects
Nests
  zoology   591.564
    s.a. spec. animals
Net
  nat. prod.
    macroeconomics   339.32
  worth
    personal finance   332.024 01
Netball
  equipment mf.   688.763 2
    soc. & econ. aspects *see*
        Secondary industries
  sports   796.32
    other aspects see Sports
Netherlandish
  languages
    linguistics   439.3
    literatures   839.3
    s.a.   *lang.*–393
  people   *r.e.n.*–393
  s.a. Low Countries; *also*
        other spec. subj. e.g.
        Arts
Netherlands   *area*–492
  s.a. Dutch
Nets
  fishing sports
    manufacturing   688.791 3
      soc. & econ. aspects *see*
        Secondary industries
    use   799.13
  hunting & shooting sports   799.202 82
    lit. & stage trmt. *see*
        Things
Nets (mathematics)   511.5
  combinatorial topology   514.223
  s.a. spec. appls. e.g.
        Engineering
Nets (surveying)   526.33
Netsukes
  dec. arts   736.68
Netted fabrics
  arts   746.046 64
    s.a. spec. proc. e.g.
        Weaving
  manufacturing
    soc. & econ. aspects *see*
        Secondary industries
    technology   677.664
  other aspects see Textiles
  s.a. spec. prod.

Netting
 textile arts 746.422 4
  s.a. spec. prod. e.g.
   Hangings
Nettle family *see* Urticales
Network
 affiliates
  broadcasting *see*
   Broadcasting stations
 analysis
  system analysis *see* Systems
   analysis
 wire telephony
  technology 621.385 1
  s.a. spec. appls. e.g.
   military use 623.733
  other aspects see
   Telephony wire
 programs
  radio performances 791.443
  television performances 791.453
Networks
 broadcast ind. *see*
  Broadcasting networks
 elect. power transmission *see*
  Circuits elect. power
  transmission
 electronic data proc. 001.644 04
  spec. subj. *s.s.*–028 544 04
Neubrandenburg Ger. *area*–431 7
Neuchâtel Switzerland *area*–494 3
Neuenburg Switzerland *area*–494 3
Neufchâtel cheeses
 dairy tech. 637.353
 other aspects see Cheeses
Neumann function 515.53
 s.a. spec. appls. e.g.
  Engineering
Neumes
 music theory 781.24
 s.a. spec. mediums
Neuquén Argentina *area*–827 2
Neuralgias
 gen. med. 616.87
 geriatrics 618.976 87
 pediatrics 618.928 7
 pub. health 614.598 7
 statistics 312.387
 other aspects see Diseases
Neurasthenia *see* Asthenic
 reactions
Neurilemma
 human anatomy & phys. 611.018 8
 other aspects see Tissue
  biology
Neuritis
 gen. med. 616.87
 geriatrics 618.976 87
 pediatrics 618.928 7
 pub. health 614.598 7
 statistics 312.387

Neuritis (continued)
 other aspects see Diseases
Neuroanatomy *see* Nervous system
  anatomy
Neurochemistry
 human phys. 612.804 2
 other aspects see Nervous
  system
Neuroendocrinology *see*
  Endocrinology
Neuroglia
 human anatomy & phys. 611.018 8
 other aspects see Tissue
  biology
Neurological
 diseases
  symptomatology 616.84
  vet. sci. 636.089 684
  s.a. spec. animals
 language disorders *see*
  Aphasias
 nursing 610.736 8
Neurology
 med. sci. 616.8
  geriatrics 618.976 8
  pediatrics 618.928
  vet. med. 636.089 68
  s.a. spec. animals
 other aspects see Medical
  sciences
 s.a. Nervous system
Neuromuscular
 diseases *see* Muscles diseases
Neurons
 human anatomy & phys. 611.018 8
 other aspects see Tissue
  biology
Neurophysiology
 human 612.8
 other aspects see Nervous
  system
Neuroptera
 culture 638.574 7
 paleozoology 565.74
 zoology 595.747
 other aspects see Insecta
Neuropteris
 paleobotany 561.597
Neuroses
 gen. med. 616.852
 geriatrics 618.976 852
 pediatrics 618.928 52
 psychology 157.3
 pub. health 614.58
 statistics 312.385 2
 other aspects see Mental
  illness
Neurosurgery
 med. sci. 617.48
  vet. med. 636.089 748
  s.a. spec. animals

Neurosyphilis *see* General
    paresis
Neuse River N.C.   *area*–756 19
Neuston   574.92
  animal   592
  plant *see* Phytoneuston
Neutral
  countries
    history
      World War 1   940.335
      World War 2   940.533 5
      s.a. spec. aspects e.g.
        Diplomatic history;
        also other spec. wars
    law of war   341.64
    regional subj. trmt.   *area*–171 83
  nationals
    law of war   341.67
  salts *see* Simple salts
Neutralist blocs
  regional subj. trmt.   *area*–171 6
  s.a. spec. countries
Neutrality
  law of war   341.64
Neutralization
  thermochemistry
    physical chem.   541.362
    applied   660.296 2
    organic   547.136 2
    s.a. spec. elements,
      cpds., prod.
  volumetric anal.
    quan. anal. chem.   545.22
    organic   547.352 2
    s.a. spec. elements &
      cpds.
Neutralized states
  internat. law   341.29
Neutrinos
  astrophysics
    gen. wks.   523.019 721 5
    acceleration   523.019 737 5
    s.a. spec. celestial bodies
  physics
    gen. wks.   539.721 5
    acceleration   539.737 5
    spec. states of matter   530.4
    s.a. spec. physical
      phenomena e.g. Heat
Neutron
  diffraction
    crystallography   548.83
    s.a. spec. substances
  radiations *see* Particle
    radiations
  stars *see* Eruptive variable
    stars
Neutrons
  astrophysics
    gen. wks.   523.019 721 3
    acceleration   523.019 737 3

Neutrons
  astrophysics (continued)
    s.a. spec. celestial bodies
  physics
    gen. wks.   539.721 3
    acceleration   539.737 3
    spec. states of matter   530.4
    s.a. spec. physical
      phenomena e.g. Heat
Nevada
  County
    Arkansas   *area*–767 52
    California   *area*–794 37
  state   *area*–793
Nevi *see* Pigmentary changes
  skin
Nevis isl.   *area*–729 73
Nevsehir Turkey   *area*–564
Nevskiaceae *see*
    Caulobacteriales
New
  Abbey Dumfries & Galloway
    Scot.   *area*–414 86
  Academy philosophy   186.2
  American version
    Bible   220.520 5
    s.a. spec. parts of Bible
  Britain   *area*–936
  Brunswick
    city N.J.   *area*–749 42
    province   *area*–715
  Caledonia   *area*–932
    colony B.C. hist.   971.102
    s.a. spec. subj. & events
      e.g. Commerce
    island   *area*–932
  Castile Spain   *area*–464
  Castle Co. Del.   *area*–751 1
  Delhi India   *area*–545 6
  Democratic Party Canada
    pol. sci.   324.271 07
    s.a. spec. subj. of concern
      e.g. Social problems
  England
    National Park N.S.W.   *area*–944 4
    Range N.S.W.   *area*–944 4
    U.S.A.   *area*–74
  English Bible   220.520 6
    s.a. spec. parts of Bible
  expenditures
    estimates
      budgeting
        pub. admin.   350.722 253 2
        central govts.   351.722 253 2
        spec. jur.   353–354
        local govts.   352.122 532
  Forest Hampshire Eng.   *area*–422 75
  formations
    physical geol.   551.305
    glacial action   551.315
    water action   551.355

New
  formations
    physical geol. (continued)
      wind action   551.375
      s.a. other spec. agents
  Galloway Dumfries & Galloway
      Scot.   *area*–414 92
  Georgia
    Solomon Isls.   *area*–935
  Granada
    history   986.105
    s.a.   *area*–861
  Guinea   *area*–95
  Hampshire   *area*–742
  Hanover Co. N.C.   *area*–756 27
  Haven
    city Conn.   *area*–746 8
    Co. Conn.   *area*–746 7
  Hebrides   *area*–934
  Ireland   *area*–936
  Jersey   *area*–749
  Jerusalem Church *see* Church
      of the New Jerusalem
  Jerusalemites
    biog. & work   289.409 2
    s.a.   *pers.*–284
  Kent Co. Va.   *area*–755 43
  Kingdom Egypt hist.   932.014
    s.a. spec. events & subj.
      e.g. Commerce
  Land RSFSR   *area*–986
  left
    pol. ideology   320.53
    soc. theology *see*
        Political ideologies
        soc. theology
  London Co. Conn.   *area*–746 5
  Madrid Co. Mo.   *area*–778 985
  Mexico   *area*–789
  Mills Derbyshire Eng.   *area*–425 11
  music
    musical style
      gen. wks.   780.904
      spec. places   780.91–.99
    s.a. spec. mediums
  nations
    pol. sci.   320.17
    results of wars
      World War 1   940.314 25
      World War 2   940.531 4
    s.a. other spec. wars
    s.a. spec. nations
  Norfolk Tas.   *area*–946 2
  Norse language
    linguistics   439.83
    literature   839.83
    s.a.   *lang.*–398 3
  Orleans
    Battle
      War of 1812 hist.   973.523 9
    Par. La.   *area*–763 35

New (continued)
  product development
    prod. management   658.575
      spec. subj.   *s.s.*–068 5
  Providence Isl. Bahamas   *area*–729 6
  Quay Dyfed Wales   *area*–429 61
  Quebec Ter.   *area*–714 17
  River
    North Carolina   *area*–756 23
    West Virginia   *area*–754 7
  Romney Kent Eng.   *area*–422 395
  Siberian Isls. RSFSR   *area*–988
  South Wales   *area*–944
  Southwest U.S.   *area*–79
  states *see* New nations
  Stone Age
    archeology   930.14
  Testament
    Bible   225
      pseudepigrapha   229.92–.95
    Greek language
      linguistics   487.4
      s.a.   *lang.*–87
    liturgy   264.3–.4
      spec. denominations   264.01–.09
  Thought   289.98
    misc. aspects see
        Miscellaneous Christian
        denominations
  Valley Egypt   *area*–622
  Westminister B.C.   *area*–711 33
  world
    vultures *see* Cathartidae
  Year
    Jewish *see* Rosh Hashanah
    soc. customs   394.268 3
    other aspects see Holidays
  York
    Bay
      oceanography   551.461 46
      regional subj. trmt.   *area*–164 78–164 79
      other aspects see
          Atlantic Ocean
    city   *area*–747 1
    county   *area*–747 1
    state   *area*–747
  Zealand
    country   *area*–931
    literature   820
    Pacific seawaters
      oceanography   551.465 78–.465 79
      regional subj. trmt. *area*–164 78–164 79
      other aspects see Pacific
          Ocean
    people   *r.e.n.*–23
    s.a. other spec. subj.
  s.a. other spec. subj.
Newark
  New Jersey   *area*–749 32
  Nottinghamshire Eng.   *area*–425 24
Newaygo Co. Mich.   *area*–774 58

Nicaraguan (continued)
  s.a. other spec. subj.
Niccolite
  mineralogy   549.32
Nice France   *area*–449 41
Nicene Creed
  Christian doctrines   238.142
  private prayers   242.723
Niches
  architectural
    construction   721.48
    design & decoration   729.34
  building   690.148
  s.a. spec. kinds of bldgs.
Nichiren Shoshu
  Buddhism   294.392 8
Nicholas
  County
    Kentucky   *area*–769 417
    West Virginia   *area*–754 69
  reign Russia hist.
    1   947.073
    2   947.08
    s.a. spec. events & subj.
      e.g. Commerce
Nickel
  arts
    decorative   739.56
    other aspects see Metals
      arts
  chemistry
    inorganic   546.625
    organic   547.056 25
    s.a. spec. groupings e.g.
      Aliphatic compounds
    technology   661.062 5
      organic   661.895
    soc. & econ. aspects *see*
      Secondary industries
    s.a. spec. prod.
  construction
    architecture   721.044 773 3
    s.a. spec. kinds of
      bldgs.
    building   693.773 32
  materials
    building   691.873 32
    engineering   620.188
      foundations   624.153 88
      naval design   623.818 28
      shipbuilding   623.820 7
      structures   624.182 8
      s.a. other spec. uses
  metallography   669.957 332
  metallurgy   669.733 2
    physical & chem.   669.967 332
    soc. & econ. aspects *see*
      Secondary industries
  mineral aspects
    econ. geol.   553.48

Nickel
  mineral aspects (continued)
    mining
      technology   622.348
      prospecting   622.184 8
    s.a. spec. minerals
  pharmacology   615.262 5
    misc. aspects see
      Pharmacology
  products
    arts *see* Nickel arts
    mf. tech.   673.733 2
    other aspects see
      Nonferrous metals
      products
  toxicology   615.925 625
    misc. aspects see
      Toxicology
  other aspects see Metal;
    also Metals
  s.a. spec. uses
Nickerie Surinam   *area*–883 1
Nicknacks *see* Ornaments arts
Nicknames *see* Names
Nicobar Isls. India   *area*–548 8
Nicola River B.C.   *area*–711 41
Nicolet Co. Que.   *area*–714 55
Nicollet Co. Minn.   *area*–776 32
Nicotiana tabacum *see* Tobacco
Nicotine *see* Alkaloids
Nidderdale North Yorkshire Eng.
     area–428 42
Nidulariales *see* Lycoperdales
Nidwalden Switzerland   *area*–494 7
Nieces   *pers.*–046
Niedersachsen Ger.   *area*–435 9
Nielloing
  arts *see* Decorative treatment
    sculpture
Nièvre France   *area*–445 6
Nigde Turkey   *area*–564
Niger
  country   *area*–662 6
    people   *r.e.n.*–966 26
  River   *area*–662
  state Nigeria   *area*–669 5
  s.a. other spec. subj. e.g.
    Arts
Niger-Congo languages
  linguistics   496.3
  literatures   896.3
  s.a.   *lang.*–963
Nigeria   *area*–669
Nigerian
  languages   409.669
    s.a. spec. langs. e.g. Ibo
  people   *r.e.n.*–966 9
  s.a. Nigeria; *also other*
    spec. subj. e.g. Arts
Nigg Grampian Scot.   *area*–412 35

Night
  flying aircraft   629.132 521 4
    military eng.   623.746
    spec. civilian aircraft
        629.132 522–.132 528
  football
    sports   796.332 6
  photography tech.   778.719
  schools
    adult ed.   374.8
  skies
    atmospheric optical phenomena
      meteorology   551.566
  time *see* Nighttime
  work
    labor econ.   331.257 4
    s.a. spec. classes of
        labor e.g. Women
    labor law *see* Labor law
Nightcaps *see* Nightclothes
Nightclothes
  comm. mf.
    soc. & econ. aspects *see*
      Secondary industries
    technology   687.165
  domestic mf.   646.475
  soc. customs   391.42
  other aspects see Clothing
Nightclub presentations
  stage performance   792.7
Nightgowns *see* Nightclothes
Nightingales *see* Turdidae
Nightmares *see* Dreams
Nightshade family *see* Solanales
Nightshirts *see* Nightclothes
Nighttime
  influence on crime   364.22
  lit. & stage trmt. *see* Times
  plants blooming in
    floriculture   635.953
    s.a. spec. plants
Nihilism
  philosophy   149.8
    indiv. phil.   180–190
    s.a. spec. branches of phil.
      e.g. Metaphysics
Niigata Japan   *area*–521 5
Niihau Isl. Hawaii   *area*–969 42
Nikolayev Ukraine   *area*–477 17
Nile
  Delta Egypt   *area*–621
  River   *area*–62
Nilotic *see* Chari-Nile
Nilpotent algebras & groups   512.55
  s.a. spec. appls. e.g.
      Engineering
Nim
  equip. mf.   688.742
    soc. & econ. aspects *see*
      Secondary industries
  recreation   794.2

Nimbarka philosophy   181.484 3
Nimrod Res. Ark.   *area*–767 38
Ninepins *see* Bowling (game)
Nineteenth century
  history   909.81
    appls. to spec. subj.   *s.s.*–090 34
  s.a. spec. countries
Ningsia-Hui Autonomous Region
    China   *area*–517 5
Ninth century
  history   909.1
    appls. to spec. subj.   *s.s.*–090 21
  s.a. spec. countries
Niobium
  chemistry
    inorganic   546.524
    organic   547.055 24
    s.a. spec. groupings e.g.
      Aliphatic compounds
  technology   661.052 4
    organic   661.895
    soc. & econ. aspects *see*
      Secondary industries
    s.a. spec. prod.
  pharmacology   615.252 4
    misc. aspects see
      Pharmacology
  toxicology   615.925 524
    misc. aspects see
      Toxicology
  other aspects see Minor
    metals
Niobrara
  Co. Wyo.   *area*–787 15
  River Neb.   *area*–782 7
Nipigon Lake Ont.   *area*–713 12
Nipissing
  District Ont.   *area*–713 147
  Lake Ont.   *area*–713 147
Nipples
  latex *see* Dipped latex
    products
Nirvana
  Buddhism   294.342 3
Nishnabotna River Ia.   *area*–777 7
Niter
  fertilizer *see* Nitrate
    fertilizers
  mineralogy   549.732
Nith River Dumfries & Galloway
    Scot.   *area*–414 86
Nithsdale Dumfries & Galloway
    Scot.   *area*–414 86
Niton *see* Radon
Nitrate fertilizers   553.64
  econ. geol.   553.64
  mining
    technology   622.364
    prospecting   622.186 4

Nitrate fertilizers (continued)
  production
    soc. & econ. aspects *see*
      Secondary industries
    technology   668.624 2
    use agric.   631.842
    s.a. spec. crops; also spec.
      types of culture e.g.
      Floriculture
    other aspects see
      Fertilizers
Nitrates
  chem. aspects *see* Nitrogen
    salts
  fertilizers *see* Nitrate
    fertilizers
  mineralogy   549.732
Nitration
  chem. eng.   660.284 46
  org. chem.   547.26
  s.a. spec. elements, cpds.,
    prod.
Nitric acid
  chem. tech.   661.24
    soc. & econ. aspects *see*
      Secondary industries
  s.a. spec. prod.
Nitrides *see* Nitrogen salts
Nitrifying
  bacteria
    fertilizers   631.847
    s.a. spec. crops; also
      spec. types of culture
      e.g. Floriculture
  crops
    fertilizers   631.847
    s.a. spec. crops; also
      spec. types of culture
      e.g. Floriculture
Nitriles
  org. chem.   547.044
    s.a. spec. groupings e.g.
      Aliphatic compounds
  synthetic drugs   615.314 4
    misc. aspects see
      Pharmacology
  synthetic poisons   615.951 44
    misc. aspects see
      Toxicology
  other aspects see Nitrogen
    compounds
  s.a. spec. prod.; also other
    spec. appls.
Nitrites *see* Nitrogen salts
Nitro
  compounds
    org. chem.   547.041
    s.a. spec. groupings e.g.
      Aliphatic compounds

Nitro
  compounds (continued)
    synthetic drugs   615.314 1
      misc. aspects see
        Pharmacology
    synthetic poisons   615.951 41
      misc. aspects see
        Toxicology
    other aspects see Nitrogen
      compounds
  dyes
    manufacturing
      chem. tech.   667.252
      soc. & econ. aspects *see*
        Secondary industries
    org. chem.   547.862
Nitrobacteriaceae *see*
  Eubacteriales
Nitrocellulose
  explosives *see* Propellant
    explosives
  glues
    chem. tech.   668.33
    other aspects see Adhesives
  textiles
    arts   746.044 61
    s.a. spec. proc. e.g.
      Weaving
    dyeing   667.346 1
    manufacturing
      soc. & econ. aspects *see*
        Secondary industries
      technology   677.461
        special-process fabrics   677.6
    org. chem.   547.856 1
    other aspects see Textiles
    s.a. spec. prod.
Nitrogen
  chemistry
    inorganic   546.711
    organic   547.04
    s.a. spec. groupings e.g.
      Aliphatic compounds
    technology   661.071 1
      soc. & econ. aspects *see*
        Secondary industries
    s.a. spec. prod.
  compounds
    chem. tech.   661.894
    synthetic drugs   615.314
      misc. aspects see
        Pharmacology
    synthetic poisons   615.951 4
      misc. aspects see
        Toxicology
    other aspects see Organic
      chemicals
    s.a. Nitrogen chemistry
  extraction from air
    chem. tech.   665.824

Nitrogen
extraction from air (continued)
  soc. & econ. aspects *see*
    Secondary industries
fertilizers
  production
    soc. & econ. aspects *see*
      Secondary industries
    technology   668.624
    use agric.   631.84
    s.a. spec. crops; also
      spec. types of culture
      e.g. Floriculture
  mineral aspects   553.93
    econ. geol.   553.93
  mining
    technology   622.393
    prospecting   622.189 3
  s.a. spec. uses; also spec.
    minerals
salts
  chem. tech.   661.65
  soc. & econ. aspects *see*
    Secondary industries
  s.a. spec. prod.
other aspects see Nonmetallic
  elements
Nitroglycerin *see* High
  explosives
Nitroguanidine *see* High
  explosives
Nitrosation
  chem. eng.   660.284 46
  org. chem.   547.26
  s.a. spec. elements, cpds.,
    prod.
Nitroso
  compounds
    org. chem.   547.041
    s.a. spec. groupings e.g.
      Aliphatic compounds
    synthetic drugs   615.314 1
    misc. aspects see
      Pharmacology
    synthetic poisons   615.951 41
    misc. aspects see
      Toxicology
    other aspects see Nitrogen
      compounds
  dyes
    manufacturing
      chem. tech.   667.252
      soc. & econ. aspects *see*
        Secondary industries
    org. chem.   547.862
Nivation
  physical geol.   551.383
Nivernais France   *area*-445 6
Nixon
  Richard M. admin.
    U.S. hist.   973.924

Nixon
  Richard M. admin. (continued)
    s.a. spec. events & subj.
      e.g. Indochinese War
      1961-75
No theater   792.095 2
Nobatia
  kingdom hist.   962.402
  s.a. spec. events & subj.
    e.g. Commerce
Nobelium
  chemistry   546.449
Nobility (social class)
  customs   390.23
  dress   391.023
  homes   392.360 23
  other aspects see Upper
    classes
Noble
  County
    Indiana   *area*-772 76
    Ohio   *area*-771 95
    Oklahoma   *area*-766 27
  gases *see* Rare gases
  s.a. Nobility (social class)
Nobles Co. Minn.   *area*-776 24
Noblus Jordan   *area*-569 53
Nocturnes
  piano music *see* Romantic
    music piano
Nodaway Co. Mo.   *area*-778 124
Nofretete reign Egypt hist.   932.014
  s.a. spec. events & subj.
    e.g. Commerce
Nograd Hungary   *area*-439 8
Noise
  aircraft
    aeronautical aerodynamics   629.132 3
    s.a. spec. appls. e.g.
      Flying
  control
    law   344.046 38
      spec. jur.   344.3-.9
    plant management   658.28
      spec. subj.   *s.s.*-068 2
    pub. admin.   350.772
      central govts.   351.772
        spec. jur.   353-354
      local govts.   352.6
  signals *see*
    Interference-signals
  soc. aspects   363.74
  sound
    engineering   620.23
    s.a. spec. appls. e.g.
      Pest control
    physics   534.355
      spec. states of matter   530.4
  work environment *see* Physical
    conditions
Nolan Co. Tex.   *area*-764 728

Nolanaceae *see* Solanales
Nomads *see* Minority groups
Nome election district Alaska
                area–798 6
Nomenclature   *s.s.*–014
Nominalism
  philosophy   149.1
    indiv. phil.   180–190
    s.a. spec. branches of phil.
        e.g. Metaphysics
Nominating conventions & meetings
  pol. sci.   324.56
  delegate selection *see*
        Nomination procedures
  finance *see* Party finance
  spec. parties   324.24–.29
Nomination procedures
  pol. sci.   324.5
  spec. parties   324.24–.29
Nomograms
  statistical method   001.422 6
  spec. subj. *see* Statistical
        method spec. subj.
Nomography
  mathematics *see* Graphs
    mathematics
Nonaffiliated broadcasting
    stations *see*
        Broadcasting stations
Nonalcoholic beverages   641.26
  comm. proc.   663.6
  home econ.
    cookery   641.62
    preparation   641.875
  other aspects see Beverages
Nonaqueous solutions
  physical chem.   541.342 3
    applied   660.294 23
    organic   547.134 23
    s.a. spec. elements, cpds.,
        prod.
Nonassociative algebras 512.24
  s.a. spec. appls. e.g.
        Engineering
Nonbeing
  metaphysics   111.5
Nonbook materials
  library trmt. *see* Special
        materials library trmt.
  s.a. Audiovisual materials;
    also
        Microreproductions
Noncellulosics
  textiles
    arts   746.044 7
    s.a. spec. proc. e.g.
        Weaving
    dyeing   667.347
    manufacturing
      soc. & econ. aspects *see*
        Secondary industries

Noncellulosics
  textiles
    manufacturing (continued)
      technology   677.47
        special-process fabrics 677.6
      org. chem.   547.857
    other aspects see Textiles
    s.a. spec. prod.
Noncombat
  services
    armed forces   355.34
    s.a. spec. mil. branches
Noncombatants
  history
    World War 1 hist.   940.316 1
    World War 2 hist.   940.531 61
    s.a. other spec. wars
  law of war   341.67
Noncommercial
  broadcasting stations *see*
        Broadcasting stations
  networks
    radio & television *see*
        Broadcasting networks
  s.a. other spec. subj.
Noncommissioned officers
  armed forces   355.338
  s.a. spec. mil. branches
Noncommunicable diseases 616.98
  pub. health   614.59
  s.a. spec. diseases
Nondestructive testing
  eng. materials   620.112 7
  s.a. spec. materials & spec.
    uses
Nondomesticated animals
  extractive industries   639
Nondominant groups *see* Minority
    groups
None *see* Office hours
Nonequation functions
  algebra   512.96
  s.a. spec. appls. e.g.
        Engineering
Nonets
  by instrument *see spec.*
      instruments
  chamber music
    recordings   789.912 57
    scores & parts   785.79
    treatises   785.709
  songs
    recordings   789.912
    scores & parts   784.85
      sacred   783.675 7
      secular   784.306 7
Non-Euclidean geometries 516.9
  s.a. spec. appls. e.g.
        Engineering

Nonobjective arts (continued)
  painting | 759.065 6
    spec. places | 759.1–.9
  sculpture | 735.230 456
    spec. places | 730.9
  s.a. other spec. art forms
Nonparametric methods
  statistical math. | 519.5
  s.a. spec. appls. e.g.
    Engineering
Nonphonetic
  shorthand systems
    Eng. lang. | 653.422
    other langs. | 653.43–.49
  s.a. other spec. subj.
Nonpoint base geometries | 516.18
  Euclidean | 516.218
  s.a. other spec. geometries;
    also spec. appls. e.g.
    Engineering
Nonpolar compounds
  chemistry | 547
Nonprofessional
  library positions | 023.3
  s.a. other spec. subj.
Nonprofit
  associations *see* Nonprofit
    organizations
  corporations
    law | 346.064
      misc. aspects see
      Organizations law
  organizations
    accounting | 657.98
    law | 346.064
      misc. aspects see
      Organizations law
    libraries | 027.68
      administration | 025.197 68
      buildings
        architecture | 727.826 8
        functional planning | 022.316 8
      catalogs *see* Library
        catalogs
      reference services | 025.527 768
      selection for | 035.218 768
      use studies | 025.587 68
      user orientation | 025.567 68
      s.a. other spec.
        activities e.g.
        Cataloging
    management | 658.048
      initiation | 658.114 8
    pub. relations | 659.288
    soc. services | 361.763
      spec. problems & groups | 362–363
      other aspects see Welfare
        services
    other aspects see
      Organizations

Nonrevenue
  rolling stock *see* Work cars
  s.a. other spec. subj.
Nonrigid
  dirigibles
    aeronautical eng.
      gen. tech. & mf. | 629.133 27
      components &
        techniques | 629.134
      models | 629.133 127
      operation | 629.132 522
    military | 623.743 7
      soc. & econ. aspects *see*
        Secondary industries
      s.a. other spec. appls.
    commerce | 387.732 7
  materials
    arch. construction | 721.044 98
      s.a. spec. kinds of
        bldgs.
    bldg. construction | 693.98
    s.a. other spec. uses
    s.a. other spec. subj.
Nonselfgoverning territories
  internat. law | 341.28
  regional subj. trmt. | *area*–171 9
Nonsporting dogs
  animal husbandry | 636.72
  other aspects see Dogs
Nonstriated muscle tissues
  human anatomy & phys. | 611.018 6
  other aspects see Tissue
    biology
Nontax revenues
  pub. finance | 336.1
  law | 343.036
    spec. jur. | 343.3–.9
  pub. admin. | 350.726
    central govts. | 351.726
    spec. jur. | 353–354
    local govts. | 352.14
Nontechnical
  graphic representations
    tech. drawing *see*
      Production illustration
        tech. drawing
  s.a. other spec. subj.
Nontheistic religions | 291.14
Non-Trinitarian concepts
  Christianity
    God | 231.044
    Jesus | 232.9
Nonverbal
  aptitude tests *see* Aptitude
    tests
  communication | 001.56
    psychology *see*
      Communication
      psychology
    sociology | 302.22

Notations
  music (continued)
    s.a. spec. mediums
    other spec. subj.   *s.s.*–014
Notes
  Christian church   262.72
  payable
    accounting trmt.   657.74
      s.a. spec. kinds of
        enterprise e.g.
          Insurance accounting
Nothingness
  lit. & stage trmt. *see*
    Philosophy
  metaphysics   111.5
Notice
  legal procedure *see* Pretrial
    procedure
Notidanoidea *see* Selachii
Notions
  clothing
    comm. mf.
      soc. & econ. aspects *see*
        Secondary industries
      technology   687.8
    domestic mf.   646.19
Notodelphyoida *see* Copepoda
Notostigmata
  zoology   595.42
  other aspects see Arachnida
Notostraca *see* Branchiopoda
Notoungulata
  paleozoology   569.75
Notre Dame Mts.   *area*–714 7
Nottingham Eng.   *area*–425 27
Nottinghamshire Eng.   *area*–425 2
Nottoway Co. Va.   *area*–755 637
Nouns *see* Words
Nourishment
  glaciers
    physical geol.   551.312
  s.a. Nutrition
Nouvelle-Québec   *area*–714 17
Nova Scotia   *area*–716
Novae *see* Eruptive variable
  stars
Novara Italy   *area*–451 6
Novaya Zemlya RSFSR   *area*–986
Novelets *see* Fiction
Novelists
  biog. & work   809.33
  s.a. spec. lits.
  other aspects see Authors
  s.a.   *pers.*–83
Novellas *see* Fiction
Novels *see* Fiction
Novelties
  manufacturing
    soc. & econ. aspects *see*
      Secondary industries
    technology   688.726

Novenas
  pub. worship   264.7
  spec. denominations   264.01–.09
Novgorod RSFSR   *area*–474 5
Novices   *pers.*–090 9
  cookery
    home econ.   641.512
    spec. subj.   *s.s.*–073
Novitiate
  monastic life
    Christianity
      men   248.894 25
      women   248.894 35
    other rel. see Personal
      religion
Novo Estado Portugal hist.   946.904 2–.904 3
  s.a. spec. events & subj.
    e.g. Commerce
Novosibirsk RSFSR   *area*–573
Nowata Co. Okla.   *area*–766 97
Nowra N.S.W.   *area*–944 7
Nowy Sacz Poland   *area*–438 6
Noxubee Co. Miss.   *area*–762 955
Nozzles
  liquid flow
    mechanics
      engineering *see* Dynamics
      physics   532.52
Nuba kingdom hist.   962.402
  s.a. spec. events & subj.
    e.g. Commerce
Nubia
  ancient region   *area*–397 8
Nubian
  Desert Sudan   *area*–625
  s.a. Chari-Nile
Ñuble Chile   *area*–833 8
Nuciculture *see* Nuts
Nuckolls Co. Neb.   *area*–782 372
Nuclear
  accidents
    disasters
      soc. action   363.349 7
      misc. aspects see
        Disasters soc. action
  gen. hist.
    collections   904.7
    s.a. hist. of spec.
      places
  insurance   368.7
    misc. aspects see
      Insurance
  astrophysics   523.019 7
    s.a. spec. celestial bodies
  bombs *see* Nuclear weapons
  chemistry *see* Radiochemistry
  energy
    engineering *see* Nuclear
      engineering
    physics *see* Nuclear physics

Nuclear (continued)
structure
  astrophysics — 523.019 74
    s.a. spec. celestial
      bodies
  physics — 539.74
    spec. states of matter — 530.4
    s.a. spec. physical
      phenomena e.g. Heat
tactical rockets
  mil. eng.
    soc. & econ. aspects *see*
      Secondary industries
    tech. & mf. — 623.454 3
warfare
  civil defense *see* Civil
    defense
  ethics *see* War ethics
  law of war — 341.63
  mil. eng.
    defense — 623.3
    offense *see* Nuclear
      weapons
  mil. sci. — 355.021 7
    strategy — 355.430 7
    s.a. spec. mil branches
weapons
  control internat. law — 341.734
  mil. eng.
    soc. & econ. aspects *see*
      Secondary industries
    tech. & mf. — 623.451 19
    s.a. spec. purposes
      e.g. Armor-piercing
      ammunition
  mil. sci. — 355.825 119
    s.a. spec. mil. branches
Nuclear-powered
automobiles
  commerce — 388.34
  engineering
    gen. tech. & mf. — 629.229 6
    maintenance — 629.287 96
    models — 629.221 96
    operation — 629.284 96
    s.a. other spec.,
      aspects e.g. Brakes
  soc. & econ. aspects *see*
    Secondary industries
  other aspects see Land
    vehicles
generation
  electrodynamic eng.
    soc. & econ. aspects *see*
      Secondary industries
    technology — 621.312 5
    s.a. spec. appls. e.g.
      Electric railroads
    other aspects see
      Electrodynamics

Nuclear-powered (continued)
submarines
  engineering — 623.825 74
    design — 623.812 574
    models — 623.820 157 4
  naval forces
    materiel — 359.83
    organization — 359.325 74
  seamanship — 623.882 574
  other aspects see Vessels
    (nautical)
Nucleation
moisture
  meteorology *see*
    Condensation
    meteorology
Nuclei
astrophysics — 523.019 723
  s.a. spec. celestial bodies
physics — 539.723
  spec. states of matter — 530.4
  s.a. spec. physical
    phenomena e.g. Heat
Nucleic acids
cytology — 574.873 28
  animals — 591.873 28
  plants — 581.873 28
  s.a. spec. organisms
org. chem. — 547.79
  s.a. spec. cpds.
Nucleolus *see* Nucleus cells
  cytology
Nucleons
astrophysics
  gen. wks. — 523.019 721 2
  acceleration — 523.019 737 2
  s.a. spec. celestial bodies
physics
  gen. wks. — 539.721 2
  acceleration — 539.737 2
  spec. states of matter — 530.4
  s.a. spec. physical
    phenomena e.g. Heat
Nucleoproteins
cytology *see* Nucleic acids
  cytology
org. chem. — 547.754
  other aspects see Proteins
Nucleosides *see* Nucleic acids
Nucleotides *see* Nucleic acids
Nucleus
cells
  cytology — 574.873 2
  animals — 591.873 2
  plants — 581.873 2
  s.a. spec. organisms
Nuclide structure *see* Nuclear
  structure
Nuda *see* Ctenophorae

Nude figures
art representation 704.942 1
  drawing tech. 743.4
  painting 757.22
  s.a. other spec. art forms
Nudibranchia *see* Acoela
  (mollusks)
Nudism
  hygiene 613.194
Nueces
  Co. Tex. *area*–764 113
  River Tex. *area*–764 1
Nueva
  Asunción Paraguay *area*–892 25
  Ecija Philippines *area*–599 1
  Esparta Venezuela *area*–875 4
  Segovia Nicaragua *area*–728 521
  Vizcaya Philippines *area*–599 1
Nuevo León Mex. *area*–721 3
Nuisance
  law 346.036
    spec. jur. 346.3–.9
Nullabor Plain S. Aust. *area*–942 38
Nullification movement
  U.S. hist. 973.561
Number
  metaphysics 119
  theoretic functions 512.73
    s.a. spec. appls. e.g.
      Engineering
  theory 512.7
    s.a. spec. appls. e.g.
      Engineering
Numbers
  coordination chem. *see*
    Coordination chemistry
  fortunetelling 133.335 4
Numbers (scriptures)
  Bible 222.14
  other aspects see Historical
    books (O.T.)
Numeration systems
  arithmetic 513.5
    s.a. spec. appls. e.g.
      Computers
Numerical
  analysis
    applied 519.4
    theoretical 511
    s.a. spec. math. branches;
     also spec. appls. e.g.
      Engineering
  computations *see* Computations
  control
    machine tools
      soc. & econ. aspects *see*
        Secondary industries
      tech. & mf. 621.902 3
      s.a. spec. appls. e.g.
        Agricultural equipment
        mf. tech.

Numerical (continued)
  data
    statistical math. 519.5
    s.a. spec. appls. e.g.
      Economics
  differentiation 515.623
    s.a. spec. appls. e.g.
      Engineering
  forecasting weather 551.634
    spec. areas 551.65
    spec. elements 551.64
  integration 515.624
    s.a. spec. appls. e.g.
      Engineering
  interpretation
    Bible 220.68
    s.a. spec. parts of Bible
    Hadith 297.124 068
    s.a. spec. Hadith
    Koran 297.122 68
      spec. parts 297.122 9
    Midrash 296.140 68
    s.a. spec. works
    Talmudic lit. 296.120 68
    s.a. spec. works
  solutions *see* Numerical
    analysis
Numerology
  parapsychology 133.335
Numidia *area*–397 2
Numididae
  hunting
    commercial 639.128 618
    sports 799.248 618
  paleozoology 568.6
  zoology 598.618
  other aspects see Aves
Numismatics 737
Numurkah Vic. *area*–945 4
Nuneaton Warwickshire Eng.
      area–424 83
Nunneries *see* Religious
    congregations
Nuns
  biog. & work
    Christianity 271.900 92
    s.a. spec. orders
  other aspects see Religious
    (members of orders)
Nuoro Sardinia *area*–459 2
Nuove musiche
  musical style
    gen. wks. 780.903 2
    spec. places 780.91–.99
    s.a. spec. mediums
Nurseries (for children)
  int. dec. 747.77
    s.a. spec. dec.
Nurseries (for plants)
  forestation 634.956 4
    s.a. spec. trees

Nurseries (for plants) (continued)
  plants grown for
    floriculture — 635.969
     s.a. spec. plants
Nursery
  rimes
    folk lit. — 398.8
  schools — 372.216
  stock
    plant propagation — 631.537
     s.a. spec. crops; also
        spec. types of culture
        e.g. Floriculture
Nurses
  biog. & work — 610.730 92
   s.a. spec. kinds of nursing
  prof. duties & characteristics — 610.730 69
    law — 344.041 4
     spec. jur. — 344.3–.9
  other aspects see Medical
    scientists
  s.a. — *pers.*–613
Nursing
  home econ. — 649.8
  homes *see* Extended care
    facilities
  law — 344.041 4
   spec. jur. — 344.3–.9
  med. sci. — 610.73
  orders
    Christianity
     church hist. — 271.07
      women's — 271.907
     ecclesiology — 262.24
     gen. wks. — 255.07
      women's — 255.907
    other rel. see Religious
     congregations
  services *see* Health services
Nursing (breast-feeding)
  home econ. — 649.3
Nusa Tenggara Indonesia — *area*–598 6
Nutation
  astronomy
    corrections — 522.9
     s.a. spec. celestial
      bodies
    theory — 521.9
     s.a. spec. celestial
      bodies
  plants
    pathology — 581.218 5
    physiology — 581.185
   s.a. spec. plants
Nuthatches *see* Sittidae
Nutmeg *see* Spices; *also*
    Laurales
Nutria *see* Hystricomorpha

Nutrients
  removal
    sewage trmt.
     technology — 628.357
    other aspects see Sewage
     treatment
Nutrition
  applied *see* Applied nutrition
  cells
    cytology — 574.876 1
     animals — 591.876 1
     plants — 581.876 1
    s.a. spec. organisms
  pathology
    gen. wks. — 574.213
     animals — 591.213
     plants — 581.213
    s.a. spec. organisms
    med. sci. — 616.39
     animals — 636.089 639
     s.a. spec. animals
     man — 616.39
  physiology
    gen. wks. — 574.13
     animals — 591.13
     microorganisms — 576.113
     plants — 581.13
    s.a. spec. organisms
    med. sci. — 612.3
     human phys. — 612.3
     vet. phys. — 636.089 23
     s.a. spec. animals
Nutritional diseases — 616.39
  geriatrics — 618.976 39
  pediatrics — 618.923 9
  pub. health — 614.593 9
  statistics — 312.339
    deaths — 312.263 9
  other aspects see Diseases
Nutritive
  adaptations
    ecology life sci. — 574.53
     animals — 591.53
     microorganisms — 576.15
     plants — 581.53
    s.a. spec. organisms
  organs
    anatomy
     gen. wks. — 574.43
      animals — 591.43
      microorganisms — 576.14
      plants — 581.43
     s.a. spec. organisms
     med. sci. — 611.3
      animals — 636.089 13
      s.a. spec. animals
      man — 611.3
    pathology
     gen. wks. — 574.223
      animals — 591.223
      plants — 581.223

Obedience
  rel. doctrines (continued)
    other rel. see Humankind
      rel. doctrines
    soc. control   303.36
    to law *see* Citizenship ethics
    other aspects see Conduct
Obesity
  gen. med.   616.398
  geriatrics   618.976 398
  hygiene   613.25
    misc. aspects see Hygiene
  pediatrics   618.923 98
  pub. health   614.593 98
  statistics   312.339 8
  other aspects see Diseases
Obion Co. Tenn.   *area*–768 13
Obituaries *see* Biographies
Obituary sermons
  Christianity   252.9
  other rel. see Preaching
Oblate monastic bldgs.
  architecture   726.777 6
  buildings   690.677 76
  other aspects see
      Religious-purpose
      bldgs.
Oblates
  rel. orders
    church hist.   271.76
      women's   271.97
    ecclesiology   262.24
    gen. wks.   255.76
      women's   255.97
Obligations *see* Duties
    (obligations)
Oblong
  books hist. & crit.   099
  s.a. other spec. subj.
Obnoxious
  organisms *see* Deleterious
      organisms
  s.a. other spec. subj.
Oboe music   788.75
  recordings   789.912 87
Oboes
  mf. tech.   681.818 7
  misc. aspects see Musical
      instruments
  musical art   788.7
Obregón Mexico hist.   972.082 2
  s.a. spec. events & subj.
    e.g. Commerce
O'Brien Co. Ia.   *area*–777 14
Obscenity
  in art
    ethics
      philosophy   176.7
      religion
        Buddhism   294.356 67
        Christianity   241.667

Obscenity
  in art
    ethics
      religion (continued)
        comp. rel.   291.566 7
        Hinduism   294.548 667
        s.a. other spec. rel.
  in literature
    ethics
      philosophy   176.8
      religion
        Buddhism   294.356 68
        Christianity   241.668
        comp. rel.   291.566 8
        Hinduism   294.548 668
        s.a. other spec. rel.
  in speech
    ethics
      philosophy   179.5
      religion
        Buddhism   294.356 95
        Christianity   241.695
        comp. rel.   291.569 5
        Hinduism   294.548 695
        s.a. other spec. rel.
  postal commun.   383.120 5
  soc. aspects   363.47
    crime   364.174
  other aspects see Moral
      issues; *also* Postal
      offenses
  s.a. Erotica
Observants *see* Franciscans
Observation
  astronomy   522
    s.a. spec. celestial bodies
  s.a. other spec. sciences
Observatories
  astronomy   522.1
    s.a. spec. celestial bodies
  s.a. other spec. sciences
Observatory
  buildings *see* Research
      buildings
  rooms
    school bldgs.
      education   371.623 4
      s.a. spec. levels of
        ed.; also Special
        education
  towers *see* Towers
    (structures)
Obsessive-compulsive neuroses
  gen. med.   616.852 27
  geriatrics   618.976 852 27
  pediatrics   618.928 522 7
  psychology   157.3
  pub. health   614.58
  statistics   312.385 227
  other aspects see Mental
    illness

Obsidian
glyptics 736.28
mineral aspects *see* Volcanic
rocks
rel. significance
Christianity 247.862 8
comp. rel. 291.37
s.a. other spec. rel.
Obsolescence
tax allowance *see*
Depreciation allowances
tax reductions
Obstacles
internat. investment 332.673 2
use in mil. training 355.544
s.a. other spec. subj.
Obstetrical
nursing
med. sci. 610.736 78
surgery
med. sci. 618.8
vet. med. 636.089 88
s.a. spec. animals
Obstetricians
biog. & work 618.200 92
prof. duties & characteristics 618.202 32
other aspects see Medical
scientists
s.a. *pers.*–618 1
Obstetrics
anesthesiology 617.968 2
vet. sci. 636.089 796 82
s.a. spec. animals
gen. wks. 618.2
vet. med. 636.089 82
s.a. spec. animals
other aspects see Medical
sciences
Obstructions
intestines
gen. med. 616.342
geriatrics 618.976 342
pediatrics 618.923 42
pub. health 614.593 42
statistics 312.334 2
deaths 312.263 42
surgery 617.554
other aspects see Diseases
obstetrics *see* Maternal
dystocia
s.a. other spec. subj.
Obtaining employment *see*
Placement labor econ.
Obwalden Switzerland *area*–494 7
Ocarina music 788.5
recordings 789.912 85
Ocarinas
mf. tech. 681.818 5
misc. aspects see Musical
instruments
musical art 788.5

Occasionalism
philosophy *see* Pantheism
philosophy
Occident
regional subj. trmt. *area*–182 1
Occidental
flower arrangements
dec. arts 745.922 4
Mindoro Philippines *area*–599 3
s.a. other spec. subj.
Occlusion disorders
dentistry 617.643
pub. health 614.599 6
statistics 312.304 764 3
other aspects see Diseases
Occult sciences *see* Occultism
Occultations
astronomy
description 523.99
theory 521.8
s.a. spec. celestial bodies
Occultism 133
rel. worship
comp. rel. 291.3
Islam 297.33
s.a. other spec. rel.
Occultists
biog. & work 133.092
s.a. spec. kinds
s.a. *pers.*–13
Occupation
military *see* Military
occupation
Occupational
classes
customs 390.4
dress 391.04
homes 392.360 4
journalism for 070.486
spec. subj. *s.s.*–023
statistics 312.94
diseases 616.980 3
geriatrics 618.976 980 3
hygiene 613.62
pediatrics 618.929 803
statistics 312.398 03
deaths 312.269 803
other aspects see Diseases
s.a. spec. diseases
ethics
philosophy 174
religion
Buddhism 294.356 4
Christianity 241.64
comp. rel. 291.564
Hinduism 294.548 64
s.a. other spec. rel.
factors
mental pub. health 362.204 2

Occupational (continued)
  fiction
    gen. wks.
      collections   808.838 4
      hist. & crit.   809.384
      rhetoric   808.384
      juvenile   808.068 384
    spec. lits.   *lit. sub.–308 4*
    indiv. authors   *lit. sub.–31–39*
    other aspects see Fiction
  hazards
    soc. path.   363.11
  health nursing
    med. sci.   610.734 6
  hygiene   613.62
  licensure
    pub. admin.
      activities   350.824 2–.824 3
      central govts.   351.824 2–.824 3
      spec. jur.   353–354
      local govts.   352.942 42–.942 43
      govt. depts. *see*
        Executive departments
  neuroses *see* Traumatic
    neuroses
  organizations *see* Nonprofit
    organizations
  registration
    pub. admin.
      activities   350.824 2–.824 3
      central govts.   351.824 2–.824 3
      spec. jur.   353–354
      local govts.   352.942 42–.942 43
      govt. depts. *see*
        Executive departments
  requirements of employees
    job analysis *see*
      Qualifications
      employees job analysis
  selection
    gen. management   658.311 2
    executives   658.407 112
    spec. subj.   *s.s.*–068 3
    pub. admin.   350.132 3
      central govts.   351.132 3
      spec. jur.   353–354
      local govts.   352.005 132 3
  safety *see* Industrial safety
  therapy   615.851 52
  s.a. spec. diseases
  s.a. other spec. subj.
Occupations
  incidence
    population statistics   312.94
  labor econ.   331.7
  s.a. spec. subj. e.g.
    Compensation
  lit. & stage trmt. *see* Social
    themes

Occupied countries
  history
    World War 2   940.533 6
    s.a. spec. aspects e.g.
      Diplomatic history
  s.a. other spec. wars; also
    spec. countries
Ocean
  basins
    regional subj. trmt.   *area*–182
  Co. N.J.   *area*–749 48
  currents
    dynamic oceanography   551.470 1
    spec. currents   551.471–.479
  Falls B.C.   *area*–711 32
  floor
    submarine geol.   551.460 83–.460 84
    s.a. spec. bodies of
      water
  liners
    engineering   623.824 32
    design   623.812 432
    models   623.820 143 2
    seamanship   623.882 432
    other aspects see Vessels
      (nautical)
  marine insurance   368.22
    misc. aspects see Insurance
  travel   910.45
    misc. aspects see Travel
  waters *see* Sea waters
  waves
    dynamic oceanography   551.470 22
    s.a. spec. bodies of
      water
  s.a. Marine; *also*
    Salt-water; *also* Sea
Oceana Co. Mich.   *area*–774 59
Ocean-floor vehicles
  engineering   629.292
  s.a. spec. appls. e.g.
    Explorations
    oceanography
Oceania   *area*–9
Oceanic
  languages
    Austronesian *see*
      Austronesian languages
    nonastronesian
      linguistics   499.1
      literatures   899.1
      s.a.   *lang.*–991
    peoples   *r.e.n.*–99
    s.a. other spec. subj. e.g.
      Arts
Oceanographers
  biog. & work   551.460 092
  other aspects see Geologists
  s.a.   *pers.*–553
Oceanographic
  engineering   620.416 2

Odonata (continued)
   other aspects see Insecta
Odontoceti
   animal husbandry   636.953
   zoology   599.53
   other aspects see Cetacea
Odontopteris
   paleobotany   561.597
Odontopteryges *see*
       Pelecaniformes
Odor
   control foods *see* Quality
      controls foods
   perception *see* Olfactory
      perception
Oedongoniales *see* Chlorophyta
Oeno Isl.   *area*–961 8
Offaly Ireland   *area*–418 6
Offenders
   biog. & activities   364.309 2
     s.a. spec. kinds of offenses
      e.g. Murder
   criminal law   345.03
     spec. jur.   345.3–.9
   criminology   364.3
   identification *see*
      Identification
      criminals
   parochial activities for
     Christianity   259.5
     other rel. see Pastoral
      theology
   welfare services   364.6
   s.a.   *pers.*–069 2
   s.a. Potential offenders
Offenses
   criminal *see* Criminal
     offenses
   mil. law   343.014
     spec. jur.   343.3–.9
   mil. sci.   355.133 4
   s.a. spec. mil. branches
Offensive
   arms
     art metalwork   739.72–.74
     customs   399
     other aspects see Ordnance
   play
     games *see spec. games*
Offerings
   rel. worship
     comp. rel.   291.34
     s.a. spec. rel.
Offertories
   liturgical music *see* Proper
      of the Mass
   organ music   786.86
     recordings   789.912 686
Office
   buildings
     architecture   725.23

Office
   buildings (continued)
     building   690.523
     other aspects see Public
      structures
   employees *see* Office
     personnel
   etiquette   395.52
   furniture
     mf. & marketing *see*
      Furniture
     office services   651.23
   holding
     ethics *see* Public
      administration ethics
     pol. right   323.5
   hours
     Christian liturgical music   783.24
     recordings   789.912 324
     s.a. Work periods
   management   651.3
   managers *see* Office personnel
   personnel
     biog. & work   651.092
     s.a. spec. kinds
     personnel admin.
      gen. management   658.304 4
       spec. subj.   *s.s.*–068 3
      pub. admin.   350.1
       central govts.   351.1
       spec. jur.   353–354
       local govts.   352.005 1
     training
      gen. management   658.312 45
       spec. subj.   *s.s.*–068 3
      pub. admin.   350.15
       central govts.   351.15
       spec. jur.   353–354
       local govts.   352.005 15
     s.a.   *pers.*–651
   services   651
Officers
   corporations
     law
      gen. wks.   346.066 42
      liability   346.031
      spec. jur.   346.3–.9
   legislative bodies
     law *see* Organization of
      legislative bodies law
     pol. sci.   328.362
      spec. jur.   328.4–.9
   mil. units   355.332
   s.a. spec. branches
   s.a. other spec. activities
Officers' exercises & maneuvers
   mil. training   355.55
   s.a. spec. mil. branches
Offices
   sanitation *see* Industrial
     sanitation

Oils (continued)
  industrial
    eng. materials   620.198
      s.a. spec. uses
    hydraulic-power tech.   621.204 24
      s.a. spec. appls. e.g.
        Turbines
    manufacturing
      soc. & econ. aspects *see*
        Secondary industries
      technology   665
        s.a. Petroleum; *also*
          Fuels
    oil-soluble paints
      technology   667.622
      other aspects see Paints
    pollution by
      soc. aspects   363.738 2
      other aspects see
        Pollutants
Oilseed plants
  agriculture   633.85
    soc. & econ. aspects *see*
      Primary industries
Oilskin *see* Waterproof fabrics
Oil-soluble
  paints
    technology   667.62
    other aspects see Paints
Ointments
  prac. pharm.   615.45
    misc. aspects see
      Pharmacology
Oise France   *area*–443 5
Oita Japan   *area*–522
Ojibway *see* Algonkian-Mosan
Okaloacoochee Slough Fla.   *area*–759 46
Okaloosa Co. Fla.   *area*–759 982
Okanagan Valley B.C.   *area*–711 42
Okanogan Co. Wash.   *area*–797 28
Okapis
  animal husbandry   636.294
  other aspects see Giraffoidea
Okayama Japan   *area*–521 9
Okeechobee
  Co. Fla.   *area*–759 53
  Lake Fla.   *area*–759 39
Okefenokee Swamp Ga.   *area*–758 75
Okehampton Devon Eng.   *area*–423 53
Okfuskee Co. Okla.   *area*–766 73
Okhotsk Sea
  oceanography   551.465 53
  regional subj. trmt.   *area*–164 53
  other aspects see Pacific
    Ocean
Okinawa   *area*–528 1
Oklahoma
  City Okla.   *area*–766 38
  Co. Okla.   *area*–766 38
  state   *area*–766
  territory   *area*–766 1

Okmulgee Co. Okla.   *area*–766 83
Okra
  agriculture   635.648
    soc. & econ. aspects *see*
      Primary industries
  foods   641.356 48
    preparation
      commercial   664.805 648
      domestic   641.656 48
    other aspects see Solanales;
      also Vegetables
Oktibbeha Co. Miss.   *area*–762 953
Olacaceae *see* Olacales
Olacales
  botany   583.26
  floriculture   635.933 26
  forestry   634.973 26
  med. aspects
    crop prod.   633.883 26
    gen. pharm.   615.323 26
      toxicology   615.952 326
    vet. pharm.   636.089 532 326
      toxicology   636.089 595 232 6
  paleobotany   561.3
  other aspects see Plants
Olancho Honduras   *area*–728 33
Oland Sweden   *area*–486
Old
  age *see* Aged people
  Bulgarian language
    linguistics   491.817 01
    literature   891.81
    s.a.   *lang.*–918 17
  Castile Spain   *area*–463 5
  Catholic Church *see* Roman
    Catholic schisms
  Egyptian *see* Egyptian
  English
    language *see* Anglo-Saxon
    sheepdog
      animal husbandry   636.73
      other aspects see Dogs
  Fletton Cambridgeshire Eng.
       area–426 51
  French language
    linguistics   447.01
    other aspects see French
      language
  Frisian *see* Old Low Germanic
  German Baptist Brethren   286.5
    misc. aspects see Baptist
  High German language
    linguistics   437.01
    other aspects see German
      language
  Icelandic
    spec. subj.   *lang.*–396 1
    s.a. West Scandinavian
      languages
  Indic *see* Sanskrit

Old (continued)
  Italian language
    linguistics   457.01
    other aspects see Italian
      language
  Kingdom Egypt hist.   932.012
    s.a. spec. events & subj.
      e.g. Commerce
  Latin language
    linguistics   477
    other aspects see Latin
      language
  Low Franconian *see* Old Low
    Germanic
  Low German *see* Old Low
    Germanic
  Low Germanic languages
    linguistics   439.1
    literatures   839.1
    s.a.   *lang.*–391
  Norse language
    spec. subj.   *lang.*–396 1
    s.a. West Scandinavian
      languages
  Northwest U.S.   *area*–77
  people *see* Aged people
  Persian language
    linguistics   491.51
    literature   891.51
    s.a.   *lang.*–915 1
  Portuguese language
    linguistics   469.701
    other aspects see
      Portuguese language
  Prussian language
    linguistics   491.91
    literature   891.91
    s.a.   *lang.*–919 1
  Rhodes Key Fla.   *area*–759 38
  Russian language
    linguistics   491.770 1
    other aspects see Russian
      language
  Saxon *see* Old Low Germanic
  School Baptists   286.4
    misc. aspects see Baptist
  soldiers' homes *see* Veterans'
    homes
  Southwest U.S.   *area*–76
  Spanish language
    linguistics   467.01
    other aspects see Spanish
      language
  Stone Age
    archeology   930.12
  Testament
    Bible   221
      Apocrypha   229.1–.7
      pseudepigrapha   229.91
    liturgy   264.3–.4
      spec. denominations 264.01–.09

Old (continued)
  world
    vultures *see* Accipitridae
    warblers *see* Sylviidae
    s.a. other spec. subj.
Old-age & survivors' insurance   368.43
  pub. admin. *see* Social
      insurance pub. admin.
  soc. law   344.023
  spec. jur.   344.3–.9
  other aspects see Insurance
Oldenburg cattle
  animal husbandry   636.234
  other aspects see Cattle
Oldham
  County
    Kentucky   *area*–769 383
    Texas   *area*–764 824
  Greater Manchester Eng. *area*–427 393
Oldmeldrum Grampian Scot.
        area–412 32
Olea europaea see Olives
Oleaceae see Loganiales
Olefins
  org. chem.
    alicyclic cpds.   547.512
    aliphatic cpds.   547.412
    s.a. spec. cpds.
  other aspects see Polyolefins
Oleomargarins
  comm. proc.   664.32
  other aspects see Fats
Olfaction
  human phys.   612.86
  other aspects see Sensory
    functions
Olfactory
  organs
    anatomy
      human   611.86
      other aspects see Sense
        organs
    physical anthropometry 573.686
    physiology
      human   612.86
      other aspects see Sensory
        functions
    tissue biology human 611.018 986
  perception
    psychology
      gen. wks.   152.166
      animals   156.216 6
      children   155.412
      s.a. psych. of other
        spec. groups
      influences   155.911 66
Oligarchies
  pol. sci.   321.5
  s.a. spec. jur.

Oligocene epoch
  geology   551.785
    s.a. spec. aspects e.g.
        Economic geology
  paleontology *see* Cenozoic era
Oligochaeta
  culture & hunting   639.754 6
  zoology   595.146
  other aspects see Worms
Oligomenorrhea *see* Menstruation
        disorders
Oligopoly
  price determination *see*
        Control of markets
  prod. econ.   338.82
  international   338.884
Oligosaccharides
  org. chem.   547.781 5
  other aspects see Sugar
Oliniaceae *see* Lythrales
Olive
  family *see* Loganiales
  oil
    comm. proc.   664.362
    other aspects see Oils
Oliver Co. N.D.   *area*–784 843
Olives
  agriculture   634.63
    soc. & econ. aspects *see*
        Primary industries
  foods   641.346 3
    preparation
      commercial   664.804 63
      domestic   641.646 3
  other aspects see Loganiales;
     also Fruits
Olivetan monastic bldgs.
  architecture   726.771 3
  building   690.677 13
  other aspects see
      Religious-purpose
      bldgs.
Olivetans
  rel. orders
    church hist.   271.13
      women's   271.97
    ecclesiology   262.24
    gen. wks.   255.13
      women's   255.97
Olivine
  mineralogy   549.62
Olmec *see* Miskito-Matagalpan
Olmsted Co. Minn. *area*–776 155
Olsztyn Poland   *area*–438 3
Olt Romania   *area*–498 2
Oltenia Romania   *area*–498 4
Olympia Wash.   *area*–797 79
Olympic
  games
    sports
      sports   796.48
      winter   796.98

Olympic (continued)
  Mts. Wash.   *area*–797 94
  Peninsula Wash.   *area*–797 94
Olyreae *see* Pooideae
Omagh N. Ire.   *area*–416 47
Omaha Neb.   *area*–782 254
Oman
  Gulf
    oceanography   551.467 36
    regional subj. trmt. *area*–165 36
    other aspects see Indian
      Ocean
  state   *area*–535 3
Omanis   *r.e.n.*–927 535
Ombudsman system
  law   342.006 7
    spec. jur.   342.3–.9
  legislative bodies *see*
      Investigative powers
      legislative bodies
  pub. admin. *see* Government
      liability pub. admin.
Omens *see* Divination
Omentum *see* Peritoneum
Omnibuses
  animal-drawn
    commerce   388.341
    services   388.413 22
  motor *see* Buses; *also* Bus
Omnipotence of God
  rel. doctrines
    Christianity   231.4
    other rel. see God
Omnipresence of God
  rel. doctrines
    Christianity   231.4
    other rel. see God
Omniscience of God
  rel. doctrines
    Christianity   231.4
    other rel. see God
Omsk RSFSR   *area*–573
Onagraceae *see* Lythrales
Onchocerciasis *see* Filarial
    diseases
Oncology
  med. sci.   616.992
    geriatrics   618.976 992
    pediatrics   618.929 92
    vet. med.   636.089 699 2
    s.a. spec. animals
    other aspects see Medical
      sciences
Ondo Nigeria   *area*–669 2
One
  old cat
    sports   796.357 8
    other aspects see Sports
  s.a. Single

One-act plays
gen. wks.
 collections   808.824 1
 hist. & crit.   809.241
 rhetoric   808.241
 juvenile   808.068 241
spec. lits   *lit. sub.*–204 1
 indiv. authors *lit. sub.*–21–29
other aspects see Drama
Onega Lake RSFSR *area*–472
Oneida
 County
  Idaho   *area*–796 41
  New York   *area*–747 62
  Wisconsin   *area*–775 25
 Lake N.Y.   *area*–747 62
Oneness *see* Unity
One-person
 cookery   641.561
 s.a. other spec. subj.
Onions
 agriculture   635.25
 soc. & econ. aspects *see*
   Primary industries
 foods   641.352 5
  preparation
   commercial   664.805 25
   domestic   641.652 5
 other aspects see
   Amaryllidales; *also*
   Vegetables
Onionskin papers
 mf. tech.   676.282 3
 other aspects see Papers pulp
   prod.
Oniscoidea *see* Isopoda
On-line catalogs
 library sci.
  spec. catalogs   016–019
  theory   025.313
On-line systems
 electronic data proc. *see*
   Networks electronic
   data proc.
Only child
 psychology   155.442
 rearing home econ. 649.142
Onondaga Co. N.Y. *area*–747 65
On-premise signs
 outdoor advertising 659.134 2
Onslow Co. N.C. *area*–756 23
On-street parking facilities
   see Parking
   facilities urban
   transp.
Ontario
 County
  New York   *area*–747 86
  Ontario   *area*–713 55
 Lake   *area*–747 9
  Canada   *area*–713 5

Ontario
 Lake (continued)
  New York   *area*–747 9
  province   *area*–713
Ontogeny *see* Development
   (biology)
Ontology   111
 misc. aspects see Philosophy
Ontonagon Co. Mich. *area*–774 985
Onychophora
 paleozoology   565.5
 zoology   595.5
 other aspects see Arthropoda
Onyx
 gem *see* Semiprecious stones
 marble   553.55
  econ. geol.   553.55
  mining
   soc. & econ. aspects *see*
    Primary industries
   technology   622.355
   prospecting   622.185 5
  s.a. spec. uses
Ooita Japan   *area*–522
Oölites *see* Sedimentary rocks
Op art *see* Optical art
Opals
 mineralogy   549.68
 other aspects see
   Semiprecious stones
Open
 clusters
  stellar astronomy
   description   523.852
   theory   521.585 2
  other aspects see Celestial
   bodies
 fires
  bldg. heating   697.1
 learning
  higher ed.   378.03
 plan
  education   371.256
   buildings   371.623 2
   s.a. spec. levels of ed.;
    also Special education
 shop
  labor econ.   331.889 2
 stacks
  library operations 025.81
 universities   378.03
Open-classroom
 instruction   371.394 1
 teaching approach 371.102 8
 s.a. spec. levels of ed.;
   also Special education
Open-country communities
 sociology   307.72
Open-field system
 land econ.   333.2

Open-hearth furnace practice
  metallurgy   669.142 2
Openings (beginnings)
  chess   794.122
Openings (buildings)
  architecture
    construction   721.82
    design & decoration   729.39
  building   690.182
    wood bldg. construction   694.2
  s.a. spec. kinds of bldgs.
Openings (jobs) *see* Job
    vacancies
Openings (physiography)
  geomorphology   551.44
  ocean floor   551.460 84
  s.a. spec. bodies of water
  regional subj. trmt.   *area*–144
Open-loop systems
  automation eng.
    soc. & econ. aspects *see*
      Secondary industries
    technology   629.82
  s.a. spec. appls.
Open-market operations
  central banking   332.114
    misc. aspects see Banking
  macroeconomics   339.53
Open-pit mining
  technology   622.31
    spec. deposits   622.33–.39
Openwork fabrics
  arts   746.046 5
  s.a. spec. proc. e.g.
      Weaving
  manufacturing
    soc. & econ. aspects *see*
      Secondary industries
    technology   677.65
  other aspects see Textiles
  s.a. spec. prod.
Opera
  buildings
    architecture   725.822
    building   690.582 2
    other aspects see Public
      structures
  glasses
    mf. tech.   681.412
      components   681.42–.43
    other aspects see Optical
      instruments
  music   782.1
    recordings   789.912 21
  performances
    ethics *see* Public
      entertainment ethics
Operating rooms
  surgery   617.917

Operation
  studies
    prod. management *see* Work
      studies prod.
      management
  s.a. spec mechanisms &
      devices
Operational calculus   515.72
  s.a. spec. appls. e.g.
      Engineering
Operations
  mathematics   511
    s.a. spec. math. branches;
      also spec. appls. e.g.
      Engineering
  number theory
    algebra   512.72
    s.a. spec. appls. e.g.
      Engineering
  on functions
    calculus   515.23
      complex variables   515.923
      real variables   515.823
    s.a. other spec. functions
      & equations; also spec.
      appls. e.g.
      Engineering
  prod. management *see* Loading
      prod. management
  research   001.424
    management use   658.403 4
    spec. appls.   *s.s.*–072
  s.a. other spec. activities
Operative surgery   617.91
  misc. aspects see Diseases
  s.a. spec. diseases
Operator
  algebras
    & groups   512.55
    s.a. spec. appls. e.g.
      Engineering
  failures
    transp. hazard
      air transp.   363.124 14
      railroad transp.   363.122 2
      vehicular transp.   363.125 1
      water transp.   363.123 1
Operators
  calculus   515.724
    s.a. spec. appls. e.g.
      Engineering
Operettas *see* Musical shows
Ophicleide music   788.455
  recordings   789.912 845
Ophicleides
  mf. tech.   681.818 45
    misc. aspects see Musical
      instruments
  musical art   788.45
Ophidia *see* Serpentes

Optical (continued)
  communication
    technology — 621.380 414
      s.a. spec. appls. e.g.
        military engineering
        623.73
      other aspects see
        Communication
  components
    cameras
      photography — 771.35
        gen. tech. — 770.282
        spec. proc. & fields — 772–778
      s.a. other spec. subj.
  crystallography — 548.9
    s.a. spec. substances
  diagnosis med. sci.
    gen. med. — 616.075 47
    surgery — 617.075 47
    s.a. spec. diseases
    other aspects see Diseases
  glass
    technology — 666.156
    other aspects see Glass
  illusions
    psychology
      gen. wks. — 152.148
        animals — 156.214 8
        children — 155.412
      s.a. psych. of other
        spec. groups
      influences — 155.911 48
  instruments
    astrophysics — 523.015 33
    s.a. spec. celestial
      bodies
    manufacturing
      soc. & econ. aspects *see*
        Secondary industries
      technology — 681.4
    physics — 535.33
      spec. states of matter — 530.4
    s.a. spec. instruments &
      appls. e.g. Telescopes
  metallography — 669.950 282
    s.a. spec. metals
  methods
    anal. chem.
      gen. wks. — 543.085
        qualitative — 544.95
        quantitative — 545.81
      organic — 547.308 5
        qualitative — 547.349 5
        quantitative — 547.358 1
      s.a. spec. elements &
        cpds.
  phenomena
    celestial bodies
      Jupiter — 523.452
      Mars — 523.432
      Mercury — 523.412

Optical
  phenomena
    celestial bodies (continued)
      moon — 523.32
      Neptune — 523.481 2
      Pluto — 523.482 2
      Saturn — 523.462
      stars — 523.82
        spec. systems — 523.84–.85
      sun — 523.72
      Uranus — 523.472
      Venus — 523.422
      s.a. other spec. bodies
    meteorology — 551.565–.567
      artificial modification — 551.686 5–.686 7
      weather forecasting — 551.646 5–.646 7
        spec. areas — 551.65
      s.a. other spec. subj.
    properties
      crystals — 548.9
        s.a. spec. substances
      earth astronomy — 525.2
      eng. materials — 620.112 95
        s.a. spec. materials &
          spec. uses
      minerals — 549.125
        spec. minerals — 549.2–.7
      solutions physical chem.
        electrolytic — 541.374 4
          applied — 660.297 44
          organic — 547.137 44
        gen. wks. — 541.341 4
          applied — 660.294 14
          organic — 547.134 14
        s.a. spec. elements,
          cpds., prod.
      s.a. other spec. subj.
    representations
      sound
        engineering — 620.21–.25
        physics — 534.46
        spec. states of matter — 530.4
    rotation
      physical chem. *see* Optical
        activity physical chem.
    scanning
      devices *see*
        Pattern-recognition
        devices
      electronic data processing
        see Inputs electronic
        data proc.
    spectroscopes
      mf. tech. — 681.414
        components — 681.42–.43
      other aspects see Optical
        instruments

Orbiting
  manned space flight
    gen. wks.
      lunar flights   629.454 4
      planetary flights   629.455
    s.a. spec. appls. e.g.
        Space warfare
Orbits
  astronomy
    description
      comets   623.63
        spec. comets   623.64
      earth   525.3
      Jupiter   523.453
      Mars   523.433
      Mercury   523.413
      moon   523.33
      Neptune   523.481 3
      Pluto   523.482 3
      Saturn   523.463
      Uranus   523.473
      Venus   523.423
      s.a. other spec. bodies
    theory   521.3
      s.a. spec. celestial
          bodies
  nuclei *see* Nuclei
  particles *see* Particles
      (matter)
  rays *see* Rays (beams)
  space flight   629.411 3
Orbits (eye sockets)
  diseases   617.78
    geriatrics   618.977 78
    pediatrics   618.920 977 8
    statistics   312.304 778
  other aspects see Eyes
Orbost Vic.   *area*–945 6
Orchard grasses
  agriculture   633.22
    soc. & econ. aspects *see*
        Primary industries
  other aspects see Pooideae;
      also Field crops
Orchards
  agriculture   634.1–.6
Orchestra
  directors
    biog. & work   785.092
    s.a.   *pers.*–785
  halls *see* Music bldgs. for
Orchestras   785.066
  s.a. spec. kinds of music
Orchestration
  music   785.028
Orchestrions
  mf. tech.   681.83
    misc. aspects see Musical
        instruments
  musical art   789.72
Orchid family *see* Orchidales

Orchidaceae *see* Orchidales
Orchidales
  botany   584.15
  floriculture   635.934 15
  med. aspects
    crop prod.   633.884 15
    gen. pharm.   615.324 15
      toxicology   615.952 415
    vet. pharm.   636.089 532 415
      toxicology   636.089 595 241 5
  paleobotany   561.4
  other aspects see Plants
Ord River W. Aust.   *area*–941 4
Order
  metaphysics   117
  probabilities   519.82
    s.a. spec. appls. e.g.
        Engineering
  work library econ.   025.23
  s.a. Public order
Ordered systems *see* Partially
      ordered systems
Orderlies
  med. sci.   610.730 698
Orders (architecture) *see*
      Architectural orders
Orders (rewards)
  mil. discipline   355.134 2
    s.a. spec. mil. branches
  numismatics   737.223
Orders (societies)
  genealogy   929.81
  gen. wks. *see* Associations
  knighthood   929.71
  religion *see* Religious
      congregations
Ordinals
  Anglican liturgy   264.037
Ordinances
  Anglican liturgy   264.035
  laws *see* Laws
  rel. worship *see* Public
      worship
Ordinary
  differential equations   515.352
    s.a. spec. appls. e.g.
        Engineering
  differentiation
    calculus   515.33
      s.a. spec. appls. e.g.
          Engineering
  language
    philosophy *see* Linguistic
        analysis philosophy
  of the Mass *see* Common of the
      Mass
Ordination
  of women
    Christian ecclesiology   262.14
    other rel. see
        Ecclesiastical theology

Ordination (continued)
  sacrament *see* Holy Orders
  sermons
    Christianity   252.7
    other rel. see Preaching
Ordnance
  depots
    armed forces   355.73
    s.a. spec. mil. branches
  factories
    armed forces   355.73
    s.a. spec. mil. branches
  law of war   341.63
  limitation internat. law   341.733
  mil. eng.
    soc. & econ. aspects *see*
      Secondary industries
    technology   623.4
      aircraft   623.746 1
      warships   623.825 1
  mil. sci.   355.82
    s.a. spec. mil. branches
  testing
    ethics *see* War ethics
    internat. law   341.733
Ordos
  Roman Catholic liturgy   264.021
Ordovician period
  geology   551.731
  s.a. spec. aspects e.g.
    Economic geology
  paleontology   560.172 4
  spec. fossils   561–569
Ordu Turkey   *area*–565
Orduña Spain   *area*–466 9
Orebro Sweden   *area*–487
Oregon
  Co. Mo.   *area*–778 875
  state   *area*–795
Orel RSFSR   *area*–473 5
Orenburg RSFSR   *area*–478 7
Orense Spain   *area*–461 5
Ores
  dressing
    mining eng.
      prod. econ.   338.2
      technology   622.7
        spec. ores   622.33–.39
    econ. geol.   553
    misc. aspects see Earth
      sciences
    mineralogy   549
  mining *see* Mining
  processing *see* Ores dressing
Oresund *see* Baltic Sea
Organ (anatomy)
  banks
    health services   362.17
    misc. aspects see Medical
      services
    veterinary care   636.083 2

Organ (anatomy) (continued)
  culture
    experimental biol.   574.072 4
    animals   591.072 4
    plants   581.072 4
    s.a. spec. organisms
    human phys.   612.028
  transplants *see* Organs
    (anatomy) transplants
Organ (music)
  cases built-in
    architecture   729.97
    rel. significance
      Christianity   247.17
      s.a. other spec. rel.
  music   786.8
  recordings   789.912 68
Organic
  chemicals
    manufacturing
      chem. tech.   661.8
      soc. & econ. aspects *see*
        Secondary industries
    s.a. spec. prod.
  chemistry   547
    soil science   631.417
    s.a. spec. crops; also
      spec. types of culture
      e.g Floriculture
  compounds
    biochemistry
      gen. wks.   574.192 4
      animals   591.192 4
      microorganisms   576.119 24
      plants   581.192 4
      s.a. spec. organisms
      med. sci.   612.015 7
      animals   636.089 201 57
      s.a. spec. animals
      man   612.015 7
  drugs
    pharmacology   615.3
    other aspects see Drugs
  evolution *see* Evolution life
    sci.
  farming   631.584
  floriculture   635.987
  s.a. spec. crops; also other
    spec. types of culture
  fertilizers
    production
      soc. & econ. aspects *see*
        Secondary industries
      technology   668.63
    use agric.   631.86
    s.a. spec. crops; also
      spec. types of culture
      e.g. Floriculture

Organic (continued)
poisons
  toxicology   615.95
    misc. aspects see
      Toxicology
psychoses
  medicine *see spec.*
    conditions e.g. Chorea
waxes *see* Waxes
s.a.other spec. subj.
Organically grown foods
agriculture *see* Organic
    farming
home econ.   641.302
Organismic psychologies   150.193 34
s.a. spec. subj. & branches of
  psych.
Organisms (biology) *see spec.*
  kinds e.g. Animals
Organists
biog. & work   786.509 2
s.a.   *pers.*–786
Organization
for Economic Cooperation &
  Development
members
  regional subj. trmt.   *area*–177
management tech.
  pub. admin.   350.007 3
  central govts.   351.007 3
  spec. jur.   353–354
  local govts.   352.000 473
of American States
  internat. law   341.245
  treaties   341.026 35
of committees
  legislative bodies
    pol. sci.   328.365 2
    spec. jur.   328.4–.9
of legislative bodies
  law   342.057
  spec. jur.   342.3–.9
  pol. sci.   328.36
  spec. jur.   328.4–.9
of management
  internal   658.402
  spec. subj.   *s.s.*–068 4
  ownership   658.114
of meetings
  law   346.062
  spec. jur.   346.3–.9
of production
  prod. econ.   338.6
of religion *see*
    Ecclesiastical theology
sociology *see* Social
    structure
s.a. other spec. subj.
Organizations   060
fraternal   366

Organizations (continued)
law
  international   341.753
  municipal   346.06
  spec. jur.   346.3–.9
prod. econ.   338.7
sociology   302.3
spec. subj.   *s.s.*–06
taxes
  law   343.066
  spec. jur.   343.3–.9
s.a. spec. kinds e.g. Labor
  unions; Corporations
Organized
crime
  soc. path.   364.106
strikes
  labor econ.   331.892 2
  s.a. other spec. subj.
Organometallic cpds.
chem. tech.   661.895
org. chem.   547.05
  s.a. spec. groupings e.g.
    Aliphatic compounds
synthetic drugs   615.315
  misc. aspects see
    Pharmacology
synthetic poisons   615.951 5
  misc. aspects see
    Toxicology
  other aspects see Organic
    chemicals
Organotherapy
pharmacology   615.36
other aspects see Drugs
Organs (anatomy)
transplants
  legal aspects   344.041 9
  spec. jur.   344.3–.9
  med. ethics
    philosophy   174.25
    religion
      Buddhism   294.356 425
      Christianity   241.642 5
      comp. rel.   291.564 25
      Hinduism   294.548 642 5
      s.a. other spec. rel.
  med. sci. *see* Plastic
    surgery
Organs (music)
mf. tech.   681.816 6
  misc. aspects see Musical
    instruments
musical art   786.6
  music *see* Organ (music)
    music
  training & perf.   786.7
s.a. Electronic organs;
    also Reed organs

Orgonomy
  therapy   615.856
    s.a. spec. diseases
Orient   *area*–5
Oriental
  architecture   722.1–.5
    misc. aspects see
        Architectural schools
  arts
    design & dec.   745.449 5
    gen. wks.   709.5
      spec. places   709.1–.9
    s.a. spec. art forms
  Christians
    biog. & work   281.092
    s.a. spec. kinds
    s.a.   *pers.*–21
  church bldgs.
    cathedrals
      architecture   726.62
      building   690.662
    gen. wks.
      architecture   726.581 5
      building   690.658 15
    other aspects see
        Religious-purpose
        bldgs.
  church music
    arts   783.026 15
    recordings   789.912 302 615
    s.a. spec. instruments;
      also spec. kinds e.g.
      Liturgical music
  religion
    pub. worship   264.015 02
    significance   246.7
  churches   281.5
    Christian life guides 248.481 5
    doctrines   230.15
      creeds   238.19
    general councils   262.515
    govt. & admin.   262.015
      parishes   254.015
    missions   266.15
    moral theology   241.041 5
    private prayers for 242.801 5
    pub. worship   264.015
    rel. associations
      adults   267.181 5
      men   267.241 5
      women   267.441 5
      young adults   267.621 5
    rel. instruction   268.815
    rel. law   262.981 5
    schools   377.815
    secondary training 207.121 5
    sermons   252.015
    theological seminaries 207.111 5
    s.a. other spec. aspects
  flower arrangements
    dec. arts   745.922 5

Oriental (continued)
  horses
    animal husbandry 636.11
    other aspects see Horses
  languages
    linguistics   490
    literature   890
    s.a.   *lang.*–9
  law   340.58
  Mindoro Philippines *area*–599 3
  philosophy   181
    s.a. spec. branches & subj.
      e.g. Metaphysics
  province Congo   *area*–675 15
  rugs
    textile arts   746.751–.759
  sores *see* Leishmaniasis
  s.a. other spec. subj.
Orientation
  employees
    personnel admin.
      gen. management 658.312 42
      executive   658.407 124 2
      spec. subj.   *s.s.*–068 3
    pub. admin.   350.15
      central govts.   351.15
      spec. jur.   353–354
      local govts.   352.005 15
  library users   025.56
Orientational perceptions
  psychology
    gen. wks.   152.188 2
    animals   156.218 82
    children   155.412
    s.a. psych. of other spec.
      groups
    influences   155.911 882
Oriente
  Cuba   *area*–729 16
  Guatemala   *area*–728 14
Orifices
  liquid flow
    mechanics
      engineering *see* Dynamics
      physics   532.52
Origami
  dec. arts   736.982
  elementary ed.   372.55
Origin
  of Bible   220.1
    s.a. spec. parts of Bible
  of Koran   297.122 1
    spec. suras   297.122 9
  of life *see* Life origin
  of species *see* Evolution life
      sci.
  of states
    internat. law   341.26
  of universe *see* Cosmogony
  s.a. other spec. subj.

Original
  documents
    storage | 651.54
  jurisdiction courts
    law | 347.02
      spec. jur. | 347.3–.9
      U.S.
        Federal | 347.732 2
        local | 347.734
          spec. localities | 347.74–.79
        state | 347.733 2
          spec. states | 347.74–.79
      other aspects see Courts
  sin
    rel. doctrines
      Christianity | 233.14
      other rel. see Humankind
        rel. doctrines
Orinoco River | *area*–87
Orioles *see* Icteridae
Orissa India | *area*–541 3
Oriya
  language
    linguistics | 491.45
    literature | 891.45
    s.a. | *lang.*–914 5
  people | *r.e.n.*–914 5
  s.a. Orissa; *also other*
        spec. subj. e.g. Arts
Orkney Isls. Scot. | *area*–411 32
Orléanais France | *area*–445
Orleans
  County
    New York | *area*–747 91
    Vermont | *area*–743 23
  Par. La. | *area*–763 35
Orléansville Algeria | *area*–653
Orlicz spaces | 515.73
  s.a. spec. appls. e.g.
        Engineering
Orlon *see* Acrylics textiles
Ormiston Gorge Nat. Park N. Ter.
        Aust. | *area*–942 91
Ormsby Co. Nev. | *area*–793 57
Ormskirk Lancashire Eng. | *area*–427 612
Ormuz Strait *see* Persian Gulf
Ornamental
  birds
    animal husbandry | 636.68
      soc. & econ. aspects *see*
        Primary industries
  fans
    dec. arts | 736.7
    s.a. spec. materials e.g.
        Ivory
    dress customs | 391.44
    rel. significance
      Christianity | 247.867
      comp. rel. | 291.37
      s.a. other spec. rel.

Ornamental (continued)
  glass
    arch. decoration | 729.8
    rel. significance
      Christianity | 247.48
      comp. rel. | 291.35
      s.a. other spec. rel.
    s.a. spec. kinds of
        bldgs.
  nails
    arts *see* Ornaments arts
  plants
    floriculture | 635.9
    misc. aspects see
        Agriculture
  woodwork
    furniture arts | 749.5
    handicrafts | 745.51
  s.a. Decorative; *also other*
        spec. subj.
Ornamentation
  bookbinding | 686.36
  s.a. other spec. occurrences
Ornaments
  arts
    decorative
      ceramics
        gen. wks.
          earthenware | 738.38
          porcelain | 738.28
          pottery | 738.24
        processes | 738.1
      glass | 748.8
      metals
        gold
          gen. wks. | 739.228
          hist. & geog. trmt. | 739.227
        iron & steel | 739.48
        platinum | 739.24
        silver
          gen. wks. | 739.238
          hist. & geog. trmt. | 739.237
        other metals | 739.5
      stone | 736.5
      wood | 736.4
    handicrafts | 745.594
    music
      music theory | 781.67
      s.a. spec. mediums
    s.a. other spec. subj.
    rel. significance
      Christianity | 247.86–.89
      comp. rel. | 291.37
      s.a. other spec. rel.
Orne France | *area*–442 3
Ornithischia
  paleozoology | 567.97
Ornithologists
  biog. & work | 598.092
  other aspects see Scientists
  s.a. | *pers.*–598

Ornithology 598
Ornithopters *see* Orthopters
Ornithosis *see* Parrot fever
Orobanchaceae *see* Personales
Orology *see* Mountains
Orphan asylums *see* Orphanages
Orphanages
  bldg. aspects *see* Young
      people welfare
      institution bldgs.
  soc. services 362.732
    misc. aspects see Young
      people soc. services to
Orphanhood
  soc. path. 362.704 4
Orphans
  soc. services 362.73
    misc. aspects see Young
      people soc. services to
  other aspects see Children
  s.a. *pers.*–069 45
Orpington London Eng. *area*–421 78
Orrell Greater Manchester Eng.
                area–427 36
Orreries
  astronomy 523.207 8
Orthochromatic photography *see*
    Monochromatic
    photography
Orthodontics
  med. sci. 617.643
  vet. med. 636.089 764 3
    s.a. spec. animals
Orthodox
  Friends 289.63
    misc. aspects see Society
      of Friends
  Judaism 296.832
    misc. aspects see Judaism
    s.a. other spec. rel. bodies
Orthoepy *see* Pronunciation
Orthogenesis
  evolution theory 575.016 3
Orthogonal
  invariants algebra 512.944
    s.a. spec. appls. e.g.
      Engineering
  polynomials 515.55
    s.a. spec. appls. e.g.
      Engineering
Orthographic projections *see*
    Projections tech.
    drawing
Orthography *see* Spelling
Orthomorphic projections
  maps 526.82
Orthopedic
  appliances
    manufacture 681.761
    use *see spec. appls. e.g.*
      Spinal column

Orthopedic (continued)
  footwear
    mf. tech. 685.38
    other aspects see Footwear
  surgery
    med. sci. 617.3
    vet. med. 636.089 73
Orthoptera
  agric. pests 632.726
    s.a. spec. types of culture
      e.g. Forestry; *also*
      spec. crops
  culture 638.572 6
  paleozoology 565.72
  zoology 595.726
  other aspects see Insecta
Orthopters
  aeronautical eng.
    gen. tech. & mf. 629.133 36
    components & techniques 629.134
    models 629.133 136
    operation 629.132 526
    soc. & econ. aspects *see*
      Secondary industries
    s.a. spec. appls. e.g.
      Racing sports aircraft
  commerce 387.733 6
    misc. aspects see Aircraft
      commerce
Orthoptics
  med. sci. 617.762
  geriatrics 618.977 762
  pediatrics 618.920 977 62
  vet. med. 636.089 776 2
    s.a. spec. animals
Orthorhombic systems
  crystallography 548.14
    s.a. spec. substances
Orthorrhapha
  culture 638.577 1
  paleozoology 565.77
  zoology 595.771
  other aspects see Insecta
Ortiz Rubio Mexico hist. 972.082 4
  s.a. spec. events & subj.
    e.g. Commerce
Oruro Bolivia *area*–841 3
Oryza sativa *see* Rice (cereal)
Oryzeae *see* Pooideae
Osage Co.
  Kansas *area*–781 643
  Missouri *area*–778 58
  Oklahoma *area*–766 25
Osaka Japan *area*–521 83
Osborne Co. Kan. *area*–781 215
Oscan *see* Osco-Umbrian
Osceola Co.
  Florida *area*–759 25
  Iowa *area*–777 116
  Michigan *area*–774 69

Oscillations
solid dynamics
  engineering   620.3
  physics   531.322
s.a. other spec. aspects
Oscillatoriaceae *see* Cyanophyta
Oscillators
electronic circuits
  tech. & mf.   621.381 533
    microelectronics   621.381 733
    microwave electronics   621.381 323
    radiowave electronics   621.381 533
    x- & gamma-ray electronics 621.381 6
  s.a. spec. appls. e.g.
    Receiving sets
  other aspects see Microwave
    electronics; Radiowave
    electronics; X-ray
    electronics
radio eng. *see* Circuits radio
  eng.
Oscillographs
radiowave electronics *see*
  Testing-devices
  radiowave electronics
s.a. other spec. uses e.g.
  Frequency measurement
  electricity
Oscilloscopes
radiowave electronics *see*
  Testing-devices
  radiowave electronics
Oscoda Co. Mich.   *area*–774 78
Osco-Umbrian
languages
  linguistics   479.9
  literatures   879.9
  s.a.   *lang.*–799
people   *r.e.n.*–799
s.a. other spec. subj. e.g.
  Arts
Osee
Bible   224.6
other aspects see Prophetic
  books (O.T.)
Oshkosh Wis.   *area*–775 65
Osiers *see* Willow
Oslo Norway   *area*–482
Osmanli *see* Turkish
Osmium
bldg. materials   691.87
chemistry
  inorganic   546.641
  organic   547.056 41
  s.a. spec. groupings e.g.
    Aliphatic compounds
technology   661.064 1
  organic   661.895
  soc. & econ. aspects *see*
    Secondary industries
s.a. spec. prod.

Osmium (continued)
construction
  architecture   721.044 77
  s.a. spec. kinds of
    bldgs.
  building   693.77
metallography   669.957
metallurgy   669.7
  physical & chem.   669.967
  soc. & econ. aspects *see*
    Secondary industries
mineralogy   549.23
  s.a. spec. minerals
pharmacology   615.264 1
  misc. aspects see
    Pharmacology
products
  mf. tech.   673.7
  other aspects see
    Nonferrous metals
    products
toxicology   615.925 641
  misc. aspects see
    Toxicology
other aspects see
  Platinum-group metals
Osmosis
kinetics *see* Transport
  phenomena
Osmotic pressure *see*
  Colligative properties
  solutions
Osmundaceae *see* Filicales
Osorno Chile   *area*–835 3
Ospreys *see* Pandionidae
Ossabaw Isl. Ga.   *area*–758 724
Osseous tissue
human anatomy & phys.   611.018 4
other aspects see Tissue
  biology
Ossetic
language
  linguistics   491.59
  literature   891.59
  s.a.   *lang.*–915 9
people   *r.e.n.*–915 9
s.a. other spec. subj. e.g.
  Arts
Ossets   *r.e.n.*–915 9
Ossett West Yorkshire Eng.
     area–428 15
Ossicles
ear
  diseases
    gen. wks.   617.842
    geriatrics   618.977 842
    pediatrics   618.920 978 42
    statistics   312.304 784 2
    deaths   312.260 478 42
  other aspects see
    Diseases

Otto engines *see* Spark-ignition
    engines
Ottoman
  Empire
    history   956
    s.a.   *area*–56
  rule
    Algeria hist.   965.02
      s.a. spec. events & subj.
        e.g. Commerce
    Egypt hist.   962.03
      s.a. spec. events & subj.
        e.g. Commerce
    Jordan hist.   956.950 3
      s.a. spec. events & subj.
        e.g. Commerce
    Lebanon hist.   956.920 34
      s.a. spec events & subj.
        e.g. Commerce
    Libya hist.   961.202
      s.a. spec. events & subj.
        e.g. Commerce
    North Africa hist.   961.023
      s.a. spec. events & subj.
        e.g. Commerce
    Palestine hist.   956.940 3
      s.a. spec. events & subj.
        e.g. Commerce
    Syria hist.   956.910 3
      s.a. spec. events & subj.
        e.g. Commerce
    Tunisia hist.   961.103
      s.a. spec. events & subj.
        e.g. Commerce
  s.a. Turkish
Ouachita
  Co. Ark.   *area*–767 66
  Mountains   *area*–766 6
    Arkansas   *area*–767 4
    Oklahoma   *area*–766 6
  Par. La.   *area*–763 87
  River La.   *area*–763 7
Ouarzazate Morocco   *area*–646
Ouija board messages
  spiritualism   133.93
Oujda Morocco   *area*–643
Oulu Finland   *area*–489 76
Oundle Northamptonshire Eng.
    area–425 54
Ouray Co. Colo.   *area*–788 22
Ouse River Eng.   *area*–428 4
Out groups soc. interaction   302.4
Outagamie Co. Wis.   *area*–775 39
Outboard
  engines shipbuilding *see*
      Internal-combustion
      engines shipbuilding
  motorboats
    engineering   623.823 13
      design   623.812 313
      models   623.820 131 3

Outboard
  motorboats (continued)
    seamanship   623.882 313
    other aspects see Vessels
      (nautical)
Outbreeding
  animal husbandry   636.082 42
    s.a. spec. animals
  genetics
    life sci.   575.132
      animals   591.15
      man   573.213 2
      microorganisms   576.139
      plants   581.15
    s.a. spec. organisms
Outcrops
  structural geol.   551.85
    s.a. spec. aspects e.g.
      Prospecting
Outdoor
  advertising   659.134 2
  clothing
    comm. mf.   687.14
    domestic mf.   646.45
    other aspects see Clothing
  cookery   641.578
  education *see* Laboratory
      method education
  employees
    public households   647.3
  evangelism
    pastoral theology
      Christianity   253.73
      other rel. see Pastoral
        theology
  furniture
    home econ.   645.8
    mf. tech.   684.18
    other aspects see Furniture
  life
    equipment mf.   688.765
    soc. & econ. aspects *see*
      Secondary industries
    sports   796.5
    other aspects see Sports
  markets
    commerce   381.18
      misc. aspects see
      Commerce
  photography tech.   778.71
  recreation centers   790.068
    s.a. spec. kinds of
      recreation
  sports
    equipment mf.   688.76
    soc. & econ. aspects *see*
      Secondary industries
    recreation   796
    other aspects see Sports

Outer
  garments
    comm. mf.   687.1
    domestic mf.
      indoor   646.43
      outdoor   646.45
      soc. customs   391.1–.3
    other aspects see Clothing
  Ketchikan election district
    Alaska   *area*–798 2
  Mongolia   *area*–517 3
  space *see* Space
Outfield play
  baseball   796.357 25
Outlaw strikes
  labor econ.   331.892 4
Outlaws *see* Offenders
Outlets (elect. lines)
  exterior wiring *see* Exterior
      wiring
  interior wiring *see* Interior
      wiring
Outlines   *s.s.*–020 2
Out-of-body experience
  spiritualism   133.9
Outpatient departments
  safety aspects *see* Health
      care facilities
  sanitation *see* Health care
      facilities sanitation
  soc. services   362.12
    misc. aspects see Hospitals
Output equip.
  computer commun. telephony
      see Computer
      communications
  computer tech. *see*
      Input-output equipment
Outputs
  electronic data proc.   001.644 3
  spec. subj.   *s.s.*–028 544 3
Outremont Que.   *area*–714 281
Ouyen Vic.   *area*–945 9
Ovarian pregnancy *see*
    Extrauterine pregnancy
Ovaries
  diseases   618.11
    geriatrics   618.978 11
    pediatrics   618.920 981 1
    statistics   312.304 811
    surgery   618.11
  plant anatomy   582.046 3
    s.a. spec. plants
    other aspects see Female
      genital organs
Ovens River Vic.   *area*–945 5
Overbreathing *see*
    Hyperventilation
Overcoats
  comm. mf.   687.144
  domestic mf.   646.452

Overcoats (continued)
  other aspects see Clothing
Overflows
  sewer systems
    soc. & econ. aspects *see*
      Secondary industries
    technology   628.21
    s.a. spec. appls. e.g.
      Floods control
Overglaze painting
  ceramic arts *see* Decorative
      treatment sculpture
  technology   666.45
Overhead
  costs
    financial management   658.155 3
    spec. subj.   *s.s.*–068 1
  lines
    elect. circuits
      electrodynamic eng.   621.319 22
      s.a. spec. appls. e.g.
        Railroads
        electrification
      other aspects see
        Electrodynamics
Overijssel Netherlands   *area*–492 1
Overindulgence
  ethics *see* Consumption ethics
Overland
  air-cushion vehicles
    soc. & econ. aspects *see*
      Secondary industries
    technology   629.322
      mil. eng.   623.748 2
  mail
    postal commun.   383.143
    other aspects see Postal
      communication
Overpasses *see* Bridges
    (structures)
Overpopulation
  soc. path.   363.91
  soc. theology
    Christianity   261.836 65
    comp. rel.   291.178 366 5
    s.a. other spec. rel.
  sociology   304.65
Overseas calls
  telephone commun. *see*
    Telephone calls
Oversewing
  bookbinding   686.35
Overshoes
  rubber
    manufacturing
      soc. & econ. aspects *see*
        Secondary industries
      technology   678.33
    s.a. spec. kinds of rubber
      e.g. Natural rubber
    other aspects see Footwear

Over-the-counter market
  investment econ.   332.643
  other aspects see Securities
          exchange
Overtime
  pay *see* Compensation scales
          pers. admin.
  work
    labor econ.   331.257 2
    *s.a. spec. classes of
        workers e.g.* Women
    other aspects see Work
          periods
Overton Co. Tenn.   *area*–768 684
Overtures
  band music *see* Band music
  orchestra music   785.5
    recordings   789.912 55
Overwater
  air-cushion vehicles
    soc. & econ. aspects *see*
          Secondary industries
    technology   629.324
    mil. eng.   623.748 4
Overweight *see* Obesity
Oviedo Spain   *area*–461 9
Ovogenesis *see* Gametogenesis
Owasco Lake N.Y.   *area*–747 68
Owen Co.
  Indiana   *area*–772 43
  Kentucky   *area*–769 393
Owenism
  economics   335.12
Owens Valley Calif.   *area*–794 87
Owensboro Ky.   *area*–769 865
Owl Creek Mts.   *area*–787 43
Owls *see* Strigiformes
Owners' liability insurance   368.56
  misc. aspects see Insurance
Ownership
  commun. systems   380.3
    gen. telecommun.   384.041
    motion pictures   384.83
    radiobroadcasting   384.543
    telegraphy   384.13
      submarine cable   384.43
      wire   384.13
      wireless   384.523
    telephony   384.63
      wire   384.63
      wireless   384.533
    television   384.554 3
      closed circuit   384.555
      community antenna   384.555 63
      subscription   384.554 7
  equity
    accounting trmt.   657.76
    *s.a. spec. kinds of
        enterprise e.g.*
        Insurance accounting
  flags *see* Flags

Ownership (continued)
  marks
    animal husbandry   636.081 2
      s.a. spec. animals
    s.a.   *s.s.*–027 7
  real property
    law *see* Land tenure law
  transp. systems   380.59
    airlines   387.71
    inland waterways   386.1
    maritime transp.   387.51
    motor transp.   388.32
    railways   385.1
      special-duty   385.5
      standard   385.1
    urban transp.   388.404 2
  s.a. Public ownership
Owsley Co. Ky.   *area*–769 176
Owyhee Co. Ida.   *area*–796 21
Oxalidaceae *see* Geraniales
Oxazines
  org. chem.   547.595
    s.a. spec. cpds.
Oxazoles
  org. chem.   547.592
    s.a. spec. cpds.
Oxdiazines
  org. chem.   547.595
    s.a. spec. cpds.
Oxdiazoles
  org. chem.   547.595
    s.a. spec. cpds.
Oxen *see* Cattle
Oxford
  County
    Maine   *area*–741 75
    Ontario   *area*–713 46
  district & city Eng.   *area*–425 74
Oxfords *see* Footwear
Oxfordshire Eng.   *area*–425 7
Oxidases *see* Oxidizing-reducing
          enzymes
Oxidation
  gen. wks.
    chem. eng.   660.284 43
    physical chem.   541.393
      applied   660.299 3
      organic   547.23
    s.a. spec. aspects e.g.
          Low temperatures
  nonalcoholic brewed beverages
    comm. proc.
      coffee   663.933
      tea   663.943
      *s.a. other spec.
          beverages*
    other aspects see Beverages
  ponds
    sewage trmt.
      technology   628.351

Oxidation
  ponds
    sewage trmt. (continued)
      other aspects see Sewage
        treatment
    s.a. spec. elements, cpds.,
      other prod.
Oxidation-reduction methods
  volumetric anal.
    quan. anal. chem.   545.23
    organic   547.352 3
    s.a. spec. elements &
      cpds.
Oxides
  chemistry *see* Oxygen
    chemistry
  mineralogy   549.5
Oxidimetry *see*
    Oxidation-reduction
    methods
Oxidizing-reducing enzymes
  biochemistry
    gen. wks.   574.192 58
    animals   591.192 58
    microorganisms   576.119 258
    plants   581.192 58
    s.a. spec. organisms
    med. sci.   612.015 18
    animals   636.089 201 518
    s.a. spec. animals
    man   612.015 18
    s.a. spec. functions,
      systems, organs
    other aspects see Enzymes
Oxney Isle Kent Eng.   *area*–422 392
Oxy cpds.
  chem. tech.   661.82–.86
  org. chem.   547.03
    s.a. spec. groupings e.g.
      Aliphatic compounds
  synthetic drugs   615.313
    misc. aspects see
      Pharmacology
  synthetic poisons   615.951 3
    misc. aspects see
      Toxicology
    other aspects see Organic
      chemicals
Oxycoccus *see* Cranberries
Oxygen
  chemistry
    inorganic   546.721
    organic   547.03
    s.a. spec. groupings e.g.
      Aliphatic compounds
  technology   661.072 1
    soc. & econ. aspects *see*
      Secondary industries
    s.a. spec. prod.
  econ. geol.   553.94

Oxygen (continued)
  extraction from air
    chem. tech.   665.823
    soc. & econ. aspects *see*
      Secondary industries
  extraction from ground
    soc. & econ. aspects *see*
      Primary industries
    technology   622.394
    prospecting   622.189 4
    s.a. spec. minerals
  pharmacology   615.272 1
    misc. aspects see
      Pharmacology
  supply
    respiration
      human phys.   612.22
      other aspects see
        Respiration
  therapy *see* Aerotherapeutics
  toxicology   615.925 721
    misc. aspects see
      Toxicology
  other aspects see Nonmetallic
    elements
  s.a. spec. uses
Oxytocin
  org. chem.   547.734 5
  other aspects see Hormones
Oyo kingdom hist.   966.901 5
  s.a. spec. events & subj.
    e.g. Commerce
Oyo Nigeria   *area*–669 2
Oyster catchers *see*
    Charadriiformes
Oyster plant *see* Salsify
Oysters
  culture   639.41
  fishing
    commercial   639.41
    law *see* Fishing law
    sports   799.254 11
  food *see* Mollusca food
  other aspects see Pelecypoda
Ozark
  Co. Mo.   *area*–778 835
  Plateau   *area*–767 1
    Arkansas   *area*–767 1
    Missouri   *area*–778 8
    Oklahoma   *area*–766 8
Ozarks Lake Mo.   *area*–778 493
Ozaukee Co. Wis.   *area*–775 92
Ozobrome process
  photographic printing   773.1
Ozocerite
  comm. proc.   665.4
    soc. & econ. aspects *see*
      Secondary industries
  mineral aspects *see* Pitch
    (carbonaceous material)

Ozone
  chem. tech.   665.89
    soc. & econ. aspects *see*
          Secondary industries
  treatment
    water supply
      technology   628.166 2
      other aspects see Water
          supply engineering
Ozotype process
  photographic printing   773.1

P

PAX *see* Telephony wire
P adic numbers *see* P-adic
    numbers
PBX *see* Telephony wire
PERT *see* Systems analysis
PETN *see* High explosives
pH
    electrolytic solutions *see*
        Hydrogen-ion
        concentration
        electrolytic solutions
PI
    macroeconomics   339.32
PPB *see* Program-performance
    budgeting
PRECIS *see* Precoordinate
    indexing
PT boats *see* Destroyer escorts
Pacas *see* Hystricomorpha
Pacemakers
    heart diseases
        gen. med.   616.128 064 5
Pacers (horses) *see* Light
    harness horses
Pacific
    Coast states U.S.   *area*–79
    Co. Wash.   *area*–797 92
    Northwest   *area*–795
    Ocean
        biology   574.925
            botany   581.925
            zoology   591.925
        s.a. spec. organisms
        fishing sports   799.166 5
        islands   *area*–9
        oceanography   551.465
            currents   551.475
            submarine geology   551.460 8
        regional subj. trmt.   *area*–164
        transocean flights   629.130 915
    region subj. trmt.   *area*–182 3
    regional organizations
        internat. law   341.246
        treaties   341.026 36
    reporter
        U.S. law   348.734 28
    War hist.   983.061
    s.a. Peaceful
Pacifism *see* Peace
Pacifists
    World War 1 hist.   940.316 2
    World War 2 hist.   940.531 62
    s.a. hist. of other spec.
        wars
Pacing-horses *see* Light harness
    horses

Packaged
    meals
        food services   642.3
        other aspects see Composite
            foods
        s.a. other spec. subj.
Packaging
    engineering
        soc. & econ. aspects *see*
            Secondary industries
        technology   688.8
        s.a. spec. kinds of packages
            e.g. Bags paper
    law   343.075
        spec. jur.   343.3–.9
    materials management   658.788 4
        spec. subj.   *s.s.*–068 7
    prod. management   658.564
        spec. subj.   *s.s.*–068 5
    sales promotion   658.823
        spec. subj.   *s.s.*–068 8
    spec. prod.
        cereal grains
            comm. proc.   664.720 9
            s.a. spec. grains
            other aspects see Cereal
                grains
        electronics
            technology   621.381 046
            s.a. spec. appls. e.g.
                Television
            other aspects see
                Electronics
        foods
            comm. proc.   664.092
            s.a. spec. foods e.g.
                Meats
            other aspects see Foods
        milk
            dairy tech.   637.135
            s.a. spec. varieties e.g.
                Whole milk
        nonalcoholic brewed beverages
            comm. proc.
                coffee   663.939
                tea   663.949
            s.a. other spec.
                beverages
            other aspects see
                Beverages
        s.a. other spec. prod.
    s.a. spec. proc. e.g.
        Bottling
Packers (agric. tools)
    agriculture   631.36
    use   635.56
    s.a. spec. crops; also spec.
        types of culture e.g.
        Floriculture

Packers (agric. tools) (continued)
mf. tech.   681.763 1
  soc. & econ. aspects *see*
     Secondary industries
Packing
  alcoholic beverages
    comm. proc.   663.14
     s.a. spec. beverages e.g.
      Wines
    other aspects see Beverages
  clothing
    home econ.   646.6
  crops
    agriculture   631.56
     s.a. spec. crops
  s.a. other spec. prod.; also
     Packaging
Pacts *see* Treaties
Padded
  toys
    handicrafts   745.592 4
    mf. tech.   688.724
    other aspects see Toys
  s.a. other spec. subj. e.g.
     Athletic gloves & mitts
Padding
  clothing *see* Notions clothing
Paddington London Eng.   *area–*421 32
Paddle tennis *see* Racket games
Paddlefishes *see*
     Acipenseriformes
P-adic numbers   512.74
  s.a. spec. appls. e.g.
     Engineering
Padiham Lancashire Eng.   *area–*427 642
Padova Italy   *area–*453 2
Padre Isl. Tex.   *area–*764 47
Padstow Cornwall Eng.   *area–*423 71
Paelignian language *see*
     Sabellian languages
Paenungulata
  animal husbandry   636.96
  hunting
    commercial   639.116
    sports
      big game   799.276
      small game   799.259 6
  paleozoology   569.6
  zoology   599.6
  other aspects see Mammalia
Paeoniaceae *see* Ranales
Pagans
  polemics against
    Christianity
      apostolic times   239.3
      later times   239.9
    Islam   297.291
    other rel. see Doctrinal
      theology
  s.a. spec. rel.

Page
  County
    Iowa   *area–*777 78
    Virginia   *area–*755 94
  design typesetting   686.225 2
Pageantry
  performing arts   791.6
Pageants
  music   782.9
  recordings   789.912 29
  performing arts   791.62
  soc. customs   394.5
Paging systems *see*
    Public-address systems
Pagodas *see* Temples
Pahang Malaysia   *area–*595 1
Pahari
  language
    linguistics   491.49
    literature   891.49
    s.a.   *lang.–*914 9
  people   *r.e.n.–*914 96
  s.a. other spec. subj. e.g.
     Arts
Pahlavi language *see* Middle
    Iranian languages
Paignton Devon Eng.   *area–*423 595
Pails
  mf. tech.   683.82
  other aspects see Household
    appliances
Pain
  human phys.   612.88
    other aspects see Sensory
     functions
  perception psych.
    gen. wks.   152.182 4
    animals   156.218 24
    children   155.412
    s.a. psych. of other spec.
     groups
    influences   155.911 824
  symptoms   616.047 2
    pathology   616.072
      dentistry   617.607 2
      neurological diseases   616.849
      surgery   617.072
    other aspects see Diseases
    s.a. spec. diseases
Painless
  childbirth
    obstetrics   618.45
    pub. health   614.599 2
    s.a. other spec. subj.
Paint
  arch. decoration   729.4
    rel. significance
      Christianity   247.44
      comp. rel.   291.35
      s.a. other spec. rel.
    s.a. spec. kinds of bldgs.

Paleo-Asiatics	*r.e.n.*–946
Paleobotanists	
biog. & work	561.092
other aspects see	
Paleontologists	
Paleobotany	561
misc. aspects see	
Paleontology	
Paleocene epoch	
geology	551.783
s.a. spec. aspects e.g.	
Economic geology	
paleontology *see* Cenozoic era	
Paleoclimatology	551.69
Paleoecology	560.45
botanical	561.1
zoological	560.45
Paleogene epochs	
geology	551.782
s.a. spec. aspects e.g.	
Economic geology	
paleontology *see* Cenozoic era	
Paleogeography	551.7
Paleography	417.7
spec. langs.	*lang. sub.*–17
s.a. spec. aspects e.g.	
Notations languages	
Paleolithic Age	
archeology	930.12
arts	709.011 2
design & dec.	745.441
painting	759.011 2
sculpture	732.22
s.a. other spec. art forms	
Paleomagnetism *see* Geomagnetism	
Paleontologists	
biog. & work	560.9
s.a. spec. kinds	
other aspects see Scientists	
s.a.	*pers.*–56
Paleontology	560
& religion	
nat. rel.	215.6
curriculums	375.56
documentation	025.065 6
libraries	026.56
misc. aspects see Special	
libraries	
library acquisitions	025.275 6
library classification	025.465 6
museums	069.956
s.a. spec. activities e.g.	
Display	
subject headings	025.495 6
other aspects see Sciences	
Paleopalynology	561.13
s.a. spec. plants	
Paleosiberian	
languages	
linguistics	494.6
literatures	894.6

Paleosiberian	
languages (continued)	
s.a.	*lang.*–946
people	*r.e.n.*–946
s.a. other spec. subj. e.g.	
Arts	
Paleozoic era	
geology	551.72
s.a. spec. aspects e.g.	
Economic geology	
paleontology	560.172
spec. fossils	561–569
Paleozoologists *see*	
Paleontologists	
Paleozoology	560
misc. aspects see	
Paleontology	
Palermo Sicily	*area*–458 23
Palestine	*area*–569 4
ancient	*area*–33
Palestinian	
arts	
architecture	722.33
misc. aspects see	
Architectural schools	
sculpture	723.3
s.a. other spec. art forms	
Talmud	296.124
s.a. other spec. subj. e.g.	
Arts	
Pali language	
linguistics	491.37
literature	891.3
s.a.	*lang.*–913 7
Palimpsests *see* Manuscripts	
Palladium	
bldg. materials	691.87
chemistry	
inorganic	546.636
organic	547.056 36
s.a. spec. groupings e.g.	
Aliphatic compounds	
technology	661.063 6
organic	661.895
soc. & econ. aspects *see*	
Secondary industries	
s.a. spec. prod.	
construction	
architecture	721.044 77
s.a. spec. kinds of	
bldgs.	
building	693.77
metallography	669.957
metallurgy	669.7
physical & chem.	669.967
soc. & econ. aspects *see*	
Secondary industries	
mineralogy	549.23
s.a. spec. minerals	

Palladium (continued)
pharmacology   615.263 6
   misc. aspects see
     Pharmacology
products
   mf. tech.   673.7
   other aspects see
     Nonferrous metals
     products
toxicology   615.925 636
   misc. aspects see
     Toxicology
   other aspects see
     Platinum-group metals
Pallets
   wooden
     mf. tech.   674.82
     other aspects see Wood
      products
Palm
   Beach Co. Fla.   *area*–759 32
   family *see* Palmales
   Sunday *see* Holy Week
Palm Valley Nat. Park N. Ter.
   Aust.   *area*–942 91
Palmaceous fruits
   agriculture   634.61–.62
     soc. & econ. aspects *see*
      Primary industries
   foods   641.346 1–.346 2
     preparation
      commercial   664.804 61–.804 62
      domestic   641.646 1–.646 2
   other aspects see Palmales;
     also Fruits
Palmae *see* Palmales
Palmales
   botany   584.5
   floriculture   635.934 5
   forestry   634.974 5
   med. aspects
     crop prod.   633.884 5
     gen. pharm.   615.324 5
      toxicology   615.952 45
     vet. pharm.   636.089 532 45
      toxicology   636.089 595 245
   paleobotany   561.45
   other aspects see Plants
Palmer
   election district Alaska   *area*–798 3
   Peninsula Antarctica   *area*–989
Palmistry
   occultism   133.6
Palmists   *pers.*–13
Palmyra
   ancient country   *area*–394
   island   *area*–969 9
Palo
   Alto Co. Ia.   *area*–777 155
   Pinto Co. Tex.   *area*–764 552

Palominos
   animal husbandry   636.13
   other aspects see Horses
Palouse River Wash.   *area*–797 39
Palpebral mechanisms eyes *see*
     Eyelids
Palpigradi
   zoology   595.452
   other aspects see Arachnida
Pamir
   language
     linguistics   491.59
     literature   891.59
     s.a.   *lang.*–915 9
     people   *r.e.n.*–915 9
   s.a. other spec. subj. e.g.
     Arts
Pamirs   *area*–586
Pamlico
   Co. N.C.   *area*–756 194
   River N.C.   *area*–756 186
   Sound
     oceanography   551.461 48
     regional subj. trmt.   *area*–163 48
     other aspects see Atlantic
      Ocean
Pampanga Philippines   *area*–599 1
Pampas *see* Plane regions
Pamphlets
   bibliographies   011.33
     spec. kinds   012–016
   catalogs
     general   017–019
     spec. kinds   012–016
   library trmt.   025.172
     acquisitions   025.282
     cataloging   025.342
     s.a. other spec. activities
     reviews   028.133
Pamphylia   *area*–392 9
Pan (animal)
   animal husbandry   636.988 44
   hunting
     commercial   639.118 844
     sports   799.278 844
   zoology   599.884 4
   other aspects see Primates
"Pan" movements
   pol. ideology   320.54
   soc. theology *see* Political
     ideologies soc.
     theology
Panama
   Canal
     body of water *see* Southeast
      Pacific Ocean
     transportation
      commerce   386.444
      govt. control   351.876 444
       spec. jur.   353–354

Panama
  Canal
    transportation (continued)
      law *see* Inland-waterway
        transp.
      other aspects see Canals
    Canal Zone   *area*–728 75
    country   *area*–728 7
  Gulf *see* Southeast Pacific
    Ocean
  province Panama   *area*–728 731
Panamanian
  literature   860
  people   *r.e.n.*–687 287
  s.a. other spec. subj. e.g.
    Arts
Panamint Valley Calif.   *area*–794 87
Pan-Arabism
  pol. ideology   320.54
  soc. theology *see* Political
    ideologies soc.
    theology
Panay Philippines   *area*–599 5
Pan-Babylonian origin
  folklore   398.192
Pancake mixes
  comm. proc.   664.753
Pancakes
  cookery   641.8
Pancarida *see* Thermosbaenacea
Panchromatic photography *see*
    Monochromatic
    photography
Pancreas
  anatomy
    human   611.37
    other aspects see Nutritive
      organs
  diseases
    gen. wks.   616.37
      neoplasms   616.992 37
      tuberculosis   616.995 37
    geriatrics   618.976 37
    pediatrics   618.923 7
    pub. health   614.593 7
    statistics   312.337
      deaths   312.263 7
    surgery   617.557
      anesthesiology   617.967 557
    other aspects see Diseases
  physical anthropometry   573.637
  physiology
    human   612.34
    other aspects see Nutrition
  tissue biology human   611.018 937
Pancreatic secretions
  human phys.   612.34
  other aspects see Digestion
Pandaceae *see* Celastrales
Pandanaceae *see* Pandanales

Pandanales
  botany   584.611
  floriculture   635.934 611
  forestry   634.974 611
  med. aspects
    crop prod.   633.884 611
    gen. pharm.   615.324 611
      toxicology   615.952 461 1
    vet. pharm.   636.089 532 461 1
      toxicology   636.089 595 246 11
  paleobotany   561.4
  other aspects see Plants
Pandas *see* Procyonidae
Pandemics *see* Epidemics
    (diseases)
Pandionidae
  hunting
    commercial   639.128 917
    sports   799.248 917
  paleozoology   568.9
  zoology   598.917
  other aspects see Aves
Pando Bolivia   *area*–844 3
Panel
  discussions *see* Public
    discussions
  heating
    buildings   697.72
  instrumentation
    automobiles
      soc. & econ. aspects *see*
        Secondary industries
      tech. & mf.   629.273
    s.a. other spec. appls.
Paneling
  int. dec.   747.3
    s.a. spec. kinds of bldgs.;
      also spec. dec.
  walls *see* Walls
  wood bldg. construction   694.6
Panels
  elect. power *see* Control
      devices electrodynamic
      eng.
  s.a. other spec. uses
Panentheism
  philosophy *see* Pantheism
    philosophy
Pangasinan Philippines   *area*–599 1
Pan-Germanism
  pol. ideology   320.54
  soc. theology *see* Political
    ideologies soc.
    theology
Pangolins *see* Pholidota
Panhandle
  Oklahoma   *area*–766 13
  Texas   *area*–764 8
Panhellenic fraternities *see*
    Greek-letter societies

Paper
  chromatography
    anal. chem. (continued)
      s.a. spec. elements &
        cpds.
  covers
    bookbinding   686.344
  cutting & folding
    dec. arts   736.98
    handicrafts   745.54
    spec. objects   745.59
  manufacturers
    biog. & work   676.209 2
    s.a. spec. prod.
    s.a.   *pers.–676*
  manufacturing *see* Papermaking
  mats
    printing *see* Plates mech.
        printing tech.
  money
    arts   769.55
    economics   332.404 4
    printing
      soc. & econ. aspects *see*
        Secondary industries
      technology   686.288
    standard
      foreign exchange   332.454
    other aspects see Money
  recycling
    mf. tech.   676.142
    other aspects see Pulp
  supports
    photosensitive surfaces *see*
        Supports photosensitive
        surfaces
  tapes
    computer tech. *see*
        Input-output equipment
    electronic data proc. *see*
        Inputs electronic data
        proc.
  textiles
    arts   746.045 7
    s.a. spec. proc. e.g.
      Weaving
    dyeing   667.357
    manufacturing
      soc. & econ. aspects *see*
        Secondary industries
      technology   677.57
      special-process fabrics   677.6
    other aspects see Textiles
    s.a. spec. prod.
  work
    child care home econ.   649.51
    elementary ed.   372.55
Paperback books
  bibliographies   011.32
  spec. kinds   012–016

Paperback books (continued)
  catalogs
    general   017–019
    spec. kinds   012–016
  publishing   070.573
  reviews   028.132
  other aspects see Books
Paperboard
  eng. materials   620.197
    foundations   624.153 97
    naval design   623.818 97
    structures   624.189 7
    s.a. other spec. uses
  mf. tech.   676.288
  other aspects see Papers pulp
      prod.
  s.a. Containers
Paperbound books *see* Paperback
      books
Paperhangers
  biog. & work   698.609 2
  s.a.   *pers.–698*
Paperhanging
  bldg. details   698.6
  int. dec.   747.3
  s.a. spec. kinds of bldgs.;
      also spec. dec.
Papermaking
  instruments & machinery
    manufacturing
      soc. & econ. aspects *see*
        Secondary industries
      technology   681.767 6
    s.a. spec. kinds
  processes *see* Papers
Papers
  eng. materials   620.197
    foundations   624.153 97
    naval design   623.818 97
    structures   624.189 7
    s.a. other spec. uses
  lit. & stage trmt. *see* Things
  noncellulosic fiber prod.
    manufacturing
      soc. & econ. aspects *see*
        Secondary industries
      technology   676.7
  photosensitive surfaces
    photography   771.532 3
    gen. tech.   770.283
    spec. proc. & fields   772–778
  pulp prod.
    manufacturing
      soc. & econ. aspects *see*
        Secondary industries
      technology   676.2
    s.a. spec. prod.
  sculpture material   731.2
    spec. periods & schools   732–735

Paraguarí Paraguay	*area*–892 123
Paraguay	
country	*area*–892
tea *see* Maté	
Paraguayan	
literature	860
people	*r.e.n.*–688 92
War hist.	989.205
s.a. other spec. subj. e.g.	
Arts	
Paraíba Brazil	*area*–813 3
Parakeets *see* Budgerigars	
Paralipomena *see* Chronicles	
Parallax	
celestial bodies	522.9
s.a. spec. celestial bodies	
corrections	
astronomy	522.9
s.a. spec. celestial	
bodies	
Parallel	
bars	
equipment mf.	688.764 4
sports	796.44
other aspects see Sports	
lines	
induction capacity	
elect. circuits *see*	
Physical phenomena	
elect. circuits	
Parallelism	
philosophy *see* Pantheism	
philosophy	
Paralysis	
manifestation of disease	
gen. wks.	616.047
neurological diseases	616.842
vet. sci.	636.089 6
s.a. spec. animals	
Paralysis agitans *see*	
Parkinson's disease	
Paralytics *see* Crippled	
Paramagnetic	
resonance	
astrophysics	523.018 836 4
s.a. spec. celestial	
bodies	
physics	538.364
spec. states of matter	530.4
Paramagnetism	
astrophysics	523.018 843
s.a. spec. celestial bodies	
physics	538.43
spec. states of matter	530.4
Paramaribo Surinam	*area*–883 5
Paramecia *see* Ciliata	
Parametric	
methods statistical math.	519.5
s.a. spec. appls. e.g.	
Enqineering	

Paraná	
River	*area*–822
Argentina	*area*–822
Brazil	*area*–816 2
state Brazil	*area*–816
Paranatural beings	
lit. & stage trmt. *see*	
Supernatural beings	
Paranoia	
gen. med.	616.897
geriatrics	618.976 897
pediatrics	618.928 97
psychology	157.2
pub. health	614.58
statistics	312.389 7
other aspects see Mental	
illness	
Paranormal phenomena	130
Paraphotic	
engineering	
gen. wks.	
soc. & econ. aspects *see*	
Secondary industries	
technology	621.36
mil. eng.	623.042
s.a. other spec. appls.	
phenomena	
astrophysics	523.015
s.a. spec. celestial	
bodies	
physics	535
spec. states of matter	530.4
radiations	
chem. reactions *see*	
Photochemistry	
spectroscopes	
mf. tech.	681.414
components	681.42–.43
other aspects see Optical	
instruments	
spectroscopy	
astrophysics	523.015 84
s.a. spec. celestial	
bodies	
physics	535.84
spec. states of matter	530.4
Paraplegia	
gen. med.	616.837
geriatrics	618.976 837
pediatrics	618.928 37
pub. health	614.598 37
statistics	312.383 7
deaths	312.268 37
other aspects see Diseases	
Paraplegics *see* Crippled	
Paraprofessional	
library positions	023.3
Paraprofessionals *see spec.*	
occupations e.g.	
paraprofessional	
teachers 371.141 24	

Parapsychologists		Parathyroid	
biog. & work	133.092	glands (continued)	
s.a. spec. kinds		diseases	
s.a.	*pers.–13*	gen. wks.	616.445
Parapsychology	133	neoplasms	616.992 44
Parasitic		tuberculosis	616.995 44
diseases		geriatrics	618.976 445
gen. wks.	574.23	pediatrics	618.924 45
animals	591.23	pub. health	614.594 45
plants	581.23	statistics	312.344 5
s.a. spec. organisms		deaths	312.264 45
med. sci.	616.96	surgery	617.539
geriatrics	618.976 96	anesthesiology	617.967 539
pediatrics	618.929 6	*other aspects see*	
pub. health	614.55	Diseases	
statistics	312.396	physical anthropometry	573.644
deaths	312.269 6	physiology	
other aspects see		human	612.44
Diseases		*other aspects see* Secretion	
s.a. spec. systems, organs,		tissue biology human	611.018 944
diseases		Paratroops	
plants		armed forces	356.166
agric. pests	632.52	Paratyphoid fever	
s.a. spec. plants; also		gen. med.	616.927 4
spec. types of culture		geriatrics	618.976 927 4
e.g. Forestry		pediatrics	618.929 274
other aspects see Pests		pub. health	614.511 4
skin diseases	616.57	statistics	312.392 74
geriatrics	618 976 57	deaths	312.269 274
pediatrics	618.925 7	*other aspects see* Diseases	
pub. health	614.595 7	Paraxonia *see* Artiodactyla	
statistics	312.357	Parazoa *see* Porifera	
deaths	312.265 7	Parcels	
other aspects see Diseases		postal commun.	383.125
Parasitiformes		*other aspects see* Postal	
zoology	575.42	communication	
other aspects see Arachnida		Parchment papers	
Parasitism		mf. tech.	676.284 5
life sci.	574.524 9	*other aspects see* Papers pulp	
animals	591.524 9	prod.	
microorganisms	576.15	*s.a.* Vellum	
plants	581.524 9	Pardons	
s.a. spec. organisms		criminal law	345.077
s.a. Medical parasitology		spec. jur.	345.3–.9
Parasitology *see* Parasitism		penology	364.65
Parasmallpox *see* Alastrim		Parental rights	
Parasols		law	346.017
dress customs	391.44	spec. jur.	346.3–.9
Parasympathetic nervous system		Parent-child relationships	
see Autonomic nervous		law	346.017
system		spec. jur.	346.3–.9
Parathyroid		*other aspects see* Family	
extracts		relationships	
pharmacology	615.362	Parenteral	
other aspects see Drugs		medication	
glands		therapeutics	615.63
anatomy		*misc. aspects see*	
human	611.44	Medication methods	
other aspects see		*s.a. spec. diseases*	
Secretory organs		therapy	615.855
		s.a. spec. diseases	

Parenthood
customs   392.3
other social aspects see
    Family relationships
s.a. Parents
Parents
ethics *see* Family ethics
psychology   155.646
s.a.   *pers.*–043 1
Parent-teacher
associations
    ed. soc.   370.193 12
relations *see* Teacher-parent
    relations
Paresis
general *see* General paresis
Paresthesia *see* Cutaneous
    sensory disorders
Paria Gulf
oceanography   551.464 66
regional subj. trmt.   *area*–163 66
other aspects see Atlantic
    Ocean
Parianeae *see* Pooideae
Paridae
hunting
    commercial   639.128 824
    sports   799.248 824
paleozoology   568.8
zoology   598.824
other aspects see Aves
Pari-mutuel horse racing   798.401
Paris France
city   *area*–443 6
department   *area*–443 61
metropolitan area   *area*–443 6
region   *area*–443 6
Parish
houses *see* Accessory rel.
    bldgs.
libraries *see* Religious
    groups libraries for;
    also Church schools
    libraries
missions
    Christianity   266.022
    other rel. see Missions
    (religion)
welfare services *see*
    Religious organizations
    welfare services
Parishes
Christian ecclesiology   262.22
local Christian church   254
local govt.
pub. admin.
    basic level   352.007 22
    intermediate level   352.007 3
Park
County
    Colorado   *area*–788 59

Park
County (continued)
    Montana   *area*–786 661
    Wyoming   *area*–787 42
Range Colo.   *area*–788 66
structures
    architecture   725.7
    building   690.57
    other aspects see Public
       structures
Parke Co. Ind.   *area*–772 465
Parker Co. Tex.   *area*–764 553
Parkersburg W. Va.   *area*–754 23
Parkes N.S.W.   *area*–944 5
Parking
aprons
    road eng.
       technology   625.889
    other aspects see Roads
areas *see* Parking facilities
buildings *see* Parking
    facilities
facilities
    civic art   711.73
    urban transp.
       commerce   388.474
       govt. control   352.918 474
       law   343.098 2
       spec. jur.   343.3–.9
lots *see* Parking facilities
turnouts roadsides
    technology   625.77
    other aspects see Roads
Parkinson's disease
gen. med.   616.833
geriatrics   618.976 833
pediatrics   618.928 33
pub. health   614.598 33
statistics   312.383 3
    deaths   312.268 33
other aspects see Diseases
Parks
civic art   711.558
govt. control
    law   346.046 783
       spec. jur.   346.3–.9
    pub. admin.   350.823 26
       central govts.   351.823 26
       spec. jur.   353–354
       local govts.   352.732
land utilization
    economics   333.783
    landscape design   712.5–.7
    reserved lands   719.32
lighting *see* Public lighting
    eng.
pub. works
    pub. admin.   350.863 2
       central govts.   351.863 2
       spec. jur.   353–354
       local govts.   352.732

Parti québécois Quebec
  pol. sci.   324.271 409 3
   s.a. spec. subj. of concern
      e.g. Social problems
Partial
  blindness *see* Blindness
  deafness *see* Deafness
  differential equations   515.353
   s.a. spec. appls. e.g.
      Engineering
  differentiation calculus   515.33
   s.a. spec. appls. e.g.
      Engineering
Partially
  blind people *see* Blind people
  deaf people *see* Deaf people
  ordered systems   511.33
   s.a. spec. math. branches;
    also spec. appls. e.g.
      Engineering
  sighted people *see* Blind
    people
Participatory democracy
  pol. sci.   323.042
Participles *see* Words
Particle
  accelerators
    pub. safety   363.189
    misc. aspects see
      Hazardous machinery
  astronomy   522.686
   s.a. spec. celestial bodies
  beams *see* Particles (matter)
    acceleration
  board
    mf. tech.   674.836
    other aspects see Wood
      products
  radiations
    biophysics
      extraterrestrial
        gen. wks.   574.191 956
        animals   591.191 956
        microorganisms   576.119 195 6
        plants   581.191 956
        s.a. spec. organisms
      med. sci.   612.014 556
        animals   636.089 201 455 6
        s.a. spec. animals
        man   612.014 556
      terrestrial
        gen. wks.   574.191 56
        animals   591.191 56
        microorganisms   576.119 156
        plants   581.191 56
        s.a. spec. organisms
      med. sci.   612.014 486
        animals   636.089 201 448 6
        s.a. spec. animals
        man   612.014 486

Particle
  radiations
    biophysics (continued)
      s.a. spec. functions,
        systems, organs
      other aspects see
        Radiations
Particle-caused respiratory
    diseases *see*
      Pneumoconiosis
Particles (linguistics) *see*
    Words
Particles (matter)
  acceleration
    astrophysics   523.019 73
      s.a. spec. celestial
        bodies
    nuclear physics   539.73
      spec. states of matter   530.4
      s.a. spec. physical
        phenomena e.g. Heat
    s.a. Dynamics
  gen. wks.
    astrophysics   523.019 721
      s.a. spec. celestial
        bodies
    nuclear physics   539.721
      spec. states of matter   530.4
      s.a. spec. physical
        phenomena e.g. Heat
  mechanics   531.16
  technology   620.43
   s.a. spec. appls. e.g.
      Electrostatic
      photoduplication
Particulates
  atmosphere
    electricity *see* Aerosols
    meteorology
    meteorology   551.511 3
      artificial modification   551.681 13
      weather forecasting   551.641 13
      spec. areas   551.65
Parties
  indoor amusements   793.2
  int. dec.   747.93
  pol. sci. *see* Political
    parties
  religion *see* Ecclesiastical
    theology
  to contracts
    law   346.022
    spec. jur.   346.3–.9
Parting properties *see*
    Mechanical properties
Partisan forces & warfare *see*
    Guerrilla
Partition frames
  wood bldg. construction   694.2

Partition-analysis	
anal. chem.	
gen. wks.	543.089 2
qualitative	544.922
quantitative	545.892
organic	547.308 92
qualitative	547.349 22
quantitative	547.358 92
s.a. spec. elements & cpds.	
Partitions	
groups	512.2
s.a. spec. appls. e.g.	
Engineering	
number theory	512.73
s.a. spec. appls. e.g.	
Engineering	
Partitions (buildings) *see*	
Walls	
Partnership associations *see*	
Unincorporated bus.	
enterprises	
Partnerships	
accounting	657.92
income taxation *see*	
Self-employment income	
taxation	
law	346.068 2
misc. aspects see	
Organizations law	
management	658.042
initiation	658.114 2
prod. econ.	338.73
public relations	659.282
taxes	
law	343.066 2
spec. jur.	343.3–.9
s.a. spec. fields of	
enterprise e.g.	
Advertising	
Partridges *see* Phasianidae	
Parts	
aircraft eng.	
soc. & econ. aspects *see*	
Secondary industries	
tech. & mf.	629.134 3
automobiles	
soc. & econ. aspects *see*	
Secondary industries	
tech. & mf.	629.24–.27
machine eng.	
soc. & econ. aspects *see*	
Secondary industries	
tech. & mf.	621.82
s.a. spec. appls. e.g.	
Transmission-devices	
other aspects see Mechanics	
s.a. other spec. subj.	
Parts (music)	
musical scores & parts *see*	
Scores (music)	
Parts of speech *see* Words	

Part-time	
enterprises *see*	
Proprietorships	
s.a. other spec. subj.	
Parturition	
disorders	
obstetrics	618.5
anesthesia	617.968 2
pub. health	614.599 2
statistics	312.304 85
deaths	312.260 485
other aspects see Diseases	
gen. wks.	
obstetrics	618.4
anesthesia	617.968 2
physiology	612.63
pub. health	614.599 2
vet. med.	
obstetrics	636.089 84
physiology	636.089 263
s.a. spec. animals	
other aspects see Diseases	
Part-whole relationships	
metaphysics	111.82
Party	
finance	
pol. sci.	324.21
spec. parties	324.24–.29
ideologies	
pol. sci.	324.23
spec. parties	324.24–.29
leadership	
pol. sci.	324.22
spec. parties	324.24–.29
meals	
cookery	641.568
organization	
gen. wks.	324.21
spec. parties	324.24.–.29
legislative bodies	328.369
spec. jur.	328.4–.9
s.a. Political	
Parulidae	
hunting	
commercial	639.128 872
sports	799.248 872
paleozoology	568.8
zoology	598.872
other aspects see Aves	
Parvobacteriaceae *see*	
Eubacteriales	
Pas, The, Man.	*area*–712 72
Pascagoula River Miss.	*area*–762 12
Pasco	
Co. Fla.	*area*–759 69
dept. Peru	*area*–852 3
Pas-de-Calais France	*area*–442 7
Pashto	
language	
linguistics	491.59
literature	891.59

Pashto	
language (continued)	
s.a.	*lang.*–915 9
people	*r.e.n.*–915 9
s.a. Afghanistan; *also other*	
spec. subj. e.g. Arts	
Pasquotank Co. N.C.	*area*–756 142
Passaic	
Co. N.J.	*area*–749 23
River N.J.	*area*–749 3
Passementerie	
arts	746.27
manufacturing	
soc. & econ. aspects *see*	
Secondary industries	
technology	677.76
other aspects see Textiles	
Passenger	
aircraft	
piloting *see* Commercial	
aircraft piloting	
airplanes *see* Commercial	
airplanes	
automobiles	
commerce	388.342
engineering	
gen. tech. & mf.	629.222
maintenance	629.287 2
models	629.221 2
operation	629.283
spec. appls.	
mil. eng.	623.747 2
s.a. other spec.	
appls.	
s.a. other spec. aspects	
e.g. Brakes	
soc. & econ. aspects *see*	
Secondary industries	
transp. services	
gen. wks.	
commerce	388.321
govt. control	351.878 321
spec. jur.	353–354
local	
commerce	388.413 21
govt. control	350.878 413 21
central govts.	351.878 413 21
spec. jur.	353–354
local govts.	352.918 413 21
other aspects see Land	
vehicles	
cars railroad *see*	
Passenger-train cars	
services	
en route *see* Passenger	
transportation	
law	
air	
international	341.756 78
municipal	343.097 8
spec. jur.	343.3–.9
Passenger	
services	
law (continued)	
bus	
international	341.756 882
municipal	343.094 82
spec. jur.	343.3–.9
gen. wks.	
international	341.756
municipal	343.093 3
spec. jur.	343.3–.9
inland-waterway	
international	341.756 68
municipal	343.096 8
spec. jur.	343.3–.9
maritime	
international	341.756 68
municipal	343.096 8
spec. jur.	343.3–.9
rail	
international	341.756 5
municipal	343.095 8
spec. jur.	343.3–.9
transp. terminals	
commerce	380.522
airports	387.736 4
bus terminals	388.33
local	388.473
ferries	386.6
ports	
inland-waterway	386.862
maritime	387.162
railroad terminals	385.262
local	388.472
special-duty	385.5
govt. control	350.875–.878
central govts.	351.875–.878
spec. jur.	353–354
local govts.	352.915–.918
law *see* Passenger	
services law	
ships	
powered	
engineering	623.824 3
design	623.812 43
models	623.820 143
seamanship	623.882 43
other aspects see Vessels	
(nautical)	
wind-driven *see* Merchant	
ships wind-driven	
terminals	
activities *see* Passenger	
services transp.	
terminals	
facilities	
inland waterways	
commerce	386.852
govt. control	350.876 852
central govts.	351.876 852
spec. jur.	353–354

Pasture
lands
govt. control (continued)
pub. admin. *see* Land
resources govt. control
pub. admin.
Pasturing
animal husbandry   636.084
s.a. spec. animals
Patagonia Argentina   *area*–827
Patanjali philosophy   181.452
Patching
roads
technology   625.761
other aspects see Roads
s.a. other spec. subj.
Patchwork
textile arts   746.46
s.a. spec. prod.
Patella *see* Lower extremities
bones
Patent
Appeals Court
U.S. law   347.732 8
leather
mf. tech.   675.2
other aspects see Leathers
medicines
therapeutics   615.886
s.a. spec. diseases
Patents   608
law
international   341.758 6
municipal   346.048 6
spec. jur.   346.3–.9
pub. admin. *see* Secondary
industries govt.
control pub. admin.
spec. articles   *s.s.*–027 2
Paternity
law   346.017 5
spec. jur.   346.3–.9
Paternosters isl.   *area*–423 49
Paterson N.J.   *area*–749 24
Pâtés
cookery   641.812
Path spaces
combinatorial topology   514.224
Pathfinder Res. Wyo.   *area*–787 86
Pathogenic
microorganisms *see*
Microbiology
organisms
econ. biol. *see* Deleterious
organisms
Pathogenicity *see* Pathology
Pathological
anatomy
biology   574.22
animals   591.22
plants   581.22

Pathological
anatomy
biology (continued)
s.a. spec. organisms
med. sci. *see* Pathology
med. sci.
s.a. Physical abnormality
development
plants agric.   632.2
s.a. spec. plants; also
spec. types of culture
e.g. Forestry
physiology
biology   574.21
animals   591.21
plants   581.21
s.a. spec. organisms
med. sci. *see* Pathology
med. sci.
s.a. other spec. subj.
Pathology
cells cytology   574.876 5
animals   591.876 5
med. sci.   611.018 15
animals   636.089 101 815
s.a. spec. animals
man   611.018 15
plants   581.876 5
s.a. spec. organisms
gen. wks.   574.2
animals   591.2
plants   581.2
s.a. spec. organisms
med. sci.
gen. med.   616.07
surgery   617.07
s.a. spec. diseases
other aspects see Diseases
Paths *see* Roads
Patiala India   *area*–545 5
Patience *see* Virtues
Patience (game)
equipment mf.   688.754 3
recreation   795.43
Patient libraries *see* Hospital
libraries
Patinating metals
arts *see* Decorative treatment
sculpture
Patio
furnishings
home econ.   645.8
furniture *see* Outdoor
furniture
gardening   635.967 1
lighting *see* Exterior
lighting
Patios
architectural
construction   721.84
design & decoration   729.39

Patios (continued)
  building   690.184
    s.a. spec. kinds of bldgs.
Patmos Greece   *area*–499 6
Patois *see* Slang
Patriarchal
  family
    soc. theology
      Christianity   261.835 85
      comp. rel.   291.178 358 5
        s.a. other spec. rel.
      sociology   306.85
  state
    pol. sci.   321.12
      s.a. spec. jur.
Patriarchs
  Christian church *see* Popes
Patricia portion Kenora Ont.
                                   area–713 1
Patrick Co. Va.   *area*–755 695
Patrilineal kinship *see* Kinship
Patriotic
  band music *see* Military band
                      music
  holidays & events
    law   344.091
      spec. jur.   344.3–.9
    soc. customs   394.268 4
  pageants
    performing arts   791.624
  societies   369.2
    members   *pers.*–369 2
  songs *see* National songs &
                      hymns
Patristic philosophy   189.2
Patristics   281.1–.4
Patrol
  police services   363.232
    misc. aspects see Law
             enforcement
Patrol-craft
  engineering   623.826 3
    design   623.812 63
    models   623.820 163
  naval forces
    materiel   359.83
    organization   359.326 3
  seamanship   623.882 63
  other aspects see Vessels
             (nautical)
Patrols
  mil. sci. *see* Reconnaissance
Patronage
  of music   780.07
  political *see* Political
             patronage
  pub. admin. *see* Civil service
Pattens *see* Footwear

Pattern
  lumber
    manufacturing
      soc. & econ. aspects *see*
             Secondary industries
      technology   674.43
  perception
    visual
      psychology
        gen. wks.   152.142 3
        animals   156.214 23
        children   155.412
          *s.a. psych. of other
             spec. groups*
        influences   155.911 423
Patternmaking
  clothing construction
    comm. mf.
      soc. & econ. aspects *see*
             Secondary industries
      technology   687.042
        s.a. spec. garments
    domestic mf.   646.407 2
  foundries
    mf. tech.   671.23
      ferrous metals   672.23
        s.a. other spec. metals
      other aspects see Foundry
             practice
  rolled metal prod.
    mf. tech.   671.821
      ferrous metals   672.821
        s.a. other spec. metals
      other aspects see Primary
             metal prod.
  s.a. other spec. appls.
Pattern-recognition
  cybernetics   001.534
  devices
    electronic eng.
      soc. & econ. aspects *see*
             Secondary industries
      tech. & mf.   621.381 959 8
        s.a. spec. appls. e.g.
             Records management
      other aspects see
             Computers
Patterns
  art *see* Abstractions art
             representation
  cultural processes
    sociology   306
    psychology   155.9
  s.a. spec. kinds; also
             Designs
Patuxent River Md.   *area*–752 41
Paul 1 reign Russia hist.   947.071
  *s.a. spec. events & subj.
             e.g.* Commerce
Paulding Co.
  Georgia   *area*–758 373

Peaches
  foods
    preparation (continued)
      domestic   641.642 5
  other aspects see Rosaceae;
      also Fruits
Peacocks *see* Peafowl
Peafowl
  animal husbandry   636.595
  sci. aspects *see* Phasianidae
  other aspects see Poultry
Peak District Derbyshire Eng.
        area–425 11
Peak hours
  highway & street traffic *see*
    Traffic patterns
Peanut oil
  comm. proc.   664.369
  other aspects see Oils
Peanuts
  agriculture
    field crops   633.368
    garden crops   635.659 6
    soc. & econ. aspects *see*
      Primary industries
  flour & meal
    comm. proc.   664.726
    other aspects see Seeds
  foods   641.356 596
    preparation
      commercial   664.805 659 6
      domestic   641.656 596
  other aspects see
    Papilionaceae; *also*
    Vegetables
Pearl
  oysters
    culture   639.412
    other aspects see Oysters
  River Miss.   *area*–762 5
  River Co. Miss.   *area*–762 15
Pears
  agriculture   634.13
    soc. & econ. aspects *see*
      Primary industries
  foods   641.341 3
    preparation
      commercial   664.804 13
      domestic   641.641 3
  other aspects see Rosaceae;
      also Fruits
Pearson
  Lester B. admin.
    Can. hist.   971.064 3
    s.a. spec. events & subj.
      e.g. Commerce
Peary Channel *see* American
    Arctic seawaters
Peas
  see spec. kinds e.g. Garden
    peas

Peasant
  art   745
    s.a. spec. art forms
    s.a. other spec. subj.
Peasants *see* Agricultural
    classes
Peat   553.21
  econ. geol.   553.21
  mining
    soc. & econ. aspects *see*
      Primary industries
    technology   622.331
    prospecting   622.182 1
  processing   662.622 1
  soil conditioners *see* Texture
    control soil
    conditioners
  other aspects see Coal
  s.a. other spec. uses
Peat mosses *see* Sphagnales
Pecans
  agriculture   634.527
  other aspects see Hickory
    nuts
Peccaries *see* Suiformes
Pecopteris
  paleobotany   561.597
Pecos
  Co. Tex.   *area*–764 923
  River   *area*–764 9
    New Mexico   *area*–789 4
    Texas   *area*–764 9
Pectins
  chem. aspects
    org. chem.   547.782
    other aspects see
      Carbohydrates
  food
    comm. proc.   664.25
    soc. & econ. aspects *see*
      Secondary industries
Pectolite
  mineralogy   549.66
Pedagogical
  algebra   512.9
  s.a. other spec. subj.
Pedal exercises
  keyboard string instruments   786.35
Pedaliaceae *see* Bignoniales
Pedalium family *see* Bignoniales
Peddlers
  retail marketing *see* Retail
    marketing
Pederasty *see* Homosexuality
Pedernales Dominican Republic
      area–729 323
Pedestals
  museum furnishings   069.31
  other aspects see Columnar
    structures

Dewey Decimal Classification

Pelvic
muscles
  human anatomy 611.736
  other aspects see Muscles
region
  human
    anatomy 611.96
    physiology 612.96
    *s.a. spec. functions,
    systems, organs e.g.
    Cardiovascular system*
  physical anthropometry 573.696
  regional med. trmt. 617.55
  *s.a. spec. systems &
  organs*
  surgery 617.55
    anesthesiology 617.967 55
    fractures 617.158
    orthopedic 617.376
    s.a. Veterinary sciences
Pelvis
  bones *see* Lower extremities
    bones
  deformities
    statistics 312.304 737 6
    surgery 617.376
      anesthesiology 617.967 376
      s.a. Veterinary sciences
    med. & surgical trmt. *see*
      Pelvic region
Pemba isl. Tanzania *area*–678 1
Pembina Co. N.D. *area*–784 19
Pembroke Wales
  city *area*–429 63
  former county *area*–429 62
Pembrokeshire Wales *area*–429 62
Pemiscot Co. Mo. *area*–778 996
Pen
  drawing
    arts 741.26
      indiv. artists 741.092
      spec. appls. 741.5–.7
      spec. subj. 743.4–.8
  names *see* Pseudonymous works
  sacs
    latex *see* Dipped latex
      products
Penaeaceae *see* Thymelaeales
Penal
  codes *see* Criminal law
  colonies
    penology 365.34
    other aspects see Penal
      institutions
  institutions
    buildings *see* Prison
      buildings
    law 344.035
      spec. jur. 344.3–.9

Penal
  institutions (continued)
    penology 365
    pub. admin.
      activities 350.849 5
        central govts. 351.849 5
          spec. jur. 353–354
        local govts. 352.944 95
      govt. depts. *see*
        Executive departments
  servitude
    penology *see* Penal
      institutions
Penalties
  employee discipline
    gen. management 658.314 4
    spec. subj. *s.s.*–068 3
    pub. admin. *see* Discipline
      employees personnel
      admin. pub. admin.
  rel. law
    Christianity
      Roman Catholic
        Codex iuris canonici 262.935
        early codes 262.92
        other denominations 262.98
      other rel. see Religious
        law
  other kinds see Punishments
Penance
  Christian doctrines 234.166
  rel. rites
    Christianity 265.6
    comp. rel. 291.34
    s.a. other spec. rel.
Penang Malaysia *area*–595 1
Penarth South Glamorgan Wales
  area–429 89
Pencil drawing
  arts 741.24
    indiv. artists 741.092
    spec. appls. 741.5–.7
    spec. subj. 743.4–.8
Pencils
  mechanical
    manufacturing
      soc. & econ. aspects *see*
        Secondary industries
    technology 681.6
  wood-cased
    mf. tech. 674.88
    other aspects see Wood
      products
Pend Oreille Co. Wash. *area*–797 21
Pender Co. N.C. *area*–756 25
Pendle Lancashire Eng. *area*–427 645
Pendlebury Greater Manchester
  Eng. *area*–427 32
Pendleton Co.
  Kentucky *area*–769 33
  West Virginia *area*–754 91

790

Pensions
labor
  economics   331.252
  s.a. spec. classes of
    workers e.g. Women
  law *see* Labor law
  pub. admin.   350.835
    central govts.   351.835
    spec. jur.   353–354
    local govts.   352.943 5
personnel admin.
  gen. management   658.325 3
  executive   658.407 253
  pub. admin.   350.5
    central govts.   351.5
    spec. jur.   353–354
    local govts.   352.005 5
veterans
  law   343.011 2
  spec. jur.   343.3–.9
  mil. sci.   355.115 1
  s.a. spec. mil. branches
Penstocks
reservoir eng.
  technology   627.882
  s.a. spec. appls. e.g.
    Military engineering
  other aspects see Liquids
    engineering
sewers   628.25
  s.a. spec. appls. e.g.
    Water drainage
Pentadiplandraceae *see*
  Celastrales
Pentaerythrite tetranitrate *see*
  High explosives
Pentalpha
equip. mf.   688.742
  soc. & econ. aspects *see*
    Secondary industries
recreation   794.2
Pentane
chem. tech.   665.773
  soc. & econ. aspects *see*
    Secondary industries
Pentaphylacaceae *see* Theales
Pentateuch
Bible   222.1
  other aspects see Historical
    books (O.T.)
Pentecost
Judaism *see* Shabuoth
Pentecostal Assemblies   289.94
  misc. aspects see
    Miscellaneous Christian
    denominations
Pentecostalism
Christian theology   230
movement Christian church hist.
     270.82
spiritual renewal   269.4

Pentecostalism (continued)
  s.a. spec. denominations;
    also Gifts of the Holy
    Spirit
Penthouse gardens   712.6
Penticton B.C.   *area*–711 42
Pentland Hills Lothian Scot.
     area–413 5
Pentodes
gas tubes
  radiowave electronics
    soc. & econ. aspects *see*
      Secondary industries
    tech. & mf.   621.381 513 5
    s.a. spec. appls. e.g.
      Radio eng. & mf.
  other aspects see
    Disruptive discharge
vacuum tubes
  radiowave electronics
    soc. & econ. aspects *see*
      Secondary industries
    tech. & mf.   621.381 512 5
    s.a. spec. appls. e.g.
      Receiving sets
  other aspects see Vacuum
    tubes
Pentosans
org. chem.   547.782
other aspects see
    Carbohydrates
Penutian *see* Macro-Penutian
Penwith Cornwall Eng.   *area*–423 75
Penybont Mid Glamorgan Wales
     area–429 71
Penza RSFSR   *area*–478 3
Penzance Cornwall Eng.   *area*–423 75
Peonies *see* Ranales
Peons   *pers.*–062 5
  misc. aspects see
    Agricultural classes
People Called Methodists   287.53
  misc. aspects see Methodist
Peoria Co. Ill.   *area*–773 52
Pepin
Co. Wis.   *area*–775 47
Lake Minn.   *area*–776 13
Pepos
agriculture   635.61
  soc. & econ. aspects *see*
    Primary industries
foods   641.356 1
  preparation
    commercial   664.805 61
    domestic   641.656 1
other aspects see
    Cucurbitales; *also*
    Vegetables

Pepper
  family
    agric. & food aspects *see*
        Condiments
    gen. wks. *see* Piperales
  shrikes
    zoology   598.8
    other aspects see
        Passeriformes
  tree *see* Sapindales
  s.a. Green peppers
Peppermint *see* Herbs; *also*
        Lamiales
Peppertype processes
  photographic printing   773.2
Pepsin *see* Enzymes
Peptic ulcers
  gen. med.   616.343
  geriatrics   618.976 343
  pediatrics   618.923 43
  pub. health   614.593 43
  statistics   312.334 3
    deaths   312.263 43
  other aspects see Diseases
Peptides
  org. chem.   547.756
  other aspects see Proteins
Peptones
  org. chem.   547.756
  other aspects see Proteins
Pequot War
  U.S. hist.   973.22
Peracarida *see* Eumalacostraca
Perak Malaysia   *area*–595 1
Peranemaceae *see* Euglenophyta
Peravia Dominican Republic
                                      area–729 373
Percentage rental
  land econ.   333.563
Perception
  epistemology   121.3
  psychology
    intellectual   153.7
    animals   156.37
    children   155.413
    s.a. psych. of other spec.
        groups
    sensory *see* Sensory
        perception
  soc. interaction   302
  theory cybernetics   001.534
  s.a. Recognition
Percheron
  animal husbandry   636.15
  other aspects see Horses
Perches (fishes) *see*
        Acanthopterygii
Perching birds *see*
        Passeriformes
Perciformes *see* Acanthopterygii
Percoidea *see* Acanthopterygii

Percolating
  filter process
    sewage trmt.
      technology   628.352
      other aspects see Sewage
          treatment
Percussion
  bands   785.067 5
    s.a. spec. kinds of music
  caps *see* Detonators
  instruments
    manufacture   681.819 01
      spec. kinds   681.819 1–.819 6
    musical art   789.01
      spec. kinds   789.1–.6
Percussion-band music   785.43
  recordings   789.912 543
Perdido River   *area*–761 21
Pere Marquette River Mich. *area*–774 61
Perennials
  floriculture   635.932
  s.a. spec. plants
Perfect
  binding   686.35
  s.a. other spec. subj.
Perfectionism
  ethical systems   171.3
    applications   172–179
Perforated
  bricks
    technology   666.738
    other aspects see
        Structural clay
        products
  s.a. other spec. subj.
Perforating-tools
  soc. & econ. aspects *see*
        Secondary industries
  tech. & mf.   621.95
    s.a. spec. appls. e.g.
        Agricultural equipment
Performance
  acting *see* Acting dramatic
        performances
  contracting
    education   371.15
      s.a. spec. levels of ed.;
        also Special education
    s.a. other spec. subj.
  evaluation
    executive management   658.401 3
  rating
    employees *see* Evaluation of
        employees
  standards
    metrology   389.63
      misc. aspects see
        Standardization
        metrology

Performance
standards (continued)
prod. management *see*
Quality controls prod.
management
surveys
pers. admin.
gen. management 658.314
executives 658.407 14
spec. subj. *s.s.*–068 3
pub. admin. 350.147
central govts. 351.147
spec. jur. 353–354
local govts. 352.005 147
tests
automobiles 629.282 4
s.a. other spec. devices
s.a. other spec. subj.
Performance (music)
music theory 781.63
s.a. spec. mediums
Performances
music 780.73
s.a. spec. mediums
other kinds see Public
performances
Performers
biog. & work 790.209 2
s.a. spec. kinds
occupational ethics 174.979
s.a. *pers.*–79
Performing arts 790.2
centers civic art 711.558
s.a. spec. arts e.g. Music
Perfume-producing plants
agriculture 633.81
soc. & econ. aspects *see*
Primary industries
Perfumes
manufacturing
chem. tech. 668.54
soc. & econ. aspects *see*
Secondary industries
soc. customs 391.63
Pericardium
anatomy
human 611.11
other aspects see
Circulatory organs
diseases
gen. med. 616.11
geriatrics 618.976 11
pediatrics 618.921 1
pub. health 614.591 1
statistics 312.311
deaths 312.261 1
other aspects see Diseases
physical anthropometry 573.611
physiology
human 612.17

Pericardium
physiology (continued)
other aspects see
Circulatory organs
tissue biology human 611.018 911
Perichoechinoida *see* Echinoidea
Peridiniales *see* Pyrrophyta
Peridiscaceae *see* Tiliales
Peridotites *see* Plutonic rocks
Peridural anesthesia *see*
Regional anesthesia
Perigee
celestial bodies *see* Orbits
Periglacial processes
physical geol. 551.38
Perimeter parking *see* Parking
facilities urban
transp.
Perimetrium
diseases *see* Periuterine
diseases
Perinatal
deaths statistics 312.24
medicine 618.32
vet. med. 636.089 832
s.a. spec. animals
other aspects see Medical
sciences
Perineal region *see* Perineum
Perineum
anatomy
human 611.96
s.a. spec. systems &
organs e.g.
Cardiovascular system
diseases
surgery 617.555
anesthesiology 617.967 555
other aspects see Diseases
physical anthropometry 573.696
physiology
human 612.96
s.a. spec. functions e.g.
Circulation (biology)
Period
fiction *see* Historical
fiction
furniture 749.2
Periodic
law
theoretical chem. 541.901
s.a. spec. elements
motions
solid dynamics *see*
Vibrations solid
dynamics
table chemistry 546.8

Permafrost (continued)
  soil mechanics
    foundation eng.   624.151 36
      s.a. spec. appls. e.g.
        Roads engineering
Permanent
  deformation
    resistance to *see*
      Plasticity
  field
    geomagnetism
      astrophysics   523.018 872
        s.a. spec. celestial
          bodies
      physics   538.72
        spec. states of matter   530.4
    fortifications mil. eng.   623.12
    magnets
      astrophysics   523.018 822
        s.a. spec. celestial
          bodies
      physics   538.22
        spec. states of matter   530.4
  mold casting
    arts *see* Casting sculpture
    metal prod.
      mf. tech.   671.253
        ferrous metals   672.253
          s.a. other spec. metals
          other aspects see Foundry
            practice
  press fabrics *see* Durable
      press fabrics
  storage
    office records   651.56
  way
    railroad eng.   625.12–.16
    military   623.631
  s.a. other spec. subj.
Permeability
  kinetics *see* Transport
      phenomena
  magnetism
    astrophysics   523.018 84
      s.a. spec. celestial
        bodies
    physics   538.4
      spec. states of matter   530.4
  soil mechanics
    foundation eng.   624.151 36
      s.a. spec. appls. e.g.
        Roads engineering
Permiaks   *r.e.n.*–945 3
Permian
  languages
    linguistics   494.53
    literatures   894.53
    s.a.   *lang.*–945 3
  people   *r.e.n.*–945 3

Permian (continued)
  period
    geology   551.756
      s.a. spec. aspects e.g.
        Economic geology
    paleontology   560.172 9
      spec. fossils   561–569
    s.a. other spec. subj. e.g.
      Arts
Permutations
  mathematics   511.64
    algebra   512.925
    arithmetic   513.25
      s.a. other spec. branches of
        math.; also spec.
        appls. e.g.
        Engineering
Permutative groups
  algebra   512.2
    s.a. spec. appls. e.g.
      Engineering
Pernambuco Brazil   *area*–813 4
Pernicious
  anemia *see* Anemias
  s.a. other spec. subj.
Pernik Bulgaria   *area*–497 73
Pernin shorthand system   653.425
Peron
  Juan admin.
    Argentina hist.
      1st   982.062
      2d   982.064
  Maria admin.
    Argentina hist.   982.064
  s.a. spec. events & subj.
    e.g. Commerce
Peronosporales
  agric. pathogens   632.452
    s.a. spec. types of culture
      e.g. Forestry; *also*
        spec. plants
  botany   589.252
  med. aspects
    gen. pharm.   615.329 252
      toxicology   615.952 925 2
    vet. pharm.   636.089 532 925 2
      toxicology   636.089 595 292 52
  other aspects see Plants
Peroxidation
  chem. eng.   660.284 43
  physical chem.   541.393
    applied   660.299 3
    organic   547.23
      s.a. spec. aspects e.g. Low
        temperatures
    s.a. spec. elements, cpds.,
      prod.
Perquimans Co. N.C.   *area*–756 144
Perranporth Cornwall Eng.   *area*–423 78
Perry Co.
  Alabama   *area*–761 44

Perry Co. (continued)
Arkansas | area–767 39
Illinois | area–773 93
Indiana | area–772 29
Kentucky | area–769 173
Mississippi | area–762 175
Missouri | area–778 694
Ohio | area–771 59
Pennsylvania | area–748 45
Tennessee | area–768 38
Persea gratissima *see* Avocados
Persecuted people *see* Afflicted
people
Persecutions
Christian church hist. | 272
Pershing Co. Nev. | area–793 53
Pershore Hereford & Worcester
Eng. | area–424 49
Persia *see* Iran
Persian
architecture | 722.52
misc. aspects see
Architectural schools
cats
animal husbandry | 636.83
other aspects see Cats
Empire Mesopotamia hist. | 935.05
s.a. spec. events & subj.
e.g. Arts
Gulf
oceanography | 551.467 35
regional subj. trmt. | area–165 35
states Arabian Peninsula area–536
other aspects see Indian
Ocean
horses
animal husbandry | 636.11
other aspects see Horses
language
linguistics | 491.55
literature | 891.55
s.a. | lang.–915 5
people | r.e.n.–915 5
period Egypt hist. | 932.016
s.a. spec. events & subj.
e.g. Commerce
rugs
textile arts | 746.755
rule Palestine hist. | 933.03
s.a. spec. events & subj.
e.g. Commerce
sculpture | 732.5
Wars hist. | 938.03
Greece | 938.03
Iran | 935.05
s.a. Iran; *also other spec.*
subj. e.g. Arts
Persimmons
agriculture | 634.45
soc. & econ. aspects *see*
Primary industries

Persimmons (continued)
foods | 641.344 5
preparation
commercial | 664.804 45
domestic | 641.644 5
other aspects see Ebenales;
also Fruits
Persistance
insurance | 368.016
s.a. spec. kinds of
insurance
Person
& offices Jesus Christ | 232.8
Co. N.C. | area–756 573
Personal
actions
legal procedures | 347.053
spec. jur. | 347.3–.9
other aspects see Legal
procedures
analysis
appl. psych. | 158.1
children | 155.418
s.a. psych. of other spec.
groups
appearance
ethics
philosophy | 177.4
religion
Buddhism | 294.356 74
Christianity | 241.674
comp. rel. | 291.567 4
Hinduism | 294.548 674
s.a. other spec. rel.
home econ. | 646.72
soc. customs | 391
s.a. Clothing
Christianity | 240
cleanliness
home econ. | 646.71
distribution
national income | 339.22
equation
corrections astronomy | 522.9
s.a. spec. celestial
bodies
machines astronomy | 522.5
s.a. spec. celestial
bodies
exemptions
customs duties | 382.782
misc. aspects see Customs
(Tariffs)
finance
economics | 332.024
grooming
accessories
manufacturing
soc. & econ. aspects
see Secondary
industries

Persons (continued)
law
  international   341.48
  municipal   346.012
   spec. jur.   346.3-.9
lit. trmt.
  folk lit.
   sociology   398.352
   texts & lit. crit.   398.22
  gen. wks.
   collections
    individuals   808.803 51
    kinds   808.803 52
   hist. & crit.
    individuals   809.933 51
    kinds   809.933 52
  spec. lits.
   collections
    individuals   *lit. sub.*-080 351
    kinds   *lit. sub.*-093 52
   hist. & crit.
    individuals   *lit. sub.*-093 51
    kinds   *lit. sub.*-080 352
  s.a. spec. lit. forms
rel. law
  Christianity
   Roman Catholic
    Codex iuris canonici   262.932
    early codes   262.92
    other denominations   262.98
   other rel. see Religious
    law
rel. worship
  comp. rel.   291.213
  s.a. spec. rel.
stage trmt.
  gen. wks.
   individuals   792.090 935 1
   kinds   792.090 935 2
  s.a. other spec. dramatic
   mediums e.g.
   Television; *also spec.*
   kinds of drama e.g.
   Tragedies (drama)
other spec. subj.   *s.s.*-092
s.a. spec. kinds e.g. Women;
  also Individuals
Person-to-group relations
  soc. interaction   302.5
Person-to-person relations
  soc. interaction   302.5
Person-to-society relations
  soc. interaction   302.5
Perspective
  arts   701.8
  s.a. spec. art forms
Perspiration
  skin biochemistry
   human phys.   612.792 1
  other aspects see
   Integumentary organs

Persuasion
  logic   168
  psychology   153.852
   animals   156.385 2
   children   155.413
   s.a. psych. of other spec.
    groups
  sociology
   communication   302.24
   control   303.34
Perth
  & Kinross Tayside Scot.   *area*-412 8
  city W. Aust.   *area*-941 1
  Co. Ont.   *area*-713 23
  Tasmania   *area*-946 3
Perthshire Scot.   *area*-412 8
Perturbations
  astronomy   521.4
  s.a. spec. celestial bodies
  space flight   629.411 4
Pertussis *see* Whooping cough
Peru
  country   *area*-85
  Current
   oceanography   551.476 1
Perugia Italy   *area*-456 51
Peruvian
  literature   860
  people   *r.e.n.*-688 5
  s.a. other spec. subj. e.g.
   Arts
Perversions *see* Sexual
  deviations
Pesach *see* Passover
Pesaro e Urbino Italy   *area*-456 77
Pescadores China   *area*-512 49
Pescara Italy   *area*-457 17
Peshawar Pakistan   *area*-549 123
Pessimism
  philosophy   149.6
  indiv. phil.   180-190
  s.a. spec. branches of phil.
   e.g. Ethics
Pest
  control
   agriculture   632.9
   s.a. spec. plants; also
    spec. types of culture
    e.g. Forestry
   home econ.   648.7
   sanitary eng.   628.96
   soc. aspects   363.78
   law   344.046
    spec. jur.   344.3-.9
   pub. admin.   350.772
    central govts.   351.772
    spec. jur.   353-354
    local govts.   352.6
  Co. Hungary   *area*-439 1

Pesticide damage
  agriculture 632.950 42
  s.a. spec. types of culture
    e.g. Forestry; *also*
    spec. plants & spec.
    pesticides
Pesticides
  pollution by
    soc. aspects 363.738 4
    other aspects see
      Pollutants
  production
    soc. & econ. aspects *see*
      Secondary industries
    technology 668.65
  use agric. 632.95
    s.a. spec. crops; also spec.
      types of culture e.g.
      Floriculture
  wastes
    pollution water-supply eng.
      technology 628.168 42
      other aspects see Water
        supply engineering
    sanitary eng.
      technology 628.746 2
      other aspects see
        Sanitary engineering
Pest-resistant construction
  buildings 693.84
  other aspects see Resistant
    construction
Pests
  agriculture 632.6
  apiculture 638.15
  floriculture 635.926
  forestry 634.966
  grape culture 634.826
    s.a. other spec. types of
      culture; also spec.
      plants
  extermination *see* Pest
    control
  resistance to
    eng. materials *see*
      Deterioration
  other aspects see Deleterious
    organisms
Pet foods
  manufacturing
    soc. & econ. aspects *see*
      Secondary industries
    technology 664.66
Petals *see* Reproductive organs
Petén Guatemala *area*–728 12
Peter (scriptures)
  Bible 227.92–.93
  other aspects see New
    Testament
Peter reign Russia hist.
  1 the Great 947.05

Peter reign Russia hist. (continued)
  2 947.061
  3 947.062
    s.a. spec. events & subj.
      e.g. Commerce
Peter Mogila
  Orthodox Confession
    Christian doctrines 238.19
Peterborough
  city Ont. *area*–713 68
  Co. Ont. *area*–713 67
  district Cambridgeshire Eng.
    area–426 51
  S. Aust. *area*–942 36
Peterculter Grampian Scot.
    area–412 35
Peterhead Grampian Scot. *area*–412 25
Petermanniaceae *see*
  Alstroemeriales
Petersburg Va. *area*–755 581
  siege
    U.S. Civil War hist. 973.737
Petersfield Hampshire Eng.
    area–422 74
Petition
  civil right 323.48
  law 342.085 4
    spec. jur. 342.3–.9
  private prayers
    Christianity 242.726
    other rel. see Prayers
      private devotions
Petiveriaceae *see* Chenopodiales
Petrels *see* Procellariiformes
Petrified
  Forest Nat. Park Ariz. *area*–791 37
  wood 561.21
Petrochemicals
  chem. tech. 661.804
  other aspects see Organic
    chemicals
Petrogenesis 552.03
Petrography 552
  misc. aspects see Earth
    sciences
Petroleum 553.282
  econ. geol. 553.282
  engineers
    biog. & work 665.509 2
    s.a. *pers.*–665
  extraction
    govt. control
      activities 351.823 88
        spec. jur. 353–354
      departments 351.082 388
        spec. jur. 353–354
    law 343.077 2
      spec. jur. 343.3–.9
    technology 622.338 2
    prospecting 622.182 82
      org. chem. 547.83

Petroleum (continued)
  processing
    soc. & econ. aspects *see*
      Secondary industries
    technology   665.5
  radiesthesia
    parapsychology   133.323 7
  resources
    economics   333.823 2
    govt. control
      law   346.046 823 2
        spec. jur.   346.3–.9
      pub. admin. *see*
        Subsurface resources
        govt. control pub.
        admin.
  supply
    law   343.092 6
      spec. jur.   343.3–.9
  synthetic
    manufacturing
      soc. & econ. aspects *see*
        Secondary industries
    technology   662.662
  tech. instruments & machinery
    manufacturing
      soc. & econ. aspects *see*
        Secondary industries
    technology   681.766 5
  s.a. spec. kinds
  s.a. Oils; *also spec. uses*
Petroleum coke
  chem. tech.   665.538 8
  other aspects see Petroleum
Petroleum Co. Mont.   *area*–786 28
Petroleum gas
  chem. tech.   665.773
  soc. & econ. aspects *see*
    Secondary industries
Petroleum-derived chemicals
  chem. tech.   661.804
  other aspects see Organic
    chemicals
Petrologists
  biog. & work   552.009 2
  other aspects see Scientists
  s.a.   *pers.*–552
Petrology   552
  misc. aspects see Earth
    sciences
Petrosaviaceae *see* Alismatales
Pets
  animal husbandry for   636.088 7
  s.a. spec. animals
Petticoats *see* Underwear
Pettis Co. Mo.   *area*–778 48
Petty officers
  naval forces   359.338
  s.a. spec. naval forces
Petunias *see* Solanales
Petuntse *see* Clays

Petworth West Sussex Eng.
         area–422 62
Pews *see* Seats ecclesiastical
    furniture
Pewsey Vale Wiltshire Eng.
         area–423 17
Pewter
  arts decorative   739.533
  other aspects see Tin
Phaeophyta
  botany   589.45
  med. aspects
    gen. pharm.   615.329 45
    toxicology   615.952 945
    vet. pharm.   636.089 532 945
    toxicology   636.089 595 294 5
  paleobotany   561.93
  other aspects see Plants
Phaëthontes *see* Pelecaniformes
Phalangers *see* Marsupialia
Phalanges
  feet *see* Lower extremities
    bones
  hands *see* Upper extremities
    bones
Phalangida
  zoology   595.43
  other aspects see Arachnida
Phalansterianism
  socialist school
    economics   335.23
Phalanxes
  mil. organization   355.31
  s.a. spec. mil. branches
Phalarideae *see* Pooideae
Phalaropes *see* Charadriiformes
Phallales *see* Lycoperdales
Phanerogamia *see* Spermatophyta
Phanerozonea *see* Asteroidea
Phantasms
  occultism   133.14
Phantoms *see* Ghosts
Phareae *see* Pooideae
Pharisees
  Judaism   296.812
  misc. aspects see Judaism
Pharmaceutical
  chemistry   615.19
    misc. aspects see
      Pharmacology
  s.a. spec. drugs
  services
    soc. welfare   362.17
    misc. aspects see Medical
      services
Pharmaceuticals *see* Drugs
Pharmacists
  biog. & work   615.409 2
  prof. duties & characteristics
    law   344.041 6
      spec. jur.   344.3–.9

Relative Index

Pharmacists (continued)
  other aspects see Medical
    scientists
  s.a.   *pers.*–615
Pharmacodynamics
  med. sci.   615.7
  misc. aspects see
    Pharmacology
Pharmacognosy
  pharmacology   615.321
  misc. aspects see
    Pharmacology
Pharmacokinetics
  med. sci.   615.7
  misc. aspects see
    Pharmacology
Pharmacologists
  biog. & work   615.109 2
  other aspects see Medical
    scientists
  s.a.   *pers.*–615
Pharmacology   615.1
  Biblical trmt.   220.861 51
  s.a. spec. parts of Bible
  curriculums   375.615 1
  documentation   025.066 151
  libraries   026.615 1
  misc. aspects see Special
    libraries
  library acquisitions 025.276 151
  library classification 025.466 151
  subject headings 025.496 151
  vet. sci.   636.089 51
  s.a. spec. animals
  other aspects see Medical
    sciences
Pharmacopeias
  pharmacology   615.11
  misc. aspects see
    Pharmacology
  s.a. spec. drugs
Pharmacy   615.4
  misc. aspects see Drugs
Pharyngeal diseases
  gen. wks.   616.32
  neoplasms   616.992 32
  tuberculosis   616.995 32
  geriatrics   618.976 32
  pediatrics   618.923 2
  pub. health   614.593 2
  statistics   312.332
  deaths   312.263 2
  surgery   617.532
  anesthesiology 617.967 532
  other aspects see Diseases
Pharyngobdellida *see* Hirudinea
Pharynx
  anatomy
  human   611.32
  other aspects see Nutritive
    organs

Pharynx (continued)
  diseases *see* Pharyngeal
    diseases
  physical anthropometry 573.632
  physiology
  human   612.31
  other aspects see Nutrition
  tissue biology human 611.018 932
Phase
  changes
  effect of heat
    astrophysics   523.013 401
    s.a. spec. celestial bodies
    physical chem. 541.363
    applied   660.296 3
    organic   547.136 3
    s.a. spec. elements, cpds., prod.
    physics   536.401
    spec. states of matter 530.4
  converters
  asynchronous *see*
    Asynchronous machinery
  diagrams
  metallurgy   669.94
  s.a. spec. metals
  elect. measurement
  technology   621.374 9
  s.a. spec. appls. e.g.
    Ignition systems & devices
  other aspects see
    Electricity
  modulators
  electronic circuits
    tech. & mf.   621.381 536 4
    microelectronics 621.381 736 4
    microwave electronics 621.381 326 4
    radiowave electronics 621.381 536 4
    x- & gamma-ray electronics 621.381 6
  s.a. spec. appls. e.g.
    Radar engineering
  other aspects see
    Microwave electronics;
    Radiowave electronics;
    X-ray electronics
  transformations
  glassmaking   666.104 2
  s.a. spec. kinds of glass
Phasemeters *see* Phase elect.
  measurement
Phaseolus
  limensis *see* Lima beans
  vulgaris *see* Kidney beans
Phases
  celestial bodies
  Jupiter   523.452
  Mars   523.432
  Mercury   523.412

Phases
  celestial bodies (continued)
    moon — 523.32
    Neptune — 523.481 2
    Pluto — 523.482 2
    Saturn — 523.462
    Uranus — 523.472
    Venus — 523.422
    s.a. other spec. bodies
Phasianidae
  hunting
    commercial — 639.128 617
    sports — 799.248 617
  paleozoology — 568.6
  zoology — 598.617
  other aspects see Aves
Phasmatodea
  culture — 638.572 4
  paleozoology — 565.72
  zoology — 595.724
  other aspects see Insecta
Phasmidia *see* Nematoda
Pheasants
  animal husbandry — 636.594
  sci. aspects *see* Phasianidae
  other aspects see Poultry
Phelps Co.
  Missouri — *area*–778 594
  Nebraska — *area*–782 392
Phenacite
  mineralogy — 549.62
Phenolics
  plastics
    chem. tech. — 668.422 2
    org. chem. — 547.843 222 2
    other aspects see Plastics
  s.a. spec. prod.
Phenols
  chem. tech. — 661.82
  org. chem. — 547.632
  other aspects see Hydroxy
      compounds
  s.a. spec. cpds.
Phenomenalism
  philosophy — 142.7
  indiv. phil. — 180–190
  s.a. spec. branches of phil.
    e.g. Metaphysics
Phenomenological schools
  psychology — 150.192
  s.a. spec. subj. & branches
    of psych.
Phenomenology
  philosophy — 142.7
  indiv. phil. — 180–190
  s.a. spec. branches of phil.
    e.g. Metaphysics
Phenotypes *see* Genetic makeup
Philadelphaceae *see* Cunoniales
Philadelphia Pa. — *area*–748 11

Philanthropists
  biog. & work — 361.740 92
  s.a. — *pers.*–361
Philanthropy
  ethics *see* Love ethics
  law *see* Welfare services law
  soc. welfare — 361.74
Philately — 769.56
Philemon
  Bible — 227.86
  other aspects see New
    Testament
Philesiaceae *see*
    Alstroemeriales
Philip
  reign
    France hist.
      1 — 944.022
      2 — 944.023
      3-5 — 944.024
      6 — 944.025
    Spain hist.
      2 — 946.04
      3 — 946.051
      4 — 946.052
      5 — 946.055
    s.a. spec. events & subj.
      e.g. Commerce
Philippians
  Bible — 227.6
  other aspects see New
    Testament
Philippine
  arts *see* Southeast Asian arts
  languages
    linguistics — 499.21
    literatures — 899.21
    s.a. — *lang.*–992 1
  people — *r.e.n.*–992 1
  Sea
    oceanography — 551.465 58
    regional subj. trmt. — *area*–164 58
    other aspects see Pacific
      Ocean
  s.a. other spec. subj.
Philippines — *area*–599
Phillip Isls. Vic. — *area*–945 2
Phillips
  Bible translation — 220.520 9
  County
    Arkansas — *area*–767 88
    Colorado — *area*–788 77
    Kansas — *area*–781 17
    Montana — *area*–786 16
Philological theory
  folklore — 398.12
Philologists
  biog. & work — 410.92
  s.a. spec. kinds e.g.
    Lexicographers; *also*
    spec. langs.

Philologists (continued)
  s.a.   *pers.*–4
Philology *see* Linguistics
Philosophers
  biog. & work   180–190
  s.a.   *pers.*–11
Philosopher's stone
  chem. theory   540.112
  lit. & stage trmt.
    folk lit.
      sociology   398.465
      texts & lit. crit.   398.26
    other aspects see Things
Philosophical anthropology   128
Philosophy   100
  appls. to spec. subj.   *s.s.*–01
  Biblical trmt.   220.81
    s.a. spec. parts of Bible
  curriculums   375.1
  documentation   025.061
  journalism   070.449 1
  libraries   026.1
    misc. aspects see Special
      libraries
  library acquisitions   025.271
  library classification   025.61
  lit. trmt.
    gen. wks.
      collections   808.803 84
      hist. & crit.   809.993 84
    spec. lits.
      collections   *lit. sub.*–080 384
      hist. & crit.   *lit. sub.*–093 84
    s.a. spec. lit forms
  of history   901
  of science   501
  rel. attitude toward
    Christianity   261.51
    other rel. see Religious
      attitudes secular
      disciplines
  stage trmt.   792.090 938 4
    s.a. spec. mediums e.g.
      Television
  subject headings   025.491
  other aspects see Disciplines
    (systems)
Philydraceae *see* Haemodorales
Phlebitis
  gen. med.   616.142
  geriatrics   618.976 142
  pediatrics   618.921 42
  pub. health   614.591 42
  statistics   312.314 2
    deaths   312.261 42
  other aspects see Diseases
Phlebotomy
  therapeutics   615.899
  s.a. spec. diseases
Phleum pratense *see* Timothy
  (grass)

Phloem
  plant
    anatomy   581.41
    pathology   581.221
  s.a. spec. plants
Phlogiston
  chem. theory   540.118
Phlorina Greece   *area*–495 6
Phlox family *see* Polemoniales
Phobias
  gen. med.   616.852 25
  geriatrics   618.976 852 25
  pediatrics   618.928 522 5
  psychology   157.3
  statistics   312.385 225
Phocidae
  animal husbandry   636.974 8
  hunting
    commercial   639.29
    sports   799.277 48
  zoology   599.748
  other aspects see Carnivora
Phocis Greece   *area*–495 1
  ancient   *area*–383
Phoenicia   *area*–394 4
Phoenician
  architecture   722.31
    misc. aspects see
      Architectural schools
  sculpture   732.944
    other aspects see
      Canaanite-Phoenician
Phoenicopteri *see* Ciconiiformes
Phoenix
  city Ariz.   *area*–791 73
  dactylifera *see* Dates (fruit)
  Islands   *area*–968 1
Phoenixes
  lit. & stage trmt.
    folk lit. texts & lit. crit.   398.245 4
    other aspects see Animals
Pholidophoroidea
  paleozoology   567.4
Pholidota
  animal husbandry   636.931
  hunting
    commercial   639.113 1
    sports   799.259 31
  paleozoology   569.31
  zoology   599.31
  other aspects see Mammalia
Phonemics *see* Phonology
Phones (linguistics) *see*
  Phonology
Phonetic
  development of words *see*
    Etymology
  shorthand systems
    Eng. lang.   653.423–.428
    other langs.   653.43–.49
  s.a. other spec. subj.

Phonetics *see* Phonology
Phonics
 reading instruction
  elementary ed.   372.414 5
Phonocardiography
 med. sci.   616.120 754 4
Phonocylinders *see* Recordings
Phonodiscs *see* Recordings
Phonofilms *see* Recordings
Phonograph records *see*
  Recordings
Phonographs *see* Reproducers
  sound
Phonology   414
 elementary ed.   372.622
 spec. langs.
  nonstandard forms *lang. sub.*–7
  standard forms   *lang. sub.*–15
Phonons
 astrophysics
  gen. wks.   523.019 721 7
   acceleration   523.019 737 7
  s.a. spec. celestial bodies
 physics
  gen. wks.   539.721 7
   acceleration   539.737 7
  spec. states of matter   530.4
  s.a. spec. physical
    phenomena e.g. Heat
Phonorecords *see* Recordings
Phonotapes *see* Recordings
Phonowires *see* Recordings
Phoronidea
 culture & hunting   639.757
 zoology   595.17
 other aspects see Worms
Phororhaci
 paleozoology   568.3
Phosphatases *see* Lipolytic
  enzymes
Phosphate fertilizers   553.64
 econ. geol.   553.64
 mining
  soc. & econ. aspects *see*
    Primary industries
  technology   622.364
   prospecting   622.186 4
 other aspects see Phosphorus
  fertilizers
Phosphates
 mineralogy   549.72
 other aspects see Phosphorus
  salts
Phosphides *see* Phosphorus salts
Phosphines
 org. chem.   547.071
  s.a. spec. groupings e.g.
    Aliphatic compounds
 synthetic drugs pharm.   615.317 1
  misc. aspects see
    Pharmacology

Phosphines (continued)
 synthetic poisons   615.951 71
  misc. aspects see
    Toxicology
 other aspects see Phosphorus
  chemistry
Phosphinic acids
 org. chem.   547.076
  s.a. spec. groupings e.g.
    Aliphatic compounds
 synthetic drugs pharm.   615.317 6
  misc. aspects see
    Pharmacology
 synthetic poisons   615.951 76
  misc. aspects see
    Toxicology
 other aspects see Phosphorus
  chemistry
Phosphites *see* Phosphorus salts
Phosphoacids
 org. chem.   547.074
  s.a. spec. groupings e.g.
    Aliphatic compounds
 synthetic drugs pharm.   615.317 4
  misc. aspects see
    Pharmacology
 synthetic poisons   615.951 74
  misc. aspects see
    Toxicology
 other aspects see Phosphorus
  chemistry
Phosphoalcohols
 org. chem.   547.073
  s.a. spec. groupings e.g.
    Aliphatic compounds
 synthetic drugs pharm.   615.317 3
  misc. aspects see
    Pharmacology
 synthetic poisons   615.951 73
  misc. aspects see
    Toxicology
 other aspects see Phosphorus
  chemistry
Phosphoaldehydes
 org. chem.   547.075
  s.a. spec. groupings e.g.
    Aliphatic compounds
 synthetic drugs pharm.   615.317 5
  misc. aspects see
    Pharmacology
 synthetic poisons   615.951 75
  misc. aspects see
    Toxicology
 other aspects see Phosphorus
  chemistry
Phosphoketones
 org. chem.   547.075
  s.a. spec. groupings e.g.
    Aliphatic compounds

Phosphoketones (continued)
  synthetic drugs pharm.   615.317 5
    misc. aspects see
      Pharmacology
  synthetic poisons   615.951 75
    misc. aspects see
      Toxicology
  other aspects see Phosphorus
    chemistry
Phosphonic acids
  org. chem.   547.077
    s.a. spec. groupings e.g.
      Aliphatic compounds
  synthetic drugs pharm.   615.317 7
    misc. aspects see
      Pharmacology
  synthetic poisons   615.951 77
    misc. aspects see
      Toxicology
  other aspects see Phosphorus
    chemistry
Phosphonium cpds.
  org. chem.   547.071
    s.a. spec. groupings e.g.
      Aliphatic compounds
  synthetic drugs pharm.   615.317 1
    misc. aspects see
      Pharmacology
  synthetic poisons   615.951 71
    misc. aspects see
      Toxicology
  other aspects see Phosphorus
    chemistry
Phosphoproteins
  org. chem.   547.754
  other aspects see Proteins
Phosphor bronze *see* Copper
Phosphorescence
  optics *see* Luminescence
    optics
Phosphoric acid
  chem. tech.   661.25
  soc. & econ. aspects *see*
    Secondary industries
  s.a. spec. prod.
Phosphorus   553.93
  chemistry
    inorganic   546.712
      technology   661.071 2
      soc. & econ. aspects
        see Secondary
        industries
      s.a. spec. prod.
    organic   547.07
      technology   661.87
      misc. aspects see
        Organic chemicals
      s.a. spec. groupings
        e.g. Aliphatic
        compounds
    s.a. Phosphorus salts

Phosphorus (continued)
  compounds *see* Phosphorus
    chemistry
  econ. geol.   553.93
  fertilizers   553.93
    production
      soc. & econ. aspects *see*
        Secondary industries
      technology   668.625
    use agric.   631.85
      s.a. spec. crops; also
        spec. types of culture
        e.g. Floriculture
  metabolism
    human phys.   612.392 4
    other aspects see
      Metabolism
  mining
    technology   622.393
    prospecting   622.189 3
  pharmacology
    inorganic   615.271 2
    organic   615.317
    other aspects see
      Pharmacology
  salts
    chem. tech.   661.43
    plant nutrition *see*
      Macronutrient elements
      plant nutrition
    soc. & econ. aspects *see*
      Secondary industries
    s.a. spec. prod.
  toxicology
    inorganic   615.925 712
    organic   615.951 7
    other aspects see
      Toxicology
  other aspects see Nonmetallic
    elements
  s.a. spec. uses; also spec.
    minerals
Phosphorylases *see* Enzymes
Photoalgraphy
  soc. & econ. aspects *see*
    Secondary industries
  technology   686.232 6
Photoaluminography
  soc. & econ. aspects *see*
    Secondary industries
  technology   686.232 6
Photobiology *see* Radiations
  biophysics
Photoceramic processes
  photographic printing   773.6
Photochemistry
  physical chem.   541.35
    applied   660.295
    organic   547.135
    s.a. spec. elements, cpds.,
      prod.

Photoconductive cells *see*
    Photoelectric devices
Photoconductivity *see*
    Photoelectric phenomena
Photocopying *see*
    Photoduplication
Photoduplication
  machines   681.65
    manufacturing
      soc. & econ. aspects *see*
        Secondary industries
    technology   681.65
  personnel
    biog. & work   686.409 2
    s.a.   *pers.–686 4*
  processes
    soc. & econ. aspects *see*
      Secondary industries
    technology   686.4
Photoelasticity *see* Optical
    properties
Photoelectric
  devices
    radiowave electronics
      soc. & econ. aspects *see*
        Secondary industries
      tech. & mf.   621.381 542
    s.a. spec. appls. e.g.
      Elevators (lifts)
    other aspects see Radiowave
      electronics
  phenomena
    astrophysics   523.018 754
    s.a. spec. celestial
      bodies
    physics   537.54
      spec. states of matter   530.4
  photometry
    astronomy   522.623
    s.a. spec. celestial
      bodies
Photoelectronic devices *see*
    Photoelectric devices
Photoemissive cells *see*
    Photoelectric devices
Photoemissivity *see*
    Photoelectric phenomena
Photoenamel processes
  photographic printing   773.6
Photoengraving
  soc. & econ. aspects *see*
    Secondary industries
  technology   686.232 7
Photoetching *see* Photoengraving
Photogrammetry   526.982
  mil. eng.   623.72
Photograph files
  police records   363.24
    misc. aspects see Police
      services

Photographers
  biog. & work   770.92
  occupational ethics   174.977
  s.a.   *pers.–77*
Photographic
  analysis
    metals   669.950 283
    s.a. spec. metals
    s.a. other spec. materials
  chemicals
    chem. tech.   661.808
    use *see* Photography
    other aspects see Organic
      chemicals
  equipment
    manufacturing
      soc. & econ. aspects *see*
        Secondary industries
    technology   681.418
    use *see* Photography
  films *see* Photosensitive
    surfaces
  papers *see* Photosensitive
    surfaces
  photometry
    astronomy   522.622
    s.a. spec. celestial
      bodies
  plates *see* Photosensitive
    surfaces
  projection
    motion-picture   778.55
    still   778.2
      stereoscopic   778.4
  spacecraft *see* Unmanned
    spacecraft
  surveying *see* Photogrammetry
Photographs
  arts   770
  identification of criminals
    see Identification
    criminals
  other aspects see Pictures
Photography
  advertising operations   659.132 3
  arts   770
  astronomy   522.63
    s.a. spec. celestial bodies
  eng. appls.
    soc. & econ. aspects *see*
      Secondary industries
    technology   621.367
    s.a. spec. appls. e.g.
      Materials engineering
  libraries   026.77
    misc. aspects see Special
      libraries
  mil. eng.   623.72
    s.a. other spec. appls.
Photogravure *see* Photengraving

Phototelegraphy *see* Facsimile
   transmission
Phototherapy   615.831
  misc. aspects see Physical
    therapies
  s.a. spec. diseases
Phototubes *see* Photoelectric
   devices
Photovoltaic cells *see*
   Photoelectric devices
Photovoltaism *see* Photoelectric
   phenomena
Photozincography
  soc. & econ. aspects *see*
    Secondary industries
  technology   686.232 6
Photronic cells *see*
   Photoelectric devices
Phra
  Budalot La reign Thailand hist.
      959.303 2
  s.a. spec. events & subj.
    e.g. Commerce
  Nang Klao reign Thailand hist. 959.303 3
  s.a. spec. events & subj.
    e.g. Commerce
Phrases (linguistics) *see*
   Grammar (linguistics)
Phraya Taksin reign Thailand
   hist.   959.302 4
  s.a. spec. events & subj.
    e.g. Commerce
Phreatoicidea *see* Isopoda
Phrygia   *area*–392 6
Phrygian languages *see*
   Thraco-Phrygian
   languages
Phrymaceae *see* Verbenales
Phthietis Greece   *area*–495 1
Phycologists
  biog. & work   589.309 2
  other aspects see Scientists
  s.a.   *pers.*–58
Phycology   589.3
Phycomycetes
  agric. pathogens   632.45
   s.a. spec. types of culture
    e.g. Forestry; *also*
    spec. plants
  botany   589.25
  med. aspects
   gen. pharm.   615.329 25
    toxicology   615.952 925
   vet. pharm.   636.089 532 925
    toxicology   636.089 595 292 5
  other aspects see Plants
Phylactolaemata
  culture   639.7
  zoology   594.72
  other aspects see Bryozoa
Phyllocarida *see* Leptostraca

Phyllocladaceae *see* Coniferales
Phyllocladus family *see*
   Coniferales
Phylloglossum *see* Lycopsida
Phyllosilicates
  mineralogy   549.67
Phylogeny *see* Evolution
Physical
  abnormality
   influence on crime   364.24
  allergies
   gen. med.   616.977
   geriatrics   618.976 977
   pediatrics   618.929 77
   pub. health   614.599 3
   statistics   312.397 7
    deaths   312.269 77
   other aspects see Diseases
  anthropologists
   biog. & work   573.092
   other aspects see
    Scientists
   s.a.   *pers.*–573
  anthropology   573
   misc. aspects see Life
    sciences
  biochemistry
   gen. wks.   574.192 83
    animals   591.192 83
    microorganisms   576.119 283
    plants   581.192 83
   s.a. spec. organisms; also
    spec. constituents
   med. sci.   612.015 83
    animals   636.089 201 583
    s.a. spec. animals
    man   612.015 83
   s.a. spec. functions,
    systems, organs
  characteristics
   influence on crime   364.24
  chemistry   541.3
   applied   660.29
   organic   547.13
   s.a. spec. elements, cpds.,
    prod.
  conditions of work
   personnel admin.
    gen. management   658.38
     executives   658.407 8
     spec. subj.   *s.s.*–068 3
    pub. admin.   350.161
     central govts.   351.161
      spec. jur.   353–354
     local govts.   352.005 161
  constitution
   celestial bodies
    comets   523.66
     spec. comets   523.64
    stars   523.86
     spec. systems   523.84–.85

Physical
  constitution
    celestial bodies (continued)
      sun   523.76
      s.a. other spec. bodies
      s.a. other spec. subj.
    crystallography   548.84–.86
    s.a. spec. substances
    diagnosis
      med. sci.
        gen. med.   616.075 4
        surgery   617.075 4
        s.a. spec. diseases
      other aspects see
        Diseases
    education   613.7
      elementary ed.   372.86
      special ed.   371.904 4
      s.a. spec. groups of
        students e.g. Blind
        people
    environments
      psychology   155.91
    evidence
      criminal investigation   363.256 2
      law
        criminal law   345.064
          spec. jur.   345.3–.9
        gen. wks.   347.064
          spec. jur.   347.3–.9
        other aspects see
          Evidence
    examinations
      employee selection *see*
        Selection procedures
      employees
        med. aspects *see* Diagnoses
    fitness
      hygiene   613.7
      programs
        pub. admin.   350.773
          central govts.   351.773
          spec. jur.   353–354
          local govts.   352.4
    geodesy   526.7
    geography   910.02
      ancient   913.02
      spec. countries   913–919
    geology   551
    gerontology   612.67
    illness
      soc. path.   362.1
      soc. theology *see* Social
        problems soc. theology
      s.a. Physically sick people
    impairments
      aged people
        psychology   155.671

Physical (continued)
  instruments
    manufacturing
      soc. & econ. aspects *see*
        Secondary industries
      technology   681.753
    s.a. spec. kinds
    location of plant
      management   658.21
      spec. subj.   *s.s.*–068 2
    metallurgy   669.9
    mineralogy   549.12
      spec. minerals   549.2–.7
    oceanography *see* Oceanography
    operations
      chem. eng.   660.284 2
      s.a. spec. prod.
      s.a. other spec. subj.
    optics
      astrophysics   523.015 2
      s.a. spec. celestial
        bodies
      physics   535.2
      spec. states of matter   530.4
    phenomena
      biophysics
        gen. wks.   574.191 2
          animals   591.191 2
          microorganisms   576.119 12
          plants   581.191 2
        s.a. spec. organisms
        med. sci.   612.014 2
          animals   636.089 201 42
          s.a. spec. animals
          man   612.014 2
        s.a. spec. functions,
          systems, organs
      celestial bodies *see*
        Physical constitution
      elect. circuits
        electrodynamic eng.   621.319 21
        s.a. spec. appls. e.g.
          Lighting engineering
        other aspects see
          Electrodynamics
      lit. & stage trmt. *see*
        Natural phenomena
      s.a. other spec. subj.
    plants *see* Plants (bldgs. &
      equip.)
    processes
      metallurgical furnaces   669.85
      s.a. spec. metals
      s.a. other spec. subj.
    properties
      chemicals *see spec.*
        chemicals
      crystals   548.84–.86
      eng. materials   620.112
        spec. materials   620.12–.19

Physical
  properties (continued)
    lumber
      mf. tech. — 674.132
    minerals — 549.12
      spec. min. — 549.2–.7
    rocks — 552.06
      spec. rocks — 552.1–.5
  requirements
    employees *see* Personal
      qualifications
  sciences — 500.2
    s.a. spec. sci.
  therapies
    gen. wks. — 615.82
    vet. sci. — 636.089 582
      s.a. spec. animals
    psychiatry — 616.891 3
      geriatrics — 618.976 891 3
      pediatrics — 618.928 913
    s.a. spec. diseases
  training *see* Physical
    education
  typology
    influence on crime — 364.24
  units
    physics — 530.8
      s.a. spec. branches of
        physics
  yoga
    hygiene — 613.704 6
  s.a. other spec. subj.
Physically
  disabled people *see* Disabled
    people
  handicapped people *see*
    Disabled people
  healthy people — *pers.*–081 2
  sick people
    soc. services *see* Medical
      services soc. welfare
    s.a. — *pers.*–081 4
    s.a. Physical illness
Physicians
  biog. & work
    med. sci. — 610.92
    vet. sci. — 636.089 092
  investments by
    financial econ. — 332.671 55
      domestic — 332.672 55
      international — 332.673 14
  prof. duties & characteristics
    law — 344.041 2
      spec. jur. — 344.3–.9
    med. sci. — 610.695 2
    vet. sci. — 636.089 069 52
  other aspects see Medical
    scientists
  s.a. — *pers.*–61
  s.a. spec. kinds

Physicists
  applied *see* Applied
    physicists
  gen. wks.
    biog. & work — 530.092
      s.a. spec. kinds
      other aspects see
        Scientists
    s.a. — *pers.*–53
Physicochemical phenomena
  glassmaking — 666.104 2
    s.a. spec. kinds of glass
  metallurgy — 669.94
    s.a. spec. metals
  plastics mf. — 668.404 2
    s.a. spec. kinds of
      plastics
  s.a. other spec. subj.
Physics — 530
  & religion
    nat. rel. — 215.3
  applied *see* Applied physics
  astronomy — 523.01
    s.a. spec. celestial bodies
  Biblical trmt. — 220.853
    s.a. spec. parts of Bible
  cells — 574.876 041
    animals — 591.876 041
    plants — 581.876 041
    s.a. spec. organisms
  curriculums — 375.53
  documentation — 025.065 3
  laboratory bldgs.
    architecture — 727.553
    building — 690.755 3
    other aspects see
      Educational buildings
  libraries — 026.53
    misc. aspects see Special
      libraries
  library acquisitions — 025.275 3
  library classification — 025.465 3
  research
    cooperation
      internat. law — 341.767 53
  soil sci. — 631.43
    s.a. spec. crops; also spec.
      types of culture e.g.
        Floriculture
  subject headings — 025.495 3
  other aspects see Sciences
Physiocracy
  econ. school — 330.152
Physiognomy(anthroposcopy) — 138
Physiographic regions
  hygiene — 613.12
    misc. aspects see Hygiene
  in art *see* Landscapes
  lit. & stage trmt.
    folk lit. soc. — 398.322
    other aspects see Places

Picea *see* Spruce trees
Picenum   *area*–374
Pichincha Ecuador   *area*–866 13
Pici *see* Piciformes
Piciformes
  hunting
    commercial   639.128 72
    sports   799.248 72
  paleozoology   568.7
  zoology   598.72
  other aspects see Aves
Pickaway Co. O.   *area*–771 815
Pickens Co.
  Alabama   *area*–761 85
  Georgia   *area*–758 255
  South Carolina   *area*–757 23
Pickering North Yorkshire Eng.
     area–428 46
Pickers *see*
     Harvesting-machinery
Picketing
  labor econ.   331.892 7
  labor law *see* Labor law
Pickett Co. Tenn.   *area*–768 687
Pickled foods
  cookery   641.616
Pickling
  foods   641.46
    commercial   664.028 6
    domestic   641.46
    other aspects see Foods
    s.a. spec. foods e.g. Meats
  preparation tech.
    biol. specimens   579.2
Picnic
  areas roadsides eng.
    technology   625.77
    other aspects see Roads
  cookery   641.578
  food services   642.3
Picrodendraceae *see* Juglandales
Pictographs *see* Nonverbal
     language
Pictorial
  arts *see* Graphic arts
  journalism   070.49
Pictou Co. N.S.   *area*–716 13
Picture
  frames
    furniture arts   749.7
    wooden
      mf. tech.   674.88
      other aspects see Wood
        products
  language *see* Nonverbal
      language
  telegraphy *see* Facsimile
      transmission
  writing *see* Nonverbal
      language

Pictures
  ed. use   371.335 2
    s.a. spec. levels of ed.;
      also Special education
  fine arts   760
  library trmt.   025.177 1
    acquisitions   025.287 1
    cataloging   025.347 1
    s.a. other spec. activities
    museology   069.57
    circulation   069.134
  spec. subj.   *s.s.*–022 2
  textiles *see* Hangings
  other aspects see Graphic
      materials; *also*
      Audiovisual materials
Piculets *see* Piciformes
Pidgin
  English   427.95
Pidyon haben
  Jewish rites   296.442 3
Pie mixes
  comm. proc.   664.753
Piecework wages *see* Incentive
     payments
Piedmont
  Plateau U.S.   *area*–75
    Alabama   *area*–761 5
    Georgia   *area*–758 4
    Maryland   *area*–752 7
    North Carolina   *area*–756 5
    South Carolina   *area*–757 3
    Virginia   *area*–755 6
  region Italy   *area*–451
Pieplant *see* Rhubarb
Pier
  buildings *see* Marine
      transportation
      buildings
  foundations
    engineering   624.158
    s.a. spec. appls. e.g.
      Military engineering
Pierce
  County
    Georgia   *area*–758 792
    Nebraska   *area*–782 56
    North Dakota   *area*–784 591
    Washington   *area*–797 78
    Wisconsin   *area*–775 42
  Franklin admin.
    U.S. hist.   973.66
    s.a. spec. events & subj.
      e.g. Commerce
Piercing
  metal prod. *see* Forging
Pieria Greece   *area*–495 6
Pierre S.D.   *area*–783 29
Piers (columns)
  structural eng.   624.16
    s.a. spec. appls. e.g. Dams

Piers (columns) (continued)
  other aspects see Columnar
    structures
Piers (docks)
  port eng.
    soc. & econ. aspects *see*
      Secondary industries
    technology   627.313
    s.a. spec. appls. e.g.
      Approach piloting
  other aspects see Port
    facilities
Pies
  comm. proc.   664.752 5
  cookery   641.865 2
Pietism
  doctrinal controversies
    Christian church hist.   273.7
Piety
  gift of the Holy Spirit
    Christian doctrines   234.12
Piezodialysis
  saline water conversion
    technology   628.167 46
    other aspects see Water
      supply engineering
Piezoelectricity
  astrophysics   523.018 724 46
    s.a. spec. celestial bodies
  physics   537.244 6
    spec. states of matter   530.4
  property of matter *see*
    Electromagnetic
    properties
Piezomagnetism *see* Magnetic
    phenomena
Pig iron
  technology   669.141 3
  other aspects see Ferrous
    metals
Pigeon English   427.95
Pigeons
  animal husbandry   636.596
  other aspects see Poultry;
    also Columbiformes
Piggyback cargo services *see*
    Unitized cargo services
Pigment
  materials   553.662
    econ. geol.   553.662
  mining
    soc. & econ. aspects *see*
      Primary industries
    technology   622.366 2
    prospecting   622.186 62
  s.a. spec. uses
  processes
    photographic printing   773
Pigmentary changes
  skin
    gen. med.   616.55

Pigmentary changes
  skin (continued)
    geriatrics   618.976 55
    pediatrics   618.925 5
    pub. health   614.595 5
    statistics   312.355
    other aspects see Diseases
Pigmentation
  biochemistry
    human phys.   612.792 7
    other aspects see
      Integumentary organs
  cytology   574.874
    animals   591.874
    plants   581.874
    s.a. spec. organisms
  physical anthr.   573.5
Pigmented cells
  connective tissues *see*
    Connective tissue
Pigments
  biochemistry
    gen. wks.   574.192 18
    animals   591.192 18
    microorganisms   576.119 218
    plants   581.192 18
    s.a. spec. organisms
    med. sci.   612.015 28
    animals   636.089 201 528
      s.a. spec. animals
    man   612.015 28
    s.a. spec. functions,
      systems, organs
  biosynthesis
    gen. wks.   574.192 97
    animals   591.192 97
    microorganisms   576.119 297
    plants   581.192 97
    s.a. spec. organisms
    med. sci.   612.015 47
    animals   636.089 201 547
      s.a. spec. animals
    man   612.015 47
  manufacturing
    comm. proc.   667.29
    soc. & econ. aspects *see*
      Secondary industries
  oil-soluble paints
    technology   667.623
    other aspects see Paints
  org. chem.   547.869
  painting material
    arts   751.2
    indiv. artists   759.1–.9
  rubber tech. *see* Compounding
    rubber
Pignuts *see* Hickory nuts
Pigs *see* Swine
Pikas *see* Lagomorpha
Pike Co.
  Alabama   *area*–761 35

Pike Co. (continued)

Arkansas	*area*–767 485
Georgia	*area*–758 453
Illinois	*area*–773 453
Indiana	*area*–772 36
Kentucky	*area*–769 23
Mississippi	*area*–762 23
Missouri	*area*–778 36
Ohio	*area*–771 847
Pennsylvania	*area*–748 24

Pikes (fishes) *see* Mesichthyes
Pila Poland   *area*–438 4
Pilasters *see* Columnar
    structures
Pile
  foundations eng.   624.154
    s.a. spec. appls. e.g.
      Bridges (structures)
  rugs
    textile arts   746.75
Piles (diseases) *see* Anus
    diseases
Pile-weave fabrics
  arts   746.046 17
    s.a. spec. proc. e.g.
      Weaving
  manufacturing
    soc. & econ. aspects *see*
      Secondary industries
    technology   677.617
  other aspects see Textiles
  s.a. spec. prod.
Pilgrimage to Mecca
  Islamic moral theology   297.55
Pilgrimages
  personal rel. experience *see*
    Religious observances
    private
  rel. rites
    Christianity   265.9
    other rel. see Public
      worship
Pillage *see* Depredation
Pillars *see* Columnar structures
Pillars of the faith
  Islamic moral theology   297.5
Pillowcases *see* Bedclothing
Pills
  prac. pharm.   615.43
    misc. aspects see
      Pharmacology
Pilot
  errors
    air transp. hazard   363.124 14
  guides
    aeronautics   629.132 54
    seamanship   623.892 9
  plants
    chem. eng.   660.280 72
    s.a. spec. prod.
  whales *see* Odontoceti

Piloting
  aeronautics
    soc. & econ. aspects *see*
      Secondary industries
    technology   629.132 52
      military   623.746 048
  manned space flight
    gen. wks.   629.458 2
    s.a. spec. appls. e.g.
      Space warfare
    s.a. spec. flights e.g.
      Lunar flights
  seamanship   623.892 2
  services
    inland ports
      commerce   386.866
      govt. control   350.876 866
        central govts.   351.876 866
        spec. jur.   353–354
        local govts.   352.916 866
      law *see* Ports
        inland-waterway transp.
        law
    seaports
      commerce   387.166
      govt. control   350.877 166
        central govts.   351.877 166
        spec. jur.   353–354
        local govts.   352.917 166
      law *see* Seaports law
        transp.
  systems
    spacecraft *see* Flight
      operations systems
      spacecraft
Pilotless aircraft
  mil. eng.   623.746 9
Pilots
  aerial
    biog. & work   629.130 92
    s.a.   *pers.*–629 1
Pilot-seat ejectors
  aircraft eng.
    soc. & econ. aspects *see*
      Secondary industries
    tech. & mf.   629.134 386
Piltdown man
  hoaxes   001.95
Pima Co. Ariz.   *area*–791 77
Pi-mesons *see* Mesons
Piña cloth *see* Bast fibers
    textiles
Pinaceae *see* Coniferales
Pinal Co. Ariz.   *area*–791 75
Pinang Malaysia   *area*–595 1
Pinar del Rio Cuba   *area*–729 11
Pindus Greece   *area*–495 3
Pine
  Co. Minn.   *area*–776 62
  family *see* Coniferales
  Mt. Ky.   *area*–769 123

Pine (continued)
trees
  forestry   634.975 1
  soc. & econ. aspects *see*
    Primary industries
  other aspects see
    Coniferales; *also*
    Trees
woods *see* Softwoods
woods region Tex.   *area*–764 15
Pineal gland
anatomy
  human   611.47
  other aspects see Secretory
    organs
diseases
  gen. wks.   616.48
    neoplasms   616.992 47
    tuberculosis   616.995 47
  geriatrics   618.976 48
  pediatrics   618.924 8
  pub. health   614.594 8
  statistics   312.348
    deaths   312.264 8
  other aspects see Diseases
physical anthropometry   573.647
physiology
  human   612.492
  other aspects see Secretion
tissue biology human   611.018 947
Pineapples
agriculture
  fiber crops
    soc. & econ. aspects *see*
      Primary industries
    technology   633.576
  food crops
    soc. & econ. aspects *see*
      Primary industries
    technology   634.774
foods   641.347 74
  preparation
    commercial   664.804 774
    domestic   641.647 74
  other aspects see
    Bromeliales; *also*
    Fruits
Pinellas Co. Fla.   *area*–759 63
Pines Isle
Cuba   *area*–729 125
New Caledonia   *area*–932
Pink family *see* Caryophyllales
Pinnacles *see* Roofs
Pinnipedia
animal husbandry   636.974 5
hunting
  commerical   639.29
  sports   799.277 45
zoology   599.745
other aspects see Carnivora

Pinochle
equipment mf.   688.754 16
  soc. & econ. aspects *see*
    Secondary industries
recreation   795.416
Pins
clothing *see* Notions clothing
numismatics   737.24
Pinus *see* Pine trees
Pioneer
Mts. Ida.   *area*–796 32
project astronautics   629.435 4
Pioneers
history *see hist. of spec.*
    places
Pions *see* Mesons
Piotrkow Trybunalski Poland
    area–438 4
Pious societies
Christianity   248.06
Pipe
fitters
  biog. & work   696.209 2
  s.a.   *pers.*–696
fitting
  buildings   696.2
organs *see* Organs (music)
Pipefishes *see* Mesichthyes
Pipeline transp.
commerce   388.5
govt. control   351.878
  spec. jur.   353–354
law
  international   341.756
  municipal   343.093
  spec. jur.   343.3–.9
other aspects see Mechanics;
    also Transportation
Pipelines
engineering
  machine eng.   621.867 2
  soc. & econ. aspects *see*
    Secondary industries
use in gas transp.   665.744
use in petroleum transp.   665.544
s.a. other spec. appls.
other aspects see Mechanics
Piperaceae *see* Piperales
Piperales
botany   583.925
floriculture   635.933 925
forestry   634.973 925
med. aspects
  crop prod.   633.883 925
  gen. pharm.   615.323 925
    toxicology   615.952 392 5
  vet. pharm.   636.089 532 392 5
    toxicology   636.089 595 239 25
paleobotany   561.3
other aspects see Plants

Pipes (conveyances)
 drainage *see* Drainage
 liquid flow mech.
  engineering *see* Dynamics
  physics   532.54
 machine eng.
  soc. & econ. aspects *see*
   Secondary industries
  tech. & mf.   621.867 2
  s.a. spec. appls. e.g.
   Water supply
 marine engine auxiliaries *see*
  Engine auxiliaries
  shipbuilding
 metal prod.
  mf. tech.   671.832
   ferrous metals   672.832
   s.a. other spec. metals
  other aspects see Primary
   metal prod.
 steam eng. *see* Transmission
  steam
 other aspects see Mechanics
Pipes (tobacco)
 manufacturing
  soc. & econ. aspects *see*
   Secondary industries
  technology   688.42
Pipestone Co. Minn.   *area*–776 26
Pipe-threading tools
 soc. & econ. aspects *see*
  Secondary industries
 tech. & mf.   621.944
 s.a. spec. appls. e.g.
  Plumbing technology
Pipewort family *see*
  Eriocaulales
Pipidae
 zoology   597.84
 other aspects see Anura
Piping
 marine engine auxiliaries *see*
  Engine auxiliaries
  shipbuilding
Pipits *see* Motacillidae
Piracy
 criminology   364.164
 law   345.026 4
  spec. jur.   345.3–.9
 soc. theology
  Christianity   261.833 164
  comp. rel.   291.178 331 64
  s.a. other spec. rel.
Pirate perch *see* Mesichthyes
Pirates' expeditions
 travel   910.453
 misc. aspects see Travel
Pisa Italy   *area*–455 5
Piscataquis Co. Me.   *area*–741 25
Pisces
 conservation tech.   639.977

Pisces (continued)
 culture
  soc. & econ. aspects *see*
   Primary industries
  technology   639.37
  other aspects see
   Agriculture
 drawing tech.   743.67
 fishing
  commercial
   soc. & econ. aspects *see*
    Primary industries
   technology   639.27
   other aspects see Fishing
    industries
  sports   799.1
 paleozoology   567
 resources
  economics   333.956
  govt. control
   law   346.046 956
    spec. jur.   346.3–.9
   pub. admin. *see*
    Biological resources
    govt. control pub.
    admin.
 zoology   597
 other aspects see Animals
Pisé *see* Sun-dried blocks
Pisidia   *area*–392 7
Pistachios
 agriculture   634.574
  soc. & econ. aspects *see*
   Primary industries
 foods   641.345 74
  preparation
   commercial   664.804 574
   domestic   641.645 74
 other aspects see Sapindales;
  also Nuts
Pistacia vera *see* Pistachios
Pistils
 plant anatomy   582.046 3
 s.a. spec. plants
Pistoia Italy   *area*–455 2
Pistols
 art metalwork   739.744 3
 hunting & shooting
  sports   799.202 833
   game   799.213
   targets   799.31
 mil. eng.
  soc. & econ. aspects *see*
   Secondary industries
  tech. & mf.   623.443
 mil. sci.   355.824 3
  s.a. spec. mil. branches
 small arms
  mf. tech.   683.432
  other aspects see Small
   arms

Pituitary
  gland
    anatomy
      human   611.47
      other aspects see
        Secretory organs
    diseases
      gen. wks.   616.47
        neoplasms   616.992 47
        tuberculosis   616.995 47
      geriatrics   618.976 47
      pediatrics   618.924 7
      pub. health   614.594 7
      statistics   312.347
        deaths   312.264 7
      other aspects see
        Diseases
    physical anthropometry   573.647
    physiology
      human   612.492
      other aspects see
        Secretion
    tissue biology human   611.018 947
  hormones
    pharmacology   615.363
    other aspects see Drugs
Pity
  psychology *see* Emotions
  virtue *see* Virtues
Pityeae
  paleobotany   561.55
Piura Peru   *area*–851 3
Pius 4 Creed
  Christian doctrines   238.2
Piute Co. Utah   *area*–792 53
Pizzas
  cookery   641.824
Place
  names   910.3
    s.a. spec. places
  settings
    table service   642.6
  treatment *see* Geographical
        treatment; *also*
        Places
Placement
  child welfare   362.73
    misc. aspects see Young
        people soc. services to
  employees
    personnel admin.
      gen. management   658.312 8
      executive   658.407 128
      spec. subj.   *s.s.*–068 3
    pub. admin.   350.14
      central govts.   351.14
        spec. jur.   353–354
      local govts.   352.005 14
  labor econ.   331.128
    law *see* Labor law

Placement
  labor econ. (continued)
    s.a. spec. classes of
        workers e.g. Women
  students
    education *see* Academic
        placement
    employment *see* Placement
        employees
Placenta
  diseases
    obstetrics   618.34
    pub. health   614.599 2
    statistics   312.304 834
      deaths   312.260 483 4
    other aspects see Diseases
  obstetrical surgery   618.87
    vet. med.   636.089 887
      s.a. spec. animals
  other aspects see Pregnancy
Placental
  dystocia
    obstetrics   618.56
      anesthesia   617.968 2
    pub. health   614.599 2
    statistics   312.304 856
      deaths   312.260 485 6
    other aspects see Diseases
  extracts
    pharmacology   615.39
    other aspects see Drugs
Placer
  Co. Calif.   *area*–794 38
  mining *see* Alluvial mining
Placers
  econ. geol.   553.13
    spec. deposits   553.2–.8
  mineralogy   549.113
    spec. minerals   549.2–.7
Places
  lit. trmt.
    folk lit.
      sociology
        legendary   398.42
        real   398.32
      texts & lit. crit.   398.23
    gen. wks
      collections
        legendary   808.803 72
        real   808.803 2
      hist. & crit.
        legendary   809.933 72
        real   809.933 2
    spec. lits.
      collections
        legendary   *lit. sub.*–080 372
        real   *lit. sub.*–080 32
      hist. & crit.
        legendary   *lit. sub.*–093 72
        real   *lit. sub.*–093 2
    s.a. spec. lit. forms

Planets
astrology | 133.53
astronomy
description | 523.4
theory | 521.54
manned flights to *see*
Planetary manned
flights
regional subj. trmt. | *area*–992
unmanned probes *see* Planetary
unmanned probes
other aspects see Celestial
bodies
Planing
mill products
manufacturing
soc. & econ. aspects *see*
Secondary industries
technology | 674.42
Planing-tools *see* Planers
Plankton | 574.92
animal | 592
plant *see* Phytoplankton
Planned
economies | 330.124
parenthood *see* Family
planning
s.a. other spec. subj.
Planning
executive management | 658.401 2
library buildings | 022.3
museum buildings | 069.22
prod. management | 658.503
spec. subj. | *s.s.*–068 5
pub. admin. | 350.007 2
central govts. | 351.007 2
spec. jur. | 353–354
local govts. | 352.000 472
sales management | 658.810 1
spec. subj. | *s.s.*–068 8
soc. welfare | 361.2
spec. problems & groups | 362–363
other aspects see Welfare
services
s.a. | *s.s.*–068
s.a. other spec. kinds
Planographic printing
graphic arts
processes | 763
products | 769
mech. printing tech.
soc. & econ. aspects *see*
Secondary industries
technology | 686.231 5
Plans
arch. design | 729.2
structural elements | 729.3
s.a. spec. kinds of bldgs.
bldg. construction | 692.1
geography | 912
spec. subj. | *s.s.*–022 3

Plant
behavior
comp. psych. | 156.9
ecology | 581.5
s.a. spec. plants
breeding *see* Plant
propagation
diseases
agriculture | 632.3
prod. econ. | 338.14
s.a. spec. plants; also
spec. types of culture
e.g. Forestry
injuries
agriculture | 632
s.a. spec. plants; also
spec. types of culture
e.g. Forestry
nutrients *see* Fertilizers
pathology *see* Pathology
pests
agriculture | 632.5
s.a. spec. plants; also
spec. types of culture
e.g. Forestry
home econ. | 648.8
sanitary eng. | 628.97
other aspects see Pests
physiology *see* Physiology
propagation
crop prod. | 631.53
s.a. spec. crops; also
spec. types of culture
e.g. Floriculture
quarantine
pest control | 632.93
s.a. spec. plants; also
spec. types of culture
e.g. Forestry
receptacles
agriculture | 631.34
use *see spec. uses e.g.*
Controlled environment
agriculture
s.a. spec. crops; also
spec. types of culture
e.g. Floriculture
mf. tech. | 681.763 1
soc. & econ. aspects *see*
Secondary industries
reserves *see* Wildlife
reserves
supports
agriculture | 631.34
use | 631.546
s.a. spec. crops; also
spec. types of culture
e.g. Floriculture
mf. tech. | 681.763 1
soc. & econ. aspects *see*
Secondary industries

Plant (continued)
  viruses
    virology — 576.648 3
    med. sci. — 616.019 4
  s.a. Botanical; *also*
      Vegetable
Plantagenets
  Eng. hist. — 942.03
  Gt. Brit. hist. — 941.03
  Ireland hist. — 941.503
  s.a. spec. events & subj.
    e.g. Courts
Plantaginaceae *see*
    Plantaginales
Plantaginales
  botany — 583.89
  floriculture — 635.933 89
  med. aspects
    crop prod. — 633.883 89
    gen. pharm. — 615.323 89
    toxicology — 615.952 389
    vet. pharm. — 636.089 532 389
    toxicology — 636.089 595 238 9
  paleobotany — 561.3
  other aspects see Plants
Plantain eaters *see*
    Cuculiformes
Plantains (fruit)
  agriculture — 634.773
    soc. & econ. aspects *see*
      Primary industries
  foods — 641.347 73
    preparation
      commercial — 664.804 773
      domestic — 641.647 73
  other aspects see
    Zingiberales; *also*
    Fruits
Plantains (weeds) *see*
    Plantaginales
Plantation songs *see* Negro
    songs U.S.
Plantations
  sociology — 307.72
Plant-culture instruments
  manufacturing
    soc. & econ. aspects *see*
      Secondary industries
  technology — 681.763 1
  s.a. spec. kinds
Planters *see* Planting-equipment
Planting
  crops
    agriculture — 631.53
    s.a. spec. crops; also
      spec. types of culture
      e.g. Floriculture
  roadside areas
    technology — 625.77
    other aspects see Roads

Planting-equipment
  agriculture — 631.33
    use — 631.53
    s.a. spec. crops; also
      spec. types of culture
      e.g. Floriculture
  mf. tech. — 681.763 1
    soc. & econ. aspects *see*
      Secondary industries
Plants
  agric. pests *see* Weeds
  arrangement
    dec. arts — 745.92
  art representation — 704.943 4
    drawing tech. — 743.7
    painting — 758.5
    s.a. other spec. art forms
  conservation tech. — 639.99
  culture — 631
    govt. control
      activities — 351.823 33
      spec. jur. — 353–354
      departments — 351.082 333
      spec. jur. — 353–354
  landscape design — 715–716
  lit. & stage trmt.
    folk lit.
    sociology
      legendary — 398.468
      real — 398.368
      texts & lit. crit. — 398.242
  other aspects see Natural
    phenomena
  resources
    economics — 333.953
    govt. control
      law — 346.046 953
      spec. jur. — 346.3–.9
    pub. admin. *see*
      Biological resources
      govt control. pub.
      admin.
Plants (bldgs. & equip.)
  functional use
    chem. eng. — 660.28
      soc. & econ. aspects *see*
      Secondary industries
    s.a. spec. prod.
    libraries — 022
    local Christian churches — 254.7
    museums — 069.21
    prisons — 365.5
    misc. aspects see Penal
      institutions
    sanitation eng. — 628.51
      soc. & econ. aspects *see*
      Secondary industries
    s.a. spec. appls. e.g.
      Industrial hygiene

Platinum (continued)
  mineral aspects
    econ. geol.   553.422
    mineralogy   549.23
    mining
      technology   622.342 4
      prospecting   622.184 22
    s.a. spec. minerals
  pharmacology   615.264 5
    misc. aspects see
      Pharmacology
  plate *see* Platinumwork
  printing-out process
    photography   772.3
  products *see* Platinumwork
  toxicology   615.925 645
    misc. aspects see
      Toxicology
  other apsects see Metal;
    also Metals
  s.a. spec. uses
Platinum-group metals
  bldg. materials   691.87
  chemistry
    inorganic   546.63
    organic   547.056 3
    s.a. spec. groupings e.g.
      Aliphatic compounds
    technology   661.063
    organic   661.895
    soc. & econ. aspects *see*
      Secondary industries
    s.a. spec. prod.
  construction
    building   693.77
  metallography   669.957
  metallurgy   669.7
    physical & chem.   669.967
  mineral aspects
    econ. geol.   553.495
    mining   622.349 5
      prospecting   622.184 95
    soc. & econ. aspects *see*
      Primary industries
  pharmacology   615.263
    misc. aspects see
      Pharmacology
  products
    mf. tech.   673.7
    other aspects see
      Nonferrous metals
      products
  toxicology   615.925 63
    misc. aspects see
      Toxicology
Platinumwork
  arts
    decorative   739.24
    other aspects see Precious
      metals arts
  mf. tech.   673.24

Platinumwork (continued)
  other aspects see Nonferrous
    metals products
Platonism
  philosophic system
    ancient   184
    modern   141.2
    indiv. phil.   180–190
    s.a. spec. branches of
      phil. e.g. Metaphysics
Platoons
  mil. organization   355.31
    s.a. spec. mil. branches
Platt Nat. Park Okla.   *area*–766 57
Plattdeutsch *see* Low German
Platte
  County
    Missouri   *area*–778 135
    Nebraska   *area*–782 52
    Wyoming   *area*–787 17
  River Neb.   *area*–782
Platters *see* Tableware
Platycopa *see* Ostracoda
Platyhelminthes
  culture & hunting   639.752 1–.752 3
  zoology   595.121–.123
  other aspects see Worms
Platypuses *see* Monotremata
Play
  groups
    sociology   302.34
    s.a. spec. organizations
  rooms *see* Recreational areas
Play (activity)
  child rearing   649.5
  recreation   790
Player pianos
  mf. tech.   681.83
    misc. aspects see Musical
      instruments
  musical art   789.72
Playgrounds
  outdoor sports   796.068
  other aspects see Parks
Playgroup movements ed.   372.216
Playhouse *see* Theater
Playing
  music theory   781.63
  s.a. spec. mediums
Playing-cards *see* Card games
Plays *see* Drama
Playwriting *see* Drama gen. wks.
  rhetoric
Pleadings
  law *see* Pretrial procedure
Pleasant Isl.   *area*–968 5
Pleasants Co. W. Va.   *area*–754 21

Plum Isl. N.Y.   *area*–747 25
Plumas Co. Calif.   *area*–794 29
Plumbaginaceae *see* Primulales
Plumbago (mineral) *see* Graphite
Plumbago (plant) family *see*
     Primulales
Plumbers
     biog. & work   696.109 2
     s.a.   *pers.*–696
Plumbing
     library bldgs.   022.8
     local govt. control   352.926
     museum bldgs.   069.29
     technology   696.1
Plumbum *see* Lead
Plums
     agriculture   634.22
       soc. & econ. aspects *see*
         Primary industries
     foods   641.342 2
       preparation
         commercial   664.804 22
         domestic   641.642 2
     other aspects see Rosaceae;
       also Fruits
Plunger pumps *see* Reciprocating
     pumps
Plural
     executives
       pub. admin.   350.003 1
       central govts.   351.003 1
       spec. jur.   353–354
       local govts.   352.008
     marriage *see* Polygamy
Pluralism
     philosophy   147.4
     indiv. phil.   180–190
     s.a. spec. branches of phil.
       e.g. Metaphysics
Plurality of worlds *see*
     Astrobiology
Plush *see* Pile-weave fabrics
Plushcapped finches
     zoology   598.8
     other aspects see
       Passeriformes
Pluto (planet)
     astronomy
       description   523.482
       theory   521.548 2
     flights to
       manned   629.455 82
       unmanned   629.435 482
     regional subj. trmt.   *area*–992 9
     other aspects see Celestial
       bodies
Plutocracies
     pol. sci.   321.5
     s.a. spec. jur.

Plutonic
     phenomena
       geophysics   551.2
     rocks
       mineralogy   549.114 3
         spec. minerals   549.2–.7
       petrology   552.3
       other aspects see Natural
         stones
Plutonium
     chemistry   546.434
Plymouth
     County
       Iowa   *area*–777 16
       Massachusetts   *area*–744 82
     Devon Eng.   *area*–423 58
     Rock chickens
       animal husbandry   636.582
       other aspects see Chickens
Plympton Devon Eng.   *area*–423 592
Plywood
     mf. tech.   674.834
     other aspects see Wood
       products
Pneumatic
     clocks
       mf. tech.   681.115
       soc. & econ. aspects *see*
         Secondary industries
     construction
       architecture   721.044 98
       s.a. spec. kinds of
         bldgs.
       buildings   693.98
     control
       automation eng.   629.804 5
       s.a. spec. appls. e.g.
         Machine tools; *also*
         spec. systems e.g.
         Closed-loop systems
     conveyor systems
       library equip.   022.9
       office use   651.79
     engineering
       physics   533.6
       soc. & econ. aspects *see*
         Secondary industries
       technology   621.51–.54
       s.a. spec. appls. e.g.
         Spacecraft
       other aspects see
         Aeromechanics
     engineers
       biog. & work   621.509 2
       s.a.   *pers.*–621
     forcing methods
       underwater foundation eng.   624.157
       s.a. spec. appls. e.g.
         Bridges (structures)
         structural eng.

Pneumatic (continued)
  tools
    soc. & econ. aspects *see*
      Secondary industries
    tech. & mf.   621.904
      s.a. spec. appls. e.g.
        Artificial road
        surfaces eng.; *also*
        spec. kinds e.g. Power
        hammers
  tubes *see* Pipes (conveyances)
  s.a. other spec. subj.
Pneumatics *see* Gases
Pneumatotherapy *see*
  Aerotherapeutics
Pneumoconiosis
  gen. med.   616.244
  geriatrics   618.976 244
  pediatrics   618.922 44
  pub. health   614.592 44
  statistics   312.324 4
    deaths   312.262 44
  other aspects see Diseases
Pneumonias
  gen. med.   616.241
  geriatrics   618.976 241
  pediatrics   618.922 41
  pub. health   614.592 41
  statistics   312.324 1
    deaths   312.262 41
  other aspects see Diseases
Pneumonic plague *see* Bubonic
  plague
Po River Italy   *area*–452
Poa *see* Bluegrasses
Poaceae *see* Graminales
Poatina Tas.   *area*–946 3
Pocahontas Co.
  Iowa   *area*–777 19
  West Virginia   *area*–754 87
Pocket
  billiards *see* Pool (game)
  gophers *see* Sciuromorpha
  mice *see* Sciuromorpha
Pocklington Humberside Eng.
          area–428 39
Pocono Mts. Pa.   *area*–748 2
Pod arrangements
  dec. arts   745.925
Podagra *see* Gout
Podiatry *see* Chiropody
Podicipediformes *see*
  Colymbiformes
Podoaceae *see* Sapindales
Podocarp family *see* Coniferales
Podocarpaceae *see* Coniferales
Podocopa *see* Ostracoda
Podophyllaceae *see* Ranales
Podostemaceae *see* Podostemales
Podostemales
  botany   583.921

Podostemales (continued)
  floriculture   635.933 921
  med. aspects
    crop prod.   633.883 921
    gen. pharm.   615.323 921
      toxicology   615.952 392 1
    vet. pharm.   636.089 532 392 1
      toxicology   636.089 595 239 21
  paleobotany   561.3
  other aspects see Plants
Podostemonaceae *see*
  Podostemales
Podostemonales *see* Podostemales
Pods
  splitting *see* Hydration
    movements
Poecilosclerida *see*
  Demospongiae
Poems (music)   781.96
  s.a. spec. musical mediums
Poetic books (O.T.)
  gen. wks.   223
    pseudepigrapha   229.912
  liturgy   264.3–.4
  spec. denominations   264.01–.09
Poetry
  gen. wks.
    collections   808.81
    crit. theory   801.951
      textual   801.959
    hist. & crit.   809.1
    rhetoric   808.1
      juvenile   808.068 1
  spec. lits.   *lit. sub.*–1
Poets
  biog. & work   809.1
  s.a. spec. lits.
  other aspects see Authors
  s.a.   *pers.*–81
Pohjois-Karjala Finland   *area*–489 75
Poinciana *see* Caesalpiniaceae
Poinsett Co. Ark.   *area*–767 96
Poinsettias *see* Euphorbiales
Point
  set topology   514.322
    s.a. spec. appls. e.g.
      Engineering
  sets   511.33
    s.a. spec. math. branches;
      also spec. appls. e.g.
      Engineering
Pointe Coupee Par. La.   *area*–763 454
Pointers (dogs)
  animal husbandry   636.752
  other aspects see Dogs
Pointillism *see*
  Neo-Impressionism
Point-of-sale advertising   659.157
Poison
  gas warfare *see* Chemical
    warfare

Poison (continued)
  hemlock *see* Umbellales
  ivy *see* Sapindales
  oak *see* Sapindales
  sumac *see* Sapindales
Poisoning
  toxicology *see* Toxicology
Poisonous
  animals
    zoology   591.69
    s.a. spec. animals
  fish flesh
    toxicology   615.945
    misc. aspects see
      Toxicology
  materials
    pub. safety   363.179
    misc. aspects see
      Hazardous materials
  mussels flesh
    toxicology   615.945
    misc. aspects see
      Toxicology
  plants
    botany   581.69
    s.a. spec. plants
Poisons
  ammunition *see* Chemical
    devices mil. eng.
  pesticides *see* Pesticides
  toxicology *see* Toxicology
Poisson integral   515.43
s.a. spec. appls. e.g.
    Engineering
Poisson's ratio
  engineering *see* Dynamics
  physics   531.381
Poisson-Stieltjes integral   515.43
s.a. spec. appls. e.g.
    Engineering
Poitou France   *area*–446
Poitou-Charentes France   *area*–446
Poker (game)
  equipment mf.   688.754 12
  soc. & econ. aspects *see*
    Secondary industries
  recreation   795.412
Pokeweed family *see*
    Chenopodiales
Polabian language
  linguistics   491.89
  literature   891.89
  s.a.   *lang.*–918 9
Poland   *area*–438
Poland-China swine
  animal husbandry   636.482
  other aspects see Swine
Polar
  easterlies *see* Planetary wind
    systems
  s.a. Arctic

Polarimeters
  mf. tech.   681.416
    components   681.42–.43
  optics *see* Polarization light
  other aspects see Optical
    instruments
Polarimetric
  analysis
    gen. wks.   543.085 6
    qualitative   544.956
    quantitative   545.816
    organic   547.308 56
    qualitative   547.349 56
    quantitative   547.358 16
    s.a. spec. elements & cpds.
  titration *see* Polarographic
    methods
Polarimetry
  astronomy   522.65
  s.a. spec. celestial bodies
  physical chem.   541.702 8
Polaris missiles
  mil. eng.
    soc. & econ. aspects *see*
      Secondary industries
    tech. & mf.   623.451 97
Polariscopic analysis *see*
    Polarimetric analysis
Polarization
  light
    astrophysics   523.015 52
    s.a. spec. celestial
      bodies
    physics   535.52
    spec. states of matter   530.4
  sound
    engineering   620.21
    s.a. spec. appls.
    physics   534.207
    spec. states of matter   530.4
Polarographic methods
  anal. chem.
    gen. wks.   543.087 2
    qualitative   544.972
    quantitative   545.32
    organic   547.308 72
    qualitative   547.353 2
    quantitative   547.349 72
    s.a. spec. elements & cpds.
Polders *see* Drainage land
    reclamation
Polecats *see* Mustelidae
Polemics
  doctrinal theology
    Christianity   239
    comp. rel.   291.2
    Islam   297.29
    other rel. see Doctrinal
      theology
Polemoniaceae *see* Polemoniales

Polishing
  metal prod.
    mf. tech. (continued)
      s.a. other spec. metals
      other aspects see Finishing
  woodwork bldgs.   698.33
Polishing-tools *see*
    Lapping-tools
Politeness *see* Courtesy
Political
  action groups
    pol. sci.   322.4
  activity
    citizenship ethics *see*
      Citizenship ethics
    civil service personnel *see*
      Employee rights civil
      service personnel
  campaigns
    election
      pol. sci.   324.9
      finance   324.78
      offenses *see*
        Electoral offenses
      strategy   324.72
      techniques   324.7
    law   342.078
      spec. jur.   342.3–.9
    literature *see* Political
      programs
    nomination *see* Nomination
      procedures
    propaganda *see* Party
      ideologies
  causes
    warfare
      mil. sci.   355.027 2
    s.a. hist. of spec. wars
  change   320.011
  clubs
    pol. sci.   324.3
    spec. parties   324.24–.29
  conditions
    ed. soc.   370.193 49
    history   900
    pol. sci.   320.9
  corruption
    criminology   364.132 3
    law   345.023 23
      spec. jur.   345.3–.9
    pub. admin.   350.994
      central govts.   351.994
        spec. jur.   353–354
      local govts.   352.002
    soc. theology
      Christianity   261.833 132 3
      comp. rel.   291.178 331 323
    s.a. other spec. rel.
  crimes *see* Political offenses
  divisions
    historical geog.   911

Political (continued)
  economy *see* Economics
  ethics *see* Political
    relationships ethics
  groups
    discrimination *see*
      Discriminatory
      practices
    status in law   342.087
      spec. jur.   342.3–.9
  history   900
    spec. wars *see* Social
      history
  ideologies   320.5
    soc. theology
      Christianity   261.7
      comp. rel.   291.177
    s.a. other spec. rel.
    s.a. Party ideologies
  institutions
    pol. sci.   320.9
    relation to soc. welfare   361.613
    soc. theology
      Buddhism   294.337 7
      Christianity   261.7
      comp. rel.   291.177
      Hinduism   294.517 7
      Islam   297.197 7
      Judaism   296.387 7
    s.a. other spec. rel.
    sociology   306.2
  justice   320.011
  machines *see* Party
    organization gen. wks.
  offenses
    criminology   364.131
    law   345.023 1
      spec. jur.   345.3–.9
    soc. theology
      Christianity   261.833 131
      comp. rel.   291.178 331 31
    s.a. other spec. rel.
  oppression
    victims of *see* Victims of
      political oppression
  organizations *see* Nonprofit
    organizations
  parties
    pol. sci.   324.2
    status in law   342.087
      spec. jur.   342.3–.9
    s.a. Party
  patronage
    pol. sci.   324.204
    spec. parties   324.24–.29
  penalties
    penology   364.68
  pins & buttons
    numismatics   737.242
  platforms *see* Political
    programs

Political (continued)
pressures
  on libraries   021.8
prisons
  penology   365.45
  other aspects see Penal
    institutions
process   324
  relation to budgeting
    pub. admin.   350.722 21
      central govts.   351.722 21
      spec. jur.   353–354
    local govts.   352.122 1
programs
  pol. sci.   324.23
  spec. parties   324.24–.29
refugees
  pol. sci.   325.21
relationships
  ethics
    philosophy   172
  religion
    Buddhism   294.356 2
    Christianity   241.62
    comp. rel.   291.562
    Hinduism   294.548 62
    s.a. other spec. rel.
rights
  law
    electoral   342.072
    other   342.085 4
    spec. jur.   342.3–.9
  pol. sci.   323.5
sabotage *see* Political
  offenses
science   320
  Biblical trmt.   220.832
  s.a. spec. parts of Bible
  curriculums   375.32
  documentation   025.063 2
  journalism   070.449 32
  libraries   026.32
    misc. aspects see Special
      libraries
  other aspects see Social
    sciences
scientists
  biog. & work   320.092
  s.a.   *pers.*–321
situation
  history   900
  pol. sci.   320.9
slogans *see* Party ideologies
songs *see* National songs &
  hymms
themes
  lit. & stage trmt. *see*
    Historical themes
unions
  regional subj. trmt.   *area*–171 2
s.a. other spec. subj.

Politicians
  biog. & work   324.209 2
  s.a. spec. pol. parties
  ethics *see* Public
    administration ethics
  s.a.   *pers.*–329
Politics *see* Political
Polk
  County
    Arkansas   *area*–767 45
    Florida   *area*–759 67
    Georgia   *area*–758 375
    Iowa   *area*–777 58
    Minnesota   *area*–776 95
    Missouri   *area*–778 77
    Nebraska   *area*–782 352
    North Carolina   *area*–756 915
    Oregon   *area*–795 38
    Tennessee   *area*–768 875
    Texas   *area*–764 165
    Wisconsin   *area*–775 17
  James K. admin.
    U.S. hist.   973.61
    s.a. spec. events & subj.
      e.g. Commerce
Polkas
  piano music   786.44
  recordings   789.912 644
Poll taxes
  pub. admin.   350.724
    central govts.   351.724
    spec. jur.   353–354
    local govts.   352.135
  pub. finance   336.25
  suffrage pol. sci.   324.62
Polled Durham cattle
  animal husbandry   636.226
  other aspects see Cattle
Pollen
  paleobotany   561.13
  s.a. spec. plants
  plant anatomy   582.046 3
  s.a. spec. plants
Pollen-plants
  bee pasturage   638.13
Pollination
  botany   582.016 62
  s.a. spec. plants
Polling
  law *see* Election procedures
    law
  pol. sci.   324.65
Pollutants
  control
    law
      international   341.762 3
      municipal   344.046 33
      spec. jur.   344.3–.9
    pub. admin.   350.823 23
      central govts.   351.823 23
      spec. jur.   353–354

Pollutants
control
pub. admin. (continued)
local govts.   352.942 323
soc. aspects   363.738
Pollution
air *see* Air pollution
control
aircraft eng. *see* Power
plants aircraft eng.
law
international   341.762 3
municipal   344.046 32
spec. jur.   344.3–.9
pub. admin.   350.823 22
central govts.   351.823 22
spec. jur.   353–354
local govts.   352.942 322
s.a. Wastes control
diseases *see* Environmental
diseases
human ecology   301.31
soc. theology
Christianity   261.836 28
comp. rel.   291.178 362 8
s.a. other spec. rel.
sociology   304.28
sanitary eng.
soc. & econ. aspects *see*
Secondary industries
technology   628.5
s.a. spec. appls. e.g.
Military engineering
soc. aspects   363.73
soil *see* Soil pollution
water *see* Water pollution
water supply *see* Water supply
water-supply eng.
technology   628.168
other aspects see Water
supply engineering
Polo
equipment mf.   688.763 53
players
biog. & work   796.353 092
s.a.   *pers.*–796 35
sports   796.353
other aspects see Sports
s.a. Water polo
Polonaises
piano music   786.44
recordings   789.912 644
Polonium
chemistry
inorganic   546.728
organic   547.057 28
s.a. spec. groupings e.g.
Aliphatic compounds
technology   661.072 8
soc. & econ. aspects *see*
Secondary industries

Polonium
chemistry
technology (continued)
s.a. spec. prod.
pharmacology   615.272 8
misc. aspects see
Pharmacology
toxicology   615.925 728
misc. aspects see
Toxicology
Polperro Cornwall Eng.   *area*–423 74
Poltava Ukraine   *area*–477 15
Poltergeists
lit. & stage trmt. *see* Ghosts
occultism   133.14
Polyacrylics *see* Acrylics
Polyamides
plastics
chem. tech.   668.423 5
org. chem.   547.843 223 5
other aspects see Plastics
s.a. spec. prod.
textiles
arts   746.044 73
s.a. spec. proc. e.g.
Weaving
dyeing   667.347 3
manufacturing
soc. & econ. aspects *see*
Secondary industries
technology   677.473
special-proc. fabrics   677.6
org. chem.   547.857 3
other aspects see Textiles
s.a. spec. prod.
Polyandry *see* Polygamy
Polyangiaceae *see*
Myxobacterales
Polybasite
mineralogy   549.35
Polycarbonates
plastics *see* Thermoplastic
plastics
Polychaeta
culture & hunting   639.754 7
zoology   595.147
other aspects see Worms
Polycladida *see* Turbellaria
Polycondensation
chem. eng.   660.284 48
physical chem.   541.393
applied   660.299 3
organic   547.28
s.a. spec. aspects e.g. Low
temperatures
s.a. spec. elements, cpds.,
prod.
Polyctenoidea *see* Heteroptera

Polycyclic current
transmission
   electrodynamic eng.   621.319 16
   s.a. spec. appls. e.g.
     Lighting airports
   soc. & econ. aspects *see*
     Secondary industries
   other aspects see
     Electrodynamics
Polycythemias
   gen. med.   616.153
   geriatrics   618.976 153
   pediatrics   618.921 53
   pub. health   614.591 53
   statistics   312.315 3
   deaths   312.261 53
   other aspects see Diseases
Polyelectrolytes
   soil conditioners *see* Texture
     control soil
     conditioners
Polyesters
   plastics
     chem. tech.   668.422 5
     org. chem.   547.843 222 5
     other aspects see Plastics
     s.a. spec. prod.
   textiles
     arts   746.044 743
     s.a. spec. proc. e.g.
      Weaving
     dyeing   667.347 43
     manufacturing
      soc. & econ. aspects *see*
       Secondary industries
     technology   677.474 3
      special-proc. fabrics   677.6
     org. chem.   547.857 43
     other aspects see Textiles
     s.a. spec. prod.
Polyethers
   plastics *see* Themoplastic
     plastics
Polyethylenes *see* Polyolefins
Polyfluoro hydrocarbons
   plastics
     chem. tech.   668.423 8
     org. chem.   547.843 223 8
     other aspects see Plastics
     s.a. spec. prod.
   textiles
     arts   746.044 748
     s.a. spec. proc. e.g.
      Weaving
     dyeing   667.347 48
     manufacturing
      soc. & econ. aspects *see*
       Secondary industries
     technology   677.474 8
      special-proc. fabrics   677.6
     org. chem.   547.857 48

Polyfluoro hydrocarbons
  textiles (continued)
   other aspects see Textiles
   s.a. spec. prod.
Polygalaceae *see* Polygalales
Polygalales
   botany   583.143
   floriculture   635.933 143
   forestry   634.973 143
   med. aspects
     crop prod.   633.883 143
     gen. pharm.   615.323 143
      toxicology   615.952 314 3
     vet. pharm.   636.089 532 314 3
      toxicology   636.089 595 231 43
   paleobotany   561.3
   other aspects see Plants
Polygamous persons   *pers.*–065 9
Polygamy
   customs   392.5
   soc. theology   291.178 358 4
     Christianity   261.835 84
     s.a. other spec. rel.
   sociology   306.84
Polyglandular diseases   616.48
   geriatrics   618.976 48
   pediatrics   618.924 8
   pub. health   614.594 8
   statistics   312.348
   deaths   312.264 8
   other aspects see Diseases
Polyglot
   dictionaries   413
     spec. subj.   *s.s.*–03
   texts
     Bible   220.51
     s.a. spec. parts of Bible
     s.a. other spec. works
Polygonaceae *see* Polygonales
Polygonales
   botany   583.917
   floriculture   635.933 917
   forestry   634.973 917
   med. aspects
     crop prod.   633.883 917
     gen. pharm.   615.323 917
      toxicology   615.952 391 7
     vet. pharm.   636.089 532 391 7
      toxicology   636.089 595 239 17
   paleobotany   561.3
   other aspects see Plants
Polygons *see* Configurations
     geometry
Polygraph tests
   criminal investigation   363.254
     misc. aspects see Evidence
   employee selection *see*
     Selection procedures
     employees
Polygyny *see* Polygamy

Polyhalite
 mineralogy 549.755
Polyhedrons *see* Configurations
 geometry
Polyhydroxy aromatics
 org. chem. 547.633
 s.a. spec. cpds.
Polyisobutylenes *see*
  Polyolefins
Polymastigida *see* Mastigophora
Polymerization
 chemistry
  engineering 660.284 48
  physical 541.393
   applied 660.299 3
   organic 547.28
  s.a. spec. aspects e.g.
   Low temperatures
  s.a. spec. elements, cpds.,
   prod.
 plastics
  chem. tech. 668.42
  org. chem. 547.843 22
  other aspects see Plastics
  s.a. spec. prod.
 textiles
  arts 746.044 73–.044 74
  s.a. spec. proc. e.g.
   Weaving
  dyeing 667.347 3–.347 4
  manufacturing
   soc. & econ. aspects *see*
    Secondary industries
  technology 677.473–.474
   special-proc. fabrics 677.6
  org. chem. 547.857 3–.857 4
  other aspects see Textiles
  s.a. spec. prod.
Polymers
 eng. materials 620.192
  foundations 624.153 92
  naval design 623.818 92
  shipbuilding 623.820 7
  structures 624.189 2
  s.a. other spec. uses
 manufacturing
  chem. tech. 668.9
  soc. & econ. aspects *see*
   Secondary industries
  s.a. spec. prod. e.g.
   Hosiery
 molecular structure
  theoretical chem. 541.225 4
   organic 547.122 54
  s.a. spec. elements &
   cpds.
 org. chem. 547.7
Polymorphism
 crystallography 548.3
 s.a. spec. substances

Polynemoidea *see*
  Acanthopterygii
Polynesia *area*–96
Polynesian
 languages
  linguistics 499.4
  literatures 899.4
  s.a. *lang.*–994
  people *r.e.n.*–994
 s.a. Polynesia; *also other*
   spec. subj. e.g. Arts
Polynomial equations 515.252
 algebra 512.942
 calculus 515.252
  complex variables 515.925 2
  real variables 515.825 2
 s.a. other spec. functions &
   equations
 s.a. spec. appls. e.g.
   Engineering
Polyolefins
 plastics
  chem. tech. 668.423 4
  org. chem. 547.843 223 4
  other aspects see Plastics
  s.a. spec. prod.
 textiles
  arts 746.044 745
  s.a. spec. proc. e.g.
   Weaving
  dyeing 667.347 45
  manufacturing
   soc. & econ. aspects *see*
    Secondary industries
  technology 677.474 5
   special-proc. fabrics 677.6
  org. chem. 547.857 45
  other aspects see Textiles
  s.a. spec. prod.
Polypedatidae
 zoology 597.89
 other aspects see Anura
Polyphaga
 agric. pests 632.764
  s.a. spec. types of culture
   e.g. Forestry; *also*
   spec. crops
 culture 638.576 4
 paleozoology 565.76
 zoology 595.764
 other aspects see Insecta
Polyphase current
 transmission *see* Alternating
   current transmission
Polyphenyl hydrocarbons
 org. chem. 547.613
 s.a. spec. cpds.
Polyplacophora *see* Crepipoda
Polypodiaceae *see* Filicales
Polypody family *see* Filicales

Pontiac's conspiracy
U.S. hist.   973.27
Pontine Isls. & Marshes   *area*–456 23
Pontoon bridges
structural eng.   624.87
    other aspects see Bridges
       (structures)
Pontotoc Co.
Mississippi   *area*–762 932
Oklahoma   *area*–766 69
Pontus ancient land   *area*–393 3
Pontypool Gwent Wales   *area*–429 97
Pontypridd Mid Glamorgan Wales
    area–429 78
Ponza Italy   *area*–456 23
Poodles
animal husbandry   636.72
    other aspects see Dogs
Pooideae
botany   584.93
floriculture   635.934 93
forage crops   633.2
    soc. & econ. aspects *see*
       Primary industries
    other aspects see Field
       crops
med. aspects
    crop prod.   633.884 93
    gen. pharm.   615.324 93
    toxicology   615.952 493
    vet. pharm.   636.089 532 493
    toxicology   636.089 595 249 3
paleobotany   561.49
    other aspects see Plants
Pool (game)
equipment mf.   688.747 3
    soc. & econ. aspects *see*
       Secondary industries
players
    biog. & work   794.730 92
    s.a.   *pers.*–794 7
recreation   794.73
Pool hall bldgs. *see* Indoor
    game bldgs.
Poole Dorset Eng.   *area*–423 37
Pools (organizations)
prod. econ.   338.87
    misc. aspects see
       Combinations
       (organizations)
Pools (water)
landscape design   714
    s.a. Swimming pools
Poor
areas regional subj. trmt.   *area*–172 4
Clares *see* Franciscans
people
    health services   362.19
       misc. aspects see Medical
          services

Poor
people (continued)
    institution bldgs.
       architecture   725.55
       building   690.555
       other aspects see Public
          structures
    soc. services   362.58
    govt. control   350.845
       central govts.   351.845
       spec. jur.   353–354
       local govts.   352.944 5
    law *see* Welfare services
       law
    other aspects see Lower
       classes
    s.a.   *pers.*–069 42
    s.a. Poverty
Pop art
gen. wks.   709.040 71
    spec. places   709.1–.9
painting   759.067 1
    spec. places   759.1–.9
sculpture   735.230 471
    spec. places   730.9
s.a. other spec. art forms
Popcorn
agriculture   635.677
    soc. & econ. aspects *see*
       Primary industries
foods   641.356 77
    preparation
       commercial   664.805 677
       domestic   641.656 77
    other aspects see
       Panicoideae; *also*
       Vegetables
Pope Co.
Arkansas   *area*–767 32
Illinois   *area*–773 991
Minnesota   *area*–776 46
Popes
biog. & work   262.130 92
Christian church govt.   262.13
coronation and election
    Roman Catholic liturgy   264.022
    other aspects see Roman
       Catholics
s.a. Papal
Poplar
borough London Eng.   *area*–421 5
trees
    forestry   634.972 3
    soc. & econ. aspects *see*
       Primary industries
    other aspects see
       Salicales; *also* Trees
woods *see* Hardwoods
Poploca *see* Macro-Otomanguean

Pornography (continued)
  soc. aspects — 363.47
  crime — 364.174
  other aspects see Moral
    issues
Porosity *see* Transport
  phenomena
Poroxyleae
  paleobotany — 561.55
Porphyries *see* Plutonic rocks
Porphyrins
  org. chem. — 547.593
  s.a. spec. cpds.
Porpoises *see* Odontoceti
Port
  Arthur Tas. — *area*–946 4
  Augusta S. Aust. — *area*–942 38
  authorities
    local govt. admin. — 352.009 2
  buildings
    engineering
      pub. admin. — 350.877 1
        central govts. — 351.877 1
          spec. jur. — 353–354
        local govts. — 352.917 1
      technology — 627.33
        s.a. spec. appls. e.g.
          Passenger services
          transp. terminals
          commerce ports
      other aspects see Port
        facilities
  Coquitlam B.C. — *area*–711 33
  facilities
    hydraulic eng.
      soc. & econ. aspects *see*
        Secondary industries
      technology — 627.3
        s.a. spec. appls. e.g.
          Military engineering
  spec. kinds
    inland-waterway
      commerce — 386.85
      govt. control — 350.876 85
        central govts. — 351.876 85
          spec. jur. — 353–354
        local govts. — 352.916 85
      law
        international — 341.756 67
        municipal — 343.096 7
          spec. jur. — 343.3–.9
      maritime *see* Seaport
        facilities
  Fairy Vic. — *area*–945 7
  Glasgow Strathclyde Scot.
    — *area*–414 28
  Hedland W. Aust. — *area*–941 3
  installations *see* Port
    facilities
  Kembla N.S.W. — *area*–944 6
  Lincoln S. Aust. — *area*–942 38

Port (continued)
  Macquarie N.S.W. — *area*–944 2
  maintenance transp.
    inland ports — 386.86
      govt. control — 350.876 86
        central govts. — 351.876 86
          spec.jur. — 353–354
        local govts. — 352.916 86
    law *see* Ports
      inland-waterway transp.
    seaports — 387.16
      govt. control — 350.877 16
        central govts. — 351.877 16
          spec. jur. — 353–354
        local govts. — 352.917 16
    law *see* Seaports law
      transp.
  Moody B.C. — *area*–711 33
  Nelson Man. — *area*–712 71
  Noarlunga S. Aust. — *area*–942 32
  Pirie S. Aust. — *area*–942 32
  Royal Isl. S.C. — *area*–757 99
  Said Egypt — *area*–621 5
  Seton Lothian Scot. — *area*–413 6
  Talbot West Glamorgan Wales
    — *area*–429 85
  s.a. Ports
Portable
  firearms
    art metalwork — 739.744 2
    mil. eng.
      soc. & econ. aspects *see*
        Secondary industries
      tech. & mf. — 623.442
  flight vehicles
    soc. & econ. aspects *see*
      Secondary industries
    tech. & mf. — 629.14
    s.a. spec. appls. e.g.
      Postal communication
  heaters
    bldg. heating — 697.24
  lamps
    mining eng. — 622.473
  lights
    nautical equip.
      soc. & econ. aspects *see*
        Secondary industries
      technology — 623.86
        design — 623.814 6
          spec. craft — 623.812
  rocket launchers
    mil. eng. — 623.442 6
  stations
    radio
      engineering — 621.384 168
      s.a. spec. appls. e.g.
        Radiotelephony
      other aspects see Radio

Position (location)
  finding
    radio
      engineering   621.384 191
       s.a. spec. appls. e.g.
        Navigation
      other aspects see Radio
    geodetic astronomy   526.64
  Positional astronomy   526.6
Position-finding devices
  navigation
    seamanship   623.892 3–.893 3
    other aspects see
      Navigation
Position-media
  advertising   659.134
Positions
  planets
    astrology   133.53
Positives
  photographic tech.   770.284
    spec. fields   778
Positivism
  philosophy   146.4
    ethical systems   171.2
      applications   172–179
    indiv. phil.   180–190
    s.a. other spec. branches of
      phil.
Positrons
  astrophysics
    gen. wks.   523.019 721 4
      acceleration   523.019 737 4
    s.a. spec. celestial bodies
  physics
    gen. wks.   539.721 4
      acceleration   539.737 4
    spec. states of matter   530.4
    s.a. spec. physical
      phenomena e.g. Heat
Posology
  pharmacology   615.14
  misc. aspects see
    Pharmacology
  s.a. spec. drugs
Post
  exchanges
    mil. quarters   355.71
    s.a. spec. mil. branches
    services   355.341
    s.a. spec. mil. branches
  office
    buildings
      architecture   725.16
      building   690.516
      other aspects see Public
        structures
    departments
      pub. admin.   351.087 3
      U.S. govt.   353.4
      other spec. jur.   354

Post (continued)
  offices
    postal commun.   383.42
    other aspects see Postal
      communication
Postage
  meters
    office use   651.759
  stamps
    arts   769.56
    investment econ.   332.63
    postal commun.   383.23
    printing
      soc. & econ. aspects *see*
        Secondary industries
      technology   686.288
      other aspects see Postal
        communication
Postage-due stamps
  prints   769.57
Postal,
  cards
    postal commun.   383.122
    other aspects see Postal
      communication
  communication   383
    govt. control   351.873
      spec. jur.   353–354
    govt. depts. *see* Post
      office departments
    law
      international   341.757 3
      municipal   343.099 2
      spec. jur.   343.3–.9
  insurance   368.2
    misc. aspects see Insurance
  offenses
    criminology   364.136
    law
      internat.   341.77
      municipal   345.023 6
      spec. jur.   345.3–.9
    soc. theology
      Christianity   261.833 136
      comp. rel.   291.178 331 36
      s.a. other spec. rel.
  organization
    law   343.099 25
      spec. jur.   343.3–.9
    postal commun.   383.4
    other aspects see Postal
      communication
  personnel
    biog. & work   383.092
    s.a.   *pers.*–383
  savings
    banks
      economics   332.22
      other aspects see Banks
        (finance)

Potash salts
  mining (continued)
    technology   622.363 6
    prospecting   622.186 36
  s.a. spec. uses
Potassium
  alkalis
    chem. tech.   661.33
    soc. & econ. aspects *see*
      Secondary industries
    s.a. spec. prod.
  bicarbonate
    chem. tech.   661.333
    soc. & econ. aspects *see*
      Secondary industries
    s.a. spec. prod.
  carbonate
    chem. tech.   661.334
    soc. & econ. aspects *see*
      Secondary industries
    s.a. spec. prod.
  chemistry
    inorganic   546.383
    organic   547.053 83
    s.a. spec. groupings e.g.
      Aliphatic compounds
    technology   661.038 3
    organic   661.895
    soc. & econ. aspects *see*
      Secondary industries
    s.a. spec. prod.
  chloride fertilizers *see*
    Potassium fertilizers
  fertilizers
    production
      soc. & econ. aspects *see*
        Secondary industries
      technology   668.623
    use agric.   631.83
    s.a. spec. crops; also
      spec. types of culture
      e.g. Floriculture
  hydroxide
    chem. tech.   661.332
    other aspects see
      Industrial chemicals
  mineral aspects *see* Minor
    metals
  pharmacology   615.238 3
    misc. aspects see
      Pharmacology
  salts plant nutrition *see*
    Macronutrient elements
    plant nutrition
  sulfate fertilizers *see*
    Potassium fertilizers
  toxicology   615.925 383
    misc. aspects see
      Toxicology
  other aspects see Alkali
    metals

Potato
  starch
    food
      comm. proc.   664.22
      soc. & econ. aspects
        see Secondary
        industries
  whisky   641.259
    comm. proc.   663.59
    other aspects see Alcoholic
      beverages
Potatoes
  agriculture
    field crops   633.491
    garden crops   635.21
    soc. & econ. aspects *see*
      Primary industries
  foods   641.352 1
    preparation
      commercial   664.805 21
      domestic   641.652 1
    other aspects see Solanales;
      also Vegetables
  s.a. Sweet potatoes
Potential
  energy
    physics   531.642
    s.a. spec. branches of
      physics
  offenders
    identification   364.41
  theory
    functional analysis   515.7
    s.a. spec. appls. e.g.
      Engineering
Potential (electricity) *see*
  Electric potentials
Potential (magnetism) *see*
  Magnetic phenomena
Potentiometers *see* Electric
  potentials measurement
Potentiometric methods
  electroanalysis
    anal. chem.
      gen. wks.   543.087 12
      qualitative   544.971 2
      quantitative   545.312
      organic   547.308 712
      qualitative   547.349 712
      quantitative   547.353 12
    s.a. spec. elements &
      cpds.
Potenza Italy   *area*–457 71
Potichomania
  handicrafts   745.546
Potomac River   *area*–752
  West Virginia   *area*–754 9
Potoos *see* Caprimulgiformes
Potosí Bolivia   *area*–841 4
Pots
  mf. tech.   683.82

Powder (continued)
 rooms
  residential int. dec.   747.78
   s.a. spec. dec.
  technology   620.43
   s.a. spec. appls. e.g.
    Electrostatic
     photoduplication
  s.a. Propellant explosives
Powdered
 milk *see* Dried milk
 soaps
  manufacturing
   chem. tech.   668.124
   soc. & econ. aspects *see*
    Secondary industries
  s.a. other spec. subj.
Powder-post beetles *see*
   Colydioidea
Powders
 animal feeds *see* Formula
   feeds
 cosmetics *see* Cosmetics
 prac. pharm.   615.43
  misc. aspects see
   Pharmacology
Powell Co.
 Kentucky   *area*–769 585
 Montana   *area*–786 86
Power
 control
  machine eng.
   technology   621.812
    s.a. spec. appls. e.g.
     Steam generation
    other aspects see
     Mechanics
 Co. Ida.   *area*–796 49
 distribution
  utilities *see* Utilities
 equipment
  textiles mf.
   soc. & econ. aspects *see*
    Secondary industries
   technology   677.028 5
    s.a. spec. kinds of
     textiles
   s.a. other spec. uses
 failure
  electrodynamic eng. *see*
    Transmission elect.
    power
 hammers
  soc. & econ. aspects *see*
    Secondary industries
  tech. & mf.   621.974
   s.a. spec. appls. e.g.
    Agricultural equipment
 of attorney
  law   346.029
   spec. jur.   346.3–.9

Power (continued)
 plants
  aircraft eng.
   soc. & econ. aspects *see*
    Secondary industries
   tech. & mf.   629.134 35
   monitoring
    instrumentation   629.135 3
  air-cushion vehicles   629.314
  automobiles
   soc. & econ. aspects *see*
    Secondary industries
   tech. & mf.   629.25
  gen. wks.
   soc. & econ. aspects *see*
    Secondary industries
   tech. & mf.   621.4
  nuclear eng. *see* Reactors
    nuclear eng.
  shipbuilding
   soc. & econ. aspects *see*
    Secondary industries
   tech. & mf.   623.87
    design   623.814 7
    spec. craft   623.812
  spacecraft *see* Propulsion
    systems spacecraft
  s.a. other spec. appls.;
    also spec. kinds e.g.
    Internal-combustion
    engines
 politics
  internat. relations
   pol. sci.   327.11
    spec. countries   327.3–.9
 residues
  number theory   512.73
   s.a. spec. appls. e.g.
    Engineering
 resources *see* Power supply
 series   515.243 2
  calculus   515.243 2
   complex variables   515.924 32
   real variables   515.824 32
   s.a. other spec. functions
     & equations; also spec.
     appls. e.g.
     Engineering
 shovels
  machine eng.
   soc. & econ. aspects *see*
    Secondary industries
   tech. & mf.   621.865
    s.a. spec. appls. e.g.
     Foundation engineering
   other aspects see Mechanics
 supply
  electronic eng.
   technology   621.381 044
    s.a. spec. appls. e.g.
     Radar

Power
  supply
    electronic eng. (continued)
      other aspects see
        Electronics
    law
      international   341.755
      municipal   343.092
      spec. jur.   343.3–.9
    pub. admin.   350.872
      central govts.   351.872
      spec. jur.   353–354
      local govts.   352.912
    soc. services   363.62
    utilities *see* Utilities
  tools
    use in home woodworking   684.083
  transformers *see* Transformers
  transmission
    machine eng.
      soc. & econ. aspects *see*
        Secondary industries
      tech. & mf.   621.85
        s.a. spec. appls. e.g.
          Agricultural equipment
        other aspects see Mechanics
    use
      agriculture   631.371
        s.a. spec. crops; also
          spec. types of culture
            e.g. Floriculture
        s.a. other spec. uses
      s.a. Electric power
Power-driven
  vessels
    engineering   623.820 4
      design   623.812 044
      models   623.820 104 4
    seamanship   623.881 4
    other aspects see Vessels
      (nautical)
    s.a. spec. kinds e.g.
      Tugboats
    s.a. other spec. subj.
Power-factor meters *see* Phase
    elect. measurement
Power-interruption insurance   368.7
  misc. aspects see Insurance
Power-machinery
  use
    agriculture   631.37
      s.a. spec. crops; also
        spec. types of culture
          e.g. Floriculture
      s.a. other spec. uses
Power-plant insurance   368.7
  misc. aspects see Insurance

Powers
  chief executives
    pub. admin.   350.003 22
      central govts.   351.003 22
      spec. jur.   353–354
      local govts.   352.008
  courts *see* Judicial powers
  legislative bodies *see*
    Legislative powers
Powers (angels) *see* Angels
Powers (mathematics) *see*
    Exponents
Power-supply equipment
  wire telephony
    soc. & econ. aspects *see*
      Secondary industries
    tech. & mf.   621.387
      s.a. spec. appls. e.g.
        shipboard use
          623.856 3
      other aspects see Telephony
        wire
      s.a. other spec. uses
Poweshiek Co. Ia.   *area*–777 596
Powhatan Co. Va.   *area*–755 612
Powys Wales   *area*–429 5
Poznan Poland   *area*–438 4
Practical
  ethics   170.44
  nurses & nursing   610.730 693
  pharmacy   615.4
    law   344.041 6
      spec. jur.   344.3–.9
    other aspects see Drugs
  politics   324.7
  s.a. other spec. subj.
Practice
  law
    criminal   345.05
      spec. jur.   345.3–.9
    gen. wks.   347.050 4
      spec. jur.   347.3–.9
    procedure *see* Legal
      procedure
  s.a. other spec. subj.
Practice-teaching   370.733
Praenestian *see* Latinian
Praesto Denmark   *area*–489 1
Pragmatic reductionism
  psychology   150.194 34
    s.a. spec. subj. & branches
      of psych.
Pragmatism
  education   370.12
  philosophy   144.3
    indiv. phil.   180–190
    s.a. spec. branches of phil.
      e.g. Ethics
Prague Czechoslovakia   *area*–437 12
Praha Czechoslovakia   *area*–437 12
Prahova Romania   *area*–498 2

Prairie
chickens *see* Tetraonidae
County
Arkansas	*area*–767 77
Montana	*area*–786 25

dogs *see* Sciuromorpha
Prairies
ecology life sci. *see*
Grasslands ecology life
sci.
other aspects see Plane
regions
Praise
private prayers
Christianity	242.721

other rel. see Prayers
private devotions
Prajadhipok reign Thailand hist.	959.304 2

s.a. spec. events & subj.
e.g. Commerce
Prakrits *see* Indic languages
Praseodymium
chemistry
inorganic	546.413
organic	547.054 13

s.a. spec. groupings e.g.
Aliphatic compounds
technology	661.041 3
organic	661.895

soc. & econ. aspects *see*
Secondary industries
s.a. spec. prod.
eng. materials	620.189 291 3

s.a. spec. uses
metallography	669.952 913
metallurgy	669.291 3
physical & chem.	669.962 913
pharmacology	615.241 3

misc. aspects see
Pharmacology
products
mf. tech.	673.291 3

other aspects see
Nonferrous metals
products
toxicology	615.925 413

misc. aspects see
Toxicology
other aspects see
Cerium-group metals
Pratt Co. Kan.	*area*–781 815

Prawns *see* Natantia
Prayer
five times daily
Islamic moral theology	297.52

gen. wks.
Christianity	248.32
comp. rel.	291.43

other rel. see Worship
of Manasses
Apocrypha	229.6

Prayer
of Manasses (continued)
other aspects see Apocrypha
private worship *see* Prayer
gen. wks.
public worship
Christianity	264.1
spec. denominations	264.01–.09

other rel. see Public
worship
Prayer desks *see* Rostral
furniture
Prayer meetings
pub. worship
Christianity	264.7
spec. denominations	264.01–.09

other rel. see Public
worship
Prayers
gen. wks. *see* Prayers public
devotions
private devotions
Christianity	242.7–.8
comp. rel.	291.43
Judaism	296.72

s.a. other spec. rel.
public devotions
Christianity	264.13
spec. denominations	264.01–.09

other rel. see Public
worship
Preachers *see* Clergy
Preaching
rel. activity
Christianity	251
comp. rel.	291.61
Islam	297.65
Judaism	296.42

s.a. other spec. rel.
Preaching orders
rel. orders
Christianity	255.04
church hist.	271.04
ecclesiology	262.24

other rel. see Religious
congregations
Pre-Aryan period India hist.	934.01

s.a. spec. events & subj.
e.g. Commerce
Preble Co. O.	*area*–771 71
Precalculus	512.1

Precambrian eras
geology	551.71

s.a. spec. aspects e.g.
Economic geology
paleontology	560.171
spec. fossils	561–569

Precast
concrete
architectural construction
with reinforcement	721.044 544

Precast
concrete
architectural construction (continued)
without reinforcement   721.044 522
*s.a. spec. structural
elements; also spec.
types of bldgs.*
bldg. construction
with reinforcement   693.544
without reinforcement   693.522
other aspects see Concretes
ferroconcrete *see* Precast
reinforced concrete
reinforced concrete
bldg. aspects *see* Precast
concrete
eng. materials   620.137
foundation   624.153 37
structures   624.183 414
other aspects see
Concretes
s.a. other spec. uses
Precedence
genealogy   929.7
Precession
astronomy
corrections   522.9
*s.a. spec. celestial
bodies*
theory   521.9
s.a. spec. celestial bodies
Precious
metals
arts
engraving *see* Metal
engraving
handicrafts   745.56
spec. objects   745.59
sculpture *see* Precious
metals sculpture
construction
architecture   721.044 72
*s.a. spec. kinds of
bldgs.*
building   693.722–.724
materials
building   691.822–.824
engineering   620.189 22–.189 24
s.a. spec. uses
metallography   669.952 2–.952 4
metallurgy   669.22–.24
physical & chem.   669.962 2–.962 4
soc. & econ. aspects *see*
Secondary industries
mineral aspects
econ. geol.   553.42
mining
technology   622.342
prospecting   622.184 2
s.a. spec. minerals

Precious
metals (continued)
products
arts *see* Precious metals
arts
mf. tech.   673.22–.24
other aspects see
Nonferrous metals
products
sculpture
dec. arts   739.2
other aspects see Metals
sculpture
stones   553.82–.86
econ. geol.   553.82–.86
mining
soc. & econ. aspects *see*
Primary industries
technology   622.382–.386
prospecting   622.188 2–.188 6
other aspects see Glyptics
s.a. spec. uses
Precipitates
gravimetric anal. *see*
Gravimetric analysis
solution components
physical chem.   541.348 5
applied   660.294 85
organic   547.134 85
*s.a. spec. elements,
cpds., prod.*
Precipitation
chem. eng.   660.284 24
s.a. spec. prod.
geol. agent   551.35
meteorology   551.577
artificial modification   551.687 7
weather forecasting   551.647 7
spec. areas   551.65
serology *see* Immune reactions
volumetric anal.
quan. anal. chem.   545.24
organic   547.352 4
*s.a. spec. elements &
cpds.*
s.a. Sedimentation
Precision
casting
arts *see* Casting sculpture
metal prod.
mf. tech.   671.255
ferrous metals   672.255
s.a. other spec. metals
other aspects see Foundry
practice
diving
sports   797.24
other aspects see Sports

Precision (continued)
  instruments
    manufacturing
      soc. & econ. aspects *see*
        Secondary industries
    technology   681
    s.a. spec. prod.
Preclassical
  Latin
    linguistics   477
    other aspects see Latin
      language
    s.a. other spec. subj.
Precocious *see* Gifted
Precognition *see* Preperception
Precoordinate
  classification
    library operations   025.42
  indexing
    library operations   025.482
    terms   025.49
  subject cataloging
    library operations   025.47
Predation
  ecology life sci. *see*
    Nutritive adaptations
      ecology life sci.
Predators
  control
    animal husbandry   636.083
    s.a. spec. animals
    wildlife conservation tech.   639.96
    s.a. spec. kinds of
      animals
Predelinquent young people
  soc. services to   362.74
    misc. aspects see Young
      people soc. services to
Predestination
  rel. doctrines
    Christianity   234.9
    other rel. see Humankind
      rel. doctrines
Prediction
  parapsychology *see* Divination
  probabilities   519.287
    s.a. spec. appls. e.g.
      Public opinion
  statistical math.   519.54
    s.a. spec. appls. e.g.
      Engineering
Preesall Lancashire Eng.   *area*–427 682
Prefabricated materials
  arch. construction   721.044 97
    s.a. spec. kinds of bldgs.
  bldg. construction   693.97
  bldg. materials   691.97
Prefectorial systems
  education   371.59
    s.a. spec. levels of ed.;
      also Special education

Preferential hiring
  labor econ.   331.889 2
  labor law *see* Labor law
  pers. admin.
    gen. management   658.311 2
    executives   658.407 112
    spec. subj.   *s.s.*–068 3
  pub. admin.   350.132 43
    central govts.   351.132 43
    spec. jur.   353–354
    local govts.   352.005 132 43
Preferred stocks
  investment econ.   332.632 25
  other aspects see Stocks
Prefixes *see* Words
Preflight activities
  manned space flight
    gen. wks.
      lunar flights   629.454 2
      planetary flights   629.455
    s.a. spec. appls. e.g.
      Space warfare
  s.a. other kinds of flight
Pregnancy
  cookery for   641.563
  human phys.   612.63
  obstetrics   618.2
    anesthesia   617.968 2
  pub. health   614.599 2
  vet. obstetrics   636.089 82
    s.a. spec. animals
  other aspects see
    Reproduction
Prehistoric
  archaeology *see* Archaeology
  geography   913.01
    spec. places   913.1–.9
  man
    physical anthr.   573.3
    s.a. spec. activities
  religions   291.042
Prehnite
  mineralogy   549.63
Prejudice
  soc. control   303.385
  other aspects see
    Discriminatory
    practices
Preliminary
  hearings
    criminal law   345.072
    spec. jur.   345.3–.9
  operations
    latex mf.
      soc. & econ. aspects *see*
        Secondary industries
      technology   678.522
      s.a. spec. kinds of
        latexes e.g. Natural
        latexes

Presbyterians
 biog. & work 285.092
  s.a. spec. denominations
 s.a. *pers.*–251
Presbyteries
 Christian ecclesiology 262.4
Preschool children
 psychology 155.423
 rearing home econ. 649.123
 s.a. *pers.*–054 3
Preschools 372.21
 misc. asepcts see Elementary
  schools
Prescience of God
 rel. doctrines
  Christianity 231.4
 other rel. see God
Prescot Merseyside Eng. *area*–427 54
Prescott & Russell United Cos.
  Ont. *area*–713 85
Prescott Co. Ont. *area*–713 86
Prescriptions
 drugs
  filling 615.4
   misc. aspects see Drugs
  writing *see* Posology
   pharmacology
Prescriptive
 linguistics *see* Applied
  linguistics
 s.a. other spec. subj.
Preseli Dyfed Wales *area*–429 62
Presentation
 in temple
  Jesus Christ doctrines 232.928
 of news
  journalism 070.412
 rel. orders 255.977
  buildings
   architecture 726.779 77
   building 690.677 977
   other aspects see
    Religious-purpose
    bldgs.
  church hist. 271.977
  ecclesiology 262.24
Presentations
 parturition
  obstetrics 618.42
   veterinary 636.089 842
   s.a. spec. animals
 pub. health 614.599 2
Preservation
 techniques
  arts 702.88
   paintings 751.6
    indiv. artists 759.1–.9
   photographic tech.
    gen. wks.
     negatives &
      transparencies 770.285

Preservation
 techniques
  arts
   photographic tech.
    gen. wks. (continued)
     positives 770.286
    spec. fields 778
    s.a. techs. in other spec.
     art forms
  foods
   commercial 664.028
    s.a. spec. kinds e.g.
     Fruits
   domestic 641.4
   library materials 025.84
   museology 069.53
    s.a. other spec. subj.
  s.a. Conservation
Preserved foods
 cookery 641.61
Preserves
 comm. proc. 664.152
 cookery 641.852
 other aspects see Sugars
Preservice training
 mil. personnel 355.223 2
  s.a. spec. mil. branches
Presidente Hayes Paraguay *area*–892 23
Presidential
 messages *see* Executive
  messages
 systems
  pol. sci. 321.804 2
   s.a. spec. jur.
Presidential-Congressional
  relations *see*
   Executive-legislative
   relations
Presidents
 of nations
  biog. & work *see hist. of*
   spec. countries
  pub. admin. 351.003 13
   U.S. 353.031
   other spec. jur. 354
   s.a. *pers.*–351 2
 other kinds see
  Administrative
  personnel; *also* Chief
  executives
Presidio Co. Tex. *area*–764 933
Presque Isle. Co. Mich. *area*–774 82
Press
 control *see* Censorship
 freedom
  civil right
   pol.sci. 323.445
  influence on crime 364.254
  journalism 070
  law 343.099 8
   spec. jur. 343.3–.9

Prestressed (continued)
  reinforced concrete
    architectural
      construction   721.044 542
      s.a. spec. structural
        elements; also spec.
        types of bldgs.
    bldg. construction   693.543
    eng. materials   620.137
      foundations   624.153 37
      structures   624.183 412
    other aspects see
      Concretes
    s.a. other spec. uses
Prestwich Greater Manchester Eng.
             area–427 38
Prestwick Strathclyde Scot.
             area–414 64
Pretoria South Africa   *area*–682
Pretrial
  procedure
    law
      criminal   345.072
      juvenile   345.087
      spec. jur.   345.3–.9
      gen. wks.   347.072
      spec. jur.   347.3–.9
      other aspects see Legal
        procedure
  release
    criminal law   345.072
    spec. jur.   345.3–.9
Preuss Range Ida.   *area*–796 45
Prevailing westerlies *see*
    Planetary wind systems
Prevention
  of crime *see* Crime prevention
  of unemployment
    labor econ.   331.137 7
    s.a. spec. classes of
      labor e.g. Women
  of violence *see* Violence
    prevention
  of war
    internat. law   341.73
  s.a. other spec. subj.
Preventive
  dentistry
    med. sci.   617.601
      geriatrics   618.977 601
      vet. med.   636.089 760 1
      s.a. spec. animals
  medicine
    pub. health   614.44
    misc. aspects see Public
      health
  s.a. other spec. subj.
Preveza Greece   *area*–495 3
Preying birds *see* Falconiformes
Price
  Co. Wis.   *area*–775 24

Price (continued)
  leadership
    prod. econ. *see* Control of
      markets
Price-demand relationship
  economics   338.521 2
  spec. ind.   338.1–.4
Price-earnings ratio
  stock valuation
    investment finance   332.632 21
Prices
  determination
    internat. comm.   382.104 4
    sales management   658.816
    spec. subj.   *s.s.*–068 8
  discrimination
    law   343.072 5
    spec. jur.   343.3–.9
  fixing
    law   343.072 5
    spec. jur.   343.3–.9
  govt. control *see* Consumption
    govt. control
  govt. procurement *see* Costs
    govt. procurement
  indexes econ.   338.528
  land econ.   333.332 3
  levels econ.   338.528
    spec. ind.   338.1–.4
  lists   *s.s.*–029 4
  macroeconomics   339.42
  prod. econ.   338.52
    primary ind.
      agriculture   338.13
      mineral ind.   338.23
      other   338.3
    secondary ind.   338.43
      commun. & transp. ind.
        see Rates
  regulation
    economics   338.526
    spec. ind.   338.1–.4
    law   343.083
      spec. commodities   343.085
      spec. jur.   343.3–.9
  stocks
    investment finance   332.632 22
  supports
    law   343.074 2
    agriculture   343.076
    spec. jur.   343.3–.9
    prod. econ. agric.   338.18
  theories
    prod. econ.   338.521
    spec. ind.   338.1–.4
Price-supply relationship
  economics   338.521 3
  spec. ind.   338.1–.4
Prickly
  heat *see* Sweat glands
    diseases

Primates (continued)
hunting
commercial
technology | 639.118
soc. & econ. aspects
see Primary
industries
sports
big game | 799.278
small game | 799.259 8
paleozoology | 569.8
zoology | 599.8
other aspects see Animals
Prime
ministers
pub. admin. | 351.003 13
spec. jur. | 354
s.a. | *pers.*–351 3
movers
soc. & econ. aspects *see*
Secondary industries
technology | 621.4
s.a. spec. appls. e.g.
Waterwheels
numbers | 512.7
s.a. spec. appls. e.g.
Engineering
Prime (prayers) *see* Office
hours
Primers (detonators) *see*
Detonators
Primes
distribution theory | 512.73
s.a. spec. appls. e.g.
Engineering
Primitive
art
preliterate | 709.011
design & dec. | 745.441
s.a. spec. art forms
untutored *see hist. of spec.*
art forms
Baptists | 286.4
misc. aspects see Baptist
Christians
biog. & work | 281.092
s.a. spec. kinds
s.a. | *pers.*–21
churches
pub. worship | 264.01
s.a. Apostolic Church
emotions
psychology | 152.432
animals | 156.243 2
children | 155.412
s.a. psych. of other spec.
groups
languages *see spec. langs.*
e.g. American native
languages
law | 340.52

Primitive (continued)
Methodist Church | 287.4
misc. aspects see Methodist
people
music
music theory | 781.71
s.a. spec. mediums
psychology | 155.81
races | *r.e.n.*–011
religion | 291.042
sociology | 301.72
spec. subj. | *pers.*–063 3
s.a. spec. groups e.g.
Australian aboriginal
people
races *see* Primitive people
remedies
therapeutics | 615.899
s.a. spec. diseases
societies
sociology | 301.72
states
pol. sci. | 321.12
s.a. spec. jur.
timepieces
mf. tech. | 681.111
soc. & econ. aspects *see*
Secondary industries
traditions
folklore | 398.1
weapons
art metalwork | 739.744 1
mil. eng.
soc. & econ. aspects *see*
Secondary industries
tech. & mf. | 623.441
s.a. other spec. subj.
Primogeniture *see* Succession
Primorski Ter. RSFSR | *area*–577
Primrose family *see* Primulales
Primulaceae *see* Primulales
Primulales
botany | 583.672
floriculture | 635.933 672
med. aspects
crop prod. | 633.883 672
gen. pharm. | 615.323 672
toxicology | 615.952 367 2
vet. pharm. | 636.089 532 367 2
toxicology | 636.089 595 236 72
paleobotany | 561.3
other aspects see Plants
Prince
Albert Sask. | *area*–712 42
Co. P.E.I. | *area*–717 1
Edward
County
Ontario | *area*–713 587
Virginia | *area*–755 632
Island
Canada | *area*–717

Prince
  Edward
    Island (continued)
      Indian Ocean   *area*–699
    George Co. Va.   *area*–755 585
    Georges Co. Md.   *area*–752 51
    Gustaf Adolf Sea *see* American
            Arctic seawaters
    of Wales
      election district Alaska *area*–798 2
      Isl. Northwest Ter.   *area*–719 5
      Strait *see* Americn Arctic
            seawaters
    Regent Inlet *see* American
            Arctic seawaters
    Rupert B.C.   *area*–711 32
    William Co. Va.   *area*–755 273 2
  Princes *see* Monarchs
  Princess Anne Co. Va.   *area*–755 51
  Princeton N.J.   *area*–749 67
    Battle U.S. Revolution
      history   973.332
  Princetown Devon Eng.   *area*–423 53
  Principal *see spec. subj.*
  Principalities (angels) *see*
            Angels
  Principals
    ed. admin.   371.201 2
    other aspects see School
            administrators
    s.a. other spec. activities
  Principe   *area*–669 93
Print
  makers
    biog. & work   769.92
    occupational ethics   174.976
    s.a.   *pers.*–76
  making
    arts   760
Printed
  advertising   659.132
  books
    hist. & crit.   094
    other aspects see Books
  circuits
    microelectronics
      soc. & econ. aspects *see*
            Secondary industries
      tech. & mf.   621.381 74
        s.a. spec. appls. e.g.
            Radar
      other aspects see
            Electronics
  matter
    postal commun.   383.123–.124
    other aspects see Postal
            communication
  media
    journalism   070.17
      s.a. spec. activities
        e.g. Reporting

Printed (continued)
    records   001.552
Printers
  biog. & work   686.209 2
  s.a.   *pers.*–686 2
Printing
  apparatus
    photography   771.4
    gen. tech.   770.284
    spec. proc. & fields   772–778
  establishments
    accounting   657.867
  functions
    library econ.   025.12
    museology   069.7
  inks
    manufacturing
      soc. & econ. aspects *see*
            Secondary industries
    technology   667.5
  machines
    manufacturing
      soc. & econ. aspects *see*
            Secondary industries
    technology   681.6
  presses
    mf. tech.   681.62
    other aspects see Printing
            machines
  processes
    gen. wks.
      soc. & econ. aspects *see*
            Secondary industries
    technology   686.2
  textiles
    arts   746.62
      soc. & econ. aspects *see*
            Secondary industries
    technology   667.38
      s.a. spec. prod.
  solutions
    photography   771.54
    gen. tech.   770.283
    spec. proc. & fields   772–778
  telegraphy
    commun. ind.
      commerce   384.14
      wire   384.14
        submarine cable   384.44
      wireless   384.524
      govt. control   351.874
        spec. jur.   353–354
      law *see* Telegraphy law
    technology   621.382 5
      s.a. spec. appls. e.g.
            Securities exchange
      other aspects see
            Telegraphy wire
Printing-out processes
  photography   772.1

857

Print-out equipment

computer eng. 621.381 953 4

  analogue 621.381 957 34

  combinations & related 621.381 959

  digital 621.381 958 34

  other aspects see Computers

  s.a. spec. uses e.g. Data

    processing

Print-outs

electronic data proc. *see*

  Outputs electronic data

  proc.

Prints

arts 769

library trmt. 025.177 1

  acquisitions 025.287 1

  cataloging 025.347 1

  s.a. other spec. activities

museology 069.57

Prionodesmacea *see* Pelecypoda

Priories *see* Religious

  congregations

Priory bldgs. *see* Monastic

  buildings

Pripet Marshes *area*–476 5

Prisms

geometry *see* Configurations

  geometry

mf. tech. 681.42

optics

  dispersing *see* Dispersion

    light optics

  refracting *see* Refraction

    light optics

Prison

administrators

  biog. & work 365.92

  s.a. spec. kinds

  other aspects see Welfare

    personnel

  s.a. *pers.*–365

areas civic art 711.556

buildings

  architecture 725.6

  building 690.56

  penology 365.5

  misc. aspects see Penal

    institutions

  other aspects see Public

    structures

camps

  armed forces *see* Prisons

    armed forces

economy 365.6

  law 344.035 6

    spec. jur. 344.3–.9

evangelism

  pastoral theology

    Christianity 253.75

    other rel. see Pastoral

      theology

Prison (continued)

inmates *see* Prisoners

labor *see* Convict labor

law *see* Penal institutions

  law

libraries 027.665

  administration 025.197 665

  buildings

    architecture 727.826 65

    functional planning 022.316 65

  catalogs *see* Library

    catalogs

  reference services 025.527 766 5

  selection for 025.218 766 5

  use studies 025.587 665

  user orientation 025.567 665

  s.a. other spec. activities

    e.g. Cataloging

s.a. Penal institutions

Prisoners

exchange

  U.S. Civil War 973.77

  U.S. Revolution 973.37

  U.S. War of 1812 973.527

  World War 1 940.473

  World War 2 940.547 3

  s.a. other spec. wars

labor econ. *see* Convict labor

labor law *see* Labor law

of war *see* War prisoners

penology *see* Prison economy

s.a. *pers.*–069 2

Prisoner's base

recreation 796.14

Prisons

accounting 657.832

psych. influences 155.962

spec. wars

  Spanish-American War 973.897

  U.S. Civil War 973.77

  U.S. Mexican War 973.627

  U.S. Revolution 973.37

  U.S. War of 1812 973.527

  Vietnamese War 959.704 37

  World War 1 940.472

  World War 2 940.547 2

  s.a. other spec. wars

s.a. Penal institutions

Privacy rights

law 342.085 8

  spec. jur. 342.3–.9

pol. sci. 323.448

Private

accounting 657.63

  s.a. spec. kinds of

    enterprise e.g.

      Insurance accounting

aircraft piloting

  soc. & econ. aspects *see*

    Secondary industries

Private
  schools (continued)
    finance
      law   344.076 7
        spec. jur.   344.3–.9
      govt. supervision & support   379.3
      law   344.072
        spec. jur.   344.3–.9
      s.a. spec. levels of ed.
    tutoring *see* Individualized
      instruction
    welfare services   361.7
      spec. problems & groups   362–363
      other aspects see Welfare
        services
    worship *see* Worship
    s.a. other spec. subj.
Privateering
  American Revolution   973.35
  s.a. other spec. wars
Privileged communications
  testimony
    law *see* Witnesses law
Privileges
  chief executives
    law   342.06
      spec. jur.   342.03–.9
    pub. admin.   350.003 28
      central govts.   351.003 28
        spec. jur.   353–354
      local govts.   352.008
  legislative bodies *see*
      Legislative privileges
  mil. discipline   355.134
  s.a. spec. mil. branches
  witnesses
    law *see* Witnesses law
  s.a. other spec. persons &
      groups
Prizes
  awards   *s.s.*–079
  research   001.44
  sales promotion *see* Sales
      promotion
Sunday schools
  Christianity   268.5
  other rel. see Religious
      instruction
  s.a. Student activities
Proanura
  paleozoology   567.8
Probabilistic processes   519.23
  s.a. spec. appls. e.g.
      Engineering
Probabilities
  gambling
    recreation   795.01
  insurance   368.01
  s.a. spec. kinds of
      insurance

Probabilities (continued)
  mathematics   519.2
  s.a. spec. appls. e.g.
      Gambling
Probability
  epistemology   121.63
Probability calculus   519.2
  s.a. spec. appls. e.g.
      Engineering
Probate law   346.052–.057
  spec. jur.   346.3–.9
Probation
  after death
    rel. doctrines
      Christianity   236.4
    other rel. see
      Eschatology
  law
    criminal   345.077
    juveniles   345.087
      spec. jur.   345.3–.9
    military   343.014 6
      spec. jur.   343.3–.9
    penology   364.63
    pub. admin.   350.849 3
      central govts.   351.849 3
        spec. jur.   353–354
      local govts.   352.944 93
    school discipline *see*
      Punishments education
Probes
  radiowave electronics *see*
      Testing-devices
      radiowave electronics
  s.a. other spec. kinds
Problem
  children *see* Delinquent
      children
  solving *see* Reasoning
Problems
  study & teaching   *s.s.*–076
Proboscidea
  agric. pests   632.696 1
  s.a. spec. types of culture
      e.g. Forestry; *also*
      spec. crops
  animal husbandry
    technology   636.961
    soc. & econ. aspects *see*
      Primary industries
  conservation tech.   639.979 61
  drawing tech.   743.696 1
  hunting
    commercial
      technology   639.116 1
      soc. & econ. aspects
        see Primary
        industries
    sports   799.276 1
  paleozoology   569.6
  zoology   599.61

Proboscidea (continued)
other aspects see Animals
Procedural rights
  criminal law — 345.056
    spec. jur. — 345.3–.9
  mil. courts — 343.014 3
    spec. jur. — 343.3–.9
  pol. sci. — 323.422
Procedure
  law *see* Legal procedure
  legislative bodies *see*
      Organization of
      legislative bodies
Procedures — *s.s.*–028
Procellariiformes
  hunting
    commercial — 639.128 42
    sports — 799.248 42
  paleozoology — 568.4
  zoology — 598.42
  other aspects see Aves
Process
  analysis
    prod. management *see*
      Production management
  design
    chem. plants — 660.281
    s.a. spec. prod.
  research
    prod. management — 658.577
    spec. subj. — *s.s.*–068 5
  theology
    Protestantism *see*
      Protestantism theology
  s.a. Evolution
Process (legal document)
  services of *see* Pretrial
      procedure
Processed
  cheese
    dairy tech. — 637.358
    other aspects see Cheeses
  s.a. other spec. subj.
Processes
  chem. plants — 660.281
  s.a. spec. prod.
  control
    prod. management *see*
      Production management
    other spec. subj. — *s.s.*–028
Processing
  butter
    dairy tech. — 637.23
  cheese
    dairy tech. — 637.33
  milk
    dairy tech. — 637.13
  s.a. Manufacturing; *also*
      other spec. subj.
Processing-centers
  library operations — 025.02

Processing-equipment
  milk
    dairy tech. — 637.132
    s.a. spec. varieties e.g.
      Whole milk
    s.a. other spec. kinds
Processing-plants
  milk
    dairy tech. — 637.131
    s.a. spec. varieties e.g.
      Whole milk
    s.a. other spec. kinds
Processionals
  Christian liturgical music — 783.29
    recordings — 789.912 329
Processions
  performing arts — 791.6
  rel. rites
    Christianity — 265.9
    other rel. see Public
      worship
  soc. customs — 394.5
Procoela
  zoology — 597.87
  other aspects see Anura
Proctology
  med. sci. — 616.35
    geriatrics — 618.976 35
    pediatrics — 618.923 5
    vet. med. — 636.089 635
    s.a. spec. animals
    other aspects see Medical
      sciences
  s.a. Anus; *also* Rectum
Procurement
  materials management — 658.72
    spec. subj. — *s.s.*–068 7
  mil. admin. — 355.621 2
    s.a. spec. mil. branches
  pub. admin. — 350.712
    central govts. — 351.712
      spec. jur. — 353–354
    local govts. — 352.162
Procyonidae
  animal husbandry — 636.974 443
  hunting
    commercial — 639.117 444 3
    sports — 799.259 744 43
  zoology — 599.744 43
  other aspects see Carnivora
Prodigies *see* Gifted
Producer
  brands
    sales promotion *see* Brands
      sales promotion
  gas
    chem. tech. — 665.772
    soc. & econ. aspects *see*
      Secondary industries
Producers' cooperatives
  economics — 334.6

Dewey Decimal Classification

Producing	
gases	
chem. apparatus	542.7
s.a. spec. appls. e.g.	
Organic chemistry	
s.a. other spec. subj.	
Product	
control	
law	344.042
spec. jur.	344.3–.9
prod. management	658.56
spec. subj.	*s.s.*–068 5
design	
prod. management	658.575 2
spec. subj.	*s.s.*–068 5
development	
prod. management	658.575
spec. subj.	*s.s.*–068 5
hazards	363.19
liability	
law	346.038 2
spec. jur.	346.3–.9
planning	
management	658.503 8
spec. subj.	*s.s.*–068 5
safety	
law	
international	341.765
municipal	344.042
spec. jur.	344.3–.9
management *see* Product	
control	
offenses *see* Public health	
offenses	
pub. meas.	363.19
govt. control	350.778
central govts.	351.778
spec. jur.	353–354
local govts.	352.4
servicing	
sales management *see*	
Customer relations	
sales management	
Production	
controls	
law	343.075
spec. jur.	343.3–.9
dramatic performances	
motion pictures	791.430 232
radio	791.440 232
stage	792.023 2
s.a. spec. kinds e.g.	
Tragedies (drama)	
television	791.450 232
economics	
cooperative	334.6
gen. wks.	338
efficiency *see* Efficiency	
prod. econ.	

Production (continued)	
govt. control	
activities	350.82
central govts.	351.82
spec. jur.	353–354
local govts.	352.942
govt. depts. *see* Executive	
departments	
illustration	
tech. drawing	604.242
spec. subj.	*s.s.*–022 1
management	658.5
spec. subj.	*s.s.*–068 5
quotas	
agriculture	
law	343.076
spec. jur.	343.3–.9
soc. aspects	306.3
s.a. spec. prod.	
Productivity	
employees	
personnel admin.	
gen. management	658.314
executives	658.407 14
spec. subj.	*s.s.*–068 3
pub. admin.	350.147
central govts.	351.147
spec. jur.	353–354
local govts.	352.005 147
labor econ.	331.118
s.a. spec. classes of labor	
e.g. Women	
prod. econ.	338.09
promotion of	
govt. control *see*	
Production govt.	
control	
Products	
economics	338.02
primary ind.	
agriculture	338.17
mineral ind.	338.27
other	338.37
secondary ind.	338.47
research technology	607.2
s.a. spec. subj. e.g.	
Aerospace engineering	
textiles mf.	
soc. & econ. aspects *see*	
Secondary industries	
technology	677.028 6
s.a. spec. kinds of	
textiles	
s.a. other spec. techs.	
Profanity	
ethics	
philosophy	179.5
religion	
Buddhism	294.356 95
Christianity	241.695
comp. rel.	291.569 5

Promotion (continued)
  employees
    personnel admin.
      gen. management   658.312 6
      executive   658.407 126
      spec. subj.   *s.s.*–068 3
      pub. admin.   350.14
        central govts.   351.14
        spec. jur.   353–354
        local govts.   352.005 14
  labor rights *see* Worker
    security
  Sunday schools
    Christianity   268.5
    other rel. see Religious
      instruction
Promotional
  activities
    corporations
      law   346.066 2
      spec. jur.   346.3–.9
  s.a. Public relations
Pronouns *see* Words
Pronunciation
  linguistics   414
    spec. langs.
      nonstandard
        forms   *lang. sub.*–7
      standard forms
        desc. & anal.   *lang. sub.*–152
        usage   *lang. sub.*–81
  vocal music   784.932
Proofreading
  printing
    soc. & econ. aspects *see*
      Secondary industries
    technology   686.225 5
Proofs
  logic *see* Logic (reasoning)
  of God's existence
    Christianity   231.042
    nat. rel.   212.1
    other rel. see God rel.
      doctrines
Propaganda
  activities
    internat. politics   327.14
      spec. countries   327.3–.9
    U.S. Civil War   973.788
    U.S. Revolutionary War   973.388
    World War 1   940.488
    World War 2   940.548 8
    s.a. other spec. wars
  films
    performing arts   791.435 3
  pub. admin.
    domestic affairs *see*
      Information services
      pub. admin.
    foreign affairs *see* Foreign
      affairs pub. admin.

Propaganda (continued)
  services
    armed forces *see*
      Psychological warfare
  soc. control   303.375
  soc. psych.   301.154
  s.a. other spec. subj.
Propagation
  biology *see* Reproduction
  crops *see* Plant propagation
    crop prod.
  s.a. Transmission
Propane
  chem. tech.   665.773
    soc. & econ. aspects *see*
      Secondary industries
Propellant explosives
  mil. eng.   623.452 6
  technology   662.26
  other aspects see Explosives
Propellants
  aircraft eng.   629.134 351
    spec. engines   629.134 352–.134 355
  s.a. other spec. vehicles
Propeller-driven planes
  aeronautical eng.
    gen. tech. & mf.   629.133 343–.133 348
    components & techniques 629.134
    models   629.133 134 3–.133 134 8
    operation   629.132 524 3–.132 524 8
    military   623.746 042
    s.a. spec. kinds e.g.
      Trainers (aircraft)
    soc. & econ. aspects *see*
      Secondary industries
    s.a. other spec. appls.
  commerce   387.733 43–.733 48
    other aspects see Aircraft
      commerce
Propellers
  aircraft eng.
    soc. & econ. aspects *see*
      Secondary industries
    tech. & mf.   629.134 36
  marine engines *see* Engine
    auxiliaries
    shipbuilding
Proper
  integrals   515.43
    s.a. spec. appls. e.g.
      Engineering
  of the Mass
    Christian liturgical music   783.23
      recordings   789.912 323
Propertied classes *see* Wealthy
    classes
Properties
  earth   551.1
  lumber
    mf. tech.   674.13

Proportional (continued)
taxation
pub. finance ... 336.293
Proportions ... 512.924
algebra ... 512.924
arithmetic ... 513.24
s.a. spec. appls. e.g.
Business arithmetic
Proprietary libraries ... 027.2
administration ... 025.197 2
buildings
architecture ... 727.822
building ... 690.782 2
functional planning ... 022.312
other aspects see
Educational buildings
catalogs *see* Library catalogs
reference services ... 025.527 72
selection for ... 025.218 72
use studies ... 025.587 2
user orientation ... 025.567 2
s.a. other spec. activities
e.g. Cataloging
Proprietorships
accounting ... 657.91
income taxation *see*
Self-employment income
taxation
management ... 658.041
initiation ... 658.114 1
prod. econ. ... 338.72
pub. relations ... 659.281
s.a. spec. fields of
enterprise e.g.
Advertising
Proprioceptive
organs
anatomy
human ... 611.8
other aspects see Sense
organs
physical anthropometry ... 573.68
physiology
human ... 612.88
other aspects see Sensory
functions
tissue biology human ... 611.018 98
perceptions
psychology
gen. wks. ... 152.188
animals ... 156.218 8
children ... 155.412
s.a. psych. of other
spec. groups
influences ... 155.911 88
Propulsion
aeronautical aerodynamics ... 629.132 38
s.a. spec. appls. e.g.
Flying

Propulsion (continued)
systems
spacecraft eng.
manned ... 629.475
unmanned ... 629.465
other aspects see
Spacecraft
other vehicles see Power
plants
Prorocentrales *see* Pyrrophyta
Prose
language *see* Languages
literature
gen. colls. ... 808.888
spec. lits. ... *lit. sub.–808*
spec. periods ... *lit. sub.–81–89*
s.a. spec. kinds e.g.
Essays
Prosecution procedure
criminal law ... 345.050 42
spec. jur. ... 345.3–.9
Prosencephalon
human phys. ... 612.825
other aspects see Brain
Prosimii
animal husbandry ... 636.981
hunting
commercial ... 639.118 1
sports ... 799.259 81
zoology ... 599.81
other aspects see Primates
Proso
agriculture
food crops ... 633.171 7
forage crops ... 633.257 17
other aspects see Millets
Prosobranchia
culture ... 639.483 2
paleozoology ... 564.32
zoology ... 594.32
other aspects see Mollusca
Prosody *see* Poetry gen. wks.
rhetoric
Prosopora *see* Oligochaeta
Prosos *see* Millets
Prospecting
mining eng.
prod. econ. ... 338.2
technology ... 622.1
Prospectors
biog. & work ... 622.109 2
s.a. ... *pers.–622*
Prospectuses ... *s.s.–029*
Prosperity
econ. cycles
prod. econ. ... 338.542
Prostaglandins *see* Hormones
Prostate
diseases
gen. wks. ... 616.65
neoplasms ... 616.992 63

Protective (continued)
  gloves
    mf. tech.   685.43
    other aspects see Handwear
  structures
    port eng.
      technology   627.24
      s.a. spec. appls e.g.
        Harbor piloting
      other aspects see Liquids
        engineering
    railroad eng.
      technology   625.13
      other aspects see
        Permanent way
  tariffs
    internat. comm.   382.73
    other aspects see Customs
      (tariffs)
Protectorates *see* Dependent
  states
Protein
  cookery   641.563 8
  metabolism disorders
    gen. med.   616.399 5
    geriatrics   618.976 399 5
    pediatrics   618.923 995
    pub. health   614.593 995
    statistics   312.339 95
    deaths   312.263 995
    other aspects see Diseases
  plastics
    chem. tech.   668.43
    org. chem.   547.843 23
    other aspects see Plastics
    s.a. spec. prod.
  synthesis
    plant nutrition
      pathology   581.213 345
      physiology   581.133 45
      s.a. spec. plants
  textiles
    arts   746.044 72
    s.a. spec. proc. e.g.
      Weaving
    dyeing   667.347 2
    manufacturing
      soc. & econ. aspects *see*
        Secondary industries
      technology   677.472
      special-process fabrics   677.6
    org. chem.   547.857 2
    other aspects see Textiles
    s.a. spec. prod.
Proteins
  appl. nutrition
    home econ.   641.12
    hygiene   613.28
  biochemistry
    gen. wks.   574.192 45
    animals   591.192 45

Proteins
  biochemistry
    gen. wks. (continued)
      microorganisms   576.119 245
      plants   581.192 45
      s.a. spec. organisms
    med. sci.   612.015 75
    animals   636.089 201 575
      s.a. spec. animals
    man   612.015 75
    s.a. spec. functions,
      systems, organs
  biosynthesis
    gen. wks.   574.192 96
    animals   591.192 96
    microorganisms   576.119 296
    plants   581.192 96
    s.a. spec. organisms
    med. sci.   612.015 46
    animals   636.089 201 546
      s.a. spec. animals
    man   612.015 46
    s.a. spec. functions,
      systems, organs
  metabolism
    human phys.   612.398
    other aspects see
      Metabolism
    org. chem.   547.75
Proteles
  animal husbandry   636.974 426
  hunting
    commercial   639.117 442 6
    sports   799.259 744 26
  zoology   599.744 26
  other aspects see Carnivora
Proteolytic enzymes
  biochemistry
    gen. wks.   574.192 56
    animals   591.192 56
    microorganisms   576.119 256
    plants   581.192 56
    s.a. spec. organisms
    med. sci.   612.015 16
    animals   636.089 201 516
      s.a. spec. animals
    man   612.015 16
    s.a. spec. functions,
      systems, organs
Proteomyxa
  culture   639.731 13
  zoology   593.113
  other aspects see Protozoa
Proterozoic era
  geology   551.715
    s.a. spec. aspects e.g.
      Economic geology
  paleontology *see* Precambrian
    eras

Providence (continued)
  of God
    rel. doctrines
      Christianity   231.5
      nat. rel.   214.8
      other rel. see God
Provident societies
  economics   334.7
Provinces
  local govt.
    pub. admin.   352.007 3
Provincial
  borrowing & debt
    law   343.037
      spec. jur.   343.3–.9
    pub. admin.   351.726
      spec. jur.   354
    pub. finance   336.343 2
  debt *see* Provincial borrowing
      & debt
  finance   336.013
    misc. aspects see Public
        finance
  governments   351
    spec. jur.   354
  libraries *see* Government
      libraries
  planning
    civic art   711.3
    economics   338.9
    soc. sci. *see* Planning soc.
        welfare
  reports of cases
    law   348.043
      spec. jur.   348.3–.9
  taxation
    pub. finance   336.201 3
      misc. aspects see Taxes
  s.a. other spec. subj.; also
      State
Provincialisms
  languages *see* Dialectology
Provincial-local relations
  constitutional law   342.042
    spec. jur.   342.3–.9
  pub. admin.   350.093
    central govts.   351.093
    spec. jur.   354
Provincial-national relations
      see
      National-provincial
      relations
Proving-grounds
  armed forces   355.74
    s.a. spec. mil. branches
Prowers Co. Colo.   *area*–788 98
Proximity
  topology   514.323
    s.a. spec. appls. e.g.
        Engineering
Prudence *see* Virtues

Prudhoe Northumberland Eng.
                           area–428 81
Prunes *see* Plums
Pruning
  plants
    crop prod.   631.542
      s.a. spec. crops; also
          spec. types of culture
          e.g. Floriculture
Pruning-equipment
  agriculture   631.34
    use   631.544
      s.a. spec. crops; also
          spec. types of culture
          e.g. Floriculture
  mf. tech.   681.763 1
    soc. & econ. aspects *see*
        Secondary industries
Prunings
  silviculture   634.953
    s.a. spec. trees
Prunus
  amygdalus *see* Almonds
  armeniaca *see* Apricots
  avium
    agriculture   634.237
    other aspects see Cherries
  besseyi
    agriculture   634.237
    other aspects see Cherries
  cerasus
    agriculture   634.237
    other aspects see Cherries
  domestica
    agriculture   634.227
    other aspects see Plums
  insititia
    agriculture   634.227
    other aspects see Plums
  persica *see* Peaches
Prussia   *area*–43
Prussian
  Old *see* Old Prussian language
  Saxony Ger.   *area*–431 8
Przemysl Poland   *area*–438 6
Psalms
  Bible   223.2
  other aspects see Poetic
      books (O.T.)
Psalteries
  mf. tech.   681.817 9
    misc. aspects see Musical
        instruments
  musical art   787.9
Psalters
  Anglican liturgy   264.038
  Roman Catholic liturgy   264.028
Psaltery music   787.9
  recordings   789.912 79
Pselaphognatha *see* Diplopoda
Pseudepigrapha *see* Apocrypha

Psychoanalytic	
systems	
psychology	150.195
s.a. spec. subj. &	
branches of psych.	
theory	
folklore	398.15
Psychodiagnoses	
clinical psych.	157.92
Psychodrama	
psychiatry	616.891 523
geriatrics	618.976 891 523
pediatrics	618.928 915 23
other aspects see Medical	
sciences	
Psychokinesis	
parapsychology	133.88
Psycholinguistics	401.9
Psychological	
causes of warfare	
mil. sci.	355.027 5
characteristics	
influence on crime	364.24
fiction *see* Realistic fiction	
warfare	
activities	
internat. politics	327.14
spec. countries	327.3–.9
Vietnamese War	959.704 38
World War 2	940.548 8
s.a. other spec. wars	
services	
armed forces	355.343 4
s.a. spec. mil.	
branches	
Psychologists	
biog. & work	150.92
s.a. spec. branches of	
psych.	
s.a.	*pers.–15*
Psychology	150
appls. to spec. subj.	*s.s.–019*
Biblical trmt.	220.815
s.a. spec. parts of Bible	
curriculums	375.15
documentation	025.061 5
journalism	070.449 15
libraries	026.15
misc. aspects see Special	
libraries	
library acquisitions	025.271 5
library classification	025.461 5
of ed.	370.15
rel. attitude toward	
Christianity	261.515
other rel. see Religious	
attitudes secular	
disciplines	
subject headings	025.491 5
other aspects see Disciplines	
(systems)	
Psychology (continued)	
s.a. Social psychology	
Psychoneuroses	
abnormal psych.	157.3–.7
Psychoneurotic	
persons	
psychology *see* Abonormal	
psychology	
speech disorders	
pub. health	614.58
other aspects see Mental	
illness	
Psychopathic personality	
pub. health	614.58
other aspects see Mental	
illness	
Psychopharmacology	
med. sci.	615.78
misc. aspects see	
Pharmacology	
Psychophysical methods	
psychology *see* Quantitative	
psychology	
Psychoses	
gen. wks.	
gen. med.	616.892–.898
geriatrics	618.976 892–.976 898
pediatrics	618.928 92–.928 98
pub. health	614.58
statistics	312.389 2–.389 8
deaths	312.268 92–.268 98
other aspects see Mental	
illness	
puerperal diseases	
obstetrics	618.76
pub. health	614.58
statistics	312.304 876
deaths	312.260 487 6
other aspects see Diseases;	
also Mental illness	
Psychosomatic medicine	616.08
s.a. spec. diseases	
Psychosurgery	
med. sci.	617.481
vet. med.	636.089 748 1
s.a. spec. animals	
Psychotherapy	
psychiatry	616.891 4
geriatrics	618.976 891 4
pediatrics	618.928 914
other aspects see Medical	
sciences	
Psychotic persons	
psychology *see* Abnormal	
psychology	
Psychotropic drugs	
addictive aspects *see*	
Addictive drugs	
pharmacodynamics	615.788
other aspects see Drugs	

Psychrometrics	
air-conditioning	
buildings	697.931 5
s.a. spec. types of	
bldgs.	
other aspects see Humidity	
Pteraspidomorphi	
paleozoology	567.2
Pteridophyta	
botany	587
floriculture	635.937
med. aspects	
crop prod.	633.887
gen. pharm.	615.327
toxicology	615.952 7
vet. pharm.	636.089 532 7
toxicology	636.089 595 27
paleobotany	561.7
other aspects see Plants	
Pteridospermae	
paleobotany	561.595
Pterobranchia	
culture	639.7
paleozoology	564.7
zoology	594.73
other aspects see	
Molluscoidea	
Pterocletes *see* Columbiformes	
Pteropoda	
culture	639.483 5
paleozoology	564.35
zoology	594.35
other aspects see Mollusca	
Pterosauri	
paleozoology	567.97
Pterostemonaceae *see* Cunoniales	
Pterygota *see* Insecta	
Ptilogonatidae	
hunting	
commercial	639.128 853
sports	799.248 853
paleozoology	568.8
zoology	598.853
other aspects see Aves	
Ptolemies reign Egypt hist.	932.021
s.a. spec. events & subj.	
e.g. Commerce	
Puberty *see* Adolescence	
Public	
accounting	657.61
s.a. spec. kinds of	
enterprise e.g.	
Insurance accounting	
accounts *see* Public finance	
administration	350
curriculums	375.35
documentation	025.063 5
ethics	
philosophy	172.2
religion	
Buddhism	294.356 22

Public	
administration	
ethics	
religion (continued)	
Christianity	241.622
comp. rel.	291.562 2
Hinduism	294.548 622
s.a. other spec. rel.	
journalism	070.449 35
libraries	026.35
misc. aspects see Special	
libraries	
other aspects see Social	
sciences	
administrators	
biog. & work	350.000 92
s.a. spec. kinds	
ethics *see* Public	
administration ethics	
investigation pub. admin.	350.992
central govts.	351.992
spec. jur.	353–354
local govts.	352.002
law	342.068
spec. jur.	342.3–.9
s.a.	*pers.*–35
behavior	
etiquette	395.53
soc. customs	390
soc. psych.	302
borrowing	
law	343.037
spec. jur.	343.3–.9
pub. admin.	350.726
central govts.	351.726
spec. jur.	353–354
local govts.	352.14
pub. finance	336.34
buildings *see* Public	
structures	
carriers	
engineering *see spec.*	
vehicles	
sanitation	363.729 3
govt. control	350.772
central govts.	351.772
spec. jur.	353–354
local govts.	352.6
law	344.046 4
spec. jur.	344.3–.9
services *see* Public	
transportation	
contracts	
law	346.023
spec. jur.	346.3–.9
conveniences *see* Comfort	
stations	
credit	
pub. finance	336.3
customs	390

Public
  lands (continued)
    revenue sources pub. finance 336.12
      misc. aspects see Nontax
        revenues
  law   342–345
  libraries   027.4
    administration   025.197 4
    buildings
      architecture   727.824
      building   690.782 4
      functional planning   022.314
      other aspects see
        Educational buildings
    catalogs *see* Library
      catlogs
    reference services   025.527 74
    selection for   025.218 74
    use studies   025.587 4
    user orientation   025.567 4
    s.a. other spec. activities
      e.g. Cataloging
  life of Jesus
    Christian doctrines   232.95
  lighting eng.
    soc. & econ. aspects *see*
      Secondary industries
    technology   628.95
    s.a. spec. appls. e.g.
      Vehicular transp.
      safety
  officials *see* Public
    administrators
  opinion
    soc. control   303.38
  order
    crimes against
      criminology   364.143
      law   345.024 3
      spec. jur.   345.3–.9
      soc. theology
        Christianity   261.833 143
        comp. rel.   291.178 331 43
      s.a. other spec. rel.
    law   344.053
      spec. jur.   344.3–.9
    pub. meas.   363.3
      govt. control   350.75
      central govts.   351.75
      spec. jur.   353–354
      local govts.   352.935
  ownership
    commun. systems
      gen. telecommun.   351.874
      motion pictures   351.874 83
      radiobroadcasting   351.874 543
      telegraphy   351.874 13
        submarine cable   351.874 43
        wire   351.874 13
        wireless   351.874 523

Public
  ownership
    commun. systems (continued)
      telephony   351.874 63
      wire   351.874 63
      wireless   351.874 533
      television   351.874 554 3
        closed circuit   351.874 555 3
        community antenna   351.874 555 63
        subscription   351.874 554 7
      spec. jur.   353–354
      land econ.   333.1
    networks
      radio & television *see*
        Broadcasting networks
    transportation systems   350.875–.878
      central govts.
        airlines   351.877 71
        inland waterways   351.876 1
        maritime transp.   351.877 51
        motor transp.   351.878 32
        railways
          gen. & standard   351.875 1
          special-duty   351.875 5
        urban transp.   351.878 4
      spec. jur.   353–354
      local govts.   352.915–.918
    s.a. Ownership; *also spec.*
      levels of govt.
  pay telephones
    wire telephony
      soc. & econ. aspects *see*
        Secondary industries
      tech. & mf.   621.386 9
      s.a. spec. appls. e.g.
        News gathering
      other aspects see Telephony
        wire
  performances   791
    bldgs. for
      architecture   725.82
      building   690.582
      other aspects see Public
        structures
    s.a. spec. kinds
  police services *see* Police
    services
  policy   350
  prosecutors
    law *see* Court officials law
  recreational land
    economics   333.11
    technology   659.2
  relations   659.2
    libraries   021.7
    local churches   254.4
    pub. admin. *see* Information
      services pub. admin.
  roads
    land econ.   333.11
    other aspects see Roads

Public (continued)
  safety
    law 344.05
      spec. jur. 344.3–.9
    offenses *see* Public health
      offenses
    pub. admin. 350.75
      central govts. 351.75
        spec. jur. 353–354
      local govts. 352.935
    soc. services 363.1
  sanitation
    engineering
      soc. & econ. aspects *see*
        Secondary industries
      technology 628.4
        s.a. spec. appls. e.g.
          Public health
      other aspects see
        Sanitation
  schools 371.01
    finance
      law .... 344.076 ?
        spec. jur. 344.3–.9
    govt. supervision & support ... 379
      law 344.071
        spec. jur. 344.3–.9
      s.a. spec. levels of ed.
  securities
    economics 332.632 3
    pub. finance 336.31
    law *see* Securities law;
      also Public debt law
    pub. admin. *see* Public debt
      pub. admin.
  service workers
    labor law *see* Labor law
  services
    library econ. 025.5
    museology 069.1
    revenue source
      pub. finance 336.19
      misc. aspects see
        Nontax revenues
  speaking
    rhetoric 808.51
      juvenile 808.068 51
    other aspects see Speaking
  speeches
    gen. wks.
      collections 808.851
      hist. & crit. 809.51
    spec. lits. .... *lit. sub.*–501
      indiv. authors ... *lit. sub.*–51–59
    other aspects see Speeches
  spending *see* Expenditures
      public
  streets
    land econ. 333.11
    other aspects see Roads

Public (continued)
  structures
    air-conditioning 697.935
    architecture 725
    building 690.5
    care 647.96
    interior decoration 747.85
    law 343.025 6
      spec. jur. 343.3–.9
    lighting
      exterior 621.322 9
      interior 621.322 5
    pub. works
      pub. admin. 350.862
        central govts. 351.862
      local govts. 352.5
  telephones *see* Public pay
      telephones
  transportation
    automobiles
      commerce 388.342 3
      engineering
        gen. tech. & mf. 629.222 3
          maintenance 629.287 23
          models 629.221 23
          operation 629.283 3
        s.a. other spec.
          aspects e.g. Brakes;
          also spec. appls.
          e.g. Busing school
            students
        soc. & econ. aspects
          see Secondary
          industries
        other aspects see Land
          vehicles
      other aspects see
        Transportation
    s.a. Public carriers
  utilities
    accounting 657.838
    law 343.09
      spec. jur. 343.3–.9
    pub. admin. 350.87
      central govts. 351.87
        spec. jur. 353–354
      local govts. 352.91
    soc. services 363.6
  utility workers
    bicg. & work 363.609 2
    s.a. spec. kinds
    s.a. *pers.*–363 6
  welfare
    powers
      legislative bodies
        law *see* Legislative
          powers law
        pol. sci. 328.341 3
          spec. jur. 328.4–.9
    services 361.6
      spec. problems & groups 362–363

Public
welfare
services (continued)
other aspects see Welfare
services
workers *see* Civil service
personnel
works 363
govt. control
activities 350.86
central govts. 351.86
spec. jur. 353–354
local govts. 352.7
departments *see* Executive
departments
law 344.06
spec. jur. 344.3–.9
worship
Christianity 264
comp. rel. 291.38
Islam 297.38
Judaism 296.4
s.a. Worship
s.a. other spec. rel.
s.a. other spec. subj.; also
Government
Public-address systems
office use 651.79
tech. & mf. 621.389 2
soc. & econ. aspects *see*
Secondary industries
s.a. spec. appls. e.g.
Disasters control
Publication
civil right
pol. sci. 323.445
s.a. Publishing
Publications
publishing 070.57
Publicity *see* Public relations
Publics
sociology 302.33
Public-service workers *see*
Civil service personnel
Publishers
biog. & work 070.509 2
occupational ethics 174.909 7
s.a. *pers.*–097
Publishing
houses
financial aspects *see*
Communications media
operations 070.5
library econ. 025.12
museology 069.7
soc. & econ. aspects *see*
Secondary industries
Pubs *see* Drinking-places
Puddings
cookery 641.864

Puddings (continued)
other aspects see Composite
foods
Puddling
furnace practice 669.141 4
Pudsey West Yorkshire Eng.
area–428 19
Puebla Mex. *area*–724 8
Pueblo
architecture 722.91
misc. aspects see
Architectural schools
Co. Colo. *area*–788 55
Puerperal diseases
obstetrics 618.7
pub. health 614.599 2
statistics 312.304 87
deaths 312.260 487
other aspects see Diseases
Puerperium
obstetrics 618.6
pub. health 614.599 2
vet. obstetrics 636.089 86
s.a. spec. animals
Puerto Plata Dominican Republic
area–729 358
Puerto Rican
literature 860
people *r.e.n.*–687 295
s.a. other spec. subj. e.g.
Arts
Puerto Rico *area*–729 5
Puffballs *see* Lycoperdales
Puffbirds *see* Piciformes
Puffins *see* Charadriiformes
Pug dogs
animal husbandry 636.76
other aspects see Dogs
Puget Sound *see* United States
Pacific seawaters
Pugilism *see* Boxing
Pulaski Co.
Arkansas *area*–767 73
Georgia *area*–758 523
Illinois *area*–773 998
Indiana *area*–772 925
Kentucky *area*–769 63
Missouri *area*–778 57
Virginia *area*–755 775
Puli
animal husbandry 636.73
other aspects see Dogs
Pulleys
mech. eng. *see* Power
transmission
mechanics 531.8
Pullovers *see* Sweaters
Pulmonary
abscesses *see* Pneumoconiosis
embolisms
gen. med. 616.249

Pulmonary
  embolisms (continued)
    geriatrics 618.976 249
    pediatrics 618.922 49
    pub. health 614.592 49
    statistics 312.324 9
      deaths 312.262 49
    other aspects see Diseases
  thromboses *see* Pulmonary
      embolisms
  tuberculosis
    gen. med. 616.995 24
    geriatrics 618.976 995 24
    pediatrics 618.929 952 4
    pub. health 614.542
    statistics 312.399 524
      deaths 312.269 952 4
    other aspects see Diseases
  valve diseases *see* Valvular
      diseases
Pulmonata
  culture 639.483 8
  paleozoology 564.38
  zoology 594.38
  other aspects see Mollusca
Pulp
  manufacturers
    biog. & work 676.109 2
    s.a. *pers.*–676
  manufacturing
    soc. & econ. aspects *see*
        Secondary industries
    technology 676.1
  s.a. spec. prod.
Pulpboards
  mf. tech. 676.183
  other aspects see Pulp
Pulpit platforms
  Christian church arch. 726.593
Pulpits *see* Rostral furniture
Pulpwood
  forest prod. 634.983
  soc. & econ. aspects *see*
        Primary industries
  s.a. spec. trees
Pulque 641.23
  comm. proc. 663.23
  other aspects see Alcoholic
      beverages
Pulsars
  astronomy
    description 523
    theory 521.5
  other aspects see Celestial
      bodies
Pulsating variable stars
  astronomy
    description 523.844 25
    theory 521.584 425
  other aspects see Celestial
      bodies

Pulsations
  geomagnetism
    physics 538.744
    spec. states of matter 530.4
Pulse
  circuits
    tech. & mf. 621.381 534
      microelectronics 621.381 734
      microwave electronics 621.381 324
      radiowave electronics 621.381 534
      x- & gamma-ray electronics 621.381 6
    s.a. spec. appls. e.g.
        Radiocontrol
    other aspects see Microwave
        electronics; Radiowave
        electronics; X-ray
        electronics
  generators
    electronic circuits *see*
        Pulse circuits
  human phys. 612.14
    misc. aspects see
        Circulation (biology)
  modulators
    electronic circuits
      tech. & mf. 621.381 536 5
        microelectronics 621.381 736 5
        microwave electronics 621.381 326 5
        radiowave
          electronics 621.381 536 5
        x- & gamma-ray
          electronics 621.381 6
      s.a. spec. appls. e.g.
          Radar engineering
      other aspects see
          Microwave electronics;
          Radiowave electronics;
          X-ray electronics
  processes
    electronic circuits *see*
        Pulse circuits
Pulse-jet engines
  aircraft eng.
    soc. & econ. aspects *see*
        Secondary industries
    tech. & mf. 629.134 353 6
Pulse-modulated systems
  radar eng. 621.384 85
    s.a. spec. appls. e.g.
        Navigation
    other aspects see Radar
Pulverization
  drying & dehydrating foods
    comm. proc. 664.028 43
    other aspects see Foods
    s.a. spec. foods e.g. Meats
Pumice
  abrasive material *see*
      Abrasive materials
  mineral aspects *see* Volcanic
      rocks

Pumping-stations
 sewerage eng.   628.29
  s.a. spec. appls. e.g.
   Water drainage
 water-supply eng.
  technology   628.144
  other aspects see Water
   supply engineering
Pumpkins
 agriculture   635.62
  soc. & econ. aspects *see*
   Primary industries
 foods   641.356 2
  preparation
   commercial   664.805 62
   domestic   641.656 2
  other aspects see
   Cucurbitales; *also*
   Vegetables
Pumps
 gen. wks.
  engineering
   soc. & econ. aspects *see*
    Secondary industries
   tech. & mf.   621.64–.69
    s.a. spec. appls. e.g.
     Water supply
     engineering
    other aspects see Dynamics
 hydraulic-power tech.
  soc. & econ. aspects *see*
   Secondary industries
  tech. & mf.   621.252
   s.a. spec. appls. e.g.
    Nautical engineering
 internal-combustion engines
   see Cooling-systems
    internal-combustion
    engines
 marine engine auxiliaries *see*
  Engine auxiliaries
  shipbuilding
Pumps (footwear) *see* Footwear
Punched cards
 computer tech. *see*
  Input-output equipment
 electronic data proc. *see*
  Inputs electronic data
  proc.
Punched-card data proc. *see*
  Automatic data proc.
Punches (beverages) *see*
  Nonalcoholic beverages
Punches (molds) *see*
  Molding-equipment
Punching-tools
 soc. & econ. aspects *see*
  Secondary industries
 tech. & mf.   621.96
  s.a. spec. appls. e.g.
   Agricultural equipment

Punctuation
 linguistics   410
  spec. langs.
   desc. & anal.   *lang. sub.*–1
   usage   *lang. sub.*–8
Punctured wounds
 statistics   312.304 714 3
  deaths   312.260 471 43
 surgical trmt.   617.143
  anesthesiology   617.967 143
  s.a. Veterinary sciences
Punic
 language *see* Canaanitic
  languages
 Wars Italy hist.   937.04
Punica granatum see
  Pomegranates
Punicaceae see Lythrales
Punishments
 armed forces   355.133 25
  s.a. spec. mil. branches
 criminal law   345.077
  juveniles   345.087
  spec. jur.   345.3–.9
 education   371.54
  s.a. spec. levels of ed.;
   also Special education
 penology *see* Penology
 rel. doctrines
  Christianity   236.2
  other rel. see Eschatology
 rel. law *see* Penalties
 soc. control   303.36
Punjab   *area*–545
 India   *area*–545
 Pakistan   *area*–549 14
Punjabi
 people   *r.e.n.*–914 2
 s.a. Panjabi
Puno Peru   *area*–853 6
Puntarenas Costa Rica   *area*–728 67
Punting
 sports
  boating   797.123
  kicking
   American football   796.332 27
    s.a. other spec. games
   other aspects see Sports
Punts *see* Hand-propelled
  vessels
Puppet masters
 biog. & work   791.530 92
 s.a.   *pers.*–791 5
Puppetry
 performing arts   791.53
Puppets
 handicrafts   745.592 24
 mf. tech.   688.722 4
 other aspects see toys
Puranas
 Hinduism   294.592 5

Purbeck
Dorset Eng.   *area*–423 36
Isle Dorset Eng.   *area*–423 36
Purchase
contracts
accounting trmt.   657.75
s.a. spec. kinds of
enterprises e.g.
Insurance accounting
real property
law *see* Acquisition of real
property law
Purchases *see* Sales
Purchasing *see* Procurement
Pure
food law *see* Product safety
law
motion   531.112
misc. aspects see Dynamics
sciences *see* Sciences
s.a. other spec. subj.
Purgatives
pharmacodynamics   615.732
other aspects see Drugs
Purgatory
rel. doctrines
Christianity   236.5
other rel. see Eschatology
Purification
ind. oils & gases   665.028 3
s.a. spec. prod.
petroleum distillates   665.534
s.a. spec. prod.
sugars & syrups
comm. proc.   664.113
cane   664.122 3
s.a. other kinds
other aspects see Sugars
water supply *see* Water supply
s.a. other spec. subj.
Purified pulp
manufacturing
soc. & econ. aspects *see*
Secondary industries
technology   676.4
Purim
customs   394.268 296
Judaism   296.436
Purines
org. chem.   547.596
s.a. spec. cpds.
Puritanism
Christian rel.   285.9
Christian life guides   248.485 9
doctrines   230.59
creeds   238.59
moral theology   241.045 9
private prayers for   242.805 9
sermons   252.059
s.a. other spec. aspects

Puritans
biog. & work   285.909 2
Purity
tests
milk
dairy tech.   637.127
s.a. other spec. prod.
Purley London Eng.   *area*–421 91
Purpose
metaphysics *see* Teleology
Purposive psychologies   150.193 3
s.a. spec. subj. & branches of
psych.
Purses
manufacturing
soc. & econ. aspects *see*
Secondary industries
technology   685.51
Purslane family *see*
Caryophyllales
Pursuit
forces
air warfare   358.43
law enforcement   363.232
misc. aspects see Law
enforcement
planes
mil. aircraft eng.   623.746 4
Pushball
equipment mf.   688.763 3
soc. & econ. aspects *see*
Secondary industries
sports   796.33
other aspects see Sports
Push-button systems
telephone commun. equip.
commerce   384.65
wire   384.65
wireless   384.535
Pushmataha Co. Okla.   *area*–766 65
Pushto *see* Pashto
Puss in corner
recreation   796.14
Pustular eruptions
gen. med.   616.52
geriatrics   618.976 52
pediatrics   618.925 2
pub. health   614.595 2
statistics   312.352
surgical trmt.   617.22
other aspects see Diseases
Put & call transactions
investment finance   332.645 2
misc. aspects see
Speculation investment
finance
Putnam Co.
Florida   *area*–759 17
Georgia   *area*–758 576
Illinois   *area*–773 375
Indiana   *area*–772 49

Pyromania (continued)
  other aspects see Mental
      illness
Pyrometallurgy
  manufacturing
    soc. & econ. aspects *see*
        Secondary industries
    technology   669.028 2
    s.a. spec. metals
Pyrometers
  use *see* Pyrometry
  other aspects see
      Measuring-instruments
Pyrometry
  astrophysics   523.013 52
    s.a. spec. celestial bodies
  chemistry *see* High
        temperatures reactions
  physics   536.52
    spec. states of matter   530.4
Pyrophyllite
  mineralogy   549.67
Pyrotechnical devices
  commun. eng.
    military   623.731 3
    nautical   623.856 13
    s.a. spec. appls. e.g.
        Navigation
Pyrotechnics *see* Fireworks
Pyrotheria
  paleozoology   569.6
Pyroxenes
  mineralogy   549.66
Pyrrhonic philosophy   186.1
Pyrroles
  org. chem.   547.593
  s.a. spec. cpds.
Pyrrophyta
  botany   589.43
  med. aspects
    gen. pharm.   615.329 43
      toxicology   615.952 943
    vet. pharm.   636.089 532 943
      toxicology   636.089 595 294 3
  paleobotany   561.93
  other aspects see Plants
Pyrus
  communis *see* Pears
  malus *see* Apples
Pythagorean philosophy   182.2
Pyuria
  gen. med.   616.633
  geriatrics   618.976 633
  pediatrics   618.926 33
  pub. health   614.596 33
  statistics   312.363 3
    deaths   312.266 33
  other aspects see Diseases

Q

Q fever
  gen. med.   616.922 5
  geriatrics   618.976 922 5
  pediatrics   618.929 225
  pub. health   614.526 5
  statistics   312.392 25
    deaths   312.269 225
  other aspects see Diseases
Qalyubiya Egypt   *area*–621
Qarawi language *see* South
        Arabic languages
Qatar
  people   *r.e.n.*–927 536 3
  state   *area*–536 3
Qattara Depression Egypt *area*–622
Qena Egypt   *area*–523
Qoran   297.122
Quabe kingdom hist.   968
  s.a. spec. events & subj.
      e.g. Commerce
Quackery
  gen. wks. *see* Frauds
  medicine   615.856
  s.a. spec. diseases
Quadrants *see* Extrameridional
      instruments
Quadraphonic systems
  tech. & mf.   621.389 336
  s.a. spec. appls. e.g.
      music 789.91
  other aspects see Reproducers
      sound
Quadratic
  equations   515.252
    algebra   512.942
    s.a. spec. appls. e.g.
        Engineering
  calculus   515.252
    complex variables   515.925 2
    real variables   515.825 2
    s.a. other spec. functions
        & equations; also spec.
        appls. e.g.
        Engineering
  programming
    mathematics   519.76
    s.a. spec. appls. e.g.
        Engineering
  transformations *see*
        Transformations
Quadrature
  calculus   515.43
    s.a. spec. appls. e.g.
        Enqineering
Quadrilaterals *see*
      Configurations geometry
Quadrilles
  dancing   793.34

Quadrilles (continued)
music *see* Dance music
Quadruple-expansion
steam engines *see*
Reciprocating engines
steam
Quadruplets
birth *see* Multiple childbirth
psychology   155.444
rearing home econ.   649.144
Quadruplex telegraphy *see*
Acoustical systems wire
telegraphy
Quails *see* Phasianidae
Quakers *see* Society of Friends
Qualifications
chief executives
pub. admin.   350.003 4
central govts.   351.003 4
spec. jur.   353–354
local govts.   352.008
clergymen
pastoral theology
Christianity   253.2
other rel. see Pastoral
theology
employees
job analysis
gen. wks.   658.306
spec. subj.   *s.s.*–068 3
pub. admin.   350.103
central govts.   351.103
spec. jur.   353–354
local govts.   352.005 103
selection *see spec. kinds*
e.g. Personal
qualifications
legislators *see* Membership
legislative bodies
pub. executives
law *see* Executive branches
law
s.a. other spec. subj.
Qualitative
analysis
chemistry *see* Qualitative
chemistry
sound
engineering   620.21–.25
s.a. spec. appls. e.g.
Musical sound
physics   534.44
spec. states of matter   530.4
chemistry   544
organic   547.34
s.a. spec. elements & cpds.
Quality
controls
air-conditioning eng.   697.932 4

Quality
controls (continued)
cereal grains
comm. proc.   664.720 4
s.a. spec. grains &
prod.
other aspects see Cereal
grains
foods
comm. proc.   664.07
other aspects see Foods
s.a. spec. foods e.g.
Meats
law *see* Production controls
mathematics   519.86
s.a. spec. appls. e.g.
Engineering
prod. management   658.562
spec. subj.   *s.s.*–068 5
s.a. other spec. subj.
engineering   620.004 5
s.a. spec. branches of eng.
standards
metrology   389.63
misc. aspects see
Standardization
metrology
prod. management *see*
Quality controls prod.
management
tests
dairy tech.
butter   637.22
cheese   637.32
milk   637.127
s.a. other spec. subj.
Quantics
algebra   512.944
s.a. spec. appls. e.g.
Engineering
Quantitative
analysis
chemistry *see* Quantitative
chemistry
sound
engineering   620.21–.25
s.a. spec. appls. e.g.
Musical sound
physics   534.45
spec. states of matter   530.4
chemistry   545
organic   547.35
s.a. spec. elements & cpds.
psychology   152.8
animals   156.28
children   155.412
s.a. psych. of other spec.
groups
Quantity
controls *see* Production
controls

Quantity (continued)
  cookery   641.57
  metaphysics   119
  prosody *see* Poetry gen. wks.
    rhetoric
  standards
    metrology   389.62
    misc. aspects see
      Standardization
      metrology
  surveying
    structural *see* Structural
      quantity surveying
  theory
    money   332.401
Quantock Hills Somerset Eng.
    area–423 85
Quantum
  chemistry
    theoretical chem.   541.28
      organic   547.128
    s.a. spec. elements &
      cpds.
  electrodynamics *see*
    Electrodynamics
  electronics *see* Electronics
  field theory
    physics   530.143
    spec. states of matter   530.4
    s.a. spec. branches of
      physics
  mechanics
    physics   530.12
    spec. states of matter   530.4
    s.a. spec. branches of
      physics
  statistical mechanics *see*
    Quantum statistics
  statistics
    physics   530.133
    spec. states of matter   530.4
    s.a. spec. branches of
      physics
  theory
    gen. wks. *see* Quantum
      mechanics
  light
    astrophysics   523.015 15
    s.a. spec. celestial
      bodies
    physics   535.15
    spec. states of matter   530.4
Quarantine
  control meas.
    law   344.043
    spec. jur.   344.3–.9
    plant pests   632.93
    s.a. spec. plants; also
      spec. types of culture
      e.g. Forestry

Quarantine
  control meas. (continued)
    pub. health   614.46
    misc. aspects see Public
      health
Quarks *see* Particles (matter)
Quarrying *see* Mining
Quarter
  granting of
    law of war   341.65
Quarter horses
  animal husbandry   636.13
  other aspects see Horses
Quartermaster *see* Supplies;
  also Supply
Quarters *see* Housing
Quartets
  by instrument *see spec.*
    instruments
  chamber music
    recordings   789.912 57
    scores & parts   785.74
    treatises   785.704
  songs
    recordings   789.912
    scores & parts   784.84
      sacred   783.675 4
      secular   784.306 4
Quartic equations *see*
    Polynomial equations
Quartz
  eng. materials   620.198
    foundations   624.153 98
    naval design   623.818 98
    structures   624.189 8
    s.a. other spec. uses
  mineralogy   549.68
Quartzites *see* Metamorphic
    rocks
Quasars
  astronomy
    description   523
    theory   521.5
  other aspects see Celestial
    bodies
Quasi contract
  law   346.029
    spec. jur.   346.3–.9
Quasi-administrative bodies
  pub. admin.   350.009
    central govts.   351.009
      spec. jur.   353–354
    local govts.   352.009
Quasi-delinquents
  criminology   364.35
Quaternary period
  geology   551.79
    s.a. spec. aspects e.g.
      Economic geology
  paleontology *see* Cenozoic era
    paleontology

Quinonization
  physical chem. (continued)
    s.a. spec. aspects e.g. Low
      temperatures
    s.a. spec. elements, cpds.,
      prod.
Quinque compilationes antiquae
  rel. law   626.924
Quinsy *see* Tonsils diseases
Quintana Roo Mex.   *area*–726 7
Quintets
  by instrument *see spec.*
      instruments
  chamber music
    recordings   789.912 57
    scores & parts   785.75
    treatises   785.705
  songs
    recordings   789.912
    scores & parts   784.85
      sacred   783.675 5
      secular   784.306 5
Quintuplets
  birth *see* Multiple childbirth
  psychology   155.444
  rearing home econ.   649.144
Quirindi N.S.W.   *area*–944 4
Quirino admin. Philippines hist.
               959.904 2
  s.a. spec. events & subj.
      e.g. Commerce
Quitman Co.
  Georgia   *area*–758 924
  Mississippi   *area*–762 453
Quito Ecuador   *area*–866 13
Quizzes
  recreation   793.73
Qumran community
  Judaism   296.815
    Dead Sea Scrolls   296.155
    other aspects see Judaism
Quoits *see* Pitching-games
Quorn S. Aust.   *area*–942 36
Quotas
  import trade   382.52
    misc. aspects see Import
      trade
Quotations   080
  literature
    gen. colls.   808.882
    spec. lits.   *lit. sub.*–802
    spec. periods   *lit. sub.*–81–89

R

R & D *see* Research &
      development
RDX *see* High explosives
RFD
  postal commun.   383.145

RFD (continued)
  other aspects see Postal
      communication
RNA *see* Ribonucleic acid
RSFSR   *area*–47
RTTY *see* Radiotelegraphy
Rabat Morocco   *area*–643
Rabbis
  Judaistic leaders   296.61
  other aspects see Clergy
Rabbit
  Ears Range Colo.   *area*–788 65
  fever *see* Tularemia
Rabbit-hair textiles
  arts   746.043 5
    s.a. spec. proc. e.g.
      Weaving
  dyeing   667.335
  manufacturing
    soc. & econ. aspects *see*
      Secondary industries
    technology   677.35
      special-process fabrics 677.6
  other aspects see Textiles
  s.a. spec. prod.
Rabbits *see* Lagomorpha
Rabies
  gen. med.   616.953
  geriatrics   618.976 953
  pediatrics   618.929 53
  pub. health   614.563
  statistics   312.395 3
    deaths   312.269 53
  other aspects see Diseases
Rabun Co. Ga.   *area*–758 123
Raccoon
  Mts. Ala.   *area*–761 6
  River Ia.   *area*–777 4
Raccoons *see* Procyonidae
Race *see* Racial
Race (competition)
  tracks
    animals
      horses   798.400 68
      other   798.8
    automobiles   796.720 68
Racehorses
  animal husbandry   636.12
  other aspects see Horses
Racemization
  physical chem. *see* Optical
      activity physical chem.
Races
  physical anthr.   572
  other aspects see Ethnic
      groups
Racetrack bldgs.
  architecture   725.89
  building   690.589
  other aspects see Public
      structures

Rachet *see* Ratchet
Racial
  characteristics
    physical anthr.   572.2
  conflict
    influence on crime   364.256
  differences
    physical anthr.   572.2
    psychology   155.82
  discrimination
    voting *see* Voting
      qualifications
  factors
    animal breeding   636.082 1
      s.a. spec. animals
  groups *see* Ethnic groups
  origins
    physical anthr.   572.2
  regions subj. trmt.   area–174
  s.a. other spec. subj.
Racine
  city Wis.   area–775 97
  Co. Wis.   area–775 96
Racing
  animal husbandry for   636.088 8
    s.a. spec. animals
  ethics
    philosophy   175.7
    religion
      Buddhism   294.356 57
      Christianity   241.657
      comp. rel.   291.565 7
      Hinduism   294.548 657
      s.a. other spec. rel.
  sports
    aircraft   797.52
    animals
      horses   798.4
      other   798.8
    automobiles   796.72
    bicycles   796.62
    boats   797.14
    men   796.426
    midget cars   796.76
    motorcycles & scooters   796.75
    soapboxes   796.62
  other aspects see Sports
Racing-cars
  engineering
    gen. tech. & mf.   629.228
      maintenance   629.287 8
      models   629.221 8
      operation   629.284 8
      s.a. other spec. aspects
        e.g. Brakes; *also*
        spec. appls. e.g.
        Automobile racing
    soc. & econ. aspects *see*
      Secondary industries

Racism
  pol. ideology   320.56
  soc. theology *see* Political
    ideologies soc.
    theology
  other aspects see Ethnic
    groups
Rack railways
  engineering
    technology   625.33
    other aspects see Mountain
      railways
Racket games
  equipment mf.   688.763 4
    soc. & econ. aspects *see*
      Secondary industries
  sports   796.34
  other aspects see Sports
Racketeering
  soc. path   364.106 7
Rackets (game)
  equipment mf.   688.763 43
    soc. & econ. aspects *see*
      Secondary industries
  players
    biog. & work   796.343
      s.a. spec. kinds
    s.a.   pers.–796 34
  sports   796.343
  other aspects see Sports
Racon
  radar eng.   621.384 892
    s.a. spec. appls. e.g.
      Military engineering
    other aspects see Radar
Radar
  aids
    mil. gunnery   623.557
      s.a. other spec. appls.
    astronomy   522.684
      s.a. spec. celestial bodies
  control devices
    air traffic *see* Air traffic
      control
  engineering
    soc. & econ. aspects *see*
      Secondary industries
    technology   621.384 8
      military   623.734 8
      nautical   623.856 48
      s.a. other spec. appls.
    navigation
      seamanship   623.893 3
      other aspects see
        Navigation
  platforms *see* Artificial
    islands
  telescopes
    astronomy   522.684
      s.a. spec. celestial
        bodies

Radar (continued)
  weather forecasting   551.635 3
    spec. areas   551.65
    spec. elements   551.64
Radcliffe Greater Manchester Eng.
         *area–*427 38
Radford Va.   *area–*755 786
Radial street patterns
  civic art   711.41
Radiant
  energy *see* Radiations
  panel heating
    buildings   697.72
  points
    astronomy
      description   523.53
      theory   521.75
    other aspects see Celestial
        bodies
Radiating systems
  acoustical eng.   620.21
  s.a. spec. appls. e.g.
      Musical sound
Radiation
  ammunition
    mil. eng.
      soc. & econ. aspects *see*
        Secondary industries
      tech. & mf.   623.459 5
  devices
    small arms
      mil. eng.
        soc. & econ. aspects
          see Secondary
          industries
        tech. & mf.   623.446
  injuries
    plants
      agriculture   632.19
      s.a. spec. plants; also
        spec. types of culture
        e.g. Forestry
    statistics   312.304 712 4
    deaths   312.260 471 24
    surgery   617.124
      anesthesiology   617.967 124
    s.a. Veterinary sciences
    s.a. Radiations effects
  of energy
    solar-energy eng.
      soc. & econ. aspects *see*
        Secondary industries
    technology   621.471
    s.a. spec. appls. e.g.
      Heating buildings
  of heat
    astrophysics   523.013 33
    s.a. spec. celestial
      bodies

Radiation
  of heat (continued)
    engineering *see*
      Transmission heat
      engineering
    physics   536.33
      spec. states of matter   530.4
  sicknesses
    gen. med.   616.989 7
    geriatrics   618.976 989 7
    injuries   617.124
    pediatrics   618.929 897
    statistics   312.398 97
      deaths   312.269 897
    other aspects see Diseases
    s.a. spec. diseases
  therapy *see* Radiotherapy
Radiations   539.2
  astrophysics   523.019 2
    s.a. spec. celestial bodies
  biophysics
    extraterrestrial
      gen. wks.   574.191 95
        animals   591.191 95
        microorganisms   576.119 195
        plants   581.191 95
        s.a. spec. organisms
      med. sci.   612.014 55
        animals   636.089 201 455
        s.a. spec. animals
        man   612.014 55
    terrestrial
      gen. wks.   574.191 5
        animals   591.191 5
        microorganisms   576.119 15
        plants   581.191 5
        s.a. spec. organisms
      med. sci.   612.014 48
        animals   636.089 201 448
        s.a. spec. animals
        man   612.014 48
    s.a. spec. functions,
      systems, organs
  chemistry *see* Radiochemistry
  diseases *see* Environmental
    diseases
  effects
    biophysics *see* Radiations
      biophysics
    eng. materials   620.112 28
      misc. aspects see
        Deterioration
      s.a. spec. materials &
      uses
    genetics *see* Radiations
      genetics
    medicine *see* Radiation
      sicknesses
    space flight   629.416
      s.a. spec. appls. e.g.
        Space warfare

Radiations (continued)
  genetics
    life sci. — 575.131
      animals — 591.159 2
      man — 573.213 1
      microorganisms — 576.139
      plants — 581.159 2
      s.a. spec. organisms
  medicine
    effects *see* Radiation
        sicknesses
    therapeutic use — 615.83–.84
      misc. aspects see
        Physical therapies
      s.a. spec. diseases
  meteorology — 551.527
    weather forecasting — 551.642 7
    spec. areas — 551.65
  particles *see* Particles
        (matter)
  physics — 539.2
    spec. states of matter — 530.4
    *s.a. spec. physical
        phenomena e.g.* Heat
  sterilization
    foods
      comm. proc. — 664.028 8
      other aspects see Foods
      s.a. spec. foods e.g.
        Meats
    *s.a. other spec. prod. &
        commodities*
    s.a. spec. kinds e.g. Heat
Radiative heating
  local bldg. heating — 697.1
Radiators
  heating equipment
    building — 697.07
    s.a. spec. kinds e.g.
        Steam heating
  internal-combustion engines
        see Cooling-systems
        internal-combustion
        engines
Radical
  theory
    algebra — 512.94
    s.a. other spec. subj.
Radicalism *see* Collectivism
Radicals
  molecular structure
    theoretical chem. — 541.224
    organic — 547.122 4
    *s.a. spec. elements &
        cpds.*
Radiesthesia
  parapsychology — 133.323
Radio — 384.5
  actors & actresses *see* Actors
  advertising — 659.142

Radio (continued)
  aids
    navigation
      seamanship — 623.893 2
      other aspects see
        Navigation
      s.a. other spec. appls.
    astronomy — 522.682
      s.a. spec. celestial bodies
    beacons
      navigation
        seamanship — 623.893 2
        other aspects see
          Navigation
  broadcasting *see*
        Radiobroadcasting
  buildings *see* Office
        buildings
  communication *see*
        Radiocommunication
  compasses
    aircraft eng. — 629.135 1
    engineering — 621.384 191
    s.a. spec. appls. e.g.
        Navigation
    navigation
      seamanship — 623.893 2
      other aspects see
        Navigation
  drama *see* Broadcast drama
  ed. use — 371.333 1
    adult ed. — 374.26
    spec. subj. — *s.s.*–071 53
    *s.a. other spec. levels of
        ed.*
  eng. & mf.
    soc. & econ. aspects *see*
        Secondary industries
    technology — 621.384 1
      military — 623.734
      nautical — 623.856 4
      s.a. other spec. appls.
  engineers
    biog. & work — 621.384 109 2
    s.a. — *pers.*–621 3
  ethics *see* Public
        entertainment ethics
  evangelism
    pastoral theology
      Christianity — 253.78
      other rel. see Pastoral
        theology
  frequency alloation *see*
        Measurement radio
  influence on crime — 364.254
  journalism — 070.19
    s.a. spec. activities e.g.
        Reporting
  manufacture *see* Radio eng. &
        mf.

Radio (continued)

music	782.86
recordings	789.912 286
networks *see* Broadcasting networks	
performers *see* Actors	
performing arts	791.44
plays *see* Broadcast drama	
preaching	
Christianity	251.07
other rel. see Preaching	
programs *see* Programs radiobroadcasting	
receivers	
automobiles	
soc. & econ. aspects *see* Secondary industries	
tech. & mf.	629.277
other aspects see Receiving sets radio	
rooms	
education *see* Instructional spaces education	
sociology	302.23
speaking *see* Public speaking	
speeches *see* Public speeches	
stations *see* Broadcasting stations	
telescopes	
astronomy	522.682
s.a. spec. celestial bodies	
towers *see* Office buildings	
waves	
biophysics	
extraterrestrial	
gen. wks.	574.191 951
animals	591.191 951
microorganisms	576.119 195 1
plants	581.191 951
s.a. spec. organisms	
med. sci.	621.014 551
animals	636.089 201 455 1
s.a. spec. animals	
man	612.014 551
terrestrial	
gen. wks.	574.191 51
animals	591.191 51
microorganisms	576.119 151
plants	581.191 51
s.a. spec. organisms	
med. sci.	612.014 481
animals	636.089 201 448 1
s.a. spec. animals	
man	612.014 481
s.a. spec. functions, systems, organisms	
other aspects see Radiations	

Radio (continued)

work	
local Christian parishes	254.3
spec. appls.	259.7
s.a. other spec. uses	
Radioactivation analysis *see* Activation analysis	
Radioactive	
air pollutants	
sanitary eng.	628.535
fallout *see* Artificial radioactivity	
isotopes *see* Radioisotopes	
materials	
pollution by *see* Pollutants	
pub. safety	363.179
misc. aspects see Hazardous materials	
phenomena	
celestial bodies	
Jupiter	523.452
Mars	523.432
Mercury	523.412
moon	523.32
Neptune	523.481 2
Pluto	523.482 2
Saturn	523.462
stars	523.82
spec. systems	523.84–.85
sun	523.72
Uranus	523.472
Venus	523.422
s.a. other spec. bodies	
s.a. other spec. subj.	
properties	
earth astronomy	525.2
s.a. other spec. subj.	
tracer tech. *see* Tracer techniques	
waste	
disposal	
law	344.046 22
spec. jur.	344.3–.9
other aspects see Wastes control	
technology	621.483 8
Radioactivity	
astrophysics	523.019 752–.019 753
s.a. spec. celestial bodies	
methods	
geophysical prospecting	622.159
physics	539.752–.753
spec. states of matter	530.4
s.a. spec. physical phenomena e.g. Heat	
Radiobiology *see* Radiations biophysics	
Radiobroadcasting	
commerce	384.54
govt. control	351.874 54
spec. jur.	353–354

Radiobroadcasting (continued)
  other aspects see
      Radiocommunication
Radiochemical methods
  anal. chem.
    gen. wks.   543.088
      qualitative   544.98
      quantitative   545.82
    organic   547.308 8
      qualitative   547.349 8
      quantitative   547.358 2
  s.a. spec. elements & cpds.
Radiochemistry
  physical chem.   541.38
    applied   660.298
    organic   547.138
  s.a. spec. elements, cpds.,
    prod.
Radiocommunication   384.5
  commerce   384.5
  engineering *see* Radio eng. &
    mf.
  govt. control
    activities   351.874 5
    departments & ministries
      see Executive
      departments
    spec. jur.   353–354
  law
    international   341.757 7
    municipal   343.099 45
    spec. jur.   343.3–.9
  other aspects see
      Communication
Radiocontrol
  air traffic *see* Air traffic
    control
  gen. wks.
    engineering   621.384 196
    s.a. spec. appls. e.g.
      Astronautics
  other aspects see Radio
Radioelements *see* Radioactivity
Radiofacsimile *see*
    Radiotelegraphy
Radiofinding equipment
  aeronautics   629.135 1
  gen. wks. *see*
      Direction-finding
  nautical eng. *see* Radio aids
  s.a. other spec. uses
Radiofrequency
  spectroscopes
    mf. tech.   681.414 8
      components   681.42–.43
    other aspects see Optical
      instruments
  spectroscopy
    astrophysics   523.018 753 4
    s.a. spec. celestial
    bodies

Radiofrequency
  spectroscopy (continued)
    engineering
      soc. & econ. aspects *see*
        Secondary industries
      technology   621.361 5
      s.a. spec. appls. e.g.
        Materials engineering
    physics *see* Radiowave
      electronics physics
    other aspects see
      Spectroscopy
Radiogenetics *see* Radiations
    genetics
Radiographic testing
  eng. materials   620.112 72
  s.a. spec. materials & spec.
    uses
Radiography
  engineering
    soc. & econ. aspects *see*
      Secondary industries
    technology   621.367 3
    s.a. spec. appls. e.g.
      Diagnoses
Radioisotope
  scanning
    med. diagnosis
      gen. med.   616.075 75
      surgery   617.075 75
      s.a. spec. diseases
    other aspects see
      Diseases
    s.a. other spec. appls.
  therapy   615.842 4
    misc. aspects see Physical
      therapies
    s.a. spec. diseases
Radioisotope-powered
  generators
    soc. & econ. aspects *see*
      Secondary industries
    tech. & mf.
      electrodynamics
      engineering   621.312 5
      s.a. spec. appls.
        e.g. Electric
        railroads
      other aspects see
        Electrodynamics
      thermal eng.   621.481
      s.a. spec. appls. e.g.
        Rocket engines
    s.a. other spec. subj.
Radioisotopes
  pollution
    water-supply eng.
      technology   628.168 5
      other aspects see Water
        supply engineering

Radioisotopes (continued)
  radiochemistry
    physical chem.   541.388 4
      applied   660.298 84
      organic   547.138 84
      s.a. spec. elements,
        cpds., prod.
    technology   621.483 7
      soc. & econ. aspects *see*
        Secondary industries
    other aspects see
        Radioactivity
    s.a. other spec. appls. e.g.
        Radioisotope therapy
Radiolaria
  culture   639.731 4
  paleozoology   563.14
  zoology   593.14
  other aspects see Protozoa
Radiological *see* Radioscopic
Radiolysis
  radiochemistry
    physical chem.   541.382
      applied   660.298 2
      organic   547.138 2
      s.a. spec. elements,
        cpds., prod.
Radionuclides *see* Radioactivity
Radiophonographs *see*
        Reproducers sound
Radioscopic
  diagnosis med. sci.
    gen. med.   616.075 7
    surgery   617.075 7
    s.a. spec. diseases
    other aspects see Diseases
  urinalysis *see* Radioscopic
        diagnosis
Radiosondes
  weather forecasting   551.635 2
    spec. areas   551.65
    spec. elements   551.64
Radiotelegraphy
  commerce   384.52
  govt. control   351.874 52
  spec. jur.   353–354
  law *see* Telegraphy law
  technology   621.384 2
    military   623.734 2
    nautical   623.856 42
    s.a. other spec. appls.
  other aspects see Radio
Radiotelephony
  commerce   384.53
  govt. control   351.874 53
  spec. jur.   353–354
  law *see* Telephony law
  technology   621.384 5
    military   623.734 5
    nautical   623.856 45
    s.a. other spec. appls.

Radiotelephony (continued)
  other aspects see Radio
Radiotherapy   615.842
  misc. aspects see Physical
        therapies
  s.a. spec. diseases
Radio-tube sets
  radio
    engineering   621.384 136 6
    s.a. spec. appls. e.g.
        Radiotelephony
    other aspects see Radio
  television
    engineering   621.388 366
    s.a. spec. appls. e.g.
        Astronautics
    other aspects see
        Television
Radiowave electronics
  astrophysics   523.018 753 4
    s.a. spec. celestial bodies
  engineering
    soc. & econ. aspects *see*
        Secondary industries
    technology   621.381 5
    s.a. spec. appls. e.g.
        Radiocommunication
  physics   537.534
    spec. states of matter   530.4
Radishes
  agriculture   635.15
    soc. & econ. aspects *see*
        Primary industries
  foods   641.351 5
    preparation
      commercial   664.805 15
      domestic   641.651 5
  other aspects see Cruciales;
        also Vegetables
Radium
  chemistry
    inorganic   546.396
    organic   547.053 96
    s.a. spec. groupings e.g.
        Aliphatic compounds
  technology   661.039 6
    organic   661.895
    soc. & econ. aspects *see*
        Secondary industries
    s.a. spec. prod.
  mineral aspects *see* Fuels
        nuclear reactors
  pharmacology   615.239 6
    misc. aspects see
        Pharmacology
  therapy   615.842 3
    misc. aspects see Physical
        therapies
    s.a. spec. diseases

Radium (continued)
  toxicology   615.925 396
    misc. aspects see
        Toxicology
    other aspects see Alkaline
        earth metals
Radius (bones) *see* Upper
    extremities bones
Radnor Powys Wales   *area*–429 54
Radom Poland   *area*–438 4
Radon
  chemistry
    inorganic   546.756
    technology   661.075 6
    soc. & econ. aspects *see*
        Secondary industries
    s.a. spec. prod.
  toxicology   615.925 756
    misc. aspects see
        Toxicology
    other aspects see Rare gases
Raeto-Romanic *see*
    Rhaeto-Romanic
Raffia
  agriculture   633.58
    soc. & econ. aspects *see*
        Primary industries
    other aspects see Palmales;
        also Unaltered
        vegetable fibers
Raffiawork
  textile arts   746.41
    s.a. spec. prod.
Raffinose
  org. chem.   547.781 5
    other aspects see Sugar
Rag pulp
  mf. tech.   676.13
    other aspects see Pulp
Rage
  ethics *see* Vices
  psychology *see* Primitive
    emotions
Ragtime
  music theory   781.572
  recordings   789.912 157 2
    s.a. spec. mediums
Ragusa Sicily   *area*–458 15
Ragweed *see* Asterales
Rahway N.J.   *area*–749 38
Rail
  fastenings
    railroad eng.
      technology   625.15
    other aspects see
        Permanent way
  transportation *see* Railroad
    transportation

Railings
  ecclesiastical furniture
    built-in arch. decoration   729.96
    rel. significance
      Christianity   247.16
      comp. rel.   291.37
      s.a. other spec. rel.
Railroad
  accessory bldgs. *see* Railroad
    buildings
  bridges *see* Bridges
    (structures)
  buildings
    architecture   725.33
    building   690.533
    other aspects see Public
      structures
  cars *see* Rolling stock
    railroads
  companies
    commerce   388.065
    govt. control   351.875
    spec. jur.   353–354
    law
      international   341.753
      municipal   346.06
      spec. jur.   346.3–.9
    investment in
      financial econ.   332.671 2
      domestic   332.672 2
      other aspects see
        Investments
  cookery   641.576
  engineers
    biog. & work   625.100 92
    s.a.   *pers.*–625
  freight station bldgs.
    architecture   725.32
    building   690.532
    other aspects see Public
      structures
  guard bldgs. *see* Railroad
    accessory bldgs.
  insurance inland marine   368.233
    misc. aspects see Insurance
  mail
    postal commun.   383.143
    other aspects see Postal
      communication
  passenger station bldgs.
    architecture   725.31
    building   690.531
    other aspects see Public
      structures
  personnel
    biog. & work   385.092
    s.a.   *pers.*–385
  police
    police services   363.287
    other aspects see Law
      enforcement

Railroad (continued)
  post offices
    postal commun.   383.143
    other aspects see Postal
        communication
  rolling stock *see* Rolling
        stock railroads
  shop bldgs.
    gen. wks. *see* Railroad
        accessory bldgs.
    terminals *see* Railroad
        terminals facilities
  signal bldgs. *see* Railroad
        accessory bldgs.
  signals
    law *see* Stationary
        facilities railroads
        law
    other aspects see
        Communication
        facilities railroads
  stations *see* Railroad
        terminals
  storage bldgs. *see* Railroad
        accessory bldgs.
  terminal bldgs. *see* Railroad
        terminals facilities
  terminals
    activities
      freight *see* Freight
          services transp.
          terminals
      passenger *see* Passenger
          services transp.
          terminals
    facilities
      commerce   385.314
        local   388.472
        special-duty   385.5
      govt. control   350.875 314
        central govts.   351.875 314
          spec. jur.   353–354
        local govts.   352.915 314
      law *see* Stationary
          facilties railroads law
  tool bldgs. *see* Railroad
        accessory bldgs.
  tracks
    commerce *see* Stationary
        facilities railroads
    engineering
      technology   625.14
      other aspects see
          Permanent way
    law *see* Stationary
        facilities railroads
        law

Railroad (continued)
  transportation
    accidents   363.122
      misc. aspects see
          Transportation
          accidents
    commerce   385
    facilities
      civic art   711.75
      govt. control   351.875
        spec. jur.   353–354
    hazards
      soc. path.   363.122
    law
      international   341.756 5
      municipal   343.095
        spec. jur.   343.3–.9
    safety
      law
        gen. wks.
          international   341.756 5
          municipal   343.095
          local   343.098 3
          spec. jur.   343.3–.9
        pub. meas.   363.122
        govt. control *see*
            Safety pub. admin.
    tunnels *see* Tunnels
    yards
      law *see* Stationary
          facilities railroads
          law
      railroad eng.
        technology   625.18
        other aspects see
            Railroads; *also*
            Railroad terminals
            facilities
Railroad-borne
  artillery *see* Field artillery
  s.a. other spec. subj.
Railroading
  technology   625.27
  other aspects see Railroads
Railroads
  construction
    mil. sci.   358.22
    s.a. Railroads engineering
  electrification
    soc. & econ. aspects *see*
        Secondary industries
    technology   621.33
    s.a. spec. appls. e.g.
        Railroad transportation
  engineering
    soc. & econ. aspects *see*
        Secondary industries
    technology   625.1
      military   623.63
      mine   622.66
    s.a. other spec. appls.

Rails
 metal prod. *see* Primary metal
  prod.
 railroad eng.
  technology   625.15
  other aspects see Permanent
   way
 roadside barriers
  technology   625.795
  other aspects see Roads
 wood bldg. construction   694.6
Rails (birds) *see* Gruiformes
Railton Tas.   *area*–946 5
Railway *see* Railroad
Rain
 meteorology   551.578 1
  artificial modification   551.687 81
  weather forecasting   551.647 81
  spec. areas   551.65
 plant injuries
  agriculture   632.16
  s.a. spec. plants; also
   spec. types of culture
   e.g. Forestry
 other aspects see Weather
Rainbow order   366.18
Rainbows *see* Condensation
   products atmospheric
   optical phenomena
Raincoats
 comm. mf.   687.145
 domestic mf.   646.453
 other aspects see Clothing
Rainfall *see* Rain
Rainford Merseyside Eng.   *area*–427 57
Rainier Mt. Wash.   *area*–797 78
Rains Co. Tex.   *area*–764 275
Rainstorms
 disasters
  soc. action   363.349 2
  misc. aspects see
   Disasters
 meteorology *see* Thermal
   convective storms
Rainy
 Lake   *area*–776 79
 River   *area*–776 79
  District. Ont.   *area*–713 117
Raised characters
 printing
  description   686.212
  technology   686.282
  soc. & econ. aspects *see*
   Secondary industries
Raised-character books
 bibliographies & reviews *see*
   Disabled people
   publications for
 library trmt.   025.179 2
  acquisitions   025.289 2
  cataloging   025.349 2

Raised-character books
 library trmt. (continued)
  s.a. other spec. activities
  publishing   070.579 2
Raising
 money
  local Christian parishes   254.8
  s.a. other spec. appls.
 s.a. other spec. subj.
Raisins *see* Grapes
Rajasthan India   *area*–544
Rajasthani
 language
  linguistics   491.479
  literature   891.479
  s.a.   *lang.*–914 79
 s.a. Rajasthan; *also other*
   spec. subj. e.g. Arts
Rajiformes *see* Batoidea
Rajshahi Bangladesh   *area*–549 24
Rakes *see* Hand tools
Raleigh
 Bay
  oceanography   551.461 48
  regional subj. trmt.   *area*–163 48
  other aspects see Atlantic
   Ocean
 city N.C.   *area*–756 55
 Co. W. Va.   *area*–754 73
Rallies
 Sunday-school services
  Christianity   268.7
  other rel. see Religious
   instruction
Ralls Co. Mo.   *area*–778 355
Ramadan
 Islamic observance   297.36
Ramadi Iraq   *area*–567 4
Ramakrishna movement
 Hinduism   294.555
 misc. aspects see Hinduism
Raman
 effect spectroscopy *see* Raman
   spectroscopy
 spectroscopes
  mf. tech.   681.414 6
  components   681.42–.43
  other aspects see Optical
   instruments
 spectroscopy
  anal. chem. *see* Visible
   light spectroscopy
   anal. chem.
  astrophysics   523.015 846
  s.a. spec. celestial
   bodies
  engineering *see* Visible
   light spectroscopy
   engineering
  physics   535.846
  spec. states of matter   530.4

Ramanujacharya philosophy   181.483
Ramayana Hinduism   294.592 2
Rambler
  houses *see* Single-story
      houses
  roses *see* Rosaceae
Rameses reign Egypt hist.   932.014
  s.a. spec. events & subj.
      e.g. Commerce
Ramie
  agriculture   633.55
    soc. & econ. aspects *see*
      Primary industries
  textiles
    arts   746.041 5
    s.a. spec. proc. e.g.
      Weaving
    dyeing   667.315
    manufacturing
      soc. & econ. aspects *see*
        Secondary industries
      technology   677.15
      special-process fabrics   677.6
    other aspects see Textiles
    s.a. spec. prod.
  other aspects see Urticales
Ramjet engines
  aircraft eng.
    soc. & econ. aspects *see*
      Secondary industries
    tech. & mf.   629.134 353 5
Ramos admin. Brazil hist.   981.062
  s.a. spec. events & subj.
      e.g. Commerce
Ramps
  architectural
    construction   721.83
    design & decoration   729.39
    s.a. spec. kinds of bldgs.
  building   690.183
    wood   694.6
  canal eng.
    technology   627.135 3
    s.a. spec. appls. e.g.
      Canal transportation
  other aspects see Liquids
    engineering
Rams (animals) *see* Sheep
Rams (hydraulics)
  hydraulic-power tech.
    soc. & econ. aspects *see*
      Secondary industries
    tech. & mf.   621.27
    s.a. spec. appls. e.g.
      Water supply
      engineering
Ramses reign Egypt hist.   932.014
  s.a. spec. events & subj.
      e.g. Commerce
Ramsey
  Cambridgeshire Eng.   *area*–426 54

Ramsey (continued)
  County
    Minnesota   *area*–776 58
    North Dakota   *area*–784 36
Ramsgate Kent Eng.   *area*–422 357
Ranales
  botany   583.111
  floriculture   635.933 111
  med. aspects
    crop prod.   633.883 111
    gen. pharm.   615.323 111
      toxicology   615.952 311 1
    vet. pharm.   636.089 532 311 1
      toxicology   636.089 595 231 11
  paleobotany   561.3
  other aspects see Plants
Ranch houses *see* Single-story
      houses
Ranches
  animal husbandry   636.01
    s.a. spec. animals
  s.a. Dude ranching
Randall Co. Tex.   *area*–764 834
Randers Denmark   *area*–489 5
Randolph Co.
  Alabama   *area*–761 57
  Arkansas   *area*–767 24
  Georgia   *area*–758 932
  Illinois   *area*–773 92
  Indiana   *area*–772 66
  Missouri   *area*–778 283
  North Carolina   *area*–756 61
  West Virginia   *area*–754 85
Random
  processes math.   519
  walks   519.282
  s.a. spec. appls. e.g.
    Engineering
Ranganathan's Colon
    Classification   025.435
  special materials   025.34
  spec. subj.   025.46
Range
  apparatus
    ordnance
      soc. & econ. aspects *see*
        Secondary industries
      tech. & mf.   623.46
  finders
    photography   771.37
    gen. tech.   770.282
    spec. proc. & fields   772–778
  land *see* Grasslands
Rangeley Lakes Me.   *area*–741 7
Ranger project astronautics   629.435 3
Rangers
  armed forces   356.167
Ranges (stoves)
  mf. tech.   683.88
  other aspects see Household
    appliances

Ranidae	
zoology	597.89
other aspects see Anura	
Rankin Co. Miss.	*area*–762 59
Ranks	
genealogy	929.7
military	355.33
s.a. spec. mil. branches	
religious *see* Governing	
leaders ecclesiology	
social *see* Social classes	
s.a. other spec. kinds	
Ransom Co. N.D.	*area*–784 315
Ranunculaceae *see* Ranales	
Rapa Isl.	*area*–962 2
Rapateaceae *see* Xyridales	
Rape	
criminology	364.153 2
law	345.025 32
spec. jur.	345.3–.9
soc. theology	
Christianity	261.833 153 2
comp. rel.	291.178 331 532
s.a. other spec. rel.	
Rape (plant)	
agriculture	
oil-producing	633.853
soc. & econ. aspects *see*	
Primary industries	
Rapeseed oil	
agriculture	633.853
soc. & econ. aspects *see*	
Primary industries	
Raphanus sativus *see* Radishes	
Raphia *see* Raffia	
Rapid	
calculations	
arithmetic	513.92
transit	
gen. wks. *see* Urban	
transportation	
railroads	
technology	625.4
other aspects see	
Railroads	
s.a. other spec. subj.	
Rapides Par. La.	*area*–763 69
Rappahannock	
Co. Va.	*area*–755 395
River	*area*–755 2
Rapping	
spiritualism	133.92
Raqqa Syria	*area*–569 12
Rare	
animals	
zoology	591.042
s.a. spec. animals	
birds	
zoology	598.042

Rare (continued)	
books	
bibliographies	011.44
spec. kinds	012–016
catalogs	
general	017–019
spec. kinds	012–016
hist. & crit.	090
library trmt.	025.171 6
acquisitions	025.281 6
cataloging	025.341 6
s.a. other spec.	
activities; also	
Rare-book libraries	
gases	553.97
chemistry	
inorganic	546.75
technology	661.075
soc. & econ. aspects	
see Secondary	
industries	
s.a. spec. prod.	
econ. geol.	553.97
extraction	
from air	
chem. tech.	665.822
soc. & econ. aspects	
see Secondary	
industries	
s.a. spec. prod.	
from ground	
soc. & econ. aspects	
see Primary	
industries	
technology	622.397
prospecting	622.189 7
pharmacology	615.275
misc. aspects see	
Pharmacology	
toxicology	615.925 75
misc. aspects see	
Toxicology	
s.a. spec. uses; also spec.	
minerals	
mammals	
zoology	599.004 2
Rare-book libraries	026.09
misc. aspects see Special	
libraries	
Rare-earth elements	
chemistry	
inorganic	546.4
organic	547.054
s.a. spec. groupings e.g.	
Aliphatic compounds	
technology	661.04
organic	661.895
soc. & econ. aspects *see*	
Secondary industries	
s.a. spec. prod.	
eng. materials	620.189 29

Rare-earth elements (continued)

metallography	669.952 9
metallurgy	669.29
physical & chem.	669.962 9
mineral aspects *see*	
Lanthanide series	
metals	
pharmacology	615.24
misc. aspects see	
Pharmacology	
products	
mf. tech.	673.29
other aspects see	
Nonferrous metals	
products	
toxicology	615.925 4
misc. aspects see	
Toxicology	

Rarefaction

gas mech.	533.52

Rarefied-gas electronics

astrophysics	523.018 753
s.a. spec. celestial bodies	
physics	537.53
spec. states of matter	530.4

Rarefying

gases	
chem. apparatus	542.7
s.a. spec. appls. e.g.	
Organic chemistry	

Raritan River N.J.	*area*–749 44
Ras al Khaimah	*area*–535 7
Ras Tafari Ethiopia hist.	963.054
s.a. spec. events & subj.	
e.g. Commerce	

Rasers

radiowave electronics	
soc. & econ. aspects *see*	
Secondary industries	
tech. & mf.	621.381 535
s.a. spec. appls. e.g.	
Television	
other aspects see Radiowave	
electronics	

Rashes *see* Integument diseases	
Rashid Syria	*area*–569 12

Rasp carving

wood *see* Wood sculpture	

Raspberries

agriculture	634.711
soc. & econ. aspects *see*	
Primary industries	
foods	641.347 11
preparation	
commercial	664.804 711
domestic	641.647 11
other aspects see Rosaceae;	
also Fruits	

Rasps *see* Filing tools

Ratchet wheels

machine eng.	
soc. & econ. aspects *see*	
Secondary industries	
tech. & mf.	621.837
s.a. spec. appls. e.g.	
Timepieces	
other aspects see Mechanics	

Ratchets

machine eng.	
soc. & econ. aspects *see*	
Secondary industries	
tech. & mf.	621.837
s.a. spec. appls. e.g.	
Agricultural equipment	
other aspects see Mechanics	

Rates

commun. ind.	
commerce	380.3
gen. telecommun.	384.041
telegraphy	384.13
submarine cable	384.43
wire	384.13
wireless	384.523
telephony	384.63
wire	384.63
wireless	384.533
television	
community antenna	384.555 63
pay	384.554 7
govt. control	351.874
spec. jur.	353–354
law *see* Telecommunication	
law	
law	343.091
spec. jur.	343.3–.9
postal commun.	383.23
law	343.099 23
spec. jur.	343.3–.9
other aspects see Postal	
communication	
transp. ind.	
commerce	380.59
air	387.712
inland waterway	386.1
maritime	387.51
motor	388.32
railway	385.12
special-duty	385.5
urban transp.	388.404 2
govt. control	350.875–.878
central govts.	351.875–.878
spec. jur.	353–354
local govts.	352.915–.918
law *see* Transportation law	

Rates (percentages)

property taxes	
pub. finance	336.222
other aspects see Property	
taxes	

Rates (taxes) *see* Local
    taxation; *also*
    Property taxes
Ratfishes *see* Chimaerae
Rathlin Isl. N. Ire.   *area*–416 15
Ratification
  of constitutions *see*
    Constitutional history
  of treaties *see* Treaties
Rating
  personnel *see* Evaluation of
    employees
  s.a. other spec. subj.
Ration
  coupons
    prints   769.57
Rational
  functions
    algebra   512.96
    s.a. spec. appls. e.g.
      Engineering
  schools psych.   150.192
    s.a. spec. subj. & branches
      of psych.
  s.a. other spec. subj.
Rationalism
  nat. rel.   211.4
  philosophy   149.7
    indiv. phil.   180–190
    s.a. spec. branches of phil.
      e.g. Metaphysics
  pol. ideology   320.512
  soc. theology *see* Political
    ideologies soc.
    theology
Rationalists
  polemics against
    Christianity   239.7
    Islam   297.297
    other rel. see Doctrinal
      theology
Rationing
  pub. admin.
    activities   350.829
      central govts.   351.829
        spec. jur.   353–354
      local govts.   352.942
    govt. depts. *see* Executive
      departments
Ratios   512.924
  algebra   512.924
  arithmetic   513.24
  s.a. spec. appls. e.g.
    Business arithmetic
Rats
  experimental animals
    med. sci.   619.93
  other aspects see Myomorpha
Rattan
  furniture
    mf. tech.   684.106

Rattan
  furniture (continued)
    other aspects see Furniture
    s.a. spec. prod.
  other aspects see Unaltered
    vegetable fibers
Rattle (musical instrument)
  music   789.4
    recordings   789.912 94
Rattles (musical instruments)
  mf. tech.   681.819 4
    misc. aspects see Musical
      instruments
  musical art   789.4
Rattlesnake ferns *see*
    Eusporangiated ferns
Rattray Tayside Scot.   *area*–412 8
Raunds Northamptonshire Eng.
           area–425 54
Ravalli Co. Mont.   *area*–786 89
Ravenglass Cumbria Eng. *area*–427 84
Ravenna Italy   *area*–454 7
Ravines *see* Depressions
    (geomorphology)
Raw
  materials
    alcoholic beverages
      comm. proc.   663.11
      s.a. spec. beverages
        e.g. Wines
      other aspects see
        Alcoholic beverages
    chem. plants   660.282
    s.a. spec. prod.
    foods
      comm. proc.   664.01
      s.a. spec. foods
      other aspects see Foods
    glassmaking   666.121
    s.a. spec. kinds of glass
    latex mf.   678.521
    s.a. spec. kinds of
      latexes e.g. Natural
      latexes
    mil. resources   355.24
    s.a. spec. mil. branches
    nonalcoholic brewed beverages
      comm. proc.
        coffee   663.931
        tea   663.941
      s.a. other spec.
        beverages
      other aspects see
        Beverages
    plastics mf.   668.411
    s.a. spec. kinds of
      plastics
    resources *see* Natural
      resources
    s.a. other spec. techs.

Raw (continued)
milk
  dairy tech.
    skim   637.147 1
    whole   637.141
  other aspects see Milk
rubber
  rubber mf.
    soc. & econ. aspects *see*
      Secondary industries
    technology   678.21
  s.a. spec. kinds of rubber
    e.g. Natural rubber
Rawalpindi Pakistan   *area*–549 142
Rawlins Co. Kan.   *area*–781 125
Rawmarsh South Yorkshire Eng.
                        area–428 23
Rawtenstall Lancashire Eng.
                        area–427 63
Ray Co. Mo.   *area*–778 19
Rayleigh Essex Eng.   *area*–426 775
Rayons
  textiles
    arts   746.044 61–.044 63
    s.a. spec. proc. e.g.
      Weaving
    dyeing   667.346 1–.346 3
    manufacturing
      soc. & econ. aspects *see*
        Secondary industries
      technology   677.461–.463
        special-process fabrics 677.6
    org. chem.   547.856 1–.856 3
    other aspects see Textiles
    s.a. spec. prod.
Rays (beams)
  astrophysics   523.019 722
  s.a. spec. celestial bodies
  physics   539.722
    spec. states of matter 530.4
  s.a. spec. physical
    phenomena e.g. Heat
Rays (fishes) *see* Batoidea
Razgrad Bulgaria   *area*–497 77
Razing
  buildings   690.26
Razor blades *see* Razors
Razorback swine
  animal husbandry 636.484
  other aspects see Swine
Razors
  manufacturing
    soc. & econ. aspects *see*
      Secondary industries
    technology   688.5
Reaction
  cross sections
    nuclear *see* Nuclear
      reactions
  kinetics *see* Reactions
  mechanisms *see* Reactions

Reaction (continued)
  rates
    chemistry *see* Chemical
      kinetics
    s.a. other spec. subj.
    steam turbines *see* Turbine
      steam engines
Reactions
  chemistry
    physical   541.39
    applied   660.299
    organic   547.139
    s.a. spec. aspects e.g.
      Low temperatures
    s.a. spec. elements & cpds.
  mechanics   531.113
    misc. aspects see Dynamics
  nuclear physics *see* Nuclear
    reactions
  s.a. other spec. subj.
Reaction-time studies
  quan. psych.   152.83
  animals   156.283
  children   155.412
  s.a. psych. of other spec.
    groups; also spec.
    appls. e.g. industrial
    fatigue studies
    658.544
Reactivity
  minerals   549.131
    spec. minerals   549.2–.7
  s.a. other spec. subj.
Reactor cores
  nuclear eng.
    tech. & mf.   621.483 1
  other aspects see Reactors
Reactors
  nuclear eng.
    soc. & econ. aspects *see*
      Secondary industries
    tech. & mf.   621.483
    s.a. spec. appls. e.g.
      Generation elect. power
  other aspects see Nuclear
    reactions
  s.a. Nuclear propulsion
Reader advisory services
  library econ.   025.54
Readers (textbooks)
  appl. ling.   418
    spec. langs.   *lang. sub.*–86
Reading
  aids library sci.   028
  appl. ling.   418
    spec. langs.   *lang. sub.*–84
  child care at home 649.58
  communication   001.543
  ethics
    philosophy   175.8

Realism
  lit. qual. (continued)
    spec. lits.
      collections   *lit. sub.*–080 12
      hist. & crit.   *lit. sub.*–091 2
    s.a. spec. lit. forms
    philosophy   149.2
    indiv. phil.   180–190
    s.a. spec. branches of phil.
      e.g. Metaphysics
    stage qual.   792.090 912
    s.a. spec. mediums e.g.
      Television; *also spec.*
      kinds of drama e.g.
      Tragedies (drama)
  s.a. other spec. subj.
Realistic
  fiction
    gen. wks.
      collections   808.838 3
      hist. & crit.   809.383
      rhetoric   808.383
      juvenile   808.068 383
    spec. lits.   *lit. sub.*–308 3
    indiv. authors *lit. sub.*–31–39
    other aspects see Fiction
  s.a. other spec. subj.
Reality
  cognition *see* Cognition
  metaphysics   111
Realization of figured bass *see*
    Thorough bass
Real-time systems
  electronic data proc. *see*
    Networks electronic
    data proc.
Realty *see* Real property
Real-valued functions   515.7
  methodology *see* Evaluation of
    functions calculus
  s.a. spec. appls. e.g.
    Engineering
Reaming-tools
  soc. & econ. aspects *see*
    Secondary industries
  tech. & mf.   621.954
  s.a. spec. appls. e.g.
    Plumbing
Reapers *see*
    Harvesting-machinery
Reaping crops
  agriculture   631.55
  s.a. spec. crops
Reapportionment
  legislative bodies   328.334 52
  spec. jur.   328.4–.9
Rear axles
  automobiles
    soc. & econ. aspects *see*
      Secondary industries

Rear axles
  automobiles (continued)
    tech. & mf.   629.245
    s.a. spec. appls. e.g.
      mil. vehicles 623.747
Reason
  epistemology   121.3
  ethical systems   171.2
    applications   172–179
  human attribute
    metaphysics   128.3
  rel. doctrines
    knowledge of God
      Christianity   231.042
    other rel. see God rel.
      doctrines
Reasoning
  depth psych.   154.24
    animals   156.4
  ed. psych.   370.152 4
  gen. psych.   153.43
    animals   156.343
    children   155.413
  s.a. psych. of other spec.
    groups
  logic   160
Rebates
  law   343.072
    spec. jur.   343.3–.9
  taxation *see* Tax reductions
Rebellion *see* Political
    offenses
Recall
  chief executives
    pub. admin.   350.003 6
      central govts.   351.003 6
      spec. jur.   353–354
      local govts.   352.008
  information theory 001.539
  memory
    psychology   153.123
    animals   156.312 2
    children   155.413
  s.a. psych. of other spec.
    groups
  pol. sci.   324.68
  prod. management *see* Product
    control
Recataloging
  library econ.   025.39
    spec. materials   025.34
Receivers
  wire telegraphy *see*
    Instrumentation wire
    telegraphy
  other kinds see Receiving
    sets

Receiverships
  accounting trmt.   657.47
    s.a. spec. kinds of
      enterprise e.g.
        Insurance accounting
  law   346.078
  spec. jur.   346.3–.9
Receiving
  antennas *see* Antennas
  equipment
    telephone commun.
      commerce   384.65
      wire   384.65
      wireless   384.525
    engineering *see* Terminal
      equipment wire
      telephony
    s.a. other spec. uses
  operations
    materials management   658.728
    spec. subj.   *s.s.*–068 7
  sets
    radio
      engineering   621.384 136
      automobiles
        soc. & econ. aspects
        see Secondary
        industries
        tech. & mf.   629.277
      s.a. other spec. appls.
        e.g. Radiotelephony
      manufacturing
        soc. & econ. aspects
        see Secondary
        industries
      technology   621.384 18
      other aspects see Radio
    television
      engineering   621.388 36
      automobiles
        soc. & econ. aspects
        see Secondary
        industries
        tech. & mf.   629.277
      s.a. other spec. appls.
        e.g. Astronautics
      manufacturing
        soc. & econ. aspects
        see Secondary
        industries
      technology   621.388 8
      other aspects see
      Television
Recent epoch
  geology   551.793
    s.a. spec. aspects e.g.
      Economic geology
  paleontology *see* Cenozoic era

Receptacles
  chem. apparatus   542.2
    s.a. spec. appls. e.g.
      Organic chemistry
    other aspects see Containers
Receptionists
  office services   651.374 3
Receptions
  food services   642.4
Receptive processes
  psychology *see* Sensory
    perceptions
Recessionals
  Christian liturgical music   783.29
    recordings   789.912 329
Recessions
  econ. cycles
    prod. econ.   338.542
    s.a. other spec. subj.
  economics   338.54
Recherche Archipelago W. Aust.
        area–941 7
Recidivists
  criminal law   345.03
    spec. jur.   345.3–.9
  criminology   364.3
Recipes
  cookery   641.5
  journalism   070.444
  s.a.   *s.s.*–021 2
Reciprocal equations
  calculus   515.253
    complex variables   515.925 3
    real variables   515.825 3
    s.a. other spec. functions &
      equations; also spec.
      appls. e.g.
      Engineering
Reciprocating
  air motors *see* Air engines
  compressors *see* Air
    compressors
  engines
    diesel *see*
      High-compression-
      ignition engines
    spark *see* Spark-ignition
      engines
    steam
      stationary
        soc. & econ. aspects
        see Secondary
        industries
        tech. & mf.   621.164
        s.a. spec. appls.
          e.g. Generation
          elect. power
      other kinds see Steam
      locomotives

Reciprocating
engines (continued)
uses
aircraft eng.
soc. & econ. aspects
see Secondary
industries
tech. & mf. 629.134 352
s.a. other spec. uses
fans & blowers *see* Piston
fans & blowers
pumps
engineering
soc. & econ. aspects *see*
Secondary industries
tech. & mf. 621.65
s.a. spec. appls. e.g.
Water supply
engineering
other aspects see Dynamics
Reciprocation
geometry *see* Transformations
geometry
Recitals
music 780.73
s.a. spec. mediums
Recitation
education 371.37
s.a. spec. levels of ed.;
also Special education
rhetoric 808.54
juvenile 808.968 54
other aspects see Speaking
Recitations
literature
gen. wks.
collections 808.854
hist. & crit. 809.54
spec. lits. *lit. sub.*–504
indiv. authors *lit. sub.*–51–59
other aspects see Speeches
Reckless driving *see* Traffic
violations
Reclaimed
rubber
rubber mf.
soc. & econ. aspects *see*
Secondary industries
technology 678.29
s.a. spec. kinds of rubber
e.g. Natural rubber
s.a. other spec. subj.
Reclamation
engineering
soc. & econ. aspects *see*
Secondary industries
technology 627.5
s.a. spec. appls. e.g.
Rice (cereal)
agriculture

Reclamation
engineering (continued)
other aspects see Liquids
engineering
soil sci.
agriculture 631.6
s.a. spec. crops; also
spec. types of culture
e.g. Floriculture
resources *see* Land
resources
Reclassification
library econ. 025.396
Recognition
employee motivation
personnel admin. 658.314 2
other aspects see
Motivation employees
memory
psychology 153.124
animals 156.312 4
children 155.413
s.a. psych. of other spec.
groups
of states & govts.
internat. law 341.26
of unions 331.891 2
s.a. Perception
Recoil
mil. gunnery 623.57
Recollects
Augustinians *see* Augustinians
Franciscans *see* Franciscans
Reconciliation
rel. doctrines
Christianity 234.5
other rel see Humankind
rel. doctrines
Reconnaissance
aircraft
mil. eng. 623.746 7
forces
air warfare 358.45
geodetic surveying 526.31
tactics
mil. sci. 355.413
s.a. spec. mil. branches
topography
mil. eng. 623.71
Reconstruction
mil. sci. 355.028
U.S. hist. 973.8
World War 1 hist. 940.314 4
World War 2 hist. 940.531 44
s.a. hist. of other spec.
wars
Reconstructionist Judaism 296.834 4
misc. aspects see Judaism
Record bldgs.
architecture 725.15
building 690.515

Recreation (continued)	
law	344.099
spec. jur.	344.3–.9
lit. & stage trmt. *see* Social	
themes	
parochial work	
Christianity	259.8
other rel. see Pastoral	
theology	
penal institutions	365.66
law	344.035 66
spec. jur.	344.3–.9
pub. admin.	
activities	350.858
central govts.	351.858
spec. jur.	353–354
local govts.	352.945 8
govt. depts. *see* Executive	
departments	
rooms *see* Recreational areas	
safety	
law	344.047 6
spec. jur.	344.3–.9
pub. meas.	363.14
govt. control *see* Safety	
pub. admin.	
specialists	
biog. & work	790.092
s.a. spec. kinds	
s.a.	*pers.–79*
other aspects see	
Recreational arts	
s.a. Amusement	
Recreational	
activities	790.1
pollution by	
soc. aspects	363.731
other aspects see	
Pollution	
areas	
civic art	711.558
furnishings	645.6
household management	643.55
residential int. dec.	747.791
s.a. spec. dec.	
arts	790
curriculums	375.79
documentation	025.067 9
journalism	070.449 79
museums	069.979
other aspects see Fine arts	
equipment	
manufacturers	
biog. & work	688.709 2
s.a.	*pers.–688*
manufacturing	
soc. & econ. aspects *see*	
Secondary industries	
technology	688.7

Recreational (continued)	
facilities	
pub. admin.	350.863 5
central govts.	351.863 5
spec. jur.	353–354
local govts.	352.735
pub. sanitation	363.729 2
govt. control	350.772
central govts.	351.772
spec. jur.	353–354
local govts.	352.6
law	344.046 4
spec. jur.	344.3–.9
soc. services	363.68
factors	
mental pub. health	363.204 2
institutions	
sociology	306.4
lands	
economics	333.78
govt. control	
law	346.046 78
spec. jur.	346.3–.9
pub. admin. *see* Land	
resources govt. control	
pub. admin.	
reading	
library sci.	028.8
services	
armed forces	355.346
s.a. spec. mil. branches;	
also hist. of spec.	
wars	
museums	069.16
therapy	615.851 53
s.a. spec. diseases	
water resources	
economics	333.784
engineering	
soc. & econ. aspects *see*	
Secondary industries	
technology	627.046
s.a. spec. appls. e.g.	
Amusement parks	
other aspects see Liquids	
engineering	
Recruitment	
mil. personnel	355.223 62
law *see* Manpower	
procurement mil. law	
s.a. spec. mil. branches	
personnel admin.	
gen. management	658.311 1
executive	658.407 111
spec. subj.	*s.s.–068 3*
libraries	023.9
pub. admin.	350.131
central govts.	351.131
spec. jur.	353–354
local govts.	352.005 131

Rectal
  anesthesia *see* General
    anesthesia
  medication
    therapeutics 615.62
      misc. aspects see
        Medication methods
      s.a. spec. diseases
Rectification
  calculus 515.43
    s.a. spec. appls. e.g.
      Engineering
    s.a. other spec. subj.
Rectifiers
  electrodynamic eng.
    soc. & econ. aspects *see*
      Secondary industries
    tech. & mf. 621.313 7
      s.a. spec. appls. e.g.
        Railroads
        electrification
  electronic circuits *see*
    Converters electronic
      circuits
  radio *see* Circuits radio
  other aspects see
    Electrodynamics
Rectilinear propagation
  light
    astrophysics 523.015 322
      s.a. spec. celestial
        bodies
    physics 535.322
    spec. states of matter 530.4
Rectories *see* Parsonages
Rectors *see* Clergy
Rectum
  anatomy
    human 611.35
    other aspects see Nutritive
      organs
  diseases
    gen. wks. 616.35
      neoplasms 616.992 35
      tuberculosis 616.995 35
    geriatrics 618.976 35
    pediatrics 618.923 5
    pub. health 614.593 5
    statistics 312.335
      deaths 312.263 5
    surgery 617.555
      anesthesiology 617.967 555
    other aspects see Diseases
  physical anthropometry 573.635
  physiology
    human 612.36
    other aspects see Nutrition
  tissue biology human 611.018 935
Recurrent novae *see* Eruptive
    variable stars

Recycling
  paper
    mf. tech. 676.142
    other aspects see Pulp
  wastes *see* Wastes control
  s.a. other spec. subj.
Red
  algae *see* Rhodophyta
  Cliffs Vic. *area*–945 9
  clovers
    agriculture 633.327
      soc. & econ. aspects *see*
        Primary industries
      other aspects see
        Papilionaceae; *also*
          Field crops
  corpuscles
    diseases
      gen. med. 616.151
        cancer 616.994 18
      geriatrics 618.976 151
      pediatrics 618.921 51
      pub. health 614.591 51
      statistics 312.315 1
        deaths 312.261 51
      other aspects see
        Diseases
    human phys. 612.111
    tissue biology
      human anatomy & phys. 611.018 5
      other aspects see Tissue
        biology
    other aspects see
      Circulatory fluids
  Cross
    nursing 610.734
    soc. welfare
      international 361.77
      national 361.763
      spec. problems & groups 362–363
      other aspects see Welfare
        services
    World War 1 hist. 940.477 1
    World War 2 hist. 940.547 71
  currants
    agriculture 634.721 7
    other aspects see Currants
  Deer River Alta. *area*–712 33
  grape wines
    gen. wks. 641.222 3
      comm. proc. 663.223
    sparkling 641.222 4
      comm. proc. 663.224
    other aspects see Wines
  ironwood family *see* Ochnales
  Lake Co. Minn. *area*–776 963

Red (continued)
  meats
    preservation
      commercial
        soc. & econ. aspects
        see Secondary
          industries
        technology   664.921–.928
        domestic   641.492
      other aspects see Meats
  River
    Co. Tex.   *area*–764 212
    of the North   *area*–784 1
      Manitoba   *area*–712 74
      Minnesota   *area*–776 9
      North Dakota   *area*–784 1
    Par. La.   *area*–763 64
    rebellion
      Canada hist.   971.051
    southern   *area*–766 6
      Louisiana   *area*–763 6
      Oklahoma   *area*–766 6
  Sea
    oceanography   551.467 33
    regional subj. trmt.   *area*–165 33
    other aspects see Indian
      Ocean
  Sea governorate Egypt   *area*–623
  seaweeds *see* Rhodophyta
Redbridge London Eng.   *area*–421 73
Redcar Cleveland Eng.   *area*–428 54
Redditch Hereford & Worcester
    Eng.   *area*–424 43
Redeemer
  Christ
    Christian doctrines   232.3
Redemption
  of first-born male
    Jewish rites   269.442 3
  pub. debt.
    pub. finance   336.363
    misc. aspects see Public
      borrowing
  rel. doctrines
    Christianity   234.3
    other rel. see Humankind
      rel. doctrines
Redemptorist monastic bldgs.
  architecture   726.776 4
  building   690.677 64
  other aspects see
      Religious-purpose
      bldgs.
Redemptorists
  rel. orders   255.64
    church hist.   271.64
    ecclesiology   262.24
Redesdale Northumberland Eng.
                                  area–428 81
Rediscount
  economics   332.84

Rediscount (continued)
  other aspects see Interest
Rediscount rates
  monetary policy   339.53
Redistricting
  legislative bodies
    law *see* Representation law
    pol. sci.   328.334 54
    spec. jur.   328.4–.9
Redox reactions *see* Reduction
    chemistry
Redruth Cornwall Eng.   *area*–423 76
Redtop
  agriculture   633.237
  other aspects see Bent
      grasses
Reducing
  negatives *see* Negatives
  personal care   646.75
Reducing-solutions
  photography   771.54
    gen. tech.   770.283
    spec. proc. & fields   772–778
Reduction
  chemistry
    engineering   660.284 43
    physical chem.   541.393
      applied   660.299 3
      organic   547.23
    s.a. spec. aspects e.g.
      Low temperatures
    *s.a. spec. elements, cpds.,
      prod.*
  ferrous ores
    metallurgy   669.14
  refuse
    technology   628.445 6
    other aspects see Refuse
      pub. sanitation
    s.a. other spec. subj.
Reductionism
  psychology   150.194
    *s.a. spec. subj. & branches
      of psych.*
Reductions in force *see* Layoffs
    of employees
Reductive algebras & groups   512.55
  s.a. spec. appls. e.g.
      Engineering
Reduvioidea *see* Heteroptera
Redwillow Co. Neb.   *area*–782 843
Redwood
  Co. Minn.   *area*–776 35
  trees *see* Coniferales
  woods *see* Softwoods
Reed
  instruments
    gen. wks.
      manufacture   681.818 056
      spec. kinds   681.818 6–.818 9

Reflection
  light
    optics (continued)
      physics   535.323
        spec. states of matter   530.4
    radiations
      meteorology *see* Radiations
        meteorology
  sound
    engineering   620.21
      s.a. spec. appls. e.g.
        Sonar
    physics   534.204
      spec. states of matter   530.4
Reflective thought
  psychology   153.422
    animals   156.342 2
    children   155.413
    s.a. psych. of other spec.
      groups
Reflectivity *see* Optical
    properties
Reflex
  actions
    biology *see* Movements
    med. sci. *see* Irritability
  disturbances
    symptomatology
      neurological diseases   616.849
      vet. sci.   636.089 684 9
        s.a. spec. animals
Reflexes
  psychology   152.322
    animals   156.232 2
    children   155.412
    s.a. psych. of other spec.
      groups
Reflexology
  psychology   150.194 4
    s.a. spec. subj. & branches
      of psych.
Reforestation
  silviculture   634.956
  s.a. spec. trees
Reform
  Judaism   306.834 6
    misc. aspects see Judaism
  legislative
    pol. sci.   328.304 6
  movements
    pol. sci.   322.44
    religion *see* Sects
    soc. action   361.24
      spec. problems & groups   362–363
  schools penology   365.42
    misc. aspects see Penal
      institutions
  s.a. other spec. subj.
Reformation
  Christian church hist.   270.6
    spec. denominations   280

Reformation (continued)
  Europe hist.   940.23
    s.a. spec. countries
Reformatories
  penology   365.34
    juvenile offenders   365.42
  other aspects see Penal
    institutions
Reformatory bldgs. *see* Prison
    buildings
Reformed
  Christians
    biog. & work   284.209 2
    s.a. spec. denominations
    s.a. American Reformed
      Christians
    s.a.   *pers.–242*
  churches
    in America   285.7
      adherents *see* American
        Reformed Christians
      buildings
        architecture   726.585 7
        building   690.658 57
        other aspects see
          Religious-purpose
          bldgs.
      Christian life guides   248.485 7
      doctrines   230.57
        creeds   238.57
      general councils   262.557
      govt. & admin.   262.057
      parishes   254.057
      missions   266.57
      moral theology   241.045 7
      music
        arts   783.026 57
        recordings   789.912 302 657
        s.a. spec.
          instruments; also
          spec. kinds e.g.
          Liturgical music
      religion
        pub. worship   264.057 02
        significance   246.7
      private prayers for   242.805 7
      pub. worship   264.057
      rel. associations
        adults   267.185 7
        men   267.245 7
        women   267.445 7
        young adults   267.625 7
      rel. instruction   268.857
      rel. law   262.985 7
      schools   377.857
      secondary training   207.125 7
      sermons   252.057
      theological seminaries   207.115 7
      s.a. other spec. aspects

Refractory materials (continued)
mining
  technology — 622.367
  prospecting — 622.186 7
  s.a. spec. uses
Refreshment buildings
architecture — 725.7
building — 690.57
  other aspects see Public
    structures
Refrigerants
refrigeration eng.
  technology — 621.564
  s.a. spec. appls. e.g.
    Deep freezing foods
  other aspects see Low
    temperatures
Refrigerating equipment
air-conditioning eng. — 697.932 2
Refrigeration
alcoholic beverages
  comm. proc. — 663.15
  s.a. spec. beverages e.g.
    Wines
  other aspects see Alcoholic
    beverages
engineering
  soc. & econ. aspects *see*
    Secondary industries
  technology — 621.56
  s.a. spec. appls. e.g.
    Preservation techniques
  other aspects see Low
    temperatures
engineers
  biog. & work — 621.560 92
  s.a. — *pers.*–621
pipes
  buildings — 696.2
shipbuilding
  soc. & econ. aspects *see*
    Secondary industries
  technology — 623.853 5
    design — 623.814 535
      spec. craft — 623.812
  s.a. other spec. appls.
Refrigerator cars *see* Freight
    cars
Refrigerators
low-temperature eng.
  soc. & econ. aspects *see*
    Secondary industries
  tech. & mf. — 621.57
  s.a. spec. appls. e.g.
    Frozen desserts
  other aspects see Low
    temperatures
Refuge areas
wildlife *see* Wildlife
    reserves

Refugees
internat. law — 341.486
political
  pol. sci. — 325.21
soc. services *see* Victims of
    political oppression
U.S. Civil War hist. — 973.715 9
World War 1 hist. — 940.315 9
World War 2 hist. — 940.531 59
  s.a. hist. of other spec.
    wars
Refugio Co. Tex. — *area*–764 119
Refuse
pub. sanitation
  law — 344.046 2
    spec. jur. — 344.3–.9
  local govt. control — 352.63
  technology — 628.44
    military — 623.754
    rural — 628.744
Regattas
sports
  misc. aspects see Sports
Regeneration
life sci.
  cells
    cytology *see* Development
      (biology) cytology
    gen. wks. — 574.31
    animals — 591.31
    plants — 581.31
    s.a. spec. organisms
  med. sci. — 612.65–.66
    animals — 636.089 265–.089 266
    s.a. spec. animals
    man — 612.65–.66
  rel. doctrines
    Christianity — 234.4
    other rel. see Humankind
      rel. doctrines
Regenerative sets
radio
  engineering — 621.384 136 6
  s.a. spec. appls. e.g.
    Radiotelephony
  other aspects see Radio
television
  engineering — 621.388 366
  s.a. spec. appls. e.g.
    Astronautics
  other aspects see
    Television
Regents
pub. admin. — 351.003 12
  biog. & work *see hist. of*
    spec. countries
  spec. jur. — 354
  s.a. — *pers.*–351 1
  s.a. Governing boards
Regge poles *see* Particles
    (matter)

Regression analysis
  statistical math.   519.536
    s.a. spec. appls. e.g.
      Engineering
Regressive taxation
  pub. finance   336.293
Regular Baptists   286.1
  misc. aspects see Baptist
Regular clerics *see* Clerks
    regular
Regulated industries *see* Public
    utilities
Regulating devices
  clockwork
    mf. tech.   681.112
      soc. & econ. aspects *see*
        Secondary industries
  s.a. other spec. subj.
Regulation
  mining eng.   622.8
  s.a. other spec. subj.
Regulations
  armed forces
    discipline   355.133
    s.a. spec. mil. branches
  s.a. Law; *also other spec.*
    subj.
Regulators
  sewers   628.25
  s.a. spec. appls. e.g.
    Water drainage
  s.a. other spec. subj.
Regulatory agencies
  law   342.066 4
    spec. jur.   342.3–.9
    spec. subj.   *law s.s.*–026 9
  pub. admin.   350.009 1
    central govts.   351.009 1
    spec. jur.   353–354
    local govts.   352.009 2
Rehabilitation
  clinical psych.   157.94
  criminal law   345.077
    spec. jur.   345.3–.9
  natural resources   333.715 3
    s.a. spec. kinds of
      resources e.g.
      Shorelands
  training
    labor econ.   331.259 2
    s.a. spec. classes of
      labor e.g. Women
  labor law *see* Labor law
  personnel admin.
    gen. management   658.312 44
    executive   658.407 124 4
    spec. subj.   *s.s.*–068 3
  pub. admin.   350.15
    central govts.   351.15
    spec. jur.   353–354
    local govts.   352.005 15

Rehabilitation (continued)
  veterans
    mil. sci.   355.115 6
    s.a. spec. mil. branches
Reign of Terror
  France hist.   944.044
  s.a. spec. events & subj.
    e.g. Commerce
Reincarnation
  metaphysics   129
  occultism   133.901 3
  rel. doctrines
    Buddhism   294.342 37
    comp. rel.   291.237
    Hinduism   294.523 7
    other rel. see Eschatology
Reindeer
  animal husbandry   636.294
  other aspects see Cervoidea
Reinforced
  concrete
    arch. construction   721.044 54
    s.a. spec. structural
      elements; also spec.
      types of bldgs.
    bldg. construction   693.54
    eng. materials   620.137
    foundations   624.153 37
    shipbuilding
      hulls   623.845 41
      structures   624.183 41
    other aspects see
      Concretes
    s.a. other spec. uses
  plastics
    chem. tech.   668.494
    other aspects see
      Plastics
  s.a. other spec. subj.
Reinforcing
  plastics mf.   668.416
    s.a. spec. kinds of
      plastics
  s.a. other spec. subj.
Reinstatement
  armed forces   355.114
    s.a. spec. mil. branches
Reinsurance   368.012
  s.a. spec. kinds of insurance
Rejuvenation
  life sci. *see* Longevity
Relapsing fevers
  gen. med.   616.924 4
  geriatrics   618.976 924 4
  pediatrics   618.929 244
  pub. health   614.574 4
  statistics   312.392 44
    deaths   312.269 244
  other aspects see Diseases

Religion
  museums (continued)
    museology   069.92
      s.a. spec. activities
        e.g. Display
    population statistics   312.9
    soc. law   344.09
      spec. jur.   344.3–.9
    subject headings   025.492
    other aspects see Disciplines
      (systems)
Religions in society *see*
    Society soc. theology
Religious
  architecture *see*
      Religious-purpose
      buildings
  art *see* Religion art
      representation
  association bldgs.
    architecture   726.9
    building   690.69
      s.a. spec. rel.
    other aspects see
        Religious-purpose
        bldgs.
  associations
    Buddhism   294.365
    Christianity   267
    comp. rel.   291.65
    Islam   297.65
    Judaism   296.67
      s.a. other spec. rel.
  attitudes
    doctrines *see* Doctrinal
        theology
    secular matters *see* Social
        theology
  beliefs *see* Doctrinal
      theology
  believers
    biog. & work   200.92
      s.a. spec. kinds e.g.
        Clergy; *also spec.*
        rel. groups
    s.a.   *pers.–2*
  calendar *see* Church year
  centers
    civic art   711.56
  concepts   200
    lit. trmt.
      gen. wks.
        collections   808.803 82
        hist. & crit.   809.033 82
      spec. lits.
        collections   *lit. sub.*–080 382
        hist. & crit.   *lit. sub.*–093 82
      s.a. spec. lit. forms

Religious
  concepts (continued)
    stage trmt.   792.090 938 2
      s.a. spec. mediums e.g.
        Television; *also spec.*
        kinds of drama e.g.
        Tragedies (drama)
  conditions   200.9
  congregations
    gen. wks.
      Buddhism   204.365 7
      Christianity   255
        church hist.   271
        ecclesiology   262.24
        organization   255
      comp. rel.   291.65
      Islam   297.65
      s.a. other spec. rel.
    rel. law *see* Persons rel.
        law
    s.a. Religious (members of
        orders)
  counselors *see* Clergy
  culture groups *see* Religious
      groups
  discipline *see* Religious law
  discourse *see* Religious
      language
  doctrines *see* Doctrinal
      theology
  education *see* Religious
      instruction
  experience
    Buddhism   294.344 2
    Christianity   248.2
    comp. rel.   291.42
    Hinduism   294.542
    Islam   297.42
    Judaism   296.71
      s.a. other spec. rel.
  factors
    mental pub. health   362.204 2
  festivals *see* Church year
  freedom
    civil right   323.442
    law   342.085 2
      spec. jur.   342.3–.9
    soc. theology
      Christianity   261.72
      comp. rel.   291.177 2
      s.a. other spec. rel.
  furniture
    built-in arch. decoration
      rel. significance
        Christianity   247.1
        comp. rel.   291.37
        s.a. other spec. rel.
  groups
    & state
      pol. sci.   322.1

Religious
  groups
    & state (continued)
      soc. theology
        Christianity   261.7
        comp. rel.   291.177
        s.a. other spec. rel.
      journalism for   070.482
      legal status   342.087
        spec. jur.   342.2–.9
      libraries for   027.67
        administration   025.197 67
        buildings
          architecture   727.826 7
          functional planning   022.316 7
        catalogs *see* Library
          catalogs
        reference services   025.527 767
        selection for   025.218 767
        use studies   025.587 67
        user orientation   025.567 67
        s.a. other spec.
          activities e.g.
          Cataloging
      s.a. Religious believers;
        also Religious
        minorities
      holidays *see* Holy days
      influences
        secular matters *see* Social
          theology
      institutions soc.   306.6
      instruction
        ecclesiastical theology
          Buddhism   294.37
          Christianity   268
          comp. rel.   291.7
          Islam   297.7
          Judaism   296.68
          s.a. other spec. rel.
        gen. ed.   377.1
        law   344.079 6
          spec. jur.   344.2–.9
        home ed.   649.7
        penal institutions   365.66
          law   344.035 66
          spec. jur.   344.3–.9
      language   200.14
        Christianity   201.4
        comp. rel.   291.014
        s.a. other spec. rel.
      law
        Buddhism   294.384
        Christianity   262.9
        comp. rel.   291.84
        Hinduism   294.594
        Islam   297.14
        Judaism   296.18
        s.a. other spec. rel.

Religious (continued)
  leaders
    biog. & work
      comp. rel.   291.609 2
      s.a. spec.kinds e.g.
        Clergy; *also spec.*
        rel. groups
    s.a.   *pers.–2*
  liberty *see* Religious freedom
  life
    personal
      Buddhism   294.344 4
      Christianity   248.4
      comp. rel.   291.44
      Hinduism   294.544
      Islam   297.44
      Judaism   296.74
      s.a. other spec. rel.
  limitations
    cookery   641.567
  medals
    numismatics   737.224
    rel. significance
      Christianity   247.872 2
      comp. rel.   291.37
      s.a. other spec. rel.
  minorities
    discrimination *see*
      Discriminatory
      practices
    soc. theology
      Christianity   621.834 6
      comp. rel.   291.178 346
      s.a. other spec. rel.
    sociology   305.6
  music *see* Sacred music
  mysticism *see* Mysticism
    religious
  mythology
    Buddhism   294.333
      sources   294.38
    Christianity   204.5
    comp. rel.   291.13
      sources   291.8
    Hinduism   204.513
      sources   294.59
    s.a. other spec. rel.
  observances
    private
      Buddhism   294.344 46
      Christianity   248.46
      comp. rel.   291.446
      Hinduism   294.544 6
      Islam   297.446
      Judaism   296.74
      s.a. other spec. rel.
    public *see* Public worship
  orders *see* Religious
    congregations

Religious (continued)
- organizations
  - welfare services   361.75
    - spec. problems & groups   362–263
    - *other aspects see* Welfare services
- pageants
  - performing arts   791.622
- plays
  - gen. wks.
    - collections   808.825 16
    - hist. & crit.   809.251 6
    - rhetoric   808.251 6
    - juvenile   808.068 251 6
  - spec. lits.   *lit. sub.*–205 16
  - indiv. authors   *lit. sub.*–21–29
  - stage presentation   792.16
  - *other aspects see* Drama
- practices
  - law   342.085 2
    - spec. jur.   342.3–.9
  - personal *see* Religious life
  - private *see* Religious observances
  - public *see* Public worship
- school bldgs.
  - architecture   727.42
  - building   690.742
  - *other aspects see* Educational buildings
- services (aids)
  - armed forces *see* Chaplain services
- services (worship) *see* Public worship
- societies *see* Religious associations
- Society of Friends *see* Society of Friends
- supremacy *see* Theocracy
- symbolism
  - art representation   704.948
    - painting   755
    - *s.a. other spec. forms*
  - religious aspects *see* Symbolism rel. significance
- therapy   615.852
  - *s.a. spec. diseases*
- training *see* Religious instruction
- virtues
  - personal rel. *see* Conduct
- wars
  - history *see* hist. of spec. places
  - religion
    - comp. rel.   291.7
    - Islam   297.72
    - *s.a. other spec. rel.*

Religious (continued)
- worship
  - private *see* Worship gen. wks.
  - public *see* Public worship
  - *s.a.* Sacred

Religious (members of orders)
- biog. & work
  - Christianity   271.009 2
  - *s.a. spec. orders*
  - comp. rel.   291.65
  - *s.a. other spec. rel.*
- meditations
  - private devotions
    - Christianity   242.694
    - *other rel. see* Meditations
- personal rel.
  - Christianity   248.894
  - *other rel. see* Personal religion
- prayers
  - private devotions
    - Christianity   242.894
    - *other rel. see* Prayers private devotions
- retreats
  - rel. practices
    - Christianity   269.694
    - *other rel. see* Spiritual renewal
- sermons for
  - Christianity   252.594
  - *other rel. see* Preaching
  - *s.a.*   *pers.*–2
  - *s.a.* Religious congregations

Religious-purpose bldgs.
- air-conditioning   697.936
- architecture   726
  - rel. significance
    - Christianity   246.9
    - comp. rel.   291.37
    - *s.a. other spec. rel.*
- building   690.6
- care   647.98
- interior decoration   747.86
- lighting
  - exterior   621.322 9
  - interior   621.322 6

Relishes
- cookery   641.812

Reluctance
- magnetism *see* Magnetic phenomena

Remains
- archaeology *see* Archaeology

Remarriage *see* Family relationships

Remedial
- education
  - adult ed.   374.012

Renal
  failure (continued)
    statistics   312.361 4
      deaths   312.266 14
    other aspects see Diseases
  hypertension *see* Hypertension
Rendering
  ind. oils & gases   665.028 2
  s.a. spec. prod.
Rendezvous
  manned space flight
    gen. wks.   629.458 3
    s.a. spec. appls. e.g.
        Space warfare
    s.a. spec. flights e.g.
        Lunar flights
Renegotiation
  contracts
    pub. admin.   350.711 3
      central govts.   351.711 3
        spec. jur.   353–354
      local govts.   352.163
Renewal theory
  probabilities   519.287
  s.a. spec. appls. e.g.
      Engineering
Renfrew
  Co. Ont.   *area*–713 81
  district Strathclyde Scot.   *area*–414 41
Renmark S. Aust.   *area*–942 33
Rennet cheeses
  dairy tech.   637.352–.354
  other aspects see Cheeses
Reno
  city Nev.   *area*–793 55
  Co. Kan.   *area*–781 83
Renovation
  home econ.   643.7
  s.a. Custodial management
Rensselaer Co. N.Y.   *area*–747 41
Rent
  economic
    land econ.   333.012
  income distribution
    macroeconomics   339.21
  real property law   346.043 44
    spec. jur.   346.3–.9
Rental
  collections
    museology   069.56
  govt. procurement *see*
      Procurement pub. admin.
  s.a. Government property
      management & disposal
  income
    macroeconomics   339.21
  land econ.   333.5
  libraries   027.3
    administration   025.197 3
    buildings
      architecture   727.823

Rental
  libraries
    buildings (continued)
      functional planning   022.313
    catalogs *see* Library
        catalogs
    reference services   025.527 73
    selection for   025.218 73
    use studies   025.587 3
    user orientation   025.567 3
    s.a. other spec. activities
        e.g. Cataloging
  subsidies
    housing meas.   363.58
    misc. aspects see Housing
Rents
  pub. revenues   336.11
    misc. aspects see Nontax
        revenues
Renunciation
  naturalization   323.623
Renville Co.
  Minnesota   *area*–776 34
  North Dakota   *area*–784 64
Reorganization
  corporations
    law   346.066 26
      spec. jur.   346.3–.9
    management   658.16
    pub. admin. *see*
        Organization management
        pub. admin.
Reorganized Church of Jesus
      Christ of Latter-Day
      Saints   289.33
  misc. aspects see Latter-Day
      Saints church
Repairs & repairing
  library materials   025.7
  s.a.   *s.s.*–028 8
Reparations
  law of war   341.66
  pub. revenues   336.182
  World War 1 hist.   940.314 22
  World War 2 hist.   940.531 4
Reparative surgery *see* Plastic
      surgery
Repatriation
  pol. sci.   323.64
Repayment
  pub. debt
    pub. finance   336.363
    misc. aspects see Public
        borrowing
Repeaters
  wire telegraphy *see*
      Instrumentation wire
      telegraphy
Repentance
  Christian sacrament *see*
      Absolution

Reproducing pianos
mf. tech. 681.83
   other aspects see Musical
     instruments
musical art 789.72
Reproduction
memory
  psychology 153.123
    animals 156.312 3
    children 155.413
    s.a. psych. of other spec.
      groups
of art 702.872
  paintings 751.5
    indiv. artists 759.1–.9
  s.a. techs. in other spec.
   art forms
of cells
  cytology 574.876 2
    animals 591.876 2
    plants 581.876 2
    s.a. spec. organisms
pathology
  gen. wks. 574.216
    animals 591.216
    plants 581.216
    s.a. spec. organisms
  med. sci. 616.6
    animals 636.089 66
    s.a. spec. animals
    man 616.6
physiology
  gen. wks. 574.16
    animals 591.16
    microorganisms 576.116
    plants 581.16
    s.a. spec. organisms
  med. sci. 612.6
    human phys. 612.6
    vet. phys. 636.089 26
    s.a. spec. animals
Reproductions *see* Reproduction
Reproductive
adaptations
  ecology 574.56
    animals 591.56
    microorganisms 576.15
    plants 581.56
    s.a. spec. organisms
organs
  drugs affecting
    pharmacodynamics 615.766
    other aspects see Drugs
  life sci.
    anatomy
      gen. wks. 574.46
        animals 591.46
        microorganisms 576.14
        plants 581.46
        s.a. spec. organisms

Reproductive
organs
  life sci.
    anatomy (continued)
      med. sci. 611.6
      animals 636.089 16
        s.a. spec. animals
      man 611.6
    pathology
      gen. wks. 574.226
      animals 591.226
      plants 581.226
      s.a. spec. organisms
    med. sci. *see*
      Reproduction
Reprography
library operations 025.129
Reptantia *see* Decapoda
  (crustaceans)
Reptile meats
preservation 641.495
  commercial 664.95
  domestic 641.495
Reptiles *see* Reptilia
Reptilia
agric. pests 632.679
  s.a. spec. types of culture
    e.g. Forestry; *also*
     spec. crops
conservation tech. 639.977 9
culture
  technology 639.39
    soc. & econ. aspects *see*
      Primary industries
  other aspects see
    Agriculture
drawing tech. 743.679
food 641.396
  cookery 641.696
hunting
  commercial
    technology 639.14
    soc. & econ. aspects
      see Primary
      industries
  sports
    big game 799.279
    small game 799.257 9
paleozoology 567.9
resources
  economics 333.957
  govt. control
    law 346.046 957
      spec. jur. 346.3–.9
    pub. admin. *see*
      Biological resources
      govt. control pub.
      admin.
zoology 567.9
other aspects see Animals
Repton Derbyshire Eng. *area*–425 19

Resedaceae *see* Resedales
Resedales
  botany — 583.124
  floriculture — 635.933 124
  med. aspects
    crop prod. — 633.883 124
    gen. pharm. — 615.323 124
      toxicology — 615.952 312 4
    vet. pharm. — 636.089 532 312 4
      toxicology — 636.089 595 231 24
  paleobotany — 561.3
  other aspects see Plants
Reserve
  Officers' Training Corps
    mil. sci. — 355.223 2
    s.a. spec. mil. branches
  requirements
    banking econ. — 332.113
      misc. aspects see Banking
  status
    armed forces — 355.113
    s.a. spec. mil. branches
Reserved lands
  landscape design — 719.3
Reserves
  armed forces
    gen. wks. — 355.37
    s.a. spec. mil. branches
    law — 343.012
      spec. jur. — 343.3–.9
  capital sources
    capital management — 658.152 26
    spec. subj. — *s.s.*–068 1
  natural resources — 333.711
  s.a. spec. kinds of
      resources e.g.
      Shorelands
  wildlife *see* Wildlife
    reserves
  s.a. Stockpiles
Reservoirs
  flood control eng. *see* Water
      storage flood control
      eng.
  hydraulic eng.
    soc. & econ. aspects *see*
      Secondary industries
    technology — 627.86
    s.a. spec. appls. e.g.
      Military engineering
    other aspects see Liquids
      engineering
  utilization
    economics — 333.916
    recreational — 333.784 5
  water-supply eng.
    technology — 628.132
    other aspects see Water
      supply engineering

Resettlement
  communities
    sociology — 307.2
Residences *see* Dwellings
Residential
  areas
    civic art — 711.58
    sociology — 307.3
  buildings
    air conditioning — 697.938
    architecture — 728
    building — 690.8
    home econ. — 643.1
    household management — 643.2
    interior decoration — 747
    lighting
      exterior — 621.322 9
      interior — 621.322 8
    sale & rental — 333.338
    sanitation — 363.729 8
      law — 344.046 4
        spec. jur. — 344.3–.9
      pub. admin. — 350.772
        central govts. — 351.772
          spec. jur. — 353–354
        local govts. — 352.6
  care
    soc. services *see*
      Institutional care
  cities planning
    arts — 711.45
  finance
    economics — 332.722
    other aspects see
      Real-estate finance
  lands
    rural *see* Rural lands
    urban *see* Urban lands
  property
    taxation — 336.225
    misc. aspects see
      Property taxes
  requirements
    voting *see* Voting
      qualifications
Residues
  number theory — 512.7
  s.a. spec. appls. e.g.
    Engineering
  petroleum
    chem. tech. — 665.538 8
    other aspects see Petroleum
  wood
    mf. tech. — 674.84
    other aspects see Wood
      products
  s.a. other spec. subj.
Resignation
  armed forces — 355.114
    s.a. spec. mil. branches

Resignation (continued)
  chief executives
    pub. admin.   350.003 6
      central govts.   351.003 6
        spec. jur.   353–354
        local govts.   352.008
  employees
    personnel admin.
      gen. management   658.313
      executive   658.407 13
      spec. subj.   *s.s.*–068 3
    pub. admin.   350.18
      central govts.   351.18
        spec. jur.   353–354
        local govts.   352.005 18
Resin-derived plastics *see*
    Natural resin-derived
    plastics
Resin-producing
  insects
    culture   638.3
    other aspects see
      Agriculture
  plants
    agriculture   633.895
    soc. & econ. aspects *see*
      Primary industries
Resins
  eng. materials   620.192 4
    naval design   623.818 924
    structures   624.189 24
    s.a. other spec. uses
  fossil *see* Fossil gums &
    resins
  manufacturing
    chem. tech.   668.37
    soc. & econ. aspects *see*
      Secondary industries
  org. chem.   547.843 4
  recovery from pulp
    technology   676.5
Resistance
  elect. measurement
    gen. tech.   621.374 2
    s.a. spec. appls. e.g.
      Ignition systems &
      devices
    radio *see* Measurement radio
    standards   621.372
    television *see* Measurement
      television
    other aspects see
      Electricity
  electrodynamics
    astrophysics   523.018 762
    s.a. spec. celestial
      bodies
    physics   537.62
      spec. states of matter   530.4
    eng. materials   620.11

Resistance (continued)
  warfare
    mil. sci.   355.021 84
    s.a. other spec. subj.
Resistance-furnaces
  elec. eng.
    soc. & econ. aspects *see*
      Secondary industries
    tech. & mf.   621.396
    s.a. spec. appls. e.g.
      Metallurgy
Resistance-welding
  metal prod.
    mf. tech.   671.521 3
    ferrous metals   672.521 3
    s.a. other spec. metals
    other aspects see Welding
Resistant construction
  buildings   693.8
  shipbuilding
    soc. & econ. aspects *see*
      Secondary industries
    technology   623.848
Resist-dyeing
  textile arts   746.66
  s.a. spec. prod.
Resistivity
  electricity
    material property *see*
      Resistance
    electrodynamics
  methods
    geophysical prospecting   622.154
  skin
    human phys.   612.791
    other aspects see
      Integumentary organs
Resistors
  microelectronics *see*
    Components
    microelectronics
  radio
    engineering   621.384 133
    s.a. spec. appls. e.g.
      Radiotelephony
    other aspects see Radio
  television
    engineering   621.388 33
    s.a. spec. appls. e.g.
      Astronautics
    other aspects see
      Television
Resolution (music)
  music theory   781.64
  s.a. spec. mediums
Resolutions (legislation)
  pol. sci.   328.377
    spec. jur.   328.4–.9

Resonance accelerators
  physics   539.733
    s.a. spec. physical
       phenomena e.g. Heat
Resonant cavities
  microwave electronics *see*
      Resonators microwave
      electronics
Resonators
  microwave electronics
    soc. & econ. aspects *see*
      Secondary industries
    tech. & mf.   621.381 332
      spec. circuits   621.381 32
    s.a. spec. appls. e.g.
      Radar engineering
  other aspects see Microwave
    electronics
Resorcinols
  org. chem.   547.633
  s.a. spec. cpds.
Resorts
  desc. & hist. *see spec.*
    places
  health *see* Physiographic
    regions hygiene
  s.a. other spec. kinds
Resource development
  internat. banking   332.153
  misc. aspects see Banking
Resources
  economic *see* Economic
    resources
  prod. econ.   338.09
  warfare
    mil. sci.   355.2
    s.a. spec. mil. branches
Respiration
  cells
    cytology   574.876 4
    animals   591.876 4
    plants   581.876 4
    s.a. spec. organisms
  pathology
    gen. wks.   574.212
    animals   591.212
    plants   581.212
    s.a. spec. organisms
    med. sci.   616.2
    animals   636.089 62
    s.a. spec. animals
    man   616.2
  physiology
    gen. wks.   574.12
    animals   591.12
    microorganisms   576.112
    plants   581.12
    s.a. spec. organisms
    med. sci.   612.2
    human phys.   612.2

Respiration
  physiology
    med. sci. (continued)
      vet. phys.   636.089 22
      s.a. spec. animals
Respiratory
  insufficiency *see* Respiratory
    system diseases
  organs
    anatomy
      gen. wks.   574.42
      animals   591.42
      microorganisms   576.14
      plants   581.42
      s.a. spec. organisms
      med. sci.   611.2
      animals   636.089 12
      s.a. spec. animals
      man   611.2
    pathology
      gen. wks.   574.222
      animals   591.222
      plants   581.222
      s.a. spec. organisms
      med. sci. *see* Respiration
  system
    anatomy *see* Respiratory
      organs
    diseases
      gen. wks.   616.2
      neoplasms   616.992 2
      tuberculosis   616.995 2
      pulmonary   616.246
      geriatrics   618.976 2
      nursing   610.736 92
      pediatrics   618.922
      pub. health   614.592
      s.a. spec. diseases
      statistics   312.32
      deaths   312.262
      surgery   617.54
      anesthesiology   617.967 54
      other aspects see
       Diseases
    drugs affecting
      pharmacodynamics   615.72
      other aspects see Drugs
    physical anthropometry   573.62
    physiology
      human *see* Respiration
      tissue biology human   611.018 92
Responsa
  Judaistic sources   296.179
Responsibility *see*
    Accountability
Responsive
  change
    management   658.406 2
    other aspects see Change

Resuscitation
  therapeutics   615.804 3
    misc. aspects see Physical
      therapies
    s.a. spec. diseases
Retail
  advertising   659.131 4
  businesses
    accounting   657.839
  cooperatives *see* Consumer
      cooperatives
  credit *see* Consumer credit
  marketing
    marketing management 658.87
    spec. subj.   *s.s.–*068 8
  salesmanship
    marketing management *see*
      Personal selling
  trade
    buildings
      architecture   725.21
      building   690.521
      other aspects see Public
        structures
    commerce   381.1
      misc. aspects see
        Commerce
    law   343.088 7
    spec. jur.   343.3–.9
Retained profits
  capital formation
    financial econ.   332.041 52
Retaining walls
  railroad eng.
    technology   625.13
    other aspects see Permanent
      way
  structural eng.   624.164
  s.a. other spec. appls.
  other aspects see Walls
Retakeoff
  manned space flight
  gen. wks.
    lunar flights   629.454 5
    planetary flights 629.455
  s.a. spec. appls. e.g.
    Space warfare
Retalhuleu Guatemala *area–*728 183
Retardation
  education *see* Failure
    education
Retarded *see* Mentally deficient
Retarding
  plant growth
    crop prod.   631.545
    s.a. spec. crops; also
      spec. types of culture
      e.g. Floriculture

Retention
  memory
    psychology   153.122
    animals   156.312 2
    children   155.413
    s.a. psych. of other spec.
      groups
Rethymne Greece *area–*499 8
Reticular tissues *see*
    Connective tissue
Reticuloses
  gen. med.   616.156
  geriatrics   618.976 156
  pediatrics   618.921 56
  pub. health   614.591 56
  statistics   312.315 6
    deaths   312.261 56
  other aspects see Diseases
Retina patterns
  identification of criminals
    see Identification
      criminals
Retinas
  diseases
    gen. wks.   617.73
      neoplasms   616.992 84
      tuberculosis   616.995 84
    geriatrics   618.977 73
    pediatrics   618.920 977 3
    pub. health   614.599 7
    statistics   312.304 773
    surgery   617.730 59
      anesthesiology   617.967 73
    other aspects see Diseases
  physiology
    human   612.843
    other aspects see Sensory
      functions
  other aspects see Eyes
Retired persons *pers.–*069 6
Retirement
  armed forces   355.114
    s.a. spec. mil. branches
  employees
    personnel admin.
      gen. management 658.313 2
      executives   658.407 132
      spec. subj.   *s.s.–*068 3
    law of pub. admin. 342.068 6
      spec. jur.   342.3–.9
    pub. admin.   350.182
      central govts.   351.182
      spec. jur.   353–354
      local govts.   352.005 182
  enterprises *see*
    Proprietorships
  guides
    personal living   646.79
  income
    gen. wks. *see* Pensions
    insurance *see* Annuities

Revenue-cutters
  naval forces (continued)
    organization   359.326 3
    seamanship   623.882 63
    other aspects see Vessels
        (nautical)
Revenues
  estimates
    budgeting
      pub. admin.   350.722 252
        central govts.   351.722 252
        spec. jur.   353–354
        local govts.   352.122 52
    pub. finance   336.02
Revenue-sharing
  law   343.034
    spec. jur.   343.3–.9
Reveries *see* Secondary
      consciousness
Reverse osmosis
  saline water conversion   628.167 44
Reversible reactions
  physical chem.   541.393
    applied   660.299 3
    organic   547.139 3
  s.a. spec. aspects e.g. Low
      temperatures
  s.a. spec. elements, cpds.,
      prod.
Reversing negatives
  photographic tech.   770.285
    spec. fields   778
Review
  study & teaching   *s.s.*–076
Reviews
  of information media   028.1
Revised
  standard version Bible   220.520 4
    s.a. spec. parts of Bible
  versions
    Bible English   220.520 4
      s.a. spec. parts of Bible
  s.a. other spec. subj.
Revivals
  Christian rel. practices   269.24
Revolution
  citizenship ethics *see*
      Citizenship ethics
  pol. sci.   321.09
Revolutionary
  groups
    pol. sci.   322.42
  unions
    labor econ.   331.886
  warfare
    mil. sci.   355.021 84
  s.a. other spec. subj.
Revolutions
  sociology   303.64

Revolutions (continued)
  s.a. spec. revolutions e.g.
    French Revolution;
    also hist. of spec.
    countries
Revolvers
  small arms
    mf. tech.   683.436
    other aspects see Small
      arms
  other aspects see Pistols
Revues *see* Musical shows
Rewards
  mil. discipline   355.134
    s.a. spec. mil. branches
  rel. doctrines
    Christianity   236.2
    other rel. see Eschatology
  soc. control   303.35
  s.a. other spec. kinds
Reweaving
  home sewing   646.25
  clothing   646.6
Reynolds Co. Mo.   *area*–778 885
Reza Shah Iran hist.   955.052
  s.a. spec. events & subj.
    e.g. Commerce
Rhabdocoela *see* Turbellaria
Rhacopteris
  paleobotany   561.597
Rhaeto-Romanic languages
  linguistics   459.9
  literatures   859.9
  s.a.   *lang.*–599
Rhamnaceae *see* Rhamnales
Rhamnales
  botany   583.279
  floriculture   635.933 279
  forestry   634.973 279
  med. aspects
    crop prod.   633.883 279
    gen. pharm.   615.323 279
      toxicology   615.952 327 9
    vet. pharm.   636.089 532 327 9
      toxicology   636.089 595 232 79
  paleobotany   561.3
  other aspects see Plants
Rhapsodies
  piano music   786.42
    recordings   789.912 642
Rhayader Powys Wales *area*–429 54
Rhea Co. Tenn.   *area*–768 834
Rheas *see* Rheiformes
Rheiformes
  hunting
    commercial   639.128 52
    sports   799.248 52
  paleozoology   548.5
  zoology   598.52
  other aspects see Aves

Rheims-Douay Bible   220.520 2
   s.a. spec. parts of Bible
Rheinland-Pfalz Ger.   *area*–434 3
Rhenish Prussia Ger.   *area*–434 2
Rhenium
   arch. construction   721.044 77
     s.a. spec. kinds of bldgs.
   bldg. construction   693.77
   bldg. materials   691.87
   chemistry
     inorganic   546.545
     organic   547.055 45
      s.a. spec. groupings e.g.
       Aliphatic compounds
   technology   661.054 5
     organic   661.895
     soc. & econ. aspects *see*
      Secondary industries
     s.a. spec. prod.
   metallography   669.957
   metallurgy   669.7
     physical & chem.   669.967
     soc. & econ. aspects *see*
      Secondary industries
   pharmacology   615.254 5
     misc. aspects see
      Pharmacology
   products
     mf. tech.   673.7
     other aspects see
      Nonferrous metals
      products
   toxicology   615.925 545
     misc. aspects see
      Toxicology
     other aspects see Minor
      metals
Rheology *see* Dynamics; *also*
     Flow phenomena
Rheostats *see* Control devices
     electrodynamic eng.
Rhetoric   808
Rheum rhaponticum *see* Rhubarb
Rheumatic
   fever
     gen. med.   616.991
     geriatrics   618.976 991
     pediatrics   618.929 91
     pub. health   614.597 23
     statistics   312.399 1
      deaths   312.269 91
     other aspects see Diseases
   heart diseases
     gen. med.   616.127
     geriatrics   618.976 127
     pediatrics   618.921 27
     pub. health   614.591 27
     statistics   312.312 7
      deaths   312.261 27
     other aspects see Diseases

Rheumatism
   gen. med.   616.723
   geriatrics   618.976 723
   pediatrics   618.927 23
   pub. health   614.597 23
   statistics   312.372 3
   other aspects see Diseases
Rheumatoid arthritis *see*
     Arthritis
Rheumatology
   med. sci.   616.723
     geriatrics   618.976 723
     pediatrics   618.927 23
     vet. med.   636.089 672 3
      s.a. spec. animals
     other aspects see Medical
      sciences
   s.a. Rheumatism
Rhine
   Confederation Ger. hist.   943.06
   Province Ger.   *area*–434 2
   River   *area*–434
Rhineland-Palatinate Ger.   *area*–434 3
Rhinencephalon
   human phys.   612.825
   other aspects see Brain
Rhinitis *see* Common cold
Rhinocarina
   paleozoology   565.36
Rhinoceroses *see* Rhinocerotidae
Rhinocerotidae
   animal husbandry   636.972 8
   hunting
     commercial   639.117 28
     sports   799.277 28
   paleozoology   569.72
   zoology   599.728
   other aspects see Mammalia
Rhinology
   med. sci.   616.212
     geriatrics   618.976 212
     pediatrics   618.922 12
     vet. med.   636.089 621 2
      s.a. spec. animals
     other aspects see Medical
      sciences
   s.a. Nose
Rhizobiaceae *see* Eubacteriales
Rhizocephala *see* Cirripedia
Rhizodiniales *see* Pyrrophyta
Rhizomastigida *see* Mastigophora
Rhizophoraceae *see* Myrtales
Rhizopoda
   culture   639.731 1
   zoology   593.11
   other aspects see Protozoa
Rhizostomeae *see* Scyphozoa
Rhode Island
   Red chickens
     animal husbandry   636.584
     other aspects see Chickens

Rhode Island (continued)
Sound
  oceanography   551.461 46
  regional subj. trmt.   *area*–163 46
  other aspects see Atlantic
      Ocean
state   *area*–745
Rhodes Greece   *area*–499 6
  ancient   *area*–391 6
Rhodesia   *area*–689 1
Rhodesian
man   573.3
people   *r.e.n.*–968 91
  black   *r.e.n.*–968 91
  white   *r.e.n.*–2
Ridgeback
  animal husbandry   636.753
  other aspects see Dogs
trypanosomiasis *see*
      Trypanosomiasis
s.a. other spec. subj. e.g.
      Arts
Rhodium
arch. construction   721.044 77
  s.a. spec. kinds of bldgs.
bldg. construction   693.77
bldg. materials   691.87
chemistry
  inorganic   546.634
  organic   547.056 34
    s.a. spec. groupings e.g.
      Aliphatic compounds
technology   661.063 4
  organic   661.895
  soc. & econ. aspects *see*
    Secondary industries
  s.a. spec. prod.
metallography   669.957
metallurgy   669.7
  physical & chem.   669.967
  soc. & econ. aspects *see*
    Secondary industries
pharmacology   615.263 4
  misc. aspects see
    Pharmacology
products
  mf. tech.   673.7
  other aspects see
    Nonferrous metals
    products
toxicology   615.925 634
  misc. aspects see
    Toxicology
other aspects see
    Platinum-group metals
Rhodobacteriaceae *see*
    Thiobacteriales
Rhodochrosite
  mineralogy   549.782
Rhododendrons *see* Ericales

Rhodonite
  mineralogy   549.66
Rhodope Greece   *area*–495 7
Rhodophyta
  botany   589.41
  med. aspects
    gen. pharm.   615.329 41
    toxicology   615.952 941
    vet. pharm.   636.089 532 941
    toxicology   636.089 595 294 1
  paleobotany   561.93
  other aspects see Plants
Rhodymeniales *see* Rhodophyta
Rhoeadales
  botany   583.122
  floriculture   635.933 122
  med. aspects
    crop prod.   633.883 122
    gen. pharm.   615.323 122
    toxicology   615.952 312 2
    vet. pharm.   636.089 532 312 2
    toxicology   636.089 595 231 22
  paleobotany   561.3
  other aspects see Plants
Rhoipteleaceae *see* Juglandales
Rhondda Mid Glamorgan Wales
                area–429 72
Rhône
  dept. France   *area*–445 82
  River   *area*–445 8
Rhône-Alpes France   *area*–445 8
Rhopalocera
  culture   638.578 9
  paleozoology   565.78
  zoology   595.789
  other aspects see Insecta
Rhubarb
  agriculture   635.48
    soc. & econ. aspects *see*
      Primary industries
  foods   641.354 8
  preparation
    commercial   664.805 48
    domestic   641.654 8
  other aspects see
    Polygonales; *also*
    Vegetables
Rhuddlan Clwyd Wales   *area*–429 32
Rhum Highland Scot.   *area*–411 85
Rhumb line course
  celestial navigation   527.53
Rhyl Clwyd Wales   *area*–429 32
Rhymes
  folk lit.   398.8
Rhyming *see* Poetry gen. wks.
      rhetoric
Rhymney
  Mid Glamorgan Wales   *area*–429 76
  Valley Mid Glamorgan Wales
                area–429 76
Rhynchobdellida *see* Hirudinea

Rhynchocephalia	
culture	639.394 5
hunting	
commercial	639.144 5
sports	799.257 945
paleozoology	567.945
zoology	597.945
other aspects see Reptilia	
Rhynocheti *see* Gruiformes	
Rhyolite *see* Volcanic rocks	
Rhysodoidea *see* Adephaga	
Rhythm	
aesthetics *see* Aesthetics	
bands	785.067 5
s.a. spec. kinds of music	
method birth control	613.943 4
perception	
psychology	153.753
animals	156.375 3
children	155.413
s.a. psych. of other spec.	
groups	
training method	
music teaching	780.77
s.a. spec. mediums	
Rhythm (music)	
music theory	781.62
s.a. spec. mediums	
Rhythm-&-blues *see* Blues	
Rhythm-band music	785.43
recordings	789.912 543
Rhythmic arts	
rel. significance	
Christianity	246.7
other rel. see Arts rel.	
significance	
Rib & fan vaults	
architectural	
construction	721.45
design & decoration	729.34
building	690.145
s.a. spec. kinds of bldgs.	
Ribaceous fruits *see* Ribes	
Ribatejo Portugal	*area*–469 45
Ribble	
River Lancashire Eng.	*area*–427 685
Valley Lancashire Eng.	*area*–427 685
Ribbons *see* Passementerie	
Ribe Denmark	*area*–489 5
Ribes	
agriculture	634.72
soc. & econ. aspects *see*	
Primary industries	
foods	641.347 2
preparation	
commercial	664.804 72
domestic	641.647 2
other aspects see Cunoniales;	
also Fruits	
Ribes rubrum *see* Currants	
Ribes uva-crispa *see*	
Gooseberries	
Ribonucleic acid	
cytology	547.873 283
animals	591.873 283
plants	581.873 283
s.a. spec. organisms	
Ribose	
org. chem.	547.781 3
other aspects see Sugar	
Ribosomes *see* Cytoplasm	
Ribs	
diseases	
surgery	617.471
anesthesiology	617.967 471
other aspects see Diseases	
fractures	617.152
orthopedic surgery	617.374
other aspects see Chest bones	
Ricciaceae *see* Hepaticae	
Rice	
County	
Kansas	*area*–781 543
Minnesota	*area*–776 555
grasses *see* Pooideae	
Lake Ont.	*area*–713 57
Rice (cereal)	
agriculture	
food crops	633.18
forage crops	633.258
soc. & econ. aspects *see*	
Primary industries	
flour & meal	
comm. proc.	664.725
foods	641.331 8
cookery	641.631 8
other aspects see Cereal	
grains	
Rich	
areas regional subj. trmt.	*area*–172 2
Co. Utah	*area*–792 13
persons *see* Wealthy classes	
soils	
plants grown in	
floriculture	635.955
s.a. spec. plants	
s.a. other spec. subj.	
Richard	
reign	
Eng. hist.	
1	942.032
2	942.038
3	942.046
Gt. Brit. hist.	
1	941.032
2	941.038
3	941.046
s.a. spec. events & subj.	
e.g. Commerce	
Richardson Co. Neb.	*area*–782 282

Richelieu
  Co. Que. *area*–714 51
  River Que. *area*–714 3
Richland
  County
    Illinois *area*–773 77
    Montana *area*–786 23
    North Dakota *area*–784 12
    Ohio *area*–771 28
    South Carolina *area*–757 71
    Wisconsin *area*–775 75
  Par. La. *area*–763 86
Richmond
  city Va. *area*–755 451
  County
    Georgia *area*–758 64
    New York *area*–747 26
    North Carolina *area*–756 34
    Nova Scotia *area*–716 98
    Quebec *area*–714 65
    Virginia *area*–755 23
  North Yorkshire Eng. *area*–428 48
  Queensland *area*–943 7
  River N.S.W. *area*–944 3
  upon Thames London Eng. *area*–421 95
Richmondshire North Yorkshire
    Eng. *area*–428 48
Ricinulei
  zoology 595.41
  other aspects see Arachnida
Ricinuleids *see* Ricinulei
Rickets
  gen. med. 616.395
  geriatrics 618.976 395
  pediatrics 618.923 95
  pub. health 614.593 95
  statistics 312.339 5
    deaths 312.263 95
  other aspects see Diseases
Rickettsiae
  microbiology 576.62
    med. sci. 616.019 2
Rickettsial diseases
  biology 574.234
    animals 591.234
    plants 581.234
  s.a. spec. organisms
  med. sci. 616.922
    geriatrics 618.976 922
    pediatrics 618.929 22
    pub. health 614.526
    statistics 312.392 2
      deaths 312.269 22
  other aspects see Diseases
  plant culture 632.8
  s.a. spec. plants; also
      spec. types of culture
      e.g. Forestry
Rickettsialpox
  gen. med. 616.922 3
  geriatrics 618.976 922 3

Rickettsialpox (continued)
  pediatrics 618.929 223
  pub. health 614.526 3
  statistics 312.392 23
    deaths 312.269 223
  other aspects see Diseases
Rickmansworth Hertfordshire Eng.
    area–425 88
Rickshaws
  commerce 388.341
  other aspects see Land
      vehicles
Riddles
  folk lit. 398.6
  recreation 793.735
Ridges *see* Elevations
      (physiography)
Riding horses
  sports 798.23
    exhibitions 798.24
  other aspects see Sports
Riding-club bldgs.
  architecture 725.88
  building 690.588
  other aspects see Public
      structures
Riding-horses
  animal husbandry 636.13
  other aspects see Horses
Riel's rebellion
  Can. hist.
    1869-1870 971.051
    1885 971.054
Riemann
  integrals
    s.a. spec. appls. e.g.
        Engineering
  surfaces 515.223
    complex variables 515.922 3
    real variables 515.822 3
    s.a. other spec. functions &
        equations; also spec.
        appls. e.g.
        Engineering
  zeta functions 515.982
    s.a. spec. appls. e.g.
        Engineering
Riemannian geometry 516.92
  metric differential 516.373
  s.a. spec. appls. e.g.
      Geodesy
Riesz spaces 515.73
  s.a. spec. appls. e.g.
      Engineering
Rieti Italy *area*–456 24
Rif
  language *see* Berber languages
  Mts. Morocco *area*–642
Rifle grenades *see* Grenades
Rifles
  artillery *see* Artillery

Rifles (continued)
  small arms
    art metalwork — 739.744 25
    hunting & shooting sports — 799.202 832
      game — 799.213
      targets — 799.31
    mf. tech. — 683.422
    mil. eng.
      soc. & econ. aspects *see*
        Secondary industries
      tech. & mf. — 623.442 5
    mil. sci. — 355.824 25
    s.a. spec. mil. branches
Rift Valley province Kenya *area*-676 27
Rifts
  structural geol. — 551.87
  s.a. spec. aspects e.g.
    Prospecting
Riga Gulf *see* Baltic Sea
Rigging
  aircraft eng.
    soc. & econ. aspects *see*
      Secondary industries
    tech. & mf. — 629.134 37
  shipbuilding *see* Gear
    shipbuilding
Right whales *see* Mysticeti
Righteousness
  Christian doctrines — 234
Rightist parties
  pol. sci. — 324.24-.29
  s.a. spec. subj. of concern
    e.g. Social problems
Rightness
  ethics
    religion
      Buddhism — 294.356
      Christianity — 241.6
      comp. rel. — 291.56
      Hinduism — 294.548 6
    s.a. other spec. rel.
Rights
  civil *see* Civil rights
  political *see* Political
    rights
  stock purchase
    investment finance — 332.632 2
    govt. control *see*
      Securities govt.
      control
    law — 346.092 2
      spec. jur. — 346.3-.9
Rights-of-way
  determination *see* Surveying
Right-to-vote *see* Political
    rights
Right-to-work
  labor econ. — 331.898
  labor law *see* Labor law
Rigid
  bodies *see* Solids

Rigid (continued)
  dirigibles
    aeronautical eng.
      gen. tech. & mf. — 629.133 25
      components &
        techniques — 629.134
      models — 629.133 125
      operation — 629.132 522
    military — 623.743 5
    soc. & econ. aspects *see*
      Secondary industries
    s.a. other spec. appls.
    commerce — 387.732 5
    misc. aspects see
      Aircraft commerce
  s.a. other spec. subj.
Rigidity
  modulus
    engineering *see* Dynamics
    physics — 531.381
    of materials — 620.112 5
    s.a. spec. materials & uses
Rigveda
  Indic rel. — 294.595 12
Riksmal *see* Norwegian
Riley Co. Kan. — *area*-781 28
Rimau-rimau
  equip. mf. — 688.742
  soc. & econ. aspects *see*
    Secondary industries
  recreation — 794.2
Rime
  meteorology — 551.574 4
    artificial modification — 551.687 44
    weather forecasting — 551.647 44
    spec. areas — 551.65
Rimes
  folk lit. — 398.8
Riming *see* Poetry gen. wks.
    rhetoric
Rimouski Co. Que. — *area*-714 771
Rims
  automobile wheels
    soc. & econ. aspects *see*
      Secondary industries
    tech. & mf. — 629.248
Ringgold Co. Ia. — *area*-777 873
Ringkobing Denmark — *area*-489 5
Rings (jewelry)
  lit. & stage trmt. *see* Things
  precious metalwork — 739.278
  other aspects see Jewelry
Rings (mathematics) — 512.4
  s.a. spec. appls. e.g.
    Engineering
Ringwood Hampshire Eng. — *area*-422 75
Ringworm *see* Parasitic skin
    diseases
Rink bldgs.
  architecture — 725.86
  building — 690.586

River
  transportation (continued)
    other aspects see
      Inland-waterway transp.
  walls
    flood control eng. *see*
      Water retention
    port. eng. *see* Protective
      structures port eng.
    reclamation eng. *see* Shore
      reclamation eng.
    other aspects see Fresh-water
Rivera Uruguay   *area*–895 34
Rivers
  Nigeria   *area*–669 4
  s.a. Streams
Riverside Co. Calif.   *area*–794 97
Riverweed family *see*
  Podostemales
Riveting
  bldg. construction   693.7
  metal prod.
    arts
      decorative   739.14
      s.a. spec. metals; also
        spec. prod. e.g.
        Jewelry
      fine *see* Direct-metal
        sculpture
    mf. tech.   671.59
      ferrous metals   672.59
      s.a. other spec. metals
    other aspects see Joining
  shipbuilding
    soc. & econ. aspects *see*
      Secondary industries
    technology   623.843 2
  s.a. other spec. appls.
Riveting-equipment
  soc. & econ. aspects *see*
    Secondary industries
  tech. & mf.   621.978
    s.a. spec. appls. e.g.
      Buildings construction
Rivets
  machine eng.
    soc. & econ. aspects *see*
      Secondary industries
    tech. & mf.   621.884
      s.a. spec. appls. e.g.
        Buildings construction
  other aspects see Mechanics
Riviera   *area*–449
  France   *area*–449
  Italy   *area*–451 8
Rivière du Loup Co. Que.   *area*–714 76
Rivulariaceae *see* Cyanophyta
Rizal Philippines   *area*–599 1
Rize Turkey   *area*–566 2

Road
  camps
    penology   365.34
    other aspects see Penal
      institutions
  oils
    chem. tech.   665.538 8
    other aspects see Petroleum
  tests
    automobiles   629.282 4
  transportation *see* Vehicular
    transp.
Roadability tests
  automobiles   629.282 5
Roadbeds
  electric railways
    technology   625.65
    other aspects see Permanent
      way
  highway eng.
    technology   625.733
    other aspects see Roads
  railroad eng.
    technology   625.123
    other aspects see Permanent
      way
Roadrunners *see* Cuculiformes
Roads
  accidents   363.125
    misc. aspects see
      Transportation
      accidents
  bridges *see* Bridges
    (structures)
  civic art   711.72–.74
  commerce   388.1
  condition
    vehicular transp. hazard 363.125 1
  construction
    mil. sci.   358.22
    s.a. Roads engineering
  deterioration *see* Roads use
  engineering
    soc. & econ. aspects *see*
      Secondary industries
    technology   625.7
      forest management   634.93
        s.a. spec. trees
      military   623.62
        s.a. other spec. appls.
  engineers
    biog. & work   625.709 2
    s.a.   *pers.*–625
  hazards
    soc. path.   363.125
  land econ.   333.772
  landscape design   713
  law
    international   341.756 82
    municipal   343.094 2
      spec. jur.   343.3–.9

Roads (continued)
  lighting
    commerce
      gen. wks. *see* Highway
        services
      urban *see* Street services
    technology *see* Public
      lighting eng.
  pub. works
    pub. admin.   350.864 2
      central govts.   351.864 2
        spec. jur.   353–354
      local govts.   352.74
  safety
    engineering *see* Safety
      engineering roads
    gen. wks. *see* Vehicular
      transp. safety
  tunnels *see* Tunnels
  use
    commerce   388.314
    local   388.413 14
  s.a. Streets; *also* Farm
    roads
Roadside
  areas eng.
    technology   625.77
    other aspects see Roads
  barriers eng.
    technology   625.795
    other aspects see Roads
  eating places *see*
    Eating-places
  park facilities *see* Highway
    services
  signs
    outdoor advertising   659.134 2
Roadsteads *see* Ports
Roan Mts. Tenn.   *area*–768 99
Roane Co.
  Tennessee   *area*–768 84
  West Virginia   *area*–754 36
Roanoke
  city Va.   *area*–755 791
  Co. Va.   *area*–755 792
  Isl. N.C.   *area*–756 175
  River   *area*–756 1
    North Carolina   *area*–756 1
    Virginia   *area*–755 6
Roasters
  electric cookery   641.586
  s.a. spec. situations,
    materials, tech.
Roasting
  cookery tech.   641.71
  nonalcoholic brewed beverages
    comm. proc.
      coffee   663.934
      tea   663.944
    s.a. other spec.
      beverages

Roasting
  nonalcoholic brewed beverages (continued)
    other aspects see Beverages
  pyrometallurgy *see*
    Pyrometallurgy
Robber flies *see* Orthorrhapha
Robbery
  criminology   364.155 2
  insurance   368.82
    misc. aspects see Insurance
  law   345.025 52
    spec. jur.   345.3–.9
  soc. theology
    Christianity   261.883 155 2
    comp. rel.   291.178 331 552
    s.a. other spec. rel.
Robbins Isl. Tas.   *area*–946 7
Robert 2
  reign France hist.   944.021
  s.a. spec. events & subj.
    e.g. Commerce
Roberts Co.
  South Dakota   *area*–783 12
  Texas   *area*–764 818
Robertson Co.
  Kentucky   *area*–769 415
  Tennessee   *area*–768 464
  Texas   *area*–764 239
Robeson Co. N.C.   *area*–756 332
Robins
  American *see* Turdidae
  European *see* Sylviidae
Robinson Gorge Nat. Park Qld.
    area–943 5
Robinvale Vic.   *area*–945 9
Robots *see* Automatons
Roby Merseyside Eng.   *area*–427 54
Rocha Uruguay   *area*–895 16
Rochdale Greater Manchester Eng.
    area–427 392
Roches
  Douvres   *area*–423 49
  moutonnées   551.315
Rochester
  Kent Eng.   *area*–422 323
  New York   *area*–747 89
  Victoria   *area*–945 4
Rock
  and roll *see* Rock (music)
  arts
    gen. wks.   709.011 3
    painting   759.011 3
    sculpture   732.23
    s.a. other spec. art forms
  asphalts *see* Bituminous
    materials
  climbing
    equipment mf.   688.765 223
    soc. & econ. aspects *see*
      Secondary industries
    sports   796.522 3

Rock
  climbing (continued)
    other aspects see Sports
  County
    Minnesota   *area*–776 25
    Nebraska   *area*–782 743
    Wisconsin   *area*–775 87
  cutting *see* Excavation
  excavation *see* Excavation
  gardens
    plants grown for
      floriculture   635.967 2
    s.a. spec. plants
  haulage *see* Excavation
  hyraxes *see* Hyracoidea
  Island Co. Ill.   *area*–773 393
  mechanics
    foundation eng.   624.151 32
    s.a. spec. appls. e.g.
      Roads engineering
  rats *see* Hystricomorpha
  River Ill.   *area*–773 3
  salt   553.632
    econ. geol.   553.632
    mining
      soc. & econ. aspects *see*
        Primary industries
      technology   622.363 2
      prospecting   622.186 32
    s.a. spec. uses
  wool *see* Insulating materials
Rock (music)   780.42
  songs   784.54
    recordings   789.912 454
  s.a. other spec. mediums
Rockbridge Co. Va.   *area*–755 852
Rockcastle Co. Ky.   *area*–769 623
Rockdale Co. Ga.   *area*–758 215
Rocket
  engines
    soc. & econ. aspects *see*
      Secondary industries
    tech. & mf.
      aircraft   629.134 354
      gen. wks.   621.435 6
        parts & accessories 621.437
      land vehicles   629.250 56
        parts & systems 629.252–.258
      marine vehicles   623.872 356
    s.a. other spec. appls.
    other aspects see Power
      plants
  fuels
    manufacturing
      chem. tech.   662.666
    soc. & econ. aspects *see*
      Secondary industries
  launchers
    mil. eng.
      soc. & econ. aspects *see*
      Secondary industries

Rocket
  launchers
    mil. eng. (continued)
      tech. & mf.   623.42
        portable   623.442 6
  planes
    aeronautical eng.
      gen. tech. & mf.   629.133 38
      components & techniques 629.134
      models   629.133 138
      operation   629.132 528
      military   623.746 045
      s.a. spec. kinds e.g.
        Trainers (aircraft)
      soc. & econ. aspects *see*
        Secondary industries
      s.a. other spec. appls.
    commerce   387.733 8
    misc. aspects see
      Aircraft commerce
  propellants
    manufacturing
      chem. tech.   662.666
    soc. & econ. aspects *see*
      Secondary industries
  propulsion *see* Rocket engines
Rocketry *see* Rocket engines
Rockets
  mil. eng.
    soc. & econ. aspects *see*
      Secondary industries
    tech. & mf.   623.454 3
Rock-fill dams
  hydraulic eng.
    soc. & econ. aspects *see*
      Secondary industries
    technology   627.83
    s.a. spec. appls. e.g.
      Military engineering
    other aspects see Liquids
      engineering
Rockford Essex Eng.   *area*–426 775
Rockhampton Qld.   *area*–943 5
Rockingham Co.
  New Hampshire   *area*–742 6
  North Carolina   *area*–756 63
  Virginia   *area*–755 922
Rockland Co. N.Y.   *area*–747 28
Rock-'n'-roll *see* Rock (music)
Rocks
  ecology
    life sci.   574.526 5
      animals   591.526 5
      microorganisms 576.15
      plants   581.526 5
    s.a. spec. organisms
  fragmentation
    frost action   551.382
  handicraft *see* Found objects
  mineralogy   549.114
    spec. minerals   549.2–.7

Rocks (continued)

petrology	552
misc. aspects see Earth	
sciences	
Rockwall Co. Tex.	*area*–764 278
Rockweeds *see* Phaeophyta	

Rocky

Mountain	
Nat. Park Colo.	*area*–788 69
trench region B.C.	*area*–711 45
Mountains	*area*–78
Canada	*area*–711
Colorado	*area*–788 3
Montana	*area*–786 5
New Mexico	*area*–789 5
Utah	*area*–792 2
Wyoming	*area*–787 2
Range Fauna Reserve Vic.	*area*–945 6

Rococo art

architecture	724.19
spec. places	720.9
other aspects see	
Architectural schools	
design & dec.	745.443
spec. places	745.449
gen. wks.	709.033
spec. places	709.1–.9
music	
gen. wks.	780.903 3
spec. places	780.91–.99
s.a. spec. mediums	
painting	759.047
spec. places	759.1–.9
s.a. other spec. art forms	

Rodentia

agric. pests	632.693 23
s.a. spec. types of culture	
e.g. Forestry; also	
spec. crops	
animal husbandry	
soc. & econ. aspects *see*	
Primary industries	
technology	636.932 3
conservation tech.	639.979 323
control	
agricultural *see* Rodentia	
agric. pests	
home econ.	648.7
sanitary eng.	628.969 3
disease carriers	
pub. health	614.438
misc. aspects see Public	
health	
drawing tech.	743.693 23
experimental animals	
med. sci.	619.93
hunting	
commercial	639.113 23
sports	799.259 323
paleozoology	569.323
zoology	599.323

Rodentia (continued)

other aspects see Animals	
Rodenticides	
production	
soc. & econ. aspects *see*	
Secondary industries	
technology	668.651
use agric.	632.951
s.a. spec. crops; also spec.	
types of culture e.g.	
Floriculture	
Rodent-resistant construction	
buildings	693.844
Rodents *see* Rodentia	

Rodeos

performing arts	791.8
Rodopi Greece	*area*–495 7

Rodrigues

island	*area*–698
Mexico hist.	972.082 4
s.a. spec. events & subj.	
e.g. Commerce	

Rods (fishing sports)

manufacturing	
soc. & econ aspects *see*	
Secondary industries	
technology	688.791 2

Rods (structural element)

structural eng.	
gen. wks.	624.177 4
concretes	624.183 44
s.a. other spec.	
materials	
naval arch.	623.817 74
s.a. other spec. appls.	
Roentgen rays *see* X rays	
Roentgenology *see* X-ray	
examinations	
Roetheln *see* German measles	
Rogaland Norway	*area*–483

Rogation Days

devotional lit.	242.37
rel. observance	263.97
Roman Catholic liturgy	624.027 2
sermons	525.67
Roger Mills Co. Okla.	*area*–766 16
Rogers Co. Okla.	*area*–766 94
Rogue River Ore.	*area*–795 21

Role theory

soc. interaction	302
Rolette Co. N.D.	*area*–784 592

Roll

aeronautical aerodynamics	629.132 364
s.a. spec. appls. e.g.	
Flying	

Rolled metal prod.

mf. tech.	671.82
ferrous metals	672.82
s.a. other spec. metals	
other aspects see Primary	
metal prod.	

Roman	
Catholic	
church (continued)	
music	
arts	783.026 2
recordings	789.912 302 62
s.a. spec.	
instruments; also	
spec. kinds e.g.	
Liturgical music	
religion	
pub. worship	264.020 2
significance	246.7
private prayers for	242.802
pub. worship	264.02
rel. associations	
adults	267.182
men	267.242
women	267.442
young adults	267.622
rel. instruction	268.82
rel. law	262.91–.93
schools	377.82
secondary training	207.122
sermons	252.02
theological seminaries	207.112
s.a. other spec. aspects	
literature	
gen. wks.	
collections	808.899 222
hist. & crit.	809.892 22
spec. lits.	
collections	*lit. sub.*–080 922 2
hist. & crit.	*lit. sub.*–099 222
s.a. spec. lit. forms	
schismatics	
biog. & work	284.809 2
s.a. spec.	
denominations	
s.a.	*pers.*–248
schisms	284.8
Christian life guides	248.484 8
church	
buildings	
architecture	726.584 8
building	690.658 48
other aspects see	
Religious-purpose	
bldgs.	
music	
arts	783.026 48
recordings	789.912 302 648
s.a. spec.	
instruments; also	
spec. kinds e.g.	
Liturgical music	
religion	
pub. worship	264.048 02
significance	246.7
doctrines	230.48
creeds	238.48

Roman	
Catholic	
schisms (continued)	
general councils	262.548
govt. & admin.	262.048
parishes	254.048
missions	266.48
moral theology	241.044 8
private prayers for	242.804 8
pub. worship	264.048
rel. associations	
adults	267.184 8
men	267.244 8
women	267.444 8
young adults	267.624 8
rel. instruction	268.848
rel. law	262.984 8
schools	377.848
secondary training	207.124 8
sermons	252.048
theological seminaries	207.114 8
s.a. other spec. aspects	
Catholics	
biog. & work	282.092
s.a.	*pers.*–22
Empire	*area*–37
law	340.54
lettering dec. arts	745.619 78
period	
Egypt hist.	932.022
Eng. hist.	936.204
France hist.	936.402
Greece hist.	938.09
Judea hist.	933.05
Spain hist.	936.603
s.a. other spec. places;	
also spec. events &	
subj. e.g. Commerce	
religion	
Catholic *see* Roman Catholic	
classical	292.07
persons in	*pers.*–292
spec. aspects	292.1–.9
Republic Italy hist.	937.02
s.a. spec. events & subj.	
e.g. Commerce	
revival architecture	724.22
spec. places	720.9
other aspects see	
Architectural schools	
sculpture	733.5
s.a. other spec. subj.	
Romance	
fiction *see* Love fiction	
languages	
linguistics	440
literatures	840
s.a.	*lang.*–4
s.a. other spec. subj. e.g.	
Arts	
Romances *see* Fiction	

Roofing
bldg. construction 695
papers
  mf. tech. 676.289
  other aspects see Papers
    pulp prod.
tiles
  technology 666.732
  other aspects see
    Structural clay
    products
Roofs
architectural
  construction 721.5
  design & decoration 729.35
building 690.15
wood bldg. construction 694.2
s.a. spec. kinds of bldgs.
Rooks Co. Kan. *area*–781 18
Rooks (chessmen) 794.143
Rooming houses *see*
  Boardinghouses
Roosevelt
County
  Montana *area*–786 22
  New Mexico *area*–789 32
Franklin D. admin.
  U.S. hist. 973.917
  s.a. spec. events & subj.
    e.g. Courts
Res. Ariz. *area*–791 55
Theodore admin.
  U.S. hist. 973.911
  s.a. spec. events & subj.
    e.g. Courts
Root
celery *see* Celeriac
crops
  agriculture
    field crops 633.4
    garden crops 635.1
  foods 641.351
    cookery 641.651
  other aspects see Field
    crops; *also*
    Vegetables
extraction 512.923
  algebra 512.923
  arithmetic 513.23
  s.a. spec. appls. e.g.
    Business arithmetic
Roots (mathematics)
number theory
  algebra 512.72
  s.a. spec. appls. e.g.
    Engineering
Roots (plants)
plant
  anatomy 581.498
  pathology 581.229 8
  physiology 581.104 28

Roots (plants)
plant (continued)
  s.a. spec. plants
  s.a. Edible roots
Rope
bridges
  structural eng. 624.52
  other aspects see Bridges
    (structures)
climbing
  sports 796.46
  other aspects see Sports
Roper River N. Ter. Aust. *area*–942 95
Ropes
eng. materials 620.197
  naval design 623.818 97
  structures 624.189 7
  s.a. other spec. uses
knotting & splicing 623.888 2
power transmission
  machine eng. 621.853
    s.a. spec. appls. e.g.
      Factory operations
  other aspects see Mechanics
sculpture material 731.2
  spec. periods & schools 732–735
shipbuilding *see* Gear
  shipbuilding
textiles
  manufacturing
    soc. & econ. aspects *see*
      Secondary industries
    technology 677.71
  other aspects see Textiles
Rope-strand cable suspension
  bridges
  structural eng. 624.55
  other aspects see Bridges
    (structures)
Roque *see* Croquet
Roraima Brazil *area*–811 4
Rorschach
tests
  indiv. psych. 155.284 2
theory
  indiv. psych. 155.264
Rosaceae
botany 583.372
floriculture 635.933 372
forestry 634.973 372
med. aspects
  crop prod. 633.883 372
  gen. pharm. 615.323 372
    toxicology 615.952 337 2
  vet. pharm. 636.089 532 337 2
    toxicology 636.089 595 233 72
paleobotany 561.3
other aspects see Plants
Rosales
botany 583.37
floriculture 635.933 37

Rosales (continued)
   forestry   634.973 37
   med. aspects
      crop prod.   633.883 37
      gen. pharm.   615.323 37
         toxicology   615.952 337
      vet. pharm.   636.089 532 337
         toxicology 646.089 595 233 7
   paleobotany   561.3
   other aspects see Plants
Rosary
   private prayers   242.74
Roscommon Co.
   Ireland   *area*–417 5
   Michigan   *area*–774 76
Rose
   chafers
      zoology   595.764 9
      other aspects see Polyphaga
   family *see* Rosaceae
Rosé wine *see* Red grape wines
Roseau Co. Minn.   *area*–776 98
Rosebery Tas.   *area*–946 6
Rosebud
   Co. Mont.   *area*–786 32
   Victoria   *area*–945 2
Rosehearty Grampian Scot. *area*–412 25
Rosemaling
   dec. arts   745.72
Roses Wars
   Eng. hist.   942.04
   Gt. Brit. hist.   941.04
   s.a. spec. events & subj.
      e.g. Courts
Rosetta stone
   paleography   493.117
Rosh Hashanah
   customs   394.268 296
   Judaism   296.431
Rosicrucian mysteries
   occultism   135.43
Rosicrucians
   biog. & work   135.430 92
   order   135.43
   s.a.   *pers.*–366 4
Roskilde Denmark   *area*–489 1
Ross
   Co. O.   *area*–771 82
   Sea
      oceanography   551.469 4
      regional subj. trmt. *area*–167 4
      other aspects see Antarctic
        waters
Ross & Cromarty Scot.   *area*–411 72
Rossarden Tas.   *area*–946 4
Rossendale Lancashire Eng. *area*–427 63
Ross-on-Wye Hereford & Worcester
        Eng.   *area*–424 45
Rostock Ger.   *area*–431 7
Rostov RSFSR   *area*–477 7

Rostral furniture
   built-in arch. decoration   729.92
   rel. significance
      Christianity   247.12
      comp. rel.   291.37
      s.a. other spec. rel.
Rotary
   clubs   369.5
      songs *see* Service club
        songs
   compressors *see* Air
      compressors
   fans & blowers
      engineering
        soc. & econ. aspects *see*
          Secondary industries
        tech. & mf.   621.62
        s.a. spec. appls. e.g.
          Ventilation
      other aspects see Dynamics
   files
      management use   651.54
   polarization of light
      astrophysics   523.015 524
      s.a. spec. celestial
        bodies
      physics   535.524
      s.a. states of matter   530.4
   pumps
      engineering
        soc. & econ. aspects *see*
          Secondary industries
        tech. & mf.   621.66
        s.a. spec. appls. e.g.
          Water supply
          engineering
      other aspects see Dynamics
   steam engines
      stationary
        soc. & econ. aspects *see*
          Secondary industries
        tech. & mf.   621.166
        s.a. spec. appls. e.g.
          Generation elect. power
      other kinds see Steam
        locomotives
   vane positive expansion motors
      see Air engines
Rotary-wing aircraft *see*
      Vertical-lift aircraft
Rotation
   celestial bodies *see* Motions
      of celestial bodies
   crop prod.   631.582
      s.a. spec. crops
   crystals
      optical crystallography 548.9
      s.a. spec. substances
   earth astronomy   525.35

Rotation (continued)
  mechanics
    solid dynamics
      engineering *see* Dynamics
      physics   531.34
Rotational flow
  fluid mech.
    engineering *see* Dynamics
    physics   532.052
    gases   533.21
    air   533.621
    liquids   532.51
Rotatoria
  culture & hunting   639.758 1
  zoology   595.181
  other aspects see Worms
Rote learning
  psychology   153.152 2
    animals   156.315 22
    children   155.413
    s.a. psych. of other spec.
      groups
Rothbury Northumberland Eng.
      area–428 87
Rother East Sussex Eng.   *area*–422 52
Rotherham South Yorkshire Eng.
      area–428 23
Rothes Grampian Scot.   *area*–412 23
Rothesay Strathclyde Scot.   *area*–414 23
Rothwell
  Northamptonshire Eng.   *area*–425 52
  West Yorkshire Eng.   *area*–428 19
Rotifera *see* Rotatoria
Rotisseries
  electric cookery   641.586
  s.a. spec. situations,
    materials, tech.
Rotor ships *see* Modern
      wind-driven vessels
Rotors
  vertical lift
    aircraft eng.
      soc. & econ. aspects *see*
        Secondary industries
      tech. & mf.   629.134 36
  s.a. other spec. kinds e.g.
      Wind engines
Rots
  plant diseases   632.4
  s.a. spec. plants; also
    spec. types of culture
    e.g. Forestry
  resistance to
    eng. materials   620.112 23
    s.a. spec. materials &
      spec. uses
Rottweiler
  animal husbandry   636.73
  other aspects see Dogs
Rouergue France   *area*–447 4

Rough
  carpentry
    bldg. construction   694.2
    s.a. other spec. appls.
  lumber prod.
    manufacturing
      soc. & econ. aspects *see*
        Secondary industries
      technology   674.28
Roulette
  ethics *see* Games ethics
  other aspects see Wheel games
Roumania   *area*–498
Roumanian *see* Romanian
Round
  dances
    recreation   793.33
  Hill Fauna Reserve N.S.W.
      area–944 9
  sculpture   731.7
    spec. periods & schools   732–735
Roundabouts *see* Intersections
    (roads & streets)
Roundhouses
  railroad transp.
    gen. wks. *see* Railroad
      accessory bldgs.
    terminals *see* Railroad
      terminals facilities
Rounds (songs) *see* Choral music
Round-table discussions *see*
    Public discussions
Roundworm-caused diseases   616.965
  geriatrics   618.976 965
  pediatrics   618.929 65
  pub. health   614.555
  statistics   312.396 5
    deaths   312.269 65
  other aspects see Diseases
Roundworms *see* Nematoda
Roussillon France   *area*–448 9
Route markers highway transp.
    see Highway services
Routes
  determination *see* Surveying
  postal service
    law   343.099 25
    spec. jur.   343.3–.9
  transp. services
    commerce
      air   387.72
      bus   388.322 1
        local   388.413 22
      maritime   387.52
      truck   388.324 2
        local   388.413 24
    govt. control   350.877–.878
      central govts.   351.877–.878
      spec. jur.   353–354
      local govts.   352.917–.918
    law *see* Transportation law

Rubidium (continued)
  pharmacology   615.238 4
    misc. aspects see
        Pharmacology
  toxicology   615.925 384
    misc. aspects see
        Toxicology
    other aspects see Alkali
        metals
Rubies   553.84
  econ. geol.   553.84
  mining
    soc. & econ. aspects *see*
        Primary industries
    technology   622.384
    prospecting   622.188 4
  synthetic
    manufacturing
      soc. & econ. aspects *see*
        Secondary industries
    technology   666.88
  s.a. spec. uses
Rubrics
  Anglican liturgy   264.032
Rubus
  allegheniensis *see*
        Blackberries
  gen. wks. *see* Cane fruits
  idaeus *see* Raspberries
  loganobaccus *see* Loganberries
  occidentalus *see* Raspberries
  roribaccus *see* Dewberries
Ruby lasers *see* Solid-state
      lasers
Rudders
  aircraft eng.
    soc. & econ. aspects *see*
        Secondary industries
    tech. & mf.   629.134 33
  shipbuilding *see* Gear
      shipbuilding
Rudolf
  Lake Kenya   *area*–676 27
  reign Germ. hist.
    2   943.034
    s.a. spec. events & subj.
        e.g. Courts
Rue family *see* Rutales
Ruffia *see* Raffia
Rugby
  football
    equipment mf.   688.763 33
    soc. & econ. aspects *see*
        Secondary industries
    sports   796.333
    other aspects see Sports
  Warwickshire Eng.   *area*–424 85
Rugeley Staffordshire Eng.   *area*–424 67
Rugmakers *see* Carpetmakers

Rugs
  fabrics
    manufacturing
      soc. & econ. aspects *see*
        Secondary industries
      technology   677.643
    other aspects see Textiles
  int. dec.   747.5
    s.a. spec. kinds of bldgs.;
        also spec. dec.
  textile arts   746.7
    other aspects see Floor
      coverings
Ruhr Ger.   *area*–535 5
Ruislip-Northwood London Eng.
             area–421 83
Ruiz Cortines Mexico hist.   972.082 8
  s.a. spec. events & subj.
    e.g. Commerce
Rule of law   340.11
Ruled surfaces
  gen. wks. *see* Surfaces
  mathematics
  integral geometry   516.362
    s.a. spec. appls. e.g.
      Engineering
Rulers *see* Monarchs
Rules
  monastic life
    Christianity
      men   248.894 28
      women   248.894 38
    other rel. see Personal
      religion
  of court *see* Court rules
  of order   060.42
  of the road
    maritime transp.
      law
        international   341.756 66
        municipal   343.096 6
        spec. jur.   343.3–.9
    safety tech.   623.888 4
  s.a. Constitutions; *also*
    other spec. subj.
Rulings *see* Decisions
Rum Highland Scot.   *area*–411 85
Rumania   *area*–498
Rumanian *see* Romanian
Rumex acetosa *see* Sorrel
Ruminantia
  agric. pests   632.697 35
    s.a. spec. types of culture
      e.g. Forestry; *also*
      spec. crops
  animal husbandry   636.2
    soc. & econ. aspects *see*
      Primary industries
  conservation tech.   639.979 735
  drawing tech.   743.697 35

Rural (continued)
development
  law   343.074 5
    spec. jur.   343.3–.9
districts
  local govt.   352.007 22
electrification
  soc. & econ. aspects *see*
    Secondary industries
  technology   621.393
    s.a. spec. appls. e.g.
      Milking
environments
  ed. soc.   370.193 46
  psychology   155.944
free delivery
  postal commun.   383.145
  other aspects see Postal
    communication
health services
  soc. welfare   362.104 25
    govt. control   350.841
      central govts.   351.841
      spec. jur.   353–354
      local govts.   352.944 1
    law *see* Welfare services
      law
lands
  economics
    conservation & use   333.76
    sale & rental   333.335
  govt. control
    law   346.046 76
    spec. jur.   346.3–.9
municipalities
  local govt.   352.007 22
parishes
  local Christian church   254.24
regions *see* Rural areas
residential areas
  civic art   711.58
sanitary eng.   628.7
  s.a. spec. appls. e.g.
    military 623.75
sociology   307.72
young people
  soc. services to   362.799
  misc. aspects see Young
    people soc. services to
s.a. other spec. subj.; also
  Agricultural
Ruscaceae *see* Liliales
Ruse Bulgaria   *area*–497 76
Rush
  County
    Indiana   *area*–772 61
    Kansas   *area*–781 48
  family *see* Juncales
  hours
    highway & street traffic
      see Traffic patterns

Rushcliffe Nottinghamshire Eng.
    area–425 29
Rushden Northamptonshire Eng.
    area–425 54
Rushes
  agriculture   633.58
  soc. & econ. aspects *see*
    Primary industries
Rushmoor Hampshire Eng.   *area*–422 725
Rushwork
  textile arts   746.41
  s.a. spec. prod.
Rushworth Vic.   *area*–945 4
Rusk Co.
  Texas   *area*–764 185
  Wisconsin   *area*–775 19
Russe Bulgaria   *area*–497 76
Russell Co.
  Alabama   *area*–761 485
  Kansas   *area*–781 51
  Kentucky   *area*–769 655
  Ontario   *area*–713 85
  Virginia   *area*–755 755
Russia   *area*–47
Russian
  blue cats
    animal husbandry   636.826
    other aspects see Cats
  communism *see*
    Marxism-Leninism
  language
    linguistics   491.7
    literature   891.7
    s.a.   *lang.*–917 1
  lettering
    dec. arts   745.619 917 1
    s.a. Cyrillic alphabet
  Orthodox Church   281.93
    misc. aspects see Eastern
      Orthodox
  people   *r.e.n.*–917 1
  Revolution 1905 hist.   947.084
  Revolutions 1917 hist.   947.084 1
  Soviet Federated Socialist
    Republic   *area*–47
  turnips *see* Rutabagas
  s.a. other spec. subj. e.g.
    Arts
Russo-Finnish War hist.   948.970 32
Russo-Japanese War hist.   952.031
Russo-Turkish War hist.   947.081
Rust
  flies *see* Cyclorrhapha
  fungi *see* Uredinales
Rusting
  resistance to
    eng. materials   620.112 23
    s.a. spec. materials &
      spec. uses
Rust-resistant paints
  technology   667.69

S

SEATO
  mil. sci.   355.031 095 9
SIDS   618.920 078
SLR cameras *see* Single-lens
    reflex cameras
STOL *see* Short-takeoff-and-
    landing airplanes
Saar River   *area*–434 2
Saarland Ger.   *area*–434 2
Saba West Indies   *area*–729 77
Sabah Malaysia   *area*–595 3
Sabbath
  rel. observance
    Christianity   263.1–.4
    Judaism   296.41
    other rel. see Times rel.
      observance
Sabbatianism
  Judaism   296.82
    misc. aspects see Judaism
Sabean *see* South Arabic
Sabellian languages
  linguistics   479.7
  literatures   879.7
  s.a.   *lang.*–797
Sabellianism
  heresies
    Christian church hist.   273.3
Sabers
  art metalwork   739.722
  other aspects see Edged
      weapons
Sabiaceae *see* Sapindales
Sabine
  Co. Tex.   *area*–764 177
  Lake La.   *area*–763 52
  language *see* Sabellian
      languages
  Par. La.   *area*–763 62
Sables *see* Mustelidae
Sabotage
  labor econ.   331.893
  mil. sci.   355.343 7
    s.a. spec. mil. branches
  political *see* Political
      offenses
  property *see* Industrial
      sabotage
  spec. wars *see* Unconventional
      warfare
Sac
  Co. Ia.   *area*–777 424
  fungi *see* Ascomycetes
Sacatepéquez Guatemala   *area*–728 162
Saccharolytic enzymes
  biochemistry
    gen. wks.   574.192 54
    animals   591.192 54

Saccharolytic enzymes
  biochemistry
    gen. wks. (continued)
      microorganisms   576.119 254
      plants   581.192 54
      s.a. spec. organisms
    med. sci.   612.015 14
      animals   636.089 201 514
        s.a. spec. animals
      man   612.015 14
    s.a. spec. functions,
        systems, organs
    other aspects see Enzymes
Saccharomycetaceae
  agric. pathogens   632.433
    s.a. spec. plants; also
        spec. types of culture
        e.g. Forestry
  botany   589.233
  med. aspects
    gen. pharm.   615.329 233
    toxicology   615.952 923 3
    vet. pharm. 636.089 532 923 3
    toxicology 636.089 595 292 33
  other aspects see Fungi
Saccharum officinarum *see* Canes
      (sugar)
Sacoglossa
  culture   639.483 5
  paleozoology   564.35
  zoology   594.35
  other aspects see Mollusca
Sacramental furniture
  built-in arch. decoration 729.91
  rel. significance
    Christianity   247.11
    comp. rel.   291.37
    s.a. other spec. rel.
Sacramentals
  pub. worship
    Christianity   264.9
    spec. denominations 264.01–.09
    other rel. see Public
        worship
Sacramento
  city Calif.   *area*–794 54
  Co. Calif.   *area*–794 53
  Mts. N.M.   *area*–789 65
  River Calif.   *area*–794 5
Sacraments
  Anglican liturgy   264.035
  Christian doctrines 234.16
  Christian rites   265
  rel. law *see* Things rel. law
Sacred
  books
    religion
      Bible *see* Bible
      Buddhism   294.382
      Christianity
        gen. wks. *see* Bible

Safety
  engineering (continued)
    roads
      technology   625.704 2
       s.a. spec. subj. e.g.
        Drainage
      other aspects see Roads
    transportation
      technology   629.042
      other aspects see
        Transportation
        engineering
    s.a. other spec. branches of
      eng. & spec. appls.
      e.g. Aerospace
       engineering
  equipment
    aircraft eng.   629.134 43
    automobiles eng.   629.276
    gen. eng.
      soc. & econ. aspects *see*
        Secondary industries
      tech. & mf.   621.992
    plant management   658.28
      spec. subj.   *s.s.*–068 2
    shipbuilding   623.865
      design   623.814 65
        spec. craft   623.812
    sports
      American football   796.332 028
      s.a. other spec.
        activities
    s.a. other spec. appls.
  gen. wks.   363.1
  law
    international   341.765
    municipal   344.047
      spec. jur.   344.3–.9
    s.a. Transportation safety
      law
  measures
    soc. services *see* Accidents
      control
    technique   *s.s.*–028 9
  personal *see* Personal safety
  programs
    employees
      personnel admin.
        gen. management   658.382
        spec. subj.   *s.s.*–068 3
        pub. admin.   350.16
        central govts.   351.16
          spec. jur.   353–354
        local govts.   352.005 16
    schools   371.77
    s.a. spec. levels of ed.;
      also Special education
  pub. admin.   350.78
    central govts.   351.78
      spec. jur.   353–354
    local govts.   352.3

Safety (continued)
  traininq
    employees
      personnel admin.
        gen. management   658.312 44
        executives   658.407 124 4
        spec. subj.   *s.s.*–068 3
        pub. admin.   350.15
        central govts.   351.15
          spec. jur.   353–354
        local govts.   352.005 15
  valves steam eng. *see*
    Transmission steam
  s.a. Public safety
Safflower oil
  comm. proc.   664.369
  other aspects see Oils
Saffron Walden Essex Eng.   *area*–426 712
Safi Morocco   *area*–646
Saga Japan   *area*–522
Sagadahoc Co. Me.   *area*–741 85
Sagas
  folklore *see* Persons lit.
  trmt. folk lit.
  Old Norse lit.   839.6
Sage *see* Lamiales
Saginaw
  Bay Mich.   *area*–774 4
  Co. Mich.   *area*–774 46
  River Mich.   *area*–774 47
Sagittariidae
  hunting
    commercial   639.128 915
    sports   799.248 915
  paleozoology   568.9
  zoology   598.915
  other aspects see Aves
Sago palm
  agriculture   633.68
    soc. & econ. aspects *see*
      Primary industries
  other aspects see Palmales;
    also Starches
Saguache Co. Colo.   *area*–788 49
Saguenay
  Co. Que.   *area*–714 17
  River Que.   *area*–714 16
Saguia el Hamra   *area*–648
Sahara (territory)   *area*–648
Sahara Desert   *area*–66
Saïda Algeria   *area*–651
Sailboating
  sports   797.124
  racing   797.14
  other aspects see Sports
Sailboats
  gen. wks. *see* Sailing-craft
  modern *see* Pleasure craft
    (nautical) sailing
Sailfishes *see* Acanthopterygii

Saint
  Lawrence (continued)
    River   area–714
      New York   area–747 56
      Ontario   area–713 7
      Quebec   area–714
    Seaway   area–714
    transportation *see* Lake
      transportation
  Louis
    city Mo.   area–778 66
    County
      Minnesota   area–776 77
      Missouri   area–778 65
  Lucia isl.   area–739 843
  Lucie Co. Fla.   area–759 29
  Malo Gulf
    oceanography   551.461 38
    regional subj. trmt.   area–163 38
    other aspects see Atlantic
      Ocean
  Martin
    island   area–729 76
    Lake Man.   area–712 72
    Par. La.   area–763 48
  Mary Par. La.   area–763 42
  Marylebone London Eng.   area–421 32
  Marys
    Co. Md.   area–752 41
    Lake O.   area–771 415
    River
      Florida   area–759 11
      Michigan   area–774 91
  Maurice Co. Que.   area–714 45
  Michael Mount Cornwall Eng.
                                  area–423 75
  Monance Fife Scot.   area–412 92
  Neots Cambridgeshire Eng.
                                  area–426 54
  Pancras London Eng.   area–421 42
  Paul
    city Minn.   area–776 581
    island   area–699
  Pierre   area–718 8
  Simons Isl. Ga.   area–758 742
  Tammany Par. La.   area–763 12
  Thomas
    city Ont.   area–713 35
    isl. Virgin Isls.   area–729 722
  Vincent
    de Paul Sisters of Charity
      see Sisters of
        Charity
    island   area–729 844
  Vitus's dance *see* Chorea
Sainte Genevieve Co. Mo.   area–778 692
Saint-Jean Co. Que.   area–714 38
Saint-John's bread *see*
        Leguminous fruits
Saint-John's-wort family *see*
        Guttiferales

Saint-Laurent
  Louis S. admin. Can. hist.   971.063 3
  s.a. spec. events & subj.
        e.g. Commerce
Saintonge France   area–446 4
Saints
  art representation
    arts   704.948 63
    s.a. spec. art forms
  Christian rel.
    paintings   247.563
    sculpture   247.3
  biog. & work
    early period   270.1–.3
    later period
      Roman Catholic   282.092
      members of orders   271.01–.98
    s.a. other spec.
        denominations
    s.a. spec. subj. e.g.
        Popes, Religious
        (members of orders)
  canonization *see* Canonization
  Christian doctrines   235.2
  private prayers to   242.75–.76
  rel. worship
    comp. rel.   291.213
    s.a. spec. rel.
  s.a.   pers.–2
Saints' days
  devotional lit.   242.37
  rel. observance   263.98
  sermons   252.67
Saint-Simonism
  socialist school
    economics   335.22
Saipan   area–967
Saitama Japan   area–521 3
Saite period Egypt hist.   932.015
  s.a. spec. events & subj.
        e.g. Commerce
Saka language *see* Middle
        Iranian languages
Sakarya Turkey   area–563
Sake   641.23
  comm. proc.   663.49
  other aspects see Alcoholic
        beverages
Sakhalin   area–577
Salacity *see* Obscenity
Salad
  dressings
    cookery   641.814
    processing   664.37
    other aspects see Oils
  greens
    agriculture   635.5
    soc. & econ. aspects *see*
        Primary industries

Saline
  waters (continued)
    s.a. spec. uses
Salinity
  sea water
    oceanography   551.460 1
      *s.a. spec. bodies of
      water*
  soil science *see* Inorganic
      chemistry soil science
Salisbury
  Plain Eng.   *area*–423 19
  town
    S. Aust.   *area*–942 32
    Wiltshire Eng.   *area*–423 19
Saliva
  human phys.   612.313
    other aspects see Digestion
Salivary glands
  anatomy
    human   611.316
      other aspects see Nutritive
        organs
  diseases
    gen. wks.   616.316
      neoplasms   616.992 316
      tuberculosis   616.995 316
    geriatrics   618.976 316
    pediatrics   618.923 16
    pub. health   614.593 16
    statistics   312.331 6
  physical anthropometry   573.631 6
  physiology
    human   612.313
      other aspects see Nutrition
  tissue biology human   611.018 931 6
Salix *see* Willow
Salmon
  fish *see* Isospondyli
  River Ida.   *area*–796 82
  River Mts. Ida.   *area*–796 78
Salmonella diseases   616.927
  geriatrics   618.976 927
  pediatrics   618.929 27
  pub. health   614.511
  statistics   312.392 7
    deaths   312.269 27
  other aspects see Diseases
Salmonoidea *see* Isospondyli
Salmopercae *see* Mesichthyes
Salon orchestras   785.066 2
  s.a. spec. kinds of music
Saloons (drinking places) *see*
      Drinking-places
Salop Eng.   *area*–424 5
Salsify
  agriculture   635.16
    soc. & econ. aspects *see*
        Primary industries

Salsify (continued)
  foods   641.351 6
    preparation
      commercial   664.805 16
      domestic   641.651 6
  other aspects see Asterales;
      also Vegetables
Salt
  flats
    ecology
      life sci.   574.526 5
        animals   591.526 5
        microorganisms   576.15
        plants   581.526 5
          s.a. spec. organisms
  Lake City Utah   *area*–792 25
  Lake Co. Utah   *area*–792 25
  lakes
    ecology life sci. *see*
        Salt-water ecology life
        sci.
    other aspects see Special
        salt-water forms
  River Ky.   *area*–769 45
Salta Argentina   *area*–824 2
Saltash Cornwall Eng.   *area*–423 74
Saltburn & Markse-by-the-Sea
  Cleveland Eng.   *area*–428 54
Saltcoats Strathclyde Scot.   *area*–414 61
Salt-free
  cookery   641.563 2
  diets
    hygiene   613.28
      misc. aspects see Hygiene
Salting
  nat. leathers
    manufacturing
      soc. & econ. aspects *see*
          Secondary industries
      technology   675.22
  s.a. other spec. subj.
Salto Uruguay   *area*–895 35
Salton Sea Calif.   *area*–794 99
Saltpeter
  fertilizer *see* Nitrate
      fertilizers
  mineralogy   549.732
Salts   553.63
  animal feeds
    animal husbandry   636.087 7
      s.a. spec. animals
  chem. tech.   661.4
  econ. geol.   553.63
  food
    manufacturing
      soc. & econ. aspects *see*
          Secondary industries
      technology   664.4
  metabolism
    human phys.   612.392 6

Salts
  metabolism (continued)
    other aspects see
      Metabolism
  metals
    chemistry
      inorganic   546.34
        spec. kinds   546.38–.68
      other aspects see Metals
        chemistry
    pharmacology   615.234
      misc. aspects see
        Pharmacology
    toxicology   615.925 34
      misc. aspects see
        Toxicology
  mining
    technology   622.363
    prospecting   622.186 3
  spec. elements *see spec.*
    elements
  other geol. aspects see
    Sedimentary rocks
  s.a. spec. prod.
  s.a. spec. uses
Salt-water
  ecology
    life sci.   574.526 36
      animals   591.526 36
      microorganisms   576.15
      plants   581.526 36
    s.a. spec. organisms
  fish culture   639.32
    s.a. spec. kinds of fish
  fishing
    industries   639.22
      misc. aspects see Fishing
        industries
    sports   799.16
    other aspects see Fishing
    s.a. spec. kinds of fish
  lagoons
    ecology life sci. *see*
      Salt-water ecology life
      sci.
    other aspects see Special
      salt-water forms
  wetlands ecology life sci.
      see Salt-water
      ecology life sci.
Saluda
  Co. S.C.   *area*–757 38
  River S.C.   *area*–757 2
Saluki dogs
  animal husbandry   636.753
    other aspects see Dogs
Salvador
  country   *area*–728 4
  Lake La.   *area*–763 33
Salvadoraceae *see* Celastrales

Salvadoran
  literature   860
  people   *r.e.n.*–687 284
  s.a. other spec. subj. e.g.
    Arts
Salvage
  law *see* Maritime law
  operations
    disaster relief   363.348
      misc. aspects see
        Disasters soc. action
    maritime transp.
      commerce   387.55
      govt. control   351.877 55
        spec. jur.   353–354
      law
        international   341.756 68
        municipal   343.096 8
          spec. jur.   343.3–.9
      underwater eng.   627.703
      s.a. spec. appls. e.g.
        Military eng.; *also*
        spec. activities e.g.
        Blasting
  s.a. Wastes
Salvation
  rel. doctrines
    Christianity   234
    other rel. see Humankind
      rel. doctrines
Salvation Army   267.15
  s.a. spec. activities e.g.
    Home missions
Salvator Rosa Nat. Park Qld.
                                area–943 5
Salvinia family *see* Filicales
Salviniaceae *see* Filicales
Salzburg Austria   *area*–436 3
Samaná Dominican Republic
                                area–729 365
Samar Philippines   *area*–599 5
Samaria Jordan   *area*–569 53
Samaritan
  language
    linguistics   492.29
    literature   892.29
    s.a.   *lang.*–922 9
  people   *r.e.n.*–922
  texts
    Bible   220.45
      s.a. spec. parts of Bible
  s.a. other spec. subj. e.g.
    Arts
Samaritans
  Judaism   296.81
    misc. aspects see Judaism
Samarium
  chemistry
    inorganic   546.415

Samarium
chemistry (continued)
  organic   547.054 15
    s.a. spec. groupings e.g.
      Aliphatic compounds
  technology   661.041 5
  organic   661.895
    soc. & econ. aspects *see*
      Secondary industries
    s.a. spec. prod.
  eng. materials   620.189 291 5
    s.a. spec. uses
  metallography   669.952 915
  metallurgy   669.291 5
    physical & chem. 669.962 915
  pharmacology   615.241 5
    misc. aspects see
      Pharmacology
  products
    mf. tech.   673.291 5
    other aspects see
      Nonferrous metals
      products
  toxicology   615.925 415
    misc. aspects see
      Toxicology
  other aspects see
    Cerium-group metals
Samaveda
  Indic rel.   294.592 13
Samba (game) *see* Rummy
Sambucus *see* Elderberries
Samhitas
  Indic rel.   294.592 1
Samnium   *area*–377
Samoa   *area*–961 3–961 4
Samoan *see* Polynesian
Samos Greece   *area*–499
  ancient   *area*–391 4
Samothrace Greece *area*–499
  ancient   *area*–391 1
Samoyed dogs
  animal husbandry 636.73
  other aspects see Dogs
Samoyedic
  languages
    linguistics   494.4
    literatures   894.4
    s.a.   *lang.*–944
  people   *r.e.n.*–944
  s.a. other spec. subj. e.g.
    Arts
Sampans *see* Hand-propelled
    vessels
Sample preparation
  anal. chem.
    gen. wks.   543.02
    qual. anal.   544.02
    quan. anal.   545.02
    organic   547.302
      qual. anal. 547.340 2

Sample preparation
  anal. chem.
    organic (continued)
      quan. anal. 547.350 2
      s.a. spec. elements & cpds.
Samples
  sales promotion *see* Sales
    promotion
Sampling theory
  statistical math.   519.52
  s.a. spec. appls. e.g.
    Engineering
Sampson Co. N.C.   *area*–756 375
Samsun Turkey   *area*–563
Samuel
  Bible   222.4
  other aspects see Historical
    books (O.T.)
Samydaceae *see* Bixales
San (African languages and
    peoples) *see* Bushman
San
  Andrés
    Mts. N.M.   *area*–789 62
    y Providencia Colombia *area*–861 8
  Antonio
    city Tex.   *area*–764 351
    River Tex.   *area*–764 1
  Augustine Co. Tex. *area*–764 175
  Benito Co. Calif.   *area*–794 75
  Bernardino
    Co. Calif.   *area*–794 95
    Mts. Calif.   *area*–794 95
  Carlos Lake Ariz. *area*–791 54
  Cristóbal Dominican Republic
        area–729 374
  Cristobal Isls. Solomon Isls.
        area–935
  Diego Co. Calif.   *area*–794 98
  Francisco
    Bay Calif.
      area   *area*–794 6
      waters *see* United States
        Pacific seawaters
    city Calif.   *area*–794 61
    Co. Calif.   *area*–794 61
  Gabriel Mts. Calif. *area*–794 93
  Jacinto Co. Tex.   *area*–764 167
  Joaquin
    Co. Calif.   *area*–794 55
    River Calif.   *area*–794 8
  Jorge Gulf
    oceanography   551.464 68
    regional subj. trmt. *area*–163 68
    other aspects see Atlantic
      Ocean
  José
    city
      California   *area*–794 74
      Costa Rica   *area*–728 63
      dept. Uruguay *area*–895 12

Sandstones (continued)
　other geol. aspects see
　　Sedimentary rocks
　s.a. spec. uses
Sandstorms *see* Dust storms
Sandusky
　Bay O. — area–771 214
　Co. O. — area–771 214
　River O. — area–771 2
Sandwell West Midlands Eng.
　　area–424 94
Sandwich
　constructions
　　structural eng.
　　　gen. wks. — 624.177 9
　　　　spec. materials — 624.18
　　　naval arch. — 623.817 79
　　　s.a. other spec. appls.
　　Kent Eng. — area–422 352
　panels
　　arch. construction — 721.044 92
　　s.a. spec. kinds of
　　　bldgs.
　　bldg. construction — 693.92
　　wood
　　　mf. tech. — 674.835
　　other aspects see Wood
　　　products
Sandwiches
　cookery — 641.84
Sandy
　soils
　　plants grown in
　　　floriculture — 635.955
　town Bedfordshire Eng. — area–425 63
Sangamon
　Co. Ill. — area–773 56
　River Ill. — area–773 55
Sangre de Cristo Range Colo.
　　area–788 49
Sanilac Co. Mich. — area–774 43
Sanitarium bldgs.
　architecture — 725.51
　building — 690.551
　other aspects see Public
　　structures
Sanitariums *see* Extended care
　　facilities
Sanitary
　affairs
　　World War 1 hist. — 940.475 2
　　World War 2 hist. — 940.547 52
　　s.a. other spec. wars
　engineering
　　local govt. control — 352.6
　　soc. & econ. aspects *see*
　　　Secondary industries
　　technology — 628
　　　military — 623.75
　　s.a. other spec. appls.

Sanitary (continued)
　engineers
　　biog. & work — 628.092
　　s.a. spec. kinds
　　s.a. — pers.–628
　landfills
　　pollution
　　　water-supply eng.
　　　　technology — 628.168 25
　　　other aspects see Water
　　　　supply engineering
　　refuse disposal
　　　technology — 628.445 64
　　　other aspects see Refuse
　　　　pub. sanitation
　　sewage disposal
　　　technology — 628.364
　　　other aspects see Sewage
　　　　disposal
　napkins *see* Surgical gauzes
Sanitation
　domestic customs — 392.36
　facilities
　　civic art — 711.8
　　home econ. — 648
　law — 344.046
　　enforcement *see* Civil laws
　　　enforcement
　　spec. jur. — 344.3–.9
　mining eng. — 622.49
　plant management — 658.28
　　spec. subj. — s.s.–068 2
　pub. admin. — 350.772
　　central govts. — 351.772
　　　spec. jur. — 353–354
　　local govts. — 352.6
　shipbuilding
　　econ. aspects *see* Secondary
　　　industries
　　social aspects — 363.72
　　technology — 623.854 6
　　　design — 623.814 546
　　　spec. craft — 623.812
　spacecraft eng. — 629.477 4
　　unmanned — 629.467 4
　　other aspects see
　　　Spacecraft
　s.a. Public sanitation; *also*
　　　other spec. appls.
Sankaracharya philosophy — 181.482
Sankhya philosophy — 181.41
Sanpete Co. Utah — area–792 563
Sanquhar Dumfries & Galloway
　　Scot. — area–414 86
Sanskrit language
　linguistics — 491.2
　literature — 891.2
　s.a. — lang.–912
Santa
　Ana
　　dept. El Salvador — area–728 412

Sapphires (continued)
  s.a. spec. uses
Saprolegniales
  agric. pathogens   632.456
    s.a. spec. types of culture
      e.g. Forestry; *also*
      spec. plants
  botany   589.256
  med. aspects
    gen. pharm.   615.329 256
      toxicology   615.952 925 6
    vet. pharm.   636.089 532 925 6
      toxicology   636.089 595 292 56
  other aspects see Plants
Saps
  forest prod.
    food   641.336
      cookery   641.636
    prod. tech.   634.986
    soc. & econ. aspects *see*
      Primary industries
    s.a. spec. trees
Saracenic architecture
  gen. wks.
    medieval   723.3
    modern   724
  spec. places   720.9
  other aspects see
    Architectural schools
Saragossa Spain   *area*–465 53
Saramacca Surinam   *area*–883 3
Sarans *see* Vinyls
Sarasota Co. Fla.   *area*–759 61
Saratoga Co. N.Y.   *area*–747 48
Saratov RSFSR   *area*–478 5
Sarawak Malaysia   *area*–595 4
Sarcodina
  culture   639.731 1
  zoology   593.11
  other aspects see Protozoa
Sarcolaenaceae *see* Ochnales
Sarcomas *see* Malignant
    neoplasms
Sarcopterygii *see* Dipnoi
Sarcoptiformes
  zoology   595.42
  other aspects see Arachnida
Sarcospermataceae *see* Ebenales
Sardinia   *area*–459
  ancient   *area*–379
Sardinian
  language
    linguistics   457.91–.93
    literature   850
    s.a.   *lang.*–56
  people   *r.e.n.*–56
  s.a. Sardinia; *also other*
    spec. subj. e.g. Arts
Sardis Reservoir Miss.   *area*–762 83
Sargasso Sea
  oceanography   551.464 62

Sargasso Sea (continued)
  regional subj. trmt.   *area*–163 62
  other aspects see Atlantic
    Ocean
Sargent Co. N.D.   *area*–784 314
Sargentodoxaceae *see*
    Berberidales
Sargodha Pakistan   *area*–549 144
Sark   *area*–423 45
Sarmatia   *area*–395
Sarpy Co. Neb.   *area*–782 256
Sarraceniaceae *see*
    Sarraceniales
Sarraceniales
  botany   583.121
  floriculture   635.933 121
  med. aspects
    crop prod.   633.883 121
    gen. pharm.   615.323 121
      toxicology   615.952 312 1
    vet. pharm.   636.089 532 312 1
      toxicology   636.089 595 231 21
  paleobotany   561.3
  other aspects see Plants
Sarthe France   *area*–441 7
Sasakian geometry   516.373
  s.a. spec. appls. e.g.
    Engineering
Sashes
  comm. mf.
    soc. & econ. aspects *see*
      Secondary industries
    technology   687.19
  domestic mf.   646.48
  soc. customs   391.4
  other aspects see Clothing
Saskatchewan
  province   *area*–712 4
  River   *area*–712 42
Saskatoon Sask.   *area*–712 42
Sassafras
  agriculture   633.82
    soc. & econ. aspects *see*
      Primary industries
  foods   641.338 2
    preparation
      commercial   664.52
      domestic   641.638 2
  tea
    comm. proc.   663.96
    other aspects see
      Nonalcoholic beverages
  other aspects see Laurales
Sassanian Empire hist.   935.07
  s.a. spec. events & subj.
    e.g. Arts
Sassari Sardinia   *area*–459 3
Satan
  rel. doctrines
    Christianity   235.47
  other aspects see Devils

Satanism
  occultism   133.422
Satellite
  cells
    nerve tissue
      human anatomy & phys.   611.018 8
      other aspects see Tissue
        biology
  communication
    commerce   384.51
    govt. control   351.874 51
      spec. jur.   353–354
    law *see* Telecommunication
      law
    technology   621.380 422
    s.a. spec. appls. e.g.
      Military engineering
    other aspects see
      Communication
  communities *see* Suburban
    areas
  states *see* Dependent states
  systems
    radio
      engineering   621.384 156
      s.a. spec. appls. e.g.
        Radiotelephony
      other aspects see Radio
    television *see*
      Communication systems
      television
Satellites
  artificial *see* Artificial
    satellites
  astronomy
    description   523.98
    theory   521.6
  other aspects see Celestial
    bodies
Satire
  gen. wks.
    collections   808.87
    crit. theory   801.957
      textual   801.959
    hist. & crit.   809.7
    rhetoric   808.7
    juvenile   808.068 7
  spec. lits.   *lit. sub.*–7
  s.a. Satirical poetry
Satirical
  opera *see* Opera
  poetry
    gen. wks.
      collections   808.817
      hist. & crit.   809.17
      rhetoric   808.17
      juvenile   808.068 17
    spec. lits.   *lit. sub.*–107
    indiv. authors *lit. sub.*–11–19
  other aspects see Poetry

Satirists
  biog. & work   809.7
  s.a. spec. lits.
  s.a.   *pers.*–87
Satisfaction
  Christian rites   265.63
Satu Mare Romania   *area*–498 4
Saturated solutions
  physical chem. *see* Solutions
    physical chem.
Saturating papers
  mf. tech.   676.284 4
  other aspects see Papers pulp
    prod.
Saturation
  org. chem.   547.122 4
Saturn (planet)
  astronomy
    gen. wks.
      description   523.46
      theory   521.546
    satellites
      description   523.986
      theory   521.66
    flights to
      manned   629.455 6
      unmanned   629.435 46
    regional subj. trmt.   *area*–992 6
    other aspects see Celestial
      bodies
Satyromania
  gen. med.   616.858 33
  geriatrics   618.976 858 33
  psychology   157.7
  statistics   312.385 833
  other aspects see Sexual
    deviations
Saucers (tableware) *see*
  Tableware
Sauces
  comm. proc.   664.58
    soc. & econ. aspects *see*
      Secondary industries
  cookery   641.814
Saudi
  Arabia   *area*–538
  Arabians   *r.e.n.*–927 538
Sauk Co. Wis.   *area*–775 76
Saul reign Palestine hist.   933.02
  s.a. spec. events and subj.
    e.g. Commerce
Sauna bldgs.
  domestic *see* Accessory
    domestic structures
  public
    architecture   725.73
    building   690.573
    other aspects see Public
      structures
Saunders Co. Neb.   *area*–782 296

Sauraism
  Hinduism   294.551 7
  misc. aspects see Hinduism
Saurashtra India   *area*–547 5
Saurauiaceae *see* Theales
Sauria *see* Lacertilia
Saurischia
  paleozoology   567.97
Sauropsida
  paleozoology   568
  zoology   598
Sauropterygia
  paleozoology   567.93
Saururaceae *see* Piperales
Sautéing
  cookery technique   641.77
Savages *see* Primitive people
Savannah
  city Ga.   *area*–758 724
  River Ga.   *area*–758 1
Savings
  accounts
    banking econ.   332.175 2
    other aspects see Bankinq
  & loan associations
    economics   332.32
    other aspects see Banks
      (finance)
  banks
    economics   332.21
    other aspects see Banks
      (finance)
  bonds *see* Public securities
  capital formation
    financial econ.   332.041 5
  capital sources
    capital management   658.152 26
    spec. subj.   *s.s.*–068 1
  departments
    commercial banks   332.12
    misc. aspects see Banking
  macroeconomics   339.43
  stamps
    prints   769.57
Savings-consumption
  relationship
    macroeconomics   339.43
Savoie France   *area*–444 8
Savona Italy   *area*–451 84
Savories
  cookery   641.812
Savoy France   *area*–444 8
Savu Sea *see* Southern Sunda
  Isls. seas
Saw (musical instrument)
  music   789.69
    recordings   789.912 969
Sawatch Range Colo.   *area*–788 4
Sawbridgeworth Hertfordshire Eng.
     area–425 83

Sawdust
  fuel
    manufacturing
      soc. & econ. aspects *see*
        Secondary industries
      technology   662.65
      mf. tech.   674.84
  other aspects see Wood
    products
Sawfishes *see* Batoidea
Sawflies *see* Hymenoptera
Sawing-tools
  soc. & econ. aspects *see*
    Secondary industries
  tech. & mf.   621.93
  s.a. spec. appls. e.g.
    Furniture manufacturing
Sawmill operations
  lumber mf.
    soc. & econ. aspects *see*
      Secondary industries
    technology   674.2
Saws *see* Sawing-tools
Saws (musical instruments)
  mf. tech.   681.819 69
  misc. aspects see Musical
    instruments
  musical art   789.69
Sawtooth
  Mts. Ida.   *area*–796 7
  Range Ida.   *area*–796 29
  Ridge Wash.   *area*–797 28
Sawyer Co. Wis.   *area*–775 16
Saxhorn music   788.425
  recordings   789.912 842
Saxhorns
  mf. tech.   681.818 42
  misc. aspects see Musical
    instruments
  musical art   788.42
Saxifragaceae *see* Saxifragales
Saxifragales
  botany   583.38
  floriculture   635.933 38
  med. aspects
    crop prod.   633.883 38
    gen. pharm.   615.323 38
      toxicology   615.952 338
    vet. pharm.   636.089 532 338
      toxicology   636.089 595 233 8
  paleobotany   561.3
  other aspects see Plants
Saxifrage family *see*
  Saxifragales
Saxmundham Suffolk Eng.   *area*–426 46
Saxon emperors
  Ger. hist.   943.022
  s.a. spec. events & subj.
    e.g. Courts
Saxony Ger.   *area*–432 1
Saxony-Anhalt Ger.   *area*–431 8

Saxophone music   788.665
  recordings   789.912 866
Saxophones
  mf. tech.   681.818 66
    misc. aspects see
      Musical-instruments
  musical art   788.66
Saxophonists
  biog. & work   788.660 92
  s.a.   *pers.–788*
Sayan Mts.   *area–575*
Sayyid dynasty
  India hist.   954.024 2
    s.a. spec. events & subj.
      e.g. Arts
Scabies *see* Parasitic skin
        diseases
Scafell Cumbria Eng.   *area–427 84*
Scalby North Yorkshire Eng.
                                   area–428 48
Scalds
  statistics   312.304 711
    deaths   312.260 471 1
  surgery   617.11
    anesthesiology   617.967 11
    s.a. Veterinary sciences
Scale
  insects *see* Homoptera
  mosses *see* Hepaticae
Scales (maps)   912.014 8
Scales (music)   781.22
  exercises
    keyboard string instruments   786.33
  s.a. spec. mediums
Scales (weighing devices) *see*
            Measuring-instruments
Scallops
  culture   639.48
  fishing
    commercial   639.48
    sports   799.254 11
  food *see* Mollusca food
  other aspects see Pelecypoda
Scalp diseases
  gen. wks.   616.546
    neoplasms   616.992 77
    tuberculosis   616.995 77
  geriatrics   618.976 546
  pediatrics   618.925 46
  pub. health   614.595 46
  statistics   312.354 6
  other aspects see Diseases
Scalping
  war customs   399
Scandal
  ethics
    philosophy   177.2
    religion
      Buddhism   294.356 72
      Christianity   241.672
      comp. rel.   291.567 2

Scandal
  ethics
    religion (continued)
      Hinduism   294.548 672
      s.a. other spec. rel.
Scandinavia   *area–48*
Scandinavian
  languages
    linguistics   439.5
    literatures   839.5
    s.a.   *lang.–395*
  people   *r.e.n.–395*
  s.a. other spec. subj. e.g.
    Arts
Scandium
  chemistry
    inorganic   546.401
    organic   547.054 01
      s.a. spec. groupings e.g.
        Aliphatic compounds
  technology   661.040 1
    organic   661.895
    soc. & econ. aspects *see*
      Secondary industries
    s.a. spec. prod.
  econ. geol.   553.494 2
  eng. materials   620.189 290 1
    s.a. spec. uses
  metallography   669.952 901
  metallurgy   669.290 1
    physical & chem.   669.962 901
  mining
    technology   622.349 42
    prospecting   622.184 942
  pharmacology   615.240 1
    misc. aspects see
      Pharmacology
  products
    mf. tech.   673.290 1
    other aspects see
      Nonferrous metals
      products
  toxicology   615.925 401
    misc. aspects see
      Toxicology
  other aspects see Metal;
    also Metals
  s.a. spec. minerals
Scanning patterns
  radar eng.   621.384 88
    other aspects see Radar
  s.a. spec. appls. e.g.
    Military engineering
Scansores
  hunting
    commercial   639.128 7
    sports   799.248 7
  paleozoology   568.7
  zoology   598.7
  other aspects see Aves

Scaphopoda
culture   639.482
paleozoology   564.2
zoology   594.2
other aspects see Mollusca
Scapolites
mineralogy   549.68
Scapula *see* Upper extremities
bones
Scarabaeoidea
zoology   595.764 9
other aspects see Polyphaga
Scarabs
glyptics   736.209 32
Scarborough
North Yorkshire Eng.   *area*–428 47
Toronto Ont.   *area*–713 541
Scarifying roads
technology   625.761
other aspects see Roads
Scarlatina *see* Scarlet fever
Scarlet fever
gen. med.   616.917
geriatrics   618.976 917
pediatrics   618.929 17
pub. health   614.522
statistics   312.391 7
deaths   312.269 17
other aspects see Diseases
Scarves
neckwear *see* Neckwear
table linens *see* Table linens
Scattering
atmospheric optical phenomena
meteorology   551.566
artificial modification   551.686 6
weather forecasting   551.646 6
spec. areas   551.65
nuclear interactions *see*
Interactions nuclear
reactions
radiations met. *see*
Radiations meteorology
Scenarios
music   781.96
s.a. spec. musical mediums
other kinds see Scripts
Scene paintings
arts   751.75
indiv. artists   759.1–.9
s.a. spec. subj., tech.,
equip.
Scenery
art representation *see*
Natural sciences art
representation
dramatic performances *see*
Settings dramatic
performances
natural *see* Natural scenes
Schaffhausen Switzerland   *area*–494 5

Schedules
ed. admin.   371.242
s.a. other spec. subj.
Scheduling
broadcasting services
commerce
radio   384.544 2
television   384.554 42
other aspects see
Broadcasting services
prod. management *see*
Sequencing
transp. services *see*
Transport functions
s.a. other spec. subj.
Scheelite
mineralogy   549.74
Schemes (mathematics)   512.33
s.a. spec. appls. e.g.
Engineering
Schenectady Co. N.Y.   *area*–747 44
Scheuchzeriaceae *see*
Alismatales
Schiffli embroidery *see* Machine
embroidery
Schipperkes
animal husbandry   636.72
other aspects see Dogs
Schisandraceae *see* Magnoliales
Schism
church authority
Christianity   262.8
other rel. see
Ecclesiastical theology
Schistosomiasis *see*
Fluke-caused diseases
Schists *see* Metamorphic rocks
Schizaeaceae *see* Filicales
Schizomids
zoology   595.453 2
other aspects see Arachnida
Schizomycetes
botany   589.9
med. aspects
gen. pharm.   615.329 9
toxicology   615.952 99
vet. pharm.   636.089 532 99
toxicology   636.089 595 299
paleobotany   561.9
other aspects see Plants
Schizophrenia
gen. med.   616.898 2
geriatrics   618.976 898 2
pediatrics   618.928 982
psychology   157.2
pub. health   614.58
statistics   312.389 82
other aspects see Mental
illness
Schizophyceae *see* Cyanophyta
Schizophyta *see* Thallophyta

School (continued)
  lunch programs   371.716
    law   344.079 42
      spec. jur.   344.3–.9
    s.a. spec. levels of ed.;
      also Special education
  lunchrooms
    food services   642.5
  milk programs *see* School
    lunch programs
  nutrition proqrams *see* School
    lunch programs
  principals
    ed. admin.   371.201 2
    misc. aspects see School
      administrators
  rooms   371.621
    s.a. spec. levels of ed.;
      also Special education
  songs   784.62
    recordings   789.912 462
  superintendents
    ed. admin.   371.201 1
    misc. aspects see School
      administrators
  supervisors
    ed. admin.   371.201 3
    misc. aspects see School
      administrators
  tablet papers
    mf. tech.   676.286
    other aspects see Papers
      pulp prod.
  week *see* School day
  year *see* Academic year
  s.a. Academic; *also*
    Educational
Schoolcraft Co. Mich.   *area*–774 935
Schoolmasters *see* Teachers
Schools   371
  accounting   657.832 7
  adult ed.   374.8
  arts styles   709
    s.a. spec. art forms
  finance
    law   344.076
      spec. jur.   344.3–.9
  fire hazards   363.379
    misc. aspects see Fire
      safety
  law   344.07
    spec. jur.   344.3–.9
  spec. subj.   *s.s.*–071
  welfare services law *see*
    Welfare services law
  s.a. spec. levels of ed.; also
    spec. kinds e.g.
      Private schools
Schooners *see* Modern
  wind-driven vessels
Schouten Isl. Tas.   *area*–946 4

Schrödinger
  representation *see* Wave
    mechanics physics
  wave equation *see* Wave
    mechanics physics
Schuyler Co.
  Illinois   *area*–773 475
  Missouri   *area*–778 262
  New York   *area*–747 81
Schuylkill
  Co. Pa.   *area*–748 17
  River Pa.   *area*–748 1
Schwerin Ger.   *area*–431 7
Schwyz Switzerland   *area*–494 7
Sciatica *see* Spinal nerves
  diseases
Science
  fiction
    gen. wks.
      collections   808.838 76
      hist. & crit.   809.387 6
      rhetoric   808.387 6
      juvenile   808.068 387 6
    spec. lits.   *lit. sub.*–308 76
    indiv. authors   *lit. sub.*–31–39
    other aspects see Fiction
  sets
    mf. tech.   688.725
    other aspects see Toys
  s.a. Sciences
Sciences   500
  & religion
    Christianity   261.55
    nat. rel.   215
    other rel. see Religious
      attitudes secular
      disciplines
  appls. to spec. subj.   *s.s.*–015
  art representation   704.949 5
    s.a. spec. art forms
  Biblical trmt.   220.85
    s.a. spec. parts of Bible
  documentation   025.065
  elementary ed.   372.35
  govt. control
    activities   350.855
      central govts.   351.855
      spec. jur.   353–354
      local govts.   352.945 5
    govt. depts. *see* Executive
      departments
  instruments
    manufacturing
      soc. & econ. aspects *see*
        Secondary industries
      technology   681.75
    s.a. spec. kinds
  journalism   070.449 5
  laboratory bldgs.
    architecture   727.55
    building   690.755

Dewey Decimal Classification

Scintillation
 of stars !see! Refraction
  radioactivity detection
   physics (continued)
    phenomena
Scioto
 Co. O.   *area*–771 87
 River O.   *area*–771 5
Scissors
 clothing construction
  domestic   646.19
 other aspects see
  Cutting-tools
Scitaminales *see* Zingiberales
Sciuromorpha
 animal husbandry   636.932 32
 huntinq
  commercial   639.113 232
  sports   799.259 323 2
 zoology   599.323 2
 other aspects see Rodentia
Scleras
 diseases
  gen. wks.   617.719
  geriatrics   618.977 719
  pediatrics   618.920 977 19
  statistics   312.304 771 9
 human phys.   612.841
 other aspects see Eyes
Scleroderma *see* Hypertrophies
  skin
Scleroparei *see* Acanthopterygii
Scoliosis *see* Spinal
  deformities
Scombroidea *see* Acanthopterygii
Sconces
 furniture arts   749.63
Scone N.S.W.   *area*–944 2
Score reading
 musical performance
  music theory   781.633
  s.a. spec. mediums
Scores (music)
 gen. wks.   780.81–.84
  s.a. spec. mediums
 library trmt.   025.178 8
  acquisitions   025.288 8
  cataloging   025.348 8
  s.a. other spec. activities
Scoring systems
 contract bridge   795.415 4
 s.a. other spec. games &
  activities e.g. psych.
   tests 153.9
Scorodite
 mineralogy   549.72
Scorpaenoidea *see*
  Acanthopterygii
Scorpion
 flies *see* Mecoptera

Scorpion (continued)
 venoms
  toxicology   615.942
  misc. aspects see
   Toxicology
Scorpiones
 zoology   595.46
 other aspects see Arachnida
Scorpions
 fake
  zoology   595.47
  other aspects see Arachnida
 gen. wks. *see* Scorpiones
 whip
  gen. wks.
   zoology   595.453 2
   other aspects see
    Arachnida
 tailless
  zoology   595.453 6
  other aspects see
   Arachnida
Scotia Sea
 oceanography   551.469 3
 regional subj. trmt.   *area*–167 3
 other aspects see Antarctic
  waters
Scotland
 country   *area*–411
  ancient   *area*–361 1
 County
  Missouri   *area*–778 312
  North Carolina   *area*–756 335
Scots   *r.e.n.*–916 3
Scott Co.
 Arkansas   *area*–767 44
 Illinois   *area*–773 455
 Indiana   *area*–772 183
 Iowa   *area*–777 69
 Kansas   *area*–781 43
 Kentucky   *area*–769 425
 Minnesota   *area*–776 54
 Mississippi   *area*–762 655
 Missouri   *area*–778 97
 Tennessee   *area*–768 71
 Virginia   *area*–755 732
Scottish
 English
  dialect
   linguistics   427.941
   other aspects see English
    language
  literature   820
 Gaelic
  language
   linguistics   491.63
   literature   891.63
   s.a.   *lang.*–916 3
  people   *r.e.n.*–916 3
  s.a. Scotland; *also other*
   spec. subj. e.g. Arts

Relative Index

Scottish (continued)
Highlands — area–411 5
Scotts Bluff Co. Neb. — area–782 98
Scottsdale Tas. — area–946 4
Scouring
  compounds
    manufacturing
      chem. tech. — 668.127
      soc. & econ. aspects *see*
        Secondary industries
  rushes *see* Sphenopsida
Scouting
  military *see* Reconnaissance
  movement *see spec. kinds e.g.*
    Boy Scouts
Scows *see* Towed vessels
Scranton Pa. — area–748 37
Scrap
  gen. wks. *see* Wastes
  metals metallurgy — 669.042
  s.a. spec. metals
  rubber *see* Reclaimed rubber
  s.a. other spec. subj.
Scrapers
  hand *see* Hand tools
  mining eng. — 622.66
Scraps
  handicrafts *see* Found objects
Scratch pad papers
  mf. tech. — 676.286
  other aspects see Papers pulp
    prod.
Scratchboard
  drawing arts — 741.29
  spec. appls. — 741.5–.7
  spec. subj. — 743.4–.8
Screamers (birds) *see*
  Anseriformes
Screening
  chem. eng. — 660.284 22
  s.a. spec. prod.
  sewage trmt.
    technology — 628.34
    other aspects see Sewage
      treatment
  water-supply trmt.
    technology — 628.162 2
    other aspects see Water
      supply engineering
  s.a. other spec. subj.
Screens
  dec. arts — 749.3
  ecclesiastical furniture
    built-in arch. decoration — 729.96
    rel. significance
      Christianity — 247.16
      comp. rel. — 291.37
      s.a. other spec. rel.
  library bldgs. — 022.9
  museum bldgs. — 069.31
Screven Co. Ga. — area–758 695

Screw
  mechanics — 531.8
Screw-cutting tools
  soc. & econ. aspects *see*
    Secondary industries
  tech. & mf. — 621.944
  s.a. spec. appls. e.g.
    Motorboats engineering
Screwdrivers
  soc. & econ. aspects *see*
    Secondary industries
  tech. & mf. — 621.972
  s.a. spec. appls. e.g.
    Furniture manufacturing
Screws
  machine eng.
    soc. & econ. aspects *see*
      Secondary industries
    tech. & mf. — 621.882
    s.a. spec. appls. e.g.
      Furniture manufacturing
  other aspects see Mechanics
Scripts
  motion pictures — 791.437
    rhetoric — 808.066 791
    drama — 808.23
  puppet plays — 791.538
    rhetoric — 808.2
  radio — 791.447
    rhetoric — 808.066 791
    drama — 808.22
  stage productions — 792.9
    rhetoric — 808.2
  television — 791.457
    rhetoric — 808.066 791
    drama — 808.22
Scripture readings
  pub. worship
    Christianity — 264.34
    spec. denominations — 264.01–.09
    other rel. see Public
      worship
Scriptures *see* Sacred books
Scrollsawing
  furniture arts — 749.5
Scrollwork
  wood handicrafts — 745.51
Scrophulariaceae *see* Personales
Scrotum
  diseases
    gen. wks. — 616.67
      neoplasms — 616.992 63
      tuberculosis — 616.995 63
    geriatrics — 618.976 67
    pediatrics — 618.926 7
    pub. health — 614.596 7
    statistics — 312.367
    deaths — 312.266 7
  other aspects see Male
    (human) genital organs

975

Scrub typhus
gen. med.	616.922 4
geriatrics	618.976 922 4
pediatrics	618.929 224
pub. health	614.526 4
statistics	312.392 24
deaths	312.269 224

other aspects see Diseases
Scrummaging
rugby	796.333 23

Scuba diving
sports	797.23

other aspects see Sports
Scullery maids *see* Household
            employees
Sculptors
biog. & work	730.92
occupational ethics	174.973 1
s.a.	*pers.–*731

Sculptural schools & styles 732–735
  spec. places
ancient	732–733
oriental	732
other	730.9

Sculpture	730

  arch. decoration *see* Relief
         (art) arch. decoration
  rel. significance
Christiantity	247.3

    other rel. see Arts rel.
        significance
Sculpturing
elementary ed.	372.53

Scunthorpe Humberside Eng.
	*area–*428 3
Scurry Co. Tex.	*area–*764 731

Scurvy
gen. med.	616.394
geriatrics	618.976 394
pediatrics	618.923 94
pub. health	614.593 94
statistics	312.339 4
deaths	312.263 94

other aspects see Diseases
Scutelleroidea *see* Heteroptera
Scyphostegiaceae *see* Urticales
Scyphozoa
culture	639.737 3
paleozoology	563.73
zoology	593.73

other aspects see Animals
Scythes *see*
        Harvesting-machinery
Scythia	*area–*395 1
Scytho-Dravidians	*r.e.n.–*948

Scytonemataceae *see* Cyanophyta
Scytopetalaceae *see* Tiliales
Sea
  anemones *see* Anthozoa
  basins
regional subj. trmt.	*area–*182

Sea (continued)
  bears *see* Otariidae
  cows *see* Sirenia
  cucumbers *see* Holothurioidea
  fans *see* Anthozoa
forces mil. sci.	359

  grapes *see* Tunicata
  hares *see* Pteropoda
  horses *see* Mesichthyes
  ice
physical geol.	551.343
Islands	*area–*757 99
Georgia	*area–*758 7
South Carolina	*area–*757 99
Lake Vic.	*area–*945 9

  lemons *see* Pteropoda
  lilies *see* Crinoidea
  lions *see* Otariidae
  mail
postal commun.	383.142

    other aspects see Postal
        communication
  mantles *see* Stomatopoda
  mats *see* Bryozoa
  mosses *see* Rhodophyta
  of Oman-Persian Gulf
Province Iran	*area–*557 5

  onions *see* Stomatopoda
  pens *see* Anthozoa
  ports *see* Seaports
  slugs *see* Pteropoda
  spiders *see* Pycnogonida
  squirts *see* Tunicata
  transportation *see* Marine
      transportation
  urchins *see* Echinoidea
  walnuts *see* Ctenophorae
  warfare
mil. sci.	359

    technology *see* Military
      engineering
  water supply sources
technology	628.116

    other aspects see Water
      supply engineering
  waters
internat. law	341.45

    intrusion
      water-supply eng.
technology	628.11

      other aspects see Water
        supply engineering
oceanography	551.460 1

    s.a. spec. bodies of
      water
  winds *see* Local wind systems
  s.a. Marine; *also*
      Salt-water; *also*
      Oceans
Seabees
naval forces	359.982

Seas
  resources
    govt. control (continued)
      s.a. spec. aspects e.g.
        Water supply soc.
        services
  temperatures
    meteorology   551.524 6
      weather forecasting   551.642 46
      spec. areas   551.65
  s.a. Oceans
Seascapes
  art representation   704.943 7
  painting   758.2
  s.a. other spec. art forms
Seashore
  flies *see* Cyclorrhapha
  s.a. Shore
Seashores *see* Physiographic
      regions
Seasickness *see* Motion sickness
Seasonal
  changes
    ecology
      life sci.   574.543
        animals   591.543
        microorganisms   576.15
        plants   581.543
      s.a. spec. organisms
    hygiene   613.13
    misc. aspects see Hygiene
  cookery   641.564
  holidays
    soc. customs   394.268 3
  houses
    architecture   728.7
    building   690.87
    other aspects see
      Residential buildings
  parties
    indoor amusements   793.22
  unemployment
    labor econ.   331.137 044
    s.a. spec. classes of
      labor e.g. Women
  variations
    econ. cycles
      prod. econ.   338.54
  s.a. other spec. subj.
Seasoning
  lumber mf.
    soc. & econ. aspects *see*
      Secondary industries
    technology   674.38
  s.a. other spec. subj.
Seasonings
  foods   641.338
Seasons
  earth astronomy   525.5
  influence on crime   364.22
  lit. & stage trmt. *see* Times

Seasons (continued)
  s.a. Seasonal
Seat
  belts *see* Safety equipment
  ejectors
    aircraft eng.
      soc. & econ. aspects *see*
        Secondary industries
      tech. & mf.   629.134 386
Seaton Devon Eng.   *area*–423 57
Seats
  automobiles
    soc. & econ. aspects *see*
      Secondary industries
    tech. & mf.   629.26
  ecclesiastical furniture
    built-in arch. decoration 729.93
    rel. significance
      Christianity   247.13
      comp. rel.   291.37
    s.a. other spec. rel.
Seattle Wash.   *area*–797 77
Seawalls
  flood control eng. *see* Water
    retention
  port eng. *see* Protective
    structures port eng.
  reclamation eng. *see* Shore
    reclamation eng.
Sea-water supply
  shipbuilding
    soc. & econ. aspects *see*
      Secondary industries
    technology   623.854 3
      design   623.814 543
      spec. craft   623.812
Seaweeds *see* Phaeophyta
Sebaceous glands
  biochemistry
    human phys.   612.792 1
    other aspects see
      Integumentary organs
  diseases   616.53
    geriatrics   618.976 53
    pediatrics   618.925 3
    pub. health   614.595 3
    statistics   312.353
    other aspects see Diseases
Sebastian Co. Ark.   *area*–767 36
Seborrhea *see* Sebaceous glands
    diseases
Secale cereale *see* Rye
Secession
  U.S. Civil War   973.713
Second
  coming of Jesus Christ
    Christian doctrines   232.6
  Empire
    France hist.   944.07
    s.a. spec. events & subj.
      e.g. Courts

Secondary (continued)
standards
elect. measurement
technology   621.372
s.a. spec. appls. e.g.
Ignition systems &
devices
other aspects see
Electricity
treatment
sewage
technology   628.351–.354
other aspects see Sewage
treatment
x rays *see* X rays
s.a. other spec. subj.
Second-class mail
postal commun.   383.123
other aspects see Postal
communication
Secondhand stores
advertising   659.196 588 7
commerce   381.1
misc. aspects see Commerce
pub. relations   659.296 588 7
retail marketing *see* Retail
marketing
Secret
agents
criminal investigation *see*
Evidence procurement
police
police services   363.283
other aspects see Law
enforcement
service
spec. wars *see*
Unconventional warfare
societies   366.1–.5
Secretarial
accounting   657.2
s.a. spec. kinds of
enterprise e.g.
Insurance accounting
bookkeeping   657.2
s.a. spec. kinds of
enterprise e.g.
Insurance accounting
Secretariat
League of Nations internat. law
    341.222 4
United Nations
internat. law   341.232 2
pub. admin.   354.103
Secretaries
office services   651.374 1
other aspects see Office
personnel
Secretary
birds *see* Sagittariidae

Secretary General
United Nations internat. law   341.232 4
s.a. other spec. occurrences
Secretion
drugs affecting
pharmacodynamics   615.74
other aspects see Drugs
pathology   574.214
animals   591.214
plants   581.214
s.a. spec. organisms
physiology
gen. wks.   574.14
animals   591.14
microorganisms   576.114
plants   581.14
s.a. spec. organisms
med. sci.   612.4
human phys.   612.4
vet. phys.   636.089 24
s.a. spec. animals
s.a. spec. functions,
systems, organs
Secretory organs
life sci.
anatomy
gen. wks.   574.44
animals   591.44
microorganisms   576.14
plants   581.44
s.a. spec. organisms
med. sci.   611.4
animals   636.089 14
s.a. spec. animals
human   611.4
pathology
gen. wks.   574.224
animals   591.224
plants   581.224
s.a. spec. organisms
med. sci. *see* Secretion
Sectionalist parties
pol. sci.   324.24–.29
s.a. spec. subj. of concern
e.g. Social problems
Section-cutting tech.
slide preparation
microscopy life sci.   578.63
animal tissues   578.93
plant tissues   578.83
Sections (plans) *see* Vertical
plane
Sects
religion
Buddhism   294.39
sources   294.385
Christianity   280
comp. rel.   291.9
sources   291.85
Hinduism   294.55
sources   294.595

Sedimentation
  sewage
    primary
      technology   628.34
      other aspects see Sewage
          treatment
    secondary
      technology   628.353
      other aspects see Sewage
          treatment
    water-supply trmt.
      technology   628.162 2
      other aspects see Water
          supply engineering
  s.a. Precipitation
Sediments
  ocean floor
    submarine geol.   551.460 83–.460 84
  physical geol.   551.304
    water action   551.354
    wind action   551.374
  s.a. other spec. aspects
Seditious libel *see* Political
        offenses
Seduction
  criminology *see* Sex offenses
Seed
  ferns
    paleobotany   561.595
  shrimps *see* Ostracoda
Seed-bearing plants *see*
        Spermatophyta
Seeders *see* Planting-equipment
Seed-hair fibers
  textiles
    arts   746.042
    s.a. spec. proc. e.g.
        Weaving
    dyeing   667.32
    manufacturing
      soc. & econ. aspects *see*
          Secondary industries
      technology   677.2
      special-process fabrics   677.6
    other aspects see Textiles
    s.a. spec. prod.
Seeding
  clouds   551.687 6
Seeding-equipment *see* Planting
        equipment
Seeding-techniques
  forestation   634.956 2
Seedless plants *see* Cryptogamia
Seeds
  animal feeds
    comm. proc.   664.762–.763
  arrangements
    dec. arts   745.928
  collecting
    forestation   634.956 2
    s.a. spec. trees

Seeds (continued)
  crop prod.   631.521
    s.a. spec. crops; also spec.
        types of culture e.g.
        Floriculture
  food
    processinq
      soc. & econ. aspects *see*
          Secondary industries
      technology   664.7
  forest prod.   634.987
    s.a. spec. trees
  forestation   634.956 2
    s.a. spec. trees
  oil
    comm. proc.   665.35
    other aspects see Oils
        industrial
  paleobotany   561.14
    s.a. spec. plants
  plant anatomy   582.046 7
    s.a. spec. plants
  plants grown from
    floriculture   635.942
      s.a. spec. plants
  use
    plant propagation   631.531
    forestry   634.956 2
      s.a. spec. crops; also
          other spec. types of
          culture e.g.
          Floriculture
  s.a. Edible seeds
Sees
  Christian ecclesiology   262.3
Sefton Merseyside Eng.   *area*–427 59
Segmented worms *see* Annelida
Segovia Spain   *area*–463 57
Segregation
  education
    ed. soc.   370.193 44
    law   344.079 8
      spec. jur.   344.3–.9
  other aspects see Social
        classes
Seiches
  dynamic oceanography   551.470 23
    s.a. spec. bodies of water
Seine
  dept. France   *area*–443 6
  River France   *area*–443 4
Seine-et-Marne France   *area*–443 7
Seine-et-Oise France   *area*–443 6
Seine-Inférieure France   *area*–442 5
Seine-Maritime France   *area*–442 5
Seine-Saint-Denis France   *area*–443 62
Seining
  sports   799.13
  other aspects see Fishing

Self-defense
  hygiene 613.66
  legal defense
    criminal law 345.04
      spec. jur. 345.3–.9
  mil. training 355.548
  s.a. spec. mil. branches
Self-denial
  private rel. experience *see*
    Asceticism
Self-destructive tendencies *see*
    Sociopathic personality
Self-development
  reading
    library sci. 028.8
Self-discipline
  private rel. experience *see*
    Asceticism
Self-education
  adult ed. 374.1
Self-employed
  labor econ. 331.125
  s.a. spec. classes of
    workers e.g. Women
Self-employment
  income
    taxation
      financial econ. 336.242 3
      law 343.052 6
        spec. jur. 343.3–.9
      pub. admin. *see* Personal
        income taxes pub.
        admin.
Self-financing
  capital formation
    financial econ. 332.041 52
Self-help
  groups
    adult ed. 374.22
  habits
    child psych. 155.418
Self-incrimination
  protection from
    procedural right
      law 345.056
        spec. jur. 345.3–.9
Selfishness *see* Vices
Self-organized infantry
  mil. sci. 356.15
Self-organizing systems
  cybernetics 001.533
Self-potential methods
  geophysical prospecting 622.154
Self-realization
  ethical systems *see*
      Perfectionism ethical
      systems
Self-reliance *see* Virtues
Self-sufficiency
  prod. econ. 338.9

Seljuks Turkey hist. 956.101
  s.a. spec. events & subj.
    e.g. Commerce
Selkirk Mts. B.C. *area*–711 43
Selkirkshire Scot. *area*–413 85
Selkup *see* Samoyedic
Selling *see* Personal selling
Selwyn Range Qld. *area*–943 7
Semaeostomeae *see* Scyphozoa
Semang *see* Mon-Khmer
Semantic development of words
    see Etymology
Semantics
  linguistics *see* Etymology
  philosophy 149.946
    indiv. phil. 180–190
  s.a. spec. branches of phil.
    e.g. Metaphysics
Semaphores
  commun. eng.
    military 623.731 2
    nautical 623.856 12
  s.a. other spec. appls.
    e.g. Railroading
Semeiology *see* Symptoms of
    disease pathology
Semen
  biol. aspects *see* Sexual
      reproduction
  med. aspects *see* Male (human)
      genital organs
Semiarid
  environments
    ecology
      life sci. 574.526 5
        animals 591.526 5
        microorganisms 576.15
        plants 581.526 5
      s.a. spec. organisms
  lands
    resources *see* Land
        resources
Semiautomatic
  switchboard systems
    wire telephony
      technology 621.385 7
      s.a. spec. appls. e.g.
        military use 623.733
      other aspects see
        Telephony wire
  switchboards
    wire telephony *see*
        Telephone switchboards
        wire telephony
  s.a. other spec. subj.
Semibituminous coal 553.24
  econ. geol. 553.24
  mining
    soc. & econ. aspects *see*
        Primary industries

Dewey Decimal Classification

Semimicro analysis
anal. chem.
gen. wks. (continued)
quantitative — 545.845
organic — 547.308 15
qualitative — 547.348 5
quantitative — 547.358 45
s.a. spec. elements & cpds.
Seminaries (theology) *see*
Theological seminaries
Seminars
ed. method *see* Discussion
method education
Seminary buildings *see*
Religious school bldgs.
Seminational rivers
internat. law — 341.442
Seminole
County
Florida — *area*–759 23
Georgia — *area*–758 996
Oklahoma — *area*–766 71
Wars
U.S. hist.
1818 — 973.54
1835-1842 — 973.57
Semiology *see* Symptoms of
disease pathology
Semionotoidea
paleozoology — 567.4
Semiotics *see* Semantics
Semipalatinsk USSR — *area*–584 5
Semiprecious stones — 553.87
econ. geol. — 553.87
mining
soc. & econ. aspects *see*
Primary industries
technology — 622.387
prospecting — 622.188 7
other aspects see Glyptics
s.a. spec. uses
Semiprivate
grounds
landscape design — 712.7
libraries *see* Proprietary
libraries
Semiquantitative anal. chem.
see Qualitative
chemistry
Semiregular variable stars
astronomy
description — 523.844 26
theory — 521.584 426
other aspects see Celestial
bodies
Semirigid dirigibles
aeronautical eng.
gen. tech. & mf. — 629.133 26
components & tech. — 629.134
models — 629.133 126
operation — 629.132 522

Semirigid dirigibles
aeronautical eng. (continued)
military — 623.743 6
soc. & econ. aspects *see*
Secondary industries
s.a. other spec. appls.
commerce — 387.732 6
misc. aspects see Aircraft
commerce
Semirings
mathematics — 512.4
s.a. spec. appls. e.g.
Engineering
Semiskilled workers
labor econ. — 331.794
labor force — 331.114 22
other aspects see
Industrial occupations
labor law *see* Labor law
other aspects see Middle
classes
Semisovereign states *see*
Dependent states
Semites — *r.e.n.*–92
Semitic
architecture — 722.3
misc. aspects see
Architectural schools
languages *see* Afro-Asiatic
languages
peoples — *r.e.n.*–92
texts
Bible — 220.4
s.a. spec. parts of Bible
Senates
pol. sci. *see* Upper houses
Senators *see* Legislators
Seneca
County
New York — *area*–747 69
Ohio — *area*–771 24
Lake N.Y. — *area*–747 69
Senegal — *area*–663
Senegalese
people — *r.e.n.*–966 3
s.a. other spec. subj. e.g.
Arts
Senegambia — *area*–663
Senescence
physical — 612.67
social *see* Aged people
sociology
Senile dementias
gen. med. — 616.898 3
geriatrics — 618.976 898 3
psychology — 157.2
pub. health — 614.58
statistics — 312.389 83
other aspects see Mental
illness

986

Separation (continued)
  processes
    chem. eng.   660.284 2
      s.a. spec. prod.
    s.a. other spec. subj.
Separators
  steam eng.
    soc. & econ. aspects *see*
        Secondary industries
    tech. & mf.   621.197
      s.a. spec. appls. e.g.
        Steam locomotives
    s.a. other spec. kinds
Sepiolite
  mineralogy   549.67
Sepoy Mutiny
  India hist.   954.031 7
Septets
  by instrument *see spec.*
        instruments
  chamber music
    recordings   789.912 57
    scores & parts   785.77
    treatises   785.707
  songs
    recordings   789.912
    scores & parts   784.85
      sacred   783.675 7
      secular   784.306 7
Septic tanks
  technology   628.742
Septicemia
  gen. med.   616.944
    geriatrics   618.976 944
    pediatrics   618.929 44
    pub. health   614.577
    statistics   312.394 4
    deaths   312.269 44
  puerperal diseases
    obstetrics   618.74
    pub. health   614.545
    statistics   312.304 874
    deaths   312.260 487 4
  other aspects see Diseases
Sepulchers *see* Mortuary tombs &
      chapels
Sepulchral bldgs. *see* Mortuary
      tombs & chapels
Sequatchie
  Co. Tenn.   *area*–768 77
  River Tenn.   *area*–768 77
Sequence *see* Proper of the Mass
Sequences   515.242
  calculus   515.242
    complex variables   515.924 2
    real variables   515.824 2
    s.a. other spec. functions &
      equations; also spec.
      appls. e.g.
      Engineering

Sequencing
  prod. management   658.53
  spec. subj.   *s.s.*–068 5
Sequential
  analysis
    statistical math.   519.54
    s.a. spec. appls. e.g.
        Engineering
  machines
    automation eng.
      soc. & econ. aspects *see*
        Secondary industries
      tech. & mf.   629.891
Sequoia
  Nat. Park Calif.   *area*–794 86
  trees
    forestry   634.975 8
    soc. & econ. aspects *see*
        Primary industries
    other aspects see
        Coniferales; *also*
        Trees
Sequoyah Co. Okla.   *area*–766 81
Seraphim *see* Angels
Serbian   *area*–497 1
Serbian
  people   *r.e.n.*–918 22
  other aspects see
      Serbo-Croatian
  s.a. Serbia
Serbo-Croatian
  language
    linguistics   491.82
    literature   891.82
    s.a.   *lang.*–918 2
  s.a. Yugoslavia; *also other*
      spec. subj. e.g. Arts
Serbs   *r.e.n.*–918 22
Serenades
  band music *see* Band music
  orchestra music *see* Romantic
      music orchestra
Serer *see* West-Atlantic
      (Niger-Congo)
Serfdom
  sociology   306.3
Serfs
  customs   390.25
    dress   391.025
    homes   392.360 25
  other aspects see Lower
      classes
  s.a.   *pers.*–062 5
Sergipe Brazil   *area*–814 1
Serials
  bibliographies   011.34
    spec. kinds   012–016
  catalogs
    general   017–019
    spec. kinds   012–016

Serials (continued)
library trmt. 025.173 2
  acquisitions 025.283 2
  cataloging 025.343 2
  s.a. other spec. activities
postal handling
  postal commun. 383.123
  other aspects see Postal
    communication
publications 050
  spec. subj. *s.s.*–05
publishing 070.572
reviews 028.134
spec. subj. *s.s.*–05
student activity 371.897 5
s.a. spec. levels of ed.;
  also Special education
Sericulture 638.2
misc. aspects see Agriculture
Series 515.243
calculus 515.243
  complex variables 515.924 3
  real variables 515.824 3
s.a. other spec. functions &
  equations; also spec.
  appls. e.g.
  Engineering
statistical method 001.422 4
  spec. subj. *see* Statistical
    method spec. subj.
Series (bibliographical)
bibliographies 011.48
  spec. kinds 012.016
catalogs
  general 017–019
  spec. kinds 012–016
s.a. spec. forms e.g. Books
Serigraphy
graphic arts
  processes 764.8
  products 769
Serious drama
gen. wks.
  collections 808.825 1
  hist. & crit. 809.251
  rhetoric 808.251
  juvenile 808.068 251
spec. lits. *lit. sub.*–205 1
  indiv. authors *lit. sub.*–21–29
stage presentation 792.1
other aspects see Drama
Sermon
on the Mount
  Christian moral theology 241.53
  Gospels 226.9
  misc. aspects see New
    Testament
outlines
  preaching
    Christianity 251.02
    other rel. see Preaching

Sermon (continued)
preparation
  preaching
    Christianity 251.01
    other rel. see Preaching
Sermons
pub. worship
  Christianity 264.6
  spec. denominations 264.01–.09
  other rel. see Public
    worship
texts
  Christianity 252
  other rel. see Preaching
Sero-bacterins
pharmacology 615.372
other aspects see Drugs
Serology *see* Immune reactions
Serous membranes
human anatomy & phys. 611.018 7
medication through
  therapeutics 615.66
  misc. aspects see
    Medication methods
s.a. spec. diseases
other aspects see Tissue
Serpent music 788.485
recordings 789.912 848
Serpentes
culture 639.396
hunting
  commercial 639.146
  sports 799.257 96
paleozoology 567.96
zoology 597.96
other aspects see Reptilia
Serpentines 553.55
econ. geol. 553.55
materials *see* Natural stones
mineralogy 549.67
mining
  soc. & econ. aspects *see*
    Primary industries
  technology 622.355
  prospecting 622.185 5
other aspects see Metamorphic
  rocks
s.a. spec. uses
Serpents (horns)
mf. tech. 681.818 48
  misc. aspects see Musical
    instruments
musical art 788.48
Serpents (reptiles) *see*
  Serpentes
Serrai Greece *area*–495 6
Serres Greece *area*–495 6
Serums
pharmacology 615.37
other aspects see Drugs

Service
club songs — 784.66
  recordings — 789.912 466
clubs — 369.5
  members — *pers.*–369 5
contracts
  law — 346.024
    spec. jur. — 346.3–.9
enterprises
  accounting — 657.83
industries *see* Service
    occupations
marks — *s.s.*–027 5
occupations
  govt. control
    activities — 350.824 3
      central govts. — 351.824 3
        spec. jur. — 353–354
      local govts. — 352.942 43
    govt. depts. *see*
      Executive departments
  labor econ. — 331.793
    active employment — 331.125 1
    aged workers — 331.398 81
    collective bargaining — 331.890 41
    employment conditions — 331.204 1
    ind. relations — 331.041
    labor force — 331.119 042
    market — 331.129 042
    need — 331.123 1
    opportunities — 331.124 1
    pensions — 331.252 9
    spec. occupations — 331.761
    strikes — 331.892 81
    unemployment — 331.137 81
    unions — 331.881 1
    wages — 331.281
    women workers — 331.481
    young workers — 331.381
  law — 343.078
    spec. jur. — 343.3–.9
  prod. econ. — 338.47
    efficiency — 338.456 1
    finance — 338.43
    mergers — 338.836 1
    organizations — 338.761
    restrictive practices — 338.826 1
of process
  law *see* Pretrial procedure
    law
periods
  armed forces — 355.11
  s.a. spec. mil. branches
pipes
  water-supply eng.
    technology — 628.15
    other aspects see Water
      supply engineering

Service (continued)
  stations
    automobiles
      soc. & econ. aspects *see*
        Secondary industries
      technology — 629.286
      s.a. spec. appls.
    technique
      tennis sports — 796.342 21
Services
  Anglican liturgy — 264.035
  commerce — 380.145
    misc. aspects see Secondary
      industries
    s.a. spec. kinds of comm.
      e.g. International
      commerce
  procurement
    pub. admin. — 350.712 6
      central govts. — 351.712 6
        spec. jur. — 353–354
      local govts. — 352.162 6
    prod. econ. — 338.02
      specific — 338.47
  religion *see* Public worship
  s.a. other spec. subj.
Serviettes *see* Table linens
Serving
  table service
    home econ. — 642.6
Servites
  rel. orders — 255.47
    church hist. — 271.47
    ecclesiology — 262.24
Servitudes
  law
    international — 341.4
    municipal — 346.043 5
      spec. jur. — 346.3–.9
Servomechanisms
  automation eng. — 629.832 3
  s.a. spec. appls. e.g.
    Gunnery
Sesame
  crops *see* Herbs
  oil
    comm. proc. — 664.369
    other aspects see Oils
    other aspects see Bignoniales
Sesquilinear forms
  algebra — 512.944
    s.a. spec. appls. e.g.
      Engineering
  geometry — 516.35
    s.a. spec. appls. e.g.
      Engineering
Session
  Court of
    Scotland
      law — 347.411 023
Session laws *see* Statutes

Set functions *see* Functions
    (mathematics)
Set theory   510.322
  s.a. spec. math. branches;
    also spec. appls. e.g.
      Electronic data
      processing
Setif Algeria   *area*–655
Sets   511.32
  s.a. spec. math. branches;
    also spec. appls. e.g.
      Electronic data
      processing
Settat Morocco   *area*–643
Setters
  animal husbandry   636.752
  other aspects see Dogs
Settings
  dramatic performances
    motion pictures   791.430 25
    stage   792.025
      s.a. spec. kinds e.g.
        Tragedies (drama)
    television   791.450 25
Setting-up exercises *see*
    Calisthenics
Settle North Yorkshire Eng.
        area–428 41
Settlements
  real estate
    law   346.043 73
    spec. jur.   346.3–.9
Settling
  water-supply trmt.
    technology   628.162 2
    other aspects see Water
      supply engineering
Setúbal Portugal   *area*–469 42
Seven
  Devils Mts. Ida.   *area*–796 26
  last words on cross
    Christian doctrines   232.963 5
  Years' War
    Europe hist.   940.253 4
    s.a. spec. countries
Seveners
  Islamic sects   297.822
  doctrines   297.204 22
  worship   297.302 2
  s.a. other spec. aspects
Sevenoaks Kent Eng.   *area*–422 36
Seventeenth century
  history   909.6
    appls. tc spec. subj.   *s.s.*–090 32
  s.a. spec. countries
Seventh
  century
    history   909.1
      appls. to spec. subj.   *s.s.*–090 21
    s.a. spec. countries

Seventh (continued)
  Day
    rel. observance
      Christianity   263.2
      other rel. see Times rel.
        observance
  Seventh-Day
    Adventists   286.73
      misc. aspects see
        Adventists
    Baptists   286.3
      misc. aspects see Baptist
Severance pay
  wage & salary admin. *see*
      Compensation scales
      pers. admin.
Severely retarded persons
  child psych.   155.452 84
  child rearing home econ.   649.152 84
  education   371.928 4
  law   344.079 128 4
    spec. jur.   344.3–.9
Severn River Gt. Brit.   *area*–424
  Wales   *area*–429 51
Severnaya Zemlya RSFSR   *area*–987
Sevier Co.
  Arkansas   *area*–767 47
  Tennessee   *area*–768 893
  Utah   *area*–792 55
Sevilla Spain   *area*–468 6
Sewage
  disposal
    engineering
      soc. & econ. aspects *see*
        Secondary industries
      technology   628.36
        military   623.753
        rural   628.74
    law   344.046 22
    spec. jur.   344.3–.9
    local govt. control   352.62
    other aspects see Wastes
      control
  districts
    local govt. admin.   352.62
  effluent
    disposal
      technology   628.362
      other aspects see Sewage
        disposal
  pollution
    water-supply eng.
      technology   628.168 2
      other aspects see Water
        supply engineering
  sludge
    disposal
      technology   628.364–.366
      other aspects see Sewage
        disposal

Sewage
  sludge (continued)
    fertilizers
      production
        soc. & econ. aspects
          see Secondary
          industries
        technology   668.636 9
    use agric.   631.869
      s.a. spec. crops; also
        spec. types of culture
        e.g. Floriculture
  treatment
    engineering
      soc. & econ. aspects *see*
        Secondary industries
      technology   628.32–.35
      military   623.753
      rural   628.74
    local govt. control   352.62
Seward
  County
    Kansas   *area*–781 735
    Nebraska   *area*–782 324
  election district Alaska   *area*–798 3
Sewellels *see* Sciuromorpha
Sewerage eng.
  law *see* Refuse pub.
    sanitation law
  soc. & econ. aspects *see*
    Secondary industries
  technology   628.2
    s.a. spec. appls. e.g.
      Wastes control
Sewers
  engineering
    soc. & econ. aspects *see*
      Secondary industries
    technology   628.23–.25
      s.a. spec. appls. e.g.
        Floods control
Sewing
  elementary ed.   372.54
  home econ.   646.2
    clothing construction   646.4
Sewing-materials
  home econ.   646.1
Sex   612.6
  cells *see* Gametogenesis
  customs   392.6
  development
    life sci.   574.36
    animals   591.36
    microorganisms   576.136
    plants   581.36
    s.a. spec. organisms
  differentiation
    life sci.   574.36
    animals   591.36
    microorganisms   576.136
    plants   581.36

Sex
  differentiation
    life sci. (continued)
      s.a. spec. organisms
  discrimination
    voting *see* Voting
      qualifications
  hormones
    biology *see* Reproduction
    human phys.   612.61–.62
    org. chem.   547.734 3
    pharmacology   615.366
    other aspects see Hormones
  human phys.   612.6
  hygiene   613.95
    elementary ed.   372.372
  instruction
    child rearing   649.65
  lit. & stage trmt. *see* Human
    qualities
  manuals   613.96
  offenses
    criminology   364.153
    law   345.025 3
      spec. jur.   345.3–.9
    soc. theology
      Christianity   261.833 153
      comp. rel.   291.178 331 53
      s.a. other spec. rel.
  population statistics   312.9
  psychology   155.3
  relations
    psychology   155.34
  rel. worship
    comp. rel.   291.212
    s.a. spec. rel.
  requirements
    employees *see* Personal
      qualifications
    voting *see* Voting
      qualifications
  other aspects see
    Reproduction
  s.a. Sexual
Sexes
  evolution
    life sci.   575.9
    animals   591.38
    plants   581.38
    s.a. spec. organisms
  soc. theology
    Christianity   261.834 3–.834 4
    comp. rel.   291.178 343–.178 344
    s.a. other spec. rel.
  sociology   305.3–.4
Sexism
  ed. soc.   370.193 45
  other aspects see Sexes
Sext *see* Office hours
Sextants *see* Extrameridional
    instruments

Sextets
  by instrument *see spec.*
      instruments
  chamber music
    recordings   789.912 57
    scores & parts   785.76
    treatises   785.706
  songs
    recordings   789.912
    scores & parts   784.85
      sacred   783.675 6
      secular   784.306 6
Sextuplets
  birth *see* Multiple childbirth
  psychology   155.444
  rearing home econ.   649.144
Sexual
  aberrations *see* Sexual
      deviations
  abnormality *see* Sexual
      deviations
  behavior *see* Sexual relations
  deviations
    medicine   616.858 3
      geriatrics   618.976 858 3
      pediatrics   618.928 583
      psychology   157.7
      statistics   312.385 83
    other aspects see
        Diseases; *also* Mental
        illness
  offenses
    criminology   364.153 6
    law   345.025 36
      spec. jur.   345.3–.9
    soc. theology
      Christianity   261.833 153 6
      comp. rel.   291.178 331 536
      s.a. other spec. rel.
    other aspects see Sexual
        relations
  disorders
    functional
      gen. med.   616.69
      geriatrics   618.976 69
      pediatrics   618.926 9
      pub. health   614.596 9
      statistics   312.369
    other aspects see
        Diseases
    s.a. Female sexual
        disorders
    sociopathic *see* Sexual
        deviations
  ethics
    philosophy   176
    religion
      Buddhism   294.356 6
      Christianity   241.66
      comp. rel.   291.566
      Hinduism   294.548 66

Sexual
  ethics
    religion (continued)
      s.a. other spec. rel.
    habits *see* Sexual relations
    manias *see* Sexual deviations
    perversions *see* Sexual
        deviations
  relations
    criminology *see* Sex
        offenses
    ethics *see* Sexual ethics
    medicine *see* Sexual
        disorders
    soc. theology
      Christianity   261.835 7
      comp. rel.   291.178 357
      s.a. other spec. rel.
    sociology   306.7
    technique   613.96
  reproduction
    pathology   574.216 6
      animals   591.216 6
      plants   581.216 6
      s.a. spec. organisms
    physiology   574.166
      animals   591.166
      microorganisms   576.166 6
      plants   581.166
      s.a. spec. organisms
  selection
    evolution
      life sci.   575.5
        animals   591.38
        plants   581.38
        s.a. spec. organisms
    s.a. Sex
Seychelles isls.   *area*-696
Seyhan Turkey   *area*-564
Seymour Vic.   *area*-945 3
Sgrafitto decoration *see*
        Decorative treatment
        ceramic
Shaba Zaïre   *area*-675 18
Shabuoth
  customs   394.268 296
  Judaism   296.438
Shackelford Co. Tex.   *area*-764 734
Shade
  plants grown in
    floriculture   635.954
    s.a. spec. plants
Shades (darkness) *see* Shadows
Shades (furnishings)
  home econ.   645.3
Shadow
  boxes
    furniture arts   749.7
  theaters
    performing arts   791.5

Shadows
  tech. drawing   604.243
  spec. subj.   *s.s.*–022 1
Shafiites
  Islamic sects   297.812
    doctrines   297.204 12
    worship   297.301 2
  s.a. other spec. aspects
Shaftesbury Dorset Eng.   *area*–423 32
Shafting
  gen. wks.
    machine eng.
      soc. & econ. aspects *see*
        Secondary industries
      tech. & mf.   621.823
      s.a. spec. appls. e.g.
        Power shovels
    other aspects see Mechanics
  marine engine auxiliaries *see*
    Engine auxiliaries
    shipbuilding
Shafts (mechanical) *see*
  Shafting
Shafts (passages)
  underground mining   622.25
    spec. deposits   622.33–.39
Shaft-sinking
  underground mining   622.25
    spec. deposits   622.33–.39
Shagbarks
  agriculture   634.527
  other aspects see Hickory
    nuts
Shah Jahan India hist.   954.025 7
  s.a. spec. events & subj.
    e.g. Commerce
Shahada
  Islamic moral theology   297.51
Shahs *see* Monarchs
Shaker
  church bldgs.
    architecture   726.589 8
    building   690.658 98
    other aspects see
      Religious-purpose
      bldgs.
  church music
    arts   783.026 98
      recordings   789.912 302 698
    s.a. spec. instruments;
     also spec. kinds e.g.
      Liturgical music
  religion
    pub. worship   264.098 02
    significance   246.7
Shakers   289.8
  biog. & work   289.809 2
  Christian life guides   248.489 8
  doctrines   230.98
    creeds   238.98

Shakers (continued)
  govt. & admin.   262.098
    parishes   254.098
    missions   266.98
  moral theology   241.049 8
  private prayers for   242.809 8
  pub. worship   264.098
  rel. associations
    adults   267.189 8
    men   267.249 8
    women   267.449 8
    young adults   267.629 8
  rel. instruction   268.898
  rel. law   262.989 8
  schools   377.898
  secondary training   207.129 8
  sermons   252.098
  theological seminaries   207.119 8
  s.a.   *pers.*–288
  s.a. other spec. aspects
Shakes
  wood roofing   695
Shakespeare
  William English drama   822.33
Shaktaism
  Hinduism   294.551 4
    misc. aspects see Hinduism
Shale oils
  comm. proc.   665.4
  soc. & econ. aspects *see*
    Secondary industries
  other aspects see Petroleum
Shales *see* Sedimentary rocks
Shallots *see* Alliaceous plants
Shallu
  agriculture
    food crops   633.174 7
    forage crops   633.257 47
  other aspects see Sorghums
Shan
  language
    linguistics   495.919
    literature   895.919
    s.a.   *lang.*–959 19
  people   *r.e.n.*–959 1
  s.a. other spec. subj. e.g.
    Arts
Shang dynasty China hist.   931.02
  s.a. spec. events & subj.
    e.g. Commerce
Shanghai China   *area*–511 32
Shanklin Isle of Wight Eng.
                area–422 85
Shanmukaism
  Hinduism   294.551 6
    misc. aspects see Hinduism
Shannon Co.
  Missouri   *area*–778 873
  South Dakota   *area*–783 66
Shansi China   *area*–511 7

Shantung
  province China   *area*–511 4
  textile *see* Wild silk
Shap Fell Cumbria Eng.   *area*–427 86
Shape
  celestial bodies *see*
        Constants celestial
        bodies
  crystals   548.12
    s.a. spec. substances
    s.a. other spec. subj.
Shaped charges
  mil. eng.
    soc. & econ. aspects *see*
        Secondary industries
    tech. & mf.   623.454 5
Shapers
  soc. & econ. aspects *see*
        Secondary industries
  tech. & mf.   621.912
    s.a. spec. appls. e.g.
        Cabinets (furniture)
        mf. tech.
Shaping
  metals
    arts
      decorative   739.14
      s.a. spec. metals; also
        spec. prod. e.g.
        Jewelry
      fine *see* Direct-metal
        sculpture
    other aspects see Metals
      products
  s.a. other spec. subj.
Share rental
  land econ.   333.563
Sharecroppers
  land econ.   333.563
  soc. & ethical aspects *see*
        Agricultural classes
Shareholders' meetings
  law   346.066 6
  spec. jur.   346.3–.9
Sharjah   *area*–535 7
Sharkey Co. Miss.   *area*–762 414
Sharks *see* Selachii
Sharkskin fabrics *see*
    Dobby-weave fabrics
Sharp Co. Ark.   *area*–767 23
Sharpsburg Battle
  U.S. Civil War hist.   973.733 6
Sharpshooters
  armed forces   356.162
Sharqiya Egypt   *area*–621
Shasta
  Co. Calif.   *area*–794 24
  Mt. Calif.   *area*–794 21
Shastri admin. India hist.   954.043
    s.a. spec. events & subj.
      e.g. Commerce

Shaunavon Sask.   *area*–712 43
Shavers
  manufacturing
    soc. & econ. aspects *see*
        Secondary industries
    technology   688.5
Shaving
  soc. customs   391.5
  technology   646.724
Shavings
  wood
    mf. tech.   674.84
    other aspects see Wood
      products
Shawano Co. Wis.   *area*–775 36
Shawnee Co. Kan.   *area*–781 63
Shear modulus
  engineering *see* Dynamics
  physics   531.381
Shearing
  animal husbandry   636.083 3
    s.a. spec. animals
  resistance to
    eng. materials   620.112 45
    spec. properties   620.112 5–.112 6
    s.a. spec. materials &
      spec. uses
  textiles *see* Finishing
    textiles
Shearing-stresses *see* Stresses
Shears
  clothing constuction
    domestic   646.19
  other aspects see
      Cutting-tools
Shearwaters *see*
    Procellariiformes
Sheaves
  combinatorial topology 514.224
    s.a. spec. appls. e.g.
      Engineering
Sheboygan Co. Wis.   *area*–775 69
Sheep
  animal husbandry   636.3
    soc. & econ. aspects *see*
      Primary industries
  products
    dairy *see* Dairy products
    meats *see* Mutton
    other prod. see spec. prod.
      e.g. Sheep's wool
  other aspects see Bovoidea
Sheepdogs
  animal husbandry   636.73
  other aspects see Dogs
Sheep's
  milk
    dairy tech.   637.17

Sheep's (continued)
  wool
    textiles
      arts   746.043 1
        s.a. spec. proc. e.g.
          Weaving
      dyeing   667.331
      manufacturing
        soc. & econ. aspects
          see Secondary
            industries
      technology   677.31
        special-process
          fabrics   677.6
      other aspects see Textiles
    s.a. spec. prod.
Sheet lightning *see* Disruptive
            discharge
Sheeting
  rubber
    manufacturing
      soc. & econ. apsects *see*
        Secondary industries
    technology   678.36
    s.a. spec. kinds of rubber
      e.g. Natural rubber
    s.a. other spec. kinds
Sheets
  bedclothing *see* Bedclothing
  rolled metal prod.
    mf. tech.   671.82
      ferrous metals   672.82
      s.a. other spec. metals
    other aspects see Primary
            metal prod.
Sheffield South Yorkshire Eng.
            area–428 21
Shefford Co. Que.   *area*–714 63
Shelburne Co. N.S.   *area*–716 25
Shelby Co.
  Alabama   *area*–761 79
  Illinois   *area*–773 798
  Indiana   *area*–772 59
  Iowa   *area*–777 484
  Kentucky   *area*–769 435
  Missouri   *area*–778 323
  Ohio   *area*–771 45
  Tennessee   *area*–768 19
  Texas   *area*–764 179
Sheldon theory
  indiv. psych.   155.264
Shelf ice
  physical geol.   551.342
Shelf West Yorkshire Eng.   *area*–428 17
Shelikof Strait *see* Alaskan
            Pacific seawaters
Shell
  carving
    dec. arts   736.6
    rel. significance
      Christianity   247.866

Shell
  carving
    rel. significance (continued)
      comp. rel.   291.37
      s.a. other spec. rel.
  model
    nuclear structure
      physics   539.743
      spec. states of matter   530.4
      s.a. spec. physical
            phenomena e.g. Heat
  parakeets *see* Budgerigars
  shock *see* War neuroses
Shellac plastics *see* Natural
            resin-derived plastics
Shellacs
  manufacturing
    soc. & econ. aspects *see*
            Secondary industries
    technology   667.79
Shellfish
  food *see* Seafoods
Shelling
  crops
    agriculture   631.56
    s.a. spec. crops
Shells (ammunition)
  artillery *see* Artillery
            projectiles
  small arms
    mil. eng.
      soc. & econ. aspects *see*
            Secondary industries
      tech. & mf.   623.455
Shells (mollusks)
  handicrafts   745.55
  spec. objects   745.59
  other aspects see Mollusca
Shells (structural element)
  structural eng.
    gen. wks.   624.177 62
    concretes   624.183 462
    s.a. other spec.
            materials
  naval arch.   623.817 762
  s.a. other spec. appls.
Shelter (housing) *see* Housing
Shelter Isl. N.Y.   *area*–747 25
Sheltered employment
  law *see* Welfare services law
  soc. welfare
    aged people   362.64
    s.a. other spec. groups
      e.g. Veterans
Shelving
  furniture *see* Cabinets
            (furniture)
  library bldgs.   022.4
Shenandoah
  Co. Va.   *area*–755 95
  Nat. Park Va.   *area*–755 9

Shenandoah (continued)
  Valley Va.   *area*–755 9
Shensi China   *area*–514 3
Shepherd dogs
  animal husbandry   636.73
  other aspects see Dogs
Shepherdia argentea *see* Buffalo
      berries
Shepparton Vic.   *area*–945 4
Sheppey Isle Kent Eng.   *area*–422 33
Shepshed Leicestershire Eng.
             area–425 47
Shepton Mallet Somerset Eng.
             area–423 83
Shepway Kent Eng.   *area*–422 395
Sherbets
  food   641.374
    cookery   641.863
  prod. tech.   637.4
    soc. & econ. aspects *see*
      Secondary industries
Sherborne Dorset Eng.   *area*–423 31
Sherbrooke Co. Que.   *area*–714 66
Sherburne Co. Minn.   *area*–776 66
Sheridan Co.
  Kansas   *area*–781 145
  Montana   *area*–786 218
  Nebraska   *area*–782 92
  North Dakota   *area*–784 76
  Wyoming   *area*–787 32
Sheriff Court
  Scotland
    law   347.411 021
Sheriff-Principal Court
  Scotland
    law   347.411 032
Sheriffs
  law *see* Court officials law
  occupational ethics   174.3
  police services   363.282
    pub. admin. *see* Law
      enforcement pub. admin.
  s.a.   *pers.*–349
  s.a. Police personnel
Sheringham Norfolk Eng. *area*–426 12
Sherman Co.
  Kansas   *area*–781 115
  Nebraska   *area*–782 44
  Oregon   *area*–795 64
  Texas   *area*–764 813
Sherman's march to the sea
  U.S. Civil War hist.   973.737 8
Sherwood Forest Nottinghamshire
      Eng.   *area*–425 24
Shetland
  Isls. Scot.   *area*–411 35
  pony
    animal husbandry   636.16
    other aspects see Horses
  sheepdog
    animal husbandry   636.73

Shetland
  sheepdog (continued)
    other aspects see Dogs
Sheyenne River N.D.   *area*–784 3
Shi Tzu
  animal husbandry   636.76
  other aspects see Dogs
Shiawassee Co. Mich.   *area*–774 25
Shielding
  nuclear reactors   621.483 23
  s.a. spec. appls. e.g.
      Military engineering
  s.a. other spec. subj.
Shields (armor)
  art metalwork   739.752
  other aspects see Defensive
      arms
Shields (protection)
  clothing *see* Notions clothing
  other appls. see Safety
    equipment
Shifnal Salop Eng.   *area*–424 59
Shifts *see* Underwear
Shiga Japan   *area*–521 8
Shigella diseases *see* Bacillary
    dysentery
Shiites
  Islamic sects   297.82
    doctrines   297.204 2
    Hadith   297.124 8
    worship   297.302
    s.a. other spec. aspects
Shikoku Japan   *area*–523
Shildon Durham Eng.   *area*–428 62
Shiloh Battle
  U.S. Civil War hist.   973.732
Shimane Japan   *area*–521 9
Shin Loch Highland Scot. *area*–411 65
Shina language *see* Dard
    languages
Shingles
  wood roofing   695
Shingles (disease)
  gen. med.   616.522
  geriatrics   618.976 522
  pediatrics   618.925 22
  pub. health   614.595 22
  statistics   312.352 2
  other aspects see Diseases
Shintoism
  art representation   704.948 995 61
  s.a. spec. art forms
  calendars   529.329 561
  cookery   641.567 956 1
  philosophy   181.095 61
  regions   *area*–176 956 1
  religion   299.561
  rel. holidays   394.268 299 561
  schools   377.995 61

Shintoist
  music *see* Shintoist sacred
      music
  sacred music
    arts   783.029 956 1
      recordings   789.912 302 995 61
      s.a. spec. instruments;
        also spec. kinds e.g.
          Liturgical music
    religion
      pub. worship   299.561 38
      significance   299.561 37
    temples & shrines
      architecture   726.195 61
      building   690.619 561
      rel. significance   299.561 35
      other aspects see
        Religious-purpose
        bldgs.
Shintoists
  biog. & work   299.561 092
  s.a. spec. kinds e.g.
    Clergy
  s.a.   *pers.*–299 56
Shinyanga Tanzania   *area*–678 27
Ship
  canals
    technology   627.137
      construction details   627.131–.136
    transportation
      interoceanic canals *see*
        Interoceanic canals
        transportation
      law *see* Inland-waterway
        transp.
      noninteroceanic canals   386.47
        govt. control   351.876 47
          spec. jur.   353–354
  canneries *see* Factory ships
  disasters   363.123
  misc. aspects see
    Transportation
    accidents
  flags *see* Flags
  railways
    engineering
      technology   625.39
      other aspects see
        Railroads
    transportation   385.77
      govt. control   350.875 77
        central govts.   351.875 77
          spec. jur.   353–354
        local govts.   352.915 77
      law *see* Railroad
        transportation law
Shipboard
  cookery   641.575 3
  hygiene   613.68
Shipbuilding *see* Vessels
    (nautical) engineering

Shipfitting
  soc. & econ. aspects *see*
    Secondary industries
  technology   623.843 3
Shiplap
  wooden
    manufacturing
      soc. & econ. apsects *see*
        Secondary industries
      technology   674.43
Shipley West Yorkshire Eng.
                              area–428 17
Shipping operations
  materials management   658.788
    spec. subj.   *s.s.*–068 7
  s.a. Transportation
Ships *see* Vessels (nautical)
Ships' stores   359.341
  s.a. spec. naval branches
Ships-in-bottles
  handicrafts   745.592 8
Shipston-on-Stour Warwickshire
    Eng.   *area*–424 89
Ship-timber beetles *see*
    Mordelloidea
Ship-to-shore commun.
  commerce *see* Radiotelephony
  port services   387.166
    govt. control   350.877 166
      central govts.   351.877 166
        spec. jur.   353–354
      local govts.   352.918 166
    law *see* Seaports law
      transp.
    traffic control *see* Traffic
      control
Shipworms *see* Pelecypoda
Shipwrecks
  travel   910.453
    misc. aspects see Travel
Shipwrights' work
  soc. & econ. aspects *see*
    Secondary industries
  technology   623.844
Shipyard bldgs. *see* Industrial
      buildings
Shipyards
  soc. & econ. aspects *see*
    Secondary industries
  technology   623.83
Shire horses
  animal husbandry   636.15
  other aspects see Horses
Shirts
  comm. mf.   687.115
    children's   687.13
  domestic mf.   646.435
  soc. customs   391.1–.3
  other aspects see Clothing

Shivaism
  Hinduism   294.551 3
    misc. aspects see Hinduism
Shizuoka Japan   *area*–521 6
Shkhauri language *see* South
    Arabic languages
Shoa Ethiopia   *area*–633
Shoalhaven
  National Park N.S.W.   *area*–944 7
  River N.S.W.   *area*–944 7
Shock
  absorbers
    automobiles
      soc. & econ. aspects *see*
        Secondary industries
      tech. & mf.   629.243
        s.a. spec. appls.
        s.a. other spec. appls.
    resistance
      materials   620.112 5
        s.a. spec. materials &
          spec. uses
    tunnels
      aircraft eng.   629.134 52
        s.a. spec. appls. e.g.
          Military engineering
    waves *see* Waves
Shock (convulsions)
  therapy
    psychiatry   616.891 2
      geriatrics   618.976 891 2
      pediatrics   618.928 912
    other aspects see Medical
      sciences
Shock (pathological)
  first aid *see* First aid
  surgical trmt.   617.21
    s.a. Veterinary sciences
Shock-resistant construction
  buildings   693.85
  shipbuilding
    soc. & econ. aspects *see*
      Secondary industries
    technology   623.848
Shoe
  buckles
    precious metalwork   739.278
    other aspects see Jewelry
  repairmen
    biog. & work   685.310 409 2
    s.a.   *pers.*–685 3
Shoeburyness Essex Eng.   *area*–426 795
Shoemakers
  biog. & work   685.310 092
    s.a.   *pers.*–685 3
Shoes
  mf. tech.   685.31
    other aspects see Footwear
Shogi *see* Japanese chess

Shooting
  sports
    game   799.21
    other   799.3
    other aspects see Sports
Shop (plant)
  technology   670.42
    s.a. spec. prod. of mf.
  training
    special ed.   371.904 4
      s.a. spec. groups of
        students
Shop (retail trade)
  buildings *see* Retail trade
    buildings
  etiquette   395.53
  sanitation *see* Industrial
    sanitation
Shoplifting *see* Larceny
Shopping
  center bldgs. *see* Retail
    trade buildings
  centers
    civic art   711.552 2
  guides *see* Consumer education
Shoran
  radar engineering   621.384 893
    s.a. spec. appls. e.g.
      Military engineering
  other aspects see Radar
Shore
  biology   574.909 46
    aquatic   574.92
    nonaquatic   574.909 46
    s.a. spec. organisms
  birds *see* Charadriiformes
  flies *see* Cyclorrhapha
  reclamation eng.
    soc. & econ. aspects *see*
      Secondary industries
    technology   627.58
      s.a. spec. appls. e.g.
        Landscape architecture
    other aspects see Liquids
      engineering
Shoreditch London Eng.   *area*–421 44
Shoreham-by-Sea West Sussex Eng.
                             area–422 69
Shorelands
  geomorphology   551.45
  reclamation *see* Shore
    reclamation
  regional subj. trmt.   *area*–146
  resources
    economics   333.917
      recreational   333.784
    govt. control
      law   346.046 917
        spec. jur.   346.3–.9

Shorelands
  resources
    govt. control (continued)
      pub. admin. *see* Land
        resources govt. control
        pub. admin.
Shorelines
  geomorphology   551.458
  other aspects see Shorelands
Shores *see* Shorelands
Shoring
  foundation eng. *see*
    Excavation foundation
    eng.
Short
  cuts
    arithmetic   513.92
    other subj.   *s.s.*–028
  stories
    gen. wks.
      collections   808.831
      hist. & crit.   809.31
      rhetoric   808.31
      juvenile   808.068 31
    spec. lits.   *lit. sub.*–301
      indiv. authors   *lit. sub.*–31–39
    other aspects see Fiction
  s.a. other spec. subj.
Shortages
  natural resources   333.711
    s.a. spec. kinds of
      resources e.g.
      Shorelands
  primary prod.
    agricultural   338.15
    mineral   338.27
    other   338.37
  prod. econ. *see*
    Maladjustments prod.
    econ.
  secondary prod.   338.47
Shortenings *see* Fats
Short-haired
  domestic cats
    animal husbandry   636.82
    other aspects see Cats
    s.a. other spec. animals
Shorthand   653
Shorthorn cattle
  animal husbandry   636.222
  other aspects see Cattle
Shortland Isls.   *area*–935
Short-order cookery   641.57
Short-range
  surface-to-surface guided
    missiles
  mil. eng.
    soc. & econ. aspects *see*
      Secondary industries
    tech. & mf.   623.451 952

Short-range (continued)
  weather forecasting   551.636 2
    spec. areas   551.65
    spec. elements   551.64
    s.a. spec. methods e.g.
      Radar
    s.a. other spec. subj.
Short-takeoff-&-landing airplanes
  aeronautical eng.
    gen. tech. & mf.   629.133 340 426
      components & techniques 629.134
      models   629.133 134 042 6
      operation   629.132 524 042 6
    s.a. spec. kinds e.g. Jet
      planes
    soc. & econ. aspects *see*
      Secondary industries
    s.a. spec. appls. e.g. Air
      transportation
  commerce   387.733 404 26
    misc. aspects see Aircraft
      commerce
Short-term
  capital *see* Working capital
  loans
    capital *see* Working capital
  securities
    pub. finance   336.32
Short-wave
  electronics
    astrophysics   523.018 753 43
      s.a. spec. celestial
      bodies
    physics   537.534 3
      spec. states of matter 530.4
    other aspects see Radiowave
      electronics
  systems
    radio
      engineering   621.384 151
      military   623.734 1
      nautical   623.856 41
      s.a. spec. appls. e.g.
      Radiotelephony
    other aspects see Radio
Shoshone Co. Ida.   *area*–796 91
Shotguns
  hunting & shooting sports   799.202 834
    game   799.213
    targets   799.31
  small arms
    mf. tech.   683.426
    other aspects see Small
      arms
Shot-peening *see* Hardening
    metal products
Shot-putting *see* Throwing
Shoulder
  belts *see* Safety equipment
  blades *see* Upper extremities
    bones

Shoulders
  diseases
    regional med. trmt.   617.572
      s.a. spec. systems &
        organs
    surgery   617.572
      anesthesiology   617.967 572
    other aspects see Diseases
  fractures   617.157
  muscles
    human anatomy   611.737
    other aspects see Muscles
  orthopedic surgery   617.397
Shoulders (highways)
  road maintenance
    technology   625.761
    other aspects see Roads
Shovels
  power *see* Power shovels
Show
  jumping horsemanship   798.250 79
Shōwa period
  Japan hist.
    early   952.033
    later   952.04
  s.a. spec. events & subj.
    e.g. Courts
Showboats
  performing arts   792.022
Showcase displays
  advertising operations   659.157
Showering
  personal care   646.71
Shows
  advertising operations   659.152
  animal husbandry for   636.088 8
    s.a. spec. animals
  s.a. Public performances
Shrapnel devices
  mil. eng.
    soc. & econ. aspects *see*
        Secondary industries
    tech. & mf.   623.451 4
Shrews *see* Insectivora
Shrewsbury & Atcham Salop Eng.
        area–424 54
Shrikes *see* Laniidae
Shrike-vireos
  zoology   598.8
  other aspects see
        Passeriformes
Shrimps
  food   641.395
  other aspects see Natantia
Shrines
  architecture   726.1
  building   690.61
  rel. significance
    comp. rel.   291.35
    s.a. spec. rel.

Shrines (continued)
  rel. worship *see* Sacred
        places rel. worship
  other aspects see
        Religious-purpose
        bldgs.
Shrinkage-controlled fabrics
  manufacturing
    soc. & econ. aspects *see*
        Secondary industries
    technology   677.688
    other aspects see Textiles
    s.a. spec. prod.
Shrink-proofing textiles *see*
        Finishing textiles
Shropshire Eng.   *area*–424 5
Shrove Tuesday *see* Mardi gras
Shrubs
  botany   582.17
  floriculture   635.976
  landscape design   715.3
  other aspects see
        Spermatophyta
  s.a. spec. plants
Shuffleboard
  equip. mf.   688.762
    soc. & econ. aspects *see*
        Secondary industries
  sports   796.2
  other aspects see Sports
Shumen Bulgaria   *area*–497 77
Shunts
  elect. measurement
    technology   621.374 2
    s.a. spec. appls. e.g.
        Ignition systems &
        devices
  other aspects see
        Electricity
Shutter & wicket dams *see*
        Movable dams
Shutters
  buildings *see* Blinds
  cameras
    photography   771.36
    gen. tech.   770.282
    spec. proc. & fields   772–778
Shuttle cars
  mining eng.   622.66
Shuttles *see spec. uses e.g.*
        Weaving
Siam
  country   *area*–593
  Gulf *see* South China Sea
Siamangs *see* Hylobatinae
Siamese
  cats
    animal husbandry   636.825
    other aspects see Cats
  language
    linguistics   495.91

Siamese
  language (continued)
    literature   895.91
    s.a.   *lang.*–959 11
    people   *r.e.n.*–959 1
    s.a. Thailand; *also other*
        spec. subj. e.g. Arts
Siberia   *area*–57
Siberian
  huskies
    animal husbandry   636.73
    other aspects see Dogs
  people *see spec. races*
  s.a. other spec. subj. e.g.
    Arts
Sibiu Romania   *area*–498 4
Sibley Co. Minn.   *area*–776 33
Siblings
  ethics *see* Family ethics
  psychology   155.443–.444
  rearing home econ.   649.143–.144
  relationships *see* Family
    relationships
  s.a.   *pers.*–045
Siblings' handbooks
  child care   649.102 45
Sibyls
  parapsychology   133.324 8
Sicily
  island   *area*–458
    ancient   *area*–378
  Strait *see* Western
    Mediterranean Sea
Sick
  animals
    services to   636.083 2
    s.a. spec. animals
  leave *see* Leaves (absence)
  people
    architectural design for 720.43
    cookery for   641.563 1
    parochial activities for
      Christianity   259.4
      other rel. see Pastoral
        theology
    recreation   790.196
      indoor   793.019 6
      outdoor   796.019 6
    soc. services *see* Health
      services soc. welfare
    treatment
      law of war   341.65
    s.a. Afflicted people;
      Mentally ill people;
      Physically sick people;
      Illness
Sickle cell anemia
  gen. med.   616.152 7
  geriatrics   618.976 152 7
  pediatrics   618.921 527
  pub. health   614.591 527

Sickle cell anemia (continued)
  statistics   312.315 27
    deaths   312.361 527
  other aspects see Diseases
Sickles *see*
    Harvesting-machinery
Sickness *see* Illness
Sidamo Ethiopia   *area*–632
Sidcup London Eng.   *area*–421 77
Side
  arms
    art metalwork   739.72
    mil. eng.
      soc. & econ. aspects *see*
        Secondary industries
      tech. & mf.   623.441
    mil. sci.   355.824 1
    s.a. spec. mil. branches
  chapels
    Christian church arch. 726.595
  effects
    drugs
      pharmacodynamics   615.704 2
    misc. aspects see
      Pharmacology
  streets *see* Streets
Sideboards *see* Cabinets
    (furniture)
Sideline markets & stores
  advertising   659.196 588 704
  pub. relations   659.296 588 704
  retail marketing   658.870 4
Sidereal
  clocks
    astronomy   522.5
    s.a. spec. celestial
      bodies
  day   529.1
  month
    moon   523.33
Siderite
  mineralogy   549.782
Side-sewing
  bookbinding   686.35
Sideshows
  circuses   791.35
Sidewalks
  road eng.
    technology   625.88
    other aspects see Streets
Sidings (railroads)
  technology   625.163
  other aspects see Permanent
    way
Sidings (walls)
  wood bldg. construction 694.2
  wooden
    manufacturing
      soc. & econ. aspects *see*
        Secondary industries
      technology   674.43

Sidmouth Devon Eng.	*area*–423 57
Sidonian architecture	722.31
misc. aspects see	
Architectural schools	
Siedlce Poland	*area*–438 4
Siege warfare	
mil. sci.	355.44
s.a. spec. mil. branches	
Siemens process	669.142 2
Siena Italy	*area*–455 8
Sienna *see* Pigment materials	
Sieradz Poland	*area*–438 4
Sierra	
County	
California	*area*–794 36
New Mexico	*area*–789 67
Leone	*area*–664
Leonean	
people	*r.e.n.*–966 4
s.a. other spec. subj. e.g.	
Arts	
Nevada Calif.	*area*–794 4
Sifakas *see* Prosimii	
Sifting	
cereal grains	
comm. proc.	664.720 4
s.a. spec. grains & prod.	
other aspects see Cereal	
grains	
Siftings	
cereal grains	
comm. proc.	664.720 8
wheat	664.722 8
s.a. other spec. grains &	
prod.	
other aspects see Cereal	
grains	
Siga Japan	*area*–521 8
Sight	
animal path.	591.218 23
med. sci.	617.7
veterinary	636.089 77
animal phys.	591.182 3
med. sci.	612.84
veterinary	636.089 284
other aspects see Sensory	
functions	
s.a. spec. animals	
Sighting apparatus	
ordnance	
soc. & econ. aspects *see*	
Secondary industries	
tech. & mf.	623.46
Sightseeing services	
transportation	
law *see* Passenger services	
law	
other aspects see Passenger	
transportation	
Sight-singing	
music	784.94

Sigillography *see* Seals	
(devices)	
Sigmoid flexure *see* Large	
intestines	
Sign language	
manual alphabet	419
study and teaching	371.912 7
s.a. Nonverbal language	
Signal	
generators	
radiowave electronics *see*	
Testing-devices	
radiowave electronics	
intensity measurement	
radio *see* Measurement radio	
television *see* Measurement	
television	
propagation	
radar engineering	621.384 81
s.a. spec. appls. e.g.	
Navigation	
other aspects see Radar	
theory	
commun. eng.	621.380 430 1
Signaling	
mil. sci. *see* Communication	
forces	
Signals	
commun. eng.	
technology	621.380 43
s.a. spec. appls. e.g.	
Military engineering	
other aspects see	
Communication	
mil. sci. *see* Communication	
forces	
railroad eng.	
technology	625.165
other aspects see Permanent	
way	
railroad transp.	
gen. wks. *see* Communication	
facilities railroads	
law *see* Stationary	
facilities railroads	
law	
road traffic controls	
road. eng.	
technology	625.794
other aspects see Roads	
transportation eng.	
technology	629.042
other aspects see	
Transportation	
engineering	
other aspects see Nonverbal	
language	
Signets	
numismatics	737.6
rel. significance	
Christianity	247.876

Signets
rel. significance (continued)
comp. rel. 291.37
s.a. other spec. rel.
Signs
advertising 659.134
painting
technology 667.9
palmistry 133.64
railroad eng.
technology 625.165
other aspects see Permanent
way
road traffic controls
road eng.
technology 625.794
other aspects see Roads
transportation eng.
technology 629.042
other aspects see
Transportation
engineering
Sikh
music *see* Sikh sacred music
sacred music
arts 783.029 46
recordings 789.912 302 946
s.a. spec. instruments;
also spec. kinds e.g.
Liturgical music
religion
pub. worship 294.638
significance 294.637
temples & shrines
architecture 726.146
building 690.614 6
rel. significance 294.635
other aspects see
Religious-purpose
bldgs.
Sikhism
art representation 704.948 946
s.a. spec. art forms
calendars 529.324 6
cookery 641.567 46
philosophy 181.046
regions *area*–176 46
religion 294.6
rel. holidays 394.268 294 6
schools 377.946
Sikhs
biog. & work 294.609 2
s.a. spec. kinds e.g.
Clergy
s.a. *pers.*–294 6
Sikkim India *area*–541 67
Sikkimese
people *r.e.n.*–914 17
s.a. other spec. subj. e.g.
Arts
Sikoku Japan *area*–523

Silage
feeds
animal husbandry 636.085 52
s.a. spec. feeds; also
spec. animals
Silencers
internal combustion engines
see Mufflers
s.a. other spec. uses
Silent
discharges
atmospheric electricity
meteorology 551.563 3
artificial modification 551.686 33
weather forecasting 551.646 33
spec. areas 551.65
s.a. other spec. subj.
Silesia *area*–438 5
Czechoslovakia *area*–437 2
Poland *area*–438 5
Silhouettes
drawing 741.7
indiv. artists 741.092
photography
technique *see* Special
effects photography
Silicates
mineralogy 549.6
other aspects see Silicon
salts
Silicides *see* Silicon salts
Silicon 553.92
chemistry
inorganic 546.683
technology 661.068 3
soc. & econ. aspects
see Secondary
industries
s.a. spec. prod.
organic 547.08
technology 661.88
misc. aspects see
Organic chemicals
s.a. spec. groupings
e.g. Aliphatic
compounds
s.a. Silicon salts
compounds
plant nutrition *see* Trace
elements plant
nutrition
other aspects see Silicon
chemistry
econ. geol. 553.92
marketing *see* Marketing
mining
prod. econ. 338.279 2
technology 622.392
prospecting 622.189 2
pharmacology
inorganic 615.268 3

Silicon
  pharmacology (continued)
    organic   615.318
    other aspects see
          Pharmacology
  salts
    chem. tech.   661.43
  toxicology
    inorganic   615.925 683
    organic   615.951 8
    other aspects see
          Toxicology
  other aspects see Nonmetallic
    elements
  s.a. spec. uses; also spec.
    minerals
Silicones
  plastics
    chem. tech.   668.422 7
    org. chem.   547.843 222 7
    other aspects see Plastics
    s.a. spec. prod.
Silicosis *see* Pneumoconiosis
Silistra Bulgaria   *area*–497 77
Silk
  books
    hist. & crit.   096.2
  textiles
    arts   746.043 9
    s.a. spec. proc. e.g.
          Weaving
    dyeing   667.339
    manufacturing
      soc. & econ. aspects *see*
          Secondary industries
      technology   677.39
        special-process fabrics 677.6
    other aspects see Textiles
    s.a. spec. prod.
Silk-cotton tree family *see*
    Tiliales
Silk-screen printing
  graphic arts *see* Serigraphy
  technology   686.231 6
    soc. & econ. aspects *see*
          Secondary industries
  textiles *see* Printing
          processes textiles
Silkworms
  culture   638.2
  other aspects see Agriculture
Silky
  flycatchers *see*
          Ptilogonatidae
  terrier
    animal husbandry   636.76
    other aspects see Dogs
Sillimanite
  mineralogy   549.62
Sills (carpentry)
  wood bldg. construction   694.2

Sills (geology)
  structural geol.   551.88
    s.a. spec. aspects e.g.
          Prospecting
Silo machinery
  agriculture   631.36
  use   631.568
    s.a. spec. crops; also spec.
      types of culture e.g.
      Floriculture
  mf. tech.   681.763 1
    soc. & econ. aspects *see*
          Secondary industries
Silos
  agriculture   631.23
    s.a. spec. crops
Silsden West Yorkshire Eng.
               area–428 17
Silt
  stream eng.
    technology   627.122
    other aspects see Liquids
      engineering
  other aspects see Sedimentary
    rocks
Silurian period
  geology   551.732
    s.a. spec. aspects e.g.
          Economic geology
  paleontology   560.172 5
    spec. fossils   561–569
Siluroidea *see* Ostariophysi
Silver
  arts *see* Silversmithing
  Bow Co. Mont.   *area*–786 68
  chemistry
    inorganic   546.654
    organic   547.056 54
    s.a. spec. groupings e.g.
      Aliphatic compounds
    technology   661.065 4
    organic   661.895
    soc. & econ. aspects *see*
      Secondary industries
    s.a. spec. prod.
  coins
    money econ.   332.404 2
    other aspects see Money
  construction
    architecture   721.044 723
    s.a. spec. kinds of
      bldgs.
    building   693.723
  letters
    books hist. & crit.   096.2
  materials
    building   691.823
    engineering   620.189 23
    s.a. spec. uses
  metallography   669.952 3

Silver (continued)
metallurgy 669.23
physical & chem. 669.962 3
soc. & econ. aspects *see*
Secondary industries
mineral aspects
econ. geol. 553.423
mineralogy 549.23
mining
technology 622.342 3
prospecting 622.184 21
s.a. spec. minerals
pharmacology 615.265 4
misc. aspects see
Pharmacology
plate *see* Silversmithing
processes
photography 772.4
products *see* Silversmithing
standard money
economics 332.422 3
other aspects see Money
toxicology 615.925 654
misc. aspects see
Toxicology
other aspects see Metal;
also Metals
Silverfish (insects)
zoology 595.713
other aspects see Apterygota
Silverpoint
drawing arts 741.25
indiv. artists 741.092
spec. appls. 741.5–.7
spec. subj. 743.4–.8
Silversmithing
arts
decorative 739.23
other aspects see Precious
metals arts
mf. tech. 673.23
other aspects see Nonferrous
metals products
Silverware
use
table setting 642.7
s.a. other spec. uses; also
Silver
Silvestrians *see* Cluniacs
Silviculture 634.95
s.a. spec. trees
Simane Japan area–521 9
Simaroubaceae *see* Rutales
Simcoe Co. Ont. area–713 17
Similarities
Euclidean geometry *see*
Euclidean geometry
Similkameen River B.C. area–711 41
Simmering
cookery tech. 641.73

Simmonds' disease *see* Pituitary
gland diseases
Simple
gas-turbine engines
soc. & econ. aspects *see*
Secondary industries
tech. & mf.
gen. wks. 621.433 2
parts & accessories 621.437
land vehicles 629.250 32
parts & systems 629.252–.258
marine vehicles 623.872 332
s.a. other spec. appls.
machines
mechanics 531.8
microscopes
physics 535.332 2
spec. states of matter 530.4
use
biology 578.42
chem. anal. *see*
Microscopic analysis
gen. sci. 502.822
s.a. other spec. appls.
oxides
mineralogy 549.52
proteins
org. chem. 547.752
other aspects see Proteins
salts metals
chemistry
inorganic 546.342
spec. kinds 546.38–.68
other aspects see Metals
chemistry
pharmacology 615.234 2
misc. aspects see
Pharmacology
toxicology 615.925 342
misc. aspects see
Toxicology
steam engines *see*
Reciprocating engines
steam
s.a. other spec. subj.
Simples
pharmacognosy 615.321
misc. aspects see
Pharmacology
Simplex telegraphy *see*
Acoustical systems wire
telegraphy
Simplexes
combinatorial topology 514.223
s.a. spec. appls. e.g.
Engineering
Simplification
management 658.406
s.a. other spec. subj.

Singleton N.S.W.   *area*–944 2
Single-wicket cricket   796.358 8
Single-wing back formation
   American football   796.332 22
Sinhalese
   language
     linguistics   491.48
     literature   891.48
     s.a.   *lang.*–914 8
   people   *r.e.n.*–914 8
   s.a. other spec. subj. e.g.
      Arts
Sink-float concentration
   ores *see* Gravity
      concentration ores
Sinkiang-Uighur Autonomous Region
      China   *area*–516
Sinking funds
   pub. finance   336.363
   misc. aspects see Public
      borrowing
Sino-Japanese
   conflict 1937-45   940.53
     1937-41   951.042
     1941-45   940.53
   War 1894-1895   952.031
Sinop Turkey   *area*–563
Sino-Tibetan languages
   linguistics   495
   literature   895
   s.a.   *lang.*–95
Sins
   moral theology
     Christianity   241.3
     other rel. see Moral
      theology
   s.a. Sin
Sintering
   metal products
     mf. tech.   671.373
      ferrous metals   672.373
      s.a. other spec. metals
     other aspects see
      Mechanical working
Sinuses *see* Nasal sinuses
Sinusitis *see* Nasal sinuses
      diseases
Siouan *see* Hokan-Siouan
Sioux
   City Ia.   *area*–777 41
   County
     Iowa   *area*–777 13
     Nebraska   *area*–782 99
     North Dakota   *area*–784 88
   Falls S.D.   *area*–783 371
   lang. & people *see*
      Hokan-Siouan
Siphonales *see* Chlorophyta
Siphonaptera
   culture   638.577 5
   paleozoology   565.77

Siphonaptera (continued)
   zoology   595.775
   other aspects see Insecta
Siphonophora *see* Hydrozoa
Siphunculata *see* Anoplura
Sir Edward Pellew Group N. Ter.
      Aust.   *area*–942 95
Sirach
   deuterocanonical book   229.4
   other aspects see Apocrypha
Siracusa Sicily   *area*–458 14
Sirenia
   animal husbandry   636.955
   hunting
     commercial   639.115 5
     sports   799.259 55
   paleozoology   569.5
   zoology   599.55
   other aspects see Mammalia
Sirocco *see* Local wind systems
Sirups (drugs)
   prac. pharm.   615.42
     misc. aspects see
      Pharmacology
Sirups (food)   641.336
   manufacturing
     soc. & econ. aspects *see*
      Secondary industries
     technology   664.1
Sisal *see* Agave fibers
Siskiyou
   Co. Calif.   *area*–794 21
   Mountains   *area*–795 25
Sistan Iran   *area*–558 3
Sisterhoods *see* Religious
      congregations
Sisters
   of Bon Secours
     convent bldgs.
      architecture   726.779 4
      building   690.677 94
     other aspects see
      Religious-purpose
      bldgs.
     rel. orders   255.94
      church hist.   271.94
      ecclesiology   262.24
   of Charity
     convent bldgs.
      architecture   726.779 1
      building   690.677 91
     other aspects see
      Religous-purpose bldgs.
     rel. orders   255.91
      church hist.   271.91
      ecclesiology   262.24
   of Mercy
     convent bldgs.
      architecture   726.779 2
      building   690.677 92

Sisters
  of Mercy
    convent bldgs. (continued)
      other aspects see
        Religious-purpose
        bldgs.
      rel. orders   255.92
      church hist.   271.92
      ecclesiology   262.24
Sisters (nuns) *see* Nuns
Sisters (siblings) *see* Siblings
Sitars *see* Lutes
Sit-down strikes
  labor econ.   331.892 6
Sites
  homes   643.12
  library bldgs.   022.1
  museum bldgs.   069.21
  s.a. other spec. subj.
Sitka election district Alaska
                        area–798 2
Sittidae
  hunting
    commercial   639.128 822
    sports   799.248 822
  paleozoology   568.8
  zoology   598.822
  other aspects see Aves
Sitting rooms *see* Living rooms
Sittingbourne Kent Eng.   *area*–422 33
Situational influences
  psychology   155.93
Sivas Turkey   *area*–565
Siwi language *see* Berber
                languages
Six Days' War 1967   956.046
Six-man football
  equipment mf.   688.763 328
    soc. & econ. aspects *see*
        Secondary industries
  sports   796.332 8
  other aspects see Sports
Sixteen soldiers
  equip. mf.   688.742
    soc. & econ. aspects *see*
        Secondary industries
  recreation   794.2
Sixteenth century
  history   909.5
    appls. to spec. subj.   *s.s.*–090 31
  s.a. spec. countries
Sixth
  century
    history   909.1
      appls. to spec. subj. *s.s.*–090 21
    s.a. spec. countries
  forms
    secondary ed.   373.238
    govt. supervision & support 379

Size
  city planning
    arts   711.43
  of celestial bodies *see*
        Constants celestial
        bodies
  of enterprise
    prod. econ.   338.64
      prod. cost   338.514 4
    spec. industries *see*
        Efficiency prod. econ.
  of nuclei *see* Nuclei
  of particles *see* Particles
        (matter)
  of rays *see* Rays (beams)
  paper *see* Finishing paper
  standards
    metrology   389.62
      misc. aspects see
        Standardization
        metrology
    prod. management *see*
        Quality controls prod.
        management
  s.a. other spec. subj.
Sizing
  coal
    fuel tech.   662.623
  ore
    mining eng.   622.74
    spec. ores   622.33–.39
  s.a. other spec. subj.
Sizuoka Japan   *area*–521 6
Skagerrak *see* North Sea
Skagit Co. Wash.   *area*–797 72
Skagway-Yakutat election district
              Alaska   *area*–798 2
Skamania Co. Wash.   *area*–797 84
Skanderborg Denmark   *area*–489 5
Skaneatales Lake N.Y.   *area*–747 65
Skaraborg Sweden   *area*–486
Skateboarding
  sports   796.21
  other aspects see Sports
Skateboards
  mf. tech.   685.362
Skates (fishes) *see* Batoidea
Skates (footwear)
  mf. tech.   685.361–.362
  other aspects see Footwear
Skating
  ice
    equipment
      manufacturing
        soc. & econ. aspects
        see Secondary
        industries
      technology   688.769 1
    sports   796.91
    other aspects see Sports

Skating (continued)
roller
  sports   796.21
  other aspects see Sports
Skeet
shooters
  biog. & work   799.313
  s.a.   *pers.*–799 3
shooting
  sports   799.313
  other aspects see Sports
Skegness Lincolnshire Eng. *area*–425 32
Skeletal
muscle tissues
  human anatomy & phys.   611.018 6
  other aspects see Tissue
    biology
organs
  anatomy
    med. sci.   611.71
      animals   636.089 171
      man   611.71
    zoology   591.47
  pathology
    zoology
      anatomical   591.227
      physiological   591.218 52
  physiology
    med. sci.   612.75
      animals   636.089 275
      man   612.75
    zoology   591.185 2
  s.a. spec. animals; also
    Bones
system *see* Skeletal organs
Skeletons
specimen preparation
  life sci.   579.1
other aspects see Skeletal
    organs
Skelmersdale & Holland Lancashire
    Eng.   *area*–427 612
Skelton & Brotton Cleveland Eng.
    area–428 54
Skeptic philosophy
ancient   186
Skepticism
nat. rel.   211.7
philosophy   149.73
indiv. phil.   180–190
  s.a. spec. branches of phil.
    e.g. Metaphysics
Sketching
arts *see* Drawing
    (delineating)
topography mil. eng.   623.71
Skew bevel gears
machine eng.
  soc. & econ. aspects *see*
    Secondary industries

Skew bevel gears
machine eng. (continued)
  tech. & mf.   621.833 2
  s.a. spec. appls. e.g.
    Differentials
  other aspects see Mechanics
Ski
tows *see* Telpherage
troops
  armed forces   356.164
Skidaway Isl. Ga.   *area*–758 724
Skidday Cumbria Eng.   *area*–427 87
Skierniewice Poland   *area*–438 4
Skiers
biog. & work   796.930 92
s.a.   *pers.*–796 9
s.a. Water skiers
Skiffs *see* Hand-propelled
    vessels
Skiing
accidents *see* Recreation
    accidents
equipment mf.   688.769 3
  soc. & econ. aspects *see*
    Secondary industries
sports   796.93
other aspects see Sports
s.a. Water skiing
Skilled workers
labor econ.   331.794
  labor force   331.114 22
  other aspects see
    Industrial occupations
labor law *see* Labor law
other aspects see Laboring
    classes
Skillets
electric cookery   641.586
  s.a. spec. situations,
    materials, tech.
Skim milk
dairy tech.   637.147
other aspects see Milk
Skimmers (birds) *see* Lari
Skimming
sewage trmt.
  technology   628.34
  other aspects see Sewage
Skin
diseases
  surgery   617.477
    anesthesiology   617.967 477
  other aspects see Diseases
drugs affecting
  pharmacodynamics   615.778
  other aspects see Drugs
personal care   646.726
other aspects see Integument
Skin-diving
sports   797.23
other aspects see Sports

Skinner system
  psychology   150.194 34
    s.a. spec. subj. & branches
        of psych.
Skipper flies *see* Cyclorrhapha
Skippers (insects) *see*
        Hesperioidea
Skips
  mining eng.   622.68
Skipton North Yorkshire Eng.
             area–428 41
Skirmishing
  mil. sci.   355.422
    s.a. spec. mil. branches
Skirts
  comm. mf.   687.117
    children's   687.13
    women's   687.12
  domestic mf.   646.437
  soc. customs   391.1–.3
  other aspects see Clothing
Skis
  mf. tech.   685.364
  other aspects see Footwear
Skittles *see* Bowling (game)
Skull
  anatomy
    human   611.715
    other aspects see Skeletal
          organs
  diseases
    surgery   617.514
      anesthesiology   617.967 514
    other aspects see Bones
         diseases
    fractures   617.155
    orthopedic surgery   617.371
    physical anthropometry 573.671 5
  physiology
    human   612.75
    other aspects see Movements
  tissue biology human 611.018 971 5
Skunk River Ia.   *area*–777 9
Skunks *see* Mustelidae
Skutterudite
  mineralogy   549.32
Sky
  art representation   704.949 52
    s.a. spec. art forms
  color
    meteorology *see* Absorption
        atmospheric optical
        phenomena
  rel. worship
    comp. rel.   291.212
    s.a. spec. rel.
Skydivers
  biog. & work   797.560 92
  s.a.   *pers.*–797 5
Skydiving
  sports   797.56

Skydiving (continued)
  other aspects see Sports
Skye and Lochalsh Highland Scot.
             area–411 82
Skylights *see* Roofs
Skyscrapers
  arch. construction   721.042
    s.a. spec. kinds of bldgs.
Slabs
  structural eng.
    gen. wks.   624.177 2
    concretes   624.183 42
    s.a. other spec.
      materials
    naval arch.   623.817 72
    s.a. other spec. appls.
Slacks *see* Trousers
Slags
  metallurgical furnaces 669.84
    s.a. spec. metals
Slander *see* Defamation
Slang   410
  spec. langs.   *lang. sub.*–7
  spec. subj.   *s.s.*–014
Slate roofing
  bldg. construction   695
Slates   553.54
  econ. geol.   553.54
  materials *see* Natural stones
  mining
    soc. & econ. aspects *see*
        Primary industries
    technology   622.354
    prospecting   622.185 4
  other aspects see Metamorphic
        rocks
  s.a. spec. uses
Slaughterhouses
  meat proc.   664.902 9
Slave
  kings
    India hist.   954.023 2
    s.a. spec. events & subj.
        e.g. Commerce
  labor
    labor econ.   331.117 34
    s.a. spec. classes of
        labor e.g. Women
  trade
    commerce   380.144
    s.a. spec. kinds of
        commerce e.g.
        International commerce
  law
    international   341.77
    municipal
      criminal   345.025
        spec. jur.   345.3–.9
      gen. wks.   343.085 4
        spec. jur.   343.3–.9

Slavery
ethics
    philosophy   177.5
    religion
        Buddhism   294.356 75
        Christianity   241.675
        comp. rel.   291.567 5
        Hinduism   294.548 675
        s.a. other spec. rel.
pol. sci.   326
sociology   306.3
Slaves
customs   390.25
    dress   391.025
    homes   392.360 25
law   346.013
    spec. jur.   346.3-.9
other aspects see Lower
        classes
s.a.   *pers.*-062 5
Slavic
languages
    linguistics   491.8
    literatures   891.8
    s.a.   *lang.*-918
people   *r.e.n.*-918
sculpture
    ancient   732.6
    later   730.94
s.a. other spec. subj. e.g.
    Arts
Slavonia   *area*-497 2
Slavs   *r.e.n.*-918
Sleaford Lincolnshire Eng.   *area*-425 35
Sledding *see* Coasting snow
    sports
Sleep
disturbances
    symptomatology
        neurological diseases   616.849
        vet. sci.   636.089 684 9
        s.a. spec. animals
human phys.   612.821
hygiene   613.79
    misc. aspects see Hygiene
psychology   154.62
    animals   156.4
other aspects see Nervous
    functions
Sleeper services
transp. systems
    law *see* Passenger services
        law
    other aspects see Passenger
        transportation
Sleepers (clothes) *see*
    Nightclothes
Sleepers (ties)
technology   625.143
other aspects see Permanent
    way

Sleeping
bags *see* Camping equipment
cars *see* Passenger-train cars
garments *see* Nightclothes
Sleepwear *see* Nightclothes
Sleet *see* Solid amorphous
    precipitation
Sleighing *see* Snow sports
Sleight-of-hand artists *see*
    Magicians (conjurers)
Slenderizing
personal care   646.75
Sleuth dogs
animal husbandry   636.753
other aspects see Dogs
Slicers *see* Cutting-tools
Slide
fasteners
    clothing *see* Notions
        clothing
preparation
    microscopy life sci.   578.6
        animal tissues   578.9
        plant tissues   578.8
rules
    manufacturing
        soc. & econ. aspects *see*
            Secondary industries
        technology   681.14
    mathematics   510.28
        s.a. spec. appls. e.g.
        Approximations
Slides
communication   001.553 4
ed. use   371.335 22
    s.a. spec. levels of ed.;
        also Special education
photographic projection   778.2
other aspects see Films
    pictorial materials
Sliding
bearings *see* Bearings
s.a. other spec. subj.
Sligo Ireland   *area*-417 2
Slime molds *see* Myxomycophyta
Slimming
personal care   646.75
Slings
hunting & shooting   799.202 82
Slip
laws   348.01
    spec. jur.   348.3-.9
        U.S.   348.731
        spec. states & localities   348.74-.79
    spec. subj.   *law s.s.*-026 2
tracing *see* Decorative
    treatment ceramic
Slipcovers
comm. mf.   684.3
domestic construction   646.21
textile arts   746.95

Small (continued)
craft (nautical)
  engineering — 623.820 2
    design — 623.812 042
    models — 623.820 104 2
  seamanship — 623.881 2
  other aspects see Vessels
    (nautical)
  s.a. spec. kinds e.g.
    Outboard motorboats
forge work — 682
fruits
  agriculture — 634.7
    soc. & econ. aspects *see*
      Primary industries
  foods — 641.347
  preparation
    commercial — 664.804 7
    domestic — 641.647
  other aspects see Fruits
game
  hunting
    sports — 799.25
groups
  sociology — 302.34
  s.a. spec. organizations
industries
  prod. econ. — 338.642
intestines
  anatomy
    human — 611.341
    other aspects see
      Nutritive organs
  diseases
    surgery — 617.554 1
      anesthesiology — 617.967 554 1
    other aspects see
      Intestines diseases
  physical anthropometry — 573.634 1
  physiology
    human — 612.33
    other aspects see
      Nutrition
  tissue biology human — 611.018 934 1
  s.a. other spec. subj.
Small-arms ammunition
mil. eng.
  soc. & econ. aspects *see*
    Secondary industries
  tech. & mf. — 623.455
Small-business loans
  economics — 332.742
  other aspects see Credit
Small-craft canals
transportation
  commerce — 386.48
  govt. control — 351.876 48
    spec. jur. — 353–354
  law *see* Inland-waterway
    transp.

Smallpox
  gen. med. — 616.912
  geriatrics — 618.976 912
  pediatrics — 618.929 12
  pub. health — 614.521
  statistics — 312.391 2
    deaths — 312.269 12
  other aspects see Diseases
Smaltite
  mineralogy — 549.32
Smell
  perception *see* Olfactory
    perception
  physiology
    human phys. — 612.86
    other aspects see Sensory
      functions
Smelting
  pyrometallurgy *see*
    Pyrometallurgy
Smilacaceae
  botany — 584.323
  floriculture — 635.934 323
  med. aspects
    crop prod. — 633.884 323
    gen. pharm. — 615.324 323
      toxicology — 615.952 432 3
    vet. pharm. — 636.089 532 432 3
      toxicology — 636.089 595 243 23
  paleobotany — 561.4
  other aspects see Plants
Smith
  County
    Kansas — *area*–781 213
    Mississippi — *area*–762 582
    Tennessee — *area*–768 52
    Texas — *area*–764 225
  Island
    Maryland — *area*–752 23
    Virginia — *area*–755 15
Smithsonite
  mineralogy — 549.782
Smithton Tas. — *area*–946 5
Smocking
  textile arts *see* Embroidery
Smog
  air pollutants
    sanitary eng. — 628.532
    soc. aspects — 363.738 7
    other aspects see
      Pollutants
Smoke
  air pollutants
    sanitary eng. — 628.532
    soc. aspects — 363.738 7
    other aspects see
      Pollutants
  signals nonverbal commun. *see*
    Nonverbal language

Smoked
  foods
    cookery   641.616
    s.a. other spec. subj.
Smokeless powder *see* Propellant
    explosives
Smoke-projecting devices *see*
    Chemical devices mil.
Smokers (apiary equipment)
  use   638.142
Smokers' supplies
  manufacturers
    biog. & work   688.409 2
    s.a.   *pers.*–688
  manufacturing
    soc. & econ. aspects *see*
        Secondary industries
    technology   688.4
Smokes
  colloid chem. *see* Aerosols
      colloid chem.
Smoking
  foods   641.46
    commercial   664.028 6
    domestic   641.46
    other aspects see Foods
    s.a. spec. foods e.g. Meats
    s.a. other spec. subj.
Smoking-tobacco *see* Tobacco
Smolensk RSFSR   *area*–476 2
Smolyan Bulgaria   *area*–497 75
Smooth muscle tissues
  human anatomy & phys.   611.018 6
  other aspects see Tissue
    biology
Smuggling *see* Revenue offenses
Smut fungi *see* Ustilaginales
Smuts
  Jan Christian admins.
    South Africa hist.
      1st   968.053
      2d   968.055
    s.a. spec. events & subj.
      e.g. Commerce
  plant diseases   632.427
    s.a. spec. plants; also
      spec. types of culture
      e.g. Forestry
Smyrna Turkey   *area*–562
Smyth Co. Va.   *area*–755 723
Snack bars
  food services   642.5
  other aspects see
    Eating-places
Snacks
  cookery   641.53
  soc. customs   394.15
Snail meats
  preservation   641.495
    commercial   664.95
    domestic   641.495

Snails *see* Gastropoda
Snake
  flies *see* Neuroptera
  Isl. Vic.   *area*–945 6
  River   *area*–796 1
    Idaho   *area*–796 1
    Oregon   *area*–795 7
    Washington   *area*–797 4
    Wyoming   *area*–787 55
  River Range Wyo.   *area*–787 55
  venoms
    toxicology   615.942
    misc. aspects see
      Toxicology
Snakebirds *see* Pelecaniformes
Snakes *see* Serpentes
Snap beans *see* Kidney beans
Snapdragon family *see*
    Personales
Snappers *see* Acanthopterygii
Snaps
  clothing *see* Notions clothing
Sneezeweed *see* Asterales
Snipe
  flies *see* Orthorrhapha
  s.a. Charadriiformes
Snipers
  armed forces   356.162
Snobbery *see* Discriminatory
    practices
Snohomish Co. Wash.   *area*–797 71
Snooker
  equip. mf.   688.747 35
    soc. & econ. aspects *see*
      Secondary industries
  recreation   794.735
Snow
  arch. construction   721.044 91
    s.a. spec. kinds of bldgs.
  atmospheric electricity *see*
      Aerosols meteorology
  bldg. construction   693.91
  carving
    dec. arts   736.94
  compaction
    airport runways
      aeronautical eng.   629.136 3
      military   623.663 7
    s.a. other spec. appls.
  control
    road eng.
      technology   625.763
      other aspects see Roads
  cover
    meteorology   551.578 46
  fences
    railroad eng.
      technology   625.13
      other aspects see
        Permanent way

Snow
  fences (continued)
    road eng.
      technology   625.763
      other aspects see Roads
  formations
    meteorology   551.578 47
      weather forecasting   551.647 847
        spec. areas   551.65
  guides
    road eng.
      technology   625.763
      other aspects see Roads
  precipitation *see* Snowfall
  removal
    airport runways
      aeronautical eng.   629.136 37
        military   623.663 7
    railroad eng.
      technology   625.17
      other aspects see
        Permanent way
    soc. services *see* Highway
      services; *also* Street
      services
    street cleaning   628.466
    s.a. other spec. appls.
  sports
    equipment mf.   688.769
    recreation   796.9
    other aspects see Sports
  surveys
    meteorology   551.579
    other aspects see Weather
Snow-compacted roads
  technology   625.792
  other aspects see Roads
Snowdonia Gwynedd Wales *area*–429 25
Snowfall
  meteorology   551.578 4
    artificial modification   551.687 84
    weather forecasting   551.647 84
      spec. areas   551.65
Snowmobiles
  sports   796.94
  other aspects see Off-road
    vehicles
Snowplows
  railroad *see* Work cars
  road eng.
    technology   625.763
    other aspects see Roads
Snowsheds
  railroad eng.
    technology   625.13
    other aspects see Permanent
      way
Snowshoeing
  equipment mf.   688.769 2
    soc. & econ. aspects *see*
      Secondary industries

Snowshoeing (continued)
  sports   796.92
  other aspects see Sports
Snowshoes
  mf. tech.   685.363
  other aspects see Footwear
Snowstorms
  disasters
    soc. action   363.349 2
    misc. aspects see
      Disasters
  meteorology   551.555
    artificial modification   551.685 5
    weather forecasting   551.645 5
      spec. areas   551.65
Snowy
  Mountains N.S.W.   *area*–944 7
  River N.S.W.   *area*–944 7
Snuff *see* Tobacco
Snuffboxes
  handicrafts   745.593 4
Snyder Co. Pa.   *area*–748 49
Soap carving
  dec. arts   736.95
Soapberry family *see* Sapindales
Soapbox racing
  sports   796.6
  other aspects see Sports
Soaps
  manufacturing
    chem. tech.   668.12
    soc. & econ. aspects *see*
      Secondary industries
Soapstones   553.55
  econ. geol.   553.55
  materials *see* Natural stones
  mining
    soc. & econ. aspects *see*
      Primary industries
    technology   622.355
    prospecting   622.185 5
  s.a. spec. uses
Soaring
  aeronautical aerodynamics   629.132 31
    s.a. spec. appls. e.g.
      Flying
  sports   797.55
    misc. aspects see Sports
Soccer
  equipment mf.   688.763 34
    soc. & econ. aspects *see*
      Secondary industries
  sports   796.334
  other aspects see Sports
Social
  accommodation
    sociology   303.6
  action
    appl. soc.   361.2
      spec. problems & groups   362–363

Social (continued)
- interaction
  - sociology — 302
- justice school
  - economics — 330.155
- law
  - international — 341.76
  - municipal — 344
- learning
  - sociology — 303.32
- maladjustments *see* Social
  - pathology
- mobility *see* Social classes
- movements
  - sociology — 303.484
- organizations *see* Nonprofit
  - organizations
- pathology — 361
  - influence on crime — 364.256
- perception
  - soc. interaction — 302
- planning *see* Planning soc.
  - welfare
- policy *see spec. subj. e.g.*
  - Welfare services
- problems — 361.1
  - soc. theology
    - Buddhism — 294.337 83
    - Christianity — 261.83
    - classical rel. — 292.178 3
    - comp. rel. — 291.178 3
    - Confucianism — 299.512 178 3
    - Germanic rel. — 293.178 3
    - Hinduism — 294.517 83
    - Islam — 297.387 83
    - Jainism — 294.417 83
    - Judaism — 296.387 83
    - Shintoism — 299.561 178 3
    - Sikhism — 294.617 83
    - Taoism — 299.514 178 3
    - Zoroastrianism — 295.617 83
    - *s.a. spec. groups of*
      - *people e.g.* Young
      - people
  - welfare — 362.042
- processes
  - sociology — 303
  - psychology — 302
- reform
  - sociology — 303.484
- reformers — *pers.–*361
- relations
  - ethics
    - philosophy — 177
    - religion
      - Buddhism — 294.356 7
      - Christianity — 241.67
      - comp. rel. — 291.567
      - Hinduism — 294.548 67
      - *s.a. other spec. rel.*

Social (continued)
- responsibility
  - ed. goal — 370.115
    - *s.a. spec. levels of ed.*
  - management — 658.408
- sciences — 300
  - Biblical trmt. — 220.83
    - *s.a. spec. parts of Bible*
  - documentation — 025.063
  - journalism — 070.449 3
  - libraries — 026.3
    - *misc. aspects see* Special
      - libraries
  - library acquisitions — 025.273
  - library classification — 025.463
  - museums
    - desc. & colls. — 300.74
    - museology — 069.93
      - *s.a. spec. activities*
        - *e.g.* Display
  - study & teaching — 300.7
    - curriculums — 375.3
    - elementary ed. — 372.83
  - subject headings — 025.493
    - *other aspects see*
      - Disciplines (systems)
- scientists
  - biog. & work — 300.92
    - *s.a. spec. kinds*
  - *s.a.* — *pers.–*301
- security
  - insurance *see* Old-age &
    - survivors' insurance
  - law — 344.02
    - spec. jur. — 344.3–.9
  - pub. admin. — 350.825 6
    - central govts. — 351.825 6
    - spec. jur. — 353–354
    - local govts. — 352.13
- taxes
  - accounting trmt. — 657.46
    - *s.a. spec. kinds of*
      - *enterprise e.g.*
      - Insurance accounting
  - pub. finance — 336.249
- services — 361
- situation *see* Civilization;
  - *also spec. subj.*
- stratification *see* Social
  - structure; *also*
  - Social classes
- structure
  - soc. theology
    - Christiantity — 261.834
    - comp. rel. — 291.178 34
      - *s.a. other spec. rel.*
  - sociology — 305
- studies
  - elementary ed. — 372.83

Sodium-free salt
  manufacturing
    soc.& econ. aspects *see*
      Secondary industries
    technology   664.4
Sodium-vapor lighting
  engineering
    soc. & econ. aspects *see*
      Secondary industries
    technology   621.327 6
    s.a. spec. appls. e.g.
      Public lighting
Sodomy *see* Sexual deviations
Sofas *see* Upholstered furniture
Sofia Bulgaria   *area*–497 73
Soft
  cheeses
    dairy tech.   637.352–.353
    other aspects see Cheeses
  drinks *see* Nonalcoholic
    beverages
  fiber crops
    agriculture   633.51–.56
    soc. & econ. aspects *see*
      Primary industries
  rock music *see* Rock (music)
  toys *see* Padded toys
Softball
  equipment mf.   688.763 578
    soc. & econ. aspects *see*
      Secondary industries
  sports   796.357 8
  other aspects see Sports
Softening processes
  water-supply trmt.
    technology   628.166 6
    other aspects see Water
      supply engineering
Software
  programming   001.642 5
  spec. subj.   *s.s.*–028 542 5
Softwoods
  mf. tech.   674.144
  properties   674.13
  structure   674.12
Sogdian language *see* Middle
    Iranian languages
Sogdiana   *area*–396
Sogn og Fjordane Norway   *area*–483
Sohag Egypt   *area*–623
Soil
  biology
    agriculture   631.46
    s.a. spec. crops; also
      spec. types of culture
      e.g. Floriculture
  ecology   574.526 404
    animals   591.526 404
    microorganisms   576.15
    plants   581.526 404
    s.a. spec. organisms

Soil (continued)
  conditioners
    production
      soc. & econ. aspects *see*
        Secondary industries
      technology   668.64
    use agric.   631.82
      s.a. spec. crops; also
        spec. types of culture
        e.g. Floriculture
  conservation
    agriculture   631.4
  content analysis
    agriculture *see* Soils
      agriculture
    engineering   624.151 4
    s.a. spec. appls. e.g.
      Roads engineering
  ecology *see* Soil biology
    ecology
  erosion *see* Erosion soil
  formation
    physical geol. *see* New
      formations physical
      geol.
  improvement
    agriculture   631.6–.8
    s.a. spec. crops; also
      spec. types of culture
      e.g. Floriculture
  wastes
    pollution water-supply eng.
      technology   628.168 41
      other aspects see Water
      supply engineering
    sanitary eng.
      technology   628.746 1
      other aspects see
        Sanitary engineering
  mechanics
    foundation eng.   624.151 36
    s.a. spec. appls. e.g.
      Roads engineering
  pollution
    control
      law   344.046 34
      spec. jur.   344.3–.9
      pub. admin.   350.823 26
        central govts.   351.823 26
        spec. jur.   353–354
        local govts.   352.942 326
    sanitary eng.
      econ. aspects *see*
        Secondary industries
      soc. aspects   363.739 6
      technology   628.55
      s.a. spec. appls. e.g.
        Crops production
  preparation *see* Tillage

Soil (continued)
  resources
    govt. control *see* Land
      resources govt. control
  roads
    engineering
      technology   625.74
      other aspects see Roads
  science   631.4
  surveys
    agriculture   631.47
      s.a. spec. crops; also
        spec. types of culture
        e.g. Floriculture
    engineering   624.151 7
Soilless culture   631.585
  s.a. spec. crops
Soils
  agriculture   631.4
    s.a. spec. crops; also spec.
      types of culture e.g.
      Floriculture
  drainage properties
    foundation eng.   624.151 36
    s.a. spec. appls. e.g.
      Roads engineering
  eng. materials   620.191
  foundations   624.151
  structures   624.189 1
  s.a. other spec. uses
  foundation eng. *see*
    Engineering geology
  influence on crime   364.22
  mineral aspects *see* Earthy
    materials
  regional subj. trmt.   *area*–148
Soil-working equip.
  agriculture   631.31
    use *see spec. uses e.g.*
      Tillage
    s.a. spec. crops; also spec.
      types of culture e.g.
      Floriculture
  mf. tech.   681.763 1
    soc. & econ. aspects *see*
      Secondary industries
Soja *see* Soybeans
Sokoto Nigeria   *area*–669 5
Sokotra   *area*–533 5
Sokotrans   *r.e.n.*–929
Sokotri
  language *see* South Arabic
    languages
  people   *r.e.n.*–929
  s.a. other spec. subj. e.g.
    Arts
Solala Guatemala   *area*–728 164
Solanaceae *see* Solanales
Solanales
  botany   583.79
  floriculture   635.933 79

Solanales (continued)
  med. aspects
    crop prod.   633.883 79
    gen. pharm.   615.323 79
      toxicology   615.952 379
    vet. pharm.   636.089 532 379
      toxicology   636.089 595 237 9
  paleobotany   561.3
  other aspects see Plants
Solano Co. Calif.   *area*–794 52
Solanum
  melongena *see* Eggplants
  tuberosum *see* Potatoes
Solar
  cells & batteries
    soc. & econ. aspects *see*
      Secondary industries
    tech. & mf.   621.312 44
    s.a. spec. appls. e.g.
      Spacecraft engineering
  day   529.1
  energy
    engineering
      soc. & econ. aspects *see*
        Secondary industries
      technology   621.47
      s.a. spec. appls. e.g.
        Solar energy-powered
        autos
    utilization
      economics   333.792 3
      govt. control
        law   346.046 792 3
        spec. jur.   346.3–.9
        pub. admin. *see* Natural
          resources govt. control
          pub. admin.
  energy-powered autos
    commerce   388.34
    engineering
      gen. tech. & mf.   629.229 5
      maintenance   629.287 95
      models   629.221 95
      operation   629.284 95
      s.a. other spec. aspects
        e.g. Brakes; *also*
        other spec. appls.
    soc. & econ. aspects *see*
      Secondary industries
    other aspects see Land
      vehicles
  engineers
    biog. & work   621.470 92
    s.a.   *pers.*–621 4
  engines
    soc. & econ. aspects *see*
      Secondary industries
    tech. & mf.   621.473
      automobiles   629.250 8
      parts & systems   629.259 5

Solid (continued)
  geometries
    analytic *see* Solid analytic
      geometry
    Euclidean *see* Solid
      Euclidean geometry
    gen. wks.   516.06
      s.a. spec. appls. e.g.
        Engineering
    s.a. other spec. geometries
  paperboard boxes
    mf. tech.   676.32
    other aspects see
      Containers
  propellant systems
    spacecraft eng.   629.475 24
      unmanned   629.465 24
    other aspects see
      Spacecraft
  solutions
    metallurgy   669.94
    s.a. spec. metals
  wastes
    disposal
      law   344.046 22
        spec. jur.   344.3–.9
      other aspects see Wastes
        control
  s.a. other spec. subj.
Solidification
  effect of heat
    astrophysics   523.013 42
    s.a. spec. celestial
      bodies
    physics   536.42
      spec. states of matter   530.4
  technology *see* Low
    temperatures
    engineering
Solidifying gases
  chem. apparatus   542.7
  s.a. spec. appls. e.g.
    Organic chemistry
Solids
  chemistry   541.042 1
    applied   660.041
  eng. mech.   620.105
    s.a. spec. appls. e.g.
      Aerospace engineering
  geometry   516.06
    s.a. spec. geometries; also
      spec. appls. e.g.
      Civil engineering
  heat expansion & contraction
    astrophysics   523.013 414
    s.a. spec. celestial
      bodies
    physics   536.414
  heat transmission *see*
    Conduction heat

Solids (continued)
  physics
    mechanics   531.2–.5
    state of matter   530.41
  sound transmission
    engineering   620.25
    s.a. spec. appls. e.g.
      Musical sound
    physics   534.22
  specific heats
    astrophysics   523.013 63
    s.a. spec. celestial
      bodies
    physics   536.63
Solid-state
  lasers
    light amplification
      soc. & econ. aspects *see*
        Secondary industries
      tech. & mf.   621.366 1
      s.a. spec. appls. e.g.
        Tracking
      other aspects see
        Amplification light
        optics
  masers
    microwave electronics
      soc. & econ. aspects *see*
        Secondary industries
      tech. & mf.   621.381 336 1
        spec. circuits   621.381 32
      s.a. spec. appls. e.g.
        Radar engineering
      other aspects see Microwave
        electronics
  physics & chem. *see* Solids
Solid-to-gas vaporization
  effect of heat
    astrophysics   523.013 445
    s.a. spec. celestial
      bodies
    physics   536.445
      spec. states of matter   530.4
Solid-to-liquid heat
      transformation *see*
      Fusion effect of heat
Solifugae
  zoology   595.48
  other aspects see Arachnida
Solihull West Midlands Eng.
         area–424 97
Solipsism
  epistemology   121.2
Solitaire
  recreation   795.43
Solitaries *see* Columbiformes
Solitary confinement
  penology   365.644
Solitude
  rel. self-discipline *see*
    Asceticism

Son
  God
    Christian doctrines — 231.2
    private prayers to
      Christianity — 242.72
Sonar
  navigation — 623.893 8
  underwater commun. devices
    soc. & econ. aspects *see*
      Secondary industries
    tech. & mf. — 621.389 53
    s.a. spec. appls. e.g.
      Military engineering
Sonatas
  gen. wks.
    music theory — 781.52
    recordings — 789.912 152
  organ music — 786.81
    recordings — 789.912 681
  piano music — 786.41
    recordings — 789.912 641
  s.a. other spec. mediums
Sonatinas
  organ music — 786.81
    recordings — 789.912 681
  piano music — 786.41
    recordings — 789.912 641
  s.a. other spec. mediums
Sonderborg Denmark — *area*–489 5
Sondrio Italy — *area*–452 5
Song
  birds
    animal husbandry — 636.68
    soc. & econ. aspects *see*
      Primary industries
    other aspects see Aves
  of Solomon
    Bible — 223.9
    other aspects see Poetic
      books (O.T.)
  of Songs *see* Song of Solomon
  of three children
    deuterocanonical book — 229.5
    other aspects see Apocrypha
Songea Tanzania — *area*–678 25
Songhai kingdom hist. — 966.2
  s.a. spec. events & subj.
    e.g. Commerce
Songs
  music
    gen. wks.
      sacred — 783.6
        hymns — 783.9
      secular — 784
      recordings — 789.912
  poetry *see* Lyric poetry
  without words
    piano music *see* Romantic
      music piano

Sonic boom
  aeronautical aerodynamics *see*
    Transonic velocity
  other aspects see Noise
Sonneratiaceae *see* Lythrales
Sonnets
  gen. wks.
    collections — 808.814 2
    hist. & crit. — 809.142
    rhetoric — 808.142
    juvenile — 808.068 142
  spec. lits. — *lit. sub.*–104 2
  indiv. authors — *lit. sub.*–11–19
  other aspects see Poetry
Sonoma Co. Calif. — *area*–794 18
Sonora Mex. — *area*–721 7
Sons
  gen. wks. — *pers.*–044 1
  of the American Revolution — 369.13
Sonsonate El Salvador — *area*–728 413
Soothsayers *see* Prophets
Soothsaying *see* Divination
Sophia reign Russia hist. — 947.05
  s.a. spec. events & subj.
    e.g. Commerce
Sophistic philosophy — 183.1
Sophonias
  Bible — 224.96
  other aspects see Prophetic
    books (O.T.)
Soprano solos *see* Women's solos
Sorangiaceae *see* Myxobacterales
Sorbian *see* Wendish
Sorbs — *r.e.n.*–918 8
Sorcerers
  rel. leaders
    comp. rel. — 291.62
    s.a. spec. rel.
Sorcery *see* Magic
Sorell Lake Tas. — *area*–946 3
Sorghum sugars & syrups
  comm. proc. — 664.133
  other aspects see Sugars
Sorghums
  agriculture
    food crops — 633.174
    forage crops — 633.257 4
    soc. & econ. aspects *see*
      Primary industries
    sugar crops — 633.62
  foods — 641.331–.336
    cookery — 641.631–.636
  other aspects see
    Panicoideae; *also*
    Cereal grains; *also*
    Sugars
Soria Spain — *area*–463 55
Soriano Uruguay — *area*–895 27
Soro Denmark — *area*–489 1
Sorophora *see* Mycetozoa

Sound	
vibrations	
biophysics (continued)	
terrestrial	
gen. wks.	574.191 43
animals	591.191 43
microorganisms	576.119 143
plants	581.191 43
s.a. spec. organisms	
med. sci.	612.014 453
animals	636.089 201 445 3
s.a. spec. animals	
man	612.014 453
s.a. spec. functions,	
systems, organs	
s.a. Audiology	
Sound-induced illness	
gen. med.	616.989 6
geriatrics	618.976 989 6
pediatrics	618.929 896
statistics	312.398 96
deaths	312.269 896
other aspects see Diseases	
s.a. spec. diseases	
Sounding devices	
sea navigation	623.893 8
Soundproofing	
aircraft eng. *see* Comfort	
equipment aircraft	
bldg. construction	693.834
Sound-resistant construction	
see Resistant	
construction	
Sounds	
linguistics *see* Phonology	
Soups	
cookery	641.813
Sour	
cherries	
agriculture	634.237
other aspects see Cherries	
s.a. other spec. subj.	
Sources	
water-supply eng.	
technology	628.11
other aspects see Water	
supply engineering	
s.a. other spec. subj.	
Souris River N.D.	*area*–784 6
Sour-milk cheeses	
dairy tech.	637.356
other aspects see Cheeses	
Soursops *see* Annonaceous fruits	
Sousaphones *see* Tubas	
South	
Africa	*area*–68
African	
literature	
Afrikaans	839.36
English	820

South	
African	
literature (continued)	
gen. wks.	
collections	808.899 68
hist. & crit.	809.896 8
Republic Transvaal hist.	968.204 5
s.a. spec. events & subj.	
e.g. Commerce	
War hist.	968.048
s.a. spec. countries &	
spec. provinces	
Africans	*r.e.n.*–968
Afrikaners	*r.e.n.*–393 6
Anglo-Saxons	*r.e.n.*–28
Negroes	*r.e.n.*–968
America	*area*–8
American native	
languages	
linguistics	498
literatures	898
s.a.	*lang.*–98
people	*r.e.n.*–98
s.a. other spec. subj. e.g.	
Arts	
Arabia Federation	*area*–533 5
Arabic languages	
linguistics	492.9
literatures	892.9
s.a.	*lang.*–929
Asia	*area*–54
Asian	
arts	
architecture	722.4
misc. aspects see	
Architectural schools	
sculpture	732.4
s.a. other spec. art	
forms	
Asians	*r.e.n.*–914
Atlantic states U.S.	*area*–75
Auckland N.Z.	*area*–931 22
Australia	*area*–942 3
Bedfordshire Eng.	*area*–425 65
Bend Ind.	*area*–772 89
Boston Va.	*area*–755 662
Cambridgeshire Eng.	*area*–426 57
Carolina	*area*–757
Central states U.S.	*area*–76
China Sea	
oceanography	551.465 72
regional subj. trmt.	*area*–164 72
other aspects see Pacific	
Ocean	
Dakota	*area*–783
Derbyshire Eng.	*area*–425 19
Esk River Tas.	*area*–946 4
Frigid Zone	*area*–116
misc. aspects see Frigid	
Zones	
Georgia Isls.	*area*–971 1

South (continued)

Glamorgan Wales   *area*–429 86

Hams Devon Eng.   *area*–423 592

Herefordshire Hereford &

    Worcester Eng.   *area*–424 45

Holland

    Lincolnshire Eng.   *area*–425 39

    Netherlands   *area*–492 3

Island N.Z.   *area*–931 5

Kesteven Lincolnshire Eng.

    area–425 38

Korea   *area*–519 5

Lakeland Cumbria Eng.   *area*–427 83

Molton Devon Eng.   *area*–423 52

Mountain Battle

    U.S. Civil War hist.   973.733 6

Ndebele Transvaal   *area*–682 95

Norfolk

    England   *area*–426 19

    Virginia   *area*–755 523

Northamptonshire Eng.   *area*–425 59

Orkney Isls.   *area*–971 1

Oset Autonomous Region Georgian

    SSR   *area*–479 5

Oxfordshire Eng.   *area*–425 79

Pembrokeshire Dyfed Wales

    area–429 63

Platte River   *area*–788 7

Pole   *area*–989

Ribble Lancashire Eng.   *area*–427 67

Sandwich Isls.   *area*–971 1

Saskatchewan River Alta.   *area*–712 33

Shetland Isls.   *area*–971 1

Shields Tyne & Wear Eng.

    area–428 75

Shropshire Salop Eng.   *area*–424 57

Slavic

    languages

       linguistics   491.81

       literatures   891.81

       s.a.   *lang.*–918 1

    peoples   *r.e.n.*–918 1

       Yugoslavs   *r.e.n.*–918 2

    s.a. other spec. subj. e.g.

       Arts

Staffordshire Eng.   *area*–424 66

Temperate Zone   *area*–126

    misc. aspects see Temperate

       Zones

Tyneside Tyne & Wear Eng.

    area–428 75

Uist Hebrides Scot.   *area*–411 4

Vietnam

    Vietnamese War participant   959.704 332

    s.a. Vietnam

Wight Isle of Wight Eng.

    area–422 85

Yorkshire Metropolitan Co. Eng.

    area–428 2

s.a. Southern; *also other*

    spec. subj.

Southall London Eng.   *area*–421 84

Southam Warwickshire Eng.

    area–424 89

Southampton

    Co. Va.   *area*–755 552

    district Hampshire Eng.   *area*–422 76

    Isl. Northwest Ter.   *area*–719 4

Southeast

    Asia   *area*–59

       Treaty Organization

          mil. sci.   355.031 095 9

    Asian

       arts

          architecture   722.4

          misc. aspects see

             Architectural schools

          sculpture   732.4

          s.a. other spec. art

             forms

       regional organizations

          internat. law   341.247 3

          treaties   341.026 373

    Asians   *r.e.n.*–95

    Europe   *area*–49

       ancient   *area*–398

    Fairbanks election district

       Alaska   *area*–798 6

    Pacific Ocean

       oceanography   551.466 1

       regional subj. trmt.   *area*–164 1

       other aspects see Pacific

          Ocean

    states U.S.   *area*–75

    s.a. other spec. subj.

Southeastern reporter

    U.S. law   348.734 25

Southend-on-Sea Essex Eng.   *area*–426 795

Southern

    Baptist Convention   286.132

       misc. aspects see Baptist

    Buddhism   294.391

       misc. aspects see Buddhism

    California   *area*–794 9

    Cameroon   *area*–671 12

    district Israel   *area*–569 49

    dynasty China hist.   951.01

       s.a. spec. events & subj.

          e.g. Commerce

    Europe   *area*–4

    Hemisphere   *area*–181 4

    Leyte Philippines   *area*–599 5

    reporter

       U.S. law   348.734 27

    Rhodesia

       history   968.910 2

       s.a.   *area*–689 1

    Sporades *see* Sporades

    states U.S.   *area*–75

    Sunda Isls. seas

       oceanography   551.465 74

       regional subj. trmt.   *area*–164 74

Southern
  Sunda Isls. seas (continued)
    other aspects see Pacific
      Ocean
  Uplands Scot.   *area*–413 7
  Yemen   *area*–533 5
  Yemenites   *r.e.n.*–927 533 5
  s.a. South; *also other spec.*
    subj.
Southgate London Eng.   *area*–421 8
Southland N.Z.   *area*–931 57
Southport
  Merseyside Eng.   *area*–427 59
  Queensland   *area*–943 2
Southsea Hampshire Eng.   *area*–422 792
Southwark London Eng.   *area*–421 64
Southwell Nottinghamshire Eng.
                                  area–425 24
South-West
  Africa   *area*–688
  Africans   *r.e.n.*–968 8
Southwest
  New U.S.   *area*–79
  Old U.S.   *area*–76
  Pacific Ocean
    oceanography   551.465 7
    regional subj. trmt.   *area*–164 7
    s.a. other spec. subj.
South-Western Region
      China   *area*–513
Southwestern reporter
  U.S. law   348.734 26
Southwick West Sussex Eng.
                                  area–422 69
Southwold Suffolk Eng.   *area*–426 41
Sovereigns *see* Monarchs
Sovereignty
  of God
    rel. doctrines
      Christianity   231.7
      other rel. see God
  of states   320.157
    internat. law   341.26
Soviet
  people   *r.e.n.*–917
  Union   *area*–47
  Asia   *area*–57
Sow bugs *see* Isopoda
Sowerby Bridge West Yorkshire
      Eng.   *area*–428 12
Sowing *see* Planting
Sows *see spec. animals e.g.*
      Swine
Sox *see* Hosiery
Soybean
  glues
    chem. tech.   668.33
    other aspects see Adhesives
  oil
    comm. proc.   664.369
    other aspects see Oils

Soybean (continued)
  plastics *see* Protein plastics
  textiles *see* Protein textiles
Soybeans
  agriculture
    field crops   633.34
    garden crops   635.655
    soc. & econ. aspects *see*
      Primary industries
  flour & meal
    comm. proc.   664.726
    other aspects see Seeds
  foods   641.356 55
    preparation
      commercial   664.805 655
      domestic   641.656 55
  other aspects see
      Papilionaceae; *also*
      Vegetables
Space
  art
    gen. wks.   709.040 79
      spec. places   709.1–.9
    painting   759.067 9
      spec. places   759.1–.9
    sculpture   735.230 479
      spec. places   730.9
    s.a. other spec. art forms
  artillery
    mil. eng.
      soc. & econ. aspects *see*
        Secondary industries
      tech. & mf.   623.419 4
  astronomy
    description   523.111
    theory   521.5
  bombardment
    mil. defense vs.   623.3
  communication
    gen. wks.
      technology   621.380 423
        s.a. spec. appls. e.g.
        Lunar flights
      other aspects see
        Communication
    radio
      engineering   621.384 197
        s.a. spec. appls. e.g.
        Astronautics
      other aspects see Radio
    television
      engineering   621.388 9
      other aspects see
        Television
  engineering   620.419
    s.a. spec. branches of eng.
    & spec. appls e.g.
      Astronautics
  environments astronautics   629.416

Space (continued)
  exploration unmanned
    soc. & econ. aspects *see*
      Secondary industries
    technology   629.435
  facilities
    mil. transp. eng.   623.69
  flight
    & religion
      nat. rel.   215.25
    soc. & econ. aspects *see*
      Secondary industries
    technology   629.41
    s.a. spec. appls. e.g.
      Space warfare
  forces
    mil. sci.   358.8
    personnel
      biog. & work   358.809 2
      s.a. hist. of spec.
        countries & spec. wars
      other aspects see
        Military personnel
      s.a.   *pers.*–358
  guided missiles
    mil. eng.
      soc. & econ. aspects *see*
        Secondary industries
      tech. & mf.   623.451 98
  hazards astronautics   629.416
  internat. law   341.47
  laboratories astronautics
    soc. & econ. aspects *see*
      Secondary industries
    technology   629.445
    s.a. spec. appls. e.g.
      Space warfare
  mail
    postal commun.   383.144
    other aspects see Postal
      communication
  medicine   616.980 214
    s.a. spec. diseases
  photography
    technique   778.35
    s.a. spec. appls. e.g.
      Eclipses
  physical theories   530.1
  physiology *see*
    Bioastronautics
  ports *see* Terrestrial
    facilities spacecraft
  probes astronautics   629.435
    s.a. spec. appls. e.g.
      Astrophysics
  projectiles in
    solid dynamics   531.555
  psychology   155.966
  regional subj. trmt.   *area*–19

Space (continued)
  research
    cooporation
      internat. law   341.767 52
  resources
    economics   333.94
    govt. control
      law   346.046 94
        spec. jur.   346.3–.9
      pub. admin. *see* Natural
        resources govt. control
        pub. admin.
  rights
    land econ.   333.339
  sciences   500.5
    s.a. spec. sci.
  shuttle astronautics
    soc. & econ. aspects *see*
      Secondary industries
    technology   629.441
    s.a. spec. appls. e.g.
      Space warfare
  stations astronautics
    soc. & econ. aspects *see*
      Secondary industries
    technology   629.442
    s.a. spec. appls. e.g.
      Space warfare
  suits
    spacecraft eng.   629.477 2
    misc. aspects see
      Spacecraft
  surveying photogrammetry   526.982 3
  transportation
    accidents   363.124
      misc. aspects see
        Transportation
        accidents
    commerce   387.8
    govt. control   351.877 8
      spec. jur.   353–354
    hazards
      soc. path.   363.124
    law
      international   341.756 79
      municipal   343.097 9
        spec. jur.   343.3–.9
    personnel
      biog. & work   387.809 2
      s.a.   *pers.*–387 8
    safety
      law
        international   341.756 7
        municipal   343.097 9
          spec. jur.   343.3–.9
      pub. meas.   363.124
        govt. control *see*
          Safety pub. admin.
  walks *see* Extravehicular
    activities manned space
    flight

Space (continued)
  warfare
    mil. sci.   358.8
    technology *see* Military
      engineering
    work environment *see* Physical
      conditions of work
  s.a. Extraterrestrial
Space (abstraction)
  metaphysics   114
  nat. rel.   215.25
  perception *see* Spatial
    perception
Space (area)
  arts   701.8
    s.a. spec. art forms
  chemistry *see* Stereochemistry
  heaters
    bldg. heating   697.2
  provision
    work environment *see*
      Physical conditions
  s.a. Spatial
Spacecraft
  accidents   363.124
    misc. aspects see
      Transportation
      accidents
  engineering
    soc. & econ. aspects *see*
      Secondary industries
    technology
      gen. wks.   629.47
        unmanned   629.46
      use
        manned flight   629.45
          mil. eng.   623.749
        unmanned flight   629.43
  gunnery
    mil. eng.   623.556
  influences
    psychology   155.966
  rendezvous astronautics   629.458 3
Spacemen *see* Astronauts
Spaces   516
  analytic *see* Analytic spaces
  combinatorial topology   514.224
  geometry   516
  topology   514.3
  s.a. spec. appls. e.g.
    Engineering
Space-time *see* Relativity
  theories
Spaghetti *see* Pastas
Spain   *area*–46
Spalding
  Co. Ga.   *area*–758 443
  town Lincolnshire Eng.   *area*–425 39
Spaniards   *r.e.n.*–61
Spaniels
  animal husbandry   636.752

Spaniels (continued)
  other aspects see Dogs
Spanish
  America   *area*–8
  American
    literature   860
    people   *r.e.n.*–68
    s.a. other spec. subj. e.g.
      Arts
  domination Italy hist.   945.07
    s.a. spec. events & subj.
      e.g. Commerce
  Guinea   *area*–671 8
  influenza *see* Influenzas
  language
    linguistics   460
    literature   860
    s.a.   *lang.*–61
  Morocco   *area*–642
  moss *see* Bromeliales
  people   *r.e.n.*–61
  plums *see* Anacardiaceous
    fruits
  Sahara   *area*–648
  Succession War
    Europe hist.   940.252 6
    s.a. spec. countries
    troops in American Revolution   973.346
  West Africa   *area*–648
  s.a. Spain; *also other spec.*
    subj. e.g. Arts
Spanish-American War
  U.S. hist.   973.89
Spanish-Moroccan War
  history   964.03
Spar varnishes
  manufacturing
    soc. & econ. aspects *see*
      Secondary industries
    technology   667.79
Sparganiaceae
  botany   584.612
  floriculture   635.934 612
  med. aspects
    crop prod.   633.884 612
    gen. pharm.   615.324 612
      toxicology   615.952 461 2
    vet. pharm.   636.089 532 461 2
      toxicology   636.089 595 246 12
  paleobotany   561.4
  other aspects see Plants
Spark
  controls
    internal-combustion engines
      see Control devices
      internal-combustion
      engines
  plugs
    internal-combustion engines
      see Ignition systems
      & devices

Special
  libraries (continued)
    buildings
      architecture | 727.8
      functional planning | 022.3
    catalogs *see* Library
      catalogs
    reference services | 025.527 6
    selection for | 025.218 6
    use studies | 025.586
    user orientation | 025.566
    s.a. spec. activities e.g.
      Cataloging
  materials
    library trmt. | 025.17
      acquisitions | 025.28
      cataloging | 025.34
      classification | 025.34
      indexing | 025.34
    s.a. other spec.
      activities
  salt-water forms
    oceanography | 551.460 9
    regional subj. trmt. | *area*–168
    other aspects see Seas
    s.a. spec. bodies of water
  services
    armed forces | 355.34
    s.a. spec. mil. branches
  subj. libraries
    buildings
      architecture | 727.83
      building | 690.783
      other aspects see
        Educational buildings
    other aspects see Special
      libraries
  s.a. other spec. subj.
Specialization
  econ. law internat. comm. | 382.104 2
  prod. econ. | 338.604 6
  sociology | 303.44
  s.a. other spec. subj.
Specialized
  courts
    law | 347.04
      spec. jur. | 347.3–.9
      U.S.
        Federal | 347.732 8
        local | 347.734
          spec. localities | 347.74–.79
        state | 347.733
          spec. states | 347.74–.79
    other aspects see Courts
  s.a. other spec. subj.
Special-purpose
  authorities
    local govt. admin. | 352.009
  districts
    local govt. admin. | 352.009

Special-purpose (continued)
  organic chemicals
    chem. tech. | 661.806–.808
    other aspects see Organic
      chemicals
  paints
    technology | 667.69
    other aspects see Paints
  railroads
    commerce | 385.5
    govt. control | 350.875 5
      central govts. | 351.875 5
      spec. jur. | 353–354
      local govts. | 352.915 5
    law *see* Railroad
      transportation law
  s.a. other spec. subj.
Specialty
  advertising | 659.13
  papers
    mf. tech. | 676.284
    other aspects see Papers
      pulp prod.
  shops
    advertising | 659.196 588 75
    pub. relations | 659.296 588 75
    retail marketing | 658.875
Species
  genetic factors
    animal breeding | 636.082 1
    s.a. spec. animals
  interfertility
    genetics | 575.134
      animals | 591.15
      microorganisms | 576.139
      plants | 581.15
    s.a. spec. organisms
Specific
  gravity
    physics mech. | 531.14
      solids | 531.54
    other states of matter
      see Mass (substance)
    spec. substances
      crystals | 548.845
      s.a. spec. crystals
      minerals *see* Mechanical
        properties minerals
  heats
    astrophysics | 523.013 63–.013 65
    s.a. spec. celestial
      bodies
    physics | 536.63–.65
      spec. states of matter | 530.4
  s.a. other spec. subj.
Specifications
  bldg. construction | 692.3
  govt. procurement
    pub. admin. | 350.712 043
      central govts. | 351.712 043
      local govts. | 352.162 043

Speculative	
philosophy	110
misc. aspects see	
Philosophy	
systems of psych.	150.192
s.a. spec. subj. & branches	
of psych.	
Speech	
disorders	
abnormal psych.	157.5
children	155.451 4
gen. med.	616.855
geriatrics	618.976 855
pediatrics	618.928 55
pub. health	614.58
statistics	312.385 5
other aspects see Mental	
illness	
elementary ed.	372.622
freedom of	
civil right	
pol. sci.	323.443
human phys.	612.78
verbal commun.	001.542
other aspects see Speaking	
Speeches	
literature	
gen. wks.	
collections	808.85
crit. theory	801.955
textual	801.959
hist. & crit.	809.5
spec. lits.	*lit. sub.*–5
other aspects see Speaking	
Speed	
control	
machine eng.	
technology	621.812
s.a. spec. appls. e.g.	
Steam locomotives	
other aspects see	
Mechanics	
drills & tests	
shorthand	653.15
s.a. spec. systems e.g.	
Gregg	
typewriting	652.307
letters	
office use	651.75
vehicular transp.	
control *see* Traffic control	
highways	388.314 4
streets	388.413 144
s.a. other spec. subj.	
Speedboats *see* Motorboats	
Speeding *see* Traffic violations	
Speedways	
automobile racing	796.720 68
Speleology *see* Caves	
Spelling	
elementary ed.	372.632

Spelling (continued)	
linguistics	411
spec. langs.	
nonstandard forms	
lang. sub.–7	
standard forms	
desc. & anal.	*lang. sub.*–152
usage	*lang. sub.*–81
Spells	
occultism	133.44
Spelthorne Surrey Eng.	*area*–422 12
Spelunkers	
biog. & work	796.525 092
s.a.	*pers.*–796 5
Spelunking *see* Caves exploring	
Spenborough West Yorkshire Eng.	
area–428 13	
Spencer Co.	
Indiana	*area*–772 31
Kentucky	*area*–769 455
Spending	
macroeconomics	339
public *see* Expenditures	
public	
Spennymoor Durham Eng.	*area*–428 62
Sperm	
cells	
gametogenesis *see*	
Gametogenesis	
histogenesis *see*	
Histogenesis	
whales *see* Odontoceti	
Spermaceti wax	
comm. proc.	665.13
other aspects see Waxes	
Spermatophyta	
botany	582
floriculture	635.93
forestry	634.97
med. aspects	
crop prod.	633.88
gen. pharm.	615.32
toxicology	615.952
vet. pharm.	636.089 532
toxicology	636.089 595 2
paleobotany	561.2
other aspects see Plants	
Sperrin Mts. N. Ire.	*area*–416 2
Spey River Scot.	*area*–411 92
Spezia Italy	*area*–451 83
Sphacelariales *see* Phaeophyta	
Sphaeropsidales *see*	
Deuteromycetes	
Sphaerosepalaceae *see* Ochnales	
Sphagnaceae *see* Sphagnales	
Sphagnales	
botany	588.1
floriculture	635.938 1
med. aspects	
crop prod.	633.888 1

Sphagnales
  med. aspects (continued)
    gen. pharm.   615.322 1
    toxicology   615.952 81
    vet. pharm.   636.089 532 21
    toxicology   636.089 595 281
  paleobotany   561.8
  other aspects see Plants
Sphagnum
  soil conditioners *see* Texture
        control soil
        conditioners
Sphalerite
  mineralogy   549.32
Sphene
  mineralogy   549.62
Sphenisciformes
  hunting
    commercial   639.128 441
    sports   799.248 441
  paleozoology   568.4
  zoology   598.441
  other aspects see Aves
Sphenophyllales
  paleobotany   561.72
Sphenopsida
  botany   587.2
  floriculture   635.937 2
  med. aspects
    crop. prod.   633.887 2
    gen. pharm.   615.327 2
    toxicology   615.952 72
    vet. pharm.   636.089 532 72
    toxicology   636.089 595 272
  paleobotany   561.72
  other aspects see Plants
Sphenopteris
  paleobotany   561.597
Spheres
  geometry *see* Configurations
      geometry
  of influence
    internat. politics   327.114
    spec. countries   327.3–.9
Spherical
  astronomy   522.7
  s.a. spec. celestial bodies
  geometries *see* Solid
      geometries
  harmonics *see* Harmonic
      analysis
  projections *see* Projections
      tech. drawing
  trigonometry *see* Trigonometry
Sphygmomanometry
  human phys.   612.140 28
  other aspects see Circulation
      (biology)

Spices
  agriculture   633.83
  soc. & econ. aspects *see*
    Primary industries
  foods   641.338 3
    preparation
      commercial   664.53
      soc. & econ. aspects
      see Secondary
      industries
      domestic   641.638 3
Spider venoms
  toxicology   615.942
  misc. aspects see
      Toxicology
Spiders
  gen. wks.
    zoology   595.44
    other aspects see Arachnida
  sun
    zoology   595.48
    other aspects see Arachnida
  weasel
    zoology   595.48
    other aspects see Arachnida
Spiderwort family *see*
    Commelinales
Spies *see* Espionage
Spigeliaceae *see* Loganiales
Spikes *see* Nails (fasteners)
Spillways
  liquid flow mech.
    engineering *see* Dynamics
    physics   532.53
  reservoir eng.
    technology   627.883
    s.a. spec. appls. e.g.
      Canal transportation
    other aspects see Liquids
      engineering
Spin
  nuclei *see* Nuclei
  particles *see* Particles
    (matter)
  rays *see* Rays (beams)
Spinach
  agriculture   635.41
  soc. & econ. aspects *see*
    Primary industries
  foods   641.354 1
    preparation
      commercial   664.805 41
      domestic   641.654 1
  other aspects see
    Chenopodiales; *also*
    Vegetables
Spinacia oleracea *see* Spinach
Spinal
  anesthesia *see* Regional
    anesthesia

Spinal (continued)
column
  anatomy
    human   611.711
    other aspects see
      Skeletal organs
  diseases
    gen. wks.   616.73
      neoplasms   616.992 711
      tuberculosis   616.995 711
    geriatrics   618.976 73
    pediatrics   618.927 3
    pub. health   614.597 3
    statistics   312.373
      deaths   312.267 3
    surgery   617.471
      anesthesiology   617.967 471
    other aspects see
      Diseases
  fractures   617.151
  orthopedic surgery   617.375
  physical anthropometry   573.671 1
  physiology
    human   612.75
    other aspects see
      Movements
  tissue biology human   611.018 971 1
cord
  anatomy
    human   611.82
    other aspects see Nervous
      system
  diseases   616.83
    geriatrics   618.976 83
    neoplasms   616.992 82
    pediatrics   618.928 3
    pub. health   614.598 3
    statistics   312.383
      deaths   312.268 3
    surgery   617.482
      anesthesiology   617.967 482
    tuberculosis   616.995 82
    other aspects see
      Diseases
  physical anthropometry   573.682
  physiology
    human   612.83
    other aspects see Nervous
      functions
  tissue biology human   611.018 982
deformities
  statistics   312.304 737 5
  surgery   617.375
    anesthesiology   617.967 375
  s.a. Veterinary sciences
irritation
  symptomatology
    neurological diseases   616.844
      vet. sci.   636.089 684 4
      s.a. spec. animals

Spinal (continued)
nerves
  diseases   616.87
    geriatrics   618.976 87
    pediatrics   618.928 7
    pub. health   614.598 7
    statistics   312.387
    other aspects see
      Diseases
  human phys.   612.819
  other aspects see Nervous
    system
Spine
  anatomy *see* Spinal column
  fungi *see* Agaricales
Spinel
  mineralogy   549.526
Spinet music
  recordings   789.912 64
  scores & parts   786.405
    spec. forms   786.41–.49
  treatises   786.404 21
Spinets
  mf. tech.   681.816 221
    misc. aspects see Musical
      instruments
  musical art   786.221
    desc. & care   786.23
  music *see* Spinet music
  training & perf.   786.304 21
    spec. kinds   786.31–.38
Spink Co. S.D.   *area*–783 217
Spinning
  angling
    sports   799.12
    other aspects see Fishing
  motion
    solid dynamics
      engineering *see* Dynamics
      physics   531.34
  textiles
    arts   746.12
    manufacturing
      soc. & econ. aspects *see*
        Secondary industries
      technology   677.028 22
      s.a. spec. kinds of
        textiles & spec. prod.
    s.a. other spec. subj.
Spinning-machines
  textiles mf.
    soc. & econ. aspects *see*
      Secondary industries
    technology   677.028 52
    s.a. spec. kinds of
      textiles
Spinor
  algebras   512.57
  s.a. spec. appls. e.g.
    Engineering

Spinor (continued)
  analysis   515.63
    s.a. spec. appls. e.g.
      Engineering
Spinsters *see* Unmarried women
Spinulosa *see* Asteroidea
Spiny
  anteaters *see* Monotremata
  rats *see* Hystricomorpha
Spiral
  gears
    machine eng.
      soc. & econ. aspects *see*
        Secondary industries
      tech. & mf.   621.833 3
        s.a. spec. appls. e.g.
          Steering gear
      other aspects see Mechanics
  nebulas *see* Galaxies
Spirals
  geometry *see* Configurations
      geometry
Spirea *see* Rosaceae
Spires *see* Roofs
Spirit
  leveling
    geodetic surveying   526.36
  photography
    occultism   133.92
  varnishes
    manufacturing
      soc. & econ. aspects *see*
        Secondary industries
      technology   667.79
Spiritism *see* Spiritualism
Spirits (alcoholic) *see*
    Alcoholic beverages
Spirits (incorporeal) *see*
    Spiritual beings
Spiritual
  beings
    rel. doctrines
      Christianity   235
      comp. rel.   291.215–.216
      Islam   297.215–.216
      Judaism   296.315–.316
      s.a. other spec. rel.
      s.a. specific types of
        spirits e.g. Evil
        spirits; *also*
        Specters
  gifts
    Christian doctrines   234.13
  powers of Mary
    Christian doctrines   232.916
  renewal
    rel. practices
      Christianity   269
      comp. rel.   291.3
      Islam   297.3
      Judaism   296.4

Spiritual
  renewal
    rel. practices (continued)
      s.a. other spec. rel.
    world
      occultism   133.901 3
Spiritualism
  comp. rel.   291.21
  occultism   133.9
  philosophy *see* Idealism
      philosophy
Spiritualistic surgery   615.852
  s.a. spec. diseases
Spiritualists
  biog. & work   133.909 2
  s.a.   *pers.*–13
Spirituals (songs) *see* Negro
    songs U.S. spirituals
Spirochaetaceae *see*
    Spirochaetales
Spirochaetales
  botany   589.99
  med. aspects
    disease organisms   616.014 9
    gen. pharm.   615.329 99
    toxicology   615.952 999
    vet. pharm.   636.089 532 999
    toxicology   636.089 595 299 9
  paleobotany   561.9
  other aspects see Plants
Spirochetal relapsing fever *see*
    Relapsing fevers
Spirotricha *see* Ciliata
Spitsbergen   *area*–981
Spleen
  anatomy
    human   611.41
    other aspects see Secretory
      organs
  diseases
    gen. wks.   616.41
      neoplasms   616.992 41
      tuberculosis   616.995 41
    geriatrics   618.976 41
    pediatrics   618.924 1
    pub. health   614.594 1
    statistics   312.341
      deaths   312.264 1
    surgery   617.551
      anesthesiology   617.967 551
    other aspects see Diseases
  physical anthropometry   573.641
  physiology
    human   612.41
    other aspects see Secretion
  tissue biology human   611.018 941
Splenic fever *see* Anthrax
Splicing *see* Knotting

Splines   511.42
  s.a. spec. math branches; also
    spec. appls. e.g.
     Engineering
Split-level houses *see*
    Single-story houses
Split-T formation
  American football   796.332 22
Spodumene
  mineralogy   549.66
Spoils system *see* Civil service
Spokane Co. & city Wash. *area*–797 37
Sponge iron
  technology   669.141 9
  other aspects see Ferrous
    metals
Sponges *see* Porifera
Spontaneous
  abortion
    mammalogy   599.021 662
    med. sci.
      obstetrics   618.33
      pub. health   614.599 2
      statistics   312.304 833
        deaths   312.260 483 3
    other aspects see
     Diseases
  generation   577
  s.a. other spec. subj.
Spools
  wooden
    mf. tech.   674.88
    other aspects see Wood
     products
Spoonbills (birds) *see*
    Ciconiiformes
Spoonbills (fishes) *see*
    Acipenseriformes
Spoons (tableware) *see*
    Tableware
Sporades Greece
  northern   *area*–499
    ancient   *area*–391 1
  southern   *area*–499 6
    ancient   *area*–391 6
Spores
  paleobotany   561.13
  plant
    anatomy   581.41
    pathology   581.221
  s.a. spec. plants
Sporoboleae *see* Pooideae
Sporochnales *see* Phaeophyta
Sporozoa
  culture   639.731 9
  zoology   593.19
  other aspects see Protozoa
Sport cars *see* Sports cars
Sporting
  dogs
    animal husbandry   636.752

Sporting
  dogs (continued)
    other aspects see Dogs
  goods
    manufacture   688.76
  use
    animal husbandry for   636.088 8
    birds
     nondomesticated   636.63
    s.a. other spec. animals
Sports
  accidents *see* Recreation
    accidents
  cars
    driving
     recreation   796.77
    other aspects see Private
     automobiles
  centers bldgs. *see* Sports
    complexes bldgs.
  child care
    home econ.   649.57
  clubs
    pol. sci.   324.3
    spec. parties   324.24–.29
  complexes bldgs.
    architecture   725.804 3
    building   690.580 43
    other aspects see Public
     structures
  ed. activities   371.89
    s.a. spec. levels of ed.;
     also Special education
  enterprises
    accounting   657.84
  equipment
    manufacturing
     soc. & econ. aspects *see*
      Secondary industries
     technology   688.76
  etiquette   395.59
  govt. control *see* Recreation
    pub. admin.
  halls *see* Sports complexes
    bldgs.
  hazards
    soc. path.   363.14
  human phys.   612.044
  hygiene   613.71
  medicine   617.102 7
  pavilions *see* Sports
    complexes bldgs.
  pins & buttons
    numismatics   737.243
  programs
    radio   791.445
    television   791.455
  recreation   796
    ethics *see* Games ethics
  rooms *see* Recreational areas

Spring
  plants flowering in
    floriculture   635.953
    s.a. spec. plants
  wheat
    agriculture
      food crops   633.117
      forage crops   633.251 7
    other aspects see Wheat
  other aspects see Seasons
Springboard diving
  sports   797.24
  other aspects see Sports
Springfield Ill.   *area*–773 56
Spring-guns
  art metalwork   739.73
Springhaas *see* Sciuromorpha
Springs (mechanical)
  machine eng.
    soc. & econ. aspects *see*
      Secondary industries
    tech. & mf.   621.824
      automobiles   629.243
      railroad rolling stock   625.21
    other aspects see Mechanics
Springs (water)
  hydrology   551.498
  water-supply sources
    technology   628.112
    other aspects see Water
      supply engineering
Springtails
  zoology   595.715
  other aspects see Apterygota
Sprinkling
  filter process
    sewage trmt.
      technology   628.352
      other aspects see Sewage
        treatment
  streets pub. sanitation eng.   628.462
Sprinters
  biog. & work   796.426
  s.a.   *pers.*–796 4
Sprinting
  sports   796.426
  other aspects see Sports
Spruce
  trees
    forestry   634.975 2
    soc. & econ. aspects *see*
      Primary industries
    other aspects see
      Coniferales; *also*
      Trees
  woods *see* Softwoods
Spur gears
  machine eng.
    soc. & econ. aspects *see*
      Secondary industries

Spur gears
  machine eng. (continued)
    tech. & mf.   621.833 1
    s.a. spec. appls. e.g.
      Automobiles engineering
    other aspects see Mechanics
Spurge family *see* Euphorbiales
Spurious knowledge   001.9
  s.a. spec. subj.
Sputniks *see* Artificial
  satellites
Squadrons
  air force organization   358.413 1
  naval organization   359.31
Squads
  mil. organization   355.31
  s.a. spec. mil. branches
Squaliformes *see* Selachii
Squaloidea *see* Selachii
Squam Lake N.H.   *area*–742 3
Squamata
  paleozoology   567.94
  other aspects see Lacertilia
Squamous epithelia
  human anatomy & phys.   611.018 7
  other aspects see Tissue
    biology
Square
  books
    hist. & crit.   099
  dances
    arts   793.34
    music *see* Dance music
Squares
  geometry *see* Configurations
    geometry
Square-wave generators
  radiowave electronics *see*
    Testing-devices
    radiowave electronics
Squaring of circles   516.204
Squash
  equipment mf.   688.763 43
    soc. & econ. aspects *see*
      Secondary industries
  players
    biog. & work   796.343
    s.a.   *pers.*–796 34
    sports   796.343
  other aspects see Sports
Squashes
  agriculture   635.62
    soc. & econ. aspects *see*
      Primary industries
  foods   641.356 2
    preparation
      commercial   664.805 62
      domestic   641.656 2
  other aspects see
    Cucurbitales; *also*
    Vegetables

Squids
  food *see* Mollusca food
  other aspects see Decapoda
      (mollusks)
Squillas *see* Stomatopoda
Squirrels *see* Sciuromorpha
Sri Lanka   *area*-549 3
Sri Lankian
  people   *r.e.n.*-914 13
  s.a. spec. subj. e.g. Arts
Stabiles
  sculpture   731.55
      spec. periods & schools   732-735
Stability
  aeronautical aerodynamics   629.132 36
      s.a. spec. appls. e.g.
          Flying
  soil mechanics
      foundation eng.   624.151 363
          s.a. spec. appls. e.g.
              Roads engineering
  structural eng. *see* Analysis
      engineering structural
      eng.
  systems eng.   620.72
      s.a. spec. appls. e.g.
          Management
  s.a. other spec. subj.
Stabilization ponds
  sewage trmt.
      technology   628.351
      other aspects see Sewage
          treatment
Stabilized
  earth materials
      architectural construction   721.044 2
          s.a. spec. structural
              elements; also spec.
              types of bldgs.
          bldg. construction   693.2
          bldg. materials   691.4
          s.a. other spec. uses
      s.a. other spec. subj.
Stabilizers
  aircraft eng.
      soc. & econ. aspects *see*
          Secondary industries
      tech. & mf.   629.134 33
Stable
  flies *see* Cyclorrhapha
  s.a. spec. subj. e.g.
      Isotopes
Stabs *see* Punctured wounds
Stachyuraceae *see* Hamamelidales
Stackhousiaceae *see* Celastrales
Stacking
  crops
      agriculture   631.55
      s.a. spec. crops
  s.a. other spec. subj.

Stacks
  library bldgs.   022.4
  steam eng. *see* Furnaces steam
      eng.
Stadiums
  architecture   725.827
  building   690.582 7
  sports   796.406 8
  other aspects see Public
      structures
Staff
  manuals
      library sci.   023.9
          s.a. spec. activities
              e.g. Cataloging
      museology   069.63
          s.a. spec. activities
              e.g. Display
      s.a. other spec. subj.
  officers
      armed forces   355.331
          s.a. spec. mil. branches
  organization
      mil. sci.   355.330 42
          s.a. spec. mil. branches
  s.a. spec. enterprises &
      activities
Staffing
  patterns
      pers. admin. *see* Personnel
          utilization
Stafford
  County
      Kansas   *area*-781 813
      Virginia   *area*-755 26
  district Eng.   *area*-424 64
Staffordshire Eng.   *area*-424 6
Staffordshire Moorlands Eng.
                                    area-424 61
Staffs
  libraries   023
  museums   069.63
  s.a. other spec. subj.
Staff-tree family *see*
      Celastrales
Stage
  fright *see* Acting
  presentations *see* Theater
Stagecoach services
  commerce   388.322 8
  govt. control   351.878 322 8
      spec. jur.   353-354
  law   343.094 8
      spec. jur.   343.3-.9
Stagecoaches
  commerce   388.341
  other aspects see Land
      vehicles

Stain techniques
  slide preparation
    microscopy life sci.   578.64
      animal tissues   578.94
      plant tissues   578.84
Stained glass
  arts   748.5
  other aspects see Glass
Staines Surrey Eng.   *area*–422 12
Staining woodwork
  buildings   698.32
Stainless steel *see* Steel
Stairs
  architectural
    construction   721.832
    design & decoration   729.39
  building   690.183 2
    wood bldg. construction   694.6
  s.a. spec. kinds of bldgs.
Stakes
  plant training *see* Poles
      plant training
Stalin
  Joseph admin.
    USSR hist.   947.084 2
    s.a. spec. events & subj.
      e.g. Commerce
Stalingrad RSFSR   *area*–478 5
Stalk-eyed flies *see*
    Cyclorrhapha
Stallions *see* Horses
Stalybridge Greater Manchester
    Eng.   *area*–427 35
Stamens
  plant anatomy   582.046 3
  s.a. spec. plants
Stamford Lincolnshire Eng.
      area–425 38
Stammerers
  child psych.   155.451 4
Stammering
  gen. med.   616.855 4
  geriatrics   618.976 855 4
  pediatrics   618.928 554
  psychology   157.5
  statistics   312.385 54
Stamp
  Act
    U.S. hist.   973.311 1
  taxes
    law   343.057
      spec. jur.   343.3–.9
    pub. admin.   350.724
      central govts.   351.724
      spec. jur.   353–354
      local govts.   352.135
    pub. finance   336.272
Stamped
  metal prod.
    mf. tech.   671.83
      ferrous metals   672.83

Stamped
  metal prod.
    mf. tech. (continued)
      s.a. other spec. metals
    other aspects see Primary
      metal prod.
  s.a. other spec. subj.
Stamping
  metal prod.
    arts
      decorative   739.14
      s.a. spec. metals; also
        spec. prod. e.g.
        Jewelry
    fine *see* Direct-metal
      sculpture
    mf. tech.   671.33
      ferrous metals   672.33
      s.a. other spec. metals
    other aspects see
      Mechanical working
  s.a. other spec. subj.
Stamping-equipment *see*
    Impressing-equipment
Stamps
  engraved
    investment econ.   332.63
    numismatics   737.6
    rel. significance
      Christianity   247.876
      comp. rel.   291.37
      s.a. other spec. rel.
  postage *see* Postage stamps
Standard
  deviation
    statistical math.   519.534
    s.a. spec. appls. e.g.
      Engineering
  money
    economics   332.420 422
    other aspects see Money
  of living
    macroeconomics   339.47
  poodle
    animal husbandry   636.72
    other aspects see Dogs
  schnauzer
    animal husbandry   636.73
    other aspects see Dogs
  time   529.75
  s.a. other spec. subj.
Standardbred horses *see* Light
    harness horses
Standard-gauge railroads
  engineering   625.1
    s.a. spec. subj. e.g.
      Permanent way
  transportation *see* Railroad
    transportation
  other aspects see Railroads

Stark Co. (continued)
  Ohio   *area*–771 62
Starke Co. Ind.   *area*–772 923
Starlings *see* Sturnidae
Starr Co. Tex.   *area*–764 485
Stars
  art representation   704.949 523 8
    s.a. spec. art forms
  astronomy
    description   523.8
    theory   521.58
  catalogs   523.890 8
  twinkling of *see* Refraction
        atmospheric optical
        phenomena
  other aspects see Celestial
        bodies
Start Point Devon Eng.   *area*–423 592
Starting-devices
  internal-combustion engines
    automobiles
      soc. & econ. aspects *see*
        Secondary industries
      tech. & mf.   629.257
    s.a. other spec. appls.
Starvation *see* Hunger
State
  & church *see* Religious groups
        & state
  & law   340.115
  banks
    economics   332.122 4
    other aspects see Banks
      (finance)
  borrowing & debt
    law   343.037
      spec. jur.   343.3–.9
    pub. admin.   351.726
      spec. jur.   353–354
    pub. finance   336.343 2
  colleges   378.053
  control of ed.
    law   344.073
      spec. jur.   344.3–.9
  courts
    U.S. law   347.733
  debt *see* State borrowing &
      debt
  departments
    U.S. govt.   353.1
    s.a. Foreign affairs
  finance
    economics   336.013
    other aspects see Public
      finance
  flags *see* Flags
  governments   351
    U.S.   353.9
    other   354
  income *see* Income

State (continued)
  labor econ.   331.117 32
    s.a. spec. classes of labor
      e.g. Women
  libraries *see* Government
      libraries
  penal institutions
    penology   365.32
    other aspects see Penal
      institutions
  planning
    civic art   711.3
    economics   338.9
    soc. sci. *see* Planning soc.
      welfare
  reports of cases
    law   348.043
      spec. jur.   348.3–.9
      U.S.   348.74–.79
      spec. subj.   *law s.s.*–026 42
  socialism
    economics   335.5
  taxation
    law   343.043
      spec. jur.   343.3–.9
    pub. finance   336.201 3
    other aspects see Taxes
  universities   378.053
  visits
    soc. customs   394.4
  s.a. other spec. subj.; also
      Government; *also*
      Public
State-federal relations *see*
      National-state
      relations
Stateless persons
  internat. law   341.486
  pol. sci.   323.632
State-local relations
  constitutional law   342.042
    spec. jur.   342.3–.9
  pub. admin.   350.093
    central govts.   351.093
    U.S. govts.   353.929 3
    other   354
Staten Isl. N.Y.   *area*–747 26
State-national relations *see*
      National-state
      relations
States (political body)
  ethics *see* Public
      administration ethics
  internat. law   341.26
  pol. sci.   320.1
  s.a. New nations; *also spec.*
      states
States of matter
  chemistry   541.04
    applied   660.04

Stations
  television (continued)
    other aspects see
      Television
  transportation *see spec. kinds*
    of terminals e.g. Bus
    terminals
  wire telephony *see* Telephony
    wire
  other see spec. kinds e.g.
    Broadcasting stations
Stations of the cross
  Roman Catholic liturgy   264.027 4
Statistical
  communication theory
    engineering   621.380 182
  forecasting weather   551.633
    spec. areas   551.65
    spec. elements   551.64
  hypothesis testing   519.56
    s.a. spec. appls. e.g.
      Engineering
  inference
    mathematics   519.54
    s.a. spec. appls. e.g.
      Engineering
  mathematics   519.5
    s.a. spec. appls. e.g.
      Economics
  mechanics *see* Statistical
    physics
  method   001.422
    spec. subj.
      research   *s.s.*–072
      technique   *s.s.*–028
  physics   530.13
    spec. states of matter   530.4
    s.a. spec. branches of
      physics
Statisticians
  biog. & work   310.92
  s.a.   *pers.*–31
Statistics   310
  libraries for   026.31
    misc. aspects see Special
      libraries
  mathematics   519.5
  populations   312
  services *see* Information
    services
  other spec. subj.   *s.s.*–021 2
Statuary
  arts   731.7
    spec. periods & schools   732–735
  rel. significance *see*
    Sculpture
Statues *see* Statuary
Status
  employee motivation
    personnel admin.   658.314 2

Status
  employee motivation (continued)
    other aspects see
      Motivation employees
  of forces
    internat. law   341.722
  of persons
    law   346.013
    spec. jur.   346.3–.9
Statute of limitations *see*
    Limitation of actions
Statutes
  law   348.022
    spec. jur.   348.3–.9
    U.S.
      Federal   348.732 2
      state & local   348.74–.79
    spec. subj.   *law s.s.*–026 32
Statutory
  actions
    legal procedure   347.053
    spec. jur.   347.3–.9
    other aspects see Legal
      procedure
  rape *see* Sex offenses
Staunton Va.   *area*–755 911
Staurolite
  mineralogy   549.62
Stauromedusae *see* Scyphozoa
Staveley Derbyshire Eng.   *area*–425 12
Stavropol RSFSR   *area*–479 7
Stawell Vic.   *area*–945 8
Steady
  flow
    fluid mech.
      engineering *see* Dynamics
      physics   532.052
      gases   533.21
      air   533.621
      liquids   532.51
  state theory cosmogony   523.18
Steaks *see spec. kinds e.g.*
    Beef
Stealing *see* Larceny
Steam
  automobiles
    commerce   388.34
    engineering
      gen. tech. & mf.   629.229 2
      maintenance   629.287 92
      models   629.221 92
      operation   629.284 92
      s.a. other spec. aspects
      e.g. Brakes; *also*
      spec. appls. e.g.
      Driving motor vehicles
    soc. & econ. aspects *see*
      Secondary industries
    other aspects see Land
      vehicles

Stems
  plant (continued)
    physiology   581.104 25
    s.a. spec. plants
  s.a. Edible stems
Stenciling
  dec. arts   745.73
  textiles *see* Printing
           processes textiles
Stencils
  mech. printing tech.
    soc. & econ. aspects *see*
           Secondary industries
    technology   686.231 6
  office use   652.4
Stenographers
  office services   651.374 1
  other aspects see Office
           personnel
Stenographic machines
  mf. tech.   681.61
  soc. & econ. aspects *see*
           Secondary industries
Stenography   653.14
  s.a. spec. shorthand systems
        e.g. Gregg
Stenomeridaceae *see*
         Dioscoreales
Stenurida paleozoology   563.94
Stepbrothers *see* Siblings
Stepchildren   *pers.*–044 1
Stephanite
  mineralogy   549.35
Stephen
  reign
    Eng. hist.   942.024
    Gt. Brit. hist.   941.024
    s.a. spec. events & subj.
        e.g. Courts
Stephens Co.
  Georgia   *area*–758 132
  Oklahoma   *area*–766 53
  Texas   *area*–764 546
Stephenson Co. Ill.   *area*–773 33
Stepney London Eng.   *area*–421 5
Stepparents *see* Parents
Steppes *see* Plane regions
Steps
  landscape design   717
  s.a. Stairs
Stepsisters *see* Siblings
Sterculiaceae *see* Tiliales
Stereochemistry   541.223
  organic   547.122 3
  s.a. spec. elements & cpds.
Stereo-multiplex systems *see*
         Frequency-modulation
         systems

Stereophonic systems
  tech. & mf.   621.389 334
  s.a. spec. appls. e.g.
        music 789.91
  other aspects see Reproducers
           sound
Stereoscopic photography   778.4
  motion pictures
    cinematography   778.534 1
    projection   778.554 1
Stereotypes
  printinq *see* Plates mech.
           printing tech.
Sterility
  female *see* Sterility
           gynecology
  gen. wks. *see* Sterility male
  gynecology   618.178
  pub. health   614.599 2
  statistics   312.304 817 8
  other aspects see Diseases
  male
    gen. med.   616.692
    geriatrics   618.976 692
    pub. health   614.596 92
    statistics   312.369 2
    other aspects see Diseases
Sterilization
  birth control meas.   613.942
  soc. aspects   363.97
  other aspects see Birth
           control
  of milk
    dairy tech.   637.133 5
    s.a. spec. varieties e.g.
         Whole milk
  pub. health control meas.   614.48
    misc. aspects see Public
         health
  spacecraft eng.
    gen. wks.   629.470 44
    unmanned   629.460 44
    life-support systems *see*
         Sanitation spacecraft
         eng.
    other aspects see
         Spacecraft
    s.a. other spec. appls.
Sterling Co. Tex.   *area*–764 871
Stern theory
  indiv. psych.   155.264
Sternum
  anatomy
    human   611.713
    other aspects see Skeletal
         organs
  diseases
    surgery   617.471
      anesthesiology   617.967 471
    other aspects see Bones
         diseases

Sternum (continued)
fractures | 617.153
orthopedic surgery | 617.374
physical anthropometry | 573.671 3
physiology
  human | 612.75
other aspects see Movements
tissue biology human | 611.018 971 3
Steroids
biochemistry
  gen. wks. | 574.192 43
    animals | 591.192 43
    microorganisms | 576.119 243
    plants | 581.192 43
  s.a. spec. organisms
  med. sci. | 612.015 73
    animals | 636.089 201 573
    s.a. spec. animals
    man | 612.015 73
  s.a. spec. functions,
    systems, organs
  org. chem. | 547.73
Sterols
biochemistry
  gen. wks. | 574.192 431
    animals | 591.192 431
    microorganisms | 576.119 243 1
    plants | 581.192 431
  s.a. spec. organisms
  med. sci. | 612.015 731
    animals | 636.089 201 573 1
    man | 612.015 731
  s.a. spec. functions,
    systems, organs
  org. chem. | 547.731
Stethoscopes
manufacturing | 681.761
  soc. & econ. aspects *see*
    Secondary industries
use med. | 616.075 4
  s.a. spec. diseases
other aspects see
    Technological
    instruments
Stettin Poland | *area*–438 1
Steuben Co.
Indiana | *area*–772 78
New York | *area*–747 83
Stevenage Hertfordshire Eng.
   | *area*–425 82
Stevens Co.
Kansas | *area*–781 725
Minnesota | *area*–776 42
Washington | *area*–797 23
Stevenston Strathclyde Scot.
   | *area*–414 61
Stewardship
Christian rel. | 248.6
Stewart
County
  Georgia | *area*–758 922

Stewart
County (continued)
  Tennessee | *area*–768 35
  Isl. N.Z. | *area*–931 575
Stewartry Dumfries & Galloway
  Scot. | *area*–414 92
Stewing
cookery tech. | 641.73
Stews
cookery | 641.823
Stibium *see* Antimony
Stibnite
mineralogy | 549.32
Stick insects *see* Phasmatodea
Sticklebacks *see* Mesichthyes
Stigmata
Christian rel. doctrines | 231.73
Christian rel. experience | 248.29
Stigonemataceae *see* Cyanophyta
Stilbeaceae *see* Verbenales
Stilette flies *see* Orthorrhapha
Still
fishing
  sports | 799.12
  other aspects see Fishing
life
  art representation | 704.943 5
    painting | 758.4
    s.a. other spec. art
      forms
Stillbirths
statistics | 312.24
Stillwater Co. Mont. | *area*–786 651
Stilton cheeses
dairy tech. | 637.354
other aspects see Cheeses
Stilts (birds) *see*
    Charadriiformes
Stilts (footwear)
mf. tech. | 685.367
Stimulants
addiction
  gen. med. | 616.864
  geriatrics | 618.976 864
  pediatrics | 618.928 64
  psychology | 157.6
  statistics | 312.386 4
    deaths | 312.268 64
heart
  pharmacodynamics | 615.711
  other aspects see Drugs
hygiene | 613.84
Stinkhorn fungi *see*
    Lycoperdales
Stipeae *see* Pooideae
Stipple engraving
graphic arts
  processes | 765.5
  products | 769
Stirling
district Scot. | *area*–413 12

Stirling (continued)
Range W. Aust.   *area*–941 2
   Nat. Park W. Aust.   *area*–941 2
Stochastic processes
probabilities   519.2
   s.a. spec. appls. e.g.
      Engineering
Stock
accounting trmt.   657.76
   s.a. spec. kinds of
      enterprise e.g.
      Insurance accounting
exchange bldgs. *see* Exchange
      buildings
exchanges *see* Securities
      exchange
farmers *see* Stockmen
issues
   capital sources   658.152 24
   spec. subj.   *s.s.*–068 1
options
   investment finance   332.645 2
   misc. aspects see
      Speculation investment
      finance
ownership plans
   wage & salary admin.   658.322 5
raisers *see* Stockmen
tickers *see* Printing
      telegraphy
Stock (materials)
control *see* Inventory control
Stockbreeding
animal husbandry   636.082
   s.a. spec. animals
Stockbridge Hampshire Eng.
                                 area–422 732
Stockbrokers *see* Brokerage
      firms
Stockholm Sweden   *area*–487
Stockings *see* Hosiery
Stockmen
biog. & work   636.009 2
   s.a. spec. kinds of stock
other aspects see
      Agricultural classes
s.a.   *pers.*–636
Stockpiles
prod. econ.
   primary prod.
      agricultural   338.15
      food   338.19
      mineral   338.27
      other   338.37
   secondary prod.   338.47
Stockport Greater Manchester Eng.
                                 area–427 34
Stocks
capital *see* Fixed capital

Stocks (continued)
investment finance   332.632 2
   govt. control *see*
      Securities govt.
      control
   law   346.092 2
labor econ.
   fringe benefits   331.255
   incentive payments   331.216 4
law *see* Labor law
s.a. spec. classes of
      workers e.g. Women
Stocksbridge South Yorkshire Eng.
                                 area–428 21
Stockton
city Calif.   *area*–794 56
Plateau Tex.   *area*–764 92
Stockton-on-Tees Cleveland Eng.
                                 area–428 51
Stockyards
animal husbandry   636.083 1
   s.a. spec. animals
Stoddard Co. Mo.   *area*–778 95
Stoic philosophy   188
Stoichiometry
industrial   660.7
   s.a. spec. prod.
theoretical chem.   541.26
   organic   547.126
   s.a. spec. elements & cpds.
Stoke Newington London Eng.
                                 area–421 44
Stoke-on-Trent Staffordshire Eng.
                                 area–424 63
Stokes Co. N.C.   *area*–756 64
Stokesley North Yorkshire Eng.
                                 area–428 49
Stolen goods *see* Larceny
Stoles
comm. mf.   687.147
domestic mf.   646.457
other aspects see Clothing
Stomach
anatomy
   human   611.33
   other aspects see Nutritive
         organs
diseases
   gen. wks.   616.33
      neoplasms   616.992 33
      tuberculosis   616.995 33
   geriatrics   618.976 33
   pediatrics   618.923 3
   pub. health   614.593 3
   statistics   312.333
      deaths   312.263 3
   surgery   617.553
      anesthesiology   617.967 553
   other aspects see Diseases
physical anthropometry   573.633

Storage
  of foods (continued)
    other aspects see Foods
    s.a. spec. foods e.g. Meats
  of gases
    chem. apparatus   542.7
    s.a. spec. appls. e.g.
      Organic chemistry
  of ind. gases
    s.a. spec. gases
  of information
    library operations   025.3
  of milk
    dairy tech.   637.135
    s.a. spec. varieties e.g.
      Whole milk
  of office records   651.53
  of petroleum   665.542
    s.a. spec. prod.
  photographic tech.
    gen. wks.
      negatives & transparencies 770.285
      positives   770.286
    spec. fields   778
  rings
    nuclear physics *see* Nuclear
      physics
  services
    transp. terminal *see*
      Freight services
  water-supply eng.
    technology   628.13
    other aspects see Water
      supply engineering
  s.a. other spec. subj.
Storage (mathematics)   519.83
  s.a. spec. appls. e.g.
    Engineering
Storax family *see* Styracales
Store (retail trade)
  buildings *see* Retail trade
    buildings
  etiquette   395.53
  sanitation *see* Industrial
    sanitation
Storehouses
  gen. wks. *see* Storage
  mil. sci.   355.75
  s.a. spec. mil. branches
Storey Co. Nev.   *area*–793 56
Stories
  Biblical events   220.950 5
  s.a. spec. parts of Bible
  musical dramas   782.086
  s.a. Fiction
Storing *see* Storage
Storks *see* Ciconiiformes
Storm
  sewer systems
    soc. & econ. aspects *see*
      Secondary industries

Storm
  sewer systems (continued)
    technology   628.212
    s.a. spec. appls. e.g.
      Floods control
  warning systems *see* Warning
    systems
Stormont Co. Ont.   *area*–713 76
Storms
  meteorology *see* Disturbances
    atmosphere meteorology
  soc. welfare action   363.349 2
  other aspects see Disasters
Story Co. Ia.   *area*–777 546
Storytelling
  child care at home   649.58
  elementary ed.   372.64
  library sci.   027.625 1
  rhetoric   808.543
    juvenile   808.068 543
  other aspects see Speaking
Stour River Eng.   *area*–423 3
Stourbridge West Midlands Eng.
      area–424 93
Stourport-on-Severn Hereford &
    Worcester Eng. *area*–424 41
Stoves
  bldg. heating   697.22
  ceramic arts   738.8
  household appliances
    mf. tech.   683.88
    other aspects see Household
      appliances
Stowmarket Suffolk Eng. *area*–426 45
Strabane N. Ire.   *area*–416 41
Strabismus *see* Ocular
    neuromuscular mechanism
    diseases
Strafford Co. N.H.   *area*–742 5
Straightening-tools
  soc. & econ. aspects *see*
    Secondary industries
  tech. & mf.   621.983
  s.a. spec. appls. e.g.
    Frames automobiles
Strain gauges
  eng. materials   620.112 302 8
  s.a. spec. materials & spec.
    uses
Strains (biology)
  genetic factors
    animal breeding   636.082 1
    s.a. spec. animals
Strains (injuries)
  statistics   312.304 717
  surgery   617.17
    anesthesiology   617.967 17
    s.a. Veterinary sciences
Strains (mechanical)
  eng. materials *see* Mechanical
    deformation

Strains (mechanical) (continued)
  solid dynamics
    engineering *see* Dynamics
    physics 531.382
Straits
  internat. law 341.446
Strange particles *see* Hadrons
Strangers
  psych. influences 155.927
  relationships with
    appl. psych. 158.27
    child 155.418
Strangford Lough N. Ire.   *area*–416 54
Strangulation *see* Asphyxiation
Stranraer Dumfries & Galloway
            Scot.   *area*–414 95
Strasburgeriaceae *see* Ochnales
Strategic
  geography
    mil. sci. 355.47
    s.a. spec. mil. branches
  missiles
    mil. eng.
    soc. & econ. aspects *see*
            Secondary industries
    tech. & mf. 623.451 9
  weapons
    control internat. law 341.738
    s.a. spec. weapons e.g.
            Bombers
Strategy
  games *see spec. games*
  mil. sci.
    mil. branches 355.43
    s.a. spec. branches
    spec. wars
      U.S. Civil War 973.730 1
      World War 1 .... 940.401
      World War 2 .... 940.540 1
    s.a. other spec. wars
Stratford-on-Avon Warwickshire
            Eng.   *area*–424 89
Strathalbyn S. Aust.   *area*–942 32
Strathclyde Scot.   *area*–414 1
Strathkelvin Strathclyde Scot.
            area–414 36
Strathmore Scot.   *area*–412 5
Stratification
  snow cover
    meteorology 551.578 466
      weather forecasting 551.647 846 6
    spec. areas 551.65
  sociology *see* Social
            structure
Stratifications
  geology
    economic 553.14
    spec. deposits 553.2–.8
    structural 551.81
    s.a. spec. aspects e.g.
            Prospecting

Stratifications (continued)
  sociology *see* Social classes
Stratified layers
  econ. geol. 553.14
  spec. deposits 553.2–.8
Stratigraphic
  geology 551.7
  paleontology 560.17
Stratosphere
  meteorology 551.514 2
  s.a. spec. aspects e.g.
            Circulation atmosphere
  regional subj. trmt.   *area*–161 3
Stratton Cornwall Eng.   *area*–423 71
Stratums *see* Stratifications
Straw pulp
  mf. tech. 676.14
  other aspects see Pulp
Strawberries
  agriculture 634.75
  soc. & econ. aspects *see*
            Primary industries
  foods 641.347 5
    preparation
      commercial 664.804 75
      domestic 641.647 5
  other aspects see Rosaceae;
            also Fruits
Streak
  minerals *see* Optical
            properties minerals
Stream of consciousness
  lit. element
    gen. wks.
      collections 808.802 5
      hist. & crit. 809.925
    spec. lits.
      collections .... *lit. sub.*–080 25
      hist. & crit. .... *lit. sub.*–092 5
    s.a. spec. lit. forms
    stage element 792.090 925
    s.a. spec. mediums e.g.
            Television; *also spec.*
            kinds of drama e.g.
            Tragedies (drama)
Streaming
  education *see* Homogeneous
            grouping education
Streamline flow
  fluid mech.
    engineering *see* Dynamics
    physics 532.052
    gases 533.21
    air 533.621
    liquids 532.51
Streams
  ecology life sci. 574.526 323
    animals 591.526 323
    microorganisms 576.15
    plants 581.526 323
    s.a. spec. organisms

Streams (continued)
 hydraulic eng.
  soc. & econ. aspects *see*
      Secondary industries
  technology   627.12
   s.a. spec. appls. e.g.
      Inland-waterway transp.
   other aspects see Liquids
      engineering
 hydrology   551.483
 internat. law   341.442
 landscape design   714
 regional subj. trmt.   *area*–169 3
 resources
  economics   333.916 2
   recreational   333.784 5
  govt. control
   law   346.046 916 2
    spec. jur.   346.3–.9
   pub. admin. *see* Water
       resources govt. control
       pub. admin.
   s.a. other spec. aspects
       e.g. Water supply soc.
       services
 temperatures
  meteorology   551.524 8
   weather forecasting   551.642 48
    spec. areas   551.65
 use
  fish culture   639.313
   s.a. spec. kinds of fish
  waste disposal
   law   344.046 26
    spec. jur.   344.3–.9
  water-supply sources
   technology   628.112
   other aspects see Water
       supply engineering
Street
 cleaning
  pub. sanitation eng.
   soc. & econ. aspects *see*
       Secondary industries
   technology   628.46
 fighting
  mil. sci.   355.426
   s.a. spec. mil. branches
 lighting *see* Public lighting
 markets
  commerce   381.18
   misc. aspects see
       Commerce
 noise
  soc. aspects   363.741
   other aspects see Noise
 organs *see* Barrel organs
 patterns
  civic art   711.41
 pianos *see* Barrel organs

Street (continued)
 railways *see* Surface rail
     systems
 services
  technology   625.76–.79
  urban transp.
   commerce   388.413 12
   govt. control   350.878 413 12
    central govts.   351.878 413 12
     spec. jur.   353–354
    local govts.   352.918 413 12
   law   343.098 2
    spec. jur.   343.3–.9
 signs
  local transp. *see* Street
      services
 urban district Somerset Eng.
                          area–423 83
 use *see* Roads use
Streetcars
 engineering
  soc. & econ. aspects *see*
      Secondary industries
  tech. & mf.   625.66
 safety *see* Railroad
     transportation safety
 terminals *see* Railroad
     terminals
 urban transp. *see* Surface
     rail systems
 other aspects see Railroads
Streets
 local transp.
  commerce   388.411
  govt. control   350.864 2
   central govts.   351.864 2
    spec. jur.   353–354
   local govts.   352.74
  law   343.098 2
   spec. jur.   343.3–.9
  pub. sanitation   363.729 1
   govt. control   352.6
   law   344.046 4
    spec. jur.   344.3–.9
 other aspects see Roads
Strelitziaceae *see* Zingiberales
Strength
 crystals   548.842
  s.a. spec. substances
 eng. materials   620.11
 structures *see* Analysis
     engineering structural
     eng.
 s.a. other spec. subj.
Strepsiptera
 culture   638.574 6
 paleozoology   565.74
 zoology   595.746
 other aspects see Insecta
Streptochaeteae *see* Pooideae

Strontium
  chemistry (continued)
    technology   661.039 4
      organic   661.895
      soc. & econ. aspects *see*
        Secondary industries
      s.a. spec. prod.
  metabolism
    human phys.   612.392 4
    other aspects see
      Metabolism
  mineral aspects *see* Minor
    metals
  pharmacology   615.239 4
    misc. aspects see
      Pharmacology
  toxicology   615.925 394
    misc. aspects see
      Toxicology
  other aspects see Alkaline
    earth metals
Strophe *see* Poetry gen. wks.
  rhetoric
Stroud Gloucestershire Eng. *area*–424 19
Structural
  analysis *see* Analysis
    engineering
  chemistry *see* Theoretical
    chemistry
  clay products
    eng. materials   620.142
    manufacturing
      soc. & econ. aspects *see*
        Secondary industries
      technology   666.73
    other aspects see Ceramic
    s.a. spec. kinds e.g.
      Bricks
  crystallography   548.81
    s.a. spec. substances
  decoration *see* Architectural
    decoration
  design *see* Design structural
    eng.
  elements
    architectural
      construction   721.1–.8
      design & decoration   729.3
      building   690.11–.18
      civic art   711.6
    s.a. spec. kinds of bldgs.
    engineering
      soc. & econ. aspects *see*
        Secondary industries
      technology   624.1
      s.a. spec. appls. e.g.
        Vessels (nautical)
        engineering
  engineers
    biog. & work   624.109 2

Structural
  engineers (continued)
    other aspects see Civil
      engineers
  formulas molecular
    theoretical chem.   541.221
    organic   547.122 1
    s.a. spec. elements &
      cpds.
  geology   551.8
    s.a. spec. aspects e.g.
      Prospecting
  materials
    buildings   691
    nuclear reactors
      soc. & econ. aspects *see*
        Secondary industries
      tech. & mf.   621.483 32
    s.a. other spec. appls.
  quantity surveying   624.104 2
    bldg. construction   692.5
    s.a. other spec. appls.
  theory   624.17
    naval arch.   623.817
    s.a. other spec. appls.
      e.g. Aircraft
  transformations
    glassmaking   666.104 2
      s.a. spec. kinds of glass
    s.a. other spec. subj.
Structuralism
  arts
    gen. wks.   709.040 77
      spec. places   709.1–.9
    painting   759.067 7
      spec. places   749.1–.9
    sculpture   735.230 477
      spec. places   730.9
    s.a. other spec. art forms
  philosophy   149.95
    indiv. phil.   180–190
    s.a. spec. branches of phil.
      e.g. Metaphysics
Structure
  atomic *see* Atomic structure
  cells
    cytology   547.872
      animals   591.872
      plants   581.872
    s.a. spec. organisms
  epistemology   121.4
  geol. deposits
    econ. geol.   553.1
      spec. deposits   553.2–.8
  lumber
    mf. tech.   674.12
  matter *see* Matter structure
  metaphysics   117
  molecular *see* Molecular
    structure
  s.a. other spec. subj.

Relative Index

Structures	
air conditioning	697.935–.938
architecture	725–728
building	690.5–.8
interior decoration	747.85–.88
landscape design	717
lighting	621.322
use *see spec. kinds e.g.*	
Agricultural structures	
Structures (mathematics)	
algebraic	512
analysis	515
combinatorial topology	514.224
geometry	516
topology	514
s.a. spec. appls. e.g.	
Engineering	
Struthioniformes	
hunting	
commercial	639.128 51
sports	799.248 51
paleozoology	568.5
zoology	598.51
other aspects see Aves	
Strychnaceae *see* Loganiales	
Strychnine *see* Alkaloids	
Stuarts	
reign	
Eng. hist.	942.06
Gt. Brit. hist.	941.06
Ire. hist.	941.506
Scot. hist.	941.103–.106
s.a. spec. events & subj.	
e.g. Commerce	
Stuccowork	
architectural construction	721.044 6
s.a. spec. structural	
elements; also spec.	
types of bldgs.	
bldg. construction	693.6
Studbooks	
animal husbandry	636.082 2
s.a. spec. animals	
Student	
activism *see* Student	
attitudes	
activities	371.89
s.a. spec. levels of ed.;	
also Special education	
associations *see* Student	
organizations	
attitudes	371.81
s.a. spec. levels of ed.;	
also Special education	
behavior *see* Student conduct	
conduct	371.81
regulation	371.51
s.a. spec. levels of ed.;	
also Special education	
employment	
higher ed.	378.365
Student (continued)	
exchanges	370.196 2
finance	
higher ed.	378.35
internat. law	341.767 3
expenditures	
higher ed.	378.38
finances	
higher ed.	378.3
law	344.079 5
spec. jur.	344.3–.9
government	371.59
s.a. spec. levels of ed.;	
also Special education	
housing	371.871
s.a. spec. levels of ed.;	
also Special education	
loans	
higher ed.	378.362
law	344.079 5
spec. jur.	344.3–.9
magazines *see* Serials	
mobility	371.291
s.a. spec. levels of ed.;	
also Special education	
newspapers	371.897 4
s.a. spec. levels of ed.;	
also Special education	
organizations	371.83
spec. subj.	371.84
s.a. spec. kinds e.g.	
Greek-letter societies;	
also spec. levels of	
ed.; also Special	
education	
periodicals *see* Serials;	
also Student	
newspapers	
placement	371.264
s.a. spec. levels of ed.;	
also Special education	
protest *see* Student attitudes	
rights	
law	344.079 3
spec. jur.	344.3–.9
transportation	371.872
s.a. spec. levels of ed.;	
also Special education	
unions	
education	371.625
s.a. spec. levels of ed.;	
also Special education	
unrest *see* Student attitudes	
yearbooks	371.897 6
s.a. spec. levels of ed.;	
also Special education	
Students	371.8
biog. & work	371.809 2
law	344.079
spec. jur.	344.3–.9

Students (continued)
parochial activities for
  Christianity   259.22–.24
  other rel. see Pastoral
    theology
personal religion
  gen. wks.
    Christianity   248.82–.83
    other rel. see Personal
      religion
  meditations for
    Christianity   242.62–.63
    other rel. see Worship
  prayers for
    Christianity   242.82–.83
    other rel. see Worship
persons   *pers.*–375
  spec. schools   *pers.*–379
  s.a. spec. levels of ed.;
    also Young people
Students' songs   784.62
  recordings   789.912 462
Student-teacher relations *see*
    Teaching
Studies (rooms) *see* Study areas
Study
  areas
    household management   643.58
    residential int. dec.   747.73
    s.a. spec. dec.
  clubs   367
  collections
    museology   069.55
  groups
    adult ed.   374.2
  rooms
    education *see* Instructional
      spaces education
    homes *see* Study areas
Study (activity)
  education   371.302 81
  s.a. spec. levels of ed.;
    also Special education
  spec. subj.   *s.s.*–07
Stuffed *see* Padded
Stuffing
  nat. leathers
    manufacturing
      soc. & econ. aspects *see*
        Secondary industries
    technology   675.24
Stunt
  flyers
    biog. & work   797.540 92
    s.a.   *pers.*–797 5
  flying
    sports   797.54
    other aspects see Sports
Stunts
  animal husbandry for   636.088 8
  s.a. spec. animals

Sturgeons *see* Acipenseriformes
Sturminster Newton Dorset Eng.
      area–423 32
Sturnidae
  hunting
    commercial   639.128 863
    sports   799.248 863
  paleozoology   568.8
  zoology   598.863
  other aspects see Aves
Sturts Stony Desert S. Aust.
      area–942 37
Stutsman Co. N.D.   *area*–784 52
Stutterers
  child psych.   155.451 4
Stuttering *see* Stammering
Stuttgart Ger.   *area*–434 7
Stylasterina *see* Hydrozoa
Style
  arts   701.8
  s.a. spec. art forms
  journalism   070.415
  manuals
    bus. commun.   651.740 2
    typesetting   686.225 2
    typewriting   652.32
  office correspondence   651.75
  s.a. other spec. subj.
Styles
  arts   709
  s.a. spec. art forms
  soc. movements   303.484
Stylidiaceae *see* Goodeniales
Stylommatophora *see* Pulmonata
Styracaceae *see* Styracales
Styracales
  botany   583.686
  floriculture   635.933 686
  forestry   634.973 686
  med. aspects
    crop prod.   633.883 686
    gen. pharm.   615.323 686
      toxicology   615.952 368 6
    vet. pharm.   636.089 532 368 6
      toxicology   636.089 595 236 86
  paleobotany   561.3
  other aspects see Plants
Styrenes
  plastics
    chem. tech.   668.423 3
    org. chem.   547.843 223 3
    other aspects see Plastics
    s.a. spec. prod.
Styria Austria   *area*–436 5
Subaqueous *see* Underwater;
    also Submarine
Subatomic *see* Nuclear
Subconscious
  depth psych.   154.2
    animals   156.4
  metaphysics   127

Submersible craft (nautical)
engineering (continued)
    models   623.820 104 5
    seamanship   623.881 5
    other aspects see Vessels
        (nautical)
    s.a. spec. kinds e.g.
        Submarines
Submission
psychology
    personality trait   155.232
Subnormal people *see* Mentally
    deficient
Subpoenas *see* Witnesses law
Subrings
    algebra   512.4
    s.a. spec. appls. e.g.
        Engineering
Subscription
books
    publishing   070.573
    other aspects see Books
  libraries *see* Proprietary
    libraries
  television *see* Pay television
Subscriptions
loan flotation
    pub. finance   336.344
    misc. aspects see Public
        borrowing
Subsets *see* Sets
Subsidence
  physical geol.   551.3
Subsidiaries *see* Combinations
    (organizations)
Subsidies
  export trade   382.6
    misc. aspects see Export
        trade
  internat. comm.   382.63
  law   343.074 2
    spec. jur.   343.3–.9
  natural resources   333.715 8
    s.a. spec. kinds of
        resources e.g.
        Shorelands
  prod. econ.   338.922
    agriculture   338.18
Subsistence theory of wages
economics   331.210 1
Subsonic
velocity
  aeronautical aerodynamics 629.132 303
    s.a. spec. phenomena e.g.
        Lift; *also spec.*
        appls. e.g. Flying
  gas flow mech.
    engineering *see* Dynamics
    physics   533.273
      air flow   533.627 3

Subsonic (continued)
vibrations
  biophysics
    extraterrestrial
      gen. wks.   574.191 942
      animals   591.191 942
      microorganisms   576.119 194 2
      plants   581.191 942
      s.a. spec. organisms
      med. sci.   612.014 542
      animals   636.089 201 454 2
        s.a. spec. animals
      man   612.014 542
    terrestrial
      gen. wks.   574.191 42
      animals   591.191 42
      microorganisms   576.119 142
      plants   581.191 42
      s.a. spec. organisms
      med. sci.   612.014 452
      animals   636.089 201 445 2
        s.a. spec. animals
      man   612.014 452
    s.a. spec. functions,
      systems, organs
  engineering   620.28
    s.a. spec. appls. e.g.
      Musical sound
  physics   534.52
    spec. states of matter   530.4
Substance
metaphysics   111.1
Substations
elect. eng.
  soc. & econ. aspects *see*
      Secondary industries
  technology   621.312 6
  wire telephony *see* Telephony
    wire
  s.a. other spec. kinds
Substitute teaching   371.141 22
  s.a. spec. levels of ed.;
    also Special education
Substitution
physical chem.   541.393
  applied   660.299 3
  organic   547.139 3
  s.a. spec. aspects e.g. Low
    temperatures
s.a. spec. elements, cpds.,
    prod.
Subsurface
materials
  road eng.
    technology   625.735
    other aspects see Roads
  mining   622.2
    spec. deposits   622.33–.39
  prospecting *see* Prospecting

Suiformes
  agric. pests   632.697 34
    s.a. spec. types of culture
      e.g. Forestry; *also*
        spec. crops
  animal husbandry
    technology   636.973 4
      soc. & econ. aspects *see*
        Primary industries
  conservation tech.   639.979 734
  drawing tech.   743.697 34
  hunting
    commercial
      technology   639.117 34
        soc. & econ. aspects
          see Primary
          industries
    sports
      big game   799.277 34
      small game   799.259 734
  paleozoology   569.73
  zoology   599.734
  other aspects see Animals
Suir River Munster Ire.   *area*–419 1
Suitcases
  manufacturing
    soc. & econ. aspects *see*
      Secondary industries
  technology   685.51
Suites (music)
  band *see* Band music
  orchestra   785.8
    recordings   789.912 58
  piano   786.48
    recordings   789.912 648
Suits
  comm. mf.   687.113
    children's   687.13
    women's   687.12
  domestic mf.   646.433
  other aspects see Clothing
Sukhothai period Thailand hist.   959.302 2
  s.a. spec. events & subj.
    e.g. Commerce
Sukkoth
  customs   394.268 296
  Judaism   296.433
Sulaimaniya Iraq   *area*–567 2
Sulawesi Indonesia   *area*–598 4
Sulfa drugs
  org. chem.   547.065
    synthetic drugs   615.316 5
    misc. aspects see
      Pharmacology
    synthetic poisons   615.951 65
    misc. aspects see
      Toxicology
Sulfate process
  wood pulp tech.   676.126

Sulfated
  hydrocarbons
    detergents mf.
      chem. tech.   668.14
      soc. & econ. aspects *see*
        Secondary industries
  oils
    detergents mf.
      chem. tech.   668.14
      soc. & econ. aspects *see*
        Secondary industries
Sulfates
  mineralogy   549.75
  other aspects see Sulfur
    salts
Sulfides
  mineralogy   549.32
  other aspects see Sulfur
    salts
Sulfinic acids
  org. chem.   547.066
    s.a. spec. groupings e.g.
      Aliphatic compounds
  synthetic drugs pharm.   615.316 6
    misc. aspects see
      Pharmacology
  synthetic poisons   615.951 66
    misc. aspects see
      Toxicology
  other aspects see Sulfur
    compounds
Sulfite process
  wood pulp tech.   676.125
Sulfites
  org. chem.   547.061
    s.a. spec. groupings e.g.
      Aliphatic compounds
  synthetic drugs pharm.   615.316 1
    misc. aspects see
      Pharmacology
  synthetic poisons   615.951 61
    misc. aspects see
      Toxicology
  other aspects see Sulfur
    compounds; *also*
      Sulfur salts
Sulfonation
  chem. eng.   660.284 47
  org. chem.   547.27
  s.a. spec. elements, cpds.,
    prod.
Sulfones
  org. chem.   547.065
    s.a. spec. groupings e.g.
      Aliphatic compounds
  synthetic drugs pharm.   615.316 5
    misc. aspects see
      Pharmacology
  synthetic poisons   615.951 65
    misc. aspects see
      Toxicology

Sulfones (continued)
  other aspects see Sulfur
    compounds
Sulfonic acids
  org. chem.   547.067
    s.a. spec. groupings e.g.
      Aliphatic compounds
  synthetic drugs pharm.   615.316 7
    misc. aspects see
      Pharmacology
  synthetic poisons   615.951 67
    misc. aspects see
      Toxicology
  other aspects see Sulfur
    compounds
Sulfosalts
  mineralogy   549.35
Sulfoxides
  org. chem.   547.065
    s.a. spec. groupings e.g.
      Aliphatic compounds
  synthetic drugs pharm.   615.316 5
    misc. aspects see
      Pharmacology
  synthetic poisons   615.951 65
    misc. aspects see
      Toxicology
  other aspects see Sulfur
    compounds
Sulfur   553.668
  chemistry
    inorganic   546.723
    organic   547.06
    s.a. spec. groupings e.g.
      Aliphatic compounds
  technology   661.072 3
    soc. & econ. aspects *see*
      Secondary industries
    s.a. spec. prod.
    s.a. Sulfur compounds
  compounds
    chem. tech.   661.896
    org. chem.   547.06
    s.a. spec. groupings e.g.
      Aliphatic compounds
    synthetic drugs pharm. 615.316
    misc. aspects see
      Pharmacology
    synthetic poisons   615.951 6
    misc. aspects see
      Toxicology
    other aspects see Organic
      chemicals
    s.a. Sulfur chemistry
  dioxide gas
    chem. tech.   665.84
    soc. & econ. aspects *see*
      Secondary industries
  econ. geol.   553.668
  metabolism
    human phys.   612.392 4

Sulfur
  metabolism (continued)
    other aspects see
      Metabolism
  mineralogy   549.27
    s.a. spec. minerals
  mining
    soc. & econ. aspects *see*
      Primary industries
    technology   622.366 8
      prospecting   622.186 68
  pharmacology   615.272 3
    misc. aspects see
      Pharmacology
  salts
    chem. tech.   661.63
    soc. & econ. aspects *see*
      Secondary industries
  plant nutrition *see*
    Macronutrient elements
    plant nutrition
    s.a. spec. prod.
  soil conditioners   631.825
    misc. aspects see Soil
      conditioners
  toxicology   615.925 723
    misc. aspects see
      Toxicology
  other aspects see Nonmetallic
    elements
  s.a. spec. uses
Sulfuric acid
  chem. tech.   661.22
  soc. & econ. aspects *see*
    Secondary industries
  s.a. spec. prod.
Sullivan
  County

Indiana	*area*–772 41
Missouri	*area*–778 235
New Hampshire	*area*–742 75
New York	*area*–747 35
Pennsylvania	*area*–748 59
Tennessee	*area*–768 96

  system psych.   150.194 34
    s.a. spec. subj. & branches
      of psych.
Sully Co. S.D.   *area*–783 284
Sulpician monastic bldgs.
  architecture   726.777 5
  building   690.677 75
  other aspects see
    Religious-purpose
    bldgs.
Sulpicians
  rel. orders   255.75
    church hist.   271.75
    ecclesiology   262.24
Sultans *see* Monarchs
Sulu
  Archipelago   *area*–599 9

Sunday-school
  buildings *see* Accessory rel.
    bldgs.
  services
    rel. instruction
      Christianity   268.7
      other rel. see Religious
        instruction
Sunderland Tyne & Wear Eng.
        area–428 71
Sundials
  mf. tech.   681.111
  time measurement   529.78
Sun-dried blocks
  architectural construction   721.044 22
    s.a. spec. structural
      elements; also spec.
      types of bldgs.
  bldg. construction   693.22
  bldg. materials   691.4
Sunflower Co. Miss.   *area*–762 47
Sunflowers
  flour & meal
    comm. proc.   664.726
    other aspects see Seeds
  other aspects see Asterales
Sung dynasty China hist.   951.024
  s.a. spec. events & subj.
    e.g. Commerce
Sunlight
  photography in   778.712
  plants grown in
    floriculture   635.954
    s.a. spec. plants
Sunnites
  Islamic sects   297.81
  doctrines   297.204 1
  worship   297.301
  s.a. other spec. aspects
Sunshine *see* Sunlight
Sunshine law *see* Freedom of
    information law
Sunspots
  astronomy   523.74
  effects
    geomagnetism   538.746
    spec. states of matter   530.4
Sunstroke *see* Heat sickness
Suomi *see* Finnish
Superannuation *see* Old-age &
    survivors' insurance;
    also Pensions
Superchlorination
  water-supply trmt.
    technology   628.166 2
    other aspects see Water
      supply engineering
Superconductivity
  astrophysics   523.018 762 3
    s.a. spec. celestial bodies

Superconductivity (continued)
  engineering   621.39
    s.a. spec. appls. e.g.
      Refrigeration
      engineering
  eng. materials   620.112 973
    s.a. spec. materials & spec.
      uses
  physics   537.623
    spec. states of matter   530.4
Superconductors
  electrodynamics *see*
    Superconductivity
Superego
  depth psych.   154.22
  animals   156.4
Superfluidity
  physics *see* States of matter
Superheaters
  steam eng.
    soc. & econ. aspects *see*
      Secondary industries
    tech. & mf.   621.197
    s.a. spec. appls. e.g.
      Steam locomotives
Superheterodyne sets
  radio
    engineering   621.384 136 6
    s.a. spec. appls. e.g.
      Radiotelephony
    other aspects see Radio
  television
    engineering   621.388 366
    s.a. spec. appls. e.g.
      Astronautics
    other aspects see
      Television
Superhuman knowledge
  rel. doctrines
    Christianity   231.4
    other rel. see God
Superintendents
  ed. admin.   371.201 1
  other aspects see School
    administrators
  s.a. other spec. activities
Superior
  city Wis.   *area*–775 12
  intelligence
    psychology   153.98
    animals   156.398
    children   155.413
    s.a. psych. of other spec.
      groups
  Lake   *area*–774 9
  Ontario   *area*–713 12
  s.a. other spec. subj.
Supermarkets
  advertising   659.196 588 78
  pub. relations   659.296 588 78
  retail marketing   658.878

Supernatural beings
  lit. trmt.
    folk lit.
      sociology   398.45
      texts & lit. crit.   398.21
    gen. wks.
      collections   808.803 75
      hist. & crit.   809.933 75
    spec. lits.
      collections   *lit. sub.*–080 375
      hist. & crit.   *lit. sub.*–093 75
    s.a. spec. lit. forms
    stage trmt.   792.090 937 5
    s.a. spec. mediums e.g.
      Television; *also spec.*
      kinds of drama e.g.
      Tragedies (drama)
Supernaturally endowed persons
  rel. leaders
    comp. rel.   291.62
    s.a. spec. rel.
Supernovae *see* Eruptive
      variable stars
Superphosphates
  fertilizers *see* Phosphorus
    fertilizers
Superposition principles
  sound *see* Synthesis sound
Supersaturated solutions
  physical chem. *see* Solutions
    physical chem.
Supersonic
  velocity
    aeronautical aerodynamics   629.132 305
    s.a. spec. phenomena e.g.
      Lift; *also spec.*
      appls. e.g. Flying
  gas flow mech.
    engineering *see* Dynamics
    physics   533.275
    air flow   533.627 5
  vibrations *see* Ultrasonic
    vibrations
Superstitions   001.96
  folklore   398.41
  s.a. spec. subj.
Supertanker
  berthing areas *see* Anchorages
    port. eng.
Supervised activities
  child care
    home econ.   649.5
Supervision
  dramatic performances
    motion pictures   791.430 23
    radio   791.440 23
    stage   792.023
    s.a. spec. kinds e.g.
      Tragedies (drama)
    television   791.450 23

Supervision (continued)
  personnel admin.
    gen. management   658.302
    spec. subj.   *s.s.*–068 3
    libraries   023.9
    pub. admin.   350.102
      central govts.   351.102
      spec. jur.   353–354
      local govts.   352.005 102
  s.a. other spec. activities
Supervisors
  ed. admin.   371.201 3
  other aspects see School
      administrators
Supervisory
  library positions   023.4
Supper
  cookery   641.53
  soc. customs   394.15
Supplementary
  budgeting
    pub. admin.   350.722 4
      central govts.   351.722 4
      spec. jur.   353–354
      local govts.   352.124
  budgets
    pub. admin.   350.722 54
      central govts.   351.722 54
      spec. jur.   353–354
      local govts.   352.125 4
  feeding
    bees   638.144
    s.a. other spec. organisms
  s.a. other spec. subj.
Supplies
  armed forces   355.8
    s.a. spec. mil. branches
  govt. manufacture *see*
      Supplies procurement
      pub. admin.
  management & disposal
    pub. admin.   350.713 5
      central govts.   351.713 5
      spec. jur.   353–354
      local govts.   352.163 5
  procurement
    pub. admin.   350.712 5
      central govts.   351.712 5
      spec. jur.   353–354
      local govts.   352.162 5
  s.a. Materials
Supply
  administration
    armed forces   355.621
    s.a. spec. mil. branches
  depots
    armed forces   355.75
    s.a. spec. mil. branches
  econ. theory   338.521 3

Supply (continued)
  logistics
    mil. sci. — 355.415
    s.a. spec. mil. branches
  management *see* Materials
    management
  natural resources — 333.711
    s.a. spec. kinds of
      resources e.g.
      Shorelands
  prod. econ.
    commun. services
      telecommunications — 384.041
        radiobroadcasting — 384.543
        telegraphy — 384.13
          submarine cable — 384.43
          wire — 384.13
          wireless — 384.523
        telephony — 382.63
          wire — 384.63
          wireless — 384.533
        television — 384.554 3
          cable television — 384.555 63
          subscription — 384.554 7
    highways
      commerce — 388.11
    transportation
      commerce
        air — 387.71
        inland waterway — 386.1
        maritime — 387.51
        motor — 388.32
        railway — 385.1
          special-duty — 385.5
        urban transp. — 388.404 2
      s.a. other spec. subj.
  services
    armed forces — 355.341
    s.a. spec. mil. branches
  ships mil.
    engineering — 623.826 5
      design — 623.812 65
      models — 623.820 165
    naval forces
      material — 359.83
      organization — 359.326 5
    seamanship — 623.882 65
    other aspects see Vessels
      (nautical)
  s.a. Supply-&-demand
Supply-&-demand
  econ. theory — 338.521
  forecasts
    prod. econ. — 338.02
      primary ind.
        agriculture — 338.17
        mineral — 338.27
        other — 338.37
      secondary ind. — 338.47
  foreign exchange rates — 332.456 2

Supply-transportation
  automobiles *see* Trucks
Support
  of music — 780.07
  vehicles *see* Vehicles
    s.a. other spec. subj.
Supporters *see* Supporting
    garments
Supporting
  garments
    comm. mf. — 687.25
    other aspects see Underwear
  structures
    underground mining — 622.28
      spec. deposits — 622.33–.39
    s.a. other spec. uses
Supports
  chem. apparatus — 542.2
    s.a. spec. appls. e.g.
      Organic chemistry
  photosensitive surfaces
    photography — 771.52
    gen. tech. — 770.283
    spec. proc. & fields — 772–778
  s.a. other spec. uses
Suppressed books
  hist. & crit. — 098.1
Supranational states
  pol. sci. — 321.04
  pub. admin. — 354.1
Suprarenal glands *see* Adrenal
    glands
Supreme
  court
    justices
      occupational ethics — 174.3
      s.a. — *pers.*–342
    of Judicature
      England
        law — 347.420 29
      reports
        U.S. law — 348.734 13
    courts
      law — 347.035
      spec. jur. — 347.3–.9
      U.S.
        federal — 347.732 6
        state — 347.733 6
          spec. states — 347.74–.79
      other aspects see Courts
    s.a. other spec. subj.
Suras Koran — 297.122 9
Surbiton London Eng. — *area*–421 94
Surety bonds insurance — 368.84
  misc. aspects see Insurance
Suretyship
  law *see* Secured transactions
    law
Surf riding
  sports — 797.172
  other aspects see Sports

Surface-to-underwater
  guided missiles
    mil. eng.
      soc. & econ. aspects *see*
        Secondary industries
      tech. & mf.   623.451 96
Surfacing
  roads
    technology
      pavements   625.8
      soil   625.75
    other aspects see Roads
  s.a. other spec. subj.
Surfactants
  manufacturing
    chem. tech.   668.1
    soc. & econ. aspects *see*
      Secondary industries
Surfboarding
  sports   797.172
  other aspects see Sports
Surfers Paradise Qld.   *area*–943 2
Surgeons
  biog. & work   617.092
  prof. duties & characteristics   617.023 2
    law   344.041 2
      spec. jur.   344.3–.9
    vet. sci.   636.089 702 32
  other aspects see Medical
      scientists
  s.a.   *pers.*–617 1
Surgeons' gloves
  latex *see* Dipped latex
      products
Surgery
  med. sci.   617
    vet. med.   636.089 7
    s.a. spec. animals
Surgical
  abortion   618.88
    vet. med.   636.089 888
    s.a. spec. animals
  assistants
    prof. duties &
      characteristics   617.023 3
    other aspects see Surgeons
  complications
    med. sci.   617.01
    misc. aspects see
      Diseases
    s.a. spec. diseases
  cottons *see* Surgical gauzes
  dressings
    use
      surgery   617.93
      misc. aspects see
        Diseases
      s.a. spec. diseases

Surgical (continued)
  gauzes
    fabric
      manufacturing
        soc. & econ. aspects
          see Secondary
          industries
        technology   677.8
      other aspects see
        Textiles
    use
      surgery   617.93
      misc. aspects see
        Diseases
      s.a. spec. diseases
  insurance   368.382 2
    misc. aspects see Insurance
  nursing   610.736 77
  sequelae
    med. sci.   617.01
    misc. aspects see
      Diseases
    s.a. spec. diseases
  shock *see* Shock
    (pathological)
  technicians
    prof. duties &
      characteristics   617.023 3
    other aspects see Surgeons
Surigao Philippines   *area*–599 7
Surinam   *area*–883
Suriname Surinam   *area*–883 6
Surnames   929.42
Surplus
  labor areas
    govt. procurement in
      pub. admin.   350.712 048
        central govts.   351.712 048
          spec. jur.   353–354
        local govts.   352.162 048
  property
    mil. admin.   355.621 3
    s.a. spec. mil. branches
    pub. revenues   336.1
    misc. aspects see Nontax
      revenues
Surpluses
  natural resources   333.711
    s.a. spec. kinds of
      resources e.g.
      Shorelands
  primary prod.
    agricultural   338.15
    mineral   338.27
    other   338.37
  prod. econ. *see*
      Maladjustments prod.
      econ.
  secondary prod.   338.47

Surrealism
  arts
    gen. wks.   709.040 63
      spec. places   709.1–.9
    painting   759.066 3
      spec. places   759.1–.9
    sculpture   735.230 463
      spec. places   730.9
    s.a. other spec. art forms
Surrey Eng.   *area*–422 1
Surry Co.
  North Carolina   *area*–756 65
  Virginia   *area*–755 562
Sürt Turkey   *area*–566 7
Surveillance
  freedom from
    civil right
      pol. sci.   323.448 2
  law enforcement   363.232
    misc. aspects see Law
      enforcement
  use of closed circuit
    television   384.555 7
Surveying   526.9
  canal eng.
    technology   627.131
    other aspects see Liquids
      engineering
  dam eng.
    technology   627.81
      spec. dams   627.82–.85
    other aspects see Liquids
      engineering
  railroad eng.
    technology   625.11
    other aspects see Railroads
  real estate
    law   346.043 2
      spec. jur.   346.3–.9
  road eng.
    technology   625.723
    other aspects see Roads
  s.a. other spec. appls.
Surveyors
  biog. & work   526.909 2
  s.a.   *pers.*–526
Surveys
  desc. research *see*
    Descriptive research
  land econ.   333.332
  marketing   380.1
    technology   658.83
  scientific   508
    s.a. spec. sci.
  s.a. other spec. appls.
Survival
  hygiene   613.69
  mil. sci.   355.54
  s.a. spec. mil. branches

Survivors
  insurance *see* Old-age &
    survivors' insurance
  soc. services
    aged *see* Aged people
      sociology
    young people *see* Young
      people soc. services
Susanna
  deuterocanonical book   229.6
  other aspects see Apocrypha
Susceptibility
  magnetism *see* Magnetic
    phenomena
Suspended sentence
  penology   364.63
Suspense
  fiction *see* Mystery fiction
  plays *see* Melodrama
Suspension bridges
  structural eng.   624.5
  other aspects see Bridges
    (structures)
Suspensions (chemistry)
  colloid chem. *see* Hydrosols
    colloid chem.
Suspensions (exclusions)
  school ed.   371.543
    s.a. spec. levels of ed.;
      also Special education
Susquehanna
  Co. Pa.   *area*–748 34
  River
    Maryland   *area*–752 74
    Pennsylvania   *area*–748
    East Branch   *area*–748 3
    West Branch   *area*–748 5
Sussex
  cattle
    animal husbandry   636.222
    other aspects see Cattle
  County
    Delaware   *area*–751 7
    England   *area*–422 5
    New Jersey   *area*–749 76
    Virginia   *area*–755 565
Sutherland Scot.   *area*–411 65
Suttapitaka Buddhism   294.382 3
Suttee
  death customs   393.9
Sutter Co. Calif.   *area*–794 34
Sutton
  borough London Eng. *area*–421 92
  Co. Tex.   *area*–764 879
  town Lincolnshire Eng. *area*–425 32
Sutton Coldfield West Midlands
    Eng.   *area*–424 96
Sutton-in-Ashfield
    Nottinghamshire Eng.
            area–425 25

Sutures
  surgical use   617.917 8
    misc. aspects see Diseases
    s.a. spec. diseases
Suturing *see* Operative surgery
Suwalki Poland   *area*–438 3
Suwanee
  Co. Fla.   *area*–759 82
  River Fla.   *area*–759 8
Svalbard   *area*–981
Svan *see* Caucasic
Svanetian *see* Caucasic
Svealand Sweden   *area*–487
Svendborg Denmark   *area*–489 4
Sverdlovsk RSFSR   *area*–478 7
Sverdrup Isls. Northwest Ter.
                area–719 5
Svetambara Jainism   294.492
Swabia Ger.   *area*–433 7
Swabian
  language
    linguistics   437.37
    literature   830
    s.a.   *lang.*–33
    s.a. Swabia; *also other*
         spec. subj. e.g. Arts
Swadlincote Derbyshire Eng.
                area–425 19
Swaffham Norfolk Eng.   *area*–426 14
Swahili language
  linguistics   496.392
  literature   896.392
  s.a.   *lang.*–963 92
Swain Co. N.C.   *area*–756 96
Swale
  district Kent Eng.   *area*–422 33
  River North Yorkshire Eng.
                area–428 48
Swaledale North Yorkshire Eng.
                area–428 48
Swallow tanagers
  zoology   598.8
  other aspects see
        Passeriformes
Swallows *see* Hirundinidae
Swamps
  drainage *see* Drainage
  ecology life sci. *see*
        Wetlands ecology life
        sci.
Swan Hill Vic.   *area*–945 9
Swan River W. Aust.   *area*–941 2
Swanage Dorset Eng.   *area*–423 36
Swans
  animal husbandry   636.68
    soc. & econ. aspects *see*
        Primary industries
Swans Lagoon Fauna Reserve Qld.
                area–943 6
Swansea West Glamorgan Wales
                area–429 82

Swanskin fabrics
  arts   746.046 24
    s.a. spec. proc. e.g.
        Weaving
  manufacturing
    soc. & econ. aspects *see*
        Secondary industries
    technology   677.624
  other aspects see Textiles
  s.a. spec. prod.
Swarming control
  apiculture   638.146
Swat Pakistan   *area*–549 122
Swatow dialect
  linguistics   495.17
  literature   895.1
  s.a.   *lang.*–951 7
Swaziland   *area*–681 3
Swazis   *r.e.n.*–968 3
Swearing
  legal procedure *see* Legal
        procedure
  profanity *see* Profanity
Sweat glands
  anatomy
    human   611.77
    other aspects see
        Integumentary organs
  diseases
    gen. med.   616.56
    geriatrics   618.976 56
    pediatrics   618.925 6
    pub. health   614.595 6
    statistics   312.356
    other aspects see Diseases
  human physiology   612.792 1
  physical anthropometry 573.677
  tissue biology human 611.018 977
Sweaters
  comm. mf.
    soc. & econ. aspects *see*
        Secondary industries
    technology   687.146
  domestic mf.   646.454
  soc. customs   391.1–.3
  other aspects see Clothing
Sweden   *area*–485
Swedenborgianism *see* Church of
        the New Jerusalem
Swedenborgians *see* New
        Jerusalemites
Swedes *see* Swedish
Swedes (vegetables) *see*
        Rutabagas
Swedish
  language
    linguistics   439.7
    literature   839.7
    s.a.   *lang.*–397
  people   *r.e.n.*–397

Swedish (continued)
  troops
    in American Revolution
      history   973.346
  turnips *see* Rutabagas
  s.a. Sweden; *also other*
      spec. subj. e.g. Arts
Sweep generators
  radiowave electronics *see*
      Testing-devices
      radiowave electronics
Sweeping
  housecleaning   648.5
  streets
    pub. sanitation eng.   628.462
Sweet
  cherries
    agriculture   634.237
    other aspects see Cherries
  cider   641.26
    comm. proc.   663.63
    other aspects see
      Nonalcoholic beverages
  clovers
    agriculture   633.366
    soc. & econ. aspects *see*
      Primary industries
    other aspects see
      Papilionaceae; *also*
      Field crops
  corn
    agriculture   635.672
    soc. & econ. aspects *see*
      Primary industries
    foods   641.356 72
    preparation
      commercial   664.805 672
      domestic   641.656 72
    other aspects see
      Panicoideae; *also*
      Vegetables
  Grass Co. Mont.   *area*–786 64
  herbs *see* Herbs
  peas *see* Leguminales
  peppers *see* Green peppers
  potatoes
    agriculture
      field crops   633.492
      garden crops   635.22
    soc. & econ. aspects *see*
      Primary industries
    foods   641.352 2
    preparation
      commercial   664.805 22
      domestic   641.652 2
    other aspects see
      Solanales; *also*
      Vegetables
  sorghums *see* Sorghums
  s.a. other spec. subj.
Sweetleaf family *see* Styracales

Sweets *see* Candies
Sweetwater Co. Wyo.   *area*–787 85
Sweida Syria   *area*–569 14
Swift
  Co. Minn.   *area*–776 41
  Current Sask.   *area*–712 43
Swifts *see* Apodiformes
Swimmers
  biog. & work   797.210 92
  s.a.   *pers.*–797 2
Swimming
  accidents *see* Recreation
    accidents
  pool bldgs.
    domestic *see* Accessory
      domestic structures
    public
      architecture   725.74
      building   690.574
      other aspects see Public
        structures
  pools
    private *see* Recreational
      areas
    pub. sanitation *see*
      Recreational facilities
      pub. sanitation
    safety aspects *see* Sports
    school buildings   371.624
    s.a. spec. levels of ed.;
      also Special education
    other aspects see
      Recreational facilities
  sports   797.21
    misc. aspects see Sports
Swimsuits *see* Sportswear
Swindles *see* Frauds
Swindon Wiltshire Eng.   *area*–423 13
Swine
  animal husbandry   636.4
    soc. & econ. aspects *see*
      Primary industries
  products
    meats *see* Pork
    other prod. see spec. prod.
      e.g. Hides
  other aspects see Suiformes
Swine flu *see* Influenzas
Swing
  bridges
    structural eng.   624.83
    other aspects see Bridges
      (structures)
  music
    recordings   789.912 157 4
    theory   781.574
    s.a. spec. mediums
Swinton South Yorkshire Eng.
      area–428 23
Swinton & Pendlebury Greater
      Manchester Eng. *area*–427 32

Swisher Co. Tex.	*area*–764 838
Swiss	
cheeses	
dairy tech.	637.354
other aspects see Cheeses	
literature	
French	840
gen. wks.	
collections	808.899 494
hist. & crit.	809.894 94
German	830
Italian	850
people	*r.e.n.*–35
timber arch.	724.7
spec. places	720.9
other aspects see	
Architectural schools	
Swiss-German language	
linguistics	437.949 4
literature	830
s.a.	*lang.*–35
Switchboard operators	
office services	651.374 3
Switchboards *see* Telephone	
switchboards	
Switches	
railroad eng.	
technology	625.163
other aspects see Permanent	
way	
wire telegraphy *see*	
Instrumentation wire	
telegraphy	
s.a. other spec. appls.	
Switching	
circuits	
tech. & mf.	621.381 537
microelectronics	621.381 737
microwave electronics	621.381 327
radiowave electronics	621.381 537
x- & gamma-ray electronics	621.381 6
s.a. spec. appls. e.g.	
Radiocontrol	
other aspects see Microwave	
electronics; Radiowave	
electronics; X-ray	
electronics	
equipment elect. power *see*	
Control devices	
electrodynamic eng.	
theory	
electronic circuits *see*	
Switching circuits	
Switzerland	
country	*area*–494
ancient	*area*–363
Co. Ind.	*area*–772 125
Swivel	
bridges *see* Swing bridges	
embroidery *see* Machine	
embroidery	

Sword dance	
recreation	793.35
Swordfishes *see* Acanthopterygii	
Swordplay *see* Fencing	
(swordplay)	
Swords	
art metalwork	739.722
other aspects see Edged	
weapons	
Sycamores *see* Hamamelidales	
Syconosa *see* Calcispongiae	
Sydney	
New South Wales	*area*–944 1
Nova Scotia	*area*–716 96
Syenites	553.52
econ. geol.	553.52
mining	
soc. & econ. aspects *see*	
Primary industries	
technology	622.352
prospecting	622.185 2
other aspects see Plutonic	
rocks	
s.a. spec. uses	
Syllabuses	*s.s.*–020 2
Syllogisms	
logic	166
Sylviidae	
hunting	
commercial	639.128 843
sports	799.248 843
paleozoology	568.8
zoology	598.843
other aspects see Aves	
Sylvite	
mineralogy	549.4
Symbioses	
ecology	574.524 82
animals	591.524 82
microorganisms	576.15
plants	581.524 82
s.a. spec. organisms	
Symbolic	
divination	
parapsychology	133.33
garments	
comm. mf.	
soc. & econ. aspects *see*	
Secondary industries	
technology	687.15
headgear	687.4
other aspects see Clothing	
logic	511.3
s.a. spec. math. branches;	
also spec. appls. e.g.	
Reasoning	
theory	
folklore	398.16
Symbolism	
art representation	704.946
paintings	753.6

Synchronous
  accelerators
    physics   539.735
      s.a. spec. physical
        phenomena e.g. Heat
  converters
    electrodynamic eng.
      soc. & econ. aspects *see*
        Secondary industries
      tech. & mf.   621.313 5
        s.a. spec. appls. e.g.
          Electric locomotives
      other aspects see
        Electrodynamics
  generators
    electrodynamic eng.
      soc. & econ. aspects *see*
        Secondary industries
      tech. & mf.   621.313 4
        s.a. spec. appls. e.g.
          Electric-power plants
      other aspects see
        Electrodynamics
  machinery
    electrodynamic eng. *see*
      Alternating-current
        machinery
Synchroscopes *see* Phase elect.
        measurement
Synchrotrons
  physics   539.735
    s.a. spec. physical
      phenomena e.g. Heat
Synclines
  structural geol.   551.86
    s.a. spec. aspects e.g.
      Prospecting
Syncretism
  philosophy   148
    indiv. phil.   180–190
    s.a. spec. branches of phil.
      e.g. Metaphysics
Syndicalism
  economics   335.82
Syndicated crime
  soc. path.   364.106 8
Syndicates
  banking econ.   332.16
    misc. aspects see Banking
  other aspects see
    Unincorporated bus.
      enterprises
Synecology
  life sci.   574.524
    animals   591.524
    microorganisms   576.15
    plants   581.524
    s.a. spec. organisms
Synentognathi *see* Mesichthyes

Synesthesia
  psychology
    gen. wks.   152.189
    animals   156.218 9
    children   155.412
    s.a. psych. of other spec.
      groups
    influences   155.911 89
Synod of Evangelical Lutheran
        Churches (Slovak)   284.132 3
    misc. aspects see Lutheran
Synods
  Christian ecclesiology   262.4
Synonyms   410
  spec. langs.
    nonstandard forms *lang. sub.*–7
    standard forms
      dictionaries   *lang. sub.*–31
      usage   *lang. sub.*–8
    spec. subj.   *s.s.*–014
Synopses   *s.s.*–020 2
Synoptic Gospels *see* Gospels
Syntax (linguistics) *see*
        Grammar (linguistics)
Synthesis
  chemistry
    engineering   660.284 4
    physical   541.39
      applied   660.299
    organic   547.2
    s.a. spec. aspects e.g.
      Low temperatures
    s.a. spec. elements, cpds.,
      prod.
    engineering   620.004 2
      s.a. spec. branches of eng.
        e.g. Electrical
        engineering
  signals
    commun. eng.
      technology   621.380 433
      s.a. spec. appls. e.g.
        Space communication
    other aspects see
      Communication
  sound
    engineering   620.21–.25
      s.a. spec. appls. e.g.
        Music bldgs. for
    physics   534.47
      spec. states of matter   530.4
    s.a. other spec. subj.
Synthetic
  asphalts *see* Bituminous
        materials
  building materials
    manufacturing
      soc. & econ. aspects *see*
        Secondary industries
    technology   666.89

Systems
  analysis (continued)
    management use   658.403 2
      pub. admin.   350.007 3
        central govts.   351.007 3
          spec. jur.   353–354
      local govts.   352.000 473
  analysts
    professional library
      positions   023.2
  electronic eng.
    soc. & econ. aspects *see*
      Secondary industries
    technology   621.381 1
     s.a. spec. appls.
  engineering   620.7
    s.a. spec. appls. e.g.
      Management
  engineers
    biog. & work   620.709 2
    s.a.   *pers.*–620 7
  s.a. other spec. appls.
Szabolcs-Szatmar Hungary *area*–439 9
Szczecin Poland *area*–438 1
Szechwan China *area*–513 8
Szolnok Hungary *area*–439 8
Szondi tests
  indiv. psych.   155.284 3

T

T formation
 American football — 796.332 22
TNT *see* High explosives
TV *see* Television
TV dinners
 food service — 642.1
Tabasco Mex. — *area*–726 3
Tabby *see* Sun-dried blocks
Tabernacles Feast *see* Sukkoth
Tabernacles (furniture) *see*
  Sacramental furniture
Tabernacles (houses of worship)
  see Temples
Tabes dorsalis *see* Locomotor
  ataxia
Tablature (music)
 music theory — 781.24
 s.a. spec. mediums
Table
 cereals
  comm. proc. — 664.756
 decor
  etiquette — 395.3
  home econ. — 642.7–.8
 furnishings
  home econ. — 642.7
 linens
  domestic mf. — 646.21
  textile arts — 746.96
 use
  home econ. — 642.7
 manners
  etiquette — 395.54
 salt
  manufacturing
   soc. & econ. aspects *see*
    Secondary industries
  technology — 664.4
 service
  home econ. — 642.6
 setting
  home econ. — 642.6
 tennis
  equipment mf. — 688.763 46
   soc. & econ. aspects *see*
    Secondary industries
  players
   biog. & work — 796.346 092
   s.a. — *pers.*–796 34
  other aspects see Sports
Tableaux
 indoor amusements — 793.24
Tablecloths *see* Table linens
Tables (furniture)
 dec. arts — 749.3
 mf. tech. — 684.13
  outdoor — 684.18
other aspects see Furniture

Tables (lists)
 of cases
  law — 348.048
   spec. jur. — 348.3–.9
  U.S.
   federal — 348.734 8
   state & local — 348.74–.79
  spec. subj. — *law s.s.*–026 48
 of laws
  law — 348.028
   spec. jur. — 348.3–.9
  U.S.
   federal — 348.732 8
   state & local — 348.74–.79
  spec. subj. — *law s.s.*–026 38
 spec. subj. — *s.s.*–021 2
 statistical method — 001.422 4
 spec. subj. *see* Statistical
   method spec. subj.
Table-tipping
 spiritualism — 133.92
Table-top photography *see*
  Special effects
  photography
Tablets
 prac. pharm. — 615.43
  misc. aspects see
   Pharmacology
Tableware
 arts
  decorative
   ceramics
    gen. wks.
     earthenware — 738.38
     porcelain — 738.28
     pottery — 738.24
     processes — 738.1
   glass — 748.8
   metals
    gold — 739.228 3
     hist. & geog. trmt. — 739.227
    iron & steel — 739.48
    platinum — 739.24
    silver — 739.238 3
     hist. & geog. trmt. — 739.237
    other metals — 739.5
   wood — 736.4
  handicrafts — 745.593
 comm. mf.
  earthenware
   technology — 666.68
   other aspects see
    Earthenware
  porcelain
   technology — 666.58
   other aspects see
    Porcelain
  s.a. other spec. materials
 rel. significance
  Christianity — 247.8
  comp. rel. — 291.37

Tableware
  rel. significance (continued)
    s.a. other spec. rel.
Taboos *see* Social customs
Tabora Tanzania   *area*–678 28
Tabulation
  statistical method   001.422 4
  spec. subj. *see* Statistical
    method spec. subj.
Taccaceae *see* Haemodorales
Tachina flies *see* Cyclorrhapha
Táchira Venezuela   *area*–871 2
Tachometers
  mf. tech.   681.118
  soc. & econ. aspects *see*
    Secondary industries
Tackles
  machine eng.
    soc. & econ. aspects *see*
      Secondary industries
  tech & mf.   621.863
    s.a. spec. appls. e.g.
      Internal transportation
  other aspects see Mechanics
Tackling
  American football   796.332 26
  other sports see spec. games
Tacna Peru   *area*–853 5
Tacoma Wash.   *area*–797 78
Tact *see* Courtesy
Tactical
  drills
    mil. sci.   355.54
    s.a. spec. mil. branches
  exercises
    mil. sci.   355.54
    s.a. spec. mil. branches
  geography
    mil. sci.   355.47
    s.a. spec. mil. branches
  rockets
    mil. eng.
      soc. & econ. aspects *see*
        Secondary industries
    tech. & mf.   623.454 3
  s.a. other spec. subj.
Tactics
  games
    recreation *see spec. games*
  mil. sci.   355.42
    s.a. spec. mil. branches
Tactile
  organs
    anatomy
      human   611.88
      other aspects see Sense
        organs
    physiology
      human   612.88
      other aspects see Sensory
        functions

Tactile
  organs (continued)
    tissue biology human   611.018 988
  perception *see* Cutaneous
    perception
Tacuarembó Uruguay   *area*–895 32
Tadcastle North Yorkshire Eng.
        area–428 45
Tadpole shrimps *see*
    Branchiopoda
Tadzhik SSR   *area*–586
Tadzhiki
  language
    linguistic   491.59
    literature   891.59
    s.a.   *lang.*–915 9
  people   *r.e.n.*–915 9
  s.a. other spec. subj. e.g.
    Arts
Tadzhikistan   *area*–586
Taeniodontia
  paleozoology   569.36
Taeniopteris
  paleobotany   561.597
Taff-Ely Mid Glamorgan Wales
        area–429 78
Taft
  William H. admin.
    U.S. hist.   973.912
    s.a. spec. events & subj.
      e.g. Commerce
Tagala *see* Philippine
Tagalog
  language
    linguistics   499.211
    literature   899.211
    s.a.   *lang.*–992 11
  people   *r.e.n.*–992 1
  s.a. Philippines; *also other*
      spec. subj. e.g. Arts
Tagus River   *area*–469 45
  Portugal   *area*–469 45
  Spain   *area*–462 8
Tahiti   *area*–962 11
Tahitian *see* Polynesian
Tahoe Lake   *area*–794 38
  California   *area*–794 38
  Nevada   *area*–793 57
Taichihuan
  equipment mf.   688.768 155
  sports   796.815 5
  other aspects see Sports
Tailem Bend S. Aust.   *area*–942 33
Tailless whipscorpions
  zoology   595.453 6
  other aspects see Arachnida
Tailoring
  comm. clothing mf.
    soc. & econ. aspects *see*
      Secondary industries
  technology   687.044

Tailoring
  comm. clothing mf. (continued)
    s.a. spec. garments
    domestic clothing mf.   646.4
Tailors
  biog. & work   646.402 092
  commercial   687.044 092
  s.a.   *pers.*–646 4
Taimyr Nat. Region RSFSR   *area*–575
Tain Highland Scot.   *area*–411 72
Taishō period
  Japan hist.   952.032
    s.a. spec. events & subj.
      e.g. Arts
Taiwan   *area*–512 49
Taiwanese
  people   *r.e.n.*–992 5
    s.a. other spec. subj. e.g.
      Arts
Tajik *see* Tadzhik
Takeoff
  accidents
    air transp.   363.124 92
    misc. aspects see
      Transportation
      accidents
  gear
    aircraft eng.
      soc. & econ. aspects *see*
        Secondary industries
      tech. & mf.   629.134 381
  procedures
    aeronautics   629.132 521 2
    spec. aircraft   629.132 522–.132 528
  astronautics
    manned   629.452
      lunar flights   629.454 3
      planetary flights   629.455
    unmanned   629.432
    s.a. spec. appls. e.g.
      Space warfare
Takeovers
  management   658.16
Talbot Co.
  Georgia   *area*–758 483
  Maryland   *area*–752 32
Talc
  mineraloqy   549.67
  refractory materials   553.676
    econ. geol.   553.676
    mining   622.367 6
      prospecting   622.186 76
    other aspects see
      Refractory materials
Talca Chile   *area*–833 5
Talented *see* Gifted
Talents
  psychic *see* Psychic
Tales *see* Fiction
Taliaferro Co. Ga.   *area*–758 616

Talismans
  Islamic worship   297.33
  numismatics   737.23
  occultism   133.44
  rel. significance
    Christianity   247.872 3
    comp. rel.   291.37
    s.a. other spec. rel.
Talking books *see* Recordings
Talking-picture photography *see*
      Sound motion-picture
      photography
Talks *see* Speeches
Tall oil
  recovery from pulp
    technology   676.5
Talladega Co. Ala.   *area*–761 61
Tallahassee Fla.   *area*–759 88
Tallahatchie Co. Miss.   *area*–762 455
Tallangatta Vic.   *area*–945 5
Tallapoosa
  Co. Ala.   *area*–761 53
  River Ala.   *area*–761 53
Tallows *see* Animal fats
Talmudic
  literature Judaism   296.12
  period Palestine hist.   956.940 2
    s.a. spec. events & subj.
      e.g. Commerce
Tama Co. Ia.   *area*–777 56
Tamar River
  Devon Eng.   *area*–423 5
  Tasmania   *area*–946 5
Tamaricaceae *see* Tamaricales
Tamaricales
  botany   583.158
  floriculture   635.933 158
  forestry   634.973 158
  med. aspects
    crop prod.   633.883 158
    gen. pharm.   615.323 158
      toxicology   615.952 315 8
    vet. pharm.   636.089 532 315 8
      toxicology   636.089 595 231 58
  paleobotany   561.3
  other aspects see Plants
Tamarinds *see* Leguminous fruits
Tamarindus *see* Leguminous
      fruits
Tamarins *see* Callithricidae
Tamarisk family *see* Tamaricales
Tamashek language *see* Berber
      languages
Tamaulipas Mex.   *area*–721 2
Tamazight lanuguage *see* Berber
      languages
Tambo River Vic.   *area*–945 6
Tambourines *see* Membranophones
Tambov RSFSR   *area*–473 5
Tamerlane
  reign Asia hist.   950.2

Tamerlane (continued)
  s.a. spec. events & subj.
      e.g. Commerce
Tameside Greater Manchester Eng.
                          area–427 35
Tamil
  language
    linguistics   494.811
    literature   894.811
    s.a.   *lang.*–948 11
  Nadu India   *area*–548 2
  people   *r.e.n.*–948
  s.a. other spec. subj. e.g.
      Arts
Tamilnadu India   *area*–548 2
Tampons *see* Surgical gauzes
Tamworth
  New South Wales   *area*–944 4
  Staffordshire Eng.   *area*–424 69
Tanagers *see* Thraupidae
Tanaidacea
  fishing sports   799.255 374
  zoology   595.374
  other aspects see
      Eumalacostraca
Tanami Desert Fauna Reserve N.
      Ter. Aust.   *area*–942 91
Tandem bicycles
  engineering
    gen. tech. & mf.   629.227 6
    maintenance   629.287 76
    models   629.221 76
    operation   629.284 76
    s.a. other spec. aspects
        e.g. Brakes
  soc. & econ. aspects *see*
      Secondary industries
Tandragee N. Ire.   *area*–416 61
Tandridge Surrey Eng.   *area*–422 18
Taney Co. Mo.   *area*–778 797
T'ang dynasty China hist.   951.01
  s.a. spec. events & subj.
      e.g. Commerce
Tanga Tanzania   *area*–678 22
Tanganyika   *area*–678 2
  Lake   *area*–678 28
Tangent space at a point
  integral geometry   516.362
  s.a. spec. appls. e.g.
      Engineering
Tangerines *see* Oranges (fruit)
Tangible
  property taxes *see* Personal
      property taxes
  risks insurance   368.062
Tangier
  Morocco   *area*–642
  Virginia   *area*–755 16
Tangipahoa Par. La.   *area*–763 13
Tango *see* Dance
Tank cars *see* Freight cars

Tankers (ships) *see* Cargo ships
      powered
Tanks (containers)
  water-supply eng.
    technology   628.13
    other aspects see Water
        supply engineering
Tanks (vehicles)
  armed forces   358.18
  mil. eng.   623.747 52
Tanners *see* Leathers
      manufacturers
Tanning nat. leathers
  manufacturing
    soc. & econ. aspects *see*
        Secondary industries
    technology   675.23
Tannin-producing plants
  agriculture   633.87
  soc. & econ. aspects *see*
      Primary industries
Tannins
  org. chem.   547.783
  other aspects see
      Carbohydrates
Tantalum
  chemistry
    inorganic   546.526
    organic   547.055 26
    s.a. spec. groupings e.g.
        Aliphatic compunds
  technology   661.052 6
    organic   661.895
  soc. & econ. aspects *see*
      Secondary industries
  s.a. spec. prod.
  eng. materials   620.189 35
  s.a. spec uses
  metallography   669.957 35
  metallurgy   669.735
    physical & chem.   669.967 35
  soc. & econ. aspects *see*
      Secondary industries
  mineral aspects
    econ. geol.   553.465
    mineralogy   549.23
    mining
      technology   622.346 5
      prospecting   622.184 65
      s.a. spec. minerals
    pharmacology   615.252 6
      misc. aspects see
          Pharmacology
    products
      mf. tech.   673.735
      other aspects see
          Nonferrous metals
          products
      s.a. spec. prod.

Tantalum (continued)
  toxicology   615.925 526
    misc. aspects see
      Toxicology
  other aspects see Metal;
    also Metals
Tantras
  Buddhist   294.385
  Hindu   294.595
Tantric
  Buddhism   294.392 5
  Hinduism   294.551 4
Tanzania   *area*–678
Tanzanian
  people   *r.e.n.*–967 8
  s.a. other spec. subj. e.g.
      Arts
Tanzanite *see* Gems
Taoism
  art representation   704.948 995 14
  s.a. spec. art forms
  calendars   529.329 514
  cookery   641.567 951 4
  philosophy   181.095 14
  regions   *area*–176 951 4
  religion   299.514
  rel. holidays   394.268 299 514
  schools   377.995 14
Taoist
  music *see* Taoist sacred music
  sacred music
    arts   783.029 951 4
    recordings   789.912 302 995 14
    s.a. spec. instruments;
      also spec. kinds e.g.
      Liturgical music
    religion
      pub. worship   299.514 38
      significance   299.514 37
    temples & shrines
      architecture   726.195 14
      building   690.619 514
    other aspects see
      Religious-purpose
      bldgs.
Taoists
  biog. & work   299.514 092
  s.a. spec. kinds e.g.
    Clergy
  s.a.   *pers.*–299 514
Taos Co. N.M.   *area*–789 53
Tap dancing
  performing arts   793.324
Tape recorders & recordings
  ed. use   371.333
  s.a. spec. levels of ed.;
    also Special education
  engineering
    soc. & econ. aspects *see*
      Secondary industries

Tape recorders & recordings
  engineering (continued)
    tech. & mf.   621.389 324
    s.a. spec. appls. e.g.
      music 789.91
  other aspects see Recordings
Tapes (adhesives)
  manufacturing
    chem. tech.   668.38
    soc. & econ. aspects *see*
      Secondary industries
Tapes (trimmings) *see*
    Passementerie
Tapestries
  fabrics
    manufacturing
      soc. & econ. aspects *see*
        Secondary industries
    technology   677.64
    other aspects see Textiles
  other aspects see Hangings
Tapestry makers
  biog. & work   746.392
  s.a.   *pers.*–746
Tapeworm-caused diseases   616.964
  geriatrics   618.976 964
  pediatrics   618.929 64
  pub. health   614.554
  statistics   312.396 4
    deaths   312.269 64
  other aspects see Diseases
Tapeworms *see* Cestoidea
Tapia *see* Sun-dried blocks
Tapioca *see* Cassava
Tapiridae
  animal husbandry   636.972 7
  hunting
    commercial   639.117 27
    sports   799.277 27
  paleozoology   569.72
  zoology   599.727
  other aspects see Mammalia
Tapirs *see* Tapiridae
Tapping-tools
  soc. & econ. aspects *see*
    Secondary industries
  tech. & mf.   621.955
  s.a. spec. appls. e.g.
    Plumbing
Taproom bldgs.
  architecture   725.72
  building   690.572
  other aspects see Public
    structures
Taprooms *see* Drinking-places
Taranaki N.Z.   *area*–931 23
Taranto
  Gulf *see* Ionian Sea
  province Italy   *area*–457 55
Tarantulas
  zoology   595.44

Tarantulas (continued)
  other aspects see Arachnida
Tarapacá Chile   *area*–831 2
Tarascan
  languages
    linguistics   497.7
    literatures   897.7
    s.a.   *lang.*–977
  people   *r.e.n.*–97
  s.a. other spec. subj. e.g.
        Arts
Tarawa   *area*–968 1
Taraxaceum officinale *see*
        Dandelions
Tardigrada
  culture & hunting   639.758 7
  zoology   595.187
  other aspects see Worms
Tardiness
  school discipline *see*
        Discipline schools
Taree N.S.W.   *area*–944 2
Tarfaya Morocco   *area*–646
Target
  ranges
    armed forces   355.73
    s.a. spec. mil branches
  selection
    mil. gunnery   623.557
    shooting sports   799.3
    misc. aspects see Sports
Targets
  shooting sports
    manufacturing
      soc. & econ. aspects *see*
          Secondary industries
      technology   688.793
    use   799.3
Tariffs *see* Customs (tariffs)
Tarija Bolivia   *area*–842 5
Tarlac Philippines   *area*–599 1
Tarn France   *area*–448 5
Tarn-et-Garonne France   *area*–447 5
Tarnobrzeg Poland   *area*–438 4
Tarnow Poland   *area*–438 6
Taro
  agric. aspects   633.68
  botanical aspects *see* Arales
  other aspects see Starches
Tarot
  parapsychology   133.324 24
Tarpons *see* Isospondyli
Tarragona Spain   *area*–467 3
Tarrant Co. Tex.   *area*–764 531
Tars
  agric. extraction   634.975 186
  other aspects see Bituminous
        materials
Tarsal bones *see* Lower
        extremities bones
Tarsiers *see* Prosimii

Tarsiiformes *see* Prosimii
Tartans
  clothing aspects *see* Clothing
  heraldry   929.6
  textile aspects *see* Textiles
Tartar
  horses
    animal husbandry   636.11
    other aspects see Horses
  suzerainty Russia hist.   947.03
    s.a. spec. events & subj.
        e.g. Commerce
  s.a. Tatar
Tartous Syria   *area*–569 13
Tarts
  cookery   641.865 2
Tartus Syria   *area*–569 13
Task forces
  naval organization   359.31
Tasman
  Peninsula Tas.   *area*–946 4
  Sea
    oceanography   551.465 78
    regional subj. trmt.   *area*–164 78
    other aspects see Pacific
        Ocean
Tasmania Australia   *area*–946
Tass wire service   070.435
Taste (aesthetics) *see*
        Aesthetics
Taste (sensation)
  control in foods *see* Quality
        controls foods
  s.a. Gustation; *also*
        Gustatory
Tatar
  ASSR   *area*–478 3
  Empire   *area*–5
    history   950.2
    s.a. spec. events & subj.
        e.g. Commerce
  Strait *see* Japan Sea
  s.a. Turkic
Tate Co. Miss.   *area*–762 85
Tatted fabrics
  arts   746.046 63
    s.a. spec. proc. e.g.
        Weaving
  manufacturing
    soc. & econ. aspects *see*
        Secondary industries
    technology   677.663
  other aspects see Textiles
  s.a. spec. prod.
Tatting
  textile arts   746.436
    s.a. spec. prod.
Tattnall Co. Ga.   *area*–758 775
Tattooing
  soc. customs   391.65
Tatura Vic.   *area*–945 4

Taunton Somerset Eng.	*area*–423 87
Taurus Mts. Turkey	*area*–564
Tautomerism	
molecular structure	
theoretical chem.	541.225 2
organic	547.122 52
s.a. spec. elements & cpds.	
Taverns *see* Drinking-places	
Tavistock Devon Eng.	*area*–423 53
Tawhid	297.14
Tax	
credits *see* Tax reductions	
deductions *see* Tax reductions	
lists genealogy	929.3
reductions	
law	343.052 3
spec. jur.	343.3–.9
pub. finance	336.206
s.a. spec. kinds of taxes e.g. Income taxes	
reform	
pub. finance	336.205
income tax	336.241 5
corporate	336.243 15
individual	336.242 15
s.a. Taxes	
Taxaceae *see* Coniferales	
Taxation	
without representation	
U.S. hist.	973.311 4
s.a. Taxes	
Taxes	
accounting	657.46
s.a. spec. kinds of enterprise e.g. Insurance accounting	
assessment *see* Assessment taxes	
collection *see* Collection of taxes	
evasion	
ethics *see* Citizenship ethics	
other aspects see Revenue offenses	
financial management	658.153
spec. subj.	*s.s.*–068 1
law	
international	341.484
municipal	343.04
spec. jur.	343.3–.9
macroeconomics	339.525
planning	
law	343.04
spec. jur.	343.3–.9
pub. admin.	350.724
central govts.	351.724
spec. jur.	353–354
local govts.	352.13
pub. finance	336.2
Taxicab	
drivers	
biog. & work	388.413 210 92
s.a.	*pers.*–388
services *see* Passenger automobiles transp. services	
Taxicabs	
commerce	388.342 32
engineering	
gen. tech. & mf.	629.222 32
maintenance	629.287 232
models	629.221 232
operation	629.283 32
s.a. other spec. aspects e.g. Brakes	
soc. & econ. aspects *see* Secondary industries	
other aspects see Passenger automobiles	
Taxidermy	579.4
Taxodiaceae *see* Coniferales	
Taxonomic	
botany	582–589
paleobotany	561.2–.9
paleozoology	562–569
zoology	592–599
s.a. other spec. subj.	
Tay River Tayside Scot.	*area*–412 8
Taylor	
County	
Florida	*area*–759 86
Georgia	*area*–758 493
Iowa	*area*–777 79
Kentucky	*area*–769 673
Texas	*area*–764 727
West Virginia	*area*–754 55
Wisconsin	*area*–775 26
Zachary admin.	
U.S. hist.	973.63
s.a. spec. events & subj. e.g. Economic conditions	
Tayport Fife Scot.	*area*–412 92
Tayside Scot.	*area*–412 5
Taza Morocco	*area*–643
Tazewell Co.	
Illinois	*area*–773 54
Virginia	*area*–755 763
Tchad *see* Chad	
Tea	
leaves	
fortunetelling	133.324 4
plant	
agriculture	633.72
soc. & econ. aspects *see* Primary industries	
foods	641.337 2
other aspects see Theales; *also* Alkaloids	

Tea (beverage)
comm. proc. — 663.94
cookery
home econ. — 641.877
other aspects see
Nonalcoholic beverages
hygiene *see* Beverages
Tea (meal)
cookery home econ. — 641.53
soc. customs — 394.15
Teacher aides — 371.141 2
s.a. spec. levels of ed.;
also Special education
Teacher-parent relations — 371.103
s.a. spec. levels of ed.;
also Special education
Teachers — 371.1
biog. & work — 371.100 92
s.a. spec. levels of ed.
exchanges — 370.196 3
internat. law — 341.767 3
govt. supervision — 379.157
law — 344.078
spec. jur. — 344.3–.9
persons — *pers.*–372
spec. schools — *pers.*–379
relations — 371.104
s.a. spec. levels of ed.;
also Special education
spec. levels of ed.
higher — 378.12
s.a. other spec. levels
spec. subj. — *s.s.*–07
other aspects see Educators
Teachers' conferences — 370.72
Teacher-staff relations — 371.106
s.a. spec. levels of ed.;
also Special education
Teacher-student relations *see*
Teaching
Teaching — 371.102
govt. supervision — 379.157
law of — 344.078
spec. jur. — 344.3–.9
spec. subj. — *s.s.*–07
elementary ed. — 372.3–.8
spiritual gift
Christian doctrines — 234.13
s.a. spec. levels of ed.;
also Special education
Teaching-aids
education — 371.32–.33
s.a. spec. levels of ed.;
also Special education
spec. subj. — *s.s.*–078
Teaching-devices *see*
Teaching-aids
Teaching-force
organization — 371.14
s.a. spec. levels of ed.;
also Special education

Teaching-load — 371.141 2
s.a. spec. levels of ed.;
also Special education
Teaching-machines
education — 371.394 45
s.a. spec. levels of ed.;
also Special education
spec. subj. — *s.s.*–078
Teaching-materials *see*
Teaching-aids
Teaching-methods — 371.3
pers. training — 658.312 404
misc. aspects see Training
personnel admin.
rel. instruction
Christianity — 268.6
other rel. see Religious
instruction
s.a. spec. levels of ed.;
also Special education
Teaching-office
rel. law *see* Things rel. law
Teaching-orders
rel. orders
Christianity
church hist. — 271.03
women's — 271.903
ecclesiology — 262.24
gen. wks. — 255.03
women's — 255.903
other rel. see Religious
congregations
Teachings of Jesus
Christian doctrines — 232.954
Teak *see* Verbenales
Team teaching — 371.148
s.a. spec. levels of ed.;
also Special education
Tear
ducts *see* Lacrimal mechanisms
eyes
gas *see* Chemical devices mil.
eng.
glands *see* Lacrimal
mechanisms eyes
Tearooms *see* Eating-places
Teasel family *see* Valerianales
Teats *see* Mammary glands
Technetium
chemistry — 546.543
technology — 661.054 3
Technical
assistance
economics — 338.91
funds
revenue source
pub. finance — 336.185
misc. aspects see
Intergovernmental
revenues
internat. law — 341.759

Tectibranchia (continued)
  zoology — 594.37
  other aspects see Mollusca
Tectonophysics — 551.8
  s.a. spec. appls. e.g.
    Prospecting
Tectosilicates
  mineralogy — 549.68
Teen agers *see* Young adults
Tees River Eng. — *area*–428 5
Teesdale Durham Eng. — *area*–428 61
Teeside Eng. — *area*–428 5
Teeth
  anatomy
    human — 611.314
    other aspects see Nutritive
      organs
  diseases
    gen. wks. — 617.63
    geriatrics — 618.977 63
    pub. health — 614.599 6
    statistics — 312.304 763
      deaths — 312.260 476 3
    other aspects see Mouth
      diseases
  physical anthropometry — 573.631 4
  physiology
    human — 612.311
    other aspects see Nutrition
  tissue biology human — 611.018 931 4
Tegre Ethiopia — *area*–634
Tegucigalpa Honduras — *area*–728 371
Tehachapi Mts. Calif. — *area*–794 88
Tehama Co. Calif. — *area*–794 27
Teheran Iran — *area*–552 5
Tehran Iran — *area*–552 5
Tehuantepec
  Canal
    transportation — 386.447
    other aspects see Canals
  Gulf *see* Southeast Pacific
    Ocean
Teignbridge Devon Eng. — *area*–423 55
Teignmouth
  Devon Eng. — *area*–423 55
  governorship India hist. — 954.031 1
  s.a. spec. events & subj.
    e.g. Commerce
Tejo River *see* Tagus River
Tekirdag Turkey — *area*–563
Tekur kingdom hist. — 966.301
  s.a. spec. events & subj.
    e.g. Commerce
Tel Aviv Israel — *area*–569 48
Telangiectasis *see* Capillaries
  diseases
Telangitis *see* Capillaries
  diseases
Telautography *see* Writing-
  telegraphy

Telecommunication
  commerce — 384
  govt. control
    activities — 350.874
      central govts. — 351.874
      spec. jur. — 353–354
      local govts. — 352.914
    departments *see* Executive
      departments
  law
    international — 341.757 7
    municipal — 343.099 4
    spec. jur. — 343.3–.9
  personnel
    biog. & work — 384.092
    s.a. spec. kinds of
      services
    s.a. — *pers.*–384
  technology — 621.38
    s.a. spec. appls. e.g.
      Military engineering
  other aspects see
    Communication
Telecontrol
  engineering — 620.46
    radio *see* Radiocontrol
    s.a. spec. appls. e.g.
      Astronautics
Telediesthesia — 133.323 9
Telegraphones *see* Recording-
  telephones
Telegraphy
  cable *see* Submarine cable
    telegraphy
  commerce — 384.1
  govt. control
    activities — 351.874 1
    spec. jur. — 353–354
    departments *see* Executive
      departments
  law
    international — 341.757 7
    municipal — 343.099 42
    spec. jur. — 343.3–.9
  stations
    commun. ind.
      commerce — 384.15
      wire — 384.15
        submarine cable — 384.45
      wireless — 384.525
    govt. control — 351.874
      spec. jur. — 353–354
    law *see* Telegraphy law
  wire
    commun. eng.
      technology — 621.382
        military — 623.732
        nautical — 623.856 2
      s.a. other spec. appls.
    other aspects see
      Communication

Telescopes (continued)

mf. tech.	681.412
components	681.42–.43

other aspects see Optical
instruments

Teletype *see* Printing
telegraphy

Television	384.55

actors & actresses *see* Actors

advertising	659.143

broadcasting *see* Television
communication

buildings *see* Office
buildings

cameras *see* Cameras
television

communication	384.55
commerce	384.55

engineering *see* Television
eng. & mf.

govt. control	351.874 55
spec. jur.	353–354

law

international	341.757 7
municipal	343.099 46
spec. jur.	343.3–.9

other aspects see
Communication

drama *see* Broadcast drama

ed. use	371.335 8
adult ed.	374.27
spec. subj.	*s.s.*–071 53

*s.a. other spec. levels of
ed.*

eng. & mf.

soc. & econ. aspects *see*
Secondary industries

technology	621.388
military	623.735
nautical	623.856 5

s.a. other spec. appls.

engineers

biog. & work	621.388 009 2
s.a.	*pers.*–621 3

ethics *see* Public
entertainment ethics

evangelism

pastoral theology

Christianity	253.78

other rel. see Pastoral
theology

frequency allocation *see*
Measurement television

influence on crime	364.254
journalism	070.19

s.a. spec. activities e.g.
Reporting

manufacture *see* Television
eng. & mf.

music	782.87
recordings	789.912 287

Television (continued)

networks *see* Broadcasting
networks

optics

engineering	621.388 13

s.a. spec. appls. e.g.
Astronautics

performers *see* Actors

performing arts	791.45
photography tech.	778.59

plays *see* Broadcast drama

preaching

Christianity	251.07

other rel. see Preaching

programs *see* Programs
television broadcasting

receivers

automobiles

soc. & econ. aspects *see*
Secondary industries

tech. & mf.	629.277

other aspects see Receiving
sets television

recorders	778.599 3
recording	778.599 2

rooms

education *see* Instructional
spaces education

sociology	302.23

speaking *see* Public speaking

speeches *see* Public speeches

stations *see* Broadcasting
stations

towers *see* Office buildings

work

local Christian parishes	254.3
specific applications	259.7

s.a. other spec. uses

Telex *see* Printing telegraphy

Telfair Co. Ga.	*area*–758 843
Telford Salop Eng.	*area*–424 56

Telford surfaces

road eng.

technology	625.86
sidewalks	625.886

other aspects see Roads

Teller Co. Colo.	*area*–788 58

Tellurides

mineralogy	549.32

Tellurium

chemistry

inorganic	546.726
organic	547.057 26

s.a. spec. groupings e.g.
Aliphatic compounds

technology	661.072 6

soc. & econ. aspects *see*
Secondary industries

s.a. spec. prod.

mineralogy	549.25

s.a. spec. minerals

Tellurium (continued)
  pharmacology   615.272 6
    misc. aspects see
      Pharmacology
  toxicology   615.925 726
    misc. aspects see
      Toxicology
    other aspects see Minor
      metals
Telophase *see* Mitosis
Telosporidia *see* Sporozoa
Telpherage
  machine eng.
    soc. & econ. aspects *see*
      Secondary industries
    tech. & mf.   621.868
    s.a. spec. appls. e.g.
      Internal transportation
    other aspects see Mechanics
Telstar *see* Communications
    satellites
Telugu
  language
    linguistics   494.827
    literature   894.827
    s.a.   *lang.*–948 27
  people   *r.e.n.*–948
  s.a. other spec. subj. e.g.
    Arts
Témiscamingue Co. Que.   *area*–714 212
Temiscouata Co. Que.   *area*–714 76
Temora N.S.W.   *area*–944 8
Tempera painting
  arts   751.43
  indiv. artists   759.1–.9
Temperaments
  theory
    indiv. psych.   155.262
    other aspects see Personality
Temperance
  Christian virtue   241.4
  ethics *see* Consumption ethics
Temperate Zones
  climate   551.691 2
  diseases   616.988 2
    geriatrics   618.976 988 2
    pediatrics   618.929 882
    statistics   312.398 82
    deaths   312.269 882
    other aspects see Diseases
  s.a. spec. diseases
  earth astronomy   525.5
  regional subj. trmt.   *area*–12
Temperate-Zone plants
  floriculture   635.952
  s.a. spec. plants
Temperature
  adaptations
    ecology *see* Weather ecology

Temperature (continued)
  changes
    deformation
      structural theory *see*
        Mechanical deformation
        structural theory
    resistance to
      eng. materials   620.112 15
        s.a. spec. materials &
          spec. uses
  control
    mining eng.   622.43
    shipbuilding
      soc. & econ. aspects *see*
        Secondary industries
      technology   623.853
        design   623.814 53
        spec. craft   623.812
    spacecraft eng.
      gen. wks.
        manned   629.470 44
        unmanned   629.460 44
      life-support systems
        manned   629.477 5
        unmanned   629.467 5
      other aspects see
        Spacecraft
      s.a. other spec. appls
  controls
    air-conditioning eng.   697.932 2
Temperatures   536.5
  astrophysics   523.013 5
    s.a. spec. celestial bodies
  effects
    biophysics
      extraterrestrial   574.191 96
        animals   591.191 96
        man   612.014 56
        plants   581.191 96
      terrestrial   574.191 6
        animals   591.191 6
        man   612.014 46
        plants   581.191 6
      s.a. spec. organisms
    hygiene   613.1
    vet. sci.   636.089 31
      s.a. spec. animals
    materials   620.112 1
      s.a. spec. materials
    physics   536.4
  extremes
    astrophysics   523.013 56–.013 57
      s.a. spec. celestial
        bodies
    physics   536.56–.57
      spec. states of matter   530.4
    thermochemistry
      physical chem.   541.368
        applied   660.296 8
        organic   547.136 8

Temperatures
extremes
thermochemistry
physical chem. (continued)
s.a. spec. elements,
cpds., prod.
geophysics
earth's crust — 551.14
earth's interior — 551.12
meteorology — 551.525
artificial modification — 551.682 5
weather forecasting — 551.642 5
spec. areas — 551.65
physics — 536.5
spec. states of matter — 530.4
precipitation
meteorology
gen. wks. — 551.577 1
hail & graupel — 551.578 7
rainfall — 551.578 11
snowfall — 551.578 41
weather forecasting — 551.647
spec. areas — 551.65
sea water
oceanography — 551.460 1
s.a. spec. bodies of
water
s.a. Heat; *also* Thermal
Tempering
glassmaking — 666.129
s.a. spec. kinds of glass
metal prod. *see* Heat
treatment
Templates
construction *see*
Patternmakinq
use in aircraft mf. — 629.134 2
use in motor vehicle mf. — 629.234
s.a. other spec. uses
Temple presentation
Jesus Christ doctrines — 232.928
Temples
architecture — 726.1
building — 690.61
rel. significance
comp. rel. — 291.35
s.a. spec. rel.
rel. worship *see* Sacred
places rel. worship
other aspects see
Religious-purpose
bldgs.
Tempo
music theory — 781.62
s.a. spec. mediums
Temporal
goods rel. law *see* Things
rel. law
power of pope
Christian ecclesiology — 262.132

Temporary
deformations
resistance to
engineering *see* Dynamics
physics — 531.382 3
fortifications mil. eng. — 623.15
groups
sociology — 302.33
magnets
physics — 538.23
spec. states of matter — 530.4
s.a. other spec. subj.
Temptation of Jesus Christ
Christian doctrines — 232.95
Ten
Commandments
Bible — 222.16
moral theology
Christianity — 241.52
Judaism — 296.385
other aspects see
Historical books (O.T.)
Thousand Isls. Fla. — *area*–759 44
Tenacity
minerals *see* Mechanical
properties minerals
Tenancy
land econ. — 333.53
law — 346.043 4
spec. jur. — 346.3–.9
Tenant-landlord relations
land econ. — 333.54
Tenants' liability insurance — 368.56
misc. aspects see Insurance
Tenby Dyfed Wales — *area*–429 63
Tenderizers
manufacturing
soc. & econ. aspects *see*
Secondary industries
technology — 664.4
Tendon sheaths
diseases
gen. wks. — 616.76
neoplasms — 616.992 75
tuberculosis — 616.995 75
geriatrics — 618.976 76
pediatrics — 618.927 6
pub. health — 614.597 6
statistics — 312.376
deaths — 312.267 6
other aspects see Diseases
human anatomy — 611.75
physical anthropometry — 573.675
physiology
human — 612.75
other aspects see Movements
tissue biology human — 611.018 975
Tendons
diseases
gen. wks. — 616.75
neoplasms — 616.992 74

Terbium
  chemistry
    technology (continued)
      soc. & econ. aspects *see*
        Secondary industries
      s.a. spec. prod.
      eng. materials   620.189 291 6
      s.a. spec. uses
    metallography   669.952 916
    metallurgy   669.291 6
      physical & chem.   669.962 916
    pharmacology   615.241 6
      misc. aspects see
        Pharmacology
    products
      mf. tech.   673.291 6
      other aspects see
        Nonferrous metals
        products
    toxicology   615.925 416
      misc. aspects see
        Toxicology
    other aspects see
      Yttrium-group metals
Terce *see* Office hours
Term papers
  preparation
    rhetoric   808.02
Terminal
  ballistics
    mil. eng.   623.516
  buildings
    airports
      aeronautical eng.   629.136 4
      military   623.664
      s.a. other spec appls.
      commerce *see* Airport
        facilities
  care
    diseases   616.029
      misc. aspects see
        Diseases
      s.a. spec. diseases &
        surgical conditions
    nursing   610.736 1
  equipment
    computer eng. *see*
      Input-output equipment
      computer eng.
  wire telephony
    soc. & econ. aspects *see*
      Secondary industries
    tech. & mf.   621.386
    s.a. spec. appls e.g.
      military use 623.733
    other aspects see
      Telephony wire
  layout
    railroad eng. *see* Railrod
      yards

Terminal (continued)
  patients
    health services   362.19
    misc. aspects see Medical
      services
Terminals
  transportation *see spec. kinds*
    e.g. Bus terminals &
      stops
Termination
  of insurance   368.016
    s.a. spec. kinds of
      insurance
  of states
    internat. law   341.26
  of treaties *see* Treaties
  s.a. other spec. subj.
Terminology   *s.s.*–014
Termite damage prevention
  wood bldg. materials   691.14
Termite-resistant construction   693.842
Termites *see* Isoptera
Terms
  chief executives
    pub. admin.   350.003 4
      central govts.   351.003 4
      spec. jur.   353–354
      local govts.   352.008
  legislators *see* Membership
    legislative bodies
  pub. executives
    law *see* Executive branches
    law
Ternary invariants
  algebra   512.944
  s.a. spec. appls. e.g.
    Engineering
Terni Italy   *area*–456 52
Ternopol Ukraine   *area*–477 18
Terns *see* Lari
Terpenes
  chemistry   547.71
    applied   661.81
    organic   547.71
Terra cotta
  architectural construction   721.044 3
    s.a. spec. structural
      elements; also spec.
      types of bldgs.
  bldg. construction   693.3
  eng. materials   620.142
    foundations   624.153 42
    other aspects see Ceramic
      materials
    s.a. other spec. uses
Terraces
  landscape design   717
Terracing
  soil conservation   631.455
    s.a. spec. crops
Terrapin *see* Turtle

Tests
  education (continued)
    s.a. spec. levels of ed.;
        also Special education
    employee selection
      gen. management   658.311 25
      spec. subj.   *s.s.*–068 3
      pub. admin.   350.132 5
        central govts.   351.132 5
        spec. jur.   353–354
        local govts.   352.005 132 5
    intelligence *see* Intelligence
            (intellect) tests
    procedural   *s.s.*–028 7
    s.a. Experimental research
Tetanus
  gen. med.   616.931 8
  geriatrics   618.976 931 8
  pediatrics   618.929 318
  pub. health   614.512 8
  statistics   312.393 18
    deaths   312.269 318
  other aspects see Diseases
Tetbury Gloucestershire Eng.
                               area–424 17
Tete Mozambique   *area*–679 5
Teton
  County
    Idaho   *area*–796 54
    Montana   *area*–786 55
    Wyoming   *area*–787 55
  Range Wyo.   *area*–787 5
Tetrabranchia *see* Nautiloidea
Tetracentraceae *see*
            Hamamelidales
Tetrafluoroethylene *see*
            Polyfluoro hydrocarbons
Tetragonal systems
  crystallography   548.14
  s.a. spec. substances
Tetrahedrite
  mineralogy   549.35
Tetrameristaceae *see* Theales
Tetraonidae
  hunting
    commercial   639.128 616
    sports   799.248 616
  paleozoology   568.6
  zoology   598.616
  other aspects see Aves
Tetrapoda
  agric. pests   632.676
  s.a. spec. types of culture
      e.g. Forestry; *also*
          spec. crops
  animal husbandry
    technology   636
    soc. & econ. aspects *see*
        Primary industries
  other aspects see
      Agriculture

Tetrapoda (continued)
  conservation tech.   639.977 6
  drawing tech.   743.676
  hunting
    commercial
      soc. & econ. aspects *see*
          Primary industries
      technology   639.1
      sports   799.24–.27
  paleozoology   567.6
  zoology   597.6
  other aspects see Animals
Tetrapodili
  zoology   595.42
  other aspects see Arachnida
Tetrodes
  gas tubes
    radiowave electronics
      soc. & econ. aspects *see*
          Secondary industries
      tech. & mf.   621.381 513 4
      s.a. spec. appls. e.g.
          Radio eng. & mf.
    other aspects see
        Disruptive discharge
  vacuum tubes
    radiowave electronics
      soc. & econ. aspects *see*
          Secondary industries
      tech. & mf.   621.381 512 4
      s.a. spec. appls. e.g.
          Receiving sets
    other aspects see Vacuum
        tubes
Tetryl *see* High explosives
Tetuan Morocco   *area*–642
Teutonic
  Knights
    rel. orders   255.49
      church hist.   271.49
      ecclesiology   262.24
  s.a. Germanic
Teviotdale Borders Scot.   *area*–413 92
Tewkesbury Gloucestershire Eng.
                               area–424 12
Texas
  County
    Missouri   *area*–778 84
    Oklahoma   *area*–766 135
  state   *area*–764
  town Qld.   *area*–943 3
Texoma Lake   *area*–766 61
Textbooks
  bibliographies   011.7
    spec. kinds   012–016
  catalogs
    general   017–019
    spec. kinds   012–016
  govt. supervision   379.156
  law   344.077
    spec. jur.   344.3–.9

Thallium (continued)
  other aspects see Minor
    metals
Thallophyta
  botany   589
  med. aspects
    gen. pharm.   615.329
    toxicology   615.952 9
    vet. pharm.   636.089 532 9
    toxicology   636.089 595 29
  paleobotany   561.9
  other aspects see Plants
Thame Oxfordshire Eng.   *area*–425 79
Thames River Eng.   *area*–422
Thamesdown Wiltshire Eng.
         area–423 13
Thanet Kent Eng.   *area*–422 357
Thanksgiving
  private prayers
    Christianity   242.724
    other rel. see Prayers
        private devotions
  sermons
    Christianity   252.68
    other rel. see Preaching
  soc. customs   394.268 3
  other aspects see Holidays
Thar Desert India   *area*–544
Thasos Greece   *area*–499
  ancient   *area*–391 1
Thatch roofing
  bldg. construction   695
Thaumaturgists
  rel. leaders
    comp. rel.   291.62
    s.a. spec. rel.
Thaxted Essex Eng.   *area*–426 712
Thayer Co. Neb.   *area*–782 335
Theaceae *see* Theales
Theales
  botany   583.166
  floriculture   635.933 166
  forestry   634.973 166
  med. aspects
    crop prod.   633.883 166
    gen. pharm.   615.323 166
    toxicology   615.952 316 6
    vet. pharm.   636.089 532 316 6
    toxicology   636.089 595 231 66
  paleobotany   561.3
  other aspects see Plants
Theater   792
  areas
    civic art   711.558
  buildings
    architecture   725.822
    building   690.582 2
    other aspects see Public
        structures
  ethics *see* Public
        entertainment ethics

Theater (continued)
  etiquette   395.53
  influence on crime   364.254
  music   782.8
    recordings   789.912 28
    orchestras   785.066 2
    s.a. spec. kinds of music
  performing arts   792
  television *see* Closed-circuit
    television
  s.a. Theatrical
Theater-in-the-round
  performing arts   792.022 8
Theaters
  accounting   657.84
Theatines
  rel. orders   255.51
    church hist.   271.51
    ecclesiology   262.24
Theatrical
  dancing
    performing arts   793.32
  make-up *see* Make-up
  performers
    biog. & work   792.092
    s.a. spec. kinds
    s.a.   *pers.*–792
  presentations
    animal husbandry for   636.088 8
    s.a. spec. animals
    library & museum services
        see Recreational
        services
  scenery
    paintings *see* Scene
        paintings
Theban supremacy Greece hist.   938.06
  s.a. spec. events & subj.
    e.g. Commerce
Thecodontia
  paleozoology   567.93
Theft *see* Larceny
Theism
  nat. rel.   211.3
Thelephoraceae *see* Agaricales
Thematic apperception tests
  indiv. psych.   155.284 4
Theobroma cacao *see* Cacao
Theocracies
  pol. sci.   321.5
  s.a. spec. jur.
Theocracy
  pol. ideology   320.55
  soc. theology
    Christianity   261.73
    comp. rel.   291.177 3
    s.a. other spec. rel.
Theodicy
  rel. doctrines
    Christianity   231.8
    nat. rel.   214

Thermal (continued)
  cracking
    petroleum   665.533
    s.a. spec. prod. e.g.
      Gasolines
  dissociations
    physical chem.   541.364
      applied   660.296 4
      organic   547.136 4
    s.a. spec. elements,
      cpds., prod.
  effects
    electric currents
      astrophysics   523.018 762 4
      s.a. spec. celestial
        bodies
      physics   537.624
      spec. states of matter   530.4
  engineering *see* Heat
    engineering
  forces
    biophysics
      extraterrestrial
        gen. wks.   574.191 96
        animals   591.191 96
        microorganisms   576.119 196
        plants   581.191 96
        s.a. spec. organisms
      med. sci.
        animals   612.014 56
           636.089 201 456
        s.a. spec. animals
        man   612.014 56
      terrestrial
        gen. wks.   574.191 6
        animals   591.191 6
        microorganisms   576.119 16
        plants   581.191 6
        s.a. spec. organisms
      med. sci.   612.014 46
        animals   636.089 201 446
        s.a. spec. animals
        human   612.014 46
      s.a. spec. functions,
        systems, organs
    eng. materials   620.112 1
      s.a. spec. materials &
        spec. uses
  insulated construction
    buildings   693.832
  methods
    anal. chem.
      gen. wks.   543.086
        qualitative   544.2
        quantitative   545.4
      organic   547.308 6
        qualitative   547.342
        quantitative   547.354
      s.a. spec. elements &
        cpds.

Thermal (continued)
  nuclear reactors
    technology   621.483 4
    s.a. spec. appls. e.g.
      Generation elect. power
    other aspects see Nuclear
      reactions
  perception
    psychology
      gen. wks.   152.182 2
      animals   156.218 22
      children   155.412
      s.a. psych. of other
        spec. groups
      influences   155.911 822
  phenomena
    celestial bodies
      Jupiter   523.452
      Mars   523.432
      Mercury   523.412
      moon   523.32
      Neptune   523.481 2
      Pluto   523.482 2
      Saturn   523.462
      stars   523.82
        spec. systems   523.84–.85
      sun   523.72
      Uranus   523.472
      Venus   523.422
      s.a. other spec. bodies
    soil physics   631.436
      s.a. spec. crops; also
        spec. types of culture
        e.g. Floriculture
      s.a. other spec. subj.
  pollution
    water-supply eng.
      technology   628.168 31
      other aspects see Water
        supply engineering
  power generation
    nuclear eng.
      soc. & econ. aspects *see*
        Secondary industries
      technology   621.481
      s.a. spec. appls. e.g.
        Public lighting eng.
  processes
    drying & dehydrating
      foods
        comm. proc.   664.028 42
        other aspects see Foods
        s.a. spec. foods e.g.
          Meats
      s.a. other spec. subj.
  properties
    crystals   548.86
      s.a. spec. substances
    earth astronomy   525.2

Thermometric titrimetry *see*
  Thermal methods
Thermometry *see* Temperatures
Thermonuclear
  reactions *see* Fusion nuclear
  reactors *see* Fusion reactors
  s.a. Nuclear
Thermopenetration
  therapeutics *see* Diathermy
    therapeutics
Thermoplastic plastics
  chem. tech. — 668.423
  org. chem. — 547.843 223
  other aspects see Plastics
  s.a. spec. prod.
Thermosbaenacea
  fishing sports — 799.255 373
  zoology — 595.373
  other aspects see
    Eumalacostraca
Thermosetting plastics
  chem. tech. — 668.422
  org.chem. — 547.843 222
  other aspects see Plastics
  s.a. spec. prod.
Thermostats
  air-conditiong eng. — 697.932 2
  heating equipment
    buildings — 697.07
    s.a. spec. kinds e.g.
      Steam heating
Thermotherapy — 615.832
  misc. aspects see Physical
    therapies
  s.a. spec. diseases
Theromorpha
  paleozoology — 567.93
Thesaurofacets
  library sci. — 025.46
Thesauruses
  library subj. vocabularies — 025.49
Theses
  preparation
    rhetoric — 808.02
  other aspects see
    Dissertations
Thesprotia Greece — *area*–495 3
Thessalonians
  Bible — 227.81–.82
  other aspects see New
    Testament
Thessaloniki Greece — *area*–495 6
Thessaly Greece — *area*–495 4
  ancient — *area*–382
Theta function — 515.984
  s.a. spec. appls e.g.
    Engineering
Thetford Norfolk Eng. — *area*–426 14
Thiazoles
  org. chem. — 547.594
  s.a. spec. cpds.

Thighs
  diseases
    regional med. trmt. — 617.582
      *s.a. spec. systems &
        organs*
    surgery — 617.582
      anesthesiology — 617.967 582
    other aspects see Diseases
  fractures — 617.158
  muscles
    human anatomy — 611.738
    other aspects see Muscles
  orthopedic surgery — 617.398
  other aspects see Lower
    extremities
Thimbles
  clothing construction
    domestic — 646.19
Thin films
  physics *see* Solids
  technology *see*
    Microelectronics
  other aspects see Surface
    phenomena
Things
  lit. trmt.
    folk lit.
      sociology
        legendary — 398.46
        real — 398.356
      texts & lit. crit. — 398.26
    gen. wks.
      collections
        legendary — 808.803 7
        real — 808.803 56
      hist. & crit.
        legendary — 809.933 7
        real — 809.933 56
    spec. lits.
      collections
        legendary — *lit. sub.*–080 37
        real — *lit. sub.*–080 356
      hist. & crit.
        legendary — *lit. sub.*–093 7
        real — *lit. sub.*–093 56
    s.a. spec. lit. forms
  rel. law
    Christianity
      Roman Catholic
        Codex iuris canonici — 262.933
        early codes — 262.92
        other denominations — 262.98
      other rel. see Religious
        law
  stage trmt.
    gen. wks.
      legendary — 792.090 937
      real — 792.090 935 6

Thirteenth century
history 909.2
  appls. to spec. subj. *s.s.*–090 22
s.a. spec. countries
Thirty Years' War
  Europe hist. 940.24
  s.a. spec. countries
Thismiaceae *see* Burmanniales
Thisted Denmark *area*–489 5
Thistles *see* Asterales
Thomas Co.
  Georgia *area*–758 984
  Kansas *area*–781 132
  Nebraska *area*–782 774
Thompson
  John Sparrow admin.
    Can. hist. 971.055
    s.a. spec. events & subj.
      e.g. Commerce
  River B.C. *area*–711 41
Thomson River Qld. *area*–943 5
Thoracica *see* Cirripedia
Thoracostei *see* Mesichthyes
Thorax
  human
    anatomy 611.94
    physiology 612.94
    s.a. spec. functions,
      systems, organs e.g.
        Cardiovascular system
  physical anthropometry 573.694
  regional med. trmt. 617.54
    s.a. spec. systems & organs
  surgery 617.54
    anesthesiology 617.967 54
    orthopedic 617.374
    s.a. Veterinary sciences
  other aspects see Regional
    anatomy
  s.a. Chest
Thorium
  chemistry
    inorganic 546.422
    organic 547.054 22
    s.a. spec. groupings e.g.
      Aliphatic compounds
  technology 661.042 2
    organic 661.895
    soc. & econ. aspects *see*
      Secondary industries
    s.a. spec. prod.
  eng. materials 620.189 292 2
    s.a. spec. uses
  metallography 669.952 922
  metallurgy 669.292 2
    physical & chem. 669.962 922
  mineral aspects *see*
    Fissionable metals
  pharmacology 615.242 2
    misc. aspects see
      Pharmacology

Thorium (continued)
  products
    mf. tech. 673.292 2
    other aspects see
      Nonferrous metals
      products
  toxicology 615.925 422
    misc. aspects see
      Toxicology
  other aspects see Metal;
    also Metals
Thornaby-on-Tees Cleveland Eng.
  area–428 51
Thornbury Avon Eng. *area*–423 91
Thorndike system
  psychology 150.194 4
    s.a. spec. subj. & branches
      of psych.
Thornhill Dumfries and Galloway
  Scot. *area*–414 86
Thorns *see* Integumentary organs
Thornton Cleveleys Lancashire
  Eng. *area*–427 682
Thornton Isl. *area*–964
Thorny-headed worms *see*
  Acanthocephala
Thorough bass
  music theory 781.32
    spec. forms 781.5
    s.a. spec. mediums
Thoroughbred
  horse
    animal husbandry 636.132
    other aspects see Horses
Thoroughfares *see* Roads
Thothmes reign Egypt hist. 932.014
  s.a. spec. events & subj.
    e.g. Commerce
Thought
  psychology 153.42
    animals 156.342
    children 155.413
    s.a. psych. of other spec.
      groups
Thousand Isls. *area*–747 58
  New York *area*–747 58
  Ontario *area*–713 7
Thrace
  ancient *area*–398
  modern *area*–495 7
    Bulgaria *area*–497 78
    Greece *area*–495 7
    Turkey *area*–563
Thracian languages *see*
  Thraco-Phrygian
  languages
Thraco-Phrygian languages
  linguistics 491.993
  literatures 891.993
  s.a. *lang.*–919 93
Thrashers *see* Mimidae

Throwing
  equipment mf. — 688.764 35
    soc. & econ. aspects *see*
      Secondary industries
  sports — 796.435
  other aspects see Sports
Thrushes *see* Turdidae
Thrust
  aeronautical aerodynamics — 629.132 33
    s.a. spec. appls. e.g.
      Flying
Thruways *see* Expressways
Thulium
  chemistry
    inorganic — 546.418
    organic — 547.054 18
      s.a. spec. groupings e.g.
        Aliphatic compounds
    technology — 661.041 8
    organic — 661.895
      soc. & econ. aspects *see*
        Secondary industries
      s.a. spec. prod.
  eng. materials — 620.189 291 8
    s.a. spec. uses
  metallography — 669.952 918
  metallurgy — 669.291 8
    physical & chem. — 669.962 918
  pharmacology — 615.241 8
    misc. aspects see
      Pharmacology
  products
    mf. tech. — 673.291 8
    other aspects see
      Nonferrous metals
      products
  toxicology — 615.925 418
    misc. aspects see
      Toxicology
  other aspects see
    Yttrium-group metals
Thumb-sucking
  symptomatology
    neurological diseases — 618.928 49
Thunder (meteorology) *see*
  Disruptive discharge
  electronics atmospheric
  electricity
Thunder Bay District Ont. — *area*-713 12
Thunderstorms *see* Thermal
  convective storms
Thurgau Switzerland — *area*-494 5
Thuribles
  rel. significance
    Christianity — 246.55
    comp. rel. — 291.37
    s.a. other spec. rel.
Thuringia Ger. — *area*-432 2
Thurniaceae *see* Juncales
Thurrock Essex Eng. — *area*-426 78
Thursday Isl. Qld. — *area*-943 8

Thurso Highland Scot. — *area*-411 62
Thurston Co.
  Nebraska — *area*-782 227
  Washington — *area*-797 79
Thutmose reign Egypt hist. — 932.014
  s.a. spec. events & subj.
    e.g. Commerce
Thyme *see* Herbs; *also*
  Lamiales
Thymelaeaceae *see* Thymelaeales
Thymelaeales
  botany — 583.933
  floriculture — 635.933 933
  forestry — 634.973 933
  med. aspects
    crop prod. — 633.883 933
    gen. pharm. — 615.323 933
      toxicology — 615.952 393 3
    vet. pharm. — 636.089 532 393 3
      toxicology — 636.089 595 239 33
  paleobotany — 561.3
  other aspects see Plants
Thymus gland
  anatomy
    human — 611.43
    other aspects see Secretory
      organs
  diseases
    gen. wks. — 616.43
      neoplasms — 616.992 43
      tuberculosis — 616.995 43
    geriatrics — 618.976 43
    pediatrics — 618.924 3
    pub. health — 614.594 3
    statistics — 312.343
      deaths — 312.264 3
    surgery — 617.546
      anesthesiology — 617.967 546
    other aspects see Diseases
  physical anthropometry — 573.643
  physiology
    human — 612.43
    other aspects see Secretion
  tissue biology human — 611.018 943
Thyratrons *see* Gas tubes
Thyristors
  gen. wks.
    soc. & econ. aspects *see*
      Secondary industries
    tech. & mf. — 621.381 528 7
      s.a. spec. appls. e.g.
        Radiocontrol
  other aspects see
    Semiconductors
Thyroid
  extracts
    pharmacology — 615.362
    other aspects see Drugs
  glands
    anatomy
      human — 611.44

Thyroid
glands
anatomy (continued)
other aspects see
Secretory organs
diseases
gen. wks. 616.44
neoplasms 616.992 44
tuberculosis 616.995 44
geriatrics 618.976 44
pediatrics 618.924 4
pub. health 614.594 4
statistics 312.344
deaths 312.264 4
surgery 617.539
anesthesiology 617.967 539
other aspects see
Diseases
physical anthropometry 573.644
physiology
human 612.44
other aspects see
Secretion
tissue biology human 611.018 944
Thyroxin
org. chem. 547.734 5
other aspects see Hormones
Thysanolaenaea *see* Pooideae
Thysanoptera
culture 638.573 1
paleozoology 565.73
zoology 595.731
other aspects see Insecta
Thysanura
zoology 595.713
other aspects see Apterygota
Tiaras
precious metalwork 739.278
other aspects see Jewelry
Tiaret Algeria *area*–651
Tibet *area*–515
Tibetan
arts *see* South Asian arts
Buddhism 294.392 3
misc. aspects see Buddhism
language
linguistics 495.4
literature 895.4
s.a. *lang.*–954 1
people *r.e.n.*–954
Terrier
animal husbandry 636.72
other aspoects see Dogs
s.a. Tibet; *also other spec.*
subj.
Tibeto-Burman languages
linguistics 495.4
literatures 895.4
s.a. *lang.*–954
Tibia *see* Lower extremities
bones

Ticino Switzerland *area*–494 7
Tick typhus
gen. med. 616.922 3
geriatrics 618.976 922 3
pediatrics 618.929 223
pub. health 614.526 3
statistics 312.392 23
deaths 312.269 223
other aspects see Diseases
Ticker tapes
financial analysis 332.632 042
Tickers *see* Printing telegraphy
Ticket services
transportation *see* Passenger
services
Tickhill South Yorkshire Eng.
area–428 27
Tickle
perception *see* Derived
sensory perception
Ticks
zoology 595.42
other aspects see Arachnida
Tidal
currents
dynamic oceanography 551.470 8
s.a. spec. bodies of
water
generation
electrodynamic eng. *see*
Hydroelectric
generation
electrodynamic eng.
waves
dynamic oceanography 551.470 24
s.a. spec. bodies of
water
gen. hist.
collections 904.5
s.a. hist. of spec.
places
seismology 551.22
Tidbinbilla Fauna Reserve
Australia *area*–947
Tide tables
earth astronomy 525.69
navigation 623.894 9
Tidelands *see* Coastal regions
Tides
dynamic oceanography 551.470 8
s.a. spec. bodies of water
earth astronomy 525.6
Tidewater
Maryland *area*–752 1
Virginia *area*–755 1
Tie plates
railroad eng.
technology 625.143
other aspects see Permanent
way

Tie-dyeing
  textile arts   746.664
    s.a. spec. prod. e.g.
      Hangings
Tien Shan   *area*–516
  China   *area*–516
  USSR   *area*–584 3
Tientsin China   *area*–511 5
Tierra del Fuego   *area*–827 6
  Argentina   *area*–827 6
  Chile   *area*–836 4
Ties (neckwear) *see* Neckwear
Ties (railroad eng.)
  technology   625.143
  other aspects see Permanent
    way
Tift Co. Ga.   *area*–758 882
Tigers
  animal husbandry   636.89
  other aspects see Cats
Tigre
  language *see* Ethiopic
    languages
  province Ethiopia   *area*–634
Tigrinya language *see* Ethiopic
    languages
Tilbury Essex Eng.   *area*–426 78
Tile
  drains
    technology   666.733
    other aspects see
      Structural clay
      products
  flooring *see* Floor coverings
  furniture
    mf. tech.   684.106
    other aspects see Furniture
    s.a. spec. prod.
  piping
    technology   666.733
    other aspects see
      Structural clay
      products
  roofing
    bldg. construction   695
Tiles
  architectural construction   721.044 3
    s.a. spec. structural
      elements; also spec.
      types of bldgs.
  bldg. construction   693.3
  bldg. materials   691.4
  ceramic arts   738.6
  eng. materials   620.142
    foundations   624.153 42
    naval design   623.818 36
    structures   624.183 6
    s.a. other spec. uses
  floor coverings *see* Floor
    coverings

Tiles (continued)
  rel. significance
    Christianity   247.886
    comp. rel.   291.37
    s.a. other spec. rel.
  rubber *see* Molded rubber
    prod.
Tilia *see* Basswood trees;
    also Linden trees
Tiliaceae *see* Tiliales
Tiliales
  botany   583.19
  floriculture   635.933 19
  forestry   634.973 19
    linden & basswood   634.972 7
  med. aspects
    crop prod.   633.883 19
    gen. pharm.   615.323 19
      toxicology   615.952 319
    vet. pharm.   636.089 532 319
      toxicology   636.089 595 231 9
  paleobotany   561.3
  other aspects see Plants
Till
  physical geol.   551.314
Tillage
  crop prod.   631.51
    grapes   634.81
    s.a. other spec. crops;
      also Mulch tillage;
      also spec. types of
      culture e.g.
      Floriculture
Tillamook Co. Ore.   *area*–795 44
Tillman Co. Okla.   *area*–766 46
Tillodontia
  paleozoology   569.35
Tilopteridales *see* Phaeophyta
Timber *see* Wood
Timbering *see* Supporting
    structures
Timbre
  perception
    psychology
      gen. wks.   152.157
      animals   156.215 7
      children   155.412
      s.a. psych. of other
        spec. groups
      influences   155.911 57
  sound
    engineering   620.21
    physics   534.34
      spec. states of matter   530.4
Time
  arts   701.8
    s.a. spec. art forms
  chronology   529

Tin

construction (continued)

  building   693.76

materials

  building   691.86

  engineering   620.185

    foundations   624.153 85

    naval design   623.818 25

    shipbuilding   623.820 7

    structures   624.182 5

    s.a. other spec. uses

metallography   669.956

metallurgy   669.6

  physical & chem.   669.966

  soc. & econ. aspects *see*

      Secondary industries

mineral aspects

  econ. geol.   553.453

  mineralogy   549.23

  mining

    technology   622.345 3

    prospecting   622.184 53

  s.a. spec. minerals

pharmacology   615.268 6

  misc. aspects see

      Pharmacology

products

  arts *see* Tin arts

  mf. tech.   673.6

  other aspects see

      Nonferrous metals

      products

roofing

  bldg. construction   695

soldiers

  handicrafts   745.592 82

toxicology   615.925 686

  misc. aspects see

      Toxicology

other aspects see Metal;

    also Metals

Tinamiformes

hunting

  commercial   639.128 55

  sports   799.248 55

paleozoology   568.5

zoology   598.55

other aspects see Aves

Tinamous *see* Tinamiformes

Tinctures

prac. pharm.   615.42

  misc. aspects see

      Pharmacology

Tingoidea *see* Heteroptera

Tinian   *area*–967

Tinsel *see* Passementerie

Tinsmithing *see* Tin products

Tintagel Cornwall Enq.   *area*–423 71

Tintwistle Derbyshire Eng. *area*–425 11

Tintype process

photography   772.14

Tioga Co.

  New York   *area*–747 77

  Pennsylvania   *area*–748 56

Tippah Co. Miss.   *area*–762 923

Tippecanoe Co. Ind.   *area*–772 95

Tipperary Ireland   *area*–419 2

Tipping

  etiquette   395.5

  labor econ.   331.216 6

    s.a. spec. classes of labor

      e.g. Women

Tipton Co.

  Indiana   *area*–772 555

  Tennessee   *area*–768 17

Tiree Strathclyde Scot. *area*–414 23

Tires

  automobile wheels

    soc. & econ. aspects *see*

      Secondary industries

    technology   629.248 2

  rubber

    manufacturing

      soc. & econ. aspects *see*

        Secondary industries

      technology   678.32

  s.a. spec. kinds of rubber

    e.g. Natural rubber

Tirol

  Austria   *area*–436 42

  Italy   *area*–453 8

Tishah b'Ab

  customs   394.268 296

  Judaism   296.439

Tishomingo Co. Miss.   *area*–762 995

Tissue

  banks

    health services   362.17

    misc. aspects see Medical

      services

    veterinary care   636.083 2

    s.a. spec. animals

  biology

    gen. wks.   574.82

    animals   591.82

    plants   581.82

    s.a. spec. organisms

    med. sci.   611.018 2–.018 9

    animals   636.089 101 82–.089 101 89

      s.a. spec. animals

    man   611.018 2–.018 9

    s.a. Histogenesis

  culture

    experimental biol. 574.072 4

    animals   591.072 4

    plants   581.072 4

    s.a. spec. organisms

    human phys.   612.028

  grafting *see* Plastic surgery

  papers

    handicrafts *see* Paper

      handicrafts

Tissue
  papers (continued)
    mf. tech. — 676.284 2
    other aspects see Papers
      pulp prod.
  respiration
    human phys. — 612.26
    other aspects see
      Respiration
  structure *see* Histology
Titanium
  chemistry
    inorganic — 546.512
    organic — 547.055 12
    s.a. spec. groupings e.g.
      Aliphatic compounds
    technology — 661.051 2
    organic — 661.895
    soc. & econ. aspects *see*
      Secondary industries
    s.a. spec. prod.
  construction
    architecture — 721.044 773 2
    s.a. spec. kinds of
      bldgs.
    building — 693.773 22
  materials
    building — 691.873 22
    engineering — 620.189 322
    foundations — 624.153 893 22
    naval design — 623.818 293 22
    shipbuilding — 623.820 7
    structures — 624.182 932 2
    s.a. other spec. uses
  metallography — 669.957 322
  metallurgy — 669.732 2
    physical & chem. — 669.967 322
    soc. & econ. aspects *see*
      Secondary industries
  mineral aspects
    econ. geol. — 553.462 3
  mining
    technology — 622.346 23
    prospecting — 622.184 623
    s.a. spec. minerals
  pharmacology — 615.251 2
    misc. aspects see
      Pharmacology
  products
    mf. tech. — 673.732 2
    other aspects see
      Nonferrous metals
      products
  toxicology — 615.925 512
    misc. aspects see
      Toxicology
  other aspects see Metal;
    also Metals
Titeri Algeria — *area*–653
Tithes
  local Christian parishes — 254.8

Titicaca Lake — *area*–841 2
  Bolivia — *area*–841 2
  Peru — *area*–853 6
Title
  indexing
    library operations
      manipulated — 025.486
      unmanipulated — 025.322
    insurance — 368.88
    misc. aspects see Insurance
  investigations
    law — 346.043 8
    spec. jur. — 346.3–.9
Titles
  genealogy — 929.7
  of ownership
    pub. regulation — 350.8
    s.a. spec. levels of
      govt.
Titling
  cinematography tech. — 778.535
  tech. drawing — 604.243
  spec. subj. — *s.s.*–022 1
Titmice *see* Paridae
Tito regime Yugoslavia hist. — 949.702 3
  s.a. spec. events & subj.
    e.g. Commerce
Titoism *see* Yugoslav communism
Titration *see* Qualitative
  chemistry
Titrimetry
  anal. chem.
    gen. wks. *see* Volumetric
      analysis
    thermometric *see* Thermal
      methods
Titteri Algeria — *area*–653
Titus (scriptures)
  Bible — 227.85
  other aspects see New
    Testament
Titus Co. Tex. — *area*–764 215
Tiverton Devon Eng. — *area*–423 54
Tlaxcala Mex. — *area*–724 7
Tlemcen Algeria — *area*–651
Tlingit *see* Na-Dene
Toads
  zoology — 597.87
  other aspects see Anura
Toasters *see* Household
    appliances
Toasting
  customs — 394.1
Toasts *see* Public speeches
Tobacco
  addiction
    gen. med. — 616.865
    geriatrics — 618.976 865
    hygiene — 613.85
    pediatrics — 618.928 65
    psychology — 157.6

Tobacco
addiction (continued)
    statistics   312.386 5
    deaths   312.268 65
agriculture   633.71
    soc. & econ. aspects *see*
           Primary industries
ethics
    philosophy   178.7
    religion
        Christianity   241.687
        comp. rel.   291.568 7
        s.a. other spec. rel.
health & safety
    soc. aspects   363.19
    misc. aspects see Product
        safety
hygiene   613.85
products
    manufacturers
        biog. & work   679.709 2
        s.a.   *pers.*–679 7
    manufacturing
        soc. & econ. aspects *see*
           Secondary industries
    technology   679.7
    soc. customs   394.14
    other aspects see Solanales;
        also Alkaloids
Tobacco-pouches *see* Smokers'
    supplies
Tobago West Indies   *area*–729 83
Tobermory Strathclyde Scot.
                  area–414 23
Tobias *see* Tobit
Tobit
    deuterocanonical book   229.22
    other aspects see Apocrypha
Tobogganing
    equipment mf.   688.769 5
        soc. & econ. aspects *see*
           Secondary industries
    sports   796.95
    other aspects see Sports
Toccatas
    organ music   786.82
    recordings   789.912 682
Tocharian languages
    linguistics   491.994
    literatures   891.994
    s.a.   *lang.*–919 94
Tochigi Japan   *area*–521 3
Toda *see* Dravida
Todd
    County
        Kentucky   *area*–769 77
        Minnesota   *area*–776 88
        South Dakota   *area*–783 62
    River N. Ter. Aust.   *area*–942 91
Todies *see* Coraciiformes

Todmorden West Yorkshire Eng.
                  area–428 12
Toes *see* Lower extremities
Toggle joints *see* Couplings
Toggling
    nat. leathers
        manufacturing
           soc. & econ. aspects *see*
              Secondary industries
           technology   675.24
Togo   *area*–668 1
Togolanders   *r.e.n.*–966 81
Toilet (personal grooming) *see*
           Personal grooming
Toilet training
    child care
        home econ.   649.62
Toilets *see* Comfort stations
Tokat Turkey   *area*–565
Tokelau   *area*–961 5
Token coins
    money econ.   332.404 3
    other aspects see Money
Tokens
    numismatics   737.3
    rel. significance
        Christianity   247.873
        comp. rel.   291.37
        s.a. other spec. rel.
Tokharian *see* Tocharian
Tokugawa period
    Japan hist.   952.025
    s.a. spec. events & subj.
        e.g. Courts
Tokushima Japan   *area*–523
Tokusima Japan   *area*–523
Tokyo Japan   *area*–521 35
Tolbukhin Bulgaria   *area*–497 77
Tolecraft
    dec. arts   745.72
Toledo
    Belize   *area*–728 24
    Ohio   *area*–771 13
    Spain   *area*–464 3
Toleration
    sociology   303.6
    other aspects see Virtues
Tolima Colombia   *area*–861 36
Tolland Co. Conn.   *area*–746 43
Tolls
    highway transp. *see* Finance
        prod. econ. highways
Tollways *see* Expressways
Tolman system
    psychology   150.194 34
    s.a. spec. subj. & branches
        of psych.
Tolna Hungary   *area*–439 7
Toltec architecture   722.91
    misc. aspects see
        Architectural schools

Tom Green Co. Tex.   *area*–764 721
Tomahawks *see* Edged weapons
Tomatoes
  agriculture   635.642
    soc. & econ. aspects *see*
      Primary industries
  foods   641.356 42
    preparation
      commercial   664.805 642
      domestic   641.656 42
    other aspects see Solanales;
      also Vegetables
Tombigbee River Ala.   *area*–761 2
Tombs *see* Mortuary tombs &
      chapels
Tomintoul Grampian Scot.   *area*–412 23
Tommy guns *see* Automatic
    firearms
Tomography *see* X-ray
    examinations
Tompkins Co. N.Y.   *area*–747 71
Tomsk RSFSR   *area*–573
Tom-toms *see* Membranophones
Tonalities
  musical sound   781.22
  s.a. spec. mediums
Tonbridge & Malling Kent Eng.
             area–422 372
Tonder Denmark   *area*–489 5
Tone
  discrimination *see* Timbre
      perception
  formation
    vocal music   784.932
  poems
    band music *see* Band music
    orchestra music *see* Program
      music orchestra music
Tonga   *area*–961 2
Tongue
  anatomy
    human   611.313
    other aspects see Nutritive
      organs
  diseases
    surgery   617.522
      anesthesiology   617.967 522
    other aspects see Mouth
      diseases
  muscles
    human anatomy   611.734
    other aspects see Muscles
  physical anthropometry   573.631 3
  physiology
    human   612.312
    other aspects see Nutrition
  tissue biology human   611.018 931 3
Tongue & Farr Highland Scot.
             area–411 62

Tongue-&-groove prod.
  wooden
    manufacturing
      soc. & econ. aspects *see*
        Secondary industries
      technology   674.43
Toning
  positives *see* Positives
Toning-solutions
  photography   771.54
  gen. tech.   770.283–.284
  spec. proc. & fields   772–778
Tonkin Gulf *see* South China Sea
Tonometry
  glaucoma treatment   617.741 075 4
  s.a. other spec. appls.
Tonsillitis *see* Tonsils
      diseases
Tonsils
  anatomy
    human   611.32
    other aspects see Nutritive
      organs
  diseases
    gen. wks.   616.314
      neoplasms   616.992 32
      tuberculosis   616.995 32
    geriatrics   618.976 314
    pediatrics   618.923 14
    pub. health   614.593 14
    statistics   312.331 4
      deaths   312.263 14
    surgery   617.532
      anesthesiology   617.967 532
    other aspects see Diseases
  physical anthropometry   573.632
  physiology
    human   612.312
    other aspects see Nutrition
  tissue biology human   611.018 932
Tonus
  muscles
    human phys.   612.741
    other aspects see Movements
  skin
    human phys.   612.791
    other aspects see
      Integumentary organs
Tooele Co. Utah   *area*–792 43
Tool engineers
  biog. & work   621.900 92
  s.a.   *pers.*–621
Toole Co. Mont.   *area*–786 12
Tooling
  bookbinding   686.36
Tools
  gen. wks.
    soc. & econ. aspects *see*
      Secondary industries

Tools
  gen. wks. (continued)
    tech. & mf.   621.9
    s.a. spec. appls. e.g.
      Carpentry
  sculpture   731.3
    spec. periods & schools   732–735
  other aspects see Equipment
  s.a. spec. kinds e.g. Hand
      tools; *also spec.*
      tools
Tooma River N.S.W.   *area*–944 8
Toombs Co. Ga.   *area*–758 782
Tooms Lake Fauna Reserve Tas.
                             area–946 4
Tooth
  sockets
    diseases *see* Gums (anatomy)
      diseases
  tissues
    diseases   617.634
      geriatrics   618.977 634
      statistics   312.304 763 4
        deaths   312.260 476 34
      other aspects see Teeth
Toothpicks
  wooden
    mf. tech.   674.88
    other aspects see Wood
      products
Toothshells *see* Scaphopoda
Toowoomba Qld.   *area*–943 3
Top
  games
    equipment mf.   688.752
      soc. & econ. aspects *see*
        Secondary industries
    recreation   795.2
    management   658.42
  minnows *see* Mesichthyes
Topaz
  mineralogy   549.62
Topcoats *see* Overcoats
Topectomy
  med. sci.   617.481
    vet. med.   636.089 748 1
    s.a. spec. animals
Topeka Kan.   *area*–781 63
Topiary work
  landscape design   715.1
Topical songs   784.68
  recordings   789.912 468
Topographic
  anatomy *see* Regional anatomy
  coordinates
    geodetic astronomy   526.61–.63
  features
    geomorphology   551.4
    surveying   526.98

Topography
  city planning
    arts   711.42
  influence on crime   364.22
  influence on precipitation
    meteorology   551.577 5
      weather forecasting   551.647 75
      spec. areas   551.65
  mil. eng.   623.71
  ocean floor   551.460 84
    s.a. spec. bodies of water
Topological
  algebras   512.55
    s.a. spec. appls. e.g.
      Engineering
  manifolds
    combinatorial topology   514.223
    s.a. spec. appls. e.g.
      Engineering
  vector spaces   515.73
    s.a. spec. appls. e.g.
      Engineering
Topology   514
  s.a. spec. appls. e.g.
    Engineerinq
Toppers *see* Harvesting
    machinery
Tops (coverings)
  automobiles
    soc. & econ. aspects *see*
      Secondary industries
    tech. & mf.   629.26
Tops (gyros)
  manufacture
    soc. & econ. aspects *see*
      Secondary industries
    technology   688.761 5
  recreation   796.15
  solid dynamics
    engineering *see* Dynamics
    physics   531.34
Torah
  Bible   222.1
    other aspects see
      Historical books (O.T.)
Torbay Devon Eng.   *area*–423 595
Torches
  lighting tech.   621.323
    s.a. spec. appls. e.g.
      Lighting airports
Torchwood family *see* Rutales
Torfaen Gwent Wales   *area*–429 97
Tories
  U.S. Revolution hist.   973.314
Torino Italy   *area*–451 2
Tornadoes
  disasters
    soc. action   363.349 2
      misc. aspects see
        Disasters

Tourist	
exemptions	
customs duties	
internat. comm.	382.782
misc. aspects see	
Customs (tariffs)	
houses *see* Dwellings	
Tourmaline	
mineralogy	549.64
Tournaments	
soc. customs	394.7
Tours *see* Travel	
Tovariaceae *see* Capparidales	
Tow Law Durham Eng.	*area*–428 64
Towboats	
engineering	623.823 2
design	623.812 32
models	623.820 132
seamanship	623.882 32
other aspects see Vessels	
(nautical)	
Towcester Northamptonshire Eng.	
	area–425 59
Towed vessels	
engineering	623.829
design	623.812 9
models	623.820 19
seamanship	623.882 9
other aspects see Vessels	
(nautical)	
Toweling *see* Towels	
Towels	
bathroom	
household equip.	643.52
domestic mf.	646.21
kitchen	
household equip.	643.3
textile arts	746.98
Tower Hamlets London Eng.	
	area–421 5
Towers	
Christian church arch.	726.597
other aspects see Roofs	
Towers (structures)	
architecture	725.97
building	690.597
other aspects see Public	
structures	
Towing services	
water transp.	
inland ports	
govt. control	350.876 866
central govts.	351.876 866
spec. jur.	353–354
local govts.	352.916 866
law *see* Ports	
inland-waterway transp.	
law	

Towing services	
water transp. (continued)	
seaports	
govt. control	350.877 166
central govts.	351.877 166
spec. jur.	353–354
local govts.	352.917 166
law *see* Seaports law	
transp.	
Town club bldgs. *see* Clubhouse	
buildings	
Towner Co. N.D.	*area*–784 38
Townhouses	
architecture	728.312
building	690.831 2
other aspects see Residential	
buildings	
Towns	
Co. Ga.	*area*–758 282
local govt.	352.007 23
Townshend Acts	
U.S. hist.	973.311 2
Townships	
local govt. admin.	352.007 22
Townsville Qld.	*area*–943 6
Toxemias *see* Bacterial diseases	
med. sci. blood	
diseases	
Toxic organisms	
econ. biol. *see* Deleterious	
organisms	
Toxicologists	
biog. & work	615.900 92
other aspects see Medical	
scientists	
s.a.	*pers.*–615
Toxicology	615.9
vet. sci.	636.089 59
s.a. spec. animals	
Toxin-antitoxins	
pharmacology	615.375
other aspects see Drugs	
Toxins	
pharmacology	615.373
other aspects see Drugs	
Toxoids	
pharmacology	615.373
other aspects see Drugs	
Toy	
dogs	
animal husbandry	636.76
other aspects see Dogs	
Manchester terriers	
animal husbandry	636.76
other aspects see Dogs	
poodles	
animal husbandry	636.76
other aspects see Dogs	
soldiers	
handicrafts	745.592 82

Toy (continued)
  theaters
    performing arts   791.5
Toyama Japan   *area*–521 5
Toys
  child care
    home econ.   649.55
  handicrafts   745.592
  latex *see* Dipped latex
      products
  manufacturing
    soc. & econ. aspects *see*
      Secondary industries
    technology   688.72
  safety
    law *see* Product safety law
    soc. aspects   363.19
      misc. aspects see Product
        safety
  soc. customs   394.3
Trabzon Turkey   *area*–565
Trace elements
  plant nutrition
    pathology   581.213 356
    physiology   581.133 56
    s.a. spec. plants
    s.a. other spec. occurrences
Tracer
  techniques
    anal. chem.
      gen. wks.   543.088 4
        qualitative   544.984
        quantitative   545.824
      organic   547.308 84
        qualitative   547.349 84
        quantitative   547.358 24
      s.a. spec. elements &
        cpds.
    radiochemistry *see* Isotopes
      radiochemistry
  testing
    eng. materials   620.112 73
    s.a. spec. materials &
      spec. uses
Trachea
  anatomy
    human   611.23
    other aspects see
      Respiratory organs
  diseases
    gen. wks.   616.23
      neoplasms   616.992 23
      tuberculosis   616.995 23
    geriatrics   618.976 23
    pediatrics   618.922 3
    pub. health   614.592 3
    statistics   312.323
      deaths   312.262 3
    surgery   617.533
      anethesiology   617.967 533
    other aspects see Diseases

Trachea (continued)
  physical anthropometry   573.623
  physiology
    human   612.2
    other aspects see
      Respiration
  tissue biology human   611.018 923
Tracheitis *see* Trachea diseases
Trachinoidea *see*
    Acanthopterygii
Trachoma
  ophthalmology
    gen. wks.   617.772
    geriatrics   618.977 772
    pediatrics   618.920 977 72
    pub. health   614.599 7
    statistics   312.304 777 2
    other aspects see Diseases
Trachylina *see* Hydrozoa
Tracing
  materials management
    receiving *see* Receiving
      operations materials
      management
    shipping   658.788 6
    spec. subj.   *s.s.*–068 7
Track
  athletics
    equipment mf.   688.764 2
      soc. & econ. aspects *see*
        Secondary industries
    sports   796.42
    other aspects see Sports
  system *see* Homogeneous
    grouping education
Tracking
  cooperation
    internat. law   341.767 52
  manned space flight
    gen. wks.   629.457
    s.a. spec. appls. e.g.
      Space warfare
    s.a. spec. flights e.g.
      Lunar flights
  unmanned space flight   629.437
    s.a. spec. appls. e.g.
      Space warfare
Tracking-systems
  spacecraft eng.
    manned   629.474 3
    unmanned   629.464 3
    other aspects see
      Spacecraft
Tracks
  railroad *see* Railroad tracks
Tract *see* Proper of the Mass
Traction systems
  elect. eng.
    soc. & econ. aspects *see*
      Secondary industries

Traction systems
  elect. eng. (continued)
    technology   621.33
    s.a. spec. appls. e.g.
      Railroad transportation
Tractors (automobiles)
  use agric.   631.372
    s.a. spec. crops
  other aspects see Work
    automobiles
Trade
  acceptances *see* Commercial
    paper
  advertising   659.131 5
  agreements
    internat. comm.   382.9
    internat. law   341.754 026
  associations
    law   346.064
    misc. aspects see
      Organizations law
  barriers
    internat. comm.   382.7
  bibliographies   015
    spec. subj.   016
  cards
    illustration   741.685
  catalogs
    spec. subj.   *s.s.*–029 4
  ethics *see* Business ethics
  promotion
    internat. banking   332.154
    misc. aspects see Banking
  schools *see* Vocational
    schools
  unions *see* Labor unions
  winds *see* Planetary wind
    systems
  s.a. Commerce
Trademarks
  law
    international   341.758 8
    municipal   346.048 8
    spec. jur.   346.3–.9
  pub. admin. *see* Secondary
    industries govt.
    control pub. admin.
  sales promotion   658.827
    spec. subj.   *s.s.*–068 8
    spec. uses   *s.s.*–027 5
Traders
  biog. & work   380.109 2
  s.a. spec. kinds
  s.a.   *pers.*–38
Trading-stamps
  sales promotion *see* Sales
    promotion
Tradition
  knowledge of God
    Christianity   231.042

Tradition
  knowledge of God (continued)
    other rel. see God rel.
      doctrines
Traditional *see spec. subj.*
Traditionalism
  philosophy   148
  indiv. phil.   180–190
  s.a. spec. branches of phil.
    e.g. Metaphysics
Traffic
  accidents   363.125
    misc. aspects see
      Transportation
      accidents
  circles *see* Intersections
    (roads & streets)
  control
    air transp.
      law
        international   341.756 76
        municipal   343.097 6
        spec. jur.   343.3–.9
    commerce   380.52
    roads & streets
      gen. wks.
        commerce   388.312 2
        govt. control   351.878 31
        spec. jur.   353–354
      law
        international   341.756 86
        municipal   343.094 6
        spec. jur.   343.3–.9
      local
        commerce   388.413 122
        govt. control   350.878 413 122
          central govts.   351.878 413 122
          spec. jur.   353–354
          local govts.   352.918 413 122
        law   343.098 2
          spec. jur.   343.3–.9
      other spec. kinds of
      transp. see Transport
      functions
  failures
    transp. hazards
      air   363.124 18
      railroad   363.122 1
      vehicular   363.125 1
      water   363.123 1
    police services   363.233 2
    govt. control   350.878 31
      central govts.   351.878 31
      spec. jur.   353–354
      local govts.   352.918 31
    law   344.052 332
      spec. jur.   344.3–.9
  controls
    road eng.
      technology   625.794
      other aspects see Roads

Traffic (continued)
flow
  highway transp.
    commerce   388.31
    govt. control   351.878 31
    spec. jur.   353–354
    law
     international   341.756 86
     municipal   343.094 6
     spec. jur.   343.3–.9
  urban transp.
    commerce   388.413 1
    govt. control   350.878 413 1
     central govts.   351.878 413 1
     spec. jur.   353–354
     local govts.   352.918 413 1
    law   343.098 2
     spec. jur.   343.3–.9
hazards
  soc. path.   363.125
load *see* Traffic volume
maintenance *see* Traffic flow
management
  shipping operations
    materials management 658.788 2
    spec. subj.   *s.s.*–068 7
noise
  soc. aspects   363.741
  other aspects see Noise
offenses *see* Traffic
    violations
patterns
  highways   388.314 3
  urban streets   388.413 143
safety *see* Vehicular transp.
    safety
signals
  roads and streets *see*
    Traffic control roads &
    streets
signs
  roads & streets *see* Traffic
  control roads & streets
violations
  criminology   364.147
  law   345.024 7
    spec. jur.   345.3–.9
  soc. theology
    Christianity   261.833 147
    comp. rel.   291.178 331 47
    s.a. other spec. rel.
volume
  highways   388.314 2
  urban streets   388.413 142
Trafficways
engineering
  soc. & econ. aspects *see*
    Secondary industries
  tech. & mf.   629.047
  military   623.6
s.a. spec. kinds e.g. Roads

Trafford Greater Manchester Eng.
          area–427 31
Tragedies (drama)
gen. wks.
  collections   808.825 12
  hist. & crit.   809.251 2
  rhetoric   808.251 2
  juvenile   808.068 251 2
spec. lits.   *lit. sub.*–205 12
  indiv. authors *lit. sub.*–21–29
stage presentation   792.12
other aspects see Drama
Tragedy
lit. qual.
  gen. wks.
    collections   808.801 6
    hist. & crit. 809.916
  spec. lits.
    collections *lit. sub.*–080 16
    hist. & crit. *lit. sub.*–091 6
  s.a. spec. lit. forms
stage qual.   792.090 916
  s.a. spec. mediums e.g.
    Television; *also spec.*
    kinds of drama e.g.
    Comedies (drama)
Tragopogon porrifolius *see*
    Salsify
Traguloidea
animal husbandry   636.973 55
hunting
  commercial   639.117 355
  sports   799.259 735 5
zoology   599.735 5
other aspects see Ruminantia
Trail B.C.   *area*–711 44
Trailer
camps
  housekeeping   647.94
  s.a. spec. activities
    e.g. Housecleaning
    (home econ.)
travel
  recreation   796.79
Trailer-park areas
civic art   711.557
  for long-term residents 711.58
  for transients   711.557
Trailers
automobile
  commerce   388.346
  dwellings
    architecture 728.79
    building   690.879
  taxation *see* Personal
    property taxes
  other aspects see
    Residential buildings
engineering
  gen. tech. & mf.   629.226
  maintenance   629.287 6

Trailers
  automobile
    engineering
      gen. tech. & mf. (continued)
        models   629.221 6
        operation   629.284 6
        s.a. other spec. aspects
          e.g. Brakes; *also*
          spec. appls. e.g.
            Travel
        soc. & econ. aspects *see*
          Secondary industries
      other aspects see Land
        vehicles
Traill Co. N.D.   *area*–784 14
Trails *see* Roads
Train
  accidents   363.122
    misc. aspects see
      Transportation
      accidents
  sheds *see* Railroad terminals
    facilities
Trainable retarded persons
  child psych.   155.452 83
  child rearing home econ.   649.152 83
  education   371.928 3
    law   344.079 128 3
      spec. jur.   344.3–.9
Trainers (aircraft)
  mil. eng.   623.746 2
Training
  armed forces   355.5
    law *see* Armed services law
    s.a. spec. mil. branches
  labor econ.   331.259 2
    s.a. spec. classes of labor
      e.g. Women
  labor law *see* Labor law
  personnel admin.
    gen. management   658.312 4
    executives   658.407 124
    spec. subj.   *s.s.*–068 3
    law of pub. admin.   342.068 6
      spec. jur.   342.3–.9
    pub. admin.   350.15
      central govts.   351.15
        spec. jur.   353–354
      local govts.   352.005 15
  plants
    crop prod.   631.546
      s.a. spec. crops; also
        spec. types of culture
        e.g. Floriculture
  veterans   355.115 2
Training-devices
  personnel training *see*
    Training-programs

Training-programs
  personnel admin.   658.312 404
    misc. aspects see Training
      personnel admin.
Training-schools penology   365.42
  misc. aspects see Penal
    institutions
Trains
  railroad rolling stock
    commerce   385.37
    local   388.42–.46
    special-duty   385.5
    other aspects see Rolling
      stock railroads
  sanitation *see* Public
    carriers sanitation
Traits
  indiv. psych.   155.23
Trajectories
  mil. eng.   623.514
  solid dynamics
    engineering *see* Dynamics
    physics   531.31
Tramp routes
  maritime transp.
    commerce   387.523
    govt. control   351.877 523
      spec. jur.   353–354
    law *see* Marine
      transportation law
Trampolining
  equipment mf.   688.764 7
    soc. & econ. aspects *see*
      Secondary industries
  sports   796.47
    other aspects see Sports
Tramps *see* Lower classes
Tramways *see* Surface rail
  systems
Trance phenomena
  psychology   154.772
  animals   156.4
Tranent Lothian Scot.   *area*–413 6
Tranquilizers
  addictive aspects *see*
    Addictive drugs use
  pharmacodynamics   615.788 2
  other aspects see Drugs
Transaction taxes
  law   343.055
    spec. jur.   343.3–.9
  pub. admin.   350.724 7
    central govts.   351.724 7
      spec. jur.   353–354
    local govts.   352.135
  pub. finance   336.27
Transactional analysis
  appl. psych.   158.2
    children   155.418
    system   158.9

Transactional analysis
  appl. psych. (continued)
    s.a. psych. of other spec.
      groups
    psychiatry   616.891 45
    geriatrics   618.976 891 45
    pediatrics   618.928 914 5
    other aspects see Medical
      sciences
Transatlantic flights
  technology   629.130 911
Transcarpathia Ukraine   *area*–477 18
Transcaucasia   *area*–479
Transcendental
  meditation
    appl. psych.   158.12
    children   155.418
    system   158.9
    s.a. psych. of other spec.
      groups
  numbers   512.73
  s.a. spec. appls. e.g.
    Engineering
Transcendentalism
  philosophy   141.3
  indiv. phil.   180–190
  s.a. spec. branches of phil.
    e.g. Metaphysics
Transcona Man.   *area*–712 74
Transcription
  linguistics *see* Notations
    languages
  shorthand notes   653.14
  s.a. spec. shorthand systems
    e.g. Gregg
Transcription (music)
  music theory   781.64
  s.a. spec. mediums
Transepts
  Christian church arch.   726.592
Transfer
  heat *see* Transmission heat
  learning
    psychology   153.154
    animals   156.315 4
    children   155.413
    s.a. psych. of other spec.
      groups
  payments
    macroeconomics   339.522
  s.a. other spec. subj.
Transference
  depth psych.   154.24
  animals   156.4
Transfers
  employees
    labor right *see* Worker
      security
    personnel admin.
      gen. management   658.312 8
      executives   658.407 128

Transfers
  employees
    personnel admin.
      gen. management (continued)
        spec. subj.   *s.s.*–068 3
      pub. admin.   350.14
        central govts.   351.14
        spec. jur.   353–354
        local govts.   352.005 14
  real property
    law   346.043 6
    spec. jur.   346.3–.9
  students   371.291 4
  s.a. spec. levels of ed.;
    also Special education
Transfiguration
  Jesus Christ
    Christian doctrines   232.956
Transfinite numbers   512.7
  s.a. spec. appls. e.g.
    Engineering
Transformation of energy
  physics   531.68
  s.a. spec. branches of
    physics
Transformations   511.33
  geometry   516.1
    Euclidean   516.21
    s.a. other spec. geometries
  number theory
    algebra   512.72
    s.a. spec. appls. e.g.
      Engineering
  s.a. other spec. branches of
    math.; also spec.
    appls. e.g.
    Engineering
Transformer substations
  elect. power *see* Modification
    elect. power
Transformers
  electrodynamic eng.
    soc. & econ. aspects *see*
      Secondary industries
    tech. & mf.   621.314
    s.a. spec. appls. e.g.
      Lighting airports
  other aspects see
    Electrodynamics
Transforms
  operational calculus   515.723
  s.a. spec. appls. e.g.
    Engineering
  s.a. Transformations
Transhipment
  ore mining eng.   622.69
Transient
  currents
    elect. circuits *see*
      Physical phenomena
      elect. circuits

Transient (continued)
  magnetism
    geomagnetism   538.74
      spec. states of matter   530.4
Transillumination
  illumination eng.
    soc. & econ. aspects *see*
      Secondary industries
    technology   621.321 5
      exterior   621.322 9
      interior   621.322 5-.322 8
    s.a. spec. kinds e.g.
      Incandescent lighting
  s.a. spec. appls. e.g.
    Lighting museum bldgs.
Transistor circuits
  technology   621.381 530 422
    microelectronics   621.381 730 422
    microwave electronics 621.381 320 422
    radiowave electronics 621.381 530 422
    x- & gamma-ray electronics 621.381 6
  s.a. spec. appls. e.g.
    Radiocontrol
  other aspects see Microwave
    electronics; Radiowave
    electronics; X-ray
    electronics
Transistorized
  circuits *see* Transistor
    circuits
  sets
    radio
      engineering   621.384 136 6
      s.a. spec. appls. e.g.
        Radiotelephony
      other aspects see Radio
    television
      engineering   621.388 366
      s.a. spec. appls. e.g.
        Astronautics
      other aspects see
        Television
Transistors
  gen. wks.
    soc. & econ. aspects *see*
      Secondary industries
    tech. & mf.   621.381 528
    s.a. spec. appls. e.g.
      Radiocontrol
  microelectronics *see*
    Components
      microelectronics
  television
    engineering   621.388 32
    s.a. spec. appls. e.g.
      Astronautics
    other aspects see
      Television
  other aspects see
    Semiconductors

Transit
  insurance   368.2
    misc. aspects see Insurance
  taxes
    pub. finance   336.263
    other aspects see Customs
      (tariffs)
Transition metals
  chemistry
    inorganic   546.62-.64
    organic   547.056 2-.056 4
    s.a. spec. groupings e.g.
      Aliphatic compounds
  technology   661.062-.064
    organic   661.895
    soc. & econ. aspects *see*
      Secondary industries
    s.a. spec. prod.
  pharmacology   615.262-.264
    misc. aspects see
      Phramacology
  toxicology   615.925 62-.925 64
    misc. aspects see
      Toxicology
  s.a. spec. metals
Transitional flow
  fluid mech.
    engineering *see* Dynamics
    physics   532.052 6
    gases   533.216
      air   533.621 6
    liquids   532.516
Transits
  astronomy   523.9
  theory   521.8
    s.a. spec. celestial bodies
Transkei Cape of Good
    Hope   *area*-687 91
Translation (linguistics) 418.02
  spec. langs.   *lang. sub.*-802
Translations
  bibliographies   011.7
    spec. kinds   012-016
  catalogs
    general   017-019
    spec. kinds   012-016
Translator programs *see*
    Software programming
Transliteration *see* Notations
    languages
Transmigration of soul *see*
    Reincarnation
Transmission
  elect. power
    electrodynamic eng.   621.319
    s.a. spec. appls. e.g.
      Electric railroads
    soc. & econ. aspects *see*
      Secondary industries
    other aspects see
      Electrodynamics

Transmission (continued)
  heat
    astrophysics   523.013 2
      s.a. spec. celestial
        bodies
    engineering
      soc. & econ. aspects *see*
        Secondary industries
    technology   621.402 2
      s.a. spec. appls. e.g.
        Heating buildings
    physics   536.2
    spec. states of matter   530.4
  light
    optics
      astrophysics   523.015 3
      s.a. spec. celestial
        bodies
      physics   535.3
      spec. states of matter 530.4
  mech. vibrations
    engineering   620.31
      s.a. spec. appls. e.g.
        Foundation engineering
  pressure
    statics *see* Statics
  radiations
    meteorology *see* Radiations
      meteorology
  sound
    engineering   620.21
      s.a. spec. appls. e.g.
        Opera buildings
    physics   534.2
    spec. states of matter   530.4
  steam
    soc. & econ. aspects *see*
      Secondary industries
    technology   621.185
      s.a. spec. appls. e.g.
        District heating
  wire telephony
    soc. & econ. aspects *see*
      Secondary industries
    tech. & mf.   621.387 8
      s.a. spec. appls. e.g.
        Military engineering
    other aspects see Telephony
      wire
  s.a. other spec. subj.
Transmission-devices
  automobiles
    tech. & mf.   629.244
    soc. & econ. aspects *see*
      Secondary industries
    s.a. spec. appls. e.g.
      Driving motor vehicles

Transmitters
  radio
    engineering   621.384 131
      s.a. spec. appls. e.g.
        Radiotelephony
    other aspects see Radio
  television
    engineering   621.388 31
      s.a. spec. appls. e.g.
        Astronautics
    other aspects see
      Television
  wire telegraphy *see*
    Instrumentation wire
    telegraphy
Transmitting
  antennas *see* Antennas
  equipment
    telephone commun.
      commerce   384.65
      wire   384.65
      wireless   384.535
    terminal *see* Terminal
    equipment wire
    telephony
Transmutations *see* Nuclear
    reactions
Transoceanic flights
  technology   629.130 91
Transonic velocity
  aeronautical aerodynamics 629.132 304
    s.a. spec. phenomena e.g.
      Lift; *also spec.*
        appls. e.g. Flying
  gas flow mech.
    engineering *see* Dynamics
    physics   533.274
    air flow   533.627 4
Transpacific flights
  technology   629.130 915
Transparency
  sea water
    oceanography   551.460 1
    s.a. spec. bodies of water
  s.a. other spec. subj.
Transpiration
  plants
    pathology   581.212 9
    physiology   581.129
    s.a. spec. plants
Transplanters *see*
    Planting-equipment
Transplanting
  plant propagation   631.536
    s.a. spec. crops; also spec.
      types of culture e.g.
      Floriculture
Transplants
  surgery *see* Plastic surgery

Transport
  aircraft
    engineering
      civilian *see* Commercial
        airplanes
      military ... 623.746 5
    functions
      commerce ... 380.52
        air ... 387.740 42
        inland waterway ... 386.240 42
          canals ... 386.404 204 2
          ferries ... 386.6
          lakes ... 386.540 42
          rivers ... 386.350 42
        marine ... 387.540 42
        rail ... 385.204 2
          local ... 388.42
          special-duty ... 385.5
        vehicular
          gen. wks.
            bus ... 388.322 042
            truck ... 388.324 042
          local
            bus ... 388.413 22
            truck ... 388.413 24
      govt. control ... 350.875–.878
        central govts. ... 351.875–.878
          spec. jur. ... 353–354
        local govts. ... 352.915–.918
      law *see spec. kinds of*
        transportation e.g.
        Inland waterway
        transportation
    phenomena
      biology *see* Membranes
        cytology
      chem. eng. ... 660.284 2
        s.a. spec. prod.
      eng. mech. *see* Dynamics
      physics mech. ... 531.113 7
        fluids ... 532.057
        gases ... 533.13
          air ... 533.63
        liquids ... 532.7
        particles ... 531.163
        solids ... 531.7
    ships military
      engineering ... 623.826 4
        design ... 623.812 64
        models ... 623.820 164
      naval forces
        materiel ... 359.83
        organization ... 359.326 4
      seamanship ... 623.882 64
      other aspects see Vessels
        (nautical)
    theory physics ... 530.136
    s.a. Transportation

Transportation
  accidents ... 363.12
    gen. hist. ... 904.7
      travel ... 910
    s.a. hist. of spec.
      places
    hazards
      soc. path. ... 363.12
      statistics ... 312.44
        deaths ... 312.274
    other aspects see Accidents
  advertising ... 659.134 4
  buildings
    architecture ... 725.3
    building ... 690.53
    other aspects see Public
      structures
  diseases ... 616.980 2
    geriatrics ... 618.976 980 2
    pediatrics ... 618.929 802
    statistics ... 312.398 02
    other aspects see Diseases
    s.a. spec. diseases
  engineering
    soc. & econ. aspects *see*
      Secondary industries
    technology ... 629.04
      military ... 623.6
    s.a. other spec. appls.
    s.a. spec. kinds e.g.
      Nautical engineering
  equipment
    agric. use ... 631.373
      s.a. spec. crops; also
        spec. types of culture
        e.g. Floriculture
    mil. sci. ... 355.83
      s.a. spec. mil. branches
    s.a. other spec. uses; also
      spec. kinds e.g. Fork
      lifts
  facilities
    civic art ... 711.7
    commerce ... 380.53
      spec. kinds ... 385–388
    govt. control *see*
      Transportation
      operations govt.
      control
    mil. resources ... 355.27
    s.a. spec. mil. branches
  fire hazards ... 363.379
    misc. aspects see Fire
      safety
  forces
    air warfare ... 358.44
  gen. wks. *see* Transportation
    operations
  insurance ... 368.2
    misc. aspects see Insurance

Trapeze work (continued)
  equipment mf.   688.764 6
    soc. & econ. aspects *see*
        Secondary industries
  sports   796.46
  other aspects see Sports
Trappers
  biog. & work   639.109 2
  s.a.   *pers.*–639 1
Trapping *see* Hunting
Trappist monastic bldgs.
  architecture   726.771 25
  building   690.677 125
  other aspects see
        Religious-purpose
        bldgs.
Trappists
  rel. orders   255.125
    church hist.   271.125
    ecclesiology   262.24
Traps
  mil. eng.   623.31
  sewers   628.25
  s.a. spec. appls. e.g.
        Water drainage
  steam eng.
    soc. & econ. aspects *see*
        Secondary industries
    tech. & mf.   621.197
    s.a. spec. appls. e.g.
        Steam locomotives
Trapshooters
  biog. & work   799.313
  s.a.   *pers.*–799 3
Trapshooting   799.313
  misc. aspects see Sports
Traralgon Vic.   *area*–945 6
Trash (art style) *see* Kitsch
Trás-os-Montes Portugal   *area*–469 2
Traumatic
  neuroses
    gen. med.   616.852 1
    geriatrics   618.976 852 1
    pediatrics   618.928 521
    psychology   157.3
    statistics   312.385 21
  shock *see* Shock
    (pathological)
Traumatology
  med. sci.   617.1
Trautonium music *see* Electronic
        music
Trautoniums
  musical art   789.99
  other aspects see Music
        instruments
Travancore-Cochin India   *area*–548 3
Travel
  cookery   641.575
  diseases   616.980 2
    geriatrics   618.976 980 2

Travel
  diseases (continued)
    pediatrics   618.929 802
    statistics   312.398 02
    other aspects see Diseases
    s.a. spec. diseases
  econ. law *see* Commerce govt.
        control law
  food services   642.3
  gen. accounts
    ancient world   913.04
    modern world   910.4
  gen. guides   910.202
  hygiene   613.68
  lit. & stage trmt. *see*
        Disciplines (systems)
  safety *see* Transportation
        safety
  scientific   508
    s.a. spec. sci.
  other aspects see Geography
Travelers
  biog. & work   910.92
    s.a. geog. of spec. places
  s.a.   *pers.*–91
Traveling
  displays
    transp. adv.   659.134 4
  shows
    performing arts   791.1
Traveling-wave tubes
  microwave electronics
    soc. & econ. aspects *see*
        Secondary industries
    tech. & mf.   621.381 335
    spec. circuits   621.381 32
    s.a. spec. appls. e.g.
        Radar engineering
  other aspects see Microwave
        electronics
Travels *see* Travel
Traverse Co. Minn.   *area*–776 435
Traversing
  geodetic surveying   526.33
Travertines *see* Limestones
Travis Co. Tex.   *area*–764 31
Trawden Lancashire Eng.   *area*–427 645
Trawlers
  engineering   623.828
    design   623.812 8
    models   623.820 18
    seamanship   623.882 8
  other aspects see Vessels
        (nautical)
Trawling
  sports   799.13
  other aspects see Fishing
Treason
  history
    U.S. Revolution   973.381

Treason
history (continued)
  s.a. hist. of spec.
    countries
  other aspects see Political
    offenses
Treasure
  Co. Mont.   *area*–786 313
  prospecting
    technology   622.19
  trove *see* Buried treasure
Treasury
  bills
    investment econ.   332.632 32
      misc. aspects see Bonds
        (securities)
    pub. finance   336.32
      misc. aspects see Public
        debt
    bonds *see* Public securities
  departments
    U.S. govt.   353.2
      other jur. see Finance
        departments
    notes *see* Treasury bills
Treaties
  internat. law   341.37
  law of war   341.66
  source of law   341.1
  texts   341.026
  s.a. spec. subj. e.g. World War 1
    940.314 1
Treatment
  refuse   628.445
    technology   628.445
    other aspects see Refuse
      pub. sanitation
  sewage *see* Sewage treatment
  water-supply eng.
    technology   628.162
    other aspects see Water
      supply engineering
  s.a. other spec. subj.
Treaty powers
  legislative bodies
    law *see* Legislative powers
      law
  pol. sci.   328.346
    spec. jur.   328.4–.9
Trebizond Turkey   *area*–565
Tredegar Gwent Wales   *area*–429 95
Tree
  diseases
    forestry   634.963
    s.a. spec. trees
  frogs
    zoology   597.87
    other aspects see Anura
  hyraxes *see* Hyracoidea

Tree (continued)
  injuries
    forestry   634.96
    s.a. spec. trees
  lily family *see* Haemodorales
  of heaven *see* Rutales
  shrews *see* Prosimii
Trees
  art representation *see* Plants
    art representation
  botany   582.16
    misc. aspects see
      Spermatophyta
    s.a. spec. plants
  floriculture   635.977
  forestry   634.9
  landscape design   715.2
  paleobotany   561.21
    s.a. spec. kinds
  rel. worship
    comp. rel.   291.212
    s.a. spec. rel.
Trees (mathematics) *see* Graphs
  mathematics
Trefoils
  agriculture   633.374
    soc. & econ. aspects *see*
      Primary industries
    other aspects see
      Papilionaceae; *also*
      Field crops
Trego Co. Kan.   *area*–781 165
Treinta y Tres Uruguay   *area*–895 22
Trellises
  use in plant training *see*
    Training plants
Tremandraceae *see* Pittosporales
Trematoda
  culture & hunting   639.752 2
  zoology   595.122
  other aspects see Worms
Trematode-caused diseases *see*
  Fluke-caused diseases
Trempealeau Co. Wis.   *area*–775 49
Trench
  fever
    gen. med.   616.922 6
    geriatrics   618.976 922 6
    pediatrics   618.929 226
    pub. health   614.526 6
    statistics   312.392 26
      deaths   312.269 226
    other aspects see Diseases
  knives *see* Edged weapons
  mouth
    gen. med.   616.312
    geriatrics   618.976 312
    pediatrics   618.923 12
    pub. health   614.593 12
    statistics   312.331 2
      deaths   312.263 12

Trench
mouth (continued)
other aspects see Diseases
warfare 355.44
s.a. spec. mil. branches
Trengganu Malaysia *area*–595 1
Trent River Eng. *area*–425
Trentino Italy *area*–453 85
Trentino-Alto Adige Italy *area*–453 8
Trento Italy *area*–453 85
Trenton N.J. *area*–749 66
Battle U.S. hist. 973.332
Trephining *see* Skull diseases
surgery
Trespass
law 346.036
spec. jur. 346.3–.9
Trestle bridges
structural eng. 624.32
other aspects see Bridges
(structures)
Treutlen Co. Ga. *area*–758 682
Treviño Spain *area*–466 7
Treviso Italy *area*–453 6
Trial
& error learning
psychology 153.152 4
animals 156.315 24
children 155.413
s.a. psych. of other spec.
groups
by jury
civil right 323.422
of Jesus Christ
Christian doctrines 232.962
Trials
law
criminal 345.07
juvenile 345.087
spec. jur. 345.3–.9
gen. wks. 347.07
spec. jur. 347.3–.9
other aspects see Legal
procedure
rel. law *see* Legal procedure
rel. law
Triangle music 789.35
recordings 789.912 93
Triangles (configurations) *see*
Configurations geometry
Triangles (music)
mf. tech. 681.819 3
misc. aspects see Musical
instruments
musical art 789.3
Triangulation
geodetic surveying 526.33
Triassic period
geology 551.762
s.a. spec. aspects e.g.
Economic geology

Triassic period (continued)
paleontology 560.176 2
spec. fossils 561–569
Tribal
communities
sociology 307.7
land
economics 333.2
state
pol. sci. 321.12
s.a. spec. jur.
Triboelectricity
astrophysics 523.018 721
s.a. spec. celestial bodies
physics 537.21
spec. states of matter 530.4
Tribology *see* Friction machine
eng.
Tribulation
Christian doctrines 236.9
Tribunals
papal admin. 262.136
other kinds see Courts
Trichechiformes
paleozoology 569.5
Trichinosis
gen. med. 616.965 4
geriatrics 618.976 965 4
pediatrics 618.929 654
pub. health 614.562
statistics 312.396 54
deaths 312.269 654
other aspects see Diseases
Trichomonadida *see* Mastigophora
Trichopodaceae *see* Dioscoreales
Trichoptera
culture 638.574 5
paleozoology 565.74
zoology 595.745
other aspects see Insecta
Trick
games
recreation 793.5
photography 778.8
Trickling
filter process
sewage trmt.
technology 628.352
other aspects see Sewage
trmt. & disposal
Tricks
manufacturing
soc. & econ. aspects *see*
Secondary industries
technology 688.726
Tricladida *see* Turbellaria
Triclinic systems
crystallography 548.14
s.a. spec. substances
Triconodonta
paleozoology 569.17

Triodes (continued)
  vacuum tubes
    radiowave electronics
      soc. & econ. aspects *see*
          Secondary industries
      tech. & mf.   621.381 512 3
        s.a. spec. appls. e.g.
          Receiving sets
      other aspects see Vacuum
          tubes
Trionychoidea *see* Chelonia
Trios
  by instrument *see spec.*
      instruments
  chamber music
    recordings   798.912 57
    scores & parts   785.73
    treatises   785.703
  songs
    recordings   789.912
    scores & parts   784.83
      sacred   783.675 3
      secular   784.306 3
Triphenylmethane dyes
  manufacturing
    chem. tech.   667.254
    soc. & econ. aspects *see*
        Secondary industries
  org. chem.   547.864
Triphylite
  mineralogy   549.72
Tripitaka
  Buddhism   294.382
Triple points *see* Phase changes
    effect of heat
Triple-expansion steam engines
    see Reciprocating
        engines steam
Triplets
  birth *see* Multiple childbirth
  psychology   155.444
  rearing home econ.   649.144
Tripods
  cameras
    photography   771.38
    gen. tech.   770.282
    spec. proc. & fields   772–778
Tripoli *see* Abrasive materials
Tripolis
  ancient   *area*–397 4
Tripolitan War
  U.S. hist.   973.47
Tripolitania   *area*–612
Tripp Co. S.D.   *area*–783 61
Trips *see* Travel
Triptychs *see* Easel paintings
Tripura India   *area*–541 5
Triremes
  engineering   623.821
    design   623.812 1
    models   623.820 11

Triremes (continued)
  seamanship   623.882 1
  other aspects see Vessels
      (nautical)
Trisaccharides
  org. chem.   547.781 5
  other aspects see Sugar
Trisection of angles   516.204
Tristan da Cunha Isl.   *area*–973
Triticum *see* Wheat
Tritium
  chemistry   546.213
Triumphs
  soc. customs   394.4
Triuridaceae *see* Triuridales
Triuridales
  botany   584.71
  floriculture   635.934 71
  med. aspects
    crop. prod.   633.884 71
    gen. pharm.   615.324 71
      toxicology   615.952 471
    vet. pharm.   636.089 532 471
      toxicology   636.089 595 247 1
  paleobotany   561.4
  other aspects see Plants
Troas ancient   *area*–392 1
Troches
  prac. pharm.   615.43
    misc. aspects see
        Pharmacology
Trochili *see* Apodiformes
Trochodendraceae *see*
        Magnoliales
Troglodytidae
  hunting
    commercial   639.128 833
    sports   799.248 833
  paleozoology   568.8
  zoology   598.833
  other aspects see Aves
Trogoniformes
  hunting
    commercial   639.128 73
    sports   799.248 73
  paleozoology   568.7
  zoology   598.73
  other aspects see Aves
Trogons *see* Trogoniformes
Trolleybuses
  commerce   388.413 223
  engineering
    soc. & econ. aspects *see*
        Secondary industries
    tech. & mf.   625.66
  other aspects see Land
      vehicles
Trolleycars *see* Surface rail
      systems

Trolling
  angling
    sports   799.12
  other aspects see Fishing
Trombidiformes
  zoology   595.42
  other aspects see Arachnida
Trombone music   788.25
  recordings   789.912 82
Trombones
  mf. tech.   681.818 2
    misc. aspects see Musical
      instruments
  musical art   788.2
Trombonists
  biog. & work   788.209 2
  s.a.   *pers.–*788
Troms Norway   *area–*484 5
Troon Strathclyde Scot.   *area–*414 64
Troop
  movements
    logistics
      mil. sci.   355.411
      s.a. spec. mil.
        branches
    ships *see* Transport ships
      military
Troops
  use in labor disputes   331.898 4
Tropaeolaceae *see* Geraniales
Tropic birds *see* Pelecaniformes
Tropical
  climates
    hygiene   613.113
      misc. aspects see Hygiene
  diseases   616.988 3
    geriatrics   618.976 988 3
    pediatrics   618.929 883
    statistics   312.398 83
    deaths   312.269 883
    other aspects see Diseases
    s.a. spec. diseases
  ecology life sci.   574.526 23
    animals   591.526 23
    microorganisms   576.15
    plants   581.526 23
    s.a. spec. organisms
  plants
    floriculture   635.952
    s.a. spec. plants
  tree fruits
    agriculture   634.6
    soc. & econ. aspects *see*
      Primary industries
    foods   641.346
    preparation
      commercial   664.804 6
      domestic   641.646
    other aspects see Fruits
  s.a. Hot-weather

Tropics *see* Torrid Zone; *also*
    Tropical
Tropisms
  plants
    pathology   581.218 32
    physiology   581.183 2
    s.a. spec. plants
Troposphere
  meteorology   551.513
    s.a. spec. aspects e.g.
      Circulation atmosphere
    regional subj. trmt.   *area–*161 2
Tropospheric wind systems
  meteorology   551.518 3–.518 5
    artificial modification
             551.681 83–.681 85
    weather forecasting 551.641 83–.641 85
      spec. areas   551.65
Trotskyism
  economics   335.433
Trotting horses
  animal husbandry   636.12
  sports *see* Horse racing
  other aspects see Horses
Troubles
  devotions for *see* Consolatory
    devotions
Troup Co. Ga.   *area–*758 463
Troupials *see* Icteridae
Trousdale Co. Tenn.   *area–*768 482
Trousers
  comm. mf.   687.113
    children's   687.13
    women's   687.12
  domestic mf.   646.433
  soc. customs   391.1–.3
  other aspects see Clothing
Trout *see* Isospondyli
Trover & conversion
  law   346.036
    spec. jur.   346.3–.9
Trowbridge Wiltshire Eng. *area–*423 15
Troy ancient   *area–*392 1
Truancy
  education   371.295
    discipline *see* Discipline
      schools
    s.a. spec. levels of ed.;
      also Special education
Trucial States   *area–*535 7
Truck
  cavalry
    armed forces   357.54
  gardening *see* Garden crops
  terminal bldgs.
    bldg. aspects *see* Motor
      vehicle transp. bldgs.
    transp. aspects *see* Truck
      terminals

Truck (continued)
  terminals
    activities *see* Freight
      services
    facilities
      gen. wks.
        commerce — 388.33
        govt. control — 350.878 3
          central govts. — 351.878 3
          spec. jur. — 353–354
          local govts. — 352.918 3
      law
        international — 341.756 883
        municipal — 343.094 83
          spec. jur. — 343.3–.9
    local
      commerce — 388.473
      govt. control — 350.878 473
        central govts. — 351.878 473
        spec. jur. — 353–354
        local govts. — 352.918 473
      law — 343.098 2
        spec. jur. — 343.3–.9
  transportation
    gen. wks.
      commerce — 388.324
      govt. control — 350.878 324
        central govts. — 351.878 324
        spec. jur. — 353–354
        local govts. — 352.918 324
    law
      international — 341.756 883
      municipal — 343.094 83
        spec. jur. — 343.3–.9
    local transit
      commerce — 388.413 24
      govt. control — 350.878 413 24
        central govts. — 351.878 413 24
        spec. jur. — 353–354
        local govts. — 352.918 413 24
      law — 343.098 2
        spec. jur. — 343.3–.9
  other aspects see Motor
    vehicle
Truckers
  biog. & work — 388.324 092
  s.a. — *pers.*–388
Trucking services *see* Freight
    transportation
Trucks
  commerce — 388.343–.344
  comm. operation
    commerce — 388.324 044
      local — 388.413 24
    govt. control
      gen. wks. — 350.878 324 044
        central govts. — 351.878 324 044
        spec. jur. — 353–354
        local govts. — 352.918 324 044

Trucks
  comm. operation
    govt. control (continued)
      local — 350.878 413 24
        central govts. — 351.878 413 24
        spec. jur. — 353–354
        local govts. — 352.918 413 24
  engineering
    gen. tech. & mf. — 629.224
    maintenance — 629.287 4
    models — 629.221 4
    operation — 629.284 4
    spec. appls
      mil. eng. — 623.747 4
      s.a. other spec. appls.
    s.a. other spec. aspects
      e.g. Brakes
    safety aspects *see*
      Vehicular transp.
    soc. & econ. aspects *see*
      Secondary industries
    use agric. *see* Transportation
      equipment
    other aspects see Land
      vehicles
Trudeau
  Pierre Elliott admin.
    Can. hist. — 971.064 4
    s.a. spec. events & subj.
      e.g. Commerce
True
  frogs
    zoology — 597.89
    other aspects see Anura
  fungi *see* Eumycophyta
  mosses *see* Musci
  s.a. other spec. subj.
Truffles
  agriculture — 635.8
    soc. & econ. aspects *see*
      Primary industries
  foods — 641.358
    preparation
      commercial — 664.805 8
      domestic — 641.658
  other aspects see
    Ascomycetes; *also*
    Vegetables
Trujillo
  administration
    Dominican Republic hist. — 972.930 53
    s.a. spec. events & subj.
      e.g. Commerce
  state Venezuela — *area*–871 4
Truk — *area*–966
Truman
  Harry S. admin.
    U.S. hist. — 973.918
    s.a. spec. events & subj.
      e.g. Courts
Trumbull Co. O. — *area*–771 38

Trumpet music	788.15
recordings	789.912 81
Trumpeters	
biog. & work	788.109 2
s.a.	*pers.–788*
Trumpets	
mf. tech.	681.818 1
misc. aspects see Musical	
instruments	
musical art	788.1
Trunk routes	
bus transp. *see* Routes	
transp. services	
Trunks (clothing) *see* Underwear	
Trunks (luggage)	
manufacturing	
soc. & econ. aspects *see*	
Secondary industries	
technology	685.51
Truro Cornwall Eng.	*area–423 78*
Truss	
arch bridges	
structural eng.	624.6
other aspects see Bridges	
(structures)	
bridges	
structural eng.	624.38
other aspects see Bridges	
(structures)	
Trusses (structural element)	
structural eng.	
gen. wks.	624.177 3
concretes	624.183 43
s.a. other spec.	
materials	
naval arch.	623.817 73
s.a. other spec. appls.	
Trust	
companies	
banking	
economics	332.26
pub. admin.	351.825
spec. jur.	353–354
other aspects see Banks	
(finance)	
services	
banking	
economics	332.178
other aspects see Banking	
Ter. of the Pacific Isls.	*area–965*
Trustees	
libraries	021.82
universities & colleges	378.101 1
s.a. other spec. kinds	
Trusteeships	
internat. law *see* Dependent	
states	
Trusts	
fiduciary *see* Fiduciary	
trusts	

Trusts (organizations)	
accounting trmt.	657.47
s.a. spec. kinds of	
enterprise e.g.	
Insurance accounting	
prod. econ.	338.85
other aspects see	
Combinations	
(organizations)	
Truth	
metaphysics	111.83
Truthfulness	
ethics	
philosophy	177.3
religion	
Buddhism	294.356 73
Christianity	241.673
comp. rel.	291.567 3
Hinduism	294.548 673
s.a. other spec. rel.	
Trypanosomiasis	
gen. med.	616.936 3
geriatrics	618.976 936 3
pediatrics	618.929 363
pub. health	614.533
statistics	312.393 63
deaths	312.269 363
other aspects see Diseases	
Trypsin *see* Enzymes	
Tsetse flies *see* Cyclorrhapha	
Tsimshian *see* Macro-Penutian	
Tsin dynasty China hist.	931.04
s.a. spec. events & subj.	
e.g. Commerce	
Tsinghai China	*area–514 7*
Tsuga *see* Hemlock trees	
Tsugaru Strait *see* Japan Sea	
Tsunami	
seismology	551.22
Tsutsugamushi disease *see* Scrub	
typhus	
Tswana *see* Bantu	
Tuamotu Isls.	*area–963 2*
Tuareg *see* Berber	
Tuataras *see* Rhynchocephalia	
Tuba music	788.485
recordings	789.912 848
Tubal pregnancy *see*	
Extrauterine pregnancy	
Tubas	
mf. tech.	681.818 48
misc. aspects see Musical	
instruments	
musical art	788.48
Tube railroads *see* Underground	
railroads	
Tuber crops	
agriculture	
field crops	633.49
garden crops	635.2

Tuber crops (continued)
foods	641.352
cookery	641.652

other aspects see Field
    crops; *also*
      Vegetables

Tuberculosis
gen. med.	616.995
geriatrics	618.976 995
pediatrics	618.929 95
pub. health	614.542
statistics	312.399 5
deaths	312.269 95

other aspects see Diseases
s.a. Pulmonary tuberculosis
Tuberoses *see* Amaryllidales
Tubers
crop prod.	631.526

  s.a. spec. crops; also spec.
    types of culture e.g.
      Floriculture
plants grown from
floriculture	635.944

  s.a. spec. plants
use
plant propagation	631.532

  s.a. spec. crops; also
    spec. types of culture
    e.g. Floriculture
s.a. Tuber crops
Tubes
metal prod. *see* Forged metal
  prod.
s.a. Vacuum tubes
Tubes (electronics)
gamma-ray *see* Gamma-ray tubes
x-ray *see* X-ray tubes
Tubes (lighting) *see* Electric
  lighting
Tubing
chem. apparatus	542.2

  s.a. spec. appls. e.g.
    Organic chemistry
rubber *see* Extruded rubber
  products
Tubuai Isls.	*area*–962 2

Tubular bridges
structural eng.	624.4

other aspects see Bridges
  (structures)
Tubulidentata
animal husbandry	636.975

hunting
commercial	639.117 5
sports	799.259 75
paleozoology	569.75
zoology	599.75

other aspects see Mammalia
Tucker Co. W.Va.	*area*–754 83
Tucson Ariz.	*area*–791 77
Tucumán Argentina	*area*–824 3

Tudors
Eng. hist.	942.05
Gt. Brit. hist.	941.05
Ireland hist.	941.505

  s.a. spec. events & subj.
    e.g. Commerce
Tufa *see* Sedimentary rocks
Tuff *see* Volcanic rocks
Tug Fork	*area*–754 4
Kentucky	*area*–769 2
West Virginia	*area*–754 4

Tug services
inland ports
commerce	386.866
govt. control	350.876 866
central govts.	351.876 866
spec. jur.	353–354
local govts.	352.916 866

law
international	341.756 67
municipal	343.096 7
spec. jur.	343.3–.9

seaports
commerce	387.166
govt. control	350.877 166
central govts.	351.877 166
spec. jur.	353–354
local govts.	352.917 166

Tugboats
engineering	623.823 2
design	623.812 32
models	623.820 132
seamanship	623.882 32

other aspects see Vessels
  (nautical)
Tughluk dynasty
India hist.	954.023 6

  s.a. spec. events & subj.
    e.g. Arts
Tuition
private	371.206
public	379.13

  s.a. spec. levels of ed.
Tula RSFSR	*area*–473 1
Tulare Co. Calif.	*area*–794 86

Tularemia
gen. med.	616.923 9
geriatrics	618.976 923 9
pediatrics	618.929 239
pub. health	614.573 9
statistics	312.392 39
deaths	312.269 239

other aspects see Diseases
Tularosa Valley N.M.	*area*–789 65

Tulip trees *see* Magnoliales
Tulips *see* Liliaceae
Tulles
fabrics
arts	746.046 54

    s.a. spec. proc. e.g.
      Weaving

Tuning
  musical instruments   781.91
    s.a. spec. instruments
Tunisia   *area*–611
Tunisian
  people   *r.e.n.*–927 611
    s.a. spec. subj. e.g. Arts
Tunnel
  diodes *see* Diodes
       semiconductors
  engineers
    biog. & work   624.193 092
    other aspects see Civil
       engineers
  vaults
    architectural
      construction   721.45
      design & decoration   729.34
    building   690.145
    s.a. spec. kinds of bldgs.
Tunneling
  underground mining   622.26
    spec. deposits   622.33–.39
Tunnels
  air conditioning   697.935 98
  architecture   725.98
  building   690.598
  construction
    mil. sci.   358.22
  highway transp.
    commerce   388.13
    law *see* Roads law
  psych. influences   155.964
  pub. works
    pub. admin.   350.864
      central govts.   351.864
      spec. jur.   353–354
      local govts.   352.74
  railroad transp. *see*
      Stationary facilities
      railroads
  structural eng.   624.193
    military   623.68
    s.a. other spec. appls.
  underground mining   622.26
    spec. deposits   622.33–.39
  s.a. other spec. occurrences
      e.g. Roads
Tuolumne Co. Calif.   *area*–794 45
Tupelo family *see* Araliales
Tupi *see* South American native
Tupper
  Charles admin.
    Can. hist.   971.055
    s.a. spec. events & subj.
      e.g. Commerce
Turbellaria
  culture & hunting   639.752 3
  zoology   595.123
  other aspects see Worms

Turbidimetric methods *see*
    Photometric analysis
Turbine steam engines
  stationary
    soc. & econ. aspects *see*
      Secondary industries
    tech. & mf.   621.165
    s.a. spec. appls. e.g.
      Generation elect. power
  other kinds see Steam
      locomotives
Turbines
  soc. & econ. aspects *see*
      Secondary industries
  tech. & mf.   621.406
    hydraulic power   621.24
  s.a. spec. appls. e.g. Jet
      engines
Turbojet
  engines
    aircraft eng.
      soc. & econ. aspects *see*
        Secondary industries
      tech. & mf.   629.134 353 3
    other aspects see Jet
      engines
  fuels
    chem. tech.   665.538 25
    other aspects see Petroleum
Turboprop
  engines
    aircraft eng.
      soc. & econ. aspects *see*
        Secondary industries
      tech. & mf.   629.134 353 2
  planes *see* Propeller-driven
      planes
Turbopumps *see* Centrifugal
      pumps
Turboramjet engines
  aircraft eng.
    soc. & econ. aspects *see*
      Secondary industries
    tech. & mf.   629.134 353 4
Turbulent flow
  aeronautical aerodynamics   629.132 32
    s.a. spec. appls. e.g.
      Flying
  fluid mech.
    engineering *see* Dynamics
    physics   532.052 7
      gases   533.217
      air   533.621 7
      liquids   532.517
Turdidae
  hunting
    commercial   639.128 842
    sports   799.248 842
  paleozoology   568.8
  zoology   598.842
  other aspects see Aves

Turf
  plants grown for
    floriculture   635.964 2
    s.a. spec. plants
Turgai USSR   *area*–584 5
Turgor movements
  plants
    pathology   581.218 4
    physiology   581.184
    s.a. spec. plants
Turgovishte Bulgaria   *area*–497 77
Turin Italy   *area*–451 2
Turing machines
  electronic eng.
    tech. & mf.   621.381 959 4
  other aspects see Computers
Turkana Lake Kenya   *area*–676 27
Turkestan   *area*–584
Turkey   *area*–561
Turkey vultures *see* Cathartidae
Turkeys
  animal husbandry   636.592
    soc. & econ. aspects *see*
      Primary industries
  products
    eggs
      food   641.375 92
        cookery   641.675 92
      prod. tech.   637.592
      soc. & econ. aspects *see*
        Primary industries
    meats
      food   641.365 92
        cookery   641.665 92
      production *see* Poultry
        products meats
    other prod. see spec.
      prod. e.g. Feathers
  other aspects see
    Meleagrididae
Turkic
  languages
    linguistics   494.3
    literatures   894.3
    s.a.   *lang.*–943
  people   *r.e.n.*–943
    s.a. other spec. subj. e.g.
      Arts
Turkish
  Cypriots   *r.e.n.*–943 5
  domination
    Cyprus hist.   956.450 2
      s.a. spec. events & subj.
        e.g. Commerce
    Iran hist.   955.02
      s.a. spec. events & subj.
        e.g. Commerce
  horses
    animal husbandry   636.11
    other aspects see Horses

Turkish (continued)
  language
    linguistics   494.35
    literature   894.35
    s.a.   *lang.*–943 5
  people   *r.e.n.*–943 5
  rugs
    textile arts   746.756 1
  Thrace   *area*–563
    s.a. Turkey; *also other*
      spec. subj. e.g. Arts
Turkmen SSR   *area*–585
Turkmenistan   *area*–585
Turkoman
  domination Iran hist.   955.02
    s.a. spec. events & subj.
      e.g. Commerce
  rugs
    textile arts   746.758
  other aspects see Turkic
Turks   *r.e.n.*–943 5
Turks & Caicos Isls.   *area*–729 61
Turku-Pori Finland   *area*–489 73
Turn-&-bank indicators
  aircraft eng.   629.135 2
    s.a. spec. appls. e.g.
      Military engineering
Turner Co.
  Georgia   *area*–758 885
  South Dakota   *area*–783 385
Turneraceae *see* Loasales
Turnices *see* Gruiformes
Turning tools
  soc. & econ. aspects *see*
    Secondary industries
  tech. & mf.   621.94
    s.a. spec. appls.
Turnip celery *see* Celeriac
Turnips
  agriculture
    field crops   633.42
    garden crops   635.125
    soc. & econ. aspects *see*
      Primary industries
  foods   641.351 25
    preparation
      commercial   664.805 125
      domestic   641.651 25
    other aspects see Cruciales;
      also Vegetables
Turnouts
  railroad eng.
    technology   625.163
    other aspects see Permanent
      way
Turnover
  employees
    pers. admin.
      gen. management   658.314
      executives   658.407 14
      spec. subj.   *s.s.*–068 3

Turnover
 employees
  pers. admin. (continued)
   pub. admin.   350.147
    central govts.   351.147
    spec. jur.   353–354
    local govts.   352.005 147
  taxes *see* Transaction taxes
Turnovo Bulgaria   *area*–497 76
Turnpikes
 early *see* Roads
 modern *see* Expressways
Turnstones *see* Charadriiformes
Turpentines
 comm. proc.   665.332
 recovery from pulp
  technology   676.5
 soc. & econ. aspects *see*
   Secondary industries
Turquoise mineralogy   549.72
Turrets *see* Towers
Turriff Grampian Scot.   *area*–412 25
Turtle
 meats
  preservation   641.495
  commercial   664.95
  domestic   641.495
 Mts. N.D.   *area*–784 6
Turtles *see* Chelonia
Tuscaloosa Co. Ala.   *area*–761 84
Tuscany Italy   *area*–455
Tuscarawas
 Co. O.   *area*–771 66
 River O.   *area*–771 66
Tuscarora Mts. Pa.   *area*–748 44
Tuscola Co. Mich.   *area*–774 45
Tussah *see* Wild silk textiles
Tutankhamen reign Egypt hist.   932.014
 s.a. spec. events & subj.
  e.g. Commerce
Tutoring *see* Individualized
  instruction
Tuva ASSR   *area*–575
Tuvalu   *area*–968 1
Tweed River Scot.   *area*–413 7
Tweeddale Scot.   *area*–413 82
Tweezers
 manufacturing
  soc. & econ. aspects *see*
   Secondary industries
  technology   688.5
Twelfth century
 history   909.1
 appls. to spec. subj.   *s.s.*–090 21
 s.a. spec. countries
Twelve patriarchs
 pseudepigrapha   229.914
 other aspects see Apocrypha
Twelve Tribes Palestine hist.   933.02
 s.a. spec. events & subj.
  e.g. Commerce

Twelvers
 Islamic sects   297.821
  doctrines   297.204 21
  worship   297.302 1
  s.a. other spec. aspects
Twelve-tone system *see* Harmony
  music theory
Twentieth century
 history   909.82
  appls. to spec. subj.   *s.s.*–090 4
 s.a. spec. countries
Twenty-first century
 history   909.83
  appls. to spec. subj.   *s.s.*–090 5
 s.a. spec. countries
Twenty-one (game)
 equipment mf.   688.754 2
 soc. & econ. aspects *see*
   Secondary industries
 recreation   795.42
Twickenham London Eng.   *area*–421 95
Twiggs Co. Ga.   *area*–758 545
Twilight
 astronomical   525.7
 meteorology *see* Scattering
   atmospheric optical
   phenomena
Twill-woven rugs
 textile arts   746.72
Twin
 Cities Minn.   *area*–776 579
 Falls Co. Ida.   *area*–796 37
Twines
 textiles
  manufacturing
   soc. & econ. aspects *see*
    Secondary industries
   technology   677.71
  other aspects see Textiles
Twining
 plants
  pathology   581.218 5
  physiology   581.185
  s.a. spec. plants
 textile arts   746.42
  s.a. spec. prod. e.g.
   Hangings
Twins
 birth *see* Multiple childbirth
 psychology   155.444
 rearing home econ.   649.144
Twisters *see* Tornadoes
Twisting
 textiles
  arts   746.12
  manufacturing
   soc. & econ. aspects *see*
    Secondary industries
   technology   677.028 22
  s.a. spec. kinds of
   textiles

Twisting (continued)
  s.a. Torsion
Two Mountains Co. Que.   *area*–714 25
Two-dimensional
  flower arrangements
    dec. arts   745.928
  s.a. other spec. subj.
Two-phase current transmission
      see
      Alternating-current
      transmission
Two-story houses *see*
      Multi-story houses
Two-way radios
  automobiles
    soc. & econ. aspects *see*
      Secondary industries
    tech. & mf.   629.277
  s.a. other spec. appls.
Two-year colleges
  higher ed.   378.154 3
Tybee Isl. Ga.   *area*–758 724
Tyldesley Greater Manchester Eng.
                           area–427 36
Tyler
  County
    Texas   *area*–764 163
    West Virginia   *area*–754 19
  John admin.
    U.S. hist.   973.58
    s.a. spec. events & subj.
      e.g. Commerce
Tylopoda
  animal husbandry   636.295–.296
  hunting
    commercial   639.117 36
    sports
      big game   799.277 36
      small game   799.259 736
  zoology   599.736
  other aspects see Ruminantia
Tympanic membranes
  diseases
    gen. wks.   617.85
    geriatrics   618.977 85
    pediatrics   618.920 978 5
    statistics   312.304 785
    deaths   312.260 478 5
  other aspects see Ears
Tyndale Bible   220.520 1
  s.a. spec. parts of Bible
Tyne & Wear Metropolitan Co. Eng.
                           area–428 7
Tyne River Eng.   *area*–428 7
Tynedale Northumberland Eng.
                           area–428 81
Tynemouth Tyne & Wear Eng.
                           area–428 79
Typecasting
  soc. & econ. aspects *see*
      Secondary industries

Typecasting (continued)
  technology   686.221
Typefaces   686.224
Typefounding
  soc. & econ. aspects *see*
      Secondary industries
  technology   686.221
Typesetters
  biog. & work   686.225 092
  s.a.   *pers.*–686 2
Typesetting
  soc. & econ. aspects *see*
      Secondary industries
  technology   686.225
Typewriters
  maintenance   681.61
    office practice   652.3
  mf. tech.   681.61
  soc. & econ. aspects *see*
      Secondary industries
Typewriting
  analysis
    criminal investigation *see*
      Documentary evidence
  technique   652.3
Typhaceae
  botany   584.613
  floriculture   635.934 613
  med. aspects
    crop. prod.   633.884 613
    gen. pharm.   615.324 613
      toxicology   615.952 461 3
    vet. pharm.   636.089 532 461 3
      toxicology   636.089 595 246 13
  paleobotany   561.4
  other aspects see Plants
Typhales
  botany   584.612–.613
  floriculture   635.934 612–.934 613
  med. aspects
    crop prod.   633.884 612–.884 613
    gen. pharm.   615.324 612–.324 613
      toxicology   615.952 461 2–.952 461 3
    vet. pharm.
          636.089 532 461 2–.089 532 461 3
      toxicology
          636.089 595 246 12–.089 595 246 13
  paleobotany   561.4
  other aspects see Plants
Typhoid fever
  gen. med.   616.927 2
  geriatrics   618.976 927 2
  pediatrics   618.929 272
  pub. health   614.511 2
  statistics   312.392 72
  deaths   312.269 272
  other aspects see Diseases
Typhoons *see* Hurricanes
Typhus *see* Rickettsial diseases
Typists
  office services   651.374 1

Typists (continued)
other aspects see Office
personnel
Typographic masterpieces
books hist. & crit.   094.4
Typography
advertising operations   659.132 4
printing   686.22
Typology
Christian doctrines   232.1
indiv. psych.   155.26
interpretation
Bible   220.64
s.a. spec. parts of Bible
Hadith   297.124 064
s.a. spec. Hadith
Koran   297.122 64
spec. parts   297.122 9
Midrash   296.140 64
s.a. spec. works
Talmudic lit.   296.120 64
s.a. spec. works
Tyrannidae
hunting
commercial   639.128 811
sports   799.248 811
paleozoology   568.8
zoology   598.811
other aspects see Aves
Tyrant flycatchers *see*
Tyrannidae
Tyre
ancient   *area*–394 4
Tyrell Lake Vic.   *area*–945 9
Tyres *see* Tires
Tyrian architecture   722.31
misc. aspects see
Architectural schools
Tyrol
Austria   *area*–436 42
Italy   *area*–453 8
Tyrone Ireland   *area*–416 4
Tyrrell Co. N.C.   *area*–756 172
Tyrrhenian Sea
oceanography   551.462 3
regional subj. trmt.   *area*–163 83
other aspects see Atlantic
Ocean
Tyumen RSFSR   *area*–573
Tywyn Gwynedd Wales   *area*–429 29

U

UFO   001.942
UHF
signals *see* Frequencies
signals
systems
radio *see* Short-wave
systems radio

UHF
systems (continued)
television *see*
Communication systems
television
UK   *area*–41
UMT
mil. sci.   355.225
UN *see* United Nations
UNESCO
internat. law   341.767
pub. admin.   350.85
s.a. spec. subj. of concern
e.g. Public libraries
UPI
wire service   070.435
U.S. *see* United States
USSR   *area*–47
Ubangi *see* Benue-Niger
Ubangi-Shari *see* Central
African Republic
U-boats *see* Submarines
Uckfield East Sussex Eng.   *area*–422 51
Udders *see* Mammary glands
Udine Italy   *area*–453 91
Udmurt
ASSR   *area*–478 1
s.a. Permian
Uganda   *area*–676 1
Ugandan
people   *r.e.n.*–967 61
s.a. other spec. subj. e.g.
Arts
Ugaritic language *see*
Canaanitic languages
Ugrians   *r.e.n.*–945 1
Ugric
languages
linguistics   494.51
literatures   894.51
s.a.   *lang.*–945 1
people   *r.e.n.*–945 1
s.a. other spec. subj. e.g.
Arts
Uige Angola   *area*–673 2
Uighur *see* Turkic
Uinta
Co. Wyo.   *area*–787 84
Mts. Utah   *area*–792 14
Uintah Co. Utah   *area*–792 21
Uist Hebrides Scot.   *area*–411 4
Ukraine   *area*–477 1
Ukrainian
language
linguistics   491.79
literature   891.79
s.a.   *lang.*–917 91
Orthodox Church   281.93
misc. aspects see Eastern
Orthodox
people   *r.e.n.*–917 91

Ultraviolet
  analysis
    anal. chem.
      gen. wks. 543.085 85
        qualitative 544.65
        quantitative 545.835
      organic 547.308 585
        qualitative 547.346 5
        quantitative 547.358 35
      s.a. spec. elements &
        cpds.
  photography
    eng. appls.
      soc. & econ. aspects *see*
        Secondary industries
      technology 621.367 2
      s.a. spec. appls. e.g.
        Materials engineering
  radiations
    astrophysics 523.015 014
      spectroscopy 523.015 844–.015 845
    biophysics
      extraterrestrial
        gen. wks. 574.191 954
          animals 591.191 954
          microorganisms 576.119 195 4
          plants 581.191 954
        s.a. spec. organisms
        med. sci. 612.014 554
          animals 636.089 201 455 4
          s.a. spec. animals
          man 612.014 554
      terrestrial
        gen. wks. 574.191 54
          animals 591.191 54
          microorganisms 576.119 154
          plants 581.191 54
        s.a. spec. organisms
        med. sci. 612.014 484
          animals 636.089 201 448 4
          s.a. spec. animals
          man 612.014 484
      s.a. spec. functions,
        systems, organs
    chemistry 541.353 4
    engineering *see* Ultraviolet
      technology
    physics 535.014
      spectroscopy 535.844–.845
    water-supply trmt.
      technology 628.166 2
      other aspects see Water
        supply engineering
    other aspects see Spectral
      regions radiations
  spectroscopes
    mf. tech. 681.414 4–.414 5
      components 681.42–.43
    other aspects see Optical
      instruments

Ultraviolet (continued)
  spectroscopy
    astrophysics 523.015 844–.015 845
      s.a. spec. celestial
        bodies
    engineering 621.361 4
      soc. & econ. aspects *see*
        Secondary industries
      s.a. spec. appls. e.g.
        Materials engineering
    physics 535.844–.845
      spec. states of matter 530.4
      other aspects see
        Spectroscopy
    technology 621.364
      mil. eng. 623.042
      s.a. other spec. appls.
    therapy 615.831 5
      misc. aspects see Physical
        therapies
      s.a. spec. diseases
Ulverston Cumbria Eng. *area*–427 83
Ulverstone Tas. *area*–946 5
Ulyanovsk RSFSR *area*–478 3
Umatilla Co. Ore. *area*–795 69
Umbagog Lake N.H. *area*–742 1
Umbellales
  botany 583.48
  floriculture 635.933 48
  med. aspects
    crop prod. 633.883 48
    gen. pharm. 615.323 48
      toxicology 615.952 348
    vet. pharm. 636.089 532 348
      toxicology 636.089 595 234 8
  paleobotany 561.3
  other aspects see Plants
Umbelliferae *see* Umbellales
Umbelliflorae *see* Umbellales
Umber *see* Pigment materials
Umbilical cord
  disorders
    obstetrics 618.58
    pub. health 614.599 2
    statistics 312.304 858
      deaths 312.260 485 8
    other aspects see Diseases
Umbrellas
  customs 391.44
  manufacturing
    soc. & econ. aspects *see*
      Secondary industries
    technology 685
Umbria Italy *area*–456 5
  ancient *area*–374
Umbrian *see* Osco-Umbrian
Umm al Qaiwain *area*–535 7
Umpiring
  American football 796.332 3
  baseball 796.357 3
  Canadian football 796.335 3

Understanding
  gift of the Holy Spirit
    Christian doctrines   234.12
  psychology *see* Perception
Undertaking *see* Dead bodies
    disposal human
Underwater
  acoustics
    sound eng.   620.25
      s.a. spec. appls. e.g.
        Sonar
  archaeology   930.102 804
    spec. oceans & seas   909.096 3–.096 7
  commun. devices
    soc. & econ. aspects *see*
      Secondary industries
    tech. & mf.   621.389 5
      s.a. spec. appls. e.g.
        Military engineering
  engineering
    soc. & econ. aspects *see*
      Secondary industries
    technology   627.7
      s.a. spec. appls. e.g.
        Underwater foundations
  foundations
    engineering   624.157
      s.a. spec. appls. e.g.
        Bridges (structures)
        structural eng.
  guided missiles
    mil. eng.
    soc. & econ. aspects *see*
      Secondary industries
    tech. & mf.   623.451 97
  mining
    technology   622.29
    spec. deposits   622.33–.39
  photography   778.73
  prospecting
    mining eng.   622.17
  treasure hunting *see* Treasure
    prospecting
  tunnels
    structural eng.   624.194
      s.a. spec. appls. e.g.
        Roads engineering
  s.a. Submarine
Underwear
  comm. mf.
    soc. & econ. aspects *see*
      Secondary industries
    technology   687.2
  domestic mf.   646.42
  soc. customs   391.42
  other aspects see Clothing
Underweight people
  cookery for   641.563
  hygiene   613.24
    misc. aspects see Hygiene

Underweight people (continued)
  medicine *see* Nutritional
    diseases
Underwriters
  biog. & work   368.012 092
  s.a.   *pers.–*368
Underwriting insurance   368.012
  s.a. spec. kinds of insurance
Undulant fever
  gen. med.   616.957
  geriatrics   618.976 957
  pediatrics   618.929 57
  pub. health   614.565
  statistics   312.395 7
    deaths   312.269 57
  other aspects see Diseases
Undulations *see* Vibrations
Unemployed persons *see* Socially
    deprived
Unemployment
  compensation
    labor econ. *see* Fringe
      benefits
  influence on crime   364.2
  insurance
    soc. insurance   368.44
      pub. admin. *see* Social
        insurance pub. admin.
      other aspects see
        Insurance
    soc. law   344.024
      spec. jur.   344.3–.9
    labor econ.   331.137
      s.a. spec. classes of labor
        e.g. Women
    labor law *see* Labor law
Unesco *see* UNESCO
Unfair econ. practices
  law
    international   341.753
    municipal   343.072
    spec. jur.   343.3–.9
Ungava Que.   *area–*714 17
Unguiculata
  animal husbandry   636.93
  hunting
    commercial   639.113
    sports
      big game   799.273
      small game   799.259 3
  paleozoology   569.3
  zoology   599.3
  other aspects see Mammalia
Ungulates *see spec. kinds e.g.*
    Horses
Unhairing
  nat. leathers
    manufacturing
      soc. & econ. aspects *see*
        Secondary industries
      technology   675.22

Unicameral legislatures
  constitutional law *see*
        Legislative branch of
        govt. law
  pol. sci.   328.39
    spec. jur.   328.4–.9
Unicellular organisms *see spec.*
      kinds e.g. Protozoa
Unicoi Co. Tenn.   *area*–768 982
Unicorn-plant family *see*
      Bignoniales
Unicorns
  lit. & stage trmt.
    folk lit. texts & lit. crit.   398.245 4
    other aspects see Animals
Unicycles *see* Monocycles
Unidentified flying objects   001.942
Unified
  catalogs
    library sci.   025.315
  field theory
    physics   530.142
      spec. states of matter 530.4
      s.a. spec. branches of
         physics
Uniflagellate
  molds
    agric. pathogens   632.458
    s.a. spec. types of
      culture e.g. Forestry;
      also spec. plants
    botany   589.258
    med. aspects
      gen. pharm.   615.329 258
      toxicology   615.952 925 8
      vet. pharm.   636.089 532 925 8
      toxicology   636.089 595 292 58
    paleobotany   561.92
    other aspects see Plants
Uniform
  algebras   512.55
  s.a. spec. appls. e.g.
      Engineering
  codes
    law texts   *law s.s.*–026 32
  flow
    fluid mech.
      engineering *see* Dynamics
      physics   532.052
      gases   533.21
        air   533.621
      liquids   532.51
  functions *see* Uniformity of
      functions
  groups   512.55
  s.a. spec. appls. e.g.
      Engineering
  spaces
    gen. wks. *see* Spaces

Uniform
  spaces (continued)
    topology   514.320 2
    s.a. spec. appls. e.g.
      Engineering
  s.a. other spec. subj.
Uniformity of functions
  calculus   515.223
    complex variables   515.922 3
    real variables   515.822 3
  s.a. other spec. functions &
    equations; also spec.
    appls. e.g.
      Engineering
Uniforms
  armed forces
    costume   355.14
    s.a. spec. mil. branches
  comm. mf.
    soc. & econ. aspects *see*
      Secondary industries
    technology   687.15
  other aspects see Clothing
Unincorporated
  banks
    economics   332.123
    other aspects see Banks
      (finance)
  bus. enterprises
    law   346.068
    misc. aspects see
      Organizations law
    management   658.044
      initiation   658.114 4
    public relations   659.284
  societies
    law   346.064
    misc. aspects see
      Organizations law
Uninsulated wires
  elect. circuits
    electrodynamic eng.
      soc. & econ. aspects *see*
        Secondary industries
      tech. & mf.   621.319 32
      s.a. spec. appls. e.g.
        Railroads
        electrification
      other aspects see
        Electrodynamics
Union
  catalogs   017–019
    library cooperation   021.642
  County
    Arkansas   *area*–767 61
    Florida   *area*–759 14
    Georgia   *area*–758 285
    Illinois   *area*–773 995
    Indiana   *area*–772 625
    Iowa   *area*–777 853
    Kentucky   *area*–769 885

Union
  County (continued)
    Mississippi   *area–*762 925
    New Jersey   *area–*749 36
    New Mexico   *area–*789 23
    North Carolina   *area–*756 755
    Ohio   *area–*771 532
    Oregon   *area–*795 71
    Pennsylvania   *area–*748 48
    South Carolina   *area–*757 41
    South Dakota   *area–*783 392
    Tennessee   *area–*768 935
  Islands   *area–*961 5
  management
    labor econ.   331.873
  of Soviet Socialist Republics
                                *area–*47
  Par. La.   *area–*763 89
  Party South Africa
    pol. sci.   324.268 04
    s.a. spec. subj. of concern
      e.g. Social problems
  racketeering
    soc. path.   364.106 7
  recognition
    labor econ.   331.891 2
  rugby *see* Rugby football
  shop
    labor econ.   331.889 2
    labor law *see* Labor law
  sympathizers
    U.S. Civil War hist.   973.717
  *s.a.*Labor unions
Unit
  method *see* Project method
  operations
    chem. eng.   660.284 2
    s.a. spec. prod.
  processes
    chem. eng.   660.284 4
    s.a. spec. prod.
  s.a. other spec. subj.
Unitarian
  Church   288.33
    misc. aspects see
        Unitarianism
  concepts *see* Non-Trinitarian
        concepts
  Universalist Association   288.32
    misc. aspects see
        Unitarianism
Unitarianism   288
  Christian life guides   248.488
  church bldgs.
    architecture   726.588
    building   690.658 8
    other aspects see
        Religious-purpose
        bldgs.

Unitarianism (continued)
  church music
    arts   783.026 8
      recordings   789.912 302 68
    s.a. spec. instruments;
        also spec. kinds e.g.
        Liturgical music
  religion
    pub. worship   264.080 2
      significance   246.7
  doctrines   230.8
    creeds   238.8
  general councils   262.58
  govt. & admin.   262.08
    parishes   254.08
  missions   266.8
  moral theology   241.048
  private prayers for   242.808
  pub. worship   264.08
  rel. associations
    adults   267.188
    men   267.248
    women   267.448
    young adults   267.628
  rel. instruction   268.88
  rel. law   262.988
  schools   377.88
  secondary training   207.128
  sermons   252.08
  theological seminaries   207.118
  s.a. other spec. aspects
Unitarians
  biog. & work   288.092
    s.a. spec. denominations
  s.a.   *pers.–*281
Unitary
  spaces   515.73
    s.a. spec. appls. e.g.
        Engineering
  states
    pol. sci.   321.01
    s.a. spec. jur.
  systems
    air-conditioning eng.   697.934 2
    s.a. spec. types of
        bldgs.
United
  Arab Emirates   *area–*535 7
  Arab Republic   *area–*62
  Brethren in Christ *see*
        Miscellaneous Christian
        denominations
  charities
    soc. welfare   361.8
    misc. aspects see Welfare
        services
  Church of Canada   287.92
    misc. aspects see Methodist
  Church of Christ   285.834
    misc. aspects see
        Congregationalism

Universalist Church
  buildings (continued)
    other aspects see
      Religious-purpose
      bldgs.
  Christian life guides   248.489 1
  doctrines   230.91
    creeds   238.91
  general councils   262.591
  govt. & admin.   262.091
    parishes   254.091
  members
    biog. & work   289.109 2
    s.a.   *pers.*–281
  missions   266.91
  moral theology   241.049 1
  music
    arts   783.026 91
      recordings   789.912 302 691
    s.a. spec. instruments;
      also spec. kinds e.g.
      Liturgical music
  religion
    pub. worship   264.091 02
    significance   246.7
  private prayers for   242.809 1
  pub. worship   264.091
  rel. associations
    adults   267.189 1
    men   267.249 1
    women   267.449 1
    young adults   267.629 1
  rel. instruction   268.891
  rel. law   262.989 1
  schools   377.891
  secondary training   207.129 1
  sermons   252.091
  theological seminaries   207.119 1
  s.a. other spec. aspects
Universals
  metaphysics   111.2
Universe
  astronomy
    description   523.1
    theory   523.101
  origin *see* Cosmogony
Universities
  higher ed.   378.155
    private   378.04
    public   378.05
Universities & colleges   378.1
  spec. subj.   *s.s.*–071 1
Universities-without-walls   378.03
University & college
  administrators
    biog. & work   378.110 92
    s.a. spec. levels of ed.
    persons   *pers.*–371
      spec. schools   *pers.*–379
    other aspects see Educators

University & college (continued)
  areas
    civic art   711.57
  buildings
    architecture   727.3
    building   690.73
    other aspects see
      Educational buildings
  libraries   027.7
    administration   025.197 7
    buildings
      architecture   727.827
      functional planning   022.317
    catalogs *see* Library
      catalogs
    reference services   025.527 77
    selection for   025.218 77
    use studies   025.587 7
    user orientation   025.567 7
    s.a. other spec. activities
      e.g. Cataloging
  publications
    bibliographies   011.54
      spec. kinds   012–016
    catalogs
      general   017–019
      spec. kinds   012–016
    s.a. spec. forms e.g. Books
  publishers *see* Institutional
    publishers
  songs   784.622
    recordings   789.912 462 2
  teachers   378.12
    biog. & work   378.120 92
    s.a. spec. levels of ed.
    persons   *pers.*–372
      spec. schools   *pers.*–379
    prof. ed.   370.712 4
      schools & courses   370.732 64
    other aspects see Educators
  teaching   378.12
  other aspects see School
  s.a. Academic
Unjust enrichment
  law   346.029
    spec. jur.   346.3–.9
Unlawful assembly *see* Public
    order crimes against
Unloading
  freight *see* Freight services
  materials management   658.788 5
    spec. subj.   *s.s.*–068 7
  ore mining eng.   622.69
  sea safety   623.888 1
Unmanned
  space flight
    soc. & econ. aspects *see*
      Secondary industries
    technology   629.43
    s.a. spec. appls. e.g.
      Space warfare

Upper
  classes (continued)
    sociology   305.52
    s.a.   *pers.*–062 1
  Egypt   *area*–623
  extremities
    bones
      anatomy
        human   611.717
        other aspects see
          Skeletal organs
      diseases
        surgery   617.471
          anesthesiology   617.967 471
        other aspects see Bones
          diseases
      fractures   617.157
      orthopedic surgery   617.397
      physical anthropometry   573.671 7
      physiology
        human   612.75
        other aspects see
          Movements
    tissue biology human   611.018 971 7
  gen. wks.
    diseases
      regional med. trmt.   617.57
      s.a. spec. systems &
        organs
      surgery   617.57
        anesthesiology   617.967 57
      other aspects see
        Diseases
      fractures   617.157
      human
        anatomy   611.97
        physiology   612.97
        s.a. spec. functions,
          systems, organs e.g.
          Cardiovascular system
        orthopedic surgery   617.397
        physical anthropometry   573.697
    muscles
      human anatomy   611.737
      other aspects see Muscles
  Franconia Ger.   *area*–433 1
  Guinea   *area*–665
  houses
    legislative bodies
      constitutional law *see*
        Legislative branch of
        govt. law
      pol. sci.   328.31
      spec. jur.   328.4–.9
  middle classes *see* Middle
    classes
  Nile Sudan   *area*–629 3
  Palatinate Ger.   *area*–433 4
  Peninsula Mich.   *area*–774 9
  Precambrian era *see*
    Proterozoic era

Upper (continued)
  Rio Grande Tex.   *area*–764 96
  Silurian epoch *see* Silurian
    period
  Volta
    country   *area*–662 5
    people   *r.e.n.*–966 25
    s.a. spec. subj. e.g. Arts
  Yukon election district Alaska
            area–798 6
Uppingham Leicestershire Eng.
            area–425 45
Uppsala Sweden   *area*–487
Uprisings *see* Revolutions;
    Riots; Wars
Upshur Co.
  Texas   *area*–764 222
  West Virginia   *area*–754 62
Upson Co. Ga.   *area*–758 486
Upton Co. Tex.   *area*–764 863
Upton-upon-Severn Hereford &
    Worcester Eng.   *area*–424 47
Ur period Mesopotamia hist.   935.01
  s.a. spec. events & subj.
    e.g. Commerce
Ural Mts.   *area*–478 7
Ural-Altaic
  languages
    linguistics   494
    literatures   894
    s.a.   *lang.*–94
  s.a. other spec. subj. e.g.
    Arts
Uralic
  languages
    linguistics   494
    literatures   894
    s.a.   *lang.*–94
  s.a. other spec. subj. e.g.
    Arts
Uralsk USSR   *area*–584 5
Uraninite
  mineralogy   549.528
Uranium
  chemistry
    inorganic   546.431
    organic   547.054 31
    s.a. spec. groupings e.g.
      Aliphatic compounds
  technology   661.043 1
    organic   661.895
    soc. & econ. aspects *see*
      Secondary industries
    s.a. spec. prod.
  eng. materials   620.189 293 1
    s.a. spec. uses
  metallography   669.952 931
  metallurgy   669.293 1
    physical & chem.   669.962 931
  mineral aspects
    econ. geol.   553.493 2

Urban (continued)
  young people
    soc. services to   362.799
      misc. aspects see Young
         people soc. services to
  s.a. City; *also other spec.*
    subj.
Urbino Italy   *area*–456 77
Urdu language
  linguistics   491.439
  literature   891.439
  s.a.   *lang.*–914 39
Ure River North Yorkshire Eng.
         area–428 48
Ureas
  fertilizers
    production
      soc. & econ. aspects *see*
        Secondary industries
      technology   668.624 1
    use agric.   631.841
    s.a. spec. crops; also
      spec. types of culture
      e.g. Floriculture
  plastics
    chem. tech.   668.422 3
    org. chem.   547.843 222 3
    other aspects see Plastics
    s.a. spec. prod.
Uredinales
  agric. pathogens   632.425
    s.a. spec. plants; also
      spec. types of culture
      e.g. Forestry
  botany   589.225
  med. aspects
    gen. pharm.   615.329 225
      toxicology   615.952 922 5
    vet. pharm.   636.089 532 922 5
      toxicology 636.089 595 292 25
  other aspects see Plants
Uremia
  gen. med.   616.635
  geriatrics   618.976 635
  pediatrics   618.926 35
  pub. health   614.596 35
  statistics   312.363 5
    deaths   312.266 35
  other aspects see Diseases
Ureters
  anatomy
    human   611.61
    other aspects see Excretory
      organs
  diseases
    gen. wks.   616.61
      neoplasms   616.992 61
      tuberculosis   616.995 61
    geriatrics   618.976 61
    pediatrics   618.926 1
    pub. health   614.596 1

Ureters
  diseases (continued)
    statistics   312.361
      deaths   312.266 1
    surgery   617.461
      anesthesiology 617.967 461
    other aspects see Diseases
  physical anthropometry 573.661
  physiology
    human   612.467
    other aspects see Excretion
  tissue biology human 611.018 961
Urethra
  anatomy
    human   611.62
    other aspects see Excretory
      organs
  diseases
    gen. wks.   616.62
      neoplasms   616.992 62
      tuberculosis   616.995 62
    geriatrics   618.976 62
    pediatrics   618.926 2
    pub. health   614.596 2
    statistics   312.362
      deaths   312.266 2
    surgery   617.462
      anesthesiology 617.967 462
    other aspects see Diseases
  physical anthropometry 573.662
  physiology
    human   612.467
    other aspects see Excretion
  tissue biology human 611.018 962
Urethritis
  gen. med.   616.624
  geriatrics   618.976 624
  pediatrics   618.926 24
  pub. health   614.596 24
  statistics   312.362 4
    deaths   312.266 24
  other aspects see Diseases
Urfa Turkey   *area*–565
Uri Switzerland   *area*–494 7
Urinalysis
  med. sci.
    gen. med.   616.075 66
    surgery   617.075 66
    s.a. spec. diseases
    other aspects see Diseases
Urinary
  calculi *see* Kidney stones
  system
    drugs affecting
      pharmacodynamics 615.761
      other aspects see Drugs
    other aspects see
      Urogenital system
Urine
  diseases   616.63
    geriatrics   618.976 63

Urine
  diseases (continued)
    pediatrics | 618.926 3
    pub. health | 614.596 3
    statistics | 312.363
      deaths | 312.266 3
    other aspects see Diseases
  human phys. | 612.461
  other aspects see Excretion
Urmston Greater Manchester Eng.
| *area*–427 31
Urns *see* Containers
Urochordata *see* Tunicata
Urodela *see* Caudata
Urogenital system
  anatomy
    human | 611.6
    other aspects see
        Reproductive organs;
        also Excretory organs
  diseases
    gen. wks. | 616.6
      neoplasms | 616.992 6
      tuberculosis | 616.995 6
    geriatrics | 618.976 6
    pediatrics | 618.926
    pub. health | 614.596
    statistics | 312.36
      deaths | 312.266
    surgery | 617.46
      anesthesiology | 617.967 46
    other aspects see Diseases
  drugs affecting
    pharmacodynamics | 615.76
    other aspects see Drugs
  physical anthropometry | 573.66
  physiology
    human | 612.46
    other aspects see
        Reproduction; *also*
        Excretion
  tissue biology human | 611.018 96
Urology
  med. sci. | 616.6
    geriatrics | 618.976 6
    pediatrics | 618.926
    vet. med. | 636.089 66
    s.a. spec. animals
    other aspects see Medical
        sciences
  s.a. Urogenital system
        diseases
Uropygi
  zoology | 595.453 2
  other aspects see Arachnida
Ursidae
  animal husbandry | 636.974 446
  hunting
    commercial | 639.117 444 6
    sports | 799.277 444 6
  zoology | 599.744 46

Ursidae (continued)
  other aspects see Carnivora
Ursuline convent bldgs.
  architecture | 726.779 74
  building | 690.677 974
  other aspects see
      Religious-purpose
      bldgs.
Ursulines
  rel. orders | 255.974
    church hist. | 271.974
    ecclesiology | 262.24
Urticaceae *see* Urticales
Urticales
  botany | 583.962
  floriculture | 635.933 962
  forestry | 634.973 962
    elm | 634.972 8
  med. aspects
    crop prod. | 633.883 962
    gen. pharm. | 615.323 962
      toxicology | 615.952 396 2
    vet. pharm. | 636.089 532 396 2
      toxicology | 636.089 595 239 62
  paleobotany | 561.3
  other aspects see Plants
Urticaria *see* Papular eruptions
Uruguay
  country | *area*–895
  River | *area*–822
    Argentina | *area*–822
    Uruguay | *area*–895
Uruguayan
  literature | 860
  people | *r.e.n.*–688 95
  s.a. spec. subj. e.g. Arts
Usage *see spec. subj.*
Usak Turkey | *area*–562
Use *see spec. subj.*
Use taxes
  law | 343.055
    spec. jur. | 343.3–.9
  pub. admin. | 350.724 7
    central govts. | 351.724 7
      spec. jur. | 353–354
    local govts. | 352.13
  pub. finance | 336.271
Useful *see spec. subj.*
User charges
  highway transp. *see* Finance
      prod. econ. highways
Usk Gwent Wales | *area*–429 98
Ustilaginales
  agric. pathogens | 632.427
  s.a. spec. types of culture
      e.g. Forestry; *also*
      spec. plants
  botany | 589.227
  med. aspects
    gen. pharm. | 615.329 227
      toxicology | 615.952 922 7

Ustilaginales
med. aspects (continued)
  vet. pharm.   636.089 532 922 7
    toxicology   636.089 595 292 27
other aspects see Plants
Ust-Orda Buryat Nat. Region
         area–575
Usulután El Salvador   *area*–728 431
Usury
  criminal *see* Financial
    offenses
  economic   332.83
  other aspects see Interest
Utah
  Co. Utah   *area*–792 24
  state   *area*–792
Ute *see* Macro-Penutian
Utensils
  cleaning
    home econ.   648.56
  kitchen
    mf. tech.   683.82
    other aspects see Household
      appliances
  s.a.   *s.s.*–028
Uterine
  hemorrhage
    obstetrics   618.54
    anesthesia   617.968 2
    pub. health   614.599 2
    statistics   312.304 854
    deaths   312.260 485 4
    other aspects see Diseases
  infections
    gynecology   618.142
    geriatrics   618.978 142
    pediatrics   618.920 981 42
    pub. health   614.599 2
    statistics   312.304 814 2
    deaths   312.260 481 42
    other aspects see
      Diseases
Uterus
  anatomy
    human   611.66
    other aspects see
      Reproductive organs
  diseases   618.14
    geriatrics   618.978 14
    neoplasms   616.992 66
    pediatrics   618.920 981 4
    statistics   312.304 814
    surgery   618.145
    other aspects see Female
      genital organs diseases
  physical anthropometry   573.666
  physiology
    human   612.62
    other aspects see
      Reproduction
  tissue biology human   611.018 966

Utica N.Y.   *area*–747 63
Utican
  architecture   722.32
    other aspects see
      Architectural schools
  s.a. other spec. subj.
Utilitarianism
  philosophy   144.6
    ethical systems   171.5
    applications   172–179
    indiv. phil.   180–190
  s.a. other spec. branches of
    phil.
Utilities
  buildings   696
  civic art   711.7
  household management   644
  library bldgs.   022.7–.8
  museum bldgs.   069.29
  plant management   658.26
    spec. subj.   *s.s.*–068 2
Utility   *s.s.*–013
Utilization *see* Consumption;
    also spec. subj.
Utopian socialism
  economics   335.02
  English   335.12
Utopias
  pol. sci.   321.07
Utrecht Netherlands   *area*–492 3
Uttar Pradesh India   *area*–542
Uttlesford Essex Eng.   *area*–426 712
Uttoxeter Staffordshire Eng.
         area–424 65
Uusimaa Finland   *area*–489 71
Uvalde Co. Tex.   *area*–764 432
Uveas
  eyes
    diseases
      gen. wks.   617.72
        neoplasms   616.992 84
        tuberculosis   616.995 84
      geriatrics   618.977 72
      pediatrics   618.920 977 2
      pub. health   614.599 7
      statistics   312.304 772
      surgery   617.720 59
      anesthesiology   617.967 72
      other aspects see
        Diseases
    physiology
      human   612.842
      other aspects see **Sensory**
        functions
Uvula *see* Mouth
Uxbridge London Eng.   *area*–421 83
Uzbek
  SSR   *area*–587
  s.a. Turkic
Uzbekistan   *area*–587

V

Vagina
 diseases (continued)
  other aspects see Female
   genital organs
  medication through *see* Mucous
   membranes medication
   through
 physical anthropometry   573.667
 physiology
  human   612.62
  other aspects see
   Reproduction
 tissue biology human   611.018 967
Vaginiperineotomy *see* Minor
  surgery obstetrics
Vagrancy
 criminology   364.148
 law   345.024 8
  spec. jur.   345.3–.9
 soc. theology
  Christianity   261.833 148
  comp. rel.   291.178 331 48
  s.a. other spec. rel.
Vagrants   *pers.*–069 2
Vahliaceae *see* Saxifragales
Vaisheshika philosophy   181.44
Vajiravudh reign Thailand hist. 959.304 1
 s.a. spec. events & subj.
   e.g. Commerce
Val
 d'Aosta Italy   *area*–451 1
 de Marne France   *area*–443 63
 d'Oise France   *area*–443 67
 Verde Co. Tex.   *area*–764 881
Valais Switzerland   *area*–494 7
Valdez-Chitina-Whittier election
   district Alaska   *area*–798 3
Valdivia Chile   *area*–835 2
Valdosta Ga.   *area*–758 865
Vale
 of Glamorgan South Glamorgan
   Wales   *area*–429 89
 of White Horse Oxfordshire Eng.
                              area–425 76
 Royal Cheshire Eng.   *area*–427 15
Valences
 molecular structure
  theoretical chem.   541.224
   organic   547.122 4
  s.a. spec. elements &
   cpds.
Valencia
 Co. N.M.   *area*–789 92
 region Spain   *area*–467 6
Valerian family *see*
   Valerianales
Valerianaceae *see* Valerianales
Valerianales
 botany   583.53
 floriculture   635.933 53

Valerianales (continued)
 med. aspects
  crop prod.   633.883 53
  gen. pharm.   615.323 53
   toxicology   615.952 353
  vet. pharm.   636.089 532 353
   toxicology   636.089 595 235 3
 paleobotany   561.3
 other aspects see Plants
Validity
 of treaties *see* Treaties
 s.a. other spec. subj.
Valises
 manufacturing
  soc. & econ. aspects *see*
   Secondary industries
  technology   685.51
Vallabhacharya philosophy   181.484 4
Valladolid Spain   *area*–462 3
Valle
 d'Aosta Italy   *area*–451 1
 del Cauca Colombia   *area*–861 52
 dept. Honduras   *area*–728 352
Valley
 breezes *see* Local wind
   systems
 County
  Idaho   *area*–796 76
  Montana   *area*–786 17
  Nebraska   *area*–782 48
 Forge winter
  U.S. Revolution hist.   973.334 1
Valleys
 geomorphology   551.442
 other aspects see Depressions
   (geomorphology)
Valois House
 France hist.   944.025
 s.a. spec. events & subj.
   e.g. Courts
Valor *see* Courage
Valparaiso Chile   *area*–832 5
Valréas France   *area*–449 2
Valuation
 assets
  accounting trmt.   657.73
   s.a. spec. kinds of
    enterprise e.g.
     Insurance accounting
  land econ.   333.332
 stocks
  investment finance   332.632 21
 taxation *see* Assessment taxes
 theory
  functional analysis   515.784
   s.a. spec. appls. e.g.
    Engineering
  s.a. other spec. subj. e.g.
    Money

Vanadium (continued)
  toxicology   615.925 522
    misc. aspects see
      Toxicology
  other aspects see Metal;
    also Metals
Van Allen radiation belts *see*
    Magnetosphere
Van Buren
  County
    Arkansas   *area*–767 29
    Iowa   *area*–777 98
    Michigan   *area*–774 13
    Tennessee   *area*–768 657
  Martin admin.
    U.S. hist.   973.57
    s.a. spec. events & subj.
      e.g. Banking
Vance Co. N.C.   *area*–756 532
Vancouver
  city B.C.   *area*–711 33
  Isl.B.C.   *area*–711 34
Vandalic *see* East Germanic
Vandalism
  criminology   364.164
  ed. problem   371.58
    s.a. spec. levels of ed.;
      also Special education
  law   345.026 4
    spec. jur.   345.3–.9
  soc. theology
    Christianity   261.833 164
    comp. rel.   291.178 331 64
    s.a. other spec. rel.
Van de Graaff electrostatic
    generators
  physics   539.732
    s.a. spec. physical
      phenomena e.g. Heat
Vanderburgh Co. Ind.   *area*–772 33
Vanga shrikes
  zoology   598.8
  other aspects see
    Passeriformes
Vanilla
  agriculture   633.82
  soc. & econ. aspects *see*
    Primary industries
  foods   641.338 2
    cookery   641.638 2
    preparation
      commercial   664.52
  other aspects see Orchidales
Vanishing animals
  zoology   591.042
    birds   598.042
    mammals   599.004 2
    s.a. other spec. animals
Vanity *see* Vices
Vans
  freight cars *see* Freight cars

Vans (continued)
  motor trucks *see* Trucks
  railroad baggage cars *see*
    Passenger-train cars
  railroad freight cars *see*
    Freight cars
  trucks *see* Trucks
Van Wert Co. O.   *area*–771 413
Van Zandt Co. Tex.   *area*–764 276
Vapor plating
  metal prod.
    mf. tech.   671.735
      ferrous metals   672.735
      s.a. other spec. metals
    other aspects see Finishing
Vaporization
  effect of heat
    astrophysics   523.013 44
    s.a. spec. celestial
      bodies
    physics   536.44
    spec. states of matter   530.4
Vaporizers
  internal-combustion engines
    see Fuel systems
    internal-combustion
    engines
Vapor-phase deposition *see*
    Vapor plating
Vapor-pressure
  lowering *see* Colligative
    properties solutions
Vapors
  specific heats
    astrophysics   523.013 65
    s.a. spec. celestial bodies
    physics   536.65
Var France   *area*–449 3
Varactors *see* Diodes
    semiconductors
Vardar Macedonia
    Yugoslavia   *area*–497 6
Varese Italy   *area*–452 2
Vargas admin. Brazil. hist.   981.061
    s.a. spec. events & subj.
      e.g. Commerce
Variable
  annuities
    insurance   368.375
    misc. aspects see
      Insurance
  costs
    financial management   658.155 3
      spec. subj.   *s.s.*–068 1
    prod. econ.   338.514 2
  pressure
    liquid flow
      mechanics
        engineering *see*
          Dynamics
        physics   532.56

Vasomotors (continued)
  other aspects see Circulatory
    fluids
Vasopressin
  chemistry   547.734 5
  human phys.   612.492
  pharmacology   615.363
  other aspects see Hormones
Vassal states *see* Dependent
    states
Vasterbotten Sweden   *area*–488
Vasternorrland Sweden   *area*–488
Vastmanland Sweden   *area*–487
Vatican
  City   *area*–456 34
  s.a. Popes
Vats *see* Containers
Vaucluse France   *area*–449 2
Vaud Switzerland   *area*–494 3
Vaudeville
  stage performance   792.7
Vaudreuil Co. Que.   *area*–714 263
Vaulting
  equipment mf.   688.764 34
    soc. & econ. aspects *see*
      Secondary industries
  sports   796.434
  other aspects see Sports
Vaults
  architectural
    construction   721.43
    design & decoration   729.34
  building   690.143
  s.a. spec. kinds of bldgs.
Vaupés Colombia   *area*–861 65
Veal *see* Beef
Vector
  algebra   512.5
    s.a. spec. appls. e.g.
      Engineering
  analysis   515.63
    s.a. spec. appls. e.g.
      Engineering
  calculus *see* Vector analysis
  geometry   516.182
    Euclidean   516.218 2
    s.a. other spec. geometries;
      also spec. appls. e.g.
      Engineering
  quantities
    kinematics   531.112
    misc. aspects see
      Dynamics
  spaces
    linear algebras   512.523
    s.a. spec. appls. e.g.
      Engineering
Vectorcardiography
  medicine   616.120 754 7

Vectors (disease carriers)
  pub. health   614.43
    misc. aspects see Public
      health
Vector-valued functions
  calculus *see* Evaluation of
    functions calculus
Vedanta philosophy   181.48
Vedas
  Indic rel.   294.592 1
Vedic
  literature   294.592 1
  period India hist.   934.02
    s.a. spec. events & subj.
      e.g. Commerce
  religion   294.509 013
  s.a. Sanskrit
Vegetable
  arrangements
    dec. arts   745.924
  drugs
    pharmacology   615.32
    other aspects see Drugs
  fats
    comm. proc.   665.3
    soc. & econ. aspects *see*
      Secondary industries
  food
    processing
      soc. & econ. aspects
      see Secondary
      industries
      technology   664.3
  fibers
    eng. materials   620.197
    foundations   624.153 97
    naval design   623.818 97
    structures   624.189 7
    s.a. other spec. uses
  foods   641.303
  glues
    chem. tech.   668.33
    other aspects see Adhesives
  juices
    comm. proc.   663.63
    other aspects see
      Nonalcoholic beverages
  manures
    fertilizers
      production
        soc. & econ. aspects
        see Secondary
        industries
      technology   668.637
      use agric.   631.87
      s.a. spec. crops; also
        spec. types of culture
        e.g. Floriculture

Veins (continued)
  diseases
    gen. wks.   616.14
      neoplasms   616.992 14
      tuberculosis   616.995 14
    geriatrics   618.976 14
    pediatrics   618.921 4
    pub. health   614.591 4
    statistics   312.314
      deaths   312.261 4
    surgery   617.414
      anesthesiology   617.967 414
    other aspects see Diseases
  physical anthropometry   573.614
  physiology
    human   612.134
    other aspects see
                Circulatory organs
  tissue biology human   611.018 914
Veins(geology)
  econ. geol.   553.19
    spec. deposits   553.2–.8
  mineralogy   549.119
    spec. minerals   549.2–.7
  structural geol.   551.88
  s.a. spec. aspects e.g.
              Prospecting
Vejle Denmark   *area*–489 5
Velloziaceae *see* Haemodorales
Vellum
  books
    hist. & crit.   096.2
  s.a. Parchment papers
Velocipedes *see* Cycles
                (vehicles)
Velocity
  kinematics   531.112
    misc. aspects see Dynamics
  of celestial bodies *see*
              Motions of celestial
              bodies
  of flow
    fluid mech.
      engineering *see* Dynamics
      physics   532.053 2
        gases   533.27
          air   533.627
        liquids   532.57
  of light
    optics
      astrophysics   523.015 24
      *s.a. spec. celestial
            bodies*
      physics   535.24
        spec. states of matter   530.4
  of nuclei *see* Nuclei
  of particles *see* Particles
                (matter)
  of rays *see* Rays (beams)

Velocity (continued)
  of sound
    engineering   620.21
    s.a. spec. appls. e.g.
              Sonar
    physics   534.202
      spec. states of matter   530.4
  theory
    money econ.   332.401
Velocity-compounded steam
                turbines
  stationary *see* Turbine steam
              engines stationary
Velour *see* Pile-weave fabrics
Velvet *see* Pile-weave fabrics
Velveteen *see* Pile-weave
              fabrics
Venango Co. Pa.   *area*–748 96
Venda Transvaal   *area*–682 91
Vendée France   *area*–446 1
Vendettas
  influence on crime   364.256
Vending machines
  automation eng. *see* Open-loop
              systems automation eng.
  food services   642.5
  retail marketing *see* Retail
              marketing
Vendor selection
  library acquisitions   025.233
  materials management   658.722
    spec. subj.   *s.s.*–068 7
Veneers
  arch. decoration *see*
              Incrustation arch.
              decoration
  wood
    mf. tech.   674.833
    other aspects see Wood
              products
Veneration
  private *see* Worship gen. wks.
  public *see* Public worship
Venereal diseases   616.951
  geriatrics   618.976 951
  pediatrics   618.929 51
  pub. health   614.547
  statistics   312.395 1
    deaths   312.269 51
  other aspects see Diseases
Venesection
  therapeutics   615.899
  s.a. spec. diseases
Venetia   *area*–453 1
  ancient   *area*–373
Venetic *see* Latinian
Veneto Italy   *area*–453
Venezia Italy   *area*–453 1
Venezuela
  country   *area*–87
  Gulf *see* Caribbean Sea

Venezuelan
  literature   860
  people   *r.e.n.*–688 7
    s.a. other spec. subj. e.g.
      Arts
Venial sin
  Christian doctrines   241.31
Venice
  city Italy   *area*–453 1
  Gulf *see* Adriatic Sea
Venison
  food   641.391
    cookery   641.691
  other aspects see Red meats
Venoms
  toxicology   615.942
    misc. aspects see
      Toxicology
Venous
  circulation
    human phys.   612.134
    other aspects see
      Circulation (biology)
  diseases *see* Veins diseases
Ventilation
  aircraft eng. *see* Comfort
    equipment aircraft
  bldg. construction   697.92
  library bldgs.   022.8
  mining eng.   622.42
  museum bldgs.   069.29
  plant management   658.25
    spec. subj.   *s.s.*–068 2
  sewers   628.23
  tunnels *see* Tunnels
    structural eng.
  work environment *see* Physical
    conditions
  s.a. Air-conditioning
Ventilation-engineers
  biog. & work   697.920 92
  s.a.   *pers.*–697
Ventilation-equipment
  household management 644.5
Ventilators
  sewers   628.25
  s.a. spec. appls. e.g.
    Water drainage
Ventnor Isle of Wight Eng.
                area–422 85
Ventricles *see* Heart
Ventriloquism
  recreation   793.8
Ventura Co. Calif.   *area*–794 92
Venus (planet)
  astronomy
    description   523.42
    theory   521.542
    transits   523.92
  flights to
    manned   629.455 2

Venus (planet)
  flights to (continued)
    unmanned   629.435 42
    regional subj. trmt.   *area*–992 2
  other aspects see Celestial
    bodies
Veps *see* Finnic
Veracruz Mex.   *area*–726 2
Veraguas Panama   *area*–728 722
Verandas
  wood bldg. construction 694.6
Verapaz Guatemala   *area*–728 15
Verbal
  aptitude tests *see* Aptitude
    tests
  communication   001.54
    psychology *see*
      Communication
      psychology
    sociology   302.22
    other aspects see
      Communication
  intelligence tests
    psychology
      group   153.933 3
      animals   156.393 33
      children   155.413
      s.a. psych. of other
        spec. groups
      individual   153.932 3
      animals   156.393 23
      children   155.413
      s.a. psych. of other
        spec. groups
  language
    commun. system   001.54
    gen. wks. *see* Languages
Verbenaceae *see* Verbenales
Verbenales
  botany   583.88
  floriculture   635.933 88
  forestry   634.973 88
  med. aspects
    crop prod.   633.883 88
    gen. pharm.   615.323 88
      toxicology   615.952 388
    vet. pharm.   636.089 532 388
      toxicology 636.089 595 238 8
  paleobotany   561.3
  other aspects see Plants
Verbs *see* Words
Vercelli Italy   *area*–451 7
Verchères Co. Que.   *area*–714 36
Verd antique marble   553.55
  econ. geol.   553.55
  mining
    soc. & econ. aspects *see*
      Primary industries
    technology   622.355
      prospecting   622.185 5
  s.a. spec. uses

Verdicts
  trials *see* Courtroom
      procedure law
Verdun Que.   *area*–714 281
Verification
  musical instruments   781.91
    s.a. spec. instruments
    s.a. Identification; *also*
      other spec. subj.
Vermes *see* Worms
Vermicelli *see* Pastas
Vermicides
  production
    soc. & econ. aspects *see*
      Secondary industries
    technology   668.651
  use agric.   632.951
    s.a. spec. plants; also
      spec. types of culture
      e.g. Floriculture
Vermiculite   553.678
  econ. geol.   553.678
  mining   622.367 8
    prospecting   622.186 78
  other aspects see Refractory
    materials
Vermiform appendix
  anatomy
    human   611.345
    other aspects see Nutritive
      organs
  diseases
    surgery   617.554 5
      anesthesiology   617.967 554 5
    other aspects see
      Intestines diseases
  physical anthropometry   573.634 5
  physiology
    human   612.33
    other aspects see Nutrition
  tissue biology human   611.018 934 5
Vermilion
  Co. Ill.   *area*–773 65
  Par. La.   *area*–763 51
Vermillion Co. Ind.   *area*–772 462
Vermont   *area*–743
Vernon
  city B.C.   *area*–711 42
  County
    Missouri   *area*–778 44
    Wisconsin   *area*–775 73
  Par. La.   *area*–763 61
Verona Italy   *area*–453 4
Verrucae *see* Hypertrophies skin
Verses *see* Poetry
Versification *see* Poetry gen.
    wks. rhetoric
Versions
  Bible   220.4–.5
    s.a. spec. parts of Bible

Versions (continued)
  obstetrical surgery   618.82
    vet. med.   636.089 882
    s.a. spec. animals
Vertebrae *see* Spinal column
Vertebrata *see* Chordata
Vertebrates *see* Chordata
Vertical
  combinations
    prod. econ.   338.804 2
    other aspects see
      Combinations
      (organizations)
  distribution
    air temperatures
      meteorology   551.525 4
        artificial modification   551.682 54
        weather forecasting   551.642 54
        spec. areas   551.65
  files
    library trmt.   025.172
      acquisitions   025.282
      cataloging   025.342
  plane
    arch. design   729.1
    structural elements   729.3
    s.a. spec. kinds of
      bldgs.
  s.a. other spec. subj.
Vertical-lift
  aircraft
    aeronautical eng.
      gen. tech. & mf.   629.133 35
        components & tech.   629.134
        models   629.133 135
        operation   629.132 525
      military   623.746 047
      s.a. spec. kinds e.g.
        Trainers (aircraft)
      soc. & econ. aspects *see*
        Secondary industries
      s.a. other spec. appls.
    commerce   387.733 5
      misc. aspects see
        Aircraft commerce
  bridges
    structural eng.   624.84
    other aspects see Bridges
      (structures)
  rotors
    aircraft eng.
      soc. & econ. aspects *see*
        Secondary industries
      tech. & mf.   629.134 36
Vertical-speed indicators
  aircraft eng.   629.135 2
    s.a. spec. appls. e.g.
      Military engineering
Vertigo *see* Dizziness
Vervain family *see* Verbenales

Verwoerd admin. South Africa
       hist. 968.058
  s.a. spec. events & subj.
      e.g. Commerce
Very-high-frequency
  signals *see* Frequencies
      signals
  systems
    radio *see* Short-wave
      systems radio
    television *see*
      Communication systems
      television
Very-low-frequency systems *see*
      Long-wave systems radio
Vesical calculi *see* Kidney
      stones
Vesicular eruptions
  gen. med. 616.52
  geriatrics 618.976 52
  pediatrics 618.925 2
  pub. health 614.595 2
  statistics 312.352
  other aspects see Diseases
Vespers
  Anglican liturgy 264.034
  other aspects see Office
      hours
Vespidae
  culture 638.579 8
  paleozoology 565.79
  zoology 595.798
  other aspects see Insecta
Vessels (containers) *see*
      Containers
Vessels (nautical)
  commerce
    gen. wks.
      inland-waterway 386.22
      marine 387.2
    govt. control
      gen. wks.
        inland-waterway 351.876 22
        marine 351.877 2
        spec. jur. 353–354
    law
      international 341.756 65
      municipal 343.096 5
      spec. jur. 343.3–.9
  engineering
    soc. & econ. aspects *see*
      Secondary industries
    tech. & mf.
      gen. wks. 623.82
      design 623.81
      s.a. spec. parts e.g.
        Hulls
  lit. & stage trmt. *see* Things
  operation
    commerce
      inland-waterway 386.240 44

Vessels (nautical)
  operation
    commerce (continued)
      marine 387.540 44
    govt. control
      inland-waterway 351.876 240 44
      marine 351.877 540 44
      spec. jur. 353–354
    law *see* Vessels (nautical)
      commerce law
  ordnance 623.825 1
  sanitation *see* Public
      carriers sanitation
Vest-Agder Norway   *area*–482
Vesteralen Norway   *area*–484 5
Vestfold Norway   *area*–482
Vestibular perceptions *see*
      Proprioceptive
      perceptions
Vestibule
  ear *see* Internal ear
Vestinian language *see*
      Sabellian languages
Vestments
  ecclesiastical *see* Symbolic
      garments
  gen. wks. *see* Outer garments
Vest-pocket books
  publishing 070.573
  other aspects see Books
Veszprem Hungary   *area*–439 7
Vetches
  agriculture 633.35
  soc. & econ. aspects *see*
      Primary industries
  other aspects see
      Papilionaceae; *also*
      Field crops
Veterans
  govt. services to 351.812
    spec. jur. 353–354
  of Foreign Wars 369.11
  soc. welfare 362.86
    law *see* Welfare services
      law
  s.a.   *pers.*–069 7
Veterans'
  benefits
    mil. sci. 355.115
  Day *see* Holidays
  homes
    architecture 725.594
    building 690.559 4
    other aspects see Public
      structures
  labor econ. 331.52
  labor law *see* Labor law
  law 343.011
    spec. jur. 343.3–.9

Veterans' (continued)
preference
personnel admin.
pub. admin. 350.132 43
central govts. 351.132 43
spec. jur. 353–354
local govts. 352.005 132 43
rights
mil. sci. 355.115
Veterinarians *see* Veterinary
scientists
Veterinary
hospital bldgs.
architecture 725.592
building 690.559 2
other aspects see Public
structures
hospitals
animal husbandry 636.083 2
s.a. spec. animals
medicine *see* Veterinary
sciences
public health 636.089 4
law 344.049
spec. jur. 344.3–.9
sciences 636.089
s.a. spec. animals
scientists
biog. & work 636.089 092
s.a. spec. kinds
s.a. *pers.*–636
services *see* Health services
shelter bldgs. *see* Veterinary
hospital bldgs.
Veto power *see* Powers chief
executives
Viaducts *see* Bridges
(structures)
Viana do Castelo Portugal *area*–469 12
Viaticum
Christian rites 265.7
Viborg Denmark *area*–489 5
Vibraphone music 789.6
recordings 789.912 96
Vibraphones
mf. tech. 681.819 6
misc. aspects see Musical
instruments
musical art 789.6
Vibration-devices
mil. eng.
soc. & econ. aspects *see*
Secondary industries
tech. & mf. 623.447
Vibration-methods
geophysical prospecting 622.159
Vibrations
aeronautical aerodynamics 629.132 362
s.a. spec. appls. e.g.
Flying

Vibrations (continued)
biophysics
extraterrestrial
gen. wks. 574.191 94
animals 591.191 94
microorganisms 576.119 194
plants 581.191 94
s.a. spec. organisms
med. sci. 612.014 54
animals 636.089 201 454
s.a. spec. animals
man 612.014 54
terrestrial
gen. wks. 574.191 4
animals 591.191 4
microorganisms 576.119 14
plants 581.191 4
s.a. spec. organisms
med. sci. 612.014 45
animals 636.089 201 445
s.a. spec. animals
man 612.014 45
s.a. spec. functions,
systems, organs
deformation
structural theory *see*
Mechanical deformation
structural theory
destructive agent
mil. eng. 623.459 6
machine eng. 621.811
s.a. spec. appls. e.g.
Hoisting-equipment
perception *see* Derived
sensory perception
resistance to
eng. materials 620.112 48
spec. properties 620.112 5–.112 6
s.a. spec. materials &
spec. uses
solid dynamics
engineering 620.3
physics 531.32
s.a. spec. kinds e.g. Sound
Vibratory system
acoustical eng. 620.21
s.a. spec. appls. e.g.
Musical sound
Vicarages *see* Parsonages
Vicars *see* Clergy
Vice
regulation *see* Moral issues
Vice-chancellors *see* Deputy
chief executives
Vicenza Italy *area*–453 5
Vice-premiers *see* Deputy chief
executives
Vice-presidents
pub. admin. *see* Deputy chief
executives

Viceroys
  pub. admin. — 351.003 12
  spec. jur. — 354
Vices
  ethics
    philosophy — 179.8
    religion
      Buddhism — 294.35
      Christianity — 241.3
      comp. rel. — 291.5
      Hinduism — 294.548
      s.a. other spec. rel.
  s.a. Sin
Vichada Colombia — *area*–861 39
Vicia
  faba *see* Broad beans
  sativa *see* Vetches
Vicksburg Siege
  U.S. Civil War hist. — 973.734 4
Victims
  of crime
    insurance — 364.48
    soc. law — 344.028
      spec. jur. — 344.3–.9
    welfare services — 362.88
    govt. control — 350.848 8
      central govts. — 351.848 8
      spec. jur. — 353–354
      local govts. — 352.944 88
    law *see* Welfare services
      law
  of political oppression
    soc. services to — 362.87
    govt. control — 351.848
      spec. jur. — 353–354
    law *see* Welfare services
      law
  of war *see* Socially deprived
Victor Emmanuel 2-3
  reigns Italy hist. — 945.09
  s.a. spec. events & subj.
    e.g. Commerce
Victor Harbour S. Aust. — *area*–942 32
Victoria
  city B.C. — *area*–711 34
  County
    New Brunswick — *area*–715 53
    Nova Scotia — *area*–716 93
    Ontario — *area*–713 64
    Texas — *area*–764 125
  Falls — *area*–689 1
  Isl. Northwest Ter. — *area*–719 3
  Lake
    Africa — *area*–678 27
    New South Wales — *area*–944 8
  queen reign
    Eng. hist. — 942.081
    Gt. Brit. hist. — 941.081
    Scotland hist. — 941.108 1
    s.a. spec. events & subj.
      e.g. Commerce

Victoria (continued)
  River N. Ter. Aust. — *area*–942 95
  state Australia — *area*–945
  Strait *see* American Arctic
    seawaters
  swine
    animal husbandry — 636.484
    other aspects see Swine
Victualing
  transp. equip.
    commerce
      aircraft — 387.736 4
      buses — 388.33
      ships & boats
        inland-waterway transp. — 386.868
        maritime transp. — 387.168
      trains — 385.26
Vicuña wool textiles
  arts — 746.043 2
    s.a. spec. proc. e.g.
      Weaving
  dyeing — 667.332
  manufacturing
    soc. & econ. aspects *see*
      Secondary industries
    technology — 677.32
    special-process fabrics — 677.6
  other aspects see Textiles
  s.a. spec. prod.
Vicuñas
  animal husbandry — 636.296
  other aspects see Tylopoda
Videotapes
  communication *see* Television
    communication
  engineering — 621.388 33
    s.a. spec. appls. e.g.
      Astronautics
  photography — 778.599
  other aspects see Television
Vidin Bulgaria — *area*–497 72
Vielle music — 787.425
  recordings — 789.912 742
Vielles
  mf. tech. — 681.817 42
    misc. aspects see Musical
      instruments
  musical art — 787.42
Vienna Austria — *area*–436 13
Vienne France — *area*–446 3
Vieques Puerto Rico — *area*–729 5
Vietcong
  Vietnamese War hist. — 959.704 332 2
Vietnam — *area*–597
Vietnamese
  language
    linguistics — 495.922
    literature — 895.922
    s.a. — *lang.*–959 22
  people — *r.e.n.*–959 2

Vietnamese (continued)
　War　959.704 3
　　s.a. hist. of spec.
　　　countries
　　s.a. Vietnam; *also other*
　　　spec. subj. e.g. Arts
Viewer access
　community antenna television
　　commerce　384.555 64
　　govt. control　351.874 555 64
　　spec. jur.　353–354
　　law *see* Television
　　　communication law
Viewfinders
　photography　771.37
　gen. tech.　770.282
　spec. proc. & fields　772–778
Vigna sinensis *see* Black-eyed
　　peas
Vigo Co. Ind.　*area*–772 45
Viking
　project astronautics　629.435 4
　s.a. Scandinavian
Vila Real Portugal　*area*–469 2
Vilas Co. Wis.　*area*–775 23
Vilcea Romania　*area*–498 2
Villa Clara Cuba　*area*–729 142
Village planning
　civic art　711.43
Villages
　local govt.
　　incorporated　352.007 23
　　unincorporated　352.007 22
　rural *see* Rural areas
Villas
　buildings
　　architecture　728.84
　　building　690.884
　　other aspects see
　　　Residential buildings
Vinalhaven Isl. Me.　*area*–741 53
Vinayapitaka
　Buddhism　294.382 2
Vincentians *see* Lazarists
Vincent's angina *see* Trench
　　mouth
Vindhya Pradesh India　*area*–543
Vindication
　religion *see* Theodicy
Vinegar
　comm. proc.　664.55
　soc. & econ. aspects *see*
　　Secondary industries
Vinegar flies *see* Cyclorrhapha
Vines
　botany　582.18
　misc. aspects see
　　Spermatophyta
　floriculture　635.974
　landscape design　715.4
　s.a. spec. plants

Vinnitsa Ukraine　*area*–477 14
Vinton Co. O.　*area*–771 837
Vinylidene chlorides
　chem. tech.　668.423 7
　org. chem.　547.843 223 7
　other aspects see Plastics
　s.a. spec. prod.
Vinyls
　plastics
　　chem. tech.　668.423 6
　　org. chem.　547.843 223 6
　　other aspects see Plastics
　　s.a. spec. prod.
　textiles
　　arts　746.044 744
　　　s.a. spec. proc. e.g.
　　　　Weaving
　　dyeing　667.347 44
　　manufacturing
　　　soc. & econ. aspects *see*
　　　　Secondary industries
　　　technology　677.474 4
　　　　special-process fabrics　677.6
　　org. chem.　547.857 44
　　other aspects see Textiles
　　s.a. spec. prod.
Vinyons *see* Vinyls textiles
Viol music　787.425
　recordings　789.912 742
Viola music　787.25
　recordings　789.912 72
Violaceae *see* Violales
Violales
　botany　583.135
　floriculture　635.933 135
　med. aspects
　　crop prod.　633.883 135
　　gen. pharm.　615.323 135
　　　toxicology　615.952 313 5
　　vet. pharm.　636.089 532 313 5
　　　toxicology　636.089 595 231 35
　paleobotany　561.3
　other aspects see Plants
Violas
　mf. tech.　681.817 2
　　misc. aspects see Musical
　　　instruments
　musical art　787.2
Violence
　ed. problem　371.58
　　s.a. spec. levels of ed.;
　　　also Special education
　lit. & stage trmt. *see* Social
　　　themes
　prevention
　　law　344.053
　　　spec. jur.　344.3–.9
　　pub. admin.　350.756
　　　central govts.　351.75
　　　spec. jur.　353–354
　　　local govts.　352.935

Violence	
prevention (continued)	
soc. services	363.3
sociology	303.6
Violent crimes	
statistics	312.46
deaths	312.276
other aspects see Crime;	
also Criminal	
offenses	
Violet family *see* Violales	
Violin music	787.15
recordings	789.912 71
Violinists	
biog. & work	787.109 2
s.a.	*pers.*–787
Violins	
mf. tech.	681.817 1
misc. aspects see Musical	
instruments	
musical art	787.1
Violoncellists	
biog. & work	787.309 2
s.a.	*pers.*–787
Violoncello music	787.35
recordings	789.912 73
Violoncellos	
mf. tech.	681.817 3
misc. aspects see Musical	
instruments	
musical art	787.3
Violones *see* Double basses	
Viols	
mf. tech.	681.817 42
misc. aspects see Musical	
instruments	
musical art	787.42
Viral diseases	
gen. wks.	574.234
animals	591.234
plants	581.234
s.a. spec. organisms	
med. sci.	616.925
geriatrics	618.976 925
pediatrics	618.929 25
pub. health	614.575
statistics	312.392 5
deaths	312.269 25
other aspects see Diseases	
plant culture	632.8
s.a. spec. plants; also	
spec. types of culture	
e.g. Forestry	
s.a. spec. systems, organs,	
diseases	
Virden Man.	*area*–712 73
Vireonidae	
hunting	
commercial	639.128 871
sports	799.248 871
paleozoology	568.8

Vireonidae (continued)	
zoology	598.871
other aspects see Aves	
Vireos *see* Vireonidae	
Virgin	
birth	
Christian doctrine	232.921
Gorda Virgin Isls.	*area*–729 725
Islanders	*r.e.n.*–969 729 72
Islands	*area*–729 72
Mary *see* Mary mother of Jesus	
Virginal music	
recordings	789.912 64
scores & parts	786.405
spec. forms	786.41–.49
treatises	786.404 21
Virginals	
mf. tech.	681.816 221
misc. aspects see Musical	
instruments	
musical art	786.221
desc. & care	786.23
music *see* Virginal music	
training & perf.	786.304 21
spec. kinds	786.3l–.38
Virginia	
Beach Va.	*area*–755 51
City Nev.	*area*–793 56
reels	
arts	793.34
music *see* Dance music	
state	*area*–755
Virginity of Mary	
Christian doctrines	232.913
Virology *see* Viruses	
Virtues	
ethics	
philosophy	179.9
religion	
Buddhism	294.35
Christianity	241.4
comp. rel.	291.5
Hinduism	294.548
s.a. other spec. rel.	
of Mary	
Christian doctrines	232.915
personal rel. *see* Conduct	
personal rel.	
Virtues (angels) *see* Angels	
Viruses	
microbiology	576.64
med. sci.	616.019 4
vet. sci.	636.089 601 94
Visas	
law	
international	341.484
municipal	342.082
spec. jur.	342.3–.9
pol. sci.	323.67

Visas (continued)
pub. admin.
  activities — 351.898
  spec. jur. — 353–354
  departments *see* Foreign
    affairs pub. admin.
    departments
Visayan Isls. Philippines — *area*–599 5
Visceral
  leishmaniasis *see*
    Leishmaniasis
  perceptions
  psychology
    gen. wks. — 152.188 6
    animals — 156.218 86
    children — 155.412
    s.a. psych. of other
     spec. groups
    influences — 155.911 886
Viscose textiles
  arts — 746.044 63
  s.a. spec. proc. e.g.
    Weaving
  dyeing — 667.346 3
  manufacturing
    soc. & econ. aspects *see*
     Secondary industries
    technology — 677.463
    special-process fabrics — 677.6
  org. chem. — 547.856 3
  other aspects see Textiles
  s.a. spec. prod.
Viscosity
  eng. mech. *see* Dynamics
  physics mech. — 531.113 4
    fluids — 532.053 3
    gases — 533.28
    air — 533.628
    liquids — 532.58
    particles — 531.163
    solids — 531.4
Viscount Melville Sound *see*
    American Arctic
    seawaters
Viscous flow *see* Viscosity
Vises *see* Holding-equipment
Viseu Portugal — *area*–469 31
Vishnuism
  Hinduism — 294.551 2
  misc. aspects see Hinduism
Visibility
  aeronautics — 629.132 4
  s.a. spec. appls. e.g.
    Flying
  atmosphere
    meteorology — 551.568
     artificial modification — 551.686 8
     weather forecasting — 551.646 8
     spec. areas — 551.656 8
  Christian church — 262.72

Visible
  files
    records management — 651.54
  light
    astrophysics — 523.015
    s.a. spec. celestial
     bodies
    biophysics
     extraterrestrial
      gen. wks. — 574.191 953
      animals — 591.191 953
      microorganisms — 576.119 195 3
      plants — 581.191 953
      s.a. spec. organisms
      med. sci. — 612.014 553
      animals — 636.089 201 455 3
      s.a. spec. animals
      man — 612.014 553
     terrestrial
      gen. wks. — 574.191 53
      animals — 591.191 53
      microorganisms — 576.119 153
      plants — 581.191 53
      s.a. spec. organisms
      med. sci. — 612.014 44
      animals — 636.089 201 444
      s.a. spec. animals
      man — 612.014 44
     s.a. spec. functions,
     systems, organs
    chemistry — 541.353 3
    s.a. Photochemistry
    physics — 535
    spec. states of matter — 530.4
  spectroscopes
    mf. tech. — 681.414 3
    components — 681.42–.43
    other aspects see Optical
     instruments
  spectroscopy
    anal. chem.
     gen. wks. — 543.085 84
      qualitative — 544.64
      quantitative — 545.834
     organic — 547.308 584
      qualitative — 547.346 4
      quantitative — 547.358 34
     s.a. spec. elements &
     cpds.
    astrophysics — 523.015 843
    s.a. spec. celestial
     bodies
    engineering — 621.361 3
    soc. & econ. aspects
     see Secondary
     industries
    technology — 621.361 3
    s.a. spec. appls. e.g.
     Materials engineering
    physics — 535.843
    spec. states of matter — 530.4

Vitamins
  metabolism (continued)
    other aspects see
      Metabolism
  org. chem. — 547.74
  pharmacology — 615.328
  other aspects see Drugs
Vitebsk Belorussia — *area*–476 56
Viterbo Italy — *area*–456 25
Viticulture — 634.8
  misc. aspects see Agriculture
Vitis vinifera *see* Grapes
Vitreous
  bodies
    diseases
      gen. wks. — 617.746
      geriatrics — 618.977 746
      pediatrics — 618.920 977 46
      statistics — 312.304 774 6
      human phys. — 612.844
    other aspects see Eyes
  glazes *see* Enamels
  humors *see* Vitreous bodies
Viverridae
  animal husbandry — 636.974 422
  hunting
    commercial — 639.117 442 2
    sports — 799.259 744 22
  zoology — 599.744 22
  other aspects see Carnivora
Vivianaceae *see* Pittosporales
Vivianite
  mineralogy — 549.72
Vivisection
  ethics *see* Experimentation
    medical ethics
Vizcaya Spain — *area*–466 3
Vizsla
  animal husbandry — 636.752
  other aspects see Dogs
Vladimir RSFSR — *area*–473 1
Vocabularies
  dictionaries *see* Dictionaries
    linguistics
  usage — 418
  spec. langs.
    nonstandard forms
      lang. sub.–7
    standard forms — *lang. sub.*–8
Vocal
  chamber music — 784.3
    recordings — 789.912 43
  cords
    diseases
      gen. wks. — 616.22
        neoplasms — 616.992 22
        tuberculosis — 616.995 22
      geriatrics — 618.976 22
      pediatrics — 618.922 2
      pub. health — 614.592 2

Vocal
  cords
    diseases (continued)
      statistics — 312.322
        deaths — 312.262 2
      surgery — 617.533
      anesthesiology — 617.967 533
      other aspects see
        Diseases
  ensemble
    music — 784.96
  expression
    music — 784.932
    psychology — 152.384 2
      animals — 156.238 42
      children — 155.412
    s.a. psych. of other spec.
      groups
  groups
    sacred music — 783.3
  music
    elementary ed. — 372.873
    recordings — 789.912
    scores, parts, treatises — 784
      dramatic — 782
      sacred — 783
    other aspects see Music
Vocalists *see* Singers
Vocation
  monastic life
    Christianity
      men — 248.894 22
      women — 248.894 32
    other rel. see Personal
      religion
Vocational
  advertising — 659.131 5
  counseling *see* Vocational
    guidance
  education — 370.113
    curriculums — 375.008 6
    govt. supervision — 379.155 2
    s.a. Professional
      education; also spec.
      levels of ed.; also
      Special education
  guidance
    education — 371.425
    s.a. spec. levels of ed.;
      also Special education
    labor econ. — 331.702
    labor law *see* Labor law
    spec. subj. — *s.s.*–023
  interest tests *see* Aptitude
    tests
  interests
    appl. psych. — 158.6
    children — 155.418
    s.a. psych. of other spec.
      groups; also spec.
      activities

Vocational (continued)
  rehabilitation
    law *see* Welfare services
      law
    soc. welfare
      aged people   362.64
      s.a. other spec. groups
        e.g. Veterans
  schools
    secondary ed.   373.24
      govt. supervision & support 379
    s.a. Vocational education
Vocations *see* Occupations
Vochysiaceae *see* Polygalales
Vodkas   641.259
  comm. proc.   663.59
  other aspects see Alcoholic
    beverages
Vogul language *see* Ugric
  languages
Voice
  human phys.   612.78
  in music   784.9
  in preaching
    Christianity   251.03
    other rel. see Preaching
  other aspects see Speaking
Vojvodina Yugoslavia   *area*–497 1
Volapük *see* Artifical
  languages
Volatiles (petrology) *see*
    Volcanic rocks
Volatilization
  quan. anal. chem.   545.46
    organic   547.354 6
  s.a. spec. elements & cpds.
Volcanic
  ashes *see* Volcanic rocks
  eruptions
    disasters
      soc. action   363.349 5
    other aspects see Disasters
  rocks
    mineralogy   549.114 2
      spec. minerals   549.2–.7
    petrology   552.2
    other aspects see Natural
      stones
Volcanoes
  geophysics   551.21
Voles *see* Myomorpha
Volga River   *area*–478
Volgograd RSFSR   *area*–478 5
Volhynia Ukraine   *area*–477 18
Volition
  psychology   153.8
    animals   156.38
    children   155.413
    s.a. psych. of other spec.
      groups

Volleyball
  equipment mf.   688.763 25
  soc. & econ. aspects *see*
    Secondary industries
  players
    biog. & work   796.325 092
    s.a.   *pers.*–796 32
  sports   796.325
  other aspects see Sports
Vologda RSFSR   *area*–472 3
Volscian language *see* Sabellian
  languages
Volta River   *area*–667
Voltage
  detectors *see* Electric
    potentials measurement
  measurement standards
    technology   621.372
    s.a. spec. appls. e.g.
      Ignition systems &
      devices
    other aspects see
      Electricity
  multipliers
    particle acceleration
      physics   539.732
  regulators
    internal-combustion engines
      see Ignition systems
      & devices
Voltaic
  cells *see* Primary batteries
  languages *see* Gur
Voltameters
  electric current measurement   621.374 4
  s.a. spec. appls. e.g.
    Ignition systems &
    devices
Voltammeters *see* Electric power
  measurement
Volterra equations   515.45
  s.a. spec. appls. e.g.
    Engineering
Voltmeters *see* Electric
  potentials measurement
Volume (sound)
  perception
    psychology
      gen. wks.   152.154
      animals   156.215 4
      children   155.412
      s.a. psych. of other
        spec. groups
      influences   155.911 54
Volumes
  calculus   515.43
  s.a. spec. appls. e.g.
    Engineering
  geometry *see* Solid geometries

Volumetric	
analysis	
quan. anal. chem.	545.2
organic	547.352
s.a. spec. elements &	
cpds.	
measuring-apparatus	
chemistry	542.3
s.a. spec. appls. e.g.	
Organic chemistry	
Voluntaries	
organ music	786.87
recordings	789.912 687
Voluntarism	
philosophy *see* Idealism	
philosophy	
Voluntary	
associations	
sociology	302.3
movements	
psychology	152.35
animals	156.235
children	155.412
s.a. psych. of other spec.	
groups	
muscle tissues	
human anatomy & phys.	611.018 6
other aspects see Tissue	
biology	
service groups	
foreign affairs admin.	
activities	351.896
spec. jur.	353–354
departments *see* Foreign	
affairs pub. admin.	
departments	
internat. assistance	361.26
internat. law	341.759
s.a. other spec. subj.	
Volunteer nurses	
social work	361.37
spec. problems & groups	362–363
other aspects see Welfare	
services	
Volunteering	
mil. personnel	355.223 62
s.a. spec. mil. branches	
Volunteers *see spec. occupations*	
e.g. volunteer nurses	
610.730 698	
Volusia Co. Fla.	*area*–759 21
Volvocales *see* Chlorophyta	
Volyn Ukraine	*area*–477 18
Von Neumann algebras & groups 512.55	
s.a. spec. appls. e.g.	
Engineering	
Voodooism	299.67
Vorarlberg Austria	*area*–436 45
Voronezh RSFSR	*area*–473 5
Voroshilovgrad Ukraine	*area*–477 16

Vorster admin. South Africa hist.	
	968.062
s.a. spec. events & subj.	
e.g. Commerce	
Vortex motions	
fluid mech.	
engineering *see* Dynamics	
physics	532.059 5
gases	533.295
air	533.629 5
liquids	532.595
Vosges	
dept. France	*area*–443 9
Mts. France	*area*–443 8
Vostok	
Island	*area*–964
spacecraft	
astronautical flights	629.454
Vote counting	
pol. sci.	324.65
Voter registration & enumeration	
law *see* Election procedures	
law	
pol. sci.	324.64
Voting	
behavior	
pol. sci.	324.9
qualifications	
law	342.072
spec. jur.	342.3–.9
pol. sci.	342.62
rights *see* Political rights	
law	
Voting-machines	
manufacturing	
soc. & econ. aspects *see*	
Secondary industries	
technology	681.14
Votyak *see* Permian	
Vowel formation	
vocal music	784.932
Vowels *see* Notations languages	
Vows	
monastic life *see* Rules	
monastic life	
Voyages	
travel	910.453
misc. aspects see Travel	
Vrancea Romania	*area*–498 1
Vratsa Bulgaria	*area*–497 72
Vulcanization	
latex mf.	
soc. & econ. aspects *see*	
Secondary industries	
technology	678.524
s.a. spec. kinds of latexes	
e.g. Natural latexes	
rubber mf.	
soc. & econ. aspects *see*	
Secondary industries	
technology	678.24

Vulcanization
  rubber mf. (continued)
    s.a. spec. kinds of rubber
      e.g. Natural rubber
Vulcanized
  papers
    mf. tech.   676.284 5
    other aspects see Papers
      pulp prod.
  rubber prod.
    manufacturing
      soc. & econ. aspects *see*
        Secondary industries
      technology   678.34
    s.a. spec. kinds of rubber
      e.g. Natural rubber
Vulgar Latin language
  linguistics   477
  other aspects see Latin
    language
Vulgarisms *see* Slang
Vulgate texts
  Bible   220.47
  s.a. spec. parts of Bible
Vultures *see spec. kinds e.g.*
    Cathartidae
Vulva
  anatomy
    human   611.67
    other aspects see
      Reproductive organs
  diseases   618.16
    geriatrics   618.978 16
    neoplasms   616.992 67
    pediatrics   618.920 981 6
    statistics   312.304 816
    surgery   618.16
    other aspects see Female
      genital organs
  physical anthropometry   573.667
  physiology
    human   612.62
    other aspects see
      Reproduction
  tissue biology human   611.018 967

W

W* algebras & groups   512.55
  s.a. spec. appls. e.g.
    Engineering
Wa *see* Mon-Khmer languages
Waadt Switzerland   *area*–494 3
Wabash
  County
    Illinois   *area*–773 78
    Indiana   *area*–772 83
  River   *area*–772 4
Wabasha Co. Minn.   *area*–776 13
Wabaunsee Co. Kan.   *area*–781 61

Wade Hampton election district
  Alaska   *area*–798 6
Wadebridge Cornwall Eng. *area*–423 71
Wadena Co. Minn.   *area*–776 87
Waders *see* Footwear
Wadmalaw Isl. S.C.   *area*–757 99
Wafers
  microelectronics *see*
    Components
    microelectronics
Waffle irons
  electric cookery   641.586
  s.a. spec. situations,
    materials, tech.
Waffles
  cookery   641.8
Wage
  earners
    labor econ.   331.125
    s.a. spec. classes of
      workers e.g. Women
  incentives *see* Incentive
    payments
  scales *see* Compensation
    scales
Wages *see* Compensation
Wagga Wagga N.S.W.   *area*–944 8
Wagoner Co. Okla.   *area*–766 87
Wagons
  commerce   388.341
  manufacturing
    soc. & econ. aspects *see*
      Secondary industries
    technology   688.6
  use agric. *see* Transportation
    equipment
  other aspects see Land
    vehicles
Wagtails *see* Motacillidae
Wahhabis
  Islamic sects   297.814
    doctrines   297.204 14
    worship   297.301 4
  s.a. other spec. aspects
Wahkiakum Co. Wash. *area*–797 91
Waiters *see* Household employees
Waitresses *see* Household
    employees
Wakayama Japan   *area*–521 8
Wake
  Co. N.C.   *area*–756 55
  death customs   393.9
  Island   *area*–965
Wakefield West Yorkshire Eng.
           area–428 15
Wakool River N.S.W. *area*–944 8
Wakulla Co. Fla.   *area*–759 89
Walachia Romania   *area*–498 2
Walaga Ethiopia   *area*–633
Walbrzych Poland   *area*–438 5
Walcott Lake ida.   *area*–796 39

Waldenses	
biog. & work	284.4
persecutions	
Christian church hist.	272.3
s.a.	*pers.–244*
Waldensian	
church bldgs.	
architecture	726.584 4
building	690.658 44
other aspects see	
Religious-purpose	
bldgs.	
churches	284.4
Christian life guides	248.484 4
doctrines	230.44
creeds	238.44
govt. & admin.	262.044
parishes	254.044
missions	266.44
moral theology	241.044 4
private prayers for	242.804 4
pub. worship	264.044
rel. associations	
adults	267.184 4
men	267.244 4
women	267.444 4
young adults	267.624 4
rel. instruction	268.844
rel. law	262.984 4
schools	377.844
secondary training	207.124 4
sermons	252.044
theological seminaries	207.114 4
s.a. other spec. aspects	
Waldensianism	
heresies	
Christian church hist.	273.6
Waldo Co. Me.	*area–741 52*
Wales	*area–429*
ancient	*area–362 9*
Walgett N.S.W.	*area–944 9*
Walker Co.	
Alabama	*area–761 76*
Georgia	*area–758 33*
Texas	*area–764 169*
Walkie-talkies *see* Portable	
stations radio	
Walking (sports)	
equipment mf.	688.765 1
soc. & econ. aspects *see*	
Secondary industries	
recreation	796.51
other aspects see Sports	
Walking sticks (insects) *see*	
Phasmatodea	
Walkouts *see* Strikes (work	
stoppage)	
Walkways *see* Roads	
Wall	
coverings	
home econ.	645.2

Wall	
coverings (continued)	
s.a. spec. kinds e.g.	
Wallpaper	
displays	
advertising operations	659.157
hangings *see* Hangings	
Walla Walla Co. Wash.	*area–797 48*
Wallabies *see* Marsupialia	
Wallace Co. Kan.	*area–781 123*
Wallachia Romania	*area–498 2*
Wallaga Ethiopia	*area–633*
Wallaroo S. Aust.	*area–942 35*
Wallasey Merseyside Eng.	*area–427 51*
Wallboards	
mf. tech.	676.183
other aspects see Pulp	
Wallenpaupack Lake Pa.	*area–748 23*
Waller Co. Tex.	*area–764 249*
Wallingford Oxfordshire Eng.	
	area–425 79
Wallington London Eng.	*area–421 92*
Wallis & Futuna Isls.	
New Caledonia	*area–932*
Wallis canton Switzerland	*area–494 7*
Wallo Ethiopia	*area–634*
Walloons	*r.e.n.–42*
Wallowa	
Co. Ore.	*area–795 73*
Mts. Ore.	*area–795 7*
Wallpaper	
handicrafts *see* Paper	
handicrafts	
home econ.	645.2
mf. tech.	676.284 8
other aspects see Papers pulp	
prod.	
Wallpapering *see* Paperhanging	
Walls	
of bldgs.	
architectural	
construction	721.2
design & decoration	729.31
building	690.12
cleaning	
home econ.	648.5
int. dec.	747.3
s.a. spec. dec.	
painting buildings	698.142
wood construction	694.2
of cells	
cytology	574.875
animals	591.875
plants	581.875
s.a. spec. organisms	
structures	
architecture	725.96
building	690.596
use	
plant training *see* Training	
plants	

War (continued)
  prisoners
    handling
      mil. tactics   355.415
        s.a. spec. mil.
          branches
    relief
      soc. welfare   361.53
    trmt. of
      law of war   341.65
  prisons
    armed forces   355.71
      living conditions   355.129 6
    s.a. spec. mil. branches
  risk insurance   368.14
    misc. aspects see Insurance
  risk life insurance   368.364
    misc. aspects see Insurance
  veterans *see* Veterans
  victims *see* Socially deprived
  s.a. Armed; Military;
      Warfare; Wars
Warble flies *see* Cyclorrhapha
Warblers *see* Sylviidae
  wood *see* Parulidae
Warburton S. Aust.   *area*–942 37
Ward
  County
    North Dakota   *area*–784 63
    Texas   *area*–764 914
  management
    med. sci.   610.733
Wardens *see* Prison
    administrators
Wardle Greater Manchester Eng.
       area–427 392
Ware Co. Ga.   *area*–758 794
Wareham Dorset Eng.   *area*–423 36
Warehouse
  buildings
    architecture   725.35
    building   690.535
    other aspects see Public
      structures
  management *see* Storage
    materials management
  receipts *see* Commercial paper
Warehouses
  location of
    management   658.21
  transp. terminals *see spec.*
    kinds of transp.
    terminals e.g.
    Railroad terminals
Warehousing
  services
    marine transp.
    law
      international   341.756 67
      municipal   343.096 7
      spec. jur.   343.3–.9

Warehousing
  services (continued)
    other spec. kinds of transp.
      see Freight services
Waretown Hertfordshire Eng.
       area–425 83
Warfare
  mil. sci.   355.02
    technology *see* Military
      engineering
  s.a. War; *also* Wars
Warley West Midlands Eng.
       area–424 94
Warm-air *see* Hot-air
Warm-blooded animals
  agric. pests   632.69
    s.a. spec. types of culture
      e.g. Forestry; *also*
        spec. crops
  animal husbandry
    technology   636
    soc. & econ. aspects *see*
      Primary industries
    other aspects see
      Agriculture
  conservation tech.   639.979
  drawing tech.   743.69
  hunting
    commercial
      technology   639.11–.12
      soc. & econ. aspects
        see Primary
        industries
    sports   799.24–.27
  paleozoology   569
  zoology   599
  other aspects see Animals
Warminster Wiltshire Eng.
       area–423 15
Warning systems
  civil defense *see* Civil
    defense
  commun. services   384.7
  govt. control   350.874 7
    central govts.   351.874 7
    spec. jur.   353–354
    local govts.   352.914 7
  law *see* Communications law
  mil. eng.   623.37
Warracknabeal Vic.   *area*–945 8
Warragul Vic.   *area*–945 6
Warrant officers
  armed forces   355.332
  s.a. spec. mil branches
Warrants
  criminal law   345.052
    spec. jur.   345.3–.9
  investment finance   332.632 2
    govt. control *see*
      Securities govt.
      control

Washing
  hides & skins
    manufacturing (continued)
      technology 675.22
  housecleaning 648.5
  negatives *see* Negatives
  positives *see* Positives
  s.a. other spec. subj.
Washing-machines
  mf. tech. 683.88
  other aspects see Household
      appliances
Washington
  city D.C. *area*–753
  burning
    War of 1812 hist. 973.523 8
  County
    Alabama *area*–761 243
    Arkansas *area*–767 14
    Colorado *area*–788 79
    Florida *area*–759 963
    Georgia *area*–758 672
    Idaho *area*–796 25
    Illinois *area*–773 88
    Indiana *area*–772 22
    Iowa *area*–777 923
    Kansas *area*–781 273
    Kentucky *area*–769 493
    Maine *area*–741 42
    Maryland *area*–752 91
    Minnesota *area*–776 59
    Mississippi *area*–762 42
    Missouri *area*–778 64
    Nebraska *area*–782 245
    New York *area*–747 49
    North Carolina *area*–756 165
    Ohio *area*–771 98
    Oklahoma *area*–766 96
    Oregon *area*–795 43
    Pennsylvania *area*–748 82
    Rhode Island *area*–745 9
    Tennessee *area*–768 97
    Texas *area*–764 25
    Utah *area*–792 48
    Vermont *area*–743 4
    Virginia *area*–755 725
    Wisconsin *area*–775 91
  District Tenn.
    history 976.803
  George admin.
    U.S. hist. 973.41–.43
    s.a. spec. events & subj.
      e.g. Public debt
  Par. La. *area*–763 11
  state *area*–797
  urban district Tyne & Wear Eng.
      area–428 71
Washita
  Co. Okla. *area*–766 42
  River Okla. *area*–766 5
Washoe Co. Nev. *area*–793 55

Washrooms *see* Comfort stations
Washtenaw Co. Mich. *area*–774 35
Wasp flies *see* Cyclorrhapha
Wasps *see* Vespidae
Waste
  materials
    photographic tech. 770.287
      spec. fields 778
  pollution
    water-supply eng.
      technology 628.168 2–.168 4
    other aspects see Water
        supply engineering
  waters
    water-supply sources
      technology 628.119
    other aspects see Water
        supply engineering
Wastelands
  resources *see* Land resources
Wastepaper pulp
  mf. tech. 676.142
  other aspects see Pulp
Wastes
  control
    cereal grains
      comm. proc. 664.720 9
        s.a. spec. grains
      other aspects see Cereal
          grains
    dyeing processes
      technology 667.36
      other aspects see Dyes
    foods
      comm. proc. 664.096
        s.a. spec. foods e.g.
          Meats
      other aspects see Foods
    gas
      chem. tech. 665.78
      other aspects see
          Industrial gases
    glass
      technology 666.14
      other aspects see Glass
    law 344.046 2
      spec. jur. 344.3–.9
    paper
      mf. tech. 676.26
        spec. papers 676.28
      other aspects see Papers
          pulp prod.
    petroleum
      chem. tech. 665.538 9
      other aspects see
          Petroleum
    plastics mf. 668.419 2
      s.a. spec. kinds of
        plastics
    prod. management 658.567
      spec. subj. *s.s.*–068 5

Water (continued)
consumption
land econ. — 333.912
control eng. *see* Hydraulics
engineering
diversion
flood control eng. — 627.45
hydraulic eng. — 627.123
other aspects see Liquids
engineering
drainage
plumbing — 696.13
droplets
atmospheric electricity *see*
Aerosols meteorology
econ. geol. — 553.7
engineering *see* Hydraulics
engineering
eng. materials — 620.198
s.a. other spec. usees
extraction
soc. & econ. aspects *see*
Primary industries
technology — 622.37
prospecting — 622.187
facilities
civic art — 711.8
features
landscape design — 714
fire extinction tech. — 628.925 2
s.a. spec. appls. e.g.
Forest fires
fixtures
buildings *see* Plumbing
fleas *see* Branchiopoda
games
sports — 797.25
other aspects see Sports
gardens
plants grown for floriculture — 635.967 4
s.a. spec. plants
gas
chem. tech. — 665.772
soc. & econ. aspects *see*
Secondary industries
s.a. spec. prod.
geol. agent — 551.35
hammer eng. — 620.106 4
heaters
buildings — 696.5
mf. tech. — 683.88
other aspects see Household
appliances
hydraulic-power tech.
soc. & econ. aspects *see*
Secondary industries
technology — 621.204 22
s.a. spec. appls. e.g.
Waterwheels
hygiene
bathing — 613.41

Water
hygiene (continued)
beverage — 613.3
other aspects see Hygiene
lit. & stage trmt.
folk lit. soc. — 398.364
other aspects see Natural
phenomena
marketing *see* Marketing
metabolism
human phys. — 612.392 3
other aspects see
Metabolism
meteorology *see*
Hydrometeorology
mines
laying
mil. eng. — 623.263
molds *see* Saprolegniales
ouzels *see* Cinclidae
pageantry
recreation — 797.203
pharmacology — 615.222
misc. aspects see
Pharmacology
pipes
buildings *see* Plumbing
pollution
control
law
international — 341.762 3
municipal — 344.046 343
spec. jur. — 344.3–.9
pub. admin. — 350.823 25
central govts. — 351.823 25
spec. jur. — 353–354
local govts. — 352.942 325
sanitary eng.
technology — 628.168
other aspects see Water
supply engineering
soc. aspects — 363.739 4
polo
sports — 797.25
other aspects see Sports
poppy family *see* Butomales
power *see* Waterpower
purification
water-supply eng.
technology — 628.162
other aspects see Water
supply engineering
radiesthesia
parapsychology — 133.323 2
receiving fixtures
plumbing — 696.12
reclamation eng.
soc. & econ. aspects *see*
Secondary industries

Water
  reclamation eng. (continued)
    technology   627.56
      s.a. spec. appls. e.g.
        Water supply
        engineering
      other aspects see Liquids
        engineering
  regional subj. trmt.   *area*–16
  rel. worship
    comp. rel.   291.212
    s.a. spec. rel.
  resources   333.91
    economics   333.91
    engineering *see* Hydraulics
      engineering
    govt. control
      law   346.046 91
        spec. jur.   346.3–.9
      pub. admin.   350.823 25
        central govts.   351.823 25
          spec. jur.   353–354
        local govts.   352.942 325
      s.a. spec. aspects e.g.
        Water supply soc.
        services
  retention
    flood control eng.
      technology   627.42
        s.a. spec. appls. e.g.
          Reclamation soil sci.
      other aspects see Liquids
        engineering
  rights
    econ. sale & gift   333.339
  safety
    law   344.047
      spec. jur.   344.3–.9
    pub. meas.   363.123
      govt. control *see* Safety
        pub. admin.
  skiers
    biog. & work   797.173 092
    s.a.   *pers.*–797 1
  skiing
    sports   797.173
    other aspects see Sports
  solutions
    physical chem.   541.342 2
      applied   660.294 22
      organic   547.134 22
    s.a. spec. elements,
      cpds., prod.
  sports   797
    misc. aspects see Sports
  storage
    flood control eng.
      technology   627.44
        s.a. spec. appls. e.g.
          Reclamation soil sci.

Water
  storage
    flood control eng. (continued)
      other aspects see Liquids
        engineering
    supply
      canals *see* Feeding canals
      engineering
        soc. & econ. aspects *see*
          Secondary industries
        technology   628.1
          military   623.751
          rural   628.72
        s.a. other spec. appls.
          e.g. Water supply
      spacecraft
        law   343.092 4
          spec. jur.   343.3–.9
      plumbing   696.12
      pub. admin.   350.871
        central govts.   351.871
          spec. jur.   353–354
        local govts.   352.61
      reserves
        landscape design   719.33
      shipbuilding
        soc. & econ. aspects *see*
          Secondary industries
        technology   623.854 2–.854 3
          design   623.814 542–.814 543
            spec. craft   623.812
      soc. services   363.61
      spacecraft eng.   629.477 3
        unmanned   629.467 3
        other aspects see
          Spacecraft
      utilities
        household management   644.6
        other aspects see
          Utilities
    table
      hydrology   551.492
    temperatures
      meteorology   551.524
        weather forecasting   551.642 4
          spec. areas   551.65
    towers
      water-supply eng.
        technology   628.13
        other aspects see Water
          supply engineering
    toxicology   615.925 22
      misc. aspects see
        Toxicology
    transportation
      accidents   363.123
        misc. aspects see
          Transportation
          accidents
      commerce   387

Water
  transportation (continued)
    engineering
      soc. & econ. aspects *see*
          Secondary industries
      tech. & mf.   629.048
        military   623.8
        s.a. other spec. appls.
    govt. control   351.877
      spec. jur.   353–354
    hazards
      soc. path.   363.123
    law
      international   341.756 6
      municipal   343.096
        spec. jur.   343.3–.9
    safety
      law *see* Water
          transportation law
      pub. meas.   363.123
        govt. control *see*
            Safety pub. admin.
    other aspects see
        Transportation
    s.a. Aquatic; *also selected*
        words beginning with
        Hydro
Water-color painting
  arts   751.422
    indiv. artists   759.1–.9
Watercress *see* Cresses
Wateree River S.C.   *area*–757 69
Waterfalls
  hydrology   551.484
  regional subj. trmt.   *area*–169 4
Waterford Ireland   *area*–419 1
Waterfowl *see* Anseriformes
Waterleaf family *see*
        Polemoniales
Water-lily family *see* Ranales
Waterloo Regional Municipality
        Ont.   *area*–713 44
Watermarks
  paper
    mf. tech.   676.280 27
    s.a. spec. papers e.g.
        Book papers
Watermelons
  agriculture   635.615
    soc. & econ. aspects *see*
        Primary industries
  foods   641.356 15
    preparation
      commercial   664.805 615
      domestic   641.656 15
  other aspects see
        Cucurbitales; *also*
        Fruits
Water-plantain family *see*
        Alismatales

Waterpower
  hydraulic-power tech. *see*
        Water hydraulic-power
        tech.
  hydroelectric generation *see*
        Hydroelectric
        generation
  land econ.   333.914
Waterproof
  construction bldgs.   693.892
  fabrics
    manufacturing
      soc. & econ. aspects *see*
          Secondary industries
      technology   677.682
    other aspects see Textiles
    s.a. spec. prod.
Water-repellent fabrics
  manufacturing
    soc. & econ. aspects *see*
        Secondary industries
    technology   677.682
  other aspects see Textiles
  s.a. spec. prod.
Water-softeners
  buildings   696.12
    hot-water supply   696.6
Water-soluble
  paints
    technology   667.63
    other aspects see Paints
  techniques
    painting arts   751.42
      indiv. artists   759.1–.9
Waterspouts (twisters) *see*
        Tornadoes
Waterton-Glacier Internat. Peace
        Park Mont.   *area*–786 52
Waterways
  hydrodynamic eng.
    soc. & econ. aspects *see*
        Secondary industries
    technology   627.042
    s.a. spec. appls. e.g.
        Floods control
    other aspects see Dynamics
  land econ.   333.915
  transportation
    commerce   386.3–.5
    govt. control   351.876 3–.876 5
      spec. jur.   353–354
    law *see* Inland-waterway
        transp. law
Waterwheels
  technology
    soc. & econ. aspects *see*
        Secondary industries
    tech. & mf.   621.21
    s.a. spec. appls. e.g.
        Grinding cereal grains

Waterwort family *see*
    Caryophyllales
Watford Hertfordshire Eng. *area*–425 892
Wath-upon-Dearne South Yorkshire
    Eng.   *area*–428 23
Watling Isl. Bahamas   *area*–729 6
Watonwan Co. Minn.   *area*–776 29
Watsonian behaviorism
  psychology   150.194 32
    s.a. spec. subj. & branches
      of psych.
Watt-hour meters *see* Energy
    elect. measurement
Wattled crows
  zoology   598.8
  other aspects see
    Passeriformes
Wattmeters *see* Electric power
    measurement
Waukesha Co. Wis.   *area*–775 93
Waupaca Co. Wis.   *area*–775 38
Waushara Co. Wis.   *area*–775 57
Wave
  action
    physical geol.   551.36
  mechanics
    physics   530.124
      spec. states of matter   530.4
    s.a. spec. branches of
      physics
  propagation
    microwave electronics
      technology   621.381 31
      s.a. spec. appls. e.g.
        Radar engineering
    other aspects see
      Microwave electronics
    radio
      engineering   621.384 11
      s.a. spec. appls. e.g.
        Radiotelephony
    other aspects see Radio
    television
      engineering   621.388 11
      s.a. spec. appls. e.g.
        Astronautics
    other aspects see
      Television
  theories
    physics   530.14
      spec. states of matter   530.4
    s.a. spec. branches of
      physics
  transmission
    microwave electronics
      technology   621.381 31
      s.a. spec. appls. e.g.
        Radar engineering
    other aspects see
      Microwave electronics

Wave
  transmission (continued)
    radio
      engineering   621.384 11
      s.a. spec. appls. e.g.
        Radiotelephony
    other aspects see Radio
    television
      engineering   621.388 11
      s.a. spec. appls. e.g.
        Astronautics
    other aspects see
      Television
Waveguide theory
  electricity
    astrophysics   523.018 712 5
    s.a. spec. celestial
      bodies
    physics   537.125
      spec. states of matter   530.4
Waveguides
  radio & microwave electronics
    astrophysics   523.018 753 4
    s.a. spec. celestial
      bodies
    physics   537.534
      spec. states of matter   530.4
    soc. & econ. aspects *see*
      Secondary industries
    tech. & mf.   621.381 331
      spec. circuits   621.381 32
      s.a. spec. appls. e.g.
        Radar engineering
    other aspects see Microwave
      electronics
Wavelength
  measurement
    radio *see* Measurement radio
    television *see* Measurement
      television
Wavell governorship India hist.   954.035 9
    s.a. spec. events & subj.
      e.g. Commerce
Waveney
  River Norfolk Eng.   *area*–426 19
  Suffolk Eng.   *area*–426 41
Waverley Surrey Eng.   *area*–422 19
Waves
  dynamic oceanography   551.470 2
    s.a. spec. bodies of water
  eng. mech. *see* Dynamics
  physics mech.   531.113 3
    fluids   532.059 3
    gases   533.293
      air   533.629 3
    liquids   532.593
    particles   531.163
    solids   531.33
Wax
  beans *see* Kidney beans

Wax (continued)
  carving
    dec. arts.   736.93
    rel. significance
      Christianity   247.869 3
      comp. rel.   291.37
      s.a. other spec. rel.
    painting *see* Encaustic
          painting
Waxes
  manufacturing
    soc. & econ. aspects *see*
          Secondary industries
    technology   665.1
  sculpturing material   731.2
    spec. periods & schools   732–735
Waxing woodwork
    buildings   698.33
Waxwings *see* Bombycillidae
Wayatinah Tas.   *area*–946 3
Waycross Ga.   *area*–758 795
Wayne Co.
  Georgia   *area*–758 756
  Illinois   *area*–773 792
  Indiana   *area*–772 63
  Iowa   *area*–777 88
  Kentucky   *area*–769 64
  Michigan   *area*–774 33
  Mississippi   *area*–762 573
  Missouri   *area*–778 92
  Nebraska   *area*–782 57
  New York   *area*–747 87
  North Carolina   *area*–756 395
  Ohio   *area*–771 61
  Pennsylvania   *area*–748 23
  Tennessee   *area*–768 39
  Utah   *area*–792 54
  West Virginia   *area*–754 47
Waynesboro Va.   *area*–755 912
Weak nuclear interactions *see*
          Interactions nuclear
          reactions
Weakley Co. Tenn.   *area*–768 24
Weald Eng.   *area*–422 5
Wealden East Sussex Eng.   *area*–422 51
Wealth
  econ. theory   330.16
  macroeconomics
    distribution   339.2
    measurement   339.3
  mental pub. health factor   362.204 2
  taxation *see* Income taxes
Wealthy classes
  customs   390.1
    dress   391.01
    homes   392.360 1
  other aspects see Upper
          classes
  s.a.   *pers.*–062 1
Weapons
  gen. wks. *see* Ordnance

Weapons (continued)
  illegal carrying *see* Public
          order crimes against
Wear Valley Durham Eng.   *area*–428 64
Weasel spiders
  zoology   595.48
  other aspects see Arachnida
Weasels *see* Mustelidae
Weather
  aeronautics   629.132 4
    s.a. spec. appls. e.g.
          Flying
  control
    govt. control *see* Air
          resources govt. control
  law
    international   341.762
    municipal   346.046 92
      spec. jur.   346.3–.9
    technology   551.58
  earth sciences   551.5
  ecology
    life sci.   574.542
      animals   591.542
      microorganisms   576.15
      plants   581.542
      s.a. spec. organisms
    soc. theology
      Christianity   261.836 25
      comp. rel.   291.178 362 5
      s.a. other spec. rel.
    sociology   304.25
  forecasting
    pub. admin.
      activities   351.855 516 3
        spec. jur.   353–354
      govt. depts. *see*
          Executive departments
    technology   551.63
  hygiene   613.11
    misc. aspects see Hygiene
  influence on crime   364.22
  lit. & stage trmt.
    folk lit. soc.   398.363
    other aspects see Natural
          phenomena
  modification *see* Weather
          control
  satellites *see* Unmanned
          spacecraft
  transp. hazard
    air   363.124 12
    rail   363.122
    vehicular   363.125 1
    water   363.123
Weather-induced illnesses   616.988
  geriatrics   618.976 988
  pediatrics   618.929 88
  statistics   312.398 8
  deaths   312.269 88
  other aspects see Diseases

Weirs (continued)
  reservoir eng.
    technology 627.883
      s.a. apec. appls. e.g.
        Canal transportation
      other aspects see Liquids
        engineering
Weismann laws *see* Genetic laws
Weld Co. Colo. *area*–788 72
Welding
  metal prod.
    arts
      decorative 739.14
        s.a. spec. metals; also
          spec. prod. e.g.
            Jewelry
      fine *see* Direct-metal
        sculpture
    manufacturing
      soc. & econ. aspects *see*
        Secondary industries
      technology 671.52
        ferrous metals 672.52
        s.a. other spec. metals
  plastics mf. 668.415
    s.a. spec. kinds of
      plastics
  shipbuilding
    soc. & econ. aspects *see*
      Secondary industries
    technology 623.843 2
Welding-equipment
  soc. & econ. aspects *see*
    Secondary industries
  tech. & mf. 621.977
    s.a. spec. appls. e.g.
      Vessels (nautical)
        engineering
Welfare 361
  buildings
    architecture 725.5
    building 690.55
    other aspects see Public
      structures
  civil right
    pol. sci. 323.46
  departments
    pub. admin. 350.084
      central govts. 351.084
        spec. jur. 353–354
      local govts. 352.944
  economics 330.155
  institution libraries 027.66
    administration 025.197 66
    buildings
      architecture 727.826 6
      functional planning 022.316 6
    catalogs *see* Library
      catalogs
    reference services 025.527 766
    selection for 025.218 766

Welfare
  institution libraries (continued)
    use studies 025.587 66
    user orientation 025.567 66
    s.a. other spec. activities
      e.g. Cataloging
  law 344.03
    spec. jur. 344.3–.9
  personnel
    biog. & work 361.92
    s.a. spec. kinds
    occupational ethics 174.936
    s.a. *pers.*–36
  programs
    labor econ. *see* Fringe
      benefits
    rel. role in *see* Society soc.
      theology
  services
    accounting 657.832
    for employees *see* Economic
      services to employees
    gen. wks.
      crime prevention 364.44
      methods 361
      penal institutions 365.66
        law 344.035 66
          spec. jur. 344.3–.9
      spec. groups 362
    govt. control 350.84
      central govts. 351.84
        spec. jur. 353–354
      local govts. 352.944
    in war
      World War 1 hist. 940.477
      World War 2 hist. 940.547 7
      s.a. other spec. wars
    law
      international 341.766
      municipal 344.031–.032
        spec. jur. 344.3–.9
      pol. sci. 323.46
    state
      economics 330.126
      soc. services 361.65
  work *see* Welfare services
Welland
  Co. Ont. *area*–713 38
  River Lincolnshire Eng. *area*–425 39
Well-being
  applied psych. 158
  parapsychology 131
  perception *see* Visceral
    perceptions
Wellesley
  governorship India hist. 954.031 2
    s.a. spec. events & subj.
      e.g. Commerce
  Isls. Qld. *area*–943 7
Wellingborough Northamptonshire
    Eng. *area*–425 58

Wheels
  automobiles
    soc. & econ. aspects *see*
        Secondary industries
    tech. & mf.   629.248
    lit. & stage trmt. *see* Things
    physics   531.8
    railroad rolling stock
      technology   625.21
      other aspects see Rolling
          stock railroads
    s.a. other spec. occurrences
Whelks *see* Gastropoda
Whey
  dairy tech.   637.3
Whig Party
  U.S.
    pol. sci.   324.273 23
    s.a. spec. subj. of concern
        e.g. Social problems
Whippets
  animal husbandry   636.753
  other aspects see Dogs
Whipscorpions
  gen. wks.
    zoology   595.453 2
    other aspects see Arachnida
  tailless
    zoology   595.453 6
    other aspects see Arachnida
Whiskies   641.252
  comm. proc.   663.52
  other aspects see Alcoholic
      beverages
Whist
  equipment mf.   688.754 13
    soc. & econ. aspects *see*
        Secondary industries
  recreation   795.413
Whistling   784.949
Whitburn Lothian Scot.   *area*–413 3
Whitby North Yorkshire Eng.
    area–428 47
Whitchurch Salop Eng.   *area*–424 53
White
  clovers
    agriculture   633.327
      soc. & econ. aspects *see*
          Primary industries
    other aspects see
        Papilionaceae; *also*
        Field crops
  corpuscles
    diseases
      cancer   616.994 19
      gen. med.   616.154
      geriatrics   618.976 154
      pediatrics   618.921 54
      pub. health   614.591 54
      statistics   312.315 4
        deaths   312.261 54

White
  corpuscles
    diseases (continued)
      other aspects see
          Diseases
      human phys.   612.112
      tissue biology
        human anatomy & phys.   611.018 5
        other aspects see Tissue
            biology
      other aspects see
          Circulatory fluids
  County
    Arkansas   *area*–767 76
    Georgia   *area*–758 277
    Illinois   *area*–773 96
    Indiana   *area*–772 93
    Tennessee   *area*–768 66
  currants
    agriculture   634.721 7
    other aspects see Currants
  Friars *see* Carmelites
  grape wines
    gen. wks.   641.222 2
      comm. proc.   663.222
    sparkling   641.222 4
      comm. proc.   663.224
    other aspects see Wines
  hair *see* Hair diseases
  Horse Vale Oxfordshire Eng.
    area–425 76
  Mts. N.H.   *area*–742 2
  Nile River   *area*–629 3
  Pine Co. Nev.   *area*–793 15
  River
    Arkansas   *area*–767 2
    Indiana   *area*–772 3
    South Dakota   *area*–783 6
    Vermont   *area*–743 65
  Russia   *area*–476 5
  Russian *see* Belorussian
  Sands Nat. Monument N.M.
    area–789 65
  Sea *see* European Arctic
      seawaters
  slave traffic
    criminology   364.15
    law
      international   341.77
      municipal   345.025
      spec. jur.   345.3–.9
    soc. theology
      Christianity   261.833 15
      comp. rel.   291.178 331 5
      s.a. other spec. rel.
  Sulphur Springs W. Va.   *area*–754 89
  whales *see* Odontoceti
White-alder family *see* Ericales
White-collar
  classes *see* Middle classes
  crime *see* Business offenses

White-collar (continued)
 workers
  labor econ. 331.792
   labor force 331.119 042
   market 331.129 042
   unions 331.880 41
  other aspects see
    Industrial occupations
 labor law *see* Labor law
Whiteface Mt. N.Y. *area*–747 53
Whitefield Greater Manchester
  Eng. *area*–427 38
Whitefish Bay Mich. *area*–747 91
Whitehaven Cumbria Eng. *area*–427 84
Whitehead N. Ire. *area*–416 17
Whitelisting
 labor econ. 331.894
 labor law *see* Labor law
Whiteside Co. Ill. *area*–773 35
Whitewash
 technology 667.63
 other aspects see Paints
Whitewashing
 buildings 698.2
Whitfield Co. Ga. *area*–758 324
Whithorn Dumfries and Galloway
  Scot. *area*–414 95
Whitley
 Bay Tyne & Wear Eng. *area*–428 79
 County
  Indiana *area*–772 75
  Kentucky *area*–769 132
Whitman Co. Wash. *area*–797 39
Whitney Mt. Calif. *area*–794 86
Whitstable Kent Eng. *area*–422 34
Whitsunday Isl. Qld. *area*–943 6
Whittlesey Cambridgeshire Eng.
  area–426 53
Whittling wood *see* Wood
  sculpture
Whole milk
 dairy tech. 637.141–.146
 other aspects see Milk
Wholesale
 businesses
  accounting 657.839
 marketing
  management 658.86
  spec. subj. *s.s.*–068 8
 trade
  commerce 381.2
   misc. aspects see
     Commerce
  law 343.088 8
   spec. jur. 343.3–.9
Whole-word methods
 reading instruction
  elementary ed. 372.414 4
Whooping cough
 gen. med. 616.204
 geriatrics 618.976 204

Whooping cough (continued)
 pediatrics 618.922 04
 pub. health 614.543
 statistics 312.320 4
  deaths 312.262 04
 other aspects see Diseases
Whyalla S. Aust. *area*–942 38
Wibaux Co. Mont. *area*–786 34
Wichita
 city Kan. *area*–781 86
 County
  Kansas *area*–781 423
  Texas *area*–764 745
Wick Highland Scot. *area*–411 62
Wickerwork plants
 agriculture 633.58
 soc. & econ. aspects *see*
   Primary industries
Wicket-keeping
 cricket sports 796.358 24
Wickham Tyne & Wear
  Eng. *area*–428 73
Wicklow Ireland *area*–418 4
Wicomico Co. Md. *area*–752 25
Widnes Cheshire Eng. *area*–427 18
Widowed persons
 psychology 155.644
 s.a. *pers.*–065 4
Widowers
 psychology 155.644 2
 s.a. *pers.*–065 4
Widows
 psychology 155.644 3
 s.a. *pers.*–065 4
Wife beating *see* Assault &
  battery
Wife-husband relationships *see*
   Husband-wife
   relationships
Wigan Greater Manchester Eng.
  area–427 36
Wight Isle Eng. *area*–422 8
Wigs
 manufacturing
  soc. & econ. aspects *see*
    Secondary industries
  technology 679
 personal care 646.724 8
 soc. customs 391.5
Wigston Leicestershire Eng. *area*–425 43
Wigtown Scot. *area*–414 95
Wilbarger Co. Tex. *area*–764 746
Wilcox Co.
 Alabama *area*–761 38
 Georgia *area*–758 845
Wild
 cinnamon family *see* Bixales
 flowers
  botany 582.13
   spec. plants *see*
     Angiospermae

Wild (continued)
  silk textiles
    arts   746.043 92
      s.a. spec. proc. e.g.
        Weaving
    dyeing   667.339 2
    manufacturing
      soc. & econ. aspects *see*
        Secondary industries
    technology   677.392
      special-process fabrics   677.6
    other aspects see Textiles
    s.a. spec. prod.
  West fiction *see* Western
    fiction
  s.a. other spec. subj.
Wildcat strikes
  labor econ.   331.892 4
Wildebeests *see* Bovoidea
Wilderness
  areas
    economics   333.782
    govt. control
      law   346.046 782
        spec. jur.   346.3–.9
      pub. admin. *see* Land
        resources govt. control
        pub. admin.
  Battle
    U.S. Civil War hist.   973.736
Wild-flower gardens
  plants grown for
    floriculture   635.967 6
  s.a. spec. plants
Wildlife
  conservation tech.   639.9
  reserves
    conservation tech.   639.95
    s.a. spec. kinds of
      animals
    economics   333.954
    govt. control *see* Animals
      resources govt. control
    landscape design   719.36
    resources *see* Animals
      resources
Wilhelmina reign Netherlands
    hist.   949.206–.207 1
  s.a. spec. events & subj.
    e.g. Commerce
Wilkes
  County
    Georgia   *area*–758 172
    North Carolina   *area*–756 82
  Land Antarctica   *area*–989
Wilkes-Barre Pa.   *area*–748 33
Wilkin Co. Minn.   *area*–776 91
Wilkinson Co.
  Georgia   *area*–758 543
  Mississippi   *area*–762 25

Will
  Co. Ill.   *area*–773 25
  human attribute
    metaphysics   128.3
    psychology *see* Volition
Willacy Co. Tex.   *area*–764 493
Willamette Valley Ore. *area*–795 3
Willemite
  mineralogy   549.62
Willesden London Eng. *area*–421 85
William
  reign
    England
      1   942.021
      2   942.022
      3   942.068
      4   942.075
    Germany
      1   943.083
      2   943.084
    Gt. Brit.
      1   941.021
      2   941.022
      3   941.068
      4   941.075
    Scotland
      3   941.106 8
      4   941.107 5
    s.a. spec. events & subj.
      e.g. Courts
Williams Co.
  North Dakota   *area*–784 73
  Ohio   *area*–771 113
Williamsburg
  city Va.   *area*–755 425 2
  Co. S.C.   *area*–757 83
Williamson Co.
  Illinois   *area*–773 993
  Tennessee   *area*–768 56
  Texas   *area*–764 289
Williamsoniaceae
  paleobotany   561.592
Willingdon governorship India
  hist.   954.035 8
  s.a. spec. events & subj.
    e.g. Commerce
Willington Durham Eng. *area*–428 64
Willow
  capital site Alaska   *area*–798 3
  family *see* Salicales
  fibers
    agriculture   633.58
      soc. & econ. aspects *see*
        Primary industries
    other aspects see Salicales
Wills
  genealogy   929.3
  law   346.054
    spec. jur.   346.3–.9
Willy-willies *see* Hurricanes

Wilmington
    city Del.   area–751 2
    Isl. Ga.   area–758 724
Wilmot Proviso   973.61
    U.S. Civil War cause   973.711 3
Wilmslow Cheshire Eng.   area–427 16
Wilpena Pound Nat. Park S. Aust.
                                        area–942 37
Wilson
    cloud chambers
        radioactivity detection
            astrophysics   523.019 777
                s.a. spec. celestial
                bodies
            physics   539.777
            spec. states of matter   530.4
                s.a. spec. physical
                phenomena e.g. Heat;
                also spec. appls.
                e.g. Civil defense
    County
        Kansas   area–781 925
        North Carolina   area–756 43
        Tennessee   area–768 54
        Texas   area–764 445
    Lake Ala.   area–761 99
    Woodrow admin.
        U.S. hist.   973.913
            s.a. spec. events & subj.
            e.g. World Wars
            history 1
Wilsons Promontory Nat. Park Vic.
                                        area–945 6
Wilting
    plants *see* Turgor movements
Wilton Wiltshire Eng.   area–423 19
Wiltshire Eng.   area–423 1
Wiluna W. Aust.   area–941 6
Wimbledon London Eng.   area–421 93
Wimborne Dorset Eng.   area–423 34
Wimmera
    district Vic.   area–945 8
    River Vic.   area–945 9
Wincanton Somerset Eng.   area–423 89
Winchelsea
    East Sussex Eng.   area–422 52
    Victoria   area–945 2
Winches
    machine eng.
        soc. & econ. aspects *see*
            Secondary industries
        tech. & mf.   621.864
            s.a. spec. appls. e.g.
            Gear shipbuilding
    other aspects see Mechanics
Winchester
    Hampshire Eng.   area–422 735
    Virginia   area–755 991
Wind
    bands   785.067 1
        s.a. spec. kinds of music

Wind (continued)
    Cave Nat. Park S.D.   area–783 95
    engines
        soc. & econ. aspects *see*
            Secondary industries
        tech. & mf.   621.45
            s.a. spec. appls. e.g.
            Water supply
            engineering
    instruments
        manufacture   681.818
        music   788
            s.a. Organs (music); *also*
                Accordions
    loads
        structural theory
            gen. wks.   624.175
            spec. elements   624.177 2–.177 9
            naval arch.   623.817 5
            s.a. other spec. appls.
    propulsion
        soc. & econ. aspects *see*
            Secondary industries
        technology   621.45
            s.a. spec. appls. e.g.
            Iceboating
    River Range Wyo.   area–787 6
    systems
        meteorology   551.518
            artificial modification   551.681 8
            weather forecasting   551.641 8
            spec. areas   551.65
    tunnels
        aircraft eng.   629.134 52
            s.a. spec. appls. e.g.
            Military engineering
    s.a. Winds
Wind-driven craft *see* Sailing
        craft
Windermere Cumbria Eng. area–427 83
Windham Co.
    Connecticut   area–746 45
    Vermont   area–743 9
Windlasses
    machine eng.
        soc. & econ. aspects *see*
            Secondary industries
        tech. & mf.   621.864
            s.a. spec. appls. e.g.
            Gear shipbuilding
    other aspects see Mechanics
Windmills *see* Wind engines
Window
    displays
        advertising operations   659.157
    furnishings
        home econ.   645.3
    glass
        technology   666.152
        other aspects see Glass

Window (continued)
  insurance   368.6
    misc. aspects see Insurance
Window-box gardening
  floriculture   635.965
    s.a. spec. plants
Windows
  automobiles
    soc. & econ. aspects *see*
        Secondary industries
    tech. & mf.   629.26
  buildings
    architectural
      construction   721.823
      design & decoration   729.38
    building   690.182 3
    int. dec.   747.3
    s.a. spec. dec.
    wood construction   694.6
    s.a. spec. kinds of bldgs.
Wind-powered generation
  electrodynamic eng.
    soc. & econ. aspects *see*
        Secondary industries
    technology   621.312 136
    s.a. spec. appls. e.g.
        Lighting engineering
  other aspects see
        Electrodynamics
Winds
  deformation
    structural theory *see*
        Mechanical deformation
        structural theory
  geol. agent   551.37
  plant injuries
    agriculture   632.16
    s.a. spec. plants; also
        spec types of culture
        e.g. Forestry
  resources *see* Air resources
  s.a. Wind systems
Windscreens *see* Windshields
Windshield wipers
  automobiles   629.276
  rubber *see* Extruded rubber
    products
Windshields
  automobiles
    soc. & econ. aspects *see*
        Secondary industries
    tech. & mf.   629.26
Windsor
  & Maidenhead Berkshire Eng.
        area–422 96
  city Ont.   *area*–713 32
  Co. Vt.   *area*–743 65
  House of
    Eng. hist.   942.08
    Gt. Brit. hist.   941.08
    Scotland hist.   941.108

Windsor
  House of (continued)
    s.a. spec. events & subj.
        e.g. World Wars
  Tableland Nat. Park Qld.   *area*–943 6
Windstorms *see* Storms
Windward Isls.   *area*–729 8
Windwheels *see* Wind engines
Wines   641.22
  comm. proc.   663.2
  cookery   641.622
  home preparation   641.872
  other aspects see Alcoholic
        beverages
Wings
  air force organization   358.413 1
  aircraft *see* Airfoils
Winkler Co. Tex.   *area*–764 913
Winn Par. La.   *area*–763 66
Winnebago
  chickens
    animal husbandry   636.581
    other aspects see Chickens
  County
    Illinois   *area*–773 31
    Iowa   *area*–777 22
    Wisconsin   *area*–775 64
    Lake Wis.   *area*–775 64
Winneshiek Co. Ia.   *area*–777 32
Winnibigoshish Lake Minn. *area*–776 78
Winnipeg
  city Man.   *area*–712 74
  Lake Man.   *area*–712 72
Winnipegosis Lake Man.   *area*–712 72
Winnipesaukee Lake N.H.   *area*–742 4
Winnowing crops
  agriculture   631.56
    s.a. spec. crops
Winona Co. Minn.   *area*–776 12
Winooski River Vt.   *area*–743 17
Winsford Cheshire Eng.   *area*–427 15
Winstanley Merseyside Eng. *area*–427 57
Winston Co.
  Alabama   *area*–761 74
  Mississippi   *area*–762 692
Winter
  cresses *see* Cresses
  Olympics
    sports   796.98
  plants flowering in
    floriculture   635.953
    s.a. spec. plants
  squashes *see* Squashes
  systems
    central air-conditioning eng. 697.933 2
    s.a. spec. types of
      bldgs.
  wheat
    agriculture
      food crops   633.117
      forage crops   633.251 7

Winter
  wheat (continued)
    other aspects see Wheat
    other aspects see Seasons
Winteraceae *see* Magnoliales
Wintergreen
  agriculture   633.82
    soc. & econ. aspects *see*
      Primary industries
  foods   641.338 2
    preparation
      commercial   664.52
      domestic   641.538 2
  other aspects see Ericales
Winton Qld.   *area*–943 5
Wipers
  automobiles   629.276
Wire
  communications
    engineering *see* Electrical
      communication
    systems
      commerce   384.6
      govt. control   351.874 6
        spec. jur.   354–354
      law *see* Telecommunication
        law
  pulleys *see* Wires mech. power
        transmission
  recordings & recorders *see*
        Recordings
  services journalism   070.435
  telegraphy *see* Telegraphy
        wire
  telephony *see* Telephony wire
  walking
    equipment mf.   688.764 6
    soc. & econ. aspects *see*
      Secondary industries
    sports   796.46
    other aspects see Sports
  s.a. Metal
Wire-cable suspension bridges
  structural eng.   624.55
  other aspects see Bridges
        (structures)
Wirehaired pointing griffon
  animal husbandry   636.752
  other aspects see Dogs
Wireless communication
  commerce   384.5
  engineering *see* Electronic
        communication
  govt. control   351.874 5
    spec. jur.   353–354
  law *see* Telecommunication law
Wirephotos *see* Facsimile
        transmission

Wires
  mech. power transmission
    machine eng.
      soc. & econ. aspects *see*
        Secondary industries
      tech. & mf.   621.854
      s.a. spec. appls. e.g.
        Materials-handling
        equip.
      other aspects see Mechanics
    metal prod.
      mf. tech.   671.842
        ferrous metals   672.842
      s.a. other spec. metals
      other aspects see Primary
        metal prod.
    sculpture material   731.2
      spec. periods & schools   732–735
    structural eng.
      gen. wks.   624.177 4
      concretes   624.183 44
      s.a. other spec.
        materials
      naval arch.   623.817 74
      s.a. other spec. appls.
    s.a. Metals
Wire-stitching
  bookbinding   686.35
Wiretapping
  criminal investigation *see*
        Evidence procurement
Wireworms *see* Elateroidea
Wirksworth Derbyshire Eng.
                               area–425 13
Wirral Merseyside Eng.   *area*–427 51
Wirt Co. W. Va.   *area*–754 26
Wisbech Cambridgeshire Eng.
                               area–426 53
Wisconsin
  Evangelical Lutheran Synod   284.134
    misc. aspects see Lutheran
  River Wis.   *area*–775
  state   *area*–775
Wisdom
  gift of the Holy Spirit
    Christian doctrines   234.12
  literature *see* Poetic books
        (O.T.)
  of God
    rel. doctrines
      Christianity   231.6
      other rel. see God
  of Solomon
    deuterocanonical book   229.3
    other aspects see Apocrypha
Wise
  County
    Texas   *area*–764 532
    Virginia   *area*–755 743

Wise (continued)
  men
    art representation *see*
      Biblical characters &
      events
      Christian doctrines   232.923
Wishaw Strathclyde Scot.   *area*–414 49
Wit *see* Humor
Witchcraft
  criminology   364.188
  law   345.028 8
    spec. jur.   345.3–.9
  occultism   133.43
  rel. worship
    comp. rel.   291.33
    Islam   297.33
    s.a. other spec. rel.
  soc. theology
    Christianity   261.833 188
    comp. rel.   291.178 331 88
    s.a. other spec. rel.
Witches
  persecutions
    Christian church hist.   272.8
Witch-hazel family *see*
    Hamamelidales
Witham
  Essex Eng.   *area*–426 715
  River Eng.   *area*–425 3
Witherite
  mineralogy   549.785
Withernsea Humberside Eng.
    area–428 38
Withholding taxes *see*
    Compensation taxation
Withlacoochee River Fla.   *area*–759 72
Withnell Lancashire Eng.   *area*–427 615
Witness bearing
  Christian rel.   248.5
Witnesses
  criminal investigations   363.254
  law
    criminal   345.066
      spec. jur.   345.3–.9
    gen. wks.   347.066
      spec. jur.   347.3–.9
  other aspects see Evidence
Witney Oxfordshire Eng.   *area*–425 71
Wittig reaction
  chem. eng.   660.284 41
  org. chem.   547.241
  s.a. spec. elements, cpds.,
    prod.
Witwatersrand   *area*–682 2
Wivenhoe Essex Eng.   *area*–426 723
Wives of clergymen
  pastoral theology
    Christianity   253.2
    other rel. see Pastoral
      theology

Wizardry
  occultism   133.43
Wizards
  rel. leaders
    comp. rel.   291.62
    s.a. spec. rel.
Wloclawek Poland   *area*–438 2
Wodonga Vic.   *area*–945 5
Woking Surrey Eng.   *area*–422 142
Wokingham Berkshire Eng. *area*–422 94
Wolfe Co.
  Kentucky   *area*–769 213
  Quebec   *area*–714 573
Wolfram *see* Tungsten
Wolframite
  mineralogy   549.74
Wollastonite
  mineralogy   549.66
Wollo Ethiopia   *area*–634
Wollondilly River N.S.W.   *area*–944 6
Wollongong N.S.W.   *area*–944 6
Wolof *see* West-Atlantic
    (Niger-Congo)
Wolverhampton West Midlands Eng.
    area–424
Wolverines *see* Mustelidae
Wolverton Buckinghamshire Eng.
    area–425 91
Wolves *see* Canidae
Woman suffrage
  pol. sci.   324.623
Womanpower *see* Manpower
Wombats *see* Marsupialia
Wombwell South Yorkshire Eng.
    area–428 25
Women
  & state
    pol. sci.   323.34
  art representation   704.942 4
    drawing tech.   743.44
    painting   757.4
    s.a. other spec. art forms
  biography
    gen. colls.   920.72
    spec. fields   *s.s.*–092
  clergy
    Christian ecclesiology   262.14
    other rel. see
      Ecclesiastical theology
  criminal offenders   364.374
  education   376
  employees *see* Women labor
  ethics   170.202 44
  etiquette   395.144
  govt. services to   350.813
    central govts.   351.813
      spec. jur.   353–354
    local govts.   352.941 3
  grooming   646.704 2
  hygiene   613.042 44
  journalism for   070.483 47

Women's
  rel. associations (continued)
    other rel. see Religious
        associations
  services
    armed forces   355.348
    s.a. spec. mil. branches
  solos
    recordings   789.912
    scores & parts   784.812
    songs
      sacred   783.675 12
      secular   784.306 12
  songs *see* Women's vocal music
  suffrage
    pol. sci.   324.623
  underwear
    comm. mf.
      soc. & econ. aspects *see*
          Secondary industries
      technology   687.22
    other aspects see Women's
        clothing; *also*
        Underwear
  vocal music
    recordings   789.912
    scores & parts   784.8
      songs
        sacred   783.675
        secular   784.306
Wondai Qld.   *area*–943 2
Wonthaggi Vic.   *area*–945 2
Wood
  arch. construction   721.044 8
  s.a. spec. kinds of bldgs.
  arch. decoration *see*
      Incrustation arch.
      decoration
  arts
    engraving *see* Wood
        engraving
    handicrafts   745.51
    spec. objects   745.59
    sculpture *see* Wood
        sculpture
  Buffalo Nat. Park Alta.   *area*–712 32
  bldg. construction   694
  bldg. materials   691.1
  County
    Ohio   *area*–771 16
    Texas   *area*–764 223
    West Virginia   *area*–754 22
    Wisconsin   *area*–775 52
  eng. materials   620.12
  foundations   624.153 2
  naval design   623.818 4
  shipbuilding   623.820 7
  structures   624.184
  s.a. other spec. uses

Wood (continued)
  engraving
    graphic arts
      processes   761.2
      products   769
  extracts
    properties   674.134
  flour
    mf. tech.   674.84
    other aspects see Wood
        products
  fuel
    manufacturing
      soc. & econ. aspects *see*
          Secondary industries
      technology   662.65
  furniture
    mf. tech.   684.104
    other aspects see Furniture
    s.a. spec. prod.
  Green London Eng.   *area*–421 88
  lice *see* Isopoda
  oils
    comm. proc.   665.33
    soc. & econ. aspects *see*
        Secondary industries
  pavements
    road eng.
      technology   625.83
      sidewalks   625.883
    other aspects see Roads
  products
    manufacturers
      biog. & work   674.809 2
      s.a.   *pers.*–674
    manufacturing
      soc. & econ. aspects *see*
          Secondary industries
      technology   674.8
    s.a. spec. prod.
  pulp
    mf. tech.   676.12
    other aspects see Pulp
  roofing
    bldg. construction   695
  sculpture
    dec. arts   736.4
    fine arts
      processes
        carving tech.   731.462
        material   731.2
      spec. periods & schools   732–735
    rel. significance
      Christianity   247.3
      comp. rel.   291.37
      s.a. other spec. rel.
  shoes
    mf. tech.   685.32
    other aspects see Footwear
  shrikes
    zoology   598.8

Words
  development *see* Etymology
  dictionaries *see* Dictionaries
  grammar *see* Grammar
      (linguistics)
  pronunciation *see*
      Pronunciation
  spec. subj.   *s.s.*–014
  spelling *see* Spelling
  usage
    linguistics   418
      spec. langs.
        nonstandard
          forms   *lang. sub.*–7
        standard
          forms   *lang. sub.*–8
      rhetoric   808
Work
  areas
    household management   643.58
    s.a. other spec. appls.
  associates
    psych. influences   155.926
  relationships with
    appl. psych.   158.26
    s.a. spec. activities
  automobiles
    engineering
      gen. tech. & mf.   629.225
        maintenance   629.287 5
        models   629.221 5
        operation   629.284 5
      s.a. other spec. aspects
        e.g. Brakes
    soc. & econ. aspects *see*
        Secondary industries
    s.a. Trucks
  cars
    railroad rolling stock
      commerce   385.32
        special-duty   385.5
      engineering
      technology
        gen. wks.   625.22
          accessory
            equipment   625.25
          running gear   625.21
          monorail   625.28
        other aspects see Rolling
            stock railroads
  days
    labor econ.   331.257 23
    s.a. spec. classes of
        labor e.g. Women
    other aspects see Work
        periods
  ethics *see* Occupational ethics
  flow design
    pub. admin.   350.007 3
      central govts.   351.007 3
      spec. jur.   353–354

Work
  flow design
    pub. admin. (continued)
      local govts.   352.000 473
  load
    court management *see*
        Judicial administration
    prod. management *see*
        Loading prod.
        management
  periods
    labor econ.   331.257
    s.a. spec. classes of
        labor e.g. Women
    labor law *see* Labor Law
    personnel admin.
      gen. management   658.312 1
      executive   658.407 121
      spec. subj.   *s.s.*–068 3
      pub. admin.   350.163
        central govts.   351.163
          spec. jur.   353–354
        local govts.   352.005 163
      pub. admin.   350.835
        central govts.   351.835
          spec. jur.   353–354
        local govts.   352.943 5
  physiology
    human   612.042
  purposes
    animal husbandry for   636.088 6
    s.a. spec. animals
  studies
    prod. management   658.542
    spec. subj.   *s.s.*–068 5
  teams
    pers. admin. *see* Personnel
        utilization
  training *see* Job training
  week
    labor econ.   331.257 22
    s.a. spec. classes of
        labor e.g. Women
Workbooks   *s.s.*–076
Worker
  control of industry
    prod. econ.   338.6
  discipline
    labor econ.   331.259 8
    s.a. spec. classes of
        labor e.g. Women
  participation *see* Employee
        participation
  security
    labor econ.   331.259 6
    s.a. spec. classes of
        labor e.g. Women
    labor law *see* Labor law
    personnel admin. *see*
        Employment conditions
    personnel admin.

Wrinkle-resistant fabrics
  manufacturing
    soc. & econ. aspects *see*
      Secondary industries
    technology   677.681
  other aspects see Textiles
  s.a. spec. prod.
Wrists
  diseases
    regional med. trmt.   617.574
      s.a. spec. systems &
        organs
    surgery   617.574
    anesthesiology   617.967 574
    other aspects see Diseases
  fractures   617.157
  orthopedic surgery   617.397
Writers *see* Authors
Writing (composition)
  communication   001.543
    misc. aspects see
      Composition (writing)
  jingles for contests   790.134
  music   781.61
    s.a. spec. mediums
Writing (manual skill) *see*
    Handwriting
Writings
  Bible   221.042
Writing-telegraphy
  technology   621.382 6
    s.a. spec. appls. e.g.
      Communication office
      services
  other aspects see Telegraphy
    wire
Writs *see* Judgments
Written
  communication   001.543
    linguistics *see* Languages
    management use   658.453
    office services   651.74
    rhetoric   808
  records
    communication   001.552
Wroclaw Poland   *area*–438 5
Wrongful death
  torts
    law   346.032 3
    spec. jur.   346.3–.9
Wrongness
  ethics
    religion
      Buddhism   294.356
      Christianity   241.6
      comp. rel.   291.56
      Hinduism   294.548 6
      s.a. other spec. rel.
Wrought iron
  technology   669.141 4
  other aspects see Iron

Wu dialect
  linguistics   495.17
  literature   895.1
  s.a.   *lang.*–951 7
Wuchereriasis *see* Filarial
    diseases
Wulfenite
  mineralogy   549.74
Württemberg Ger.   *area*–434 7
Würtz-Fittig reaction
  chem. eng.   660.284 41
  org. chem.   547.21
  s.a. spec. elements, cpds.,
    prod.
Wyandot Co. O.   *area*–771 26
Wyandotte
  chickens
    animal husbandry   636.583
    other aspects see Chickens
  Co. Kan.   *area*–781 39
Wychavon Hereford & Worcester
    Eng.   *area*–424 49
Wycliffe Bible   220.520 1
  s.a. spec. parts of Bible
Wycombe Buckinghamshire Eng.
              area–425 95
Wye River Wales   *area*–429 5
Wymondham Norfolk Eng. *area*–426 19
Wyndham W. Aust.   *area*–941 4
Wynyard Tas.   *area*–946 5
Wyoming
  County
    New York   *area*–747 93
    Pennsylvania   *area*–748 35
    West Virginia   *area*–754 45
  state   *area*–787
  Valley Pa.   *area*–748 32
Wyperfeld Nat. Park Vic. *area*–945 9
Wyre
  Forest Hereford & Worcester
    Eng.   *area*–424 41
  Lancashire Eng.   *area*–427 682
Wythe Co. Va.   *area*–755 773

X

X rays
  astrophysics   523.019 722 2
    s.a. spec. celestial bodies
  biophysics
    extraterrestrial
      gen. wks.   574.191 955
      animals   591.191 955
      microorganisms 576.119 195 5
      plants   581.191 955
      s.a. spec. organisms
    med. sci.   612.014 555
    animals   636.089 201 455 5
      s.a. spec. animals
    man   612.014 555

X rays
  biophysics (continued)
    terrestrial
      gen. wks. — 574.191 55
        animals — 591.191 55
        microorganisms — 576.119 155
        plants — 581.191 55
        s.a. spec. organisms
      med. sci. — 612.014 485
        animals — 636.089 201 448 5
        s.a. spec. animals
        man — 612.014 485
      s.a. spec. functions,
          systems, organs
    physics — 539.722 2
      spec. states of matter — 530.4
      s.a. spec. physical
          phenomena e.g. Heat
    other aspects see Radiations
  s.a. X-ray
Xanthe Greece — *area*–495 7
Xanthophyceae
  botany — 589.486
  med. aspects
    gen. pharm. — 615.329 486
      toxicology — 615.952 948 6
    vet. pharm. — 636.089 532 948 6
      toxicology — 636.089 595 294 86
  paleobotany — 561.93
  other aspects see Plants
Xanthorrhoeaceae *see* Agavales
Xenarthra *see* Edentata
Xenon
  chemistry
    inorganic — 546.755
    technology — 661.075 5
      soc. & econ. aspects *see*
          Secondary industries
      s.a. spec. prod.
  pharmacology — 615.275 5
    misc. aspects see
        Pharmacology
  toxicology — 615.925 755
    misc. aspects see
        Toxicology
  other aspects see Rare gases
Xenopterygii *see*
        Acanthopterygii
Xeroderma *see* Hypertrophies
        skin
Xerography
  office use — 652.4
  soc. & econ. aspects *see*
      Secondary industries
  technology — 686.44
Xiphosura
  paleozoology — 565.392
  zoology — 595.392
  other aspects see Arthropoda

X-ray
  analysis
    anal. chem.
      gen. wks. — 543.085 86
        qualitative — 544.66
        quantitative — 545.836
      organic — 547.308 586
        qualitative — 547.346 6
        quantitative — 547.358 36
      s.a. spec. elements &
          cpds.
    astronomy — 522.686
    s.a. spec. celestial bodies
    circuits
      astrophysics — 523.018 753 53
      s.a. spec. celestial
          bodies
      physics — 537.535 3
        spec. states of matter — 530.4
      technology — 621.381 6
      s.a. spec. appls. e.g.
          Radiography
    electronics
      astrophysics — 523.018 753 5
      s.a. spec. celestial
          bodies
      physics — 537.535
        spec. states of matter — 530.4
      technology — 621.381 6
        soc. & econ. aspects *see*
            Secondary industries
      s.a. spec. appls. e.g.
          Radiography
    equipment
      pub. safety — 363.189
        misc. aspects see
            Hazardous machinery
    examinations
      med. sci.
        gen. med. — 616.075 72
        surgery — 617.075 72
        s.a. spec. diseases
        other aspects see
            Diseases
    metallography — 669.950 283
      s.a. spec. metals
    photography *see* Radiography
    spectroscopes
      mf. tech. — 681.414 8
        components — 681.42–.43
      other aspects see Optical
          instruments
    spectroscopy
      astrophysics — 523.018 753 52
      s.a. spec. celestial
          bodies
      engineering
        soc. & econ. aspects *see*
            Secondary industries

X-ray
  spectroscopy
    engineering (continued)
      technology   621.361 6
        s.a. spec. appls. e.g.
          Materials engineering
    physics   537.535 2
      spec. states of matter   530.4
    other aspects see
      Spectroscopy
  testing
    eng. materials   620.112 72
      s.a. spec. materials &
        spec. uses
  therapy   615.842 2
    misc. aspects see Physical
      therapies
    s.a. spec. diseases
  tubes
    astrophysics   523.018 753 55
      s.a. spec. celestial
        bodies
    physics   537.535 5
      spec. states of matter   530.4
    technology   621.381 6
      s.a. spec. appls. e.g.
        Radiography
  s.a. X rays
Xylem
  plant
    anatomy   581.41
    pathology   581.221
    s.a. spec. plants
Xylography *see* Wood engraving
Xylophone music   789.6
  recordings   789.912 96
Xylophones
  mf. tech.   681.819 6
  misc. aspects see Musical
    instruments
  musical art   789.6
Xyridaceae *see* Xyridales
Xyridales
  botany   584.36
  floriculture   635.934 36
  med. aspects
    crop prod.   633.884 36
    gen. pharm.   615.324 36
      toxicology   615.952 436
    vet. pharm.   636.089 532 436
      toxicology   636.089 595 243 6
  paleobotany   561.4
  other aspects see Plants

Y

Y.W.C.A. *see* Young Women's
    Christian Associations
Y.W.H.A. *see* Young Women's
    Hebrew Associations
Yacht club bldgs.
  architecture   725.87
  building   690.587
  other aspects see Public
    structures
Yachting *see* Boating
Yachts *see* Pleasure craft
    (nautical)
Yadkin
  Co. N.C.   *area*–756 66
  River N.C.   *area*–756 68
Yaghnobi language
  linguistics   491.59
  literature   891.59
  s.a.   *lang.*–915 9
Yahya Khan admin. Pakistan hist.
               954.904 6
    s.a. spec. events & subj.
      e.g. Commerce
Yajurveda
  Indic rel.   294.592 14
Yakima
  Co. Wash.   *area*–797 55
  River Wash.   *area*–797 55
Yaks
  animal husbandry   636.293
  other aspects see Bovoidea
Yakut
  ASSR   *area*–575
  s.a. Turkic
Yakutat election district Alaska
               area–798 2
Yallourn Vic.   *area*–945 6
Yalobusha Co. Miss.   *area*–762 82
Yam family *see* Dioscoreales
Yamagata Japan   *area*–521 1
Yamaguchi Japan   *area*–521 9
Yamaguti Japan   *area*–521 9
Yamal-Nenets Nat. Region RSFSR
               area–573
Yamanashi Japan   *area*–521 6
Yamanasi Japan   *area*–521 6
Yamaska Co. Que.   *area*–714 54
Yambol Bulgaria   *area*–497 78
Yamhill Co. Ore.   *area*–795 39
Yams
  agriculture   635.23
    soc. & econ. aspects *see*
      Primary industries
  foods   641.352 3
  preparation
    commercial   664.805 23
    domestic   641.652 3
  other aspects see
    Dioscoreales; *also*
    Vegetables
Yancey Co. N.C.   *area*–756 873

Yangtze River	*area*–512
Yankton Co. S.D.	*area*–783 394
Yannina Greece	*area*–495 3
Yap	*area*–966
Yaracuy Venezuela	*area*–872 6
Yard sales	
commerce	381.19
misc. aspects see Commerce	
Yardmen *see* Household employees	
Yarmouth	
Co. N.S.	*area*–716 31
Isle of Wight Eng.	*area*–422 85
Yarns	
clothing *see* Notions clothing	
textile prod.	
manufacturing	
soc. & econ. aspects *see*	
Secondary industries	
technology	677.028 62
s.a. spec. kinds of	
textiles	
Yaroslavl RSFSR	*area*–473 1
Yarra River Vic.	*area*–945 2
Yarram Vic.	*area*–945 6
Yarrangobilly Caves N.S.W.	
	area–944 7
Yarrawonga Vic.	*area*–945 4
Yass N.S.W.	*area*–944 7
Yates Co. N.Y.	*area*–747 82
Yavapai Co. Ariz.	*area*–791 57
Yaw	
aeronautical aerodynamics	629.132 364
s.a. spec. appls. e.g.	
Flying	
Yawara	
judo *see* Judo	
jujitsus *see* Jujitsus	
Yawls *see* Modern wind-driven	
vessels	
Yaws *see* Parasitic skin	
diseases	
Yazoo	
Co. Miss.	*area*–762 49
River Miss.	*area*–762 4
Yazoo-Mississippi Delta	*area*–762 4
Yea Vic.	*area*–945 3
Yearbooks	
school journalism *see* Student	
yearbooks	
Yearly Conference of People	
Called Methodists	287.53
misc. aspects see Methodist	
Year-round systems	
central air-conditioning eng.	697.933 4
s.a. spec. types of bldgs.	
Years	
time interval	529.2

Yeasts	
leavens	
manufacturing	
soc. & econ. aspects *see*	
Secondary industries	
technology	664.68
plants *see* Saccharomycetaceae	
Yell Co. Ark.	*area*–767 38
Yellow	
fever	
gen. med.	616.928
geriatrics	618.976 928
pediatrics	618.929 28
pub. health	614.541
statistics	312.392 8
deaths	312.269 28
other aspects see Diseases	
Medicine Co. Minn.	*area*–776 37
River China	*area*–511
Sea	
oceanography	551.465 56
regional subj. trmt.	*area*–164 56
other aspects see Pacific	
Ocean	
Yellow-dog contracts	
labor econ.	331.894
labor law *see* Labor law	
Yellow-eyed grass family *see*	
Xyridales	
Yellow-green algae *see*	
Xanthophyceae	
Yellowstone	
Co. Mont.	*area*–786 39
Nat. Park Wyo.	*area*–787 52
River Mont.	*area*–786 3
Yemen	*area*–533 2
Southern	*area*–533 5
Yemenites	*r.e.n.*–927 533 2
Yenisei language *see* Samoyedic	
languages	
Yeniseian *see* Paleosiberian	
Yeovil Somerset Eng.	*area*–423 89
Yeppoon Qld.	*area*–943 5
Yeso Japan	*area*–524
Yew family *see* Coniferales	
Yezidis	
religion	299.159
Yi dynasty Korea hist.	951.902
s.a. spec. events & subj.	
e.g. Commerce	
Yiddish language	
linguistics	437.947
literature	839.09
s.a.	*lang.*–37
Yield point	
solid dynamics	
engineering *see* Dynamics	
physics	531.382 5

Young	
adults	
publications for (continued)	
catalogs	
general	017–019
spec. kinds	012–016
reviews	028.162 55
s.a. spec. forms e.g.	
Books	
reading	
library sci.	028.535
rearing home econ.	649.125
customs	392.14–.15
recreation	790.192
indoor	793.019 2
outdoor	796.019 2
sermons	
Christianity	252.55
other rel. see Preaching	
sexual behavior	301.417 5
soc. services to	362.796
misc. aspects see Young	
people soc. services to	
Sunday school divisions	
Christianity	268.433
other rel. see Religious	
instruction	
other aspects see Young	
people; *also* Adults	
s.a.	pers.–055
s.a. Young men; *also*	
Young women	
adults' rel. associations	
Christianity	267.6
other rel. see Religious	
associations	
animals	
animal husbandry	636.07
s.a. spec. animals	
s.a. Young of animals	
Co. Tex.	*area*–764 545
employees	
personnel admin.	
gen. management	658.304 2
spec. subj.	s.s.–068 3
pub. admin.	350.1
central govts.	351.1
spec. jur.	353–354
local govts.	352.005 1
men	
ethics	170.202 232
etiquette	395.123 2
hygiene	613.042 33
sex	613.953
journalism for	070.483 36
meditations for	
Christianity	242.632
other rel. see Worship	
personal rel.	
Christianity	248.832

Young	
men	
personal rel. (continued)	
other rel. see Personal	
religion	
prayers for	
Christianity	242.832
other rel. see Worship	
psychology	155.532
sexual behavior	301.417 532
soc. services to	362.792
misc. aspects see Young	
people soc. services to	
other aspects see Men	
Men's	
Christian Associations	267.3
camps	
sports	796.542 2
s.a. other spec.	
activities	
Hebrew Associations	296.673
s.a. spec. activities	
e.g. Recreation	
of animals	
zoology	591.39
s.a. spec. animals	
s.a. Young animals	
people	
law *see* Minors law	
parochial activities for	
Christianity	259.2
other rel. see Pastoral	
theology	
publications for	
bibliographies	011.62
spec. kinds	012–016
catalogs	
general	017–019
spec. kinds	012–016
reviews	028.162
s.a. spec. forms e.g.	
Books	
reading	
library sci.	028.5
soc. path.	362.704 2
soc. services to	362.7
govt. control	350.847
central govts.	351.847
spec. jur.	353–354
local govts.	352.944 7
law *see* Welfare services	
law	
soc. theology	
Christianity	261.834 23
comp. rel.	291.178 342 3
s.a. other spec. rel.	
societies	
pol. sci.	324.3
spec. parties	324.24–.29
sociology	305.23

Yttrium-group metals
mining (continued)
   technology   622.349 47
   prospecting   622.184 947
s.a. spec. uses; also spec.
    minerals
other aspects see Metal;
    also Metals
Yüan dynasty
  China hist.   951.025
s.a. spec. events & subj.
    e.g. Arts
Yuba Co. Calif.   *area*–794 35
Yucatán
  Channel *see* Mexico Gulf
  state Mex.   *area*–726 5
Yucca Flats Nev.   *area*–793 34
Yuccas *see* Liliaceae
Yugoslav
  Banat   *area*–497 1
  communism
    economics   335.434 4
    pol. ideology   320.532 3
    soc. theology *see*
       Political ideologies
       soc. theology
  people   *r.e.n.*–918 2
s.a. Serbo-Croatian; *also*
    other spec. subj. e.g.
      Arts
Yugoslavia   *area*–497
Yugoslavs   *r.e.n.*–918 2
Yukaghir *see* Paleosiberian
Yukian *see* Hokan-Siouan
Yukon
  River   *area*–798 6
    Alaska   *area*–798 6
    Canada   *area*–719 1
  Territory   *area*–719 1
Yukon-Koyokuk election district
      Alaska   *area*–798 6
Yuma Co.
  Arizona   *area*–791 71
  Colorado   *area*–788 78
Yunnan China   *area*–513 5
Yurak language *see* Samoyedic
    languages
Yvelines France   *area*–443 66

Z

ZBB *see* Zero-base budgeting
Z transform
  operational calculus   515.723
  s.a. spec. appls. e.g.
     Engineering
Zacapa Guatemala   *area*–728 132
Zacatecas Mex.   *area*–724 3
Zacharias *see* Zechariah
Zaïre
  county   *area*–675 1

Zaïre (continued)
  district Angola   *area*–673 2
  river   *area*–675 1
Zakarpatskaya Ukraine *area*–477 18
Zakat
  Islamic moral theology   297.54
Zakynthos Greece   *area*–495 5
Zala Hungary   *area*–439 7
Zambales Philippines   *area*–599 1
Zambezi River   *area*–679
Zambézia Mozambique *area*–679 6
Zambia   *area*–689 4
Zambian
  people   *r.e.n.*–968 94
  s.a. other spec. subj. e.g.
    Arts
Zamboanga Philippines *area*–599 7
Zamiaceae *see* Cycadales
Zamora Spain   *area*–462 4
Zamora-Chinchipe Ecuador *area*–866 44
Zamosc Poland   *area*–438 4
Zanichelliaceae *see* Najadales
Zante Greece   *area*–495 5
Zanzibar   *area*–678 1
Zanzibaris   *r.e.n.*–967 81
Zapata Co. Tex.   *area*–764 483
Zaporozhye Ukraine   *area*–477 17
Zapotec *see* Macro-Otomanguean
Zaragoza Spain   *area*–465 53
Zavala Co. Tex.   *area*–764 437
Zaydites
  Islamic sects   297.824
    doctrines   297.204 24
    worship   297.302 4
    s.a. other spec. aspects
Zea mays
  everta *see* Popcorn
  gen. wks. *see* Corn
  saccharata *see* Sweet corn
Zealand Denmark   *area*–489 1
Zealots
  Judaism   296.81
    misc. aspects see Judaism
Zebras
  animal husbandry   636.18
    soc. & econ. aspects *see*
       Primary industries
  products
    dairy products *see* Dairy
      products
    other prod. see spec. prod.
      e.g. Hides
  other aspects see Equidae
Zebus
  animal husbandry   636.291
  other aspects see Bovoidea
Zechariah
  Bible   224.98
  other aspects see Prophetic
    books (O.T.)
Zeehan Tas.   *area*–946 6

Zirconia *see* Refractory
    materials
Zirconium
  chemistry
    inorganic | 546.513
    organic | 547.055 13
    s.a. spec. groupings e.g.
      Aliphatic compounds
    technology | 661.051 3
      organic | 661.895
    soc. & econ. aspects *see*
      Secondary industries
    s.a. spec. prod.
  materials
    building | 691.873 5
    engineering | 620.189 352
    s.a. spec. uses
  metallography | 669.957 35
  metallurgy | 669.735
    physical & chem. | 669.967 35
    soc. & econ. aspects *see*
      Secondary industries
  minerals aspects
    econ. geol. | 553.465
    mining
      technology | 622.346 5
      prospecting | 622.184 65
    s.a. spec. uses; also spec.
      minerals
  pharmacology | 615.251 3
    misc. aspects see
      Pharmacology
  products
    mf. tech. | 673.735
    other aspects see
      Nonferrous metals
      products
  toxicology | 615.925 513
    misc. aspects see
      Toxicology
  other aspects see Metal;
    also Metals
Ziryen *see* Permian
Zither music | 787.85
  recordings | 789.912 78
Zithers
  mf. tech. | 681.817 8
  misc. aspects see Musical
    instruments
  musical art | 787.8
Zoantharia *see* Anthozoa
Zodiac
  astrology | 133.52
  astronomy | 523
  lit. & stage trmt.
    folk lit.
      sociology | 398.362
      texts & lit. crit. | 398.26
    other aspects see Natural
      phenomena

Zodiacal light
  astronomy
    description | 523.59
    theory | 521.54
Zohar
  Judaism | 296.16
Zonal regions
  earth astronomy | 525.5
  ecology life sci. | 574.526 2
    animals | 591.526 2
    microorganisms | 576.15
    plants | 581.526 2
    s.a. spec. organisms
  subj. trmt. | *area*–11–13
  s.a. spec. regions e.g.
    Frigid Zones
Zone melting
  electrometallurgy *see*
    Electrometallurgy
Zones
  earth *see* Zonal regions
Zonguldak Turkey | *area*–563
Zoning
  area planning | 711
  law | 346.045
    spec. jur. | 346.3–.9
  local govt. admin. | 352.961
Zonta clubs | 369.5
Zoogenous diseases *see* Zoonoses
Zoological
  garden bldgs.
    architecture | 727.559
    building | 690.755 9
    other aspects see
      Educational buildings
  gardens | 590.744
    landscape design | 712.5
  laboratory bldgs.
    architecture | 727.559
    building | 690.755 9
    other aspects see
      Educational buildings
  sciences | 590
    Biblical trmt. | 220.859
    s.a. spec. parts of Bible
    curriculums | 375.59
    documentation | 025.065 9
    libraries | 026.59
    misc. aspects see Special
      libraries
    library acquisitions | 025.275 9
    library classification | 025.465 9
    subject headings | 025.495 9
    other aspects see Sciences
Zoologists
  biog. & work | 591.092
  s.a. spec. kinds
  other aspects see Scientists
  s.a. | *pers.*–59